Ex Libris

Randy Manning

8212 © APCo

MANUAL OF
Climbers and Wall Plants

MANUAL OF
Climbers and Wall Plants

Consultant Editor J K BURRAS
Series Editor MARK GRIFFITHS

TIMBER PRESS
Portland, Oregon

Derived from
The New Royal Horticultural Society Dictionary of Gardening
Editor in Chief Anthony Huxley
Editor Mark Griffiths, Managing Editor Margot Levy
in four volumes, 1992

First edition published 1994 by
THE MACMILLAN PRESS LTD,
London and Basingstoke

Associated companies in Auckland, Delhi, Dublin, Gaborone,
Hamburg, Harare, Hong Kong, Johannesburg, Kuala Lumpur,
Lagos, Manzini, Melbourne, Mexico City, Nairobi, New York,
Singapore, Tokyo.

First published in North America in 1994 by
Timber Press, Inc.
The Haseltine Building
133 S.W. Second Avenue, Suite 450
Portland, Oregon 97204-3527, U.S.A.

ISBN 0-88192-299-4

Printed and bound in Great Britain by
Mackays of Chatham PLC

Contents

Preface

The New RHS Dictionary Manuals aim to survey the major groups of garden plants. These groups may be botanical (for example Orchids; Grasses), formed on the basis of more general similarities (Cacti and Succulents; Bulbs), or united by only the loosest of characters and their common use in gardens. Of all the Manuals, none covers a group so varied in its members and uses as the present volume. It contains 300 genera of climbing plants drawn from 72 families – a multitude assembled from habitats of almost every type, from desert to rainforest, exhibiting habits from xerophyte to epiphyte, tree to bulb and from almost every climate. What defines this group is a need for support in the quest for light and nourishment. There are other opportunists and passengers in the Plant Kingdom – the epiphytes and parasites, for example – but climbers are among the great strategists, proving that there is always room at the top, achieving their goals by hook, prickle, root, tendril, adhesive disc and twining stem, scrambling, sprawling, sticking and strangling. Annuals and perennials, herbs, shrubs and trees, bulbs, cacti, ferns and orchids are among their number. In this volume can be found plants tender and hardy, grown for foliage, flower and fruit, plants suitable for trees and trellis, pea-sticks and pergolas, house walls and hot-house rafters.

Amid such an abundance of vines, lianes, twiners and clamberers, it is hard to generalize about what makes a climber, and all the more so in view of the range of uses to which we put these plants. Scandent shrubs like *Bougainvillea* and *Streptosolen* can be grown as standards or even free-standing specimens: in cultivation, not all climbers need support. The genus *Hedera*, essentially climbing, contains many important cultivars, some creeping, some stiffly erect. These are included here for the sake of completeness. *Ficus pumila* and many of the scandent aroids are usually grown indoors as relatively young creeping or trailing plants, but, with maturity, prove themselves to be true climbers of considerable stature. These too are treated here, whereas strictly low-growing creepers and trailers are excluded. A predominantly climbing genus like *Hoya*, *Clematis* or *Jasminum* may contain several non-climbing members. These are covered in the accounts that follow, either because they are of importance to the development of the genus in cultivation, or because they furnish a fuller picture of the genus. Some shrubs (for example *Abeliophyllum*, *Cestrum*, *Clianthus* and *Forsythia suspensa*) are semi-scandent, producing long stems that eventually lean into their supports or merely sprawl. In cultivation, these quasi-climbers tend to need some physical support and are included here for that reason. *Fremontodendron* and other shrubs that are effectively self-supporting, but almost invariably treated as wall plants in cultivation, are also described in the main A to Z sequence.

As a grouping, wall shrubs are even more ambiguous than climbers. They may be free-standing (e.g. *Acacia*) or marginally scandent (e.g. *Itea*). They come to be associated with walls for a number of reasons. Many are rather tender and will only succeed in cool temperate cultivation given the shelter of a warm, sunny wall (e.g. *Acca* and *Erythrina*). Others are displayed to best advantage against walls and other structures and may be trained to simulate the climbing habit (e.g. *Chaenomeles* and *Pyracantha*). Shrubs and trees like *Ceanothus* and *Magnolia grandiflora* come into horticulture with a reputation for tenderness and excellent potential for wall training, only to prove themselves hardier than expected and quite capable of standing upright. They continue to be planted against walls for tradition's sake and because, quite simply, they look good used in this way. Wall shrubs, then, comprise what is at best an artificial and debatable category. Gardeners in milder climates may find the association of many of these plants with sheltered walls a nonsense. For these reasons, they are handled in this Manual in a brief and separate listing, although the Introduction gives them due horticultural attention.

This work focuses on plants grown for ornament. The many climbing crop plants, notably in the Leguminosae and Cucurbitaceae, are retained here, but their cultivation and cultivars are given only in outline. Readers requiring more detailed treatments are referred to *The New RHS Dictionary of Gardening*. The myriad cultivars of climbing rose, likewise, are beyond the scope of this work – only a selection appears here.

Much of the text of *The Manual of Climbers and Wall Shrubs* derives from *The New RHS Dictionary of Gardening*. The Introduction, however, is newly written by Ken Burras who, for many years the Superintendent of one of the world's oldest surviving walled gardens, was supremely placed to oversee the preparation of this volume. A debt of gratitude is also due to those authors whose words have been taken virtually unchanged from the *Dictionary*, especially David Frodin, David Hunt and Victoria Matthews, and to Peter Rose, who prepared a new account of *Hedera*. Our work has been vastly expedited by the kindness of Dr. Brent Elliott and his colleagues at the Lindley Library of the Royal Horticultural Society, and by the Keeper and Librarian of the Royal Botanic Gardens, Kew. Thanks are also due to Gabriel Weston.

The publishers wish to thank the artists whose drawings were first published in *The New Royal Horticultural Society Dictionary of Gardening* and are reproduced here: Lorna Minton (*Campsis* and *Campsidium*), Susanna Stuart-Smith (*Ceropegia*; *Nepenthes*), Christine Grey-Wilson (*Clematis*), Elisabeth Dowle (*Hedera*), Pauline Dean (*Lonicera*), Joanna Langhorne (*Passiflora*), Vana Haggerty (*Beaumontia*; *Strophanthus*; *Wisteria*) and Glenn Rodrigues (*Akebia*; *Holboellia*; Lardizabalaceae; *Tecomaria*). All other illustrations were newly commissioned for this volume and were drawn by Camilla Speight.

Mark Griffiths   London 1994

Introduction

There are few gardens which could not be made more interesting and attractive by the judicious use of climbers and wall plants. By means of a variety of leaf and stem adaptations, climbers exploit surfaces and space not available to other forms of garden plants. Often at crucial points in the garden scene, they can add a vertical dimension, as when furnishing pergolas or arbours; on walls and fences they may provide a backcloth to ground level plantings and, in the mixed border (utilizing free standing posts), their use gives the emphasis of height and provides all-important focal points. Walls and fences may offer sheltered and often very necessary environments for a range of delightful climbers otherwise too tender for a given locality. In the same way and with a modest amount of attention to pruning and securing to suitable anchorage points, a wide variety of shrubs may be used to clothe walls and fences.

In larger gardens, individually landscaped areas or 'rooms' can be created by training climbers on partitions of heavy-duty trellising. Arbours furnished with climbing roses, *Clematis* or *Wisteria* may serve as entrance gateways – connecting vistas which nonetheless retain the surprise element within the room. Pergolas may serve the same purpose, or they can provide a distinct and special feature, possibly furnished with alternate plants of *Wisteria* and *Laburnum* to create a tunnel vista which shows the pendulous flower racemes to best effect. Summerhouses, gazebos, stone ornaments, balustrades, vases and statues all add a mature and romantic atmosphere to quieter parts of the garden when partially clothed with climbers such as roses, *Clematis,* honeysuckle and ivy. The use of trees and shrubs as supports for climbers is a well established and popular gardening technique, particularly in the wild and semi-wild garden. With the application of a little knowledge of the growth habit of the host and visitor plant, many attractive and trouble-free combinations can be achieved. The more vigorous climbing roses such as 'Kiftsgate', 'Wedding Day' and 'Climbing Cecile Brunner' are ideal for colonizing trees. Climbing honeysuckles, Russian Vine (*Polygonum baldschuanicum*) and the more vigorous *Clematis* such as *C.montana* may also be used in this way, whilst the delicate *C.viticella* and its forms are particularly attractive in combination with heathers. The welcome revival of the conservatory has led to a demand for suitable plants. Gardening in conservatories would be unthinkable without the inclusion of a range of climbing and wall plants. The range of climbers which may be grown expands considerably with the provision of even a modest amount of background heating.

BOTANICAL ASPECTS OF CLIMBING PLANTS: TRUE CLIMBERS   Throughout the natural world, climbing plants are adapted in ways which permit the exploitation of the more rigid stem structures of other plants, thus allowing them to present their leaves and flowers to light, air, moisture and appropriate pollinating agents. These adaptations may consist of nothing more than long *scandent stems* which (as in the tropical *Allamanda* or the hardy *Jasminum nudiflorum*) thread their way through and are supported by the branches of adjacent shrubs and trees. In *hook climbers* (such as *Rosa, Rubus* and some species of *Bougainvillea*), the sprawling stems are furnished with thorns or spines which anchor them among the branches of the host plant. The stems of the Rangoon Creeper (*Quisqualis indica*), are supported by *persistent petioles* which, following the shedding of the leaf blade, becomes woody, reflexed and thorn-like.

Liane is a term usually applied to the numerous species of woody climbers inhabiting tropical forests, but they also occur, though less abundantly, in temperate woodlands. Twining lianes (such as *Wisteria*) possess stem tips which rotate, seeking support, and then secure themselves by spiralling in a clockwise or anti-clockwise direction around the stems of other woody plants. The Japanese Wisteria is an example of a clockwise twiner whilst the Chinese Wisteria spirals in an anti-clockwise direction. By this means, climbers are able to leave the shade of the forest floor and to ascend, via neighbouring trees, to the topmost canopy of the forest. Some climbers with spiralling habits, such as bindweed and the perennial hop, are *herbaceous twiners* with stems arising annually from a perennial underground root system. Some spiralling climbers are true annuals.

Adventitious root climbers produce small but numerous roots on one side of their woody stems (as in ivy and *Hydrangea petiolaris)*; these adhere to the bark of trees and to rock, stone and even brick surfaces. *Aerial roots*, produced by tropical climbers such as *Monstera* and *Philodendron*, also assist in supporting the stems by fastening on to other plants.

More specialized climbers such as *Clematis, Tropaeolum, Rhodochiton* and *Lathyrus*, possess *sensitive petioles* and (or) leaves which clasp almost any structure with which they come into contact. In *Gloriosa* and *Littonia* the *leaf tips* are extended, sensitive and tendrilous, taking support from shrubs and ground vegetation. *Sensitive tendrils* may also be *modified leaflets* (as in *Cobaea*), or modified *axillary stems* (as in *Passiflora* and *Vitis*), whilst in the case of *Smilax* they are *modified stipules*. The much-branched tendrils of Virginia Creeper are furnished with terminal *adhesive discs* which attach tenaciously to most surfaces. Perhaps the most remarkable climbing adaptation occurs in the carnivorous *Nepenthes*, where the leaf midrib is extended beyond the leaf blade and functions as a tendril. This supports not only the terminal pitcher (which together with its fluid contents may attain considerable weight), but also the stems which, in some species, climb to great heights. In the forests of Borneo this allows their use as ropes for slinging foot bridges.

WALL SHRUBS Walls provide opportunities for cultivating a range of shrubs which, by reason of their growth habit or climatic requirements, are less successfully grown as free-standing plants. The shelter and warmth provided by garden walls with favoured aspects has long been exploited for the growing of more tender plants. Fruits such as fig, grapes, 'apricocks', pears, peaches and nectarines would ripen in such situations. Of these, only the grape is a true climber but, by suitable pruning and training techniques, it was soon appreciated that fruits with natural bush or tree habits could be adapted and contained against walls, thriving in the microclimate they provide.

By the Middle Ages, grafting techniques were well established and restricted forms of trees, on suitable understocks, admirably suited to this form of cultivation, appeared. Fans, espaliers, cordons and more fanciful tree shapes became popular. Records and illustrated books of monastic and castle gardens indicate the wide range and variety of ornamental shrubs cultivated, and although we have to wait until the reign of Elizabeth I for evidence of a reasonable variety of roses, there can be little doubt that these plants too were grown on garden walls at the time.

Plant introductions from around the world have, since those early days, resulted in a wide range of shrubby plants suitable for wall cultivation. From the New World in 1734 arrived *Magnolia grandiflora*, possibly the most magnificent evergreen plant traditionally grown against south- or west-aspect walls in the British Isles. North America, especially Western California, also contributed *Ceanothus, Carpenteria, Fremontodendron, Garrya, Ribes speciosum* and *Dendromecon rigida*. From Central and South America came *Abelia floribunda, Azara, Abutilon* (*Cornyabutilon*) *vitifolium, A.megapotamicum, Escallonia*, the two species of *Crinodendron* and the exotic Cock's Spur Coral Tree (*Erythrina crista-galli*). We have the Mediterranean region to thank for the deliciously fragrant *Argyrocytisus (Cytisus) battandieri*. From China, Japan, Korea and the Himalayas came a range of potential wall shrubs including *Camellia sasanqua, Abeliophyllum distichum, Buddleja asiatica, Chaenomeles speciosa* (and its derivatives), *Forsythia suspensa, Itea ilicifolia* and *Xanthoceras* while from Australasia came *Acacia baileyana* and *A.dealbata, Callistemon* (the Bottle Brushes), *Leptospermum* (the New Zealand Tea Tree) and the Parrot's Bill or Lobster Claw (*Clianthus puniceus*).

SELECTION OF SITES Many wall shrubs require protection from frost when grown out-of-doors in cool temperate regions like the British Isles and much of North America. Such protection can often be provided by south- or west-facing walls. Among climbers, such plants might include the Brazilian Cruel Plant (*Araujia sericofera*), the evergreen *Clematis armandii* and the winter-flowering *Clematis cirrhosa* var. *balearica. Clematis texensis* (from Texas) and its hybrids also require frost protection and a sunny aspect if they are to thrive. The Chilean *Eccremocarpus scaber*, again, requires a sheltered wall aspect and this is also the case with the elegant Colombian *Passiflora antioquiensis. Solanum jasminoides* 'Album', *Sollya heterophylla, Trachelospermum asiaticum* and *T.jasminoides* are other climbing plants which, if they are to give of their best, require the shelter of sunny walls when grown out-of-doors in zones 8 and under. There are, of course, a few border-line hardy climbers and wall shrubs which prefer not only the protection of a wall, but also a degree of shade; these include the Chilean woodland plants *Berberidopsis corallina* and *Lapageria rosea*.

Outside the subtropics and tropics, totally non-hardy climbers require the protection of glasshouses, conservatories or dwelling rooms. Ideally, the degree of protection should be matched with the temperature and humidity conditions prevailing in the habitats from which the plants originate. Plants from the tropical regions of the world, such as *Allamanda*, the calabash or bottle gourd

(*Lagenaria siceraria*), the loofah (*Luffa cylindrica*), *Manettia, Nepenthes*, the granadilla (*Passiflora quadrangularis*), the rainforest members of the Arum family (*Philodendron, Monstera* and *Scindapsus*) and the exotic green-flowered Jade Vine (*Strongylodon macrobotrys*), all require perennially warm, and humid conditions. In temperate regions, heated glasshouses are the rule, but surprising successes are occasionally achieved in dwelling rooms by careful attention to temperature, light and humidity requirements. Other non-hardy climbers with less exacting heat requirements will survive in unheated or barely frost-free glasshouses in cool temperate zones. These include *Agapetes, Antigonon leptopus*, the Kangaroo Vine (*Cissus antarctica*), the Primrose Jasmine (*Jasminum mesnyi*) and the supremely fragrant *Jasminum polyanthum*. In addition to true annual climbers such as *Ipomoea (Quamoclit) coccinea* and the Morning Glory (*Ipomoea purpurea*), certain frost-tender perennials are traditionally grown outside as annuals during the summer months in the British Isles. These include the curious black-flowered *Rhodochiton atrosanguineum* and the Cup and Saucer Vine (*Cobaea scandens*). Seed is usually sown under glass early in the year and the resulting plants are moved to the outdoor garden when danger of frost is past.

SUPPORTS FOR CLIMBERS   There are no restrictions as to the kinds of walls which may be furnished with climbing plants. Stone, brick, concrete-rendered, all are suitable. Self-clinging climbers with adhesive pads (as in *Parthenocissus*) or with adventitious roots (as in *Hedera, Schizophragma* and *Hydrangea petiolaris*) will adhere directly to wall surfaces without additional support. Walls treated with emulsion- based paints are, however, unsuitable for climbers of this kind because of the ease with which the paint is pulled from the wall by the weight and/or movement of the climbing stems. Windy, exposed sites may also present problems: self-clinging climbers may have difficulty in establishing themselves if buffeted or may even be blown off the wall at some later stage in their development. In such cases, it may be necessary to secure the stems by tying them to wall nails.

Concern is expressed from time to time (particularly by architects and building surveyors) about the possible damage inflicted on walls by climbing plants. There is no doubt that adventitious roots may, over time, have a damaging effect on cement mortar used in the construction of brick or stone walls. In addition, stems occasionally become established between brick and stone joints and their subsequent growth and expansion may damage the wall. Ivy is undoubtedly responsible for most problems of this kind, but this usually only happens when plants have been allowed to grow unchecked for many years and have developed stems of a substantial thickness. Periodic inspections accompanied by the pruning out of offending branches will alleviate these problems. This is also the case with liane-type climbers (*Wisteria*, honeysuckle, etc.) grown against buildings, where the woody stems may become established and thicken around gutters and downspouts. Non-clinging climbers and wall plants require support and attachment to walls for which various techniques and materials are used. Inspections of old kitchen garden walls (where nail holes generally permeate brickwork and mortar) reveal the extent to which individual wall fastenings were used for wall-trained fruits and climbers. Lead-headed cast iron nails were particularly common and these products are still obtainable. Modern alternatives include hardened steel nails and galvanized 'vine eyes'. In the 19th century, peach and nectarine houses were usually built as 'lean-to' structures against south- or west-facing walls. It was customary to fix vertical metal bars at suitable intervals along the wall; these supported horizontal wires to which the plant stems were fastened. This technique is still used today, even out of doors, although it is more usual to dispense with vertical bars and fix horizontal wires directly to galvanized vine eyes or to galvanized or zinc-plated eyed screws. Long runs of wire will benefit from the addition of adjustable strainers allowing periodic tightening of the wires. Whichever system is adopted, it is advisable to drill and plug the walls to receive the screws or nails to ensure firm fixing and lessen the risk of damage to the wall. The specification of wire used should be appropriate to the kind of plant it is intended to support. Generally speaking, galvanized wire of between 1.5mm and 2.5mm diameter is satisfactory for the majority of climbing and wall plants. For large-growing specimens such as *Wisteria* and *Magnolia*, multi-strand wire of to 3mm may be used.

Alternative supports for plants against walls or fencing include cedar wood, plastic or plastic-coated trellis (whether rigid or expanding), fastened directly to the wall or fence via a spacer, which allows climbing plants room to twine and facilitates the tying of plants to the trellis with garden twine, tarred string or plastic strap ties.

Timber fencing and trellising should not be treated with creosote, which is inimical to plant life, but with a modern preservative instead.

FREE-STANDING POSTS, TRELLIS, PERGOLAS AND ARBOURS   Such structures are traditionally intended for furnishing with climbing plants and may be constructed of timber or a combination of timber and brick or stone; although bowers and arbours are available purpose-made of heavy gauge wire, metal rods or even rigid polystyrene. As with garden posts, timbers used in the construction of features of this kind require treating with suitable preservatives. Modern commercial treatments, including water-based, high pressure tanalising, are usually applied at the sawmill or factory, but 'do it yourself' timber preservatives are available, without recourse to creosote. Timber posts may be prevented from rotting at ground level by using metal spikes with ferrules designed for square or round section posts. These are stocked by most garden centres and are designed as supports to be driven into the ground for fence post repairs. They are, however, ideal for supporting timber posts above the ground which are intended for pillar roses or climbing plants.

PREPARATION OF SITES AND PLANTING   Planting sites against walls or buildings can, initially, be dry and inhospitable places for plants, not least because of overhanging roofs and gutters which prevent rain from reaching the border. In addition, south- and west-facing walls particularly draw a considerable amount of moisture which is rapidly lost to the atmosphere. Dry soils are hungry soils – time and effort are well spent in the thorough preparation of planting sites. If possible, avoid planting directly against a wall (a minimum of 30cm/1ft away is advisable) and, ideally, the top spit (one spade's depth of soil) should be removed over an area approximately 1m long by 50cm/20in. wide for each plant. Fork over the second spit, ensuring the ground is thoroughly broken up to aid drainage, and incorporate organic fertilizer such as bonemeal. Lightly firm this spit and cover with a layer of well rotted manure or compost. Prior to planting, thoroughly mix with the removed first layer of topsoil a generous quantity of well rotted manure or organically based planting compost and then replace it; on heavy clay soils, it is advisable to replace the excavated soil with a medium-fertility loam-based mix such as John Innes No. 3.

This would be a suitable ground preparation for most plants against walls and fences. Away from walls (posts, pergolas, arches, etc.), a more generous (1m/3ft square) area of ground should be excavated; this is true also of sites for plants intended to colonize trees. In the latter case, ensure that the site is well away from the dry conditions at the base of the tree trunk and lead the stems back into the tree stem and branches as they develop, giving support as necessary.

Most climbing plants and shrubs obtained from garden centres or nurseries are container-grown and care should be taken in removing the plant from its pot. Do not pull the plant out. Soft plastic containers can be cut away from the root ball; otherwise, completely invert the plant in its pot and tap the rim of the pot sharply on a solid object such as the top of a fork or spade driven firmly into the ground – this usually detaches the root ball from the pot quite easily.

Ensure the roots are moist by completely immersing the root ball in a bucket of water for a few minutes and, prior to planting, carefully tease away a selection of roots from the perimeter of the root ball. Determine the correct depth of the planting hole by placing the plant in position, ensuring sufficient depth has been allowed for a final covering of about 5cm/2in. of soil above the existing surface roots. Progressively firm the previously prepared topsoil as it is replaced around the roots of the plant and leave the surface above the roots slightly concave to facilitate watering. A final mulch of well rotted manure or organic compost will assist in conserving moisture during dry periods, but care should be taken to ensure that the root balls of newly planted specimens are never allowed to dry out. This is particularly important in the first growing season following planting.

TRAINING AND PRUNING   Self-clinging climbers (with adhesive discs or adventitious roots) will attach themselves to walls without assistance. Other climbers with spiralling stems or tendrils generally require some tying in of the early shoots to allow the stems to reach and begin colonizing the support or trellis provided. Thorn-assisted and scandent-stemmed climbers, together with wall shrubs, will need to be secured to suitable wall fixings or to fences and posts at fairly regular intervals. Care should be taken to ensure that straps, ties of plastic coated wire, or even strong string, do not ultimately constrict and cause damage as the stems increase in girth. The force exerted by the increase in stem girth of liane-type climbers is considerable and they will require regular inspection and training to prevent stems from spiralling around each other, lifting tiles, encircling gutters and downspouts or forcing trellis from walls. Initial training, in what may be called the formative years, will consist of controlling development by the removal of superfluous growth and encouraging shoots to grow in a desired direction by pruning back to appropriate axillary buds. The aim should be to produce a balanced framework neatly covering the allocated space.

The pruning of established climbers and wall plants varies from little or no regular pruning, as in the case of vigorous roses colonizing trees and older plants of *Magnolia grandiflora,* to the regular summer and winter pruning of *Wisteria.*

A prerequisite of any pruning regime is the careful and complete removal of dead, damaged and diseased wood. With most wall subjects, the opportunity should be taken to thin crowding shoots and to replace, as appropriate, old non-flowering growth with young actively growing shoots originating low down on the plant (but, of course, avoiding sucker growths originating from the stock on budded or grafted plants). Regular pruning regimes are generally determined by the age of wood on which a particular plant flowers or fruits. Wall shrubs such as *Jasminum nudiflorum,* which flower in early spring on wood of the previous year's growth, are pruned immediately after flowering, cutting back the old flowering shoots to within two or three buds of the base. This treatment encourages young lateral growths which will flower the following season. Summer-flowering climbers and wall plants such as *Passiflora caerulea* and *Rosa* 'Golden Showers' are best pruned hard in March to encourage a generous supply of young flowering shoots in the same year. Well established plants of *Wisteria* are pruned twice each year, to encourage the development of lateral flowering spurs. Summer pruning, usually in July, consists of pruning back long trailing laterals to approximately 15cm/6in. This is followed by late autumn or winter pruning of the same laterals to within two or three buds of the base.

WINTER PROTECTION   The selection of sites with appropriate aspects is of fundamental importance in the successful cultivation of borderline-hardy climbing and wall plants. Even so, some degree of additional winter protection may be desirable and worthwhile. Favoured walls in larger 19th-century gardens were occasionally provided with glass overhangs, from which cotton blinds could be suspended, giving protection to rare and tender plants during hard weather. Fibreglass fleece sheeting is the modern-day equivalent and is available from garden centres, where it is extensively used to protect young growth of certain plants against spring frosts and cold winds.

Non-hardy climbers and wall shrubs which are able to produce new shoots from a perennial rootstock (as in *Erythrina* and *Clematis texensis* 'Étoile Rose'), may be protected by a mound of leaf litter or chip bark applied over the root system before the onset of winter. Long straw and dried bracken are also useful forms of winter protection when used around the bases of stems. A wigwam of canes supporting hessian sacking is another form of hard weather protection for basal shoots.

CONTAINER-GROWN CLIMBERS AND WALL PLANTS   A range of climbers and even some wall plants may be successfully grown in tubs, pots and other containers. Free-standing displays are possible, using triangular trellis panels or canes, making them particularly suitable as patio or conservatory features.

For long life, tubs and other wooden containers should be constructed of oak. Commercially made planters are available with polythene or fibreglass linings and these considerably extend the life of the wooden surrounds. Traditional clay and plastic pots, or fibreglass and even concrete aggregate receptacles may be used. Watering regimes will vary according to the kind of container used, the aspect chosen and the degree of establishment of the plant's root and stem system.

Plants such as *Clematis*, which require cool root conditions, are probably better suited to wooden or clay containers. Low-growing hummock-forming bedding plants, alpines and shrublets may be established around the edge of the containers to provide essential summer shade for the root system.

Good drainage is particularly important and suitable sized holes should be present in the base of the container; these are traditionally covered with small stones or broken crocks (pot shards), brick-rubble, etc., to a depth of not less than 6cm/2.5in. A shallow cover of moss or dried leaves will prevent the soil from blocking the drainage system. Loam-based compost is preferable as a medium for perennial climbers and mixtures close to the John Innes No.3 formulation are close to ideal, except for lime-haters. Soilless composts are difficult to wet once dry, and, as the base fertilizer content is usually of a limited duration, they are more suitable for annual climbers and temporary displays. Even with loam-based composts, the gradual depletion of soil nutrients must be taken into consideration and regular feeding with proprietary liquid feeds during the growing season is advisable. For best results, spring top-dressing with a similar loam-based compost is also essential and, after a year or two, complete repotting will probably be required.

Wall Shrubs

Abelia Caprifoliaceae. 15 species, small to medium-sized evergreen or deciduous shrubs from Asia and Mexico (*A.floribunda*). Branches slender, arching. Leaves small, neat, dark green emerging red-bronze, sometimes attractively variegated (*A.*'Goldsport'). Flowers in small clusters from spring to early autumn, tubular, white, shell pink, lilac, rose or red, often with contrasting bronze-pink calyces.

Abutilon Malvaceae. 150 species, mostly evergreen shrubs and trees from the tropics and subtropics. Growth slender and virtually scandent in *A.megapotamicum*, stout and erect in *A.ochsenii*, *A.vitifolium* and their hybrid, *A.×suntense*. Leaves small, dark, ovate-lanceolate in *A.megapotamicum* (also variegated cultivars), broad, lobed and hairy in the other three listed here. Flowers produced in summer, large, pendulous, lantern-like, yellow with a dark red calyx in *A.megapotamicum*, broader and spreading, lavender to white in the others.

Acacia Leguminosae. 1000+ species, trees and shrubs of cosmopolitan distribution, most abundant in Australia and Africa. Two widely used as wall shrubs – *A.baileyana*, a small, compact tree with very finely pinnate, steely blue-grey foliage and mildly fragrant, ball-like heads of lemon yellow flowers, and *A.dealbata*, the Florist's Mimosa, a far larger tree with looser, sea-green or grey leaves and larger sprays of strongly scented, bright yellow flowers.

Acca Myrtaceae. 2 species, evergreen shrubs and small trees. *A.sellowiana* (*Feijoa sellowiana*) is most often grown, a small tree with broad, leathery dark green leaves and flowers carried in summer with conspicuous red stamens. The flowers and the egg-shaped fruit are edible. Variegated cultivars are sometimes offered.

Aloysia Verbenaceae. 37 species, aromatic, semi-evergreen shrubs. The South American *A.triphylla* (*Lippia citriodora*), Lemon Verbena, is most commonly grown, a low, compact bush with narrow leaves strongly scented of lemon when crushed and small, white or lilac-tinted flowers in slender spikes.

Argyrocytisus Leguminosae. 1 species, *A.battandieri* (*Cytisus battandieri*), a tall, rangy evergreen shrub from Morocco with silvery, trefoil-like leaves and cone-shaped racemes of pineapple-scented, golden yellow flowers in summer.

Azara Flacourtiaceae. 10 species, evergreen shrubs and small trees from South America. Grown for their glossy, dark green leaves (very small and rounded in *A.microphylla* to longer and lanceolate in *A.lanceolata*), carried on arching, spray-like branches and small, dull yellow flowers – often scented and followed by berry-like, purple-black fruit.

Buddleja Loganiaceae. *c*100 species, evergreen or deciduous trees and shrubs of cosmpolitan distribution, typically with rather small tubular flowers in narrow thyrsoid panicles on slender, arching branches. Many species ornamental and grown in open garden situations. Some tender species are semi-scandent and ideal for walls in cool conservatories and glasshouses (*B.indica*, leaves large, broad, wavy, flowers white to pale yellow; *B.madagascariensis*, leaves narrow, long, flowers orange-yellow); others are of more free-standing habit and near-hardy, but favour wall-training outdoors in zone 8 (*B.asiatica*, leaves ovate, floccose, flowers white, fragrant; *B.bhutanica*, leaves connate-perfoliate, flowers white, fragrant; *B.candida*, leaves silvery, felted, flowers violet; *B.crispa*, leaves grey-green, wavy, woolly, flowers lilac with a white or orange throat; *B. × lewisiana*, (*B.asiatica × B.madagascariensis*), flowers white to yellow- orange; *B. × pikei*, (*B.alternifolia × B.crispa*), leaves downy, wavy, flowers fragrant, mauve-pink with yellow throat; *B.yunnanensis*, flowers lilac).

Bupleurum Umbelliferae. 100 species of perennial herbs, subshrubs and shrubs with leathery leaves and compound umbels of small, yellow-green flowers. Many of the genus herbaceous, the Thorow-waxes; *B.fruticosum* from S.Europe an evergreen, sprawling shrub, however, with leathery, sea-green oblanceolate leaves and fine heads of yellow flowers.

Calceolaria Scrophulariaceae. *c*300 species, herbs, subshrubs and shrubs from Central and South America, grown for their showy, pouch- or slipper-like flowers. Most familiar as the tender, colourful hybrids of the Herbeohybrida and Fruticohybrida Groups, also the tufted, 'alpine' *C.darwinii* and *C.uniflora*, some Slipper Flowers are, nonetheless, shrubby and suited to cultivation on conservatory walls and in very sheltered, sunny locations outdoors in zones 8 and 9. The species most often seen is *C.integrifolia*, from Chile – a clammy, sprawling shrub with narrow, toothed and densely hairy leaves and cymes of bright yellow flowers in summer.

Caldcluvia Cunoniaceae. 11 species, evergreen shrubs and trees scattered throughout the Southern Hemisphere. *C.paniculata* is sometimes grown on sheltered walls in cool temperate climates. A native of Chile, it makes a large, erect shrub with long, tough oblong-elliptic leaves, toothed and prominently veined. The small, white, fragrant flowers are carried in corymbs in summer.

Callistemon Myrtaceae. 25 species, evergreen shrubs from Australia with long, arching branches densely clothed with narrow leaves. The flowers have colourful stamens (pink, crimson, scarlet, ruby, cream or yellow) and are carried in a crowded cylindrical arrangement, surrounding the most recently ripened length of branch – hence the common name, Bottlebrush Bush. Species most often grown include *C.citrinus* (foliage lemon-scented, flowers red, also 'Splendens' a particularly fine, scarlet selection); *C.linearis* (leaves narrow, flowers scarlet); *C.pallidus* (flowers cream to yellow-green);

C.rigidus (leaves rigid, flowers deep red); *C.salignus* (leaves and branches slender, willowy, flowers cream to pale yellow, sometimes pink or red); *C.sieberi* (leaves small, narrow, flowers pale yellow, good cold-hardiness); *C.speciosus* (leaves narrow, rigid, pointed, flowers deep red); *C.subulatus* (leaves small, rigid, silky at first, flowers crimson, good cold-hardiness).

Camellia Theaceae. *c*250 species, Asiatic, evergreen trees and shrubs with glossy, tough lanceolate to ovate-elliptic leaves and large flowers in a wide range of forms and colours from yellow to white to pink through deepest red. The Camellia is too extensively developed and cultivated to require any but the briefest treatment here. Traditionally, many species, hybrids and cultivars have been grown against walls to safeguard against wind scorch of the foliage and to escape the damage done to buds and flowers by late frosts. Increasingly, Camellias are grown in the open garden and as free-standing specimens in tubs and planters – especially in milder areas, like inner cities, or where shelter is afforded by the surrounding trees and shrubs. These plants do, nonetheless, make excellent wall shrubs, favouring rather damper, cooler and more shady locations than most. This method of cultivation is recommended especially for the more tender species and cultivars, notably the delicate *C.sasanqua*.

Cantua Polemoniaceae. 6 species, evergreen shrubs and trees from cool, mountainous regions in South America. *C.buxifolia*, the Magic Flower or Sacred Flower of the Incas is a small shrub with large, drooping tubular flowers – purple-pink in the throat, bright cerise to scarlet at the limb, sometimes with golden lines. It will survive in milder districts of zone 8, given the protection of a south- or southwest-facing wall.

Carpenteria Hydrangeaceae. 1 species (*C.californica*, the Tree Anemone), a small to medium-sized evergreen shrub native to California. Large white flowers with golden stamens are produced from mid to late summer.

Ceanothus Rhamnaceae. *c*50 species, evergreen and deciduous shrubs or small trees native to North America and northern Mexico.The majority of cultivated species originate from the Southwest US, have small, persistent, dark green leaves and dense panicles of small flowers in shades of blue, lilac, pink or white. Some are procumbent or prostrate (*Cc.divergens, gloriosus, prostratus*), others are essentially erect and free-standing (the deciduous, large-leaved and -flowered *C.×delileanus* and its selections like 'Gloire de Versailles', for example), many, however, are spreading or hummock-forming shrubs typical of dry, chaparral scrub and are among the most popular and resilient of wall shrubs. The larger evergreen *Ceanothus* species and hybrids include *Cc.cyaneus, griseus, impressus,* × *lobbianus,* × *mendocinensis, thyrsiflorus* and × *veitchianus*. They will tolerate dry, impoverished conditions and full sunlight, quickly covering walls and creating a dense mass of dark foliage. They may be trained (or reined-in) using strong wires.

Chaenomeles Rosaceae. 3 species, spiny deciduous shrubs from East Asia with rounded flowers in shades of white, pink, red and orange-red followed by aromatic, yellow quince-like fruit. The Japanese or Flowering Quinces (Japonica) are beautiful shrubs, flowering in early spring and often on bare wood. They are available in a wide range of hybrids and cultivars and will tolerate most situations. Free-standing speci-mens will usually form multi-stemmed, spreading mounds; they may also be pruned to make informal hedges; but the Japonica is undoubtedly seen to best advantage when grown against walls and pruned hard into fans and espaliers. As wall shrubs, *Chaenomeles* have no particular requirement for brilliantly sunny and heavily protected sites and will enliven even the gloomiest places.

Chimonanthus Calycanthaceae. 6 species, deciduous and semi-evergreen shrubs from China. *C.praecox*, the Wintersweet, is a medium-sized shrub with undistinguished foliage. In winter, however, its bare branches are covered in nodding, waxy flowers; these are of dull, semi-translucent yellow with purple markings, but are gloriously fragrant. It flowers parsimoniously if the new growths are not thoroughly ripened. The flowers are damaged by persistent frosts and damp and are most powerfully scented in full sunlight – for these reasons, the Wintersweet is often grown against sunny, sheltered walls.

Choisya Rutaceae. 9 species, evergreen, aromatic shrubs with tough, glossy, digitately compound leaves and terminal cymes of white, orange blossom-like flowers produced in spring and again in the autumn. They hail from the SW United States and Mexico but are altogether hardy. Because of their provenance, however, they tend to be used against sunny walls and there is little doubt that they perform better thus treated. *C.ternata*, the Mexican Orange Blossom is widely grown, as is its yellow-leaved form, 'Sundance'. *C.arizonica* is a choicer, if rather refractory plant, with very narrow leaflets. 'Aztec Pearl', the hybrid between the two, inherits the large and fragrant flowers of one and the slender leaflets of the other.

Colletia Rhamnaceae. 17 species, shrubs from South America with robust flattened stems clothed with formidable spines derived from the stem wings. Leaves lacking or very small and ephemeral. Flowers small, white, fragrant, produced in great abundance, covering the branches in summer. *C.hystrix* and *C.spinosissima* are olive green with long, slender spines; *C.paradoxa* (*C.cruciata*) has very broad spines of a striking, chalky blue-grey. They require sunny, sheltered and rather dry conditions against walls, to which they may be tied as their stems elongate and become weighty with thorns.

Colquhounia Labiatae. 3 species, evergreen, medium-sized shrubs from E Asia. *C.coccinea* has densely white-felted growth and whorls of scarlet to fiery orange flowers in summer. It requires a sunny, sheltered site on a light soil and may be pruned hard back after flowering or in late winter, when much of the top growth may have been killed by frost already.

Corokia Cornaceae. 3 species, small, evergreen, tree-like shrubs native to New Zealand, with twiggy, densely tangled branchlets of a dark, ashy grey, small dark leaves with silver indumentum, tiny yellow flowers and scarlet fruit. Valued for their intricate habit and strong silver/black tones. In cold, windy and damp regions they require the shelter of a south-facing wall.

Cotoneaster Rosaceae. Over 70 species, evergreen or deciduous trees and shrubs native to Europe, North Africa and Asia, characteristically with small, cream flowers and attractive fruits resembling minute apples in shades of red, orange, yellow, white, pink, purple and black. Of the many species, hybrids and cultivars of horticultural importance, several are grown on walls, not for the sake of protection but to maximize their spreading or sprawling habit. Small species can be fanned or encouraged to creep over retaining walls and the footings of house walls, for example, *C.adpressus, C.cochleatus, C.congestus, C.conspicuus, C.* 'Coral Beauty', *C.dammeri, C.* 'Gnom', *C.* 'Herbstfeuer', *C.* 'Lowfast', *C.microphyllus, C.nanshan, C.radicans* and, of course, *C.horizontalis,* with rigid, herring-bone fans clothed in small, richly coloured leaves and vivid fruit. Larger plants can be trained on walls or planted as hedges alongside them, their arching branches encouraged to cover their surfaces and cascade over their tops. Suited to this use are *C.* 'Hybridus Pendulus'and *C. salicifolius.*

Crinodendron Elaeocarpaceae. 2 species, large evergreen shrubs from South America. *C.hookerianum,* the Chile Lantern Tree has rod-like branches with dark, leathery, lanceolate leaves and hung with lantern-like, fleshy scarlet flowers. *C.patagua* is more delicate in appearance, its hanging, fringed bells a pure white .

Daphne Thymelaeaceae. *c*50 species, small evergreen or deciduous shrubs from Europe, North Africa and Asia. The Daphnes are grown for their small, often fragrant flowers and, in some species and cultivars, for their ornamental fruit and foliage. Most are hardy but benefit from the protection of a sheltered and sunny wall or fence.The following are often grown in this way – *D* × *burkwoodii* (densely branched and rounded with small leaves and sweetly fragrant pale pink flowers), *D.genkwa* (sparse habit with lilac-mauve flowers on bare branches) and *D.odora* (evergreen with glossy, laurel-like leaves and heavily scented, waxy, mauve-pink flowers in late winter. Includes 'Aureomarginata', attractively variegated.).

Dendromecon Papaveraceae. 1 species, *D.rigida,* the Tree or Bush Poppy, a native of California. A large evergreen shrub with long, narrow, rather stiff leaves and poppy-like, yellow flowers carried throughout the summer.

Desfontainia Loganiaceae. 1 species, a bushy, evergreen shrub native to Chile and Peru, with holly-like leaves and tubular flowers in shades of vermilion, scarlet and fiery orange.It thrives on cool, acid soils rich in leafmould, with the shade and shelter of a wall.

Drimys Winteraceae. 30 species, evergreen trees and shrubs native to South America, Asia and Australasia. Two species are sometimes grown against walls on acid soils – *D.lanceolata,* the Pepper Tree, an aromatic shrub or small tree from Australia with a narrowly erect habit, bronze new growth, purple-red branches, large, tough leaves and masses of small, green-white flowers in spring, and *D.winteri* from South America, an erect, multi-stemmed shrub or tree with aromatic bark, handsome dark and leathery leaves with silver undersides and fragrant ivory flowers in late spring.

Eriobotrya Rosaceae. 10 species, large shrubs and trees from East Asia. The most commonly grown is *E.japonica,* the Loquat or Japanese Medlar, a large shrub or broad-crowned tree with stout, tawny-haired branches, very bold, corrugated, leathery deep green leaves, panicles of small, muskily scented, off-white flowers and edible, egg-shaped, yellow fruit. Large, free-standing specimens of the Loquat can be seen throughout the South of England; it is, however, far more likely to produce leaves of fine quality and perhaps even fruit if grown against a warm and sunny wall.

Erythrina Leguminosae. Over 100 species of evergreen or deciduous herbs, shrubs and trees found throughout the Tropics and Subtropics, with prickly stems, compound leaves and very showy, pea-like flowers in erect racemes. In cool temperate climates, the species usually grown is the spectacular *E.crista-galli,* the Cockspur Coral Tree, a South American native with thorny stems, trefoil leaves and long, erect racemes of deep scarlet flowers. It should be planted at the foot of a south-facing wall in full sunlight. In winter, the crown must be thickly mulched with leaf litter and straw or dry bracken. Hard frosts will kill the last year's growth of erect stems which should be removed along with the dry mulch in late spring. Plants used in this way, (stooled, in effect) produce dense stands of strongly upright, free-flowering growth each year.

Escallonia Grossulariaceae. *c*50 species, evergreen shrubs with resinous, aromatic dark green foliage and panicles or racemes of small flowers in shades of white, rose, cerise and scarlet. They are widely grown as free-standing specimens and for hedging in milder regions (especially on the coast). Several of the finer species and cultivars suffer where prolonged hard frosts and cold winds are common and perform better given the protection of a wall, among them *E.bifida, E.grahamiana, E.laevis, E.leucantha, E.revoluta* and *E.tucumanensis.* Others (e.g. *E.* 'Donard Brilliance', *E.*× *langleyensis, E.* 'St.Keverne', *E.* × *virgata*) have a strongly arching habit used to best advantage on walls.

Garrya Garryaceae. 18 species, evergreen shrubs and trees native to the Americas. *G.elliptica,* the Silk Tassel Bush from California is a large shrub with leathery, undulate, sea green leaves and long silky grey catkins produced in late winter (particularly long in the cultivar 'James Roof'). This species and the hybrids *G.* × *issaquahensis* and *G.*× *thuretii* are vulnerable to wind scorch, winter wet and prolonged frosts and tend to be grown with some wall protection.

Grevillea Proteaceae. *c*250 evergreen trees and shrubs mostly native to Australia, usually with narrow, semi-rigid leaves and dense terminal clusters of small, tubular flowers with long, exserted styles.Some are near-hardy and will grow outdoors in mild districts given the protection of a south-facing wall, among them *G.alpina* (low-growing, silvery with red and cream flowers), *G.* 'Canberra Gem' (flowers bright pink, waxy, produced throughout the year), *G.juniperina* (bright green, flowers yellow, pink or red), *G.rosmarinifolia* (leaves grey-green, needle-like, flowers pink to red with cream) and *G.* × *semperflorens* (flowers orange-yellow and red tipped with green).

Hibiscus Malvaceae. Over 200 species, herbs, shrubs and trees found in warm regions throughout the world. The hardy species and cultivars do not require wall protection. The genus is listed here, however, because one species, the tender *H.schizopetalus,* is often treated as a wall shrub or even as a climber under glass. It bears hanging, lantern-like flowers with deeply laciniate petals in shades of red and pink along very slender branches. Best tied in to pillars, wires or trellis in conservatories and cool to intermediate glasshouses.

Indigofera Leguminosae. *c*700 species, herbs, shrubs and trees widespread in warm regions, usually with palmately or pinnately compound leaves and narrow racemes or spikes of pea-like flowers. The shrubby species flower freely against south-facing walls on free-draining soils in mild areas. Hard frosts may kill the year's growth to the ground, but plants will usually regenerate quickly, especially if mulched with straw or bracken, producing dense stands of flower-laden stems by summer. Most of the species in temperate cultivation require this treatment and bear flowers in shades of pink, crimson or scarlet. *I.heterantha* (*I. gerardiana*), from the N.W. Himalaya is perhaps the most worthy, growing to 2m against a wall, with fine, grey-downy foliage and packed terminal racemes of pale pink or rose-purple flowers throughout the summer. The tender, pink-flowered subshrub, *I.tinctoria* is the source of true indigo.

Itea Iteaceae. 10 species, evergreen or deciduous trees and shrubs native to E North America and NE Asia. *I.ilicifolia*, from W China, is a small to medium-sized evergreen shrub with slender branches, olive to dark green holly-like leaves and very long, narrow, tassel-like racemes of minute yellow-green flowers in summer. Slightly tender, its lax, semi-scandent stems should be backed by a south-facing wall.

Jovellana Scrophulariaceae. 6 species, subshrubs and shrubs from Chile and New Zealand with pouched, slipper-like flowers closely resembling those of the related *Calceolaria*. *J.violacea*, a compact, Chilean shrub with mauve flowers spotted with violet, may survive outdoors in very mild localities if planted in perfectly draining soil at the foot of a sun-soaked, sheltered wall.

Kerria Rosaceae. 1 species, *K.japonica*, the Jew's Mallow or Japanese Rose, a deciduous, suckering shrub native to China. It forms a dense clump of erect to arching, green, rod-like stems covered in spring with bright yellow flowers. *Kerria* is by no means tender. Its customary use as a wall shrub probably arises from the need to contain and control (by roping together and tying in) its many slender stems. In the open garden, these become lax and prone to wind damage. Reflected heat from walls will also promote earlier and freer flowering and longer, greener stems.

Leptospermum Myrtaceae. 79 species, densely branched evergreen trees and shrubs from Australasia, characteristically with small, narrow, rather rigid leaves often with a red-bronze tint and myrtle-like flowers in shades of white, cream, rose, cerise and deep red. The most commonly grown species is *L.scoparium*, the Tea Tree, a New Zealand native with white flowers; it has spawned numerous cultivars, most of which will thrive outdoors with wall protection, as will many other species in this genus.

Magnolia Magnoliaceae. 125 species, deciduous or evergreen trees and shrubs native to the Americas and E Asia. Two Magnolias are grown as wall shrubs (or trees) – *M.grandiflora*, the magnificent Bull Bay from the South Eastern United States, is a long-established feature of many grand buildings in the British Isles, with large, persistent, glossy dark green leaves and deliciously scented, waxen white blooms. The Chinese *M.delavayi* is less commonly cultivated – an evergreen tree or large shrub (especially where cut back by harsh winters) with very large, oblong-cordate leaves of a leathery sage green and fleshy ivory flowers. This

species is a valuable foliage plant with all the exotic impact of the larger-leaved *Ficus* species.

Mahonia Berberidaceae. 70 species, evergreen shrubs native to North and Central America and East Asia, with tough, prickly, pinnate or 3-parted leaves and terminal racemes or panicles of small flowers in shades of yellow, orange and cream. In cool temperate climates, several of the asiatic species are slightly tender and are planted near walls where protection from harsh winds , snow and prolonged frosts is provided. The site need not be south-facing, indeed some shade is preferable. These include the very robust and rich yellow-flowered *M.acanthifolia, M.napaulensis* and *M.siamensis*, the rigidly erect and regimented *M.lomariifolia* and the smaller and finer *M.confusa* and *M.fortunei*. The asiatic species tend to be strongly erect and scarcely branching; far more complementary to walls are those Mahonias from the SW United States and Mexico of a lower, shrubbier habit and a still more pronounced need for shelter. Among these are *M.fremontii, M.nevinii* and *M.trifoliolata* with beautiful blue-green foliage and short clusters of pale yellow flowers. They require perfectly drained soils and full sun against a south-facing wall.

Michelia Magnoliaceae. *c*45 species, evergreen shrubs and trees native to East Asia. They are closely related to *Magnolia*, usually with smaller, waxy flowers in shades of cream and ivory and often deliciously scented. Three species are sometimes attempted on moist, acid to neutral soils against south-facing walls in very mild regions: *M.compressa*, an erect shrub or small tree with persistent, glossy leaves 5–10cm long and fragrant 5cm diameter flowers ivory stained purple-red in the centre; *M.doltsopa* a small, semi- evergreen tree with large, leathery leaves and 5cm diameter, white, fragrant flowers; *M.figo*, the Banana Shrub, a densely branched evergreen shrub with relatively small, glossy dark green leaves and 3cm diameter ivory flowers tipped or edged in purple-pink and strongly scented of banana flavouring.

Olearia Compositae. 130 species, herbs and evergreen shrubs or trees mostly Australasian, with leathery leaves often white-hairy beneath and daisy-like flowers in white, purple or yellow. This genus contains many 'Daisy Bushes' popular in cultivation, most of which are hardy, withstanding even the harshest saline winds in maritime regions. They do, however, have a marked preference for rather dry, warm soils and sunny locations, outside which their wood fails to ripen adequately and their tough silvery foliage and profuse flowering will deteriorate.

Phygelius Scrophulariaceae. 2 species, evergreen or semi-evergreen shrubs or subshrubs native to South Africa and grown for their erect, pyramidal panicles of drooping, tubular flowers. In cool temperate zones, they are used more or less as herbaceous perennials, the soft annual shoots cut back by frosts to a woody stock: this is particularly the case with the many colourful hybrids grouped as *P.* × *rectus*. The Cape Fuchsia, *P.capensis*, will nonetheless make a slender-stemmed, semi-scandent shrub trained on a sunny wall in a sheltered position, soon attaining 2 metres and covered in summer with scarlet blooms.

Piptanthus Leguminosae. 2 species, evergreen shrubs native to the Himalayas, with dark green stems, narrow, trifoliolate leaves and racemes of showy, yellow, pea-like flowers in late spring. Both *P.nepalensis* with deep green, more or less glabrous leaves, and the silky-tomentose *P.tomentosus* will grow in the open garden, making medium-sized, multi-stemmed shrubs. Away from the shelter of a south-facing wall, their hollow stems may nevertheless be killed off by temperatures of −15°C /5°F or lower.

Pittosporum Pittosporaceae. *c*200 species, evergreen trees and shrubs from the Southern Hemisphere and East Asia. Most of the species in cultivation require some wall protection in zones 8 and under. Of the three most popular, *P.crassifolium* with broad, thick leaves and dark purple-red flowers will grow unprotected, as will the widely cultivated *P.tenuifolium*. Both, however, luxuriate in warm and sheltered positions, as are essential for the third, *P.tobira*, a medium-sized shrub with tough leaves and waxy cream flowers scented of orange blossom.

Prostanthera Labiatae. 50 species, the Mint Bushes, evergreen, strongly aromatic shrubs from Australia with neat foliage and small, two-lipped white, pink, mauve, purple-blue or red flowers in great abundance. Although usually grown in the conservatory or cool glasshouse, they may succeed outdoors in mild localities, given a south-facing wall.

Punica Punicaceae. 2 species, shrubs and small trees widespread in Europe, the Middle East and Southwest Asia. *P.granatum*, the Pomegranate, is grown for its showy scarlet flowers and edible fruit. It will survive as a shrub against a sun-drenched wall in milder locations in zone 8. Its cultivar 'Nana,' a charming dwarf tree with abundant flowers, is somewhat hardier and better suited to cool temperate gardens.

Pyracantha Rosaceae. 7 species, stiffly branched and viciously thorny evergreen shrubs from Europe and Asia, usually with oblong-obovate, dark green leaves, masses of small cream flowers and ornamental fruit in tones of red, orange and yellow. The Firethorns are quite hardy and will thrive as free-standing, if rather rangy, multi-stemmed shrubs; they are traditionally treated as wall shrubs, however, and this is undoubtedly the best way in which to encourage and enjoy a fine display of fruit from late summer to winter. They will take to any wall other than the most sun-baked of southerly aspects and are especially useful for providing a dense, evergreen and decorative covering even on north and east-facing walls. Establish by creating a fan or espalier framework, to which unwanted and over-luxuriant shoots may be trimmed back after flowering. Eventually, a strong, woody structure will build up, requiring little or no tying in and persisting for many years. Virtually all species and cultivars are suitable.

Ribes Grossulariaceae. 150 species, small to medium-sized evergreen or deciduous trees and shrubs, including the flowering and edible currants and the gooseberry. Two ornamentals are grown against walls − *R.speciosum*, the Fuchsia-Flowered Gooseberry, a thorny evergreen from California with small, glossy, lobed leaves and pendulous, deep red flowers which narrow to the long, protruding stamens, and *R.viburnifolium*, again from California, a thornless, lax-stemmed evergreen with glossy, aromatic foliage and short erect

racemes of flesh pink to brick red flowers followed by red fruit. Both are slightly tender, requiring warm soils, full sunlight and shelter from wind. Their slender, semi-scandent stems should be tied in to wires and carefully pruned and/or replaced with new growths to maintain vigour.

Salvia Labiatae. *c*900 species, annual, biennial or perennial herbs, subshrubs and shrubs of cosmopolitan distribution, often aromatic and with spikes of whorled, tubular, two-lipped flowers. With the exception of the Common Sage, *S.officinalis*, most of the shrubby Salvias need the shelter of a south-facing wall in zone 8, with full sun and well drained, warm soils.

Sophora Leguminosae. *c*52 species, evergreen or deciduous shrubs and trees with pinnate leaves and pea-like flowers. The New Zealand Kowhai, *S.tetraptera*, is a small shrub with fine foliage and clusters of showy tubular, yellow flowers. It is usually grown against a south-facing wall in full sun. The related *S.microphylla*, a Chilean native with smaller leaflets, is hardier, but also responds well to wall treatment.

Sutherlandia Leguminosae. 5 species, South African shrubs with rod-like stems, pinnate leaves, slender racemes of pea-like flowers and inflated, bladdery pods. *S.frutescens*, the Duck or Balloon Plant, produces purple-pink to scarlet flowers in summer.

Tibouchina Melastomataceae. 350 species, hairy herbs and shrubs from South America with showy flowers. *T.urvilleana* (*T.semidecandra*), the Glory Bush, is a Brazilian native, a large shrub with velvety leaves and silky, deep purple flowers. It is not hardy, but is sometimes trained on walls in conservatories and cool to intermediate glasshouses.

Vestia Solanaceae. 1 species, an erect, small, evergreen shrub native to Chile with glossy, foetid leaves and nodding, tubular, yellow-green flowers in spring and summer. Plant at the foot of a sheltered wall in sun or semi-shade.

Vitex Verbenaceae. 250 species, trees and shrubs, mostly evergreen with digitately compound leaves and panicles or racemes of small flowers. The two species described here, *V.agnus-castus* and *V.negundo*, hail from the Mediterranean and Middle East to East Asia respectively. In temperate cultivation, they are small to medium-sized, deciduous, tree-like shrubs with attractively gnarled bark and slender, elegant branches. The first, the long-cultivated Chaste Tree, produces strongly aromatic, grey-downy leaves and, in late summer and autumn, slender racemes of fragrant, mauve flowers. The second is larger, with 3–5, not 5–9, leaflets per leaf and lax panicles of lavender flowers, again in late summer. Both require full sun, freely draining, light soils and the shelter of a south-facing wall.

Xanthoceras Sapindaceae. 2 species, small, erect, deciduous trees native to China, often multi-stemmed with yellow wood, pinnate leaves and erect, terminal panicles of Horse Chestnut-like flowers. *X.sorbifolium* (flowers white stained yellow to red at centre) is quite hardy but usually flowers profusely only if given the heat and shelter of sun-drenched walls to ripen its wood and promote bud development.

Pests and Diseases

PESTS

Aphids, including the common greenfly, attack a wide range of ornamental plants both outdoors and under glass. A disagreeable problem associated with infestations of aphids is the presence of honeydew, a sugary substance secreted by most species, which settles on leaf surfaces directly below feeding colonies. This sticky exudation is familiar to car owners who park beneath aphid-infested lime trees during the summer months. Ants are frequently seen feeding on honeydew in close proximity to aphids and, indeed, are known to protect the colonies from predators. Honeydew is a convenient medium for the growth of Sooty Mould fungus which eventually blackens the surfaces of leaves affected by it. In addition to stem-feeding aphids, root-feeding species are occasionally encountered, these are most usually evident when re-potting or potting-on plants under glasshouse conditions.

Control measures. It is particularly important to prevent the serious build-up of colonies of aphids before infestations disfigure and distort leaves and stems. Frequent inspections are the rule, particularly in the early spring months when newly arrived winged females can multiply so rapidly on succulent young growth. Plant-derived insecticides containing derris, nicotine or pyrethrum, include Bioresmethrin, Permethrin and Rotenone. They control by contact with the insects and are regarded as more environmentally friendly than chemical-based insecticides. The latter may include formulations of diazinon, malathion and HCH which are generally more persistent in their action. Other compounds such as dimethoate, heptenophos and menazon are systemic, i.e. absorbed by and translocated throughout the plant, rendering toxic the sap on which the aphids feed. Systemic insecticides have the advantage of being effective over several weeks.

Under glasshouse conditions, fumigation is often a very efficient method of controlling the build-up and spread of aphid populations. As with spraying treatments, repeated applications at 10–14-day intervals may be necessary to maintain insect-free plants.

Woolly Aphis (*Eriosoma lanigerum*) can be troublesome on a range of wall plants including *Cotoneaster* and *Pyracantha*. The aphids, which secrete a protective covering of cotton-wool-like wax, colonize branches and bark crevices resulting in swollen and deformed stems with open lesions through which fungal and bacterial infections may become established. Some cultivars of apple such as 'Blenheim Orange' appear to be particularly susceptible to Woolly Aphis when grown as cordons or espaliers against walls.

Control measures. Small infestations may be treated by painting the colonies with diluted methylated spirit or malathion. More extensive infestations should be controlled by spraying with HCH or a systemic insecticide such as dimethoate, following the pruning out and burning of severely infected stems and branches. Forceful hosing of the colonies with water will considerably reduce the infestations prior to spraying and hold them in check thereafter.

Mealybug (*Pseudococcus* spp.). These well known insect pests of plants in protected cultivation are similar to Woolly Aphis in producing a protective cover of cottonwool-like wax. Honeydew secretions and associated Sooty Mould fungus are features of established colonies. The control measures recommended for Woolly Aphis are suitable. Biological control is also possible by the use of an Australian species of ladybird beetle, *Cryptolaemus montrouzeri*, the adults and larvae of which feed avidly on the mealybugs.

Scale Insects. Several species may be encountered on outdoor plants in Britain and North America including **Peach** or **Brown Scale** (*Parthenolecanium corni*), **Mussel Scale** (*Lepidosaphes ulmi*) and **Horse Chestnut Scale** (*Pulvinaria regalis*). All are sap-feeding insects and it is the female of the species which is apparent as colonies of white to yellow or brown scales, usually 2–5mm in length. Though mobile in the nymph stage, when mature, the females lose their legs and become immobile, feeding by sucking by the plant sap via their stylets. In the outdoor garden, eggs are usually laid in late summer and, following the death of the female, are protected by her persistent scaly skin until the nymphs hatch and emerge to colonize young stems and foliage. Under glass, other species such as **Soft Scale** (*Coccus hesperidum*) and **Hemispherical Scale** (*Saissetia coffeae*), may be encountered attacking climbers and wall shrubs such as *Camellia, Clerodendrum* and *Stephanotis*.

Control measures. Hand removal or brushing of small colonies with dilute methylated spirit or spray malathion is effective. Systemic insecticide sprays should be used on large plants or extensive colonies of mature scales. A parasitic mite, *Metaphycus*, which feeds on the nymph stage of scale insects is a new and promising biological method of control.

Red Spider Mites (*Tetranychus* spp.). In Britain and North America, these pests are usually found under glass attacking a wide range of plants. Hot, dry conditions favour the build-up and spread of the mites, which may vary in colour according to the plants on which they are found. They are particularly mobile and occur in large colonies feeding on plant sap. The first indications of infection are pepperings of small, pale-coloured spots on the upper surfaces of the leaves, followed by a more general discoloration and premature defoliation. The mites are usually found on the undersurface of the leaves but, in severe infestations, they may colonize most parts of the plant above ground .

Control measures. A forceful daily hosing of the undersurface of the leaves will keep the mites at bay. Established infestations may be dealt with by disposing of badly infected plants or foliage and regular spraying with derris or dimethoate. A predatory mite, *Phytoseiulus persimilis*, is increasingly used as a biological control, but regular introductions of the predator are needed. As with all biological controls, this predator cannot be used in tandem with chemical pesticides, the one killing the other.

Glasshouse Whitefly (*Trialeurodes vaporariorum*). Under glass, this insect attacks a range of climbing and wall plants and is particularly difficult to control. The life cycle from eggs to adult can, depending upon temperature, be completed in a matter of 21 days and, as each adult female may produce up to 200 eggs, it will be appreciated how quickly infestations can build up. Adults and larvae normally feed on the undersurface of leaves but their presence may be detected when the foliage is disturbed as the adults take to the air with a distinct circular flight motion. As with aphids, honeydew is secreted as a waste product; this, in turn, may become colonized by Sooty Mould fungus.

Control measures. Because of the rapid life cycle, regular applications of an appropriate insecticide such as pyrethrum, bioresmethrin or HCH, at 10-to 14-day intervals, is necessary, either as a spray or a fumigant. The parasitic species of a chalcid wasp *Encarsia formosa*, is widely used as a method of biological control, but its success depends upon temperatures in excess of 21°C/70°F and of repeated introductions of the wasp during the growing season. Adult whitefly are attracted to the colour yellow and may be ensnared by the use of yellow cards coated with a suitable sticky substance (such as clean engine oil) and suspended in the greenhouse. Carnivorous Butterworts such as *Pinguicula moranensis* may be grown among susceptible plants with considerable benefit.

Tarsonemid Mites, including **Strawberry** and **Cyclamen Mite** (*Tarsonemus pallidus*) and **Broad Mite** (*Polyphagotarsonemus latus*). These minute insects, almost invisible to the naked eye, may be found infesting climbers under glass. Bad attacks can cause stunting and discoloration of leaves and distortion of flowers. The mites may be spread by handling infected foliage and by vegetative propagation of infected plants.

Control measures. Dusting mildly affected plants and foliage with green flowers of sulphur can be useful but it is probably better to remove and burn more seriously infested plants. Vapourizing with flowers of sulphur is effective, but great care should be taken to use only purpose-designed vapourizers which do *not* ignite the sulphur.

Vine Weevil (*Otiorhynchus sulcatus*). This is an increasingly troublesome pest of glasshouse plants. The female weevil is capable of laying several hundred eggs in the compost at the base of potted or border plants, usually during late spring. The white, crescent-shaped, legless larvae, which emerge in about 14 days, feed on roots, tubers, etc. over a period of about 12 weeks. The adults, with their angled antennae, typical of weevils, emerge in summer and autumn under glass and feed after dark on the leaves of a variety of plants.

Control measures. Spray or fumigate against adult stages with HCH and incorporate HCH dust with border or potting compost against larval stages. A microscopic parasitic eelworm *Steinernena bibionis*, is a promising biological control when applied in a spray.

DISEASES

Fire Blight (*Erwinia amylovora*). A bacterium which can be particularly serious on shrubby members of the family Rosaceae. Among wall plants affected are species and cultivars of *Cotoneaster, Pyracantha* and *Chaenomeles*; certain apple and pear cultivars grown as cordons or espaliers are also susceptible. Infection normally occurs during the spring and summer months, via the shoots or even through the flowers. Leaves and flowers are affected, shoots turn brown, as though scorched by fire (hence the common name); leaves wilt and wither but remain attached to the shoot.

Control measures. The removal and burning of affected plants.

Rose Blackspot (*Diplocarpon rosae*). A well known fungal disease confined to roses; most cultivars and some species may be affected. Large brown or blackish coalescing blotches appear on the leaves from late spring and will, in severe cases, cause yellowing of the leaves followed by severe defoliation.

Control measures. With susceptible cultivars, it is advisable to spray with a suitable fungicide, as a preventative measure, at 10-day intervals from late spring until late summer. Prune out early in spring any shoots showing early signs of infection. Sprayings at two week intervals with Captan or the more recent systemic fungicides such as Benomyl should prove effective.

Powdery Mildews. A range of fungal organisms commonly infecting climbing and wall plants in the garden and underglass. Of particular concern are those infecting *Clematis*, rose and peach (*Shaerotheca pannosa*), vines (*Uncinula necator*), Cucurbitaceae (*Spharotheca fulginea*) and apple cultivars (*Podosphaera leucotricha*). Infestations may, depending on weather conditions, be particularly serious, discolouring and distorting leaves and shoots which become covered with a typical white, powdery coating of mycelium and conidial spores.

Control measures. Under glass, good ventilation is essential, combined with regular spraying with Benomyl or Dinocap. In the garden, the early pruning out of affected shoots followed by repeat sprayings of Benomyl or Dinocap at two-week intervals is recommended.

Rose Dust (*Phragmidium mucronatum*) appears in spring as small orange pustules on the branchlets, leafstalks and upper leaf surfaces, followed by a similar infection of the under surface of the leaves.

Control measures. Spray at two-week intervals throughout the growing season using fungicides such as Thiram and Zaneb. Combination sprays may be useful to combat Blackspot, Rust and Powdery Mildew.

Cankers, which may be of fungal or bacterial origin, attack a wide range of woody plants. Typical symptoms include cracked and broken bark leading to extensive lesions prone to secondary infections and which, in the case of apple cultivars, may encourage infestations of insect pests such as Woolly Aphis.

Clematis Wilt (*Ascochyia clematidea*). This fungal organism is probably the main cause of the collapse and dieback of *Clematis* shoots. Occasionally the whole plant is affected at or about flowering time, when the collapse may also be accompanied by a blackening of the shoot tips.

Control measures. Cut back infected plants to a point at or just below ground level; plant with several nodes of the stem bases buried to ensure that following this treatment, new and uninfected shoots will sprout from below ground level. Paint cut shoots with Medo fungicide and spray new growths with an appropriate copper-based fungicide.

VIRUSES

Of the virus-induced diseases which may affect certain climbing plants and wall shrubs, the more common are **Cucumber Mosaic Virus** (occasionally encountered on *Asclepias, Passiflora, Stephanotis* and *Hoya*), **Camellia Yellow Mottle Virus, Tobacco Mosaic Virus** (infecting Solanaceae), **Pelargonium Leaf Curl Virus** and **Wisteria Vein Mosaic Virus**. Destruction of infected plants, control of insect vectors (which may introduce and/or spread viruses), care in selecting uninfected propagation material and hygienic propagating techniques are all the measures that can usefully be taken.

Climbers

A to Z

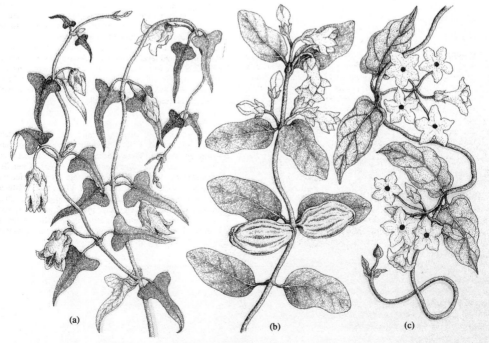

Araujia   (a) *A.angustifolia* (b) *A.sericofera* (c) *A.graveolens*

Temperature Conversion

$$°C = 5/9 \ (°F -32) \qquad °F = 9/5 \ °C +32$$

Celsius	−18°	−10	0	10	20	30	40

Fahrenheit	0°	10	20	32	40	50	60	70	80	90	100

Conversions of Measurements

Length			
	1 millimetre	=	0.0394 inch
	1 centimetre	=	0.3937 inch
	1 metre	=	1.0936 yards
	1 kilometre	=	0.6214 miles

Range of Average Annual Minimum Temperature for each Climatic Zone

Zone	°F	°C
1	< −50	< −45.5
2	−50 to −40	−45.5 to −40.1
3	−40 to −30	−40.0 to −34.5
4	−30 to −20	−34.4 to −28.8
5	−20 to −10	−28.8 to −23.4
6	−10 to 0	−23.3 to −17.8
7	0 to +10	−17.7 to −12.3
8	+10 to +20	−12.2 to −6.7
9	+20 to +30	−6.6 to −1.2
10	+30 to +40	−1.1 to +4.4
11	> +40	> +4.4

Abeliophyllum Nak. (*Abelia* (Caprifoliaceae); Gk *phyllon*, leaf. The foliage of this genus is said to resemble that of *Abelia*.) WHITE FORSYTHIA. Oleaceae. 1 species, a deciduous sprawling shrub to 2m. Shoots tetragonal, tinted maroon at first, becoming warty, glabrous. Leaves to 5cm, opposite, entire, ovate, apex acuminate, rounded at base, minutely downy; petiole to 4mm. Flowers produced before leaves, white, sometimes tinted pink, highly fragrant, in short axillary racemes on branchlets; calyx and peduncle dark maroon; petals to 1.2cm, 4, oblong, notched at apex; stamens 2, anthers yellow. Fruit a nutlet, rounded, winged. Late winter to early spring. Korea. Z8.

CULTIVATION A graceful shrub with slender, arching branches tinted maroon when young and covered by fragrant white blossom in late winter. The foliage appears after the flowers and is not very exciting. Slightly tender, it should be planted against a south-facing wall and used somewhat after the fashion of *Forsythia suspensa*, a shrub it will never match in vigour. Most well drained, fertile soils will suit. Cut back flowered stems by half to two-thirds as soon as all blossom has faded. Propagate by layering in autumn or spring, or by half-ripe cuttings inserted in a propagating case in summer.

A.distichum Nak.
'Roseum': flowers flushed pink.

Abeliophyllum distichum

Acanthocereus (Berger) Britt. & Rose. (From Gk *akantha*, thorn, and *Cereus*, referring to the sharp spines.) Cactaceae. 6 or more species of cacti, mostly shrubs or weakly scandent, one tree-like with trunk to 60cm diam.; stems segmented or not, sometimes rooting at the tips, ribbed; ribs usually 3–5. Flowers funnelform, 12–25 × c6–12cm, nocturnal, white; floral areoles with felt and usually short stiff spines; tube elongate, typically stiff, erect; perianth broad. Fruit globose or ovoid, 4–8cm, red or green, spiny, splitting when ripe, in one species 8–12cm, green, naked, indehiscent; seeds broadly oval, to 4.8 × 3.6mm, black-brown, shiny. Tropical America and the Caribbean region. Z9.

CULTIVATION Large cacti with showy white flowers headily scented at night: several species have climbing stems, notably *A.tetragonus*, and may be tied in to walls or allowed to ramble freely in dry, sunny areas of Mediterranean and subtropical gardens. Otherwise, grow in a heated greenhouse (min. 10–15°C/50–60°F); use 'standard' cactus compost: moderate to high inorganic content (more than 50% grit), pH 6–7.5. Shade in hot weather, maintain low humidity; keep dry from mid-autumn until early spring, except for light misting on warm days in late winter.

A.acutangulus (Pfeiff.) Backeb. & F. Knuth. See *A.tetragonus*.

A.baxaniensis (Karw.) Britt. & Rose. See *A.tetragonus*.

A.colombianus Britt. & Rose (*A.guatemalensis* hort.; ?*A.pitajaya* (Jacq.) Dugand ex Croizat; ?*Cereus pitajaya* (Jacq.) DC.).
Similar to *A.tetragonus* and perhaps not distinct. Shrubby, erect, 2–3m, branching freely from the base; stems 9cm broad, red-brown at first, later shiny green; ribs 3, wing-like; areoles 5cm apart, large; central spines 1–3, 4–5.5cm, very stout; radial spines 5–8, short. Flowers 25cm, white; tube 23.5cm, including the dilated throat; flowering areoles spineless. Colombia.

A.guatemalensis hort. See *A.colombianus*.

A.horridus Britt. & Rose.
Stout shrub; stems 8–10cm diam., somewhat grey-green; ribs 3, or 5–6 on young growth, deeply crenate; areoles 3–6cm apart, large; central spines 1(–2), to 8cm, very stout; radial spines 1–6, to 1cm, conic. Flowers 18–20cm; tube 12cm, including the throat, 4cm broad at apex. Fruit 3.5cm, light red, thick-skinned, spiny, splitting at maturity; pulp red. Guatemala and perhaps Mexico.

A.occidentalis Britt. & Rose.
Similar to *A.tetragonus*. Shrubby, forming dense thickets; stems weak and slender, 4–5cm diam., dull green, often bronzed; ribs 3–5, margins slightly sinuate; areoles 1–3cm apart, brown-felted; spines numerous, equal, to 7cm, tinged yellow. Flowers 14–18cm. W Mexico.

A.pentagonus (L.) Britt. & Rose. See *A.tetragonus*.
?**A.pitajaya** (Jacq.) Dugand ex Croizat. See *A.colombianus*.

A.subinermis Britt. & Rose.
Low shrub, to 1m; stem-segments stout, 5–7cm broad, shining green; ribs 3–4; areoles 3–4cm apart; spines 0 or 6–10, to 1.5cm. Flowers 15–22cm; tube somewhat spiny; outer tepals tinged red, inner tepals white. Fruit globose to short-oblong, 4cm, dull red. S Mexico.

A.tetragonus (L.) Hummelinck (*A.pentagonus* (L.) Britt. & Rose; *A.acutangulus* (Pfeiff.) Backeb. & F. Knuth; *A.baxaniensis* (Karw.) Britt. & Rose; *Cereus pentagonus* L.).
Gaunt shrub with stems to 3m or more, arching to clambering and sometimes rooting at the tips, eventually forming thickets; seg. 30–100×2.5–9cm; ribs 3–5, deep, wing-like. Areoles 2.5–4cm apart; spines 5–8, the longest to 4cm, stout. Flowers 17–25×c10cm; tube to 15cm, pale green. Fruit usually 3–6×2.5–4cm. Summer. Widespread in coastal areas of the southern US. (Florida and Texas), West Indies, Mexico, Venezuela.

Aconitum L. (Classical Latin name derived from Gk *akoniton*, a name used by Theophrastus and Nicander for a poisonous plant growing on sheer cliffs.) MONK'S-HOOD; WOLF'S BANE. Ranunculaceae. About 100 species of annual, biennial or perennial herbs. Roots generally tuberous, occasionally long and clustered. Stems erect to scrambling or scandent. Leaves basal and rosulate or cauline and alternate, ovate to suborbicular, lamina deeply palmately divided into 3–7 lobes or leaflets, themselves more or less lobulate or dentate. Inflorescence a raceme or racemose panicle; pedicels bearing a bracteole; flowers bilaterally symmetric; sepals 5, the most conspicuous part of the flower, petal-like, uppermost hemispheric to cylindric, large, erect, forming a hood ('helmet'); petals 2–10, small, concealed within sepals, uppermost pair with long nectar-secreting spurs projecting into the helmet; stamens numerous. Fruit a group of 3–5 follicles; seeds angled or winged, sometimes with transverse plates or folds. Temperate regions of the Northern Hemisphere. Z6.

CULTIVATION   In addition to the many border perennials familiar as Monk's Hood or Wolf's Bane, *Aconitum* contains several climbing or scrambling species. These are slender, intricate plants with finely cut foliage and, usually, smaller inflorescences than are found in their free-standing counterparts. The trailing Wolf's Banes succeed planted on the edges of shrubberies and woodland gardens where they scramble freely among the surrounding vegetation, or allowed to entwine themselves through trellises and in the stems of larger, woody climbers (i.e. *Parthenocissus*, *Clematis*). They favour a moist, humus-rich soil in part-shade or full sun. Once established, their long tuberous roots should not be disturbed and the plants will require little maintenance other than to cut away dead growth in winter and gently to guide new growth in spring. The crowns should be mulched with garden or mushroom compost in spring and, in cold areas, with straw, bracken or leaf litter in late autumn. All parts are extremely toxic. Propagate by division in autumn, or by seed sown in cold frames.

A.hemsleyanum Pritz.
Roots tuberous. Stems glabrous, scrambling to twining. Leaves ovate, deeply 3–5-lobed more than two-thirds of way to middle, dark green above, distinctly paler beneath, glabrous or sparsely lanate; lobes broadly dentate. Inflorescence a group of widely spreading racemes, long-stalked; pedicels glabrous or sparsely crisped-hairy, particularly toward apex; flowers large, dark purple-blue to indigo; helmet hemispheric-cylindric, downy, sepals not clawed, ciliate; petals 2, long-clawed, spur hooked. Summer. C & W China.

A.japonicum hort. non Thunb. See *A.uncinatum*.

A.reclinatum Gray. TRAILING WOLF'S BANE.
Stem to 3m, slender, weak, trailing or scandent, erect, to 1m. Leaves 10–20cm diam. reniform, deeply 5-cleft, segments cuneate-obovate, acutely coarsely incised above middle. Inflorescence elongate, usually compound, lax; pedicels finely pubescent; flowers white; helmet 1.5×0.5cm, subconical, almost horizontal, elevated dorsally into slender subcylindric projection. Summer. E US (Virginia to Georgia).

A.uncinatum L. (*A.japonicum* hort. non Thunb.) WILD MONK'S HOOD.
Roots tuberous. Stems 60–120cm, ascending, twining or scrambling, thin, weak. Leaves 5–10cm diam., ovate, deeply 3–5-lobed, dark green above, paler beneath, glabrous, lobes trapezoid, broad, sparsely dentate. Inflorescence a short, somewhat umbellate raceme, lax, few-flowered; pedicels clad with long, straight, spreading or deflexed hairs; flowers deep blue; helmet to 2.5×2cm, rounded-conical, lower margin somewhat curved, scarcely beaked; spur inclined, somewhat spiral. Summer. E US (Pennsylvania to Indiana and Kentucky, Virginia, Georgia).

A.vilmorinianum Komar.
Roots tuberous, thick with yellow fibres. Stems 2m, erect below, twining or scrambling above, branched, crisply pubescent above. Leaves broadly ovate, divided into 3 (occasionally 5) leaflets, pale green, sparsely pubescent on veins or glabrous, leaflets lanceolate to ovate, regularly dentate or lobed, tapered to base, distinctly stalked. Inflorescence racemose, flexuous; pedicels glabrous or sparsely crisped-hairy; flowers to 3.75cm, few, indigo, hairy; helmet taller than wide,

rounded at apex, lateral edge of opening concave, beak short, deflexed. Autumn. W & C China.

A.volubile Pall.
Roots tuberous. Stems 45–120cm, downy, twining or scrambling in upper part, thin, weak, to 4m in climbing plants, pilose above. Leaves 3–9 × 5–15cm, suborbicular, ternately lobed, hairy, lobes deeply divided, lobules linear-lanceolate.

Inflorescence 12–20cm, racemose, often single-flowered; pedicels spreading- or somewhat deflexed-pilose; flowers 2–3cm, purple and green or light blue (tinged blue and green); helmet hemispheric-conic, higher than wide, lateral edge of opening concave, beak spreading; spurs short, blunt, bent near apex. Summer–autumn. E Asia (Siberia, Mongolia, China, Japan).

Acridocarpus Guillem., Perrott. & A. Rich. (From Gk *akris*, locust, and *karpos*, fruit; the fruit is said to resemble a locust.) Malpighiaceae. 30 species of trees or shrubs, sometimes climbing. Leaves entire, glabrous or sericeous, often glandular beneath; stipules absent. Inflorescence a terminal or axillary raceme or corymb; calyx 5-lobed; petals 5, yellow, unguiculate, subentire, unequal; stamens 10, filaments short; carpels 3, united in sharply 3-lobed ovary, styles 2–3, elongate, divergent. Samaras 2–3, confluent at base, expanded above into straight or oblique vertical wing thickened on upper margin. Tropical Africa, Madagascar, New Caledonia. Z10.

CULTIVATION *A.natalitius* is a showy climber suited to walls, pergolas and large host trees in semi-shade in subtropical and tropical gardens. In cool regions, it will thrive in a warm glasshouse or conservatory (minimum temperature 10–13°C/50–55°F) in tubs or beds of sharply drained, medium-fertility loam-based soil. Admit bright filtered light and water freely when in full growth. New stems will require tying-in to wires or trellis; prune out older, exhausted branchlets after flowering. Increase by cuttings inserted in a heated case.

A.natalitius A. Juss.
Climber; branches tomentose becoming glabrous. Leaves 7.5–12.5 × 2.5–5cm, alternate, oblong-obovate, obtuse, glabrous, coriaceous, glossy above. Racemes terminal, 15cm, elongate, rusty-tomentose; flowers pale yellow; petals 1cm, crenate; ovary 2-styled. Fruit broadly winged, wings obliquely obovate, 1.5cm. Summer. S Africa (Natal).

Actinidia Lindl. (From Gk *aktis*, a ray, alluding to the styles which radiate like spokes of a wheel.) Actinidiaceae. Some 40 species of scandent shrubs, mostly dioecious, deciduous, with solid or lamellate pith. Leaves alternate, simple, dentate. Flowers solitary or in axillary cymes, usually white; sepals and petals usually 5, rounded; stamens numerous, anthers often purple or yellow. Fruit a many-seeded berry. Summer. E Asia.

CULTIVATION Twining shrubs grown for their foliage, to some extent their flowers and, in several cases, for their edible fruit. In China, where they are known as *yang-tao*, they have been cultivated since at least AD 770. *A.deliciosa*, the Kiwi Fruit, or Chinese Gooseberry, has egg-shaped, bristly fruit, with translucent green flesh perfumed rather like a strawberry and tasting like a muscat grape. It is also a handsome ornamental with downy young growth and, in summer, cup-shaped white flowers. It was introduced to Britain by Robert Fortune in 1847. More important was its introduction to New Zealand in 1906, where it soon became a major crop. It is also grown in subtropical and warm temperate regions of France, Italy, Australia, South Africa, Israel, the US, Chile and Japan. When dormant, it is known to withstand temperatures of –8°C/18°F, although young growth will suffer severe damage at only –2°C/29°F. To fruit well, *A.deliciosa* requires winter chilling to induce flower development (600–1100 hours below 7°C/45°F), a frost-free period of growth of 8–9 months, and a long, warm and sunny summer, to ripen fruit. Vines begin to bear fruit 2–4 years after planting and may continue to produce for 40 years and more. Male and female plants are required for pollination; where space is limited, plant a female on to which a small male branch has been grafted. Pollination is by insects, or by hand when grown under glass.

In cool-temperate climates, most *Actinidia* species are probably better known as ornamentals – strongly twining climbers used as wall plants or scrambling through old trees. The leaves of *A.kolomikta* emerge chocolate and lime green, their tips beautifully splashed with cream and pink; male plants are reputed to show better variegation, especially on slightly alkaline soils. Some species, such as *A.kolomikta* and *A.polygama*, attract cats, and should be protected from their attentions when young. The foliage of the Silver Vine, *A.polygama*, bronzed when young, later develops silvery or creamy variegation. Both withstand temperatures of at least –17°C/1°F.

Plant all species in deep and well drained loamy soils, rich in organic matter and preferably neutral or, in the case of *A.deliciosa*, slightly acidic. *Actinidia* grows well in part shade, but if cultivated for fruit, site in full sun with shelter from wind which will snap and bruise young growth and cause wind scar in the fruit. Where necessary, prune ornamentals in winter.

In colder climates, *A.deliciosa* requires the protection of the cool glasshouse (min. 7°C/45°F), if grown for fruit. Plant in the dormant season into the greenhouse border or in large pots of medium-fertility loam-based mix. Cut back to 30cm/12in. after planting, and train on a strong trellis or wires; create an open framework by trimming back the shoots when the vine has reached the required height and training the laterals horizontally, stopping them when they fill the allocated space. Fruit production begins in the third year, on laterals that emerge from the main framework. Restrict these to seven nodes beyond the fruit, and remove any subsequent sublaterals. Feed weekly during the growing season. Thin established plants in winter, and renew three-year-old fruiting laterals by cutting back to a dormant bud. Kiwi fruit are very sensitive to ethylene, and must be stored apart from fruit which produce it. Under commercial conditions, Kiwi fruit has a potential storage life of nine months at freezing point and with relative humidity of 90%; domestically, 4–6 weeks post-harvest storage is optimal for after-ripening and development of flavour.

Propagate cultivars from semi-ripe cuttings taken in late summer, in a closed case with bottom heat of 20–25°C/68–77°F – also by layering in winter. Sow seed in spring or autumn; seedlings are variable and in *A.deliciosa* appear to be predominantly male. Commercially, selected cultivars are grafted (cleft or whip-and-tongue grafts) on seedling rootstocks.

In temperate climates, *Actinidia* is largely free from serious pests and diseases. In warmer regions, especially in fruit-producing areas, they may be attacked by leafroller caterpillars, greedy scale, thrips, passion-vine hopper and rootknot eelworm and may suffer from botrytis (*Pseudomonas viridiflava*), bacterial blossom rot (*Sclerotinia* spp.) and *Phytophthora*.

A.arguta (Sieb. & Zucc.) Planch. ex Miq. TARA VINE; YANG-TAO.
Twining to 10m. Branchlets glabrous, rarely hairy at first. Pith white to pink-brown, lamellate. Leaves to 8–15 × 4–8cm, broadly ovate to ovate-oblong, base cordate to rounded, apex briefly acuminate, margins serrate, membranous to papery, mid-green, glabrous or somewhat hairy beneath, especially on veins or in vein axils. Flowers to 2.5cm diam., in axillary umbel-like racemes, white, fragrant; anthers deep red-purple. Fruit to 2.5cm, oblong to subglobose, fleshy, yellow-green, edible. Temperate E Asia. 'Ananasnaya': very hardy, vigorous; flowers attractive, fragrant; fruit small in large clusters. 'Issai': self-fertile. 'Meader Female': female clone, to be pollinated by 'Male' or 'Meader Male'. 'Podsnaja': late-ripening, fruit sweet. 'Rannaja': early-ripening (i.e. mid to late summer), fruit sweet. 'Uroshainaja': fruit very sweet, produced in abundance even by young plants. var. **arguta**. Leaves 8–12 × 4.5–7.5cm, elliptic-ovate to broadly ovate, base rounded to subcordate, thin-textured, glabrous or with veins hairy beneath. Inflorescence somewhat hairy. China, Korea, Japan. var. **cordifolia** (Miq.) Dunn (*A. cordifolia* Miq.). Leaves 4–9 × 5–10cm, broadly ovate, base cordate, papery, veins bristly. Inflorescence brown-tomentose. Japan, Korea. var. **rufa** (Sieb. & Zucc.) Maxim. (*A.rufa* (Sieb. & Zucc.) Planch.) New growth rusty-tomentose. Leaves 6–10 × 5–10cm, ovate to broadly ovate, base cordate to truncate, membranous, ultimately glabrous or with hairs in vein axils beneath. Japan, Korea. Z4.

A.callosa Lindl.
Twining to 8m. Branchlets ultimately glabrous, initially grey or rusty-tomentose with conspicuous, long yellow lenticels. Pith orange, lamellate. Leaves to 5–13 × 3–7cm, ovate to oblong, apex acuminate, rounded to obliquely cuneate at base, finely toothed, papery, wholly glabrous or hairy in vein axils. Flowers to 2.5cm diam., white or cream-white, fragrant, solitary or in axillary cymes; anthers yellow. Fruit to 2.5cm diam., oblong-ovoid, green, spotted grey or red-brown and tinged red. China to Java. Z7.

A.callosa var. *henryi* Maxim. See *A.henryi*.
A.chinensis hort. non Planch. See *A.deliciosa*.
A.cordifolia Miq. See *A.arguta* var. *cordifolia*.

A.coriacea (Finet & Gagnep.) Dunn.
Semi-evergreen, twining to 10m. Branchlets red-brown, more or less glabrous. Pith solid, white or yellow. Leaves to 10–16 × 3–5cm, oblong to ovate-oblong or lanceolate, apex acuminate, base cuneate or subcordate, sharply and finely dentate, the teeth with red-tinted glandular tips, thickly leathery, glabrous, dark above, pale green beneath. Flowers to 2cm diam., solitary or in axillary racemes, red-tinted or pink with pale edges; filaments red, anthers yellow. Fruit to 2cm diam., brown spotted white, ovoid to globose. China. Z6.

A.deliciosa C.S. Liang & A.R. Fergusson (*A.chinensis* hort. non Planch.) KIWI FRUIT; CHINESE GOOSEBERRY; YANGTAO.
Twining to 10m. Shoots red-pubescent. Pith lamellate, white-yellow. Leaves to 6–20 × 5–17cm, broadly ovate to elliptic, apex rounded, sometimes emarginate, base cordate, finely dentate, ciliate, densely white stellate-pubescent beneath. Flowers to 4cm diam., cream-white becoming yellow with yellow anthers, borne on axillary branches. Fruit to 6.5cm, oblong-globose or ellipsoid, densely brown-bristly, flesh green, edible. China. var.*setosa* from Taiwan is densely

bristly throughout with thinner-textured ovate leaves with an acute to short-acuminate apex. 'Blake': fast-cropping and self-fertile; recommended for smaller gardens. 'Tomuri': stems red, hairy; leaves oval, dark green; flowers less abundant, large, cream, produced late in season. Commercially, female cvs like 'Bruno' (fruit elongated) and 'Hayward' (fruit large) are used, with male pollinators such as 'Male', 'Matua' and 'Tomuri' included in plantations. Z7.

A. × fairchildii Rehd. (*A.arguta* × *A.deliciosa*)
Garden hybrid intermediate between parents.

A.gagnepainii Nak. See *A.kolomikta* var. *gagnepainii*.

A.hemsleyana Dunn.
Twining to 10m. Sterile branches long, arching, densely bristly at first and narrow-leaved. Fertile branches lateral, shorter, more finely hairy and bristly. Pith lamellate. Leaves 8–15(–20) × 3–5(–10)cm, oval-oblong to lanceolate-oblong, base cuneate, thin-textured, glabrous or with rusty hairs along veins beneath, dark green above, blue-green beneath. Flowers green-white. Fruit to 2.5cm, oblong-ovoid, brown-pubescent to glabrous. E China. Z6.

A.henryi (Maxim.) Dunn (*A.callosa* var. *henryi* Maxim.).
Rampant twiner. Branchlets striped, brown-villous at first, bristly. Pith off-white, lamellate. Leaves 8–14 × 3–6.5cm, oblong-ovate, apex acuminate, base usually cordate, margins serrulate, thin-textured, dark green above, paler beneath, glabrous except for finely bristly veins. Flowers to 1.5cm diam., white, in axillary clusters with red-hairy stalks; anthers yellow. China (Yunnan). Z7.

A.holotricha Finet & Gagnep.
Tall twiner. Branches lax, brown-bristly at first. Pith white, lamellate. Leaves 9–13 × 6–8cm, broadly oblong-ovate, apex acuminate, base rounded to truncate, margins sharply denticulate, thin-textured, veins bristly throughout. Flowers to 2cm diam., yellow; anthers yellow. Fruit poorly known. SW China. Z7.

A.kolomikta (Rupr. & Maxim.) Maxim.
Weakly climbing to 7m. Branchlets brown, more or less smooth. Pith brown, lamellate. Leaves to 6–15 × 3–12cm, ovate to ovate-oblong, apex acuminate, base cordate, serrate, membranous, usually glabrous, pale green beneath, splashed and banded bronze to chocolate, white and pink above, especially in male plants. Flowers to 1.5cm diam., white, fragrant; anthers yellow. Fruit to 2.5cm diam., ovoid-globose, yellow-green, sweet, edible. Temperate E Asia. 'Arctic Beauty': very hardy; leaves to 12cm, emerging purple-bronze, maturing pink, white and green; flowers small, white, fragrant. 'Arnold Arboretum': fruit sweet, small. 'Krupnoplodnaya': very hardy; leaves red in summer. These females can be pollinated by male 'All-Purpose'. var. **gagnepainii** (Nak.) Li (*A.gagnepainii* Nak.) Leaves larger, usually with some bristly hairs on veins throughout, erroneously said to lack colourful variegation. W China. Z4.

A.lanceolata Dunn.
Pith brown, lamellate. Leaves to 6.5cm, papery, ovate-lanceolate or lanceolate, puberulent above, white-stellate beneath. Flowers to 1cm diam., green, in axillary cymes; anthers yellow. Fruit to 1cm, ovoid. China. Z6.

A.melanandra Franch.
To 7m. Branchlets tinted red-brown, initially with fine white hairs and a blue tint. Pith off-white, lamellate. Leaves to 6–9 × 3–4cm, ovate to ovate-oblong or oblong-lanceolate, apex acuminate, base rounded or cuneate, margins serrulate, thin-textured, glabrous above, blue-green and glabrous except for tufts of rusty hairs in vein axils beneath. Flowers to 2.5cm diam., white, solitary or in axillary cymes; filaments black-red, anthers purple. Fruit to 3cm, ovoid, glabrous, pruinose, red-brown. Japan, China. Z6.

A.polygama (Sieb. & Zucc.) Maxim. (*A.repanda* Honda; *A.volubilis* (Sieb. & Zucc.) Miq.). SILVER VINE.
Twining to 5m. Branchlets glabrous. Pith white, solid Leaves 7–12 × 5–8cm, ovate or ovate-oblong, apex acuminate, base acute or rounded to subcordate, serrulate, glabrous above, usually bristly on veins, silvery white to creamy yellow throughout or above only, in patches or flecks. Flowers to 3cm, solitary or in clusters of 2 or 3, white, fragrant; anthers yellow in typical plants. Fruit to 2.5cm diam., ovoid-globose, apex somewhat beaked, yellow, translucent, sour. Temperate E Asia. var. **lecomtei** (Nak.) Li. Differs from the typical plant in leaves glabrous beneath, anthers brown, not yellow. W China. Z4.

A.purpurea Rehd.
Differs from *A.arguta* in leaves longer, narrower. Flowers to 1.5cm diam. Fruit ovoid-oblong, flushed purple, sweet-tasting. China. Z6.

A.repanda Honda. See *A.polygama*.

A.rubricaulis Dunn.
Tall climber. Branchlets red-brown, glabrous, with conspicuous lenticels. Pith solid, off-white. Leaves 8–10 × 1.2–3.8cm, oblong-lanceolate to oblong-ovate, base cordate, apex acumi-nate, margins sparsely and often glandular-serrate, thick-textured, glabrous, dark green above, pale beneath. Flowers to 2cm diam., off-white, solitary and in clusters; anthers yellow. Fruit to 1.8cm, ovoid, yellow. SW China. Z6.

A.rufa (Sieb. & Zucc.) Planch. See *A.arguta* var *rufa*.
A.rufa var. *parvifolia* Dunn. See *A.melanandra*.

A.strigosa Hook.f. & Thoms.
Twiner. Branchlets red-brown with pale lenticels, bristly and brown-pubescent at first. Pith white, lamellate. Leaves 7–13 × 4–7cm, ovate to oblong-ovate, apex acuminate, base rounded, oblique, margins coarsely toothed, tough-textured, veins bristly beneath. Flowers to 2cm diam., white, paired or few in cymes; anthers yellow. India (Sikkim, E Himalaya). Z7.

A.tetramera Maxim.
Tall twiner resembling *A.polygama* but differing from all species in its 4-parted flowers. Branchlets grey to rusty brown. Pith lamellate, brown. Leaves 5–10 × 2.5–4cm, narrowly oblong-ovate, apex acuminate, base obliquely cuneate, serrulate, tough-textured, glabrous or with sparsely hairy veins beneath, often flecked white or pink. Flowers 4-merous, white tinted pink; anthers yellow. Fruit to 2cm, ovoid, brown dotted white, glabrous. W China. Z6.

A.venosa Rehd.
Tall vine. Branchlets purple-brown with pale lenticels, soon glabrous. Pith white, lamellate. Leaves 5–15 × 3–6cm, ovate to ovate-oblong, apex acuminate, base rounded to cordate, margin serrulate, thin-textured, dark green above, paler beneath, finely hairy at first, veins conspicuously and prominently reticulate. Flowers yellow-white in tawny-hairy cymes. Fruit to 1.5cm diam., ovoid, brown, glabrous. W China. Z6.

A.volubilis (Sieb. & Zucc.) Miq. See *A.polygama*.

Actinostemma Griff. (From Gk *aktis*, ray, and *stemma*, wreath, i.e. stamens.) Cucurbitaceae. 1 species, a monoecious, scandent herb. Base sometimes woody. Stems partially pubescent; tendrils simple or bifid. Leaves 5–10 × 3–7cm, hastate, cordate, coarsely serrate, orbicular to reniform, acuminate, occasionally 3–5-lobed, petiolate. Male inflorescence a panicle or raceme, to 12cm; female flower solitary; calyx tubular, segments 5, slender, glandular, linear-lanceolate; corolla green-yellow, tubular, segments narrow, 5–6mm; stamens 5, free; ovary unilocular, stigmas 2. Fruit ovoid, softly spiny, about 1cm diam.; seeds 2–4, compressed obovoid. India to E Asia. Z10.

CULTIVATION An ally of the cucumber climbing by tendrils and cultivated for the culinary oil expressed from its fruit. This plant is sometimes found in botanic gardens where it is grown under glass or as an annual in sheltered situations and used in demonstrations of economic plants.

A.lobatum (Maxim.) Maxim. See *A.tenerum*.

A.tenerum Griff. (*A.lobatum* (Maxim.) Maxim.). GOKIZURU.

Adenia Forssk. Passifloraceae. Some 93 species of herbaceous perennial shrubs. Stems climbing or sprawling, sometimes shrubby, with tendrils, thorns or spines, usually arising from a massively swollen caudiciform rootstock. Leaves simple, entire, lobed or palmately divided, base with up to 2 glands; stipules minute. Inflorescence axillary, cymose; bracts minute; flowers usually unisexual, campanulate to tubular or infundibular, glabrous usually green or yellow; hypanthium cupular or tubular; sepals usually 5, overlapping, persistent; petals usually 5, usually fimbriate or laciniate; disc glands 5, near base of hypanthium, ligulate; male flowers with usually 5 stamens, anthers basifixed; female flowers usually smaller than male flowers, ovary superior, placentas 3–5, ovules numerous, styles 3–5. Fruit a 3–5-valved capsule, stipitate, pericarp fleshy to coriaceous, yellow to green or bright red. Africa to Asia.

CULTIVATION Unusual caudiciform shrubs grown for their swollen bases crowned with tangled thorny branches; their habitually stark appearance is relieved, sometimes only for a few months each year, by bright green palmate leaves and small pale flowers resembling *Passiflora*. They have become popular as indoor bonsai. Pot in an extremely gritty loam-based medium. Water sparingly except when in leaf or when it is desirable to initiate growth. Minimum temperature 15°C/60°F in full sunlight and dry airy conditions. Propagate by seed. Stem cuttings will succeed but, as with so many woody caudiciforms, may fail or take years to produce the attractive caudex. Scale and mealybug may be pests under glass.

A.digitata (Harv.) Engl.
Climber to 3m. Leaves to 18×17cm, deeply 3–5-lobed to -foliolate; leaflets to 15×4cm, 3–5-lobed or entire, ovate or linear, acute to rounded; petiole to 9cm, basal glands 2. Inflorescence 5–20-flowered in males, 1–10-flowered in females, peduncles to 7cm; male flowers tubular-infundibular, hypanthium to 3.5× 4mm, calyx tube to 12mm, lobes to 11mm, ovate to oblong, fimbriate, petals to 12mm, lanceolate, filaments to 9mm, anthers to 6mm; female flowers tubular-infundibular, hypanthium to 4×4mm, calyx tube to 8mm, lobes to 7mm, ovate to oblong, petals to 7mm, linear to lanceolate, gynophore to 4mm, ovary to 6mm. Fruit to 5.5×3.5cm, ovoid to oblong, pericarp bright yellow to red; seeds to 8mm. Africa.

A.fruticosa Davy.
Shrub to 6m, glabrous. Leaves to 8×8cm, simple to 3–5-foliolate; leaflets to 6 × 4cm, ovate or orbicular, subacute to rounded, entire; petiole to 5cm basal gland, 1. Inflorescence solitary in leaf-axils or grouped on short shoots, peduncle to 1cm, 2–5-flowered in males, 1–3-flowered in females; male flowers campanulate, hypanthium to 2.5 × 4.5mm, sepals to 9mm, lanceolate, petals to 8mm, oblong to lanceolate, serrulate, filaments to 4mm, anthers to 6.5mm; female flowers similar, sepals to 7mm, petals to 4mm, gynophore to 3mm, ovary to 4mm. Fruit 1–2 per inflorescence, to 20 × 18mm, subglobose. S Africa.

A.pechuelii (Engl.) Harms.
Bushy shrub to 1.5m, mostly leafless, lacking tendrils, pruinose, glabrous, thorny. Leaves to 6×2cm, coriaceous, entire to shallowly 3-lobed, ovate-oblong to lanceolate; petiole to 2mm, basal glands 2. Inflorescence 1–3-flowered in males and females; male flowers campanulate, hypanthium to 2×4mm; sepals to 5mm, elliptic to oblong, petals to 5mm, lanceolate, serrulate, filaments to 2mm, anthers to 4.5mm; female flowers similar, sepals to 4mm, petals to 2.5mm, gynophore to 1mm, ovary to 2mm. Fruit 1 per inflorescence, to 2mm, subglobose to ellipsoid. S Africa.

A.spinosa Davy.
Thorny shrub to 1.5m. Leaves to 3.5 × 3cm, subcoriaceous, simple, broadly ovate to elliptic, obtuse, entire, basal glands 1 or 2; thorns to 4cm. Flowers solitary or few on short shoots, peduncle to 5mm, 2–6-flowered in males, 1–3-flowered in females; male flowers tubular-campanulate, hypanthium to 3 × 4mm, sepals to 18mm, lanceolate, petals to 10mm, lanceolate, serrulate, filaments to 5.5mm, anthers to 5mm; female flowers similar, hypanthium to 1.5mm, sepals to 8mm, petals to 3.5mm, gynophore to 2mm, ovary to 5mm. Fruit 1–2 per inflorescence, to 2.5 × 1.5cm, subglobose. S Africa.

Adenocalymma Mart. ex Meissn. (From Gk *aden*, gland and *kalymma*, covering: the leaves and flowers often have prominent dark glands.) Bignoniaceae. 34 species of lianes. Stems 4-ribbed; branches terete. Leaves usually trifoliolate, terminal leaflet often replaced by simple tendril. Inflorescence an axillary or terminal raceme, bracteate, bracts usually deciduous; calyx cupular, truncate to bilabiate, sometimes denticulate, peltate-glandular; corolla yellow, tubular-funnelform to tubular-campanulate, slightly pubescent outside; anthers glabrous; ovary narrow-cylindric, lepidote or puberulent; ovules 2-seriate; disc pulviniform. Fruit an oblong capsule, valves parallel, slightly compressed, woody, lenticellate; seeds in 2 wings, or without wings, thick, corky; wings brown at base, hyaline at edges. Mexico to Argentina, mostly in Brazil. Z10.

CULTIVATION As for *Clytostoma*.

A.alboviolaceum Loes. See *Mansoa hymenaea*.

A.apurense (HBK) Sandw.
Leaflets 3, oblong-elliptic, shortly mucronate, base acute, short-pilose beneath; leaves on young branches simple. Flowers to 6cm; calyx glabrous; corolla 5.7cm, limb *c*3cm diam., densely pubescent outside. Brazil.

A.calderonii (Standl.) Seib. See *A. inundatum*.
A.ciliolatum Blake. See *Mansoa hymenaea*.

A.comosum (Cham.) A. DC.
Stems punctate. Leaflets 3, ovate to lanceolate, shorter and wider than *A.longeracemosum*; leaves, bracts, calyx lobes glandular. Racemes densely bracteate; flowers 5cm diam. at mouth, bilabiate, upper lip 2-lobed, lower lip 3-lobed. Brazil.

A.dusenii Kränzl. CIPO-CRUZ-AMARELO.
Branches pubescent, glabrescent. Leaflets 15 × 1.5–5.5cm, ovate or oblong-elliptic, apex rounded to acuminate and mucronate, base rounded to subcordate, sometimes cuneate, midrib pubescent or glabrous above, sparsely pubescent at least on midrib beneath, leathery; pseudostipules 5–7mm, acute, glandular. Inflorescence 12cm diam., densely pubescent; bracts 6–11mm; calyx truncate or irregularly lobed, puberulent and glandular; corolla 4.5–6cm, cream to yellow, pubescent outside and inside lobes, limb to 3.5cm diam. Capsule 14×5cm, oblong, acute, densely pubescent and glandular, median line conspicuous; seeds in wing. 1.6–2.5 × 2.5cm. Brazil.

A.floribundum DC. See *Cuspidaria floribundum*.
A.friesianum Kränzl. See *Arrabidaea corallina*.
A.grenadense Urban. See *A.inundatum*.
A.hintonii Sandw. See *A.inundatum*.
A.hosmeca Pittier. See *Mansoa hymenaea*.

A.inundatum Mart. ex DC. (*A.calderonii* (Standl.) Seib.; *A.grenadense* Urban; *A.hintonii* Sandw.).
Stem 10cm diam.; branches usually black, glabrous to lepidote, lenticellate. Leaflets 4.5–17 × 2.2–8.8cm, 2-3 ovate to ovate-elliptic, apex acute to acuminate, base rounded, truncate or subcordate, membranous to papery, grey, shining. Inflorescence bracts 1 × 1cm; calyx 1–2 × 5–8 × 4-6mm, 5-lobed, bilabiate; corolla 2.5–6.9 × 0.9–1.9cm at mouth, tube 6–7×4–5mm, lobes 1–2cm, tips relfexed, puberulent outside. Capsule 9.5–27 × 2.5–3.1 × 4.1–2.2cm, oblong, rounded, not flattened, rugose, grey; seeds 1.7–2.1 × 5.1–7.6cm; wings thin. Mexico to N Venezuela, Brazil, Grenada.

A.laevigatum Mart. ex DC. non Bur. & Schum. See *A.marginatum*.
A.laevigatum Bur.& Schum. non Mart. ex DC. See *Mansoa hymenaea*.

A.longeracemosum Mart. ex DC. Leaflets to 25cm, usually 3, oblong-lanceolate, apex acuminate and mucronate, base attenuate, obtuse; petiole to 2.5cm. Raceme, rachis, pedicels, calyx, corolla puberulent-velutinous; calyx 5-toothed; bracts glandular; corolla golden, lobes incurved. Brazil.

A.macrocarpum Donn. See *Mansoa hymenaea*.

A.marginatum (Cham.) DC. (*A.laevigatum* Mart. ex DC. non Bur. & Schum.).
Leaflets 2–13 × 2.5–8cm, elliptic to ovate-elliptic, apex acuminate or rounded, emarginate, base rounded to cordate, leathery or rigid-papery, margin cartilaginous; pseudostipules *c*5mm, elliptic, glandular. Inflorescence densely pubescent; bracts 1mm; calyx truncate, denticulate, glandular-indumentose; corolla 3–5.5cm, densely pubescent outside, limb to 5cm diam., papillose-puberulent inside. Fruit 14–35 × 2–3.3cm, tetragonal, crooked, glabrescent. Brazil to Paraguay, Uruguay, N Argentina (subtropical). var. **apterospermum**

Sandw. Leaflets usually 8 × 4.5cm, rounded or emarginate at apex. Capsule 14 × 3.3cm; seeds not in wing. Brazil (tropical Atlantic).

A.obovatum Urban. See *Mansoa hymenaea.*
A.portoricense Stahl. See *Arrabidaea chica.*
A.splendens Bur.& Schum. See *Mansoa difficilis.*

Adlumia Raf. ex DC. (For John Adlum (1759–1836), US soldier and grape-breeder, he developed the most important of the early American grapes, 'Catawba', at his nursery in Georgetown, D.C.) Fumariaceae. 1 species, a herbaceous, biennial vine, climbing to 5m or more. Leaves pale green, delicate, fern-like, 3–4-pinnate, lowermost leaves to 25cm or more; stem leaves far smaller, ultimate pinnae less than 1cm long, irregularly lobed; petioles aiding climbing. Flowers pale pink or white, similar to those of *Dicentra*, bisexual, 1.5cm, narrow-cordate to ovate, in 5–10cm-long, pendulous axillary panicles; petals 4, spongy, in pairs, outer pair pouched basally, acute, inner pair enclosing stamens and ovary; stamens 6, united at base into a tube attached to corolla, apically united into 2 bundles. Fruit an oblong capsule containing few seeds, enclosed by persistent corolla. Summer. NE America, Korea. Z6.

CULTIVATION   Found growing in moist woodland, usually in mountainous areas, *A.fungosa* is an attractive biennial vine cultivated for its delicate foliage and drooping panicles of small, spurred pink or white flowers. It is hardy to −17°C/1°F, but needs shelter from strong winds and protection from full sun. Grow in lightly shaded wild gardens or woodland gardens where the soil is moist and rich in humus and the atmosphere cool and humid. It forms a low bushy plant during the first year, and climbs to 3–4m/10–13ft during the second year. Provide support, for example light brush wood, or grow through other shrubs. Propagate from seed sown in early spring; it will self-sow where growing conditions are suitable.

A.fungosa (Ait.) Greene ex BSP (*A.cirrhosa* Raf.; *Fumaria fungosa* Ait.). CLIMBING FUMITORY; MOUNTAIN FRINGE; ALLEGHENY VINE.

For illustration see Fumariaceae.

Agapetes D. Don ex G. Don f. (From Gk *agapetos*, lovable, referring to the attractive flowers.) Ericaceae. About 95 species of evergreen, scandent, semi-epiphytic shrubs; twigs smooth or hispid, lenticels sometimes present. Leaves alternate, subsessile, coriaceous. Flowers solitary and axillary or in several-flowered cymes, beautifully coloured; calyx tube spheric to hemispheric, 5-winged or 5-ribbed; corolla tubular or goblet-shaped to campanulate, pentagonal, limb with 5 short erect or reflexed lobes; stamens 10, anthers spurred. Fruit a berry, 5-winged. E Asia to N Australia (NE India, SW China, Burma, New Guinea, Fiji, New Caledonia & NE Australia). Z9.

CULTIVATION   These small shrubs succeed best in cool glasshouses or conservatories in light shade and buoyant, humid conditions. Where frosts occur only very rarely, they can be attempted outdoors in the shelter of a wall. Pot tightly in an acidic, leafy mixture with coarse bark. Water and syringe plentifully throughout the growing season; keep plants rather drier as the flowers open (usually in winter). The smaller species (especially *A.rugosa*, *A.serpens* and their hybrid offspring) can be grown in baskets where their arching branches hung with brilliant flowers can be seen from below. *A.macrantha*, perhaps the most beautiful of the genus, can be trained against walls in conservatory beds. Both its dark foliage and cool candy-pink bells barred with blood red commend it. Propagate by air-layering.

A.affinis (Griff.) Airy Shaw (*A.glabra* (Griff.) C.B. Clarke). Shrub, erect, short. Leaves strongly pseudo-verticillate, 10–20 × 3–5cm, oblong-lanceolate, rounded at base, entire or obscurely crenate, glabrous, coriaceous. Flowers in clusters in leaf axils; inflorescence minutely pubescent; peduncles long; corolla cylindric, straight, then inflated, to 1.5cm, pale green to white, or brick red. Himalaya to Assam.

A.buxifolia Nutt. Shrub to 1.5m, evergreen; branches spreading, pilose. Leaves 2.5–3 × 1.2cm, elliptic-oblong to ovate-oblong, crenate in distal part, subacute at apex, cuneate at base, bright glossy green, coriaceous. Flowers in leaf axils, solitary or in pairs or rarely in corymbs; pedicels slender, 1cm, pilose; corolla greatly exceeding calyx, tubular, 2.5cm, bright red, waxy. Fruit white. Spring. Bhutan.

A.glabra (Griff.) C.B. Clarke. See *A.affinis.*

A.'Ludgvan Cross' (*A.rugosa* × *A.serpens*.) Intermediate between parents, branches less rigid than in *A.rugosa*, less pendulous than in *A.serpens*. Leaves to 3.5cm, ovate, acuminate. Flowers carmine red with white V-markings. Fruit mauve. Garden origin.

A.macrantha Benth. & Hook. f. (*A.variegata* var. *macrantha* (Benth. & Hook. f.) Airy Shaw). Shrub to 2m, erect to arching; stems minutely pubescent when young, glabrescent with age with lenticels. Leaves

8–12 × 2–3cm, laurel-like, lanceolate-elliptic, acuminate at apex, cuneate at base, entire, smooth, mid-vein prominent above; petiole 4–6 × 3mm. Flowers in fascicles of 3–7 on trunk and older branches, pendulous; pedicels 3cm; calyx rounded, 7mm, white, lobes 3mm; corolla cylindric-urceolate, 4.5 × 2.5cm, white to pink, conspicuously V-marked in dark red, lobes white or green, 1cm, strongly reflexed. Winter. NE India. Differs from *A.variegata* in its larger flowers.

A.mannii Hemsl. Shrub to 80cm, erect or sprawling; twigs minutely pubescent. Leaves 1.5–2 × 0.6–0.8cm, elliptic, obtuse to retuse at apex, cuneate at base, entire. Flowers generally solitary in upper leaf axils; pedicels 6mm, mostly glabrous; calyx 3.5mm, green, pubescent, lobes triangular; corolla tubular, slightly contracted at mouth, 1cm, pale green to off-white with darker green mouth. Fruit globose, 12mm, dark red, fleshy. Winter–spring. Burma, Assam, Yunnan.

A.moorei Hemsl. Shrub to 2.5m, erect; stems glabrous. Leaves 7 × 3cm, lanceolate-elliptic, acute at apex, broadly truncate to rounded at base, entire, mid vein prominent beneath; petiole 3–4mm, sparsely pubescent Inflorescence racemose, erect, 12–20-flowered; peduncle 5mm, densely brown-scaly; pedicels 8–12mm, hairy; calyx 8mm, green, flushed red where exposed, tube rounded, limb slightly angled; corolla brilliant orange-red, tips green on opening but becoming yellow then red with age, 2.5cm, tube cylindric, convex above, strongly angled, 16mm, lobes triangular-acuminate, curved outwards, 13mm, exterior pubescent at tip. Spring. Burma.

A.obovata (Wight) Hook. f.
Shrub, low and spreading, to 60cm; stems coarsely brown-setose. Leaves 1.4–1.8 × 0.5–0.6cm, spathulate, rounded at apex, cuneate at base, smooth; petiole 1.5mm. Flowers solitary in upper leaf axils; pedicels 1.5–2mm, glabrous; calyx 3mm, tube rounded, lobes deltoid; corolla campanulate, 6mm, green flushed dull red, glabrous, tube moderately angled, 4mm, lobes reflexed in upper half, 3mm. Fruit black, fleshy. Winter. Assam (Khasi Hills).

A.rugosa (Hook.) Sleumer (*Pentapterygium rugosum* Hook.).
Shrub, stiffly erect, 30–90cm. Leaves 7–10cm, ovate-lanceolate, acuminate at apex, somewhat cordate at base, dentate, deep green above, paler beneath, flushed red when young, very rugose above. Inflorescence racemose, axillary, few-flowered, pendulous; corolla 5-angled, white with purple marbling or deep red bands between angles, contracted and tinged green at mouth. Fruit globose, 8mm, red to purple. Spring. Khasi Hills.

A.serpens (Wight) Sleumer.
Shrub, 50–70cm, but can be trained to 3m, with a thickened base, then lenticellate; stems arching or pendulous, elongate, ferruginous-hispid. Leaves rather crowded, 1.8–2cm, lanceolate to oblong-ovate, margins revolute, dark green sometimes flushed purple above, paler beneath; petiole 1–2mm. Flowers solitary or rarely in 2s or 3s, distributed along stem in leaf axils, numerous, pendulous; calyx winged, pale green sometimes flushed or edged in red; corolla 2cm, bright red with darker crimson V-shaped markings, tube slightly inflated,

lobes triangular, recurved, 3mm. Fruit globose, 12mm, white flushed purple, darkening with age, soft. Winter–spring. Nepal, Bhutan, N Assam. 'Nepal Cream': flowers ivory.

A.setigera (Wallich) D. Don ex G. Don.
Shrub. Leaves to 15 × 7cm, lanceolate, somewhat cuneate at base, acute to acuminate at apex, shortly stoutly petiolate to sessile. Inflorescence lateral, of corymbose racemes, many-flowered, rather densely glandular-setose and minutely pubescent; calyx lobes subulate, 3–4mm; corolla 2.5cm, red, cylindric, distinctly curved or oblique, lobes short, triangular. Winter. India (Pundua Mts).

A.speciosa Hemsl.
Shrub to 1m+, glabrous throughout; base and rootstock swollen. Leaves crowded, 6–11 × 3–4.5cm, lanceolate to broadly oblong, subcordate at base, acute at apex, deep green, slightly glossy, coriaceous. Inflorescence racemose, strongly contracted, from upper leaf axils; pedicels to 3cm; calyx 3–4mm; corolla distinctly 5-angled, 3–4cm × 1.2–1.5cm, crimson with darker V-shaped markings, lobes recurved, 7mm, green or tinged yellow. Winter. Probably Burma.

A.variegata (Roxb.) G. Don.
Shrub, rather large, glabrous throughout; branches long, vigorous. Leaves mostly crowded near branch tips, 15–20cm, broadly lanceolate, acute to acuminate at apex, tapered to base, dentate, dark green above, paler beneath; veins prominent, somewhat reticulate beneath; petiole very short. Inflorescence of pendent axillary corymbs, on old wood; peduncles red; corolla 2.5cm, tubular-campanulate, pale red or rarely yellow-green with deeper red transverse and longitudinal markings. Winter. Assam. *A.macrantha* differs principally in its larger flowers of a clearer pink.

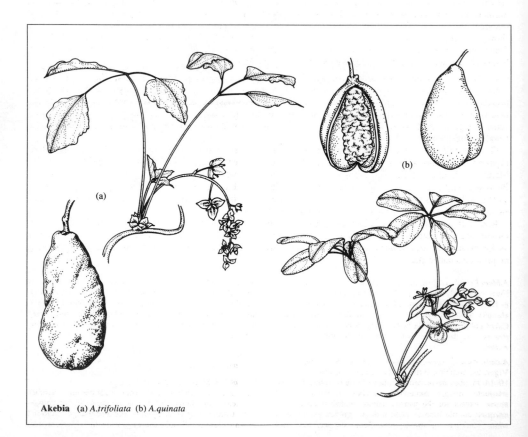

Akebia   (a) *A.trifoliata* (b) *A.quinata*

Akebia Decne. (Latinized form of *akebi*, the Japanese name for these plants.) CHOCOLATE VINE. Lardizabalaceae. 2 species of evergreen or deciduous twining, ultimately shrubby perennial climbers. Leaves alternate, digitate, composed of 3 to 5 leaflets. Flowers unisexual: male and female flowers in the same pendulous axillary raceme, the larger, pistillate flowers at the base, the smaller, staminate ones at the tip; petals absent; sepals 3–4, rounded, petaloid, chocolate brown to maroon-red or deep purple. Fruits fleshy, ovoid-oblong, violet or purple; seeds black or red-brown. Japan, China, Korea. Z5.

CULTIVATION Cultivated for their elegant foliage and dark flowers. They are fast growing (particularly *A.quinata*, which can become invasive) and will thrive on a trellis or pergola, trained against a wall or fence, or allowed to ramble through other plants. *Akebia* requires a moisture-retentive and well drained soil but is unfussy as to pH. They can be grown in full sun or partial shade, and although hardy to –20°C/–4°F when mature, benefit from winter protection when young. Seed requires stratification prior to germination under glass. Stem cuttings require bottom heat and frequent misting or high humidity and can be slow to root.

A.lobata Decne. See *A.trifoliata*.

A.×pentaphylla Mak. (*A.quinata × A.trifoliata*.)
Leaflets 4 or 5 (occasionally 6 or 7), oval to ovate, bright green, shallowly crenate or entire. Flowers slightly fragrant, intermediate in form and colour between parents: male flowers stalked at flowering, female flowers 1.4–4cm wide. Spring. Japan. A natural hybrid, also arising in cultivation.

A.quinata Houtt.
Fast-growing, semi-evergreen or deciduous. Leaflets 3–5cm, 5, glabrous, oblong or ovate, notched at the apex, otherwise entire, dark green above, blue-green beneath; petioles 7–12cm, slender. Flowers strongly vanilla-scented; males 4–15 per raceme, 0.5–1cm wide, sepals pale plum purple, reflexed, females usually 2, 2–3cm wide, sepals 3 or 4, dark chocolate to maroon, pedicel longer than in male. Fruit 5–10cm, ovoid-oblong, dark purple, pruinose, containing numerous red-brown or black seeds embedded in white pulp. Spring. China, Korea, Japan.

A.trifoliata (Thunb.) Koidz. (*A.lobata* Decne.).
Deciduous climber to 9m. Leaflets 3–6cm, 3, ovate to broadly elliptic, margin shallowly lobed or, rarely, entire, apex notched, glossy emerald green. Flowers unscented: males 7–20 per raceme, to 0.5cm wide, appearing stalkless at flowering, sepals reflexed, pale purple, females 2 or 3, 1.5–2cm wide, sepals spreading or reflexed, dark purple. Fruit 7–13cm, ovoid-oblong, pale purple, containing numerous black seeds embedded in white pulp. Spring. China, Japan.

Allamanda L. (For F. Allamand (1735–*c*1795), a Swiss physician and botanist who collected plants in Surinam and sent seed of this plant to Linnaeus.) Apocynaceae. 12 species of evergreen erect or, more usually, scandent shrubs. Leaves whorled, alternate or opposite, entire, base with axillary glands. Flowers large and showy, in terminal cymes; calyx leafy, lobes 5, lanceolate; corolla funnelform, tube narrow, limb 5-lobed, flared; stamens inserted on corolla, free, included; ovary single-celled, ovules many. Fruit a globose or oblong, bivalvate, dehiscent, capsule covered with spines. Tropical America. Z10.

CULTIVATION In subtropical gardens *Allamanda* species are grown as cover for pergolas, pillars and fencing. Although mature specimens may survive several degrees of frost, in cooler climates they need the year-round protection of a glasshouse or to be overwintered in pots under glass. Occurring in mangrove swamp and on lowland river banks, *A.cathartica* will grow as a climber or sometimes as a small tree, and is valued for its handsome foliage and striking yellow flowers. The more shrubby *A.schottii* is also valued for its prickly fruit, used in floral arrangements.

Grow in full sun, but with shade from the strongest summer sun, in a well drained but moisture-retentive, high-fertility, loam-based mix with additional leafmould, screened well rotted manure and coarse sharp sand. Maintain a humid but buoyant atmosphere; water plentifully when in growth but keep almost dry in winter. Provide a winter minimum temperature of 13–15°C/55–60°F. Encourage a bushy habit by pinching out young stem tips. Provide support and tie in as growth proceeds. Prune in late winter by cutting back the previous year's stems to 1–2 nodes and remove old, weak and straggling growth.

Root soft stem tip cuttings in late spring/early summer in equal parts sharp sand and leafmould in a shaded closed case with bottom heat at 21°C/70°F. Also by ripewood cuttings. Graft more weakly growing species such as *A.blanchetii* on to *A.cathartica* 'Hendersonii'. Propagate *A.schottii* by seed. Whitefly and red spider mite may be problems under glass.

A.blanchetii A. DC. (*A.purpurea* hort.). PURPLE ALLAMANDA.
Erect or weakly climbing. Young branchlets hairy. Leaves 8–12cm, usually in whorls of 4, oblong or obovate-oblong, abruptly acuminate, downy above, more densely so beneath. Calyx pubescent; corolla 6–9cm long, 5–6cm across at limb, rose-purple, darker in throat, tube not basally swollen. S America.

A.cathartica L.COMMON ALLAMANDA; GOLDEN-TRUMPET.
Vigorous, climbing shrub to 16m. Leaves in whorls of 3–4, 10–14cm, obovate-lanceolate, apex obtuse or subacute, base attenuate, margin somewhat undulate, leathery, glossy above, except for the usually villous midrib. Calyx lobes unequal; corolla limb to 12.5cm diam., golden yellow with white markings in throat, tube 3cm, slender, base not swollen, lobes obovate with rounded tips. S America. 'Grandiflora': flowers freely produced, exceptionally large. 'Hendersonii': flowers orange-yellow with white spots in throat, exterior tinged bronze, lobes thick and waxy. 'Nobilis': leaves large and strongly whorled; flowers very large, pure gold.

A.neriifolia Hook. f. See *A.schottii*.
A.purpurea hort. See *A.blanchetii*.

A.schottii Pohl. BUSH ALLAMANDA.
Erect, glabrous shrub to 1.5m. Branches sometimes clambering. Leaves in whorls of 2–5, oblong, apex long acuminate-acute. Corolla deep golden-yellow streaked orange-red to rich brown within; corolla tube short and wide, to 1.25cm, swollen

at base, limb to 5.5cm diam. S America. Commonly confused with *A.cathartica*, from which it may be distinguished by the neater habit, and rather broad and shallow flowers with orange or red-brown tints, particularly in the throat.

A.violacea Gardn. & Fielding. See *A.blanchetii*.

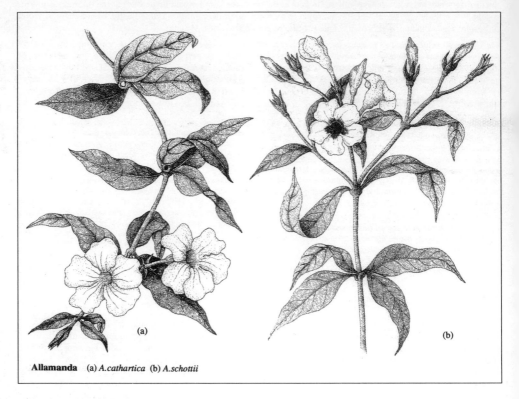

Allamanda (a) *A.cathartica* (b) *A.schottii*

Aloe L. (From the Gk name, allied to Heb. *allal*, bitter, or Arab. *alloch*). Liliaceae (Aloeaceae). About 325 species of perennial herbs, shrubs or trees, stemless or with thin, clambering stems or well developed trunks, branched or unbranched. Leaves usually in rosettes, occasionally in an open spiral, rarely in 2 or 3 ranks, sessile, the base clasping the stem, thickened, often very succulent, mostly hard-toothed or spiny at the margins and sometimes on the surface, which is uniform in colour or blotched. Flowers in lateral or terminal racemes or panicles, on often very elevated scapes; pedicels short or long; perianth usually red, yellow or orange, tubular, tepals 6, outer segments free to base or connate into a tube, apices acute to obtuse, straight or, more usually, spreading to recurved, inner segments sometimes free, usually dorsally adnate to the outer segments for about half their length; style slender, filaments and style lengthening, the 3 inner filaments lengthening before the 3 outer, anthers and stigma usually exserted; ovary oblong, usually green, 3-sided. Fruit an oblong to globose, papery or woody capsule. S Africa, Tropical Africa, Madagascar, Arabian Peninsula, Cape Verde Is. Z9.

CULTIVATION The genus *Aloe* is large and diverse, containing small tufted plants, medium-sized shrubs, massive rosette plants and candelabra-like trees. It is unsurprising, then, that some of its members should have developed a loosely scandent habit. These are slender-stemmed plants of the bush and forest margins where they require the support of surrounding vegetation or sprawl over rocks and soil.

In Mediterranean and subtropical gardens, the following two climbing Aloes can be encouraged to scramble through shrubs and trees, tied into trellis-work or wires on walls, or wound around pillars. They grow well on all but the dampest soils and are ideally suited to baked, sunny and starved conditions where their succulent foliage (finer than that of most Aloes) and brilliant flowers will provide interest throughout the year.

Under glass or in the home or conservatory, pot firmly into any moderately fertile, mineral-based soil that is sufficiently porous to allow free drainage – coarse sand, crushed brick, perlite and other additions will assist. Small quantities of organic matter (leafmould, coir or garden compost) may be incorporated provided its breakdown will not sour the potting residue, in which the Aloe should be left undisturbed for several years at least.

Provide full sun and ventilate fully whenever weather permits. Tie in to trellis or wire netting on walls, rafters and pillars. In spring and summer, plants should be thoroughly soaked whenever they dry out; reduce water to a minimum during the winter months (winter minimum temperature 7–10°C/45–50°F). Vigorously growing plants benefit from a bimonthly liquid feed. Increase by stem cuttings or offsets. Sometimes affected by scale insect and mealybug.

A.ciliaris Haw. CLIMBING ALOE.
Climber, stem slender, to 5m, clothed with the ciliate or auriculate remains of the sheathing leaf bases. Leaves distant, borne on the terminal 30–60cm of the stems to 10–15 × 1.5cm, spreading to recurved, linear-lanceolate, long-acuminate, flat to slightly channelled above, convex beneath, margins white-toothed. Inflorescence, usually unbranched, to 30cm; pedicels to 5mm; perianth scarlet, green tinged with yellow at the mouth, to 30mm, outer segments free for 6mm, inner segments free; anthers and stigma exserted to 4mm. S Africa (Cape Province).

A.tenuior Haw.
Rootstock large, subtuberous below, somewhat woody above, especially at ground level. Stems few to several, branched, 1–3m, mature stems usually bare below the lax terminal rosette, climbing, or supported by bushes, or spreading to arching in the open. Leaves to 15 × 1.5cm, linear-lanceolate, thin to slightly fleshy, glaucous-green, basally sheathing, the sheaths obscurely green-lined, flat becoming slightly channelled above, convex beneath, margins white, very narrow, teeth minute, white. Inflorescence to c30cm, unbranched or with 1–2 short branches; racemes cylindric, slightly tapered, rather laxly flowered, about equalling the peduncle in length, about 15cm; pedicels to 5mm; perianth yellow, 11–14mm, cylindric, outer segments free for less than half their length, inner segments free; anthers and stigma exserted 4–6mm. S Africa (Cape Province,Transkei).

Ampelopsis Michx. (From Gk *ampelos*, grape, and *opsis*, appearance, due to its resemblance to the grape vine, *Vitis*.) Vitaceae. About 25 species of deciduous shrubs or woody vines. They differ from *Vitis* in their bark, which is not frayed, and their white, not brown pith, and from *Parthenocissus* in their tendrils, which lack holdfasts. Tendrils often present, opposite the leaves. Leaves simple or compound. Flowers usually 5-merous, cymose, small, tinged green; calyx saucer-shaped, shallowly lobed, scarious; stamens erect and well developed in male flowers, shorter and usually obsolete in females; pistil surrounded at base by a 4-lobed cupulate disc, reduced and sterile in male flowers. Fruit a thinly fleshed, 1–4-seeded berry. N America, Asia.

CULTIVATION   These vigorous climbers are useful for clothing sunny or partly shaded walls or pergolas, the larger species, such as *A.chaffanjonii*, with good autumn colours in reds and yellows, are particularly striking when trained to cascade from the lower branches of large trees or high stumps in parts of the garden where they can grow unconfined. Smaller species, such as *A.orientalis*, with a lax shrubby habit, will scramble through large shrubs or can be grown in large containers. *Ampelopsis* climbs by coiling tendrils, although large plants frequently cannot support the weight of their foliage and will need tying in.

They are grown primarily for their foliage, and for the yellow, orange or deep blue berries which ripen only in hot summers followed by a mild autumn. *A.aconitifolia* is valued for the light texture of its finely divided leaves, the slower-growing *A.megalophylla* is remarkable for the very large, pinnate leaves and leaflets. *A.brevipedunculata*, with luxuriant hop-like foliage, is particularly attractive when bearing masses of blue-green to deep blue fruits, which it does more readily if confined at the root; var. *maximowiczii* produces a wide variety of leaf shapes. The leaves of the less vigorous *A.brevipedunculata* 'Elegans', sometimes grown as a house plant, are splashed with white and pink, complemented by the pink young shoots.

With the exceptions of the slightly tender *A.cantoniensis* and *A.brevipedunculata* 'Elegans', most are extremely winter-hardy, especially if given a long hot summer to ripen their wood. *A.humulifolia*, *A.cordata* and *A.aconitifolia* are grown in regions where winter temperatures frequently fall below −25°C/−13°F. Plant in a warm, sheltered position in a deep, moderately fertile loamy soil in sun or part shade. *A.brevipedunculata* 'Elegans' gives better and more persistent variegation in part shade. Keep within bounds by pruning back the young growth in late winter or early spring to within 1–2 buds of the main framework to build up a spur system. Propagate species by seed sown outside in autumn, or stratify in damp sand for six weeks at or slightly below 5°C/40°F and sow in spring. Propagate cultivars by leaf bud cuttings in mid summer: treat with rooting hormones and root in a closed case with bottom heat. Greenwood or semi-ripe cuttings taken in summer may also succeed. Vine weevil sometimes troubles container-grown plants.

A.aconitifolia Bunge (*Vitis aconitifolia* (Bunge) Hance; *Vitis dissecta* Carr.).
Vine; stems slender, young shoots glabrous. Leaves very variable, palmately 3–5-parted, 5–12cm diam., deep glossy green above, paler beneath, central leaflet sessile; leaflets 2.5–7.5cm, lanceolate to rhombic, deeply coarsely dentate to 3–5-lobed, fresh green, glabrous above, with tufted pubescence in vein axils beneath; petiole 1–5cm. Inflorescence of numerous forked cymes. Fruit 5–6mm diam., rounded-obovate, blue at first, turning yellow or dull orange to brown. Late summer–early autumn. N China, Mongolia. var. **glabra** Diels. Leaves glabrous, generally 3-parted, segments lobed or dentate. Z4.

A.aegeriophylla (Bunge) Boiss. See *A.vitifolia*.

A.arborea (L.) Koehne (*A.bipinnata* Michx.; *Vitis arborea* L.; *Cissus arborea* (L.) Gray). PEPPER VINE.
Vine, high-climbing; shoots flexuous, rather angular, slender, tinged purple, more or less glabrous; tendrils slender, forked, sometimes lacking on bushy plants. Leaves 10–20cm, broadly deltoid, 2–3-pinnate, dark green and glabrous above, downy on veins beneath at first, becoming glabrous; leaflets 1.2–4.5 × 0.8–3cm, ovate to rhombic, acute, at apex, cuneate at base, subsessile or shortly petiolate, deeply dentate, teeth few, large, triangular. Flowers in panicles much shorter than leaves, in compact subumbellate clusters on each principle fork. Fruit 8mm diam., dark purple. Summer. E US (Virginia inland to Illinois, S to Florida, Texas & Mexico). Z7.

A.bipinnata Michx. See *A.arborea*.

A.bodinieri (Lév. & Vaniot) Rehd. (*A.micans* Rehd.; *Vitis bodinieri* Lév. & Vaniot; *Vitis flexuosa* var. *wilsonii* hort.; *Vitis micans* (Rehd.) Bean; *Vitis repens* Veitch).
Robust vine to 6.5m; shoots often tinged purple on sunny side when young, glabrous. Leaves 6–12cm, 3-lobed, often shallowly so, rounded to triangular-ovate, shallowly cordate to truncate at base, acute at apex, coarsely triangular-dentate,

glittering green above, pale or somewhat glaucous beneath, glabrous throughout; petiole 4–7.5cm, tinged purple. Inflorescence crowded, in branching clusters; peduncle slender, 2.5–5cm. Fruit 4–5mm diam., flattened-globose, dark blue. Summer. C China (Hupeh, Sichuan). var. *cinerea* Rehd. Leaves grey-tomentose. Z5.

A.brevipedunculata (Maxim.) Trautv. (*A.heterophylla* var. *amurensis* Planch.; *Cissus brevipedunculata* Maxim.; *Vitis davidiana* (Carr.) Nichols.; *Vitis heterophylla* Thunb.).
Vine, climbing vigorously; young shoots roughly hairy. Leaves 5–15 × 5–15cm, 3-lobed or occasionally 5-lobed, side lobes spreading, cordate at base, coarsely mucronate-crenate, dark green and very sparsely pubescent above at first, setose beneath; petiole 0.75cm to length of lamina, hairy at first. Inflorescence once or twice forked, each fork terminated by a cyme. Fruit 6–8mm diam., amethyst purple to bright blue. Summer; fruits September–October. China, Japan, Korea, E Russia. Treated by some authors as a variety of *A.glandulosa*. var. *maximowiczii* (Reg.) Rehd. (*Vitis heterophylla* var. *maximowiczii* Reg.; *Vitis heterophylla* Thunb.; *A.heterophylla* (Thunb.) Sieb. & Zucc. non Bl.). Young shoots glabrous or slightly downy; leaves very variable, broadly cordate and unlobed to deeply 3–5-lobed, glabrous or slightly downy beneath. Fruit porcelain blue. China, Japan, Korea. Z4. 'Citrulloides' (var. *citrulloides* (Dipp.) Bail.; *A.citrulloides* (Dipp.) Lebas; *Vitis citrulloides* Koch): Leaves deeply and narrowly 5-lobed, some of the lobes lobed again. 'Elegans' (var. *elegans* (Koch) Bail.; *Vitis elegans* Koch; *Vitis elegantissima* Jaeger; *A.tricolor* hort.; *A.variegata* hort.): The form commonly cultivated as a pot plant; smaller; shoots tinged pink; leaves splashed pink, white, green or yellow. Z9.

A.brevipedunculata var. *citrulloides* (Dipp.) Bail. See *A.brevipedunculata* var. *maximowiczii* 'Citrulloides'.
A.brevipedunculata var. *elegans* (Koch) Bail. See *A.brevipedunculata* var. *maximowiczii* 'Elegans'.

A.cantoniensis (Hook. & Arn.) Planch.
Vine, climbing high. Leaves pinnate or somewhat bipinnate with lowest pinnae bearing 3–5 leaflets and upper ones entire; leaflets ovate to ovate-oblong, serrate, laterals more or less oblique and rounded or obtuse at base, terminal leaflet 3–7 × 1.5–3cm, acute at base, subcoriaceous, glabrous, glaucous beneath, distinctly petiolulate. Inflorescence corymbose; peduncle often tortuous, 4–8cm. Fruit ovoid-globose, black tinged blue. S China to Peninsular Malaysia. Z9.

A.chaffanjonii (Lév.) Rehd. (*Vitis chaffanjonii* Lév. & Vaniot; *A.watsoniana* Wils.).
Similar to *A.megalophylla*. Vine, glabrous throughout. Leaves to 30cm, pinnate, lustrous green above, claret purple beneath, brilliantly coloured in autumn, smooth; leaflets 3.5–11 × 2–5cm, 5–7, ovate to oblong, rounded to broadly tapered at base, long-acuminate at apex, sparsely dentate. Fruit to 8mm diam., red turning black. China (Hupeh). Z5.

A.citrulloides (Dipp.) Lebas. See *A.brevipedunculata* var. *maximowiczii* 'Citrulloides'.

A.cordata Michx. (*Cissus ampelopsis* Gray).
Vine, climbing high; bark warted, glabrous or very slightly downy; tendrils forked, few or absent on fertile branches. Leaves 6–12cm, unlobed or shallowly lobed, ovate-deltoid, acutely serrate, broadly truncate to subcordate at base, acuminate at apex, glabrous or nearly so except at base; petiole long, downy. Inflorescence a slender-stalked, repeatedly forked panicle, 4–8cm. Fruit 7–10mm diam., blue or slightly tinged blue-green. Summer. E & C US (Iowa to Kansas S to South Carolina & Florida). Z4.

A.delavayana Planch. (*Vitis delavayana* (Planch.) Franch. ex Bean).
Vine; stems swollen at nodes, tinged pink and hairy when young. Leaves palmately 3–5-lobed or 3–5-parted, leaflets 3.5–10 × 2–3.5cm, narrowly ovate, tapered to both ends, coarsely dentate, rather rough above, pubescent at least on veins beneath

when young, central leaflet short-stalked, lateral leaflets sessile, asymmetric, sometimes lobed on lower side and oblique at base; petiole tinged pink. Fruit small, dark blue. W China. Z5.

A.engelmannii hort. ex Rehd. in Bail. See *Parthenocissus quinquefolia* var. *engelmannii*.
A.glandulosa var. *brevipedunculata* auct. See *A.brevipedunculata*.
A.hederacea (Ehrh.) DC. See *Parthenocissus quinquefolia*.
A.henryana (Hemsl.) Rehd. in L.H. Bail. See *Parthenocissus henryana*.
A.heterophylla (Thunb.) Sieb. & Zucc. non Bl. See *A.brevipedunculata* var. *maximowiczii*.
A.heterophylla var. *amurensis* Planch. See *A.brevipedunculata*.
A.himalayana Royle. See *Parthenocissus himalayana*.
A.hoggii Nichols. See *Parthenocissus tricuspidata*.

A.humulifolia Bunge (*Cissus davidiana* Carr.; *Vitis davidiana* (Carr.) Nichols.).
Vine to 6.5m; shoots often tinged purple on exposed side when young, glabrous. Leaves 6–12cm, 3–5-lobed with rounded sinuses, rarely unlobed, rounded to triangular-ovate, shallowly cordate to truncate at base, acute at apex, coarsely triangular-dentate, lustrous bright green above, white tinged blue beneath, thick and rather firm, glabrous; petiole 4–7.5cm, tinged purple. Inflorescence slender-stalked, crowded, in branching clusters. Fruit flattened-globose, 4–5mm diam., pale yellow becoming pale blue. Summer; fruits October. N China. Z5.

A.japonica (Thunb.) Mak. (*A.serjaniifolia* Bunge; *Paullinia japonica* Thunb.; *Vitis serjaniifolia* (Reg.) Maxim.).
Vine, creeping; stems slender, young shoots glabrous; roots tuberous. Leaves ternately 3–5-parted to pinnate, 5–12cm, dark green above, pale glossy green beneath, glabrous; leaflets 2.5–7.5cm, 3–5, lanceolate, sparsely to coarsely dentate, the lowest pair themselves pinnately divided; rachis broadly winged. Fruit 6mm, pale violet-blue with darker spots. Summer; fruits September to October. China, Japan, Korea. Z7.

A.leeoides (Maxim.) Planch. (*Vitis leeoides* Maxim.).
Woody vine; branches glabrous, marked with lenticels; tendrils bifid. Leaves 12–30cm, ternately 2–3-pinnate, more or less glabrous; lowest leaflets ternately parted or lobed, others ovate to oblong, acuminate at apex, acute at base, sparingly adpressed-dentate, short-stalked. Inflorescence large. Fruit globose, red. Summer. Japan, Ryukyu Is., Taiwan. Z7.

A.lowii Cook. See *Parthenocissus tricuspidata* 'Lowii'.

A.megalophylla (Veitch) Diels & Gilg (*Vitis megalophylla* Veitch).
Vine, climbing vigorously, 10–12m, glabrous throughout; shoots somewhat glaucous when young. Leaves 45–60 × 35–50cm, bipinnate, or pinnate above, pinnae 7–9 on larger leaves, lowest 1–2 pairs again pinnate, terminal leaflet 5–15 × 2.5–7.5cm, ovate to ovate-oblong, coarsely mucronate-dentate, deep green above, strongly glaucous beneath. Inflorescence sparse, slender, branched, each branch terminated by a 10–15cm cyme. Fruit top-shaped, 6mm diam., dark purple, ripening black. Summer. W China. Z5.

A.micans Rehd. See *A.bodinieri*.

A.orientalis (Lam.) Planch. (*Cissus orientalis* Lam.; *Vitis orientalis* (Lam.) Boiss.).
Laxly bushy shrub or vine; shoots slightly ribbed, glabrous; tendrils few. Leaves variable, pinnate to bipinnate or biternate; leaflets 2.5–7.5 × 1.5–5cm, usually 9, ovate, rhombic or obovate, tapered to base, coarsely dentate above, dull dark green above, paler grey-green beneath, glabrous throughout, or sometimes with minute tufts of hair in vein axils beneath. Inflorescence cymose, long-stalked; flowers 4-parted. Fruit rounded top-shaped, 6mm diam., pale red. Asia Minor, Syria.

A.quinquefolia (L.) Michx. See *Parthenocissus quinquefolia*.
A.saint-paulii hort. ex Rehd. See *Parthenocissus quinquefolia* var. *saint-paulii*.

A.sempervirens hort. ex Veitch. See *Cissus striata*.
A.serjaniifolia Bunge. See *A.japonica*.
A.tricuspidata Sieb. & Zucc. See *Parthenocissus tricuspidata*.
A.variegata hort. See *A.brevipedunculata* var. *maximowiczii* 'Elegans'.
A.veitchii hort. See *Parthenocissus tricuspidata* 'Veitchii'.

A.*vitifolia* (Boiss.) Planch. (*Cissus vitifolia* Boiss.; *A.aegeriophylla* Bunge; *Vitis aegeriophylla* (Bunge) Boiss.; *Vitis persica* Boiss.).
Close to *A.bodinieri* but wholly glabrous and lacking tendrils. Shoots erect, weakly striate. Leaves 4–7cm broad, entire to obscurely 3-lobed, broadly deltoid to ovate, broadly cuneate to somewhat truncate at base, irregularly coarsely dentate with acuminate triangular teeth, shortly petiolate. Fruit 3–5mm diam., globose, black tinged blue. Iran, Turkestan to NW Himalaya. Z6.

A.watsoniana Wils. See *A.chaffanjonii*.

Amphicarpaea Elliott ex Nutt. HOG PEANUT. (From Gk *amphi*, both, and *karpos*, fruit, referring to the dimorphic fruit.) Leguminosae (Papilionoideae). 3 species of annual or perennial, herbaceous, twining vines. Leaves trifoliolate, petiolate; stipules persistent, lanceolate, papery; leaflets elliptic to ovate, occasionally unequal at base. Flowers dimorphic: papilionaceous flowers in axillary racemes to 20cm long; pedicels to 1cm, with basal ovate bracts; sepals 5, forming a tube at base; corolla deep red, purple, light mauve or white, standard ovate to rounded, clawed, wings auriculate, clawed; stamens 9, united for half their length; apetalous flowers lower on plant, smaller than papilionaceous flowers; stamens 1–2; style reflexed. Fruit of flowers on upper part of plant linear-oblong, laterally compressed, 3–4-seeded; fruit of flowers on lower part of plant often subterranean, fleshy, strigose; seeds 1. Africa, Asia, N America.

CULTIVATION *A.bracteata* occurs in cool, moist, woodland habitats from Quebec to Montana as far south as Texas and Florida. It is a variable species well suited to the wild garden and is sometimes grown in collections of native plants and in conservation plantings. It is also sometimes included in botanical collections, especially those with an economic or historical bias; the subterranean fruit and fleshy roots are very nutritious and were once a valuable food source for Native Americans, especially in the Missouri valley. Grow in moist, humus-rich soils in shade. Propagate by seed, or by division.

A.*bracteata* (L.) Rickett & Stafleu.
Annual twining herb to 1.5m, glabrous to pubescent. Petioles to 10cm; stipules 1 × 0.5cm, broadly lanceolate to ovate, acute; leaflets to 8.25cm (lateral leaflets unequal at base), ovate to deltoid, acute, dark green above, lighter beneath, adpressed-hairy. Papilionaceous flowers in axillary racemes to 15cm long; bracts ovate to pandurate; calyx tube to 0.5cm, gibbous at base, lobes 4, lanceolate-deltoid; corolla purple-maroon, standard to 1.5 × 0.5cm, margins involute, claw to 0.5cm. Fruit 1-seeded, linear-oblong, laterally compressed, curved, often subterranean, margins pubescent. Summer–early autumn. E US, SE Canada. Z7.

Amphilophium Kunth. (From Gk *amphilophos*, crested on all sides, referring to the corolla limb.) Bignoniaceae. 7 species of cane-like climbers. Branches hexagonal with conspicuous edges; pseudostipules leafy. Leaves 2–3-pinnate, terminal pinnae often replaced with trifid tendril. Panicles terminal; calyx campanulate, double, tube thick, expanded; corolla thick, tubular, bilabiate, divided to middle, upper lip 2-lobed, lower lip 3-lobed, glabrous or slightly pubescent outside. Fruit an oblong-elliptic capsule, valves parallel, slightly compressed, woody, smooth or tuberculate; seeds thin, puberulent, in membranous wing. Americas. Z10.

CULTIVATION A robust liane with fragrant purple flowers for the warm glasshouse or conservatory; cultivation as for *Anemopaegma*.

A.macrophyllum HBK. See *A.paniculatum* var. *molle*.
A.molle Schldl. & Cham. See *A.paniculatum* var. *molle*.
A.mutisii HBK. See *A.paniculatum*.

A.*paniculatum* (L.) HBK (*A.mutisii* HBK; *A.paraguariense* Hassl. ex O. Schulz; *A.purpureum* Brandg.; *A.vauthieri* DC.; *A.xerophilum* Pittier; *Bignonia paniculata* L.; *Endoloma purpureum* Raf.).
Stem 10cm diam. Branches lepidote or pubescent, especially on edges; pseudostipules leafy, 3–10 × 3–6mm. Leaves 2-pinnate, some with terminal tendril; pinnae 2.5–15 × 2.1–10.7cm, ovate to suborbicular, membranous, apex acuminate to obtuse, base truncate to cordate, lepidote; petiole 2.3–7cm; petiolules 0.6–4.3cm, tetragonal to hexagonal, scurfy-pubescent. Peduncle lepidote and pubescent; flowers fragrant; calyx 0.7–1.2 × 0.8–1.5cm, densely lepidote, often pubescent at base; corolla 2.4–3.5 × 0.7–1.6cm, white-yellow, becoming purple, upper lobes 1mm, lower lobes 0.3–1.8cm, viscid outside, glabrous or pubescent; stamens didynamous, filaments 1.4–1.8cm; staminode 3–5mm; pistil 2.4–2.7cm; ovary pubescent Capsule oblong, slightly lenticellate, densely lepidote; seeds 1–1.9 × 2.7–3cm. Mexico to N Argentina. var. *molle* (Schldl. & Cham.) Standl. (*A.macrophyllum* HBK; *A.molle* Schldl. & Cham.). Densely soft-pubescent throughout. Mexico to Peru.

A.paraguariense Hassl. ex O. Schulz. See *A.paniculatum*.
A.purpureum Brandg. See *A.paniculatum*.
A.vauthieri DC. See *A.paniculatum*.

Anemopaegma Mart. ex Meissn. (From Gk *anemos*, wind, and *paigma*, sport: the wind plays with these lianas.) Bignoniaceae. 43 species of lianes. Branches terete, with pseudostipules leafy or absent. Leaves with 2–5 pinnae, often with simple or trifid terminal tendril. Inflorescence terminal or axillary raceme; calyx cupular, truncate, margin glandular; corolla yellow, tubular-campanulate, glabrous or glandular-lepidote inside or outside; ovary ellipsoid, lepidote or puberulent; ovules 2–6-seriate. Fruit oblong-elliptic to orbicular capsule, valves parallel, usually strongly compressed, smooth; seeds flat, rounded in membranous, hyaline wing, or without wing, larger, and brown. Americas, Mexico to Brazil and Argentina. Z10.

CULTIVATION Where frost is common, these vigorous vines are suitable only for large pots or tubs in the humid atmosphere of the warm glasshouse or conservatory, where they are grown for their smooth, leathery, evergreen foliage and their profusion of short-lived blooms. The very pretty flowers of *A.chrysoleucum* are rose-scented. *A.carrerense*, from the lowland forests of Trinidad, is less commonly cultivated but equally worthy.

Grow in a well drained fibrous loam with additional organic matter, in full sun to part shade; *A.chrysoleucum* prefers light shade. Maintain a minimum night temperature of 10–15°C/50–60°F, and water plentifully when in growth; reduce water in winter. Prune in spring to encourage lateral buds to break; trim back all the previous season's growth and remove weak shoots. Propagate by seed or by softwood cuttings of sideshoots with short internodes rooted in moist sand in a closed case with bottom heat.

A.belizeanum Blake. See *A.chrysoleucum.*

A.carrerense Armitage.
Leaflets 6.25×7.5cm, 2, ovate, with terminal tendril. Flowers 3.25×6.25cm, funnelform, pale to deep yellow. Capsule flat, elliptic, 6.25–10cm, apex and base acute; seeds in flat wing. Trinidad.

A.chamberlaynii (Sims) Bur. & Schum.
Leaflets 5–14 × 2.5–5.5cm, oblong-ovate to lanceolate, apex acute, tendrils trifid. Racemes 2–8 flowered; calyx truncate, 7–8mm; corolla pale yellow, to 5cm. Brazil.

A.chrysoleucum (HBK) Sandw.
Leaflets 5.5–15×2.7.1cm, with or without simple tendril, narrowly elliptic, apex acute, base cuneate, membranous to leathery. Inflorescence axillary, often only 1–3-flowered; calyx 7–12×7–10mm, glabrous, margin finely ciliate; corolla lobes 1.1–2cm, cream inside, yellow outside, glandular-lepidote, tube yellow, with orange stripe below, 6–10.3 × 1.1–2.2cm at mouth. Capsule 6.2–12.2 × 2.9–6cm, ellipsoid, slightly flattened, rough, with persistent calyx; seeds 1.4–1.8 × 1.9–2.4cm, not winged. Mexico to N Brazil.

A.grandiflorum Sprague. See *A.paraense.*
A.lehmanii Sandw. See *A.puberulum.*
A.macrocarpum Standl. See *A.chrysoleucum.*
A.pachypus Schum. See *Mansoa hymenaea.*

A.paraense Bur. & Schum.
Leaflets 2 or 3, ovate to oblong-ovate, base obtuse or rounded, apex cuspidate or pointed; pseudostipules leafy. Flowers yellow or cream, densely lepidote inside, glabrous outside. Trinidad, Guyana, Peru, Brazil.

A.puberulum (Siebert) Miranda.
Leaflets 8–13×5.6–7.5cm, 2 together with terminal trifid tendril or scar, ovate-elliptic, apex acute, base rounded, papery, puberulent beneath, shining above. Inflorescence puberulent; calyx 6–8 × 8–9mm, leathery, glandular puberulent; corolla 5–5.4 × 1.5–1.6cm, tubular–campanulate, tube 4–4.3cm, lobes 0.8–1cm. Fruit 12–21×6.5–8cm, oblong-elliptic, puberulent and glandular-lepidote, flattened. Spring–summer. Mexico to E Ecuador.

A.punctulatum Pittier & Standl. See *A.chrysoleucum.*

A.rugosum (Schldl.) Sprague.
Branches subterete to angular; stem minutely glandular-pubescent. Leaflets 2, 5–7.5 × 3.1–5cm, broadly ovate, base obtuse, rugose, shining above, tendrils simple. Calyx to 7mm, truncate; corolla 6.25cm, glabrous. Capsule ovate, strongly compressed, apex acute, narrowed to base. Venezuela.

A.scandens Méllo ex Schum. See *A.chamberlaynii.*
A.tonduzianum Kränzl. See *Cydista aequinoctialis* var. *hirtella.*

Anredera Juss. (Derivation unknown.) Basellaceae. 10 species of lianes or twining herbs arising from tuberous rootstocks. Leaves ovate, cordate or elliptic, fleshy. Flowers small, bisexual or unisexual, in axillary spikes or racemes; bracteoles 2, often fused to perianth; perianth segments 5, basally united; stamens 5, filaments curved outward when in bud; style simple or trifid. Fruit globose, enclosed by perianth S America, naturalized S Europe. Z9.

CULTIVATION Grown for the pendent racemes of sweetly fragrant white flowers in autumn, *A.cordifolia* is a slender, fast-growing, drought-resistant plant that is useful in frost-free zones for screening or for covering archways and pergolas. In cool temperate zones, it is grown in the cool glasshouse, or treated as a half-hardy annual.

Plant in full sun or in good indirect light, in a well-drained and humus-rich soil. Give the support of wire or trellis and ensure plentiful water when in growth, reducing until almost dry in autumn and winter. Provided that the roots are not frosted, the plant will regenerate from the base in spring; where hard and persistent frosts are likely, dig up the tuberous roots and overwinter in a cool, dry place. Where necessary prune in spring to just above ground level, or cut back the previous season's growth by half. Propagate by tubers removed from the stem in spring, or by softwood cuttings taken in early winter.

A.cordifolia (Ten.) Steenis (*Boussingaultia cordifolia* Ten.; *Boussingaultia gracilis* Miers; *Boussingaultia gracilis* var. *pseudobaselloides* (Hauman) Bail.; *Boussingaultia gracilis* f. *pseudobaselloides* Hauman). MADEIRA VINE; MIGNONETTE VINE.
Tuber oblong, scaly at first. Stems twining, to 6m. Leaves 2.5–10cm, ovate-lanceolate, base cordate, thinly fleshy, glabrous, mid to dark green; petioles to 2.5cm, often bearing tubers in axils. Racemes to 30cm; flowers white, fragrant; style deeply trifid. Brazil to Paraguay to N Argentina. Most material in cultivation labelled as *A.baselloides* is *A.cordifolia*; *A.baselloides* (HBK) Baill. has an undivided style.

Antigonon Endl. (From Gk *anti*, against, and *gonia*, an angle, referring to the flexuous stems.) Polygonaceae. 3 species of perennial lianes with tendrils. Stems slender, jointed, flexuous, pubescent or glabrous. Leaves alternate, cordate to deltoid, acute to acuminate, petiolate, entire. Racemes branching, terminating in tendrils; flowers perfect; perianth of 5 papery sepals, the 3 outer sepals broader than the 2 inner, red-pink or green-white; stamens 8, 2–3mm, filaments united below; styles 3; ovary 3-angled. Fruit an achene within enlarged perianth, bluntly 3-angled, slightly shiny, brown. Mexico, C America. Z10.

CULTIVATION A fast-growing and decorative climber for clothing buildings, arbours and screens in the tropics, *A.leptopus* was widely used there during World War II to camouflage anti-aircraft emplacements. In cooler climates, it is suitable for a large tub or border in the intermediate glasshouse or conservatory; trained directly beneath the glass it provides useful shade in high summer.

Grow in a sandy, well drained and moderately fertile, loam-based mix. Provide wire support and position in full sunlight; water plentifully when in growth, reduce water in winter, when a minimum temperature of 10–15°C/50–60°F is necessary. Large specimens resent root disturbance; prune hard back in spring to restrain over vigorous growth and thin out crowded stems. Top growth may be damaged by lower temperatures and killed by the lightest frosts, but provided roots are given sufficient protection, growth will re-emerge in spring and flower that year. Propagate from seed in spring sown at 13–16°C/55–60°F. Root stem cuttings in summer in damp sand or perlite in a closed case with bottom heat at 15°C/59°F.

A.guatemalense Meissn. (*A.macrocarpum* Britt. & Small). Resembles *A.leptopus* but leaves broadly cordate, 3–9 × 2.5–7cm, pubescent. Sepals orbicular, at anthesis about 1cm, closely tomentose, pink. Fruit obscurely 3-angled. Mexico, Guatemala, Costa Rica, W Indies.

A.leptopus Hook. & Arn.CORAL VINE; CONFEDERATE VINE; MEXICAN CREEPER; CHAIN OF LOVE; ROSA DE MONTANA. Vigorous vine to 12m, roots tuberous. Leaves deltoid or cor-

date, acute to acuminate, 3–14 × 2–12cm, glabrous to pubescent beneath; petiole 1–2.5cm. Flowers 6–20 in axillary and terminal racemes or panicles; sepals cordate, in fruit 8–25 × 4–20mm, coral-pink to -red, outer surface minutely pubescent. Fruit about 1cm, apex strongly angled. Summer–early autumn. Mexico. 'Album': flowers white.

A.macrocarpum Britt. & Small. See *A.guatemalense*.

Araujia Brot. (From the Brazilian vernacular name for the plant.) Asclepiadaceae. 4 species of evergreen twining shrubs. Leaves opposite, simple, oblong to triangular-oblong, broadly cuneate to sagittate base. Flowers fragrant, white or pink, waxy, borne sparsely in axillary umbels or cymes; corolla salverform or campanulate, often streaked maroon inside, tube, inflated at base, lobes 5, semi-erect; anthers terminating in a small inflexed projection, each containing a single pollinium of waxy, sticky pollen; stigma often 2-beaked at apex. Fruit a leathery follicle or pod, deeply grooved, sometimes inflated; seeds tipped with a tuft of silky hairs. S America.

CULTIVATION Twining shrubs for the cool to intermediate glasshouse or conservatory, or, in the case of *A.sericofera*, the protection of a south-facing wall with a winter mulch in favoured areas where only mild frosts occur. *A.sericofera* earns its soubriquet, the Cruel Plant, by trapping moths at night – their proboscides become caught in the glutinous pollen masses of each headily fragrant flower until the rising sun, drying out the pollinia, releases the hapless pollinator.

Plant in a medium-fertility loam-based mix such as John Innes no.3. Water and feed freely throughout the growing season; keep barely damp in the winter months. Under glass, bright filtered sunlight will suit in summer, full sunlight at other times. Train on canes, trellis and posts. Increase by cuttings of ripe wood in late autumn, or by seed. The 'cruelty' of *Araujia* to moths hardly compares with that visited on *Araujia* by mealybug and whitefly.

A.albens G. Don. See *A.sericofera*.

A.angustifolia Steud. (*Physianthus megapotamicus* Mart.). To 6m. Leaves narrow-lanceolate, base hastate, apex acuminate. Flowers solitary, green-white to purple; corolla rotate to campanulate, lobes toothed. Autumn. Uruguay. Z10.

A.graveolens Mast. (*Physianthus auricomus* Graham; *Schubertia graveolens* Lindl.). Stout climber covered with coarse, spreading yellow hairs; malodorous when bruised. Leaves obovate, to 11.5×6cm, narrowing to cordate base. Flowers in umbellate clusters, white, fragrant, funnel-shaped, 5–6cm diam. Autumn. Brazil. Z9.

A.sericifera auct. See *A.sericofera*.

A.sericofera Brot. (*A.albens* G. Don; *A.sericifera* auct.; *Physianthus albens* Mart.; *Schubertia albens* Mart.). CRUEL PLANT. Robust; stem to 10m, covered with pale down when young, producing copious latex if damaged. Leaves oval-oblong, cuneate at base, 5–10 × 2–5cm, pale green; petiole 1–3cm. Flowers 2–8 in an asymmetric raceme, waxy, white to ivory, fragrant; corolla tube 1.5cm × 3cm; sepals undulate. Fruit a large, grooved pod, 12.5 × 5–7.5cm. Summer–autumn. S America, naturalized Australia (Queensland). Z9.

Argyreia Lour. (From Gk *argyreios*, silvery, referring to the silver-hairy leaf undersurfaces of some species.) Convolvulaceae. About 90 species of mainly woody climbers to 20m+ with herbaceous growing tips, a few species erect, glabrous to hairy. Leaves petiolate, entire, usually orbicular. Inflorescence 1- to many-flowered, axillary, cymose, lax to capitate; sepals 5, often dorsally pubescent, herbaceous to subcoriaceous, often persistent in fruit; corolla funnel-shaped, tubular or campanulate, entire to lobed, usually with hairy midpetaline bands; stamens included or exserted; stigma 2-lobed. Fruit berry-like, indehiscent, fleshy, leathery or mealy, red, orange, yellow or purple when ripe; seeds 1–4, usually glabrous. Tropical Asia to Australia (Queensland, 1 species). Z9.

CULTIVATION The showy flowers of *A.nervosa*, the most commonly grown species, are beautifully set off by heart-shaped, silver-backed leaves, making a close screen of overlapping foliage on trellising and other supports in tropical and subtropical gardens. *Argyreia* species are vigorous lianes in their natural habitat of jungle and forested ravine and in cultivation require supports stout enough to carry their weight. Careful attention must be given to training, especialy in hot humid conditions, when rapid growth will form am impenetrable tangle if it becomes enmeshed in other plants. Give full sun and moderately fertile, well drained soil. Also, for borders in large intermediate glasshouses, with a winter minimum of 13°C/55°F; thin the previous year's growth in spring. Propagate from seed in spring when available. Alternatively from softwood/greenwood cuttings with bottom heat in spring/summer. Susceptible to red spider mite and whitefly under glass.

A.beraviensis (Vatke) Bak. See *Stictocardia beraviensis*.

A.capitata (Vahl) Choisy.
Woody climber to 15m, young growth with brown or yellow patent hairs. Leaves 7.5–18cm on hairy 5–16cm petioles, ovate to orbicular, occasionally oblong-lanceolate, apex acuminate, base cordate, brown- or yellow-hairy. Inflorescence capitate, dense, on a stout, patent-hairy, 3–30cm peduncle; corolla 4.5–5.5cm, funnel-shaped, maroon, pale violet or pink, sometimes white. Indonesia and Malaysia to Vietnam and Bangladesh.

A.nervosa (Burm. f.) Bojer. WOOLLY MORNING GLORY.
Woody climber to 10m, containing white latex. Leaves 18–27 cm, ovate to orbicular, apex obtuse, acute or with a short cusp, base cordate, densely white, grey or yellowish-hairy beneath. Inflorescence subcapitate, on a long, stout, white-tomentose peduncle; corolla 6–6.5cm, tubular to funnel-shaped, lavender, base of tube darker, midpetaline bands and tube densely woolly outside. India, Bangladesh; pantropically cultivated and naturalized.

A.tiliifolia Wight. See *Stictocardia campanulata*.

Aristolochia L. (From Gk *aristos*, best, and *lochia*, childbirth; under the Doctrine of Signatures, the foetus-like flowers of *A.clematitis* commended its use as an abortifacient and as a calmative in childbirth.) BIRTHWORT; DUTCHMAN'S PIPE. Aristolochiaceae. About 300 species of lianes, scramblers, shrubs or perennial herbs. Woody stems sometimes thick with corky and fissured bark. Leaves alternate, entire or 2–7-lobed, with palmate to pinnate venation, often deeply cordate or subhastate at base; pseudostipules present in some species; petiole sulcate. Flowers consisting of calyx only, often of fantastic shape, malodorous, zygomorphic or rarely actinomorphic, solitary, fasciculate or in inflorescences which may be cymose, racemose, spicate, paniculate, axillary or cauligerous; perianth (calyx) straight, curved or S-shaped, usually inflated at base (utricle), contracted above utricle into cylindric or funnel-shaped tube (syrinx) graduating into limb, limb entire or 3–6-lobed: perianth may have 2 additional structures: at junction of tube and utricle, the syrinx projects into the utricle and a circular flange or annulus forms at junction of tube and limb; stamens usually 4, 5 or 6 (to 10), adnate to style column to form gynostemium concealed within utricle; style column 5–6 lobed; ovary indistinguishable from pedicel, oblong to elongate, angular, 5–6-locular; bracteole may be present at base of pedicel. Fruit capsular, dehiscent or indehiscent; seeds usually numerous, deltoid or triangular, often winged or flat. Cosmopolitan, temperate and tropical.

CULTIVATION Natives of moist woodlands, *Aristolochia* species bear unusual and often malodorous flowers, sometimes of extraordinary shape, size and marking. Few flowers are so showy or sinister as those of *A.cymbifera* or *A.grandiflora* which hang like tattered and stained rags. In other species, the limb is not so large and flaccid that it conceals the slender, curving tube that earns these plants the name Dutchman's Pipe. Hardly conventionally beautiful, the flowers are nonetheless alluring in a range of colours from flesh to bronze or ivory veined and mottled pink, mauve or black, often with glossy annuli and dark lashes. *Aristolochia* species are frequently recommended for the rapid covering of porches, pergolas and summerhouses, but care should be taken to avoid the strongest-smelling species. Few are truly odourless: even *A.littoralis*, often recommended for tropical gardens, should be used with care in enclosed spaces – the flowers are not foetid but the leaves are rank when crushed.

Most can be grown in the intermediate glasshouse (minimum temperature 15°C/60°F); a few, such as *A.littoralis*, are hardy where temperatures regularly drop below –5°C/23°F, and may regenerate from the base if frosted. The hardier *A.macrophylla*, *A.manshuriensis*, *A.sempervirens* and *A.tomentosa* will tolerate temperatures to –10°C/14°F.

Grow in full sun or part shade, in a well drained loamy soil rich in organic matter; water sparingly during the winter and plentifully in the growing season. Provide support; prune to shape or to confine the plants in late winter or early spring. Propagate from softwood cuttings – hardy species in midsummer, greenhouse species in early spring – using a rooting hormone and bottom heat at 21–23°C/70–75°F, in a soilless propagating medium. Alternatively, divide rootstocks in autumn. Seed requires three months of cold stratification (5°C/40°F), or may be sown when ripe in autumn. Soak seed in hand-hot water for 48 hours and surface-sow at 25–30°C/77–86°F. Prone to attack from red spider mite and aphids.

A.altissima Desf. See *A.sempervirens*.
A.brasiliensis Mart. & Zucc. See *A.labiata*.

A.californica Torr.
Vigorous deciduous climber to 5m. Leaves 4–12 × 3–10cm, broadly cordate, acute to obtuse at apex, strigose above, tomentose beneath; petioles to 5cm. Flowers solitary, axillary, bracteolate, geniculate, dull purple; utricle U-shaped, unevenly inflated, to 3cm, not differentiated into utricle and tube, abruptly narrowed at limb; annulus and syrinx absent;

limb 3-lobed, smooth, 2 × 2cm, lobes concave, divergent Summer. California. Z8.

A.clypeata Lind. & André. See *A.gigantea*.

A.chrysops (Stapf) Hemsl. (*Isotrema chrysops* Stapf).
Climber to 5m. Stems woody, felty when young. Leaves variable, 10–15 × 4–7cm, broadly ovate, cordate, hastate and lanceolate, grey-downy above. Flowers solitary, syrinx recurved, narrowed midway, exterior yellow, downy, interior yellow, glabrous, limb 2–3cm diam., 3-lobed, annulus promi-

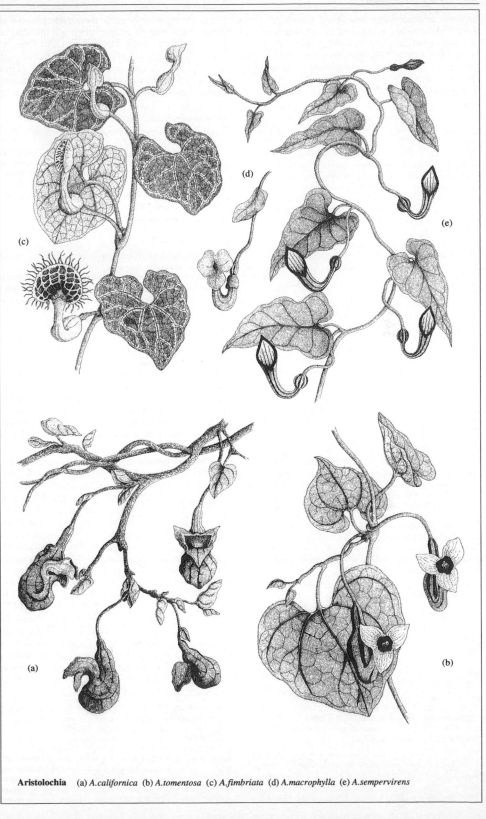

Aristolochia (a) *A.californica* (b) *A.tomentosa* (c) *A.fimbriata* (d) *A.macrophylla* (e) *A.sempervirens*

nent, rim golden yellow with a ring of maroon in centre. Summer. China. Z8.

A.cymbifera Mart. & Zucc.
Evergreen climber to 7m+. Bark grey, ridged, corky. Young branches pea green, flexible. Leaves to 15 × 10cm, reniform, grey-green; petioles clasping; pseudostipules present. Flowers ivory to white, mottled and intricately veined chocolate to maroon; utricle strongly saccate, to 8cm; tube to 4cm, slightly recurved, basally impressed; upper lip to 18cm across, suborbicular, cleft, flaccid and often folded, hanging over lower lip, minutely and closely veined, lower lip lanceolate, carinate-replicate, beak-like, ciliate, green-white marked brown. Summer. Brazil. Z10.

A.durior Hill. See **A.macrophylla**.
A.elegans Mast. See **A.littoralis**.

A.fimbriata Cham.
Glabrous climber to 2m+. Leaves to 9cm diam., suborbicular, cordate to reniform, conspicuously veined, often in a paler tone of silver or yellow. Flowers with strongly curved tube ascending from utricle, tube green; limb erect, 2.5cm across, more or less circular, deeply and finely fringed, exterior green-brown, interior purple-brown veined yellow. Autumn. Brazil. Z10.

A.galeata Mart. & Zucc. See **A.labiata**.

A.gigantea Mart. & Zucc. (*A.clypeata* Lind. & André).
Vigorous liane. Leaves 12–16 × 10–15cm, broadly triangular, acuminate, base subtruncate, deep green, glabrous above, white-tomentose beneath. Flowers cauliferous, geniculate, purple and yellow-orange; bracteoles absent; utricle swollen, obpyriform, 10cm, syrinx absent; tube not sharply differentiated from utricle and limb, U-shaped, 4cm; limb 1-lobed, abruptly spreading from tube, broadly cordate, 16 × 14cm, unappendaged, exterior white netted purple, interior maroon broken with white or ivory. Panama. Z10.

A.gigas Lindl. See **A.grandiflora**.

A.grandiflora Sw. (*A.gigas* Lindl.; *A.sturtevantii* hort.; *A.grandiflora* var. *sturtevantii* Will. Wats.). PELICAN FLOWER.
Vigorous glabrescent liane. Leaves 10–20 × 8–15cm, triangular cordate, apex acute to acuminate, base deeply cordate, deep green, paler beneath, strigose beneath at first. Flowers solitary, axillary, bracteolate, twice geniculate (at tube flexure and annulus), variable in size (largest and most colourful in var. *sturtevantii*.), blotched with purple, white, yellow, red and green; utricle obpyriform, gibbous, 6–17cm, syrinx cylindric, to 4cm, directed obliquely into utricle; tube bent at middle, 7–15cm; annulus thin, sharp-edged; limb abruptly spreading from tube and annulus, 1-lobed, essentially heart-shaped viewed face on, with a dark eye and a ribbon-like appendage hanging from its lower margin, 20–50 × 50–300cm (including length of appendage). Summer. C America, Caribbean. Z10.

A.kaempferi Willd. (*A.lineata* Duchart; *Hocquartia kaempferi* (Willd.) Nak.).
Scandent shrub, 2–3m high; young branches and leaves soft-pubescent. Leaves often polymorphic, 8–15cm, cordate-orbicular, sometimes 3-lobed, obtuse to subactue, cordate, subcoriaceous, glabrate above, grey-white-pubescent beneath. Flowers solitary in axils, pedicels 4–5cm, densely pubescent; syrinx recurved near middle, lobes 3, orbicular, glabrous inside, green-yellow, brown-striate, valvate and covering the throat in bud. Early summer. Japan. Z8.

A.× kewensis Will. Wats. (*A.labiata* × *A.trilobata*.)
Vigorous climber, intermediate between parents. Leaves triangular-cordate, almost as large as in *A.labiata*, veins tinged red. Flowers dull yellow, netted red-brown; tail-like lip crimson. Summer. Garden origin. Z10.

A.labiata Willd. (*A.ringens* Link & Otto non Vahl; *A.labiosa* Ker-Gawl.; *A.brasiliensis* Mart. & Zucc.; *A.galeata* Mart. & Zucc.). ROOSTER FLOWER.
Robust rather glaucous liane. Leaves 7–12 × 7–15cm, glabrous, broadly cordate, apex obtuse, ; green above, grey

beneath; pseudostipules large, sessile, clasping, ruffled. Flowers axillary, solitary, lacking bracteoles, geniculate, mottled red, yellow, green and purple; utricle subglobose, 7cm, syrinx absent, tube straight, emerging at sharp angle from utricle, 4cm, annulus absent; limb with 2 superposed lobes, upper lobe suborbicular, narrowly clawed, ruffled, deflected, pendent, 13–15 × 14–18cm, lower lobe stiffly erect, narrowly lanceolate, 10–15cm. Summer. S America. Z10.

A.labiosa Ker-Gawl. See **A.labiata**.
A.lineata Duchart. See **A.kaempferi**.

A.littoralis Parodi (*A.elegans* Mast.). CALICO FLOWER.
Vigorous glaucous liane. Leaves 7–9 × 6–10cm, cordate to reniform, apex obtuse, basally cordate, smooth, green above, grey-green beneath, heavily glaucous; pseudostipules auriculate, clasping, pale green. Flowers solitary, axillary, lacking bracteoles, geniculate, green-yellow and deep black-purple; utricle subcylindric, 3.5cm, syrinx absent; tube bent, 3cm, ivory, annulus absent; limb ivory marbled and veined purple or maroon, with a yellow throat, 1-lobed, orbicular, abruptly spreading from tube, 10 × 10cm. S America, naturalized C America and S US. Z9.

A.macrophylla Lam. (*A.durior* Hill; *A.sipho* L'Hérit.). DUTCHMAN'S PIPE.
Glabrescent deciduous liane, to 9m. Leaves 7–50 × 7–45cm, broadly cordate, apex obtuse to acute, base cordate, glabrous above, finely puberulent to glabrous beneath; petiole to 7.5cm. Flowers solitary, axillary, bracteolate, geniculate, green spotted with purple, brown and yellow, limb bordered purple-brown; utricle cylindric, 0.5cm, syrinx absent; tube curved upward, narrowing to limb, 2.5cm, annulus diminutive, slightly raised or absent; limb smooth, 3-lobed, 2 × 2cm, lobes subequal concave, divergent, unappendaged. Summer. E US (Appalachians). Z7.

A.macroura Gomes. See **A.trilobata**.

A.manshuriensis Komar.
Differs from *A.macrophylla* in downy young shoots and leaf undersides. Flowers yellow, flushed purple; tube to 5cm long; limb 3cm across, with abruptly acuminate points. Manchuria, Korea. Z7.

A.moupinensis Franch.
Deciduous climber. Stems initially downy. Leaves 10–12 × 6–10cm, cordate, apex acute, downy. Flowers solitary on slender bracteate pedicels, syrinx 4–5cm, pale green, compressed, downy, reflexed to expose yellow throat, lobes 3, spreading, yellow spotted purple, edged green. Summer. W China. Z8.

A.ringens Vahl non Link & Otto.
Vigorous, glaucous, evergreen liane, 7m+. Leaves 7–12 × 7–15cm, glabrous, broadly cordate, apex obtuse, green above, grey beneath; pseudostipules large, sessile, clasping, ruffled. Flowers axillary, solitary, produced on young wood, lacking bracteoles, geniculate, mottled red, yellow, green and veined purple; utricle subglobose, woolly within, 7cm, syrinx absent; tube straight, emerging from utricle at sharp angle, 4cm; annulus absent; limb with 2 superposed lobes, upper lobe obovate-spathulate, projecting forwards but not hanging loosely downwards as in *A.cymbifera*, 8 × 4–5cm, lower lobe 16–20cm, lanceolate, more or less rigid, projecting forwards, chute-like. Summer. C America, Caribbean, Florida. Z9.

A.ringens Link & Otto non Vahl. See **A.labiata**.

A.sempervirens L. (*A.altissima* Desf.).
Evergreen climber to 5m, occasionally procumbent. Leaves 10 × 6cm, triangular-ovate, cordate, glabrous, leathery, basal sinus shallow. Flowers 2–5cm, resembling a small pitcher, yellow striped purple, tube strongly curved; limb entire, acute, erect, purple or dull brown-purple, especially on margin. Spring. Mediterranean (S Italy to Crete). Z8.

A.sipho L'Hérit. See **A.macrophylla**.
A.sturtevantii hort. See **A.grandiflora**.

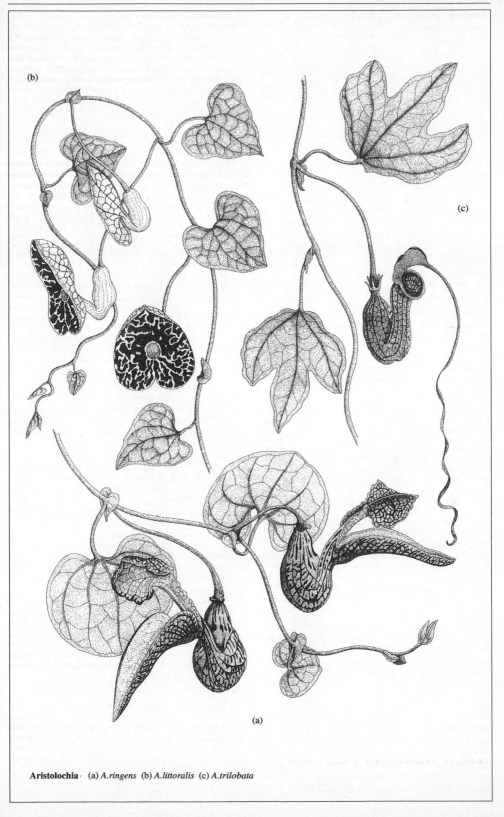

(b)

(c)

(a)

Aristolochia (a) *A.ringens* (b) *A.littoralis* (c) *A.trilobata*

A.tomentosa Sims.
Tomentose liane to 10m. Leaves 9–20×8–15cm, broadly cordate, apex acute to obtuse, shallowly cordate at base, finely pubescent above, tomentose beneath. Flowers axillary, solitary, lacking bracteoles, geniculate, purple, yellow and green; utricle cylindric, 0.7cm; tube constricted, sharply bent, 1.5cm, annulus prominent, purple, rugose; limb smooth, 3-lobed, lobes convex, unequal, strongly revolute, 2 × 2cm. Summer. SE–SC US. Z8.

A.trilobata L. (*A.macroura* Gomes).
Glabrous, vigorous liane. Leaves 10–15 × 3–15cm, deeply to obscurely palmately 3-lobed, truncate at base; pseudostipules suborbiculate, clasping. Flowers axillary, solitary, green mottled brown, terminal lobe and tail deep brown, lacking bracteoles, geniculate; utricle ellipsoid, 4–5cm, syrinx absent; tube bent upwards, 5–7cm, annulus absent: limb 1-lobed, smooth, narrowly triangular, 15–20 × 2–2cm, including length of tail-like appendage which hangs from its apex, the whole resembling a *Nepenthes* or *Sarracenia* pitcher. Summer. Eastern C America, Caribbean. Z9.

Arrabidaea DC. (For Bishop Antonio de Arrabida, *c*1827, editor of *Flora Fluminensis.*) Bignoniaceae. About 50 species of lianes, rarely small trees of shrubs. Branches terete; pseudostipules small, inconspicuous. Leaves usually trifoliolate, but terminal leaflet often replaced by simple tendril, juvenile leaves often simple. Inflorescence a terminal or axillary panicle, densely flowered; calyx cupular, truncate or bilabiate, finely 5-denticulate, pubescent; corolla red or pale pink to purple, rarely white, campanulate to salverform, lobes pubescent outside; ovary narrowly cylindrical to trigonal, finely scaly, ovules 2–seriate; disc cupular-pulviniform. Fruit a linear capsule, compressed, valves parallel, smooth, rarely verrucose, usually with prominent median nerve; seeds with 2 wings, wings usually hyaline. Americas (Mexico, W Indies, to Argentina). Z10.

CULTIVATION As for *Clytostoma.*

A.acuminata (Johnst.) Urban. See *A.corallina.*
A.acutifolia DC. See *A.chica.*
A.barquisimetensis Pittier. See *A.corallina.*

A.chica (Humb.& Bonpl.) Verl. (*A.larensis* Pittier; *A.rosea* DC.).
Stem with prominent lenticels, glabrous or slightly puberulent, young branches tinged red. Leaflets 3.3–11.5 × 1.3–5.5cm (terminal leaflet larger), ovate to narrow-ovate, apex acute to acuminate, base truncate to cuneate, membranous, puberulent on veins beneath; petiole 1.5–7.1cm. Inflorescence branches puberulent; corolla 1.6–3 × 0.5–1.4cm, at mouth of tube, tube 1.1–2.1cm, lobes 0.6–1.2cm. Fruit 12–23 × 0.9–1.2cm, linear, acute, smooth, scaly. Spring–autumn. Mexico to Argentina.

A.corallina (Jacq.) Sandw. (*A.acuminata* (Johnst.) Urban; *A.barquisimetensis* Pittier; *A.guaricensis* Pittier; *A.obliqua* var. *hirsuta* (DC.) Dugland; *A.praecox* Hassl.; *A.rhodantha* Bur.& Schum.; *A.rotundata* (DC.) Bur.ex Schum.; *A.spraguei* Pittier).
Stem with prominent lenticels, glabrous or glabrescent. Leaflets 3.1–18.2 × 2.3–11.6cm, ovate, apex acute to obtuse, base cordate to truncate, or cuneate, membranous to leathery, pubescent or glabrescent; petioles 2.3–3.6cm. Inflorescence puberulent; corolla tube campanulate, 2.7–4.6 × 2.1–2.8 × 0.8–1.2cm at mouth, lobes 0.5–1cm, lilac to purple-red, white inside. Fruit 12–47 × 1.6–2cm, glandular-punctate. Mexico to Argentina.

A.corymbifera Bur. ex Schum. See *A.selloi.*
A.dichotoma (Vell.) Bur. See *A.selloi.*

A.floribunda (HBK) Loes. ANIBAK.
Branches white-tuberculate, puberulent. Leaflets to 6.25cm, oblong-elliptic, apex acute, base tapered, glabrous, shining. Flowers 1.7cm, purple, funnelform. Fruit linear. Mexico.

A.guaricensis Pittier. See *A. corallina.*
A.guatemalensis Schum.& Loes. See *Cydista aequinoctialis* var.*hirtella.*

A.isthmica Standl. See *Cydista aequinoctialis.*
A.larensis Pittier. See *A.chica.*

A.littoralis (HBK) Wendl.
Branches glabrous, branchlets hairy. Leaflets to 13cm, 2–3, ovate, apex acute to acuminate, base rounded, soft-pubescent. Flowers red, downy-pubescent outside, funnelform. Fruit 20–35 × 1–1.3cm. Spring–summer. Mexico.

A.magnifica Sprague ex Steenis. See *Saritaea magnifica.*

A.mollis Bur.ex Schum.
Leaflets to 12.5cm, 3, ovate, downy-pubescent, base subcordate. Flowers small, downy-pubescent; inflorescence terminal. French Guyana.

A.mollissima (HBK) Bur. ex Schum.
Stem to 3cm diam. Leaves rarely simple; leaflets 3–10 × 2–7cm, 2–3, ovate to suborbicular, apex obtuse, base truncate to rounded, membranous, pubescent. Inflorescence axillary and terminal; flowers fragrant; corolla dark purple or, rarely, white, tube 2–5 × 0.8–1.6cm. Fruit 14–19 × 1–2cm, linear, pubescent. Venezuela.

A.obliqua var. *hirsuta* (DC.) Dugland. *See A.corallina.*
A.ovalifolia Pittier. See *A.corallina.*
A.praecox Hassl. See *A.corallina.*
A.pseudochica Kränal. See *Cydista aequinoctialis.*
A.rhodantha Bur.& Schum. See *A.corallina.*
A.rosea DC. See *A.chica.*
A.rotundata (DC.) Bur.ex Schum. See *A.corallina.*

A.selloi (Speng.) Sandw. (*A.dichotoma* (Vell.) Bur.).
Leaves 10 × 8cm with 2–3 leaflets, ovate to elliptic, apex strongly acuminate, base rounded to cordate, glabrous, puberulent on venation; petiole pilose, 1.5–3cm. Inflorescence 7–10cm, glabrous; pedicels 5–10mm; corolla pink to violet, tube 2–3cm, exterior pubescent, limb 2–2.5cm diam., interior pubescent. Fruit 18–40 × 1–1.6cm, apex attenuate, glabrous, slightly verrucose. N Brazil, Paraguay, Peru, Uruguay, N Argentina.

Artabotrys R. Br. (From Gk *artos,* bread, cake, and *botrys,* bunch of grapes.) TAIL GRAPE. Annonaceae. 100 species of scandent shrubs, often climbing by means of toughened, modified peduncles, leaf-opposed and shaped like hooks. Leaves alternate, entire, oblong-lanceolate, glossy. Flowers solitary, paired or in clusters, on long woody peduncles, fragrant; petals 6, in whorls, the inner petals somewhat smaller, valvate, yellow or white, swollen at base, concealing numerous crowded stamens or pistils; ovary bilocular. Fruit clustered, on toughened receptacle; seeds 2, oblong. Old World Tropics. Z10.

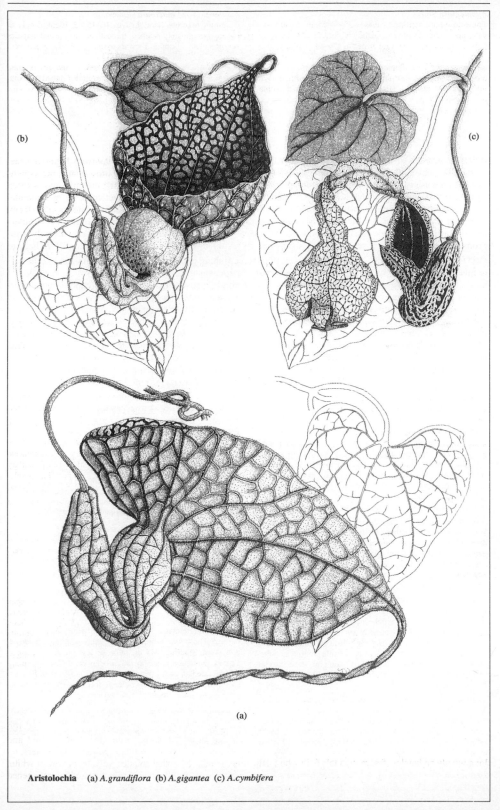

Aristolochia   (a) *A.grandiflora* (b) *A.gigantea* (c) *A.cymbifera*

CULTIVATION Vigorous shrubs climbing by hooks and suited to damp, semi-shaded positions in warm glasshouses and conservatories, or on walls, trellises and through thickets outside in Zone 10. Grown for the small but exquisitely scented blooms. These are harvested for essential oils and for making a stimulant infusion.

A.hexapetalus (L.f.) Bhand. CLIMBING ILANG-ILANG.
Shrub, climbing to 4m; shoots initially glabrescent. Leaves 10–20cm, oblong-lanceolate. Flowers highly fragrant, sometimes paired; sepals reflexed, yellow-white; outer petals to 2.5cm, ivory to brown, midrib hooked at base below; ovaries

8–12. Fruit to 4cm, ovoid-globose, abruptly pungent, in clusters to 30cm. S India. Sri Lanka, introduced throughout Old World Tropics.

A.odoratissimus R.Br. See A.hexapetalus.
A.uncinatus (Lam.) Merrill. See A.hexapetalus.

Asarina Mill. TWINING SNAPDRAGON. (From the Spanish vernacular name for the related *Antirrhinum*.) Scrophulariaceae. 16 species of diffuse, sprawling or twining perennial herbs, sometimes grown as annuals. Leaves generally scattered, sometimes subopposite or alternate, petiolate; petioles sometimes twining. Flowers axillary; sepals 5, free or united at base; corolla tubular-funnelform, limb bilabiate, with ventral basal pouch and prominent ventral ridges sometimes united into a palate; stamens 4 didynamous, anthers often adhering and dehiscing in unison; stigmas united, small, somewhat capitate. Fruit a capsule, globose, rupturing above; seeds irregular cylinders, with numerous thick, corky wing-ridges of lines of tubercles. Mexico & SW US, S Europe. Z9.

CULTIVATION The Twining Snapdragons are trailing and climbing plants grown for late summer colour in well drained spots on rock gardens in mild, sheltered areas: *A.procumbens* is suited to spilling over the cool face of partly shaded rocks, planted walls or raised beds. Where conditions suit it will spread by underground runners and may become invasive. Other species such as *A.scandens* and *A.antirrhinifolia* are climbing plants found in more arid situations and, in cold areas, are best cultivated as frost-tender perennials, allowed to twine their leaf-stalks on twiggy sticks, slender bamboo canes or similar supports in a sunny glasshouse or conservatory. Ventilate freely during the summer and shade from the strongest sun. In frost-free areas, these species are compact, non-woody climbers for patio trellising. Elsewhere, plant out in late spring after the last frosts into fertile, preferably alkaline soils. Water plentifully during the summer and feed pot-grown plants fortnightly with a dilute liquid fertilizer. Root softwood tip cuttings of non-flowering shoots taken in late summer, in a closed propagating case, and overwinter young plants in frost-free conditions. Alternatively, propagate from seed sown in early spring under glass.

A.antirrhinifolia (Humb. & Bonpl.) Pennell. VIOLET TWINING SNAPDRAGON.
Plant glabrous; stems much branched, diffuse, extensively twining. Leaves 1.5–2.5cm, ovate-hastate, apex acuminate, base narrowly cordate; petioles 1–3cm, somewhat twining. Pedicels 1–3cm, slender, somewhat incurved and flexuous; calyx lobes 1–1.3cm, linear-lanceolate, entire; corolla 2–2.5cm, tube pale and dull coloured, lobes purple to violet, palate white tinged yellow, marked with dark lines. Spring–summer. SW US (California to Texas) to S Mexico.

A.barclayana (Lindl.) Penn. (*Maurandya barclayana* Lindl.).
Vine, to 3m+; stem rather woody at base. Leaves 2cm, cordate to broadly hastate, long acute, angular, entire, glabrous; petioles twining. Calyx glandular-pilose, long-attenuate; corolla funnelform, without palate, lobes 3–7cm, spreading, rounded, white or pink darkening to deep purple, purple downy without, tube tinged green. Summer. Mexico.

A.erubescens (D. Don) Penn. (*Maurandya erubescens* (D. Don) A. Gray). CREEPING GLOXINIA.
Vine, densely softly glandular-pubescent throughout, grey-green; stems woody at base. Leaves 4–7.5cm, more or less deltoid, dentate, petioles twining. Pedicels twining; calyx lobes 2–2.5cm, broad, foliaceous; corolla 7cm, glandular-pubescent, lobes obtuse or notched, rose-pink, tube swollen on one side, white, marbled within. Summer. Mexico. 'Alba': flowers white.

A.filipes (A. Gray) Pennell. (*Antirrhinum filipes* A. Gray). YELLOW TWINING SNAPDRAGON.
Plant glabrous, slightly glaucous; stems branched, diffuse, twining around supports. Leaves 3–5cm, lanceolate, entire, lower ovate, shorter, narrowed to base; petioles 2–6mm.

Pedicels 3–7cm, very slender, twining around supports; sepals 0.3–0.4cm, lanceolate; corolla 1–1.2cm, yellow, palate raised, golden yellow with black spots. Spring. SW US (Oregon to California and Utah).

A.lophospermum (L.H. Bail.) Penn. (*Lophospermum scandens* D. Don; *Maurandya lophospermum* L.H. Bail.; *Maurandya scandens* (D. Don) A. Gray non (Cav.) Pers.).
Similar to *A.erubescens*, except slightly pubescent to glabrate; corolla rose-purple, more or less punctate without, tube not swollen at one side, white. Summer. Mexico.

A.procumbens Mill. (*Antirrhinum asarina* L.).
Plant glandular-pubescent; stems ligneous at base, procumbent. Leaves to 5×6cm, ovate-cordate to reniform, crenate-dentate, rarely somewhat palmatifid; petiole to 5cm. Flowers solitary; pedicels 1.5–2cm; sepals 1–1.3cm, somewhat unequal, lanceolate, acute, united at base; corolla 3–3.5cm, tube white with faint purple veins, lobes pale yellow or sometimes pale pink, palate deep yellow. SW Europe (S France, NE Spain).

A.purpusii (Brandg.) Penn. (*Maurandya purpurea* hort.).
Perennial herb with tubers, usually glabrous, rarely glandular-pubescent; stems 30–45cm, more or less prostrate, slender. Leaves triangular-ovate to deltoid, lower leaves sometimes coarsely dentate, long-petiolate. Pedicels longer than flowers; calyx lobes 1cm, broadly oblong, foliaceous; corolla 4cm, purple-carmine, without palate. Mexico.

A.scandens (Cav.) Penn. (*Maurandya scandens* (Cav.) Pers.).
Similar to *A.barclayana* except calyx glabrous; corolla funnelform with spreading lobes 4–5cm, pale violet to lavender or pink, tuber paler. Mexico.

Asparagus L. (Classical name for *A.officinalis*.) Liliaceae (Asparagaceae). To 300 species of perennial, rhizomatous herbs, shrubs or climbers, usually with fusiform tubers. Stems erect, spreading, or climbing. True leaves small, scale-like, emerging at the nodes, with hardened bases, often spine-like; leaves subtend green leaf-like, or thread-like cladophylls, solitary or in clusters of 3–50 at the nodes of the leaf-axils. Flowers small, bisexual or functionally unisexual, green, white or yellow, solitary, paired or borne in clusters among the cladophylls, occasionally in terminal umbels, or in racemes borne on the older shoots; flower stalks distinctly jointed; tepals 6, widely spreading or basally united to form campanulate perianth; stamens 6, free, filaments borne at base of tepals; anthers versatile; ovary superior, 3-celled. Fruit usually a globose 1–6-seeded berry. Old World.

CULTIVATION With the exception of the edible *A.officinalis*, the genus *Asparagus* is grown exclusively for its fine, ferny foliage. A fair proportion of its members have slender, elongated stems which sprawl, scramble or actively entwine themselves in surrounding shrubs, trees or, in cultivation, through trellis, wires or on sticks. Of the species described below, only *A.verticillatus* is fully hardy. This is a fleshy-rooted perennial with a semi-woody rootstock and closely branched wiry stems climbing to 3m. The branches are dense with fine foliage and hung in late summer with glossy black berries, especially in the free-flowering selection 'Floribundus'. This native of Eastern Europe requires a free-draining, gritty or sandy soil, good sunlight, protection from strong winds and the support of fences, posts, trellis or host plants.

The two most commonly encountered species described below are *A.setaceus*, the Asparagus Fern, with exceptionally finely feathered fern-like foliage on slender, rambling stems, and *A.asparagoides*, an unusual Asparagus in that its cladophylls ('leaves') are decidedly leafy and 'myrtle-like'. Both of these species are much-used in floristry and both have several cultivars, some with a non-climbing, bushy habit. Other species of particular interest include those with long, leaf-like cladophylls and woody grey stems, among them *A.drepanophyllus* and *A.falcatus*. Bold plants with large heads of airy foliage, they will climb or scramble with age and under optimum conditions; otherwise they make excellent hanging plants or tolerant foliage screens for office and other interior plantings.

Plant the tender species in a fertile, loam-based mix with additional grit or sharp sand; water and feed plentifully when in growth and ventilate freely. During the colder months when growth virtually ceases, reduce water supplies and withold fertilizer. Bright, filtered light is ideal, but most of these plants will tolerate light or even heavy shade, (they will, however, produce long, weak growth to reach the light). Full sunlight will fade and damage foliage, especially in the case of *A.setaceus* and the other ferny-leaved species. A minimum temperature of 7°C/46°F is recommended, as are good humidity levels, achieved by regular misting in warm weather. Increase by seed, or by dividing stem clumps when repotting. The growths, even in the case of 'woody' species like *A.falcatus*, are only in effect annual or biennial stems produced from a basal crown. They will usually attain their allotted size and begin to deteriorate after a few years, at which point they should be cut out cleanly at the base to make room for new shoots. Largely pest-free.

A.aethiopicus L. (*A.tenuifolius* Hook.f.)
Close to *A.falcatus*. Stem to 7m, woody, terete, climbing. Cladophylls 1–4 × 0.1–0.2cm, flat, rigid, ascending, mucronate, borne in clusters of 3–6. Flowers white, racemose, perianth to 3mm. Fruit a crimson, globose berry, 5–7mm. C & S Africa. Z9.

A.africanus Lam.
Roots fibrous. Stems to 3m, glabrous, climbing terete, woody, much-branched. Leaves with hardened bases which project obliquely downwards as small spines; cladophylls 0.5–1cm, subulate, rigid, borne in clusters of 8–20. Flowers usually bisexual, white, small, mostly borne in axillary umbels of 2 or 3; perianth 2.5–3mm; peduncles 5–8mm, straight, jointed in the lower half. Fruit a 1-seeded, red berry, to 6mm. S Africa. Z9.

A.asparagoides (L.) Druce (*Medeola asparagoides* L.; *A.medeoloides* (L.) Thunb.). SMILAX (of florists).
Stem to 1.5m, bright green, twining, glabrous or slightly ridged. Leaves with hardened bases, scarcely projecting; cladophylls 1.5–3.5 × 0.8–2cm, ovate-acuminate, solitary, alternate, leathery, round or cordate at base, with several longitudinal veins. Flowers bisexual, solitary or paired in leaf-axils; peduncles 5–8mm, jointed in the upper half; tepals 5–7 mm; stamens orange. Fruit a red, 1–4-seeded berry, 6–8mm. S Africa. 'Aureus': foliage golden-yellow. 'Myrtifolius' (BABY SMILAX); habit small, elegant; cladophylls to 2cm. Z10.

A.crispus Lam.
Herbaceous. Root tuberous. Stem to 1m, green, flexuous, climbing or drooping, much-branched. Leaves with rather soft, spine-like, basal projections; cladophylls 0.3–0.9 × 0.05–0.1cm, 3-angled, reflexed, linear, borne in clusters of 2 or 3. Flowers bisexual, white, soliary, fragrant; perianth 4–5mm; peduncles 6–11mm, jointed in the upper half; anthers

orange or vermilion. Fruit a pale, pink or white, ovoid, 3- to 9-seeded berry; seeds black. S Africa. Z9.

A.deflexus auct. See *A.scandens* var. *deflexus*.

A.drepanophyllus Welw.
Tuberous. Stems to 10m, terete, woody, climbing, with faint, papilose ridges. Main lower branches lacking; upper branches in a single horizontal plane. Leaves with hardened bases which project as small, sharp spines; cladophylls with papillose margins, flat, the central cladophyll 2–7 cm, the laterals somewhat smaller. Flowers green, campanulate, borne in erect racemes on older shoots; peduncles deflexed; perianth to 4mm. Fruit a bright scarlet, 3-lobed, 1-seeded berry. W & C Africa. Z9.

A.falcatus L. SICKLE THORN.
Stems to 12m or more, climbing, terete, woody, glabrous, grey-brown. Leaves project almost vertically downwards as small, blunt, rigid, spines; cladophylls 5–9 × 0.5–0.7cm, bright green, linear-oblong to linear-lanceolate, falcate, with a conspicuous midrib, in clusters of 1–3. Flowers bisexual, white, fragrant, borne in axillary racemes on the older wood; perianth 2.5–4mm. Fruit a brown, 1- or 2-seeded berry, to 5mm. S Africa, E Africa, Ceylon. Z10.

A.medeoloides (L.) Thunb. See *A.asparagoides*.
A.plumosus Bak. See *A.setaceus*.

A.racemosus Willd. (*A.tetragonus* Bresl.)
Tubers elliptic. Stems to 7m or more, climbing, spineless, grey to brown, branched above; mains stems robust with fine, papillose ridges. Leaves with hardened bases, modifying at more or less right angles into long, sharp spines; cladophylls , 1–2 × 0.1cm, often falcate, with 3 or 4 grey-green, ridge-like angles, borne in clusters of 3 to 8. Flowers bisexual, 0.5cm

diam., white or pink, fragrant, borne in racemes on the older, bare wood; perianth 2–4mm. Fruit a black or red, several-seeded berry. S Africa, E Africa, Asia. Z9.

A.retrofractus L.
Stem scrambling or weakly climbing, becoming brown and glabrous with age; branches very flexuous; spines absent or few, always absent from the ultimate branchlets. Cladophylls to 2.5cm. in dense clusters, subulate, curved, ascending, bright green. Flowers white, in axillary umbels. Fruit an orange, 1-seeded berry. S Africa. Z9.

A.scandens Thunb.
Herbaceous perennial. Stems to 2.5m, scrambling or climbing, terete, weak, much-branched above, glabrous or with slight ridges. Leaves with small, hardened bases which scarcely project; cladophylls 0.5–1.5 × 0.1–0.2cm, linear-lanceolate, flat, glabrous, light green, borne in whorls of 2 or 3, emerging in a single plane when 3, one of them longer than the other 2, the whole, branchlets included, making a 'frond'. Flowers usually bisexual, white, nodding, axillary, mostly solitary, occasionally borne in clusters or 2 or 3; perianth 3–4mm, spreading, peduncles 8–12mm, jointed in the upper half. Fruit a scarlet, 1-seeded berry. var. **deflexus** Bak. (*A.deflexus* auct.) Branches deflexed, very flexuous; flowers and cladophylls smaller. S Africa Z9.

A.setaceus (Kunth) Jessop (*A.plumosus* Bak.). ASPARAGUS FERN, LACE FERN.
Evergreen. Stems climbing or scrambling, woody or wiry, green, glabrous. Leaves with hardened bases which modify downwards into small, sharp spines; cladophylls to 1cm, very finely filiform, bright green or dark green, finely pointed, borne in clusters of 8–20 branchlets in a single plane to form a flat 'frond', triangular in outline. Flowers bisexual, white, solitary, terminal, perianth to 3mm; peduncles 2–5mm, jointed at about the middle. Fruit a red, 1–3-seeded berry. S & E Africa. 'Cupressoides': habit compact, narrowly pyramidal; cladophylls also held erect. 'Nanus': habit more compact, upright, cladophylls more numerous, shorter. 'Pyramidalis': loose pyramidal habit. 'Robustus': strong-growing. Z9.

A.ternifolius Hook.f. See *A.aethiopicus*.
A.tetragonus Bresl. See *A.racemosus*.

A.verticillatus L.
Herbaceous. Roots long, fleshy; rootstock woody. Stems to 3m, climbing, erect, glabrous, woody, much-branched with short, hard, sharp prickles, grooved and ridged; branches 45–90cm, slender. Leaves with hardened bases projecting downwards as small spines; cladophylls 1–6 × 0.05–0.15cm, with 3 papillose angles, filiform, in whorls of 10–20 per node. Flowers unisexual, axillary, in whorls of 1–10 per node; perianth 2.5–4mm, funnelform; peduncles deflexed, jointed above middle. Fruit a 1–3-seeded black berry, 5–8mm diam. SE Europe to Siberia. 'Floribundus': flowers and berries freely produced. Z6.

Asteranthera Klotzsch & Hanst. (From Gk *aster*, star, and *anthos*, flower, referring to the flower shape.) Gesneriaceae. 1 species, an evergreen, woody, scrambling vine, to 4.5m in habitat, young shoots pale-pilose. Leaves to 3×2cm in unequal, opposite pairs, ovate-orbicular to ovate-elliptic, pilose, dentate, teeth 2–5 per side. Flowers axillary, solitary or paired, on bracteate peduncles to 5cm; calyx 5-lobed; corolla to 6cm, bright red, tube narrow, widening to 2-lipped limb, limb to 3cm across, perpendicular to tube, upper lip 2-lobed, lower lip 3-lobed, marked with yellow; stamens 4, exserted, anthers clustered. Fruit a fleshy capsule, green, marked red. Summer. Chile. Z9.

CULTIVATION In the wild, *Asteranthera* experiences constant high humidity and soil moisture and grows in full sun, often in association with *Desfontainea*. Grow in sunny sheltered positions on acidic soils, provided with plentiful moisture and allow to climb or scramble. It is not reliably frost-hardy, especially in combination with winter wet, but stocks may be assured by semi-ripe cuttings or by division; plants root easily at the nodes. Propagate also by seed, which is tiny and difficult to handle.

A.ovata Hanst.

Bauhinia L. (For Jean Bauhin (1541–1613) and Gaspard Bauhin (1560–1624), Swiss botanists: the bilobed leaves characteristic of the genus symbolize the two brothers.) MOUNTAIN EBONY; ORCHID TREE. Leguminosae (Caesalpinioideae). Some 250–300 species of trees, shrubs or lianes, often armed or with tendrils. Leaves alternate, simple, reniform to bilobed, with palmate veins, rarely entire or bifoliolate; stipules deciduous. Thorns recurved, solitary or in pairs. Flowers usually in terminal, simple, few-flowered or compound corymbose racemes; hypanthium elongate-cylindric, calyx spathe-like, entire or finely dentate at apex inflated, 5-lobed; petals 5, showy; stamens 10 or fewer. Fruit oblong, usually straight, leathery to woody. Tropics and subtropics of Old and New World. Z9–10.

CULTIVATION A large genus of shrubs or trees grown in tropical and subtropical gardens, very sheltered locations outdoors in zone 9 and, otherwise, in the large intermediate to warm glasshouse or conservatory (minimum winter temperature 15°C/60°F, except for *B.yunnanensis*, which will overwinter in frost-free cool house conditions). The species described below are either large vines climbing by tendrils or semi-scandent shrubs. They are prized mostly for their showy 'orchid-like' blooms; *B.vahlii*, however, is a spectacular foliage plant – a robust liane producing very large kidney-shaped, downy leaves in addition to the attractions of its pure white flowers. The tendrilous climbers can be trained on pergolas and trellis or through host trees; other species can be allowed to ramble through surrounding vegetation or tied into walls.

Grow in full sun in fertile, moisture-retentive but well drained soil; apply a general fertilizer annually. Under glass, plant in beds or tubs filled with sandy, medium-fertility, loam-based mix with additional organic matter. Prune after flowering to restrict size or to thin out congested and exhausted growth. Propagate by seed, simple layering or grafting. Cuttings of semi-ripe wood with most leaves removed will root in moist sand in a closed case with gentle bottom heat.

B.binata Blanco (*B.hookeri* hort. pro parte).
Shrub. Branches climbing, often with tendrils. Leaves bifoliolate; leaflets to 4cm, ovate, pale green beneath. Flowers in dense, terminal or axillary corymbs; pedicels to 1cm; calyx to 1cm, ovoid, lobes 5, reflexed; petals to 2.5cm, obovate or spathulate, hairy on outer surfaces, white; stamens red. Fruit to 20 × 3cm, subsessile, oblong to falcate, flattened, corky. Spring. Insular SE Asia (coastal regions).

B.championii Benth.
Liane, with tendrils. Leaves simple, bilobed to half the length, lobes obtuse, hairy beneath. Flowers very small, in axillary racemes to 10cm long; petals white; fertile stamens 3. Fruit to 7.5×2.5cm. Hong Kong.

B.corymbosa Roxb. ex DC. (*B.glauca* Benth. non hort.; *B.scandens* auct.; *Phanera corymbosa* (Roxb. ex DC.) Benth.) PHANERA.
Climber, with tendrils. Young shoots with red-brown hairs. Leaves to 4cm, pale green beneath, suborbicular-cordate, bilobed nearly to base, lobes obtuse. Tendrils nodal, solitary or in pairs. Flowers fragrant in dense, terminal racemes; pedicels to 1cm; hypanthium to 2cm, calyx to 0.5cm, ovoid, 5-lobed; petals to 1.5cm, white to pink or white streaked with pink; fertile stamens 3, red. Fruit to 15 × 1.5cm, stipitate, oblong, compressed. S China.

B.fassoglensis Kotschy ex Schweinf.
Vine, with tendrils, downy to glabrous. Leaves to 12cm, simple, emarginate or bilobed to one-third of the length, obcordate to reniform, lobes obtuse; stipules to 1cm; tendrils nodal, solitary, forked at apex into 2 spiralling branches. Flowers in loosely flowered, axillary racemes; pedicels to 3cm; calyx to 1.5cm, ovoid, 5-lobed; petals to 3cm, obovate, yellow; fertile stamens 2. Fruit to 10 × 6cm, asymmetrically oblong, flattened, glabrous, woody. Summer–early autumn. Africa.

B.galpinii N.E. Br. (*B.punctata* Bolle). PRIDE OF THE CAPE; CAMEL'S FOOT.
Spreading or climbing shrub to 3m, glabrous. Leaves to 5cm, simple, emarginate or bilobed to one-third of the length, lobes obtuse. Flowers 6–10 in short axillary racemes; pedicels to 3cm; calyx to 5cm, spathe-like, splitting into 5 lobes; petals to 4cm, broadly obovate, clawed, orange or red, margin rugose; fertile stamens 3, red. Fruit to 10×2.5cm, stipitate, oblong or oblanceolate, flattened, woody. Spring–autumn. S Africa.

B.glabra Jacq.
Climber. Stems and tendrils often laterally compressed. Leaves lustrous, bilobed to three-quarters of the length and cordate, or bifoliolate, lobes or leaflets acute. Inflorescence terminal, simple or compound; hypanthium to 1.5cm, calyx to 1cm, ellipsoid becoming campanulate, dentate, 5-lobed; petals to 2cm, clawed, white or white with purple streaks; stamens 10. Fruit to 10 × 3cm, obovate to oblong, compressed. Summer–winter. Tropical America.

B.glauca Benth. See *B.corymbosa*.
B.glauca hort. non Benth. See *B.hupehana*.
B.hookeri hort. See *B.binata*.

B.hupehana Craib (*B.glauca* hort.).
Climbing shrub, often with tendrils, hairy becoming glabrous. Leaves to 8cm, simple, bilobed to one-third of the length,

ovate, lobes obtuse; tendrils laterally compressed, spiralling. Inflorescence terminal or axillary, many-flowered; flowers scented; pedicels to 3cm; calyx ellipsoid, 5-lobed; petals to 1.5cm, obovate, clawed, white or pink or white tinted rose; fertile stamens 3. Fruit to 25 × 3cm, oblong, laterally compressed. Spring–early summer. China.

B.mollicella Blake. See *B.aculeata*.

B.pauletia Pers. RAILWAY FENCE BAUHINIA.
Spiny shrub or small tree to 7m, occasionally climbing, pubescent. Leaves to 6cm, simple, bilobed to one-third of the length, suborbicular to cordate; spines usually nodal, solitary or in pairs, reflexed. Inflorescence terminal, few- to many-flowered; pedicel to 1cm; calyx to 10cm, spathe-like, mucronate; petals to 10cm, filiform, pale green; fertile stamens 5, rarely more. Fruit to 20×1.5cm, stipitate, oblong, laterally compressed; stipe to 5cm. Winter. Northern S America, Antilles, Mexico.

B.petersiana Bolle.
Shrub with spreading branches, or liane. Young shoots short-hairy. Leaves to 6cm, simple, bilobed, to half the length, cordate to truncate, glabrous above, lobes spreading, obtuse. Inflorescence terminal, corymbose, few-flowered; pedicels to 3cm; calyx to 7cm, oblanceolate, spathe-like, mucronate, splitting; petals to 8cm, oblanceolate, clawed, white, margins ruffled; fertile stamens 5, filaments to 10cm, red, hairy. Fruit to 30×5cm, stipitate, oblanceolate, curving. Summer. Africa.

B.piliostigma hort. See *B.fassoglensis*.

B.porosa Boiv. ex Baill.
Shrub with climbing branches, glabrate. Leaves to 10cm, simple, entire or bilobed to half the length, orbicular to ovate. Inflorescence terminal, loosely flowered; petals subequal, cream to pale yellow, clawed. Fruit to 20cm, stipitate, oblong, coriaceous. Summer–early autumn. Madagascar.

B.punctata Bolle. See *B.galpinii*.
B.reticulata DC. See *B.fassoglensis*.
B.saigonensis Pierre ex Gagnep. See *B.yunnanensis*.
B.scandens auct. See *B.corymbosa*.

B.vahlii Wight & Arn. MALU CREEPER.
Liane to 35m. Bole grooved. Leaves to 30 × 30cm, simple, bilobed to a quarter of the length, suborbicular-cordate, woolly beneath, lobes obtuse. Tendrils to 10cm, forked at apex. Inflorescence terminal, simple or compound, many-flowered; pedicels to 3cm; calyx to 1cm, splitting into 2 reflexed segments; petals to 2.5cm, obovate, clawed, white to cream, pubescent becoming glabrous, margins wavy; stamens 3. Fruit to 30cm, oblong, laterally compressed, woody. Summer. India.

B.yunnanensis Franch. (*B.saigonensis* Pierre ex Gagnep.).
Evergreen shrub or liane, glabrate. Leaves bifoliolate; leaflets to 3.5cm, ovate, pale green beneath. Tendrils in pairs, compressed, circinnate. Inflorescence terminal on axillary branches, many-flowered; pedicels to 4cm; calyx to 1cm, splitting into 5 reflexed segments; petals to 1.5cm, clawed, pink to light mauve, sometimes veined rose; fertile stamens 3. Fruit to 12 × 2cm, stipitate, oblong, laterally compressed, somewhat coriaceous. Summer. SE Asia.

Beaumontia Wallich. (For Diana Beaumont (*d*1831) of Bretton Hall, Yorkshire.) Apocynaceae. 9 species of evergreen vines. Leaves opposite, entire, thin-textured with small glands in vein axils. Flowers showy, fragrant, in crowded axillary and terminal corymbs; calyx 5-parted; corolla funnelform or campanulate, tube short, lobes 5, twisted; stamens attached toward throat, filaments slender, anthers sagittate. Fruit thick woody follicles. China, Indomalaysia. Z10.

CULTIVATION   In the eastern Himalaya *B.grandiflora* grows through trees and over rocks and shrubs in altitudes as high as 150–1400m/490–4590ft, often in full sun, rooting deeply in the alluvial deposits of dry river beds. It is a beautiful shrubby vine for tub or border plantings in the glasshouse or conservatory, bearing large fragrant white trumpet flowers in abundance from late spring into summer. It requires hot moist conditions in summer, with cool, dry conditions in winter. Grow in full light in a fertile but well drained medium and maintain a warm, close environment in summer. Water plentifully when in full growth, sparingly at other times. Maintain a minimum winter night temperature of 7–10°C/45–50°F; once wood is well ripened, slightly lower temperatures will assist flower bud initiation. Provide support and prune after flowering to thin the previous year's growth and to remove any that is shading the lower stems. Propagate by semi-ripe cuttings taken with heel in late summer, root in a sandy propagating mix in a closed case with bottom heat, or by seed.

B.grandiflora Wallich (*B.jerdoniana* Wight; *B.longiflora* Hook.). NEPAL TRUMPET FLOWER; MOONFLOWER; MOONVINE; HERALD'S TRUMPET; EASTER LILY VINE.
Woody twiner to 5m or more. New growth tinted pink-bronze; branchlets initially rusty-tomentellous. Leaves 10–28cm, broadly oblong-ovate, apiculate, glossy, glabrous above, downy beneath, rusty-pubescent at first. Calyx lobes 5, large, ovate, tips tinted red; corolla tube 7.5–13×2.5–6.5cm, funnelform-campanulate, white, exterior tinted green at base, interior somewhat deeper in colour. India to Vietnam.

B.jerdoniana Wight. See *B.grandiflora*.
B.longiflora Hook. See *B.grandiflora*.

Beaumontia grandiflora

Behnia Didr.(For Professor W.F.G. Behn, friend and expedition companion of Danish botanist Didrik Didrichsen (1814–1867).) Liliaceae (Luzuriagaceae). 1 species, a climbing perennial similar in habit to *Asparagus asparagoides*. Rhizome compact, roots swollen. Stems terete, slender, much-branched, flexuous, glabrous. Leaves 5–7.5cm, alternate, ovate to narrowly ovate-acuminate, strongly parallel- and reticulate-veined, glossy, coriaceous, sessile. Inflorescence a few-flowered, short, lax, axillary cyme; peduncle thin, flexuous; bracts small; perianth segments 2cm, basally united to form a short tube, spreading above, white-green; stamens arising from lower part of perianth tube, filaments terete, anthers versatile; ovary ovoid; stigma tripartite. Fruit globose, fleshy; seeds 3–15, hard, black. S Africa. Z9.

CULTIVATION   As for the tender *Asparagus* species.

B.reticulata Didr.

Benincasa Savi. (For Count Benincasa (*d*1596), Italian botanist.) Cucurbitaceae. 1 species, an annual, monoecious, downy-pubescent vine. Tendrils 2–3-fid, slender. Leaves palmate, deeply cordate, suborbicular, 5–7-lobed, pilose above, hispid beneath, 10–25×10–25cm; petiole eglandular, villous, subtended by probract.

Flowers solitary, axillary, yellow; calyx lobes 5, serrate, reflexed, lanceolate; corolla rotate to campanulate, 5-lobed; stamens 3, anthers flexuous; ovary inferior, oblong-ovoid, 2–4cm, rudimentary in male flowers; style 1; stigmas 3; pedicel pubescent. Fruit very large, fleshy, indehiscent, globose or oblong, hispid, glaucous, pubescent, becoming waxy, glabrous; seeds many, horizontal, ovoid-oblong, white, 10×6mm. Indomalaya, widely cultivated in Old World tropics. Z10.

CULTIVATION   As for *Trichosanthes*, except that multiple plantings and cross-pollination are not required. The wax gourd produces such enormous fruits that it is best cultivated as prostrate groundcover unless the fruits can be well supported. High temperatures and bright light are needed to develop the waxy bloom on the fruit.

B.cerifera Savi. See *B.hispida*.

B.hispida (Thunb.) Cogn. (*B.cerifera* Savi; *Cucurbita hispida* Thunb.). WAX GOURD; WHITE GOURD; ASH GOURD; CHINESE WATER MELON; TUNKA; ZIT-KWA.

Berberidopsis Hook.f. (From *Berberis* (Berberidaceae) and Gk *opsis*, appearance.) CORAL PLANT. Flacourtiaceae. 1 species, a glabrous, scrambling, sometimes twisting, evergreen shrub with long terete branches, to 5m. Leaves to 10cm, alternate, petiolate, simple, oblong, base round, apex acute, dull to glossy dark green above, somewhat glaucous beneath, tough margins sharply dentate. Flowers near-hemispherical, to 1.75cm diam. on a short apical raceme or clustered in axillary pairs toward branch tips, pendulous on slender red pedicels to 3.5cm; bracteoles and tepals fleshy, concave above, orbicular, 9–15, crimson to deep sealing-wax red and glossy; stamens 7–10; ovary 1-celled with a 3-lobed stigma. Fruit a many-seeded berry. Summer–autumn. Chile, very rare in the wild. Z8.

CULTIVATION   A native of moist woodland habitats in Chile, *B.corallina* is grown for its decorative, toothed, bright evergreen leaves and the beautifully contrasting, deep red, pendulous flowers, carried for long periods from summer through until early autumn. It will flourish on a north- or west-facing wall, or on trees and large shrubs. Hardy to –10°C/14°F but prone to wind scorch. In areas of prolonged low temperatures, protect wall-grown specimens with hessian or evergreen branches and mulch at the roots; frost-damaged plants will shoot from the base. Plant in a cool position, sheltered from cold winds, in well drained soils enriched with organic matter, and mulch with well rotted manure or compost. *Berberidopsis* will tolerate slightly calcareous soils, given ample organic matter; shallow chalk soils are not suitable. In the cold glasshouse, use a lime-free growing medium and plant in the border rather than in tubs, to minimize temperature fluctuations at the root. Water plentifully when in growth; keep fairly dry in winter. Prune carefully in

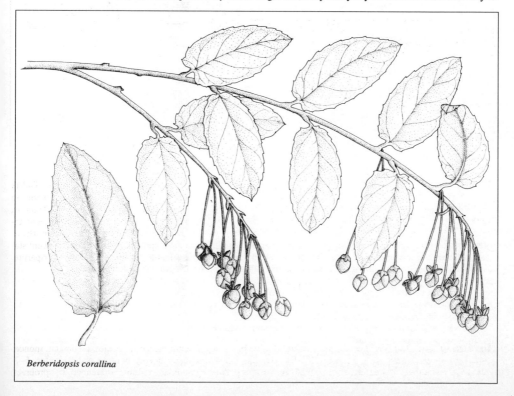

Berberidopsis corallina

spring to remove old, weak and crossing branches or later, to relieve overcrowding. Propagate by semi-ripe cuttings in a closed case with bottom heat, or by simple layering.

B.corallina Hook. f.

Berchemia Necker ex DC. (For M. Berchem, 17th-century French botanist.) Rhamnaceae. 12–22 species of woody, perennial, deciduous, climbing or scandent plants, rarely trees or shrubs, to 6m. Leaves petiolate, with small, caducous stipules; lamina entire, pinnately many-veined. Inflorescence fasciculate, paniculate or a raceme-like thyrse, axillary or terminal; flowers small, many; sepals 5, apically thickened above; petals 5, white, nectariferous disc thick or thin; stamens 5. Fruit an elongate drupe, 2–3× times longer than thick, leathery-fleshy, with 1 stone. Spring or summer. S Asia, E Africa, S US, Mexico, Guatemala.

CULTIVATION Suitable for walls with wire support, for covering fences or for growing through large shrubs, *Berchemia* species are graceful scrambling plants with elegant, prominently veined foliage and, in long hot summers, an abundant display of small but attractive fruits. The neat foliage of *B.racemosa* gives good, clear yellow autumn colour. *B.racemosa* and *B.scandens* will tolerate temperatures to about −15°C/5°F, possibly more with shelter from cold drying winds. Grow in moisture-retentive but well drained fertile soil, in sun where soil remains permanently moist, or in light shade. Thin out old and congested growth in winter. Propagate by seed sown in autumn or spring, by semi-ripe cuttings or by root cuttings in winter; also by simple layering of young stems in winter.

B.flavescens Wallich.
Climber, 1.5–3m, young growth with dark, patent hairs or glabrous. Leaves 5–15×2.5–6cm on 1.2–2.5cm petioles, vein pairs 9–16, base attenuate, shiny green above, paler beneath. Inflorescence 3–10cm, terminal, pyramidal, paniculate; flowers borne on current year's wood, on 3–4mm pedicels; Fruit 8mm, botuliform. India (Himalaya), Nepal, Tibet, W China. Z5.

B.giraldiana Schneid.
5–6m, climbing or scandent, young shoots arching. Leaves 3–7cm, on 0.6–1.8cm petioles, vein pairs 9–11, apex acute or acuminate, base rounded or slightly cordate, glabrous or sparsely downy beneath. Inflorescence to 20cm, pyramidal, terminal, paniculate. Fruit 8mm, botuliform, red when immature, black at maturity. Summer. China (Hupeh, Sichuan, Shansi). Z6.

B.lineata DC.
Climber to 5m, habit elegant, twigs finely downy. Leaves 1–3 × 0.3–1.5cm, vein pairs 4–9, oval-ovate, base and apex rounded, dark green above, pale, grey-green beneath. Inflorescence axillary or terminal; flowers 2mm, on 3–6mm pedicel; sepals linear, erect, enclosing white petals. Fruit 8mm, cylindrical or ovoid, blue-black at maturity. N India, China, Taiwan. Z8.

B.racemosa Sieb. & Zucc.
Scandent plant to at least 4m, stems flexible, glabrous. Leaves 3–6cm, vein pairs 6–9, ovate, base slightly cordate, dark green above, paler and sometimes glaucous beneath. Inflorescence to 15cm, terminal, paniculate, pyramidal; flowers very small, green-white. Fruit 8mm, globose, red at first, black at maturity. Late summer. Japan, Taiwan. 'Variegata': leaves variegated cream. Z6.

B.scandens (Hill) K. Koch (*B.volubilis* (L. f.) DC.). SUPPLEJACK; VINE RATTANY.
Climber to 5m, twigs glabrous, twining. Leaves 2–8cm on 0.4–1.3cm petioles, vein pairs 9–12, narrowly ovate-elliptic to elliptic, base rounded or cuneate, apex usually acute, rarely weakly so or blunt, often mucronate, glabrous, dark green above, paler beneath, margins undulate. Inflorescence 1–3cm, axillary or terminal, racemose or paniculate, often shorter than leaves; flowers on 1–3mm pedicels, buds pyramidal; sepals 1.5–2mm, very narrowly deltoid to subulate; petals 1–1.5mm, oblanceolate, green-white. Fruit 5–8mm long, 3–4mm diam., oblong, dark blue to black. Spring. US (Virginia to Texas and Missouri), Mexico (Chiapas), Guatemala. 'Variegata': leaves variegated cream to white. Z7.

B.volubilis (L. f.) DC. See *B.scandens*.

Bignonia L. (For the Abbé Bignon (1662–1743), Librarian to Louis XIV.) Bignoniaceae. 1 species, a glabrous evergreen vine, climbing by tendrils to 20m. Leaves opposite, jugate, with a terminal trifid tendril or scar; leaflets 5–10cm, often only 1 pair, oblong-lanceolate, semi-rigid, apex acuminate, obtuse, base cordate, entire. Inflorescences cymose, axillary, 2–5-flowered, or flowers solitary; calyx campanulate, 5-lobed; corolla tubular-funnelform, 4–5cm, deep orange to scarlet, limb bilabiate, trumpet-shaped; stamens didynamous, villous at base, included, anthers glabrous; ovules 1–3-seriate; ovary sessile or shortly stalked. Fruit a capsule, linear, flattened, 15cm; seeds elliptic, winged. Summer. N America. Z6.

CULTIVATION *B.capreolata* occurs in rich, moist woodlands. In areas free from prolonged winter frosts, it makes a handsome specimen on a sheltered sunny wall, or when clothing a fence or large tree. It can be allowed to sprawl as groundcover, although it may not flower when grown in this way. In colder climates *Bignonia* is suited to the cool glasshouse or conservatory. Grown for the striking orange-red flowers carried in abundant small clusters in summer, *Bignonia* becomes a beautiful, high climbing evergreen vine when conditions suit (in cooler conditions it may drop its leaves in winter). *B.capreolata* 'Atrosanguinea' is an attractive form with long, narrow leaves and rich purple-brown blooms.

Grow in a well drained, fertile medium with additional organic matter, in full sun outdoors but with protection from direct summer sun under glass. Ventilate freely when conditions allow, spray over with fresh water when not in flower, and water plentifully when in growth. Maintain a winter minimum temperature of 5–10°C/40–50°F; given long hot summers to ripen wood, plants grown outside will tolerate temperatures to

Bignoniaceae (a) *Pandorea jasminoides* (b) *Bignonia capreolata* (c) *Distictis buccinatoria* (d) *Eccremocarpus scaber*

–5°C/23°F. Grown as groundcover, *Bignonia* will tolerate lower temperatures. Restricting the roots by tub cultivation, rather than direct border plantings, will limit over-vigorous growth and encourage flowering. Cut back the previous season's growth by two thirds in early spring, and remove weak shoots in mid-summer. Propagate by seed, layering or by leaf-bud cuttings in summer, rooted in a mix of equal parts peat and grit in a closed case with bottom heat at 21°C/70°F. Very susceptible to mealybug.

B.acuminata Johnst. See *Arrabidaea corallina*.
B.aequinoctialis L. See *Cydista aequinoctialis*.
B.apurensis HBK. See *Adenocalymma apurense*.
B.australis Ait. See *Pandorea pandorana*.
B.balbisiana DC. See *Arrabidaea corallina*.
B.boliviana Rusby. See *Arrabidaea corallina*.
B.buccinatoria Mair. See *Distictis buccinatoria*.
B.callistegioides Cham. See *Clytostoma callistegioides*.
B.capensis Thunb. See *Tecomaria capensis* ssp. *capensis*.

B.capreolata L. (*B.crucigera* L.; *Doxantha capreolata* Miers; *Anostichus capreolatus* (L.) Bur.; *Campsis capreolata* hort.). CROSS-VINE; QUARTERVINE; TRUMPET FLOWER. 'Atrosanguinea': leaves narrow, long; flowers dark purple, tinted brown.

B.chamberlaynii Sims. See *Anemopaegma chamberlaynii*.
B.cherere Lindl. See *Distictis buccinatoria*.
B.chica Humb. & Bonpl. See *Arrabidaea chica*.
B.chinensis Lam. See *Campsis grandiflora*.
B.chrysoleuca HBK. See *Anemopaegma chrysoleucum*.
B.cinerea DC. See *Distictis laxiflora*.
B.colombiana Morong. See *Arrabidaea corallina*.
B.comosa Cham. See *Adenocalymma comosum*.
B.corallina Jacq. See *Arrabidaea corallina*.
B.crucigera L. See *B.capreolata*.
B.cuprea Cham. See *Arrabidaea chica*.
B.dichotoma Vell. See *Arrabidaea selloi*.
B.dichotoma Jacq. See *Arrabidaea corallina*.
B.difficilis Cham. See *Mansoa difficilis*.
B.diversifolia HBK. See *Cydista diversifolia*.
B.echinata Jacq. See *Pithecoctenium crucigerum*.
B.erubescens S. Moore. See *Arrabidaea chica*.
B.glabrata HBK. See *Arrabidaea corallina*.
B.grandiflora Thunb. See *Campsis grandiflora*.
B.hibiscifolia Cham. See *Arrabidaea corallina*.
B.hostmannii E. Mey. See *Cydista aequinoctialis*.
B.hymenaea DC. See *Mansoa hymenaea*.
B.ignea Vell. See *Pyrostegia venusta*.
B.jasminoides hort. non Thunb. See *Pandorea jasminoides*.

B.lactiflora Vahl. See *Distictis lactiflora*.
B.laxiflora DC. See *Distictis laxiflora*.
B.littoralis HBK. See *Arrabidaea littoralis*.
B.magnifica hort. See *Saritaea magnifica*.
B.marginata Cham. See *Adenocalymma marginatum*.
B.meonantha Sweet. See *Pandorea pandorana*.
B.mollis Vahl. See *Arrabidaea mollis*.
B.mollissima HBK. See *Arrabidaea mollissima*.
B.muricata HBK. See *Pithecoctenium crucigerum*.
B.nitidissima DC. See *Cydista aequinoctialis*.
B.obliqua HBK. See *Arrabidaea corallina*.
B.pandorae Sims. See *Pandorea pandorana*.
B.pandorana Andrews. See *Pandorea pandorana*.
B.pandorea Vent. See *Pandorea pandorana*.
B.paniculata L. See *Amphilophium paniculatum*.
B.perforata Chom. See *Stizophyllum perforatum*.
B.picta HBK. See *Cydista aequinoctialis*.
B.pterocarpa Cham. See *Cuspidaria pterocarpa*.
B.purpureum Lodd. See *Clytostoma binatum*.
B.radicans L. See *Campsis radicans*.
B.rotundata DC. See *Arrabidaea corallina*.
B.rugosa Schldl. See *Anemopaegma rugosum*.
B.sarmentosa var. *hirtella* Benth. See *Cydista aequinoctialis* var. *hirtella*.
B.scandens Vell. See *Anemopaegma chamberlaynii*.
B.selloi Spreng. See *Arrabidaea selloi*.
B.speciosa Graham. See *Clytostoma callistegioides*.
B.spectabilis Vahl. See *Cydista aequinoctialis*.
B.tagliabuana hort. See *Campsis* × *tagliabuana*.
B.trifoliata Vell. See *Adenocalymma longeracemosum*.
B.tweediana Lindl. See *Macfadyena unguis-cati*.
B.unguis-cati L. See *Macfadyena unguis-cati*.
B.variabilis Jacq. See *Pleonotoma variabile*.
B.venusta Ker-Gawl. See *Pyrostegia venusta*.
B.villosa Vahl ex Spreng. See *Arrabidaea corallina*.
B.villosa Vahl. See *Cydista aequinoctialis*.
B.violacea hort., not DC. See *Clytostoma callistegioides*.

For illustration see Bignoniaceae.

Billardiera Sm. (For J.J.H. de Labillardière (1755–1834), French explorer and botanist.) Pittosporaceae. 8 species of perennial, evergreen vines of slender habit, climbing to about 5m. Leaves alternate, entire, usually lanceolate. Inflorescence 1- to several-flowered, at branch tips; flowers 5-merous, pendulous, more or less campanulate; petals mostly yellow, some purple, connate for about half their length; anthers shorter than filaments, not fused around style. Fruit a berry, edible in some species, seeds many. Australia. Z8.

CULTIVATION   Grown for its flowers and beautifully coloured fleshy fruits, in frost-free areas and in mild coastal gardens *B.longiflora* will cover cool walls or fences and is especially attractive when allowed to clamber through other shrubs. In cool temperate zones, grow in the cool glasshouse or conservatory. Plant in humus-rich, moist but well drained, lime-free soils in a position that ensures a cool root run. Provide support and shelter from cold winds and shade from the hottest summer sun. Where prolonged frosts are likely, protect roots with a mulch of bracken litter. Prune in spring to remove weak, dead and overcrowded growth. Under glass, provide support, water plentifully when in full growth, less at other times, and maintain a winter minimum temperature of 5–7°C/40–45°F, with rare dips to freezing permissible on sheltered walls. Propagate by seed, which germinates prolifically if sown fresh but may take up to a year to germinate if allowed to dry out. Take stem cuttings of desirable colour variants in early summer, or basal cuttings of younger growth in autumn. Also by simple layers.

B.longiflora Labill. APPLEBERRY; BLUEBERRY; PURPLE APPLEBERRY.
Climber to 2m, glabrous or with young growth finely hairy. Leaves 1.5–4.5cm, on slender petioles, oblanceolate to narrowly elliptic or lanceolate, apex obtuse. Flowers solitary, 1.5–3.5cm; pedicels to 1cm; petals oblanceolate, yellow-green at first, later pink or purple. Fruit to 2.5cm, oblong-globose, brilliant cobalt to violet blue, rarely red, pink or white ('Fructu-albo', 'Alba'). Summer. Tasmania.

For illustration see Pittosporaceae.

Blechnum L. (From the classical Greek name, *blechnon*, for a fern or ferns in general.) HARD FERN. Blechnaceae. Some 200 terrestrial or occasionally epiphytic ferns. Rhizomes ascending or erect and often stout (tree fern 'trunks' in *B.brasiliense* and *B.gibbum*, among others), or else more or less elongate and running, sometimes stoloniferous, usually densely covered with scales. Fronds often emerging red, bronze or pink, mostly 1-pinnate, or rarely simple, usually glabrous, monomorphic or dimorphic with the divisions of the fertile fronds strongly contracted. Sori elongate-linear, usually continuous, borne near or against the costa on an elongate transverse veinlet parallel to the costa; indusium narrowly linear, continuous or nearly so, firm, opening toward the costa. Cosmopolitan, mainly S hemisphere. Z10 for the species listed below.

CULTIVATION   *Blechnum* encompasses a great number of ferns ranging widely in habit and hardiness. Among the tender species, several are vigorous climbers, their rhizomes travelling long distances over tree trunks, rocks and other supports. The three listed below will succeed in sheltered, shady and damp semi-woodland situations in zone 10. They should be planted in an open soil rich in garden compost or leafmould and encouraged to root on the stems of supporting plants, where their rather tough and coarsely cut fronds will form a dense covering. Under glass, they require a minimum winter temperature of 10°C/50°F in humid, shady conditions. They work well if established in beds and allowed to climb on damp walls, chicken-wire cylinders filled with a bark-based mix or even left to thread themselves through hanging wires or chains. Frequent syringing and a weak fortnightly foliar feed are beneficial during summer. They must never be allowed to dry out completely. Increase by detaching lengths of rooted rhizome.

B.attenuatum (Sw.) Mett. CLIMBING BLECHNUM.
Rhizome creeping, often ascending, long, densely scaly; scales linear, attenuate, up to 2.5cm, brown, often with a black central stripe; stipe to 10cm, pale to red-brown. Frond blades to 60cm, alternate, dimorphic; sterile frond blades pinnatisect, 50–100 × 10 × 30cm, pinnate at base, broadly lanceolate, very attenuate below, pinnae horizontal. *c*15–23 × 1–1.5cm, close together, with a narrow acute sinus, becoming gradually smaller downwards, acuminate or truncate and emarginate, entire, or sub-serrate. Fertile frond blades with more remote pinnae, 6–10 × 0.1–1.5cm. sessile, linear, apiculate or acuminate. Australia (NSW), New Zealand, Norfolk Is., Polynesia, Chile.

B.filiforme Ettingsh.
Rhizome long, stout, branched, climbing to a great height, clothed with squarrose scales. Sterile fronds numerous, scattered along rhizome, pinnate, of two forms: those on the ground or on the lower part of the rhizome small, 7.5–15 × 1.5–2.5cm, linear or linear-lanceolate; pinnae 0.5–1.5cm, oblong to orbicular-oblong, sharply and deeply toothed. Fronds from the upper part of the rhizome much larger, 30–75 × 7.5–1.5cm, lanceolate, pendulous, coriaceous, dark green,

glabrous or more or less scaly along the rachis and costae; stipes short, scaly at the base. Pinnae numerous, 4–7.5 × 1.5cm, lanceolate, falcate, narrowed upwards into a finely acuminate point, shortly stipitate and truncate or rounded or cordate at the base, margins regularly and finely crenate-dentate. Fertile fronds from near the top of the rhizome, ovate or ovate-oblong in outline; pinnae numerous, 7.5–15 × 0.25cm, very narrow-linear or almost filiform. Indusium very narrow. New Zealand, Fiji.

B.polypodioides (Sw.) Kuhn.
Rhizome scandent, greatly elongate, to 10m+, sub-woody, densely scaly, scales to 1.7cm, linear-attenuate, red-brown, mostly with a black median line and denticulate-ciliate margins. Fronds crowded or somewhat distant, dimorphic; sterile blades 30–45 × 2.5–5cm. linear to lanceolate, tapering at both ends, pinnatisect, segments 25–75 pairs, 2.5 × 0.6–1cm, narrowly oblong-deltate, broad at base, acuminate or more or less falcate at apex, margins entire or minutely toothed, revolute, veins simple or 1-forked at base, ending in large tips near margin; stipes to 10cm. Fertile fronds lanceolate to ovate, pinnate, abruptly reduced at base, to 15cm broad; pinnae to 4cm, distant, linear, pod-like; stipes to 15cm. C America, S Mexico, Greater Antilles. Z10.

Bomarea Mirb. (For Jacques Christophe Valmont de Bomare (1731–1807), a French patron of science.) Liliaceae (Alstroemeriaceae). Over 100 species of rhizomatous perennial herbs. Roots slender with tubers borne at tips. Stems long, twining. Leaves cauline, usually lanceolate. Flowers in terminal, simple or compound umbels, long-stalked, drooping; perianth tubular-campanulate, tepals obovate to oblanceolate, equal or whorled in two unequal series; stamens 6, erect, borne at base of tepals and equal in length to them, anthers basifixed; style slender, 3-fid; ovary superior, 3-celled. Fruit a 3-celled capsule; seeds orange or red, numerous. S America. Z9.

CULTIVATION   Grown for their handsome umbels of brightly coloured and beautifully marked flowers, *Bomarea* species are tuberous-rooted, vining perennials for the cool glasshouse or conservatory. In favoured areas in Zone 8 they might also be tried in a sheltered, moist and slightly acid border, where their vining stems could climb and seek shade in shrubs like *Crinodendron* and *Lomatia*. Protect crowns of plants grown outdoors with bracken and straw in winter. Pot-grown specimens may spend the summer out of doors if brought in before first frosts; the stems usually die back during winter, when plants should be kept cool, almost dry and frost free; cut back old flowered growth to ground level as the leaves begin to fade.

Under glass, grow with support of wire or trellis in a light, fertile, loam-based mix, rich in organic matter and with additional sharp sand. Provide good ventilation, a minimum temperature of 5–7°C/40–45°F, and admit full light or bright filtered light in high summer. Water plentifully and liquid feed when in full growth, withdrawing water gradually to keep almost dry in winter. Propagate by careful division or by seed, in a soilless propagating mix, potting on seedlings into individual pots at 5–8cm/2–3in. high; germination takes about three weeks at 18–23°C/65–75°F.

B.acutifolia (Link & Otto) Herb.
Close to *B.shuttleworthii*. Leaves lanceolate to ovate-lanceolate, pubescent on veins beneath; outer tepals red, not spotted.

B.caldasiana Herb. See *B.caldasii*.

B.caldasii (HBK) Asch. & Gräbn. (*B.caldasiana* Herb.; *B.kalbreyeri* hort.).
Stem to 4m. Leaves to 15 × 2.5cm, oblong-acute, almost glabrescent or puberulent beneath; petiole distinct. Flowers 20–60 in a simple umbel; tepals unequal, outer 2–2.5cm, dull orange-red to red-brown, inner 2.5–3.5cm, bright yellow to orange, occasionally flecked green, brown or red. Northern S America.

B.cardieri Mast.
Stem to 4m. Leaves to 18 × 7cm, oblong-lanceolate, acuminate. Flowers to 40; umbels compound; tepals 5.5–6.5cm, equal, outer pink, finely flecked mauve inside, with a short, green, horn-like projection on the back just below apex, inner pink, occasionally green, spotted mauve. Colombia.

B.conferta Benth. See *B.patacocensis*.

B.edulis (Tussac) Herb.
Leaves to 12.5 × 2.5cm, lanceolate, glabrous or puberulent beneath. Flowers in compound umbels; tepals nearly equal, 2.5–3cm, outer pink, inner bright green or yellow, spotted purple or dark pink. W Indies, C America, Northern S America.

B.frondea Mast.
Close to *B.patacocensis*, with outer tepals yellow, and inner tepals bright yellow, spotted dark red.

B.kalbreyeri hort. See *B.caldasii*.

B.multiflora (L.f.) Mirb.
Stem puberulent. Leaves to 10cm. Flowers 20–40, in simple umbels; tepals approximately 2.5cm, equal, outer tinged red, inner red-yellow with brown flecks. Northern S America.

B.oligantha Bak.
Similar to *B.multiflora* but with flowers 6–8 per umbel.

B.patacocensis Herb. (*B.conferta* Benth.).
Stem to 5m, puberulent. Leaves to 15cm, oblong-lanceolate, puberulent beneath. Flowers 20–60, in simple umbels; tepals unequal, outer to 3.3cm, orange or crimson, inner to 6.5cm, chrome-yellow or crimson, flecked chocolate or violet, with orange tips. Andes of Colombia and Ecuador. Plants grown under this name are often *B.racemosa*.

B.racemosa Killip.
Distinguished from *B.patacocensis* by its deep red stem, scarlet outer tepals, 5–6.3cm, and scarlet inner tepals, spotted brown with yellow base, 6.3–7.5cm; pedicels stout, tomentulose, to 10cm. S America.

B.salsilla (L.) Herb.
Stem to 2m, glabrous. Leaves lanceolate to oblong. Flowers small, purple, in compound umbels; tepals equal, 1–1.5cm, crimson or purple-red, tinged green at tips. Chile.

B.shuttleworthii Mast.
Leaves to 15 × 5cm, ovate-lanceolate, glabrous beneath. Umbel compound; tepals equal, to 5cm, outer orange-red with dark spots towards the tip, inner yellow at the base with green, dark-spotted tips and a red midrib. Colombia.

Bougainvillea Comm. ex Juss. (For L.A. de Bougainville (1729–1811), the first Frenchman to cross the Pacific. In 1768 he embarked on a voyage of discovery to the South Seas, taking with him the King's Botanist Philibert Commerson, whose assistant Jean Baré was in fact one Jeanne Baret and thus, on her return from Mauritius after Commerson's death in 1773, the first woman to circumnavigate the globe.) Nyctaginaceae. 14 species of climbing shrubs and small trees, glabrous or pubescent, some with stiff, curved thorns at leaf axils. Leaves alternate, petiolate, ovate to broadly elliptic. Flowers small, white to yellow, axillary, solitary or in clusters of 3 subtended by persistent, showy, leaf-like bracts; perianth tubular, fusiform, 5-ridged, the ridges terminating in star-like rays on the expanded limb; stamens 8, unequal, usually exserted. Fruit an elongated 5-lobed achene, fusiform to pyriform. S America. Z9.

CULTIVATION　In tropical and subtropical gardens, *Bougainvillea* is unsurpassed for covering trellis and pergolas, bearing brilliantly coloured bracts which surround small, pale flowers over long periods. Many respond to training as standards, in the open garden or in pots under glass. In subtropical zones, shrubby, less vigorous species such as *B.glabra* are often used as informal hedging. In constantly humid climates, *Bougainvillea* remains evergreen.

　B.glabra and offspring tend to flower continuously and are best grown where they experience virtually no dry season. For maximum flower production, they should be fed and watered throughout the year. This group flowers even on young plants and, with the *B.×* *buttiana* hybrids which flower more seasonally, make the best container-grown specimens.

　B.spectabilis, its cultivars and hybrids with *B.glabra* require a dry season to promote flowering. Under glass, water and feed plentifully at first to produce strong growth, then reduce both to induce flowering. In the open garden, grow in full sun in rich, well drained soils. In habitat or grown among trees, plants of the *B.spectabilis* group will climb by means of thorns; in cultivation they require regular tying to a support framework.

　Even in favoured areas in cool temperate zones, *Bougainvillea* species are unlikely to survive in the open and are best grown in large pots or tubs in a cool glasshouse or conservatory, with a minimum night temperature of 7°C/45°F for all but *B.spectabilis*, which requires 10°C/50°F. In large glasshouses, grow in a bed 60cm/24in. deep, with a rubble base for drainage and containing sharply draining, moderately fertile loam-based mix. *Bougainvillea* can also be grown in large pots, with appropriate support, and often flowers better with a confined root run; in pots, *B.glabra* and *B.spectabilis* may easily be restricted to about 1.5–2.5m/5–8ft.

　Grow in high-fertility loam-based mix in well ventilated but humid conditions, damping down and syringing regularly in warm weather. Water plentifully during the growing season, sparingly from late autumn into spring, keeping the medium just moist. As strong growth recommences, increase humidity and temperatures by about 10°C/18°F, apply top dressing and then liquid-feed weekly. Flowering may last longer if temperatures can be lowered during the development of flower buds. Spur-prune established specimens (except in the case of *B.peruviana*, which resents pruning) in early spring, and remove weak growth. *B.glabra* is reported to respond well to hard pruning. Deadhead in autumn. Root greenwood cuttings in late winter with bottom heat at 20°C/68°F. Air layer in spring. In subtropical climates, cuttings may be inserted directly into the flowering position, if not exposed or excessively sunny and arid. Susceptible to scale insect, mealybug and red spider mite, especially under glass.

B.brasiliensis Rausch. See *B.spectabilis*.

B.×buttiana Holtt. & Standl. (*B.glabra×B.peruviana.*)
Puberulent woody climber to 12m. Leaves to 11.5 × 8cm, ovate, apex acuminate, glabrous, midrib pubescent. Bracts undulate to crispate, purple to orange, 3.5 × 3.2cm, glabrous, veins puberulent; perianth tube to 2 × 0.2cm, constricted below middle, angled, pubescent. Garden origin.

B.glabra Choisy in DC. PAPER FLOWER.
Strong climber. Leaves to 13 × 6cm, elliptic, narrow at base, apex acute, glabrous to sparsely pubescent, usually glossy above, paler beneath with raised pubescent venation. Bracts white or purple-magenta, fading with age, weakly undulate, sometimes persisting after flowering; perianth tube inflated, pentagonal, short-pubescent with hairs curving upwards. Summer. Brazil.

B.peruviana Humb. & Bonpl.
Stoutly thorny, glabrous vine. Leaves to 10.5 × 8cm, broadly ovate. Bracts pale magenta to pink, deepening with age, wrinkled, to 3.5 × 2cm, glabrous; perianth tube slender, to 1mm diam., glabrous, angles obscure; lobes flared, pubescent below, glabrous above. Columbia, Ecuador, Peru. 'Ecuador Pink', 'Lady Hudson' and 'Princess Margaret Rose' are all very close to the type.

B.spectabilis Willd. (*B.brasiliensis* Rausch.).
Robust climber with prominent, hooked thorns. Leaves10 × 6cm, ovate, tomentose throughout or velutinous beneath only. Bracts 5–6cm, purple or pink, fading with age; perianth tube obscurely angled, long-pubescent. Spring. Brazil.

B. Spectoglabra Group. Hybrids between *B.spectabilis* and *B.glabra*, see below.

B.cultivars. 'Afterglow': habit loose-upright, canes arching; thorns many, short straight; bracts broadly elliptic with distinct tip, 3.5 × 2.5cm, deep orange when young, pink-orange in age. 'Alba': habit loose-upright, canes arching; thorns many, short, recurved; bracts narrowly elliptic to oblong, 3.5 × 2cm, white with green-tinted veins. 'Asia': habit loose, open; thorns few; bracts elliptic, 3.7×2.7cm, purple. 'Barbara Karst': habit loose-upright; thorns many, medium length, straight; bracts elliptic to nearly round, 3.7×3cm, purple-red. 'Betty Hendry': habit rounded, open; thorns many, long, straight; bracts broadly ovate, 5×3.5cm, purple-red. 'Bois de Rose': habit loose-upright, open; thorns many, medium-length, straight, stout; bracts nearly round, to 4.2×3.8cm, red-orange when young, rose-purple in age. 'Brilliant': habit dwarf, rounded, dense, twiggy; thorns few, short, slender; bracts elliptic, 3.7×2.7cm, red. 'Camarillo Fiesta': habit low, loose, open; thorns many, short, recurved; bracts broadly elliptic, 4×3.5cm, deep orange-red, somewhat browner when young. 'C.B. Red Seedling': habit loose, open; thorns few; bracts elliptic, 4×3.2cm, orange-red when young, ageing red-purple. 'Closeburn': habit low-spreading, dwarf; thorns few or absent; bracts broadly ovate, 3.5 × 2.7cm, orange-red. 'Convent': habit loose-upright, open; thorns many, medium length, stout, slightly recurved; bracts ovate-elliptic, 4.5 × 3cm, twisted, light purple. 'Crimson Lake': closely resembles 'Mrs Butt'. 'Cypheri': bracts to 4.5cm, deep flamingo pink, not persistent. 'David Lemmer': habit rounded; thorns few, straight, slender; bracts broadly elliptic to nearly round, 5 × 4cm, red to dark red in age. 'Double Pink': habit loose, open; thorns few, short; bracts 'double', ovate, the largest 2.5 × 1.6cm, red-purple, lighter toward the base, not persisting and fading to brown. 'Double Pink/White': habit loose, open; thorns many, medium length, recurved; bracts 'double',

broadly elliptic, 3×2cm, red-purple, shading to white at base, exposed tips pink. 'Dudley Delap': habit low-spreading, dense, pubescent; thorns few; bracts elongate, ovate, 4.2 × 3cm, red. 'Dulcie Daborn': habit rounded, loose, open; thorns few, short, straight, slender; bracts nearly round, 3.7×3.4cm, red.

'Easter Parade': habit loose-upright; thorns many, short, recurved; bracts narrowly ovate, 4.5 × 2.5cm, lavender-pink. 'Elizabeth Angus': habit very vigorous, loose, open, with strong arching canes; thorns many, long, stout, recurved; bracts broadly ovate, 5 × 3.7cm, light purple. 'Fascelle's Purple': habit very vigorous, loose-upright, with arching canes; thorns many, long, straight; bracts ovate, 4.8 × 3.2cm, red-purple. This red-purple class includes 'New River', 'Sanderiana' ('Brasiliensis') and 'Solar no. 1'; 'Fascelle's Purple' has the largest bracts. 'Fascelle's Strawberry': habit dense, moderately spreading; thorns few, long, straight, slender (old inflorescences are 'thorny' also); bracts broadly ovate, 2.8 × 2.5cm, deep dusty-rose. 'Formosa': shrubby; bracts magenta; perianth tube 5–6mm diam.'Glabra Cypheri': habit rounded; thorns many, stout, recurved; bracts ovate-elliptic, 4.3×2.7cm, magenta. 'Glabra India': habit very vigorous, dense, rounded; thorns few, short, recurved; bracts broadly elliptic, 5 × 4cm, light purple; resembles a larger, more vigorous 'Sanderiana' ('Brasiliensis'). 'Golden Glow': habit loose-upright, open, with arching canes; thorns many (on strong canes), long, recurved; bracts nearly round, 3 × 2.5cm, golden-orange when young to lighter orange in age. 'California Gold', 'Golden Dawn', 'Golden Glow' and 'Lyman's Yellow' are all very close. 'Helen Johnson': habit rounded, dense; bracts to 3.5 × 3cm, ovate to round, purple-red. 'Hugh Evans': habit very vigorous, dense, upright; thorns many, medium length, recurved; bracts nearly elliptic, 3.5 × 3cm, orange when young, ageing rose-pink.

'India Flame': habit low-spreading, open; thorns many, medium length, straight, stout; bracts ovate-elliptic, 4.5–5 × 3.2–3.5cm, deep orange when young, ageing medium rose-purple. 'Isabel Greensmith': habit loose, open; thorns many, long, stout, recurved; bracts ovate-elliptic, cordate and asymmetrical at base, deep orange when young, ageing deep rose. 'Jamaica Queen': habit rounded, dense; thorns few, short, slender; bracts elliptic, 3.5×2.5cm, deep rose when young, ageing deep purple. 'Jane Snook': habit low-spreading, dense, with small twigs; thorns few, short, recurved; bracts elliptic-oblong, 5 × 3.7cm, lavender. 'Jewell': habit loose; thorns few, long, slender; bracts ovate-elliptic, 3.5×2.7cm, purple-red. 'Key West': habit loose, open; thorns short, recurved, slender; bracts elliptic-ovate, 3.5 × 2.8cm, light purple. 'Killie Campbell': habit rounded, dense; thorns few; bracts broadly elliptic to nearly round, 3.6 × 3cm, rose-purple. 'Lacquer Red': habit loose-upright, open; thorns many, short, slender; bracts broadly elliptic, 3.7 × 2.2cm, red. 'Lady Elizabeth': habit loose-upright, open; thorns many, short, recurved, slender; bracts elliptic, 3.5 × 2.5cm, rounded to shallowly cordate at base, light purple.'Lady Huggins': bracts pale red-purple; perianth tube to 3mm diam. 'Lady Mary Baring': habit loose-upright, with arching canes; thorns many, long, slightly recurved; bracts elliptic to nearly round, 3×2.5cm, yellow-orange when young, ageing paler orange. 'Lady Wilson': bracts cerise, less than 3.5cm, brick red. 'Lateritia': habit loose-upright, open; thorns many, long, recurved, stout; bracts ovate to elliptic, 3.8–4.2 × 2.8–3.3cm, orange red. 'Lemmer's Special no.2': habit loose-upright, rounded, open; thorns few, short; bracts nearly round, 3.2 × 3cm, purple-red. 'Lion's Club': habit rounded, open; thorns many on canes, few on slender twigs, short, straight, stout; bracts ovate-elliptic, 4.5×3.5cm, orange-red to deep purple with age. 'Louis Wathen': bracts apricot to red, stamens not enclosed.

'Magnifica': bracts vivid purple, not persistent, to 4.5cm or longer; leaves shining, dark green. 'Mahara' ('Carmencita'): habit loose-upright, open; thorns many, medium-long, slightly recurved; bracts 'double', broadly ovate, 1.5–2.2 × 1.1–1.7cm, uniformly purple-red. 'Mary Palmer': habit rounded, dense, no long arching canes; thorns moderately numerous, recurved; bracts broadly elliptic, 4.2 × 3cm, pink or, in some plants, with an admixture of white bracts also. 'Minyata': habit low-spreading, dense; thorns few, short, slender; bracts ovate-elliptic, 3.2 × 3.2cm, dull red-orange. 'Miss Luzon': bracts scarlet to blood red; perianth tube open in flower. 'Miss Manila': habit loose; thorns few, long, straight, slender; bracts elliptic to nearly round, 4 × 3.7cm, orange to rose; resembles 'Bois de Rose', but young bracts are more orange. 'Mrs Butt': habit loose-upright, open; thorns many, short, slender; bracts elliptic, 3.5 × 2.5cm, uniformly dark red. 'Mrs Helen McLean': bracts apricot to amber; stamens enclosed. 'Mrs Leano': bracts bright red, to 4cm, not persistent; somewhat drought-tolerant. 'Natalii no.6': habit low-spreading; thorns few, short, straight, slender; bracts nearly round, 4.3–4.7 × 4cm, red to deep red in age. 'New River': habit upright, dense, with strong arching canes; thorns many, recurved, strong, stout; bracts ovate, 3.6 × 2.7cm, light purple. 'Penang': bracts elliptic, abruptly attenuate, dark violet. 'Pigeon Blood': bracts oxblood; perianth tube open in flower. 'Pink Beauty': bracts to 4cm, damask pink to pale magenta. 'Poultonii Special': habit loose-upright, open; thorns many, short, recurved, stout; bracts nearly round, 4.5–5 × 4.2cm, red-purple. 'Poultonii': habit low-spreading, dense; thorns many, short, straight; bracts broadly elliptic to nearly round, 3.6 × 2.5cm, purple-red. 'Rainbow': bracts coral red, becoming multicoloured as they fade. 'Red Glory': habit rounded, loose, open; thorns few, short, straight; bracts elliptic, 4.3 × 3.2cm,

purple-red. 'Rhodamine': habit rounded; thorns few, long, straight, slender; bracts oblong-elliptic, 3.7 × 2.8cm, red-purple. 'Rosa Catalina': habit loose, upright, open; thorns many, long, recurved, stout; bracts nearly round, 3 × 2.6–2.8cm, red-purple. 'Roseuille's Delight': habit upright, open; thorns many, short, slightly recurved; bracts 'double', ovate, 2.5 × 1.7cm, mostly red-orange, fading to orange-pink but also to red-purple. 'Sanderiana' ('Brasiliensis'): habit loose-upright or climbing, foliage dense; thorns many, long, recurved; bracts ovate, 3.5 × 2.7cm, uniformly deep violet-purple with green veins; commonly confused with 'Solar no.1' and 'Fascelle's Purple'. 'Scarlet O'Hara' ('San Diego Red'?): habit loose-upright; thorns many, short, recurved; bracts nearly round, 4.3–5 × 3.9–4.5cm, dark red. 'Scarlet Queen': bracts purple red; perianth tube closed in flower. 'Solar no.1': habit loose-upright; thorns many, long, recurved; bracts ovate, 4–4.5 × 2.7–3cm, light purple; close to 'Sanderiana'. 'Snow White': bracts white, persistent. 'Sun Oija': habit rounded, open; thorns few, straight, slender; bracts ovate-elliptic, 4.5 × 3.7cm, red-purple. 'Susan Hendry': habit loose; thorns many, long, straight, stout; bracts nearly round, 3.5 × 3cm, dark red; cf. 'Scarlett O'Hara'. 'Sweetheart': habit loose, upright, open; thorns many, long, slightly recurved, stout; bracts broadly elliptic, 4 × 3.2cm, red. 'Temple Fire': habit dwarf, low-spreading, slow-growing; thorns more or less absent; bracts broadly ovate, 4 × 3.5cm, red-purple. 'Texas Dawn': habit loose, open, with tall, arching canes; thorns many, long, recurved, stout; bracts elliptic, 3 × 2.5cm, red-purple. 'Thomasii': bracts to 6cm, pink. 'Variegata': leaves variegated grey-green and cream; several variegated forms derived from different species and crossings are probably in cultivation – this is best treated as a group name. 'William Poulton': habit low-srpeading, dense, dwarf; thorns few, short, straight; bracts nearly round, 2.7 × 2.5cm, red to red-purple in age.

Bowiea Harv. & Hook. f. (For James Bowie (c1789–1869), a gardener at Kew who collected in Brazil and S Africa.) Liliaceae (Hyacinthaceae). 3 species of perennial bulbous herbs with deciduous twining stems. Bulbs large, globose, succulent, composed of large, closely packed concentric scales. Stems succulent, green, very slender, scrambling, twining and branching freely and intricately. Leaves small, short-lived, photosynthesis achieved by the mass of thin stems and green bulb scales. Flowers produced on twisting racemes at the ends of the twining shoots, small, green-white or yellow. Fruit fleshy. Southern & Tropical Africa. Z10.

CULTIVATION Bizarre bulbs for the succulent house or a dry bright windowsill, minimum temperature 7°C/45°F. Sit the squat green bulb in a small pot or pan, a quarter buried in a gritty mixture suitable for succulents. Water very sparingly and then only to avoid shrivelling or growth abortion. As temperature and light increase, an elaborate, slender, lime green stem will emerge from the bulb apex and twine through any support provided. *B.volubilis* is the most commonly encountered species. It can be relied upon to produce one or two such growth flushes within a year. After fruiting, reduce water and allow the stem to die off.

B.kilimandscharica Mildbr. (*Schizobasopsis kilimandscharica* (Mildbr.) Barschus).
Close to *B. volubilis*; bulb smaller, to 10cm diam. Flowers yellow-hyaline. Fruit to 3cm, pointed. Tanzania (Kilimanjaro area).

B.volubilis Harv. & Hook. f. (*Schizobasopsis volubilis* (Harv. & Hook. f.) J.F. Macbr.). CLIMBING ONION.
Bulb light shining green, growing above soil level, to 20cm diam. Stems long-twining, thin, bright glossy green. Fruit to 1.4cm, blunt. S Africa.

Bryonia L. (From Gk *bruein*, to burgeon, referring to spring growth from the tuber.) BRYONY. Cucurbitaceae. About 12 species of dioecious, rarely monoecious, climbing, perennial herbs. Roots fleshy or tuberous. Tendrils simple. Leaves 3–5-lobed or -angular, petiolate. Flowers white or green to yellow; calyx tube campanulate, lobes oblong; male flowers racemose or fasciculate; stamens 3 or 5, anthers free or attached, flexuous, oblong; pistillode absent; female inflorescence racemose or corymbose, occasionally solitary; staminodes 3 or 5; ovary ovoid; style slender. Fruit a berry, small, indehiscent; seeds ovoid to oblong, margin crenate. Temperate Europe to W Asia and N Africa. Z6.

CULTIVATION Hedgerow herbs in temperate regions, perennating through tubers and often thought attractive for their berries. Rarely cultivated but easily encouraged by scattering ripe seed at the base of hedgerows. In the open ground, seed can be sown in early spring and plants trained up a tripod of canes.

B.alba L. WHITE BRYONY.
To 4m. Root thick, yellow. Leaves 5-lobed, sometimes 5-angled. Flowers white to pale green, to 2cm diam. Fruit black, to 1cm. Europe to Iran.

B.amplexicaulis Lam. See *Solena amplexicaulis*.

B.cretica ssp. *dioica* L. See *B.dioica*.

B.dioica Jacq. (*B.cretica* ssp. *dioica* L.). RED BRYONY; WILD HOP.
Root fleshy; tendrils simple. Leaves 5-lobed, rough. Flowers pale green. Fruit red, to 0.5cm diam. Summer. Europe, N Africa, W Asia.

B.grandis L. See *Coccinia grandis*.

B.laciniosa hort. See *Diplocyclos palmatus*.

Caesalpinia L. (For Andrea Cesalpini (1524/25–1603), Italian botanist, philosopher, and physician to Pope Clement VIII, author of *De Plantis* (1583) and other works.) Leguminosae (Caesalpinioideae). 70+ species of shrubs, trees and perennial herbs, some climbing, sometimes thorny. Leaves alternate, bipinnate; stipules short-lived and small or conspicuous and persistent. Flowers in terminal, often paniculate racemes; calyx with short tube, 5-toothed; corolla segments 5, subequal, clawed, standard often smallest; stamens 10, markedly exserted, filaments long, somewhat declinate; pistil sessile, stigma inconspicuous, ovary few-ovulate. Fruit an ovate to lanceolate, laterally compressed legume, valves usually thick to membranous, sometimes glandular. Tropics & subtropics.

CULTIVATION A large genus found for the most part in tropical dry open scrub or lowland rainforest, *Caesalpinia* is valued for its finely divided foliage and brilliant flowers, often with showy stamens. The one climbing species commonly cultivated is *C.decapetala*, the Mysore Thorn, a vigorous vining shrub with thorny branches, ferny foliage and erect racemes of pale yellow flowers. From China and Japan, var. *japonica*, differs in its hairless racemes of flowers, the uppermost petal of which tends to be striped red. The Mysore Thorn, and its Japanese variety especially, are hardier than other members of the genus, tolerating short winter lows of –10°C/14°F. In very sheltered locations in zone 8, or in Mediterranean or subtropical gardens, they will quickly cover sunny walls, trellises or pergolas. In colder regions, they will thrive in cool glasshouses or conservatories, planted in beds or tubs and trained on walls or pillars. Grow in full sun in any moderately fertile, well drained and loam-based soil. Water and feed freely during spring and summer, less so in winter. Prune lightly after the main summer flowering to restrict growth, and more aggressively in late winter to remove weak or crossing branches and establish the desired framework. Propagate by seed, pre-soaked in warm water for 24 hours; or by softwood cuttings in sand in a closed case with bottom heat.

C.decapetala (Roth) Alston (*C.sepiaria* Roxb.; *Biancaea sepiaria* (Roxb.) Tod.). MYSORE THORN.
Climbing shrub to 3m. Branches often vine-like, often with sharp decurved thorns. Petiole to 30cm, often prickly; pinnae 6–10 pairs; leaflets to 1.5 × 0.8cm, 7–12 pairs, obovate-elliptic to oblong, rounded, clearly veined. Flowers many, in erect axillary and terminal racemes, raceme-axes puberulent, congested in bud with conspicuous, lanceolate bracts; pedicels to 2.5cm, slender, not jointed; calyx lobes to 1cm, imbricate, unequal; corolla rotate, petals pale yellow, sometimes spotted red, unequal, suborbicular; filaments some-times strongly exserted, pink, villous. Fruit to 10 × 3cm, dehiscent, oblong, with a slender beak, valves coriaceous to subligneous, few-seeded. Summer (principally, but flushes of flowers sometimes produced throughout the year). Tropical Asia. Z9. var. *japonica* (Sieb. & Zucc.) Ohashi (*C.japonica* Sieb. & Zucc.). Usually prickly. Leaflets 2.5 × 1.25cm, 4–8 pairs. Racemes laxer than in type, subglabrous; pedicels to 3.5cm; upper petal striped red. Japan, China. Z8.

C.japonica Sieb. & Zucc. See *C.decapetala* var. *japonica*.

C.sepiaria Roxb. See *C.decapetala*.

Caiophora Presl. Loasaceae. (*Cajophora*). 65 species of annual or short-lived perennial herbs, covered with bristly, stinging hairs. Stems terete, usually twining. Leaves opposite, pinnately lobed. Flowers usually solitary, axillary; petals deeply concave above, yellow, red or white; stamens numerous, clustered opposite petals. Fruit a twisted capsule, opening by spiralling valves. S America. Z9.

CULTIVATION A beautiful twiner for the conservatory or the dry or silver garden, where it can be used to scramble through shrubs. Coral flowers and ingeniously spiralled seed pods compensate for the viciously stinging foliage. Treat as an annual, sown under glass in early spring and planted out before twining begins, or establish as a perennial in sheltered spots, allowing that the stems will die back to rather weedy stocks that will need dry-mulch protection in temperatures below –25°C/–8°F.

C.lateritia Benth. (*Blumenbachia lateritia* (Klotzsch) Griseb.; *Loasa aurantiaca* hort.; *Loasa lateritia* (Klotzsch) Gillies ex Arn.).
Biennial or short-lived perennial herb. Stems to 3m, slender, tightly twining. Leaves 8–18 × 2.5–4cm, cordate to ovate-lanceolate, pinnately lobed or toothed, densely covered in soft hairs interspersed with sharp stinging bristles, dull pale green. Flowers solitary or paired in axils, nodding, on slender, erect pedicels to 8cm; calyx lobes to 0.75cm, triangular-ovate; petals to 3cm, peach to brick-red. Argentina.

Calamus L. (From Gk *kalamos*, reed, reed-pen, stem.) RATTAN PALM; WAIT-A-WHILE PALM. Palmae. Some 370 species of palms, erect and high-climbing with the stem becoming bare and producing axillary sucker shoots, or stemless. Leaves pinnate, sometimes opposed by a sharply toothed and whip-like cirrus which aids climbing; sheath often armed with spines; petiole flat above, convex beneath, armed, or absent; rachis armed; pinnae single-fold, entire, occasionally praemorse, linear-lanceolate or cuneate, regularly spaced or grouped along rachis, sometimes discolorous, with bristles, scales, hairs or spines. Inflorescences borne on leaf sheaths, amid persistent, tubular, spiny bracts; flagella present in non-cirrate species; female inflorescence branched × 2, male inflorescence branched × 3; flowers white to cream. Male flowers solitary, symmetrical; sepals 3, joined; petals 3, basally connate; stamens 6. Female flowers paired with a sterile male flower, larger than male flowers; calyx tubular; petals basally connate; staminodes 6, filaments joined into ring, anthers empty. Fruit to 1.8cm diam., globose, usually yellow and 1-seeded; epicarp covered in vertical rows of reflexed scales. Tropical Africa, Asia, Malay Archipelago, New Guinea, NE Australia to Fiji. Z10.

CULTIVATION Vigorous, often ferociously armed climbing palms from the Old World Tropics, *Calamus* species have many non-ornamental uses: the stems of *C.rotang*, Malacca, are used for walking sticks, umbrella handles, furniture and barbarous acts of corporal punishment. The leaves of many species are used for thatch, the cirri of some to make fine trapping mesh and the fruits of others for the table. Typically, *Calamus* produces a clump of slender, scrambling stems clothed with spines and attractive pinnate leaves. Opposed to the leaves are long, whip-like developments of the leaf sheaths called cirri or flagella. Armed with hooks and spines, the cirri serve as grappling hooks-cum-non-twining tendrils, anchoring the stems in the surrounding vegetation. In humid tropical and subtropical gardens, *Calamus* is a striking climber, allowed to naturalize in damp, wooded sites. Under glass, it requires tub or bed cultivation in a warm glasshouse or conservatory. Plant in an open, fertile bark-based mix in semi-shade. Water, feed and mist frequently in warm weather. Train through larger glasshouse shrubs or tie into trellis, rafters and pillars. Cut out overgrown or exhausted canes cleanly at the base, taking care to avoid the stem thorns and cirri of which will tear flesh and rip clothing.

Of the species described below, the Australian natives are perhaps the most attractive and amenable – *C.australis* with large leaves composed of narrowly lanceolate pinnae, *C.muelleri*, a smaller plant with less spiny leaf sheaths and fewer, oblanceolate pinnae, and *C.caryotoides* with leaflets resembling ragged-edged fishtails. Propagate by division of the clump, or by seed sown on damp sand in a warm, closed case (germination is slow.)

C.australis Mart. LAWYER CANE; WAIT-A-WHILE.
Tall and scrambling. Stems many, *c*1.5cm diam. Leaf sheaths armed with long, rust-coloured, needle-like spines, blades to 1m; petioles sparsely armed, cirrus long, flagellate, with strong, hooked spines. Australia, NE Queensland.

C.caryotoides Cunn. ex Mart. FISHTAIL LAWYER CANE.
Stems slender, clustered. Leaf sheaths armed with short spines; blades to 30cm, sessile; pinnae 8–10, cuneate, apices truncate, serrate, armed with spines, terminal pinnae usually fused into fishtail shape. Australia, NE Queensland.

C.ciliaris Bl.
Climbing by leafless axillary branches armed with reflexed spines, lacking cirri. Leaves to 90cm; petiole 10–15cm, channelled above, convex beneath, sparsely spined; pinnae 40–50 each side of rachis, hairy. India.

C.muelleri H.A. Wendl. & Drude. WAIT-A-WHILE.
Scrambling. Stems many, 8–12mm diam. Leaf sheaths clothed with weak, grey spines; blades to 60cm; pinnae 11–14, lanceolate, margins spiny, apical flagella slender with small, sharp hooks. E Australia, NE NSW, SE Queensland.

C.rotang L. (*C.roxburghii* Griff.). RATTAN CANE.
Leaves to 80cm, lacking cirri; pinnae alternate or suboppoite, lanceolate-acuminate, glossy above, papery, to 30cm, margins ciliate, 2 terminal pinnae free. Sri Lanka, S India.

C.roxburghii Griff. See *C.rotang*.

Calystegia R. Br.(From Gk *kalyx*, calyx, and *stege*, covering, due to the bracteoles which partially or completely surround the calyx.) BINDWEED. Convolvulaceae. About 25 species of perennial, climbing or scrambling herbs, spreading rapidly via branching rhizomes. Stems to 5m, containing white latex. Leaves petiolate, bases often lobed. Flowers axillary, solitary or in small clusters, with 2 large bracteoles which may partially or totally conceal the calyx; corolla large, tubular or funnel-shaped, white or pink, sometimes yellow-hued, sometimes ciliate; stigma with 2 swollen, elongate lobes. Fruit a subglobose capsule; seeds glabrous. Widely distributed in temperate and subtropical zones, often introduced and naturalized. Many of the species hybridize with others. Some taxa, e.g. *C.sepium* ssp. *sepium*, are troublesome weeds. All need careful management in cultivation due to their invasive nature. The name *C.soldanella* is often found in the horticultural literature but the true plant, (L.) R. Br., tends not to flower in cultivation.

CULTIVATION The slender, tough rhizomes of *Calystegia* species make them potentially invasive in gardens, especially in warm climates and on rich soils: with their showy flowers, they are nevertheless attractive and especially useful for clothing unsightly structures or boundary fencing where other plants are not endangered by their spread. The double-flowered form of *C.hederacea* is possibly the most attractive, but will require a sheltered site to survive winters in cool-temperate regions. Grow in full sun in any soil and propagate from seed in spring or by division when dormant.

C.hederacea Wallich (*C.japonica* (Thunb.) Miq.; *C.pellita* (Ledeb.) G. Don; *Convolvulus japonicus* Thunb.; *Convolvulus pellitus* Ledeb.).
Herbaceous climber. Stems to 5m. Leaves narrowly sagit-
tate to lanceolate, to 10cm, on long petioles, densely hairy, with basal lobes. Flowers solitary, on winged peduncles, to 3.5cm diam., rose-pink. Summer–autumn. E Asia; naturalized E US. 'Flore Pleno' (*C.pubescens*

Lindl.; *Convolvulus pellitus* f. *pellitus* Ledeb.): flowers double, sterile, to 5cm diam. and 3.5cm long, bright rose-pink, corolla divided into many narrow, petal-like lobes. Z5.

C.japonica (Thunb.) Miq. See *C.hederacea*.

C.macrostegia (Greene) Brummitt (*Convolvulus macrostegius* Greene).
Herbaceous climber. Stems 1–4m, becoming woody at base. Leaves 4–10cm, deltoid-hastate, somewhat fleshy, sparsely hairy, basal lobes with 2–3 coarse, spreading teeth, apices acute or acuminate. Flowers usually solitary, on 10–20cm peduncles, with membranous, ovate-rounded to suborbicular bracteoles, 2–3cm, tinted pink; calyx totally concealed; corolla white at first, later pink, 5–6cm. W US (California, coastal islands). ssp. **cyclostegia** (House) Brummitt (*Convolvulus cyclostegius* House). Leaves 2–5cm, triangular-lanceolate to ovate. Peduncles 3–10cm; bracteoles 1–1.5cm, sometimes purple; corolla 2.5–4.5cm, white with purple stripes on outside, sometimes pink when old. Z8.

C.occidentalis (A. Gray) Brummitt (*Convolvulus occidentalis* A. Gray).
Tall climber. Leaves 1–4cm, triangular-hastate, basal lobes broad, 2-toothed, apex blunt. Flowers 1–3 per peduncle, with 5–10mm long, lanceolate to oblong-lanceolate bracteoles well below calyx; sepals 6–12mm, unequal; corolla 3–4cm, white, yellow-brown or pink, purple with age. US (S California). Z8.

C.pellita (Ledeb.) G. Don. See *C.hederacea*.
C.pubescens Lindl. See *C.hederacea* 'Flore Pleno'.

C.pulchra Brummitt & Heyw.
Climber. Stems hairy, at least when young. Leaves dull green, sagittate, sinus parallel-sided and oblong. Peduncle winged; bracteoles 15–25mm wide, overlapping and almost concealing calyx, base sac-like, apex rounded to emarginate; corolla 5–7.5cm diam., pink. Summer–autumn. NE Asia, or perhaps a hybrid of European garden origin. Z5.

C.sepium (L.) R. Br. (*Convolvulus sepium* L.). BINDWEED; HEDGE BINDWEED; WILD MORNING-GLORY; RUTLAND-BEAUTY.
Glabrous climber. Leaves on petioles to 10cm, sagittate, sinus acute with divergent sides. Peduncle wingless, bracteoles 1–3 × 0.5–2cm, barely overlapping, usually acute at apex; calyx not concealed; corolla 3–7cm diam., white or pink. Widely distributed in Europe, naturalized elsewhere. ssp. **spectabilis** Brummitt. Glabrous or with stems and petioles hairy. Leaf sinus rounded. Bracteoles 12–24mm wide, strongly keeled; corolla usually 5–6cm diam., pink. Summer–autumn. USSR (Siberia), or perhaps a naturalized garden hybrid of *C.sepium* and *C.pulchra*. Z4.

C.silvatica (Kit.) Griseb.
Climber, wholly glabrous. Leaves sagittate, with a rounded sinus, sides parallel or divergent. Peduncles not winged; bracteoles 14–38mm, almost totally concealing calyx, base sac-like; corolla 5–9cm diam., white, centre band of each lobe sometimes flushed pink on outside. Summer–autumn. S Europe, N Africa, naturalized further north. Z7.

C.tuguriorum (Forst. f.) R. Br. ex Hook. (*Convolvulus tuguriorum* Forst. f.).
Slender climber, glabrous to puberulent. Leaves 1–4cm, thin, ovate-cordate or deltoid, apex acute or acuminate, sinus broad and shallow; petioles slender, to 4cm. Peduncles terete, sometimes very narrowly winged; bracteoles ovate-cordate to suborbicular, apiculate; sepals broad-ovate, subequal, apex obtuse to subacute, sometimes apiculate; corolla 2.5–5cm diam., white to pink. Summer–autumn. New Zealand, S Chile. Z5.

Camoensia Welw. ex Benth. (For Luis de Camoëns (1524–1580), Portuguese poet, author of *The Lusiades*.) Leguminosae (Papilionoideae). 2 species of shrubs or lianes climbing to 20m+. Leaves trifoliolate; stipules spinose; leaflets large, coriaceous; stipels subulate. Flowers large, in erect, stout-peduncled, axillary racemes; bracts and bracteoles short, caducous; calyx obconical-campanulate, lobes 5 thick, overlapping, 2 posterior lobes connate; standard large, broad-orbicular, wings and keel small, oval to cuneate; stamens 10, connate below, separate above, anthers uniform, linear, dorsifixed; ovary long-stipitate, 2–3-ovulate, sometimes pubescent, style long, thin, stigma capitate. Fruit a broad, linear, flattened but thick, dehiscent legume, bivalved, 3–4-seeded; seeds obovoid, transverse, flattened. Tropical W Africa (Gulf of Guinea). Z10.

CULTIVATION Stout and vigorous woody climbers found in the wild scrambling through tropical forest to heights of 20m/65ft; they are widely grown in tropical zones as ornamentals. When in bloom, *C.scandens* is one of the most exquisitely beautiful of tropical climbers. The clusters of large milk-white flowers are frilled, gilded and fragrant; they are usually borne in winter, but in favourable conditions will be produced again in summer. The velvety red pods are also decorative.

Grow in full sun in a freely draining, high-fertility, loam-based mix, with additional organic matter and sharp sand; maintain high humidity and a minimum temperature of 16–18°C/60–65°F, and provide strong support of trellis or wires. Water plentifully when in growth. Prune after flowering in winter, removing overcrowded branches and cutting back flowered shoots to within 5–8cm/2–3in. of their base. Propagate from seed in a sandy, soilless propagating mix; germinate at 23–25°C/75–77°F. Root semi-ripe cuttings in sand in a closed case with bottom heat at 25°C/77°F.

C.maxima (Welw.) Benth. See *C.scandens*.

C.scandens (Welw.) J.B. Gillett (*C.maxima* (Welw.) Benth.).
Large spiny liane. Petioles to 10cm; leaflets to 15 × 7.5cm, ovate- or obovate-acuminate, subglabrous, glossy; stipels acicular. Flowers 2–5, in pendulous, axillary racemes with short, red or brown-red tomentum; bracts to 1cm, lanceo-late, acicular, caducous; pedicels 1cm, with bracteoles at apex; hypanthium to 12cm, tomentose, lobes to 4cm; corolla to 12cm, white, edged yellow or gold, standard to 8cm diam., suborbicular, frilled, wings and keel narrow-oblanceolate. Fruit to 15 × 3cm, valves woody and velvety; seeds 2cm.

Campsidium Seem. (Diminutive of *Campsis*.) Bignoniaceae. 1 species, an evergreen woody vine to 15m. Leaves 10–15cm, opposite, imparipinnate; petiole channelled above; pinnae 2–4cm, 11–13, oblong-elliptic, entire or apex serrate. Flowers in loose terminal racemes; bracts linear-subulate; calyx 5-lobed, campanulate, green, lobes triangular; corolla 3cm, tubular-ventricose, scarlet-orange, pubescent within, lobes 5, equal, rounded, dentate; stamens 4, equal or 2 exserted, 2 included; ovary glabrous, style stout; stigma 2-lobed. Fruit an elliptic-oblong capsule to 10cm, valves leathery with papery endocarp. C & S Chile. Z10.

CULTIVATION   As for *Tecomanthe*.

C.chilense Reisseck & Seem. See *C.valdivianum*.

C.valdivianum (Philippi) Bull (*C.chilense* Reisseck & Seem.; *Tecoma valdiviana* Philippi).

Campsis Lour. TRUMPET VINE; TRUMPET CREEPER. (From Gk *kampsis*, bending; the stamens are curved.) Bignoniaceae. 2 species of deciduous vines to 13m, climbing by aerial roots. Leaves imparipinnate, opposite; pinnae ovate- to lanceolate-elliptic, apex acuminate, margins serrate. Inflorescence a terminal cyme or panicle; calyx 5-lobed; corolla funnelform-campanulate, tube curved and expanded at apex, orange; stamens 4. Fruit a capsule, 2-valved, dehiscent. E Asia, N America.

CULTIVATION   Native to moist woodlands of eastern North America, *C.radicans* often grows as an aggressive weed in its native zones, widely distributed in cultivated fields, roadsides and on trees. Although *Campsis* may be grown as a bush or hedge with hard pruning, it is more commonly used as a climber, to cover large areas of south- or south-west-facing walls and fences. It is valued for its beautifully coloured and exotic flowers carried late in the season into autumn. *C.grandiflora* bears its blossom in larger, looser clusters. *C.g.* 'Thunbergii' will tolerate saline winds. *C.radicans* is hardy to –20°C/–4°F, *C.grandiflora* to –10°C/14°F; the hybrid *C.× tagliabuana* is intermediate between its parents in most respects, including hardiness.

Grow in moist, well drained soil in a warm, sheltered site in light shade or with full sun to ripen wood and maximize flowering in zones at the limits of hardiness. *C.radicans* will become rampant on very rich soils. Cut back to within 15cm/6in. of ground level when planting to encourage basal growth; when plants have filled allotted space, prune in late winter/early spring, by cutting back the previous season's growth to 2–3 buds of the framework. Remove suckers from grafted plants. Tie in to give additional support – the aerial roots may not be strong enough to carry the weight. Take leaf-bud cuttings immediately after bud break in spring or in summer, root in a closed case with bottom heat at 21°C/70°F. Germinate seeds at 10–13°C/50–55°F, stratification at 5°C/40°F for two months may give more even germination. Take 3–4cm/1.25–1.5in. root cuttings in mid to late winter and root in a closed case at 13–16°C/55–60°F. Increase also by simple layering. Cultivars are budded on to year-old seedling stock when dormant. *C.radicans* and

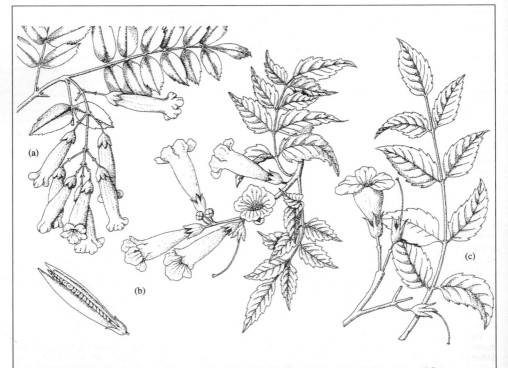

Campsis and Campsidium   (a) *Campsidium valdivianum* (b) *Campsis radicans*, fruit (c) *Campsis grandiflora*

C.× *tagliabuana* are also propagated by hardwood cuttings in the cold frame in late autumn. These tend to produce a heavy callus and root slowly. *Campsis* may be affected by leaf spot, powdery mildew, scale insect, whitefly and mealybug.

C.capreolata hort. See *Bignonia capreolata*.
C.chinensis (Lam.) Voiss. See *C.grandiflora*.
C.dendrophila Seem. See *Tecomanthe dendrophila*.

C.grandiflora (Thunb.) Schum. CHINESE TRUMPET VINE. Scandent shrub, to 6m; aerial roots few or absent. Pinnae 4–7cm, 7–9, wholly glabrous. Inflorescence a loose panicle; calyx deeply divided, lobes lanceolate, to 2cm; corolla tube funnelform, limb to 6cm diam., orange outside, rich yellow inside. Summer–autumn. Japan, China. 'Thunbergii': flowers orange, corolla tube short, lobes reflexed, somewhat hardier, late-flowering. Z7.

C.hybrida Zab. See *C.*× *tagliabuana*.

C.radicans (L.) Seem. TRUMPET CREEPER; VIRGINIA JASMINE. Scandent shrub to 10m; aerial roots abundant. Pinnae to 6cm, 9–11, glabrous but midrib pubescent beneath. Flowers in clusters of 4–12; calyx campanulate, lobes triangular, short; corolla to 7cm, tubular-funnelform, pale orange, yellow

inside, limb scarlet to 4cm diam. Summer. SE US. 'Crimson Trumpet': vigorous climber; leaves lush deep green; flowers large, deep velvety red. 'Flava' ('Yellow Trumpet'): leaves pale green; flowers rich yellow. 'Praecox': flowers scarlet. 'Speciosa': habit shrubby, poor climber; leaflets elliptic; flowers small, flaming orange. Z4.

C.× *tagliabuana* (Vis.) Rehd. (*C.hybrida* Zab.; *Tecoma hybrida* hort. ex Dipp.; *Tecoma intermedia* hort. ex Beissn.; *Tecoma tagliabuana* Vis.). (*C.grandiflora* × *C.radicans*.) Intermediate between the parents. Shrubby. Leaves 20–35cm, rachis pilose; pinnae to 8×4.5cm, 7–11, lightly pubescent above and on veins beneath, serrate. Panicles loose; corolla tubular-campanulate, tube to 6.5cm, base narrow, widening to 3cm across at throat, orange outside, scarlet inside, limb to 6.5cm diam., lobes to 3.8×2.4cm. 'Coccinea': flowers brilliant red. 'Mme Galen': vigorous; leaflets to 15, small, dark green; flowers to 8cm wide, rich deep apricot, with darker veins. Z4.

Camptosema Hook. & Arn. (From Gk *kamptos*, curved, and *semeia*, standard, referring to the curved appendages at the base of the standard.) Leguminosae (Papilionoideae). Some 12 species of perennial shrubs or subshrubs, climbing or suberect. Leaves trifoliolate, rarely 1-, 5-, or pinnately 7-foliolate; stipules caducous; leaflets smooth, subcoriaceous, stipellate. Flowers in axillary, fasciculate racemes; bracts caducous; bracteoles small, often deciduous; calyx tubular, 4-lobed, 2 upper lobes connate; standard ovate-oblong, basally auricled, wings oblong, somewhat adnate to the oblong keel; stamens 10, vexillary stamen free at base, connate with others above, anthers elliptic, uniform; ovary stipitate, many-ovulate; style subulate, incurved, glabrous; stigma small, terminal. Fruit a stipitate, tardily dehiscent legume, bivalved; seeds small, flattened. S America (especially Brazil). Z9.

CULTIVATION *Camptosema* species are found in moist lowland woodland; in their native zones, their nectar-rich flowers are particularly attractive to hummingbirds. Grown for its long, slender racemes of rich, ruby-red flowers, *C.rubicundum* is an elegant climber that is particularly suitable for smaller gardens in essentially frost-free, warm temperate climates, such as those of California. If cut back by light frosts, it will re-shoot from the base. Prune to thin tangled or exhausted shoots. Under glass, cultivate as for *Camoensia*.

C.rubicundum Hook. & Arn. (*Dioclea glycinioides* hort.; *Kennedya splendens* Meissn.). SCARLET WISTERIA. Tall climbing shrub. Shoots slender. Leaves trifoliolate; leaflets to 5×2cm, oblong or narrow-oval, base and apex rounded, often emarginate, glabrous. Flowers in slender

racemes to 25.5cm; calyx cylindric, 4- or 6-lobed, lobes unequal; corolla deep ruby red, standard to 2.5cm, somewhat hooded, wings and keel oblong, 1.6cm. Fruit linear, coriaceous; seeds elliptic. Summer. Brazil, Argentina.

Canarina L. (From the habitat of *C.canariense*, the Canary Islands.) Campanulaceae. 3 species of herbaceous perennials, differing from *Campanula* in having 6-merous flowers and fruit an edible berry. Canary Is., Tropical E Africa.

CULTIVATION *C.canariensis*, from shady ravines and wooded areas, is a handsome climbing or trailing plant for the cool to intermediate glasshouse of conservatory, particularly valued for its waxen pale orange bell flowers, beautifully veined in crimson and carried on the tips of lateral growths from late autumn to spring. *C.abyssinica* and *C.eminii* are smaller plants but no less beautiful. Grow in bright filtered light in a fertile, perfectly drained, humus-rich medium, comprising equal parts loam, leafmould, screened well rotted manure and sharp sand; ensure ample root room. Water moderately when in growth and keep just dry when dormant. Maintain good ventilation when weather allows and a minimum temperature of 7–10°C/45–50°F for *C.canariensis*, 10–13°C/50–55°F for other species. Provide support for *C.canariensis* and cut back exhausted growth when dormant. Repot as growth resumes. Root tubers of *C.abyssinica* and *C.eminii* may be stored dry when dormant. Propagate by seed, division or by basal cuttings in sand in a closed case with gentle bottom heat.

C.abyssinica Engl.
As for *C.eminii*, but leaves smaller, base cordate, corolla shorter, pedicels spiralling half way up, filaments basally dilated. Abyssinia, Kenya, Uganda. Z10.

C.campanula L. See *C.canariensis*.

C.canariensis (L.) Kuntze (*C.campanula* L.). CANARY BELL-FLOWER.
To 1.2m, stems semi-scandent; rootstock fleshy. Leaves opposite, narrowly ovate to linear, base hastate to cordate, serrate, petiolate. Flowers pendulous, borne singly at tip of axillary branches; calyx lobes leafy, recurved; corolla cam-

panulate, lobes recurved, orange-yellow, with russet to maroon lines. Canary Is. Z9.

C.eminii Asch. AFRICAN BELLFLOWER.
Glabrous herb, branchlets slender, drooping or trailing, fleshy. Leaves to 8cm, opposite, elongate-ovate, crenate at base or lobed, petiolate. Flowers terminal; pedicels slender, drooping; calyx striped red; corolla tubular in lower half, inflated upwards, lobes deltoid, dull to sulphur yellow, striped green. Kenya. Z10.

Canavalia DC. (From *canavali*, the name of one species in Malabar.) Leguminosae (Papilionoideae). Some 51 species of perennial herbs or lianes. Stems scandent or procumbent. Leaves petiolate, trifoliolate; stipules and stipels small, caducous. Flowers large, in axillary racemes; calyx campanulate, lobes 5, lower 3 and upper 2 each forming a lip; standard round, reflexed, keel blunt or beaked, incurved; ovary generally multi-ovular, style narrow, curved, stigma terminal, small; stamens 10, 9 joined in a tube, 1 partly free, anthers homogeneous. Fruit a legume, flat or swollen, filiform or oblong, often with costae or wings along the upper seam, ligneous, usually dehiscent; seeds 4–15, ovoid, condensed, ellipsoid or reniform. Tropics and Subtropics, mainly Americas. Z10.

CULTIVATION   Cultivated in tropical and subtropical zones for their edible beans which contain dangerous toxins and need special preparation, *Canavalia* species occur in woodland and in sandy and rocky coastal habitats. In temperate zones they can be trained up pillars and along rafters in the warm glasshouse, grown for the ornamental value of their large flowers. Plant in a well drained medium with additional organic matter, in dappled sunlight with a minimum night temperature of 16–18°C/60–65°F. Water moderately when in growth, less in winter. Sow scarified seeds in spring or autumn, at the base of their support.

C.africana Dunn (*C.virosa* (Roxb.) Wight & Arn.).
Perennial, scandent or procumbent, 3–15m; stems rusty-downy at first, later glabrous. Leaflets 6–16.5 × 3.8–12cm, ovate-obtuse or rounded, downy throughout; rachis 1.5–3.5cm; petiole 4–13cm; stipules 2.5mm. Racemes 6–21cm; peduncles 12–28cm; standard to 3×1.7cm, oblong, pale purple, veined white, flushed green at base, wings and keel pale purple-red, white toward base. Fruit to 18×3cm condensed, filiform to oblong; seeds 1–2×0.7–1cm, oblong-ellipsoid, brown or mahogany, marbled black. E Africa.

C.ensiformis (L.) DC. CHICKSAW LIMA BEAN; JACK BEAN; WONDER BEAN; GIANT STOCK BEAN.
Annual bush or climber to 2m. Leaflets to 20cm. Corolla purple-pink, standard to 2.5cm or longer. Fruit to 40×3cm, linear, buff-brown; seeds white. S America.

C.gladiata (Jacq.) DC.
Annual, twining or erect, resembling *C.ensiformis* but fruits wider (to 5cm across) and seeds deep red, coral or chocolate-brown. Old World Tropics.

C.virosa (Roxb.) Wight & Arn. See *C.africana*.

Capparis L. (From *kapparis*, name used by Dioscorides.) CAPER. Capparidaceae. Some 250 species of evergreen shrubs or small trees, often scandent, glabrous or pubescent with simple or stellate hairs. Leaves spirally arranged, simple, herbaceous to coriaceous, usually stipulate, short-petiolate. Inflorescence terminal or axillary, usually a raceme or a panicle, 1- to many-flowered, bracteate; flowers white or yellow to purple-brown, often fragrant, pedicellate; sepals 4, free or slightly united at base, often dimorphic, valvate or imbricate; petals 4, equal or slightly unequal, imbricate, mostly obovate; stamens long, showy, several to 100 or more, exceeding petals; gynophore subequal to stamens, ovary unilocular, placentas 2–6, ovules few to many, stigma usually obscure. Fruit an elongate to globose berry, unilocular, sometimes dehiscent; seeds 1 to many, obliquely reniform. Subtropics, Tropics. Z10 unless specified.

CULTIVATION   *Capparis* species are grown for their large showy flowers, sweetly scented in *C.lasiantha* and graced with long showy stamens. The pickled flower buds of *C.spinosa* are capers. In warm temperate and subtropical climates, they are attractive ornamentals suited to training on walls or through other shrubs and trees. In cooler regions, *Capparis* requires the protection of the glasshouse with a minimum temperature of about 12°C/54°F, although *C.spinosa* is sometimes grown as a frost-tender annual. Grow in full sun in a freely draining soil. Under glass, grow in well crocked pots with a medium-fertility, loam-based mix with additional sharp sand, and water carefully and moderately when in growth. Propagate by ripe seed sown fresh, or by semi-ripe cuttings in sand in a closed case.

C.lasiantha R. Br. ex DC. NATIVE ORANGE; SPLIT JACK.
Shrub or climber to 3m, branches orange-brown to grey-tomentose, spiny. Leaves to 6.5 × 2cm, ovate or elongate, obtuse to rounded, rounded at base, coriaceous, blue-green above, yellow-green beneath, short-petiolate. Flowers fragrant, solitary in leaf axils or in rows of 2 or 3; pedicels to 2cm; sepals to 8 × 4mm, outer sepals ovate or navicular, acute, inner sepals elliptic; petals 1.6 × 0.4cm, obovate, white; stamens 20–22, filaments to 3cm; gynophore to 3cm, pubescent below, ovary to 3mm, ellipsoid. Fruit to 4 × 2cm, ellipsoid to globose, yellow. Australia.

C.rupestris Sibth. & Sm. See *C.spinosa* var. *inermis*.

C.spinosa L. COMMON CAPER.
Prostrate or straggling, spiny, deciduous shrub. Leaves to 6× 5.5cm, elliptic or suborbicular, obtuse to rounded, truncate to rounded at base; petiole to 1.5cm; stipular thorns present. Flowers solitary, axillary; pedicels to 7.5cm; sepals to 28mm, ovate, glabrescent, posterior sepals larger, deeply saccate; petals pure white or white tinted red beneath, upper petals to 5.5×4cm, subrhomboid, lower petals to 3.5 ×3.5cm; stamens white, 100–190, filaments to 5cm, sometimes purple-red; gynophore to 7cm, ovary to 8mm, oblong, glabrous, placentas 5 or 6. Fruit to 5×1.5cm, ellipsoid to fusiform, olive-green. S Europe and Asia to Malesia, and Pacific (*C.mariana* Jacq.& *C.cordifolia* Lam.), Australia (var. *nummularia* (DC.) Bail.). var. *inermis* Turra (*C.rupestris* Sibth. & Sm.). Stipular thorns absent. W Mediterranean to N India. Z8.

Cardiospermum L. (From Gk *kardia*, heart, *sperma*, seed: the seed has a heart-shaped white spot near the hilum.) Sapindaceae. 14 species of herbs or shrubs climbing by tendrils. Leaves alternate, mostly biternately compound, leaflets coarsely toothed to pinnatifid. Flowers zygomorphic, bracteate, small, in axillary corymbs with a pair of opposite tendrils; sepals 4–5, free, imbricate, unequal; petals 4, white, unequal; stamens 8, filaments with spreading, soft, straight hairs; style with 3 linear branches; ovary 3-chambered. Capsule subglobose, membranous, inflated; seeds cordate-globose, black. Tropical Africa, America and India. Z9.

CULTIVATION Vigorous, extensively branching vines which may be grown in the open in tropical or subtropical regions for their interesting, bladder-like fruits; the soft, ferny foliage is useful for covering trellising, pergolas, fences and other supports. *C.grandiflorum* occurs in moist or dry thicket and forest, climbing by tendrils into the tree canopy: its showy flowers are larger than those of *C.halicacabum* and scented. *C.halicacabum* is normally encountered in the wild as a short-lived plant, sprawling over and entwining grasses or other shrubs on wasteground or thicket by rivers, streams and on lagoon banks: it has become naturalized in many areas, including the southern US and Australia. Normally grown as an annual, in areas where temperatures do not drop below 5°C/40°F, it may be sown *in situ*: in colder regions, sow under glass about two months before planting out. Grow in any well drained, fertile ground in full sun; water plentifully in dry weather. Propagate from seed sown in spring at 18–21°C/65–70°F; germination is good, occurring about three weeks from sowing. Also from softwood cuttings in spring.

C.caillei A. Chev. See *C.grandiflorum*.

C.grandiflorum Sw. HEARTSEED. (*C.caillei* A. Chev.). Herbaceous vine to 8m. Stems pubescent, sulcate. Leaves 15–20cm, leaflets toothed, papery, hairy beneath. Flowers to 1cm diam., cream, fragrant. Fruit 7 × 4cm, ovoid, almost triangular, usually glabrous. Tropical America and Africa. f. *hirsutum* (Willd.) Radlk.Stems and petiole hirsute to setose.

C.halicacabum L. BALLOON VINE; HEART PEA. Woody vining perennial to 2m. Stem slender, grooved. Leaves 8–12cm, oblong-acuminate; leaflets to 4 × 3cm, glabrous, deeply toothed, elongate-ovate. Flowers to 0.8cm diam., white, unscented. Fruit to 2.5 × 2.5cm diam., ovoid-globose, obscurely 3-angled, very inflated, pubescent. Tropical India, Africa, America.

Cayratia Juss. (From the native name, *cáy rat long*.) Vitaceae. 45 species of herbs, shrubs or vines close to *Vitis* and *Parthenocissus*. Tendrils opposite leaves, forked 1–3 times, sometimes terminating with adhesive holdfasts. Leaves alternate, digitately or pedately compound; leaflets 3–12, margins dentate-crenate to serrate. Inflorescence of corymbose cymes or umbellate, axillary, apparently terminal or opposite leaves, long-pedunculate; flowers small, 4-merous; calyx subtruncate; petals free, patent or reflexed, green; receptacle cupular, adnate to ovary base, with thin margins; ovary 2-celled with 2 ovaries per cell; style terete; stigma small. Fruit a berry, globose to depressed-globose, thickly discoid or transversely ellipsoid; seeds 2–4 with 1–2 deep cavities on ventral side. Old World Tropics and Subtropics. Z10.

CULTIVATION Tender vines resembling *Parthenocissus*, they are useful for covering walls and trees outdoors in zone 10 and for the intermediate to warm glasshouse or conservatory elsewhere. Cultivation as for *Tetrastigma*.

C.acuminata (A. Gray) A.C. Sm. (*Cissus acuminata* A. Gray; *Vitis acuminata* (A. Gray) Seem.). Vine, slender, subglabrous. Leaves pedately 5-foliolate, or with one or both of lateral leaflets undivided; leaflets 4–6cm, ovate to ovate-oblong or rhombic, acute at base, long-acuminate at apex, irregularly mucronate-serrate, membranous; petioles slender, 4–7.5cm; petiolule of central leaflet to 1.5cm, those of laterals shorter. Inflorescence cymose, small, laxly flowered; peduncle slender, 5cm. Fiji.

C.japonica (Thunb.) Gagnep. (*Vitis japonica* Thunb.; *Columella japonica* (Thunb.) Alston). Vine with elongate rhizome; tendrils bifid. Leaves pedately 5-foliolate; leaflets 3–8cm, ovate to ovate-orbicular, generally acute or acuminate at apex, acute to obtuse at base, aristate-serrate, glabrous or finely pubescent beneath; petiolules very unequal, 0.5–3.5cm. Inflorescence axillary or terminal, with 3

main branches, 6–10cm. Fruit globose, white or perhaps blue-black. Summer. E Asia, Malaysia, New Caledonia, Australia.

C.oligocarpa (Lév. & Vaniot) Gagnep. (*Cissus oligocarpa* (Lév. & Vaniot) L.H. Bail.; *Vitis oligocarpa* Lév. & Vaniot; *Columella oligocarpa* (Lév. & Vaniot) Rehd.). Scandent shrub, more or less softly cinereous-pubescent Branches terete, grooved; tendrils hair-like, forked. Leaves pedately compound; leaflets lanceolate-ovate, obtuse to rounded at base, slenderly elongate-acuminate at apex, sometimes glabrescent, central leaflet 6–11cm, laterals 3–5 cm, veins reticulate; petioles slender; petiolules of lateral leaflets 0.2–1cm, of central 1.5–5cm. Inflorescence generally axillary, subumbellate, 4cm diam.; peduncle 2–3cm. Fruit globose, 6–8mm, yellow then black. China, Vietnam.

C.thomsonii (Lawson) Süsseng. See *Parthenocissus thomsonii*.

Celastrus L. (From *kelastros*, an ancient Greek name for *Phillyrea latifolia*.) BITTERSWEET; SHRUBBY BITTERSWEET. Celastraceae. Some 30 species of shrubs, mostly deciduous, often scandent or twining. Twigs slender, smooth or lenticellate with solid or chambered pith. Leaves usually ovate, pubescent or glabrous, alternate, sharply or bluntly toothed. Flowers in large, terminal panicles or axilliary cymes, small, white, pale green or pale red, unisexual in some species; calyx 5-toothed; petals 5, oblong-ovate; stamens 5; disc entire or undulate; ovary superior, 2–4 locular, style rather short, stigma 3-lobed. Fruit a capsule, small, 3-valved, dehiscent, woody; seeds 1–2 per valve, winged at the apex, with fleshy orange or red aril. Africa, America, Australia, E & S Asia, Pacific.

CULTIVATION Vigorous twining and scandent shrubs, they will cover walls, fences, stumps and host trees with densely tangled slender branches enlivened in autumn and winter by persistent fruit which split to reveal brilliantly coloured seeds. In addition to their vivid seed coatings, most *Celastrus* species have good, clear yellow fall colour, while the foliage of *C.glaucophyllus* and *C.hypoleucus* is blue green and that of *C.rosthornianus* highly polished and thick-textured. Many are dioecious and a plant of each sex will be required for successful fruiting. With the exception of the tender *C.australis*, *Celastrus* will tolerate temperatures as low as −15°C/5°F. Plant in full sun or semi-shade on any fertile, damp soil; attach to the support at first. Seed sown in spring will germinate readily but, of course, produce plants of unknown sex. Root cuttings taken in late winter and placed in a cold frame will succeed, as will simple layering.

C.angulatus Maxim. (*C.latifolius* Hemsl.)
Shrub, climbing to 7.25m; young twigs angular, pith chambered. Leaves 10–18 × 8–14cm, broadly elliptic-ovate, briefly acuminate, crenate, glabrous. Panicles to 15cm, terminal, pendulous; flowers small, pale green. Fruit to 9mm diam., yellow, carried abundantly in pendulous trusses, valves orange within; aril red. Summer. NW & C China. Z5.

C.articulatus Thunb. See *C.orbiculatus*.

C.australis Harv. & F. Muell.
Scandent shrub to 7m, glabrous. Leaves to 10cm, ovate-lanceolate to oblong-elliptic or lanceolate, entire or minutely dentate, attenuate at base; petiole short. Panicles terminal or rarely in upper axils, narrow, loose, to 5cm; flowers white, 6mm diam. Fruit to 6mm thick; aril orange-yellow. Australia (Victoria). Z9.

C.dependens Wallich. (*C.paniculatus* Willd.)
Twining shrub, resembling *C. scandens*; young twigs brown, conspicuously lenticellate; pith chambered. Leaves 7.5–12cm, oblong, acuminate, finely crenate, shining deep green above; petiole to 10mm, often shorter. Panicles to 17cm. Fruit close to *C.scandens*. Himalaya to SW China. Z8.

C.flagellaris Rupr.
Twining shrub to 8m; young twigs hollow, red-tinted, with persistent hooked stipular thorns. Leaves to 5cm, broadly ovate, shortly tapering, serrulate, pale green, scaberulous above; petiole to 3cm, slender. Flowers 1–3 in axillary, sessile cymes, small, green. Fruit yellow-green, to 6mm diam.; aril orange-red. Summer. China, Japan, S. Korea. Z4.

C.gemmatus Loes.
Twining shrub to 12m, resembles *C. orbiculatus* but winter buds conic-ovoid, to 12mm. Leaves to 11cm, elliptic, tapering finely, serrulate or crenulate, glossy green above, veins finely reticulate beneath. Inflorescence corymbose, sparse, short-stalked. Fruit 1cm diam., close to *C. orbiculatus*. C & W China. Z7.

C.glaucophyllus Rehd. & Wils.
Scandent shrub to 10m, pith chambered. Leaves to 10cm, elliptic-obovate, acuminate, attenuate to the base, sparsely crenate, glaucous above, markedly so beneath. Flowers green, inconspicuous, clustered in axils and in short terminal racemes. Fruit to 1cm, ovoid at first, yellow; aril scarlet. W China. Z8.

C.hookeri Prain.
Vining to 6m; young twigs initially rusty-pubescent, soon glabrous. Leaves elliptic to ovate, apex narrow, rounded or cuneate at base, coarsely toothed, veins rusty-pubescent beneath; petiole to 7cm, usually shorter. Flowers in axillary clusters and racemes, peduncles short; filaments glabrous. Fruit abundant, to 6mm, orange; aril red. Himalaya, China. Z6.

C.hypoglaucus Hemsl. See *C.hypoleucus*.

C.hypoleucus (Oliv.) Loes (*C.hypoglaucus* Hemsl.).
Twining to 5m; twigs initially glaucescent. Leaves to 14cm, oblong-elliptic, briefly acuminate, remotely serrulate, dark green above, glaucous blue-green beneath; petiole to 12mm. Flowers to 6mm diam., in axillary cymes and loose terminal panicles to 12cm, pale yellow. Fruit to 8mm diam., ultimately yellow, ripening particularly late; aril red. Summer. China. Z8.

C.latifolius Hemsl. See *C.angulatus*.

C.loeseneri Rehd. & Wils.
Twining to 6m; twigs initially smooth, red-brown, obscurely punctate, pith chambered. Leaves 5–11cm, oval to broad ovate to elliptic-lanceolate, acuminate, crenate, deep green above, paler beneath, thick. Flowers few, clustered in axillary short-stalked cymes, sometimes on short, leafless, lateral brances, rarely in a terminal raceme, small, white tinged green. Fruit 8mm diam., yellow; aril red. C China. Z6. The name *C.loesneri* is sometimes misapplied to *C.orbiculatus*.

C.orbiculatus Thunb. (*C.articulatus* Thunb.) ORIENTAL BITTERSWEET.
Densely twining shrub to 12m; twigs tangled, slender, soon hardening, light brown, rod-like, pith solid. Leaves 5 to 10cm, broadly elliptic, to semiorbicular, abruptly tapered, finely crenate to serrate, pale green throughout. Flowers 6mm diam., clustered 2–4 in axillary cymes, pale green. Fruit globose, 3-valved, deep yellow within, massed in bead-like bunches in autumn; aril coral pink to red. NE Asia, naturalized N America. Z4. var. *punctatus* (Thunb.) Rehd. (*C.punctatus* Thunb.). Less vigorous; leaves smaller, elliptic-ovate to elliptic oblong. 'Diana': female form.

C.paniculatus Willd. See *C.dependens*.
C.punctatus Thunb. See *C.orbiculatus var. punctatus*.

C.rosthornianus Loes.
Twining to 5m; young twigs very slender, pith chambered. Leaves to 8cm, narrow-elliptic to elliptic-lanceolate, acuminate, cuneate, denticulate, pale green, highly lustrous, smooth above, thick-textured; petiole to 6mm. Flowers 1–3 in small but numerous subsessile axillary cymes, white tinged green. Fruit 6mm diam., ochre to apricot; aril red. C & W China. Z5.

C.rugosus Rehd. & Wils.
Twining to 6m; young twigs angular or striated, glabrous, densely punctate, pith chambered. Leaves to 13cm, ovate to oblong, short-acuminate, coarsely rugulose above, veins glabrous or pubescent, reticulate beneath; petiole to 1.5cm. Flowers clustered 1–3 in axillary cymes or terminal racemes, small, pale green. Fruit abundant, orange-yellow; aril bright red. China. Z6.

C.scandens L. WAXWORK; AMERICAN BITTERSWEET; STAFF VINE.
Twining to 7m; twigs tough, terete, glabrous, pith solid. Leaves to 10cm, ovate-oblong, tapering toward apex, serrate, base cuneate. Flowers small, unisexual or bisexual, in terminal racemes or panicles to 10cm, pale yellow. Fruit globose, 8mm diam., yellow, aril carmine-red. N America (Quebec, south to New Carolina and New Mexico). 'Indian Brave': male form. 'Indian Maiden': female form. Z2.

C.spiciformis Rehd. & Wils. var. *laevis* (Rehd. & Wils.) Rehd. (*C.vaniotii* (Lév.) Rehd.)
Scandent shrub to 3m, glabrous. Leaves to 10cm, oval or ovate, sometimes ovate-lanceolate, acuminate, shallowly dentate, pale and often glaucescent beneath; petiole to 1.5cm. Flowers in terminal panicles to 13cm, small, creamy-white. Fruit to 6mm, orange-yellow; aril shining dark brown. China. Typical plants of *C.spiciformis* are unlikely to be in cultivation; they differ from var. *laevis* in the leaves which are downy beneath. Z6.

C.vaniotii (Lév.) Rehd. See *C.spiciformis*. var. *laevis*.

Ceratosanthes Burm. ex Adans. (From Gk *keras*, horn, and *anthos*, flower.) Cucurbitaceae. Some 5 species of dioecious, perennial herbs, from tuberous roots. Stems climbing or trailing. Tendrils simple. Leaves palmately lobed, variable, often withering early. Male flowers in racemose or subumbelliform clusters, white, opening at night; calyx elongated, slightly expanded at apex, 5-lobed; corolla 5-lobed, lobes bifid at apex; stamens 3, free, inserted on throat of calyx tube; female flowers in small umbelliform clusters, resembling males; ovary globose to fusiform; stigmas bifid or 2-parted. Fruit baccate, indehiscent, red; seeds several, subglobose. S America, W Indies. Z10.

CULTIVATION   As for *Trichosanthes*. Can also be grown as groundcover in a glasshouse or conservatory border.

C.palmata (L.) Urban (*Trichosanthes palmata* L.; *Trichosanthes tuberosa* Roxb. non Willd.).
Stems to 5m, arising from a large tuber. Leaves 1–9cm, broadly ovate, pentagonal or reniform, base cordate, palmately 3–5-lobed, scabrid-punctate above; petioles 1–4.5cm, sparsely pubescent. Male flowers white, 4–40 in racemes, peduncles 1.5–14cm, pedicels to 7mm, glandular-pubescent; calyx 13–27mm, slightly pubescent, lobes spreading, 1–4mm, green; corolla lobes to 20× 3.5mm; female flowers solitary or 2–4, on peduncle to 10cm, pedicels 1–8mm; ovary ellipsoid. Fruit solitary or in pairs, ovoid or ellipsoid, 15–30× 10–19mm, red, smooth; seeds c4mm. Northern S America (Lesser Antilles, Trinidad, Guyana, Surinam, Venezuela, N Colombia).

Ceropegia L. (From Gk *keros*, wax, and *pege*, fountain, in reference to the form and the waxy appearance of the flowers.) Asclepiadaceae. 200 species of perennials, climbing or erect, often with a caudex, swollen tubers or fleshy, fusiform roots. Leaves opposite, occasionally in whorls of 3, in the case of non-succulent species always well developed, usually petiolate, cordate to lanceolate especially in climbing species, usually linear to almost filiform in erect species, in succulent species well developed or smaller, reduced to scales or caducous. Flowers in a cyme or solitary, pedicellate or sessile, arising laterally between the petioles; calyx composed of 5 sepals, the 5 petals of the corolla united to form a tube which is usually longer than wide, swollen at base and cylindric or funnel-shaped in the central and upper parts, straight or curved, tips of corolla lobes often remaining united creating a lantern-like structure. Fruit a follicle, lanceolate to cylindric, pointed, glabrous; seeds flat with a tuft of silky hairs. Canary Is., Tropical & SE Africa, Madagascar, Comoro, Tropical Arabia, Himalaya, W & S China, India, Sir Lanka, Indonesia, Philippines, New Guinea, Australia (Queensland). Z10.

CULTIVATION   *Ceropegia* species are found in almost all types of subtropical and tropical habitat, from desert to rainforest. Cultivation must be matched to the habitat from which the plant originates. Almost all found in cultivation, however, tend to be more or less succulent and it is to these that the following notes apply.

The genus shows a wide diversity in shape and colour of leaf, flower and stem structure, which makes many of them excellent plants for greenhouse decoration or as house plants in temperate parts of the world. In tropical and subtropical zones, the climbing species can make interesting additions to trellis pergolas and walls, particularly in areas of low rainfall. The Sweetheart Vine, *C.linearis* ssp. *woodii* is a popular trailer and basket plant with slender cascading stems, succulent heart-shaped leaves and curious flowers. All are tender and need a minimum winter temperature of 12–13°C/54–55°F. Some species from particularly warm areas, such as Madagascar, are better at 16°C/60°F minimum.

When grown as glasshouse plants, they require intermediate or warm conditions with medium to low humidity, particularly in winter, and bright filtered light in summer. When grown in pots, gritty, free-draining, loam-based medium should be used. The root system is often tuberous or fusiform; wide and relatively shallow pots suit the former, and standard to extra deep (e.g. long toms) suit the latter. Pot or re-pot in early spring, and water very sparingly or not at all until re-established. Rest succulents between mid-autumn and early spring, watering only to prevent excessive shrivelling. Water rapid-growing, leafy species sparingly in spring and autumn, moderately in summer. Water slow-growing succulent species sparingly at all times. Apply a weak liquid feed monthly when in growth.

Propagate by cuttings, seed, or by tubers, which are produced at the nodes along the stems of some species, most notably *C.linearis*. Cuttings should be taken just below a node and consist of 2–3-node tip-cuttings of mature young shoots. The most common pest is mealybug. Whitefly may affect leafy young growths. Basal rot will occur in overwet conditions; stems thus affected should be used for cutting material.

C.africana R. Br. (*C.wightii* Graham & Wight).
Stems slender, trailing or erect from small tubers, the stems themselves proliferous, producing small tubers. Leaves ovate, elliptic or lanceolate, fleshy. Corolla glabrous outside, tube 1–2.5cm, exterior tinged green, brown-violet-striate toward the mouth, interior glabrous, lobes linear, 0.6–1.2cm, joined at the tip, with dark purple hairs inside along the keel; outer corona lobes of staminal column deeply cupular, inner lobes broad and laterally flattened. S Africa (E & W Cape).

C.albertina S. Moore. See *C.aristolochioides* ssp. *albertina*.

C.ampliata E.Mey.
Stems moderately thick and succulent, tall and often twining or snaking, grey-green, leafless or with scale-like leaves (these often ovate or elliptic in cultivated plants). Corolla tube 2.5–5cm, broadly cylindric with a swollen base, exterior pale green, interior with a transverse purple band, lobes to 0.9cm, oblong-lanceolate, dark green, joined at tips. S Africa (Southern Cape).

C.arabica H. Huber.
Roots tufted, fleshy; stems glabrous, twining, usually leafless. Corolla glabrous outside, tube 2.5–3.5cm, exterior marked purple, interior glabrous, hairs only in the widened

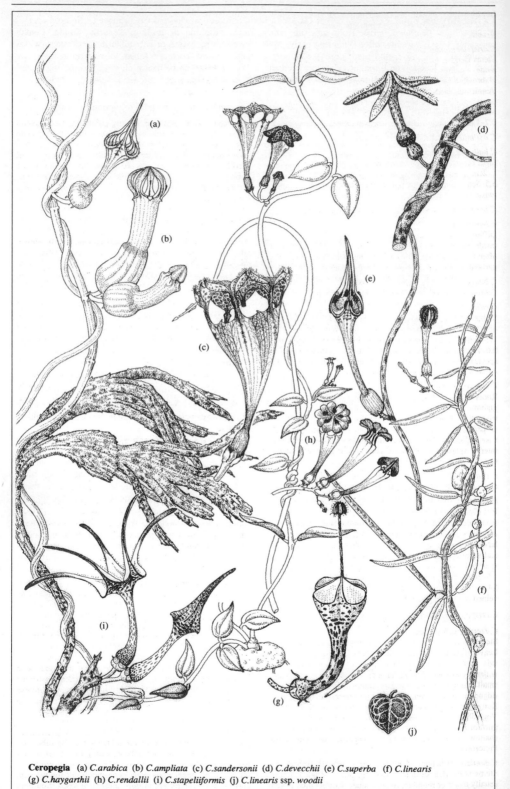

Ceropegia   (a) *C.arabica* (b) *C.ampliata* (c) *C.sandersonii* (d) *C.devecchii* (e) *C.superba* (f) *C.linearis*
(g) *C.haygarthii* (h) *C.rendallii* (i) *C.stapeliiformis* (j) *C.linearis* ssp. *woodii*

funnel-shaped mouth, lobes triangular or narrow-linear, 1.5–2.5cm, white-pubescent within, tips joined, glabrescent. Arabia.

C.aristolochioides Decne.
Stems slender, glabrous, slightly succulent. Leaves petiolate, ovate, usually cordate at base. Corolla dark purple outside, glabrous, tube to 1.5cm, interior hairy in central part only, mouth widened, funnel-shaped, lobes 0.4–0.8cm, broad-ovate, glabrous. Senegal to Ethiopia. ssp. *albertina* (S. Moore) H. Huber (*C.albertina* S. Moore). Corolla lobes 0.7–1.6cm, oblong-linear, narrower at the mouth.

C.assimilis N.E. Br. See *C.cancellata*.

C.ballyana Bullock.
Stem robust, twining. Leaves ovate or elliptic, fleshy; petiole 1–2cm. Flowers green-white spotted red-brown; corolla tube 3.5–5cm, lobes 6–7cm, linear from triangular base, apices twisted together. Kenya.

C.barbertonensis N.E. Br. See *C.linearis* ssp. *woodii*.

C.barklyi Hook. f.
Differs from *C.africana* in having corolla lobe hirsute on the inside slender section, lobes equalling or exceeding tube, often twisted together for much of their length, interior hairy, particularly toward the base. S Africa (Eastern Cape).

C.boussingaultiifolia Dinter. See *C.nilotica*.
C.brownii Ledger. See *C.denticulata* ssp. *brownii*.

C.cancellata Rchb. (*C.assimilis* N.E. Br.).
Stems slender, twining, from small tuber. Leaves ovate-oblong to linear, fleshy. Corolla glabrous outside, tube 1.2–2cm, green, interior hairy in central part, lobes 0.6–1.2cm, linear, purple-brown, glabrous, united at tips. This species appears to be midway between *C.africana* and *C.linearis*. S Africa (Cape Province).

C.carnosa E. Mey.
Roots fleshy, fusiform, tufted; stem slender, twining, glabrous. Leaves small, fleshy, ovate to ovate-lanceolate or triangular. Corolla glabrous outside, cream spotted and striped red-brown, tube 1.2–1.9cm, interior hirsute toward the base and the slightly widened mouth, lobes 0.4–0.6cm, ovate, interior sparsely white-hairy, same colour as tube, united at tips. S Africa (Natal, E Cape).

C.connivens Dyer. See *C.fimbriata* ssp. *connivens*.
C.constricta N.E. Br. See *C.nilotica*.

C.crassifolia Schltr. (*C.crispata* N.E. Br.; *C.thorncroftii* N.E. Br.; *C.tuberculata* Dinter).
Roots a cluster of thick, fleshy, fusiform tubers; aerial growth annual, consisting of a twining stem to 3m, with large, circular-ovate leaves to 8×8cm. (Cape plants have stems to 1m and narrow-lanceolate to linear leaves.) Corolla green-white, speckled red-brown or purple, exterior glabrous, tube 1.5–3cm, the funnel-shaped opening moderately widening, lobes 0.5–1.2cm, broad-ovate, interior sparsely hirsute, veined red-brown. Namibia to Natal.

C.crispata N.E. Br. See *C.crassifolia*.

C.decidua E.A. Bruce.
Stems short, to 15cm, thin, twining, from a small round tuber. Leaves variously ovate to lanceolate. Corolla glabrous outside, papillose inside swollen basal part of tube, lobes linear widening to spathulate at tip, tips united, sometimes with a small canopy, lobes 4–6mm, interior purple-ciliate, tube ridged in line with centre of lobes for upper third of its length. Kenya to Cape Province. ssp. *pretoriensis* R.A. Dyer. Vegetatively similar to type, but longitudinal ridge on upper third of corolla tube absent; outer corona lobes forming much shallower cup. Confined to the Transvaal (in and around Pretoria).

C.denticulata Schum. (*C.nilotica* var. *simplex* H. Huber).
Stems somewhat succulent, twining, often 4-angled. Leaves usually ovate or rhombic, finely dentate. Corolla tube 2–4cm, green- or yellow-white, base much swollen, not constricted,

lobes prolonged from a triangular base into a linear beak 1–2cm long, sometimes slightly spathulate to widened at tips, margins long purple-ciliate. Kenya, Uganda, Tanzania. ssp. *brownii* (Ledger) Bally (*C.brownii* Ledger). Differs in obliquely constricted, swollen base of corolla tube. Widespread in tropical Africa.

C.devecchii Chiov. (*C.variegata* var. *cornigera* H. Huber).
Stems climbing, succulent, glabrous pale green, subcylindric or obtusely 3-angled; upper internodes 3–7cm, nodes thickened, 0.3–0.6cm diam.; branches few, horizontally spreading. Leaves reduced to ovate-triangular, acute scales to 0.4×0.2cm. Raceme subterminal, few-flowered; corolla large, showy, green-white, base and tube sparsely spotted pale purple, lobes and processes with dark purple spots merging to form a purple edge, lobes white within with a dark purple transverse band near tip, yellow-green above the band, processes pure white within. exterior glabrous, base inflated, 1.2–1.5 × 0.7–0.8cm, with a constriction forming a thickened annulus inside, tube to 1 × 0.3cm, cylindric, widening funnel-like at apex, interlobal processes spreading-deflexed, tips obtuse, slightly recurved, 2–2.3cm × 4–5mm, canaliculate, open above, stiffly and minutely ciliate. Somalia, Ethiopia, Yemen. var. *adelaidae* Bally. Stems grey-green mottled red. Leaves much reduced, sessile, claw-shaped, black, reflexed at tip, spiny, 3–4mm long, 3mm wide at base. Corolla tube 3cm, exterior white-green spotted red, lobes 4.5×4.5cm, erect, broadly triangular, apiculate, green at base, brown toward apex, interlobal processes canaliculate, acute, 3×0.7cm; horizontal, exterior glabrous, white-green, interior pale green with lines of hairs, margins bristly. Kenya, N Tanzania.

C.distincta N.E. Br.
Stems stout, slightly succulent, twining. Leaves ovate or elliptic. Corolla exterior glabrous, tube 1.5–3cm, hirsute inside at base and in the dilated, funnel-shaped mouth, middle part glabrous, lobes ovate at base, gradually extending to a broad-spathulate tip, around 1cm, white-ciliate. Zanzibar.

C.distincta ssp. *lugardae* (N.E. Br.) H. Huber. See *C.lugardae*.

C.estelleana R.A. Dyer. See *C.fimbriata*.

C.filiformis (Burchell) Schltr. (*Systrepha filiformis* Burchell; *C.infundibuliformis* E. Mey.).
Roots fleshy, tufted; stems twining, glabrous. Leaves narrow, linear to almost thread-like. Inflorescence on a short pedicel; corolla glabrous throughout, tube 1.2–2.4cm, exterior off-white to pale green with purple bands and blotches, swollen, unspotted at base, widening slightly toward the mouth, lobes filiform, 1.2–2cm, dark purple, united at tips. S Africa (N Cape).

C.fimbriata E. Mey. (*C.estelleana* R.A. Dyer).
Roots fusiform; stems very succulent, twining, glabrous. Leaves absent or reduced to 1cm scales. Flowers usually solitary, foul-smelling; corolla exterior glabrous, tube 3–5cm, inflated in lowest quarter, then abruptly narrowing to 0.2cm above and gradually widening to the funnel-shaped mouth 0.9cm wide, lobes widening to spathulate above, united to form an umbrella-shaped canopy 1–2cm across, the edge of the spathulate sector of the lobes with purple, clavate, motile hairs attached. S Africa (restricted to Eastern Cape near Grahamstown). ssp. *connivens* (Dyer) P.V. Bruyns (*C.connivens* Dyer). Corolla tube less constricted above swollen base of tube than in the type, clavate hairs borne only on strut below broadened apex of corolla lobes. Restricted to Karroo area. ssp. *geniculata* (Dyer) P.V. Bruyns (*C.geniculata* Dyer). Corolla tube similar to ssp. *connivens*, but only widening to a narrow funnel, lobes at least 3× as long as wide, sometimes equalling tube, with a conspicuous 'knee' one-quarter of the way up, clavate motile hairs found only in area of knee. Southern Cape.

C.galeata H. Huber.
Stems very succulent, twining, glabrous. Leaves scale-like. Corolla 4cm, glabrous, outside yellow-green or light ochre-yellow blotched brown or olive green, inflated to spherical in the lower half, then abruptly constricted to the tube above and widening again to the funnel-shaped upper part, lobes with a triangular, laterally plicate base, then broadly obovate above, united for upper third to form a canopy 2–2.5cm across, margin purple-ciliate. Kenya.

C.galpinii Schltr. See *C.rendallii*.
C.geniculata Dyer. See *C.fimbriata* ssp. *geniculata*.
C.hastata N.E. Br. See *C.linearis* ssp. *woodii*.

C.haygarthii Schltr.
Stems stout, slightly succulent, perennial, twining. Leaves ovate or elliptic. Corolla exterior glabrous, tube 1.5–3cm, with a much-widened, funnel-shaped neck, lobes with a broad, rounded, almost hemispheric base, narrowing to a filiform stalk 0.5–1.4cm long then widening into an ovate tip. S Africa (widespread in Cape Province).

C.infundibuliformis E. Mey. See *C.filiformis*.

C.leroyi Rauh & Marn.-Lap.
Vegetative stem prostrate, 5–10×0.5cm, finely tuberculate; flowering stem extended, twining, to 50cm tall. Leaves 2–2.5cm, linear-lanceolate. Corolla tube much broadened in lower third, slender and terete above, 2.5–3cm, lobes linear, 6–12mm, tips united. SW Madagascar.

C.linearis E. Mey.
Stems thin, twining or cascading, from depressed globose tubers; tubers also develop on stem nodes, especially when stems are prostrate-growing. Leaves triangular-ovate, lanceolate or linear, fleshy. Corolla exterior glabrous, tube 1.2–1.5cm, exterior light green with purple longitudinal stripes, interior of middle section dark-hirsute, lobes narrow-linear to slightly spathulate and uniting toward tips, at least twice as long as corolla tube is wide, dark purple-brown, margins with purple ciliate hairs, corolla tube not widening significantly at junction with lobes. S Africa (S Cape Province). ssp. **tenuis** (N.E. Br.) P.V. Bruyns (*C.tenuis* N.E. Br.). Corolla lobes not more than twice as long as the tube mouth is wide. Cape. ssp. **woodii** (Schltr.) H. Huber (*C.woodii* Schltr.; *C.barbertonensis* N.E. Br.; *C.hastata* N.E. Br.; *C.schoenlandii* N.E. Br.). HEARTS ENTANGLED; SWEETHEART VINE; HEARTS ON A STRING. Stems slender, glabrous, twining, pendent or creeping, forming tubers at the nodes. Leaves to 1.25cm diam., fleshy, rounded-reniform, cordate, dull purple beneath, sea green above, often with purple and grey-green markings. Corolla exterior glabrous, tube 1–2cm, exterior dull pink or light green, interior of middle section hirsute, tube widening to funnel-shaped at junction with lobes, lobes narrow-linear, spathulate, widening toward tips, 0.5–0.7cm, purple-brown, margins and interior keel with purple ciliate hairs. Zimbabwe to E Cape.

C.lugardae N.E. Br. (*C.distincta* ssp. *lugardae* (N.E. Br.) H. Huber).
Stems stout, slightly succulent, twining. Leaves ovate or elliptic. Corolla exterior glabrous, sometimes with a fine down, lobes triangular-ovate at base, gradually extending to a linear or spathulate tip, 1.5–2cm. Angola, N Namibia, Botswana, Tropical E Africa south of Equator.

C.monteiroi Hook. f. See *C.sandersonii*.
C.mozambicensis Schltr. See *C.nilotica*.

C.multiflora Bak.
Stems annual, to 90cm, from a tuber to 10cm diam., slender, twining, glabrous. Leaves fleshy, round-ovate, elliptic, lanceolate or linear. Inflorescence many-flowered; corolla green-white, tube 1.2–2.6cm, exterior glabrous, interior hirsute, lobes 0.5–1.5cm, filiform from a triangular base, interior hairy at base, lower half projecting obliquely outward, upper half directed almost horizontally inward, tips remaining united. S Africa (N Cape, Transvaal). ssp. **ten-**

taculata (N.E. Br.) H. Huber (*C.tentaculata* N.E. Br.). Corolla lobes usually separating. Angola, Namibia, Zimbabwe.

C.nilotica Kotschy (*C.boussingaultiifolia* Dinter; *C.constricta* N.E. Br.; *C.mozambicensis* Schltr.; *C.plicata* E.A. Bruce).
Stems somewhat succulent, twining, often 4-angled. Leaves usually ovate or rhombic, often finely dentate. Inflorescence cymose; corolla tube 2–4cm, green- or yellow-white, blotched red-brown, transversely constricted above swollen base, glabrous above, hirsute below, lobes broadly oblong-ovate or triangular, 6–12mm, with a large basal yellow or white blotch, the middle with a purple-brown transverse band, then green or red-brown above, interior with fine, short, purple hairs. Kenya, Sudan, Tropical Africa south of Equator.

C.nilotica var. *simplex* H. Huber. See *C.denticulata*.

C.pachystelma Schltr.
Tuber to 10cm diam.; stems slender, twining, downy. Leaves broad, almost cordate, pilose, fleshy. Corolla bronze or yellow-green to off-white, downy outside, tube 1.2–2.4cm, interior of middle section short-pubescent, lobes narrow-linear, 0.5–1.2cm, light brown below, red above, pubescent throughout, or sometimes glabrescent within. Mozambique, Natal, Transvaal, Namibia. ssp. **undulata** (N. E. Br.) H. Huber (*C.undulata* N.E. Br.). Corolla lobes 0.8–1.2cm, widening to spathulate tip.

C.patersoniae N.E. Br. See *C.zeyheri*.
C.plicata E.A. Bruce. See *C.nilotica*.

C.racemosa N.E. Br.
Roots fleshy, thickened, tufted; stems slender, twining, not succulent, short-hairy. Leaves broad-ovate to linear. Fl. elongated; corolla red-brown, tube 1–2cm, exterior glabrous, interior evenly hairy, a little widened at mouth, lobes long-ovate, 0.5–1.2cm, interior sparsely white-hairy. Tropical Africa.

C.rendallii N.E. Br. (*C.galpinii* Schltr.).
Main tuber large; stems 8–15cm, slender, twining and bearing small tubers at nodes, or erect and remaining dwarf, glabrous or minutely downy. Leaves fleshy, ovate or linear. Corolla exterior glabrous, tube 1.2–2cm long on the interior middle section, lobes narrow-linear in basal half, widening above to spathulate, united to form an umbrella-shaped canopy 0.7–0.9cm across, margins obscurely 10-lobed, sparsely ciliate with purple hairs. S Africa (Orange Free State, Transvaal).

C.robynsiana Werderm.
Resembles *C.ballyana*. Stem robust, twining. Leaves ovate or elliptic, fleshy; petiole 1–2cm. Corolla tube 2.5–3cm, lobes 2cm. Congolese Republic.

C.rupicola Deflers.
Stems terete, pale green, to 1m tall, to 2cm thick, erect, tips sometimes twining. Leaves broadly ovate, slightly fleshy, pale green, deciduous, leaving a raised circular leaf scar, margins short-hairy. Inflorescence to 15-flowered, produced near tips of stems; peduncle 1cm; flowers red-brown, to 5cm, half of which is a narrow tube slightly widened and curved at base, lobes broad but strongly replicate and joined at tip to form a solid-looking cage, margins slightly ciliate with fine white hairs. N Yemen. var. *strictantha* N.P. Tayl. Flowers cream blotched red-brown. Yemen.

C.sandersonii Hook. f. (*C.monteiroi* Hook. f.).
Stems robust, very succulent, twining. Leaves cordate. Flowers green; corolla tube 3.5–5cm, interior of swollen portion hairy, otherwise almost glabrous, lobes united to form an umbrella-shaped canopy to 2.5cm diam., margin shortly 10-lobed, blotched dark green, covered with white motile hairs. Mozambique, S Africa.

C.schoenlandii N.E. Br. See *C.linearis* ssp. *woodii*.

C.senegalensis H. Huber.
Stems slender, twining, glabrous. Leaves usually linear, with minute cilia along margins and along underside of midrib.

Corolla exterior glabrous, tube 1.2–2.4cm, interior of middle section hirsute, lobes narrow-linear, almost filiform, 0.8–1.5cm, interior densely hirsute. Senegal.

C.serpentina E.A. Bruce. See *C.stapeliiformis* var. *serpentina*.

C.somaliensis Chiov.
Stems slender, twining, slightly fleshy, glabrous. Leaves small, ovate, downy or glabrescent. Corolla exterior downy, tube 1–2cm, hairy inside base and funnel-shaped mouth, glabrous in middle section, lobes narrowing from ovate base to a thread-like stalk and widening to a spathulate tip, almost equalling tube, interior white-hairy. Somalia, Kenya.

C.stapeliiformis Haw.
Stems to 1.5m tall, shrubby, very succulent, 1–1.5cm thick, mottled grey-brown; upper flowering stem elongated, twining, glabrous, 5mm thick. Leaves small, ovate, scale-like. Inflorescence several-fld; corolla tube 2–4cm, exterior off-white, or green-white blotched black-purple, lobes linear, from a triangular base, 2.5cm, free, spreading, white, tipped and edged yellow-green, black-purple or dark brown. S Africa (E Cape). var. *serpentina* (E.A. Bruce) H. Huber (*C.serpentina* E.A. Bruce). Stems more slender than in the type, longer. Flowers longer, lobes slimmer, often remaining joined for part of length. Transvaal.

C.superba D.V. Field & I.S. Collenette.
Tubers long-fusiform; stems sparsely branched, semi-succulent, twining, to 2m, 0.2–0.3cm diam. Leaves 0.6 × 0.2cm, minute, linear-lanceolate, caducous. Pedicel 6–15mm; corolla 6–8cm, base abruptly narrowed to a cylindric portion to 0.3cm diam., widening to c1cm at mouth, interior and exterior glabrous except at mouth, lobes to 3cm, base deltoid then replicate and narrow-linear, united at tip, tube and base of lobes dull white with pale purple spots arranged in lines, replicate portion of lobes bright green inside, base with broad, transverse, purple band. Saudi Arabia, S Yemen.

C.tabulifera Deflers. See *C.variegata*.
C.tentaculata N.E. Br. See *C.multiflora* ssp. *tentaculata*.
C.tenuis N.E. Br. See *C.linearis* ssp. *tenuis*.
C.thorncroftii N.E. Br. See *C.crassifolia*.
C.tuberculata Dinter. See *C.crassifolia*.
C.undulata N.E. Br. See *C.pachystelma* ssp. *undulata*.

C.variegata (Forssk.) Decne. (*C.tabulifera* Deflers).
Stems very succulent, twining or creeping, almost leafless, mottled green-grey-brown. Flowers tinged with pale green or pink, spotted dark red-brown; corolla tube 3.5–4.5cm, base inflated, longer and narrower than in the related *C.devecchii*, interlobal projections also much smaller, protruding only 0.5cm either side of tube, lobes 1–1.5cm, base triangular-ovate, above which the almost filiform projections are twisted helically together to form a tip 0.5cm long. Arabia.

C.variegata var. *cornigera* H. Huber. See *C.devecchii*.
C.wightii Graham & Wight. See *C.africana*.
C.woodii Schltr. See *C.linearis* ssp. *woodii*.

C.zeyheri Schltr. (*C.patersoniae* N.E. Br.).
Roots fleshy, fusiform; stems twining, glabrous, usually leafless. Leaves, when present, to 1cm, small, ovate or lanceolate. Corolla tube 2–5cm, lobes pale green-white with deltoid base then a long, narrow, straight strut terminating in an ovate-lanceolate tip, all of which join together, lobes almost equalling tube, bright green-hairy, particularly in lower half. S Africa (S Cape).

Cestrum L. (From Gk *kestron*.) Solanaceae. Some 175 species of pungently scented, evergreen or deciduous shrubs, often with long, slender branches requiring support. Leaves alternate, simple. Flowers in axillary or terminal corymbs or cymes usually forming leafy panicles; calyx tubular to campanulate-urceolate, to 7mm, 5-lobed, persistent; corolla tubular to funnel-shaped, limb 5-lobed; stamens 5, included, attached to base of corolla; ovary 2-chambered; stigma bilobed. Fruit a 2-chambered, succulent berry; seeds to 11. Tropical & subtropical S America. Z9. Species with more or less urceolate red to orange corollas formerly included in *Habrothamnus*.

CULTIVATION   A genus of shrubs grown for their attractive tubular flowers and, in the case of *C.laurifolium*, for bold, leathery evergreen foliage. These are not true climbers; the stems of many species, however, are slender and arching and will ramble in habitat or respond favourably to wall and pillar training in cultivation. In cool-temperate areas where temperatures do not fall much below –5°C/23°F in winter, the more frost-tolerant species (e.g. *C.parqui* and Mexican species) may be planted against west- and south-facing walls. *C.parqui* often thrives in the open in sheltered gardens; even when cut back by frost, it should shoot from the base in spring. Protect with a covering of matting or evergreen prunings in winter. Where old wood has survived, two or three flushes of bloom can be expected from early summer to autumn.

In colder areas, grow in the cool to intermediate glasshouse (minimum night temperature of 10°C/50°F for the frost-tolerant Mexican species and *C.parqui*, 13–16°C/55–60°F for those from the Tropics). Best when planted directly into glasshouse borders, they may also be grown in large pots or tubs. Plant in the open in spring into any reasonably fertile, freely draining soil; give full sun or part shade. Feed and water well in the first two years. Young plants should be pinched to produce bushy specimens; otherwise, prune in spring to restrict size or to remove from ground level the less floriferous 2–3-year-old wood.

Under glass grow in large pots of a medium- to high-fertility, well drained, loam-based mix. Ventilate freely whenever temperatures exceed 16°C/60°F; give some protection from fierce sun in summer; water moderately during the growing season. After flowering, reduce temperatures slightly and keep the growing medium fairly dry for 4–6 weeks, then prune hard back, and root-prune if plants are to remain in the same size pot. When roots have filled the new pots, feed fortnightly with a dilute liquid fertilizer, pinching lateral growths occasionally until late summer. Container-grown plants may be plunged in the open during summer or planted directly into borders. Propagate by 8–10cm/3–4in. lateral semi-ripe or greenwood cuttings in summer, rooted under mist or with bottom heat of about 20°C/68°F.

C.album Ferrero ex Dunal. See *C.diurnum*.
C.angustifolium Lodd. See *C.laurifolium*.

C.aurantiacum Lindl. (*Habrothamnus aurantiacus* Seem.).
Arborescent or climbing glabrous shrub, to 2m. Stems erect, terete. Leaves to 11 × 7cm, ovate to lanceolate entire, malodorous if crushed, acute to acuminate; petiole long. Panicles pyramidal, leafy, to 10cm across; flowers to 3cm, glabrous, bright orange; calyx to 9 × 4mm, lobes 5, subulate;

corolla tube to 1.8cm. Summer. Guatemala. 'Album': flowers white.

C.corymbosum Schldl. (*C.tinum* St.-Lager).
Close to *C.endlicheri* and possibly synonymous with it. To 2m. Branches rigid. Leaves to 10 ×3.5cm, elliptic to oblanceolate, coriaceous; base cuneate; petiole decurrent. Inflorescence corymbose, to 5cm, to 25-fld; flowers sessile to short-stalked, to 2.5cm; calyx to 3mm, lobes 5, unequal, to 1mm; corolla red, funnelform, to 2cm; lobes toothed, ovate-acuminate. Brazil.

C.× cultum Francey. (*C.elegans* × *C.parqui*.)
To 3m. Leaves 8.5 ×2cm, ovate to lanceolate, base acute, apex long-acute; petiole decurrent. Inflorescence terminal, paniculate, subcorymbose, densely flowered, to 6.5 ×7cm; flowers to 2.5cm; calyx to 6mm, lobes to 6, triangular; corolla tube cylindric, neck funnel-shaped, glabrous, violet. Garden origin. 'Cretian Blue': flowers violet-purple, abundant.

C.diurnum L. non Weston (*C.album* Ferrero ex Dunal). DAY JESSAMINE.
Evergreen, glabrous shrub, to 3m. Stems slender, erect. Leaves to 10×4cm, oblong to oblong-elliptic, glossy, entire, abruptly acute to obtuse; petiole short. Inflorescence axillary, spicate, 10cm; flowers clustered to 20, fragrant by day; calyx campanulate, 3mm; corolla 2cm, white occasionally tinged green, funnel-shaped, lobes reflexed. W Indies.

C.diurnum Weston non L. See *C.laurifolium*.

C.elegans (Brongn.) Schldl. (*C.purpureum* (Lindl.) Standl.; *C.paniculatum* Schldl.; *Habrothamnus elegans* Brongn.).
Evergreen, arborescent shrub, to 3.5m. Branches pendent, soft-pubescent Leaves to 10cm, ovate-oblong to lanceolate, downy, olive green, entire, apex acuminate, base cordate. Panicles corymbose, dense, pendent; calyx 5-lobed, to 8mm; corolla tubular, red to purple, to 2.5cm, limb lobes reflexed, acute. Fruit ellipsoid purple-red. Summer–autumn. Mexico. var. **longiflorum** Francey. Flowers to 2.5cm and over. var. **smithii** Bail. Flowers pink.

C.endlicheri Miers.
Shrub, to 180cm, glabrous. Stems erect, to 3mm diam. Leaves to 15×3cm, ovate-lanceolate short-stalked, apex acuminate. Inflorescence paniculate, to 15×10cm; flowers short-stipitate, scarlet-red; calyx conic, to 6mm; corolla funnel-shaped, to 2.5cm, limb to 8mm, lobes to 2cm, triangular, acuminate. Summer. S America. Close to *C.corymbosus*.

C.fasciculatum (Schldl.) Miers (*Meyenia fasciculata* Schldl.).
Resembles *C.elegans*, but exterior of flowers glabrous Evergreen shrub, to 2m. Stems slender, sparsely branched. Leaves to 7×4cm, ovate to lanceolate, undulate, base acute, apex acute to short-acuminate. Inflorescence terminal, clustered, to 8cm wide; flowers to 1.8cm, clustered, exterior pubescent, carmine to red-purple; calyx to 11mm, pubescent, lobes to 5, triangular. Spring. Mexico.'Newellii' (*C.newellii* hort.): flowers crimson; calyx and corolla glabrous; possibly a hybrid of *C.elegans* × *C.fasciculatum*.

C.laurifolium L'Hérit. (*C.venetatum* Lam.; *C.diurnum* Weston non L.; *C.angustifolium* Lodd.).
To 4m. Leaves 5–20cm, petiolate, oblong-elliptic to ovate, glabrous, coriaceous, margins slightly revolute, apex obtuse to rounded, rarely acute to short-acuminate. Inflorescence paniculate, axillary, to 6-flowered; calyx to 4mm, interior glabrous, exterior pilose, lobes 5, unequal, triangular; corolla to 2.5cm, funnelform, green to yellow-green. Fruit violet. Antilles, Cuba, naturalized Lebanon.

C.newellii hort. See *C.fasciculatum* 'Newellii'.

C.nocturnum L. LADY OF THE NIGHT; NIGHT JESSAMINE.
Evergreen shrub, to 4m. Stems scandent to spreading; shoots slender. Leaves to 13 × 3cm, alternate, narrow-lanceolate, apex acuminate. Inflorescence axillary, slender, paniculate to racemose, to 13cm; flowers nocturnally fragrant; calyx to 5mm, tubular, glabrous; corolla slender, to 2.5cm, pale green to ivory. Fruit white. Summer–autumn. W Indies.

C.paniculatum Schldl. See *C.elegans*.

C.parqui L'Hérit. WILLOW-LEAVED JESSAMINE.
Deciduous, glabrous shrub, to 3m. Stems branched. Leaves to 14 × 5cm, linear-lanceolate to elliptic, apex acute, base cuneate; petiole short. Inflorescence cymose, axillary or terminal, to 13cm, forming terminal leafy panicles; flowers nocturnally fragrant; calyx to 7mm, lobes to 2mm; corolla to 2.5cm, yellow-green to yellow, lobes ovoid, to 6mm. Fruit violet-brown. Summer. Chile.

C.psittacinum Stapf.
Scandent, evergreen shrub. Shoots and leaves softly pubescent. Leaves to 10×5cm, elliptic to oblong, base cuneate to rounded, apex acute to obtuse. Flowers in axillary or terminal racemes forming a pyramidal panicle; calyx tubular to funnel-shaped; corolla vivid orange, to 1.4cm, funnel-shaped, lobes ciliate, rounded to ovoid. Autumn. C America.

C.purpureum (Lindl.) Standl. See *C.elegans*.

C.roseum HBK.
Evergreen shrub, to 180cm. Shoots soft-pubescent. Leaves to 10 × 5cm, undulate, oblong to ovate, soft-pubescent, base acuminate. Inflorescence axillary or terminal, corymbose; corolla to 3cm, rose to purple; limb to 13mm, lobes spreading, acute; stamens equal, to 2cm. Fruit red. Mexico.'Illnacullin': flowers rose-pink.

C.tinum St.-Lager. See *C.corymbosus*.
C.venetatum Lam. See *C.laurifolium*.

Chamaedorea Willd. (From Gk *chamai*, lowly, on the ground, and *dorea*, a gift: the fruits are easily reached.) Palmae. Some 100 species of small palms. Stems solitary or clustered, usually slender and cane-like, erect, or procumbent, occasionally climbing, clothed with fibrous leaf bases or smooth, green and ringed, sometimes absent. Leaves pinnate or entire and emarginate, reduplicate; petiole flat above, convex beneath; pinnae 1- to many-fold, acuminate, glabrous. Inflorescences interfoliar, branched × 1 or × 2, amid 3, papery, overlapping bracts; flowers solitary, rarely arranged in clusters: male flowers with sepals united into cap, petals free or joined, stamens 6, pistillode prominent; female flowers with sepals 3, petals 3, ovary 3-celled, only one developing, female inflorescence yellow to orange. Fruit 0.5–2cm, spherical to ellipsoid, red or black, with basal stigmatic remains. C & S America. Z10.

CULTIVATION A genus of small palms occurring predominantly on moist humus-rich soils in the shady understorey of rainforest. They are among the most elegant and undemanding of palms, widely used in interior decoration and grown in the home and conservatory. The climbing species twine and ramble loosely around and through surrounding vegetation, their long bamboo-like stems clothed with arching, dark green, pinnate fronds. In tropical and subtropical gardens, they are attractive additions to the lath house, the fringes of woodland gardens and the boles of large specimen trees. In cooler regions, they are suitable for training on pillars and rafters in the large, shady, warm glasshouse or conservatory, or for moss poles and bark/moss-filled mesh cylinders in the home. A minimum temperature of 10°C/50°F is necessary, together with light shade. Water and feed copiously and syringe foliage in the early morning whenever possible in warm weather; reduce water supplies in winter. Pot in large containers or beds in an open, bark-based mix with additional leafmould or garden compost. Propagate by seed.

C.elatior Mart. (*C.resinifera* Wendl.; *C.scandens* Liebm.) Stems to 4m×2cm, cane-like, weakly climbing, clump forming. Leaf blades to 3m, entire with apex deeply emarginate, becoming pinnate, pinnae 35×3cm, linear-lanceolate, apex and base attenuate sometimes curved. Inflorescence bracts 3–4; male inflorescence 20cm, rachillae slender, spreading or reflexed; female inflorescence to 40×30cm, orange-pink to brown. Fruit to 1cm, globose, black, glaucous. Mexico, Guatemala.

C.resinifera Wendl. See *C.elatior*.

C.scandens Liebm. See *C.elatior*.

C.seifrizii Burret. Stem scandent. Leaf blade to 40cm; pinnae 14.5 – 24 × 1cm, 14 per side, base decurrent; petiole 5cm. Inflorescence bracts 5, rachillae to 3cm, 5; male flowers fragrant. Fruit 0.8cm, rugose. Yucatan.

Chiococca P. Browne. (From Gk *chion*, snow, and *kokkos*, berry, referring to the colour of the fruit.) Rubiaceae. Some 8 species of shrubs or trees. Stems erect to climbing and vine-like, terete, glabrous or pubescent. Leaves petiolate, opposite, lustrous and leathery to membranous, glabrous; stipules persistent, apex cuspidate. Flowers in axillary, secund, simple or branched panicles or racemes, white to cream or yellow, fragrant; calyx tube ovoid to turbinate, constricted, glabrous or pubescent, limb persistent, lobes 5; corolla campanulate to funnelform, tube glabrous at throat, lobes 5, spreading or reflexed, valvate in bud; stamens 5, inserted at or near base of corolla tube, anthers basifixed, included or exserted, linear; ovary 2-celled, style filiform, stigma simple or 2-lobed, cylindric to club-shaped, ovules solitary in each cell, pendent, compressed. Fruit a berry, globose or subglobose, leathery, white; seeds pendent, compressed, testa membranous, embryo plane, endosperm fleshy. Tropical and subtropical New World. Z10.

CULTIVATION   An attractive genus of tropical evergreens, usually climbers, grown for their fragrant flowers. The flowers of *C.alba* are pure white and scentless on emergence in late winter, becoming creamy and fragrant as they mature. They give way to white berries. Grow in the warm glasshouse, with high humidity and part shade, in a mix of equal parts loam, coir and sharp sand. Propagate from seed sown in spring, or from nodal softwood cuttings in sand in a closed case with bottom heat.

C.alba (L.) Hitchc. (*Lonicera alba* L.; *C.racemosa* L.; *C.anguifuga* DC.). SNOW BERRY; WEST INDIAN SNOW BERRY. Evergreen shrub or tree, to 6m. Stems climbing and vine-like, glabrous or pubescent, lenticellate, bark grey to brown. Leaves to 10×5cm, ovate, lanceolate, or elliptic to oblong, apex acute or narrowly acute, base attenuate to obtuse and decurrent, lustrous above and leathery, glabrous; petioles to 1cm; stipules to 2mm, adpressed, mucronate. Flowers in pedunculate, axillary, few- to many-flowered panicles or racemes, white ageing ivory to pale yellow, ultimately strongly fragrant; pedicels to 1mm; calyx tube to 3mm, glabrous or minutely pubescent, lobes to 1mm, deltoid, apex acute or subulate; corolla tube to 6mm, exterior glabrous, lobes to 3mm, deltoid; anthers to 3mm. Fruit to 8×6mm, subglobose, succulent, glabrous, white, crowned by persistent calyx limb. Florida and W Indies, C to S America.

C.anguifuga DC. See *C.alba*.

C.racemosa L. See *C.alba*.

Chorizema Labill. (From Gk *choros*, a dance, and *zema*, a drinking or food vessel: Labillardière and his party were close to death by thirst and exhaustion when they came across a spring of fresh water and this plant in the same place: he danced for joy. The name has also been said to derive from Gk *chorizonema* – *choris*, separate, *nema*, thread, referring to the separate stamen filaments.) Leguminosae (Papilionoideae). Some 18 species of twiners or small shrubs. Leaves alternate, simple, entire, or sharply toothed or lobed. Flowers pea-like in axillary or terminal racemes; bracts narrow and tapering, scant; pedicel short; calyx lobes subequal, the upper lobes partially fused; petals all short-clawed, standard emarginate, exceeding wings and keel, wings straight, obovate, keel blunt or attenuate, straight or incurved; ovary downy, sometimes stalked, 4- to many-ovuled, style incurved, stigma oblique or cylindriform; stamens 10, distinct. Fruit a short, stout legume. Australia, naturalized California. Z9.

CULTIVATION   *Chorizema* species occur on gravelly soils in coastal regions and along river courses in dry, warm-temperate climates that are frost-free or almost so. They can be trained against walls or trellis, or allowed to scramble in the border or rockery. In cooler zones, they are grown in the cool glasshouse or conservatory. They are light-textured climbers or shrubs of lax habit grown for their attractive foliage and exuberantly coloured flowers. *C.cordatum* produces its brightly coloured blooms throughout the year and is well suited to pot cultivation and, like *C.ilicifolium*, will scramble through shrubs or twine up wires or trellis. They are also grown in hanging baskets. Some species, such as *C.dicksonii*, will tolerate light frosts, where summers are long and hot enough for growth to ripen fully.

Plant in neutral to slightly acid soils that are well drained, moisture-retentive and rich in organic matter. Grow in full sun. but with some protection from the strongest summer sun and from strong winds and maintain an organic mulch over the shallow roots. Grow containerized specimens in a high-fertility loam-based mix with additional organic matter such as leafmould. Ventilate freely and water moderately when in growth, with regular applications of dilute liquid fertilizer during the growing season. Maintain a winter minimum temperature of 5–10°C/40–50°F. Pot-grown plants may be moved to a position in light dappled shade during summer.

Propagate by seed sown in spring; immerse in boiling water and soak for 12–24 hours (repeat for seed that does not swell); also by semi-ripe cuttings in summer.

C.cordatum Lindl. HEART-LEAVED FLAME PEA; AUSTRALIA FLAME PEA; FLOWERING OAK.
Semi-scandent or dense upright shrub, 1–3.5 × 1–2m. Branches numerous, delicate. Leaves to 5cm, ovate, apex soft, acuminate, base cordate, margins sometimes minutely spiny-dentate or lobed. Flowers to 1.5cm, in terminal racemes to 15cm long; standard red, orange and yellow, keel magenta or mauve. Summer–early winter. Western Australia. Several colour forms are grown, including some with yellow standards.

C.dicksonii R.A. Graham. YELLOW-EYED FLAME PEA.
Small many-branched shrub, 1–1.5 × 1.2m. Leaves to 2cm, linear, pungent, glabrous, conspicuously veined, curved. Flowers 2cm diam., in lax terminal racemes; standard orange-red with a vivid central yellow flash, keel orange-red. Late summer–early winter. Western Australia.

C.diversifolium A. DC.
Climbing shrub, shoots slender, wiry, sometimes twining. Leaves 2.5–5cm, ovate, obovate or lanceolate, entire. Flowers in sparse racemes to 10cm long; standard to 1.5cm diam., orange-yellow, wings purple-red. Late spring. W Australia.

C.elegans hort. See *C.ilicifolium.*

C.ilicifolium Labill. (*C.elegans* hort.; *C.varium* Benth.). HOLLY FLAME PEA.
Herb or shrub, 50cm–1m tall, erect or spreading, generally glabrous. Leaves 2–8cm, ovate-acuminate or narrow-oblong, holly-like, subsessile or sessile, rounded or subcordate at base, margins sinuous or notched, glossy, leathery, patterned with tracery of veins. Racemes to 15cm, sinuous, 5- to many-flowered, terminal or axillary; standard orange-red and yellow, reflexed and nearly tubular, sometimes incised, wings oblong-obovate, straight, keel rose-mauve. Spring–summer. Western Australia.

C.varium Benth. See *C.ilicifolium.*

Cionosicyos Griseb. (Gk *kion*, pillar, and *sikyos*, cucumber.) Cucurbitaceae. 3 species of monoecious, perennial, herbaceous or partially woody climbers. Tendrils bifid or simple. Leaves simple or palamately 3–7-lobed, with glands near base. Flowers solitary, occasionally in racemes, axillary, white to pale green, 1–4cm across; receptacle campanulate; sepals 5; corolla campanulate, lobes 5, divided almost to base, ovate to oblong, to 2cm; stamens 3, free, anthers usually coherent; ovary inferior, ovules many. Fruit globose, smooth; pericarp thick; seeds ovate to oblong-ovate. C America, Caribbean. Z10.

CULTIVATION As for *Coccinia.*

C.excisus (Griseb.) C. Jeffrey.
Stems glabrous. Leaves broad, angular-ovate or cordate-ovate, glabrous above, sparsely pubescent on veins beneath, lobulate or occasionally angulate, lobules 3–7; petiole 1–4cm. Flowers solitary, white to pale green-yellow; petals papillose, smaller in female; ovary pubescent. Fruit globose, green, sometimes becoming red, 3–5cm, 5–7-seeded. C America, Cuba.

Cissus L. GRAPE IVY; TREEBINE; IVY. (From the Gk *kissos*, ivy, referring to the climbing habit of most species.) Vitaceae. About 350 species of herbs, shrubs or vines, some xerophytic with succulent caudices and roots. Stems woody, herbaceous or swollen to fleshy trunks; tendrils opposite leaves or absent. Leaves simple or lobed to digitately 3–7-foliolate, entire to dentate, thin and herbaceous to succulent; stipules present. Inflorescence generally a terminal or leaf-opposed compound cyme made up of umbels; flowers small, white to green, bud not constricted in middle; calyx entire, obconic to saucer-shaped, 4-lobed;petals cucullate at apex, deflexed after anthesis, caducous; stamen filaments short; disc annular, entire or lobed, more or less adnate to ovary; style simple, subulate; stigma subulate or subcapitate. Fruit a berry, flesh dry, generally inedible; seed usually 1, oblong to ovoid or subglobose, often abruptly narrowed at one end. Tropics & Subtropics.

CULTIVATION With the exception of *C.trifoliata*, which occurs in rocky habitats, frequently at the mouth of caves, most *Cissus* species are found in tropical and subtropical forest and woodland; *C.hypoglauca* and *C.antarctica* occur in the rainforest littoral of Southeast Australia. They are grown primarily for their lush, glossy foliage, although in favourable conditions some also produce attractively coloured berries. In temperate climates they are used as climbing or trailing house- or conservatory plants; *C.antarctica*, *C.striata* and *C.rhombifolia* perform well in hanging baskets. In mild maritime climates with little or no frost, *C.striata* is sometimes grown as a screen in sheltered situations out of doors. *C.rhombifolia* and its cultivar 'Ellen Danica' are commonly grown in interior landscapes and as houseplants, valued for their handsome, coarsely toothed, glossy leaves; it is an extremely tolerant species, especially with regard to low light levels and dry atmospheres; *C.antarctica* is also shade-tolerant, suffering leaf scorch in direct sunlight. *C.discolor* has beautifully quilted leaves, marked with silver above and wine red beneath; it has higher temperature and humidity requirements than most other species and needs a warm glasshouse or conservatory. The genus includes several of succulent habit – *C.quadrangularis*, with its distinctive angular and segmented succulent stems, and *C.cactiformis*, a succulent climber, its light green stems edged brown, bearing foliage only on the young growth. *C.tuberosa* is a caudiciform succulent, often with finely divided foliage. It makes a striking indoor bonsai.

Grow in a well drained sandy medium with additional organic matter, in bright indirect light, with a minimum temperature of 7–10°C/45–50°F, although higher temperatures to about 21°C/70°F will improve leaf size and quality; give *C.discolor* high humidity and a minimum temperature of 15–18°C/60–65°F. Water moderately when in growth, with regular applications of liquid feed; keep just moist during winter. Prune only to remove overcrowded growth and to restrict size. Encourage dense growth by pinching out the tips occasionally in spring. Tie in shoots to support as growth proceeds. Propagate by 5cm/2in. stem cuttings in late spring early summer, root in sand in a closed case with bottom heat, or by layering. Also by seed sown in spring.

C.acida Chapm., Jacq. or L. See *C.trifoliata*.

C.acuminata A. Gray. See *Cayratia acuminata*.

C.adenopoda Sprague. PINK CISSUS. Tuberous-rooted herbaceous climber; stems slender. Leaves trifoliolate, stalked; leaflets 8–17cm, elliptic-ovate, coarsely serrate, setose-pilose throughout, purple-green-hairy above, red-hairy with prominent veins beneath. Flowers pale yellow in a loose panicle. Fruit purple-black. Tropical W Africa. Z10.

C.albonitens hort. ex Nichols. See *C.sicyoides* 'Albonitens'.

C.amazonica Lind.
Stately vine. Stems woody. Leaves simple, ovate and to 15cm on mature plants, linear and to 5cm on young specimens, acuminate at apex, glaucous green above, light maroon to red beneath, smooth and glabrous, veins silvery-white above, red beneath, particularly prominent on young leaves. Flowers and fruit not known. Reputedly Amazon, but known only in cultivation. Z10.

C.ampelopsis Gray. See *Ampelopsis cordata*.

C.antarctica Vent. (*C.baudiniana* Brouss.; *C.glandulosa* Poir.; *Vitis antarctica* (Vent.) Benth.). KANGAROO VINE.
Vine, evergreen. Stems woody; branches pubescent when young; tendrils present. Leaves 7–10×3–5cm, simple, ovate to oblong, long acuminate at apex, somewhat cordate at base, margins entire to sinuate or irregularly dentate, green and glossy above, glabrous, tough and coriaceous. Inflorescence dense, umbellate cymes, tomentose-pubescent; flowers few, green, pubescent. Fruit black. Summer. Australasia. 'Minima': dwarf, slow-growing form; branches mostly horizontal. Z10.

C.arborea Gray. See *Ampelopsis arborea*.

C.baudiniana Brouss. See *C.antarctica*.

C.brevipedunculata Maxim. See *Ampelopsis brevipedunculata*.

C.cactiformis Gilg (*Vitis succulenta* Galpin).
Vine, climbing to treetops in wild, to 3×1m trained against greenhouse wall, succulent, of striking appearance. Stems acutely 4–5-angled, 3–4cm diam., very fleshy, strongly constricted at nodes, grey-green, winged on angles, wings undulating, to 2cm broad, green; adventitious roots developing at nodes; tendrils simple. Leaves simple, more or less orbicular, 3-lobed to unlobed, small, ephemeral. Inflorescence paniculate, to 20cm. Fruit black. Tropical & Southern Africa. Z10.

C.capensis Willd. See *Rhoicissus capensis*.

C.capriolata (D. Don) Royle. See *Tetrastigma serrulatum*.

C.chontalensis (Seem.) Planch.
Vine, climbing, glabrous. Branchlets angular. Leaves 3-foliolate, beautiful bright green, central leaflet elliptic, laterals obliquely ovate, acuminate, dentate. Inflorescence compound, cymose; flowers scarlet. Winter. Nicaragua (Chontales Mts). Z10.

C.cirrhosus (Thunb.) Willd. See *Cyphostemma cirrhosum* .

C.cucumerifolia Planch.
Leaves orbicular to broadly ovate, generally more or less deeply cordate at base, simple to somewhat lobed, densely pilose to tomentose beneath, tomentum often very short and strongly adpressed. Flower buds large, much longer than broad; petals coriaceous, glabrous; calyx strongly expanded, cupulate. Malawi. Z10.

C.davidiana Carr. See *Ampelopsis humulifolia*.

C.dinteri Schinz. See *C.nymphaeifolia*.

C.discolor Bl. (*C.javana* DC.; *C.velutina* Lind. ex Hook.; *Vitis discolor* (Bl.) Dalz.). REX BEGONIA VINE.
Vine, glabrous or subglabrous throughout, of spectacular appearance. Stem slender, obscurely 5–6-angled, flushed red near apex; tendrils bifid. Leaves 6–25×3–21cm, ovate-oblong to lanceolate, cordate or truncate at base, acuminate at apex, lustrous dark green above with double row of grey-green, silvery-white or pale pink blotches between veins, dark red beneath, sometimes sparsely hairy on veins. Inflorescence often secund, with 4–5 main branches; peduncle to 1.5cm; pedicels red; calyx at least partially red; petals 2mm, green, often tinged red at apex. Fruit globose, dark red tinged black. SE Asia to Australia. 'Mollis': leaves minutely hirsute; flowers carmine-red, cymes large, stalks tall. Z10.

C.endresii Veitch (*Vitis endresii* (Veitch) Nichols.).
Vine, climbing vigorously. Shoots tinged crimson when young; tendrils present, flushed crimson. Leaves 18–20×15cm, obovate, cordate at base, acuminate at apex, flushed crimson when young, when mature bright satiny green above, darker near veins, ferruginous beneath, veins prominent, tinged red. Costa Rica. Z10.

C.erosa Rich. (*Vitis erosa* Bak.).
Stems quadrangular, grooved or narrowly winged, subglabrous; tendrils numerous. Leaves trifoliolate, glabrous, subcoriaceous; leaflets 5–15×2.5–6cm, lanceolate to ovate, cuneate at base, serrate with mucronate teeth, veins slightly prominent. Inflorescence cymose, hirtellous; flowers scarlet. Tropical America. Z10.

C.glandulosa Poir. See *C.antarctica*.

C.gongylodes (Burchell ex Bak.) Planch. (*C.pterophora* (Bak.) Nichols.; *Vitis pterophora* Bak.; *Vitis gongylodes* Burchell ex Bak.).
Vine, climbing high, villous. Stems strongly winged, rather succulent. Leaves 3-foliolate, 5–18cm; leaflets rhombic-obovate, terminal leaflet sometimes 3-lobed, lateral leaflet obliquely ovate, acute to acuminate, serrate, large, sessile, pilose, undulate-rugose, veins reticulate, impressed; petioles long; stipules large, purple tinged brown. Inflorescence composed of several dense globular cymes; peduncles divaricately branched. Autumn. Brazil, Paraguay & Peru. At the end of each growing season fleshy club-shaped stem sections 12.5–15cm long develop at ends of branches, finally dropping to ground, where they root and proliferate. Z9.

C.henryana hort. See *Parthenocissus henryana*.

C.hereroensis Schinz. See *Cyphostemma hereroense*.

C.himalayana Walp. See *Parthenocissus himalayana*.

C.hypoglauca A. Gray (*Vitis hypoglauca* (A. Gray) F. Muell.).
Vine, climbing high. Shoots ferruginous-tomentose when young; tendrils absent. Leaves generally 5-foliolate, digitate; leaflets ovate to lanceolate, acuminate at apex, obtuse at base, scarcely minutely dentate, light green above, glaucous beneath particularly when young, coriaceous, glabrous; petiolules slender. Cymes axillary, short, rather dense; flowers numerous, very small, attractive, yellow. Fruit globose, dark blue tinged black. Australia (NSW, Victoria). Z10.

C.hypoleuca Harv.
Vine, weakly climbing. Stems weak, striate, minutely pubescent or glandular. Leaves pedately 5-foliolate, long-petiolate; leaflets broadly lanceolate, acute to acuminate, margins shallowly broadly mucronate-dentate, green and glabrous above, paler and densely white-tomentose beneath. Inflorescence cymose, diffuse, tomentose with spreading branches. S Africa. Z9.

C.incisa (Nutt. in Torr. & A. Gray) Dur. See *C.trifoliata*.

C.javalensis (Seem.) Planch.
Leaves simple, cordate at base, acuminate at apex, mucronate-dentate, green and velvety-pubescent above, tinged purple and glabrous beneath, veins tinged purple.

Cissus (a) *C. gongylodes* (b) *C. lindenii* (c) *C. antartica* (d) *C. rhombifolia* (e) *C. rhombifolia* 'Ellen Danica' (f) *C. discolor*

Inflorescence cymose, compound; flowers bright scarlet. Nicaragua. Z10.

C.javana DC. See *C.discolor*.

C.lindenii André.
Vine, woody below, glabrous throughout. Adventitious roots arising from base of petiole, long, rather fleshy, descending to soil and rooting there. Branches terete, somewhat warty; tendrils present. Leaves 15–20×14–16cm, ovate, cordate at base, long acuminate at apex, laxly serrate with mucronate teeth, bright deep green above with silvery blotches between veins, paler beneath, veins prominent beneath, tinged pink near base; petiole 10–15cm, terete, somewhat twisted, with scattered translucent vesicles. Colombia. Z10.

C.mandaiana hort. See *C.rhombifolia* 'Mandaiana'.

C.mexicana Mattei.
Vine. Branches angled, velvety; tendrils moderately few. Leaves trifoliolate; leaflets acute at apex, mucronate-serrate, velvety, white-villous particularly on veins beneath, central leaflets largest, rhombic to ovate-subrhombic, laterals obliquely ovate, semi-cordate on outer side at base; petiolule of central leaflet longer than those of laterals. Inflorescence cymose, much-branched, pedunculate; flowers scarlet, pedicellate; petals adhering to calyptra; disc yellow. Mexico. Z9.

C.mexicana DC. non Mattei. See *Parthenocissus quinquefolia*.

C.neilgherrensis Wight. See *Parthenocissus himalayana*.

C.nymphaeifolia (Welw. ex Bak.) Planch. (*C.dinteri* Schinz).
Herb. Leaves simple, suborbicular to ovate, entire or variously dentate or shallowly lobed, cordate at base, to 15cm diam., ferruginous-tomentose on both sides when young, glabrescent above. Inflorescence ferruginous-tomentose; flower buds glabrous or almost so. Namibia, Angola. Z10.

C.oblonga (Benth.) Planch. (*Vitis oblonga* Benth.).
Vine, evergreen. Stems terete, grey-pubescent; tendrils generally simple, pubescent Leaves 7.5×3.5cm, simple, oblong-ovate, truncate to shallowly cordate at base, acute to obtuse at apex, margins entire or occasionally serrate towards apex, usually glabrous when mature; petiole 2cm, usually glabrous; stipules triangular, pale grey to pale ferruginous-pubescent. Inflorescence umbellate; peduncle with 2–3 main branches, 1cm. Fruit very dark purple to black. Australia (Queensland). Z10.

C.obtectum Wallich. See *Tetrastigma obtectum*.

C.oleracea Bol.
Glabrous perennial. Rhizome subterranean, simple, 5–7.5cm diam., woody, with several obpyriform tubers. Stems several, laxly procumbent, simple or very rarely branched, sinuous, leafy, to 60cm, succulent. Leaves to 19× 15cm, alternate, simple, broadly ovate to rarely suborbicular, acutely dentate, glaucous, thick and fleshy; petioles thick, 5mm; stipules lanceolate-falcate, 8mm. Inflorescence cymose, axillary, divaricately branched, long-stalked. S Africa. Z9.

C.oligocarpa (Lév. & Vant.) L.H. Bail. See *Cayratia oligocarpa*.

C.orientalis Lam. See *Ampelopsis orientalis*.

C.pterophora (Bak.) Nichols. See *C.gongylodes*.

C.quadrangula Salisb. or L. See *C.quadrangularis*.

C.quadrangularis L. (*C.quadrangula* Salisb. or L.; *Vitis quadrangularis* (L.) Wallich ex Wight & Arn.).
Herb or vine, much-branched, succulent. Stem acutely quadrangular, narrowly winged, thick, green, conspicuously constricted at nodes, internodes 6–10cm; tendrils entire. Leaves 3–8×3–8cm, on apical part of stem only, ovate to deltoid, entire or 3–5-lobed, obtuse at apex, cordate or truncate at base, green both sides, succulent; stipules erecto-patent. Inflorescence with 3–4 main branches, to 5cm; peduncles 1.5–2.5cm; petals green tinged yellow or pink. Fruit dark red tinged black. Africa, S Asia, Malaysia. Z10.

C.quinata (Ait.) Planch.
Scandent plant with tendrils. Stem generally slender. Leaves 3–5-foliolate, distinctly petiolate, fleshy; leaflets coarsely serrate, glabrous or sparsely pilose on veins beneath. Flower buds about half length of pedicels, both glabrous or with scattered short glandular hairs. S Africa. Z9.

C.rhombifolia Vahl (*C.rhomboidea* E. Mey.; *Vitis rhombifolia* Bak.).VENEZUELA TREEBINE.
Vine, climbing, evergreen. Stems fulvous-villous when young, wingless; tendrils forked. Leaves pedately 3-foliolate, fulvous-villous when young, glabrescent; leaflets 2.5–10cm, rhombic-ovate, cuneate at base, acute at apex, remotely sharply dentate, dark glossy green above, rusty-pubescent on veins beneath; petioles rusty-villous. Inflorescence 20–30-flowered cymes; peduncles short, glandular-pubescent; flowers green-hairy. Tropical America. 'Ellen Danica': vigorous, bushy; leaves large, deeply lobed and much incised, rich, glossy green. 'Mandaiana' (*C.mandaiana* hort.): stems erect, becoming scandent when older; tendrils absent when young; leaves more leathery and glossy. Z10.

C.rhomboidea E. Mey. See *C.rhombifolia*.

C.rocheana Planch. See *C.trifoliata*.

C.rotundifolia (Forssk.) Vahl (*Saelanthus rotundifolius* Forssk.).
Climbing shrub, much-branched. Stem 4–5-angled, woody, rather thin, pubescent; tendrils present. Leaves persistent, very broadly ovate to orbicular or reniform, generally more or less deeply cordate at base, subentire to sparingly undulate-dentate, folded and often splitting along main vein, large, green tinged blue, thick and fleshy, glabrous or occasionally sparsely pilose on veins beneath. Pedicels moderately thick, eglandular. Fruit cherry-sized. E Africa to S Arabia. Z10.

C.serrulata Roxb. See *Tetrastigma serrulatum*.

C.sicyoides L. PRINCESS VINE.
Vine, scrambling over rocks or climbing into trees to some height. Leaves 4–15×3–10cm, simple, ovate, obtuse to subcordate at base, acute to acuminate at apex, remotely finely bristle-toothed, thinly fleshy, deep green above, paler beneath, glabrous to densely minutely pubescent, with scattered transparent dots, veins conspicuous; petioles 5–12mm. Inflorescence decompound in open subglobose cymes, 2–5× 2–5cm; petals 2mm, yellow or white. Fruit black. Tropical Africa & America, north to N Mexico; Galápagos. 'Albonitens' (*C.albonitens* hort. ex Nichols.): leaves with brilliant silvery-white metallic lustre above. Z10.

C.striata Ruiz & Pav. (*Vitis striata* (Ruiz & Pav.) Miq.; *Ampelopsis sempervirens* hort. ex Veitch). MINIATURE GRAPE IVY.
Vine, climbing, small, evergreen, elegant. Stems slender, angled, hairy; tendrils very slender, threadlike. Leaves copiously produced, palmately 5-foliolate, 4–7.5cm across, membranous to somewhat coriaceous; leaflets 1.2–3.6 × 0.6–1.8cm, obovate to oblanceolate, coarsely dentate toward apex, tapered to base, subsessile, dark green and glabrous throughout, with a short gland terminating each tooth; petiole 2–4cm. Inflorescence small, cymose; flowers green. Fruit abundant, globose, maroon to black. Chile & S Brazil. Z9.

C.thomsonii (Lawson) Planch. See *Parthenocissus thomsonii*.

C.trifoliata (L.) L. (*C.incisa* (Nutt. in Torr. & A. Gray) Dur. ex Desm.; *C.acida* Chapm., Jacq. or L.; *C.rocheana* Planch.). MARINE IVY; MARINE VINE; POSSUM GRAPE.
Vine to 10m. Stem slender, striate, succulent when young; tendrils long, stout. Leaves 3-foliolate to 3-partite, rigid and succulent; leaflets broadly ovate to obovate, cuneate at base, margins with 1–2 shallow lobes or deeply serrate particularly towards apex. Inflorescence of umbellate clusters; petals 3mm; pedicels recurved. Fruit dark purple, almost black. Summer. S US (Missouri and Kansas to Texas and Arizona), N Mexico. Z9.

C.tuberosa Moc. & Sessé ex DC.
Vine, growing vigorously; caudex swollen, misshapen, skin smooth. Stems somewhat grooved, with internodes fattened,

terminal sections often becoming detached from parent and acting as propagating units, pubescent or glabrate; tendrils long, with adhesive terminal discs; aerial roots produced, often extending to ground-level. Leaves 4–9cm, simple, obovate, coarsely serrate to palmately lobed, with deeply incised lobes, sparsely pubescent or glabrous, long-petiolate. Mexico. Z10.

C.velutina Lind. ex Hook. See *C.discolor.*
C.vitifolia Boiss. See *Ampelopsis vitifolia.*
C.voinieriana (Pierre ex Nichols. & Mottet) Viala. See *Tetrastigma voinierianum.*

Citrullus Schräd. ex Ecklon & C. Zeyh. (From Gk *kitron*, citron; the fruits were thought to resemble those of *Citrus.*) Cucurbitaceae. 3 species of annual or perennial herbs, trailing or climbing, monoecious or dioecious; tendrils simple, branched, or absent. Leaves simple, usually deeply pinnately lobed, bracteate. Flowers solitary in axils; calyx tube short; corolla 5-lobed, yellow, campanulate; male flowers with stamens 3, anthers flexuous; female flowers with ovary inferior, pubescent, subglobose; staminodes present. Fruit broad-cylindric to subspherical, indehiscent, pericarp firm, mesocarp fleshy; seeds many, ovate, compressed. Asia, Africa. Z9.

CULTIVATION   A bitter purgative is derived from the dried pulp of *C.colocynthis*, the 'gall' of ancient times. *C.lanatus* is the water melon, producing edible fruits and seeds. Its protein-rich seed is ground for flour and caked for livestock. A vining annual known in cultivation for about 4000 years, it is now cultivated not only in the tropics and subtropics but also in warm temperate regions of the Mediterranean and occasionally in cool zones in warm, sheltered sites or in the hot glasshouse. Many cultivars are available, and selection of those which mature in 80–85 days, such as 'Fordbrook Hybrid', 'New Hampshire Midget', and 'Sugar Baby', allows their cultivation as far north as Long Island, New York.

Grow on well drained, light soils with added manure and hoof and horn: also as individuals on compost heaps, where they benefit from the bottom heat. In warm, settled weather, sow six seeds together on mounds 3.5m/11ft apart for long-season cultivars; 1.8m/6ft apart for short-season cultivars: bush cultivars are planted closer still. After germination, they are thinned out to 1–2 per mound. Alternatively, start three weeks earlier under glass (15–21°C/60–70°F) and transplant to open sites. Water regularly just before wilting point is reached. Cultivate soil shallowly and mulch to conserve moisture – black plastic effectively absorbs heat and warms the ground. Limit the number of fruits per plant by pinching young fruits out at 3–5-day intervals. Ripe watermelons produce a dull muffled sound when struck. Plants are susceptible to striped cucumber beetle.

C.colocynthis (L.) Schräd. (*Cucumis colocynthis* L.). COLOCYNTH; BITTER APPLE; VINE OF SODOM.
Perennial, trailing. Rootstock woody, tuberous. Stems shortly pubescent, later scabrous; tendrils usually simple. Leaves palmate, ovate, scabrid-pubescent beneath, 1–8 × 1–6cm, rarely longer, lobes 3–5, midlobe lobulate; petiole densely pubescent; stipules to 5mm, caducous. Male flowers pale yellow, calyx and corolla to 8mm, pedicel long; female flowers with pubescent ovary, pedicel longer than male. Fruit to 5cm diam., globose, smooth, striped green; seeds yellow-brown, to 6×3mm. N Africa to Afghanistan and Pakistan; widely cultivated.

C.fistulosus Stocks. See *Praecitrullus fistulosus.*

C.lanatus (Thunb.) Matsum. & Nak. (*Momordica lanata* Thunb.; *Cucurbita citrullus* L.). WATER MELON.
Annual coarsely villous monoecious climber or trailer. Tendrils stout, branching, pubescent. Leaves pinnately lobed, ovate, denticulate, smooth, with translucent patches above, pubescent beneath, lobes 3–5, ovate, obtuse. Flowers yellow, about 3cm diam. Fruit globose to cylindric, mottled or striped light and dark green, to 1m×40cm, flesh crystalline pink to red (yellow to orange in some cultivars); seeds ovate, about 10 × 5mm, black or dark red, often marked or marbled. Namibia; widely naturalized and cultivated.   var. *citroides* (L.H. Bail.) Mansf. CITRON; PRESERVING MELON. Fruit smaller, with white flesh, seeds never marked or marbled. Used only for preserving.

C.vulgaris Schräd. ex Ecklon & Zeyh. See *C.lanatus.*

Clematis L. (From Gk *clema*, a tendril; name used by Dioscorides for several scandent plants.) VIRGIN'S BOWER; LEATHER FLOWER; VASE VINE. Ranunculaceae. 200+ species of deciduous or evergreen, semi-woody to woody climbers or woody-based erect to sprawling perennials. Leaves usually opposite, sometimes alternate, simple, ternate or 1–2-pinnate; petiole often twisted and clasping. Flowers unisexual or bisexual, campanulate to discoid, solitary or in fascicles or panicles; sepals 4–8, petaloid, valvate; petals absent; staminodes sometimes petaloid; stamens numerous, filaments often dilated; styles elongate, usually plumose-pubescent, ovule pendulous. Fruit numerous achenes with long, persistent, often plumose styles. N & S Temperate regions, mountains of Tropical Africa..

CULTIVATION   Clematis have long been cultivated in Japan, and have been cultivated in Europe since the 16th century. Japanese cultivars, mainly those of the Patens Group, were introduced into European gardens in the mid-19th century. Nurserymen and plant breeders took the opportunity of using these earlier-flowering cultivars in a vast breeding programme, crossing them with European species and cultivars and other large-flowered clematis introduced from China, mainly during the period 1855–80. Many of the cultivars raised at that time are still popular today.

Clematis species and cultivars have many uses in the modern garden. The vigorous species such as *C.montana* are ideal for growing over buildings and through large trees. The herbaceous species are suitable for growing with a range of shrubs, especially roses. The less vigorous climbers, such as *C.alpina* and

C.macropetala, are superb for growing against exposed north- or east-facing walls or fences. *C.viticella* and its colourful cultivars are best suited for growing over shrubs or small trees and even over winter- or summer-flowering heathers and other groundcover plants.

The winter-flowering evergreen species, particularly *C.cirrhosa* and its forms like var. *balearica* and the heavily marked 'Freckles', are more suited to the sheltered garden or, in cold districts, the conservatory or cool glasshouse. Very sheltered spots and conservatories can be graced by the winter- and spring-flowering evergreen New Zealand species (*C.colensoi*, *C.petriei*, *C.afoliata* and *C.marmoraria*). The beautiful scrambling *C.phlebantha* from the Himalayas will produce a mound of interlaced stems covered with potentilla-like leaves and starry white flowers if planted against a sheltered south-facing wall, while *C.armandii* – a spectacular evergreen bearing large, glossy, 3-lobed leaves and trusses of sweetly scented white flowers – is far hardier in cool temperate areas than is often believed and will thrive on a north-facing wall. As one of the few evergreen climbers to offer both handsome foliage and a fine display of blooms, it is fast gaining popularity.

The large-flowered clematis cultivars fall into two basic groups: those that flower on ripened stems of the previous season and those that flower on the current season's growth from midsummer onwards. Compact and free-flowering, the early large-flowered types can, for purposes of cultivation, be split again into sections. The very early flowering types (typical of the *C*.Patens Group) such as 'Miss Bateman', are ideal for growing in containers or small gardens. The double and semi-double large-flowered cultivars, such as *C*.'Vyvyan Pennell', are more suited to growing through wall-trained shrubs such as *Pyracantha* because of the weight of their flowers. The later, early summer-flowering cultivars with large flowers and vigorous habit, such as *C*.'Marie Boisselot', fare better grown through large free-standing shrubs or small trees.

The second group of large-flowered cultivars, such as the popular *C. × jackmanii* which flowers on the current season's growth, is superb for growing through wall-trained shrubs, either deciduous or evergreen, or through climbing or rambler roses or free-standing species roses, where they can be chosen to flower at the same time, or before or after the host plant.

Species and cultivars can be chosen to enhance the conservatory, garden room or garden, almost throughout the year. Winter sees the flowers of *C.cirrhosa* and its forms in the protected environment or sheltered garden, followed by the more hardy large-leaved evergreen *C.armandii* and the extremely winter-hardy *C.alpina* and *C.macropetala* with colourful lantern-like flowers on exposed walls and fences during mid-spring. Late spring sees the myriad small flowers of *C.montana* and its forms grace trees and fences. The early large-flowered cultivars start during late spring and early summer, including all those clematis that produce their main crop of flowers from the ripened stems of the previous season. These are followed by the summer-flowering large-flowered cultivars, such as *C*.Jackmanii Group, and the later-flowering species and their cultivars, such as *C.viticella*, including the herbaceous types such as *C.integrifolia*, all of which flower on the current season's stems. *C.alpina* and its allies will often flower a second time in early autumn, with the late flowers of *C.tangutica* and its forms and subspecies. *C.× jouiniana* will often flower into November in Great Britain. Some species are scented; the best are *C.armandii*, *C.flammula* (almond-scented), *C.heracleifolia* var. *davidiana*, *C.× jouiniana* and the heavily scented *C.recta*. The flowers of pale, large-flowered cultivars such as *C*.'Nelly Moser' fade badly if planted in a south-facing position. Dark reds, blues and purples are best for planting in direct sunlight.

In addition to the climbing species and cultivars, there are several herbaceous species which are particularly useful as medium to large subjects for the herbaceous border. For the sake of completeness, their sometimes semi-scandent habit and their importance in breeding programmes, they are treated here. *C.douglasii* var. *scottii* from the grasslands of North America will produce slender, semi-sprawling stems furnished with delicate pinnate leaves and mauve, urn-shaped flowers on swan's neck stalks. It is quite hardy and performs best on gritty dry soils in full sun; prune back hard to the woody base in winter. *C.integrifolia*, *C.recta* and *C.stans* bear weakly erect stems ranked with pinnate leaves and open, nodding, star-shaped flowers in shades of violet, mauve and off-white. The herbaceous and subshrubby clematis are non-clinging, variable in height and can be placed most successfully in a herbaceous border or mixed shrub border. The robust *C.heracleifolia* will also grow in semi-shady conditions. The slender-stemmed taller species, such as *C.recta*, need the support of twigs or sticks if placed at the back of a border, although they can also be allowed to flop on to the ground.

All these species may be susceptible to winter wet. *C.× jouiniana* and *C.ranunculoides* are altogether more robust: their freely branching, erect stems are crowded with coarsely lobed leaves and scattered with small, sky-blue flowers. The large-leaved forms of *C.heracleifolia* are particularly useful for filling gaps in large shrub borders, being subshrubby in habit. The dense foliage of *C.heracleifolia* 'Mrs. Robert Brydon' can also be used as groundcover or for densely covering a pergola or archway up to about 250cm/8ft. As the leaf-stalks do not cling to supports they need tying as required. The herbaceous species and their cultivars flower on the current season's stems. Some are highly scented, such as *C.recta* and *C.heracleifolia* var. *davidiana*, which also has slightly scented foliage in the autumn. Some forms of *C.integrifolia* 'Alba' are also sweetly scented.

C. × jouiniana (*C.heracleifolia* × *C.vitalba*) and its forms might be termed semi-herbaceous, producing a sprawling mass of vigorous stems, persistent dark green leaves and scented, hyacinth blue flowers. They are best used for covering paving, breaking up the outlines of borders and for covering tree-stumps and drain-covers. They can also be trained onto a wall or other support.

The New Zealand species and their many cultivars are fine plants for the conservatory or frost-free glasshouse in cool-temperate areas; they may also be grown successfully in virtually frost-free gardens in a sunny well

Clematis (a) *C.orientalis* (b) *C.serratifolia* (c) *C.tangutica* ssp. *obtusiuscula* (d) *C.tangutica* (e) *C.intricata* (f) *C.tibetana* ssp. *vernayi* 'Orange Peel' (g) *C.alpina* (h) *C.alpina* 'Frances Rivis' (i) *C.macropetala*

drained site. *C.afoliata* and *C.paniculata* will certainly survive mild frosts. When grown in containers, the potting medium should be gritty and well drained and not be allowed to become overwet during the winter months. Some cultivars make ideal plants for the alpine house, such as *C.* × *cartmanii* 'Joe'. Some, such as forms of *C.forsteri*, have an extremely strong scent. All are evergreen and flower on the previous season's ripened stems. They therefore require only the removal of dead and weak stems after flowering each year.

Climbing clematis, if grown in containers, can be planted at most times of the year, assuming that soil conditions are favourable, namely, not frozen, too dry nor too wet. However, spring and autumn are the best times to plant. Clematis are successful in acid as well as alkaline soils.

Clematis can be expected to grace their supports for many years, therefore thorough initial soil preparation is essential. Unless the soil is rich in nutrients and has plenty of fibre, a hole of approximately 45×45cm/18×18in. should be dug, and all uncongenial soil removed. This should be replaced with a mixture of old potting soil, good topsoil and leafmould or garden compost, mixed with a little bonemeal. On sandy or very free-draining soils, rotted straw or garden compost can be added to help retain moisture. Clematis will grow perfectly well on heavy clay soils, provided grit or coarse sand is added to create good drainage. Clematis do not like to be grown in poorly drained, heavy soils.

If the planting site is to be near to the base of a tree, large shrub or hedgerow, the exact position should be chosen away from the main feeder roots of the supporting plant so that they will not encroach on the root system of the newly planted clematis. If the planting site is at the base of a wall, the clematis should be planted to avoid the bone-dry strip of soil near the wall.

To avoid damage by animals or infection by the disease clematis wilt, all climbing clematis should be planted with the top of the root ball 8cm/3in. below the soil surface. This will help to build up a good root crown of growth buds. The plant should be watered before it is removed from its container and immediately afterwards. If planting is carried out during the spring months, careful attention should be paid to watering until the plant has become established.

Clematis in the wild grow from behind rocks or from the base of shrubs or scrub where their root systems are shaded from direct sunlight. Clematis in cultivation also benefit from a shaded root system and this can be attained by planting a low growing shrub such as lavender, heather or *Hebe* near the base of the clematis without encroaching too much on its root system. A small slab of stone or slate can also achieve the same result.

When clematis are to be grown in tubs or containers, wooden or stone material should be chosen with a minimum diameter and depth of 45cm/18in., avoiding plastic which becomes too hot in summer. A soil-based medium should be used if possible. The container should have good drainage and be raised off the ground. Small stones can be placed in the bottom and a little well rotted garden compost can be added before the container is filled with potting medium. Watering will be necessary every day during prolonged dry weather. Bedding plants or summer-flowering annuals should be planted in the container to help maintain a shaded, cool root system.

All newly planted clematis should be pruned hard the first spring after planting, especially those planted in containers. This will encourage the plants to become bushy and well furnished at the base. All growth, whatever species or cultivar, should be removed down to a strong pair of leaf axil buds 30cm/12in. above soil level.

Most clematis are of a climbing habit and this is achieved by the petiole, which twists itself around its support. Clematis are not clinging and will not attach themselves to a bare wall. If they are provided with a support, whether it be wire, trellis or another plant, they will loosely attach themselves or may be easily tied on. As clematis put on new growth each year, they should be trained onto or over their supports to make sure that they have some guidance until they firmly attach themselves. This also applies to clematis grown over ground cover plants, where their main stems can be pegged.

Herbaceous clematis will thrive in a fertile sandy loam in full sun. Some, notably *C.douglasii* var. *scottii*, need very good drainage and do best in full sun. Emerging stems of *C.stans* and *C.recta* may require the support of pea-sticks in mid-spring. All the herbaceous species benefit from a mulch of garden compost or well rotted farmyard manure in late winter, although care must be taken not to smother the tender basal buds. Prune flowered growths to two basal buds in winter.

PRUNING. For the purpose of pruning, climbing clematis fit into three basic groups according to whether they flower on old or previous season's wood or that of the current year. Of species it can, however, be remarked that pruning can be limited to the removal of exhausted or congested growth, or to keeping within boundaries, after flowering.

Group 1. Types which produce short flower-stalks direct from the previous season's leaf axil buds; the spring-flowering species *C.alpina, C. macropetala* and *C.montana*. Remove any dead or damaged stems after flowering and, as the growing season progresses into summer and autumn, train new growth into the support if it can be reached, keeping stems within their allocated space.

Group 2. The early large-flowered cultivars, the double and semi-double and the large-flowered types which flower before midsummer (i.e. Florida, Lanuginosa and Patens Groups). These produce stems of varying lengths from 15cm/6in. to 60cm/24in. with a single flower at the end. These stems grow away from the axillary buds which will have ripened the previous season. Remove dead and shorter damaged stems down to a strong pair of buds during late winter or very early spring. Tie in the old growth and new growth as it appears so that it can support the large flowers.

Group 3. These produce all their flowers in clusters or panicles at the end of the current season's growth (i.e. Jackmanii, Texensis and Viticella Groups). Remove all top growth down to just above the base of the previous season's stems during late winter and very early spring. New growth will be visible at this time; prune just above where it commences. All top growth should be trained and tied in to its support during the growing season.

MAINTENANCE. An annual mulch of well rotted garden compost or farmyard manure is advantageous during late winter. Avoid placing the mulch over the root crown. A mulch of coir mixed with bonemeal or balanced garden fertilizer can also be used. This will also help to keep roots cool. Watering should be maintained during dry spring and summer weather. Liquid feeding will also assist spring growth and help provide extra food for a second flush of growth after flowering. Do not feed just before and during flowering as this will shorten the flowering period, but maintain a good supply of water. Liquid feed and plenty of water must be applied to all container-grown plants during spring, summer and early autumn. These should be only sparingly watered during late autumn and winter to allow the growing wood to ripen before winter.

PROPAGATION. All *Clematis* species can be successfully propagated from seed. Seeds should be sown soon after harvesting; to ensure good germination, cold frames can be used. Cultivars, both large- and small-flowered, should be reproduced from layering, cuttings or possibly from grafting. Layering can be carried out during late winter or early spring with old stems, or in early summer with current season's growth. Herbaceous clematis can be increased by division or, with more difficulty from cuttings. *C.heracleifolia* and its cultivars increase easily by layering.

Cuttings may be taken before flowering during late spring or from the very early spring-flowering types in early summer. Internodal cuttings of soft to semi-ripe wood are best; one of the pair of leaves should be removed. Insert the cuttings in a light, sandy potting mixture. The prepared cuttings should be kept moist until they have rooted and protected from direct sunlight. A cold frame or propagation unit can be used. Nodal cuttings of *C.armandii* will root in a cool mist unit. Potting on can be carried out the following spring for the large-flowered cultivars or during midsummer for the easier and faster-rooting species.

Grafting for the more difficult large-flowered cultivars is possible on to a rootstock of *C.viticella* or *C.vitalba* during early spring. A propagation unit or cold frame can be used; a cleft-graft is generally preferred. A grafted plant should be potted on with the union well below soil level to allow the scion to form roots.

PESTS AND DISEASES. Clematis are largely free from major pests. However, preventative action should be taken to avoid a build-up of aphids during the spring as they will damage new growth and flower buds. Earwigs may chew holes in leaves and flower buds of a Clematis growing near a building with crevices in which these night prowlers tend to hide. Slugs and snails can cause damage in the early spring to fresh young growth by skinning stems. Mice and rabbits can also cause damage to young growth and even destroy established plants. Mildew can be unsightly during mid- and late summer.

Clematis wilt was once a major trouble. Due to the availability of much stronger plants and cleaner propagation practices, this is less of a problem than in the past. If the plant should suddenly collapse while in full flower, or perhaps just before flowering commences and the growing tips turn black, all top growth should be removed down to soil level and burnt. If the clematis was planted deeply enough, it should start to grow again from below soil level. The wilt is caused by a fungus and can be controlled by spraying with an appropriate fungicide at monthly intervals. In gardens where wilt is or has been a problem, preventative spraying should commence in mid-spring and continue until late summer. Herbaceous *Clematis* do not suffer from clematis wilt.

C.addisonii Britt.
Low shrub to 1m. Branches erect, later procumbent, blue-green, glabrous. Leaves to 8cm, glaucous, lower leaves simple, broad-ovate, subsessile, sometimes lobed, obtuse, upper leaves simple to 2–4-foliolate, sometimes to 6-foliolate; leaflets ovate. Flowers urceolate, solitary, terminal and axillary, pendulous; sepals purple, stout, lanceolate, recurved. Achenes rhomboid to subspherical, ribbed, lanuginose; styles to 5cm, brown-pubescent. Spring–summer. Eastern N America (Virginia, N Carolina). Z6.

C.aethusifolia Turcz.
Erect or scandent perennial to 60cm. Stems slender, somewhat ribbed, sparsely adpressed pubescent. Leaves to 20.5cm, bright green, 3-, 5- or 7-pinnatisect, segments deeply lobed or trifoliate; leaflets to 3cm, linear to obovate or oblong, broad-tapered at base, coarsely and irregularly-dentate, lanuginose. Flowers to 2cm, narrow-campanulate, pendulous, in 1–3-flowered, axillary cymes; peduncles erect, slender, to 5cm; sepals pale yellow to cream-white, to 2cm, narrow-oblong, acute, white-lanuginose at margins; filaments filiform, lanuginose. Achenes ribbed, lanuginose, with white-plumose styles to 2cm. Summer. N China, Korea. Z5. var. *latisecta* Maxim. Leaves larger, segments more round to ovate; leaflets to 4cm.

C.afoliata Buch. (*C.aphylla* Col.).
Semi-scandent, almost leafless shrub to 2m, erratically branched. Branches slender, wire-like, striate; branchlets

somewhat ribbed, dark green, glabrous. Leaves trifoliolate, sometimes present when young; leaflets minute, ovate or triangular; petiole slender, to 10cm, green. Flowers 2.5cm diam., solitary and 2–6-grouped in axillary cymes. Peduncles slender, to 5cm, pubescent; sepals green-white, 4–6, lanceolate, patent, sericeous outside. Achenes rufous, pubescent, with sericeous styles to 2cm. Spring–summer. New Zealand. Z8.

C.akebioides (Maxim.) hort. ex Veitch.
Close to *C.orientalis*. Leaves pinnate, leaflets 5–7, glaucous, thick-textured, obtuse, bluntly and irregularly toothed to obscurely lobed. Inflorescence sessile or short-stalked; flowers clustered in axils; sepals yellow, sometimes stained red or purple beneath, to 2.5cm, fairly thickly textured, ovate, erect or spreading. W China. Z5.

C.albicoma Wherry.
Close to *C.ochroleuca*. Branches to 60cm, erect, initially downy, later glabrous. Leaves 4–5cm, ovate, entire, ultimately glabrous, net-veined. Flowers solitary at branch tips, nodding, campanulate; sepals purple, tips recurved. Achenes with downy tails to 3cm long. Spring. NE US. Z5.

C.alpina (L.) Mill. (*Atragene alpina* L.).
Deciduous climber to 2.5m. Stems somewhat ribbed, glabrous. Leaves to 15cm, biternate; leaflets 9, to 5 × 1.5cm, ovate-lanceolate, coarse-serrate, lanuginose at base. Flowers solitary, pendulous, stellate-campanulate; peduncles to

10cm; sepals 4, to 4cm × 12.5mm, blue or mauve, oblong, sericeous below; staminodes petaloid, white, spoon-shaped, to 2cm. Achenes with sericeous styles to 4cm. Spring. N Europe & mts of C & S Europe, N Asia. 'Bluebell': as 'Pamela Jackman', flowers blue. 'Burford White': to 4m; flowers large, clear white, bell-shaped, tepals pointed; vigorous. 'Columbine': flowers pale lavender, almost campanulate; sepals long and acute. 'Columbine White': to 4m; leaves pale; flowers white, on upright stems. 'Frances Rivis' ('Blue Giant'): sepals to 5 × 2cm, ovate, rich sky blue; staminodes to 1.5 × 0.3cm. 'Grandiflora': flowers large, mauveblue. 'Helsingborg': flowers deep purple; stamens petaloid, dark purple. 'Inshriach': flowers small on slender, swannecked pedicels; sepals narrow, decurved to spreading, sometimes slightly twisted, dark lilac to pale mauve, staminodes equal, to three-quarters length of sepals green-white tipped mauve, many in a tight central boss. 'Jacqueline du Pré': flowers large, warm pink, interior soft pink with silverpin edging, staminodes blush pink. 'Pamela Jackman': flowers to 8cm diam., dark azure; sepals to 4.5 × 1.5cm; staminodes tinted blue. 'Pauline': flowers Oxford blue flushed violet, centre white. 'Rosy Pagoda': flowers pale pink. 'Ruby': flowers soft red, staminodes cream. 'Willy': flowers pale pink, deep pink at base of stamens, early-flowering. var. *ochotensis* (Pall.) S. Wats. Leaves similar to those of var. *sibirica*; sepals indigo, more acute; staminodes narrow to broadly spathulate, downy, usually rounded. E Siberia, Sachalin, Kamchatka, Korea, Japan. var. *sibirica* (L.) Schneid. (*Atragene sibirica* L.; *C.sibirica* (L.) Mill.). Leaflets more coarsely and irregularly serrate, pale cream. Sepals yellow-white, rarely flushed blue, elliptic-lanceolate, long-acuminate; staminodes pale cream, spathulate, narrower and dense-pubescent N Norway and Finland to E Siberia, C Urals and Manchuria. 'Graveye': flowers large, milky yellow, very early-flowering. 'White Moth': flowers semi-double, white. Z5.

C.alpina var. *occidentalis* (Hornem.) A. Gray. See *C.occidentalis*.
C.alpina var. *thibetica* hort. See *C.alpina* 'Frances Rivis'.
C.aphylla Col. See *C.afoliata*.

C.apiifolia DC.
Deciduous climber to 4.5m. Stems slender, somewhat lanuginose. Leaves trifoliolate, occasionally pinnate with the lower segments trifoliolate; leaflets to 7.5cm, thin, broad-ovate to ovate-lanceolate, cordate to tapered at base, deeply incised and often trilobed, subglabrous, pubescent on veins beneath. Flowers 1.6cm diam., in axillary panicles to 15cm; sepals dull white, patent, dense-lanuginose outside; stamens glabrous. Achenes with sericeous styles. Autumn. China, Japan. Z7.

C.aristata R. Br.
Climber. Stems initially downy. Leaves long-petioled, 1–2 × ternate; leaflets coriaceous, toothed or entire. Flowers in axils, forming a panicle-like inflorescence; sepals 2–2.5cm, 4–5, white or ivory, oblong or oblong-lanceolate, spreading, glabrous or downy; anthers oblong with an aristate appendage. Achenes ovoid, glabrous or downy; styles to 5cm, plumose. Summer. Australia. Z7.

C.armandii Franch.
Evergreen climber to 9m. Stems minutely-lanuginose when young. Leaves tough, coriaceous, trifoliolate; leaflets to 15 × 6.5cm, oblong-lanceolate to ovate, acute, rounded or somewhat cordate at base, entire, emerging bronze-pink, soon rich glossy green, glabrous, prominently veined; petiole to 10cm; petiolules to 2.5cm, twisted. Flowers to 6.5cm diam., in groups of 3 in dense axillary clusters; peduncles bracteate at base; sepals pure white or cream-white, later rose, 4–7, narrow-oblong, 2.5cm × 8.5mm. Achenes ovoid, appressedpubescent with plumose styles to 3cm. Spring. C & W China. 'Apple Blossom': leaves strongly tinted bronze when young; flowers cup-shaped, pink in bud, fading to white. 'Snowdrift': leaves large, new leaves tinted copper after

flowering; flowers large, on drooping stalks, white, waxy, very fragrant.

C.× aromatica Lenné & Koch. (*C.flammula* × *C.integrifolia*.)
Erect subshrub to 2m. Stems slender. Leaves simple, trilobed or 5-foliolate; leaflets to 3cm, ovate to broad-oval, entire, glabrous. Flowers 4cm diam., in lax terminal cymes; peduncles 5cm, somewhat lanuginose; sepals dark violet, 4, oblong, patent, lanuginose at margins; filaments white or yellow, pubescent at apex. Achenes sericeous-pubescent. Summer–autumn. Z4.

C.australis T. Kirk.
Climber. Branchlets slender, grooved, pubescent. Leaves trifoliolate; leaflets to 4cm, pinnatifid to pinnate. Flowers unisexual, solitary or few-clustered in panicles; sepals white or pale yellow, 5–8, 2cm, sericeous. Achenes pubescent when young. New Zealand. 'Green Velvet': hybrid with *C.petriei*; leaves dark green, crenately lobed; flowers downy, emerald green. Z8.

C.baldwinii Torr. & A. Gray (*Viorna baldwinii* (Torr. & A. Gray) Small). PINE HYACINTH.
Erect herb to 60cm. Leaves to 10cm, mostly simple, sometimes trifoliolate above, elliptic to lanceolate or linear. Flowers purple or purple-pink, urceolate, 2.5cm, pendulous. Achenes with persistent styles to 12.5mm. S US (Florida). Z7.

C.balearica Rich. See *C.cirrhosa* var. *balearica*.

C.barbellata Edgew.
Climber to 4m, similar to *C.montana*, readily identified by flower colour. Branches cylindric, glabrous or subglabrous. Leaves trifoliolate; leaflets to 8cm, ovate-lanceolate, acute, rounded at base, abundantly lobed and irregularly sharp-serrate. Flowers campanulate, solitary or several-grouped, axillary; sepals 4, oblong-ovate, to 4cm, somewhat outspread, lanuginose, dull purple to brown-violet; filaments dilated, lanuginose, anthers long-pubescent at apex. Achenes rhomboid, glabrous, with plumose styles. Spring–summer. W Himalaya. 'Pruinina': flowers plum, lantern-shaped, stamens petaloid, white; late-flowering.

C.bergeronii Lav. See *C.× eriostemon* 'Bergeronii'.

C.brachiata Thunb.
Climber. Leaves 5-foliolate, rarely bipinnate; leaflets rounded to ovate, coarse-serrate. Flowers numerous; sepals cream or white, to 2.5cm. S Africa. Z9.

C.brevicaudata DC.
Vigorous climber. Stems many, densely tangled. Leaves 5–7-foliolate, lower lobes ternate, upper lobes simple; leaflets to 7cm, ovate-lanceolate, long-acuminate, sinuate-serrate, glabrous or somewhat pilose. Flowers to 2cm diam., in many-flowered axillary cymes, grouped into large, terminal panicles; pedicels pubescent; sepals white or somewhat yellow, to 1.5cm, exterior pubescent; filaments glabrous. Achenes compressed, strong-pubescent, with plumose styles to 3cm. Summer. Japan, China, W Mongolia. Z5.

C.buchananiana DC.
Vigorous climber. Young shoots pubescent Leaves pinnately 5–7-foliolate; leaflets to 10cm, broad-ovate, cordate at base, coarse-serrate or sometimes lobed, pubescent. Flowers tubular, to 3cm, in a long, leafy, paniculate inflorescence; sepals 4, to 2.5cm, cream-white to pale yellow, stout, linear-oblong, recurved at apex, fine-pubescent inside, lanuginose and ribbed outside; filaments dense-pubescent. Achenes lanate, with persistent styles to 5cm. Summer–autumn. Himalaya (Pakistan to SW China). Z6.

C.buchananiana Finet & Gagnep., non DC. See *C.rehderiana*.
C.caerulea var. *odorata* hort. See *C.× aromatica*.
C.calycina Ait. See *C.cirrhosa* var. *balearica*.

C.campaniflora Brot.
Deciduous climber to 6m. Stems slender, somewhat lanuginose when young. Leaves 5- or 7-ternate; leaflets to 7.5cm, narrow-lanceolate, ovate or oval, simple or sometimes lobed,

Clematis (a) *C.florida* 'Sieboldii' (b) *C.chrysocoma* (c) *C.rehderiana* (d) *C.montana* (e) *C.veitchiana* leaf

glabrous. Flowers bowl-shaped, solitary or several grouped together, pendulous; peduncles to 7.5cm, lanuginose; sepals white tinged violet, 4, 2cm, oblong, abruptly acuminate and recurved, semi-expanded, lanate; style glabrous or tomentose; filaments subglabrous. Achenes rounded-ovate, with somewhat lanuginose styles to 8.5mm. Summer. Portugal. Z6.

C.cartmanii hort. (*C.marmoraria* × *C.paniculata*.)
Bushy dwarf intermediate between parents with finely dissected dark green leaves and large panicles of white flowers. Garden origin. 'Joe' (male selection): dwarf tufted to mat-forming shrub; branches glabrous, purple-tinted; flowers to 4cm diam., white, to 30 per panicle.

C.catesbyana Pursh.
Climber. Stems minute-pubescent. Leaves biternate; leaflets membranous, lobed or entire. Flowers 2.5cm diam., in cymose panicles; sepals white, linear to cuneate. SE US (South Carolina, Florida, Louisiana). Z8.

C.chinensis Retz.
Deciduous climber. Stems ribbed, subglabrous and sparsely-lanuginose. Leaves pinnately 5-foliolate; leaflets to 7.5cm, ovate or cordate, usually cordate at base, glabrous, except for midrib lanuginose, 3- or 5-veined. Flowers to 2cm diam., in many-flowered cymose panicles; sepals white, 4, very narrow, lanuginose on margins. Achenes densely appressed-pubescent, with slender, densely white-downy styles to 4cm. Autumn. C & W China. Z6.

C.chrysocoma Franch.
Deciduous climber to 2.5m. Stems densely brown-yellow villous-lanuginose when young. Leaves trifoliolate, densely brown-yellow-villous to lanuginose; petioles to 5cm, dense brown-yellow villous-lanuginose; leaflets to 4.5 × 4.5cm, broad-ovate or rhomboid to narrow-obovate, trilobed, sometimes only coarsely and irregularly serrate, lateral leaflets to 2.5cm, sessile; petiolules of terminal leaflets to 6.5mm.

Flowers 4.5cm diam., solitary; peduncles to 7.5cm, densely brown-yellow-villous to lanuginose; sepals white tinged pink, 4, broad-oblong, abruptly acuminate, densely sericeous beneath; stamens forming a cluster 2.5cm diam. Achenes with gold-brown-pubescent plumose styles to 3cm. Summer–autumn. China (Yunnan). 'Rosea': flowers soft pink, sepals winged, stamens yellow. Z7.

C.chrysocoma var. **sericea** (Franch.) Schneid. See *C.spooneri*.

C.cirrhosa L. (*C.balearica* Pers., non Rich.).
Evergreen climber to 4m. Stems striate or smooth, sometimes sericeous-pubescent when young. Leaves to 5cm, simple, dentate or trilobed, or ternate or biternate with dentate or lobed leaflets, glossy dark green; petioles twining. Flowers pendulous, broad-campanulate, to 7cm diam., solitary or in axillary fascicles, subtended by a small cuplike pair of bracteoles; pedicels slender, to 5cm; sepals ovate, to 2.5cm, cream, rarely spotted red, sericeous outside; filaments alate, glabrous. Achenes with plumose styles to 5cm. Winter–spring. S Europe, Mediterranean. 'Wisley Cream': leaves light green; flowers cream. var.*balearica* (Rich.) Willk. & Lange (*C.calycina* Ait.). Sepals pale cream, always spotted and flecked red-maroon within. 'Freckles': flowers large, cream, intensely flecked and spotted maroon to violet within, on exceptionally long, slender pedicels. Z7.

C.coccinea Engelm. See *C.texensis*.
C.coerulea Lindl. See *C.patens*.

C.colensoi Hook. f.
Evergreen climber, much-branched. Branches slender, slightly pubescent when young. Leaves 7 × 8cm, triangular, ultimately pinnatisect or pinnately trifoliolate; leaflets rounded at apex. Flowers 10-grouped, axillary; sepals green, 6, narrow-lanceolate, sericeous. Spring–summer. New Zealand. Z8.

C.columbiana (Nutt.) Torr. & A. Gray (*Atragene columbiana* Nutt.).
Semi-woody climber. Branchlets slender. Leaves pinnately trifoliolate; leaflets 4cm, thin, ovate, acute, cordate at base, entire or coarse-serrate. Flowers solitary; sepals purple or blue, lanceolate, to 5cm. Fruit with persistent styles to 5cm. N America (British Columbia south to Colorado & Oregon). Z4.

C.connata DC.
Vigorous deciduous climber to 8m. Stems somewhat ribbed. Leaves 3- or 5-foliolate, with paired petiole bases forming a large disc-like process around the stem at each node; leaflets to 12.5×7.5cm, ovate, sometimes trilobed, apex finely acuminate, base cordate, coarse-serrate, glabrous or lanuginose, bright green. Flowers campanulate, pendulous, in axillary panicles to 12.5cm; sepals soft yellow, oblong, to 2.5cm, acute and recurved at apex, fine-lanuginose inside; filaments pubescent. Achenes lanuginose, with sericeous-plumose styles to 3cm. Summer–autumn. Himalaya, SW China. Z6.

C. County Park Hybrids. (*C.petriei* × *C.marmoraria.*)
'Pixie': evergreen, trailing subshrub. Leaves to 4cm, trifoliolate; leaflets lobed. Flowers pale yellow-green in a congested panicle. Male selection. Spring. 'Fairy': female selection, differs from 'Pixie' in 8–10 staminodes, silky golden styles; fruit with downy achenes. Z6.

C.crispa L. (*C.simsii* Sweet). BLUE JASMINE; MARSH CLEMATIS; CURLY CLEMATIS; CURLFLOWER.
Climbing deciduous shrub to 2.5m. Leaves to 20.5cm, pinnately 3-, 5- or 7-foliolate; leaflets to 7.5×4cm, often trifoliolate or lobed, thin, lanceolate to broad-ovate, cordate at base, entire, glabrous. Flowers campanulate, solitary, terminal, pendulous; peduncles to 7.5cm; sepals to 5cm×12.5mm, connate below, distinct and spreading at tips, lavender, almost white at margins, thin and sinuate, somewhat lanuginose outside. Achenes sericeous or subglabrous, with only somewhat plumose styles. Summer. SE US. 'Distorta' (*C.distorta* Lav.): sepals curled. Z5.

C.delavayi Franch.
Erect shrub to 1.5m. Leaves to 10cm, pinnate; leaflets to 3.5× 1.5cm, sessile, lanceolate to elliptic-ovate, acute, entire, deep green above, silver-white and densely sericeous beneath. Flowers to 3cm diam., 3–6-grouped in terminal cymes; sepals 4–6, white, obovate, densely pubescent outside. Summer. China. Europe. Z5.

C.dioscoreifolia Alév. & Vaniot. See *C.terniflora.*
C.distorta Lav. See *C.crispa* 'Distorta'.

C.×divaricata Jacq. (*C.integrifolia* × *C.viorna.*)
Erect, non-climbing shrub. Leaves pinnate or simple and irregularly lobed; leaflets 3–7, sessile, glabrous beneath. Flowers to 2.5cm, short-stalked, nodding, campanulate; sepals red-lilac, spreading. Summer. Garden origin. Z6.

C.douglasii Hook.
Herbaceous, non-climbing perennial to 60cm. Shoots densely pubescent when young, later glabrous; branches angular, furrowed. Leaves simple below, 2–3-pinnate above; leaflets oblong, lanceolate or ovate, entire, sometimes sparsely serrate, villous. Flowers tubular or campanulate, 2.5cm, solitary, terminal, sometimes also axillary, pendulous; pedicels long, swan-necked; sepals 4, deep mauve to violet, thick, oblong, 2.5cm, reflexed, paler outside; stamens 2.5cm+. Achenes rhomboid, with persistent, brown, plumose styles to 5cm. Spring–summer. Northwest America.var. *scottii* (T.C. Porter) Coult. To 1m. Leaves grey-green, bipinnate; leaflets narrow-lanceolate, downy beneath. Flowers to 4cm, urceolate; sepals 4, strongly recurved at tips, lavender to pale magenta, downy. British Columbia, Washington east to Montana, Wyoming. 'Rosea': flowers rose pink. Z6.

C.×durandii Kuntze. (*C. ×jackmanii* × *C.integrifolia.*)
Robust erect to semi-scandent shrub to 180cm. Leaves to 15× 7.5cm, simple, ovate, acute, tapered or somewhat cordate at base, glossy green, glabrous or subglabrous, conspicuously 3–5-veined; petioles to 5cm. Flowers to 11.5cm diam., usually 3-grouped; sepals deep violet-blue, usually 4, to 6, patent or reflexed, obovate, 4cm diam., slightly undulate at margins; stamens yellow, filaments pubescent, villous at apex, achenes with long, sericeous styles. Summer–autumn. 'Pallida': flowers paler, violet-rose. Z5.

C.erecta L. See *C.recta.*

C. × eriostemon Decne. (*C.integrifolia* × *C.viticella.*)
Sprawling semi-woody shrub to 3m. Branches striate, brown, glabrous or slightly pubescent Leaves pinnately 7-foliolate; leaflets elliptic, acute, entire, deep green, terminal leaflets usually slightly lobed; petiole to 4cm. Flowers 1–3-grouped, terminal; peduncles to 10cm; sepals 4, dark violet to lavender, spathulate, 4 × 2.5cm, abrupt-acuminate and reflexed, conspicuously 3-veined. Achenes with pubescent styles to 3cm. Bergeronii' (*C.bergeronii* Lav.): to 3m; leaves thick; leaflets large, oval, wide; flowers almost campanulate, grouped to 3, sepals spathulate-cuneate, to 3 × 1.5cm, mauve; flowers clusters rounded. 'Hendersonii': to 2.5m; stems slender; leaves pinnate; flowers to 6.5cm diam., solitary, violet; sepals patent, 2cm diam.; summer–autumn. 'Intermedia': as 'Hendersonii', but stems thicker; flowers similar to *C.integrifolia*, violet blue. Z4.

C.fargesii Franch. (*C.potaninii* var. *fargesii* (Franch.) Hand.-Mazz.)
Deciduous climber to 6m. Young shoots strongly ribbed, purple, lanuginose. Leaves to 23cm, bipinnate, 5–7-foliolate; petioles lanuginose; leaflets to 5 × 4cm, ovate, deeply irregularly- and coarsely-serrate, sometimes trilobed, rounded at base, sericeous-lanuginose, dull green, lateral leaflets sessile or subsessile, to 2.5 × 2cm. Flowers to 6.5cm diam., axillary, 1–3-grouped; pedicels to 18cm; sepals 6, obovate, to 2cm diam., short-acuminate, pure white above, yellow and lanuginose outside; filaments glabrous, anthers pale yellow. Achenes with plumose styles. Summer–autumn. China. Z6.

C.fasciculiflora Franch.
Evergreen climber to 6m. Leaves trifoliolate; leaflets oval-oblong, to 10cm. Flowers yellow-white, exterior lanate-pubescent, in dense axillary clusters; peduncles to 2cm; filaments much longer than anthers. Achenes glabrous. SW China. Z8.

C.finetiana Lév. & Vaniot.
Semi-evergreen climber to 4m. Branches glabrous. Leaves trifoliolate; petioles to 7.5cm; leaflets to 10 × 5cm, thin, somewhat coriaceous, narrow-ovate, acute, rounded or somewhat cordate at base, entire, bright green, glabrous, 3-veined. Flowers to 4cm diam., axillary, in 3-flowered, sometimes to 7-flowered inflorescence; peduncles to 5cm, glabrous; bracts lanceolate, small; sepals pure white, green-white outside, 4, lanceolate, 1.5cm, acute, patent, subglabrous; filaments glabrous, much shorter than sepals, anthers yellow. Achenes pubescent, with brown, plumose styles. Summer. C & W China. Possibly not distinct from *C.pavoliniana*. Z8.

C.flammula L.
Scandent woody-based deciduous subshrub to 5m. Leaves 3- or 5-foliolate; leaflets narrow-lanceolate to rounded, 2–3-lobed or trifoliolate, bright green, glabrous, often coriaceous. Flowers very fragrant, to 2.5cm diam., in lax, many-flowered, bracteate, axillary panicles to 30.5cm; peduncles dense-pubescent; sepals pure white, 4, to 1.2cm, oblong, obtuse, densely pubescent on margins; filaments to 4mm, glabrous, anthers to 4mm. Achenes strongly compressed, ovoid, 6.5mm, with white-plumose, 3cm styles. Summer–autumn. S Europe, N Africa, W Syria, Iran, Turkey. Z6.

C.flammula var. *rubromarginata* Cripps. See *C.terniflora.*
C.flammula var. *robusta* Carr. See *C.terniflora.*

C.florida Thunb.
Deciduous or semi-evergreen climber to 4m. Stems tough, wiry. Leaves to 12.5cm, ternate, each division trifoliolate;

leaflets to 5cm, ovate to lanceolate, entire or serrate, shiny deep green above, pubescent beneath. Flowers white or cream, sometimes lined or tinted green, to 7.5cm diam., flat, solitary, axillary; peduncles to 10cm, lanuginose, bracteate; bracts 2, sessile, lobed, foliate; sepals 4–6, ovate, acuminate, patent; staminodes (when present) deep violet, to 2.5cm, transitional to stamens; stamens patent, filaments white, anthers deep violet; styles deep violet. Achenes compressed, rhomboid, purple, with persistent, sericeous, plumose styles. Summer. China, Japan. 'Alba Plena': flowers double, staminodes and sepals white flushed green, exterior with central green stripe. 'Sieboldii' ('Bicolor'): flowers white with purple staminodes forming anemone centre. Z7.

C.foetida Raoul.
Evergreen climber. Young shoots grooved, fulvous-tomentose. Leaves to 9 × 12cm, glabrous or sparse-pubescent, trifoliolate; petioles to 9cm, pubescent; leaflets to 9cm, ovate, obtuse to acute, entire to sinuate, rarely crenate-lobed or serrate, thinly coriaceous, deep green. Flowers to 2.5cm diam., in axillary, dichasial cymes; pedicels bracteate; bracts paired, connate; sepals yellow, 5–8, imbricate, to 2.3cm, ovate-oblong, glabrous above, pilose beneath; filaments glabrous, anthers to 1.5mm; staminodes few. Achenes to 4mm, pubescent, with 2.5cm styles. New Zealand. Z8.

C.forrestii W.W. Sm. See C.napaulensis.

C.forsteri J.F. Gmel.
Evergreen climber. Leaves to 16 × 14cm, glabrous or subglabrous, trifoliolate; leaflets to 7cm, lanceolate to broad-ovate, entire, crenate-dentate, deeply pinnatifid, bi-pinnatisect or pinnate, coriaceous, bright green. Flowers pure yellow, solitary or 2–6-grouped, axillary, unisexual; pedicels bracteate; bracts paired, connate; sepals 5–8, white, imbricate, lanceolate, ovate or narrow-oblong, to 3cm, glabrous or sericeous; filaments glabrous, anthers 3mm; staminodes few. Achenes to 5mm, with styles to 3.5cm. Summer. New Zealand. 'Tempo': male selection, very vigorous; flowers to 4cm diam., pale green becoming white. Z8.

C.×francofurtensis Rinz. (C.florida × C.viticella.)
Close to C.viticella. Leaves bipinnate; leaflets ovate, acute, downy beneath. Flowers large; sepals 6, purple, interior pure white; stamens violet. Summer. Garden origin. Z6.

C.fremontii Wats. (Viorna fremontii (Wats.) Heller).
FREMONT'S CROWFOOT.
Robust, erect perennial to 50cm, somewhat branched. Stems lanate. Leaves to 10cm, simple, subsessile, tough, ovate-lanceolate to broad-ovate, entire or subentire, sparsely villous-tomentose, conspicuously reticulately veined. Flowers 2.5cm, glabrous outside, pendulous, solitary, terminal; sepals purple, 4, thick, reflexed at apex, tomentose at margins. Achenes lanate at base, with styles to 2.5cm. Summer. NW America. Z4.

C.fruticosa Turcz.
Similar to C.recta. Subshrub to 50cm, closely branched. Leaves lanceolate, entire or toothed, dark green, glabrous. Flowers 1–4 per cluster; sepals to 2cm, 4, yellow, spreading. Summer. C Asia to Mongolia and China. Z5.

C.fusca Turcz.
Climber to 3m. Young branches angled, lanuginose. Leaves to 20cm, pinnately 5–7-foliolate; leaflets to 6cm, ovate, apex acute, base rounded or cordate, entire, glabrous or somewhat lanuginose beneath, terminal leaflet often absent. Flowers urceolate, pendulous, solitary; pedicels stout, to 2.5cm, densely rufous-pubescent; sepals dull purple to violet inside, densely rufous-pubescent outside, 4–6, oblong-ovate, to 2.5cm, acuminate and reflexed at apex, lanate; filaments grey-brown-pubescent. Achenes with yellow-brown-sericeous-pubescent, plumose, 3cm styles. Summer. NE Asia. var. *violacea* Maxim. Flowers violet. Korea. Z5.

C.fusca hort. non Turcz. See C.japonica.
C.gebleriana Bongard. See C.songarica.

C.gentianoides DC.
Prostrate or creeping to 120cm. Leaves simple or trifoliolate; leaflets lanceolate or lanceolate-ovate. Flowers solitary or few-clustered; sepals white, 4, oblong. Tasmania. Z9.

C.glauca Willd.
Scandent shrub to 4m. Branches slender, glabrous. Leaves pinnate or bipinnate; leaflets to 5cm, elliptic to lanceolate, 2–3-lobed, blue-green. Flowers 4cm diam., solitary or paired, axillary, in paniculate inflorescence; peduncles to 8cm; sepals yellow, ovate-lanceolate, to 2cm, acuminate, broad-patent, not reflexed, glabrous or subglabrous outside, sometimes pubescent inside, dense short-lanuginose at margins. Achenes compressed, pubescent, with plumose styles to 9cm. Summer–autumn. W China to Siberia. Z4.

C.glauca auctt. non Willd. See C.intricata and C.ladakhiana.
C.glauca var. akebioides (Maxim.) Rehd. & Wils. See C.akebioides.

C.glycinioides DC.
Differs from C.aristata in leaves always with 3, thinner-textured, broad and sparsely toothed leaflets and smaller flowers with anthers not appendaged. Australia. Z7.

C.gouriana Roxb.
Vigorous climber. Young shoots pubescent Leaves 5- or 7-foliolate; leaflets to 8cm, ovate-oblong, long-acuminate, usually subcordate at base, often entire, shiny above, pubescent when young; petiolules to 1cm. Flowers white, to 2cm diam., in large panicles. Achenes pubescent. Himalaya, China. Z6.

C.gouriana var. finetii Rehd. & Wils. See C.peterae.

C.gracilifolia Rehd. & Wils.
Deciduous climber to 4m. Stems ribbed, grey, densely adpressed-lanuginose when young; branches striate. Leaves ternate or pinnately 3-, 5- or 7-foliolate; petioles somewhat lanuginose; leaflets to 4cm, subsessile, ovate, acute, coarse-serrate or trilobed, somewhat lanuginose. Flowers to 5cm diam., 2–4-grouped, axillary; pedicels slender, to 7.5cm, lanuginose; sepals white, 4, obovate, patent, lanuginose outside. Achenes glabrous, with plumose, 2.5cm styles. Summer. W China. Z5.

C.grata Wallich.
Vigorous climber to 10m. Stems very grooved; young branches pubescent Leaves pubescent, pinnately 5-foliolate; leaflets to 6cm, broad-ovate, coarsely and deeply-dentate, sometimes lobed, pubescent beneath. Flowers 2cm diam., in many-flowered, terminal and axillary panicles; sepals 4, cream white, ovate-oblong, to 1cm, patent, glabrous inside, lanate outside. Achenes pubescent, with plumose styles to 4cm. Autumn. Himalaya. var. **grandidentata** Rehd. & Wils. To 9m. Stems ribbed, lanuginose. Leaves 15cm+, tri- or 5-foliolate; petioles lanuginose; leaflets to 7.5cm, ovate, acuminate, rounded or tapered at base, coarsely and irregularly dentate, grey-lanuginose, especially beneath, terminal leaflet often deeply 3-lobed; petiolules 8.5mm. Flowers 2.5cm diam., 3-grouped, in small, axillary and terminal panicles; sepals 4–5, white, narrow-oblong, glabrous or subglabrous inside, tomentose outside. Achenes glabrous, with sericeous styles. Spring–summer. China. Z5.

C.grata var. argentilucida (Lév. & Vaniot) Rehd. See C.grata var. grandidentata.

C.graveolens Lindl.
Climber to 4m. Close to C.orientalis but with more finely divided leaves, spreading sepals and a heavy scent. Leaves 1–3-pinnate, glaucous; leaflets irregularly lobed or dentate. Flowers 1–3-grouped in axillary cymes; sepals 4, yellow, ovate-obovate, often notched at apex, 3–4cm, patent, densely fine-pubescent at margins; filaments pubescent, dilated above. Achenes rhomboid, with plumose styles. Summer. Himalaya. Z7.

C.grewiiflora DC.
Climber. Stems lanate. Leaves pinnately 3- or 5-foliolate; leaflets to 10cm, broad-ovate, acute, tapered or cordate at

base, usually deep 5-lobed, serrate, densely lanate. Flowers broadly campanulate, 4cm, pubescent inside, densely tomentose outside, in many-flowered panicles; sepals tawny-yellow, 4, yellow, ovate, to 3cm, somewhat recurved at apex; filaments filiform, lanuginose. Summer. Himalaya, Burma. Z8.

C.× guascri Lem. (*C.patens × C.viticella.*)
Tall climber. Branches downy at first. Leaflets 5, glabrous. Flowers to 8cm diam., solitary; sepals 4–6, obovate, 3-veined, violet-red, downy beneath. Spring. Garden origin. Includes such 'classic' cultivars as 'Minor' (blue tinted carmine), 'Albert Victor' (lavender), 'Fair Rosamond' (pink-white) and 'The Queen' (lilac-blue). Z7.

C.henryi Oliv.
Climber to 4m. Leaves simple, ovate-oblong, to 12cm, apex acute or long-acuminate, base cordate, entire or sparse-denticulate, 5-veined; petioles to 5cm. Flowers solitary, axillary; sepals 4, light pink, somewhat brown outside, oblong-elliptic, to 3cm, acute, patent; stamens to 3cm, filaments densely pubescent. Achenes oblong, pubescent, with short, plumose styles. Winter. China, Vietnam, Taiwan. Z6.

C.heracleifolia DC.
Woody-based perennial herb to 1.5m; stems erect, ribbed, rufous, lanuginose. Leaves trifoliolate; leaflets to 6.5×6.5cm, rounded-ovate, somewhat cordate or truncate at base, irregularly and shallowly sparse-setose-serrate, with pale hairs, terminal leaflet to 12.5 × 12.5cm. Flowers tubular, to 2.5cm, in dense, short, axillary clusters; pedicels to 2.5cm, lanuginose; sepals 4, deep blue, recurved at apex, lanuginose. Achenes with plumose styles. Summer–autumn. C & N China. 'Campanile': to 1.5m; flowers 2cm, numerous, densely clustered; flowers mid-blue. 'Côte d'Azur': hyacinth blue. 'Jaggards': flowers deep blue. var. *davidiana* (Verl.) Hemsl. To 1m. Leaves coriaceous. Flowers fragrant, in dense fascicles; sepals spreading, indigo-blue. 'Manchu': flowers deep blue. 'Wyevale': leaves broad, much divided; flowers small, deep blue, hyacinth-like, fragrant, clustered. var. **ichangensis** Rehd. & Wils. Leaflets rounded at base, pubescent, especially beneath. Flowers blue, exterior silver-pubescent, interior dark blue. C & N China. Z3.

C.heracleifolia var. *stans* (Sieb. & Zucc.) Kuntze. See *C.stans.*

C.hilarii Spreng.
Vigorous climber. Leaves pinnately compound; leaflets to 7.5cm, coriaceous, trilobed or tridentate. Flowers white, to 2.5cm diam., in few-flowered panicles. Fruit with styles to 7.5cm. S America (Brazil to Argentina). Z9.

C.hirsutissima Pursh. See *C.douglasii.*

C.hookeriana Allan.
Closely resembles *C.paniculata*, but leaflets deep-lobed, sepals green-yellow to light yellow, and staminate flowers to 2.5cm diam. New Zealand. Z8.

C.indivisa Willd. See *C.paniculata.*

C.integrifolia L.
Erect herbaceous perennial or subshrub to 1m. Stems simple or somewhat branched, white-pubescent. Leaves to 9×5cm, sessile, simple, coriaceous, ovate-lanceolate, acute, entire, green, glabrous above, pubescent beneath, especially on veins, prominently veined. Flowers stellate-campanulate, flat, solitary, rarely 2–3-grouped, pendulous, terminal, occasionally axillary; pedicels 4cm; sepals dark violet or blue, rarely white, usually 4, lanceolate, to 5cm, short-acuminate, patent, glabrous, lanuginose and recurved toward margins, sinuate; filaments dilated, yellow, lanuginose. Achenes rhomboid, with plumose, yellow-lanuginose styles. Summer. C Europe, SW Russia, W & C Asia. 'Alba': flowers white. 'Olgae': flowers clear light blue, sepals long and recurved, sweetly scented. 'Pastel Blue': flowers delicate powder blue. 'Pastel Pink': flowers soft light pink. 'Rosea': flowers sugar pink, underside darker, scented. 'Tapestry': flowers large, mauve to rich red, sepals mauve. Z3.

C.integrifolia var. *pinnata* hort. See *C.× divaricata.*

C.intricata Bunge.
Close to *C.akebioides*, from which it differs in its foliage (closer to *C.orientalis*), sepals fully outspread, never reflexed, sometimes flushed purple beneath. N China, S Mongolia. Sometimes offered as *C.glauca*. Z5.

C. × jackmanii T. Moore. (Probably *C.lanuginosa × C.viticella.*)
Climber to 4m. Leaves simple to trifoliolate; leaflets to 12cm, broad-ovate, apex acute, base somewhat cordate, deep green and glabrous above, paler and light-pubescent beneath. Flowers rich velutinous violet-purple, numerous, to 12.5cm diam., in 3-flowered cymes; peduncles to 14cm; sepals 4–6, broad-obovate, outspread, pubescent outside; filaments green-white, anthers brown. Achenes compressed, rhomboid, with persistent, long, plumose styles. Summer–autumn. 'Alba': flowers palest grey, double (single later in season). 'Purpurea Superba': flowers deep violet. 'Rubra': flowers red to plum, double, single later in season. Z5.

C.japonica Thunb.
Scandent downy subshrub. Leaves ternate, petiolate; leaflets 5–8cm, subsessile, coarsely toothed. Flowers to 3cm, 1 to few-clustered, nodding, campanulate; peduncles to 10cm with a pair of small bracts at midpoint; sepals purple-red to maroon, 4 broadly lanceolate, somewhat fleshy, glabrous except for downy margin; stamens to half length of sepals Summer. Japan. Z6.

C.× jeuneiana Symons-Jeune. (*C.armandii × C.finetiana.*)
Vigorous scandent evergreen with foliage like *C.armandii*. Flowers to 2.5cm diam., 3–5-clustered, in often to 30-flowered, axillary cymes; sepals 5–6, white, silver-pink beneath, oval-lanceolate. Summer. Z8.

C.× jouiniana Schneid. (*C.heracleifolia* var. *davidiana × C.vitalba.*)
Very vigorous, sprawling, semi-evergreen, woody-based perennial or semi-scandent shrub to 4m. Stems strongly ribbed, somewhat lanuginose. Leaves 3- or 5-foliolate; leaflets to 10cm, intermediate between parents, ovate, coarse-dentate, weakly pubescent Flowers fragrant, 3cm diam. in corymbs to 15cm, forming terminal and axillary panicles to 60cm; sepals 4, white to ivory deepening to opal then lilac or sky blue toward tips, strap-shaped, 2cm, acute, expanded but somewhat recurved. Achenes sometimes absent, rhomboid, with short, plumose styles. Autumn. Garden origin. 'Mrs Robert Brydon': leaves coarse; flowers small, off-white, somewhat tinted blue, clustered. 'Oiseau Bleu': to 90cm, open habit; leaves small; flowers mauve to pink. 'Praecox': vigorous; flowers pale blue flushed silver. Z4.

C.kamtschatica Boug. See *C.fusca.*

C.koreana Komar.
Prostrate deciduous shrub. Leaves trifoliolate, thinly pubescent; leaflets to 8cm, cordate-ovate, long-acuminate, somewhat cordate at base, coarse-dentate, often trilobed or ternate. Flowers to 3.5cm, solitary; pedicels to 15cm; sepals dull violet, elliptic-lanceolate, to 3cm, lanuginose on margins; staminodes spathulate, 2cm. Summer. Korea. Z6.

C.kousabotan Decne. See *C.stans.*

C.ladakhiana Grey-Wilson.
Climber to 3m, stems somewhat pubescent, tinged brown-purple. Leaves pinnate to bipinnate, leaflets narrow, acuminate. Flowers occasionally solitary, mostly grouped 3–7 in axils; pedicels 1.5–12cm; sepals spreading, narrowly elliptic, yellow to orange-yellow, usually with darker markings. Summer. India (Kashmir & Kumaon), China (Xizang). Z6.

C.lanuginosa Lindl.
Deciduous climber to 2m+. Branches pubescent. Leaves to 10cm, simple, ovate, apex acuminate, base cordate, lanuginose, or trifoliolate with leaflets to 12.5 × 7.5cm, thick, ovate to oval-lanceolate, acute, cordate at base, glabrous above, densely soft-grey-lanate beneath. Flowers to 20cm diam., ter-

Clematis (a) *C.afoliata* (b) *C.hookeriana* (c) *C.paniculata* male plant in flower, female flower and leaf of *C.paniculata* var. *lobata* (d) *C.phlebantha*

minal, solitary or 2–3-grouped in cymes; pedicels ebracteate, lanate; sepals white to pale lilac, 6–8, ovate or obovate, to 10cm, imbricate, expanded, lanuginose outside. Achenes ribbed, with sericeous styles to 7.5cm. Spring–autumn. China. Rarely found in cultivation but a parent of many hybrids. 'Candida': flowers large, white, heavy texture; sepals broad and round; anthers creamy white. Z6.

C.lasiandra Maxim.
Vigorous deciduous climber, to 4m. Stems slender, angular, glutinous when young, sparsely pubescent Leaves to 20.5cm, ternate or biternate, trifoliolate and deeply trilobed or 7- or 9-foliolate; petioles pubescent at base; leaflets to 10cm, ovate to lanceolate, long slender-acuminate, oblique at base, irregularly serrate, sparsely lanuginose and deep green above, glabrous and lighter beneath. Flowers campanulate, 1.25cm, 3-grouped, sometimes solitary or paired, in axillary cymes to 5cm; peduncles to 7cm; sepals white, violet-traced, oblong, reflexed at apex, subglabrous outside; stamens yellow-white, filaments densely sericeous-pubescent. Achenes with long plumose styles. Autumn. C & W China, Japan. Z6.

C.lasiantha Nutt.
Climber to 5m. Branchlets lanate. Leaves usually trifoliolate; petioles to 5cm; leaflets to 5cm, broadly ovate, rounded to subcordate at base, coarsely serrate to trilobed, teeth rounded, strigose-pubescent, especially beneath; petiolules to 1cm. Flowers 1-, 3- or 5-grouped; peduncles to 12cm, bracteate; sepals white, broad-oblong, to 2.5cm, sericeous-lanate; filaments somewhat compressed. Achenes pubescent, with plumose, 2.5cm styles. W US (California). Z8.

C.× lawsoniana Moore & Jackm. (*C.lanuginosa* × *C.patens*). See *C.*Lanuginosa Group.
C.leiocarpa Oliv. See *C.uncinata.*

C.ligusticifolia Torr. & A. Gray.
Climber to 6m. Leaves pinnately 5–7-foliolate; leaflets to 7cm, tough, ovate to lanceolate, apex long-acuminate, base cuneate, coarsely dentate and often trilobed, yellow-green, glabrous or slightly setose. Flowers 2cm diam., unisexual, in corymbose panicles; sepals white, to 1.5cm, patent, lanuginose. Achenes pilose, grouped in large clusters, with white, plumose styles to 6cm. Summer–autumn. Western N America. var. **californica** S. Wats. Leaves lanuginose or velutinous beneath. Z5.

C.linearifolia Steud. See *C.microphylla.*

C.macropetala Ledeb.
Deciduous climber, to 1m. Stems slender, angular, lanuginose when young. Leaves to 15cm, biternate; petioles slender; leaflets to 4×2cm, ovate to lanceolate, apex acute, base rounded or tapered, sometimes cordate, irregularly coarsely serrate and lobed, glabrous or subglabrous. Flowers to 10cm diam., pendulous, solitary, axillary; pedicels slender, 7.5cm+; sepals blue or violet-blue, 4, oblong-lanceolate, to 5cm×8.5mm, acute, exterior densely pubescent; staminodes numerous, in several rows, lanuginose, outer violet-blue, narrow-elliptic, acute, inner blue-white, linear; stamens many, anthers pale yellow. Achenes ovoid, with slender, plumose, 4cm styles. Spring–summer. N China (Kansu), E Siberia, Mongolia. 'Ballet Blanc': flowers very double, small, white; seedling of 'Maidwell Hall'. 'Blue Bird' (*C.macropetala* × *C.alpina* var. *sibirica*): vigorous; flowers semi-double, large, deep lavender. 'Jan Lindmark': flowers pale purple. 'Maidwell Hall' ('Lagoon'): flowers semi-double, to 5cm diam., deep blue. 'Markham's Pink' ('Markhamii'): flowers strawberry pink, nodding. 'Rosy O'Grady' (*C.macropetala* × *C.alpina*): flowers to 7cm diam., semi-double, deep bright pink, sepals long and pointed. 'White Swan' (*C.macropetala* × *C.alpina* var. *sibirica*): flowers large, to 12cm diam., pure white. 'Snow Bird': flowers white, late-flowering. Z5.

C.mandschurica Rupr. (*C.recta* var. *mandshurica* Maxim.).
Decumbent or scandent perennial Close to *C.terniflora*, with rather woody stems and bipinnate leaves. Leaves pinnatisect,

upper leaves often ternate; leaflets somewhat coriaceous, lanceolate-ovate, apex short-acuminate, base cuneate or cordate, sparsely pubescent and prominently veined beneath. Flowers small, many, in terminal and axillary inflorescences; pedicels bracteate; bracts narrow, small; sepals white, oblong, to 1.5cm, tapered toward base, densely white-pubescent on margins below; anthers linear, glabrous. Achenes compressed, glabrous, with styles to 3cm. Summer. Japan, China. Z7.

C.marata J.B. Armstr.

Low evergreen climber. Branches very slender. Leaves to 7×4cm, dull green, pubescent, trifollolate; petioles to 4.5cm; leaflets to 2.5cm, linear, entire or 3+-lobed, lobes spathulate, sometimes pinnatifid, coriaceous. Flowers green-yellow, to 2.5cm diam., solitary or 2–4-grouped; bracts 1–2-paired, connate, spathulate, pubescent; sepals 4, sometimes 5, imbricate, ovate-oblong, to 1.5cm × 6mm, glabrous above, pubescent below; filaments glabrous, anthers 2mm; staminodes few. Achenes to 5mm, glabrous, with styles to 2.5cm. New Zealand. Z8.

C.marmoraria Sneddon.

Prostrate, suckering evergreen shrub to 6cm tall, the smallest Clematis species, loosely resembling a rigid clump of parsley. Branches open, terete, obscurely ribbed. Leaves 1–4cm, trifoliolate; leaflets deeply and closely divided, glossy green, rigid, thick, glabrous. Flowers to 2cm diam., solitary or clustered, long-stalked, erect; sepals 5–8, green-white becoming creamy white; stamens 40–50, filaments green, flattened, anthers cream. Achenes 40–50, to 3mm, downy. New Zealand. Z8.

C.maximowicziana Franch. & Savat. See C.terniflora.

C.meyeniana Walp.

Vigorous evergreen climber to 5m+. Stems wiry, purple-brown, glabrous. Leaves trifoliolate; petioles to 10cm; leaflets broad-ovate to lanceolate, to 12.5×7.5cm, apex short- to slender-acuminate, base cordate or rounded, tough, coriaceous. Flowers 2.5cm diam., in large, lax, many-flowered panicles; sepals white, 4, narrow-oblong, 1.2cm, emarginate, entire, lanate at margins, conspicuously 3-veined; anthers gold-yellow. Achenes with sericeous, 3cm styles. Spring. SE China. Z8.

C.microphylla DC.

Climber. Leaves bi- or tri-ternate; petioles long; leaflets linear or lanceolate-oblong. Flowers cream, in short panicles; sepals 4, to 2.5cm. Fruit with styles to 4cm. Australia. Z9.

C.montana Buch.-Ham. ex DC.

Very vigorous, climber, to 8m. Young branches somewhat pubescent, later glabrous. Leaves trifoliolate; petioles to 9cm; leaflets to 10cm, ovate-lanceolate, apex acute and sometimes somewhat deep-trilobed, tapered or rounded at base, serrate, rarely entire, glabrous; petiolules short. Flowers 5cm diam., 1–5-grouped, axillary; pedicels to 21cm (usually shorter), pubescent; sepals white or pink, 4, rarely 5, elliptic, to 4cm, obtuse or acute, patent, glabrous or subglabrous inside, pubescent on veins outside, lanuginose on margins. Achenes rhomboid, glabrous, with white, plumose styles to 1.5cm. Spring–summer. C & W China, Himalaya. 'Alba': leaves light green; flowers off-white. 'Alexander': flowers large, to 10cm diam., creamy white; stamens yellow; scented. 'Peveril': flowers to 8cm diam., pure white, stamens long and shimmering. 'Vera': leaves dark green; flowers pink, fragrant. f. grandiflora Rehd. Exceptionally vigorous, to 12m; flowers white, abundant. China. var. rubens Kuntze. Young leaves tinged purple-bronze; flowers 5–6cm diam., pink-red. China. 'Elizabeth': flowers palest pink; stamens yellow; vanilla-scented. 'Freda': less vigorous; leaves bronze; flowers cherry pink edged crimson. 'Lilacina' (C.montana f. grandiflora × C.montana var. rubens): flowers pale mauve. 'Marjorie': vigorous; flowers semi-double, creamy pink tinted orange, staminodes petal-like, salmon. 'Mayleen': leaves tinted bronze; flowers large, to 7.5cm diam., pink, stamens gold. 'Odorata': flowers palest pink,

sweetly scented, abundant. 'Perfecta' (C.montana f. grandiflora × C.montana var. rubens): vigorous; branches deep brown tinted red; flowers to 9cm diam., white flushed lilac. 'Picton's': flowers small, deep satin pink, anthers gold. 'Pink Perfection': vigorous; flowers profuse, small, deep pink, sepals round. 'Superba' (possibly C.montana var. rubens × C.'Mrs Geo. Jackman'): vigorous; flowers large, white. 'Tetrarose': tetraploid; stems tinted ruby; leaves bronze; flowers large, to 10cm diam., rich rosy mauve. 'Undulata': strong-grower; flowers white, flushed mauve, sepals undulate. var. wilsonii Sprague. Flowers small, white, fragrant, borne in great profusion. China. Z6.

C.montana var. sericea Franch. See C.spooneri.

C.nannophylla Maxim.

Erect deciduous shrub 120cm+, of dense habit. Young branches slender, striate, strongly ribbed, adpressed-grey-pubescent Leaves to 6.5cm, trilobed or deeply pinnatisect; leaflets narrow, sharp-acuminate, glabrous or subglabrous. Flowers to 3cm diam., solitary, sometimes 3-grouped, rarely paired, terminal; sepals golden yellow, brown at centre, 4, ovate or oval, to 12.5mm diam. Achenes with 2.5cm styles. China. Z7.

C.napaulensis DC. (C.forrestii W.W. Sm.).

Evergreen vine to 7m. Young branches grooved, grey. Leaves 3- or 5-foliolate; leaflets to 9 × 4cm, slender, oval-lanceolate, acute, entire, sparsely dentate or trilobed, glabrous, terminal leaflet largest. Flowers narrow-campanulate, 2.5cm, 6–10-grouped, in axillary clusters; pedicels to 4cm, bracteate; bracts cupulate, 6.5mm, lanuginose; sepals cream-yellow, 4, ovate, to 2.5cm, somewhat patent, sericeous-lanuginose; stamens very numerous, to 2.5cm, anthers purple. Achenes with white-sericeous, 2.5cm+ styles. Winter–spring. SW China, N India. Z8.

C.nutans Royle.

Woody scrambler to 5m. Leaves pinnately 5–7-foliolate; leaflets to 8cm, oblong, ovate, or lanceolate, usually 3–5-lobed, lobes acute or obtuse, lanuginose. Flowers campanulate, pendulous, in paniculate inflorescence; sepals pale yellow, 4, oblong, to 4cm, lanuginose outside; filaments filiform, lanuginose towards base, anthers short. Achenes compressed, rhomboid, with long, plumose styles. Summer. Himalaya. Z8.

C.nutans hort., non Royle. See C.rehderiana.

C.nutans var. thyrsoidea Rehd. & Wils. pro parte. See C.rehderiana.

C.occidentalis (Hornem.) DC. (C.alpina var. occidentalis (Hornem.) A. Gray; C.pseudoalpina (Kuntze) J. Coult. & A. Nels.; C.verticillaris DC.). BELL RUE.

Climbing or trailing shrub to 2.5m. Young stems grooved or furrowed, glabrous. Leaves trifoliolate; leaflets 5–7cm, lanceolate-ovate, base cordate, margins entire to 2–3-lobed, often serrate, thinly downy beneath at first. Flowers to 7.5cm diam., solitary, long-stalked, nodding; sepals to 6cm, 4, lanceolate, blue to violet or rosy mauve, spreading, prominently veined, veins and margins downy; staminodes petaloid, narrow-spathulate. Achenes with styles 4cm, plumose. Spring. Northeast and Northwest N America. var. dissecta (C.L. Hitch.) Pringle. Seldom attaining 1m. Leaflets deeply cut. Sepals to 3.25cm, rosy mauve to indigo, acuminate. Washington State (Cascade Mts). var. grosseserrata (Rydb.) Pringle. Usually exceeding 3m. Leaflets usually entire, rarely 2–3-lobed; sepals to 6cm, indigo, rarely white, acuminate to attenuate. Saskatchewan, Yukon, Colorado. Z6.

C.ochotensis (Pall.) Poir. See C.alpina var. ochotensis.

C.ochroleuca Ait. (Viorna ochroleuca (Ait.) Small). CURLY-HEADS.

Perennial or subshrub to 60cm. Young shoots sericeous. Leaves to 10 × 5cm, simple, sessile, ovate, obtuse, entire or sometimes lobed, glabrous above, lanate beneath. Flowers campanulate, 2cm, erect, solitary, terminal, sometimes also axillary; sepals 4, thick, ovate, 2.5cm+, recurved at apex, lanate, white inside, dull yellow and grey-pubescent outside, sometimes maroon. Achenes erect, rhomboid, with yellow-brown, plumose styles to 6cm. Spring–summer. Eastern N America (Pennsylvania to Georgia). Z6.

C.odorata hort. See *C.× aromatica*.
C.'Orange Peel'. See *C.tibetana* ssp. *vernayi*.
C.oreophila Hance. See *C.meyeniana*.

C.orientalis L.
Deciduous vine or scrambler to 8m. Stems striate; branches thin, glabrous. Leaves to 20cm, pinnately 5–7-foliolate, rarely 3- or 9-foliolate; leaflets oblong to broad-elliptic, acute or acuminate, abruptly narrowed at base, trilobed, entire or dentate, subcoriaceous, grey-green, glabrous to sericeous, glaucous. Flowers to 5cm diam., solitary or in 3- to many-flowered, terminal and axillary, bracteate panicles; peduncles to 10cm, pubescent; sepals yellow or green-yellow, 4, oblong or elliptic, to 1.4cm, acuminate, patent, later recurved, thick and fleshy, sericeous, lanate at margins; stamens with filaments dilated above, maroon, pilose, anthers to 5mm, yellow. Achenes rhomboid, somewhat ribbed at margins, dark brown, lanuginose, with plumose, dense, long-erect-pubescent styles to 5.5cm. Summer–autumn. Aegean, Ukraine, SE Russia, Iran, W Himalaya, W China, Korea. Z6.

C.orientalis hort. non L. See *C.tibetana* ssp. *vernayi*.
C.orientalis var. *acutifolia* Hook. f. & Thomps. See *C.ladakhiana*.
C.orientalis var. *akebioides* Maxim. See *C.akebioides*.
C.orientalis var. *daurica* (Pers.) Kuntze. See *C.ladakhiana*.
C.orientalis var. *glauca* Maxim. See *C.intricata*.
C.orientalis var. *serrata* Maxim. See *C.serratifolia*.
C.orientalis var. *tangutica* Maxim. See *C.tangutica*.

C.paniculata Gmel. (*C.indivisa* Willd.).
Evergreen climber 9m+. Branchlets stout, glabrous; young shoots furrowed, soft-pubescent Leaves trifoliolate; petioles to 7.5cm; leaflets to 7.5 × 5cm, ovate, apex obtuse, base rounded or somewhat cordate, entire, crenate or lobed, coriaceous, shiny green, glabrous; petiolules to 2.5cm. Flowers to 10cm diam., unisexual, pistillate flowers smaller, in lax, many-flowered, axillary panicles to 30.5cm; pedicels slender, to 11.5cm, lanuginose, bracteate; bracts 2, small; sepals white, 6–8, narrow-oblong, to 12.5mm; filaments yellow, anthers rose. Achenes lanuginose, with plumose 5cm+ styles. Spring–summer. New Zealand. var. *lobata* Hook. Leaves lobed. Z5.

C.paniculata Thunb., non Gmel. See *C.terniflora*.

C.parviflora Cunn.
Evergreen woody climber. Leaves to 16 × 16cm, tawny-pubescent, especially beneath, trifoliolate; petioles to 8cm, pilose; leaflets to 8cm, thin, ovate, acute to obtuse, entire to serrate, sometimes deeply lobed to dissected. Flowers in axillary, dichasial cymes; peduncles bracteate; bracts paired, connate, fulvous-pubescent; sepals yellow, 5–8, imbricate, narrow-oblong to elliptic-oblong, to 2.2cm, glabrous above, pubescent beneath; filaments glabrous, anthers 1mm; staminodes few. Achenes to 4mm, pubescent, with styles to 3cm. New Zealand. Z8.

C.patens Morr. & Decne. (*C.coerulea* Lindl.).
Deciduous climber to 4m. Leaves pinnately 3–5-foliolate; petioles lanuginose; leaflets to 10 × 6.5cm, ovate or oval-lanceolate, acute, entire, glabrous above, slightly pubescent beneath. Flowers to 15cm diam., solitary, terminal; pedicels ebracteate, lanuginose; sepals cream white, violet or bright blue, 6–8, somewhat imbricate, elliptic-obovate, to 8cm, long-acuminate; anthers purple-brown. Achenes conspicuously ribbed, dark brown, with long, persistent, yellow-sericeous-pubescent, plumose styles. Spring–summer. Japan, China. 'Fortunei': flowers to 12cm diam., milky white turning pink, double. 'Standishii': flowers to

14cm diam., pale lilac with metallic lustre, centre lilac-rose. Z6.

C.pauciflora Nutt.
Low-growing climber. Leaves 3- or 5-foliolate; leaflets cordate to cuneate-obovate, to 2cm, usually tri-dentate or -lobed, glabrous to sericeous-tomentose. Flowers solitary or in few-flowered panicles; sepals lanceolate-oblong, 12.5mm. SW US (S California), N Baja California. Z9.

C.pavoliniana Pamp.
Evergreen climber, 4.5m. Stems glabrous. Leaves trifoliolate; petioles to 7.5cm; leaflets to 7.5cm, narrow-ovate, rounded or cordate at base, entire, glabrous. Flowers to 4cm diam., 3–7-clustered, axillary; sepals pure white, 4, lanceolate. Summer. China. Z7.

C.peterae Hand.-Mazz. (*C.gouriana* var. *finetii* Rehd. & Wils.).
Woody climber. Stems pubescent Leaves pinnate; leaflets to 7.5cm, ovate or elliptic, acuminate, rounded or slightly cordate at base, entire or 1–4-dentate, pubescent. Flowers in many-flowered, lax panicles; sepals white or yellow-white, oblong, to 1.25cm. Achenes with 2.5cm styles. China. Z7.

C.petriei Allan.
Sprawling woody vine to 4m, thin-branched. Branches pubescent when young. Leaves bi- or tri-pinnate; leaflets to 3 × 2cm, tough, coriaceous, ovate-oblong, obtuse, truncate at base, entire or 1–2-dentate, teeth blunt. Flowers axillary, solitary or in few-flowered, small, bracteate panicles; bracts ovate, small, sometimes somewhat connate at base; sepals yellow-green, 6–8, ovate-oblong, 2cm, lanuginose. Achenes ovoid, strong-ribbed, dark red, glabrous when mature, with styles to 3cm. Summer–autumn. New Zealand (South Is.). 'Limelight': male selection with purple foliage and lime green flowers. 'Princess': female selection, similar to 'Limelight' but with smaller flowers and showy seed heads. Z8.

C.phlebantha L.H. Williams.
Erect to trailing or sprawling bush to 1.5m. Stems longitudinally ribbed and lanate when young, bark exfoliating in thin strips. Leaves to 7.5cm, opposite, imparipinnate, 7-, sometimes 5- or 9-, leafy; petioles and rachis lanate; leaflets 1.5 × 1.5cm, sessile or subsessile, acute, broad-cuneate at base, green and sericeous above, densely white-lanate beneath, terminal leaflet 5-lobed, lateral leaflets usually trilobed, lobes triangular or broad-triangular. Flowers to 4.5cm diam., solitary, axillary; pedicels to 8cm, often bracteate; bracts 2, simple or leafy and trilobed; sepals white, 5–7, red-veined, elliptic to obovate, to 2 × 1cm, acute or somewhat mucronate, cupped in back, densely lanate outside; anthers yellow. Achenes pubescent, with plumose styles. Spring–summer. W Nepal. Z7.

C.pitcheri Torr. & A. Gray. (*C.simsii* Britt. & Br., non Sweet).
Deciduous climber to 3.5m+. Stems lanuginose when young. Leaves pinnately 3–7-foliolate; leaflets to 7.5 × 4cm, ovate, 2–3-lobed or trifoliolate, rounded or somewhat cordate at base, thick, lanuginose beneath, reticulate-veined, terminal leaflet often reduced to a tendril. Flowers urceolate, solitary; pedicels to 10cm, lanuginose; sepals 4, thick, green-yellow inside, violet outside, ovate, to 3cm, acuminate, somewhat reflexed, margins converging and lanuginose. Achenes subcircular, narrowed at apex, with somewhat lanuginose, 2cm styles. Spring–autumn. SE US (Indiana to Missouri, Nebraska and Texas). Z4.

C.platysepala (Trautv. & C.A. Mey.) Hand.-Mazz. See *C.alpina* var. *ochotensis*.

C.potaninii Maxim.
Woody-based climber to 3m. Leaves biternate; leaflets to 7cm, ovate, apex acuminate, rounded or tapered at base, irregularly lobed or serrate. Flowers solitary or paired in axillary, bracteolate cymes; bracteoles small; sepals white, sometimes

yellow-flushed, 6, obovate, to 4cm, mucronate, patent, lanuginose outside; filaments somewhat dilated above, anthers yellow. Achenes rhomboid, glabrous, with plumose styles. Summer. SW China. var. *souliei* Finet & Gagnep. Flowers larger. Z7.

C.potaninii var. *fargesii* (Franch.) Hand.-Mazz. See *C.fargesii*.

C.pseudoalpina (Kuntze) J. Coult. & A. Nelson. See *C.occidentalis*.

C.×pseudococcinia Schneid. (*C.×jackmanii* × *C.texensis*.)
Similar to *C.texensis* but to 3m with flowers campanulate, sepals 4–6. 'Admiration': sepals salmon, interior white. 'Countess of Onslow': pink tinted mauve, sepals with central. red bar. 'Duchess of Albany': deep pink, erect, centre tinted brown, ventral side striped white. 'Duchess of York': pink, midstripe darker. 'Grace Darling': pale carmine pink, profuse. 'Sir Trevor Lawrence': bright crimson edged light violet, stamens cream. See also *C.* Texensis Group. Z5.

C.pseudoflammula Schmalh. ex Lipsky.
Erect perennial to 70cm, resembling an herbaceous *C.flammula*. Stems fistulose, flexuous above, finely costate, somewhat pubescent. Leaves to 25cm, bipinnate; petioles pubescent; leaflets to 5cm, oblong-ovate or oblong-linear, usually entire, sometimes deeply bipartite, glabrous or somewhat pubescent, prominently veined beneath. Flowers 2cm diam., erect; sepals creamy white, narrow-obcuneate, to 1.8cm, glabrous, except tomentose margins; anthers glabrous. Achenes flat with long, plumose-pubescent styles. Summer. S Russia, S & E Ukraine. Z5.

C.pubescens Benth.
Climber. Leaves trifoliolate; leaflets acuminate, subcordate at base, entire or coarsely serrate, sericeous. Flowers small, solitary, paired or 3-grouped; sepals white, ovate, soft-pubescent. Mexico. Z9.

C.quinquefoliolata Hutch.
Vigorous, tall, evergreen climber. Stems ribbed, lanuginose; branches striate. Leaves pinnately 5-foliolate; petioles 15cm; leaflets to 10 × 3.5cm, lanceolate to ovate-lanceolate, apex obtuse or short-acuminate, rounded or cordate at base, glabrous except lanuginose, grooved midrib above. Flowers to 5cm diam., axillary, in 3-, 5- or 7-flowered cymes; sepals milk white, 4–6, narrow-oblong, to 6.5mm, lanceolate, especially on margins beneath; stamens many, anthers yellow. Achenes sericeous, with dense buff-sericeous styles to 7.5cm. Autumn. China. Z8.

C.ranunculoides Franch.
Erect perennial herb to 50cm or climber to 2m. Branches angular, striate, tinted red, pubescent to subglabrous. Leaves trifoliolate or pinnately 5-foliolate, or simple and trilobed; petioles to 15cm, often much curled; leaflets rounded-obovate or ovate, to 5cm, coarsely dentate, pubescent. Flowers pendulous, solitary and axillary, or few-grouped and terminal; peduncles short, slender, pubescent; sepals purple to pink, 4, oblong, 1.5cm, broadly spreading, much reflexed, lanuginose, 3-ribbed dorsally; stamens 1cm. Achenes compressed, 3cm, lanuginose. Spring–autumn. China. Z6.

C.recta L.
Erect perennial to 1.5m, densely branched. Stems fistulose, finely grooved, short-pubescent above. Leaves to 15cm, pinnately 5–7-foliolate; petioles sulcate, glabrous or somewhat pubescent; leaflets to 9cm, oval-lanceolate, apex acuminate, base cuneate or somewhat cordate, entire, glabrous and deep blue-green above, lighter and prominently veined beneath; petiolules short. Flowers 2cm diam., erect, in many-flowered, terminal panicles; sepals milky white, 4, narrow-ovate or oblong-obcuneate, to 1.8cm, patent, glabrous, except tomentose margins; anthers glabrous. Achenes compressed, rhomboid, ribbed, subglabrous, with short, plumose-pubescent styles. Summer. S & C Europe. 'Grandiflora': flowers large, very abundant. 'Peveril': stems upright, to 90cm; flowers pro-

fuse, scented. 'Plena': flowers double. 'Purpurea': branches and leaves flushed bronze to red. Z3.

C.recta var. *mandshurica* Maxim. See *C.mandschurica*.
C.recta f. *fruticosa* (Turcz.) O. Kuntze. See *C.fruticosa*.

C.rehderiana Craib (*C.nutans* hort., non Royle; (*C.nutans* var. *thyrsoidea* Rehd. & Wils. pro parte; *C.buchananiana* Finet & Gagnep., non DC.).
Very vigorous, scandent, woody, deciduous, to 7.5m. Stems angular, lanuginose. Leaves to 23cm, pinnately 7- or 9-foliolate; leaflets to 7.5 × 5cm, broad-ovate, apex acute, cordate or rounded at base, often trilobed, coarsely serrate, lanuginose above, sericeous-lanuginose and prominent-veined beneath; petiolules to 4cm, pubescent Flowers campanulate, pendulous, in several-flowered, erect, lanuginose, ribbed panicles to 23cm; bracts ovate to elliptic, sometimes deeply trilobed, sepals soft primrose yellow or pale green, 4, to 2cm, ribbed, reflexed, glabrous inside, velutinous outside; stamens to 2cm, thin-pubescent. Achenes compressed, orbicular-ovoid, lanuginose, with sericeous, plumose, 2cm styles. Summer–autumn. W China. Z6.

C.reticulata Walter.
Woody climber to 3m. Stems slender. Leaves pinnately 3–7-foliolate; leaflets to 7cm, broadly ovate to ovate-lanceolate, acute or obtuse and mucronate, entire, coriaceous, slightly pubescent and coarsely reticulate-veined beneath. Flowers campanulate or urceolate, 2cm, pendulous, solitary, axillary; peduncles bracteate; sepals lilac inside, grey-yellow and pubescent outside, 2cm, reflexed. Achenes with plumose styles. Summer. SE US (S California to Florida & Texas). Z6.

C.scottii T.C. Porter. See *C.douglasii* var. *scottii*.

C.serratifolia Rehd.
Deciduous scrambler to 3m. Stems thin, ribbed, glabrous. Leaves biternate; leaflets to 7.5cm, ovate to lanceolate, apex long-acuminate, oblique at base, serrate, thin, glabrous, bright green; petiolules to 2.5cm. Flowers widely star-shaped, solitary, paired or 3-grouped in bracteate cymes, axillary; bracts small; sepals soft yellow, violet-tinged or -veined, 4, lanceolate or narrow-oblong, 2.5cm, acuminate, patent, glabrous outside, villous inside and on margins; stamens purple, filaments somewhat dilated, long-ciliate below. Achenes compressed, ovoid, cuneate at base, pubescent with plumose, 5cm styles. Summer–autumn. Korea, NE China. Z6.

C.sibirica (L.) Mill. See *C.alpina* var. *sibirica*.
C.simsii Sweet. See *C.crispa*.
C.simsii Britt. & A. Br., non Sweet. See *C.pitcheri*.

C.songarica Bunge.
Erect or semi-scandent woody-based perennial to 1.5m. Stems slender, ribbed, glabrous. Leaves to 10×3cm, simple, linear to lanceolate, entire to serrate-dentate, thick, somewhat fleshy, blue-green, glaucous, glabrous, distinctly 3-veined; petioles to 3cm. Flowers to 2.5cm diam., numerous, pendulous, solitary or paired, sometimes 3-grouped in paniculate inflorescence, terminal or axillary; pedicels slender, to 5cm; sepals yellow-white, oblong-obovate or elliptic, to 2cm, glabrous inside, lanuginose outside; filaments narrow-linear, glabrous. Achenes compressed, densely pubescent, with plumose-pubescent styles to 3cm. Summer–autumn. Mongolia, Korea, S Siberia, Turkestan. Z6.

C.spooneri Rehd. & Wils. (*C.chrysocoma* var. *sericea* (Franch.) Schneid.).
Deciduous climber to 6m. Shoots lanuginose. Leaves trifoliolate; petioles to 10cm; leaflets to 7cm, oval or ovate, coarse-serrate, yellow-sericeous beneath. Flowers to 6cm diam., solitary or paired, axillary; pedicels to 18cm; sepals pure white, 4, rounded-oval or obovate, to 2.5cm diam., yellow-sericeous-pubescent outside. Spring. China. Z6.

C.spooneri 'Rosea'. See *C.× vedrariensis* 'Rosea'.
C.standishii Van Houtte. See *C.patens* 'Standishii'.
C.stanleyi Hook. See *Clematopsis stanleyi*.

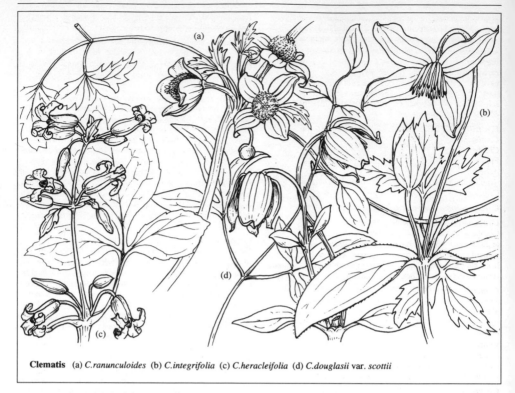

Clematis (a) *C.ranunculoides* (b) *C.integrifolia* (c) *C.heracleifolia* (d) *C.douglasii* var. *scottii*

C.stans Sieb. & Zucc. (*C.heracleifolia* var. *stans* (Sieb. & Zucc.) Kuntze; *C.kousabotan* Decne.).
Deciduous erect shrub or subshrub or climber to 180cm. Stems stout, furrowed, densely grey-lanuginose. Leaves trifoliolate; petioles lanuginose; leaflets to 15 × 14.5cm, broad-ovate, coarsely serrate, lanuginose on veins, distinctly veined. Flowers tubular, 2 × 2cm, unisexual, clustered and axillary, and in branched, bracteate, usually terminal panicles to 25cm+; bracts foliate; sepals white, 1cm, recurved, blue inside, white and tomentose outside. Japan. Z4.

C.stenophylla Fraser. See *C.microphylla*.
C.stenosepala DC. See *C.glycinioides*.

C.tangutica (Maxim.) Korsh. (*C.orientalis* var. *tangutica* Maxim.).
Climber to 3m. Branches pubescent when young. Leaves pinnate or bipinnate; leaflets to 8cm, oblong to lanceolate, sometimes 2–3-lobed, irregularly dentate, teeth pointing outward, bright green. Flowers campanulate to lantern-shaped, to 3.4cm, pendulous, usually solitary; pedicles erect, to 15cm, pubescent; sepals golden yellow, 4, oval-lanceolate, to 4cm, apex slender-acuminate, later broad-patent, exterior and margins sericeous. Achenes with long-plumose styles. Summer–autumn. Mongolia, NW China. 'Bill Mackenzie' (possibly *C.tangutica* × *C.tibetana* ssp. *vernayi)*: vigorous; flowers very large, yellow, nodding, long-lasting. 'Corry' (*C.tangutica* ssp. *obtusiuscula* × *C.tibetana*): flowers large, very open, lemon. 'Drake's Form': flowers large. 'Lambton Park': flowers large, to 7cm diam., yellow, nodding. ssp. *obtusiuscula* (Rehd. & Wils.) Grey-Wilson. More lanuginose throughout; leaflets smaller, less serrate. Flowers rich yellow, solitary, opening widely; sepals shorter, to 3cm, obtuse-elliptic or short-acuminate. China (W Sichuan). Z5.

C.tenuiloba A. Gray.
Procumbent vine. Leaves biternate; leaflets to 2.5cm, usually pinnatisect, segments ovate or lanceolate. Sepals blue or pur-

ple, to 4cm, acuminate, patent. Achenes with 5cm styles. W US (S Dakota, Arizona). Z4.

C.ternata Mak. See *C.japonica*.

C.terniflora DC. (*C.maximowicziana* Franch. & Savat; *C.flammula* var. *robusta* Carr.)
Erect perennial to 5m; stems tangle-forming, semi-woody, somewhat lanuginose when young. Leaves pinnately 3–5-foliolate; leaflets to 10cm, cordate or ovate, entire, glabrous or subglabrous, dark green; petiolules long. Flowers 3cm diam., in many-flowered forked panicles to 10cm; sepals white, 4, linear. Achenes with grey-plumose styles to 4cm. Autumn. Japan. Z6.

C.terniflora var. *mandschurica* (Rupr.) Ohwi. See *C.mandschurica*.

C.texensis Buckl. (*C.coccinea* Engelm.).
Scandent subshrub or perennial to 2m. Branches rufous, glabrous or subglabrous. Leaves glaucous, pinnately 4–8-foliolate; leaflets to 8cm, ovate to rounded, sometimes 2–3-lobed, usually cordate at base, entire, tough, blue-green, glabrous, with small, thorny tips, distinctly reticulate-veined, terminal leaflet reduced to a tendril; petiolules 8cm. Flowers urceolate, to 3 × 2cm, much narrowed towards mouth, solitary, pendulous; pedicels ribbed, to 15cm; sepals scarlet-red or carmine, thick, narrow-ovate, somewhat reflexed, margins lanuginose. Achenes with plumose, 4cm styles. Summer–autumn. SW US (Texas). 'Major': flowers to 3cm, exterior scarlet, interior pale yellow or white, thick. 'Passiflora': flowers to 2cm, scarlet throughout, rather more thinly textured. Z5.

C.thunbergii Steud.
Scandent. Leaves pubescent, pinnate or ternate; leaflets ovate, serrate or cut. Flowers to 5cm diam., in many-flowered panicles; sepals lanceolate, acuminate, patent. S Africa. Z9.

C.tibetana Kuntze.
Climber resembling *C.orientalis*, from which it differs in the finely cut, smooth and glaucous foliage and thickly textured

pale yellow flowers. N India. ssp. *vernayi* (Fisch.) Grey-Wilson. Leaves markedly glaucous. Flowers to 5cm, solitary or in threes, nodding, narrow-campanulate then outspread; sepals green-yellow to burnt orange, thickly fleshy, somewhat rugulose; stamens dark purple. Nepal, Tibet. ssp. *vernayi* is easily distinguished by its remarkably thick sepals. These have led to its being named 'Orange Peel Clematis', a soubriquet which has also been applied as a cultivar name to a selection of this subspecies with especially thickened sepals of a rich yellow-orange. Z6.

C.× triternata DC. (*C.× violacea* A. DC.). (*C.flammula* × *C.viticella*.)
Climber to 4m. Leaves simple or bipinnate; leaflets entire. Flowers 3cm diam., in terminal panicles; sepals lilac, 6. Achenes with pubescent styles. Garden origin. 'Rubromarginata' (*C.flammula* var. *rubro-marginata* Cripps.): flowers white, edged wine red, profuse. Z6.

C.troutbeckiana Spring. See *C.versicolor*.

C.tubulosa Turcz.
Climbing shrub. Leaves petiolate, divided with 3 leaflets, leaflets ovate to rhomboidal, sharply serrate. Inflorescence paniculate-corymbose, axillary, sessile or shortly peduncu-late; flowers campanulate; sepals pale blue-lilac, slightly recurved at tips. Late summer. China. Z6.

C.uncinata Benth. (*C.leiocarpa* Oliv.).
Semi-evergreen climber to 4.5m. Stems slender, furrowed, glabrous. Leaves 3- or 5-divided, each division trifoliolate; leaflets to 10cm, ovate to ovate-lanceolate, acute, entire, glabrous, blue-green and somewhat glaucous beneath, 3–5-veined. Flowers 2.5cm diam., in many-flowered, leafless cymes, grouped into terminal and axillary panicles to 30cm diam.; sepals creamy white, narrow-oblong; anthers linear, yellow. Achenes glabrous. Summer. C China. Z6.

C.× vedrariensis Vilm. (*C.verrierensis* hort.). (*C.chrysocoma* × *C.montana* var. *rubens*.)
Closely resembles *C.montana* var. *rubens*. Vigorous evergreen climber, 6m. Young shoots furrowed, lanuginose. Leaves trifoliolate; petioles to 5cm, lanuginose; leaflets to 6.5×4cm, ovate, apex acute, rounded or broad-cuneate at base, often trilobed, coarsely serrate, terminal leaflet largest, dull purple-green and pale-pubescent above, especially on veins, lighter and denser pubescent, especially when young, beneath. Flowers to 6.5cm, solitary, axillary; pedicels slender, to 12.5cm, pubescent; sepals rose, lilac or pink, 4, occasionally 5–6, rounded-oval, to 2.5cm diam., short-acuminate, patent; stamens yellow. Spring–summer. Garden origin. 'Hidcote': flowers small, deep pink. 'Highdown': flowers pink. 'Rosea': (*C.spooneri* 'Rosea'): flowers large, to 10cm diam., pale pink. Z6.

C.veitchiana Craib.
Closely resembles *C.rehderiana*. Climber to 3m. Leaves deeply incised, bipinnate, 7–9-foliolate; leaflets to 6cm, often 20+, ovate to oval-lanceolate, tri-foliolate or -lobed, sericeous beneath. Flowers yellow-white, campanulate, in bracteate panicles; bracts subulate, 6.5mm. Autumn. W China. Z6.

C.venosa (Carr.) K. Koch. See *C.× francofurtensis*.
C.verrierensis hort. See *C.× vedrariensis*.

C.versicolor Small (*C.troutbeckiana* Spring). LEATHER FLOWER.
Scandent, woody, to 3.5m. Stems subcylindric, blue, glabrous. Leaves 8-foliolate; petioles slender; leaflets to 6cm, oval-oblong, apex blunt, cordate at base, often 2–3-lobed, entire, tough-coriaceous, blue-green, glabrous, glaucous and strongly reticulate-veined beneath. Flowers ovoid-campanulate, 2.5cm, pendulous, solitary; pedicels bibracteate basally; sepals purple or blue, 4, thin, lanceolate, 2cm, recurved, glabrous, dense-pubescent at margins. Achenes rhomboid, with long, white, plumose, 5cm styles. Summer. S US (Missouri, Arkansas). Z5.

C.viorna L. LEATHER FLOWER; VASE VINE.
Scandent woody-based shrub or subshrub to 3m. Leaves 5–7-foliolate; leaflets to 7×5cm, ovate to elliptic-lanceolate, often cordate at base, entire or somewhat lobed, deep green, glabrous. Flowers urceolate, pendulous, solitary; pedicels stiff, to 7.5cm; sepals violet or dull purple, 4, very thick, coriaceous, to 3cm, acute, recurved, grey-white-pubescent at margins. Achenes rhomboid, with brown-plumose styles to 5cm. Spring–summer. Eastern N America (Pennsylvania to Georgia and Indiana). Z4.

C.virginiana L. WOODBINE; LEATHER FLOWER; VIRGIN'S BOWER; DEVIL'S DARNING-NEEDLE.
Deciduous semi-woody climber to 6m. Young stems furrowed, subglabrous. Leaves trifoliolate, rarely 5-foliolate; petioles to 7.5cm; leaflets to 9cm, broad-ovate, apex acuminate, rounded or somewhat cordate at base, coarse- and irregular-serrate or lobed, glabrous; petiolules to 6.5mm, somewhat lanuginose when young. Flowers to 3cm diam., in many-flowered, axillary panicles to 15cm; sepals dull white, 4, rarely 5, thin, oblong or spathulate, to 1.5cm, patent, pubescent outside. Achenes with sericeous, white, plumose styles to 4cm, forming silver heads 6.5cm diam. Summer–autumn. Eastern N America. Z4.

C.vitalba L. TRAVELLER'S JOY; OLD MAN'S BEARD.
Deciduous semi-woody climber to 30m. Stems furrowed, lanuginose. Leaves pinnately 5-foliolate, rarely trifoliolate; leaflets ovate, rarely linear-lanceolate, base subcordate, dentate or subentire, sparsely pilose to glabrous. Flowers 2cm diam., in bracteate, axillary panicles; pedicels densely pubescent; sepals green-white, oblong, to 11mm, obtuse, dense-white-tomentose; filaments glabrous, anthers to 2mm. Achenes slightly compressed, with long, plumose styles. Summer. Europe, Lebanon, Caucasia, N Iran, Afghanistan. Z4.

C.viticella L.
Deciduous semi-woody climber to 3.5m. Stems slender, obscurely striate, furrowed, rufous, somewhat lanuginose when young. Leaves to 12.5cm, pinnately trifoliolate; leaflets to 6.5cm, lanceolate to broad-ovate, often 2–3-lobed, entire, somewhat coriaceous, densely pubescent, especially beneath, veins prominent. Flowers 4cm diam., somewhat pendulous, solitary, or several-flowered in branched inflorescence, terminal or axillary; pedicels to 10cm; sepals blue, purple or rose-purple, 4, oblong-obovate, apex acuminate, to 4×3cm, undulate, sericeous outside; filaments dilated, glabrous. Achenes compressed, rhomboid, ribbed, broad, short, sericeous-pilose when young, later subglabrous, with very short, glabrous styles. Summer–autumn. S Europe. 'Coerulea': flowers violet. 'Marmorata': sepals 4, small, blue-grey. 'Nana': bushy, non-climbing. 'Plena': flowers double, violet. 'Purpurea': flowers plum. 'Purpurea Plena Elegans': flowers to 8cm diam., very double, deep violet. 'Rubra': flowers deep carmine. 'Rubra Grandiflora': flowers large, sepals 6, carmine red. f. *albiflora* (Kuntze) Rehd. Flowers pure white. Z6.

C.wilfordii (Maxim.) Komar. See *C.serratifolia*.

C.cultivars.
FLORIDA GROUP. Woody climbers, 2.5–3.5m, flowering spring to summer on previous year's wood; flowers usually semi-double or double, spring–summer but usually single later in the season, 15–22cm diam., white to lilac and deep violet. 'Belle of Woking' (double, mauve flushed silver, rosette form, stamens yellow), 'Duchess of Edinburgh' (double, small, to 15cm diam., rose-shaped, white), 'Haku Ookan' (flowers semi-double, rich violet, stamens white), 'Kathleen Dunford' (large, to 22cm diam., semi-double, rosy purple, stamens gold), 'Miss Crawshay' (small, to 15cm diam., semi-double, mauve-pink, stamens gold), 'Proteus' (semi-double, deep coral pink), 'Sylvia Denny' (double, white, stamens pink).

JACKMANII GROUP. Woody climbers, 2–6m, flowering summer to autumn, on new shoots; flowers 12–20cm diam., sepals usually 4, wide to narrow and pointed, shell pink, red, blue to purple. 'Comtesse de Bouchard' (strong-growing; flowers almost circular, satin pink flushed lilac, abundant, stamens cream), 'Gipsy Queen' (flowers to 15cm diam., rich purple with 3 red stripes, abundant), 'Hagley Hybrid' (flowers cup-shaped, sepals pointed, shell pink, abundant, stamens brown), 'Madame Baron Veillard' (vigorous; sepals pointed, lilac-pink, profuse, long-lasting, stamens white), 'Madame Edouard André' (low; sepals acuminate, deep claret, stamens cream), 'Madame Grange' (sepals incurving, purple-tinted bronze with brown midstripe, silky pink beneath), 'Mrs Cholmondeley' (vigorous, to 5m; flowers to 22cm diam., sepals long and narrow, lavender, profuse, anthers brown; long-flowering), 'Niobe' (sepals pointed, dark velvety ruby, darker in bud, stamens gold), 'Perle d'Azur' (vigorous, to 5m; flowers sky blue, sepals slightly corrugated, semi-pendent, profuse, stamens green), 'Rouge Cardinal' (low; flowers to 18cm diam., 6 recurving and blunt sepals deep crimson, darker in bud, stamens brown), 'Star of India' (to 6m; flowers to 12cm diam., plum with red midstripe, abundant, stamens yellow).

LANUGINOSA GROUP. Woody climbers, 2.5–5m, flowering on short side-shoots on current year's growth; flowers very large, loosely arranged, summer to autumn, appearing consecutively, single or double, 15–22cm diam., white through cream to lavender or deep red. 'Beauty of Worcester' (small, double, deep blue tinted violet, stamens creamy white), 'Bracebridge Star' (flowers lavender with crimson midstripe, stamens plum), 'Edith' (clear white, stamens dark red), 'Fair Rosamond' (flowers small, to 15cm diam., white flushed blue with red midstripe, stamens purple; scented), 'General Sikorski' (flowers blue, edges crenulate, stamens gold), 'Henryi' (robust; flowers large, to 20cm diam., to 8 acuminate sepals creamy white, stamens coffee-coloured; long-flowering), 'Horn of Plenty' (cup-shaped, rosy purple with darker midstripe, stamens plum), 'Lady Caroline Nevill' (semi-double, soft lilac with darker midstripe, stamens beige), 'Marie Boisselet' ('Madame le Coultre'); (vigorous, to 5m; sepals to 6, overlapping, flat, palest pink fading to pure white; anthers pale yellow to pale brown), 'Nelly Moser' (large, to 22cm diam., sepals pointed, palest lilac with carmine mid-stripe, anthers rusty-red), 'Silver Moon' (palest pearly lilac, stamens yellow), 'William Kennet' (vigorous; sepals to 8, overlapping, edges crimped, lavender blue with darker mid-stripe, abundant).

PATENS GROUP. Woody climbers, 2–3.5m, flowering in spring on old wood; flowers with pointed sepals, usually single, 15–25cm diam., sepals wide and overlapping to pointed, flat to wavy edged, white to purple, often with darker midstripe. 'Barbara Dibley' (small; sepals long, deep red to violet, midstripe darker, stamens plum), 'Barbara Jackman' (small, to 16cm diam., 6 broad, acuminate sepals, violet with dark pink to red midstripe, anthers cream), 'Bees Jubilee' (pinky mauve, midstripe deep carmine stamens brown), 'Captain Thuilleaux' ('Souvenir de Captain Thuilleaux'); (sepals pointed, cream with broad strawberry midstripe, anthers brown), 'Countess of Lovelace' (double, lilac-blue, rosette-form), 'Daniel Deronda' (semi-double, violet-blue, stamens cream), 'Dawn' (compact, flowers large, pearly pink sepals overlapping, stamens carmine), 'Doctor Ruppell' (rose madder with carmine midstripe, stamens gold), 'Elsa Spath' ('Xerxes') (flowers large, to 20cm diam., sepals to 6, deep violet with dark purple midstripe, stamens plum), 'Gillian

Blades' (flowers large, to 22cm diam., pure white, sepals flat with frilled edges), 'H.F. Young' (to 3.5m; sepals pointed and overlapping, Wedgwood blue, stamens cream, early-flowering, abundant), 'Lasurstern' (to 3.5m; to 22cm diam., sepals narrow, wavy-edged, rich blue, anthers white; long-flowering), 'Lincoln Star' (to 2m; sepals pointed, raspberry pink, centre plum, anthers burgundy), 'Lord Nevill' (dark violet blue, crenulate, stamens red), 'Miss Bateman' (flowers small, to 15cm diam., stellate, 8 overlapping sepals creamy white, stamens rusty red), 'Mrs George Jackman' (semi-double, sepals overlapping and elliptic, creamy white, abundant, anthers brown), 'Prins Hendrik' (to 25cm diam., sepals pointed and wavy-edged, lavender, stamens purple), 'Richard Pennell' (flowers saucer-shaped, sepals overlapping, rosy purple, anthers red and gold), 'The President' (to 18cm diam., saucer-shaped, 8 sepals, purple with paler midstripe, stigma and filaments off-white), 'Vyvyan Pennell' (double, large, deep violet, later single and bluer, stamens buff), 'Wada's Primrose' ('Moonlight', 'Yellow Queen'); (flowers small, to 15cm diam., primrose with yellow anthers), 'Walter Pennell' (double, deep pink flushed mauve, stamens buff).

TEXENSIS GROUP. Non-scandent erect to sprawling shrubs or woody-based semi-herbaceous perennials, flowering abundantly on young shoots over a long summer period; flowers campanulate. 'Duchess of Albany': flowers tubular, nodding, bright pink to lilac at margins; summer-early autumn. 'Etoile Rex': flowers to 5cm, nodding, bell-shaped, cerise to mauve, margin silver-pink; summer-early autumn. 'Gravetye Beauty': flowers cerise to scarlet, tubular-campanulate, then outspread. 'Lady Bird Johnson': flowers dusky red, later edged purple, stamens creamy yellow. 'The Princess of Wales': flowers deep vivid pink, stamens creamy yellow.

VITICELLA GROUP. Woody climbers, 2.5–6m, flowering abundantly, short flower season, flowers appearing consecutively, 15cm diam., single to double, white to red and deep purple with coloured midstripe or veins. 'Alba Luxurians' (creamy white, sepals tipped green, centres dark; vigorous), 'Ascotiensis' (large, to 20cm diam., bright blue, sepals pointed, stamens green), 'Duchess of Sutherland' (small, claret with lighter midstripe, stamens gold), 'Ernst Markham' (to 15cm diam., sepals blunt-tipped, vibrant petunia red, profuse, stamens gold), 'Etoile Violette' (flowers deep purple, sepals blunt-tipped, stamens gold), 'Huldine' (vigorous, to 6m; flowers to 10cm diam., pearly white with lilac midstripes beneath, profuse), 'Kermesina' (flowers wine red, stamens brown), 'Lady Betty Balfour' (to 6m, vigorous; deep violet-blue, stamens yellow. late-flowering), 'Little Nell' (to 5cm diam., white with creamy midstripe shading to lavender at margins, abundant), 'Madame Julia Correvon' (to 8cm diam., ruby red, sepals twisted and recurved), 'Margot Koster' (to 2.5m; flowers to 10cm diam., deep lilac-pink, sepals spaced, abundant), 'Mary Rose' (flowers small, double, spiky, dusky amethyst, profuse), 'Minuet' (large, cream, sepals edged lavender; stems long and erect), 'Mrs Spencer Castle' (small, double, heliotrope pink, stamens gold), 'Royal Velours' (flowers deep velvety purple), 'Venosa Violacea' (sepals boat-shaped, violet with paler centre, veins dark purple), 'Ville de Lyon' (vigorous; sepals wide and rounded, carmine-red edged darker, profuse; stamens gold), 'Voluceau' (petunia red, stamens yellow).

Clematoclethra Franch. (From the Gk *klematis*, climbing plant, and the genus *Clethra*, referring to the climbing habit and the resemblance to the genus *Clethra*.) Actinidiaceae. Some 10 species of twining, scandent shrubs differing from *Actinidia* in their solid stem pith and flowers with 10 stamens and a single style. Usually dioecious, deciduous. Leaves alternate, simple, exstipulate, usually dentate, petiolate. Flowers solitary or in axillary cymes, white; sepals 5, imbricate, persistent; petals 5; stamens 10, filaments white; ovary 5-locular, with some 10 ovules per locule, style slender. Fruit a fleshy berry usually 5-seeded. C & W Asia. Z6.

CULTIVATION   A genus of twining woody Asian climbers closely related to *Actinidia*, *Clematoclethra* is grown for the dense cover provided by its foliage in summer, for the small, white, scented flowers and the ornamental clusters of black or red berries. They are not strikingly showy plants, but are useful climbers for wires and trellis on walls, or for training through trees. They favour light shade or filtered sunlight and moist soils rich in organic matter. Otherwise undemanding, they will tolerate low temperatures and will require only occasional tying-in and pruning to remove excessive, exhausted or frost-damaged growth. Propagate by simply layering or by semi-ripe cuttings inserted in a frame.

C.actinidioides Maxim. To 10m or more; branches glabrous. Leaves to 8cm, oval-oblong, base rounded to cordate, finely dentate, glabrous except for tufted hairs in vein axils beneath. Flowers grouped in 3's or solitary. Fruit black. W China.

C.hemsleyi Baill. Tall twiner; young shoots tomentose, soon glabrous. Leaves to 10cm, ovate, long-acuminate, base more or less cordate, thin-textured, finely glandular-dentate, veins brown-pubescent beneath; petiole to 8cm. Flowers 8–12 per long-stalked cyme. Fruit black. W China.

C.integrifolia Maxim. Shoots to 8m; branches ± glabrous. Leaves to 6.5cm, ovate to ovate-oblong, margin entire but bristly, thus appearing dentate, base rounded, smooth and glaucous beneath. Flowers solitary or clustered, fragrant. Fruit black. W China.

C.lasioclada Maxim. Shoots to 6m; branches pilose. Leaves to 10cm, ovate, long-acuminate, bristly-dentate, rounded to cordate at base, midrib pubescent above, sparsely pubesc. and light green beneath. Flowers to 13mm diam., in axillary cymes. Fruit to 8mm diam., globose, black. W China.

C.scandens Franch. Shoots to 8m, densely brown-setose. Leaves to 12.5cm, ovate-lanceolate to oblong, acute to long-acuminate, slightly bristly-dentate, rounded or narrowed at base, midrib setose above, with setose veins beneath; petiole to 3cm, setose. Flowers to 8mm diam., in axillary cymes. Fruit to 8mm diam., red, globose. W China.

Clematopsis Bojer ex Hutch. (*Clematis*, plus Gk *opsis*, appearance.) Ranunculaceae. Some 18 species related to *Clematis* and *Anemone*. They differ from *Clematis* in having leaves sometimes alternate and flowers with closely overlapping rather than valvate sepals. This distinction has been questioned and the species recombined in *Clematis* (see Bibliography). Tropical and S Africa, Madagascar. Z10.

CULTIVATION As for container-grown *Clematis*, in a cool glasshouse or conservatory.

C.stanleyi (Hook.) Hutch. (*Clematis stanleyi* Hook.) Tall, robust, scandent shrub, branches initially pubescent becoming woody. Leaves to 15cm, variable, 1–3-pinnate; leaflets oblong-cuneate, with linear to oblong segments, or incised to toothed, sericeous. Flowers to 6cm diam., pink to pale blue-purple, solitary on erect then drooping stalks to 10cm; sepals imbricate, broadly ovate, thick, ribbed, tomentose. Fruit an achene with silver plumose styles. Summer. S Africa.

Clerodendrum L. (From Gk *kleros*, lot, chance, and *dendron*, tree, referring to the variable medical properties of some species.) Verbenaceae. Some 400 species of woody trees, shrubs or vines, usually unarmed, glabrous or pubescent. Leaves opposite or whorled, simple, entire or dentate, exstipulate. Inflorescence of terminal or axillary cymes, sometimes arranged in panicles or corymbs; flowers usually large, showy; calyx campanulate or tubular, truncate or 5-dentate to 5-partite, often accrescent; corolla salverform, tube cylindrical, straight or curved, limb 5-lobed, spreading or reflexed; stamens 4, long-exserted, didynamous, inserted in corolla tube, anthers bilocular; ovary imperfectly 4-locular, style terminal, elongate. Fruit a drupe, obovoid or globose, 4-lobed or 4-sulcate, usually separating into 4 pyrenes. Tropical and subtropical regions, mostly Asia and Africa. Z10 .

CULTIVATION A large genus of shrubs, some of the most beautiful and popular among them climbers. The blooms are characterized by the prominent stamens and, often, by the slender, elongated tube of the corolla, sometimes invested by an enlarged calyx in a contrasting colour, as in the graceful, pendulous flower sprays of *C.thomsoniae*, with pure white calyces and deep red corollas. The climbing species are tropical and subtropical in origin and will flourish outdoors in zone 10 or on walls and trellises under glass in cool regions (minimum winter temperature 10°C/50°F). *C.thomsoniae* and *C.splendens* also make free-flowering houseplants for well lit rooms where the atmosphere is not too dry, trained on a wigwam or frame of canes. Grow all the species listed below in full sun with shade from the hottest summer sun, in a large pot or in the glasshouse border in a high-fertility, loam-based mix with additional leafmould and sharp sand. Maintain good ventilation, water plentifully and feed fortnightly when in full growth, reducing water gradually as light levels and temperatures fall: keep almost dry in winter. Cut back after flowering only when necessary to thin out overcrowded growth, to shape or restrict to allotted space. Propagate by seed sown in spring, bysoftwood cuttings or semi-ripe cuttings rooted in a sandy propagating mix in a closed case with bottom heat; also by root cuttings in spring and by removal of rooted suckers.

C.aculeatum (L.) Schldl. (*Volkameria aculeata* L.). Vine-like shrub, often much-branched, branches to 3m, puberulent, spinescent. Leaves to 7.5×2.5cm, lanceolate or elliptic-obovate to oblong, obtuse or acuminate, base cuneate, glabrous or puberulent above, puberulent beneath; petioles to 1.2cm. Cymes axillary, few-flowered; peduncles to 2.5cm; pedicels to 14mm, puberulent; calyx to 3mm, lobes reflexed, triangular, acute; corolla white, tube to 18mm, lobes to 8mm, reflexed; stamens purple, to 3.5cm. W Indies.

C.cephalanthum Oliv. in Hook. Evergreen climber to 18m, more or less glabrous. Stems hollow between joints, often inhabited by ants in habitat. Leaves 10–30cm, ovate-lanceolate, apex acuminate. Flowers in broad terminal cymes to 24cm diam.; calyx to 2cm, purple-red; corolla white, tube to 8cm, very slender, limb to 3.25cm, lobes oblong; stamens exserted some 3cm, red. Summer. Zanzibar. Z10.

C.scandens Beauv. See *C.umbellatum*.

C. × speciosum Dombr.(*C.splendens* × *C.thomsoniae.*) JAVA GLORY BEAN; PAGODA FLOWER.
Resembles *C.thomsoniae* except calyx pale red or pink; corolla deep rose shaded violet.

C.splendens G. Don ex James.
Twining shrub to 2m, glabrous. Leaves to 18×8cm, opposite, broadly ovate to oblong, acute to acuminate, base subcordate or rounded, entire, usually glabrous, lustrous dark green above, paler beneath; petiole to 2cm. Cymes arranged in a terminal panicle, densely many-flowered; peduncle to 5cm; calyx to 1cm, lobes triangular, acute, red; corolla bright red to scarlet, tube to 2cm, glabrous or puberulent, lobes to 2cm, obovate; stamens exserted some 1.8cm. Tropical Africa.

C.thomsoniae Balf.f. BAG FLOWER; BLEEDING HEART VINE.
Twining shrub to 4m, evergreen, glabrous. Leaves to 17× 10cm, ovate to ovate-oblong, acute or acuminate, base subcordate to rounded, entire; petiole to 2.5cm. Cymes terminal and axillary, 8 to 20-flowered, pubescent; pedicels to 5mm; calyx white, to 2.5cm; corolla dark red, tube to 2cm, glandular-pubescent, lobes to 1cm. Tropical W Africa.

C.umbellatum Poir. (*C.scandens* Beauv.).
Evergreen climber, downy throughout. Stems 4-angled. Leaves 8–10cm, ovate, apex acuminate, base cordate, downy. Flowers in 5–10cm diam. axillary corymbs; corolla white tinted rose, tube to 1.25cm, limb to 2.5cm diam., lobes obovate; stamens exserted some 2.5cm. Summer to winter. Tropical Africa. Z10.

Clianthus Sol. ex Lindl. (From Gk *kleos*, glory, and *anthos*, flower.) Leguminosae (Papilionoideae). 2 species of evergreen, glabrous or pubescent, trailing perennial shrubs or subshrubs (*C.formosus* often short-lived). Branches long, scandent or procumbent, becoming woody especially at base. Leaves alternate, imparipinnate; leaflets small, numerous. Flowers papilionaceous, in short, pendulous, axillary racemes or on erect peduncles; calyx green, campanulate, 5-lobed or toothed; standard broad, sharply acuminate, sharply reflexed, wings exceeded by standard and keel, oblong or thread-like, keel carinate, very sharply acuminate, upcurved, like a lobster claw, equal to or exceeding standard; stamens 10, 9 connate, 1 free, anthers uniform; ovary stalked, many-ovuled, style delicate, incurved. Fruit a legume, narrowly oblong, distended, rounded, beaked; seeds numerous, reniform. Australia, New Zealand.

CULTIVATION *Clianthus* occurs in scrub or on rocky and sandy hills. *C.formosus*, Sturt's Desert Pea, is a silvery trailer producing umbels of black-eyed scarlet flowers on erect stalks. *C.puniceus*, long-cultivated by the Maori, is also found in sheltered coastal habitats in its native New Zealand, where some specimens are said to be over 100 years old. It is grown for its graceful pinnate leaves and the unusual and beautifully formed claw-like flowers. The brilliant red blooms change colour with age and sunlight. Hardy to about −10°C/14°F, perhaps more with perfect drainage, *C.puniceus* can be grown as a wall shrub, trained on trellis or wires against a south- or southwest-facing wall, with shelter from cold winds.

Grow in full sun or light, dappled shade, in well drained soils. Give a thick, dry mulch of bracken litter or leafmould in autumn. Plants cut down by frost may regenerate from the roots in spring. In containers, grow in an open, gritty, loam-based mix; water moderately when in growth and very sparingly in autumn and winter. Maintain good ventilation and a minimum night temperature of 7–10°C/45–50°F. Prune in early summer after flowering to remove deadwood and to establish a flowering framework for the following season. Propagate from seed in spring, at 16–18°C/60–65°F; *C.puniceus* 'Albus' comes true from seed. Semi-ripe cuttings taken in summer will root in a closed case with bottom heat.

C.puniceus (G. Don) Sol. ex Lindl. GLORY PEA; PARROT'S BEAK; PARROT'S BILL; LOBSTER CLAW.
Evergreen shrub to 5m; main stem erect; branches divaricate, long, arching to scandent, slowly becoming woody; branchlets downy. Leaves 7–15cm; leaflets 1–3cm, 13–25, narrow-oblong, blunt or retuse, deep green, glabrescent above, canescent beneath, sessile. Flowers to 7.6cm, 6–15 in drooping racemes on 7.6–10cm peduncles; corolla typically scarlet, sometimes vermilion, coral-pink or white, lustrous, standard 4–5cm, acute, ovate, wings sharp-tipped, narrow and tapering to each end, falcate, less than half keel length, keel 6.5cm, falcate, sharply acuminate. Summer–late autumn. New Zealand (North Is.) 'Albus': flowers white tinted green to ivory, sparse. 'Flamingo': flowers deep rose pink. 'Magnificus': flowers small, deep red. 'Red Admiral': flowers red, profuse. 'Red Cardinal': leaves soft green; flowers red. 'White Heron': flowers pure white, abundant. Z8.

Clitoria L. (The small incurved keel, which is often held uppermost within the enlarged, funnel-like standard, might be thought suggestive of the clitoris.) Leguminosae (Papilionoideae). 70 species of herbs or shrubs; stems climbing, erect or prostrate. Leaves alternate, trifoliolate or imparipinnate; leaflets 1–9, usually 3 or, more rarely, 1; stipules persistent, furrowed. Flowers solitary or in axillary fascicles or in few-flowered, pedunculate, axillary racemes; bracts 2–6, persistent, upper pairs connate, bracteoles large; calyx tubular-infundibuliform, lobes 5, upper 2 basally connate; standard orbicular or broadly obovate, larger than other petals, not spurred, keel often uppermost, incurved, short but conspicuous, sharp-tipped, wings oblong to falcate; stamens 10, connate or vexillary stamen free and 9 connate, anthers usually uniform; ovary stalked, ovules many, style incurved, barbate on inner surface. Fruit compressed, linear to linear-oblong, dehiscing along both sutures, 2-valved; seeds ovate or subglobose, compressed, testa smooth or sticky. Tropics. Z10.

CULTIVATION The most commonly grown species is *C.ternatea*, a slender herbaceous or semi-woody vine with pinnate leaves and sail-like flowers in shades of bright blue, usually stained white and yellow. This and its smaller counterpart, *C.heterophylla*, require a minimum temperature of 10°C/50°F in humid, semi-shaded conditions. They are suitable for pot or bed cultivation in a medium-fertility loam-based mix in conservatories, glasshouses and porches, where they should be trained on wires, trellis or canes. In Mediterranean and subtropical gardens, they will thrive on sheltered walls. *C.amazonum*, with quilted pale crimson flowers, requires higher temperatures and humidity. *C.mariana* is native to the eastern United States from New Jersey to Texas and is also found in Mexico. A small twiner with pale blue or lilac flowers, it will grow through pea sticks or surrounding shrubs in well drained, sunny sites in gardens in zones 6 and upwards wherever summers are hot and humid. Elsewhere, for example Western Europe, it may be advisable to provide a sheltered site on a south-facing wall and, given that the stems may be cut back by hard frosts, to mulch the crowns with bracken in winter. Propagate all species by seed or mound layering – the latter often occurs spontaneously as plants branch and sucker below the soil surface.

C.amazonum Mart.
Almost erect or tall climbing shrub. Leaflets to 12.5cm, 3, ovate, tapering to a point at apex, pale beneath; petioles short. Flowers few, in short racemes; corolla white or pale rose-purple, standard to 7.5cm, marked with dark lines. N Brazil.

C.heterophylla Lam.
Twining herb. Leaflets usually 5 per leaf, sometimes as many as 9, glabrous, orbicular, oval, lanceolate or rarely linear. Flowers resemble those of *C.ternatea*, but are smaller. Tropical Asia.

C.mariana L.
Twining or trailing, to 1m, glabrous or short-downy. Leaflets 3–5×1.5–2.5cm, 3, ovate to lanceolate, apex sharp-tipped to blunt and often emarginate, base blunt to rounded, glabrous above, glabrous to short-downy beneath; petioles 2.5–6cm.

Flowers 1–3 in axillary racemes; corolla pale blue or lilac, standard 4–6 × 3–4cm. Summer. US (New Jersey, S to Florida, Texas), Mexico.

C.ternatea L. BLUE PEA; BLUE VINE; BUTTERFLY PEA; PIGEON WINGS.
Herbaceous vine, trailing or scandent, virtually glabrous, 45cm–3m. Leaves 6–12cm, leaflets 1–6.7×0.3–4cm, usually 5 or 7, elliptic-ovate, sharp-tipped to rounded at base and apex, glabrescent above, downy beneath; petiole 1–3cm. Flowers axillary, single or paired; corolla 3–5cm, standard 1.5–3.5cm diam., clear blue, white stained yellow at centre, sometimes more strongly marked or pure white. Late summer–early autumn. Tropical Asia, naturalized throughout tropics and subtropics. 'Blue Sails': flowers semi-double, deep blue. 'Semi-double': flowers semi-double, rich blue.

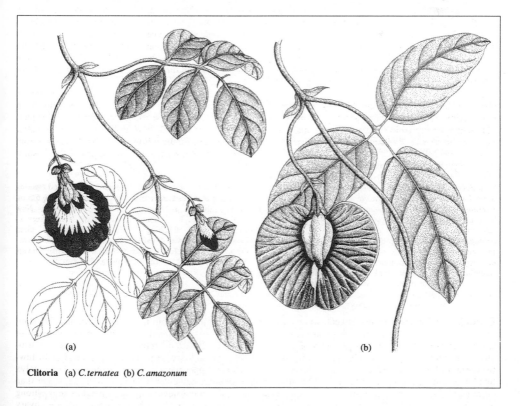

Clitoria   (a) *C.ternatea*   (b) *C.amazonum*

Clytostoma Miers (From Gk *klytos*, glorious, and *stoma*, mouth, referring to the flowers.) Bignoniaceae. 9 species of evergreen vines. Leaves opposite, pinnate; leaflets 2, rarely 3; petiolules short; rachis extended into tendril. Flowers in axillary or terminal pairs or panicles; calyx campanulate, lobes 5, subulate; corolla funnelform-campanulate, lobes 5, imbricate; stamens usually 4; ovaries conical, tuberculate, 2-locular. Fruit a bilocular silique, valves parallel, armed with spiny bristles, many-seeded, each seed enclosed in a wing. Spring–summer. Tropical America. Z10.

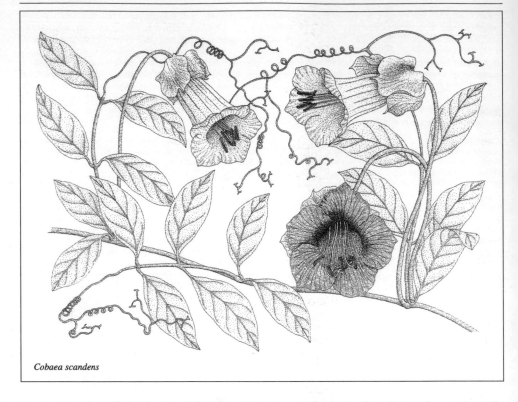

Cobaea scandens

CULTIVATION In tropical and subtropical gardens, *Clytostoma* species are excellent climbers for covering walls and fences; *C.callistegioides* is also used as groundcover. In cooler zones, they are easily grown plants for the cool to intermediate glasshouse or conservatory. *C.callistegioides* is vigorous, with bronzed young leaves and attractive clusters of bright pink blooms carried at intervals from late spring through summer. They are sometimes followed by large, spiny seed pods. Grow in a well drained but moist soil outdoors or in glasshouse beds or in containers of a medium-fertility loam-based mix with additional organic matter and coarse sand. They will tolerate some shade but need at least part day sun and under glass some protection from direct sun at the hottest part of the day. Maintain a humid atmosphere and a winter minimum between 10–13°C/50–55°F. *Clytostoma* withstands hard pruning: remove congested growth in early spring or after flowering. Propagate by semi-ripe or greenwood cuttings of strong side shoots with 2–3 nodes, root in a closed case with bottom heat at 21–24°C/70–75°F. Sow seed or layer in spring.

C.binatum (Thunb.) Sandw. (*C.purpureum* Rehd.; *Bignonia purpurea* Lodd.).
Leaflets to 8cm, elliptic to oblong-obovate, apex acuminate, green above, paler beneath, margin entire, sometimes dentate. Flowers clustered or in pairs; calyx lobes triangular; corolla rosy-mauve or pale purple, with a paler or white throat, tube 2.5cm, lobes ovate, spreading. Uruguay.

C.callistegioides Bur. & Schum. (*Bignonia speciosa* Graham; *Bignonia picta* Lindl.; *Bignonia callistegioides* Cham.).
ARGENTINE TRUMPET VINE; LOVE-CHARM; PAINTED TRUMPET.
Young leaves and stems soft-pubescent, leaflets to 8cm, oblong-elliptic, glabrous, shining above, reticulate veins conspicuous beneath, apex acuminate, margin undulate. Flowers paired; calyx lobes subulate; corolla 7cm, tube yellow striped lilac, lobes purple, spreading, ovate, apex obtuse, margins sinuate. S Brazil, Argentina.

C.purpureum Rehd. See *C.binatum*.

Cobaea Cav. (For the Jesuit priest and naturalist Bernardo Cobo (1572–1659), who visited Mexico and Peru.) Polemoniaceae (Cobaeaceae). About 20 species of herbaceous or shrubby perennial climbers, to at least 10m. Leaves pinnate, alternate, with a terminal tendril; tendrils finely and copiously branched, coiling tightly. Flowers solitary in axils, bright green to violet or deep purple, usually fragrant; calyx leafy, 5-lobed; corolla 5-lobed, campanulate to salverform or with lobes free; stamens 5, exserted; filaments long. Fruit a fleshy capsule; seeds many, flat, winged. Mexico to Tropical S America. Z9.

CULTIVATION Found in mountain habitats in Mexico and widely naturalized in tropical America, *C.scandens* is a fast growing climber commonly grown as an annual for covering arches, pillars and pergolas or to scramble through large shrubs. It is also suitable as a perennial for the larger glasshouse or conservatory. The large cup-shaped blooms are carried over long periods from late summer: the corolla is green and musk-scented on emergence, flushing violet-purple with maturity. While this species is perhaps one of the most familiar climbers of all, there are other members of the genus which have been grown at other times and may still be cultivated in Central and South America. Among them, *C.minor* is a charming 'dwarf' (to 2m/6ft) with smaller, spreading, pale purple flowers; *C.trianaei* resembles a large, persistently green-flowered *C.scandens*, and *C.penduliflora* produces curious hanging flowers with deeply cut, twisted segments. The cultural requirements for all these species are the same. Grow in moisture-retentive but well drained soil in full sun with shelter from strong wind. On freely draining soils and in containers, water plentifully when in full growth. Under glass, prune hard back after flowering in late autumn and maintain a minimum night temperature of 4–5°C/39–40°F. Propagate by seed sown in early spring at 15–21°C/60–70°F in individual small pots or by softwood stem cuttings. Red spider mite and aphids may attack, especially under glass.

C.minor Mart. & Gal.
Small, delicate climber. Leaves to 7cm; leaflets usually 6, to 2.5cm, oblong-ovate. Calyx lobes to 1.75cm, triangular-subulate; corolla rotate, segments to 3cm, oblong-obovate, free and spreading, pale violet becoming darker toward base with a pale green stripe in tube. S Mexico.

C.penduliflora Hook. f.
Tall robust climber; branches angled. Leaves to 20cm; leaflets to 8cm, usually 6, ovate-oblong, apex acute to acuminate. Flowers pendulous on drooping pedicels to 20cm long; calyx lobes to 3.5cm, oblong-lanceolate, swollen at base; segments to 8cm, distinct, linear-lorate, wavy and twisted, hanging downward, dull violet; stamens far-exserted with long, spreading filaments parting corolla segments. S America.

C.scandens Cav. CUP AND SAUCER VINE; MEXICAN IVY; MONASTRY BELLS; VIOLET IVY.
Glabrous climber to at least 8m. Leaves with large, leafy stipules at base, leaflets to 10cm, 4–6 per leaf, oblong or elliptic,

tendrils hook-tipped. Peduncles to 25cm, pedicel twisted after anthesis; flowers erect in bud, horizontal at anthesis; calyx leafy, green, saucer-like, subtending 'cup' of corolla; corolla campanulate, to 5cm long, 4cm diam., segments broadly obovate, tips reflexed, green-cream and musky-scented at first, later violet then deep purple with a honey-like fragrance. Summer–autumn. Mexico (Puebla), but widely naturalized, especially in the Neotropics. 'Alba': flowers white. In some forms the corolla remains green-cream, and some variegated forms are in cultivation.

C.trianaei Hemsl.
Differs from *C.scandens* in corolla to 7.5cm long, more narrowly campanulate-funnelform, segments larger and broader, dull green with red-violet veining, tips not or scarcely reflexed. Colombia, Ecuador.

Coccinia Wright & Arn. (From Lat. *coccineus*, scarlet, referring to the bright red fruit.) Cucurbitaceae. About 30 species of dioecious climbers or trailers, usually tuberous-rooted. Stems glabrous or scabrous. Tendrils usually simple; probracts present. Leaves simple to palmately 5-angled or 5-lobed, occasionally glandular beneath. Male inflorescence a cluster or raceme, or flowers sometimes solitary; flowers white or yellow; calyx short, campanulate, 5-lobed; corolla campanulate, acutely 5-lobed, long; stamens 3, inserted at base of calyx tube, filaments connate or coherent; pistillode absent; female flowers solitary, rarely racemose, resembling males except with 3 staminodes; ovary ovoid or oblong to fusiform; stigmas 3. Fruit a berry, soft, globose to elongate, indehiscent, occasionally ribbed; seeds many, compressed, ovate, margined. Tropical Africa to India and Malesia. Z9.

CULTIVATION   Tuberous-rooted to caudiciform perennial climbers from the dry tropics of the Old World, found in deciduous bushland, savannah, dry evergreen forests and thickets. Grown for their colourful fruits, bright green foliage and, in some species, curiously enlarged rootstocks and stem bases, in temperate zones they require glasshouse cultivation in temperate zones in intermediate to hot conditions, medium humidity and bright, filtered light. Pot in a medium-fertility soil-based mix in early spring and water moderately throughout growth, training on a strong trellis. *C.grandis* is very demanding of space. Control red spider mite as described under *Trichosanthes*. Plants of each sex are required for fruit production. Sow seed in early spring in bottom heat at 20°C/68°F to renew plants. If cultivated as perennials, grow in the glasshouse border, water very sparingly in winter and top-dress with fresh compost in early spring.

C.cordifolia hort. See *C.grandis*.

C.grandis (L.) Voigt (*Bryonia grandis* L.; *C.indica* Wright & Arn.; *C.cordifolia* hort.). IVY GOURD; SCARLET-FRUITED GOURD.
Perennial climber, rarely prostrate, to 20m. Rootstock tuberous. Stem branched, terete, glabrous or scaly. Leaves broadly ovate, cordate to 5-angled or 3–5-lobed, 5–10 × 5–10cm, glabrous, glossy; petiole striate, to 5cm. Flowers white, pale yellow or yellow-orange, to 4cm, solitary or paired. Fruit ovoid, to 5cm, becoming bright red, beaked; seeds oblique, compressed, about 6 × 4mm. Tropical Africa and Asia to N Australia, introduced to Tropical America.

C.indica Wright & Arn. See *C.grandis*.

C.palmata (Sonder) Cogn. (*Cephalandra palmata* Sand. in Harv. & Sand.).
Perennial climber, mostly glabrous, to 8m. Rootstock much enlarged or caudex-like. Stems sulcate. Tendrils bifid. Leaves palmate, ovate-oblong, deep green and occasionally scabrid above, paler, often glandular beneath, 4–12×4–12cm, lobes 5, deeply divided, ovate to ovate-lanceolate, acuminate, minutely dentate; petiole to 6cm. Flowers pale yellow, to 2cm, males in racemes. Fruit narrow, oblong-fusiform, becoming red, 5–8cm; seeds rugose, to 8×4 × 1.5mm. S & E Africa.

C.sessilifolia (Sonder) Cogn.
Perennial herbaceous climber. Stems smooth, to 5m+. Leaves often sessile, palmate, to 12cm, lobes 5, oblong-lanceolate, acute, dentate or lobulate. Flowers pale yellow to pale orange, males in racemes; corolla distinctly veined. Fruit red, to 9cm. S Africa.

Cocculus DC. (Diminutive form of Gk *kokkos*, a berry, referring to the small drupes.) Menispermaceae. MOONSEED. 11 species of deciduous or evergreen climbers, shrubs and small trees. Leaves alternate, sometimes lobed. Flowers unisexual, inconspicuous, borne in axillary panicles or racemes; sepals 6, often pubescent; petals 6, usually cleft; male flowers with 6–9 stamens, females flowers to 0 to 6 staminodes and 3–6 distinct carpels. Fruit a small drupe, globose, red or black; seeds horseshoe- or halfmoon-shaped. S & E Asia, Africa, N America.

CULTIVATION Grown primarily for their glossy foliage and autumn fruits, *Cocculus* species are useful for growing through trees, hedges, trellis and other supports. Hardy to about –15°C/5°F, grow in well drained but moisture-retentive and fertile soils in sun or part shade. Prune if necessary to confine to allotted space in later winter/early spring. Propagate by semi-ripe cuttings in a closed case or by seed; vining species also by root cuttings.

C.carolinus (L.) DC. CAROLINA MOONSEED; RED MOONSEED; CORAL BEADS; SNAILSEED.
Deciduous twiner to 4m. Stems pubescent. Leaves 5–10cm, ovate to cordate, sometimes obscurely 3–5-lobed, 3–7-veined, downy beneath; petiole equalling blade. Flowers to 0.5cm diam., green-white, the males in short panicles, the females in racemes. Fruit 0.5–0.75cm diam., bright red. SE US.

C.orbiculatus (L.) DC. (*C.trilobus* (Thunb.) DC.).
Close in general appearance to *C.carolinus*. Leaves 4.25–10cm, ovate to broadly ovate, sometimes cordate-hastate or shallowly 3-lobed, 3–5-veined. Flowers very small, cream to off-white or yellow-green, in axillary clusters. Fruit to 0.75cm diam., black, pruinose. Temperate & Tropical E Asia (India to Japan, south to Java).

C.trilobus (Thunb.) DC. See *C.orbiculatus*.

Codonopsis Wallich. (From Gk *kodon*, bell, and *opsis*, appearance, alluding to shape of corolla.) BONNET BELLFLOWER. Campanulaceae. Some 30 species of more or less foetid perennial herbs with thick tuberous or fusiform roots. Leaves opposite or alternate, petiolate. Flowers nodding, usually solitary and terminal on short branches; calyx lobes 5, large, broad; corolla broadly elongate-campanulate to funnelform, urceolate or star-shaped, often with colourful spots and tessellation within, lobes 5; stamens free from corolla; ovary inferior or subinferior. Capsules loculicidally dehiscent. Himalaya to Japan and Malesia.

CULTIVATION *Codonopsis* species frequently occur in alpine brush and on rocky slopes, to altitudes of 2100–3600m, with some, for example *C.clematidea*, at altitudes of 4200m/1360ft. They are suitable for herbaceous gardens, woodland gardens and rock gardens, the climbing species such as *C.clematidea* and *C.tangshen* being eminently suited to situations whereby they can twine through pea-sticks or light shrubbery. *C.convolvulacea*, although hardy to –15°C/5°F, has a fragile beauty perhaps best expressed in the alpine house. *C.gracilis*, *C.javanica* and *C.viridis* are slightly tender, requiring a sheltered south-facing wall in zones 8 or under, with a dry winter mulch over the crowns and tubers, or the protection of a cool glasshouse. They are valued for their nodding bell-shaped blooms, in a colour range from soft china blue through periwinkle blue and often with exquisitely patterned interiors, with *C.lanceolata* showing paler and more subtle slate blues. Most of the readily available species will tolerate temperatures to between –10 and –15°C/14–5°F, but where cold is prolonged will need a thick protective mulch in winter. *C.clematidea* is slightly less cold-tolerant. Grow on light, fertile, humus-rich and well drained soils, in sun in zones with cool summers and where the soil remains moist throughout the growing season, elsewhere in semi-shade or dappled shade. Propagate by careful division or by seed in spring, prick out when large enough to handle and pot on successively until large enough to plant out.

C.affinis Hook. f. & Thoms.
Slender, foetid perennial herb of twining habit, to 2m, branchlets pubescent. Leaves 5–16cm, oblong to elliptic, cordate, entire to denticulate, deep green, shiny, initially closely pubescent, petiolate. Flowers solitary or in branched clusters at tips of branchlets; corolla to 1.5cm, tubular-campanulate, purple or green, lobes recurved, often hairy, deltoid, purple. C Himalaya, from Nepal to Sikkim. Z7.

C.benthamii Hook.f.& Thoms.
Close to *C.macrocalyx* and *C.tubulosa*, but hairier with leaves lanceolate to ovate-lanceolate and green to yellow-green flowers 1.6–2cm long. Himalaya (Nepal to Bhutan, S Tibet). Z6.

C.cardiophylla Diels ex Komar.
Resembling *C.clematidea*, distinguished by more cordate leaves which have a thin, white, slightly thickened margin. Flowers smaller, to 2cm, lavender marked purple at base. Summer. China (Hubei) to Tibet. Z4.

C.clematidea (Schrenk ex Fisch. & C.A. Mey.) C.B. Clarke.
Erect to semi-scandent perennial to 80cm, branches eventually sprawling and flexuously curved upwards. Leaves to 2.5cm, narrowly ovate to acuminate, petiolate, veins prominent beneath, scarcely pubescent. Flowers usually solitary, nodding, terminal; calyx lobes linear, recurved, green suffused blue; corolla 1.7–3cm, campanulate, pale or milky blue with tangerine and black markings at base within, lobes short, broadly triangular, somewhat recurved. Summer. C Asia, from S USSR to W Himalaya. Z4.

C.convolvulacea Kurz.
Perennial, twiner to 3m; rhizome swollen; stems slender, glabrous. Leaves 2.5–6cm, lanceolate-ovate, alternate, occasionally with a cordate base, entire to denticulate, coriaceous, long-petiolate. Flowers solitary on long pedicels, terminal or on short lateral shoots; corolla 4–5cm diam., rotate-campanulate, divided almost to base into oblanceolate lobes, azure to violet-blue (white in 'Alba'). SW China and N Himalaya. Z5.

C.convolvulacea var. *forrestii* (Diels) Ballard. See *C.forrestii*.

C.forrestii Diels (*C.convolvulacea* var. *forrestii* (Diels) Ballard; *C.tibetica* auct.).
Close to *C.convolvulacea*. To 3.5m, usually shorter, scrambling. Leaves 3–10cm, broadly oval, base cordate, glaucous beneath, serrate, short-petiolate. Flowers 4.6–6.5cm, lavender blue with a claret basal spot within. Summer. China (N Yunnan). Z7.

C.gracilis (Lem.) Book.f. & Thoms. (*Leptocodon gracilis* Lem.)
Tuberous-rooted perennial herb. Stems to 1m. slender, glabrous, twining. Leaves 0.8–2cm, broadly ovate, sparsely bluntly toothed, pale green, slightly hairy, stalked. Flowers solitary, nodding, terminal or axillary; corolla 3–5cm, narrowly funnel-shaped, blue, tube flaring at mouth, lobes very short, broadly triangular. Himalaya (E Nepal to Assam). Z8.

C.handeliana Nannf. See *C.tubulosa*.
C.japonica Miq. See *C.lanceolata*.

C.javanica (Bl.) Hook.f. & Thoms. (*Campanumoea cordata* Maxim.; *Campanumoea javanica* Bl.).
Vigorous twining tuberous perennial herb to 3m; stems slender, green, glabrous. Leaves 2.5-6cm, cordate-ovate, bluntly toothed to entire, glabrous or somewhat hairy, long-stalked. Flowers usually solitary on short lateral shoots; corolla 1.4–3.5cm, broadly campanulate, white tinted green or ivory, cut to 1/3 depth into spreading, ovate-triangular lobes. E Himalaya, SW China, SE Asia to Java. Z9. Cf. *C.viridis*.

C.lanceolata (Maxim.) Benth. & Hook. f. (*C.japonica* (Sieb. ex Morr.) Miq.; *C.ussuriensis* (Rupr.) Hemsl.; *Campanumoea japonica* Sieb. ex Morr.; *Glosocomia lanceolata* Maxim.; *Glosocomia ussuriensis* Rupr.).
Glabrous foetid perennial twiner to 3m, stems green tinged purple. Leaves to 5cm, crowded toward end of lateral branchlets, elliptic-lanceolate to linear-oblong, usually entire, occasionally undulate, membranous, glaucous beneath. Flowers pendulous, solitary or paired, terminal on short lateral branches; corolla 1.5–2.5cm, campanulate, lobes deltoid, not recurved, green flushed purple to dusky purple or lilac with purple or violet markings within. Autumn. China. Z7.

C.macrocalyx Diels.
Stems 60–80cm, weakly twining, sparsely branched, smooth. Leaves 3–9cm, alternate, oblong-ovate, lobed to crenate, glaucous beneath, sparsely hairy. Flowers with calyx leafy, inflated, corolla 2–4cm, tubular-campanulate, somewhat constricted, yellow-green marked purple at base. W China. Z6.

C.nepalensis Grey-Wilson.
Very close in general appearance to *C.convolvulacea* and possibly much confused with it in cultivation. This species differs in its thinner-textured, ovate-cordate, entire to slightly toothed leaves to 5.5cm; its larger, mid-blue flowers (6.5–9cm diam.) with corolla rotate, divided almost to base into broadly ovate lobes, hairy below within. Differs also in the broadly turbinate to depressed-globose fruit (not narrowly pyriform as in both *C.convolvulacea* and *C.forrestii*). Nepal. Z7.

C.pilosula (Franch.) Nannf.
Differs from *C.tangshen* in its smaller leaves and flowers. Twining to 1.7m. Leaves to 2cm, lanceolate to cordate at base, pilose. Flowers on lateral branchlets; calyx lobes lanceolate; corolla to 2.5cm, campanulate, green flushed with dull purple. N China. Z6.

C.rotundifolia Benth.
Vigorously twining to 3m. Leaves 2–7cm, ovate to lanceolate, sometimes cordate at base, subentire to toothed or sinuate, sparsely dark-pubescent, petiolate, varying in length. Flowers solitary, terminal or axillary; calyx with large, leafy lobes; corolla 2–3cm, campanulate, swollen in middle, yellow-green or green-white with conspicuous purple-black net venation, lobes recurved, triangular. Himalaya. Z7.

C.tangshen Oliv.
Twining to 2m, glabrous or scaberulous. Leaves 2.5–6cm, fleshy, broadly lanceolate, coarsely dentate, pubescent, petiolate. Flowers solitary, usually terminal; calyx lobes ovate, green; corolla 3–4cm, campanulate, yellow to olive green strongly net-veined and spotted purple at base within. Summer. W China. Z4.

C.tibetica auct. See *C.forrestii*.

C.tubulosa Komar. (*C.handeliana* Nannf.).
Similar to *C.macrocalyx*. Twining perennial herb to 1.5m, glabrous. Leaves ovate-lanceolate, usually opposite, short-petiolate. Flowers solitary, terminal or lateral; calyx lobes to 1.4cm, ovate; corolla 3.5–4.3cm, narrowly tubular-campanulate, waisted above base, tinged with lime to yellow, with faint purple venation within, lobes ovate-triangular, forward-pointing, not at all reflexed. SW China. Z7.

C.ussuriensis (Rupr.) Hemsl. See *C.lanceolata*.

C.vinciflora Komar.
Delicate, twining perennial herb to 1m; stems very slender, glabrous, not usually branched. Leaves small, thin-textured, lanceolate to ovate, toothed, glabrous, green above, glaucescent beneath. Flowers solitary, terminal or on short lateral shoots toward stem apex; corolla 3–4cm diam., rotate, blue to lilac-blue, divided almost to base into elliptic to oblanceolate lobes. Differs from *C.convolvulacea* in less vigorous habit, smaller, thinner, toothed leaves and smaller flowers. The tubers, divested of their thin covering, are smooth; those of *C.convolvulacea* are finely warty. W & SW China, Himalaya (Sikkim to Bhutan and Assam). Z8.

C.viridiflora Maxim.
Differs from *C.clematidea* in stem and leaves somewhat hairy; calyx lobes not reflexed; corolla 1.6–2cm, yellow-green. C China. Z7.

C.viridis Wallich.
Vigorously twining, rather foetid perennial herb to 4m; stems slender, glabrous. Leaves 2–7cm, alternate, cordate to ovate or ovate-triangular, subentire to toothed, slightly hairy, long-stalked. Flowers terminal or axillary, solitary; corolla 2–3.5cm, inflated-campanulate, pale green or green-white, lobe edges and interior slightly spotted purple-red, lobes triangular, recurved. Differs from *C.javanica* in its slender, distant (not lanceolate-elliptic, spreading) calyx lobes and semi-inferior (not superior) ovary. Himalaya (Pakistan to Nepal, Bhutan, Assam). Z9.

Combretum Loefl. (Name in Pliny for an unidentified climbing plant.) Combretaceae. Some 250 species of trees or shrubs, sometimes scandent. Leaves opposite or whorled, sometimes alternate, glabrous or pubescent, often scaly, usually petiolate. Inflorescence a raceme or a panicle, terminal or axillary, glabrous or pubescent, few- to several-flowered; flowers usually bisexual; calyx tube adnate to ovary, glabrous or pubescent, lobes 4 or 5, filiform or subulate to deltoid; petals 4 or 5, sometimes absent, exceeding calyx lobes, glabrous or pubescent; stamens 8 to 10, often in 2 series, usually exserted; style free, usually exserted, ovary inferior, unilocular, ovules 2. Fruit usually indehiscent, 4 or 5-winged, carinate or angled, sessile or stipitate, 1-seeded. Tropics (except Australia). Z10.

CULTIVATION Vigorous woody climbers grown for their showy spikes of small, sometimes fragrant flowers, with conspicuous stamens and attractive brightly coloured fruits. In temperate zones, grow in the warm glasshouse or conservatory, where they perform best planted directly into the border. Plant in a freely drain-ing, humus-rich, soilless medium with additional loam. Admit bright filtered light, with partial shade in summer; water plentifully when in growth, less at other times, syringe frequently before flowering and maintain a minimum temperature of 16°C/60°F. Train on wires against walls and across glasshouse and con-servatory roofs; also against pillars and the trunks of large trees. Prune immediately after flowering to remove congested growth and spur back to a framework. Propagate by semi-ripe cuttings in sand in a closed case with bottom heat. Red spider mite may be a problem under glass. Mealy bug and scale insect may also infest congested growth. All three pests can usually be held in check by thorough pruning and frequent hos-ing down.

C.afzelii Engl. & Diels in Engl. See *C.grandiflorum.*

C.bracteosum (Hochst.) Brandis (*Poivrea bracteosa* Hochst.). HICCOUGH NUT.
Small tree, shrub or climber to 8m; branches glabrous, spineless. Leaves to 10cm, opposite or subopposite, simple, ovate, acuminate, rounded or narrowed at base, usually glabrous, dull green above, pale green beneath. Inflorescence a dense raceme, short, axillary and terminal; flowers small, bright red-scarlet; bracts large, foliaceous; calyx 5-lobed, lobes dentiform; petals 5. Fruit ovate or rounded, smooth, slightly 5-angled, wings absent, 1-seeded. S Africa.

C.celastroides Welw. ex Lawson.
Small tree or shrub, often rambling. Stem much-branched, smooth, grey. Leaves to 6 × 2.5cm, opposite, simple, broadly lanceolate or ovate, obtuse or emarginate, narrowed or rounded at base, somewhat chartaceous, lepidote and velutinous beneath, smooth above, short-petiolate. Inflorescence to 10cm, lax, terminal and axillary; flowers yellow; pedicels often pubescent. Fruit small, subglobose, tinted bright red, winged. Angola.

C.coccineum (Sonn.) Lam. (*C.purpureum* Vahl.).
Shrub or climber, glabrous or glabrescent when young. Leaves to 24 × 12cm, oblong. Inflorescence a raceme or a panicle, terminal, elongate; bracts small, rigid, linear, caducous; flowers to 2.5cm; pedicel short or elongate; calyx tubular, exterior glabrous, interior slightly scaly, lobes short, triangular; petals to 4 × 2.5mm, red, persistent, narrowly oblong, acute, attenuate at base, glabrous; sta-mens exserted, red. Fruit to 8mm, orbicular, compressed, 4 or 5-winged, wings papery. Madagascar.

C.comosum G. Don.
Scandent shrub, puberulous when young. Leaves oblong or elliptic, acute or acuminate, subcordate at base, glabrous or pubescent, short-petiolate. Inflorescence to 15cm, a panicle, terminal, spreading; flowers to 12mm, red, short-pedicel-late; bracts ovate, acute; bracteoles lanceolate, acute; calyx lobes 5, broadly subulate; petals to 9mm, lanceolate or elliptic-lanceolate. Fruit to 20 × 15mm, rose when young, glabrous, emarginate, with 4 chartaceous wings, short-stipi-tate. Sierra Leone.

C.decandrum Roxb.
Evergreen shrub, scandent; branches orange-brown, pubes-cent. Leaves chartaceous, oblong to oblong-lanceolate, acuminate, glabrous, veins sometimes puberulent, entire; petiole pubescent. Inflorescence a panicle, terminal or axil-lary, densely orange-brown-pubescent; flowers small, white; bracts to 3cm, white or pale green, glabrous or pubescent; calyx tube elliptic-oblong, 5-lobed, densely orange-brown pubescent; petals 5, obovate-oblong. Fruit to 2.5cm, oblong, 5-winged, glabrous. India, Burma.

C.flagrocarpum Herb. ex C.B. Clarke.
Scandent or straggling shrub,tomentose or villous when young, sometimes scaly or glandular. Leaves to 20 × 9cm, ovate or oblong-elliptic to lanceolate, obtuse to long-acumi-nate, pubescent, becoming glabrescent with age. Inflorescence 10–15cm, a raceme or a panicle, terminal or axillary; flowers to 6mm diam., yellow. Fruit to 4cm, rotund. Summer–winter. Burma, NE India.

C.grandiflorum G. Don.(*C.afzelii* Engl. & Diels in Engl.).
Scandent shrub, young branches pubescent Leaves to 10 × 5cm, opposite, ovate-elliptic, acuminate, glabrous or pubes-cent; petioles short, pubescent. Inflorescence short, axillary and terminal spikes; flowers red, large, showy; bracts ovate; calyx tube to 2cm, lanceolate, interior glabrous, exterior slightly pubescent, lobes triangular, acute; petals bright red, narrowly obovate to oblanceolate; stamens usu-ally 10, exserted. Fruit to 20 × 12mm, subrotund, emar-ginate, short-stipitate. N Africa.

C.latifolium Bl.
Branchlets glabrous, scaly, red when young. Leaves to 20 × 13cm, opposite, chartaceous to subcoriaceous, elliptic to ovate-elliptic, acuminate, base cuneate to rounded; petiole to 2cm. Inflorescence a panicle to 20cm, terminal or axil-lary, velvety; bracts small, soon deciduous; flowers green-white, sessile; calyx tube to 6mm, lobes 4, to 3 × 2mm, tri-angular, acute; petals 4, to 2 × 2mm, subrotund, glabrous, short-clawed, slightly emarginate; stamens 8, filaments to 4mm; style to 1cm. Fruit to 3cm diam., subrotund, 4-winged, viscid-glandular, short-stipitate. India, Burma, Ceylon, Indochina, Thailand, Malaysia, New Guinea.

C.microphyllum Klotzsch. FLAMECREEPER; BURNING BUSH
Small tree or vigorous scrambler. Leaves to 6 × 5cm, oppo-site or alternate, ovate, oblong or suborbiculae, apex rounded or apiculate, rounded at base, pubescent; petiole velutinous. Inflorescence an axillary raceme, shorter than lvs; flowers bright red-scarlet, pubescent; petals minute; stamens elongate. Fruit to 2cm, yellow-green becoming red, ellipsoid, 4-winged. Mozambique.

C.paniculatum Vent.
Evergreen climber to 10m, glabrescent. Leaves to 18 × 9.5cm, alternate or opposite, elliptic-oblong, apex rounded or acuminate, subcordate to obtuse at base, chartaceous, glabrous or glabrescent; petiole to 3cm. persisting as a thorny hook. Inflorescence a panicle, terminal or axillary; bracts to 4mm, narrowly elliptic-ovate; flowers red, sessile or subsessile; calyx tube to 5mm, pubescent, lobes denti-form; petals to 2.5 × 2.5mm, ovate to subrotund; filaments to 4mm, red; style to 8mm. Fruit to 2.5 × 2cm, ellipsoid-oblong to subrotund, slightly pubescent, 4 or 5-winged, pink or orange. Tropical Africa.

C.purpureum Vahl. See *C.coccineum.*

C.racemosum Beauv.
Shrub to 4m, often scandent; branchlets puberulent, spineless. Leaves to 10cm, alternate or opposite, elliptic-lanceolate, acuminate, rounded at base, glabrous, short-petiolate. Inflorescence a dense panicle; bracts ovate; bracteoles white, linear-lanceolate; calyx tube lanceolate, pubescent, lobes 4, dentiform, interior glabrous; petals red, obovate. Fruit to 2cm, elliptic, 4-winged, short-stipitate. W Africa.

Congea Roxb. Verbenaceae. Some 7 species of scandent shrubs. Leaves opposite, simple, entire. Flowers white, pink or rose, in small, capitate, involucrate cymes, usually arranged in a terminal panicle; calyx tubular, persistent, 5-toothed; corolla labiate, upper lip erect, 2-lobed, lower lip spreading, 3-lobed; stamens 4, long-exserted, didynamous, inserted in throat, anthers dorsifixed, bilocular; ovary bilocular, with 2 pendent ovules per locule, style capillary, stigma bifid. Fruit a coriaceous capsule, indehiscent, 1-seeded. SE Asia. Z10.

CULTIVATION   As for *Clerodendrum*.

C.tomentosa Roxb. LAVENDER WREATH; SHOWER ORCHID.
Large shrub, short-tomentose. Leaves to 20cm, ovate to ovate-elliptic or ovate-oblong, acute or acuminate, base rounded or obtuse, tomentose to subglabrous beneath; petiole pubescent. Flowers white, sessile; bracts 3 per cyme, to 2.5cm, white to lilac, ovate to elliptic-oblong, acute or obtuse,

short-tomentose; calyx pubescent, lobes lanceolate, acute; corolla tube interior pubescent to glabrous. Burma, Thailand.

C.velutina Wight.
Differs from *C.tomentosa* in having 4 bracts per cyme, these purple-rose and silvery-velutinous. Burma, S Thailand, N Malaysia.

Convolvulus L. (From Lat. *convolvere*, to twine.) BINDWEED. Convolvulaceae. About 250 species of annual or perennial, erect, climbing or scrambling herbs and shrubs to 2m, some containing latex. Stems herbaceous to woody. Leaves sessile to petiolate, usually entire. Flowers solitary or in axillary or terminal clusters; pedicels with tiny and much-reduced leaf-like bracteoles, never enclosing calyx; corolla funnel-shaped, dorsally hairy, midpetaline areas often a different colour to limb; stamens included; stigma 2-lobed, lobes linear and thread-like or club-shaped. Fruit a dry capsule, usually 4-seeded. Widely distributed in most temperate and subtropical regions, with a few tropical species. Separated from *Calystegia* mainly on the basis of its tricolpate pollen and 2-locular ovary; see Lewis and Oliver (1965). Some, e.g. *C.arvensis* L., are troublesome weeds.

CULTIVATION   *Convolvulus* originates in the dry heat of Mediterranean-type climates: the most ornamental thrive in warm, sheltered gardens where temperatures do not fall much below –5°C/23°F. Many are invasive, but the spread of more rampant species like *C.althaeoides* is limited in cold areas by the dieback of otherwise naturally evergreen foliage: use tiles or slates to control wandering root systems. *Convolvulus* species are used on sunny rock gardens, banks and at border fronts, grown for their flowers or for the beautiful silver foliage in *C.althaeoides* ssp. *tenuissimus*. In areas where winter temperatures fall much below –5°C/23°F, the more tender species may be overwintered in well-crocked pots of low-fertility, loam-based mix in the cold glasshouse or conservatory. Climbers, scramblers and trailers may be used to clothe low walls or trellising supports (requiring a framework around which to twine themselves): *C.sabatius* suits hanging baskets and troughs, in a medium-fertility loam-based mix with additional leafmould and regular liquid feed.
    Plant all species after the last frosts: give full sun in a sheltered position and sharply drained, low to medium fertility soils. Those normally grown as annuals (e.g. *C.pentapetaloides*) are sown *in situ*; where temperatures allow, sow in autumn and give cloche protection over the winter. Deadhead regularly for a succession of flower. In cold areas overwinter stock plants under glass, or provide a winter mulch to give protection to the root zone. Propagate by seed in spring at 15–18°C/60–65°F; also by semi-ripe heel cuttings in summer, rooted in a well drained medium with moderate humidity or by division of herbaceous perennials in spring. Susceptible under glass to red spider mite. In addition to the twining, scrambling, sprawling and trailing species described below, *Convolvulus*, of course, contains such celebrated garden plants as the silver-leaved *C.cneorum* and the blue-and-yellow-flowered *C.tricolor* (not to be confused with *Ipomoea tricolor*). Being bushy in habit and free-standing, these are not treated here.

C.althaeoides L.
Perennial herb to 1m, pubescent throughout; stems slender, climbing or trailing. Leaves grey-green, ovate-cordate, petiolate, upper often cordate to sagittate but very variable, often deeply lobed. Inflorescence axillary, 1–3- (occasionally 5-)flowered, peduncles longer than bracts; sepals variable, rounded to acute at apex; corolla 2.5–4cm diam., pink to pink-purple, widely funnel-shaped. ssp. **althaeoides** Hairs mostly patent, of more robust habit. Leaf lobes shallower and wider. Sep. 7–10mm. Summer. S Europe. ssp. **tenuissimus** (Sibth. & Sm.) Stace (*C.tenuissimus* Sibth. & Sm.; *C.elegantissimus* Mill.). Hairs dense, virtually all adpressed, silvery and soft-textured. Leaf lobes narrower and deeper. Flowers often solitary, sepals 6–9mm. Summer. S Europe. Z8.

C.arvensis L. FIELD BINDWEED.
Perennial herb to 2m, glabrous or pubescent Stems climbing or trailing, slender. Leaves petiolate, shape varying from linear to ovate or ovate-oblong, sagittate to hastate, margins usually entire. Inflorescence axillary, 1–3-flowered, peduncles about same length as bracts; sepals blunt or emarginate; corolla 1–2.5cm diam., funnelform, white or pink with pink midpetaline areas. Summer, autumn. Europe, Asia, widely naturalized elsewhere. Can be a highly invasive weed; if cultivated needs careful management. Z5.

C.canariensis L.
Woody climber to about 2m. Leaves 4–9cm, oval-oblong, densely hairy, with raised veins above. Inflorescence axillary, cymose, 7–9-flowered; sepals densely hairy; corolla pale blue. Canary Is. Z9.

C.cyclostegius House. See *Calystegia macrostegia* ssp. *cyclostegia*.

C.elegantissimus Mill. See *C.althaeoides* ssp. *tenuissimus*.

C.floridus L. f.
Woody climber or shrub to 4m. Leaves 2–14cm, linear-lanceolate, oblong-linear or oblong, sometimes spathulate, covered in short, dense hairs. Inflorescence terminal, paniculate, many-flowered; flowers sessile, about 1cm diam., white or pale pink. Canary Is. Z9.

C.imperialis hort. See *Ipomoea × imperialis*.

C.incanus Vahl.
Perennial to 1m, prostrate or climbing, tinged grey, silky pubescent Leaves 2–5cm, hastate, oblong-ovate or linear-sagittate, basal lobes occasionally forked or toothed. Inflorescence 1–3-flowered, peduncle 2.5cm, bracts paired, 4mm, linear-filiform; corolla 1–2cm, pink to white, acutely lobed, stigmas filiform to linear. Spring, summer. US (Nebraska and Colorado to Texas and Arizona). Z4.

C.japonicus Thunb. See *Calystegia hederacea.*
C.macrostegius Greene. See *Calystegia macrostegia.*
C.major hort. See *Ipomoea purpurea.*
C.mauritanicus Boiss. See *C.sabatius.*
C.occidentalis A. Gray. See *Calystegia occidentalis.*

C.ocellatus Hook. (*C.randii* Rendle).
Erect to prostrate perennial, brown- to silver-pubescent. Leaves to 5cm, linear-oblong, occasionally 5-lobed. Inflores-cence axillary, 1-flowered; corolla pink, mauve or white with a maroon central spot. Summer. S Africa. Z8.

C.pellitus f. pellitus Ledeb. See *Calystegia hederacea.*
C.pellitus f. anestius Ledeb. See *Calystegia hederacea* 'Flore Pleno'.

C.pentapetaloides L.
Prostrate annual or short-lived perennial to 30cm. Leaves oblanceolate to linear or oblong. Inflorescence 1-flowered; sepals elliptic-ovate, blunt, with a small mucro, glabrous; corolla 7–10mm diam., blue with a yellow centre. Summer. Portugal to Turkey. Z8.

C.randii Rendle. See *C.ocellatus.*

C.sabatius Viv. (*C.mauritanicus* Boiss.).
Perennial with a branching, woody stock, 10–50cm, with ascending to trailing, sparsely to densely pubescent, simple or branched herbaceous growth. Leaves to 4cm, petiolate, oblong-ovate to orbicular, base cuneate to truncate, entire. Inflorescence axillary, 1–3-flowered, peduncle not exceeding bracts in length; calyx hairy, outer sepals acute, inner acuminate; corolla 1.5–2.2cm diam., funnelform, pale to clear blue to lavender pink, tube usually paler, often cream or yellow at base. Summer. Italy, N Africa. Z8.

C.scammonia L. SCAMMONY.
Deciduous glabrous perennial; stems angled, trailing. Leaves lanceolate-cordate to sagittate. Inflorescence 3-flowered; flowers large, ebracteate, campanulate, cream or pale red. E Mediterranean, Asia Minor. Z7.

C.scoparius L. f.
Shrub to 1m+. Leaves 0.5–5cm, linear-filiform, often caducous, with short hairs, often glandular. Inflorescence 5–6-flowered, terminal or axillary; corolla white or pink. Canary Is. Z9.

C.sepium L. See *Calystegia sepium.*
C.tenuissimus Sibth. & Sm. See *C.althaeoides* ssp. *tenuissimus.*
C.tuguriorum Forst. f. See *Calystegia tuguriorum.*

For illustration see Ipomoea

Corallocarpus Welw. ex Hook. f. (From Gk *korallion*, coral red, and *karpos*, fruit.) Cucurbitaceae. 13 species of monoecious climbing or trailing perennial herbs. Rootstock tuberous. Aerial parts mostly coarsely hairy. Tendrils simple. Leaves simple, palmate, ovate to reniform, cordate; lobes minutely apiculate, obtuse. Male inflorescence racemose, crowded at apex; flowers small, green or yellow; calyx tube campanulate, lobed; petals united at base, connate; stamens 3, free, inserted in mouth of tube; disc basal, fused to tube; female flowers in fascicles or solitary, similar to males except staminodes 5 or absent, subulate; disc obscure; ovary inferior; stigma 2–3-lobed. Fruit a berry, ovoid to ellipsoid, green and red, dehiscent; seeds small, obliquely pyriform to subglobose. Africa, Madagascar, India.

CULTIVATION   As for *Coccinia*, but multiple planting not required for fruit set.

C.boehmii (Cogn.) C. Jeffrey (*Kedrostis boehmii* Cogn.).
Stems sparsely to densely lanate, becoming glabrous with papery bark forming at base. Leaves densely shortly pubescent, sinuate-toothed, 2–5×3–7cm, lobes 3; petiole to 5cm. Male inflorescence a subcapitate raceme, female inflorescence a cluster or short raceme, coaxillary with male; calyx tube pubescent within; petals spreading, to 2mm. Fruit 1–5, subspherical, beaked, minutely pubescent; seeds rugose or scaly. Tropical Africa. Z10.

Corydalis Vent. (From GK *korydalis*, the crested lark; the flower resembles the shape of its head.) Fumariaceae (Papaveraceae). About 300 species of annual or perennial herbs, with rhizomes or tubers. Stems sometimes woody at the base, often much-branched. Leaves basal and alternate on stems, compound, usually biternate, rarely simple, broadly triangular in outline, usually glaucous; leaflets often further divided; petioles sometimes winged. Flowers in racemes, terminal or opposite leaves with a bract below each flower; petals 4, in pairs, the upper and lower, outer pair with reflexed apical lips and basal spur, the inner pair convergent, enclosing stamens and style; stamens 6. Fruit a dehiscent capsule enclosing many black seeds. Northern temperate regions, especially the Sino-Himalayan area, and S Africa.

CULTIVATION   A genus of hardy herbs, most of them small perennials with clumps of ferny foliage and racemes of bright, tubular crested and spurred flowers close in appearance to those of the allied genera *Adlumia* and *Dicentra*. Like those two genera, *Corydalis* also contains climbing species – vigorous but slender-stemmed annuals or short-lived perennials which entangle themselves in surrounding shrubs and are valued for their fine leaves and subtly attractive flowers. The two listed below can be naturalized in semi-shaded, damp, leafy sites in shrubberies and woodland fringes or at the foot of old walls unlikely to become too hot or dry. Seed should be sown *in situ* in spring. Given little or no encouragement, both species will readily colonize and spread and may become a nuisance.

C.claviculata (L) DC. CLIMBING CORYDALIS.
Annual. Stem to 1m, climbing, slender, weak. Leaves long-petioled, once or twice pinnate, leaflets entire, reduced to a tendril at apex. Flowers to 0.6cm, to 10, in racemes opposite leaves; petals pale yellow-white, streaked with pink, inner petals tipped dark red, spur short, downward-curving; floral bracts linear. Summer. Europe. Z6.

C.vesicaria (L.) Pers.
Annual, climbing, to 1m. Stem slender, branching. Leaves long-petioled, bipinnate, leaflets entire or cut, elliptic, becoming reduced as tendrils. Flowers to 0.5cm, few, in axillary racemes; petals yellow, outer petals broadly winged, spur very short, obtuse; floral bracts lanceolate. Spring–summer. S Africa. Z8.

For illustration see Fumariaceae.

Cucumeropsis Naudin. (From Lat. *cucumis*, cucumber, and Gk *opsis*, appearance; the fruit resembles the cucumber.) Cucurbitaceae. 1 species, a herbaceous climber, to 4m. Stems sparsely crispate. Leaves simple, ovate-cordate or somewhat reniform, punctate, denticulate, obtuse or acute, sometimes slightly lobed, 6–12 × 7–14cm; petiole slightly pubescent, 2–10cm. Male inflorescence racemose or umbelliform, 4- to 12-flowered, sometimes bracteate; peduncle to 12cm; calyx campanulate, pubescent within, lobes lanceolate; petals small, united at base, pale yellow; stamens 3, inserted in throat of receptacle; disc cupulate; pedicel to 14mm; female flowers solitary, ovary cylindric, 1–2cm; calyx pubescent within; lobes lanceolate; petals to 7 × 4mm. Fruit a berry, cylindric ellipsoid, cream-white, striped green, about 19 × 9cm; stalk to 1cm; seeds large, ovate, compressed, white, to 2cm. W Africa. Z10.

CULTIVATION   As for *Momordica*.

C.edulis (Hook. f.) Cogn. See *C.mannii*.

C.mannii Naudin (*Cladosicyos edulis* Hook. f.; *C.edulis* (Hook. f.) Cogn.).

Cucumis L. (Lat. *cucumis*, cucumber.) Cucurbitaceae. About 30 species of herbs, climbing or trailing, annual or perennial, monoecious or andromonoecious. Stem hispid or scabrid. Tendrils simple. Leaves simple, occasionally divided, palmate, angled or 3–7-lobed, usually scabrid or hispid. Male flowers solitary or borne in short, lateral clusters, yellow, 1–2cm diam.; calyx tubular, lobed; lobes filiform; petals 5, joined near base; stamens 3, free, inserted on perianth tube, anthers flexuous; nectary cup central; disc subglobose; female flowers solitary, occasionally clustered, similar to male flowers except staminodes 3; ovary ovoid or globose, pubescent, nectary ring at base of style; disc annular. Fruit indehiscent, fleshy, smooth or spiky; seeds lenticular, acute. Tropical Africa, Asia, introduced to New World Tropics. Z10.

CULTIVATION   An economically important genus, *Cucumis* embraces the melons (save the Water Melon) and the cucumber, together with the more exotic Kiwano and the West Indian Gherkin. For a full treatment of these crops see 'Cucumbers', 'Gourds' and 'Melons' in *The New RHS Dictionary of Gardening* (1992).

C.acutangula L. See *Luffa acutangula*.

C.africanus L. f.
Monoecious annual trailer. Stems grooved, hirsute to pilose, becoming scabrid, to 1m. Leaves 2–10cm, palmate, ovate, cordate, setose, lobes 3–5 rarely 7, broadly elliptic to lanceolate, obtuse to acute, dentate to subentire, median lobe largest, often lobulate; petioles hispid, to 7cm. Male flowers solitary or in racemes; receptacle hirsute; sep. subulate to filiform, to 4mm; corolla yellow, 10–15mm; female flowers solitary, similar to male except ovary fusiform to oblong. Fruit variable, ellipsoid to subcylindric, spiny, pale green with purple bands. S Zimbabwe to S Africa.

C.africanus Thunb. non L. f. See *C.zeyheri*.

C.anguria L. (*C.erinaceus* hort.; *C.grossulariiformis* hort.). WEST INDIAN GHERKIN; BUR GHERKIN; GOAREBERRY; GOOSEBERRY GOURD.
To 2.5m. Stems slender, angled, rough, pubescent Leaves to 8cm, broadly ovate, cordate, veins pubescent, lobes 3–5, rounded, often lobulate, basal lobes asymmetric. Male flowers solitary or cymose; calyx tube about 3cm; petals yellow, 5–6 × 3–4cm; female flowers solitary, perianth similar to male; ovary ellipsoid, to 5 × 8mm, bristly; pedicel 13–95mm. Fruit ovoid or oblong, to 5 × 4cm, prickly, grey-green with green stripes, becoming yellow. Tanzania to the Transvaal. var. *longipes* (Hook. f.) Meeuse. Fruit concolorous, with dense subulate spines. W & S Africa.

C.chito E. Morr. See *C.melo*.
C.cognatus Cogn. See *C.melo*.
C.colocynthis L. See *Citrullus colocynthis*.
C.conomon Thunb. See *C.melo* Conomon Group.

C.dipsaceus Ehrenb. ex Spach. HEDGEHOG GOURD; TEASEL GOURD.
Annual. Roots fibrous. Stem slender, grey-green, hispid. Leaves 2–10 × 3–10cm, broad-ovate to reniform-ovate, scabrid-pubescent especially on veins beneath, occasionally shallowly 3-lobed; petiole pubescent, 3–1cm. Male flowers 1–4; calyx tube to 5mm, pale green; petals yellow with green nerves, to 10 × 5mm; female flowers solitary, petals larger than male; ovary ellipsoid, bristly. Fruit firm, soft-spiny, ellipsoid, 2–5cm; stalk stout, about 1cm. Arabia, NE Africa.

C.dudaim L. See *C.melo* Dudaim Group.
C.erinaceus hort. See *C.anguria*.
C.flexuosus L. See *C.melo* ssp. *melo* var. *flexuosus*.
C.grossulariiformis hort. See *C.anguria*.

C.melo L. (*C.cognatus* Cogn.) MELON.
Annual, occasionally perennial, trailing or prostrate. Stems angular and hirsute to terete and glabrous. Leaves 5–15 × 5–15cm, membranous, subreniform, obtuse, 5-angled or shallowly 3–5-lobed, soft villous throughout, the veins especially, lobes broad, rounded; petiole hispid-pubescent, 3–10cm. Male flowers in fascicles; females solitary; calyx tube villous, 5–8mm, lobes subulate; corolla 1–2cm; ovary ellipsoid to cylindric, pubescent. Fruit 3–10 × 2–7cm, highly variable in cultivation; seeds white, emarginate, oblong, compressed. Cultivated throughout warmer regions. ssp. *melo* (*C.melo* var. *cultus* Kurz). SWEET MELON; MUSK MELON. Annual. Leaves softly pubescent. Flowers 2–3cm. Fruit subspherical to ellipsoid. Many cultivars varying in fruit characteristics cultivated throughout the tropics and subtropics.

Cantalupensis Group. CANTELOUPE. Fruit medium-sized, rind hard, rough, not netted, flesh sweet, fragrant.

Chito Group. MANGO MELON; ORANGE MELON; MELON APPLE; VINE PEACH. Fruit yellow or orange, lemon- or orange-shaped and -sized, flesh white, scarcely edible.

Conomon Group. ORIENTAL PICKLING MELON. Fruit smooth, globose to club-shaped, fleshy, white or green, rather hard; used for pickling.

Dudaim Group. DUDAIM MELON; QUEEN ANNE'S POCKET MELON; STINK MELON. Fruit small, marbled, very fragrant.

Inodorus Group. HONEYDEW MELON; WINTER MELON. Fruit large, rind smooth or wrinkled, flesh white or green, somewhat fragrant.

Reticulatus Group. MUSK MELON; NETTED MELON; PERSIAN MELON. Fruit medium-sized to large, rind with coarse netted markings, flesh orange and muskily fragrant.

var. *flexuosus* (L.) Naudin (*C.flexuosus* L.). SERPENT MELON; SNAKE MELON. Fruit elongated, furrowed, to 90cm. ssp. *agrestis* (Naudin) Greb. Ovary densely puberulous, with adpressed forward-pointing hairs. Cult. in India and Pakistan. var. *momordica* (Roxb.) Cogn. (*C.momordica* Roxb.). PHOOT; KACHRA; SNAP MELON. Fruit ovoid to cylindric, glabrous, yellow, 30–60×7–15cm. *C.melo* var. *cultus* Kurz. See *C.melo* ssp. *melo*.

C.metuliferus Naudin. AFRICAN HORNED CUCUMBER. Annual, climbing or trailing. Stem hispid-pubescent. Leaves 4–10cm, broadly ovate, cordate, usually 3-lobed, serrate, long-pubescent especially on nerves beneath, lobes ovate-triangular; petioles long-pubescent. Male flowers in clusters, 1–4-flowered, to 1cm; female flowers solitary, 2–6cm; calyx tube pale green; petals 6–15 × 2–10cm; ovary pale green with fleshy spines. Fruit to 10cm, oblong, orange marked red with blunt, conical spines to 12mm when ripe. Tropical Africa to S Africa.

C.momordica Roxb. See *C.melo* ssp. *agrestis* var. *momordica*.

C.odoratissimus Moench. See *C.melo*.

C.prophetarum L. GLOBE CUCUMBER. Climber or trailer to 2m. Stems scabrid, somewhat thickened. Leaves 1–5×1–6cm, ovate to suborbicular, cordate to truncate, sinuate-toothed, usually deeply 3–5-lobed; petiole hispid, to 9cm. Male flowers in clusters of 1–6; calyx tube green, to 5mm; petals yellow, to 7m; female flowers solitary; tube to 4mm, petals to 8mm; ovary ellipsoid, softly papillose. Fruit subglobose to ellipsoid, 2–7cm; stalk 1–4cm; seeds elliptic in outline, compressed. Tropical Africa to Pakistan and India. ssp. *dissectus* (Naudin) C. Jeffrey (*C.figarei* var. *dissectus* Naudin).To 1.4m. Stems

scabrid. Leaves to 9×8cm. Fruit softly aculeate. Zaire to NE Africa and Arabia.

C.sacleuxii Paill. & Boiss. Stems long- and short-pubescent, irritant. Leaves 3–9 × 4–11cm, palmate, broadly ovate, densely pubescent, longer irritant hairs on venation beneath, serrate, lobes 5–7, triangular, acute to obtuse. Male flowers 1–3; pedicel to 1.5cm; petals yellow, rounded, to 10mm; female flowers on bristly pedicel; petals to 12mm; ovary fusiform, pubescent, to 1.5cm. Fruit obovoid to ellipsoid, terete, smooth except for scattered spines, green striped yellow, 6–8 × 4–5cm; seed about 7mm. E Africa, Madagascar.

C.sativus L. CUCUMBER; GHERKIN; KHIRA. Trailing. Stems rough, hairy, angular. Leaves 12–18cm, triangular-ovate, often 3–8-lobed, hispid or scabrid, lobes acute; petiole 1–2cm. Male flowers clustered in axils, female flowers usually solitary; sep. spreading; corolla about 2.5cm; ovary hispid, fusiform. Fruit clustered, globose to oblong or short-cylindric, tuberculate or prickly when young, highly variable in size and form; seeds about 11mm.

C.zeyheri Sonder (*C.africanus* Thunb. non L. f.). Herbaceous perennial trailer or climber. Base woody. Stems herbaceous, slender, angular, to 2m. Leaves 3–10 × 2–7cm, firm, palmate, ovate-elliptic to oblong, lobes 3–5, acute to obtuse, lanceolate to obovate, denticulate, median lobe longest, often lobulate, scabrid or setose. Male flowers fascicled or solitary, to 2cm; female flowers solitary, to 3cm; receptacle pubescent, 3–4mm; sep. subulate, erect to 4mm; corolla slightly pubescent, 3–5mm; ovary ellipsoid to oblong, setose. Fruit ellipsoid, yellow, spiny. Angola, Zimbabwe, S Africa.

Cucurbita L. (Lat. word for a type of gourd.) Cucurbitaceae. 27 species of monoecious, annual or perennial herbs. Stems prostrate or climbing; tendrils opposite leaves, simple or 2-5-branched. Leaves alternate, entire to lobed, large, palmately ribbed, scabrous to pubescent. Male flowers large, yellow to yellow-white, solitary or clustered in axils; calyx campanulate, 5-lobed; corolla campanulate, 5-lobed; stamens 3, inserted on calyx tube, filaments free, anthers connate, forming a conspicuous body; female flowers solitary, on short peduncles; corolla similar to male, but staminodes 3; ovary inferior, oblong or globose, 3-locular, occasionally falsely 5-locular; stigma 3, 2-lobed. Fruit a berry (pepo), indehiscent, with tough, hard rind, variable in shape and colour, flesh thick, succulent, edible; seeds numerous, ovate or ovate-oblong, margin often thickened, white, tawny or black. Tropical and Warm America. Z10 unless specified.

CULTIVATION One of the most economically important genera in the Cucurbitaceae, *Cucumis* contains the pumpkins, squashes, marrows and courgettes, and several species which produce gourds used both practically and ornamentally. The variation within each of these crops is too wide-ranging to be treated here, as are their cultural requirements, for which the reader is referred to 'Gourds', 'Pumpkins' and Squashes' and 'Marrows' in *The New RHS Dictionary of Gardening* (1992) and to Herklots, *Plantsman* (1986).

C.andreana Naudin. Annual vine. Stems long-running, to 20m, rooting at nodes. Leaves 3-lobed, green marbled white; petiole long, setose. Male flowers smaller than in *C.pepo*, yellow; calyx lobes linear, acute; corolla to 9cm, lobes acute. Fruit obovoid, 6–15cm, green striped white and yellow; seeds to 5mm, numerous, black. Uruguay, Argentina.

C.argyrosperma hort. ex L.H. Bail. (*C.mixta* Pang.). SILVER-SEED GOURD; CUSHAW. Annual. Stems long-running, smooth, glabrous; tendrils 3–4-fid, short. Leaves *c*20cm, cordate-ovate or cordate-reniform, shallowly lobed, obtuse, scarious, slightly pubescent, denticulate. Male flowers yellow; *c*6cm; calyx narrow, lobes 2–3cm; corolla striped green. Fruit 15–20cm, globose to ovoid, rind hard, grey-white striped and marked green; peduncle angular, enlarged; seeds to 3cm, flat, deep-margined. Mexico. Z9.

C.citrullus L. See *Citrullus lanatus*.

C.cordata S. Wats. Pubescent perennial. Stems slender, angled; tendrils short, coiled. Leaves 4–8 × 5–10cm, ovate, cordate, 3–5-lobed, nearly to middle, lobes rounded or acute, lobulate, pubescent, more densely so below, irregularly toothed; petiole to 5cm, hispidulous. Flowers solitary; female flowers *c*7cm; calyx lobes short; ovary oblong, slightly pubescent. Fruit globose, *c*8cm, green with 5 clear, pale stripes, and secondary stripes and marks; peduncle angled; seeds ovate, *c*11mm. Summer. Baja California, Mexico. Z9.

C.digitata A. Gray. Perennial. Stems trailing, slender, angled, pilose; tendrils short, branched. Leaves suborbicular, pedately 5-lobed, lobes 5–10cm, linear-lanceolate, acuminate, 2 lateral lobes again divided, slightly hirsute above, closely hairy below, margins often with few angles or teeth. Male flowers yellow; calyx tube to 3cm, cylindrical, lobes 7–10mm, narrow; corolla to 8cm. Fruit 8–9cm, subglobose, dark green striped white-green; peduncle slender; seeds *c*1cm, white. Arizona, New Mexico, S California. Z4.

C.ficifolia Bouché (*C.melanosperma* A. Braun ex Gasparr.).
CIDRA; SIDRA; FIG-LEAVED GOURD; MALABAR GOURD.
Perennial vine. Stems stout, setose to pilose, becoming
woody at base; tendrils many times divided. Leaves
15–25cm, subreniform to orbicular-ovate, shallowly to
deeply lobed, or sinuate, basal sinus deep; petiole 5–20cm,
stout. Male flowers yellow to pale orange; calyx tube
5–7mm, lobes linear; corolla lobes spreading; cor. of female
flowers to 12cm diam. Fruit 15–35cm, ovoid to globose,
green striped white, flesh white; seeds c1.5cm, ovate-orbicular, black. Mexico to Chile.

C.foetidissima Kunth (*C.perennis* (James) A. Gray).
CALABAZILLA; MISSOURI GOURD; BUFFALO GOURD; FOETID
WILD PUMPKIN.
Perennial. Stems to 6m, rooting at nodes; tendrils stout, short.
Leaves 15–30cm, triangular-ovate, base cordate or truncate,
acute, occasionally lobed, grey-green, scabrous above, entire
to sinuate-dentate. Male flowers 10–12cm; calyx tube
15–20mm, lobes linear, to 3mm; corolla ribbed; female flowers 9–10cm. Fruit 6–7cm, oblong to globose, green striped and
marked cream; seeds c12mm. Nebraska to California, Mexico.

C.hispida Thunb. See *Benincasa hispida*.
C.lagenaria L. See *Lagenaria siceraria*.
C.leucantha hort. See *Lagenaria siceraria*.

C.lundelliana L.H. Bail.
Annual to perennial vine, sparsely hirsute or glabrous. Stems
prostrate or scandent, slender; tendrils often simple. Leaves
5–9 × 4–7cm, broadly ovate, cordate, deeply 5-lobed, lobes
obtuse, short-pilose above; petiole 2–12cm, slender, denticulate. Male flowers 6–7.5cm, solitary, yellow to orange-yellow; calyx 5–9mm, lobes narrow, linear; corolla lobes obtuse
or acute. Fruit c7 × 6cm, globose-oblong, green or yellow-
tinged, glabrous; seeds 10–12mm with wrinkled margin.
Guatemala, SE Mexico, British Honduras.

C.maxima Duchesne ex Lam. AUTUMN SQUASH; WINTER
SQUASH; PUMPKIN.
Annual. Stems often long-running, striate, slightly hirsute or
setose. Leaves orbicular to reniform, obtuse, occasionally
with rounded lobes, often sinuate. Flowers light to bright yellow, faintly scented; calyx tube obovate, lobes narrow, short;
corolla lobes spreading, obtuse, soft. Fruit variably globose,
oblong, compressed-cylindric, yellow, red, orange, or green;
peduncle cylindric, smooth, spongy; seeds white or pale-
coloured. Summer. S America, widely cultivated. Z9.

C.melanosperma A. Braun ex Gasparr. See *C.ficifolia*.
C.melopepo L. See *C.pepo*.
C.mixta Pang. See *C.argyrosperma*.

C.moschata (Duchesne ex Lam.) Duchesne ex Poir. PUMPKIN;
CANADA PUMPKIN; CROOKNECK SQUASH; WINTER SQUASH.
Annual vine. Stems softly hairy. Leaves broad-ovate to suborbicular, often shallowly 5-lobed, green marked white. Male
flowers large, yellow; calyx lobes leafy, large; corolla lobes

spreading, subacute. Fruit very variable, often oblong or
crookneck, on expanded, ridged peduncle. Spring–summer.
US to S America. Fruit ripens in autumn and winter, many
cultivated forms.

C.okeechobeensis (Small) L.H. Bail.
Annual vine. Stems climbing, slender, hirsute, glabrescent;
tendrils simple or 3–4-branched. Leaves 12–20cm, suborbicular to reniform, base cordate, apex short-triangular, 5–7-
angled, slightly pubescent below, sharp-toothed; petiole
pubescent becoming glabrous. Male flowers white to cream;
calyx tube campanulate, lobes small; corolla c6cm, lobes
curving. Fruit 7–8cm, subglobose, green, marked white, flesh
white, bitter; seeds 11–12mm. Florida..

C.palmata S. Wats.
Perennial vine. Stems sulcate, grey, hispidulous; tendrils usually short, branched. Leaves 6–10cm diam., suborbicular in
outline, cordate, palmately 5-lobed, lobes cut below middle,
narrow, acuminate, terminal lobe longer, 5–6cm, tough,
canescent, short-hirsute; petiole shorter than leaf. Male flowers to 8cm; calyx tube 2–2.5cm; corolla ribbed, pubescent;
female flowers to 8cm; corolla ribbed. Fruit 8–9cm, subglobose, dull green, banded and marked green-white; peduncle
stout; seeds 10–12mm, white. S California.

C.pepo L. (*C.melopepo* L.). AUTUMN PUMPKIN; SUMMER
PUMPKIN; AUTUMN SQUASH; SUMMER SQUASH; VEGETABLE
MARROW; MARROW; COURGETTE; ZUCCHINI
Highly variable hispid annual. Stems short or trailing, prickly,
occasionally soft-hairy. Leaves triangular or ovate-triangular,
cordate, often deeply 5-lobed, lobes obtuse, large, hispid.
Flowers c10cm diam., orange-yellow; corolla large, lobes
erect, acute. Fruit variable in shape and size, often orange or
green when mature; peduncle strongly angled, 5–8-ridged,
short; seeds tawny. Spring–summer. US, widely cultivated.

C.perennis (James) A. Gray. See *C.foetidissima*.
C.siceraria Molina. See *Lagenaria siceraria*.

C.sororia L.H. Bail.
Climbing annual, resembling *C.texana*. Leaves 3-lobed or
3–5-angled, more scabrous beneath; petioles strigose and
downy. Calyx and corolla more hairy than *C.texana*. Fruit
longer than wide, mottled not striped; seeds c9 × 4–5mm. S
Mexico.

C.texana (Scheele) A. Gray (*Tristemon texanum* Scheele).
Climbing annual. Stems slender, angled, pilose; tendrils 2–5-
branched, slender, spiralling. Leaves 12–14cm, ovate-pyrami-
dal in outline, base cordate, 5-lobed nearly to middle, sinuses
closed, scabrous above, denticulate. Male flowers 7–8cm,
pale yellow, on long pedicels; calyx tube pilose, lobes narrow; corolla slightly pilose, veined; female flowers slightly
shorter. Fruit c6cm diam., variable, ovoid to pyriform, green,
striped pale green; peduncle to 5cm, sulcate; seeds 9–10 ×
5–7mm. Texas.

Cuspidaria DC. (Probably referring to the cuspidate capsules of some species, e.g. *C.pterocarpa*.)
Bignoniaceae. 8 species of lianes. Branches subterete, finely fluted, with glandular patches at nodes. Leaves unijugate, with or without simple tendril, or trifoliate, or simple; pseudostipules inconspicuous or lacking.
Inflorescences axillary or terminal thyrses; bracts and bracteoles small, deciduous; calyx campanulate, 5-den-
tate; corolla funnelform-campanulate, limb slightly oblique; stamens included; anthers markedly curved, ciliate;
disc pulvinate; ovary ovoid-ellipsoid, glandular-scaly; ovules 2–4-seriate. Fruit linear-oblong capsule, 4-winged,
woody; seeds transverse oblong, in membranous wing. Tropical Americas. Z10.

CULTIVATION   As for *Bignonia*.

C.floribunda (DC.) A. Gentry (*Adenocalymma floribunda*
DC.).
Leaflets 7.5 × 5cm, ovate, base attenuate, apex acuminate,
glabrous. Corolla 2.5cm, crimson. Bolivia.

C.pterocarpa (Cham.) DC. (*Bignonia pterocarpa* Cham.;
Nouletia pterocarpa (Cham.) Pichon). CIPO-CRUZ.
Leaflets 4–11 × 2–6cm, ovate-lanceolate to ovate, apex acumi-
nate, base acute or rounded, margin ciliate, veins pubescent.
Corolla 3.5–5.5cm, lilac-pink or white. Brazil, Paraguay, NE
Argentina.

Cyclanthera Schräd. (From Gk *kyklos*, circle, and *anthera*, anther.) Cucurbitaceae. 15 species of monoecious, annual or perennial vines. Stems closely grooved, glabrous to pubescent. Tendrils simple to compound, often bifid, glabrous to pubescent. Leaves lanceolate to orbicular, simple to 3–9-lobed, petiolate. Male flowers small, in axillary racemes or narrow panicles; calyx 5-lobed; corolla 5-lobed, rotate, yellow-white or tinged green; stamens 1, with anthers connate into head, and anther locules united in 2 horizontal rings; female flowers larger than males, commonly solitary; ovary ovoid, with 1–3 carpels, style 1. Fruit explosively dehiscent or occasionally indehiscent, spiny or setose, rarely smooth; seeds ovoid, few to many, slightly compressed, margin often appendaged. S US to Argentina. Z10.

CULTIVATION   As for *Sechium*.

C.brachybotrys (Poepp. & Endl.) Cogn. (*Momordica brachybotrys* Poepp. & Endl.).
Stems puberulent at nodes, otherwise glabrous. Tendrils bifid. Leaves 7–12cm diam., 3-lobed, lobes triangular to oblong, crenate, lateral lobes shorter, punctate-scabrous above, paler and scabrous beneath; petiole 2–4cm. Male flowers on filiform peduncles; calyx 1.5mm diam., lacking teeth; corolla yellow-white or tinged green; female flowers subsessile. Fruit to 3cm, slightly spiny. Peru.

C.brachystachya (Ser.) Cogn. (*C.explodens* Naudin).
Stems to 3m, glabrous. Tendrils unequally bifid. Leaves 5–10cm diam., ovate to suborbicular, strongly 3–5-angled or -lobed, basal sinus deep, square, apex acute; petiole c3cm. Male flowers axillary, in short, delicate inflorescence; calyx green-white; sepals absent or obscure; corolla white, c1.5–2.5mm diam.; female flowers solitary, axillary. Fruit 2–4cm, spiny, explosively dehiscent. Summer. Mexico to Colombia, Ecuador.

C.explodens Naudin. See *C.brachystachya*.

C.pedata (L.) Schräd.
Annual vine to 4.5m. Stems glabrous. Tendrils bifid. Leaves 2.5–20cm, broadly ovate to orbicular, pedately 5-lobed, lobes lanceolate, glabrous, serrulate to dentate, basal sinus rounded; petiole 1–8cm. Male flowers axillary, in panicles, 10–20cm; corolla white, lobes c2mm; female flowers solitary in axils. Fruit to 16×6cm, indehiscent, sparsely setose, green-white. C & S America.

C.tonduzii Cogn. ex Dur. & Pittier.
Stems slender, glabrous, pubescent at nodes. Tendrils bifid. Leaves 5-foliate; leaflets 4–12cm, obtuse, acute, denticulate to crenate, often deeply lobed or 3-sect, punctate-scabrous above, glabrous beneath; petiole 3–10cm. Flowers white; male flowers 20–30 per peduncle; calyx 3mm diam.; corolla segments c2mm. Fruit 2–2.5×1–1.5cm, densely spiny. Costa Rica.

Cydista Miers. (From Gk *kydistos*, most glorious, referring to the flowers.) Bignoniaceae. 4 species of lianes. Branches terete or tetragonal; pseudostipules leafy or absent. Leaves simple or unijugate, sometimes tipped with simple tendril. Inflorescences axillary or terminal racemes or panicles, few-flowered; calyx cupular, truncate or irregularly bilabiate, lepidote to puberulent or hirsute; corolla tubular-funnelform, lepidote and often lightly puberulent outside; stamens and anthers glabrous, straight, divaricate; ovary narrowly cylindric, lepidote or puberulent; ovules 2-seriate; disc obsolete. Fruit a linear capsule, compressed. Americas. Z10.

CULTIVATION   As for *Clytostoma*.

C.aequinoctialis (L.) Miers (*Arrabidaea isthmica* Standl.; *Arrabidaea pseudochica* Kränzl.; *Bignonia aequinoctialis* L.; *Bignonia hostmannii* E. Mey; *Bignonia nitidissima* DC.; *Bignonia picta* HBK; *Bignonia spectabilis* Vahl; *Bignonia villosa* Vahl; *C.amoena* Miers; *C.spectabilis* (Vahl) Miers).
BEJUCO COLORADO; BEJUCO DE DANTA; VAQUERO BLANCO.
Stem to 8cm diam. Branches glabrous to pubescent Leaflets 5.4–16.2×2.2–9.2cm, ovate, apex acuminate to obtuse, base cuneate to truncate, membranous or papery, lepidote, pubescent, especially on veins; petioles 0.9–4.5cm; petiolules 0.8–3.9cm. Inflorescence paniculate; flowers fragrant; calyx 4–10×4–9cm, truncate to 5-lobed or bilabiate, lepidote or pubescent, sometimes glandular; corolla 2.5–7.6×0.6–2.2cm, white to lilac, lined chestnut, throat yellow, tube 1.9–5cm, lobes 0.6–2.6cm, glandular-lepidote outside, puberulent inside. Mexico, W Indies, to Brazil. var. *hirtella* (Benth.) A. Gentry (*Anemopaegma tonduzianum* Kränzl.; *Arrabidaea guatemalensis* Schum. & Loes.; *Bignonia sarmentosa* Bertol.; *Bignonia sarmentosa* var. *hirtella* Benth.; *C.pubescens* Blake; *C.sarmentosa* (Bertol.) Miers; *Levya nicaraguensis* Bur. ex Baill.). Leaflets conspicuously hairy on veins beneath; calyx and inflorescence conspicuously hairy. Mexico to N Colombia.

C.amoena Miers. See *C.aequinoctialis*.
C.praepensus (Miers) Sandw. See *Mansoa difficilis*.
C.pubescens Blake. See *C.aequinoctialis* var. *hirtella*.
C.sarmentosa (Bertol.) Miers. See *C.aequinoctialis* var. *hirtella*.
C.spectabilis (Vahl) Miers. See *C.aequinoctialis*.

Cynanchum L. (From Gk *kynos*, dog, and *ancho*, to strangle: some species are poisonous.) Asclepiadaceae. 100 species of perennial herbs. Stems climbing or erect with twining tips. Leaves opposite or whorled. Flowers cymose, 5-merous, corolla usually rotate, deeply lobed, corona small; anthers with apical membranous appendages. Fruit a slender or thick follicle. Tropics & Subtropics.

CULTIVATION   A diverse genus of climbing and sprawling herbs, the tropical species with succulent stems should be treated as for *Ceropegia*. Those from cooler climates are close to *Vincetoxicum* in both appearance and requirements.

C.acuminatifolium Hemsl. See *C.ascyrifolium*.

C.ampanihensis Jum. & Perrier (*C.humbertii* Choux).
Stems to 1m × 2mm, creeping or somewhat climbing; branches numerous, fusiform, 3–8cm long, 2–3mm thick, flushed purple-red. Leaves 1.5×0.7mm, scale-like, triangular. Inflorescence paired, 5-flowered, to 6mm across; corolla lobes 5, strongly reflexed, 2.5–3×1.5–2mm; corona 6×3mm, outer lobes with sharply pointed, 3mm spine, inner lobes with 2mm spines. Madagascar. Z10.

C.aphyllum (Thunb.) Schltr. (*Asclepias aphyllum* Thunb.; *Sarcocyphala gerrardii* Harv.; *Sarcostemma tetrapterum* Turcz.; *C.sarcostemmatoides* Schum.).
Stems scrambling, branching freely, rooting at nodes; branches 1.5–3mm thick, internodes 10–40cm. Leaves 3×1mm. Flowers in sparse umbels produced from a tuberculate projection; corona green striped brown. Southern & Tropical Africa, SW Madagascar. Z10.

C.ascyrifolium (Franch. & Savat.) Matsum. (*C.acuminatifolium* Hemsl.) CRUEL PLANT, MOSQUITO PLANT.
Crisped-hairy herb to 1m; stems erect, often twining above. Leaves to 15cm, ovate or elliptic, acuminate. Cymes axillary, paniculate, corolla white, to 1.25cm diam., corona lobes slightly shorter than stigma. Fruit to 15cm, broadly lanceolate. Japan, NE Asia. Z8.

C.compactum Choux.
Stolons subterranean; stems 20–30cm tall, 3–5mm thick, grey-green, sometimes red-violet; in habitat stems are annual, but in cultivation they are longer-lived and elongated to 50cm, forming dense clumps, internodes 1–3cm. Leaves reduced to scales 1–1.3mm long. Flowers to 8mm diam., borne in short-stalked terminal clusters of 10–15, yellow-green; corona white. SC Madagascar. var. *imerinense* Descoings. Differs in having stems more slender; flowers smaller; growth form more attractive. Madagascar. Z10.

C.crispum Jacq. See *Fockea crispa*.

C.humbertii Choux. See *C.ampanihensis*.

C.laeve (Michx.) Pers. (*Ampelamus albidus* (Nutt.) Britt.; *Gonolobus laevis* Michx.). HONEY VINE; BLUE VINE; SAND VINE.
Twining herb to 2m. Leaves to 9cm, triangular, deeply cordate with a broad sinus. Cymes axillary, raceme-like, shorter than leaves, corolla white, to 1cm diam., lobes more or less erect, corona lobes deeply bifid, much longer than stigma. Fruit to 15cm, lanceolate. SE US (Pennsylvania south to Georgia and Texas). Z8.

C.macrolobum Jum. & Perrier.
Shrub to 40cm, branching irregularly from base; stems 6mm thick, surface prominently verrucose due to peeling waxy surface. Inflorescence terminal, few-flowered; flowers green-maroon-brown, 1.3cm diam.; corolla lobes 5mm, radiating, with a central groove; corona lobes dentate at tips. SW Madagascar. Z10.

C.mahafalense Jum. & Perrier.
Stems liana-like, 4–6mm diam., several metres long, twining, grey, internodes 15cm. Leaves minute, caducous. Flowers 4–5mm diam., terminal on short spurs, 3–5 together; corolla tube to 1.5mm, campanulate, lobes beige, oval-oblong, with 3 wine red veins; corona white, with 10 dentate lobes. SC Madagascar.

C.marnieranum Rauh.
Low, much-branched shrub; stems succulent, erect to creeping, 5–7mm thick, dark to olive green, covered with irregularly spaced tubercles and short white hairs. Leaves to 1.5mm, deciduous. Inflorescence 3–5-flowered; pedicels 3–6mm; corolla lobes 5–6mm, bright yellow, remaining united at the tips when the flower first opens, giving the appearance of a tubeless *Ceropegia*; corona white, 1.5–2mm tall. The most easily recognizable species and the one most frequently seen in cultivation. C Madagascar. Z10.

C.nigrum (L.) Pers. See *Vincetoxicum nigrum*.

C.nodosum (Jum. & Perrier) Descoings (*Mahafalia nodosum* Jum. & Perrier).
Stems clambering, cylindric, 4–10mm thick, glabrous but covered with thick, white, cracking layer of wax, thickened at nodes, internodes to 1cm. Flowers 8–13 in small umbels. S Madagascar. Z10.

C.perrieri Choux.
Shrub, branching from base, 80–160cm; stems erect, terete or slightly angular, 9–13mm thick, grey-green, surface smooth or rough, nodes prominent. Inflorescence usually 5-flowered, borne near stem tips; flowers small; corolla lobes insignificant, fused at base, recurved, with a deep central nerve on upper surface; corona white, incurved to form a distinct pentangle. Madagascar. Z10.

C.pycneuroides Choux.
Stolons creeping, subterranean; stems erect, unbranched, 40–60cm tall, to 2.5cm thick at base; bark green. Leaves to 6cm × 3mm, long-acicular, arranged in 5–7 oblique rows, remaining on plant for 1–2 years. Inflorescence borne beside leaf base; corolla lobes green-white, joined to form a short tube at base, oval, oblong, 4–6×2–3mm. C Madagascar. Z10.

C.rauhianum Descoings.
Stems to 80cm, scarcely branching, 4-angled to subterete, 6–10mm thick, glabrous with a waxy layer, constricted at nodes, segments 4–5cm. Inflorescence terminal, many-flowered; corolla 4mm diam., lobes 4.5–5 × 2mm, brown-green, oval-oblong, obtuse, papillose above, with a central groove; corona white, distinctly pentangular. SE Madagascar. Z10.

C.rossii Rauh.
Forming dense, 1m-wide mats of creeping growths; stems 4-angled, dark green, lanate; flowering stems erect, more rounded. Leaves scale-like, caducous. Flowers solitary or paired, never clustered; corolla lobes 4 × 2.5mm, strongly reflexed, olive green edged cream-white above, yellow-green beneath, hairy when young. S Madagascar. Z10.

C.sarcostemmatoides Schum. See *C.aphyllum*.

C.vincetoxicum (L.) Pers. See *Vincetoxicum officinale*.

Cyphostemma (Planch.) Alston. (From Gk *kyphos*, curved, and *stemma*, wreath.) Vitaceae. 150 species of perennial succulent and non-succulent caudiciform shrubs, climbers and vines; most spp. in cultivation caudiciform and succulent. Some species forming large swollen trunks, often clavate, tapering, not segmented, lacking tendrils; others with or without a subterranean caudex, stems erect to clambering or prostrate with rudimentary tendrils at first. Leaves clustered at ends of shoots, more or less fleshy, glabrous or felted, deciduous, simple, pinnate or tripartite, less often palmate or digitate. Inflorescence a lax corymb; flowers small, usually yellow-green; corolla almost cylindric, constricted midway; stigmas 2-lobed. Fruit a variously coloured fleshy berry, usually with only one large seed. Southern & E Africa, Madagascar. Z9.

CULTIVATION Succulent plants for the sunny conservatory or intermediate glasshouse, *Cyphostemma* species are grown for their unusual appearance and habit of growth. The glossy, bright green foliage emerges from the top of obese and gouty, club-shaped stems which as they mature become almost woody with thin, peeling, papery bark. They usually drop their leaves in late summer, and may then enter a long resting period, failing to produce leaves the following spring; continue to water as normal during the summer and maintain over winter in an almost dry state, they should then resume normal growth the following season. Grow in full sun in a freely draining, sandy potting mix with additional grit for drainage and a little organic matter. Water sparingly when in growth and keep dry in winter. Maintain a minimum temperature of 10°C/50°F, although plants will survive temperatures as low as 4°C/39°F in dry, well ventilated conditions; in this case the growing tip may die out but if cut back to healthy tissue should regenerate in spring. Propagate by seed in spring, or from cuttings.

C.cirrhosum (Thunb.) Descoings (*Vitis cirrhosa* Thunb.; *Cissus cirrhosus* (Thunb.) Willd.).
Stems succulent, compressed, curved in different directions with tufted hairs, bark grey. Leaves petiolate, obovate, pointed, sharply serrate, bracts sessile or amplexicaul, tendrils simple. Flowers white. S Africa (W Cape).

C.cornigerum Descoings.
Stems 2×0.4m, fleshy, succulent, very sappy, bark green, branches climbing, glandular at first, later glabrous. Petioles 2–6cm; leaves tripartite, leaflets 4.5–7.5 × 3.5cm, almost round, crenate, veins puberulous beneath. S Africa (SW Cape).

C.hereroense (Schinz) Descoings (*Cissus hereroensis* Schinz).
Caudex thick, tuberous, to 70cm; stems 30–50cm, 2–4, fleshy, prostrate, usually more or less flexuous, branches few, shortly grey-papillose. Leaves 5–7-partite, sessile, leaflets 8–10×1.5cm, lanceolate to narrow-lanceolate, coarsely crenate-serrate, lower surface grey-papillose. Namibia.

C.laza Descoings.
Stem 1–2×0.7–1m, narrowly conic, fleshy, bark parchment-like, branches 3–5m, 2–3, thickened at base, prostrate to clambering, white-felted when young. Leaves 7–16 × 5–11cm, pinnatifid. Madagascar.

Decumaria L. (From Lat. *decimus*, tenth, referring to the number of parts of the flower.) Hydrangeaceae. 2 species of deciduous or semi-evergreen shrubs climbing by means of adhesive aerial rootlets. Close in many respects to *Hydrangea anomala* and *Schizophragma hydrangeoides*, from which they may be distinguished by the inflorescence, composed wholly of similar, fertile flowers. Branchlets initially pubescent. Leaves opposite, ovate to oblong or orbicular, simple, entire or toothed, petiolate, estipulate. Inflorescence an umbellate, terminal or axillary panicle of small white flowers; sepals 7–10, calyx tube united to ovary; petals 7–10; stamens 20–30; ovary inferior, style very short, stigma capitate. Fruit a turbinate, several-seeded capsule, ribbed at base, dehiscing between ribs. W China, SE US.

CULTIVATION   Both are climbers suited to wall plantings or for growing through trees and over stumps; *D.barbara* is also sometimes grown as groundcover. Semi-deciduous, *D.barbara* will tolerate temperatures to –15°C/5°F; the evergreen *D.sinensis*, suited to east- or west-facing walls, is slightly less cold-tolerant. Grow in moist but well drained fertile soil, *D.barbara* in sun to semi-shade, *D.sinensis* in semi-shade. Prune after flowering to remove excess outward-facing growth on wall-grown plants, and to remove damaged growth after a severe winter. Propagate by semi-ripe nodal cuttings in a closed case with bottom heat; also by seed or layering in autumn.

D.barbara L. CLIMBING HYDRANGEA; WOOD VAMP.
To 10m. Leaves 5–10cm, ovate to ovate-oblong, usually tapering and obscurely toothed toward apex, initially slightly downy, becoming glossy, dark green above, puberulous beneath. Panicles 5–8cm diam., terminal, broad, rather domed; flowers sweetly fragrant. SE US. Z7.

Decumaria barbara

D.sinensis Oliv.
Seldom exceeding 4m. Leaves 3–7cm, sometimes persistent, obovate to orbicular, obtuse and sometimes serrate in apical half, matt mid-green. Panicles 3–8cm diam., terminal or axillary, flat-topped; flowers muskily scented. C China. Z8.

Delairea Lem. (For M. Delaire, 19th-century French botanist.) Compositae. 1 species, a succulent, climbing herb to 6m. Stems woody at base, much-branched. Leaves to 10 × 8cm, deltoid to orbicular-reniform, lobed, pubescent beneath, auriculate at base, lobes deltoid, acute; petioles to 11cm, with 2 basal, winged auricles. Capitula discoid, many, in dense corymbs; phyllaries c3mm, keeled, with 2–4 shorter, supplementary bracts; florets yellow; ovary bristly. Distinguished from *Senecio scandens* by the absence of ray florets. Spring–summer. S Africa, naturalized elsewhere. Z9.

CULTIVATION An evergreen, twining climber, grown primarily as a house or conservatory plant for its foliage, although moderately ornamental in bloom, bearing yellow groundsel-like flowers. In drier, mediterranean-type climate zones that are essentially frost-free (to –3°C/27°F), *Delairea* is used for screening and groundcover; it has naturalized in California. Otherwise, grow under glass, in sun or partial shade, in a medium-fertility, loam-based mix; water moderately when in full growth and maintain a minimum temperature of 5–7°C/40–45°F. Propagate by seed, layering or semi-ripe cuttings in summer.

D.odorata Lem. (*Senecio mikanioides* Otto ex Harv.).
GERMAN IVY; PARLOUR IVY.

Derris Lour. (From Gk *derris*, a leather covering, referring to the leathery pods.) Leguminosae (Papilionoideae). Some 40 species of woody climbers, trees or shrubs. Leaves imparipinnate or trifoliolate. Inflorescence terminal or axillary, a raceme or panicle; flowers many, usually clustered; calyx campanulate, subentire or denticulate, 2 upper teeth more or less connate; standard ovate to obovate, glabrous or pubescent, wings adhering to keel, keel slightly curved; stamens usually connate, occasionally 1 free, anthers equal; ovary subsessile, ovules few, style curved and tapering. Fruit flat, elliptic to narrow-oblong, pinioned along both sutures, or only the dorsal suture, flimsy to leathery; seeds 1, smooth or corrugated, oblong to reniform. Old World Tropics. Z10.

CULTIVATION *Derris* is found along muddy river banks and in low-altitude forest and mangrove swamps. The swollen roots of several species – particularly *D.elliptica* – contain rotenones; in chopped form, they were used as fish poisons; powdered derris root is widely used in horticulture as an insecticide. *Derris* is sometimes included in botanical collections for educational purposes; *D.scandens* is an attractive ornamental climber bearing a profusion of long pendulous racemes of pale flowers in addition to the handsome foliage which emerges a pale pink and deepens to bronze before turning dark green. These vigorous, woody twiners are suitable for training on wires or trellis in the warm greenhouse or conservatory, or, in the tropics and subtropics, through the branches of large trees in damp, shady, sheltered situations. Under glass, grow with a minimum night temperature of 16–18°C/60–65°F and bright indirect light in a free-draining, moisture-retentive, loam-based mix with additional organic matter; water moderately when in growth. Propagate from scarified seed, by 20–30cm/8–12in. semi-ripe cuttings or by single-node softwood cuttings, treated with rooting hormone and placed in a closed case with bottom heat.

D.elliptica (Wallich) Benth.TUBA ROOT; DERRIS ROOT.
Woody climber to 20m; stems rusty-pubescent at first, later glabrous, tough, coated with dark fissured bark. Leaves to 25cm, emerging bronze, hardening bright green; leaflets to 10 × 5cm, to 11, obovate, acute, coriaceous, nerves pubescent beneath. Racemes to 18cm, axillary; flowers white tinted rose-mauve. Burma to New South Wales.

D.scandens Benth. MALAY JEWEL VINE.
Climber to 20m; branchlets and leaves initially cinereous. Leaves 34–76cm; leaflets to 5cm, to 19, coriaceous, oblong or obovate-oblong, emerging bronze-pink, bright green, short-stalked. Racemes to 60cm, numerous, axillary; flowers pale rose. E India to Malay Peninsula, China, N Australia.

Dicentra Bernh. (From Gk *dis*, two, and *kentron*, spurred, referring to the 2-spurred flowers.) BLEEDING HEART. Fumariaceae (Papaveraceae). 19 species of annual or perennial deciduous herbs, arising from taproots, bulblets, tubers or rhizomes. Stemless or with stems 1–20 or more, erect, ascending or climbing. Leaves arranged in basal rosettes or alternately on upright stems, usually ternately decompound and long-petioled; leaflets subsessile, ovate to oblong-lanceolate, glabrous and occasionally glaucous, entire or serrate. Flowers in panicles, racemes or corymbs, or solitary, axillary or leaf-opposed, pendulous, heart-shaped in outline; sepals 2, rudimentary; petals 4 in 2 pairs: outer pair spurred at base and usually pouched, inner pair tongue-shaped, with convex inner faces and crested apices, forming a hood covering the anthers and ovary; stamens group in 2 bundles of 3, each bundle opposite an outer petal, filaments united almost to the anthers. Fruit fleshy or membranous capsules; seeds small, black or brown, usually sticky glandular. Asia, N America.

CULTIVATION Attractive, slender herbs with ferny foliage and trusses of heart-shaped yellow flowers, the following *Dicentra* species will thrive on moist, leafy soils, twining through sheltered shrubberies or on wires against walls unlikely to become too dry and scorched. They will tolerate temperatures to –15°C/5°F; in cold areas, protect crowns of perennial species with a dry mulch. Propagate by division of perennials; by seed of *D.torulosa* sown *in situ* in spring.

D.macrocapnos Prain (*D.scandens* auct.; *Dactylicapnos macrocapnos* (Prain) Hutch.)
Climbing perennial herb; stems to 1m, grooved, glabrous. Leaves decompound, to 8cm; petioles 3cm; basal leaves often modified into branched tendrils; lateral leaflets slightly smaller, broadly ovate, entire, equally or unequally acute, rounded or truncate at base, obtuse, apiculate at apex, glabrous. Flowers yellow, 2.2cm long, in leaf-opposed racemes 6cm long, bracteate; petals 22mm, crested at back. Himalaya.

D.scandens auct. See *D.macrocapnos*.

D.scandens (D.Don) Walp.
Climbing perennial. Stems several, 3–4m. Terminal leaflets tendril-like, others ovate to lanceolate, acute to strongly oblique at base, glabrous, 3–35 × 2-25mm, entire. Flowers in 2–14-flowered racemes, pendent, yellow or white, tipped pink or light purple, cordate in outline; outer petals 13–22 × 2-4mm, apices reflexed, spur 1–5mm: inner petals 13–18 × 3mm, crest exserted by 2mm. Summer. Himalaya. Z5.

D.thalictrifolia Wallich. See *D.scandens*

D.torulosa Hook.f. & Thoms. (*D.thalictrifolia* Wallich).
Climbing annual. Stems several, 2–4m. Leaves biternately decompound; terminal leaflets often tendril-like; leaflets glabrous, 3–33 × 2–10mm, margins entire, base oblique. Flowers pendent in 2–6-flowered corymbs; corolla lemon-yellow, elongate-cordate in outline; outer petals 10–14 × 1.5–3mm, apex reflexed by 2mm, spur 2mm; inner petals 9–12×2mm, crest exserted by 1–2mm. Summer. Nepal to SE China.

For illustration see Fumariaceae.

Dichelostemma Kunth. (From Gk *dichelos*, with two prongs, and *stemma*, garland.) Liliaceae (Alliaceae). 7 species of cormous perennial herbs, distinguished from *Brodiaea* by the leaves distinctly keeled beneath and conspicuously veined, the coloured bracts, the fertile stamens sometimes to 6 (always 3 in *Brodiaea*) and the stigma lobes short, not spreading. Corm tunic fibrous, dark brown. Leaves 2–5, long-linear, grassy, outspread to sprawling, usually shorter than scape, keeled beneath, channelled above. Scapes slender; flowers in an umbel, subtended by spathe valves; perianth campanulate; fertile stamens 3–6, inserted on inner perianth lobes; staminodes 3, inserted on outer lobes, sometimes with reduced anthers; ovary superior; style inflated toward apex, narrowly 3-winged. Fruit a loculicidal capsule; seeds long-ovoid, 3-angled, angles prominently ridged. Summer. W US.

CULTIVATION   This remarkable native of California produces clumps of rather undistinguished, grassy foliage from small corms, followed in mid to late spring by long flowering stems topped by umbels of nodding, pale pink flowers. These stems may be over a metre long and will twine and coil through surrounding shrubs and brushwood, or through supports such as pea-sticks and canes. It will survive outdoors in zone 8 if grown on perfectly drained, gritty soils with the protection of a sunny, south-facing wall and a dry mulch in winter. Otherwise, plant the corms at a depth of 5cm/2" in half pots of a sandy and gritty loam-based mix. Grow in the cool glasshouse, conservatory or alpine house. Admit full sunlight and ventilate freely. Water from mid spring to late summer; keep dry at other times. Support emerging scapes on birch twigs stuck in the soil. Propagate by detached cormlets.

D.californicum (Torr.) Alph. Wood. See *D.volubile*.

D.volubile (Kellogg) A.A. Heller (*Brodiaea volubilis* (Kellogg) Bak.; *Stropholirion californicum* Torr.). SNAKE LILY; TWINING BRODIAEA.
Scape to 150cm, clambering and twining; pedicels slender, spreading or pendent in flower, turning upwards in fruit; perianth to 2cm, pale to rose pink, tube 6-angled; staminodes white. California. Z8.

Dimorphanthera (Drude) F. Muell. ex J. J. Sm. Ericaceae. Some 70 species of evergreen scandent shrubs, many of them epiphytic. Branches long, arching to clambering, attaching themselves with short adventitious roots. Leaves leathery, dark green, elliptic to lanceolate. Flowers fleshy and waxy, tubular-campanulate, clustered in axils toward stem tips. Spring–summer. Malesia, New Guinea especially. Z9.

CULTIVATION   Magnificent evergreen shrubs for the cool greenhouse or conservatory, or for cool, airy and humid positions in subtropical gardens. They resemble larger and more luxuriant *Agapetes* species and have similar cultural requirements, but tend to favour slightly lower temperatures (minimum 10°C/50°F) and a more humid, montane-type atmosphere. The stems will root on brick walls and the trunks of course-barked trees and palms. They succeed best, however, if planted among mossy rocks, which they will soon cover with leathery dark green foliage lit up in spring and summer by waxy bell-shaped flowers. As yet, these plants are little-known in cultivation – undeservedly so, for they should thrive in Camellia house-type conditions, certainly associate well with Vireya Rhododendrons and experience little hardship in cool to intermediate orchid houses. Propagate by lengths of rooted stem.

D.amoena Sleum.
Clambering shrub to 3m. New growth hairy, bronze-red-tinted. Leaves to 25 × 10cm, oblong, entire. Flowers massed in axils; corolla tubular, to 4×1cm, rose to flesh pink or crimson. New Guinea.

D.dryophila Sleum.
Large liane, to 20m, entirely glabrous. New growth tinted red-bronze. Leaves to 25cm, ovate-lanceolate to elliptic. Flowers 3–5 per axillary cluster, pendulous; corolla tubular to 5×2cm, brilliant crimson. SW New Guinea.

D.kempteriana Schlecht.
Clambering liane. Leaves to 22 × 6cm, elliptic to broadly lanceolate, somewhat spirally arranged, rose-tinted when young. Flowers profusely borne; corolla to 3cm, campanulate, coral pink to crimson. New Guinea, New Britain.

D.megacalyx Sleum.
Clambering liane, rooting freely and broadly similar in appearance to *Hydrangea seemanii*. Leaves to 20cm, oblong-lanceolate, glabrous, leathery, dark green. Flowers in axillary clusters; corolla funnelform, to 3.5 × 2cm, fiery orange-red. New Guinea.

Dioscorea L. YAM. (For Dioscorides, 1st-century Greek physician and herbalist, author of *Materia medica.*) Dioscoreaceae. Some 600 species of monoecious or dioecious, scandent herbs. Stems twining, arising from tuberous roots. Leaves usually alternate, sometimes opposite, simple to palmately compound, base often cordate, axils sometimes bearing bulbils. Flowers small, usually green-white: males in small, axillary racemes, perianth campanulate, stamens 6; female flowers in spikes or spike-like racemes, opening widely, perianth deeply 6-lobed. Fruit a 3-angled or 3-winged capsule, dehiscent; seeds strongly compressed, winged. Tropical and subtropical regions. Z10 unless otherwise stated.

CULTIVATION   *Dioscorea* contains several species of great economic importance: the massive root tubers of *D.alata* and *D.batatus* are yams, cultivated throughout the tropics as sources of staple starch foods. They are also fast-growing dark green foliage cover for pergolas, fences and expanses of bare earth. Of the species listed below, only *D.balcanica* is fully hardy – an attractive herbaceous perennial producing long twining stems clothed with dark green, heart-shaped leaves and bearing drooping spikes of colourful fruit. It should be grown through shrubs in semi-shaded, damp situations. The remainder require fertile, well drained soils with full sun to part-shade and minimum temperatures of 13–16°C/55–60°F when in growth. Water sparingly as growth begins, increasing when in full growth. Withold water as foliage begins to yellow and store over-wintering tubers in their pots and in dry conditions with a minimum temperature of 7–10°C/45–50°F. Plants that produce small tubers, or no tubers at all (for example *D.bulbifera*), or seem likely to carry their stems and foliage over several seasons (e.g. *D.discolor*) ought not to be given a full winter rest. Support on wires or canes, or allow *D.alata* and *D.batatas* to creep. *D.amarantoides* produces dense panicles of small flowers. *D.discolor* is perhaps the most beautiful member of the genus - a luxuriant climber for shaded corners of the warm glasshouse, it carries large, quilted leaves zoned with satiny pale and dark green, patterned with silver-white and purple-red. Species hailing from dry, rocky places in Southern Africa tend to develop a large, woody exposed tuber top which resembles a domed or pyramidal caudex, fissured in *D.macrostachyra*, spectacularly cracked and plated in *D.elephantipes*. The vegetative growths of these caudiciforms tend to be short-lived and lush, in strong contrast to their desiccated, corky bases. These species should be grown in a sandy free-draining mix in full sunlight. Water moderately when in growth (usually a period of 2–3 months in spring and summer), very sparingly at other times. Propagate most species by division of the dormant tuber in spring; by detached aerial tubers for *D.alata*, *D.batatas* and *D.bulbifera*, and by seed for the caudiciform species.

D.alata L. WHITE YAM; WATER YAM.
Tubers to 2.5m, ovoid-cylinfdrcal Stem 4-winged or 4-angled, frequently with small axillary tubers. Leaves ovate to oblong, base cordate, glabrous, 7–9-nerved. Male flowers in branched spikes; female flowers in simple spikes. India to Malay Peninsula.

D.amarantoides Presl.
Stem somewhat angled. Leaves to 10 × 5cm, alternate, ovate-lanceolate to cordate, 7-nerved. Male flowers in a dense panicle to 40cm. Peru.

D.balcanica Kosanin.
Tuberous roots to 2cm diam. Stem to 150cm, cylindrical, twining clockwise. Leaves to 7 × 6cm, cordate or ovate, shortly acuminate, 9-nerved, long-petiolate. Fruiting spike to 7cm, drooping; fruit to 2.5cm diam. Balkans. Z6.

D.batatas Decne. CHINESE YAM; CINNAMON VINE.
Tuberous roots to 90cm, clavate or cylindrical. Stem somewhat angled, twining clockwise, green or green-purple, bearing small, axillary tubers. Leaves to 8cm, opposite, ovate, base cordate, 7–9-nerved, short-petiolate. Flowers white, in axillary racemes, cinnamon-scented. Temperate E Asia, naturalized US. Z5.

D.bulbifera L. AIR POTATO.
Tuberous roots small, globose, sometimes absent. Stem to 6m, bearing axillary, subspherical or angled tubers. Leaves to 25 × 18cm, usually alternate, sometimes opposite, ovate, base cordate, cuspidate; petiole to 14cm. Male flowers in spikes to 10cm; female flowers in spikes to 25cm. Tropical Africa and Asia.

D.cotinifolia Kunth.
Tuberous roots to 9 × 5cm. Stem twining anticlockwise. Leaves to 8 × 5cm, usually alternate, sometimes opposite, broadly ovate, subcordate or truncate at base; petiole to 3cm. Male flowers in racemes to 7.5cm; female flowers in racemes to 15cm. S Africa.

D.discolor Kunth.
Tuberous roots to 7cm diam. Stem slightly angled. Leaves to 15cm, ovate-cordate, apex cuspidate, patterned dark satiny green and lustrous light green above with a silvery white midrib and zones of silver-white, red-purple beneath. Flowers inconspicuous. Tropical S America.

D.elephantipes (L'Hérit.) Engl. (*Testudinaria elephantipes* (L'Hérit.) Burchell). ELEPHANT'S FOOT; HOTTENTOT BREAD; TORTOISE PLANT.
Tuberous roots to 90cm, exterior woody, fissured and faceted with trapezoid plates which enlarge and build up visible corky layers over the years. Stems to 6m, twining clockwise. Leaves to 6cm broad, alternate, suborbicular-cordate to reniform, shortly mucronate, 7–9-nerved. Male flowers in simple or branched racemes to 7.5cm; female flowers in simple racemes. S Africa.

D.hastifolia Nees.
Tuberous roots to 12 × 3cm. Stem to 9m, cylindrical, twining anti-clockwise. Leaves to 8cm, alternate, linear to linear-lanceolate or hastate. Male flowers in racemes to 8cm; female flowers in short, few-flowered racemes. W Australia.

Dioscorea (a) *D. elephantipes* (b) *D. discolor*

D.macrostachya Benth. (*Testudinaria macrostachya* (Benth.) Rowley).
Tuberous roots to 20cm diam., deeply corrugated. Stem somewhat angled, twining clockwise. Leaves to 20 × 18cm, ovate, acuminate, base cordate, long-petiolate. Male flowers in few-flowered clusters, in racemes to 30cm; female flowers solitary, in racemes. C America.

D.trifida L.f. CUSH-CUSH; YAMPEE.
Tuberous roots small. Stems sharply angled or narrowly winged, twining clockwise. Leaves to 25cm, 3-lobed, cordate, puberulent above, pilose veins beneath. Male flowers in racemes; female flowers in spikes. S America, W Indies.

Diplocyclos (Endl.) T. Post & Kuntze. (From Gk *diploos*, double, and *kyklos*, circle.) Cucurbitaceae. 4 species of monoecious climbing, perennial herbs; tendrils 2-fid. Leaves simple, palmate, lobes 5. Flowers small, white to pale yellow, in leaf axils, male flowers clustered, female flowers solitary; calyx campanulate, lined by nectary, 5-lobed; corolla 5-lobed, campanulate, entire; stamens 3, inserted on calyx (staminodes in female flowers); disc annular; ovary inferior, cylindric (pistillode absent in male flowers); style 1, slender, stigmas 3. Fruit a berry, subovoid, red, variegated, solitary or clustered, fleshy, thin-walled; seeds pyriform with double-grooved margin. Tropical Africa to Tropical Asia and Pacific Is. Z10.

CULTIVATION   As for *Momordica*.

D.palmatus (L.) C. Jeffrey (*Bryonia palmata* L.).
Stem glabrous, slender, becoming ridged and white-spotted. Rootstock fleshy. Leaves broadly ovate, 4–14 × 4–15cm, glabrous, deeply lobed, lobes 3–5, linear-lanceolate to elliptic, entire or sinuate. Flowers white or pale yellow, male flowers in clusters coaxillary with smaller female flowers. Fruit green or red, with white stripes, in clusters of 1–5, ovoid, 1.5 × 2.5cm; seeds about 6 × 4mm. Tropical Africa, Tropical Asia to N Australia.

Diplopterygium (Diels) Nak. Gleicheniaceae. About 20 species of scandent, thicket-forming, terrestrial ferns. Rhizomes long-creeping, slender, wiry, much-branched, scaly. Primary pinnae to 2m, bipinnatifid; pinnules elongate, pinnatifid, cut almost to main vein; dormant bud covered by overlapping scales; veins free, forked once. Sori numerous on ultimate segments; sporangia 2–5 per sorus. Tropical and warm temperate Asia to W Pacific. Z10.

CULTIVATION   A very vigorous fern for beds in large warm glasshouses and conservatories or humid, shaded areas of subtropical and tropical gardens where its invasive habit will not be too vexatious. It resembles a giant dark green bracken, but with rhizomes and tiered, branching fronds which scramble into surrounding vegetation forming dense tangles. Grown in semi-shade in moist, close conditions in an open, bark-based medium. Propagate by division.

D.longissimum (Bl.) Nak. (*Gleichenia longissima* Bl.) GIANT SCRAMBLING FERN.
Large scrambling fern forming dense thickets to 6m high; stipes 30–100cm, green, smooth and glossy. Fronds rusty-scaly all over when young, persistently so beneath; primary pinnae 60–100cm; pinnules sessile, oblique, rounded at apex, dark green above, glaucous beneath; dormant bud covered by dark brown scales with pale margin. Pacific region, Australia to China.

Dipogon Liebm. (From Gk *di-*, two, and *pogon*, beard.) Leguminosae (Papilionoideae). 1 species, a perennial vine. Stems woody at base; branches narrow, long, somewhat pubescent. Leaves alternate; leaflets to 4cm, rhomboid, acute, glaucous beneath; stipules entire, somewhat deltoid. Flowers to 1.25cm, in pendulous axillary clusters of 3–6; bracts acute, hirsute, narrow and tapering to each end; calyx campanulate, pubescent, lips 2, upper lip 2-toothed, lower lip 3-toothed; corolla rose to mauve or white, standard rounded, reflexed, keel falcate, obtuse, clawed, partly connate, wings blunt, clawed, falcate; stamens 10, filaments narrow, glabrous, anthers spherical; ovary filiform, glabrous, ovules 4-8, style curved. Fruit to 2.5cm, condensed, glabrous stipitate, tinged brown; seeds 4–5 black. S Africa. Z9.

CULTIVATION   *D.lignosus* is a slender climber grown for the decorative clusters of rosy purple flowers; it is also a useful green manure in warm countries and bears edible pods like snap beans. Cultivate as for *Lablab*.

D.lignosus (L.) Verdc. AUSTRALIAN PEA.

Dischidia R.Br. (Gk *dischides*, twice-cleft: the corona segments are bifid.) Asclepiadaceae. 80 species of evergreen climbers or trailers with milky sap, some of them myrmecophytes. Stems usually slender, rooting at nodes. Leaves of two types – opposite, fleshy, circular to ovate-lanceolate, or developed into inflated 'pitchers' which play host to ants. Detritus, collected by the ants, excreted by them or accumulating naturally, fills the pitcher, as does rainwater. Fine adventitious roots then penetrate the pitcher, which provides a source of water and nutrients for the plant. Flowers usually small, in terminal or axillary umbel-like racemes, 5-merous; corolla urceolate-ovoid with a narrow throat, fleshy; corona of 5, 2-lobed segments in a single whorl. SE Asia, W Pacific, tropical Australia. Z10.

CULTIVATION   *Dischidia* is a genus of *Hoya*-like vines for cultivation in the shaded intermediate to warm glasshouse (minimum temperature 13–15°C/55–60°F), or in the home in growing cases and in the more humid rooms – i.e. bathroom or kitchen. The species most frequently seen is *D.rafflesiana* – not a beautiful or showy plant, but a fascinating curiosity and an outstanding example of myrmecophily, the symbiotic association of plants with ants. Irrespective of whether ants are present, this slender trailing vine will develop grossly inflated, heavily veined, dull green sacs in contrast to its otherwise delicate habit. It is strongly epiphytic and will not succeed in pots. Plant in a mix of coarse bark, perlite and coir or leafmould in sphagnum-lined baskets and encourage the stems to trail and root, and then cascade. Where high levels of humidity are guaranteed, or if this plant can be regularly misted, make a pouch of moss or coconut fibre filled with the bark medium, plant it with the *Dischidia* and tie onto a slab of cork or a raft of the type used for epiphytic orchids. The stems will then trail and root freely and the pitchers be more naturalistically displayed. Baskets or cork slabs should be suspended in semi-shade and kept moist either by plunging or by misting throughout the spring and summer. At this time a weak fortnightly liquid feed is beneficial. During the colder, darker months, merely mist every second day. Propagate by sections of rooted stem.

D.rafflesiana Wallich.
Stems slender, climbing, twining or pendulous. Unmodified leaves to 2.5cm, ovate-orbicular, fleshy; 'pitchers' 5–12cm, roughly shaped like a purse or a lamb's heart, dull pale green, heavily textured and obscurely veined, often filled with roots arising from the opposite axil. Flowers to 0.75cm, yellow-white, fleshy, tinted purple in throat. SE Asia to Australasia.

Distictis Mart. ex Meissn. (From Gk *di-*, twice, and *stiktos*, spotted: the seeds are very flat and look like 2 rows of spots in the fruit.) Bignoniaceae. 9 species of lianes. Branches hexagonal, often with leafy pseudostipules. Leaves 2-foliolate, often ending with a trifid tendril. Flowers few, in terminal racemes or panicles; calyx cupular, truncate or 5-toothed, margin glandular; corolla tubular or tubular-campanulate, pubescent outside; anthers glabrous; ovary oblong, puberulent; disc annular-pulvinate. Fruit a convex or biconvex capsule, oblong-elliptic, apex and base acute, valves unequal; seeds in 2 rows. Mexico, W Indies. Z9.

CULTIVATION   Where temperatures seldom fall below freezing, *D.buccinatoria* can be grown to great effect against a south- or southwest-facing wall, or used to cover tree stumps and pillars. In colder regions they are more safely grown with the protection of the cool glasshouse or conservatory, although on well drained soils and with a long hot summer to ripen wood, *D.buccinatoria* will tolerate temperatures to –5°C/23°F. They are grown for their large and showy trumpet-shaped flowers, carried in profusion over a long period in summer: those of *D.laxiflora* are a rich purple in bud, opening to lavender and fading to almost white; they are, in addition, vanilla-scented.

Grow in well drained but moisture-retentive soils with plentiful organic matter. Provide good ventilation and a minimum temperature of 5–7°C/40–45°F, for *D.lactiflora* and *D.laxiflora*. Water plentifully when in growth reducing as light levels and temperatures fall in winter. Prune to within 15cm/6in. of the base at planting time and remove congested growth in spring. Tie in new growth as necessary; adhesive pads may only be formed in contact with rough surfaces and may not be strong enough to support the plant's weight. Propagate by seed, by greenwood or semi-ripe cuttings or by layering.

D.buccinatoria (DC.) A. Gentry (*Bignonia buccinatoria* Mairet; *Phaedranthus buccinatorius* (DC.) Miers; *Pithecoctenium buccinatorium* DC.).
Leaflets 10cm, ovate-lanceolate, apex acuminate, glabrous above, minutely white-scaly beneath. Corolla 7.5–8cm, *c*1.9cm diam. at apex, tubular-funnelform, purple-red, yellow in throat, yellow-tomentose. Mexico.

D.cinerea (DC.) Greenman. See *D.laxiflora*.

D.lactiflora (Vahl) DC. (*Bignonia lactiflora* Vahl; *Macrodiscus lactiflora* Bur. ex Baill.).
Leaflets to 6cm, ovate, glabrous, scaly beneath, rigid, veins prominent. Corolla 2.5cm, white, throat yellow, glabrous to pubescent but velvety outside. W Indies, St Domingo, Puerto Rico.

D.laxiflora (DC.) Greenman (*Bignonia laxiflora* DC.; *Bignonia cinerea* DC.; *D.cinerea* (DC.) Greenman; *Pithecoctenium cinereum* DC.; *Pithecoctenium laxiflorum* DC.).
Leaflets 2–7 × 1–4cm, ovate-elliptic, apex acute or obtuse, sometimes apiculate, base truncate or rounded, scaly throughout, puberulent to glabrescent above, puberulent beneath. Corolla 4.5–7.5 × 1.3–2.5cm, tubular-campanulate, magenta, lobes 1–1.5cm, tube exterior pale-puberulent. Spring–summer. Mexico, Nicaragua.

D.'Rivers'.
Leaves dark green. Flowers dark mauve with gold throat, late-flowering.

For illustration see Bignoniaceae.

Dolichandra Cham. (From Gk *dolichos*, long, and *aner*, man, stamen referring to the long, exserted stamens.) Bignoniaceae. 1 species, a glabrous liane. Stems finely fluted, with glandular patches. Leaves bifoliolate, with or without terminal, trifid tendril; leaflets 3–7 × 1–3.5cm, oblong-lanceolate to oblong-ovate, apex acute and mucronate, leathery, margin crispate; pseudostipules inconspicuous. Inflorescence a 1–6-flowered cyme; bracts and bracteoles leafy, 10–15 × 6–10mm; calyx 2cm, slender, mucronate; corolla 5–7cm, tubular, decurved, vermilion to purple-vermilion, interior yellow, obliquely bilabiate, upper lip 2-lobed, lower lip 3-lobed; stamens exserted, anthers glabrous; staminode included; disc pulvinate; ovary oblong-ovoid, glabrous; ovules many-seriate. Fruit 11 × 2cm, an oblong to narrowly ellipsoid capsule, rugose, woody; seeds transverse oblong, in wing. Brazil, Paraguay, Uruguay, Argentina. Z10.

CULTIVATION   A vigorous climber grown for the brilliant red, tubular flowers, carried in small clusters and in pleasing contrast with the dark leathery foliage. Grow under glass as for *Bignonia* with a minimum temperature of about 10°C/50°F. Propagate by stem cuttings of three joints taken in spring and rooted in a closed case with bottom heat.

D.cynanchoides Cham.

Dregea E. Mey. Asclepiadaceae. 3 *Hoya*-like climbing shrubs. Warm regions of Old World.

CULTIVATION   A handsome climbing shrub with large, heart-shaped leaves and nodding umbels of starry flesh-pink or white flowers. *Dregea sinensis* is supposedly rather tender, performing well in beds or tubs of a medium-fertility, loam-based mix in a cool glasshouse or conservatory; it will, however, tolerate sharp but not prolonged frosts. Outdoors, it favours a very sheltered situation in full sun to semi-shade. It should be allowed to clamber through the branches of trees, or tied to trellis. Propagate by seed or semi-ripened cuttings inserted in a case.

D.sinensis Hemsl. (*Wattakaka sinensis* (Hemsl.) Stapf).
Climbing shrub to 3m. Leaves to 10cm, broadly ovate, cor-date, grey-felted beneath. Flowers 1.5cm diam., 10–25 in axillary, long-stalked, downy umbels to 9cm diam., pink or white; calyx deeply 5-lobed, stamens 5. Seed pods to 7cm. China. Z9.

Dyssochroma Miers (From Gk *dyssoos*, ruined, and *chroma*, colour, in reference to the flowers.) Solanaceae. 2 species of climbing subshrubs or small trees. Leaves alternate, elliptic, acuminate, entire, leathery. Flowers large, pendulous, pedunculate, often solitary at ends of branchlets; calyx of 5 acute, lanceolate, equal lobes, con-nivent, becoming free; corolla funnelform, with 5 equal long-lanceolate, recurved lobes; stamens straight, exserted, equal; style 2-lobed, erect; ovary conical, 2-locular, with many ovules. Brazil. Z10.

CULTIVATION   Clambering shrubs for tropical and subtropical gardens or large tubs in the intermediate glasshouse or conservatory, *Dyssochroma* species produce showy, drooping blooms in shades of cool green and olive. Cultivate as for *Solandra*..

D.eximia Benth. & Hook. f.
Moderately branched shrub. Leaves oval, narrowing to a short point, glossy, leathery; petiole to 1.2cm, stout. Flowers paired, to 15cm, drooping, funnelform; peduncle to 2.5cm; calyx to 4.5 × 4.5cm; corolla to 15cm, yellow-green, with 5 broadly acuminate, recurved lobes, spreading to 15cm across 3-nerved; stamens 5, slightly exceeding tube.

D.viridiflora (Miers) Sims (*Solandra viridiflora* Miers).
Deciduous shrub, to 1m. Leaves to 11 × 5cm, in dense fasci-cles, elliptic-oblong, slender-pointed; petiole to 2cm, sulcate. Flowers drooping, terminal, solitary; peduncle to 2cm; calyx 3.5 × 3.5cm; corolla to 10cm green, cylindrical portion of tube included within the calyx, lobes to 3.5 × 1cm, recurved, 3-nerved; stamens exserted to 4.5cm beyond mouth of the tube.

Eccremocarpus Ruiz & Pav. (From Gk *ekkremes*, pendent, and *karpos*, fruit.) GLORY FLOWER. Bignoniaceae. 5 species of evergreen or herbaceous vines. Leaves opposite, bipinnate or twice pinnatisect, with terminal ten-drils. Inflorescences racemose, terminal; calyx 5-lobed, campanulate; corolla tube long, narrow or somewhat ventricose, throat swollen but suddenly contracted at mouth, limb small entire or bilabiate; fertile stamens 4. Fruit an ovate to elliptic capsule; seeds in suborbicular wing. Chile and Peru. Z8.

CULTIVATION   *E.scaber*, the species most commonly seen in cultivation, is a valuable tendril-climber for cover-ing walls, fences and pergolas, and will scramble through shrubs, bearing a succession of exotic and brightly coloured blooms throughout the summer until first frosts. Although perennial, it will flower in its first year from seed if sown early. In a warm and sheltered position with good drainage, it will re-sprout from the base, even where temperatures have fallen to –5°C/23°F and below. In cool temperature zones, *Eccremocarpus* species are also amenable to tub cultivation in the cool glasshouse or conservatory.

   Grow in well drained and fertile, neutral to slightly acid soils in full sun; although *E.scaber* will tolerate part-day shade, flowering is more profuse in sun. Mulch with a deep dry layer of bracken litter in zones at the limits of hardiness. Remove overcrowded growth and frost-damaged stems in spring. Propagate from seed under glass in late winter; germinate at 13–16°C/40–50°F and prick out into individual pots to harden off before planting out after danger of frost is passed. For earlier blooms, sow in late summer and overwinter at about 5–7°C/40–45°F. Propagation is also possible by leaf bud or soft tip cuttings when leaves have fully expanded in early summer – root in a closed case with bottom heat at 20°C/68°F.

*E.*Anglia Hybrids.
Flowers yellow, orange, pink, scarlet and crimson.

E.longiflorus Humb. & Bonpl.
Stem clothed with red indumentum. Leaves 2–3-pinnate, pin-nae entire, ovate, rarely notched at apex; petiole pubescent. Flowers on long, drooping stalks; calyx red; corolla longer than in *E.scaber*, 3–4× calyx length, slightly curved, yellow; limb lobes green, obtuse, reflexed. Summer. Peru.

E.scaber Ruiz & Pav. (*Calampelis scaber* D. Don).
1–3m, stems ribbed. Leaves to 7cm, ternately 2–3-pinnate, pin-nae alternate, base cordate, margin entire or dentate, glabrous or scabrid-pubescent. Inflorescence to 15cm; flowers to 2.5cm;

corolla scarlet to orange; pedicels to 1.2cm. Summer. Chile. 'Aureus': flowers golden yellow. 'Carmineus': flowers deep red. 'Roseus': flowers bright pink to red.

For illustration see Bignoniaceae.

Echinocystis (Michx.) Torr. & A. Gray. (From Gk *echinos*, hedgehog, and *kystis*, purse, alluding to the spiny fruit.) Cucurbitaceae. 1 species, a monoecious, climbing, tuberous, perennial herb. Stems to 6m. Tendrils 2–3-fid. Leaves palmate, 3–5-lobed. Male inflorescence an axillary panicle; female flowers solitary or paired, coaxillary with male; calyx lobes 6, bristly; corolla green-white, lobes 6, slender, to 5mm; stamens 3, coherent; ovary 2-celled. Fruit a pod to 5cm, ellipsoid or globose, spinose, dehiscing through apex, 5cm. N America. Z7.

CULTIVATION A fast-growing vine native to North America, the Prickly Cucumber is grown for its round, prickly fruit (far from edible) and the speed with which it will cover arbours, pergolas, fences and tree trunks. Given a long, hot summer, it will form tubers and perform as a perennial; otherwise sow seed under glass in early spring and plant out in early summer, or sow in situ in late spring. *Echinocystis* requires a richly fertile soil and copious supplies of water.

E.fabacea Naudin. See *Marah fabaceus.*

E.lobata (Michx.) Torr. & A. Gray. WILD CUCUMBER; WILD BALSAM APPLE; MOCK CUCUMBER; PRICKLY CUCUMBER.

E.macrocarpa Greene. See *Marah macrocarpus.*

E.oregana (Torr. & A. Gray) Cogn. See *Marah oreganus.*

Eleutherococcus Maxim. (From Gk *eleutheros*, free, and *kokkos*, pip, here referring to the pyrenes.) Araliaceae. About 30 species of generally deciduous and often bristly or prickly shrubs or trees to 7m, sometimes more or less scandent or sprawling; branches generally slender. Leaves digitately (1–)3–5-foliolate, the bases more or less sheathing the twigs but without stipules. Inflorescences terminal, simple or compound, often on side or short shoots. Flowers in umbels or heads, solitary or in clusters with the central or terminal unit always larger; pedicels not jointed at the base of the ovary; petals and stamens usually 5; ovary 2–5-locular; styles free or variously united. Fruits drupaceous, black or purple-black at maturity, remaining inferior, ellipsoid or round or more or less compressed laterally; pyrenes 2–5. S & E Asia, Japan, the Ryukyus, Taiwan and the Philippines (Luzon); most diverse in C & W China.

CULTIVATION *Eleutherococcus* species add an exotic note to shrub border planting in temperate gardens, with their bold, compound foliage and clusters of black fruit: in positions sheltered from north and east winds, they will usually survive temperatures from –10° to –15°C/14–5°F and are tolerant of poor soils and pollution. Tolerant of shearing, *E.sieboldianus* (the most commonly cultivated species) is frequently used for hedging in cool and warm temperate areas, where it will withstand urban pollution: clip once or twice annually. Grow in any well drained, humus-rich soil in full sun for the best results. Specimen shrubs may be pruned to thin crowded wood and to shorten ungainly growth in late winter. Propagate from ripe seed in autumn and by root cuttings in late winter; alternatively by suckers and semi-ripe cuttings with bottom heat in summer.

E.giraldii (Harms) Nak. (*Acanthopanax giraldii* Harms). Shrub to 3m, sometimes sprawling; branches densely covered with spreading or reflexed bristle-like prickles, or occasionally unarmed. Leaves 3–5-foliolate, the petiole to 8cm, often bristly-spiny; leaflets to 5 × 2.5cm, nearly sessile, very thin, usually glabrous when mature, oblong-obovate to obovate to oblanceolate, base attenuate, margins irregularly biserrate. Inflorescence on both main and short shoots terminal, usually a solitary umbel, the main axis to 2cm, with or without long hairs or bristles; umbels glabrous; petals white tinged green. Fruit black, 8mm diam.; styles 5, their lower parts united into a column. Summer. North central China. Z6.

E.gracilistylus (W.W. Sm.) S.Y. Hu (*Acanthopanax gracilistylus* W.W. Sm.; *Acanthopanax spinosus* auct., non (L. f.) Miq.). Slenderly twiggy, scandent or prostrate bushy armed shrub to 3m or so, similar to *E.sieboldianus* but with leaflets more finely toothed and styles slenderly elongate, spreading, and wholly or mostly free from one another in fruit; twigs unarmed or with a few reflexed prickles at the nodes; styles 2. Flowers green. Summer. China, Vietnam. Sometimes confused with the closely related *E.spinosus*. Z6.

E.rehderianus (Harms) Nak. (*Acanthopanax rehderianus* Harms). Scandent shrub to 3m, superficially similar to *E.sieboldianus* but with inflorescence appearing at ends of both long and short shoots; leaflets sessile or subsessile, crenate-serrate in the upper third, at least above the widest part. Inflorescence simple, umbellate as in *E.sieboldianus* but commonly with 2 additional

single flowers in the basal portion of the peduncular axis. Fruit black, subglobose, 5mm; stylar column less than 1mm, with 4–5 stigmata diverging at apex. C China (W Hupeh). Z6.

E.sessiliflorus (Rupr. & Maxim.) S.Y. Hu (*Acanthopanax sessiliflorus* (Rupr. & Maxim.) Seem.). WANGRANGKURA. Vigorous spreading shrub to 5m with sprawling branches, eventually pyramidal. Leaves 3(–5)-foliolate; petiole to 12cm, sometimes with one or more prickles; leaflets sessile, obovate, to 18 × 7cm, glabrous, the lateral ones more or less oblique, primary lateral veins sometimes splitting in two not far from midrib, irregularly serrate. Inflorescence simple or compound, compact, a terminal umbel head-like, solitary or surrounded by a cluster of 2–4 similar head-like umbels; all parts hairy, including, when young, the 'heads'; petals dull purple. Fruit black, 10–15mm, crowded together on very short stalks; styles mostly united into a column, only the stigmata distinct. Late summer. NE Asia (N and NE China, Korea, Soviet Far East). Of outstanding appearance in autumn for its abundance of black fruit in usually simple heads at the ends of the twigs. Z4.

E.sieboldianus (Mak.) Koidz. (*Acanthopanax sieboldianus* Mak.; *Acanthopanax spinosus* auct., non (L.f.) Miq.; *Aralia pentaphylla* Sieb. & Zucc., non Thunb.; *Acanthopanax pentaphyllus* (Sieb. & Zucc.) Marchal). Scandent shrub to 3m, with slim, vigorously arching, cane-like primary branches armed at the nodes; short shoots developing from old wood. Leaves (3–)5(–7)-foliolate, rhombic-elliptic, toothed. Inflorescence simple, terminating short shoots but appearing axillary in relation to the long shoots; umbels solitary on long glabrous stalks; flowers green-white; ovary 5-locular, styles partly united. Fruit black, nearly globose, 6–8mm across. Late spring to early summer. E China; Japan (introduced). 'Variegatus' (*Acanthopanax sieboldianus* f. *variegatus* (Nichols.) Rehd.): growth more sparse; leaflets with creamy-white perimeter. Z4.

E.simonii (Schneid.) Hesse (*Acanthopanax simonii* Schneid.). Weakly growing, bushy armed shrub to 3m; twigs glabrous, sometimes green, with strong spines clustering almost ring-like around the nodes and scattered, recurved, slender long prickles elsewhere. Leaves (3–)5-foliolate; petioles to 7cm though usually shorter; leaflets to 12×4cm, rather unequal in size, very shortly stalked to nearly sessile, narrowly elliptic or obovate, more or less bristly-hairy throughout, the bristles on the ventral midrib sometimes conspicuous, apex long-acute, biserrate. Inflorescence simple or compound, relatively small and compact; terminal umbel to 3cm diam., solitary or with a crowded basal whorl of 2–5 lateral umbels; main axis to 7–8cm, all parts glabrous; petals green, glabrous. Fruit black, subglobose, 5–6mm diam.; stylar column 1.5mm, the stigmata fused. Early summer. C China. Z6.

E.spinosus (L. f.) S.Y. Hu (*Acanthopanax spinosus* (L. f.) Miq.; *Aralia pentaphylla* Thunb.). Shrub to 3.5m or so, similar to *E.sieboldianus*, but with somewhat smaller leaves, shorter inflorescence and 2 partly free styles. Leaflets cuneiform, entire, wavy or shallowly and sparsely toothed. Inflorescence axis to 4cm or so; umbels many-flowered. Fruit black; lower half of styles united into a column. Summer. Japan. Closely related to, and formerly confused with *E.gracilistylus*. In Japan used for hedges, at least in Edo (Tokyo) in the time of Hiroshige.

E.trichodon (Franch. & Savat.) Ohashi (*Acanthopanax trichodon* Franch. & Savat.). A strongly branching shrub to 3m, superficially resembling *E.sieboldianus* but with inflorescence at ends of both long and short shoots and ovary 2-locular; stems unarmed or only slightly prickly; petiole and upper side of main vein minutely spiny; margins unevenly doubly serrate, the teeth ending in a bristle; inflorescence simple, umbellate, the axis purple-red, to 5cm long, glabrous, sometimes bearing additional single flowers; fruit purple-black, 6–7cm, the styles 2, mostly fused into a column. Japan. Z6.

E.trifoliatus (L.) S.Y. Hu (*Acanthopanax trifoliatus* (L.) Voss; *A. aculeatus* (Ait.) Witte). Scandent or erect armed shrub to 7m, the prickles scattered, often recurved; branches grey. Leaves usually 3-foliolate, petioles short, prickly, blades to 8×4.5cm, shortly stalked, rhombic to obovate to oblanceolate, apex acute or obtuse, margins coarsely to finely toothed, upper surface glabrous, the midrib beneath often bristly. Inflorescence terminal, paniculate, sometimes partly leafy, main axis elongate; terminal umbel surrounded at least by a whorl of lateral umbels on peduncles to 7cm, with similar umbels sometimes also present lower down the main axis and in upper leaf axils. Flowers green; ovary 2-locular; styles partly united into a column. Fruit laterally compressed, to 4mm long. S and E Asia, Taiwan, Philippines (Luzon); in China north to Hubei. Z7.

E.wilsonii (Harms) Nak. Similar to *E.giraldii* but plant unarmed or with bristly spines only at the nodes and leaflet margins visibly only simple serrate. Umbels solitary. Fruit black, globose, 6–7mm across; styles 3–5, partly united into a column. W China (W Sichuan, Yunnan). Z5.

Elytropus Muell. Arg. Apocynaceae. 1 species, a vigorous evergreen twiner to 5m. Stems slender, bristly. Leaves opposite, elliptic to elliptic-oblong, acuminate, with bristly hairs throughout, ciliate. Flowers small, white tinted lilac, solitary or paired, axillary. Fruit green ripening yellow. Spring. Chile, Argentina. Z8

CULTIVATION Plant in semi-shade or full sun on moist soils rich in organic matter and allow to twine through shrubs ands trees in semi-wooded locations or train on wires or trellis against walls. Easily damaged by frost and hard winds. Propagate by nodal cuttings of semi-ripe shoots taken in summer and inserted in a case.

E.chilensis Muell.Arg.

Epipremnum Schott. (From Gk *epi*, upon, and *premnon*, a trunk.) Araceae. 8 evergreen lianes, to 30m+, dimorphic with juvenile and adult phases; adhesive roots emerging from stem. Leaves entire to pinnate, occasionally perforated, ovate to oblong and lanceolate, coriaceous; main and minor veins parallel in adult leaves; petioles long, geniculate, sheathing at base. Peduncle short, solitary; spathe cymbiform, not forming tube, deciduous, yellow to green or purple; spadix short, stout, included, covered by hermaphrodite flowers; perianth absent; stamens 4; ovary unilocular, ovules 2 or 4; seeds hard coated, reniform. SE Asia to W Pacific. Z10.

CULTIVATION Tropical climbers grown – usually in their juvenile state – for their glossy heart-shaped leaves, these often attractively marbled and perforated. In tropical and subtropical gardens, they are used as groundcover, trailers and for clothing tree trunks, to which they attach themselves by long adventitious roots. Under glass, they require a minimum winter temperature of 10°C/50°F, semi-shade, moderate to high humidity and an open, bark-based mix. That said, the cultivars of *E.aureum* are often to be seen in the home, in offices and in public buildings, contending bravely with dehydrated moss-poles and neglected hydroponic planters. Propagate by rooted lengths of stem.

E.aureum (Lind. & André) Bunting(*Pothos aureus* Lind. & André; *Rhaphidophora aurea* (Lind. & André) Birdsey; *Scindapsus aureus* (Lind. & André) Engl.). GOLDEN POTHOS; DEVIL'S IVY; HUNTER'S ROBE. To 15m when adult, stems green, striped yellow or white. Juvenile leaves 15–30cm, ovate, cordate, bright green, irregularly variegated yellow or white; adult leaves to 80cm, ovate to ovate-oblong, cordate, irregularly pinnatisect, segments few to many, oblong, truncate, variegated; petioles short, stout. Peduncle 12cm; spathe and spadix to 15cm. Solomon Is. 'Marble Queen': leaves entire, green boldly streaked white and moss green, petioles white; stalks streaked green. 'Tricolor' (*Pothos tricolor* hort.): leaves entire, variegated white, petioles and stalks off-white.

E.giganteum Schott.
To 30m+, stems to 7.5cm diam. Leaves 30–60 × 15–30cm, entire, oblong, obtuse, cordate, coriaceous, glossy bright green, veins many; petiole to 60cm, sheathing, geniculate. Spathe to 25cm, subcylindric, cuspidate, dull green or purple, yellow within; spadix equalling spathe. Malaysia, Thailand.

E.mirabile Schott. TONGA PLANT.
Stems climbing, 2.5cm diam., with persistent scarious remains of cataphylls. Leaves 30–50×20–30cm, entire when juvenile, pinnatifid when adult, cordate, perforated along midrib, segments 4–10 per side, truncate, acute or acuminate, dark green; petiole to 38cm. Spathe to 12cm, green, yellow within; spadix sessile, obtuse, green. Malaysia, Polynesia to Australia.

E.pinnatum (L.) Engl. (*Rhaphidophora pinnata* Schott.; *Monstera nechodomii* hort.).
To 20m, stems 1–4cm diam., green or brown, with persistent scarious cataphyll remains. Juvenile leaves oblong-lanceolate, entire or occasionally pinnatifid or perforate; adult leaves to 100 × 45cm, elliptic-oblong, perforate or with translucent spots along midrib, irregularly pinnatifid, segments oblong, 8–14 per side. Spathe to 23cm, green. Malaysia to New Guinea.

E.cultivars. 'Exoticum': leaves oblique-lanceolate, to 20cm long, thin, matt dark green, splashed silver.

Ercilla A. Juss. (For Don Alonso de Ercilla (1533–95), of Madrid.) Phytolaccaceae. 2 species of evergreen climbers, attaching themselves adventitious roots with disc-like holdfasts. Leaves alternate, thick, leathery, entire, petiolate. Flowers small, bisexual, in dense axillary spike-like racemes; calyx 5-lobed; stamens 4–8. Fruit a berry. Americas, S Africa. Z8.

CULTIVATION With shelter from cold winds *E.spicata* gives dense, evergreen cover on the ground or on shaded walls and is well suited to rambling through trees. Grown for the neat, pale-veined foliage and the small, densely flowered spikes of blossom produced in spring. In favourable climates these are followed by purple-red berries. Tolerant of temperatures to between –5 and –10°C/23–14°F. Grow in a well drained but moisture-retentive, lime-free soil in sun to part shade. Provide wire supports for wall-grown specimens; tie in as growth proceeds – the aerial roots are not strong enough to support a heavy mass of top-growth. Prune after flowering to remove older, crowded stems. Propagate by nodal stem cuttings in mid-summer, 8–10cm/3–4in. long, treat with a hormone rooting compound and root in a closed case with bottom heat.

E.spicata (Hook. & Arn.) Moq. (*E.volubilis* Juss.; *Bridgesia spicata* Hook. & Arn.; *Phytolacca volubilis* Heimerl).
Twining shrub, to 6m. Leaves to 5cm, many, alternate, ovate-cordate to oblong, fleshy, glossy, dark green, short-petioled.

Flowers inconspicuous, in sessile spikes to 4.5cm; calyx 5-lobed, purple or green; petals absent; stamens 8–12, white. Berries dark purple, 4–8 per flower. Peru, Chile.

E.volubilis A. Juss. See *E.spicata*.

Euonymus L. (*Evonymus*) (From the ancient Gk name *euonymon dendron*, hence to Lat. meaning 'of good name' – an ironic allusion to its toxicity.) Celastraceae. Over 170 species of deciduous or evergreen, erect, procumbent or scandent shrubs or trees; branches usually 4-sided. Leaves opposite, rarely alternate, simple, entire or serrate, glabrous. Flowers bisexual or unisexual, axillary in cymes or solitary, small, rather inconspicuous; calyx 4–5-lobed; petals attached below the disc, usually entire; stamens 5, the filaments sometimes absent; disc discoid, 4- or 5-lobed; ovary below the disc and adnate to it, 3–5-locular; style short. Fruit a capsule, 3–5-valved, with 1–2 seeds per locule; seeds entirely or partially enclosed in an aril, the endosperm fleshy. Asia, Europe, N & C America, Madagascar, Australia.

CULTIVATION The spindle trees are grown variously for their brilliant fall colour or tough evergreen, often variegated foliage, or wide habit range, or ornamental fruit. Only three species in general cultivation can strictly be termed climbers or wall shrubs: these are similar in overall appearance, carrying rather leathery foliage on slender branches which tend to creep and root unless introduced to a support. *E.fortunei* is most commonly grown – an invaluable evergreen for ground-cover in one of its many semi-prostrate or bushy forms or wall work in some of its cultivars, where handsome variegated or tinted foliage is combined with bright scarlet, orange or pink fruit. *E.obovatus* is a small deciduous creeper with interlacing stems and striking 'strawberry-like' fruit. Like *E.fortunei*, it will take to the footings of walls and the lower boughs of shrubs with little persuasion. Both of these species tolerate a wide variety of soils and sites, surviving minimum temperatures of –15°C/5°F, chalk and urban pollution. Variegated cultivars of *E.fortunei* will produce finer foliage in bright, fertile and sheltered conditions – as also favour the production of showy fruit in *E.obovatus*. *E.wilsonii* is rather more tender, requiring minimum temperatures no lower than –10°C/14°F and a sheltered position on a damp, slightly acid, leafy soil. Increase all by nodal cuttings taken between summer and autumn.

E.carlesii hort. See *E.fortunei* 'Carlesii'.
E.carrierei Vauv. See *E.fortunei* 'Carrierei'.
E.coloratus hort. See *E.fortunei* 'Coloratus'.

E.fortunei (Turcz.) Hand.-Mazz.
Evergreen climbing shrub to 5m, with aerial roots, or procumbent along the ground; branches finely warty, green. Leaves to 6cm, variable, basically ovate-elliptic, apex acute, base broadly cuneate, finely serrate, thinly coriaceous, veins distinct beneath. Flowers 4-merous, about 5mm diam.; calyx teeth entire; petals. elliptic, pale green. Fruit to 6mm wide,

smooth to obscurely warted, aril yellow to orange or pink to red. Summer. China. 'Berryhill': to 70cm, strong, erect; leaves green. 'Carlesii' (*E.carlesii* hort.): upright shrub, to 1m; leaves coarse, thick, glossy; fruit abundant. 'Carrierei' (*E.carrierei* Vauv.): bushy, low, climbing when supported; leaves to 5cm, elliptic-oblong, acute, glossy; fruit very abundant. 'Coloratus' (*E.coloratus* hort.): strongly climbing or trailing; leaves rather coarsely serrate, large, tinted deep purple above in autumn, red-tinted beneath. 'Dart's Blanket': low creeping; leaves thick, leathery, green, tinged crimson in winter. 'Dart's Carpet': to 35cm; branches creeping; leaves small, dark green tinged bronze-red in winter. 'Dart's Dab': to 35cm; branches spreading; leaves small, dull green. 'Emerald Charm': habit erect; leaves glossy green; fruit yellow-white, seeds orange. 'Emerald Gaiety': hardy, compact shrub; leaves green eged silver. 'Emerald 'n' Gold': leaves variously variegated, green, gold, and pink. 'Golden Prince' ('Gold Tip'): small, compact shrub; tips of young branches gold; leaves green tinged yellow. 'Gracilis': branches ascending; leaves variegated white, yellow or pink or combinations of these. 'Kewensis' (*E.kewensis* hort. ex Hesse): stems slender, prostrate; leaves very small, dull green with paler veins. 'Marginatus': trailing or climbing by rootlets, dense; leaves small, ovate, margined cream; flowers white tinged green; fruit pink. 'Minimus' (*E.fortunei* f. minimus (Simon-Louis) Rehd.): similar to 'Kewensis' but somewhat larger. Procumbent, rooting along branches, forming dense mats; branches erect, dense, thin, usually not more than 5cm high; leaves to 6mm, elliptic to rounded. 'Pulchellus' (*E.pulchellus* Carr.; *E.japonicus* 'Microphyllus'): leaves narrow-oblong to lanceolate-oblong, small. 'Reticulatus': leaves veined white. 'Robustus': upright; leaves large, pale green. 'Silver Gem': tall, compact; leaves edged white, speckled red. 'Silver Queen': compact; leaves large, later tinged pink, broad cream margin. 'Uncinatus': leaves small, oval, margins serrate, grey-green with grey veins. 'Vegetus' (*E.fortunei* var. vegetus (Rehd.) Rehd.): broad and bushy, occasionally climbing with support; branches thick, easily broken; leaves elliptic to rounded, apex rounded, crenate, dull light green, thick; fruit abundant. var. **radicans** (Miq.) Rehd. (*E.radicans* Sieb. ex Miq.; *E.repens* Carr.) Stems slender, trailing and rooting.

Leaves to 3.5cm, ovate-elliptic, shallowly toothed. Most cultivars are derived from this variety. Z5. *E.echinatus* Wallich from Himalaya differs from *E.fortunei* in its densely prickly green fruits. It is scarcely cultivated.

E.fortunei f. **minimus** (Simon-Louis) Rehd. See *E.fortunei* 'Minimus'.

E.fortunei var.*acutus* hort. See *E.fortunei* 'Pulchellus'.

E.fortunei var. **vegetus** (Rehd.) Rehd. See *E.fortunei* 'Vegetus'.

E.kewensis hort. ex Hesse. See *E.fortunei* 'Kewensis'.

E.microphyllus hort. ex Carr. See *E.fortunei* 'Pulchellus'.

E.obovatus Nutt. RUNNING STRAWBERRY BUSH.
Deciduous shrub, prostate, rarely more than 30cm high, glabrous; branches rooting, climbing if supported. Leaves to 6cm, obovate-elliptic, crenate, light green. Cymes 1–3-flowered; flowers 5-merous; peduncle slender; petals red tinged green, rounded. Fruit usually 3-lobed, to 1.8cm wide, carmine-red, warty; aril red. N America. 'Variegatus': leaves variegated green and white. Z3.

E.pulchellus Carr. See *E.fortunei* 'Pulchellus'.

E.radicans Sieb. ex Miq. See *E.fortunei* var. radicans.

E.repens Carr. See *E.fortunei* var. radicans.

E.wilsonii Sprague.
Evergreen shrub, climbing to 6m. Leaves to 14cm, lanceolate, apex acuminate, shallowly dentate, base cuneate, veins distinct beneath; petiole to 1.2cm. Cymes loose, to 8cm diam.; flowers pale yellow. Fruit 4-lobed, 2cm wide, covered with awl-shaped spines to 5mm; aril yellow. Summer. W China. Z9.

× **Fatshedera** Guill. (*Fatsia japonica* 'Moseri' × *Hedera hibernica*.) Araliaceae. An evergreen shrub of loose sprawling habit, to 1.2m. Leaves palmately and deeply 5-lobed, dark lustrous green. Young leaves and petioles pubescent with rust-coloured, scale-type hairs. Flowers small, green-white, umbellate in panicles; stamens sterile. Fruit absent. Autumn. Garden origin (France, 1910). Z7.

CULTIVATION Less demanding of space and altogether neater than *Fatsia japonica*, an excellent evergreen shrub for positions where winter temperatures do not fall below about −15°C/5°F: flowers usually appear too late in the season to open. Although not self-clinging like its *Hedera* parent, it does show a slight tendency to climb and may be tied in to clothe trellising, pillars or other supports. Also useful as a conservatory or houseplant when grown with the support of bamboo canes: plants under glass may reach 3m/10ft or more, but the variegated cultivars are generally less vigorous and require good light conditions. May be grown as a standard specimen when grafted on to a rootstock of *Hedera hibernica*. Grown as a houseplant, it will thrive even in dry air conditions where temperatures do not fall below 20°C/68°F. Fruit is not set: take greenwood cuttings in summer, cutting through rather than below the node and then removing tops 1cm/¹/₂in. above the first node, leaving the cutting with two nodes and one leaf. Pinch and hard prune young plants to promote bushiness.

× *F.lizei* Guill.
'Pia': leaves undulate. 'Anna Mikkels': leaves variegated yellow. 'Variegata': leaves variegated cream.

Ficus L. (Lat. name for the edible fig.) FIG. Moraceae. About 800 species of deciduous or evergreen monoecious or dioecious lactiferous trees, shrubs and woody root-climbing vines, many of them beginning life and sometimes remaining as epiphytes or also overwhelming and strangling their host and becoming free-standing; stems and twigs thick to thin, unbranched and palmoid to highly branched with flattened sprays of foliage; stipules enclosing buds at first, small to large, persistent or quickly falling but leaving distinctive ring-like scars at the nodes. Leaves simple (rarely palmately or pinnately lobed and then mostly in saplings), thin to thick, spirally arranged, alternate (and sometimes distichous) or occasionally opposite, pinnately or more or less palmately veined, very varied in size, form, surfaces, venation details and pubescence and sometimes quite showy. Flowers minute, unisexual, their perianth reduced, wholly enclosed, from 2 to several thousand within a fleshy receptable (the fig); male flowers with 1–7 stamens; female flowers with ovary and style; gall flowers sterile, providing homes for fig-wasps of *Blastophaga*, *Ceratosolen* and other genera. Receptacles of varying sizes and maturing with differing colours and other markings, sessile or pedunculate, sometimes subtended by persistent or caducous bracts, naked or more or less covered with bracteate scales, globose, oblate, pyriform or oblong, the apex topped by a small, sometimes elevated ostiole enclosed by bracteoles. Seeds small, more or less numerous. Tropics and subtropics.

CULTIVATION   *Ficus* is cultivated as an ornamental for the beauty of its foliage. The amazing diversity of habit within the genus ranges from low-growing, small-leaved creepers to vigorous vines and tall shrubs or trees. Many begin life as epiphytes, most notably the 'strangler figs'. The seed, initially lodged in stem or branch, produces a plant with a mass of aerial roots which, in seeking nutrient at ground level cuts off the host's sustenance and eventually kills it, by which time the *Ficus* roots have coalesced to form the 'pseudo-trunk' which supports it for the remainder of its life. The banyans extend huge roots a great distance from their branches, which then develop as trunk-like prop roots. Because they often begin life in the crowns of host trees, producing twining, clasping roots and stems, strangler figs like the famous Banyan (*F.benghalensis*) and the ubiquitous Weeping Fig (*F.benjamina*) might be classed as climbers of sorts, their activities not entirely dissimilar to those of very old specimens of *Hedera*. Essentially, however, their stem and branch growth is not climbing, and this is certainly true of plants in cultivation.

Other *Ficus* species can truly be said to climb. Small, creeping vines such as *F.pumila, F. punctata* and *F.sagittata* (cool to intermediate glasshouse) and *F.villosa* (hot glasshouse) are self-rooting climbers suited to walls and pillars in conservatories, glasshouses and interior landscapes: *F.sagittata* and *F.pumila* make good basket plants, *F.punctata* may be allowed to scramble up the trunks of palms. A north-facing conservatory wall suits *F.pumila* which will occasionally survive outdoors in sheltered temperate gardens where temperatures rarely fall below freezing. In cool shady conservatories, few climbers provide better wall cover than a mature plant of *F.pumila*. It may be trained in a fan or feather pattern through careful pruning and subsequently trimmed like an ivy to create a dense dark green growth overlaying gnarled and long-lived branches. Such specimens are features of many of the older surviving conservatories; one of the finest can be seen at Dumbarton Oaks, Georgetown, D.C. All of these species may be planted in the open garden in subtropical and tropical regions: grow in part shade in any well drained but humus-rich soil. As glasshouse subjects or houseplants, they require a minimum winter temperature of 4°C/39°F. Maintain high humidity by damping down glasshouse paths regularly in the summer months and give medium to bright indirect light in a draught-free environment.

In cool temperate climates, the Common Fig, *F.carica*, is often grown as a wall shrub on relatively starved and shallow soils in south-facing aspects. Ancient specimens adorn the walls of many fine houses and institutions. This treatment usually provides conditions favourable to wood and fruit ripening and should be considered by gardeners wishing to produce edible figs in small domestic gardens. For the cultivation and cultivars of *F.carica*, see 'Figs' in T*he New RHS Dictionary of Gardening* (1992).

Propagate in spring and summer from seed (sown at 20°C/68°F) or by layering and air-layering, or by detaching and potting rooted lengths of stem.

Ficus is susceptible to anthracnose, leaf-spot and *Agrobacterium radiobacter* var. *tumefaciens* or crown gall (although the latter is rarely serious enough to require treatment). Spray with the appropriate fungicide. Edible figs and ornamental *Ficus* may be attacked by the fig cyst eelworm (*Heterodera fici*); infested plants show a loss of vigour. As eelworms only attack the roots, the plants may be regenerated from cuttings raised in a sterilised medium. The foliage may become infested with several types of scale insect, especially the soft scale (*Coccus hesperidum*), the hemispherical scale (*Saissetia coffaea*) and the oleander scale (*Aspidiotus nerii*); also by mealybugs (*Pseudoccus* spp.) and by a tarsonemid mite, the strawberry mite (*Tarsonemus pallidus*).

F.acuminata Roxb. See *F.subulata*.
F.acuminata auct. non Roxb. See *F.parietalis*.
F.barbata Miq. See *F.villosa*.

F.carica L. COMMON FIG.
Deciduous shrub or tree to 9m, the crown rounded, sometimes branching from base. Twigs stout, initially puberulent, soon glabrous, with prominent scars; buds glabrous. Leaves alternate, 3(–5)-lobed, rough to the touch above, pubescent beneath, to 20(–30)×18cm across, broadly ovate to orbicular, lobes somewhat elongate, with dentate or dentate-crenate margin; petiole to 7cm. Figs axillary among leaves, solitary, shortly peduncled, pear-shaped or almost globose, glabrous, green to maroon or brown (rather variable), 2–5cm diam. Cyprus, Turkey and Caucasus to Turkamen Reublic and Afghanistan, but established elsewhere (ssp. *carica*); Syria, Turkey, Iraq and Iran (ssp. *rupestris* (Hausskn.) Browicz). All figs in cultivation are ssp. *carica*. Wild plants with male flowers have been referred to its var. *caprificus* Tausch & Rav. Z7.

F.cerasiformis Desf. See *F.parietalis*.
F.confusa Elmer. See *F.subulata*.

F.erecta Thunb.
Large, many-stemmed straggling shrub or small tree to 4.5m, the prostrate parts, if any, freely rooting. Twigs to 4mm thick, elongate, glabrous; stipules relatively soon falling, to 8mm. Leaves alternate, flat, entire save for some teeth near apex, slightly rough to the touch but otherwise glabrous, to 20×10cm, very thin, symmetric, obovate to narrowly obovate, widest point usually above the middle, apex acute to just obtuse, gradually

passing into an acuminate tip, base usually obtuse or rounded; venation slightly palmipinnate, the basal pair subtrinerved, other main veins 6–8 per side; petiole to 4cm. Figs solitary, axillary among leaves, usually pedunculate, glabrous, sometimes stipitate, globose or pear-shaped, to 1.7cm diam.; peduncles to 2cm. China, Taiwan, Ryukyu Is., Japan and Korea. Includes *F.sieboldii* (Miq.) Corner, with linear to oblong-lanceolate leaves. Some plants grown in California are var. *beecheyana*. var. **beecheyana** (Hook. & Arn.) King. HEAVENLY FAIRY FRUIT. Differs in hispid-villous pubescence of most parts and rougher leaf surface, the bases are alo more angular and commonly subcordate, and the figs larger (to 2.5cm across). China (including Hong Kong), Ryukyu Is., Taiwan. Z9.

F.falcata Thunb. See *F.punctata*.
F.foveolata Wallich ex Miq. See *F.sarmentosa*.
F.foveolata var. *nipponica* (Franch. & Savat.) King. See *F.sarmentosa* var. *nipponica*.
F.macrocarpa Bl. non Hueg. ex Kunth & Bouché. See *F.punctata*.

F.montana Burm. f. (*F.quercifolia* Roxb.) OAKLEAF FIG.
Lax shrub or half-climber; branches mostly sprawling or decumbent, often rooting. Twigs initially hollow, more or less shortly hispid, ending in minutely pubescent buds to 0.8cm long. Leaves alternate, wavy or irregularly indented or (in younger plants) lobed, glabrous and smooth or slightly scabrous above, scabrous beneath, to 15×7.5cm, thin, symmetric, oblong, apex acute, base rounded or sometimes subcordate; venation prominent beneath, basal veins 2, spread-

ing, lateral veins 6–10 per side; petioles to 1.8cm. Figs solitary or in pairs in axils towards twig ends, pedunculate, urn-shaped, green, surface rough with white flecks and tubercular scales, to 0.8×0.5cm; peduncle to 1.1cm. SE Asia to Java and Borneo. The related *F.heteropoda* (Philippines, Sulawesi and Moluccas) and *F.copiosa* (Sulawesi to Micronesia, Solomon Is. and Australia) are occasionally cultivated; the leaves are usually opposite. *F.montana* will fruit when only 0.6m tall; in cultivation lobed juvenile leaves may persist. Z10.

F.nipponica Franch. & Savat. See *F.sarmentosa* var. *nipponica.*

F.parietalis Bl. (*F.acuminata* auct. non Roxb.) SHARP-POINTED FIG.
Initially an epiphytic shrub, later a handsome climber with long, thick, coiling stems or superseding its host and arborescent to 15m. Twigs lateral, slender, densely rusty-brown-hairy. Leaves alternate, *F.entire*, glabrous above, rough-pubescent beneath, to 18×9cm, distinctly asymmetric, thinly coriaceous, elliptic, apex obtuse, gradually passing into a distinctly caudate tip, base oblique, obtuse; venation palmipinnate, rather widely spaced above the basal veins, distinctly elevated beneath, basal veins 1(–2) pairs, the upper extending close to margins to one to two-thirds the blade length, other main veins 2–6 or so per side, ascending, arching, connected by 3–7 strong cross-veins; petiole to 2cm, pubescent as the twigs. Figs axillary, solitary, globose or ovoid, pendent on a stipe, to 2×2.2cm, warty, yellow to bright orange, hispid-tomentose; stipe to 1.8cm. SE Asia to Java, Borneo and Palawan and Balabac in the Philippines. Z10.

F.pumila L. (*F.repens* auct. non Willd.;*F.scandens* Lam.; *F.stipulata* Thunb.) CREEPING FIG; CLIMBING FIG; CREEPING RUBBER PLANT.
Root-climber with freely growing fertile shoots. Juvenile phase with slender brown glabrous rooting stems ultimately spreading over large surfaces; stipules to 1cm, persistent; leaves glabrous, entire, to 5×3cm, thinly coriaceous, asymmetric, ovate to elliptic, apex rounded, tip blunt, base oblique, cordate; petiole to 4mm. Adult phase erect or spreading; twigs ridged; stipules silky; leaves entire, glabrous above, glabrous or sparsely pubescent beneath with prominent venation, to 10.5×5cm, generally symmetric, coriaceous, oblong to elliptic to ovate, apex narrowly rounded to obtuse, tip blunt, base rounded to slightly cordate; venation palmipinnate, strongly reticulate, with 1 inconspicuous and 1 prominent pair of basal veins, the latter extending up into blade for as much as one third, and 3–5 short lateral veins on each side; petiole to 2.5cm. Figs axillary towards ends of twigs, mostly solitary, pyriform to oblong or somewhat cylindrical on thick stalks and with a broad, distinct apex, green with white flecks, maturing purple, densely hairy, to 6.2×4cm; stalks to 1.1cm. E Asia (N Vietnam to China and Japan). 'Minima': very slender, small, slow-growing; leaves to 1cm. 'Quercifolia': leaves pinnately lobed. 'Sonny': very small, spreading; leaves round to oval, irregularly waved, with variable cream margins. 'Variegata': vigorous, tufted; leaves marbled white to cream. Z9.

F.punctata Thunb. (*F.falcata* Thunb.; *F.macrocarpa* Bl. non Hueg. ex Kunth & Bouché.) SICKLE-LEAVED FIG.
Much-branched evergreen creeping shrub or root-climber, initially resembling *F.pumila* but adult foliage less sharply distinct. Creeping stems slender, rooting at nodes, light brown-hairy. Juvenile leaves dainty, distichous, entire, glabrous, paler and tessellated beneath, to 0.8×0.6cm, asymmetric, coriaceous, narrowly oblong to oblong-lanceolate to elliptic-obovate, sometimes rhomboid, always falcate, apex obtuse to rounded, tip blunt, base oblique, rounded, midrib always to one side, sometimes very close to the inner margin; intermediate and adult leaves developing on rootless, freely growing lateral shoots, rather larger but otherwise not strongly distinct from juveniles, slightly oblique to all but symmetric, to 4.7×2.5cm, linear-oblong to obovate-lanceolate to elliptic-obovate, base narrowed, obtuse to rounded; venation pinnate, strongly contrasting beneath, lateral veins 3–5, ascending anastomosing; petiole to 9mm. Figs on short leafless shoots to 3.5cm long

arising from old wood, pedunculate, globose to pyriform, beaked, finely velvety-hispid, peach-pink, to 11×8cm,; peduncle to 2cm. SE Asia (S Thailand) to Java, Borneo and Sulawesi. Grown for the shape and distinctively contrasting surfaces and colours of the juvenile foliage. The large pear-figs, not usually produced in indoor cultivation, are the feature by which this species is soonest distinguished from *F.pumila*. Z10.

F.quercifolia Roxb. See *F.montana.*
F.radicans Desf. See *F.sagittata.*
F.ramentacea Roxb. See *F.sagittata.*
F.repens auct. non Willd. See *F.pumila.*
F. reticulata (Miq.) Miq. See *F.sarmentosa.*

F.sagittata Vahl. (*F.radicans* Desf.; *F.ramentacea* Roxb.)
Wiry climbing or trailing evergreen creeper with rooting stems, later a powerful climber, often becoming free-standing. Twigs initially pubescent, soon glabrous. Foliage dimorphic; juvenile leaves soon glabrescent, not bullate, to 8cm, ovate, shallowly cordate, stipules to 2.5cm, awl-shaped, conspicuous; adult leaves entire, glabrous beneath except initially for the veins, the surface finely reticulate, to 20cm or more, symmetric or slightly asymmetric, ovate or oblong-lanceolate, apex acute, passing into an acuminate tip, base rounded or slightly cordate; venation pinnate, the 6–8 main veins ascending, relatively straight; petioles to 1cm, the stipules c8mm, awl-shaped. Figs axillary, solitary or paired, very shortly pedunculate, globose, initially pubescent, later glabrous, ripening red, to 1.4cm across; peduncles 2–3mm. Himalaya, S China and Andaman Is. through SE Asia to Palau, the Philippines, Maluku and Timor. 'Variegata': leaves grey-green with creamy-white variegation. Z10.

F.salicifolia Mig see *F.subulata.*

F.sarmentosa Hamilt. ex Sm. (*F.foveolata* Wallich ex Miq.;
Dimorphic climber, similar to *F.pumila* but differing in more limited development of basal veins, sharper leaf apices and figs generally in pairs; juvenile leaves star-shaped, to 2×2cm; adult leaves to 15×6cm, narrowly lanceolate. Nepal to China, Taiwan, Ryukyu Is., Japan and Korea. Plants in cultivation are var. **nipponica** (Franch. & Savat.) Corner (*F.nipponica* Franch. & Savat.), which differs in shorter peduncles (0–4mm as against 5–15mm in var. *sarmentosa*). E Himalaya & SE Asia to China, Taiwan, Ryukyu Is. and Japan. 'Variegata': leaves irregularly margined cream. Z9.

F.scandens Lam. See *F.pumila.*
F.stipulata Thunb. See *F.pumila.*

F.subulata Bl. (*F.acuminata* Roxb.; *F.confusa* Elmer; *F.salicifolia* Mig.)
Largely glabrous, dioecious, semiscandent or straggling basket-rooted shrub or low-level epiphyte; twigs initially puberulous, slender with long, awl-shaped stipules. Leaves dark green above, alternate, entire, glabrous, 10–25cm, asymmetric, elliptic-lanceolate, widest usually below middle, apex narrowed, acute, tip caudate-acuminate, base acute to obtuse; venation pinnate, lateral veins 7–10 per side; petiole to 0.75cm. Figs axillary, solitary or in pairs, almost sessile, becoming orange-red, to 1.25cm diam. E Himalaya and S China through SE Asia and Malesia (including the Philippines, but absent from Johore, Singapore, the Riau Is., Banka, and eastern Lesser Sunda Is.) to the Solomon Is. Z10.

F.villosa Bl. (*F.barbata* Miq.) VILLOUS FIG.
Dimorphic trailing or scandent shrub or strong, high-climbing liane. Twigs stout, purple-brown, densely villous; stipules to 4cm, persistent for a few nodes. Juveniles leaves entire, hairy beneath, to 17×9.5cm, papery to thinly leathery, broadly ovate, apex acute, tip slightly acuminate, base cordate; adult leaves dark green, to 25.5×13cm, leathery, oblong to ovate, sometimes asymmetric, densely villous-hairy all over beneath or only on the veins, sparsely hairy or almost glabrous above, apex obtuse or acute, tip acuminate, base rounded to cordate;

venation pinnate, with 7–9 spreading or ascending lateral veins well-elevated beneath on each side, the lowest pair somewhat prominent; petiole rather short in relation to the blade. Figs in fascicles in leaf axils, globose or apically flat-tened, beaked, moderately hairy, green to orange-yellow, about 1cm diam.; stalks 5–7mm. Malaysia, Indonesia and the Philippines. Z10.

Fockea Endl. (For Gustav Woldemar Focke (early 19th century), German physician and plant physiologist.) Asclepiadaceae. 10 species of perennial caudiciform succulents. Stem tuberous or napiform, branches thin, twining or erect. Leaves oblong, margins undulating. Flowers to 4cm diam., borne in leaf axils, solitary or several together in dense clusters, dioecious; petals narrow, starfish-like. Southern Africa (Angola to the Karroo).

CULTIVATION Native to the dry veld of southern and southwestern Africa, their cultivation is as for *Ceropegia* but they will take full sun and large amounts of water during the summer. As the caudex can become massive, so they must have a large deep pot. Propagate by seed.

F.angustifolia Schum.
Caudex large; stems several, 50–70cm, erect or climbing, minutely hairy. Leaves 1.5–10 × 0.2–0.6cm, linear. Flowers in clusters of 2–6, lobes green. S Africa (Cape Province).

F.capensis Endl. See *F.crispa*.

F.crispa (Jacq.) Schum. (*Cynanchum crispum* Jacq.; *F.capensis* Endl.).
Puberulous throughout. Caudex napiform, large, almost entirely subterranean; stems thin, twining or prostrate. Leaves 2–3 × 1–2cm, oval-acuminate, undulate-crispate. Flowers 2–3 together, green-grey with small brown blotches. S Africa (Karroo).

F.dammarana Schltr.
Caudex more or less thickened; branches laxly felty-haired when young. Leaves 1.2–2.3 × 3–6cm, linear-lanceolate, acuminate. Flowers few. Namibia.

F.edulis (Thunb.) Schum. (*Chymocormus edulis* (Thunb.) Harv.; *F.glabra* Decne.).
Caudex large; branches more or less glabrous. Leaves oblong to ellipticalyx Flowers solitary or in groups of 2–3; petals curved, lime green; corona white with long lobes. S Africa.

F.glabra Decne. See *F.edulis*.

F.multiflora Schum.
Caudex large; branches stout, gnarled. Leaves small, flat, white-felted beneath. Flowers numerous, in clusters. S Angola.

Folotsia Costantin & Bois. Asclepiadaceae. Leafless succulents. Stems climbing or shrubby, smooth, segmented, terete. Flowers in umbel-like clusters; corona lobes large, united at base, forming a pentagon. Madagascar. Z10.

CULTIVATION As for *Ceropegia*.

F.aculeata (Descoings) Descoings (*Prosopostelma aculeatum* Descoings).
Stems to 30–40cm, trailing, thin, branching from the base, white-powdery. Flowers few; corolla large, papillose within, white, tube 3.5mm, lobes triangular-oblong, bifid. S Madagascar.

F.floribunda Descoings (*Prosopostelma grandiflorum* Choux).
Forms a profusely branched shrub of intricately entwined branches to 3m across and 1.5m tall but will produce stems to 3m long when climbing in trees. Shoots 1.5cm thick, intense green, internodes 10–15cm. Inflorescence many-flowered, flowers rose-scented, lobes 8–9mm long, 4mm wide at base, off-white, corona forming a pentangle with its edges opposite the sepals. N Madagascar.

F.grandiflora (Jum. & H. Perrier) Jum. & H. Perrier (*Decaderia grandiflorum* Jum. & H. Perrier).
Trailing, branches green, becoming white. Flowers around 20 in sessile umbels at the nodes; corolla round, large, lobes 7 × 2mm, triangular, pointed. Madagascar.

Forsteronia G. Mey. (For Thomas Furley Forster (1761–1825), British naturalist.) Apocynaceae. Some 50 species of woody climbing vines with milky sap. Leaves opposite or whorled, entire. Flowers bisexual in axillary or terminal dichasial or thyrsiform inflorescences; corolla funnelform, limb flared; stamens carried on corolla tube, anthers exserted; ovary carries 5 nectaries at its base. Fruit a pair of follicles with comose seeds. Tropical America.

CULTIVATION A tropical liane with evergreen, leathery foliage and dense heads of red or pink, funnel-shaped flowers. It requires the support of a trellis, pergola or host tree. Grow in full sunlight in a fertile, moist but well drained, loam-based soil with additional coir, garden compost or leafmould. Place in a humid but buoyant atmosphere and water plentifully when in full growth, sparingly as light levels and temperatures drop in winter. Maintain a minimum temperature of 16–18°C/60–65°F when in growth, slightly less when dormant. Increase by seed or ripewood cuttings in early spring, rooted in moist sand in a closed case with bottom heat.

F.corymbosa (Jacq.) G. Mey.
To 6m or more. Leaves opposite, to 7.5cm, obovate to elliptic, apex obtuse to acuminate, coriaceous; petioles to 1cm. Flowers red to salmon pink, borne in dense, usually terminal inflorescence, tube 2–3mm, lobes 4–5mm. Fruit 10–15cm, robust, apex obtuse, the follicles widely spreading. Cuba, Hispaniola.

Forsythia Vahl. (For William Forsyth (1737–1804), Superintendent of the Royal Gardens, Kensington.) Oleaceae. 6 species of deciduous shrubs. Branches golden-green, covered with lenticels. Leaves opposite, usually simple, rarely divided ×3, serrate or entire, glabrous; petioles short. Flowers yellow, borne before leaves, singly or clustered to 6, from scaly buds at joints of previous year's growth; calyx 4-lobed, green; corolla deeply divided into 4 oblong lobes, united below in a short tube; stamens 2; stigma heterostylous, twice divided. Fruit a woody capsule, somewhat inflated, bearing many winged seeds. E Asia, C Europe.

CULTIVATION Among the most colourful and floriferous of early spring-flowering shrubs, *F.suspensa* is effectively a climber – its long, arching main branches require the support of walls, fences and larger shrubs and trees, allowing the mass of branchlets to cascade. Plant when dormant in almost any soil. It will tolerate part shade but bloom more prolifically in sun. The slender branches of *F.suspensa* should be allowed to develop in weeping profusion unhindered wherever possible. Older plants may be rejuvenated by thinning by one-third to one-half every 2–3 years, allowing light into the centre and promoting better flowering in areas with cool summers. Propagate by half-ripe cuttings in summer in a case or cold frame, or by hardwood cuttings outside in autumn. Seed can be sown in spring although fruits are rarely borne in cool-temperate zones. Birds may destroy flower buds in cold areas. *Forsythia* is susceptible to leaf spot fungi (*Marssonina forsythiae* and *Phyllosticta forsythiae*), *Armillaria* root rot, attack by capsid bugs; forsythia gall (which may disfigure but not damage) and bacterial blight (*Pseudomonas syringae*).

F.suspensa (Thunb.) Vahl.
To 3m, often with slender, arching, smooth branches. Leaves sometimes trifoliolate. Flowers slender-stalked. Early spring. China. var. **fortunei** (Lindl.) Rehd. Shrub to 3m, erect, arching as growth matures. Leaves to 9 × 5cm, simple or 3-lobed on vigorous shoots, ovate, serrate. Flowers solitary or paired; corolla lobes deflexed, deep yellow, twisted. Mid-spring. China. var. **sieboldii** Zab. Shrub to 2.5m, semi-pendent, sometimes creeping. 'Atrocaulis' (f. *atrocaulis* Rehd.): very vigorous, new growth tinted black-purple, flowers creamy pale yellow. 'Aurea': leaves yellow. 'Decipiens': erect; flowers solitary, long-stalked, numerous, corolla deep yellow, lobes spreading, margins somewhat involute. 'Nymans': close to 'Atrocaulis', flowers larger, bright pale yellow; young plants quick to flower; flowers produced later than most. 'Pallida': more upright in growth, flowers pale yellow, solitary. 'Variegata': leaves variegated yellow. Z5.

Fremontodendron Cov. (For Major-General John Charles Frémont (*d.* 1890), American explorer, botanist and horticulturist.) FREMONTIA; FLANNEL BUSH; CALIFORNIA BEAUTY. Sterculiaceae. 2 species of more or less evergreen spreading shrubs and trees, stellate-pubescent; inner bark mucilaginous. Leaves alternate, unlobed or palmately 3-, 5-, or 7-lobed, subentire. Flowers solitary, showy, on short pedicels; calyx petaloid, 5-lobed, glandular-pitted at the base inside; bracts usually 3, at the base of the calyx; petals

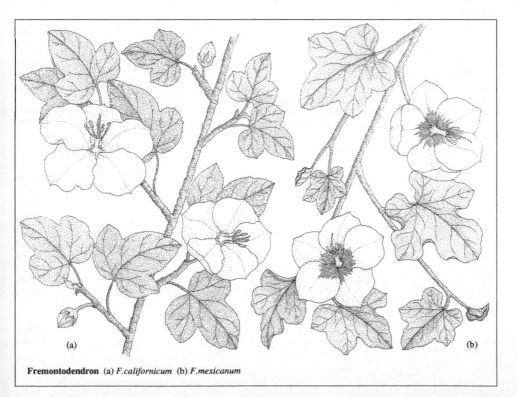

Fremontodendron (a) *F.californicum* (b) *F.mexicanum*

absent; staminal tube divided into 5 parts in the upper half, each with linear 1-celled anthers; style filiform, exceeding the staminal tube. Fruit a capsule, 4–5-valved, 4–5-celled, each cell 2–3-seeded; seeds dark. Southwest N America. Z8.

CULTIVATION Handsome evergreens, grown for their beautiful flowers with conspicuous golden-yellow petaloid calyces, carried from late spring through until mid-autumn. *F.*'California Glory' and 'Ken Taylor' are hardier than the species and, given a sheltered position on a warm south- or southwest-facing well, may be grown in gardens where temperatures occasionally fall as low as −15°C/5°F. *Fremontodendron* species are tolerant of chalk soils and are particularly useful for poor dry soils; rich fertile soils results in excessive growth at the expense of flowering. Grow in full sun in light, well drained soils of low to moderate fertility; provide shelter from cold drying winds, especially at the limits of hardiness. Propagate by softwood or semi-ripe cuttings in a sandy propagating mix with gentle bottom heat.

Fremontodendron has hybridized with its ally in the Sterculiaceae, *Chiranthodendron pentadactylon*, the Handflower or Monkey's or Devil's Hand Tree, a tall Mexican and Guatemalan tree with broad, felty, linden-like leaves and cup-shaped flowers with bright red stamens which take the form of an outstretched, clawed hand. The hybrid is a broadly erect tree with large pale green leaves and dark amber flowers, the 'hands' are deep wine red. It is hardier than *Chiranthodendron* and likely to perform well in Mediterranean-type climates or against extremely sheltered south-facing walls in zones 8–9.

F.californicum (Torr.) Cov. (*Fremontia californica* Torr.).
Shrub to 7m, branches spreading, foliage and flowers mostly on short spur-like branchlets. Leaves to 5cm, suborbicular to elliptic-ovate, unlobed to 3-lobed, 1–3-veined at the base, dull green and sparsely stellate-pubescent above, densely tawny-stellate beneath; petioles 1–4.5cm. Calyx 3.5–6cm diam., shining golden yellow, basal glands long-hairy. Capsule 2.5–3.5cm, ovoid, densely pubescent; seeds dull black. California, W Arizona, N Baja California. ssp. *decumbens* (R.M.Lloyd) Munz. PINE HILL FREEMONTIA. Low-spreading bush branching at 45°, to 2 × 2m. Leaves medium-sized, 3-lobed, grey-hairy. Flowers deep golden yellow to orange-brown. El Dorado County. ssp. *napense* (Eastw.) Munz (*Fremontia napensis* Eastw.). Compact bush, branches whip-like, wiry, to 1.5m; leaves 3-lobed, rounded, to 2.5cm; flowers to 3cm diam., cup-shaped, often rose-tinged, ultimately brilliant orange, scarlet beneath.

F.decumbens R.M. Lloyd. See *F.californicum* ssp. *decumbens*.

F.mexicanum Davidson (*Fremontia mexicana* (Davidson) Macbr.).
Close to *F.californicum*, differing in 5-lobed leaves and narrower sep. Shrub to 6m; branches stiff, densely stellate-tomentose; bark yellow, later becoming dark. Leaves 2.5–7cm, thick, suborbicular, cordate and 5–7-veined at the base, shallowly 5-lobed, sparsely stellate-pubescent above, densely tawny-tomentose beneath; petiole 2–4cm. Flowers sometimes partly obscured by foliage; calyx 6–9cm diam., shallowly campanulate, orange-yellow, becoming red at base outside, glands glabrous or glabrate. Seeds glossy black. S California and N Baja California. 'California Glory' (*F.californicum* × *F.mexicanum*): hardier than either parent, growth strong; flowers shell-shaped, flat, lemon tinged red on exterior, nectaries softly haired. 'Ken Taylor' (*F.californicum* ssp. *decumbens* × *F.*'California Glory'): habit dwarf; flowers orange-yellow all year. 'Pacific Sunset': vigorous, to 6m; leaves angularly lobed; flowers bright yellow with tail-like tips. Z9.

F.napense (Eastw.) R.M.Lloyd. See *F.californicum* ssp. *napense*.

Freycinetia Gaudich. (For Admiral Freycinet (1779–1842), French circumnavigator.) Pandanaceae. 175 species of dioecious, climbing or scrambling evergreen shrubs. Stems slender, often several, ringed with persistent leaf bases, diffusely branched, sometimes producing aerial roots. Leaves decussate to spiralling towards branch tips, linear-lanceolate, slightly concave above, apex narrowed to a fine point, base sheathing, margin and midrib beneath usually spiny-toothed, leathery, dark green often tinted red from base, venation parallel. Spadices club-shaped, subtended by coloured, fleshy bracts; flowers small, lacking calyx or corolla; female flowers with small staminodes; ovary superior. Fruit an oblong-ellipsoid to globose syncarp of fleshy berries, often pendulous. Sri Lanka to SE Asia, Australia, New Zealand, Pacific Is. Z10.

CULTIVATION Tall, slender, multi-stemmed evergreen shrubs for shady positions in subtropical and tropical gardens where their scrambling stems can be allowed to range freely. They are valued for their glossy, *Dracaena*-like foliage and highly coloured, waxen floral bracts. Otherwise, grow in semi-shade and high humidity in an intermediate to warm glasshouse or conservatory, in tubs or beds of open coarse bark mixed with additional leafmould and garden compost. They require frequent misting and may need pruning and some support when growing vigorously. Propagate by air-layering or division. Sometimes affected by scale insect.

F.banksii Cunn.
Scrambling to 30m or more. Stems 0.5cm across, abundantly branched. Leaves 60–90 × 2.5cm, margin minutely toothed. Inflorescence bracts thick, white or pale lilac, fleshy. Individual berries each 8mm. New Zealand.

F.multiflora Merrill.
Tall scrambling shrub. Leaves 30 × 2cm, smooth, glossy dark green, recurved. Inflorescence bracts orange to brick-red, boat-shaped, waxy. Individual berries each to 5mm. Philippines.

Fumariaceae   (a) *Adlumia fungosa*   (b) *Dicentra scandens*   (c) *Corydalis claviculata*

Gelsemium Juss. (From It. *gelsomino*, jasmine.) YELLOW JESSAMINE. Loganiaceae. 3 species of evergreen, twining, glabrous shrubs. Leaves opposite, entire; stipules small. Flowers sweetly fragrant, 5-parted, in axillary or terminal, 1- to few-flowered clusters; corolla funnelform, lobes short, overlapping. Fruit a 2-valved capsule; seeds flattened, winged. All parts usually contain toxic alkaloids. Americas, SE Asia.

CULTIVATION   Twining evergreens from both moist and dry woodland in the wild, *Gelsemium* species are grown for their narrow glossy leaves and handsome, fragrant, funnelform, yellow flowers, carried in spring through to late summer. In zones that are frost-free or almost so, they are suitable for training on trellis and pergolas or for growing on steep banks. In zones at the limits of their hardiness, they need the shelter of a warm south- or southwest-facing wall; in these conditions, where long hot summers ensure ripening, they may tolerate temperatures to −10°C/14°F or below. Otherwise grow in the cool glasshouse or conservatory.

Grow in full sun or light shade in any well drained, moisture-retentive, moderately fertile soil; high levels of nitrogen result in excessive vegetative growth at the expense of flowering. Under glass, provide cool to intermediate conditions and plant in a medium-fertility loam-based mix in direct sun; water moderately when in growth, otherwise sparingly. Under glass they will flower more profusely if restricted at the roots. Prune hard back after flowering, to keep within bounds, remove deadwood and thin crowded shoots. Propagate by seed in spring at 18–21°C/65–70°F, or by semi-ripe cuttings in a closed case with gentle bottom heat. Mealybug, scale insect and white fly may be problems under glass; control with appropriate insecticides or biological controls.

G.amboinense Kuntze. See *Tecomanthe dendrophila*.
G.dendrophilum Kuntze. See *Tecomanthe dendrophila*.

G.rankinii Small.
Similar to *G.sempervirens* but leaf bases more rounded; pedicels scaly only at base; flowers unscented; sepals acuminate, persistent in fruit.   Fruit to 1.2cm, long-beaked. N Carolina to Florida and Alabama. Z8.

G.sempervirens (L.) St.-Hil. CAROLINA JASMINE; CAROLINA YELLOW JESSAMINE; CAROLINA WILD WOODVINE; FALSE JASMINE; EVENING TRUMPET FLOWER
Stems slender, to 6m. Leaf petioles short; lamina to 5×3.5cm, oblong or ovate-lanceolate, base narrow, shiny green. Flowers fragrant, axillary; sepals obtuse, deciduous in fruit; corolla yellow with orange centre, to 3cm long, 2.5cm+ wide; pedicels short and scaly throughout. Fruit to 2cm, short-beaked. Late spring–early summer. S US, Mexico, Guatemala. Z9.

Gerrardanthus Harv. ex Hook. f. (For W.T. Gerrard (*d*1866), who collected in Natal, Zululand and Madagascar.) Cucurbitaceae. 5 species of dioecious perennial climbers. Rootstock semi-tuberous. Stems often succulent, swollen, becoming partially lignified. Tendrils apically bifid. Leaves simple, ovate, cordate, entire or 3–5-lobed. Inflorescence a panicle, female inflorescence with few flowers; calyx tube shallow, slightly cupular with dentiform lobes; petals 5, unequally rotate; stamens 5, paired, 1 reduced; anther adpressed, staminodes in female often absent; ovary trigonous, elongate, pistillode absent in male; styles 3, occasionally 1. Fruit obconical, dry, coriaceous, trigonous; seeds fusiform with membranous wing. C, E & S Africa. Z9.

CULTIVATION An impressive member of the Cucumber family for the cool to intermediate, dry glasshouse or porches and pergolas in xeriscapes in zones 9 and over. Climbing stems clothed with lobed, smooth mid green leaves arise from a massive caudex. Plant in a gritty, loam-based medium in large clay pots, tubs or borders in full sun. Water and feed moderately when in growth, hardly at all when at rest. Propagate by seed (stem cuttings will root but tend not to form a caudex).

G.macrorhiza Harv. ex Benth. & Hook. f.
Stems basally swollen, subglobose, to 50cm diam., becoming woody; branches climbing freely. Leaves glabrous, 3–7-lobed, 3–8×3–8cm, lobes entire. Corolla tinted brown, 1.2cm diam.; styles 3. Fruit obconical, cylindric, yellow-brown, somewhat ribbed, to 7cm; seeds brown, compressed, to 25× 7mm, wing pale brown. S & E Africa.

G.megarhiza Decne. See *G.macrorhiza*.

Gloriosa L. GLORY LILY; CLIMBING LILY; CREEPING LILY. Liliaceae (Colchicaceae). 1 species, a tuberous, perennial herb, related to *Sandersonia* and *Littonia*, climbing by means of tendrils at leaf tips. Tubers narrow or thick, irregularly cylindric, red-brown. Stems to 2.5m, 1–4 per tuber, simple or sparsely branched, slender, twining, glossy bright green. Leaves 5–8cm (excluding terminal tendril), ovate-lanceolate to oblong, apex acuminate, apex finely tapering, often to a tendril to 3–5cm long (if uncoiled), glossy bright green, pliable. Flowers solitary, on long pedicels in leaf axils, usually angled downwards; tepals 6, 4–10× 2.5–3cm, narrow-lanceolate to spathulate, acuminate, spreading, usually bowed at centre and gently but distinctly reflexed at tip, yellow to red or purple or bicoloured, margins often incurved, undulate or crisped; stamens 6, slender, spreading, anthers to 1cm, versatile; style 3-branched, bent at base at right angle to the ovary. Fruit a capsule. Summer–autumn. Tropical Africa and Asia. Z10. All parts are toxic. The several 'species' of *Gloriosa* are now treated as variants of *G.superba*. They vary in height and attitude of stems, the development of leaf tendrils, colour and shape of tepals.

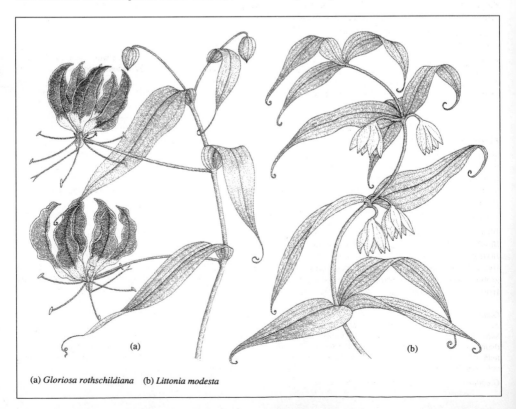

(a) *Gloriosa rothschildiana*   (b) *Littonia modesta*

CULTIVATION   A beautiful, slender climbing herb, clinging by means of tendrils, *G.superba* is grown for its exotic, brilliantly coloured blooms. It is relatively easily grown in the cool glasshouse or conservatory in cool temperate zones. In frost-free climates these plants are used as sprawlers or climbers for sunny situations in freely draining soils, showing useful tolerance of nutritionally poor soils.

Grow in full sun in a freely draining, fertile, loam-based mix with additional sharp sand and screened, well rotted garden compost. Support the climbing stems on pea sticks, a cane frame or a wire hoop, water plentifully and feed fortnightly with dilute liquid feed when in full growth, with a minimum temperature of 8–10°C/46–50°F. Pot-grown specimens may be moved out of doors for the warm summer months. Withhold water as growth ripens and dies back in late summer/early autumn; store the long, narrow tubers in their pots in dry, frost-free conditions. Repot every 1–2 years either in late winter with heat or in early spring. Propagate by seed sown in a sandy propagating mix in late winter with gentle bottom heat, by careful division in spring, or be offsets. Aphids may be a pest under glass.

G.abyssinica Rich. See *G.superba* 'Abyssinica'.
G.carsonii Bak. See *G.superba* 'Carsonii'.
G.rothschildiana O'Brien. See *G.superba* 'Rothschildiana'.
G.simplex L. See *G.superba* 'Simplex'.

G.superba L.
The typical plant is described below as *G.*'Superba'. 'Abyssinica' (*G.abyssinica* Rich.): stems 45–60cm; tepals 5–7.5cm, red centrally banded gold, especially at base, not crisped. 'Carsonii' (*G.carsonii* Bak.): stems to 90cm; tepals broad, purple-red, edged yellow, strongly reflexed, margins undulate, not crisped. 'Citrina': tepals citron yellow tinted or striped claret. 'Grandiflora': like 'Simplex', but tepals larger, golden-yellow. 'Greeneae': tepals smooth, straight, yellow

tinted copper. 'Rothschildiana' (*G.rothschildiana* O'Brien): stem to 250cm; tepals 7.5–10cm, scarlet fading to ruby or garnet, yellow at base and in central stripe, strongly recurved – the largest and finest form. 'Simplex' (*G.simplex* L.): small; tepals spathulate, yellow-green turning deep orange and yellow, margin not crisped. 'Superba' (*G.superba* L.): stems to 180cm; tepals narrow, closely undulate and crisped, reflexed, yellow-green turning deep rich orange and red. 'Superba Lutea': tepals yellow, tightly crisped. 'Verschuurii' (*G.verschuurii* Hoog): stems to 150cm; tepals to 9cm, thick, reflexed, undulate, vivid crimson, yellow at margins and base. 'Virescens': tepals smooth, clear yellow.

G.verschuurii Hoog. See *G.superba* 'Verschuurii'.

Gmelina L. (For J. Gottlieb Gmelin (1709–55), German naturalist.) Verbenaceae. Some 35 species of trees or shrubs, often scandent when young, often armed with axillary spines. Leaves opposite, simple, entire or lobed. Inflorescence of few-flowered cymes or racemes, often arranged in a terminal panicle; flowers large, showy; calyx persistent, obconical-campanulate, truncate or 4 to 5-dentate, often with large glands; corolla tube infundibular, limb oblique, bilabiate, upper lip entire or 2-lobed, lower lip 3-lobed; stamens 4, usually included, didynamous, inserted below middle of corolla tube; ovary 4-locular. Fruit a succulent drupe, 1- to 4-seeded. Africa, Mascarenes, Australasia and Indomalaya. Z10.

CULTIVATION   As for *Clerodendrum*.

G.hystrix Schult. ex Kurz. See *G.philippensis*.

G.philippensis Cham.(*G.hystrix* Schult. ex Kurz). WILD SAGE. Shrub; branches pendent to scandent, spiny. Leaves to 10× 6cm, ovate-elliptic to obovate, acute or obtuse, glaucous with peltate scales beneath, veins pubescent; petiole to 4cm.

Racemes to 20cm, many-flowered; bracts to 4×3cm, ovate or obovate, green or red-purple; calyx with 2–4 glands; corolla yellow, to 5.5cm, irregularly campanulate, exterior pubescent. India, Philippines.

Grewia L. (For Nehemiah Grew (1641–1712), plant anatomist.) Tiliaceae. Some 150 species of climbers, shrubs or trees; branches stellate-tomentose. Leaves simple, alternate, 3–9-nerved, entire or serrate, with persistent stipules. Flowers fairly small, solitary, or borne in few-flowered axillary or terminal cymes; sepals 5, stellate-tomentose outside; petals 5, usually with nectariferous claws; stamens numerous, distinct; ovaries 5-celled, with 8 or more ovules. Fruit a small, 1- to 2-seeded drupe, fleshy or fibrous, with 1–4 lobes. S & E Asia, Africa, Australia. Z10 .

CULTIVATION   A comparatively large genus containing shrubs and trees. *G.asiatica* (Phalsa) is grown in India for its pleasantly acid, edible fruits; it and others are used also as sources of fibre. Most of the species will thrive in any fertile, well drained soil in full sunlight in zones 9 to 10, and several of the shrubby species have found favour in Mediterranean-type gardens. The three described below are sprawling to climbing shrubs with attractive foliage and pink, mauve, white or yellow flowers. They require to be tied into walls or trellises. In cooler zones, grow them in intermediate to hot glasshouse conditions in a mix of equal parts loam and peat. Propagate from seed or by layering.

G.caffra Meissn.
Spreading or climbing evergreen shrub, 2–3m. Leaves to 8cm, moss-green, glabrate, acute or acuminate. Flowers 4cm diam., axillary, pale lavender pink, stamens yellow, prominent. Fruit globose, without lobes, glabrous or sparsely pubescent. E & S Africa.

G.orientalis L. (*G.columnaris* Sm.).
Trailing or erect evergreen shrub. Leaves 7.5cm, ovate to oblong, shortly acuminate, scabrous beneath, with 3 veins from the base. Flowers few, terminal or axillary cymes, white or yellow. Fruit to 1.5cm diam., tinged purple, with 4 shallow lobes. India.

G.columnaris Sm. See *G.orientalis*.

G.similis Schum.
Climbing shrub to 4.5m. Leaves to 10cm, ovate to ovate-elliptic. Flowers in axillary cymes to 3–6, mauve. Fruit deep orange, 4-lobed. India.

Gurania Cogn. (Anagram of the related genus *Anguria*.) Cucurbitaceae. About 75 species of herbaceous climbers or trailers, dioecious, annual or perennial. Tendrils simple. Leaves simple, palmate, membranous to subcoriaceous. Male inflorescence a raceme or capitulum; receptacle tubular; sepals elongate, narrow, tinged red, exceeding petals; petals free, ligulate, yellow; stamens 2, free, subsessile; pistilode absent; female flowers solitary or clustered, similar to male except staminodes 0–2; ovary cylindric, bilocular; style bifid; stigmas 2. Fruit long, cylindric, fleshy; seeds many, compressed, ovate. Tropical America. Z10.

CULTIVATION A vigorous cucurbit suited to large pots or beds of fertile loam in the warm glasshouse, where it will quickly grow into the rafters and twine through glazing bars, producing long, cylindric ornamental fruit. Cultural requirements as for *Momordica*, but cross-pollination is usually needed for fruit production.

G.makoyana (Lem.) Cogn. (*Anguria makoyana* Lem.).
Stout, perennial climber. Stems and tendrils villous. Leaves membranous to subcoriaceous, pilose, suborbicular, deep green above, paler beneath, 15–35 × 18–4cm, lobes 3, rounded, acuminate, minutely denticulate. Male inflorescence capitate, female inflorescence a few-flowered cluster; recepta-cle tube to 1cm; sepals erect, linear, acuminate, pubescent, about 2cm shorter in female; petals erect, fused, ellipsoid, papillose, to 8mm; ovary cylindric, pilose, about 2cm; style thick. Fruit cylindric, acute at both ends, green; seeds numerous, cream, ovate, 8×2mm. Guatemala, Honduras.

Gynostemma Bl. (From Gk *gyne*, woman, and *stemma*, garland.) Cucurbitaceae. 2 species of dioecious or monoecious trailing perennial herbs. Stems often somewhat woody at base. Tendrils bifid, occasionally simple. Leaves usually palmately lobed. Inflorescence an axillary panicle or raceme; flowers green or white, bracteate; calyx small, rotate, 5-lobed; corolla rotate, lobes 5, deeply divided, lanceolate; stamens 5, partially connate, staminodes in female; ovary 2–3-locular, pistillode absent in male. Fruit a globose berry, 1–3-seeded, black; seeds compressed. S & E Asia. Z8.

CULTIVATION As for *Echinocystis*.

G.pentaphyllum (Thunb.) Mak. SWEET TEA VINE.
Annual or perennial to 8m. Stem puberulent. Tendrils simple. Petiole to 7cm; leaflets 3–7, lanceolate to ovate, acuminate to obtuse, serrate, oblique, terminal leaflet to 8 × 3cm, laterals smaller. Inflorescence to 15cm, pubescent; flowers yellow-green; ovary globose; styles 3. Fruit dark green to near black, smooth, with white line, to 0.8cm diam. Japan.

Hardenbergia Benth. (For Countess von Hardenberg, sister of the celebrated traveller Baron von Hügel (1795–1870); a patron of horticulture and an active traveller in the tropics, he collected plants in Western Australia in 1833.) Leguminosae (Papilionoideae). AUSTRALIAN SARSPARILLA 3 species of vines and subshrubs. Leaves alternate, with a single leaflet or trifoliolate to imparipinnate, leaflets very variable in shape. Flowers in pairs or small clusters in long, axillary racemes, small, violet or purple, sometimes white or pink, standard broadly orbicular, spotted yellow or green, wings adherent to keel, almost equaling standard; stamens 10, 1 free. Fruit linear; seeds arillate. Allied to *Kennedya*, but flowers many and smaller, and keel obtuse, shorter than wings. Australia, Tasmania. Z9.

CULTIVATION *Hardenbergia* spp. are characteristic of the dry sclerophyll vegetation of their native zones and are found in a dense scrub comprising mainly evergreen shrubs and dwarf trees. *H.comptoniana* is commonly found in coastal scrub, and often occurs scrambling through the trees in the jarrah (*Eucalyptus marginata*) forests of western Australia. They are vigorous climbers, grown for their attractive violet or mauve-pink flowers carried in late winter and early spring. In favourable climates, where winter temperatures do not fall much below −5°C/23°F, they are well suited to growing over arch, fence or pergola, or will trail over a retaining wall. In cooler zones, they may be pot-grown in the cool glasshouse or conservatory, with a minimum winter temperature of 7–10°C/45–50°F. Grow in moist, well drained, lime-free soils in sun or light dappled shade. In containers in a moderately fertile medium that drains freely and is rich in organic matter will suit. Water moderately and feed monthly with dilute liquid feed when in growth, and keep just moist in winter. Container-grown plants with integral support may be plunged outdoors in summer. Propagate by seed sown in spring at 20°C/68°F, presoaked for 24 hours prior to sowing and covered with fine grit. Also by tip-cuttings in late spring, rooted in moist sand or vermiculite, in a closed case with bottom heat. Scale insects are sometimes a pest.

H.comptoniana Benth. (*H.digitata* Lindl.). WESTERN AUSTRALIAN CORAL PEA; BLUE CORAL PEA.
Evergreen vine to 3m. Stem slender, vigorous, twining. Leaves 3–5-foliolate; leaflets 6 × 3cm, narrow-lanceolate to ovate, acuminate. Flowers in dense, axillary or terminal racemes to 12.5cm long, blue to purple, standard 4mm diam. with white, green-spotted blotch at base, wings obovate. Fruit to 5 × 1cm, narrowly cylindric, turgid; seeds 6×3mm, ellipsoid, brown, pale-arillate. Summer. W Australia.

H.digitata Lindl. See *H.comptoniana*.
H.monophylla (Vent.) Benth. See *H.violacea*.

H.violacea (Schneev.) F.C. Stearn (*H.monophylla* (Vent.)
Benth.; *Kennedya ovata* Sims; *Kennedya monophylla* Vent.).
VINE LILAC; PURPLE CORAL PEA; FALSE SARSAPARILLA.
Evergreen climbing shrub to 2m+. Stems vigorous and twining, or prostrate and not rooting. Leaves 8×2.5cm, simple, ovate to oblong-lanceolate, leathery. Flowers about 30, in pendulous axillary racemes, purple, white, pink, or lilac, standard 8.5mm diam., cordate, emarginate, spotted yellow or green at centre, wings obovate, purple. Fruit 4cm, linear, turgid; seeds to 5×2.5mm, reniform.   Spring. E Australia, Tasmania.'Rosea': flowers pink. 'Violacea': habit lowmounding or vining; leaves lustrous; flowers bright lavender with primrose eye, in long racemes, spring. 'White Crystal': flowers pure white, late winter.

Harrisia Britt. (For William Harris, Superintendent of Public Gardens and Plantations in Jamaica, early 20th century.) Cactaceae. About 20 species of shrubs, some tree-like, to 7m, or scandent; stems usually slender, ribbed, not segmented, not rooting aerially; ribs 4–12. Flowers nocturnal, funnelform, 12–22 × c8–12cm, white; floral areoles with hair-spines or merely felted; tube elongate; perianth-limb broad. Fruit fleshy, areolate and scaly and/or spiny, yellow or orange and not splitting (subg. *Harrisia*) or red and usually splitting (subg. *Eriocereus*); seed broadly oval, 1.5–2.5 × 1.2–1.8mm, black-brown, semi-matt, periphery crested with larger cells; relief low-domed; hilum medium, basal, deeply impressed, forming a chamber. SE US (Florida), the Caribbean region, Brazil, Bolivia, Paraguay, Argentina. Z10.

CULTIVATION   Grow in an intermediate glasshouse (min. 10–15°C/50–60°F), use `standard' cactus compost: moderate to high inorganic content (more than 50% grit), pH 6–7.5; shade in hot weather; maintain low humidity; keep dry from mid-autumn until early spring, except for light misting on warm days in late winter.

H.aboriginum Small. See *H.gracilis*.

H.adscendens (Gürke) Britt. & Rose (*Eriocereus adscendens* (Gürke) A. Berger).
Shrub, woody at base; stems much branched or clambering to 5–8m×2–5cm; ribs 7–10, low, rounded; areoles raised on elongate tubercles; leaf-rudiments present; spines usually 10, 2–3cm, stout. Flower 15–18cm, white. Fruit 5–6cm diam., globose to elongate, tuberculate, red, splitting unilaterally when red; pulp juicy, white. E Brazil.

H.bonplandii (Parmentier ex Pfeiff.) Britt. & Rose. See *H.pomanensis*.

H.earlei Britt. & Rose.
Prostrate shrub; stems 2–3m, eventually 4–6cm diam., nearly terete; young stems 2–3cm diam.; ribs 5–7, dark green; areoles 2–4cm apart; spines 5–8, 4–5cm, ascending. Flower c20cm, white. Fruit 6–7cm diam., depressed-globose, yellow, nearly smooth. Cuba.

H.eriophora (Pfeiff.) Britt. (*H.fragrans* Small).
Like *H.gracilis*. Ribs 9–12. Spines 8–15, the longest 1.2–4.4cm. Flower 15–17.5×7.5–10cm; floral areoles with white hairs 10–15mm; inner tepals entire. Summer. Cuba, SE US (Florida).

H.fragrans Small. See *H.eriophora*.

H.gracilis (Mill.) Britt. (*H.aboriginum* Small; *H.simpsonii* Small).
Erect or sprawling shrub; stems 1–5m×2.5–4cm, not segmented; ribs 9–11, rounded; areoles c12mm apart; spines 7–16, up to 2.5cm, rigid. Flower 15–20×10–12cm; floral areoles with white or brown hairs 6–8mm; inner tepals irregularly toothed. Fruit 3–4×3–6cm, depressed-globose, orange-red or yellow. Summer. Jamaica, SE US (Florida).

H.guelichii (Speg.) Britt. & Rose (*Eriocereus guelichii* (Speg.) A. Berger).
Clambering shrub, reputedly to 25m; stems 3–5cm diam., segmented, 3–4 angled; spines c6, 1 stouter and longer than the rest. Flower large; scales of pericarpel and tube c2cm; floral areoles nearly naked. Fruit 4–7cm diam., strongly tuberculate, with persistent scales, spineless. Summer. N Argentina.

H.jusbertii (Rebut ex Schum.) Borg (*Eriocereus jusbertii* (Rebut ex Schum.) Riccob.).
Stems suberect; ribs 4–6, broad; spines c7–11, less than 5mm. Flower 18cm, white with brown-green tube. Fruit to 6cm diam., depressed-globose, red. A plant of uncertain status, possibly a hybrid or a variant of *H.pomanensis*. It is known only in cultivation, and commonly used as a grafting stock.

H.martinii (Labouret) Britt. & Rose (*Eriocereus martinii* (Labouret) Riccob.).
Sprawling or clambering shrub, to 2m or more; stems 1.5–2.5cm diam.; ribs 4–5; areoles seated on broad tubercles, c15–25mm apart; central spine 1, 2–4cm, stout, radial spines 1–3, to 3mm. Flower 15–22×15–17cm; pericarpel and tube with small subulate scales 2–3mm; floral areoles felted and more or less hairy; inner tepals white or pale pink. Fruit c3cm, globose, red, splitting down one side, tuberculate and very shortly spiny. Summer. Argentina.

H.nashii Britt.
Slender shrub to 2–3m; stems divergent, 3–4cm diam.; ribs 9–11, rounded; areoles 20–25mm apart; spines 3–6, to 15mm. Flower 16–20cm; scales of tube to 15mm, acuminate. Fruit 6–8 × 4–5cm, ellipsoid, strongly tubercled at first. Hispaniola.

H.pomanensis (F.A. Weber) Britt. & Rose (*Eriocereus pomanensis* (F.A. Weber) A. Berger; *H.bonplandii* (Parmentier ex Pfeiff.) Britt. & Rose; *Eriocereus bonplandii* (Parmentier ex Pfeiff.) Riccob.).
Stems erect at first, then sprawling or clambering to 3m or more, 3–8cm diam., 4(–5)-angled, articulate, glaucescent; areoles 12–14mm apart; spines rigid, pink-tinged at first, later nearly white, tipped almost black; central spine 1, 1–2.5cm, radial spines 5–8, c1cm. Flower c15cm; tube with acute scales 1cm or more; floral areoles hairy. Fruit 3–5cm, globose, red, splitting laterally to expose the spongy white funicles and black seeds. Summer. S Brazil and Paraguay to N Argentina. Specialists disagree on the identity of the original *H.bonplandii*, and the name is therefore best avoided.

H.portoricensis Britt.
Slender shrub to 2–3m; stems suberect, 3–4cm diam.; ribs 11, rounded; areoles 15–20mm apart; spines 13–17, to 3cm. Flower c15cm; scales of tube to 15mm, acuminate. Fruit 4–6cm diam., ovoid to globose, yellow, tubercled at first, becoming smooth or nearly so. Puerto Rico.

H.regelii (Weingart) Borg (*Eriocereus regelii* (Weingart) Backeb.).
Status uncertain. Perhaps a variety of *H.martinii*.

H.simpsonii Small. See *H.gracilis*.

H.tetracantha (Labouret) D. Hunt (*Roseocereus tetracanthus* (Labouret) Backeb.; *Trichocereus tetracanthus* (Labouret) Borg).

Shrub or small tree to 4m; stems 6–10cm diam., blue- or grey-green; ribs 7–9, somewhat tubercled below the areoles; central spine 1, radial spines 4–7. Flower 18–22cm; scales of pericarpel acute; floral areoles with dense curled hairs. Fruit ovoid. Bolivia.

H.tortuosa (Forbes ex Otto & A. Dietr.) Britt. & Rose (*Eriocereus tortuosa* (Forbes ex Otto & A. Dietr.) Riccob.).

Intermediate between *H.pomanensis* and *H.martinii*; stems 2–4cm diam., 6–7-ribbed, the ribs somewhat tuberculate and the grooves between slightly zig-zag; central spine 1, 3–4cm, radial spines 5–10, to 2cm. Flower 12–15cm; scales of pericarpel short; areoles of pericarpel with felt and an occasional short spine; scales of tube acute, c1cm; areoles of tube hairy; inner tepals white to pale pink. Fruit 3–4cm, globose, red, tubercled and with a few short spines. Summer. Argentina.

Hedera L. (Lat. name for the plant.) IVY. Araliaceae. 11 species of evergreen, woody, climbing or creeping plants with distinct sterile juvenile and fertile arborescent stages. Stems of juvenile stage climbing, supported by aerial rootlets; stems of arborescent stage without aerial rootlets. Leaves alternate, simple, those of juvenile stage conspicuously lobed or cordate, those of arborescent stage more nearly entire, base cordate, obtuse or broadly cuneate, all leaves glabrous and often waxy and shining above, stellate-hairy or scaly beneath. Flowers small, perfect, in globose umbels which are solitary or in compound racemes or panicles; pedicels stellate-hairy or scaly; calyx 5-lobed, 1–3mm, yellow-green; stamens 5, alternate with petals ovary 4–5-celled; styles fused into single column, stigma 5-lobed. Fruit a subglobose drupe, 4–7mm, with persistent style at apex, black, sometimes orange, yellow or cream. Europe, Asia, N Africa.

CULTIVATION Ivies are valued as coverage for walls, sheds and even unsightly tree stumps; ivy-clad buildings have considerable charm. For large expanses of wall the larger-leaved kinds such as *H.colchica* and *H.hibernica* are the most suitable; for smaller areas the diversity of leaf shape and variegation of the many cultivars of *H.helix* can be used to advantage. Variegated ivies look particularly well against red-brick backgrounds and add immensely to the winter beauty of the garden. The yellow-green leaved clones such as *H.helix* 'Buttercup' associate well with purple-leaved shrubs or blue-flowered plants, while against white walls the winter purple of the leaves of *H.helix* 'Atropurpurea' can make a dramatic contrast.

Preference for shade and its creeping habit make ivy an excellent groundcover plant and one whose variegated cultivars can be used with great effect to brighten dark corners. The sulphur-cream *H.hibernica* 'Sulphurea' underplanted with autumn crocus (*Colchicum* spp.) makes an attractive colour combination and will guard the flowers against mud splash.

Concern is sometimes expressed as to the effects of ivy on trees or buildings. Ivy is not parasitic and, while the growth of ivy on trees of value or beauty is to be deprecated, an unloved tree may well be given up to it. When such a tree becomes ivy-laden it makes a most pleasing winter picture and a refuge for birds. On sound buildings and walls, ivy is harmless but can become unwieldy and harbour insects. To obviate this it should be clipped over in late spring every other year or so. Walls and fences that are very weak can be pulled down if a mass of ivy becomes heavy with snow or rain; clipping prevents this.

For fence or boundary screening, ivy takes up less space than a conventional hedge and is particularly useful for clothing chain-link or wire fencing. A vigorous clone such as *H.helix* 'Digitata' should be planted at 90cm/36in. intervals. The resultant 'fedge' may be clipped in spring like a hedge.

The non-climbing forms of *H.helix*, 'Congesta' and 'Erecta', and the slow-growing, rock-hugging 'Conglomerata' make good feature plants for rock garden or patio. In completely shaded town gardens, ivy will grow perfectly well and here the variegated kinds can be utilized as climbers or potplants to brighten a dark site.

Although the Victorians used ivies widely for indoor decoration it was the appearance in the US in 1921 of a clone of *H.helix* with short internodes that gave rise to the present extensive use of ivies as house plants. This interest has also led to a revival of the technique of producing 'standard' ivies through side-grafting small-leaved trailing kinds on the single 45cm–1m stems of × *Fatshedera*, the vigorous hybrid between *Hedera hibernica* and *Fatsia japonica* 'Moseri'.

In ivy topiary, wire frames fashioned as globes, birds, animals, etc. are stuffed with moss which has been soaked in a dilute fertilizer solution. Rooted cuttings of short-jointed clones such as *H.helix* 'Ivalace' or the variegated 'Goldchild' are then inserted and the whole sprayed frequently with water to keep the moss moist and deter red spider mites. As the plants grow they are trimmed and clipped to produce the ivy-clad figure.

Ivies are readily propagated using nodal cuttings of juvenile growth with one or two leaves. Woody shoots of the adult stage are less easy and may require mist facilities. Cuttings are best taken between June and October when the young growth has hardened sufficiently. Inserted in sharp sand in lightly shaded frames they root rapidly and may then be potted into a medium-fertility soil-based mix. When well rooted and growing they may be planted out or, if specimen or conservatory plants are required, potted on into larger pots and then trained either to canes in the form of a trellis or on to moss poles. In the conservatory or the home, ivies should never be placed in direct sunlight or be allowed to dry out. During summer a balanced liquid feed every 14 days is beneficial.

Soil preparation for ivies growing outside should be generous, as for any permanent planting. In non-lime areas the inclusion of chalk, lime or mortar rubble can be advantageous but is not essential. Plants intended to climb need to be guided by being tied to a cane leading to their support. If this is not done the ivy will initially creep along the ground, possibly ascending at a point not envisaged by the planter. Ivies growing outside are relatively free of disease. Under glass they may be subject to red spider mite and scale insects.

Hedera   (a) *H.hibernica* leaf of juvenile state (above), leaf of arborescent state (below)   (b) *H.hibernica* 'Sulphurea'
(c) *H.azorica* leaf of juvenile state, above leaf of arborescent state, below   (d) *H.hibernica* 'Variegata'   (e) *H.canariensis*
'Gloire de Marengo'   (f) *H.canariensis*   (g) *H.canariensis* leaf of juvenile state   (h) *H.maderensis*

Leaves are either unlobed or lobed, the space between the lobes, the sinus, is either shallow and wide giving a broader leaf or narrow and deep giving a more 'fingered' leaf. The hairs which often define a species are minute, present mainly on young growth and either spread star-like (stellate) or like minute scales (scale-like).

H.algeriensis Hibb. See *H.canariensis*.

H.azorica Carr. Leaves with 5–7 bluntly acute lobes, 9–11 × 10–12cm, centre lobe only slightly longer than laterals, sinuses shallow, light matt green. hairs stellate, 3–5-rayed, white and so extensive as to give young stems and leaves a felted appearance. Azores.

H.canariensis Willd. (*H.algeriensis* Hibb.) Juvenile leaves unlobed, occasionally 3-lobed, 10–15 × 8–12cm, bluntly acute, base cordate, margin entire, mid-green and glossy, stems purple-red. Adult leaves elliptic-lanceolate, hairs scale-like, 1–15 rays. Flowers 10–20 on umbels. Berry black. Canary Is., N Africa. Z8. 'Gloire de Marengo': as species but leaves variegated with areas of silvery-grey and cream-yellow; a popular house-plant but an outside climber in favoured districts. 'Margino Maculata': as the species but extensively mottled cream-yellow variegation. 'Montgomery': leaves 3-lobed, stems and petioles wine-red; sometimes listed as *H.algeriensis*. 'Ravensholst': as the species but with large, mostly 3-lobed leaves, centre lobe acute and broad, some leaves unlobed and elliptical; dark glossy green. 'Striata': as the species but vigorous and a darker green with a very slight yellow variegation at the leaf centre. McAllister and Rutherford have proposed that the name *H.canariensis* should be given to a new ivy found on Teneriffe ('New work on Ivies', *Journal International Dendrology Society* and *British Ivy Society Journal* 1982) and that the long-accepted ivy described by Willdenow in 1804 be redesignated *H.algeriensis*, based on the view that Willdenow had been examining Algerian material. This amounts effectively to a name-swap, and one that has caused considerable confusion in botanical and horticultural circles. Whilst that position was adopted in *The New RHS Dictionary* (1992) and the *Index of Garden Plants* (1994), pending the emergence of further evidence, the more traditional stance is taken here.

H.colchica K. Koch PERSIAN IVY; BULLOCK'S HEART IVY; COLCHIS IVY.
Leaves ovate, generally unlobed, 6–12 × 6–8cm, apex acute, base cordate, margin entire, dark green. All plant parts resinous-scented when crushed. Adult leaves lanceolate; hairs scale-like, 12–20 rays. Inflorescence umbellate-corymbose; calyces triangularly toothed. Berry black. Caucasus to Asiatic Turkey. 'Dentata' (ELEPHANT'S EARS): leaves pendent, larger than the type, 15–20 × 15–18cm, base auriculate, the margins carrying widely spaced fine teeth, light green. 'Dentata Variegata': similar to 'Dentata' but leaves smaller, 15–20 × 10–12cm, light green variegated with areas of grey-green and irregular marginal areas of cream-yellow. 'Sulphur Heart' ('Paddy's Pride'): similar to 'Dentata Variegata' but leaves a deeper green with an irregular central splash of yellow. Z6.

H.helix L. COMMON IVY; ENGLISH IVY.
Juvenile leaves 3–5-lobed, 5–8cm, leathery, entire with cordate base and pale venation, young stems and leaves with white-stellate, 4–6-rayed hairs. Leaves of arborescent stage elliptic, entire, less than 5cm wide. Flower pedicels, peduncle and calyx bearwhite-stellate hairs. Fruit to 9mm, black, rarely orange. Europe and E Russia.The most variable of the species, *H.helix* has yielded many horticulturally useful clones. var. *baltica*: As type but exceptionally cold-resistant. 'Angularis': leaves 5-lobed, centre lobe prolonged and acuminate, laterals bluntly acute, dark green in summer, colouring purple in winter. 'Atropurpurea': leaves 3-lobed, centre lobe prolonged and acuminate, laterals blunty acute, dark green in summer, purple in winter. 'Buttercup': leaves 5-lobed, apex acute, base cordate, light green, butter yellow in sunlight. 'Cavendishii' : leaves 3-lobed, apex acuminate, mid-green, dappled grey-green, margin cream-yellow; stems light green.

'Chrysophylla' ('Spectabilis Aurea'; 'Aurea Spectabilis'): leaves 3-lobed, lobes acute, leaf base truncate, mid to deep green, slightly suffused yellow; can be confused with 'Angularis Aurea', whose leaves are thinner and lighter green. 'Congesta' : non-climbing, erect; leaves 3-lobed, dark green, in a distichous arrangement. 'Conglomerata': creeping but producing short upright shoots; leaves unlobed, margins undulate and waved. 'Dealbata' ('Discolor'): leaves triangular, 3-lobed, dark green mottled cream-white. 'Digitata': leaves 5-lobed, deeply divided, cente lobe only slightly longer than laterals. 'Erecta': non-climbing, erect; leaves 3-lobed; stems green; larger in all parts than 'Congesta'. 'Eva': leaves small with grey-green centre, splashed deep green, margined cream. 'Fantasia': leaves 5-lobed, apex acute, base deeply cordate, bright green heavily mottled cream-yellow. 'Goldchild': leaves 3–5-lobed, base cordate, mid-green with bright yellow, mostly marginal variegation. 'Goldheart': leaves 3-lobed, centre lobe longer and acuminate, dark green with prominent yellow splash in the leaf centre. 'Glacier': leaves 3-lobed, apex acute, mid-green overlaid grey-green with occasional cream variegation. 'Glymii': leaves unlobed, ovate-acuminate, glossy, becoming deep purple in winter. 'Green Ripple': leaves 5-lobed, light green, veins prominent on leaf surface giving a rippled effect.

'Ivalace': leaves 5-lobed, margins strongly undulate, convolute at the sinus giving a crimped and laced effect, dark green and glossy. 'Kolibri': leaves 3–5-lobed, light green with flecks of grey-green and areas of cream variegation. 'Little Diamond': leaves unlobed, apex acute, base attenuate, producing a diamond-shaped leaf, grey-green, white variegation slight and mainly at the edge. 'Manda's Crested': leaves 3– 5-lobed, lobes convolute with blunt, downward-pointing apices giving a curly effect. 'Maple Leaf': leaves 5-lobed, apex acuminate, centre lobe 1.5 times length of laters, edges irregularly indented, mid-green. 'Melanie': similar to 'Parsley Crested' but having the crested leaf edged coloured violet-purple. 'Midas Touch': leaves unlobed, deltoid or triangular, apex bluntly acute, base cordate, dark green, irregularly variegated bright yellow. 'Minor Marmorata' (SALT AND PEPPER IVY): leaves 3-lobed, small (3–5cm), dark green, spotted and splashed cream-white. 'Parsley Crested': leaves unlobed, ovate to almost circular, margins crimped and crested, light green. 'Pedata' (BIRD'S FOOT IVY): leaves 5-lobed, centre lobe prolonged and narrow, basal lobes back-pointing, dark green, veins grey-white. 'Professor Friedrich Tobler': leaves with 3–5 narrow (0.5–1cm) lobes divided almost to the centre vein, dark green. 'Shamrock': leaves 3-lobed, centre lobe broad, lateral lobes sometimes folded in pleated fashion alongside centre lobe, dark green. 'Spetchley': leaves 3-lobed, very small (0.5–2cm), centre lobe prolonged, dark green. 'Tres Coupé': leaves 3-lobed, centre lobe twice the length of laterals deeply cut, mid to dark green. 'Tricolor': leaves unlobed, triangular, small (2–4cm), grey-green with cream-yellow edge that is slightly pink in summer, intensifying to purple in winter. 'William Kennedy': leaves 3-lobed but laterals often reduced to give a single-lobed small (1.5–3cm) leaf. var. *poetarum* Nyman (*H.poetica*; *H.helix* var. *poetica*). POET'S IVY; ITALIAN IVY. Leaves 5-lobed, 5–7 × 6–8cm, the two basal lobes much reduced giving a somewhat 'square' appearance to the light green leaf; grown for the novelty of its dull orange berries.

H.helix 'Hibernica'. See *H.hibernica*.

H.hibernica (Kirchn.) Bean (*H.helix* 'Hibernica'). IRISH IVY.
Young leaves 5-lobed, 5–9 × 8–14cm, lobes triangular and bluntly acute, centre lobe larger, base cordate, dark green, with stellate hairs tending to lay in parallel fashion rather than the haphazard fashion of *H.helix*. Adult leaves ovate-elliptic. Berry black, not freely produced. Atlantic coast of GB,

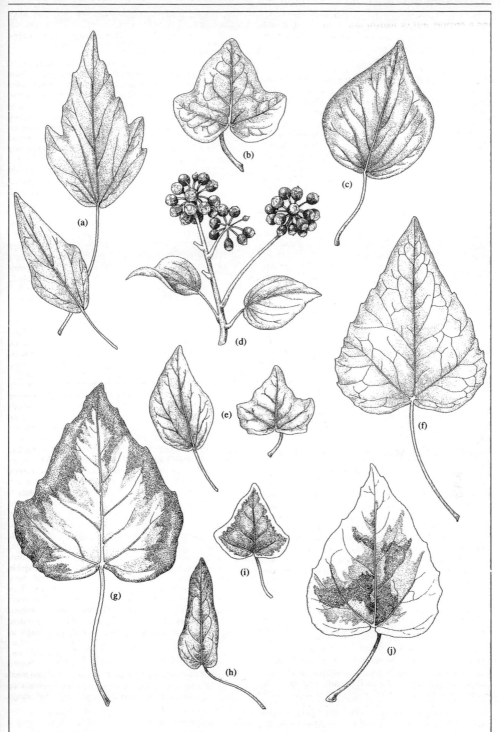

Hedera   (a) *H.nepalensis* leaf of juvenile state (above), leaf of arborescent state (below) (b) *H.colchica* leaf of juvenile state (c) *H.colchica* leaf of arborescent state (d) *H.colchica* fruiting heads (e) *H.rhombea* leaf of juvenile state (right), leaf of arborescent state (left) (f) *H.colchica* 'Dentata' (g) *H.colchica* 'Sulphur Heart' (h) *H.pastuchovii* (i) *H.rhombea* 'Variegata' (j) *H.colchica* 'Dentata-variegata'

Ireland, W France, Spain, Portugal. 'Deltoidea' (SWEETHEART IVY): leaves sometimes 3-lobed but more often deltoid and unlobed, base strongly cordate with overlapping lobes giving an almost heart-shaped leaf, dark green. 'Hamilton': leaves 5-lobed, centre lobe only slightly longer than laterals, mid green, edge thickened. 'Helford River': leaves 5-lobed, centre lobe prolonged and acuminate, mid-green with grey-white veins. 'Lobata Major': leaves 3-lobed, lateral lobes at right angles to the long-acuminate central lobe. 'Rona': leaves 5-lobed, mid-green with freckled and diffused yellow variegation; less green leaf intrusion than with 'Variegata'. 'Rottingdean': leaves 5-lobed, digitate, centre lobe slightly longer than laterals, sinuses narrow and convolute at the clefts, dark green. 'Sulphurea': leaves irregularly 3–5-lobed, grey-green, edged and splashed sulphur yellow. 'Variegata': leaves 5-lobed, dark green, some leaves entirely yellow or parti-coloured, often defined by the veins, variegation striking but all-green leaves predominant. Z7.

H.maderensis K. Koch ex Rutherford ssp. **maderensis**. Juvenile leaves 3-lobed, occasionally unlobed, 4–5 × 6–7cm, sinuses very shallow orabsent, lobes obtuse, base truncate or slightly cordate, mid to dark green, very glossy at first. Hairs scale-like with 10–16 rays. Madeira. Z9.

H.maroccana McAllister. MOROCCAN IVY. Stems and petioles purple-red. Leaves 3-lobed, 7–9 × 7cm, centre lobe twice as long as laterals, sinuses shallow, apex acute, base cuneate or truncate, dark green; hairs scale-like, rays 6–8. Morocco. 'Spanish Canary': leaves very large; hardy and fast-growing. Z8.

H.nepalensis K. Koch (**H.himalaica** Tobler; **H.cinerea** (Hibb.) Bean). HIMALAYAN IVY. Juvenile leaves ovate to lanceolate, 6–10 × 4–5cm, obscurely lobed, lobes often little more than3–6 marginal indentations, apex acute, base truncate, matt olive-green, hairs scale-like, 12–15-rayed. Adult leaves elliptic-lanceolate, unlobed. Berry dull orange. Himalaya to Kashmir. 'Suzanne': differs from type in 5-lobed leaves, the short basal lobes back-pointing to give a 'bird's foot' effect, dark green. var. **sinensis** Tobler. Juvenile leaves unlobed, rarely 3-lobed, ovate-acuminate, base cuneate, maroon at first rapidly maturing to matt mid-green. Adult leaves elliptic-ovate. N & E China.

H.pastuchovii Woron. (**H.pastuchowii**). Juvenile leaves narrowly ovate, 4–9 × 3–4cm, unlobed, apex acuminate, base slightly cordate, dark green, glossy, slightly leathery, hairs scale-like with 8–12 rays, sparse. USSR, Iran.

H.rhombea (Miq.) Bean (**H.japonica** Paul). JAPANESE IVY. Juvenile leaves ovate to triangular, unlobed, 2–4 × 4–5cm, apex acute, mid-green, leathery, stems green, hairs scale-like, rays 10–18. Japan. 'Pierrot': leaves similar but smaller, stems thin and wiry, possibly a Taiwanese botanical variety. 'Variegata': similar to the type but with slightly smaller leaves with a distinctive rim of white variegation at the leaf edge; more useful and much more widely grown than the type. Z7.

H.roegneriana Hibb. See **H.colchica**.

Heliophila L. (From Gk *helios*, sun, and *philos*, loving.) Cruciferae. 71 species of annual to perennial herbs and subshrubs, to 3m. Stems erect, decumbent or climbing. Leaves variable: entire, lobed, pinnately or nearly bipinnately divided; minute stipules sometimes present. Flowers usually in a raceme; sepals 4, sometimes saccate at base; petals 4, usually clawed, lanceolate to round, often with basal appendage, white to blue or pink; stamens 6, free. Fruit a silique or silicle, rounded to linear, sometimes torulose, round in section or somewhat compressed, dehiscent; seed compressed, often winged. Summer. S Africa. Z9.

CULTIVATION The Cape Stocks are grown for their colourful flowers and attractive foliage, usually as flower border annuals; *H.scandens*, however, is a woody-based perennial climber with fleshy leaves and racemes of large, rose-tinted flowers. It favours a well drained soil and an open, sunny position in drier areas in zones 9 and 10. In colder regions, grow in the cool to intermediate glasshouse or conservatory in pots of sandy and gritty loam-based mix; train on wires or canes; position in direct sunlight with low humidity; ventilate freely in summer; water sparingly in winter and maintain a minimum temperature of 10°C/50°F. Increase by seed sown in late winter.

H.scandens Harv. Perennial woody or woody-based twining climber, to 3m. Leaves 4–8cm, broad-elliptic to lanceolate, glabrous, fleshy, acute or obtuse; petiole narrow. Racemes corymbose, becoming lax in fruit; sepals 4.5–6.5mm; petals 8.5–14mm, white tinted rose, circular-obovate. Fruit 25–40 × 8–13mm, elliptic, compressed, net-veined, style narrow-winged.

Hibbertia Andrews (For George Hibbert (1757–1837), a patron of botany, he had a private botanic garden at Clapham, London, England and employed James Niven to collect plants in South Africa.) BUTTON FLOWER; GUINEA GOLD VINE. Dilleniaceae. Some 125 species of evergreen shrubs, ericoid or scandent. Leaves alternate, sometimes perfoliate, linear to obovate; petioles, where present, usually terminal; sepals and petals 5; stamens numerous. Fruit a 1– to several-seeded follicle; seeds arillate. Madagascar, Australasia, Polynesia. Z10.

CULTIVATION Valued for their handsome foliage, often beautifully coloured on emergence, and the simple and brightly coloured blooms carried over several months in summer. *Hibbertia* species are suitable for outdoor cultivation in warm temperate, essentially frost-free climates, although given the shelter of a warm south- or southwest-facing wall, they may tolerate very light and short-lived frosts. In cooler regions, they are elegant specimens for the cool glasshouse or conservatory. Grow in sun or part shade in any moderately fertile, well drained but retentive soil; provide support, tying-in as growth progresses. Under glass, admit bright filtered light, ensuring shade from the hottest summer sun, and use a freely draining, medium-fertility, loam-based mix. Water plentifully and feed fortnightly when in full growth, reducing water as light levels and temperatures fall in autumn. Maintain a winter minimum temperature of 5–10°C/40–50°F. Prune to thin out congested growth in early spring. Propagate by semi-ripe cuttings in a sandy propagating mix, or by layers.

Hedera helix   (a) *H.helix* leaf of arborescent state   (b) *H.helix* inflorescence   (c) *H.helix* leaf of juvenile state
(d) 'Atropurpurea'   (e) 'Parsley Crested'   (f) 'Congesta'   (g) 'Goldheart'   (h) 'Pedata'   (i) 'Conglomerata'   (j) 'Eva'
(k) 'Glacier'   (l) 'Ivalace'   (m) 'Gnome'   (n) 'Green Ripple'   (o) 'Manda's Crested'   (p) 'Maple Queen'
(q) 'Professor H. Tobler'   (r) 'Shamrock'   (s) 'Buttercup'

H.dentata R. Br. SNAKE VINE; TOOTHED GUINEA FLOWER
Shrub or subshrub. Stems trailing or twining, initially downy. Leaves to 5cm, ovate-oblong, apex obtuse or acuminate, margins sometimes sparsely and shallowly prickle-toothed, base rounded. Flowers to 5cm diam.; petals deep yellow, obovate, mucronate, outspread. Australia (NSW).

H.perfoliata Endl.
Glabrous shrub, erect or trailing. Leaves 2.5–7 × 1.25–3cm, ovate, perfoliate, entire or sparsely toothed. Flowers to 3cm diam.; petals obovate, primrose to golden yellow. W Australia.

H.scandens (Willd.) Dryand. ex Hoogl. (*H.volubilis* Andr.; *Dillenia scandens* Willd.; *Dillenia speciosa* Thunb.). SNAKE VINE; GOLD GUINEA PLANT; GUINEA FLOWER, GUINEA GOLD VINE; BUTTON FLOWER.Shrub to 1.25m, procumbent or twining. Branches initially sericeous. Leaves 5–10 × 1.5–3cm, obovate to lanceolate, base cuneate, glabrous above, sericeous beneath; petiole winged, stem clasping. Flowers to 5cm diam., malodorous, at tips of downy lateral branchlets; petals golden yellow, obovate. Australia (Queensland, NSW).

Hidalgoa La Ll. & Lex. (For Michael Hidalgo (early 19th century), eminent Mexican.) CLIMBING DAHLIA. Compositae. About 5 species of subshrubby perennial herbaceous lianes, climbing by means of the petioles. Leaves opposite, pinnately divided into 3 or more leaflets, entire or toothed. Capitula radiate, usually solitary; ray florets yellow or red, disc florets yellow, usually sterile. Fruit a cylindrical cypsela; pappus absent. Mexico, C America. Z10.

CULTIVATION As for *Mutisia*.

H.ternata La Ll.
Perennial to 50cm. Leaves to 10×7cm, ovate, 3-pinnate, segments coarsely toothed, central leaflet to 7.5cm, lateral segments smaller; petioles to 5cm. Capitula to 5cm diam., solitary or few, terminal or axillary; ray florets 5, orange. Mexico.

H.wercklei Hook.f. (*Childsia wercklei* J.L. Childs).
Subshrub to 1m+. Leaves to 6 × 5cm, ovate, 3-pinnate, toothed, teeth tipped red-brown; petiole to 5cm. Capitula to 6cm diam., solitary, axillary; ray florets 10, scarlet above, yellow beneath. Costa Rica.

Hiptage Gaertn. (From Gk *hiptamai*, to fly; the samaras are winged.) Malpighiaceae. 20–30 species of erect or climbing shrubs. Leaves opposite, simple, coriaceous, eglandular or glandular beneath, petiolate; stipules absent. Inflorescence a terminal or axillary, simple or compound raceme; flowers numerous, fragrant; peduncles bracteate, pedicels 2-bracteolate; sepals 5, unequal, glandular; petals 5, unguiculate, unequal, erose or fimbriate, sericeous externally; stamens 10, 1 larger than others, filaments connate at base; ovary 3-lobed, stigmas 1–2. Samaras 1–3, 2–3-winged. Tropical Asia to Fiji. Z10.

CULTIVATION As for *Acridocarpus*.

H.benghalensis (L.) Kurz.
Large shrub or tall climber, white- or yellow-sericeous in all parts. Leaves to 20cm, lanceolate to ovate-lanceolate. Flowers 10–30 in racemes, pink or white, marked yellow, very fragrant. Sri Lanka, SE Asia to Philippines and Taiwan.

H.madablota Gaertn.
Tall climber, glabrous except inflorescence Leaves 10–15cm, oblong or ovate-lanceolate, apex acuminate, coriaceous,

glossy above. Racemes axillary, to 15cm; flowers to 2.5cm diam., very fragrant; petals fimbriate, white, the fifth marked yellow at base. Sri Lanka and India to Burma and Malaysia.

H.obtusifolia DC.
Large shrub to 6m, close to *H.madablota* but smaller in all parts. Leaves oblong, obtuse. Flowers fragrant white, fifth petal flushed pink, with yellow base, others white. S China.

Hodgsonia Hook. f. & Thoms. (For B.H. Hodgson (1800–1894).) Cucurbitaceae. 1 species, a dioecious climber. Stems to 30m. Leaves coriaceous, palmate, broad, glabrous, lobes 3–5, entire to denticulate, acute, 14–18cm. Male flowers in racemes, females solitary; calyx tubular, often rusty-pubescent outside, 5-lobed, to 9cm; petals 5, to 5cm, obovate, truncate with curling apical filaments to 9cm long, off-white tinted yellow with rusty hairs; stamens 3, filaments short, anthers connate, exserted; ovary globose, unilocular; style 1, long; stigmas 3. Fruit globose, grooved, firm, red-brown, tomentose, 5–11cm; seeds usually 6, flat, ellipsoid, veined. SE Asia. Z10.

CULTIVATION As for *Trichosanthes*. One of the most showy cucurbits in flower and fruit but extremely vigorous, requiring a large glasshouse even when grown as an annual. The inside of the seed is edible and an oil may be derived from it used, among other purposes, for roasting opium.

H.heteroclita Hook. f. & Thoms. See *H.macrocarpa*.

H.macrocarpa (Bl.) Cogn. (*H.heteroclita* Hook.f. & Thoms.).

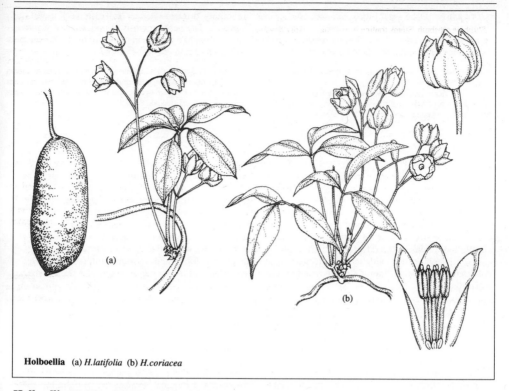

Holboellia (a) *H.latifolia* (b) *H.coriacea*

Holboellia Wallich. (For Frederik Ludvig Holboell (fl. 1847), a superintendent at the Copenhagen Botanic Garden.) Lardizabalaceae. About 5 species of evergreen, twining shrubs. Leaves long-petioled composed of 3–9 palmately arranged leaflets. Flowers axillary corymbs or racemes, unisexual; petals reduced to nectaries, sepals petaloid, 6, fleshy, male flowers with 6 distinct, free stamens; female flowers with 3 carpels and 6 rudimentary stamens. Fruit a fleshy, indehiscent berry; seeds black, glossy, embedded in pulp. N India to China. Closely related to *Stauntonia*, which differs in its thin sepals and united stamens. Z8.

CULTIVATION *Holboellia* species are grown for their handsome, evergreen foliage and small, delicately coloured flowers, either to drape a wall or cover a tree stump; alternatively, they may be used to climb small trees, trellis or a tripod system in a border. *H.coriacea* is considered to be the hardiest species, but may suffer damage during prolonged spells below –5°C/23°F. To keep the plant within suitable proportions, weaker growths and dead wood can be removed in spring. They succeed on most garden soils, either in sun or shade. Fruits are not readily produced, particularly in northern areas, and hand pollination may be required. Increase by seeds, cuttings and layering.

H.coriacea Diels.
To 7m, young shoots often red. Leaflets 3, central leaflet larger, 5–15cm, ovate to obovate or lanceolate, lateral leaflets ovate, entire, coriaceous, dark green, distinctly veined. Male flowers white, 1.2cm long, borne in a terminal cluster of corymbs; female flowers larger, 3–4 in lower leaf axils, sepals white-green delicately flushed purple, carpels cylindric. Fruit 5cm, oblong or ovate-oblong, purple. Summer. C China.

H.fargesii Reaub.
Differs from *H.coriacea* in its 5–9 leaflets (blue-green beneath) and flowers 2cm long. Summer. C China.

H.hexaphylla hort. See *Stauntonia hexaphylla*.

H.latifolia Wallich.
To 5m, branches and twigs glabrous, glaucous. Leaflets 4–12cm, 3–7, digitately arranged, ovate-oblong, tip acute or acuminate, base rounded or cuneate, glabrous, central leaflet with longer petiolule than lateral leaflets; petiole 4–8cm. Raceme 3–12cm of 3–7 fragrant flowers: male flowers green-white, female flowers purple, 1–2cm diam. Fruit 5–10cm, an oblong to ovoid-oblong berry, with apex and base rounded, red to purple. Spring. Himalaya. var. **angustifolia** (Wallich) Hook. f. & Thoms. Leaflets 7–9, narrower. Distribution as for *H.latifolia*, doubtfully distinct.

Holmskioldia Retz. (For Theodor Holmskiold (1732–94), Danish botanist.) Verbenaceae. Some 10 species of scandent shrubs. Leaves opposite, simple. Inflorescence a short terminal panicle or an axillary raceme; calyx usually red, rotate-campanulate, membranous, tube short, limb spreading, entire or subentire; corolla tubular, bilabiate, tube elongate, slightly curved, upper lip 2-cleft, lobes erect-spreading, lower lip 3-cleft, lobes reflexed; stamens 4, exserted, didynamous; ovary 4-locular, with 1 pendent ovule per locule. Fruit a 4-lobed capsule. Tropical Africa, Asia. Z10.

CULTIVATION Once established *Holmskioldia* species are highly drought-tolerant and extremely useful for plantings in poor sandy soils in tropical and subtropical gardens. The best-known is *H.sanguinea*, a vigorous scrambler with scarlet tubular flowers subtended by 'hat'- or 'saucer'-like calyces in orange or red. In cooler climates, they need warm glasshouse protection (min. 16°C/60°F), and treatment as for *Clerodendrum*.

H.sanguinea Retz. CUP AND SAUCER PLANT; MANDARIN'S-HAT; CHINESE-HAT PLANT.
Leaves to 7.5cm, membranous, ovate or ovate-elliptic, acuminate, base rounded, slightly serrate, minutely pubescent beneath when young; petiole to 2.5cm, slender, puberulent.

Flowers to 2.5cm, pedicel slender, filiform, puberulent; calyx to 1.8cm diam., net-veined, glabrous, brick-red to orange, becoming green-brown with maturity; corolla scarlet. Fruit obovate, black. Himalaya.

Hoya R. Br. (For Thomas Hoy (*c*1750–1822), gardener at Syon House, London.) PORCELAIN FLOWER; WAX FLOWER. Asclepiadaceae. Variable genus of some 200–230 species of perennial, evergreen, branching climbers and epiphytes, some more shrubby or succulent. Stems usually woody; branches of some species exude latex if damaged. Petioles short, stout, with an apical extra-floral nectary; leaves opposite, variable in shape and size, often leathery or fleshy, mostly glabrous, entire. Inflorescence axillary, pendent, nectariferous umbellate racemes or cymes; peduncles 3–10cm, often persisting over several seasons and bearing successive umbel-like clusters of flowers; flowers few to many, pentamerous, often fragrant, waxy; calyx small, corolla lobes thick, often reflexed, usually white, pink or pale yellow; central corona formed by appendages at the filament bases, with lobes which alternate with corolla lobes and surround anthers often highly coloured; pollen in pollinia. Fruit subcylindric, elongated, horn-like; seeds dense, comose. Asia, Polynesia, Australia.

CULTIVATION Vigorous evergreens, usually climbers, grow for their handsome foliage and large pendent heads of waxy flowers, often deliciously fragrant, as in *H.australis* and *H.carnosa* and its cultivars. Suitable for clothing pergolas, trellises and arches in the humid tropics (or subtropics, for *H.carnosa*, *H.globulosa*, *H.lanceolata* ssp.*bella*, *H.sikkimensis* and *H.polyneura*), in temperate climates they succeed in the warm glasshouse or conservatory or as houseplants. Most need the support of wire, trellis or hoops, preferably wadded with a moisture-retentive material such as sphagnum, but slender shrubby species such as *H.lanceolata* ssp.*bella* are amenable to cultivation in hanging baskets. Grow in a coarse, open, fertile medium that is freely draining but moisture-retentive, rich in fibrous organic matter, with additional coarse sand and charcoal. Provide bright light, but shade from the hottest sun to avoid foliage scorch, and maintain a humid but buoyant atmosphere; water plentifully and liquid feed fortnightly when in full growth keeping just moist in winter. The tropical species require minimum temperatures of 16–18°C/60–65°F, subtropical species require minima of 10–13°C/50–55°F. Some species bear successive flushes of flowers on the same stalk over several seasons, so remove only the individual flowers as they wither. Propagate by semi-ripe cuttings in a shaded closed case with gentle bottom heat or by layers. Mealybug can be a problem under glass. The non-climbing species are retained here for the sake of completeness.

H.acuta Haw. (*H.parasitica* (Roxb.) Wallich ex Wight).
Slender vine. Leaves 10cm, ovate-lanceolate, base cuneate, apex acute, pale green. Umbels to 40-flowered, convex; peduncles 3–5cm; pedicels 3cm; corolla 1.5cm diam., white, hairy within; corona dark pink above, white below. Summer. India to Malaysia and Indonesia. Z10.

H.archboldiana Norman.
Robust vine. Leaves 20–30cm, shiny, oblong, base cordate, apex acute. Umbels to 15cm diam., 8–12-flowered; peduncle stout, 1.5cm; pedicels about 7, 4cm; calyx lobes small, ovate; corolla 3.5cm diam., lobes triangular, reflexed, red-pink tipped white; corona lobes 6mm, hard and yellow-brown to black when dry. New Guinea. Z10.

H.australis R. Br. ex Traill (*H.bandaensis* hort.; *H.dalrympleana* Muell.; *H.darwinii* hort.; *H.keysii* Bail.).
Succulent, epiphytic climber to 5m. Leaves to 12cm, obovate or suborbicular, acute, thick, dark green. Umbels 4cm diam.; flowers 10–40 per umbel, honeysuckle-scented; corolla lobes broad, white, waxy, flat and glabrous with papillose margins; corona red-purple, cup-shaped. Summer. Australia. Z9.

H.bandaensis hort. See *H.australis*.
H.bella Hook. See *H.lanceolata* ssp. *bella*.

H.carnosa (L. f.) R. Br. WAX PLANT.
Succulent, glabrous climber to 6m or more, often epiphytic in wild. Leaves to 8cm, elliptic-obovate, base tapering to cordate, apex blunt to bluntly acute, dark green, sometimes flecked white. Flowers on short peduncles, umbels rounded; corolla 1.5cm diam., lobes recurved, white to flesh-pink,

densely papillose above; corona waxy white with a red centre. Summer. India, Burma, S China. 'Alba': flowers white. 'Exotica': leaves variegated yellow and pink, margins green. 'Picta': leaf margins creamy white. Further leaf colour variants occur, including some with only sparse and faint silver mottlings or yellow zones. Z9.

H.carnosa var. *compacta* hort. See *H.compacta*.
H.carnosa var. *picta* (Sieb.) Bl. See *H.carnosa* 'Picta'.

H.compacta C.M. Burton (*H.carnosa* var. *compacta* hort.; *H.* 'Hindu-rope').
Pendulous shrub. Leaves folded with under surfaces exposed and upper surfaces concealed. Flowers almond-scented, similar to those of *H.carnosa* but corona lobes broader and shorter. Origin unknown.

H.coriacea Bl.
Vigorous climber. Leaves to 12cm, ovate or ovate-elliptic, dark green, leathery, slightly fleshy. Umbels large, dense, to 40-flowered, on reflexed peduncles to 8cm; pedicels 5cm, hairy; flowers 1.5cm diam., colour varying with position of plant; corolla lobes ivory, buff yellow or very pale brown; corona white with crimson or maroon centre. India and Burma to Indonesia. Z10.

H.coronaria Bl.
Climber to 3m, thick-stemmed, slow-growing, pubescent. Leaves to 10cm, oval, mucronate, almost glabrous above, margins revolute; petioles terete, hairy. Umbels large, to 10-flowered; peduncles to 3cm; flowers to 2cm diam., strongly scented at night; corolla lobes pale green-white to creamy yel-

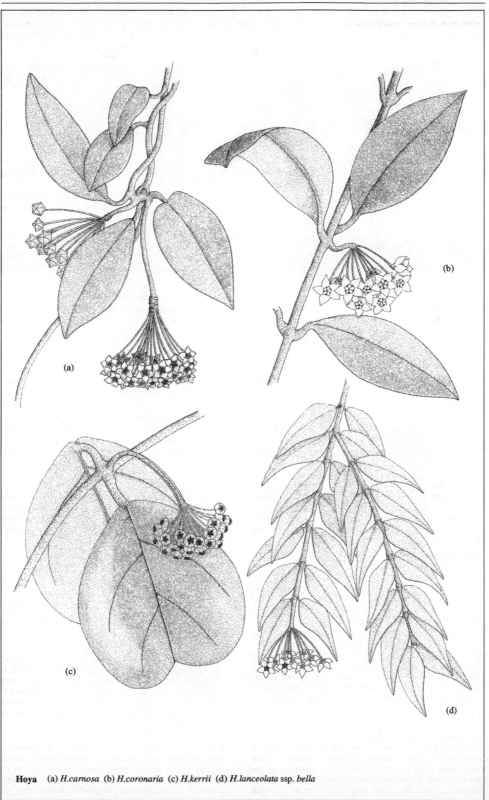

Hoya   (a) *H.carnosa* (b) *H.coronaria* (c) *H.kerrii* (d) *H.lanceolata* ssp. *bella*

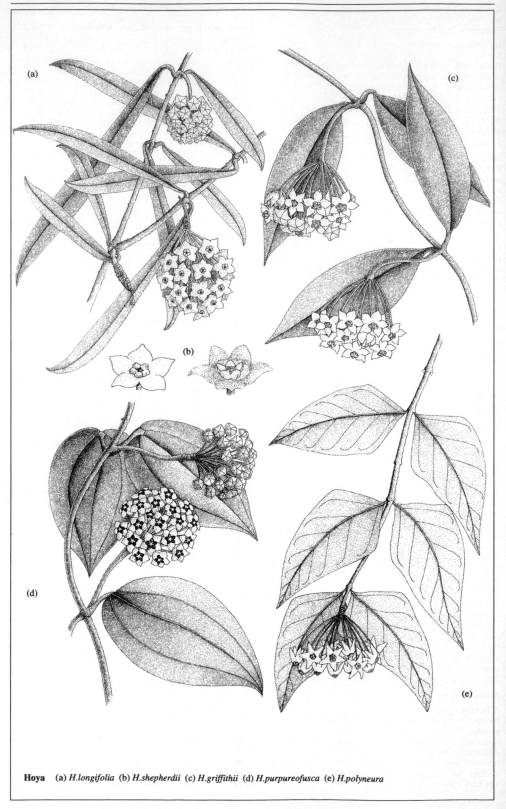

Hoya (a) *H.longifolia* (b) *H.shepherdii* (c) *H.griffithii* (d) *H.purpureofusca* (e) *H.polyneura*

low, forming a shallow bell shape; corona with 5 basal crimson spots. Summer. S Indonesia, Malaysia, Thailand, Philippines, New Guinea. Z10.

H.cumingiana Decne.
Erect, shrubby climber. Leaves to 7cm, sessile, cordate, flat, closely set together, bright green and glabrous above, slightly downy beneath. Umbels pendent, on short peduncles; flowers 12–15 per umbel, sweet-scented; corolla lobes glossy, yellow-green, reflexed; corona yellow with dark maroon or red centre. Spring–early summer. Malaysia. Z10.

H.dalrympleana Muell. See *H.australis*.
H.darwinii hort. See *H.australis*.

H.fraterna Bl.
Robust, sprawling, with thick, terete stems. Leaves to 30cm, broadly elliptic, base subcordate, thick, leathery, dark green above, acute, margins revolute. Umbels large, dense, to 20-flowered; peduncle thickened at base; flowers to 2.5cm diam.; corolla red-pink; corona bright yellow to buff, shiny. Indonesia. Z10.

H.fusca Wallich.
Large, branching vine. Leaves to 22cm, oblong, with thick petioles, flat, thick and leathery, base obtuse, apex mucronate. Umbels dense, hemispherical, many-flowered; peduncle thick, half as long again as petioles; flowers to 2cm diam.; calyx small, lobes ovate; corolla lobes bright yellow, lanceolate, margins reflexed; corona truncate, dark brown. Summer. Nepal to S China and Thailand. Z9.

H.fuscomarginata N.E. Br. See *H.pottsii*.

H.globulosa Hook. f.
Climber with downy stems and branches. Leaves to 15cm, oblong, puberulent, leathery, base rounded, apex slender-acute. Umbels globose, many-flowered; corolla lobes cream-yellow or straw-yellow; corona with a pink base, apex cream. Spring, summer. N India, Nepal, Tibet. Z9.

H.griffithii Hook.f.
Climber, stems twining. Leaves 10–25cm, short-petiolate, oblanceolate to elliptic. Umbels many-flowered; peduncles stout, 2.5–4.5cm; flowers 2.5–4cm diam.; corolla lobes dark rose-red, with 2 faint pink stripes per lobe; corona waxy-white. Summer. NE India to S China. Z9.

H.'Hindu-rope'. See *H.compacta*.

H.imperialis Lindl.
Fast-growing, robust climber to over 6m, stems and branches covered by a thick down. Leaves 15–22cm, elliptic to narrow-oblong, thick, leathery, base cordate, apex mucronate, revolute, margins wavy. Umbels to 20cm diam., 7–12-flowered; peduncles 10–12cm; flowers 7cm diam.; pedicels curved, about 8cm; corolla lobes spreading, dark rusty-brown or magenta to maroon and finely hairy above, green beneath, fleshy, waxy; corona creamy white, prominent, blunt. Summer. Indonesia, Malaysia. Z10.

H.kerrii Craib.
Climber to 3m, stems smooth, pale. Leaves to 10cm or longer, on stout petioles, broadly obovate to orbicular-cordate, dark green, paler and downy beneath, leathery, apex blunt and deeply emarginate, ciliate. Umbels to 20-flowered; flowers 1.2cm diam., densely hairy inside; corolla creamy white; corona rose-purple. Summer. Thailand, Laos. Z10.

H.keysii Bail. See *H.australis*.

H.lacunosa Bl.
Stems and branches terete, thin. Leaves fleshy, on short, stout petioles, dimorphic, either to 3cm, thick, ovate, or to 7cm, oblanceolate, with ridged margins. Peduncles reflexed, 5cm, concave; umbels to 30-flowered; pedicels 0.4–2.5cm; corolla lobes to 8mm, white-green, with dense, tiny, soft hairs, apices strongly reflexed; corona yellow. Spring, early summer. Thailand, Malaysia, Indonesia. Z10.

H.lanceolata Wallich ex D. Don. ssp. **lanceolata** (*H.sikkimensis* hort.).
Shrub-like, to 1m, stems flaccid, pendulous, short-hairy. Leaves to 2.5cm, variable but usually lanceolate, densely set, base rounded, fleshy, green. Umbels 3–7-flowered; flowers sweetly scented; corolla snow white, lobes to 6mm, flat or slightly reflexed, hairy; corona rose-red to amethyst-violet, translucent, thick-lobed. Summer. Himalaya. ssp. **bella** (Hook.) D.H. Kent (*H.bella* Hook.; *H.paxtonii* hort. ex Williams). MINIATURE WAX PLANT. To 45cm, stems arching, minutely and densely pale-downy. Leaves to 3cm, on very short petioles, dark to rather pale green, ovate-lanceolate, thinly fleshy, revolute, base rounded. Umbels 8–9-flowered; flowers 1.5cm diam., very sweetly scented, pendent; corolla lobes to 7mm, waxy-white, acute, margins slightly incurved; corona amethyst-violet, segments ovate to cymbiform. Summer. Himalaya to N Burma. 'Krinkle-Kurl': leaves twisted and curled, folded lengthways. Z9.

H.lasiantha (Bl.) Korth.
Climber. Leaves to 16cm, elliptic, short-acute, papery. Peduncle to 6cm; umbel convex, to 40-flowered; pedicels curving, to 5cm; corolla lobes about 1.5cm, yellow to pale orange, strongly reflexed, bases with dense, long hairs; corona orange. Summer. S Thailand, Malaysia, Indonesia. Z10.

H.latifolia G. Don.
Stems long, climbing. Leaves to 25cm, ovate to oblong-ovate, thick, leathery, copper-coloured when young. Peduncles stout, bases warty, to 7.5cm; umbels many-flowered; corolla pink. S Thailand, Malaysia, Indonesia. Z10.

H.linearis Wallich ex D. Don.
Epiphyte. Stem woody with slender, grey-green, pendent branches to over 1.6m long. Leaves closely set, 2.5–5cm, very narrow, linear in outline, subcylindric, deeply grooved beneath, revolute, finely hairy, dark green above, paler beneath, short-petiolate. Umbels small, terminal, lax; flowers slightly fragrant, 1cm diam.; corolla ivory-white; corona yellow, tinged pink, translucent. Summer–autumn. Himalaya. var. **sikkimensis** Hook.f. Stems weaker, more flaccid. Umbels 10–13-flowered; flowers about 1.3cm diam.; corolla glabrous within, lobes recurved. Summer–autumn. Himalaya to N Burma. Z9.

H.longifolia Wallich. STRING BEAN PLANT.
Close to *H.shepherdii*. Epiphyte. Stems to 1cm, slender. Leaves 6–15cm, linear-lanceolate, acuminate, dark green, fleshy; petioles thick, geniculate near apex making leaves almost pendent. Umbels 5cm diam., few-flowered; flowers delicate, 1–4cm diam., fragrant; corolla white, sometimes flushed pink, not usually hairy as in *H.shepherdii*; corona rose-pink or red. Early summer. Himalaya to S Thailand and Malaysia. Z9.

H.macgillivrayi Bail.
Leaves to 20cm, broadly ovate or ovate, base cordate, apex cuspidate, glabrous, dark green, copper when young, petioles to 3cm. Umbels 4–12-flowered, peduncles to 11cm; pedicels to 4cm; flowers 8cm diam., cup-shaped; corolla lobes dark red, bases sometimes white, acute, with recurved margins; corona dark red, occasionally white-centred, to 2.4cm diam., lobes 4–6mm, linear. Australia (Queensland). Z9.

H.macrophylla Bl.
Shrub-like, scrambling climber, glabrous. Leaves to 25cm, ovate-lanceolate or elliptic-lanceolate, fleshy, base rounded, apex acute, pale green, with 3 longitudinal yellow veins. Umbels globose or subglobose, many-flowered, on purple peduncles to 7.5cm; flowers about 1.2cm diam.; corolla lobes white, fleshy, papillose at base inside; corona creamy white. Indonesia. Z10.

H.motoskei Teijsm. & Binnend.
Vigorous climber quickly attaining 5m. Leaves to 6cm, with irregular silver flecks, broadly elliptic or orbicular, leathery,

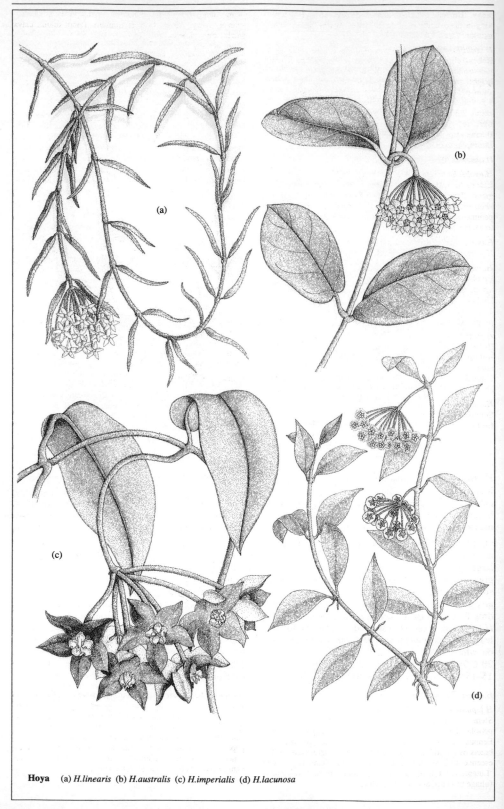

Hoya   (a) *H.linearis* (b) *H.australis* (c) *H.imperialis* (d) *H.lacunosa*

waxy. Umbels rounded, dense; flowers strongly scented, long-lasting; corolla white to pale creamy pink; corona maroon. Japan, Okinawa. Z9.

H.multiflora Bl. (*Centrostemma multiflorum* (Bl.) Decne.).
Robust climber to 80cm, often loosely shrubby in habit. Leaves to 10cm, linear to elliptic, tapering at both ends, bright green, often blotched white, tough and leathery, short-petiolate. Flower clusters terminal, to 40-flowered, on 1.5–5cm peduncles; flowers strongly scented; corolla lobes about 2.5cm, creamy white to straw-yellow with orange tips, reflexed; corona white, prominent. Late summer. Burma to Thailand, China, Malaysia, Indonesia and Philippines. Z10.

H.obscurinerva Merrill. See *H.pottsii*.

H.ovalifolia Wight & Arn. ex Wight.
Leaves to 4–10×2–5cm, elliptic to rhomboid, narrow, dark green, fleshy, revolute, short-petiolate. Umbels large, dense, about 12-flowered, on stout peduncles; pedicels equalling peduncles; corolla bright yellow; corona red. Summer. India to Malaysia. Z9.

H.parasitica (Roxb.) Wallich ex Wight. See *H.acuta*.
H.paxtonii hort. ex Williams. See *H.lanceolata* ssp. *bella*.

H.polyneura Hook.f. FISHTAIL HOYA.
Epiphytic shrub. Leaves to 10cm, broadly rhombic-ovate, acute, dark green, attractively veined in a darker or paler tone. Umbels axillary, short-petioled, to 15-flowered; flowers 1.2cm diam. or more; corolla white to cream; corona red to purple. Himalaya to S China. Z9.

H.pottsii Traill (*H.trinervis* Traill; *H.fuscomarginata* N.E. Br.; *H.obscurinerva* Merrill).
Robust climber to 3m. Leaves to 7cm, cordate or oblong, apex narrowly acute, rusty-red above, white-green beneath. Umbels globose; flowers fragrant; corolla pale yellow, slightly hairy; corona purple-centred. N India to China. Z9.

H.pubicalyx Merrill. RED BUTTONS.
Scrambling shrub. Leaves 10–14cm, oblong to oblong-ovate, fleshy, leathery, apex acuminate, base obtuse. Umbels to 9cm

diam., many-flowered; peduncles stout; pedicels slender, sparsely hairy, 3.5cm; flowers fragrant, 1.8cm diam.; calyx small, lobes oblong-ovate to ovate-lanceolate; corolla lobes 6mm, broadly triangular, spreading, apices recurved, densely papillose inside; corona red-brown, stellate. Philippines. Z10.

H.purpureofusca Hook.
Robust climber to over 5m, glabrous, branches terete. Leaves 8–13cm, ovate, fleshy, dark green mottled with silver-pink, acute. Umbels large, dense, globose or almost so, on peduncles shorter than leaves; flowers on slender pedicels.; corolla lobes red-brown to ash-grey, densely white-hairy above; corona pink to purple. Summer. Indonesia. Z10.

H.rubida Schltr.
Epiphyte in branches and on trunks of trees. Leaves to 6cm, ovate, thick, fleshy, dark glossy green above, paler beneath. Umbels to 25-flowered; flowers 1.2cm diam.; corolla glossy, bright maroon; corona red. New Guinea. Z10.

H.sana Bail. See *H.australis*.

H.serpens Hook.f.
Pendent shrub, stems coarse. Leaves to 5cm, ovate to broadly elliptic, papillose on both surfaces, hairy, subsessile. Umbel on a long peduncle; corolla to 1.2cm diam., white to pink, hairy inside; corona red. Himalaya to Burma. Confused with other miniature species. Z10.

H.shepherdii Short ex Hook.
Close to *H.longifolia*, differing principally in the hairy corolla. Climber, stems terete, hairy. Leaves 5–15cm, fleshy, channelled and dark green above, paler beneath, linear-lance-olate; petiole geniculate near its apex. Umbels to 5cm diam., many-flowered; calyx small, lobes triangular, corolla 1cm, white to pink, margins hairy; corona white, red or pink-centred. Summer. India. Z9.

H.sikkimensis hort. See *H.lanceolata*.
H.trinervis Traill. See *H.pottsii*.
H.variegata Sieb. ex Morr. See *H.carnosa* 'Picta'.

Humulus L. (From Lat. *humus*, soil, referring to the creeping habit.) HOP. Cannabidaceae. 2 species of twining, herbaceous perennials, dioecious, scabrous, producing a latex sap. Leaves opposite, broadly ovate-cordate, palmately 3–7-lobed. Male inflorescence a loose axillary panicle, female inflorescence a short bracteolate spike, becoming cone-like, 2 small flowers per bract, bracts ovate, membranous to papery, overlapping; perianth segments 5, stamens 5, ovary superior, stigmas 2. Fruit an achene. Temperate Europe, N America, C & E Asia. Z5.

CULTIVATION   Rapidly growing twiners with long herbaceous stems and large, lobed leaves, *Humulus* species are especially useful as temporary screening plants on trellis or wires, and for scrambling through hedging and large open shrubs. Valued for their often strikingly coloured foliage, in autumn *H.lupulus* also produces its fragrant straw-coloured inflorescences, used in brewing and, air-dried, to make swags and garlands. The young shoots are edible in salads or cooked as for spinach. *H.lupulus* is hardy at least to −15°C/5°F. *H.japonicus* is usually grown as annual in cool temperate climates, rapidly forming a green screen that makes an admirable backdrop for more brightly coloured flowers. Grow in any moderately fertile well drained soil in sun or part shade; *H.l.* 'Aureus' colours best in sun, when few foliage climbers can rival the beauty of its fresh gold to sulphur leaves. Propagate cultivars of *H.lupulus* by greenwood leaf-bud cuttings in mid-summer taken from material on which leaves have fully expanded. Apply 0.2% I.B.A. and root in a closed case with bottom heat at 20°C/70°F. Progeny from seed is highly variable. Sow *H.japonicus in situ* in spring, or earlier under glass at 15–18°C/60–65°F. Lower the temperature on germination and plant out when danger of frost is passed.

H.americanus Nutt. See *H.lupulus*.

H.japonicus Sieb. & Zucc. JAPANESE HOP.
Stem very rough. Leaves deeply 5–7-lobed, strongly serrate; petioles longer than blades. Male inflorescence a panicle. Female inflorescence an ovoid spike on a long peduncle, bracts ovate-orbicular, green. Fruit scarcely larger than inflorescence, to 2cm, dull green, tinged purple. Temperate E Asia. 'Lutescens': foliage pale gold to lime green. 'Variegatus': foliage blotched and streaked white.

H.lupulus L. (*H.americanus* Nutt.). COMMON HOP; EUROPEAN HOP; BINE.
Stem rough. Leaves 3–5-lobed, coarsely toothed; petioles usually shorter than blades. Male inflorescence an axillary panicle; female inflorescence a round axillary spike; bracts papery, orbicular, to 2cm. Fruit much larger than inflorescence, 3–5cm, straw-coloured. N temperate regions, widely naturalized. 'Aureus': leaves golden yellow.

Hydrangea L. (From Gk *hydor*, water, and *aggeion*, vessel; an allusion to the cup-shaped fruit.) Hydrangeaceae. 23 species of deciduous or evergreen shrubs, small trees or climbers. Bark often flaking when mature. Leaves usually rounded-ovate and toothed, opposite or in whorls of 3. Fertile flowers bisexual, radially symmetric, in panicles or corymbs; sepals 4 or 5, small, inconspicuous; petals 4 or 5; stamens 8 or 10 or rarely more; ovary inferior or half-inferior, 2–5-celled, containing many ovules. Fruit a 2–5-celled, many-seeded capsule. Many species bear larger, sterile flowers; in these the showy part is the enlarged calyx, and they are often borne at the outside of the corymbose inflorescences. China, Japan, the Himalayas, Philippines, Indonesia and N & S America.

CULTIVATION *Hydrangea* includes several true climbers. These are slender-stemmed shrubs which attach themselves to trees and walls with clinging ivy-like aerial roots. The two deciduous species listed here are among the most popular of hardy climbers, tolerant of low winter temperatures, most soils, shade and atmospheric pollution. With some initial support, they will soon form a dense and interwoven network of attractive red-brown branches clothed with luxuriant dark green foliage and broad heads of lacy white flowers. They are particularly well suited to urban gardens where they will clothe partition walls and basement areas even if planted in a confined area of well prepared fertile soil or in large tubs. The two evergreen species are altogether more tender and demand damp, slightly acidic soils rich in organic matter in shaded and sheltered sites. These are handsome climbers with tough dark green leaves and fine white flowers. Although American, they grow and contrast well with 'exotic' Asiatics such as *Trachycarpus, Phyllostachys* and *Rhododendron sinograde* and can be used as a backdrop or carpet for Rousseau-esque plantings in secretive city gardens. All of these climbers require little pruning other than to remove unwanted extension growth in summer or to restrict the spread of wall-grown plants; cut back outward-growing lateral shoots to a suitable bud in spring. This may best be done over several seasons to minimize loss of flowers. Sow seed under glass in early spring. Root basal softwood cuttings of non-flowering shoots treated with 0.8% I.B.A. in a closed case with bottom heat at 21°C/70°F.

H.altissima Wallich. See *H.anomala*.

H.anomala D. Don (*H.altissima* Wallich).
Deciduous climber by means of aerial roots, to 12m. Shoots hairless or hairy, later very rough and peeling. Leaves 7.5–13 ×4–10cm, ovate, apex shortly acuminate, cordate at base, coarsely toothed, hairless except for downy tufts in the vein axils beneath; petioles 1.5–7.5cm. Corymbs fairly flat, 15–20cm across, with few, white, peripheral sterile flowers each 1.5–3.7cm across, and numerous, small, cream fertile flowers; petals united, falling as a cap; stamens usually fewer than 15. Early summer. Himalaya, China. Z5.

H.anomala ssp. *petiolaris* (Sieb. & Zucc.) E. McClintock. See *H.petiolaris*.

H.petiolaris Sieb. & Zucc. (*H.anomala* ssp. *petiolaris* (Sieb. & Zucc.) E. McClintock; *H.scandens* Maxim. non (L.f.) Serr.).
Deciduous climber to 20m, climbing by means of aerial roots. Shoots at first finely hairy or glabrous, later rough and peeling. Leaves 3.5–11 × 2.5–8cm, ovate-rounded, shortly acuminate, more or less cordate at base, finely toothed, glabrous above, sometimes pubescent beneath, especially on the veins; petioles 0.5–4cm. Corymbs flat, 15–25cm across, with to 12 white, peripheral sterile flowers, each 2.5–4.5cm across; fertile flowers small, numerous,

off-white; petals united, falling as a cap; stamens usually more than 15. Summer. Japan, USSR (Sakhalin), Korea, Taiwan. Z5.

H.rehderiana Schneid. See *H.aspera*.
H.scandens Maxim. non (L.f.) Ser. See *H.petiolaris*.

H.seemanii Riley.
An evergreen climber or creeper with leathery dark green elliptic leaves and white flowers. It differs from *H.serratifolia* in its inflorescence – a single terminal corymb (not many superimposed corymbs) with large sterile flowers. Mexico. Z8.

H.serratifolia (Hook. & Arn.) Philippi (*H.integerrima* (Hook. & Arn.) Engl.).
Evergreen climber, to 30m in favourable situations. Shoots at first with fine pubescence, later glabrous, and bearing aerial roots. Leaves 5–15×2.5–7.5cm, elliptic, apex acuminate, base tapered and often cordate, almost always entire, leathery, glabrous; petioles 0.5–4.5cm. Inflorescence terminal and axillary, to 15 × 9cm, composed of numerous small corymbs, each at first enclosed by 4 papery bracts; flowers normally all small, fertile, white, although some variants exist with 1 or few white sterile flowers; petals free, falling individually; filaments long. Summer. Chile, Argentina. Z8.

Hylocereus (A.Berger) Britt. & Rose. (From Gk *hyle*, wood, and *Cereus*, alluding to their wooded habitats.) Cactaceae. Perhaps 16 species of epiphytic, climbing or scrambling cacti, often to 5m or more; stems usually 3-winged or angled, segmented, green or glaucous, the margins often horny, often producing aerial roots; areoles with short spines or rarely spineless. Flowers usually very large, funnelform, nocturnal, white or rarely red; pericarpel and tube stout; scales usually broad, triangular; floral areoles usually naked or nearly so; stamens numerous in a continuous series; style thick, stigma-lobes sometimes bifid. Fruit large, globose, ovoid or oblong, fleshy, with broad scales; seeds oval or broadly oval, $c2.5 × 1.5–2$mm, black-brown, smooth; hilum medium, oblique, superficial; mucilage-sheath present, covering entire seed. Central America, the West Indies, Colombia and Venezuela. Z10.

CULTIVATION Grow in an intermediate heated greenhouse (minimum 10–15°C/50–60°F), in an 'epiphyte' compost: equal parts organic/inorganic matter, below pH 6; shade all summer; maintain high humidity; reduce watering in winter.

H.antiguensis Britt. & Rose. See *H.trigonus*.

H.calcaratus (Weber) Britt. & Rose.
Stems 4–7cm diam., rather soft, green; ribs 3, thin, prominently lobed; spines 2–4, small, bristly, white. Flowers 35–37 × 20–30cm, white, opening in the evening and lasting nearly 48 hours, fragrant; upper scales papery. Fruit not known. Costa Rica. This species has one of the largest of all cactus flowers.

H.costaricensis (Weber) Britt. & Rose.
Stems stout, 5–10cm diam., glaucous; margins straight or undulate, not horny; spines 2–4, short, stout, brown, accompanied by 2 deciduous hair-like bristles. Flower-buds purple; flowers c30cm, fragrant; outer tepals narrow, tinged red, inner pure white. Fruit 10cm, oblong, scarlet. Costa Rica, Nicaragua.

H.escuintlensis Kimnach.
Stems to 5m; segments 10–30 × 3–4cm, shallowly lobed, dark green, margins horny; leaf-rudiments 1–2mm; areoles 2–4cm apart; spines 1–2, 1–1.5mm, subulate. Flowers 28–31 × 24–36cm; scales narrowly deltoid; outer tepals green-yellow, sometimes maroon-tinged, inner tepals creamy white; stigmas often bifid. Fruit 9 × 6.5cm, oblong, purple-red, with recurved scales; pulp white or pale pink. Guatemala. More free-flowering than most species. First distributed as *H.guatemalensis*.

H.extensus (Salm-Dyck ex DC.) Britt. & Rose.
Stems slender, 1.5cm diam.; ribs low, obtuse; areoles remote; spines 2–4, 1–2mm, dark brown, accompanied by fine bristles. Flowers large; tube green; outer tepals green-yellow, inner tepals white, tinged pink. Fruit not known. Trinidad.

H.guatemalensis (Eichlam) Britt. & Rose.
Very similar to *H.costaricensis*. Stems 2–7cm broad, glaucous; ribs 3, low-undulate; margins horny; areoles up to 2cm apart; spines 2–4, to 3mm, conic. Flowers 30cm; outer tepals pink, inner white; stigmas entire. Fruit 6–7cm in diam., covered with large scales. Guatemala.

H.lemairei (Hook.) Britt. & Rose.
Stems 2–3cm diam., grey-green; ribs low, slightly elevated at the areoles, not horny; areoles 2–2.5cm apart; spines usually 2, very short, conic. Flowers 27cm; tepals white, tinged pink near base; stigmas bifid. Fruit 6–7cm, oblong, purple; splitting when ripe to expose white pulp. Trinidad, Surinam.

H.minutiflorus Britt. & Rose.
Stems 1.5–3.5cm wide, deep green; ribs 3, low, acute, crenate; margins not horny; areoles 2–4cm apart; spines usually 1–3, minute, brown. Flowers only 3–3.5 × 8–9cm, very fragrant; tube 1 cm or less, with oblong or ovate scales, purple or green at base; floral areoles sometimes setose; outer tepals with red midvein and tip, inner very narrow, white. Fruit 4.5cm, globose, magenta, tuberculate; areoles with spines and hair-spines to 4mm; pulp white. Seeds 2–2.25 ×

1.25–1.5mm, brown, keeled. September. S. Mexico to Honduras.

H.monacanthus (Lem.) Britt. & Rose.
Areoles c3cm apart; spines 1–2, minute. Flowers 28 × 17cm; scales large; outer tepals tinged green, inner tepals white; stigmas sometimes bifid. Colombia, Panama.

H.napoleonis (Graham) Britt. & Rose. See *H.trigonus*.

H.ocamponis (Salm-Dyck) Britt. & Rose (*H.purpusii* (Weingart) Britt. & Rose).
Stems glaucous; ribs 3–4, acute, rather deeply undulate; margins horny; areoles 2–4cm apart; spines 3–8, 5–12mm, acicular. Flowers 25-32 × 20-25cm; pericarpel covered with ovate, acute, purple-margined scales; outer tepals green or purple, inner white. Fruit unknown. Mexico.

H.polyrhizus (Weber) Britt. & Rose.
Stems slender, 3–4cm diam., white and later green; ribs 3, low; margins nearly straight, not horny. Spines 2–4, 2–4mm, brown, accompanied by 2 deciduous hair-spines. Flower-buds, purple; flowers 25–30cm, fragrant; pericarpel covered with ovate red- or purple margined scales; outer tepals red, inner nearly white; stigmas not bifid. Fruit 10cm, oblong, scarlet. Panama to Ecuador.

H.purpusii (Weingart) Britt. & Rose. See *H.ocamponis*.

H.stenopterus (Weber) Britt. & Rose.
Stems 4cm broad, soft, light green; ribs 3, low, thin; areoles slightly raised; spines 1–3, small, yellow. Flowers 9-12 × 13–15cm; tube short; scales overlapping, orbicular to narrowly ovate, margins purple, tepals purple-red. Costa Rica.

H.triangularis (L) Britt. & Rose.
Closely related to *H.undatus*, but a more slender-stemmed plant with the stem-wings not horny. Flowers c20cm; scales broad, imbricate. Cuba, Hispaniola, Jamaica.

H.trigonus (Haw.) Safford (*H.antiguensis* Britt. & Rose; *H.antiguensis* Britt. & Rose).
Stems elongate, 2–4cm diam., 3-angled, green, margins shallowly crenate, not horny; areoles at apices of crenations; spines 2, 4 or 8, 4–7mm, becoming dark brown. Flowers 14–25 × c21cm; scales small, narrow, not overlapping; floral areoles often with short spines; tepals white. Fruit 7–10 × 3–5cm, oblong-ovoid, red; scales fleshy. Puerto Rico to Grenada.

H.undatus (Haw.) Britt. & Rose.
Epiphytic or climbing to 5m or more; stems usually segmented, 3-winged, 4–7.5cm diam., margins crenate, horny; areoles in the sinuses, usually 4-5cm apart; spines 0–3, 3–6mm, conical, grey-brown. Flowers 25–30 × 15–25cm; scales broad, imbricate; tepals white. Fruit 10–15 × 10–12cm, globose-long; scales long-pointed, to 25mm, fleshy. Summer. Tropical America. Widely cultivated in the tropics for the edible fruit.

Hymenopyramis Wallich ex Griff. (From Gk *hymen*, seed capsule, and *pyramis*, pyramid.) Verbenaceae. Some 6 species of scandent shrubs. Leaves opposite, simple. Inflorescence a terminal or axillary panicle, bracteate; flowers minute; calyx 4-toothed, enlarging in fruit; corolla infundibular, limb 4-lobed; stamens exserted, inserted in throat, anthers erect, bilocular; ovary bilocular, with 2 ovules per locule, style capillary, stigma bifid. Fruit a globular capsule. India, SE Asia. Z10.

CULTIVATION   As for *Clerodendrum*.

H.bracteata Wallich.
Leaves to 12.5cm, chartaceous, ovate or ovate-oblong to ovate-lanceolate, acuminate, entire, glabrous above, white or grey-velutinous beneath; petiole slender, densely puberulent.

Inflorescence puberulent, terminal and axillary; flowers white; pedicel capillary, puberulent, elongating in fruit; corolla obliquely campanulate. Fruit pilose. India, SE Asia.

Ibervillea Greene ex Small. Cucurbitaceae. 4 species of dioecious, perennial vines. Stems glabrous, often massively swollen at base. Tendrils simple. Leaves reniform to broadly ovate, deeply 3–5-lobed, lobes coarsely lobed or toothed. Male flowers in racemes or clusters, or solitary, green-yellow; calyx cylindrical to campanulate, shortly 5-lobed; corolla with 5 oblong to linear lobes; stamens 3, inserted at throat of calyx tube, connective not produced, anthers straight, oblong; female flowers solitary; ovary with 2–3 placentas, stigma trifid. Fruit ovoid to globose, red or brightly coloured; seeds several, slightly swollen. SW US and N Mexico. Z10.

CULTIVATION   As for *Kedrostis*.

I.lindheimeri (A. Gray) Greene (*Sicydium lindheimeri* A. Gray). WILD BALSAM; HIERBA DE-VIBORA
Climbing or trailing herb; stems slender, 2–4m, little-branched. Leaves to 12cm, seg. 3–5, cuneate to rhombic-ovate, toothed to lobed, *c*1cm wide, scabrous; petiole 3.5cm. Male flowers yellow, 5–8 per raceme; calyx cylindric, 6–8mm, slightly puberulent. Fruit globose, 25–35mm diam., orange-red; seeds round, *c*6mm. Summer. Texas to S California and N Mexico.

I.sonorae (S. Wats.) Greene.
Climbing herb resembling *I.lindheimeri*, but with very swollen caudex in old age, leaves more dissected, 2–3-parted nearly to base, segments coarsely sinuate-toothed; fruit and ovary more attenuate toward apex, seeds many, obovate to oblong-obovate, more compressed, with rugose-tuburculate surface. Summer. N Mexico.

Ipomoea L. (From Gk *ips*, a worm, used by Linnaeus for *Convolvulus*, and *homoios*, resembling.) MORNING GLORY. Convolvulaceae. A large and variable genus of 450–500 species of annual to perennial herbs, shrubs or small trees, woody to herbaceous, usually climbing, but can be erect, ascending, prostrate or even floating in water, sometimes containing latex (mostly woody species); height to at least 3m (climbers) and 8m (trees). Leaves usually petiolate, entire to lobed, sometimes compound, often variable on the same plant, with pseudostipules in some species. Inflorescence axillary, flowers solitary or in dichasial cymes or sometimes panicles; sepals variable, herbaceous or chartaceous to coriaceous, often sub- or unequal and enlarged in fruit, glabrous or pubescent; corolla usually actinomorphic, subentire to lobed, rarely deeply, funnel-shaped or campanulate, sometimes tubular or hypocrateriform, purple, pink, red or white (yellow in a few species); stamens included to exserted, hairy at base; stigma 2- or 3-lobed, capitate. Fruit a dry, dehiscent capsule, 4- or 6-valved; seeds glabrous to long-pubescent, to 4–6, rarely to 10; pollen spinulose, pantoporate, globose. Widely distributed in Tropical and Subtropical regions. Many herbaceous species which are perennial in areas in which they are native can be grown as annuals in temperate zones.

CULTIVATION   *Ipomoea* species occur in tropical and subtropical areas as vigorous lianas or weak-stemmed sprawling plants of grassland, scrub and beach; many are widely naturalized by roadsides or railways. Several species have economic uses. The most widespread of these is the sweet potato, *I.batatas*; its root tuber is an important carbohydrate source in the tropics, especially Papua New Guinea and Central America. Several other species are used in traditional medicine in other regions. Many contain lysergic acid derivatives, and the seeds of *I.tricolor* were used as a hallucinogen by the Aztecs; this is the most commonly cultivated Morning Glory today. *I.pes-caprae* is sometimes used as a sand-binder in arid zones and *I.carnea* ssp. *fistulosa* is a rough hedge or streambank stabilizer in the hot Terai of India and Nepal. Where climate allows, many are valuable in the open garden for their showy flowers and vigorous climbing habit used to clothe walls, trellising or natural hosts. Rampant species (e.g. *I.indica*, *I.alba*) are best confined to garden boundaries or used for covering unsightly garden structures. Apart from *I.tricolor*, the ubiquitous Morning Glory, other popular species include *I.alba*, the spectacular Moonflower, a woody-based perennial with huge white blooms and *I.coccinea*, *I.quamoclit* and *I.×multifida* – vigorous vines, though delicate in appearance, with small flowers in brilliant tones of crimson and scarlet. The last two, with finely divided leaves, are especially attractive. The Spanish Flag, *I.lobata* is a weakly twining annual or short-lived perennial with erect spikes of uncharacteristically tubular flowers which pass with age through scarlet, yellow and cream. Subtropical gardens and large heated conservatories might accommodate the two robust, semi-woody species, *I.mauritiana* and *I.horsfalliae*; both have large, palmately lobed leaves, the first with narrowly funnel-shaped deep red or purple-pink flowers, the second with wider blooms in shades of pink with a darker 'eye'.

Optimum yields of *I.batatas* are obtained from crops grown in moderate rainfall areas (750–1250mm/30–50in./per annum); a low humidity at maturity is beneficial. A temperature range of 22–25°C/72–77°F is preferable and good light levels are essential for healthy growth. The sweet potato is a short-day plant: less than 11 hours of sunlight/day induce flowering, but day-length variation appears to have a limited effect on tuber initiation and development. There are soft-fleshed and dry-fleshed edible cultivars; the skin colour varies from purple and red to yellow, and the flesh colour from orange to white. Besides these there are 'industrial' cultivars grown for their high starch content.

In warm climates, grow in well drained sandy loams at pH 5.5–6.5. In wet areas, plants are grown on ridges or mounds. Propagate by stem cuttings from the terminal shoots inserted to half their depth after removal of the lower leaves. Plant cuttings in ridges 75cm/30in. apart with 25–30cm/10–12in. between plants, or on mounds at similar spacing. Plants may also be raised from seed, although the progeny are variable, and from tubers. Irrigation is rarely required, except after planting and during exceptionally dry periods since cuttings are normally inserted at the beginning of the rains. Organic manure is beneficial, applied before planting and combined with an NPK application. Later dressings of a high-potash NPK fertilizer encourage tuber development.

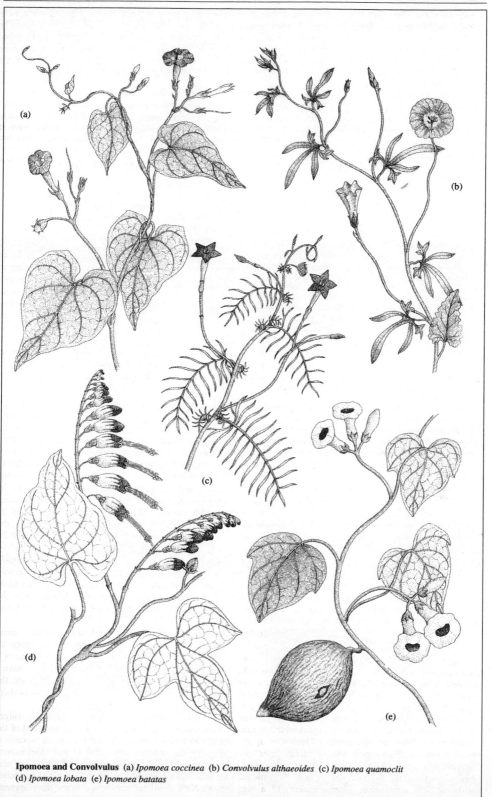

Ipomoea and Convolvulus (a) *Ipomoea coccinea* (b) *Convolvulus althaeoides* (c) *Ipomoea quamoclit* (d) *Ipomoea lobata* (e) *Ipomoea batatas*

Deficiencies of boron, magnesium or calcium may need correcting on some soils. Sweet potatoes need frequent rotation, since they suffer from many diseases and also from nematodes. The tubers mature in 80–200 days from planting, depending on the vigour of the cultivar. Single plants may produce 40–50 tubers, weighing from 100g to 1kg. Tubers, which need tender handling at harvesting, may be cured at a temperature of 27–29°C/80–85°F and a relative humidity of 85–90% for 4–7 days and then stored for 140 days or more at a temperature of 13–16°C/55–60°F and a relative humidity of 85–90%. Storage diseases are numerous and stored tubers must be regularly examined.

In cool-temperate areas grow under glass (min. 7–10°C/45–50°F) in pots and tubs: grow vigorous species in borders where space allows or treat fast-growing, soft-stemmed twiners as frost-tender annuals. Plant in fertile, well drained loam in a warm, sunny site and provide support. In frost-free areas, sow *in situ*. Under glass, give a high-fertility, loam-based mix and medium to high humidity; water plentifully during the growing season. Prune semi-woody species in late winter or spring to thin out old congested growth. Propagate from seed sown singly in pots in spring at 18°C/65°F: nick seeds or soak for 12 hours in tepid water to promote rapid germination. Perennials also by softwood or semi-ripe cuttings in summer. Susceptible to whitefly or red spider mite.

I.acuminata (Vahl) Roem. & Schult. See *I.indica.*

I.alba L. (*I.bona-nox* L.; *Calonyction aculeatum* (L.) House). MOONFLOWER; BELLE DE NUIT.
Perennial herbaceous climber, woody at base with age, 5–30m, glabrous, containing white latex, often developing fleshy protruberances on the stem. Leaves 5–15cm, on 5–20cm peduncles, ovate or orbicular, entire or 3-lobed, apex caudate, base cordate. Inflorescence 1–8-flowered on 1–24cm peduncles; flowers on 0.7–1.5cm pedicels, nocturnally fragrant; sepals 0.5–2cm, ovate to elliptic, fleshy, apex caudate; corolla 9–15cm long, 8–14cm diam., hypocrateriform with a long tube, white, midpetaline areas and tube green outside; stamens exserted; stigma 2-lobed. Fruit 2–3cm long, 1–2cm diam., ovoid to subglobose, with a 7–10mm mucro; seeds 8–10mm, dark brown to black, glabrous. Summer. Pantropical. 'Giant White': flowers very large, pure white. Z9.

I.batatas (L.) Poir. SWEET POTATO.
Perennial herbaceous climbers with tuberous rootstock, usually rather fleshy and succulent, with abundant purple pigmentation of stem and leaves. Leaves 5–10cm, cordate to ovate, entire, toothed or 3-lobed. Inflorescence not present in some clones, where present few-flowered; sepals 0.8–1.5cm, somewhat chartaceous, oblong to ovate, apex usually acuminate; corolla 4–7cm, funnelform, lavender to pale purple, base of tube darker inside, sometimes white. Fruit rare, ovoid. Pantropical. Often grown in water for attractive foliage. Z9.

I.biloba Forssk. See *I.pes-caprae.*
I.bona-nox L. See *I.alba.*
I.brasiliensis (L.) Sweet. See *I.pes-caprae.*

I.cairica (L.) Sweet (*I.palmata* Forssk.; *I.cavanillesii* Roem. & Schult.).
Herbaceous perennial to 1.8m, with tuberous rootstock, prostrate or climbing, glabrous, occasionally with hairy axils. Leaves 3–10cm on 2–6cm petioles, palmately 5-lobed, basal lobes sometimes bifid, ovate to orbicular in outline, lobes to 4cm, elliptic or lanceolate to ovate, pseudo-stipulate. Inflorescence 1- to many-flowered, on a 0.5–8cm peduncle, lax; pedicels 1.2–3cm; sepals to 0.6cm, ovate, apex obtuse to acute with a short mucro, margins translucent; corolla 3–6cm, funnel-shaped, red, purple or white with tube purple inside and a purple hue on outside of limb, sometimes wholly white; stamens included; stigma 2-lobed. Fruit 1–1.2cm diam., glabrous; seeds 4.2–6mm, dark, densely short-hairy with long, comose hairs on axils. Tropical and subtropical Africa and Asia, widely introduced elsewhere. Z8.

I.carnea Jacq. (*I.crassicaulis* Benth.).
Shrubs or climbers to 2.5m, containing white latex, base woody, growing tips herbaceous, hollow, glabrous to short-hairy. Leaves 10–25cm, on 2.5–15cm petioles with 2 basal extrafloral nectaries, ovate to lanceolate or suborbicular, apex long-acuminate, base truncate to shallowly cordate. Inflorescence 1- to several-flowered, paniculate, at branch apices, on 5–15cm peduncles; sepals to 0.6cm, suborbicular, subcoriaceous; corolla 5–8cm long, 8–12cm diam., pink to pink-purple, tube dark purple at base, funnel-shaped, with tiny hairs outside, especially in midpetaline areas. Fruit 2cm long, 1–1.5cm diam., ovoid to subglobose; seeds covered in long brown hairs. ssp. *carnea* Habit climbing. Leaves ovate to suborbicular, short-pubescent US (Florida) to Paraguay. ssp. *fistulosa* (Mart. ex Choisy) D. Austin (*I.fistulosa* Mart. ex Choisy). Habit erect and shrubby. Leaves lanceolate-elongate, mostly glabrous. Summer. Pantropical by introduction. Z9.

I.cavanillesii Roem. & Schult. See *I.cairica.*

I.coccinea L. (*Quamoclit coccinea* (L.) Moench). RED MORNING GLORY; STAR IPOMOEA.
Annual herb to 2–4m, glabrous. Leaves 2–14cm, ovate, entire or coarsely toothed, base cordate, apex acute or acuminate. Inflorescence 2–8-flowered, on 1–13cm peduncles; flowers on 0.5–1.5cm pedicels, pendent in fruit; sepals to 0.5cm, oblong to elliptic, fleshy, apex truncate with a subterminal mucro; corolla 1.5–2.5cm, limb 1.7–2cm diam., scarlet, tube buff-yellow inside; stamens exserted; stigma 2-lobed. Fruit to 0.7cm diam., subglobose, 1–4-seeded. Summer. US (Pennsylvania to Georgia and Kansas). Z7.

I.coccinea var. *hederifolia* (L.) A. Gray. See *I.hederifolia.*
I.congesta R. Br. See *I.indica.*
I.crassicaulis Benth. See *I.carnea.*
I.digitata Auct. non L. See *I.mauritiana.*
I.dissecta Pursh. See *Merremia dissecta.*
I.fistulosa Mart. ex Choisy. See *I.carnea* ssp. *fistulosa.*

I.hederacea (L.) Jacq. (*Pharbitis hederacea* (L.) Choisy).
Annual herbaceous climber to 3m, densely covered in long, erect hairs. Leaves 3–12cm, ovate to suborbicular, usually 3-lobed, rarely entire or 5-lobed, apex acute or acuminate, base cordate. Inflorescence 1–5-flowered, dense; sepals 1.5–2.5cm, elliptic to lanceolate with a long, recurved linear acumen, densely patent-pubescent; corolla 2–4cm, limb 2–3cm diam., funnel-shaped, usually blue, sometimes purple, tube white, occasionally wholly white; stamens included; stigma 3-lobed. Fruit 0.8–1.2cm diam., subglobose; seeds densely short-hairy, black. Very closely related to *I.nil.* Summer. S US to Argentina. 'Roman Candy': to 1.5m; leaves green and white; flowers cerise and white. Z8.

I.hederifolia L. (*Quamoclit hederifolia* (L.) G. Don; *I.coccinea* var. *hederifolia* (L.) A. Gray; *Quamoclit coccinea* var. *hederifolia* (L.) House).
Annual herb to 1.6m, glabrous. Leaves 2–15cm, 3- or 5- (rarely 7-) lobed in cultivated forms, rarely entire, usually coarsely toothed, apex acute or acuminate, base cordate. Inflorescence 10–40cm, 3–16-flowered, on 2.5–30cm peduncles; pedicels 0.3–1cm; sepals to 0.4cm, oblong to elliptic, apex blunt or truncate with a subterminal mucro, fleshy; corolla 2.5–4.5cm, limb 1.8–2.5cm diam., subhypocrateriform, red or orange, tube buff-yellow inside; stamens exserted; stigma 2-lobed. Fruit to 0.8cm diam., 1–4-seeded; seeds to 0.4cm, with 2 lines of dark hairs on the back. Summer. Pantropical, introduced in Africa and Asia. Z9.

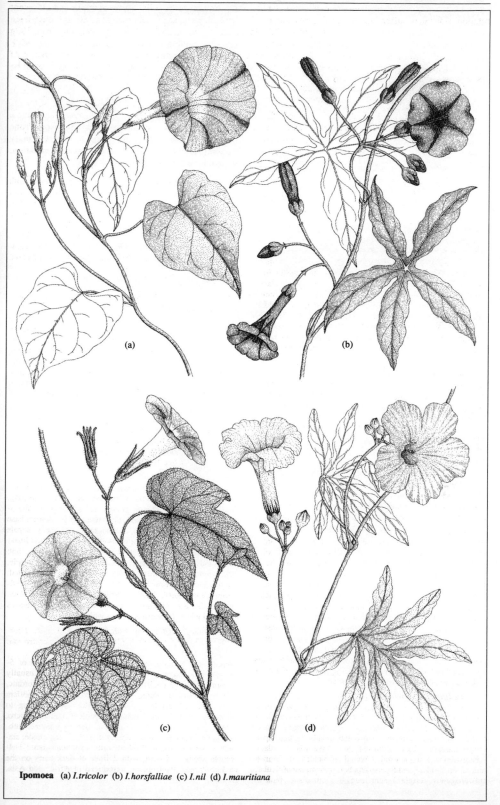

Ipomoea   (a) *I.tricolor* (b) *I.horsfalliae* (c) *I.nil* (d) *I.mauritiana*

I.horsfalliae Hook.
Perennial woody climber to 8m. Leaves 5–20cm on
2.5–13cm peduncles, orbicular in outline, palmately 3–5-
lobed, with the longest central lobe ovate, elliptic or elliptic-
oblong, apex acuminate, others ovate-lanceolate to linear-
lanceolate, glabrous. Inflorescence 8–30cm on 1.5–14cm
peduncles, few- to several-flowered, laxly branched;
pedicels 8–15cm; sepals 0.7–1cm, ovate-elliptic or elliptic,
apex obtuse, purple to almost black apart from base; corolla
about 4cm, limb *c*4–5cm diam., hypocrateriform, red to
maroon, with 5 rounded lobes; stamens exerted; stigma 2-
lobed. W Indies, sometimes introduced in other tropical
regions. 'Briggsii': floriferous, corolla magenta to crimson.
Z10.

I.× imperialis hort. (*Convolvulus imperialis* hort.; *Pharbitis
imperialis* hort.). IMPERIAL JAPANESE MORNING GLORY.
Probably a hybrid of or selection from *I.nil*. Differs in having
larger, double flowers, often with fringed or fluted limbs.
Summer. Garden origin. Z9.

I.indica (Burm.) Merrill (*I.acuminata* (Vahl) Roem. &
Schult.; *I.learii* Paxt.; *I.congesta* R. Br.). BLUE DAWN FLOWER.
Herbaceous climber to 6m, perennial; stems almost glabrous
or with adpressed hairs, much-branched. Leaves 5–17cm on
2–18cm petioles, ovate to orbicular, entire or 3-lobed, apex
acuminate, base cordate. Inflorescence 1- to few-flowered,
dense, on 4–20cm peduncles; pedicels 0.25–0.8cm; sepals
1.4–2.2cm, lanceolate to ovate, apex narrowly triangular-
acuminate, herbaceous, adpressed-pubescent to glabrous;
corolla 5–7cm, limb 6–8cm diam., funnel-shaped, blue or
purple, rarely white; stamens included; stigma 2-lobed. Fruit
to 1cm diam., globose to apically flattened; seeds 1–4, brown,
glabrous. Pantropical. A troublesome weed in some tropical
and subtropical regions. Z9.

I.learii Paxt. See *I.indica*.

I.lobata (Cerv.) Thell. (*Mina lobata* Cerv.; *I.versicolor*
Meissn.; *Quamoclit lobata* (Cerv.) House). SPANISH FLAG.
Annual or short-lived perennial to 5m, herbaceous, glabrous
or sparsely hairy. Leaves 3–16cm, ovate, entire or deeply and
palmately 3-lobed, margin coarsely toothed, base cordate,
lobes elliptic to ovate or obovate, apices acute or acuminate.
Inflorescence a 5–30-flowered, secund, erect raceme; pedicels
0.3–0.7cm; sepals 2–3.5mm, elliptic to subovate, with a subapical mucro, glabrous, fleshy; corolla 1.8–2.2cm, narrowly
tubular-urceolate, curving and forward-pointing with a
5–7mm narrow tube and a 15–17mm urceolate limb, with 5
triangular lobes at apex, scarlet before opening, fading to yellow, then white with red-tinted tips; stamens exerted; stigma
2-lobed. Fruit 7mm diam., subglobose; seeds hairy. Summer.
Mexico. The only species with bilaterally symmetrical flowers. Z9.

I.mauritiana Jacq. (*I.digitata* auct. non L.).
Perennial woody climber to 5m, growing tips herbaceous,
roots tuberous, glabrous. Leaves 5–8cm, orbicular in outline,
palmately 3–9-lobed, lobes ovate with acuminate apices.
Inflorescence 2.5–20cm, few- to many-flowered; pedicels
1–2.5cm; sepals 0.6–1.2cm, orbicular or elliptic, leathery,
glabrous, convex and clasping corolla base; corolla 4–6cm,
funnel-shaped, pink to pale maroon, tube darker at base; stamens included; stigma 2-lobed. Fruit 1.2–1.4cm, ovoid, with
comose black seeds. Pantropical. Long confused with *I.digi-
tata*, a rare endemic of Hispaniola. Z9.

I. × multifida (Raf.) Shinn. (*I.× sloteri* (House) Ooststr.).
(*Quamoclit × sloteri* House). (*I.coccinea × I.quamoclit.*)
CARDINAL CLIMBER.
Annual climber to 1m, glabrous. Leaves 2–4.5cm, deltoid-
ovate in outline, deeply 3–7-lobed, lobes linear or linear-lanceolate, sometimes themselves lobed. Inflorescence 1- to few-
flowered; sepals 0.5–1.2cm, oblong-elliptical, obtuse, with a
subterminal mucro, fleshy; corolla 2.5–5cm, scarlet to crimson,
subhypocrateriform, limb 2–2.5cm diam.; stigma 2-lobed; stamens exerted. Rarely sets fruit. Summer. Garden origin. Z9.

I.nil (L.) Roth (*Pharbitis nil* (L.) Choisy).
Annual herb to 5m, climbing, densely covered in long erect
hairs. Leaves 4–14cm on 3–16cm petioles, broadly ovate to
orbicular, entire or 3-lobed. Inflorescence 1–5-flowered on
2.5–12cm peduncles; pedicels 0.5–1cm; sepals 17–25mm,
elliptic to lanceolate, apical acumen long, erect, very narrowly triangular, base densely covered with erect pubescence;
corolla 3–6cm, limb 4–5cm diam., funnel-shaped, blue, rarely
purple or red, tube white; stamens included; stigma 3-lobed.
Fruit 0.8–1.2cm diam., subglobose; seeds black, with dense,
short pubescence. Summer. Pantropical. 'Chocolate': corolla
pale chocolate-brown. 'Early Call': corolla large, limb to 7cm
diam., scarlet with a white tube. 'Flying Saucers': large round
flowers, marbled sky-blue and white. 'Limbata': corolla violet-purple with a white margin. Platycodon Flowered White:
flowers white. Platycodon Mixed: flowers single and semi-
double, red, purple edged white or white, abundant. 'Scarlett
O'Hara': corolla red. 'Scarlet Star': flowers cerise with white
star, abundant. Spice Island Mix: non-climbing; leaves variegated with white; corolla colour variable. Z9.

I.palmata Forssk. See *I.cairica*.

I.pandurata (L.) G. Mey. WILD SWEET POTATO VINE; WILD
POTATO VINE; MAN OF THE EARTH.
Prostrate or climbing herbaceous perennial to 10m, roots
tuberous. Leaves to 15cm, ovate or pandurate, sometimes 3-
lobed, base cordate. Inflorescence 1–5-flowered; corolla to
10cm diam., broadly funnel-shaped, white, tube purple at
base. Summer. US (Connecticut to Florida and Texas). Z7.

I.pes-caprae (L.) R. Br. (*I.biloba* Forssk.; *I.pes-caprae* ssp.
brasiliensis (L.) Ooststr.; *I.brasiliensis* (L.) Sweet). BEACH
MORNING GLORY; RAILROAD VINE.
Prostrate perennial; stem extensive, rooting at nodes, semi-
succulent, glabrous. Leaves 3–10cm, fleshy, ovate, elliptic,
orbicular, obovate or transverse-elliptic to reniform, apex
emarginate. Inflorescence 1- to few-flowered, on 3–16cm
stout peduncles; pedicels 1.2–4.5cm; sepals 0.5–1cm, ovate to
broadly elliptic or orbicular, apex obtuse with a small mucro,
subcoriaceous; corolla 3–5cm, funnel-shaped, pink to pale
purple, darker purple at tube base; stigma 2-lobed; stamens
included. Fruit 1.2–1.7cm diam., erect; seeds black with
dense, short brown pubescence. Pantropical. Z10.

I.purpurea (L.) Roth (*Convolvulus major* hort.; *Pharbitis
purpurea* (L.) Choisy). COMMON MORNING GLORY.
Annual climbing herb to 2.5m, usually hairy. Leaves 2–10cm
on 2–15cm petioles, broadly ovate or orbicular, entire or 3-
lobed, short-hairy above and beneath. Inflorescence 1–5-
flowered on 3–18cm peduncles; pedicels 0.8–1.5cm, pendent
in fruit, sepals 0.8–1.6cm, oblong-lanceolate, apex acute to
obtuse, occasionally short-acuminate with bristly hairs at
base, herbaceous; corolla 3–5cm, funnel-shaped, blue, purple,
pink, red, white, or with stripes of these colours on a white
background, tube white or pink-purple; stigma 3-lobed; stamens included. Fruit 0.7–1.2cm diam.; seeds 1–6, black,
glabrous. Summer. Origin probably Mexico, now pantropical
by introduction. var. *purpurea*. Leaves entire. var. *diversifolia* (Lindl.) O'Don. Leaves entire or 3(–5)-lobed on same
plant. 'Alba': flowers white. 'Huberi': leaves marked silver;
flowers pink to purple, edged white. 'Violacea': flowers deep
violet, double. Z9.

I.quamoclit L. (*Quamoclit vulgaris* Choisy; *Quamoclit pen-
nata* (Desr.) Bojer). CYPRESS VINE; STAR-GLORY; INDIAN PINK.
Annual climber to 3m; stems slender, glabrous. Leaves
1–9cm, elliptic to ovate in outline, deeply pinnatisect with
9–19 pairs of linear lobes, pseudostipulate. Inflorescence 1–5-
flowered on 1.5–14cm peduncles; pedicels 0.8–2.5cm, club-
shaped; sepals 0.4–0.7cm, elliptic to oblong, apex blunt with
a short subterminal mucro, fleshy; corolla 2–3cm, hypocrateriform, limb 1.8–2cm diam., distinctly and stellately 5-lobed,
scarlet, occasionally white; stigma 2-lobed; stamens exerted.
Fruit to 1cm, ovoid, mucronate (remains of style), 1–4-
seeded. Summer. Tropical America, much naturalized elsewhere. Platycodon Flowered Red Picotee: corolla with a

white margin, often semi-double. Relli-Valley Strain: leaves fern-like; flowers plum, pink and occasionally white. Z9.

I.rubrocaerulea Hook. See *I.tricolor*.

I. × *sloteri* (House) Ooststr. See *I.* × *multifida*.

I.tricolor Cav. (*I.rubrocaerulea* Hook.). MORNING GLORY. Annual or perennial climbing herb to 4m, glabrous. Leaves 3.5–7cm on 1.5–6cm petioles, ovate, apex long-acuminate, base cordate. Inflorescence 1- to several-flowered, on stout, fistulose, 3–9cm peduncles; pedicels 1.5–1.8cm; sepals 0.5–0.6cm, narrowly triangular to ovate-lanceolate, green and leathery with white margins, keeled on back; corolla 4–6cm, funnel-shaped, bright sky-blue, tube white, golden-yellow at base inside; stamens included; stigma 2-lobed. Fruit ovoid to subconical, mucronate (remains of style); seeds 1–4, brown or black, minutely hairy. Summer. Mexico and C America,

widely introduced elsewhere. 'Blue Star': flowers sky-blue striped dark blue. 'Crimson Rambler': flowers crimson with white throats. 'Heavenly Blue': corolla very intense sky-blue. 'Heavenly Blue Improved': flowers large, bright blue with paler centre. 'Flying Saucers': corolla marbled with blue and white. 'Pearly Gates': corolla marbled with white and blue. 'Rainbow Flash': dwarf, 40 × 15cm; flowers rose, carmine, white and deep blue. 'Summer Skies': flowers light sky-blue. 'Wedding Bells': flowers rose-lavender. Z9.

I.tuberosa L. See *Merremia tuberosa*.

I.versicolor Meissn. See *I.lobata*.

I.violacea L.
A moth-pollinated species, not widely cultivated. The name is often used for *I.tricolor* due to confusion over Linnaean typification.

Jasminum

Jasminum L. (Latinized form of Persian *yāsmīn*.) JASMINE; JESSAMINE. Oleaceae. About 200 shrubs and small trees, many sprawling, scandent or twining, evergreen or deciduous. Stems terete to angled. Leaves opposite or alternate, imparipinnate, trifoliolate or with only one leaflet, thus 'simple'. Flowers often fragrant, solitary or clustered in axils, or in cymes or cymose panicles; calyx small, campanulate to turbinate with 5 or more lobes; corolla tubular with 4 or more spreading lobes; stamens 2. Fruit a 2-valved berry, usually black and with only one carpel developing. Old World tropics, subtropics and temperate regions.

CULTIVATION   Grown for their often heavily fragrant flowers, the genus *Jasminum* comprises species for a number of garden situations, from *J.parkeri*, with tiny yellow flowers in early summer, which forms low, dense and evergreen hummocks suitable in scale for the rock garden, to the free-standing semi-evergreen *J.humile*, a fine wall shrub, bearing large and fragrant flowers from early spring to late autumn. The twining climbers, such as *J.officinale* (Jessamine or Common Jasmine) and the tropical species, *J.rex*, will scramble over trelliswork, shrubs, trees or other supports.

The rambling or scandent shrubby species, which require tying with shoots carefully trained and spaced, can be used as wall shrubs, or trained over pergolas, arches, arbours and fences. *J.nudiflorum* is also useful as a soil-stabilizer on steep banks; it will cascade over a retaining wall and, with other frost-hardy species, is tolerant of urban pollution. A sunny site is best for free flowering, but *J.officinale* and *J.nudiflorum* tolerate the shade of a north-facing wall. *J.mesnyi*, with spectacular semi-double flowers, and *J.polyanthum*, vigorous and intensely fragrant, for south- or southwest-facing walls in areas with little or no frost, make excellent conservatory plants in colder zones. *J.polyanthum* may also be grown as a house plant trained on wire hoops or canes. Species designated zone 10 need frost-free conditions, those in zones 8 and 9 need to be sited against warm walls, or given greenhouse protection. Zone 8 species are best in sheltered sites, especially in areas where severe winter spells can be expected.

Cultivate frost-tender species in a cool glasshouse or conservatory border (minimum temperature 5°C/40°F) or in 30cm/12in. pots of a medium-fertility loam-based mix, with wires or other support. (*J.polyanthum* requires a temperature drop of 10°C/18°F to induce flowering.) Water plentifully in summer, sparingly in winter, and ventilate freely when possible. *J.rex* requires a minimum temperature of 18°C/65°F, and succeeds best with part-day shade. Tie in leaders of scandent species in a fan formation after planting. Cut back flowered growth of *J.nudiflorum* immediately after flowering; remove weak growth and tie in as necessary. Thin, but do not shorten, shoots of *J.officinale* after flowering. Other species require no regular pruning, other than thinning of overgrown plants.

Propagate by semi-ripe cuttings in late summer–early autumn, overwintering at 7–10°C/45–50°F. Take cuttings of *J.mesnyi* and *J.polyanthum* with a heel, and root with bottom heat of 16°C/60°F. Also by layers, and seed sown when ripe. Subject to attack by one or more species of polyphagous aphids, and by mealybugs. Grey mould may infect frost-damaged plants, causing dieback.

J.affine Carr. See *J.officinale* 'Affine'.

J.angulare Vahl.
Evergreen climbing shrub. Leaves opposite; leaflets 3, rarely 5, ovate to lanceolate, terminal leaflet longer, narrow, slightly acuminate. Flowers unscented, borne at axils in threes, to 3cm diam.; calyx bell-shaped, teeth 7, shorter than tube; corolla white, lobes 5, oval to lanceolate. S.Africa. Z9.

J.angustifolium var. *laurifolium* (Roxb.) Ker-Gawl. See *J.laurifolium*.

J.azoricum L. (*J.fluminense* hort. non Vell.)
Evergreen climbing shrub. Shoots terete, twining. Leaves opposite; leaflets 3, ovate, acute, undulate, cordate at base, terminal leaflet larger. Flowers fragrant, long-stalked, borne in terminal panicles; calyx tubular, 5-toothed, to 2.5mm;

corolla white, tube to 0.5cm, lobes to 6, 1cm long. Late summer. Azores. Z9.

J.bahiense DC. See *J.fluminense*.

J.beesianum Forr. & Diels.
Deciduous or semi-evergreen, sprawling shrub. Young stems minutely pubescent, slender, downy at nodes, sulcate, slightly twining. Leaves opposite, simple, ovate-lanceolate, 2–5cm, olive green, slightly downy. Flowers 1–3 per axil, small, fragrant, pale pink to deep rose. Produces abundant shining black berries which persist in winter. Early summer. China. Z7. A form of *J. beesianum* with longer leaves and larger, pale pink flowers is often seen, this may be a distant backcross with *J.* × *stephanense*. The typical *J.beesianum* is altogether smaller, with darker flowers.

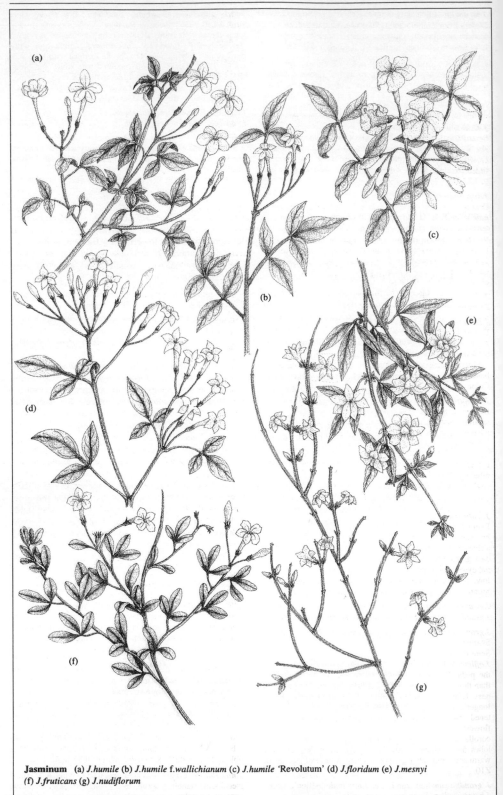

Jasminum (a) *J.humile* (b) *J.humile* f.*wallichianum* (c) *J.humile* 'Revolutum' (d) *J.floridum* (e) *J.mesnyi* (f) *J.fruticans* (g) *J.nudiflorum*

J.bignoniaceum Wallich ex G.Don.
Differs from *J.humile* in shorter, broader lateral leaflets, the broader corolla tube and short corolla lobes. Shrub or small tree. Leaves alternate; leaflets (1–3–)5–9, to 2cm, elliptic to obovate. Flowers yellow, nodding, in umbel-like clusters terminating lateral shoots; calyx teeth far shorter than tube; corolla yellow with short, broad lobes. India, Sri Lanka. Z10.

J.blinii Lév. See *J.polyanthum*.
J.dianthifolium hort. See *J.simplicifolium* ssp. *suavissimum*.

J.dichotomum Vahl.
Scrambling or climbing evergreen shrub to 8m. Leaves opposite, simple, to 10cm, ovate to broadly lanceolate. Flowers in crowded corymbs; calyx lobes very small; corolla white tinted red on exterior, especially in bud, tube to 2.5cm, lobes to 1.25cm, 5-9, oblanceolate. Tropical Africa. Z10.

J.dispermum Wallich in Roxb.
Deciduous or semi-evergreen climber differing from *J.officinale* in short (not long, slender) calyx lobes and long, narrow, terminal leaflet. Leaves opposite; leaflets 5-7, lanceolate-acuminate, lateral leaflets to 5cm, terminal leaflet to 10cm. Flowers in axillary and terminal cymes, fragrant; calyx to 1cm, teeth 5, short; corolla white often tinted pale red or pink on exterior, especially in bud, tube to 1.8cm, lobes to 0.7cm, obovate. N India to Yunnan. Z9.

J.diversifolium Kobuski. See *J.subhumile*.
J.farreri Gilmour. See *J.humile* f. *farreri*.

J.floridum Bunge.
Differs from *J.humile* in longer, narrower calyx-lobes. Erect, semi-evergreen shrub; branches square in section, glabrous, semi-pendent, green. Leaves alternate; leaflets 3–5, 1–3.5cm, oval to ovate, acuminate, glabrous, shining green above, pale beneath. Flowers in cymes, profuse, yellow. Late summer. China. Z9.

J.fluminense Vell. (*J.bahiense* DC.)
Evergreen climbing shrub differing from *J.angulare* in smaller calyx and broad inflorescence. New growth somewhat hairy or glabrous. Leaves opposite; leaflets 3, the terminal leaflet to 5cm long, lateral leaflets smaller, pubescent throughout. Flowers fragrant, short-stalked in broad lax cymes; calyx small with 5–6 very short teeth; corolla white, tube to 2.5cm, lobes 5–6, shorter than tube. Tropical Africa, Arabia; naturalized Maldives, Brazil. Z10.

J.fluminense hort. non Vell. See *J.azoricum*.

J.fruticans L.
Evergreen or semi-evergreen shrub to 1.25m, erect with branches densely set, slender, striped green, angular. Leaves alternate; leaflets 1–2cm, 3, tough, narrow-oblong, obtuse, dark green, glabrous, minutely ciliate. Flowers to 5 per terminal cyme; calyx with slender lobes equalling tube; corolla yellow, tube to 1.25cm, lobes 5, obtuse, to half length tube. Summer. Mediterranean, Asia Minor. Z8.

J.giraldii hort. See *J.humile* f. *farreri*.
J.gracile Andrews. See *J.simplicifolium* ssp. *australiense*.

J.grandiflorum L. CATALONIAN JASMINE; ROYAL JASMINE; SPANISH JASMINE.
Semi-evergreen or evergreen climbing shrub differing from *J.officinale* in its large flowers, arranged in open cymes with the pedicel of the flower central to each dichotomy shorter than those on either side, its confluent leaflets and its tenderness. Leaves opposite; leaflets 5–7, to 2cm (terminal leaflet longer), ovate, lateral leaflets somewhat confluent on flattened rachis. Inflorescence terminal, cymose-paniculate; flowers intensely fragrant; calyx teeth to 1.8cm, linear; corolla white, exterior sometimes tinted red, tube to 2cm, lobes 5–6, oblong. S Arabia, NE Africa, widely grown in warm and temperate regions elsewhere. Source of jasmine oil. Z10.

J. grandiflorum hort. non L. See *J.officinale* 'Affine'.
J.heterophyllum Roxb. See *J.subhumile*.

J.heterophyllum var. *subhumile* (W.W. Sm.) Kobuski. See *J. subhumile*.

J.humile L. ITALIAN JASMINE.
Evergreen or semi-evergreen shrub to 6m, erect, occasionally tree-like. Leaves alternate; leaflets to 7, to 4cm, ovate-lance-olate. Flowers sometimes scented, in near-umbellate clusters; calyx teeth very small, rectangular; corolla yellow, tube to 2cm, lobes to 1cm, rounded, spreading. Summer. Middle East, Burma, China. 'Revolutum' (*J.revolutum* Sims; *J.humile* var. *revolutum* (Sims) Stokes; *J.reevesii* hort.; *J.triumphans* hort.). Semi-evergreen, robust shrub, glabrous. Leaflets 3–7, terminal leaflet to 6cm, laterals to 4cm. Flowers 2.5cm wide, yellow, fragrant, 6–12 together, stamens slightly protruding. Summer. f. *farreri* (Gilmour) P. Green (*J.farreri* Gilmour; *J.giraldii* hort.). Evergreen, spreading shrub to 1.5m; young shoots angular, pubescent, flushed red at first, hardening green. Leaves 5–12cm; leaflets 3, oval-lanceolate, distinctly narrow-acuminate, terminal leaflet to 10cm, laterals slightly shorter, dull green, coarse above, pubescent beneath. Inflorescence hairy; flowers yellow, to 12 per terminal cyme. Summer. Upper Burma. f. *wallichianum* (Lindl.) P. Green (*J.wallichianum* Lindl.; *J.pubigerum* var. *glabrum* DC.; *J.humile* var. *glabrum* (DC.) Kob.). Shoots most angular. Leaflets 7–13, to 5cm, ovate-lanceolate, terminal leaflet long, narrow-acuminate. Flowers pendent; corolla 1 cm. Nepal. Z8.

J.humile var. *glabrum* (DC.) Kob. See *J.humile* f. *wallichianum*.
J.humile var. *revolutum* (Sims) Stokes. See *J.humile* 'Revolutum'.

J.laurifolium Roxb. (*J.angustifolium* var. *laurifolium* (Roxb.) Ker-Gawl.).
Evergreen slender climber with narrowly elliptic-lanceolate leaves and starry white flowers with glabrous calyces. Assam, Bangladesh. This species is most commonly represented in cultivation by the following form. f. *nitidum* (Skan) P.S. Green (*J.nitidum* Skan; *J.gracile* var. *magnificum* Graf.). ANGEL HAIR JASMINE; ANGEL WING JASMINE; WINDMILL JASMINE; STAR JASMINE; CONFEDERATE JASMINE. Stems slightly hairy. Leaves to 8cm, simple, opposite, elliptic-lanceolate to ovate-lanceolate, glossy bright green above. Flowers fragrant, star-like in sparse cymes terminating short branches; calyx pilose, tube shorter than lobes, lobes to 0.8cm, slender, spreading; cor. white, often tinted red in bud and on exterior, tube to 2cm, slender, lobes to 1.5cm, 9–11, linear-lanceolate, radiating at right angles to tube. India? (*not* Admiralty Is.), widely cultivated in Tropics and Subtropics.

J.leratii Schlect. in Engl. (*J.ligustrifolium* hort. non Lam.).
Evergreen climber. Leaves 5-8cm, simple, opposite, ovate to lanceolate. Flowers in terminal or axillary sparse to crowded panicles; calyx teeth small, scarcely exceeding tube; corolla white, tube to 2cm, lobes to 1.25cm, 5–7, lanceolate. New Caledonia, Loyalty Is. Z10.

J.ligustrifolium hort. non Lam. See *J. leratii*.

J.mesnyi Hance (*J.primulinum* Hemsl.). PRIMROSE JASMINE.
Evergreen rambling shrub to 2m, related to *J.nudiflorum*. Shoots square in section. Leaves opposite; leaflets 3, 2.5–7cm, lanceolate, dark glossy green. Flowers 3–5cm wide, solitary on very short axillary shoots with small, leafy bracts; calyx lobes 5–6, narrow-acuminate, glabrous or minutely downy; corolla usually semi-double, bright yellow, lobes to 1cm across, obtuse. Summer. W China. Z8.

J.multiflorum (Burm.f.) Andrews (*J.pubescens* (Retz.) Willd.). STAR JASMINE. Evergreen pubescent climber. Leaves to 5cm, opposite, simple, ovate, base rounded to cordate. Flowers large, fragrant, in sparse to crowded clusters; calyx lobes to 1.25cm, with long yellow hairs; corolla white, lobes oblong-lanceolate, 5–8, to half length of tube. India. Z10.

J.nudiflorum Lindl. (*J.sieboldianum* Bl.). WINTER JASMINE.
Deciduous, rambling shrub, to 3 × 3m, spreading, requiring support. Branches long, slender, arching to pendent, glabrous,

Jasminum (a) *J.rex* (b) *J.polyanthum* (c) *J.sambac* (d) *J.officinale* (e) *J.dispermum* (f) *J.azoricum* (g) *J.beesianum* (h) *J.angulare*

square in section. Leaves opposite; leaflets 3, 1–3cm, oval-oblong, dark green, glabrous, ciliate. Flowers borne before leaves, singly in axils of previous year's growth; corolla to 3cm wide, yellow, 6-lobed. Winter–early spring. N China. 'Aureum': leaves yellow, liable to revert to green. 'Nanum': dwarf, slow-growing, compact. Z6.

J.officinale L. COMMON JASMINE; TRUE JASMINE; JESSAMINE. Deciduous climbing shrub to 10m. Shoots sprawling to twining, slender, green, square in section. Leaves opposite; leaflets 5–9, 1–6cm, elliptic, acuminate, sessile except long-stalked terminal leaflet. Flowers to 5 per subumbellate cyme, cymes clustered terminally, highly fragrant; calyx teeth 5, narrow-linear, 5–15mm; corolla white, tube to 2cm, lobes 4–5, shorter than tube, +/– triangular-ovate. Summer–early autumn. Asia Minor, Himalaya, China. Z7. 'Affine' (*J.affine* Carr.; *J.officinale* f. *affine* (Carr.) Rehd.). Flowers larger, more profuse, exterior pink; corolla lobes broader. 'Aureum': leaves blotched golden yellow; less hardy. 'Inverleith': leaves 2–5cm; leaflets 3–7, lanceolate, terminal leaflet to 2.5cm, often deeply lobed, bases confluent and decurrent on rachis. Inflorescence 3–5-flowered; corolla tube to 1.5cm, cylindrical-funnelform, exterior strongly tinted pink-red, lobes 5, to 1cm, broadly ovate, apiculate, pure white above, tinted red beneath, especially in bud.

J.parkeri Dunn. Evergreen twiggy dwarf shrub, to 30cm, forming a dense mat or mound. Young shoots sulcate, pubescent, later glabrous. Leaves alternate, to 2.5cm; leaflets 3–5, 0.3–0.6cm, ovate-acuminate, sessile. Flowers borne singly or, rarely, in pairs, terminally or at axils, yellow, 1.5cm wide. Summer. NW India. Z7.

J.polyanthum Franch. (*J.blinii* Lév.). Deciduous or evergreen climbing and twining shrub to 8m. Leaves opposite; leaflets 5–7, lanceolate, narrow-acuminate at apex, terminal leaflet to 8cm, laterals shorter, coriaceous, 3-nerved. Flowers in axillary panicles, sparse or numerous, highly fragrant; corolla to 2cm, white within, exterior flushed pink, lobes obovate. Summer. China (Yunnan). Z9.

J.primulinum Hemsl. See *J.mesnyi.*
J.pubescens (Retz.) Willd. See *J.multiflorum.*
J.pubigerum var. *glabrum* DC. See *J.humile* f. *wallichianum.*
J.reevesii hort. See *J.humile* 'Revolutum'.

J.rex S.T. Dunn. Glabrous climber. Leaves opposite, simple, to 16cm, dark glossy green, broadly ovate, acuminate. Flowers on slender, drooping stalks, 2–3 per axillary cyme, unscented; calyx lobes to 0.5cm, 6, linear, twice length of calyx tube; corolla white, salverform, tube to 2.5cm, lobes 8(–9), ovate-oblong, equalling tube. Summer. Thailand. Z10.

J.revolutum Sims. See *J.humile* 'Revolutum'.

J.sambac (L.) Ait. ARABIAN JASMINE. Evergreen twiner, shoots pubescent, angular. Leaves opposite or whorled in threes, semi-rigid, shiny, glabrous or hairy, broad-ovate to 8cm, acute, conspicuously veined. Flowers in clusters 3–12; highly fragrant; calyx lobes narrow; corolla waxy white, pink with age, tube 1.2cm, lobes to 1.5cm, 6–9, oblong. Flowers continuously. Widespread due to long cult.; may originate in wild in India. 'Grand Duke of Tuscany'('Flore Pleno'): flowers double, corolla lobes rounded, like a small *Gardenia.* Z10.

J.sieboldianum Bl. See *J.nudiflorum*

J. simplicifolium Forst.f. Evergreen climber or tree close to *J.leratii*, with oblong leaves and white flowers with 6–9, narrower corolla segments. Z10. The typical form of this species is confined to Tonga and Fiji. Two subspecies are more widely grown, the first with calyx lobes equal to or shorter than the tube, the second with calyx lobes longer than the calyx tube. ssp. *australiense* P.S. Green (*J.gracile* Andrews; *J.simplicifolium* Sims non Forst.; *J. volubile* Jacq.). Scrambling shrub to 2m, or climber to 10m, or tree-like. Stems glabrous. Leaves (2–)3–6(–9)cm, ovate-lanceolate to

narrowly elliptic, apex acute to obtuse, subcoriaceous, dark glossy green above, veins prominent. Inflorescence cymose, paniculate, terminal on long and lateral shoots, flowers also sometimes axillary, fragrant; calyx tube 2mm, more or less entire or with 5–8 triangular teeth to 1mm; corolla white, tube 8–10mm, lobes 5–8, 6–8mm, lanceolate, acute. Queensland, New South Wales, Lord Howe Is., Norfolk Is., Papua New Guinea. ssp. *suavissimum* (Lindl.) P.S.Green (*J.suavissimum* Lindl.; *J.dianthifolium* hort.). Subshrub or shrub erect to 50cm, or trailing scrambler. Stems slender, glabrous or minutely puberulous at first. Leaves (1–)2.5–5(–7)cm, linear to very narrowly lanceolate or narrowly elliptic, apex slender, acute, somewhat revolute, veins obscure. Inflorescence terminal, 1–9-flowered, cymose; flowers slender-stalked and sweetly fragrant; calyx tube 1–2mm, lobes 1–5mm, 5–6, narrowly linear; corolla white, tube 6–13mm, lobes (6–)7–9(–11)mm, (3–)7–8, lanceolate, acute. Queensland, New South Wales. Hybrids are recorded between these two subspecies.

J.simplicifolium Sims non Forst.f. See *J.simplicifolium* ssp. *australiense.*

J.sinense Hemsl. Evergreen woody climber. Stems terete, initially densely and sometimes rather rusty-tomentose. Leaves opposite, trifoliolate; leaflets 4–10cm (terminal leaflet largest), ovate to broadly ovate, olive to mid green, densely tomentose beneath, less so above. Inflorescence densely corymbose, tomentose, terminal on long and side shoots; flowers fragrant; calyx pilose, tube 2–3mm, lobes 1.5–3mm, subulate-triangular; corolla white, tube 2.5–4cm, slender, lobes 0.8–1cm, 5–6, oblong-elliptic, spreading, margins somewhat reflexed and twisted. S & SW China. Z10.

J.smilacifolium Griff. ex C.B. Clarke in Hook.f. Large climbing shrub. Leaves to 18cm, ovate to ovate-lanceolate, apex acute to acuminate, base obtuse to rounded, thick, glossy. Inflorescence cymose, to 20-flowered; corolla white often stained pink-red, tube to 2.5cm, lobes to 2cm, acute. Malacca. Z10.

J. × stephanense Lemoine (*J.beesianum* × *J.officinale.*) Fast-growing climber, twining, to 5m; stems often yellow-green or cream at first, glabrous, ridged, slender. Leaves simple or 3–5-lobed; leaflets pale olive green, pubescent beneath. Flowers pale pink, small, in sparse cymes. Mid-summer. Garden origin, also said to occur wild in W China. Z7.

J.subhumile W.W.Sm. (*J.heterophyllum* Roxb.; *J.heterophyllum* var. *subhumile* (W.W. Sm.) Kobuski; *J.diversifolium* Kobuski). Shrub or small tree attaining 3m. Shoots obscurely angled, glabrous to densely pubescent. Leaves alternate, simple or trifoliolate; leaflets (or single blade) 2–12cm, glabrous lanceolate or narrowly to broadly ovate. Inflorescence +/– cymose-paniculate terminating lateral shoots; flowers fragrant; calyx glabrous, tube 1–2mm, lobes 0–0.75mm; corolla yellow, tube 9–12mm, lobes 4–9mm, rounded. Himalayas, India, Burma, W China.

J.tortuosum Willd. Climber. Leaves opposite; leaflets to 4cm, 3, linear-lanceolate to linear-oblong. Flowers 3–5 per cluster terminating lateral branchlets and long shoots; calyx lobes to 4mm, 5–6, triangular; corolla white, tube to 2.5cm, lobes to half length tube, usually 6. S Africa. Z10.

J.trinerve Vahl Climber. Branches terete, glabrous. Leaves ovate, apex long-acuminate, distinctly 3-nerved from base; petiole jointed in middle. Flowers terminal or axillary, solitary or clustered; calyx lobes subulate; corolla white, tube to 2.5cm, lobes 6–8, linear-lanceolate, shorter than tube. Java. Z10.

J.triumphans hort. See *J.humile* 'Revolutum'.
J. volubile Jacq. See *J.simplicifolium* ssp. *australiense.*
J.wallichianum Lindl. See *J.humile* f.*wallichianum.*

Juanulloa Ruiz & Pav.(For Jorge Juan (1713–73) and Antonio Ulloa (1716–95), Spanish travellers in S America.) Solanaceae. Some 10 species of epiphytic or climbing and rooting shrubs. Leaves simple, entire, glabrous to tomentose, coriaceous. Inflorescence a cluster, short raceme or panicle; flowers yellow or orange to red; calyx large, campanulate, occasionally fleshy, and ridged, lobes oblong to lanceolate; corolla tubular, inflated on one side, throat contracted, exterior tomentose, lobes 5, obtuse; stamens 5, equal, included or slightly protruding; anthers elongate; ovary superior, 2-chambered. Fruit an indehiscent berry, succulent or dry; seeds compressed. C & S America. Z10.

CULTIVATION   A semi-epiphyte or tree-top climber flowering high in the forest canopy, *J.mexicana* may be grown in the open garden in frost-free climates and is an attractive plant for clothing trellises with its leathery, evergreen leaves and drooping flame-coloured flowers. Give a fertile soil in full sun. In cool temperate areas, grow in a freely draining, medium-fertility loam-based mix in the intermediate glasshouse (minimum temperature 13°C/55°F) with medium to low humidity. Propagate from seed or by cuttings.

J.aurantiaca Otto & Dietr. See *J.mexicana.*
J.eximia Hook. See *Dyssochroma eximia.*

J.mexicana (Schldl.) Miers (*J.aurantiaca* Otto & Dietr.; *J.parasitica* Ruiz & Pav.).
Vine or epiphytic shrub to 3m. Leaves oblong, to 20cm, tomentose, apex acuminate. Inflorescence terminal, a short raceme or cluster; flowers pendent; calyx to 1.5cm diam., waxy, angled, pale orange, lobes 5, acuminate; corolla to 4cm, tubular, 5-ribbed, narrowed at throat, waxy, brilliant orange, lobes ovate, to 0,5cm, interior glabrous; anthers to 1cm; style slender. Peru, Colombia, C America. Z8.

J.parasitica Ruiz & Pav. See *J.mexicana.*

Justicia L. (For James Justice (*fl.* 1730–63), great Scottish horticulturist.) Acanthaceae. Some 420 species of perennial herbs, subshrubs or shrubs. Stems ascending to erect, glabrous or pubescent, jointed. Leaves opposite, oblong-ovate to ovate, usually entire. Flowers borne in axillary or terminal spikes, cymes or panicles, subtended by bracts; sepals 5, varying in shape, size and colour; corolla tubular campanulate, white to scarlet to mauve, often with lines within, tube short, straight or curved, corolla limb bilabiate; stamens 2; ovary 2-locular; stigma entire, capitate. Fruit a 2- or 4-seeded capsule. Tropical and subtropical N and S hemispheres, and temperate N America.

CULTIVATION   A showy, purple-flowered scrambler for use on walls and pergolas in sunny subtropical and tropical gardens, or, in cooler zones, cultivation in glasshouses and conservatories (minimum winter temperature 10°C/50°F). Plant in a well drained, fertile, loam-based soil. Water, feed and syringe regularly during warm weather, less often at other times. Tie in new leads and cut out weak, exhausted growth. Propagate by short, semi-ripe stem cuttings with most of the leaves removed and inserted in a case with bottom heat.

J.cydoniifolia (Nees) Lindau (*Adhatoda cydoniifolia* Nees). BRAZILIAN BOWER PLANT.
Climbing shrub, scrambling to 3m or more, pubescent. Leaves to 15cm, ovate, dark green, petiole to 2.5cm. Flowers 1–2 on short axillary peduncles at end of branches; calyx to 0.5cm; corolla tube short, more or less equalling calyx, upper lip arched and hood-like, white with purple margin, lower lip large, rich deep purple with white median stripe. Summer–autumn. Brazil. Z10. Plants grown under the name *Adhatoda cydoniifolia* are sometimes *Megaskepasma erythrochlamys*, a non-climber.

Kadsura Juss. (Japanese name for *K.japonica.*) Schisandraceae. 22 species of twining, evergreen, monoecious shrubs. Leaves entire or obscurely toothed, lacking stipules; petioles slender. Flowers unisexual, usually borne singly at axils; sepals and petals indistinguishable, 9–15; stamens 20–80, the filaments fused forming a fleshy head bearing the anthers. Fruit a fleshy berry, 2–3-seeded, many, forming a head (not a spike as in *Schisandra*). E & SE Asia.

CULTIVATION   Twining, evergreen vines grown for their attractive foliage, small but scented flowers, and for the scarlet berries. *Kadsura* is frost hardy to –5°C/5°F, but in colder areas is grown in cool to intermediate conditions in the glasshouse or conservatory. In the open, plant in a sheltered position, in sun or part shade, on moderately fertile, well drained neutral to acid soils. Otherwise, cultivate as for *Schisandra*.

K.japonica (L.) Dunal.
Glabrous climber to 4m. Leaves 4–11 × 2.5–6.5cm, elliptic to ovate-lanceolate, remotely toothed, deep green. Flowers to 1.5cm diam., ivory to cream; pedicel to 3cm. Fruiting head to 3cm+; berries scarlet. Japan, Korea. 'Variegata': leaves edged yellow to cream. Z7.

Kedrostis Medik. Cucurbitaceae. Some 23 species of prostrate or climbing, perennial herbs, usually monoecious and often with massively swollen caudiciform bases. Leaves entire or lobed; tendrils usually simple. Flowers white, yellow or green, small; male flowers in a raceme or a corymb; calyx campanulate, lobes 5, ovate to linear-lanceolate; corolla rotate, lobes 5, stamens 3 or sometimes 5, unilocular or bilocular, free or coherent, filaments short; female flowers solitary or in small clusters; calyx and corolla similar to those in male flowers; staminodes 3 or absent; ovary ovoid, rostrate, placentas 2 or 3, stigmas 2 or 3, ovules few- to many. Fruit a berry, indehiscent, fleshy, ovoid or subglobose, sessile or subsessile, rostrate, few to several-seeded, testa smooth. Africa to tropical Asia. Z10

CULTIVATION Remarkable Cucurbits with grotesquely swollen caudiciform bases and slender vining stems with attractively cut foliage; they require a minimum temperature of 10°C/50°F, a sharply draining soil high in grit and sand, full sunlight and dry, airy conditions. When in growth (usually for only a few months), they demand good water supplies and a weak fortnightly feed; at other times, especially in cool, dull weather, keep virtually dry, watering only to prevent shrivelling of the caudex. These are among the most spectacular of the caudiciforms and excellent additions to collections of cacti and succulents.

K.africana (L.) Cogn.
Base caudiciform, greatly swollen, succulent; climbing stems to 6m, slender. Leaves to 10cm diam., orbicular to cordate, usually glabrous, deeply pinnately or palmately lobed, segments filiform to elliptic; petiole to 1.2cm. Flowers minute, white to yellow-green: male inflorescence to 8cm; few- to 12-flowered; calyx lobes to 2mm, narrowly triangular to linear; corolla lobes to 2cm, finely papillose; female inflorescence to 6mm; ovary glabrous. Fruit to 15mm diam., subglobose, glabrous, few-seeded, red when ripe. Africa.

K.boehmii Song. See *Corallocarpus boehmii.*

K.foetidissima (Jacq.) Cogn. (*Trichosanthes foetidissima* Jacq.).
Base becoming swollen; climbing stems to 2m, often branched, usually pilose or pubescent. Leaves to 12 × 9cm, ovate-cordate to suborbicular, unlobed or slightly 3–5-lobed, obtuse to cuspidate, entire to undulate or dentate, usually pubescent throughout; petioles to 6cm. Flowers white to yellow-green: male flowers 1–7, in racemes, peduncle to 3cm, pubescent; pedicels to 1cm; calyx usually pubescent; corolla to 5mm, usually pubescent; female flowers solitary, in same axils as male flowers, sessile; ovary pilose. Fruit to 22mm, ovoid, red when ripe, long-pubescent beak to 15mm. Tropical Africa to tropical Asia.

Kennedya Vent. (For Lewis Kennedy (1775–1818), a founding partner of Lee & Kennedy, nurserymen of Hammersmith, London.) CORAL PEA. Leguminosae (Papilionoideae). Some 16 species of woody or herbaceous perennial climbers. Stems trailing or climbing, sometimes twining, usually pubescent or villous. Leaves alternate; stipules persistent, often conspicuous; leaflets 3, very rarely 1 or 5, alternate. Flowers in axillary pedunculate umbels or racemes, single, paired or in threes, large, showy; calyx lobes about equal to tube, upper 2 united except at the tips; standard obovate to orbicular, occasionally callused or auricled, keel incurved; stamens 10, 1 free, anthers equal; ovary several-ovulate; style slender. Fruit a cylindric legume, compressed or turgid; seeds arillate. Australia, Tasmania, New Guinea. Z10.

CULTIVATION *Kennedya* species occur on low-fertility podzols, on coastal limestone, in scrubland and plains, and are found scrambling through jarrah (*Eucalyptus marginata*) forest. They are grown primarily for their generous shows of pea flowers, soft black-purple with a central yellow blotch in *K.nigricans*, bright coral in the fast growing and drought-resistant *K.rubicunda*, and a dazzling scarlet pink in *K.prostrata*. In frost-free regions, *Kennedya* species are beautiful ornamentals grown as climbers or for groundcover; *K.prostrata* is very fast growing and *K.coccinea* is well adapted to covering dry, sunny banks. In cooler zones, they are well suited to the cool glasshouse or conservatory, trained up pillars and along rafters or scrambling through shrubs.

Grow in well drained soils, in full sun in a warm sheltered position. Under glass, pot in a sandy, medium-fertility, loam-based mix, provide the support of wire or trellis, and maintain a winter minimum temperature of 5–10°C/40–50°F. Water moderately when in growth, and keep dry but not arid in winter. Prune after flowering to remove overcrowded growth. Propagate by seed sown in spring at 21°C/70°F; germination may be erratic at lower temperatures. Immerse seed in boiling water and soak for 12 hours before sowing. Take semi-ripe cuttings in summer.

K.beckxiana F. Muell.
Coarse, woody, twining to 3m. Stipules small, base broad; leaflets to 5cm, 3, lanceolate-ovate; stipels linear. Flowers 1–5 in a loose umbel, 3cm diam.; standard narrow-obovate, red, yellow-patched at base. Summer. W Australia.

K.coccinea Vent. (*K.dilatata* A. Cunn. ex Lindl.). CORAL VINE.
Prostrate or twining, robust, often woody, to 2m. Stipules narrow, deltoid, tapering, prominently veined; leaflets to 1.5cm, usually 3, linear-lanceolate to cuneate, leathery, coarse, sometimes lobed; stipules linear, small. Flowers 4–20 in umbels, red, young buds rusty-pubescent; standard to 1.6cm, orbicular, spotted-yellow edged purple at base. Spring. Australia, Tasmania.

K.dilatata A. Cunn. ex Lindl. See *K.coccinea.*

K.eximia Lindl.
Prostrate, sometimes twining, sericeous, to 1m. Stipules broad, acute, veined, deciduous; leaflets to 2.5cm, 3, ovate, obovate or lanceolate, clearly veined. Flowers 1–6 in umbel or short raceme, scarlet; standard to 1.7cm, broadly obovate, rarely orbicular. Spring–summer. W Australia.

K.glabrata (Benth.) Lindl.
Slender, twining to 50cm, glabrous or sparsely addressed-pubescent. Stipules broad, veined; leaflets to 2.5cm, 3, obovate or cuneate, truncate, mucronate. Flowers in umbels, scarlet; standard to 1.3cm diam., suborbicular, emarginate. Spring–summer. W Australia.

K.macrophylla (Meissn.) Benth.
Coarse, twining, to 3m, patent-pubescent, initially sericeous. Stipules very broad, often united, to 2.5cm diam.; leaflets to 6cm, 3, obovate-orbicular, obtuse; stipules lanceolate. Flowers racemose on axillary peduncles, red; standard orbicular, to 1.3cm diam. Spring. Australia.

K.marryattae Lindl. See *K.prostrata.*
K.monophylla Vent. See *Hardenbergia violacea.*

K.nigricans Lindl. BLACK CORAL PEA; BLACK BEAN.
Robust, woody climber to 6m, glabrous or subpubescent, capable of prolific growth but usually stunted. Stipules cuneate, striate, 3mm; leaflets to 12.5cm, 1 or 3, ovate, tough; stipules linear, bristly. Flowers in racemes, to 4cm, violet-purple or black and yellow-splotched; standard narrow-obo-

vate, folded back over calyx, 3 × 1cm. Spring–summer. W Australia.

K.ovata Sims. See *Hardenbergia violacea.*

K.procurrens Benth.
Stems pubescent, prostrate. Stipules broadly lanceolate; leaflets to 5cm, 3, ovate to elliptical, mucronate, minutely pubescent above, pubescent beneath. Flowers to 2cm, borne in short, terminal racemes on long peduncles; standard to 1.5cm, pale red to mauve or violet, broadly obovate, emarginate. Australia (Queensland).

K.prostrata R. Br. (*K.marryattae* Lindl.). RUNNING POSTMAN; SCARLET RUNNER.
Prostrate or trailing with occasionally branching runners, to 25cm, hirsute to densely pubescent Stipules cordate, 5mm, leafy; leaflets to 13cm, 3, rarely 1 or 2, ovate-orbicular. Stipules acute, 2mm, bristly. Flowers 1–2, on a peduncle to

2.5cm, bright scarlet to pink; standard narrow, obovate, yellow-callused at base. Autumn. W Australia.

K.rubicunda (Schneev.) Vent. DUSKY CORAL PEA.
Evergreen vine to 3m. Stem robust, twining or mat-forming; branches slender, hirsute. Stipules small. Leaflets 15cm, 3, ovate, dull green, hirsute. Flowers in slender umbels, 4cm, dark red; standard abruptly reflexed at middle, with a large, pale blotch at base. Spring. Australia (NSW, Victoria).

K.splendens Meissn. See *Camptosema rubicundum.*

K.stirlingii Lindl.
Prostrate or suberect, rarely twining, to 2m, hirsute, basal portions becoming woody when old. Stipules large, leafy. Leaflets to 6cm, 3, obovate-lanceolate. Peduncle 1–3-flowered; flowers brick-red; standard orbicular, 1.5cm diam. Spring. W Australia.

Lablab Adans. (From a Hindu plant name.) Leguminosae (Papilionoideae). 1 species, a perennial herb, to 6m. Stems usually twining. Leaves alternate, trifoliolate; petiole slender, narrow-ridged above, base pulvinate; stipules lanceolate to triangular; leaflets to 15 × 15cm, ovate to triangular or rhombic, downy to glabrous, apex acute or acuminate; petiolules pulvinate. Inflorescences to 40cm, axillary, erect; flowers in clusters of 5, white or purple; calyx 4-lobed, upper 2 sepals joined; standard to 1.5cm, reflexed, notched, wings obovate; stamens 10. Fruit to 15 × 5cm, oblique-oblong, margin warty; seeds 3–6, rounded, slightly flattened. Tropical Africa, widely cultivated in India, SE Asia, Egypt, Sudan. Z9.

CULTIVATION   The pods and seeds of *L.purpureus* are a popular vegetable on the Indian subcontinent. This fast-growing, short-lived climber has ornamental value too, in its fragrant, pea-like flowers and maroon pods. In temperate zones it is suitable for the cool glasshouse or conservatory, trained on wires and pillars; it is also grown as an annual outdoors, on trellis, fence or cane supports. Grow outdoors in well drained soils in full sun, planting out only when danger of frost is passed. Under glass, use a freely draining, soilless mix and maintain a minimum winter temperature of 7–10°C/45–50°F; water plentifully when in growth, but avoid waterlogged and stagnant conditions in the pot. Apply liquid feed weekly when growing strongly. In warm zones, with a temperature range of 18–30°C/65–85°F and moderate rainfall (up to about 900mm/36in. per annum), *Lablab* is grown for its edible cultivars. Short-day, long-day and daylength-neutral cultivars are available; some are drought-resistant. Well drained soils with a high organic content and pH 5.5–6.0 are preferred. Sow seed on ridges, 6–8 seeds per station, later thinning to four, or at 30–45cm/12–18in. intervals in rows 75–90cm/30–36in. apart. Vigorously climbing forms, which may reach 6m/20ft, require stakes or other support. Apply fertilizers high in P and K, and top-dress regularly. Young pods are harvested 70–120 days after sowing, and may be stored at a relative humidity of 90% at 1–2°C/34–36°F; they can also be preserved by salting. Yields of 250–450g/m^2 (8–14oz/yd^2) can be obtained. In cool temperate zones, use daylength-neutral or long-day cultivars. Sow seed in early spring in a soilless propagating mix at 18–22°C/65–72°F, and transfer to growing bags or 25cm/10in. pots when plants are 10–12cm/4–5in. high. Regular watering, and applications of a balanced NPK fertilizer, such as that used for tomatoes, will be suitable.

L.niger hort. See *L.purpureus.*

L.purpureus (L.) Sweet (*L.niger* hort.; *Dolichos lablab* L.; *Dolichos soudanensis* hort.). DOLICHOS BEAN; HYACINTH BEAN; BONAVIST; LUBIA BEAN; SEIM BEAN; INDIAN BEAN; EGYPTIAN BEAN.
'Giganteus': flowers large, white.

Lagenaria Ser. (From Gk *lagenos*, flask, referring to the shape of the fruit.) WHITE-FLOWERED GOURD; CALABASH GOURD; BOTTLE GOURD. Cucurbitaceae. 6 species of annual or perennial herbs, climbing or scandent, robust, monoecious. Tendrils simple or bifid. Leaves simple, ovate with a cordate base or 3–5-lobed; petiole bearing pair of glands below lamina. Male flowers solitary or in racemes, large, white; calyx tubular, lobes 5, small, narrow; petals 5, free, obovate, entire; stamens 3; anthers often coherent, thecae triplicate, contorted; female flowers solitary, campanulate, large, white; staminodes 3; ovary pubescent; stigmas 3, bilobed. Fruit to 1m, cylindric, bent, shaped like a club, skittle or a crook-necked flask, indehiscent, epicarp hard, mesocarp fleshy; seeds many, oblong, compressed. Pantropical, widely naturalized. Z10.

CULTIVATION   Strong-growing annual climbers grown for their calabash gourds. The fruit of *L.siceraria* is edible when young and its hard exterior is used to make various receptacles. Cultivate as *Trichosanthes* except that multiple planting and cross-pollination are not required. The large flowers open in the evenings and are also attractive. Sometimes troubled by whitefly.

L.leucantha Duchesne. See *L.siceraria*.
L.longissima hort. See *L.siceraria*.

L.siceraria (Molina) Standl. (*L.vulgaris* Ser.; *Cucurbita lagenaria* L.; *Cucurbita siceraria* Molina; *Cucurbita leucantha* hort.).
To 10m, viscid-pubescent annual. Leaves ovate-cordate, rarely lobed, sinuate-toothed, pubescent, 3–23×4–23cm; petiole 3–13cm. Flowers solitary; male peduncle to 12cm, female shorter; petals obovate, 3–4.5 × 2–4cm, male larger than female; ovary villous. Fruit smooth, green to green-yellow, pubescent, subglobose to lageniform; seeds white, slightly 2-horned, to 2cm. Pantropical, domesticated separately in the Old and New Worlds. The many cultivated variants of *L.siceraria* are named according to their appearance and the use to which they are put, e.g. SUGAR TROUGH GOURD; HERCULES' CLUB; BOTTLE GOURD; DIPPER; KNOBKERRY; TRUMPET GOURD.

L.vulgaris Ser. See *L.siceraria*.

Lapageria Ruiz & Pav. (For Joséphine Tascher de la Pagérie (1763–1814), wife of Napoleon Bonaparte and an enthusiastic patron of gardening.) CHILEAN BELLFLOWER; CHILE BELLS; COPIHUE. Liliaceae (Philesiaceae). 1 species, an evergreen climbing monocot, spreading strongly by subterranean stolons. Stems to 10m, thickly wiry, becoming woody at base, twining, branching toward summit, clothed with sharp scale-like bracts. Leaves 6–12×2.5cm, alternate, ovate or ovate-lanceolate to subcordate, acute, glossy dark green, leathery, with 3–5 prominent parallel veins; petioles to 1cm. Flowers 1–3, campanulate, pendulous, short-stalked, solitary or a few clustered in the axils of upper leaves; tepals 6.5–9.5cm, oblong-elliptic, 6 in 2 whorls, each with a basal pouched nectary, outer tepals flesh pink to magenta, crimson or white, broader than inner and rather heavily textured, inner tepals brighter, often faintly spotted or streaked crimson; stamens 6, free or slightly joined at base; style longer than stamens, clavate, apex slightly lobed. Fruit a many-seeded, oblong-ovoid, edible berry; seeds pale yellow or yellow-brown. Summer–winter. Chile. Z9.

CULTIVATION   One of the most handsome climbers, *L.rosea* is the national flower of Chile, grown for its nodding, waxy rose flowers, carried from summer into autumn. Given the protection of a partially shaded and sheltered wall, it will grow outside where temperatures seldom fall below –5°C/23°F; otherwise it makes a fine specimen for the borders of the cold glasshouse or conservatory. Grow in cool, well drained but moisture-retentive, humus-rich, lime-free soils in light shade or where direct sunlight reaches the leaves for short periods only. Under glass grow in bright filtered light, ensuring protection from bright sunlight especially during high summer. Propagate by layering in spring or autumn or by seed, pre-soaked for about 48 hours before sowing.

L.rosea Ruiz & Pav.
'Beatrice Anderson': flowers deep red. 'Flesh Pink': flowers flesh coloured. 'Nash Court Pink': flowers pink, marbled darker. 'Nash Court Red': flowers red. 'Penheale': flowers dark red. 'Superba': flowers brilliant crimson. var. *albiflora* Hook. Flowers white.

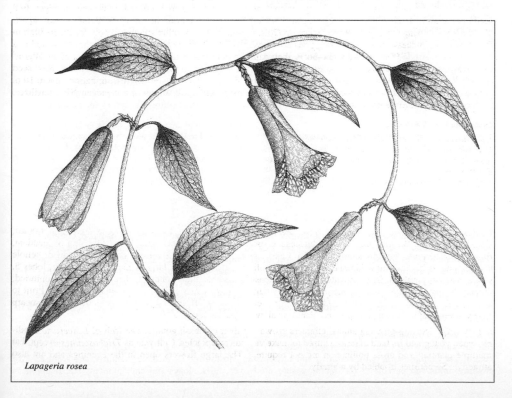

Lapageria rosea

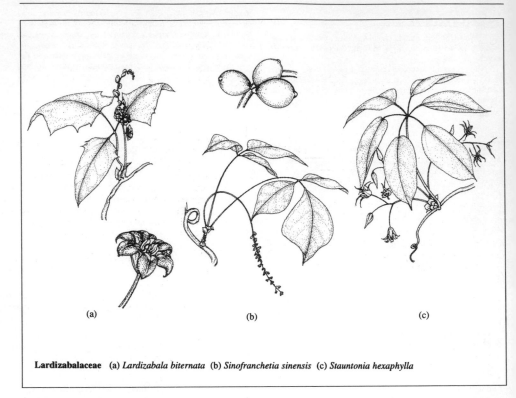

Lardizabalaceae (a) *Lardizabala biternata* (b) *Sinofranchetia sinensis* (c) *Stauntonia hexaphylla*

Lardizabala Ruiz & Pav. (For Miguel de Lardizabel y Uribe, 18th-century Spanish naturalist.) Lardizabal-aceae. 2 species of evergreen, monoecious climbers. Leaves alternate. Flowers unisexual, sepals 6, petaloid, nectaries 6, petaloid; male flowers in drooping to ascending raceme with 6 united stamens; female flowers solitary, with 6 staminodes and 3–6 carpels. Fruit developing from 1 carpel, a many-seeded berry. Chile.

CULTIVATION A handsome twining climber with dark green compound leaves and slender spikes of small dark male flowers. Where pollination is successful (flowers are unisexual and the plants themselves sometimes dioecious), dark mauve-blue fruit follow the solitary female flowers. Hardy to –10°C/14°F, this vine nevertheless prefers a shady protected site in well drained soils rich in decayed matter. A pleasing if rather subtle candidate for city gardens and sheltered groves. Propagate by seed in spring or stem cuttings in spring and autumn.

L.biternata Ruiz & Pav.
Twining to 4m. Leaves ternate, biternate or triternate, dark glossy green above, paler with distinct reticulate venation beneath, coriaceous, leaflets 5–10cm, 3–9, ovate, the central leaflet largest, lateral leaflets often sessile, margins entire or shallowly crenate, with 1–2 thorny teeth. Male flowers in axillary, pendulous to ascending spikes, 7.5–10cm long, sepals 6, fleshy, arranged in 2 whorls, broadly ovate, green edged dark brown-purple, petals small, lanceolate, white, farinose, stamens 6, connate, carpels rudimentary; female flowers solitary, axillary, 1.5–1.8cm long, pedicel 2.5cm, slender, carpels 3 (rarely 6); stamens 6, free, sterile. Fruit 6cm, ovoid-oblong, dark purple. Winter. Chile. Z8.

Lathyrus L. (Name used by Theophrastus, from the Ancient Greek name for the pea or pulse, combining *la-*, very, and *thoures*, a stimulant: the seeds were said to have excitant or irritant properties.) Leguminosae (Papilionoideae). VETCHLING; WILD PEA. 110+ species of annual or perennial herbs, often climbing by means of leaf tendrils. Stems usually winged. Leaves usually paripinnate, occasionally reduced to grass-like phyllodes; stipules often leaf-like; leaflets usually distinctly parallel-veined. Flowers papilionaceous in axillary racemes, or solitary, axillary; calyx actinomorphic to 2-lipped; keel usually obtuse; stamens 10, 1 free; style pubescent below. Fruit a narrow-oblong, flat, dehiscent legume, 2+-seeded. Eurasia, N America, mts of E Africa and temperate S America.

CULTIVATION Grown primarily for their decorative qualities; those described have handsome flowers, are often fragrant and most will tolerate temperatures below –15°C/5°F. Some are useful as green manure and in erosion control, for example *L.hirsutus*, *L.sativus* and *L.sylvestris*. Most climb by means of tendrils, and are useful for clothing trellis and pergola or for trailing unsupported over walls, slopes and embankments etc. *L.japonicus* ssp.*maritimus*, a sprawling native of sand and shingle beaches, is especially useful for hot, sunny banks, and is sometimes grown on the rock garden with due consideration for its vigour. *L.splendens*, with rich red-crimson blooms, *L.nervosus*, with periwinkle blue flowers, and *L.pubescens* are suitable for similar uses where winter temperatures do not fall much below zero for prolonged periods; *L.nervosus* thrives best in zones with cool moist summers.

The perennial, clump-forming species are included here for the sake of completeness. They are suited to the flower border (in particular those without tendrils formerly included in *Orobus*) some of these are suitable in scale for the rock garden, among them *L.gmelinii* (*L.aureus* hort.) with rich, deep orange yellow flowers, *L.hirsutus*, *L.niger* and *L.vernus*. The last is especially delightful in late winter when its light bunches of emerging stems packed with rose, blue and mauve blooms bring relief to the woodland garden and the foreground of herbaceous borders.*L.palustris* is well adapted to the bog garden and, with *L.venosus*, to other damp situations that approximate to their natural habitat; similarly, *L.sylvestris* is eminently suited to wild gardens and native plant collections. *L.latifolius*, the Everlasting Sweetpea, is a favourite plant for cottage gardens.

Grow *Lathyrus* species in any moderately fertile, well drained soil in sun, or in light dappled shade for *L.rotundifolius*, *L.grandiflorus*, *L.venosus* and *L.sylvestris*. *L.latifolius*, *L.vernus*, *L.niger* and *L.luteus* are tolerant of part day shade. Provide appropriate support (i.e. canes, trellis or host-shrubs for climbers; for semi-scandent or erect perennials, a few birch twigs pushed into the ground around their crowns should suffice), deadhead throughout the season and cut back in autumn to ground level. An annual application of a general fertilizer may be given on very poor soils.

Propagate from pre-soaked seed under glass in early spring or *in situ* in spring, also by division in early spring. This last method is most successful with *L.vernus* and the non-climbing species; many of the climbing perennials do not transplant well and even seed-grown specimens are best planted out when young and left undisturbed.

L.odoratus (Sweetpea) has been subjected to much horticultural improvement on both sides of the Atlantic, giving rise to a range of types suited to a variety of horticultural purposes. The tall types, 2–3m/6–10ft or more in height, with long-stemmed blooms, are grown for cutting and exhibition; they are judged on trueness of colour, freshness, placement, size and form of bloom, and its proportion to stem length, and on presentation. Tall sweetpeas include the Grandiflora types, commonly known as 'old-fashioned' sweetpeas, raised mostly before 1900 by Henry Eckford. Old-fashioned types are valued for their dainty and beautifully scented flowers in a range of intense colours, but they have been largely superseded by the Spencer types, originating in the early years of the 20th century primarily from 'Countess Spencer' and 'Gladys Unwin', and differing from earlier types in the much enlarged, frilled or waved standards. The multitude of modern Spencer Sweetpeas show almost infinite variation in size and degree of waviness or frilling, length of stem, number and spacing of flowers in the raceme, some with doubling of the standard, and with a colour range including selfs, bicolours, picotees and those with flecks and ripples of contrasting colour. Other talls include the Early Multiflora Giganteas, earlier-flowering than Spencer types, the Cuthbertson Floribundas, also earlier, with a reputation for tolerance of hot weather, and the Galaxy and Mammoth series; all show an increased number of blooms per stem.

Dwarf types are plants of bushy habit reaching heights of 15–30cm/6–12in., with large but short-stemmed flowers, less useful for cutting but well suited to tubs, pots and boxes, and as edging and bedding plants; they require little or no support other than perhaps a layer of pea sticks to keep the foliage off the soil in wet seasons. These include the Little Sweetheart series. The Cupid and Patio series are classified as dwarf prostrate forms, usually achieving heights of above 10cm/4in. The Snoopea series are prostrate but slightly taller, 30cm/12in. Semi-dwarfs or intermediates, to 100cm/39in. in height, include the Jet Set, Knee High and Continental series. They have the advantage of being largely self-supporting, with longer-stemmed flowers than dwarf types.

Sweetpeas are grown using the natural system where a supply of cut flowers is required, on the cordon system for larger blooms for cutting and exhibition, and under glass for early blooms. Under the natural system, plants are grown in rows, sown into soil prepared in autumn by the incorporation of well rotted manure or compost, with pea sticks or netting for support for tall types. Sow seed in autumn, and overwinter in the cold frame, or sow in spring under glass or *in situ*. In mild winter areas, seed may be sown *in situ* in autumn. All side shoots are left on, faded blooms are removed, and feeding and watering as necessary will prolong the flowering season.

For cordon culture, ground preparation is more thorough. In autumn prepare a bed, two spits (45cm/18in.) deep, and a metre wide (for a double row), incorporating well rotted animal manure by double digging. The addition of bonemeal in new beds is beneficial and where necessary apply lime to achieve pH 6.5–7. The site should be sunny and open and rows ideally run north to south; shelter to north and east is desirable. Sow presoaked or chipped seed in autumn or early winter, into well crocked pots or boxes of loam-based propagating mix, or into a 4:1:1 mix of loam, leafmould and sharp sand. Overwinter in a well ventilated cold frame, giving protection of frame lights only when temperatures drop below zero; where temperatures drop below –2°C/28°F, protect with additional hessian sacks or similar material. In late winter/early spring, stop plants to encourage grown of side shoots, harden off for planting out in mid-spring or late spring (depending on sowing date).

The cordon consists of a framework of wires between stout posts with a cane for each plant tied into the framework. Plant firmly at the base of the cane, and when plants are established and have reached 25–30cm/10–12in., select the strongest leader and tie in to the cane; exceptionally vigorous cultivars are grown on with two leaders. All subsequent side-shoots and tendrils are removed, either at the base or by removing the growing tip beyond the first pair of leaves. Tie in at each leaf joint, with wire rings or raffia, and remove the first few flower stems.

Plants in full bloom may be given a fortnightly application of high phosphate fertilizer, (e.g. 5:15:5 NPK), but all additional feeding must be done judiciously to avoid oversoft, pest- and disease-prone growth. An organic mulch of spent hops, straw or very well rotted manure will retain moisture and keep the plants weed free. It is common practice to 'drop' plants which may reach the top of their canes well before the end of the flowering season, to obtain improved quality blooms at a convenient height for cutting. Remove ties, lay plants carefully along the row, and gently bend the top 30–40cm/12–16in. of growth upwards, re-attaching to a conveniently placed cane. Plants resume flowering in about 14–16 days.

For early blooms in the cold glasshouse, autumn-sown plants are brought under glass in winter and planted out into a prepared site in the glasshouse border, or into large pots of a medium-fertility loam-based mix. Provide a minimum temperature of 5–10°C/40–50°F, good ventilation, and bright indirect light; reduce water when temperatures are low to avoid bud drop. Early-flowering cultivars are most suitable for glasshouse cultivation; those in the peach/salmon pink colour range retain their colour particularly well grown under these conditions.

The foliage of *Lathyrus* species may become infested by thrips, especially onion thrips (*Thrips tabaci*), polyphagous aphids particularly the peach potato aphid (*Myzus persicae*) and gall midge, the pea midge *Continaria pisi*. The flowers may be damaged by bumble bees or become infested with pollen beetles (*Meligethes*). Seedlings are vulnerable to slugs and snails and roots may be injured by symphylids and the larvae of fungus gnats. Mice may remove and/or resow seed at sowing time. Birds, especially sparrows take seedlings on emergence.

A foot and root rot, in which roots and stem bases are discoloured and eventually decay, can be caused by the fungi *Aphanomyces euteiches*, *Rhizoctonia solani* or *Thielaviopsis basicola*. Seedlings should be raised in a sterile medium but if the disease does occur a systemic fungicide drench may give some control. White mould, which resembles powdery mildew, is caused by the fungus *Ramularia deusta*; a white, powdery growth occurs on the stems and on both leaf surfaces. The disease is favoured by damp conditions and sulphur or dithiocarbamate fungicides have been recommended for its control. Sweetpeas can also be affected by crown gall (*Agrobacterium tumefaciens*), damping-off (*Phytophthora* and *Pythium*), downy mildew (*Peronospora viciae*), fasciation (*Corynebacterium fascians*), grey mould (*Botrytis cinerea*), powdery mildew (*Erysiphe polygoni*), sclerotinia rot (*Sclerotinia sclerotiorum*) and wilt (*Fusarium* spp.). Several aphid-transmitted viruses including bean yellow mosaic, pea venation mosaic and pea mosaic affect sweetpeas, causing such symptoms as leaf vein-clearing, mottling and yellowing as well as flower colour breaks. Aphid control is unlikely to give fully effective control and any obviously affected plants should be discarded. White clover mosaic virus, which causes leaf mottling and flower distortion, is easily transmitted by contact if healthy plants are handled after touching affected ones. Bud drop sometimes occurs as a result if overwatering, sudden temperature drops or from too little sun.

L.angustifolius Martrin-Donos. See *L.latifolius*.
L.angustifolius Medik. non Martrin-Donos. See *L.sylvestris*.
L.acutifolius Vogel. See *L.pubescens*.
L.affinis Guss. See *L.aphaca*.
L.americanus (Mill.) Kupicha. See *L.nervosus*.
L.andicola Gand. See *L.pubescens*.

L.aphaca L. (*L.affinis* Guss.; *L.polyanthus* Boiss. & Bl.; *L.pseudoaphaca* Boiss.). YELLOW VETCHLING.
Annual to 1m; stem angled. Mature leaves terminate in a tendril; stipules to 5×4cm, paired, leaf-like, hastate, grey-green; leaflets 1 pair on juvenile leaves, absent on mature leaves. Flowers to 18mm, usually solitary, yellow; peduncles to 5cm. Fruit to 3.5cm×0.8cm, brown, glabrous, 6–8-seeded. Late spring–summer. W & C Europe.

L.armitageanus Westc. ex Loud. See *L.nervosus*.
L.asiaticus (Zalk.) Kudrj. See *L.sativus*.

L.aureus (Steven) Brañdza.
Sparsely pubescent. Leaflets 2.5–5cm across, in 3–6 pairs, oval to ovate, with brown glands beneath. Flowers in racemes: corolla 1.7–2.2cm, brown to yellow-orange. Fruit glandular at first. Balkans. Z6.

L.aureus hort. non (Steven) Brañdza. See *L.gmelinii*.
L.azureus hort. See *L.sativus*.
L.californicus Douglas. See *L.japonicus* ssp. *maritimus*.

L.cyaneus (Steven) K. Koch (*Orobus cyaneus* Steven).
Perennial, some 30.5cm. Stem ascending or suberect, angular. Stipules to 1.5×0.5cm, lanceolate-linear, sagittate; leaflets to 8×1.2cm, in 1–3 pairs, linear-lanceolate. Racemes 1–15-flowered; corolla to 2.5cm, blue-lilac, white at base. Fruit to 4.5cm, linear, acuminate at apex, brown, slightly inflated. Summer. Caucasus. Z6.

L.davidii Hance.
Perennial to 120cm; stems erect or ascending, glabrous. Leaves terminate in a 2- or 3-branched tendril; stipules to

6×2.5cm, semi-sagittate or -cordate; leaflets to 8×4cm, 3–4 pairs, rhomboid-oval, or oval-oblong. Racemes many-flowered; peduncles to 10cm; corolla yellow-white, later ochre. Fruit 10 × 0.6cm, hairy to glabrous, many-seeded. Summer. Manchuria, N China, Korea, Japan. Z6.

L.drummondii hort. See *L.rotundifolius*.
L.dumetorum Philippi. See *L.pubescens*.
L.ewaldii (Meinsh.) Meinsh. See *L.laevigatus*.

L.gmelinii (Fisch. ex DC.) Fritsch non Rouy (*L.luteus* (L.) Peterm. non Moench; *Orobus gmelinii* Fisch. ex DC.; *Orobus luteus* L.).
To 1.5m; stems erect, glabrous or somewhat pubescent Stipules to 3 × 1.5cm, semi-sagittate, ovate or ovate-lanceolate, acuminate, dentate at base; leaflets to 10 × 5cm, 3–6 pairs, broad-lanceolate, acuminate, slightly glaucous beneath. Racemes 4–15-flowered; calyx campanulate, subglabrous; corolla to 3cm, light- to orange-yellow, brown-striped. Fruit to 8 × 0.9cm, slightly curved, glabrous, 12–15-seeded. Summer. C & S Urals, mts of C Asia. The name *L.luteus*, a synonym of this species, is misapplied to *L.aureus*. Z4.

L.gmelinii (Fisch. ex DC.) Rouy non Fritsch. See *L.laevigatus*.
L.gramineus A. Gray. See *L.nissolia*.

L.grandiflorus Sibth. & Sm. (*Pisum graecum* Quézel & Contandr.). TWO-FLOWERED PEA; EVERLASTING PEA.
Perennial to 2m; stems angled, not winged, scabrous to pubescent. Leaves terminating in a 3-branched tendril; stipules linear, occasionally sagittate, to 10 × 1.5mm; leaflets to 5 × 3.5cm, 1 pair, occasionally 3 pairs, ovate, weakly parallel-veined. Racemes 1–4-flowered; corolla to 3cm, standard violet, growing paler towards the margin, keel pink, wings purple. Fruit to 9 × 0.7cm, brown, glabrous, 15–20-seeded. Summer. S Italy, Sicily, S Balkans. Z6.

L.heterophyllus L.
Resembles *L.latifolius*, but with 2–3 pairs of leaflets, and flowers smaller, to 2.5mm. Summer. C & W Europe. Z6.

L.hirsutus L. SINGLETARY PEA; CALEY PEA; ROUGH PEA; WINTER PEA; AUSTRIAN PEA.
Perennial to 50cm; stems angular, not winged. Leaves not terminating in a tendril; stipules to 3 × 1.5cm, lanceolate to ovate-orbicular, sagittate or semi-sagittate; leaflets to 4×2cm, 1 pair, lanceolate to suborbicular, acute. Racemes 2–6-flowered; corolla to 2cm, blue-violet. Fruit 4 × 0.5cm, linear, pubescent, usually 6-seeded. SE Europe. Z7.

L.incurvus Rchb. See *L.palustris*.
L.inermis Rochel ex Friv. See *L.laxiflorus*.

L.japonicus Willd. CIRCUMPOLAR PEA; BEACH PEA; SEA PEA.
Perennial to 90cm; stems angled, not winged. Leaves occasionally not terminating in a tendril; stipules to 2.5×2cm, triangular-hastate; leaflets to 4 × 2cm, 2–5 pairs, elliptic, pinnately-veined. Racemes 2–7-flowered; corolla to 2.5cm, purple, becoming blue. Fruit to 5 × 1cm, brown, glabrescent, 4–11-seeded. Summer. Coasts of W & N Europe, China, N America; inland in NW Russia and N Norway. Seeds viable 4–5 years in sea-water. ssp. **maritimus** (L.) P.W. Ball (*L.californicus* Douglas; (*L.japonicus* var. *glaber* (Ser.) Fern.). Racemes 5–12-fld; corolla to 18mm. Coasts of W Europe & Baltic, N America. Z3.

L.japonicus var. *glaber* (Ser.) Fern. See *L.japonicus* ssp. *maritimus*.

L.laetiflorus Greene (*L.strictus* Torr. & A. Gray).
Perennial to 2m; stems not winged. Leaves terminate in a tendril; stipules ovate-lanceolate to lanceolate; leaflets to 5 × 4.5cm, 4–6 pairs, narrow-linear to ovate. Racemes 5–12-flowered; calyx to 1.5cm; corolla to 2.5cm, white or pink-flushed, to blue or crimson. Fruit to 8×0.8cm. Summer. W US (California). Z8.

L.laevigatus (Waldst. & Kit.) Gren.(*L.ewaldii* (Meinsh.) Meinsh.; *L.gmelinii* (Fisch. ex DC.) Rouy non Fritsch).
To 70cm. Stem erect, angular, occasionally few-branched, glabrous or soft-hairy. Stipules to 2.5 × 0.8cm, lanceolate or ovate-lanceolate; leaflets to 7 × 3cm, 2–6 pairs, elliptic to ovate, usually short-acuminate, blue-green beneath. Racemes 3–17-flowered; calyx tubular-campanulate; corolla 2.5cm, yellow. Fruit to 7 × 0.8cm, black, glabrous, 11–14-seeded. Summer. C Europe to N Spain, N Balkans and N Ukraine. Z5.

L.latifolius L. (*L.angustifolius* Martrin-Donos; *L.megalanthus* Steud.; *L.membranaceus* C. Presl). PERENNIAL PEA; BROAD-LEAVED EVERLASTING PEA.
Perennial to 3m; stems prostrate or climbing, broad-winged, coarsely pubescent, downy or glabrous. Leaves terminate in a 3-branched tendril; stipules to 6 × 1cm, lanceolate to ovate, semi-hastate, conspicuously nerved; leaflets to 15 × 5cm, 1 pair, linear to elliptic, acute, thin-mucronate at apex, blue-green, reticulate-veined. Racemes long-stalked, 5–15-flowered; calyx broad-campanulate; corolla to 3cm diam., magenta-purple, pink, or white. Fruit to 11 × 1cm, brown, glabrous, 10–15-seeded. Summer. C & S Europe, naturalized N America. 'Albus' ('Snow Queen'): flowers white. 'Blushing Bride': flowers white flushed pink. 'Pink Beauty': flowers dark-purple and red. 'Red Pearl': flowers carmine red. 'Rosa Perle' ('Pink Pearl'): vigorous; flowers pink, long-lasting. 'Splendens': flowers deep-pink. 'White Pearl' ('Weisse Perle'): flowers white. Z5.

L.laxiflorus (Desf.) Kuntze (*L.inermis* Rochel ex Friv.; *Orobus laxiflorus* Desf.).
Glabrous or pubescent perennial. Stem to 50cm, not winged. Leaflets 2–4 × 1–2cm, each leaf with one pair, lanceolate to suborbicular. Racemes with 2–6 flowers; corolla 1.5–2cm, violet. Fruit 3–4 × 0.5cm, pubescent. SE Europe. Z7.

L.linifolius (Reichard) Bässler (*Orobus linifolius* Reichard). var. **montanus** (Bernh.) Bässler (*L.montanus* Bernh.).
Stem to 50cm, winged. Leaflets 1–5(–10) × 0.1–1.2(–1.6)cm, in 1–4 pairs, oval or linear. Racemes with 2–6 flowers; corolla 1–1.6cm, deep pink to blue. Fruit 2.5–4.5 × 0.5cm, russet, glabrous. W & C Europe. Z6.

L.luteus (L.) Peterm. non Moench. See *L.gmelinii*.
L.magellanicus Lam. See *L.nervosus*.
L.megalanthus Steud. See *L.latifolius*.
L.membranaceus C. Presl. See *L.latifolius*.
L.montanus Bernh. See *L.linifolius* var. *montanus*.
L.myrtifolius Muhlenb. See *L.palustris*.

L.nervosus Lam. (*L.magellanicus* Lam.; *L.americanus* (Mill.) Kupicha; *L.armitageanus* Westc. ex Loud.). LORD ANSON'S BLUE PEA.
Vigorous perennial to 60cm. Stem not winged. Leaves terminate in a 3-branched tendril; stipules to 2.5 × 1.8cm, sagittate, oval or suborbicular; leaflets to 4cm, 1 pair, ovate to ovate-oblong. Racemes long-stalked, 3–7-flowered; calyx glabrous; corolla to 2.2cm, indigo. Fruit to 6 × 0.5cm, black, glossy. Summer. S America. Z9.

L.neurolobus Boiss. & Heldr.
Perennial to 50cm. Lower leaves lacking tendrils, upper leaves with simple tendril; stipules to 3mm, linear; leaflets to 12×0.4cm, 1 pair, oblong. Racemes 1–2-flowered; corolla to 1cm, blue. Fruit to 3 × 0.4cm, brown, glabrous, with prominent longitudinal veins, 3–6-seeded. Crete. Z8.

L.niger (L.) Bernh. (*Orobus niger* L.). BLACK PEA.
Perennial to 80cm. Stem erect, angular. Stipules to 10 × 0.2cm, semi-sagittate, linear-lanceolate; leaflets to 3.5 × 1.2cm, 3–6 pairs, elliptic or oblong-oval, mucronate at apex, grey-green beneath, obscurely-nerved. Racemes 3–6-flowered; calyx broad-campanulate, short-ciliate at margin; corolla to 1.5cm, lilac-violet. Fruit to 5 × 0.5cm, sessile, somewhat inflated, 10–12-seeded. Summer. Europe, Caucasus, Syria, N Africa. Z6.

L.nissolia L. (*L.gramineus* A. Gray). GRASS VETCHLING.
Annual to 90cm; stems erect or ascending, not winged, glabrous. Leaves simple, reduced to a blade-like midrib, without a tendril, acuminate; stipules to 2mm, filiform. Racemes 1–2-flowered; calyx tubular-campanulate; corolla to 1.8cm, crimson. Fruit sessile, to 6 × 0.4cm, pale-brown, glabrous or pubescent, 12–20-seeded. Late spring–early summer. W, C & S Europe.

L.occidentalis Nutt. ex Torr. & A. Gray. See *L.palustris*.

L.odoratus L. SWEETPEA.
Annual to 2m; stems somewhat downy. Stipules to 2.5 × 0.4cm, lanceolate, semi-sagittate; leaflets to 6 × 3cm, 1 pair, oval to ovate-oblong, to 6 × 3cm. Racemes 1–3-flowered; calyx campanulate; corolla to 3.5cm, typically purple but, of course, now highly developed and much varied. Fruit to 7 × 1.2cm, brown, downy, 8-seeded; seeds smooth, black-brown. Summer. Crete, Italy, Sicily. For cultivars and seed races see note on cultivation above. var. **nanellus** L.H. Bail. Plants compact, not climbing.

L.ornatus Nutt. ex Torr. & A. Gray.
Erect perennial to 30cm or more. Leaflets in 4–7 pairs, linear. Racemes 3–5-flowered; flowers 2.5cm, purple. US (South Dakota to Wyoming and Oklahoma). Z3.

L.palustris L. (*L.pilosus* Cham.; *L.incurvus* Rchb.; *L.myrtifolius* Muhlenb.; *L.occidentalis* Nutt. ex Torr. & A. Gray; *Orobus myrtifolius* (Muhlenb.) Hall; *Orobus myrtifolius* Alef.). MARSH PEA.
Perennial to 120cm; stems ascending or climbing, narrow-winged. Leaves terminate in branched tendrils; stipules to 2 × 0.8cm, lanceolate or ovate, semi-sagittate; leaflets to 8 × 1.6cm, in 2–5 pairs, linear to lanceolate. Racemes long-stalked, 2–8-flowered; calyx to 1.2cm, campanulate; corolla to 2.2cm, purple-blue. Fruit to 7 × 1cm, brown, glabrous, 8–10-seeded. Summer. Europe to E Asia, Japan and E North America. Z5.

L.petiolaris Vogel. See *L.pubescens*.

L.pilosus Cham. See *L.palustris*.

L.polyanthus Boiss. & Bl. See *L.aphaca*.

L.pratensis L. COMMON VETCHLING; MEADOW VETCHLING; YELLOW VETCHLING.
Perennial to 120cm. Leaves terminate in a tendril; stipules to 3×1.2cm, linear to lanceolate, rarely ovate; leaflets 4×1cm, 1 pair, linear-lanceolate to elliptic. Racemes long-stalked, 2–12-flowered; calyx 0.8cm, tubular-campanulate, sparsely white-pubescent; corolla to 1.6cm, yellow. Fruit to 3.5×0.6cm, sessile, black, occasionally pubescent, 8–10-seeded. Late spring–summer. Europe, N Africa to Asia, Siberia and Himalaya. Z4.

L.pseudoaphaca Boiss. See *L.aphaca*.

L.pubescens Hook. & Arn. (*L.acutifolius* Vogel; *L.andicola* Gand.; *L.dumetorum* Philippi; *L.petiolaris* Vogel).
Vigorous climber to 3m+; stems pubescent, glandular. Leaves terminate in a 3-branched tendril; stipules to 3×1.5cm, semi-sagittate, ovoid-lanceolate; leaflets to 7.5×2.5cm, 1 pair, occasionally 2 pairs, elliptic-lanceolate. Racemes 6–16-flowered; peduncles to 18cm; calyx villous; corolla 2.5cm diam., lilac or indigo. Fruit to 7.5×0.6cm, 8–10-seeded. Summer. Chile, Argentina. Z9.

L.roseus Steven (*Orobus roseus* (Steven) Ledeb.).
Perennial to 1.5m; stems erect, angular, not winged, glabrous. Leaves not usually terminating in a tendril; stipules to 1.5cm, semi-sagittate, lanceolate or subulate; leaflets to 5×3.5cm, 1 pair, ovate-orbicular, pinnately-veined. Racemes 1–5-flowered; calyx short-campanulate; corolla to 2cm, rose-pink. Fruit to 5.5 × 1cm, pale-brown, glabrous, 5–11-seeded. Summer. Turkey, Caucasus. Z6.

L.rotundifolius Willd. (*L.drummondii* hort.). PERSIAN EVER-LASTING PEA.
Perennial to 1m; stems angular, glabrous. Leaves terminate in a 3-branched tendril; stipules to 2.5×0.6cm, hastate, oblong-lanceolate, acuminate; leaflets to 6 × 4.5cm, 1 pair, ovate-orbicular. Racemes 3–8-flowered; calyx to 1cm, broad-campanulate; corolla to 2cm, deep pink. Fruit to 7×1cm, sessile, brown, glabrous, 8–10-seeded. Summer. E Europe, W Asia. Z6.

L.sativus L. (*L.asiaticus* (Zalk.) Kudrj.; *L.azureus* hort.). INDIAN PEA; RIGA PEA; DOGTOOTH PEA; KHESAI.
Annual to 1m; stems angular. Stipules to 2.5×0.5cm, lanceolate, semi-sagittate; leaflets to 15×1cm, 1–2 pairs, linear to lanceolate, acuminate. Flowers solitary on stalks to 3cm long; calyx short-campanulate; corolla to 2.5cm, white, pink or blue. Fruit to 4 × 1.8cm, brown, glabrous, 2–6-seeded. Europe.

L.splendens Kellogg. PRIDE OF CALIFORNIA.
Shrubby perennial to 3m; stems angled, not winged. Leaves terminate in a branched tendril; stipules narrow-lanceolate; leaflets to 7×5cm, 3–5 pairs, narrow-linear to ovate-oblong. Racemes 4–12-flowered; calyx to 1.2cm, pubescent; corolla to 4cm, rose, violet, or magenta-red. Fruit to 8×1cm, beaked. US (California), Baja California. Z8.

L.strictus Torr. & A. Gray. See *L.laetiflorus*.

L.sylvestris L. (*L.angustifolius* Medik.). FLAT PEA; NARROW-LEAVED EVERLASTING PEA.
Perennial to 2m; stems prostrate or climbing, angular, winged. Leaves with a branched tendril; stipules to 3×0.5cm, linear to lanceolate, semi-sagittate; leaflets to 15 × 4cm, 1

pair, linear to lanceolate. Racemes long-stalked, 3–12-flowered; calyx to 0.7cm, broad-campanulate, to 7mm; corolla to 2cm, purple-pink mottled purple and green. Fruit to 7×1cm, brown, glabrous, 10–15-seeded. Summer. Europe (except extreme N and extreme S), Middle East. 'Wagneri': flowers deep red. Z6.

L.tingitanus L. TANGIER PEA.
Annual to 120cm; stems winged, glabrous. Stipules to 2.5× 1.2cm, lanceolate to ovate, semi-sagittate or -hastate; leaflets to 8×1.8cm, 1 pair, linear-lanceolate to ovate. Racemes 1–3-flowered; calyx 1cm; corolla to 3cm, rose-pink. Fruit to 10 × 1cm, brown, glabrous, somewhat coriaceous, 6–8-seeded. S & E Iberian Peninsula, Sardinia, Azores.

L.tuberosus L. EARTH CHESTNUT; TUBEROUS PEA; FYFIELD PEA; EARTH NUT PEA; DUTCH-MICE; TUBEROUS VETCH.
Perennial to 120cm; stems ascending or prostrate, 4-angled, not winged, glabrous, from a creeping rootstock which produces small, fleshy and edible tubers. Leaves terminate in a 3-branched tendril; stipules to 2 × 0.4cm, linear to lanceolate, semi-sagittate; leaflets to 4.5 × 1.5cm, 1 pair, oblong-ovate, weakly parallel-veined. Racemes long-stalked, 2–7-flowered; calyx to 0.7cm, broadly campanulate; corolla to 2cm, rose-pink. Fruit 4×0.7cm, brown, glabrous, 3–6-seeded. Summer. Europe (except N and extreme S). Z6.

L.variegatus (Ten.) Gren. & Godron. See *L.venetus*.

L.venetus (Mill.) Wolf. (*L.variegatus* (Ten.) Gren. & Godron; *Orobus venetus* Mill.).
Resembles *L.vernus*, but stipules ovate-orbicular, leaflets ovate-orbicular, acute, very short-acuminate; flowers more numerous, 6–30 on racemes, corolla smaller, to 1.5cm; fruit dotted with brown glands. SE & EC Europe. Z6.

L.venosus Muhlenb. ex Willd.
Perennial to 1m; stems stout, erect or climbing, strongly 4-angled, not winged, pubescent. Leaves terminate in a well developed, usually simple tendril; stipules linear-lanceolate to lanceolate; leaflets to 6×3cm, 4–7 pairs, oblong-ovate, glabrous to densely short-pubescent. Racemes 5–25-flowered; calyx to 1.4mm, usually densely pubescent; corolla to 2cm, purple. Fruit to 6×0.8cm, glabrous or pubescent. Late summer. N America. Z4.

L.vernus (L.) Bernh. (*Orobus vernus* L.). SPRING VETCH.
Bushy herbaceous perennial to 60cm, usually shorter; stems several erect, angular, not winged. Leaves terminate in a point, not a tendril; stipules to 2.5 × 0.8cm, ovate-lanceolate, rarely linear, semi-sagittate; leaflets to 10 × 3cm, 2–4, oval to lanceolate, acuminate, weakly parallel-veined. Racemes terminal and axillary, 3–15-flowered, to 25.5cm; calyx to 1cm, gibbous; corolla to 2cm, red to rose-mauve becoming violet then blue to aquamarine. Fruit to 6 × 0.8cm, brown, glabrous, 8–14-seeded. Winter–spring. Europe (except extreme N). 'Albiflorus': flowers blue-white. 'Alboroseus': flowers rose-white. 'Roseus': flowers rose-blue. Z4.

L.vestitus Nutt. ex Torr. & A. Gray.
Perennial to 40cm. Leaflets 3.5cm, in 5 pairs. Flowers white veined pink or purple, pink to violet blue or purple-red, fading yellow. Fruit 5cm, pubescent. US (Oregon, California). ssp. **puberulus** (Wight ex Greene) Hitchc.Taller, usually twining, pubescent. Flowers pink to pale purple. US (California). Z8.

L.violaceus auct. See *L.laetiflorus* and *L.vestitus*.

Leptocereus (Berger) Britt. & Rose. (From Gk *leptos*, slender, and *Cereus*, referring to the thin ribs.) Cactaceae. To 12 species of trees and shrubs, sometimes prostrate or scandent, to 8–10m, much branched; stems usually segmented, ribbed; ribs 3–8. Flowers 2–5×1.5–3cm, tubular-campanulate, diurnal or nocturnal, in one species clustered at the felted apex of terminal segments, almost white or pale green, yellow or pink; floral areoles spiny to nearly naked; epignyal tube short; perianth-limb short, spreading or rotate. Fruit 1.5–10×1.5–6cm, globose to oblong, fleshy, spiny to nearly naked; seeds *c*2.5×1.6–1.7mm, oval or broadly oval, black-brown or brown, dull, rugose or ruminate, periphery undifferentiated or crested with larger cells; relief flat or low-domed; hilum medium, oblique, impressed. Cuba, Hispaniola and Puerto Rico.

CULTIVATION Grow in an intermediate greenhouse (min. 10–15°C/50–60°F), use 'standard' cactus compost: moderate to high inorganic content (more than 50% grit), pH 6–7.5; shade in hot weather; maintain low humidity; keep dry from mid-autumn until early spring, except for light misting on warm days in late winter.

L.weingartianus (Hartmann ex Dams) Britt. & Rose. Decumbent or climbing shrub, sometimes to 10m, eventually with a woody trunk; rootstock tuberous; distal branches 1–2cm thick; ribs 4–7; areoles 15mm apart; central spines 6, to 1.5cm, radial spines 10–12, shorter, yellow to red-brown. Flower *c*4cm. Summer. Z10.

Littonia Hook.(For Dr Samuel Litton (1779–1847), Professor of Botany at Dublin.) Liliaceae (Colchicaceae). Some 8 species of perennial, tuberous and rhizomatous, climbing herbs. Stems scrambling to erect, loosely snaking, unbranched. Leaves alternate or opposite above, in whorls of 3 to 5 below, lanceolate, tendrilous at apex, sessile. Flowers orange, campanulate, nodding, axillary, solitary in leaf axils, with pedicel occasionally borne just below leaf; tepals 6, separate, free almost to the base, not spreading widely, with basal, nectar-bearing scale; stamens 6, anthers basifixed, versatile; style simple, straight. Fruit a loculicidal, 3-valved capsule; seeds globose, brown. S Africa, Arabia. Z9.

CULTIVATION Scrambling or climbing understorey herbs of woodland and scrub, grown for their deep golden flowers which are followed by attractive seed pods. In mild sheltered gardens, *L.modesta* will survive mild winters, or can be lifted and stored in frost-free conditions over winter, otherwise it needs protected cultivation as for *Gloriosa*.

L.modesta Hook. Tuber 3cm diam. Stem to 1.2m. Leaves bright emerald, linear to ovate-lanceolate, glabrous, ending in tendril. Pedicels short, to 5cm; tepals orange yellow, lanceolate, tapering, sharply-tipped. S Africa. var. **keitii** Leichtlin. Stem branched, flowers abundant.

For illustration see Gloriosa.

Loasa Adans. (From the native name in S America.) Loasaceae. 105 species of annual, biennial or perennial herbs or subshrubs covered in fiercly stinging hairs. Habit bushy, decumbent or twining. Leaves entire, lobed or decompound. Flowers nodding to decurved, solitary and axillary or in short racemes or panicles; petals 5, spreading yellow, white or cinnabar-red, deeply concave above, carinate beneath (i.e. on uppermost surface), appearing saccate and inflated, each with a colourful basal nectar-scale. Mexico to S America. Z10.

CULTIVATION As for *Caiophora*.

L.aurantiaca hort. See *Caiophora lateritia*.
L.lateritia (Klotzsch) Gillies ex Arn. See *Caiophora lateritia*.

L.triphylla Juss. Annual to 40cm. Stems erect to loosely twining. Leaves to 6cm, alternate, trifoliolate or simple in upper regions of plant, the lobes deeply and irregularly toothed or serrate. Flowers to 1.8cm diam.; petals white; nectar-scales yellow barred red and white, forming a crown of colourful concentric rings. S America. var. **papaverifolia** (HBK) Urban & Gilg. Lower leaves with 2–4 slender, irregularly toothed, pinnate lobes each side. Flowers to 2.5cm diam. var. **volcanica** (André) Urban & Gilg (*L.volcanica* André). Leaves more shallowly lobed than in type. Flowers to 5cm diam.

L.volcanica André. See *L.triphylla* var. *volcanica*.

Lonicera L. (For Adam Lonitzer (1528–86), German naturalist, author of a herbal (*Kreuterbüch*) much reprinted between 1557 and 1783.) HONEYSUCKLE; WOODBINE. Caprifoliaceae. About 180 species of deciduous or evergreen, bushy, scandent, twining or creeping shrubs. Bark often exfoliating. Leaves opposite, usually simple, entire, sometimes pinnately lobed, sessile or shortly petioled, sometimes with connate stipules, upper leaf pairs often fused, forming a disc. Flowers epigynous, paired and axillary or in usually 6-flowered whorls in terminal spikes or panicles, bracteate; sepals 5; corolla tubular to campanulate, tube often basally swollen, bilabiate with upper lip 4-lobed, or with regular 5-lobed limb and lobes imbricate; stamens 5, included or exserted; ovary inferior. Fruit a many-seeded berry, white, yellow, red or black. N Hemisphere.

CULTIVATION A large, diverse and generally long-lived genus, *Lonicera* species have a wide range of applications in the garden; most are grown for their attractive flowers, many of which are sweetly scented. The berries are often attractive to birds.
  The climbing and twining species are used for covering trelliswork, walls, fences, pergolas and old tree stumps. This group includes the woodbine, *L.periclymenum*, the Common Honeysuckle of hedgerow and woodland, and its cultivars, which are among the most fragrant of the genus, but there are many others worthy of cultivation. *L.tragophylla*, with showy bright yellow blooms, for shady positions, is hardy in southern New England, and *L.×brownii*, the unscented Scarlet Trumpet Honeysuckle, has a number of fine cultivars including

'Dropmore Scarlet', which produces brightly coloured tubular flowers from summer to early autumn. *L.hilde-brandtiana*, the frost-tender Giant Burmese Honeysuckle, is the largest of the genus; its creamy flowers fading to orange are up to 15cm/6in. long, followed by egg-shaped fruit up to 2.5cm/1in. in diameter. The twining *L.japonica* 'Aureoreticulata', its leaves netted with gold, is also used for groundcover but needs strict control, being a rampant species likely to swamp less vigorous neighbours.

Plant the evergreen climbers in spring, deciduous species in their dormant season, in a moist but well drained soil enriched with organic matter. Give a light annual mulch of leafmould or well rotted compost; excess nitrogen will generate vigorous foliar growth at the expense of flowers, in which case apply sulphate of potash at 14g/m²('/₂ oz/yd²) in spring.

Lonicera will grow in sun or part shade. In habitat, the climbers generally grow with their roots in shade and their shoots reaching up to the sun, and in partial shade they appear to be less susceptible to attack by aphids. Plant *L.hildebrandtiana* in the glasshouse or conservatory border, using wires as support. Keep barely moist in winter with minimum temperature 5–7°C/40–45°F; water freely in the growing season and provide good ventilation and full sun throughout spring, summer and autumn. Prune young plants of all species by shortening stems to encourage branching and establish a good framework. Thereafter prune to keep within bounds, and thin out old wood to prevent excessive crowding after flowering, or for late summer-flowerers in early spring.

Propagate from semi-ripe cuttings in summer, or by hardwood cuttings in late autumn, also by simple layering in late autumn. Aphid infestations cause distortion of flower trusses and young shoots.

L.acuminata Wallich.
Scandent or rarely creeping shrub. Branchlets pubescent. Leaves 10×4.5cm, oblong, long-acuminate, cordate at base, scattered-pubescent or glabrescent; petioles 5mm, pubescent. Flowers in terminal, many-flowered capitula, and also often on axillary 2-flowered peduncles; bracteoles 1.5mm, ciliate; calyx tube glabrous, sepals glabrous or ciliate; corolla to 2cm, yellow to red; tube funnelform, 8.5mm, setose-pubescent, lobes pubescent or glabrous; style fulvous-pubescent. Fruit black. Summer. Himalaya (Nepal to Sikkim). Z5.

L.affinis Hook. & Arn.
Scandent, semi-evergreen shrub to 7m. Branches terete, glandular, white-puberulent when young. Leaves to 9×5cm, ovate or oblong-elliptic, acute or short-acuminate, rounded at base, glabrous above, glandular-pubescent beneath; petioles to 1cm, glandular, white-puberulent when young. Flowers white, becoming yellow, paired, terminal; peduncles to 7mm, axillary; bracts 2mm, lanceolate-deltoid, patent; bracteoles free, somewhat pilose; glabrous, sep. narrow-deltoid; corolla bilabiate, narrow, to 6cm, glabrous outside; style glabrous. Fruit 7mm diam., glabrous, blue-black, white-pruinose. Spring–summer. Japan, China. Z6.

L.albiflora Torr. & A. Gray. WHITE HONEYSUCKLE.
Of bushy habit, to 2.5m, somewhat scandent. Branches twining. Leaves to 3cm, rarely to 6.5cm, rigid, suborbicular to oval or obovate, apex rounded, base rounded to broadly cuneate, glabrous or pubescent, somewhat glaucous, uppermost pair connate at base. Flowers white or yellow-white, glabrous or pilose outside, corolla 1.5–3cm, bilabiate; style and filaments glabrous. Fruit orange. Spring. Southern N America. Z6.

L.alseuosmioides Gräbn.
Scandent evergreen shrub. Young branchlets slender, glabrous. Leaves to 6×0.85cm, narrow-oblong, apex and base acuminate, glabrous, margins revolute and adpressed-pubescent. Flowers in short broad panicles; corolla 1.25cm, funnelform, tube exceeds limb, inside purple and pubescent, outside yellow and glabrous. Fruit to 6.5mm diam., globose, black, purple-pruinose. Summer–autumn. W China (Sichuan). Z6.

L.× americana (Mill.) K. Koch (*Periclymenum americanum* Mill.; *L.caprifolium* var. *major* Carr.; *L.italica* Schmidt; *L.grata* Ait.). (*L.caprifolium × L.etrusca.*)
Resembles *L.caprifolium* in growth and foliage, but lower leaves more acute. Young stems purple, glabrous. Flowers fragrant, yellow, tinted maroon, in crowded whorls from axils of connate leaves and small bracts, often in 25×20cm panicles; corolla 5cm, tube slender, glandular, pubescent outside. Fruit red. Summer. S & SE Europe, NW Yugoslavia. 'Atrosanguinea': flowers deep red outside. 'Quercifolia':

leaves lobed, sometimes with yellow margin or red-striped. 'Rubella': flowers light purple outside, buds more deeply coloured. Z6.

L.balearica (DC.) DC. (*L.implexa* f. *balearica* DC.).
Like *L.implexa*, but leaves oval or obovate to oblong, lower leaves truncate to cordate at base. Flowers fewer per whorl than in *L.implexa*. Mediterranean. Z8.

L.brachypoda DC. See *L.japonica* var. *repens*.
L.breweri A. Gray. See *L.conjugalis*.

L.× brownii (Reg.) Carr. (*L.etrusca* var. *brownii* Reg.; *L.sempervirens* var. *brownii* (Reg.) Lav.). (*L.sempervirens × L.hirsuta.*) SCARLET TUMPET HONEYSUCKLE.
Resembles *L.sempervirens*. Scandent deciduous shrub to 3m. Leaves elliptic, blue-green and somewhat pubescent beneath, uppermost leaf pairs connate; petiole glandular. Flowers orange-scarlet in capitula; corolla resembles that of *L.hirsuta*, bilabiate, glandular pubescent outside. Spring–summer. Gardin origin. 'Dropmore Scarlet': vigorous; flowers long trumpet-shaped, bright scarlet, midsummer-early autumn, long lasting. 'Fuchsioides': flowers orange-scarlet, bilabiate. 'Plantierensis': flowers large, coral-red, tipped orange. 'Punicea': flowers orange-red outside; slow-growing. 'Youngii': flowers deep crimson. Z5.

L.calcarata Hemsl.
Tall scandent shrub. Leaves to 14cm, ovate to elliptic-lanceolate, acuminate. Flowers red-yellow, axillary, paired; corolla 3cm, with a 1.5cm spur; filaments pilose at base; style pilose at base; ovary 5-celled. China. Z6.

L.caprifolium L. ITALIAN WOODBINE; ITALIAN HONEYSUCKLE.
Scandent deciduous shrub to 6m. Branchlets subglabrous. Lower leaves with short petioles, upper leaves sessile, to 10× 5cm, obovate or oval, apex rounded, base acuminate, subglabrous, glaucous, especially beneath, terminal pair fused. Flowers yellow-white, pink-tinged, fragrant, in 4–10-flowered, sessile whorls from axils of terminal 3 pairs of leaves; corolla bilabiate, upper lip erect to reflexed, 4-lobed, to 5cm, tube slender. Fruit orange-red. Spring–summer. Europe, W Asia. 'Pauciflora': corolla tube to 3cm, purple or rose outside, off-white inside. 'Praecox': leaves grey-green; flowers cream, often tinted light red, later turning yellow, early-flowering. Z5.

L.caprifolium var. *major* Carr. See *L.× americana*.
L.chinensis Wats. See *L.japonica* var. *repens*.

L.ciliosa (Pursh) Poir. WESTERN TRUMPET HONEYSUCKLE.
Twining evergreen shrub. Leaves to 10cm, ovate or oval, apex and base acuminate, ciliate, blue-green and glaucous beneath, terminal pair connate forming an acutely tipped elliptic disc; petioles to 12.5mm. Flowers to 4cm, yellow to orange-scarlet, pubescent outside, in terminal, 1–3-whorled spikes; corolla distinctly bilabiate, swollen at base. Fruit 5mm

Lonicera   (a) *L.tragophylla* (b) *L.caprifolium* (c) *L.pericylmenum* (d) *L. × tellmanniana* (e) *L.splendida*
(f) *L. × americana*

diam., red. Summer. North America. Z5. var. *occidentalis* (Hook.) Nichols (*L.occidentalis* Hook.) Flowers slightly larger; corolla-tube glabrous, dark orange outside. Z5.

L.confusa (Sweet) DC.
Twining deciduous to semi-evergreen shrub. Branchlets brown, softly short-pubescent. Leaves elliptic to oblong, to 7cm, pubesc. and ciliate, deep green above, becoming glabrous, grey-green beneath. Flowers white, later yellow, fragrant, axillary and terminal, in short, dense panicles; bracteoles subulate; corolla 4cm, slender, glandular-pubescent outside. Fruit black. Summer–autumn. E China. Z8.

L.conjugalis Kellogg (*L.breweri* A. Gray; *L.sororia* Piper). Straggling deciduous shrub to 1.5m, much-branched. Stem slender; branchlets strigulose. Leaves to 4cm, oblong-ovate to oblong-obovate, acute, slender, pale green and subglabrous above, lighter and pubescent beneath, ciliate; petioles to 3mm. Flowers dull purple, paired, axillary, on middle and upper part of branches; peduncles to 2.5cm, slender; bracts minute or absent, calyx teeth obsolete; corolla to 8mm, bilabiate, white-pubescent. Fruit to 6mm, bright red. Summer. W US (California). Z8.

L.delavayi Franch. See *L.similis* var. *delavayi*.

L.dioica L.(*L.glauca* Hill).
Spreading or twining deciduous shrub to 1.5m. Stems glabrous when young. Leaves to 9 × 5cm, oval or oblong, apex and base acuminate, glabrous when young, intensely glaucous beneath, upper pairs connate into disc. Flowers yellow-green, tinged purple, *c*1.5cm, in terminal clusters; corolla bilabiate, gibbous, glabrous outside; style usually glabrous. Fruit red. Spring–summer. Northeast America. Z5.

L.douglasii Koehne, non DC. See *L.glaucescens*.

L.etrusca Santi.
Scandent semi-evergreen shrub to 4m. Young shoots maroon, glabrous. Leaves to 8 × 5cm, oval or obovate, apex rounded, rounded or broad-tapered at base, glaucous, blue-green and usually pubescent beneath, upper leaves connate. Inflorescence terminal spikes, often in groups of 3; flowers closely packed in whorls, yellow tinted red, becoming deep yellow; peduncle to 4cm; bracteoles broad; corolla bilabiate, 5cm, tube narrow, occasionally glabrous or glandular; stamens much exserted. Fruit 6mm diam., red. Summer. Mediterranean region. 'Donald Waterer': flowers red and white, yellowing with age, fragrant. 'Michael Rosse': flowers cream and pale yellow, later darkening, slightly fragrant. 'Superba': shoots flushed red; flowers cream, later orange, in large terminal panicles; strong-growing. Z7.

L.etrusca var. *brownii* Reg. See *L.× brownii*.

L.flava Sims. YELLOW HONEYSUCKLE.
Somewhat scandent deciduous shrub to 2.5m, often bushy. Stems glabrous; branchlets grey-green pruinose. Leaves to 8cm, broad-elliptic to elliptic, apex acute, bright green above, blue-green and densely pruinose beneath, uppermost pair connate into a disc. Inflorescence terminal, pedunculate, flowers grouped in 1–3 superimposed and spreading whorls, fragrant, yellow, later orange; corolla bilabiate, upper lip 3-lobed, tubular not gibbous, 3cm. Fruit 6.5mm diam., red. Spring–summer. SE US (S Carolina). Z5.

L.flexuosa Thunb. See *L.japonica* var. *repens*.

L.giraldii Rehd.
Scandent evergreen to 2m. Branches twining, tangled, densely yellow-hairy when young. Leaves to 7 × 2.5cm, narrow-oblong, acuminate, cordate at base, dense-pubescent; petiole to 8.5mm, pubescent Flowers maroon, in capitate terminal clusters at branch tips; corolla 2cm, yellow-pubescent, tube slender, enlarged slightly at base. Fruit purple-black, pruinose. Summer. China (Sichuan). Z6.

L.glabrata Wallich.
Vigorous evergreen climber; new shoots hairy. Leaves lanceolate, base cordate, apex acuminate, hairy, glossy dark green. Flowers in terminal clusters and axillary pairs, somewhat fra-

grant; corolla bilabiate yellow tinged red becoming white tinged pink. Fruit black. Summer and autumn. Himalaya. Z7.

L.glauca Hill. See *L.dioica*.

L.glaucescens (Rydb.) Rydb. (*L.douglasii* Koehne, non DC.). Closely resembles *L.dioica*. Twining deciduous shrub. Shoots glabrous. Leaves to 8cm, elliptic to oblong, blue-green and pubescent beneath, uppermost pair fused. Flowers light yellow, red and short-pubescent inside, 2cm, tube opening slightly to apex; style pubescent. Fruit pale red. Spring–summer. Northeast N America (Canada to Nebraska). Z3.

L.grata Ait. See *L.× americana*.

L.griffithii Hook. f. & Thoms.
Deciduous twining shrub to 5m. Bark exfoliating; young shoots glabrous. Leaves to 5 × 2.5cm, broad-ovate, oblong or rounded, green, glabrous, glaucous, often deeply lobed; petiole to 1.25cm. Flowers rose to white, in terminal clusters of 2–3 whorls; sepals lanceolate, spreading, persistent; corolla-tube bilabiate, 2.5cm, finely-glandular-pubescent outside; stamens glabrous; style villous. Spring. Afghanistan. Z8.

L.× heckrottii Rehd. (? *L.sempervirens* × *L.× americana*.)
Scarcely scandent deciduous shrub, lax, spreading. Leaves to 6cm, subsessile, oblong or elliptic, glaucous beneath, uppermost pairs connate at base. Flowers fragrant, abundant, rich pink outside, sparsely pubescent and yellow inside, 4cm, in whorls on terminal spikes; corolla bilabiate, tube slender. Fruit red. Typical selection sometimes called L. 'American Beauty'. Summer. Garden origin. 'Goldflame': leaves dark green; flowers yellow inside, flushed strong purple (a dark selection of the cross). Z5.

L.henryi Hemsl.
Scandent evergreen or semi-deciduous shrub. Shoots slender, densely-strigose. Leaves to 9×4cm, oblong-lanceolate to oblong-ovate, acuminate, rounded or cordate at base, deep green above, lighter and somewhat shiny beneath, ciliate, pubescent on veins, occasionally subglabrous; petiole to 1.25cm. Flowers 2cm, maroon or yellow, usually paired, crowded in panicles, spikes, or heads, axillary and terminal corolla bilabiate; filaments pilose at base. Fruit purple-black. Summer. W China. Z4.

L.hildebrandtiana Collett & Hemsl. GIANT BURMESE HONEYSUCKLE; GIANT HONEYSUCKLE.
Vigorous scandent evergreen, sometimes semi-deciduous, to 25m. Leaves to 12 × 10cm, broad-ovate, oval or rounded-oval, apex abruptly acuminate, base broadly acuminate, deep green above, lighter and glandular beneath; petiole to 2cm. Flowers cream white, changing to gold then amber, fragrant, paired, axillary, or grouped in large inflorescence; corolla-tube narrow, to 16 × 10cm, bilabiate, upper lip 4-lobed, lower lip recurved. Fruit ovoid, to 2.5cm. Summer. China, SE Asia. Z9.

L.hirsuta Eaton (*L.pubescens* Sweet). HAIRY HONEYSUCKLE.
Twining deciduous shrub. Young shoots slender, glandular-pubescent. Leaves to 10 × 5cm, oval, deep dull green above, grey beneath, pubescent, especially beneath, ciliate, upper leaves fused forming disc. Inflorescence terminal or axillary spikes of flowers in 2–3 dense whorls; corolla-tube bilabiate, to 3cm, yellow-orange, glandular-pubescent outside, base saccate. Fruit yellow-red. Summer. NE America. Z3.

L.hispanica Boiss. & Reut. See *L.periclymenum* var. *glaucohirta*.

L.hispidula Douglas ex Torr. & A. Gray.
Procumbent, sometimes scandent, deciduous shrub. Branches sarmentose; branchlets usually hispid. Leaves to 6cm, oval-oblong, apex abrupt-acuminate or acute, rounded to subcordate at base, pubescent to glabrous above, soft-pubescent beneath, ciliate, uppermost leaf pair fused into disc. Flowers closely whorled in spikes; corolla white becoming red, bilabiate, tube 1.5cm, glabrous or slightly pubescent. Fruit red. Summer. Western N America (British Columbia to California). Z6.

L.implexa Sol. MINORCA HONEYSUCKLE.
Scandent evergreen 2.5m+. Young shoots slender, purple, glabrous or setose. Leaves to 7 × 2.5cm, sessile, elliptic to oblong, acuminate or blunt, glabrous, strongly glaucous beneath, leaf pairs on flowering shoots mostly fused into rhombic discs. Flowers yellow, pink-suffused outside, white inside, becoming yellow, in the axils of the 3 uppermost leaf pairs; corolla to 4.5cm, tube pubescent inside; style pubescent above. Summer. Mediterranean. Z9.

L.implexa f. **balearica** DC. See **L.balearica**.

L.interrupta Benth. CHAPPARAL HONEYSUCKLE.
Twining evergreen shrub, of bushy habit. Branchlets glabrous, glaucous. Leaves to 4cm, orbicular to elliptic, entire, glabrous or somewhat pubescent, green above, glaucous beneath, uppermost leaf pairs connate at base. Flowers to 2cm, sessile, yellow, in interrupted spikes to 16cm; corolla funnelform, gibbous, glabrous outside; filaments pubescent. Fruit 5mm diam., subglobose, red. Summer. SW US (Arizona and S California). Z8.

L.italica Schmidt. See **L.× americana**.

L.japonica Thunb. JAPANESE HONEYSUCKLE; GOLD-AND-SIL-VER FLOWER.
Evergreen or semi-evergreen climbing vigorously to 9m. Branches terete, hollow, glandular, prominently patent-pubescent when young. Leaves to 8 × 3cm, oblong to ovate-elliptic, apex acute or obtuse, mucronate, usually rounded at base, entire, sinuately incised or lobed on juvenile or very vigorous shoots, light green beneath, thinly lanate, villous, or sometimes glabrous, margins ciliate; petioles to 8mm. Flowers white, becoming yellow, paired, intensely fragrant; peduncles to 1cm; bracts foliaceous, ovate, to 2cm; bracteoles 1mm, elliptic, pilose; calyx-tube glabrous, sepals 1mm, ovate, ciliate; corolla to 4cm, bilabiate, soft-pubescent outside, tube narrow. Fruit to 7mm diam., blue-black, separate. Spring–summer. Japan, Korea, Manchuria, China; naturalized SE US. var. **repens** (Sieb.) Rehd. (*L.brachypoda* var. *repens* Sieb.; *L.flexuosa* Thunb.; *L.japonica* var. *flexuosa* (Thunb.) Nichols.; *L.brachypoda* DC.; *L.chinensis* Wats.; *L.japonica* var. *chinensis* (Wats.) Bak.). Stems sometimes tinted red or maroon. Leaves soon glabrous, often deeply lobed markedly purple-tinged on veins beneath. Flowers white becoming yellow, upper lip lobed. 'Aureoreticulata' ('Reticulata'): habit compact, creeping, climbing or ground-covering, to 3m high, to 3m wide; leaves small, bright green, with golden reticulate veins, sometimes lobed; otherwise like var. *repens*. 'Dart's World': habit spreading and bushy, to 25cm high, to 1.2m wide; stems dark maroon; leaves to 7 × 3cm, ovate, dark green, tinted blue and pubescent with red veins beneath; flowers to 4cm, 2-lipped, interior white, exterior often flushed rosy red, later yellow and strong red, in pairs. 'Halliana': leaves pubescent when young, rich green; flowers white, sometimes tinted red, later yellow, upper lip divided almost to middle. 'Hall's Prolific': habit climbing, to 6m high, to 3m wide; leaves ovate; flowers white, later cream to yellow, strongly scented, profuse, even when young. 'Purpurea': leaves tinted purple; flowers maroon outside, white inside. 'Variegata': leaves variegated yellow. Z4.

L.japonica var. **chinensis** (Wats.) Bak. See **L.japonica** var. *repens*.

L.japonica var. **flexuosa** (Thunb.) Nichols. See **L.japonica** var. *repens*.

L.occidentalis Hook. See **L.ciliosa** var. *occidentalis*.

L.periclymenum L. WOODBINE; HONEYSUCKLE.
Twining shrub to 4m. Young shoots glabrous or pubescent, hollow. Leaves to 6.5 × 4cm, ovate, oval or obovate, apex usually acuminate, occasionally obtuse, base acuminate, lightly pubescent becoming glabrous, glaucous and blue-green beneath, uppermost pair separate. Flowers fragrant, red and yellow-white, to 5cm, glandular-glutinous outside, in 3–5-whorled terminal spikes; corolla bilabiate. Fruit round,

bright red. Summer. Europe, Asia Minor, Caucasus, W Asia. var. **glaucohirta** Kunze (*L.hispanica* Boiss. & Reut.).Leaves ovate to elliptic, acute, pubescent, grey-blue beneath. Spain, Morocco. 'Aurea': leaves variegated yellow. 'Belgica': habit bushy, to 3m high, to 3m wide; leaves glabrous, thick, elliptic-oblong; flowers white, flushed purple outside, later yellow, scented, in large clusters; fruit large, red, abundant. 'Belgica Select': a fast-growing selection of 'Belgica'. 'Berries Jubilee': leaves tinted blue, glaucous grey beneath; flowers yellow; fruit bright red; vigorous grower. 'Graham Thomas': flowers large, white, later yellow tinted copper, long-lasting. 'Munster': flowers dark pink in bud, white streaked pink on opening, ultimately cream. 'Quercina': leaves 'oak-like', sinuately toothed to lobed, sometimes variegated white. 'Serotina' ('Late Red') LATE DUTCH HONEY-SUCKLE: leaves narrow; flowers dark purple outside, later fading, yellow inside, profuse; fruit red. 'Serotina Florida': habit compact; flowers dark red outside, yellow and white inside, crimson in bud, scented; fruit translucent red; slow-growing. 'Serpentine': twigs slender, deep maroon when young; leaves narrow, tinted pale blue beneath; flowers to 7cm, interior cream, exterior light mauve with white edge, later yellow; buds deep maroon, in clusters to 10, arranged in rings; fruit red, profuse, dense. Z4.

L.periclymenum f. **serotina** Ait. See **L.serotina**.

L.prolifera (Kirchn.) Rehd. (*Caprifolium proliferum* Kirchn.; *L.sullivantii* A. Gray). GRAPE HONEYSUCKLE.
Deciduous twiner or a shrub to 180cm; of lax, patent habit. New shoots glaucous. Leaves to 10 × 6.5cm, thick, oval, obovate or oblong, pruinose above, glaucous and lightly pubescent beneath, upper leaves connate, forming round disc. Flowers pale yellow, usually in 4 superimposed whorls; corolla-tube 3cm, pubescent inside, glabrous outside, slightly expanded. Fruit to 12.5mm diam., scarlet. Summer. C North America (Ohio to Tennessee & Mo.) Z5.

L.pubescens Sweet non Stokes. See **L.hirsuta**.

L.reticulata Champ.
Twining evergreen, rarely deciduous, shrub. Branches short-pubescent or glabrous. Leaves to 7cm, oblong-ovate, obtuse, rounded to subcordate at base, glabrous above, tomentose and strongly reticulate beneath; petioles to 1.5cm. Flowers in axillary pairs, usually in terminal panicles or racemes; bracts subulate; sepals ovate-lanceolate; corolla to 6cm; style glabrous; ovaries glabrous. Fruit usually black,

L.sempervirens L. TRUMPET HONEYSUCKLE; CORAL HONEY-SUCKLE.
Vigorous scandent evergreen shrub. Young shoots glabrous. Leaves to 8 × 5cm, oval or slightly obovate, deep green and glabrous above, blue-green, glaucous and often pubescent beneath, 1–2 uppermost pairs of leaves connate, forming a circular or oblong disc; petiole to 6.5mm. Flowers rich scarlet-orange outside, more yellow inside, in 3–4 superimposed whorls; corolla to 5cm with 5 equal lobes. Fruit bright red. Spring–autumn. E & S US (Connecticut to Florida & Texas). var. **minor** Ait. Semi-evergreen. Leaves elliptic to oblong-lanceolate. Flowers more abundant, orange-red to scarlet, smaller, narrower. 'Magnifica': flowers red outside, interior yellow; semi-evergreen. 'Sulphurea' ('Flava'; f. *sulphura* (Jacques) Rehd.): to 10m; flowers bright yellow, long- and late-flowering. 'Superba' ('Red Coral', 'Red Trumpet', 'Rubra', 'Dreer's Everlasting'): leaves ovate-elliptic, glabrous above; flowers bright scarlet; deciduous. Z3.

L.sempervirens var. **brownii** (Reg.) Lav. See **L.× brownii**..

L.serotina (Ait.) Gaud. See **L.periclymenum** 'Serotina'.

L.similis Hemsl.
Scandent semi-evergreen shrub. C & W China (Hupeh, Sichuan), India, Burma. usually seen in the form var. **delavayi** (Franch.) Rehd. (*L.delavayi* Franch.). Scandent, evergreen, glabrous shrub. Leaves to 6cm, lanceolate, apex acute, base

Lonicera (a) *L.henryi* (b) *L.giraldii* (c) *L.alseuosmoides* (d) *L.confusa* (e) *L.similis* var. *delavayi* (f) *L.biflora*
(g) *L.japonica* 'Halliana' (h) *L.affinis* (i) *L.arizonica* (j) *L.glaucescens* (k) *L.dioica* (l) *L.japonica* (m) *L.ciliosa*

round to cordate, bright green above, white lanate beneath. Inflorescence racemose at branchlet tips; flowers to 8cm, in axillary pairs, white becoming yellow; corolla bilabiate; stamens and style strongly exserted, tube slightly expanded. Fruit black. SW China. Z8.

L.sororia Piper. See *L.conjugalis.*

L.splendida Boiss.
Vigorous scandent evergreen. Leaves to 5cm, oval to oblong, glabrous, rarely pilose, glaucous blue-grey, upper pair connate. Flowers yellow-white, becoming red, in terminal, sessile clusters of densely compound whorls; corolla to 5cm, bilabiate, fine-pubescent outside. Summer. Spain. Z8.

L.subaequalis Rehd.
Scandent deciduous shrub. Branches glabrous. Leaves to 10cm, oval to oblong-obovate, apex obtuse, tapered at base, glabrous, uppermost pair connate into an elliptic disc; petiole short. Flowers in sessile whorls; corolla to 3cm, funnelform, pubescent inside, glandular outside; stamens inserted close to mouth of tube; filaments glabrous, anthers linear-oblong; style glabrous, exceeding the corolla. W China (Sichuan). Z6.

L.subspicata Hook. & Arn.
Scandent evergreen shrub to 2.5m. Branchlets puberulent. Leaves to 4 × 1cm, linear-oblong to oblong, rounded both ends, entire, coriaceous, grey-pubescent, especially beneath, uppermost pairs connate into a disc; petioles to 5mm. Flowers yellow or cream whorled in short, leafy spikes to 12cm; sepals broad-lanceolate, 1mm; corolla bilabiate, to 1cm, glandular-pubescent, tube gibbous; filaments pubescent at base. Fruit to 7mm ellipsoid, yellow or red. Summer. W US (California). Z8.

L.sullivantii A. Gray. See *L.prolifera.*

L.× tellmanniana hort. (*L.sempervirens* × *L.tragophylla.*)
Vigorous, deciduous, scandent shrub. Branchlets glabrous, green-brown. Leaves to 10cm, ovate to oblong, becoming deep green above, white-pruinose beneath, upper pair fused into an elliptic disc. Inflorescence terminal whorls; corolla tube to 4.5cm, rich orange to coppery gold. Summer. Garden origin. In the US, this is known as 'Redgold'. Z5.

L.tragophylla Hemsl.
Deciduous, vigorous, scandent shrub. Branchlets hollow; flowering shoots 15–20cm. Leaves to 14cm, sessile or subsessile, oblong, glaucous green and midrib pubescent beneath, uppermost 1–3 pairs fused into elliptic or rhombic discs. Flowers 1–2 whorls in a terminal head; inflorescence glabrous; corolla 7–8cm, tube 3× length of limb, lightly hairy inside, orange to yellow, often tinted red above. Fruit red. Summer. China. Z6.

L.yunnanensis Franch.
Evergreen, scandent shrub, to 4m; shoots glabrous. Leaves 3–4cm, oblong to lanceolate, almost glabrous, uppermost pair fused into disc. Flowers in whorls, gathered into spikes, occasionally solitary; calyx bilabiate; corolla to 2.5cm, yellow, glabrous, tube swollen, interior pubescent China (Yunnan). var. **tenuis** Rehd. Smaller. Leaves to 3cm, lightly pubescent beneath. Flowers in single whorls; corolla to 2cm, white become yellow. SW China. Z7. The name *L.yunnanensis* has also been applied to *L.* 'Yunnan', a selection of the non-climbing *L.nitida.*

Luffa Mill. (Arabic *louff*, name given to *L.cylindrica.)* LOOFAH; DISHCLOTH GOURD; RAG GOURD; STRAINER VINE. Cucurbitaceae. 6 species of annual climbers, occasionally trailing, monoecious or dioecious, scabrous or hairy. Tendrils 2–6-fid. Leaves simple, palmately angled or lobed, glandular; probracts glandular. Male inflorescence a raceme; flowers large, conspicuous, white to yellow; calyx tube campanulate, lobed; petals 5, free; stamens 3–5, filaments and anthers free; female flowers solitary, similar to male except staminodes absent; ovary ribbed, tuberculate or spiny; stigmas 3. Fruit elongate, cylindric, glabrous or spinose, fleshy becoming dry, dehiscent through terminal operculum; seeds compressed, black, narrowly winged. Pantropical, probably introduced to Americas. Z9.

CULTIVATION Annual climbers grown throughout the tropics for their large golden-yellow flowers and edible young fruits and commercially for their fibrous fruits ('loofah sponges'); the exposed and dried vascular system of the dried fruit of *L.cylindrica* is the bathroom loofah. The young fruits of *L.acutangula* are eaten in the Orient. They occur in the wild in woodland and grassland. Cultivate as for *Trichosanthes* except that multiple planting and cross-pollination are not required. Prepare the sponges by steeping mature fruit in running water until the skin and seed contents have broken down and can be washed away.

L.acutangula (L.) Roxb. (*Cucumis acutangula* L.). ANGLED LOOFAH; SING-KWA.
Climber. Stem 4–5-angled. Tendrils 4–7-fid. Leaves palmate, glabrous, about 17 × 11cm; lobes 5–7, acuminate; petiole 8–12cm. Male inflorescence a raceme to 15cm, borne on long peduncle; female flowers solitary; pedicels bracteate, bearing nectaries; calyx tube pubescent, 5-lobed; corolla yellow, to 5cm diam., bearing nectaries in female; stamens 3; ovary 10-angled. Fruit deeply 10-angled, to 30cm or more, about 10cm diam.; seeds rugose, emarginate, to 12 × 8cm. Pakistan, widely cultivated throughout Tropics. var. **amara** (Roxb.) Clark (*L.amara* Roxb.). Leaves smaller, softly villous. Fruit to 8cm; seeds smaller. India, Pakistan, Yemen.

L.aegyptiaca Mill. See *L.cylindrica.*
L.amara Roxb. See *L.acutangula* var. *amara.*

L.cylindrica (L.) M. Roem. (*Momordica cylindrica* L.; *L.aegyptiaca* Mill.). LOOFAH; VEGETABLE SPONGE.
Climber or trailer to 15m. Stems finely pubescent. Tendrils 3- to 6-fid. Leaves palmate, ovate-cordate, 6–18×6–20cm, lobes 3–5, ovate, sometimes slightly lobulate, sparsely serrate or entire, midlobe largest. Male raceme glandular-bracteate, 12–35cm; female flowers on peduncle to 3cm; calyx tube pubescent within, lobes acute, to 12mm; petals yellow, rounded, to 4.5cm; stamens 3 or 5, absent in female; ovary cylindric, densely pubescent, slightly 10-ribbed, absent in male. Fruit ellipsoid to cylindric, glabrous, to 50cm; seeds lenticular, to 12×8×3mm, smooth, narrowly winged. Tropical Asia and Africa.

L.gigantea hort. See *L.cylindrica.*
L.macrocarpa hort. See *L.cylindrica.*
L.marylandica hort. See *L.cylindrica.*

L.operculata (L.) Cogn. (*Momordica operculata* L.).
Stems climbing or trailing, striate. Tendrils bifid. Leaves palmate, subreniform, scabrous, to 15cm, lobes 3–5, narrowing at base, entire or slightly denticulate, midlobe largest. Male raceme 5–30-flowered, to 20cm; pedicels glandular-bracteate, to 3m (female flowers sessile); sepals triangular to ovate-acuminate, to 3mm; petals to 1cm; stamens 3, anthers sometimes partially connate, staminodes sometimes present in female; ovary fusiform, tomentose, spinose, absent in male; style linear, sometimes 3-parted. Fruit about 6cm, ellipsoid to fusiform, dry, operculate, fibrous, slightly ribbed, spinose; seeds white to dark brown, compressed. Mexico to Colombia and Peru.

Luzuriaga Ruiz & Pav. (For Don Ignatio M.R. de Luzuriaga, Spanish botanist of the early 19th century.) Liliaceae (Luzuriagaceae). 4 species of trailing, creeping or climbing perennial herbs with rooting, rather shrubby stems, with simple or branched leafy lateral shoots. Leaves jointed to stems, very short-stalked, lower surface dark green, facing upwards because of twisted petiole, veins parallel, 3 to many, upper surface glaucous except for green veins (lowest leaves of lateral shoots often reduced to scales). Flowers solitary or a few together, axillary, pedicels equalling perianth; tepals 6, free, white; stamens 6; ovary superior, 3-celled; style simple. Fruit a berry. Peru, Chile, Falkland Is., New Zealand. Floral parts spotted orange-brown when dry. Z9.

CULTIVATION These climbers originate in moist, cool woodlands in South America and New Zealand. Their habit is broadly similar to that of *Lapageria*, as are their cultural requirements, but the two species listed below are altogether more delicate in appearance. Closely branched slender stems twine and creep over mossy surfaces, damp walls, trunks and compost-filled wire cylinders. They are clothed in 'ferny' dark green foliage and small white flowers – the overall effect akin to that of a fragile jasmine. Although tolerant of light and short-lived frosts, they are more safely grown in the cool glasshouse, in a moist, fibrous soilless medium in shade. Propagate by semi-ripe cuttings in a closed case with bottom heat.

L.erecta Kunth. See *L.polyphylla*.

L.polyphylla Hook. f. (*L.erecta* Kunth). Much-branched, shrub-like, scrambling or twining. Leaves 1.25–2.5cm, elliptic to oblong, mostly subtending flowers. Flowers to 2cm diam., white, sometimes spotted red-brown, broadly campanulate, solitary; filaments longer than anthers, anthers dorsifixed, reflexed. Summer. Chile.

L.radicans Ruiz & Pav. Stems slender, vining, sparsely branched. Leaves 1–3.5cm, linear-oblong to elliptic-ovate or ovate-lanceolate. Flowers to 3.25cm diam., pure white, fragrant, star-shaped, spreading, solitary or 2–3 together, fragrant; filaments thick, anthers yellow, connivent, much longer than filaments, basifixed, erect. Summer. Chile, Peru.

Lycium L. (From Gk *lykion*, from Lycia, Asia Minor; name of a species of *Rhamnus* transferred to this genus by Linnaeus.) BOXTHORN; MATRIMONY VINE. Solanaceae. About 100 species of deciduous and evergreen shrubs, often spiny; stems slender, erect or spreading, often scrambling. Leaves entire; petioles short. Flowers solitary or clustered in leaf axils, many, small, dull white, green or purple; calyx 3–5-toothed, bell-shaped; corolla funnel-shaped, 5-lobed; stamens 5, exserted, often with a circle of basal hairs; style 1. Fruit a showy bright red berry; seeds few to many. Cosmopolitan; temperate and subtropical regions.

CULTIVATION Interesting if unspectacular flowering shrubs. Given a warm season to ripen fruit, they are primarily valued for their berries, providing a long-lasting display of colour in the autumn and early winter on an arching, elegant branch system. *L.chinense* is so prolific even in the cool British climate that it has become naturalized along the south coast of England from bird-sown seed. *L.pallidum* rarely fruits well after cool British summers. They are remarkably tolerant of maritime conditions. *L.carolinianum* and *L.barbarum* survive temperatures down to about −5°C/23°F; *L.pallidum* will tolerate temperatures down to about −17°C/1°F; the most commonly grown species, *L.chinense* and *L.barbarum*, usually withstand winter minimums of −23°C/−10°F. On the edge of their zones of hardiness, specimens often succeed when trained as wall plants or espaliers against a framework of wire. Many species, notably *L.barbarum* and *L.chinense*, make good informal hedges, responding well to shearing and providing a thorny and impenetrable barrier. Other garden uses include shrub plantings for stabilizing banks and clothing unsightly tree stumps and retaining walls with tangled and cascading stems.

Avoid situations where the freely suckering rootstocks are likely to invade nearby flower borders. Prune in late winter or early spring to confine to the space allocated, or to thin old, crowded or weak wood; shear hedging plants two to three times in the growing season. Espaliers should be pruned after fruiting in winter or early spring. Propagate from seed sown in spring and by rooted suckers. Alternatively, increase by hardwood cuttings in autumn or spring, layering, or by semi-ripe cuttings rooted with gentle bottom heat in summer. *L.pallidum* is the most difficult to propagate, suckering only occasionally and being notoriously hard to root from cuttings.

L.barbarum L.(*L.halimifolium* Mill.; *L.vulgare* Dunal; *L.flaccidum* Koch). COMMON MATRIMONY VINE; DUKE OF ARGYLL'S TEA TREE.
Deciduous, erect or spreading shrub, to 3.5m. Branches narrow, usually spiny, arching or sprawling, glabrous. Leaves to 5cm, narrowly oblong-lanceolate, apex acute or obtuse, base cuneate grey-green. Flowers in clusters of 1–4, on long pedicels; calyx with 2–3 obtuse lobes; corolla tube to 9mm, slightly exceeding lobes, dull lilac to mauve. Fruit to 2cm, ovoid, orange-red or yellow. SE Europe to China. Z6. A widespread and variable shrub, the taxa *L.chinense* and *L.europaeum* are maintained here as they represent distinct plants in cultivation; however, both of these names are commonly applied to material typical of *L.barbarum* and *vice versa*.

L.carnosum hort., non Poir. See *L.chinense*.

L.carolinianum Walter. CHRISTMAS BERRY.
Spiny shrub to 1.5m, evergreen, glabrous. Stems erect, branches spreading to sprawling. Leaves to 2cm, clustered,

clavate in outline or spathulate-clavate, obtuse, entire, fleshy. Pedicels to 15cm; calyx to 4mm, lobes triangular-ovate, acute; corolla tube to 0.6cm, lobes ovate, occasionally white, lobes ovate to oblong-ovate, obtuse or notched, to 0.6cm; filaments villous at base. Fruit subglobose, to 1.2cm diam., red. S Carolina to Florida and Texas. Z8.

L.chilense Bertero (*L.grevilleanum* Miers).
To 2m, deciduous, much-branched; branches often procumbent, mostly unarmed. Leaves to 2cm, oblong, base cuneate, sometimes glandular-pubescent throughout. Flowers usually solitary, to 1cm diam.; pedicels short; calyx 5-lobed, white-pubescent; corolla to 0.8cm, yellow, pubescent outside, lobes 5, purple within, equalling tube. Fruit to 0.8cm diam., globose, orange-red. Chile. Z9.

L.chinense Mill. (*L.rhombifolium* Dipp.). CHINESE MATRIMONY VINE.
Shrub to 4m, deciduous; branches arching or procumbent, usually unarmed. Leaves to 8cm, rhombic-ovate to ovate-

lanceolate, apex acute or obtuse, base cuneate, bright green, glabrous; petioles to 1cm. Flowers 1–4; pedicels to 12mm; calyx 3 to 5-toothed, lobes acute; corolla purple, to 1.5cm. Fruit to 2.5cm, ovoid to oblong, scarlet to orange-red. China. See *L.barbarum*. Z6.

L.europaeum L. (*L.mediterraneum* Dunal).
Rigid deciduous shrub to 4m, with stout thorns usually on long, arching branches. Leaves to 5×1cm, oblanceolate, grey-green, smooth, rarely with soft or stiff hairs. Flowers solitary or in clusters of 2 or 3; calyx 3mm, 3-fid with unequally toothed segments; corolla 1.3cm, narrowly funnelform, pink or white, lobes 0.3–0.4cm; stamens usually exserted, filaments not pubescent. Fruit to 0.8cm, globose to ovoid, red. Mediterranean, Portugal. See *L.barbarum*. Z9.

L.flaccidum Koch. See *L.barbarum*.

L.gracile Meyen. See *L.chilense*.
L.grevilleanum Miers. See *L.chilense*.
L.halimiifolium Mill. See *L.barbarum*.
L.intricatum Boiss. See *L.europaeum*.
L.mediterraneum Dunal. See *L.europaeum*.
L.ovatum Lois. See *L.chinense*.

L.pallidum Miers. Much-branched, erect, deciduous shrub to 2m; branches spreading, spiny. Leaves to 3cm, oblanceolate, thick, fleshy. Flowers solitary or in pairs, nodding; pedicels short; calyx with 5 acute lobes; corolla to 2cm, pale yellow-green, marked or flushed purple-pink, lobes rounded, one third length of tube; stamens and styles exserted. Fruit to 1cm diam., globose, scarlet. Arizona and Utah to Mexico. Z6.

L.rhombifolium Dipp. See *L.chinense*.
L.vulgare Dunal. See *L.barbarum*.

Lygodium

Lygodium Sw. (From Gk *lygodes*, flexible, twining, referring to the climbing habit.) CLIMBING FERN. Schizaeaceae. About 40 species of scandent ferns. Rhizome subterranean. Stipes long, twining; rachises elongate, slender, twining, wiry, pinnae borne in distant pairs on short stalks, pinnately or palmately lobed, pinnules entire or serrate. Sporangia arranged laxly in a row flanking midvein of sporangiophores (contracted marginal segments); indusium hood-shaped, opening longitudinally; annulus subapical, lateral; spores tetrahedral. Tropics. Z10 unless specified.

CULTIVATION Ferns of wide distribution, inhabiting forests, their elongated fronds climbing through trees and shrubs by means of twining pinnules and rachis and their overall appearance being remarkably 'unfernlike'. Growth can be up to 10–12m/32–40ft. with the uppermost fronds frequently growing in full sun. Glasshouse protection is required in cold climates for all except *L.palmatum* and *L.japonicum*, the two most commonly cultivated species – the former with small, palmate frond divisions in dark green, the latter with intricately feather-cut bright green fronds. In extremely sheltered, damp locations, both these species are hardy to –15°C/5°F; even if their fronds are lost in winter, heavily mulched crowns will produce a new flush in mid to late spring, quickly forming a beautiful screen of lacy pinnules. *L.japonicum* is one of the finest foliage climbers for the cool or cold glasshouse, conservatory or large, well lit rooms in the home, where the foliage is carried throughout the year. Individual fronds may persist and continue growing for two years, after which time they tend to deteriorate and ought to be cut out at the base and discarded. *Lygodium* species are useful for hiding unsightly structures, growing up trellises and supports and providing shade for other plants. Most other species require warm glasshouse treatment. The root system of all species is extensive and specimens are better planted out into a soil of neutral to slightly acid pH; they become stunted and less likely to climb if restricted in a container. Where plants are containerized, use a medium suitable for terrestrial ferns. High humidity, bright filtered sunlight and good air circulation will ensure strong growth in the warm glasshouse. Water copiously throughout the growing season, and feed at two-week intervals. Growth will slow down in winter, so water moderately; *L.japonicum* may stop altogether and the fronds die down, during which time water should be applied sparingly to avoid rot. Mulch with organic matter before growth commences. Hard scale is a pest on *Lygodium*, and emerging croziers must be protected from slugs and snails.

Propagate from spores or by division. Serpentine layering is also a possibility: an active growing frond is pinned out or weighed down at each node onto the soil surface where it may root and shoot out as a new plant. Fronds may also be layered individually.

L.articulatum A. Rich.
Sterile fronds bipinnatifid, segments 5–7.5cm, 4, ligulate-oblong, obtuse at apex, distinctly auriculate at base, shortly petiolate, fertile fronds multi-dichotomous; sporangiophores short, densely clustered, lamina much reduced. New Zealand.

L.circinatum (Burm. f.) Sw. (*L.dichotomum* Sw.; *L.pedatum* Sw.)
Pinnules deeply digitate, into 5–6 lobes, or 1–2-forked, sterile pinnules with ultimate division 10–30 × 1–2cm; sporangiophores 2–4mm in short, densely clustered spikes, close-set in marginal rows. Tropical Asia and Australasia.

L.dichotomum Sw. See *L.circinatum*.

L.flexuosum (L.) Sw. (*L.pinnatifidum* Sw.)
Pinnules linear-lanceolate, subacute at apex, articulate at base, short-stalked, terminal segments 8–15×1–2cm, ligulate-oblong, with 3–4 similar segments each side, occasionally hastate or pinnate below, fertile fronds smaller than sterile; sporangiophores to 6mm, triangular, marginal; sporangia 3–5mm. Tropical Asia and Australasia.

L.forsteri Lowe. See *L.reticulatum*

L.hastatum (Willd.) Desv. See *L.volubile*

L.japonicum. (Thunb.) Sw.
Pinnules 10–20×8–18cm, deltoid, terminal segments pinnatifid or hastate, lateral segments 2–3 per side, very unequal, long-stalked, pinnate in lower part, margins entire, serrate or minutely crenate; sporangiophores to 12mm. Japan to Australia. Z9.

L.microphyllum (Cav.) R. Br. (*L.scandens* Sw.). CLIMBING MAIDENHAIR FERN; SNAKE FERN.
Fronds to 3m; primary rachis 1.5mm diam., secondary rachis 4mm, terminating in dormant bud, producing 1 pair or lateral branches, tertiary rachis to 15cm, pinnately branched, pinnules 3–6 each side, stalked, glabrous, sterile pinnules lanceolate-ovate, cordate at base, fertile pinnules ovate to deltate; sporangiophores 4–6mm; spores reticulate. Tropics, widespread in Old World, naturalized Jamaica and Florida. Z9.

L.palmatum (Bernh.) Sw.
Fronds 40–90cm, sterile pinnae 2–4×3–6cm on stalk 2cm, deeply palmately lobed, deeply cordate at base, sinus nearly closed, glabrous, lobes to 25×12mm, to 6, entire, rounded at

apex, fertile pinnae apical, dichtomously branched several times, axes snaked or narrowly marginate, terminal segments numerous, 3–5 × 1.5mm; rachis 1mm diam., dark brown at base, paler upwards, sparsely pilose at base; sporangia 6–10 per segment E US (New Hampshire to Florida). Z8.

L.pedatum Sw. See *L.circinatum.*
L.pinnatifidum Sw. See *L.flexuosum*

L.reticulatum Schkuhr. (*L.forsteri* Lowe)
Pinnules 15–22 × 1–15cm, with terminal segments and 6 subequal segments each, ligulate-oblong or cordate-hastate, rounded or cordate at base, articulate at base, 5–7 × 1–2cm,

lowest shortly stalked; sporangia in close rows along segment margins. Australia, Polynesia.

L.scandens Sw. See *L.microphyllum.*

L.volubile Sw. (*L.hastatum* (Willd.) Desv.)
Ultimate sterile pinnules 4–10×0.5–1.5cm, alternate, 2–4 per side, oblong-lanceolate, cuneate or truncate at base, acute to acuminate at apex, margins minutely crenate-serrate, fertile pinnules usually shorter than sterile; sporangiophores to 10mm, often very shortly pilose at base; spores minutely punctate, obscurely cristate-tuberculate. C America, W Indies, northern S America.

Macfadyena A. DC. (For James MacFadyen (1798–1850), Scottish botanist, author of *Flora Jamaica* (1837).) Bignoniaceae. 3 species of climbing vines. Branches slender, subterete with glandular patches between nodes. Leaves bifoliolate with terminal, trifid, claw-like tendril; pseudostipules small, subulate. Inflorescences axillary cymes or thyrses, often reduced to 1–3 flowers; calyx truncate to spathe-like, split at middle, or bilabiate to irregularly lobed, membranous; corolla yellow, tubular-campanulate, broadly 5-lobed; anthers glabrous; ovary oblong, lepidote, puberulent or glabrescent; ovules 2–4-seriate; disc annular-pulvinate. Fruit a narrow, linear capsule, flattened, valves parallel, smooth; seeds slender, 2-winged. Mexico, W Indies to Uruguay.

CULTIVATION   A vigorous climber grown for its yellow, foxglove-like flowers, *Macfadyena* will grow outdoors in frost-free regions or places where several degrees of frost are sometimes recorded. *M.unguis-cati*, a spectacular plant when covered in its beautiful golden yellow blooms, has also been used as groundcover and in erosion control. In cool temperate zones, cultivate as for *Bignonia* in the cool to intermediate glasshouse or conservatory. Cut back at planting to 60–100cm/24–39in., pinching out shoot tips as they reach 1.3–1.6m/4–5ft to build up a framework. Prune established plants immediately after flowering, remove overcrowded and outward-facing growth, and give stems the additional support of ties.

M.unguis-cati (L.) A. Gentry (*Bignonia tweediana* Lindl.; *Bignonia unguis-cati* L.; *Doxantha acutistipula* Miers; *Doxantha adunca* Miers; *Doxantha dasyonyx* (Blake) Blake; *Doxantha exoleta* (Vell.) Miers; *Doxantha lanuginosa* Miers; *Doxantha mexicana* Miers; *Doxantha praesignis* Miers; *Doxantha serrulata* Miers; *Doxantha tenuicaula* Miers; *Doxantha unguis* (L. emend. DC.) Miers). ANIKAB; BEJUCO EDMURCIELAGO; MANO DE LAGURIJA.
Climber; stem c6cm diam., pseudostipules ovate, striate. Claws of leaf tendrils swollen; young leaves 1–2 ×0.4–0.8cm,

narrow-ovate to lanceolate, apex mucronate; adult leaves 5–16×1.2–6.9cm, narrow-ovate to ovate, membranous, lepidote, glabrous or puberulent especially on veins, glandular on veins beneath; petiole 1.1–4.7cm; petiolules 0.5–2.5cm. Inflorescence usually 1–3(–15)-flowered; calyx 5–1.8 × 0.8–1.8cm, margin sinuate; corolla yellow striped orange in throat, 4.5–10×1.2–2.4cm at mouth, tube 3.3–6.9cm, lobes 1.2–3.1cm. Capsule 26–95 × 1–1.9cm, linear, apex tapered. Mexico and W Indies to Argentina. Z8.

Mandevilla Lindl. (For H.J. Mandeville, British Minister at Buenos Aires, who introduced *M.laxa.*) Apocynaceae. Some 120 species of tuberous, perennial herbs, subshrubs and, more usually, woody lianes with milky sap. Leaves opposite, entire. Inflorescence a lateral raceme; calyx 5-parted; corolla funnelform to salverform, tube cylindric to ovoid, throat campanulate, lobes 5, orbicular to oblong-elliptic; stamens enclosed within throat, anthers connivent. Fruit paired cylindric follicles. C & S America. Many species formerly placed in the genus *Dipladenia.* Z10 unless specified.

CULTIVATION   Handsome climbers for warm climates on pergolas, arbours and as wall specimens with support, or in the glasshouse or conservatory border in cooler zones. *M.laxa*, showing some tolerance of frost, is suitable for a warm, sheltered wall in favoured temperate gardens; it breaks freely from old wood and given suitable protection (hessian, matting, etc.) may regenerate from the base even if cut down by frost. *Mandevilla* species are grown for their showy, funnel-shaped, often sweetly scented blooms, produced over long periods in spring or summer.

Grow in a coarse, well drained but moisture-retentive medium, rich in organic matter, with full sun but with shade from the strongest summer sun. *M.laxa* can be grown in the cold house, kept frost-free; other species perform better at minimum temperatures of 7–10°C/45–50°F. Young plants of *Mm.* × *amabilis, sanderi* and *splendens* grow well and flower freely in well lit, warm rooms in the home and are often offered for sale as houseplants trained on wire hoops. Water plentifully and liquid feed occasionally when in growth and flower. Provide support and mist over frequently, especially in warm bright weather or if grown in the home. Reduce water as light levels and temperatures drop in autumn to keep almost dry in winter. Prune in late winter/early spring to thin old and crowded growth and spur back remaining stems.

Propagate by semi-ripe stem cuttings in summer or by softwood nodal cuttings, 8–10cm/3–4in. long. Treat with 0.5% I.B.A., and root in a closed case with bottom heat at 20°C/68°F. Red spider mite, mealybug and whitefly may be pests under glass.

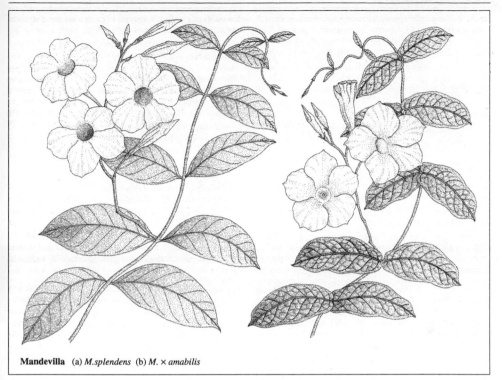

Mandevilla   (a) *M.splendens* (b) *M.* × *amabilis*

M.×amabilis (hort. Buckl.) Dress (*Dipladenia* × *amabilis* hort. Buckl.). (*M.splendens* × ?)
Twiner to 4m. Leaves 10–20cm, oblong-acute, rugose, short-petioled. Flowers 9–12.5cm diam., funnelform, rose pink, rosy crimson at centre, throat yellow, lobes rounded, short-acuminate. Garden origin.

M.×amoena hort. (*M.×amabilis* × *M.splendens*.)
A backcross with more abundantly produced, darker blooms to 10cm diam. Probably synonymous with *M.*'Alice du Pont' and *M.*'Splendens Hybrid' (sic.).

M.boliviensis (Hook. f.) Woodson (*Dipladenia boliviensis* Hook. f.). WHITE DIPLADENIA.
Slender-branched shrubby climber to 4m. Leaves to 10cm, glossy green, elliptic to obovate-elliptic, apex caudate-acuminate, base obtuse; petioles to 2cm. Flowers 3–7 per raceme; corolla to 5cm, funnelform, white, throat golden yellow, lobes to 4cm, acuminate. Bolivia, Ecuador.

M.laxa (Ruiz & Pav.) Woodson (*Echites laxa* Ruiz & Pav. *M.suaveolens* Lindl.; *M.tweediana* Gadeceau & Stapf). CHILEAN JASMINE.
Climber to 4m. Stems verruculose, wiry. Leaves 5–7cm, oblong, base cordate, apex acuminate, glossy green above, purple or grey-green beneath with tufts of pale hair in axils; petioles 1.25–5cm. Flowers highly fragrant; corolla to 5cm diam., white to ivory, tube downy within. Argentina. Z9.

M.sanderi (Hemsl.) Woodson (*Dipladenia sanderi* Hemsl.).
Twining shrub to 5m. Leaves to 6cm, broadly oblong-elliptic, apex briefly acuminate, base rounded, coriaceous, glabrous; petiole to 1cm. Raceme equalling leaves, 3–5-flowered; corolla rose pink, funnelform, throat to 4.5cm, lobes to 3.5cm, acuminate. Brazil. 'Rosea' (BRAZILIAN JASMINE; SAVANAH FLOWER): leaves to 5cm, ovate, lustrous green above, bronze-green beneath; flowers to 8cm, salmon pink, throat and tube yellow within.

M.splendens (Hook.f.) Woodson (*Dipladenia splendens* (Hook.f.) A. DC.; *Echites splendens* Hook.f.). PINK ALLAMANDA.
Twining shrub to 6m. Stems initially downy. Leaves to 20cm, broadly elliptic, apex acuminate, base subcordate, thin-textured, very finely downy. Raceme equalling leaves, 3–5-flowered; corolla 7.5–10cm diam., funnelform, rose pink, tube to 4cm, lobes to 3.25cm, rounded, briefly acuminate, spreading. SE Brazil. 'Rosacea': flowers rose-pink, flushed and bordered deeper rose, tube yellow within, ringed bright rose at throat.

M.suaveolens Lindl. See *M.laxa*.
M.tweediana Gadeceau & Stapf. See *M.laxa*.

Manettia Mutis. (For X. Manetti (*b* 1723), Keeper of the botanic garden at Florence.) Rubiaceae. Some 80 species of evergreen herbs or subshrubs, usually climbing and twining. Leaves opposite, petiolate, stipulate. Flowers axillary and solitary, or in pedunculate, few-flowered panicles or cymes; calyx tube turbinate or obovoid to campanulate, limb persistent, lobes usually 4, often with intervening teeth; corolla tubular to funnelform, tube plane or curved; occasionally pubescent, lobes usually 4, erect or reflexed; stamens usually 4, inserted at throat, anthers oblong, included or exserted; ovary 2-celled, style filiform, stigma occasionally 2-lobed, club-shaped, ovules many. Fruit a capsule, obovoid to turbinate, 2-celled and -grooved, leathery to papery; seeds many, compressed, winged. Tropical America. Z10.

CULTIVATION Evergreen, twining climbers with soft, or sometimes slightly shrubby stems, grown for their vibrantly coloured, tubular flowers and glossy foliage. *M.luteorubra* and *M.cordifolia* are both commonly known as the Fire Cracker Vine, a reference to the bright orange and scarlet of the blooms, in the first tipped with yellow. Grow in bright, indirect light, on trellis or other support, in the glasshouse or conservatory, min. 7–10°C/45–50°F. Pot in a well drained, medium-fertility, loam-based mix, with added leafmould. Water plentifully when in growth, reducing water as temperatures fall in autumn. Avoid persistent wetting of foliage, especially in bright sunlight or cold weather. Cut back if necessary in spring. *Manettia* species are also grown in temperate zones as annuals, planted outside for summer display, in humus-rich soils with part shade in summer. Specimens of *M.luteorubra*, achieved by growing three cuttings together on a wigwam structure, soon make sturdy and highly decorative houseplants. Most will degenerate after a few years, making frequent propagation desirable: take softwood cuttings of new growth in spring, or semi-ripe cuttings in summer. Susceptible to attack by white fly.

M.asperula Benth. See *M.cordifolia*.
M.bicolor Hook. f. non Paxt. See *M.luteorubra*.

M.coccinea (Aubl.) Willd. (*Nacibea coccinea* Aubl.; *M.costaricensis* Wernham).
Climbing herb to 2m. Stems 4-angled, glabrous to short-pubescent. Leaves to 10cm, usually shorter, ovate or lanceolate or oblong, apex acute or narrowly acute, base acute or obtuse and decurrent, thin-textured, lustrous, rough above, glabrous to short-pubescent beneath. Flowers axillary and solitary, or in pedunculate, few-flowered cymes or racemes; peduncles to 5cm; calyx tube to 5mm, glabrous or pubescent, lobes to 1.4cm, linear to oblanceolate, attenuate, recurved, margin ciliate, glabrous or pubescent; corolla salverform, pink to scarlet spotted red, tube to 2.3cm, exterior and throat yellow-pubescent, densely so within, lobes to 0.5cm, ovate or deltoid to oblong, apex acute, glabrous. Summer. W Indies and Cuba to Northern S America.

M.cordifolia Mart. (*M.grandiflora* Vell.; *M.asperula* Benth.; *M.micans* Poepp. & Endl.). FIRECRACKER VINE.
Climbing herb, to 4m. Stems terete. Leaves to 8cm, ovate to ovate-lanceolate, apex acute or narrowly acute, base rounded to cordate, thin-textured, lustrous above, glabrous or pubescent beneath; petioles short. Flowers solitary or in a crowded leafy panicle (*M.micans*); calyx lobes lanceolate to oblong, apex acute; corolla to 5cm, vivid red or dark orange fading to yellow at lobes (*M.micans*), tubular, tube distended above, interior pubescent . Winter–summer. S America (Bolivia to Argentina, Peru).

M.costaricensis Wernham. See *M.coccinea*.

M.discolor hort. See *M.luteorubra*.
M.glabra Cham. & Schldl. See *M.cordifolia*.
M.grandiflora Vell. See *M.cordifolia*.
M.inflata Sprague. See *M.luteorubra*.

M.luteorubra Benth. (*M.inflata* Sprague; *M.bicolor* Hook.f. non Paxt.; *M.discolor* hort.). BRAZILIAN FIRE CRACKER; TWINING FIRE CRACKER; FIRECRACKER VINE.
Climbing perennial herb or shrub to 4m in cult. Stems strongly twining, somewhat 4-angled, intricately branched, slender, shortly and coarsely pubescent throughout, somewhat viscid, pale green. Leaves 2.5–10cm, ovate-rhombic to ovate-lanceolate, acute, pale to dark green, subcoriaceous. Flowers solitary, rarely paired, axillary, short-stalked; calyx lobes to 1.25cm, foliose, erect to reflexed; corolla to 5cm, tubular-cylindric, narrowing toward limb, bright red, hispidulous, lobes yellow, short, recurved. Paraguay, Uruguay.

M.micans Poepp. & Endl. See *M.cordifolia*.

M.reclinata L.
Climbing herb to 1m. Stems terete, glabrous. Leaves to 7cm, ovate to elliptic, apex narrowly acute, base acute or obtuse, thin-textured, occasionally sparsely pubescent; petioles to 1cm. Flowers axillary and solitary, or in umbellate panicles; pedicels to 3cm, peduncles to 3.5cm; calyx tube to 0.8cm, turbinate, pubescent, limb persistent, lobes to 0.9cm, unequal, linear to lanceolate, pubescent; corolla red, tube to 2cm, exterior minutely pubescent, interior pubescent, lobes to 0.5cm, ovate, narrowly acute. W Indies and Cuba, Mexico to Northern S America.

For illustration see Rubiaceae.

Mansoa DC. (For Antonio Luiz Patricio da Silva Manso (1778–1848). Brazilian botanist and author of works on medicinal plants.) Bignoniaceae. About 15 species of lianes. Branches subterete to tetragonal, glabrescent or pubescent, with or without glandular patches between nodes; pseudostipules subulate. Leaves trifoliate, terminal leaflet often replaced by a simple or branched tendril. Inflorescence an axillary or terminal raceme or panicle; calyx cupular to tubular-campanulate, truncate or 5-ribbed with ribs ending in broad or subulate teeth *c*5mm, puberulent-lepidote; corolla tubular, 5-lobed; anthers glabrous or downy; ovary cylindrical, glandular-papillose; ovules 2–4 seriate. Fruit a linear-oblong capsule, flattened, valves parallel, woody, densely pubescent or tuberculate; seeds 2-winged, wings membranous, rarely absent. Mexico to Brazil. Z10.

CULTIVATION As for *Pandorea*.

M.alliacea (Lam.) A. Gentry. BEJUCO DE AJO.
Vegetation smells strongly of onions. Leaflets 5–10 × 1.5–5cm, ovate-elliptic, apex acuminate or obtuse, base truncate or attenuate, shining above. Flowers in groups of 6–25, dark to pale purple; corolla 4–6×0.5×2cm. Americas.

M.difficilis (Cham.) Bur. & Schum.
Leaflets 5–11×3–6cm, oblong-ovate, apex acute to acuminate, base rounded to cordate, leathery, shining, punctate. Corolla 5.5–9cm, violet, purple or vermilion, limb 6.5cm diam., puberulent. Brazil.

M.hymenaea (DC.) A.Gentry.
Vegetation smells strongly of onions. Leaflets 4.8–9.4 × 3.3–7.5cm, ovate to narrow-ovate, apex obtuse to acute, base truncate to cordate, usually glabrous. Inflorescence puberulent; corolla 4.1–5×0.8–1.5cm at mouth, pale lilac to purple, pink or white, tube 3–3.6cm, lobes 0.6–1.3cm, tube glabrous, lobes puberulent. Mexico to Brazil.

Marah Kellogg. (Derivation obscure.) BIGROOT; MANROOT. Cucurbitaceae. 7 species of monoecious, herbaceous vines. Tubers large, globose to cylindric. Tendrils simple to 3-fid. Stems striate. Leaves suborbicular, palmate, cordate, 5–7-lobed; petioles long. Male inflorescence a raceme or peduncle, axillary, deciduous; calyx teeth small or rudimentary; corolla campanulate to rotate, glandular, segments 4–8, usually 5; anthers 3; filaments fused; female flowers solitary, co-axillary with male; calyx and corolla similar to male except larger; ovary inferior; locules usually 4. Fruit a capsule, globose to fusiform, pendulous, often spinose, dehiscent, turgid becoming dry; seeds large. Western N America. Z8.

CULTIVATION   As for *Coccinia*, but in cool to intermediate conditions. Multiple planting is not required for fruit set.

M.fabaceus (Naudin) Greene (*Echinocystis fabacea* Naudin). Stems to 7m, sparsely pubescent. Leaves palmate, suborbicular, to 5–10×5–10cm, glabrous to scabrous, lobes 5–7, acute or obtuse, occasionally mucronate, 1–3cm deep. Male inflorescence 5–25cm; calyx teeth obscure; corolla green-white, to 0.5×1cm, with marginal trichomes; ovary globose, tapering. Fruit globose, densely spinose, 4–5cm; seeds lenticular, light brown, ridged, to 2.4×2.0×1.5cm. California.

M.macrocarpus (Greene) Greene (*Echinocystis macrocarpa* Greene). CHILICOTHE.
Stems 1–7m, deeply striated. Leaves palmate, suborbicular, scabrous above, hispid beneath, lobes 5–7, acute or obtuse. Male inflorescence 5–40cm, calyx lobes 2.5mm, smaller in female, deltoid to linear-lanceolate, occasionally obsolete; corolla cupular, white. Fruit cylindric, beaked, 8–12×6–9cm,

spines dense, flattened, 0.5–3cm; seeds oblong, somewhat flattened, brown with dark equatorial line, 0.9–2.5cm. California, Baja California.

M.oreganus (Torr. & A. Gray) Howell (*Sicyos oreganus* Torr. & A. Gray; *Echinocystis oregana* (Torr. & A. Gray) Cogn.).
Stems 1–7m, often sparsely pubescent. Tendrils 2–3-fid. Leaves palmate, suborbicular, cordate, entire to subcrenulate or denticulate, glabrous to pubescent, 8–35cm diam., lobes 5–7, shallow, acute, obtuse or acuminate; petiole pubescent, 4–12cm. Calyx lobes broadly triangular to subulate; corolla to 1.2 × 1.7cm, white, male slightly smaller. Fruit striped, sparsely spinose, seeds discoid, to 2×1.2cm, red-brown. SW US to S Canada.

Marcgravia L. Marcgraviaceae. 45 species of epiphytic shrubs with two forms of growth and foliage, much after the fashion of *Hedera*. The sterile shoots creep, attaching themselves closely to the host plant by means of short adhesive roots; these shoots are clothed with closely ranked leaves which overlap and lie flush to the surface like shingles, a phenomenon also found in some climbing Araceae and *Ficus*. The fertile shoots produce few or no adventitious roots and scramble or arch away from the host, their pendulous branches more loosely furnished with larger, stalked leaves and terminating in dense, umbel-like racemes. Flowers of two types – the outermost fertile with 4 sepals and 4–5 petals united in a circumscissile cap and 10 to many stamens; the innermost sterile and abortive with persistent bracts modified into stalked, pitcher-like nectaries. Fruit a 4–12-celled, globose, many-seeded capsule. Tropical America. Z10.

CULTIVATION   *M.rectiflora* is an attractive evergreen ivy-like shrub for use on trees or walls in damp, shaded situations in subtropical and tropical gardens, or in the conservatory or warm glasshouse (minimum winter temperature 15°C/60°F). Its juvenile growth will form a close cover of small, mid to dark green leaves clinging to trunks, cork-clad posts or brick. The fertile branches develop in the plant's uppermost reaches and hang down, weighted with laurel-like leaves and umbels of curious green 'flowers' – in fact slender pitcher-like nectaries developed from the bracts that subtend the short-lived true flowers. Plant at the foot of the host or support in an open mix of bark, charcoal and leafmould. Water and nutrients are mostly taken through the self-clinging stems. These require frequent hosing or misting outside the wet tropics. Keep within bounds by trimming the tips of sterile shoots or pruning the fertile branches. Propagate by air layering fertile branches or rooting detached portions of 'shingle' growth in a warm, humid case. Under glass, *Marcgravia* is sometimes afflicted by scale insect and by mealybug.

M.rectiflora Triana & Planch.
Evergreen epiphytic shrub climbing to 15m (usually to 3m under glass). Leaves of sterile shoots to 3cm, elliptic to oblong, sessile, waxy mid-green with a bronze or rusty tinge when young, closely adpressed to host and often overlapping;

leaves of fertile shoots to 10cm, oblong-lanceolate, apex acuminate, base shortly stalked, leathery, mid-green. Flowers in terminal umbels, insignificant; nectaries to 2cm, cylindric-clavate, whorled, waxy, mid-green. W Indies.

Marianthus Hueg. ex Endl. (From Maria and Gk *anthos*, flower, dedicating the flower to the Virgin Mary.) Pittosporaceae. 15 species of perennial, evergreen, procumbent shrubs or woody climbers, to 5m; stems slender. Leaves alternate, entire or with the lower leaves lobed. Inflorescence a terminal or axillary cluster; flowers 5-merous; petals connivent at base and appearing fused, red, blue or white. Fruit a capsule, compressed, membranaceous; seeds many, unwinged. Australia. Z8.

CULTIVATION   As for *Billardiera*.

M.erubescens Putterl.
Climber to 5m. Leaves leathery, broad. Flowers many, 2.5cm, brilliant red. Late spring. W Australia.

M.ringens (J.L. Drumm. & Harv.) F.J. Muell.
Climber to 3m. Leaves broad, leathery, dark green. Flowers many, *c*2.5cm, orange. Spring. W Australia.

For illustration see Pittosporaceae.

Melothria L. (From Gk *melothron*, bryony.) Cucurbitaceae. About 10 species of monoecious or dioecious herbaceous climbers or trailers, perennial, occasionally annual. Tendrils simple. Leaves entire or palmately lobed, often scabrid or hispidulous. Male inflorescence a raceme or corymb; male flowers small, pedicellate; receptacle campanulate; sepals small, denticulate; corolla white, yellow or pale green, deeply divided; stamens 3, usually free, anthers occasionally coherent; pistillode globose; female inflorescence a cluster or solitary; flowers similar to male except staminodes 3, ovary globose to fusiform, triloculate with disc at base of style. Fruit a berry, long-stalked, small, indehiscent; seeds many, compressed, often emarginate, smooth or rugose, creamwhite. Subtropical and tropical Americas. Z10.

CULTIVATION   as for *Coccinia*, but multiple planting is not required for fruit set.

M.indica (L.) Lour. See *Zehneria indica*.
M.indica Lour. See *Zygosicyos indica*.
M.japonica (Thunb.) Maxim. See *Zehneria indica*.
M.maderspatana (L.) Cogn. See *Mukia maderaspatana*.

M.pendula L.
Scandent. Stems slender, often rooting at nodes. Leaves slender, pubescent, ovate-cordate to triangular, angulate, entire or, sometimes, shallowly lobulate, acuminate, scabrous above, paler and pubescent beneath. Male raceme 2–7-flowered; female flowers solitary on filiform pedicels; corolla yellow; ovary oblong; stigma slightly lobed. Fruit subglobose to ellipsoid or ovoid, to 2cm, purple dappled green; seeds obovate, to 4mm. S US to S America.

M.punctata Cogn. See *Zehneria scabra*.
M.scabra (L. f.) Naudin. See *Zehneria scabra*.

Menispermum L. (From Lat. *menis*, a tiny half-moon-like device inscribed at the opening of books, and *spermum*, seed, referring to the shape of the seed.) MOONSEED. Menispermaceae.
2 species of woody-based dioecious twiners. Stems slender, tangled, rampant, suckering, pale green, frequently persisting for a few seasons and becoming woody, otherwise herbaceous and of annual duration. Leaves variable in shape, obscurely 5–7-lobed, peltate, petiole long, inserted near basal sinus. Flowers inconspicuous, yellow-green in axillary stalked racemes or panicles; sepals 4–10, exceeding petals; petals 6–9; stamens in male flowers 9–24, in females, 6, sterile; carpels 2–4. Fruit to 1cm diam., dark red-purple to black, subglobose, hanging in grape-like bunches; seeds crescent-shaped. Eastern N America, E Asia.

CULTIVATION   Vigorous, suckering climbers forming a dense tangle of twining shoots clothed in attractive foliage, suitable for walls (with support), trellis and host trees, although they require thoughtful placement if they are not to out-compete less vigorous neighbours. Where plants of both sexes are grown together, the female may bear long racemes of small, glossy, black fruits containing the crescent-shaped seeds that give rise to the common name, Moonseed. Although in habitat *M.canadense* may experience temperatures to –30°C/–22°F and below, in mild maritime climates *M.canadense* may produce softer growth that is cut to the ground where winter temperatures fall much below –5 to –10°C/23–14°F; plants will re-sprout from the base in spring, and, where not cut by frost, may even need to be kept in check by pruning to the base in late autumn or early spring. Grow in partial shade or full sun in any moderately fertile soil that does not dry out excessively in summer. Propagate by seed, by removal of suckers, or by ripewood cuttings in the cold frame or cool glasshouse in autumn.

M.canadense L. YELLOW PARILLA.
Stems to 6m, usually persistent. Leaves 5–20cm, ovate-cordate to suborbicular, entire or obscurely 5–7-lobed, dark green above, somewhat paler and initially downy beneath. Racemes long. Fruit pruinose, purple-red to blue-black. Eastern N America. Z5.

M.davuricum DC. (*M.dauricum* auct.).
Distinguished from *M.canadense* by its annual or, rarely, persistent aerial stems, its shorter, more crowded and frequently paired racemes, leaves to 10cm, more evidently peltate and sharply lobed, and larger, black fruit. E Asia. Z4.

Merremia Dennst. (For the German naturalist, Blasius Merrem (*d*1824).) Convolvulaceae. 60–80 species of perennial, herbaceous of woody climbers, occasionally erect to procumbent, a few cm high to 20cm+. Leaves petiolate, entire, lobed with to 9 leaflets. Inflorescence axillary, 1- to few-flowered, with lanceolate or linear bracts; sepals usually subequal; corolla campanulate or funnel-shaped, entire or lobed; filaments glandular at base, anthers spirally twisted after dehiscence; stigma globose or biglobose. Fruit a dry capsule; seeds 1–6, pubescent or glabrous. Pantropical. Separated from *Ipomoea* largely on the basis of its smooth (rather than spinulose) pollen grains. Z9.

CULTIVATION   *M.tuberosa* is a rampant plant, best used on garden boundaries or to cover unsightly garden structures; the fruits are useful in dried flower arrangements. Cultivation as for the tender perennial species of *Ipomoea*; most easily propagated from seed.

M.aurea (Kellogg) O'Donnell.
Slender, tuberous climber to 2.5m. Leaves compound, ovate to orbicular in outline, axils hairy, leaflets 5, 2–4 × 0.5–2cm, entire, subsessile. Flowers solitary, on glabrous pedicel; sepals to 1cm, oblong to oval, blunt, unequal; corolla 5–10cm diam., 3–8cm long, funnel-shaped, golden-yellow, mid-petaline areas darker. Mexico (Baja California).

M.dissecta (Jacq.) Hallier f. (*Ipomoea dissecta* (Jacq.) Pursh).
Herbaceous climber to at least 8m; stems hairy at first, later glabrous. Leaves divided almost to base into 7–9, 10cm, lanceolate lobes, glabrous or sparsely hairy, margins coarsely and sinuately toothed. Inflorescence 1–4-flowered, on a 5–7cm peduncle; corolla 3–4.5cm long, to 5cm diam.,

broadly funnel-shaped, white with a purple or magenta tube. S US to Tropical S America.

M.tuberosa (L.) Rendle (*Ipomoea tuberosa* L.).WOOD ROSE; YELLOW MORNING GLORY; SPANISH WOODBINE.
Large, stout woody climber to 20m. Leaves 8–15cm, deeply 7-lobed almost to base, glabrous, lobes elliptic to lanceolate, entire, apices acuminate; petioles long. Inflorescence 1- to several-flowered; peduncles 10–20cm; corolla 5–6cm, campanulate, bright yellow. Mexico to Tropical S America, introduced in many other tropical regions.

Metrosideros Banks ex Gaertn. (From *metra*, middle, and *sideros*, iron, in reference to the hard wood of the genus.) Myrtaceae. 50 species of aromatic shrubs, trees or woody climbers. Leaves opposite, simple, pinnately veined, gland-dotted. Flowers in axillary or axillary and terminal, cymose, usually pedunculate inflorescences, these sometimes reduced to a single flower, often aggregated into compound inflorescences, sometimes ramiflorous; sepals 5, imbricate; petals 5; stamens numerous, 2 or more times as long as petals, rarely less, usually highly coloured; ovary 3-celled. Fruit a leathery capsule; seeds narrowly linear to filiform. Spring–summer. S Africa, Malesia, Australasia, Pacific Is. Z9.

CULTIVATION The best-known representative of this genus is the Christmas Tree, *M.excelsa*, a large broad-domed tree with leathery leaves and brilliant red flowers. Several species are, however, vines, inhabitants of cool, damp woodlands where their narrow stems creep over the trunks and rocks, clothing them with small, close-fitting dark green leaves somewhat after the fashion of *Ficus pumila*. Unlike the Creeping Fig, this dense evergreen coat is illuminated by small flowers, their bright colour imparted by long, showy stamens – carmine and scarlet in the most commonly grown species, *M.carminea* and *M.fulgens*, white to delicate pink in the others listed here.

These plants are too seldom cultivated: few climbers offer so compact a cover of fine evergreen foliage *and* flowers. They are, moreover, ideally suited to areas of the cool glasshouse or conservatory which few other plants would tolerate, thriving in moist, almost chilly shade.Where frosts are light and short-lived, they might be attempted outdoors – for example in favoured regions of Eire, Western Scotland and the Scilly Isles – planted in humid, sheltered and wooded places of the sort that suits *Crinodendron*, *Hoheria*, *Dicksonia* and the hardier Proteaceae. Under glass, plant in light shade in an open, slightly acid mix rich in leafmould; ventilate freely; water copiously throughout the year, misting the foliage in hot weather. Train on moss poles, old brick walls, pillars and tree-fern trunks. Propagate by simple layering or by semi-ripe cuttings taken in summer and rooted in a closed case with bottom heat.

M.aurea hort. See *M.fulgens.*

M.carminea Oliv. AKAKURA.
Liane to 15m+. Branchlets, inflorescence and receptacle setose to pubescent. Leaves 1.5–3.5cm, elliptic to ovate-oblong to broad-ovate, obtuse to subacute, coriaceous; petioles 0.1cm. Inflorescence in terminal compound cymes; flowers numerous; pedicels 5mm; sepals broad-oblong, 2mm; petals suborbicular, shortly clawed, 5 × 4mm, margins usually toothed; stamens 10–15mm, brilliant carmine. New Zealand.

M.colensoi Hook. f.
Slender liane to 6m+. Branchlets subterete, setose to pubescent Leaves to 1.5–2cm, ovate-lanceolate, acute to acuminate, densely pubescent when young, subsessile. Inflorescence of terminal and lateral, small, few-flowered cymes; pedicels usually setose, 3mm; receptacle c5mm, more or less funnelform, pubescent; sepals narrow-triangular, acute; stamens c10mm, pink to white. New Zealand.

M.diffusa Forst. f. (*Melaleuca diffusa* Forst. f.). SMALL RATA VINE.
Slender liane to 6m+. Branchlets indistinctly 4-angled, finely pubescent. Leaves 0.7–2.5cm, oblong to ovate-lanceolate to ovate-oblong, usually acute to apiculate, somewhat pubescent when young, subsessile. Inflorescence of few-flowered lateral cymes, usually below leaves; pedicels to 5mm, pubescent; receptacle turbinate, c3mm, abruptly expanded above; sepals ovate-triangular; stamens slender, 7–9mm, white to pink. New Zealand.

M.florida Sm. See *M.fulgens.*

M.fulgens Sol. ex Gaertn. (*M.scandens* (Forst. & Forst. f.) Druce; *M.florida* Sm.; *M.speciosa* sensu Colenso). AKA; RATA VINE.
Liane to 10m+; bark separating in flakes. Leaves 3.5–6cm, elliptic-oblong, obtuse, glabrous; petiole stout, to 0.5cm. Inflorescence of terminal cymes; receptacle obconical to urceolate, glabrous, c12mm, ribbed; sepals oblong, obtuse; stamens scarlet, 20–25mm. New Zealand. 'Aurata': stamens pale yellow.

M.perforata (Forst. & Forst. f.) A. Rich. FLOWERY RATA VINE.
Rather slender liane to 15m+. Branchlets terete, somewhat setose. Leaves 0.6–1.2cm, broad-ovate to broad-oblong to suborbicular on same plant, glabrous, pale beneath and more or less setose, margins revolute, subsessile. Inflorescence of axillary few-flowered cymes, crowded toward apex of branchlets; peduncles and pedicels pubescent to setose; receptacle broad-turbinate; sepals broad, obtuse; petals suborbicular, white or pink; stamens 8–10mm, white to pink. New Zealand.

M.scandens (Forst. & Forst. f.) Druce. See *M.fulgens.*
M.speciosa sensu Colenso. See *M.fulgens.*

Mikania Willd. (For J.G. Mikan (1743–1814), Professor of Botany at Prague, or his son J.C. Mikan (*d*1844), plant collector in Brazil.) Compositae. About 300 species of evergreen, perennial, woody or herbaceous lianes. Leaves usually opposite, entire to dentate. Capitula discoid, small, clustered in spikes, racemes or panicles; involucre cylindric to ovoid; phyllaries 4–5, usually striate; florets hermaphrodite. Fruit a 5-angled cypsela; pappus bristles usually white or tinged yellow, scabrid. Tropics, especially New World. Z10.

CULTIVATION As for *Delairea*. Most species are frost-tender and need glasshouse protection in cool temperate zones.

M.amara Willd. See *M.parviflora*.
M.apiifolia DC. See *M.dentata*.

M.dentata Spreng. (*M.ternata* (Vell.) Robinson; *M.apiifolia* DC.).
Woody, clothed in purple hairs. Leaves palmately lobed, lobes 5–7, oblong-rhombic to oblanceolate-rhombic, entire to pinnatifid or 3-lobed, dark green above, purple beneath. Capitula clustered in lax corymbs; florets white tinged yellow. Pappus off-white. C & S Brazil.

M.hemisphaerica Schultz-Bip. ex Bak.
Herbaceous, glabrous throughout. Leaves to 10cm, simple, ovate, cordate at base, acuminate, margins serrate-dentate; petiole to 5cm. Capitula in a corymbose panicle; florets white flushed with pink. Pappus rufescent. Brazil.

M.parviflora (Aubl.) Karst. (*M.amara* Willd.).
Herbaceous to woody. Leaves large, ovate, entire to remotely dentate, apex acuminate, base acute or decurrent, glabrous or nearly so. Capitula in cymes; florets pale lime green or pale blue. Pappus pale brown. C & Tropical S America.

M.scandens (L.) Willd. WILD CLIMBING HEMP-WEED; CLIMBING HEMP-VINE.
Herbaceous, subglabrous. Leaves to 10cm, triangular to hastate, base deeply cordate, margins entire or remotely repand-dentate, apex acuminate, glabrous to slightly scabrous or pubescent; petioles long. Capitula in dense corymbs, strongly vanilla-scented; florets white, tinged yellow, or lilac to purple. Pappus off-white. Summer. Tropical America.

M.ternata (Vell.) Robinson. See *M.dentata*.
M.guaco Humb. & Bonpl. See *M.parviflora*.

Millettia Wight & Arn. (For J.A. Millett, 18th-century botanist who made the first collection of *Millettia* in Canton, China.) EVERGREEN WISTERIA. Leguminosae (Papilionoideae). Some 90 species of lianes, shrubs or trees. Leaves imparipinnate; stipules small, stipels present; leaflets in few to several pairs, opposite or alternate, oblong-lanceolate, generally persistent, often coriaceous. Flowers papilionaceous, usually in terminal and lateral panicles or racemes; bracts and bracteoles usually falling before anthesis; calyx campanulate, either truncate or with 5 teeth, upper dental pair connate; standard large, keel blunt, incurved, clawed; wing oblong-falcate, usually auricled and clawed; stamens 9, usually monadelphous, anthers equal, ovate; ovary thread-like, occasionally hirsute, usually sessile, ovules 3–11, style downy at base, glabrous at apex, stigma terminal, small. Fruit linear or oblong, swollen or flat, valves 2, ligneous or coriaceous; seeds 1 to few, reniform or orbicular. E Asia, India, Africa, Madagascar.

CULTIVATION   The climbing members of the genus *Millettia* are mostly tall, twining lianes, although *M.dura* will assume the habit of either a small free-standing tree or a clambering shrub according to location. As has often been said, they resemble evergreen Wisterias, usually with leathery foliage of a darker green and more intensely coloured flowers. In tropical and subtropical regions, they are used after the fashion of *Wisteria*, trained on pillars, pergolas and house walls. Outside zones 9 and 10, they are usually grown in tubs or borders in the glasshouse or conservatory (minimum temperature 10°C/50°F), where they will tolerate most soils and respond well to bright, filtered sunlight, full ventilation and copious supplies of water and feed when in growth. *M.reticulata* and *M.nitida* have been grown successfully outdoors where temperatures fall as low as −15°C/5°F: they ought, perhaps, to be more confidently attempted on sheltered, sunny walls in zone 8. The Australian Evergreen Wisteria, *M.megasperma*, will endure mild or infrequent frosts and is an excellent climber for Mediterranean-type climates. Pruning and propagation as for *Camoensia*.

M.dura Dunn.
Small tree or climbing shrub to 13m. Young stems brown-pubescent. Leaves initially rusty-pubescent; leaflets 8–9cm, 15–19, lanceolate-oblong, apex tapering to a point, glabrous above except on midrib and margins, downy beneath. Flowers in rusty-pubescent, drooping panicles 10–20cm long; corolla mauve, standard *c*2.5cm. Fruit 14–20cm, linear-oblong, glabrous. E Africa. Z10.

M.megasperma Benth. AUSTRALIAN EVERGREEN WISTERIA.
Tall *Wisteria*-like twining liane. Leaflets to 5cm, dark green, tough, glossy. Flowers purple in drooping subterminal racemes. Fruit to 15cm, woody, velutinous. Queensland, New South Wales. Z9.

M.nitida Benth.
Tall liane. Branchlets initially rusty-pubescent. Leaflets 0.5–7.5cm, usually 5, ovate or elliptic-oblong, apex tapering to a short tip, leathery, glabrous, lustrous above. Flowers large, densely packed in downy panicles; corolla purple, standard *c*2.5cm, sericeous beneath. Fruit 7–10cm, rusty-pubescent, torulose. S China, Hong Kong, Taiwan. Z9.

M.reticulata Benth.
Tall twining liane. Leaflets to 9cm, 5–9, lanceolate-elliptic, apex blunt, base cordate, glabrous, subcoriaceous. Flowers fragrant, rose to mauve or lavender blue, to 1.5cm, packed in erect, terminal panicles to 20 × 20cm. S China, Taiwan. Z9.

Mitraria Cav. (From Lat. *mitra*, mitre, referring to the shape of the fruit.) Gesneriaceae. 1 species, a climbing or straggling, evergreen perennial herb or subshrub; stem villous to glabrous, obscurely tetragonal becoming somewhat woody at base, branching dense, tangled. Leaves to 2cm, opposite in equal pairs, ovate, acute, dentate, lustrous dark green, coriaceous, hairy. Flowers solitary on arching to drooping, hairy stalks; floral bract 1, bilobed; calyx 4- or 5-lobed, lobes to 1.2cm, lanceolate, free, slightly enclosed by floral bract; corolla to 3cm, tubular, scarlet or orange-red, inflated about halfway up, narrowing to mouth, pilose, limb lobed, lobes to 0.7cm, rounded, slightly reflexed; stamens 4, anthers united in pairs; ovary superior. Fruit a capsule, green flushed red. Summer–autumn. Chile. Z8.

CULTIVATION   An unusual small shrubby gesneriad with flame-coloured flowers, it will succeed planted at the foot of a sheltered, shady wall and trained on wires or trellis. Plant in an open but moist soil rich in leafmould and low in pH. A cool root-run is essential, as is protection from scorching winds and sun. Not fully hardy, this plant responds well to the temperature range and location-types that suit *Asteranthera*, *Berberidopsis* and *Lapageria*. Propagation as for *Asteranthera*.

M.coccinea Cav.

Momordica L. (From Lat. *mordere*, to bite; the seeds have praemorse tips.) Cucurbitaceae. 45 species of monoecious or dioecious, annual or perennial scramblers. Tendrils simple or bifid. Leaves palmate or pedate with 3–7 lobes or leaflets, dentate or undulate. Flowers solitary (males sometimes in corymbs or racemes); peduncle of male flower conspicuously bracteate; calyx tubular; corolla showy, rotate or campanulate, yellow or white, deeply lobed; stamens 3, occasionally 2, free, inserted in throat of tube, anthers flexuous, partially coherent, absent in female; ovary oblong or fusiform, usually ribbed, tuberculate or papillose. Fruit pendulous, ripening yellow or orange, bursting and expanding in a starlike configuration at maturity, oblong, dehiscent or indehiscent, tuberculate or ridged; seeds compressed with grooved margin, often glossy red, suspended in a white, pulpy mass. Africa, Indomalesia, naturalized Americas. Z9.

CULTIVATION   Perennial tendril climbers from the moist tropics of the Old World, particularly Africa and found in bushland, savannah and sometimes colonizing disturbed ground. Grown for their tuberculate fruit, splitting in several species to reveal showy, scarlet-pulped seeds. *M.balsamina* and *M.charantia* bear fruits which are edible when green. The flowers of *M.cochinchinensis* are showy and hooded, while those of *M.charantia* are strongly vanilla-scented in the morning.

In cool temperate zones all need glasshouse cultivation as annuals in hot conditions, high humidity and bright filtered light. The potting compost must be well drained but rich: a mix of 2:2:1:1 sterilized loam/well rotted manure/coir/grit is ideal. Plant in early spring. *M.cochinchinensis* and *M.rostrata* are dioecious, and plants of each sex are needed for seed production. Water plentifully throughout growth and liquid feed fortnightly, training the growth on to wires or a trellis. Control red spider mite as described under *Trichosanthes*. Collect seed in the autumn for spring sowing with bottom heat at 20°C/68°F.

M.balsamina L. BALSAM APPLE.
Climber or trailer to 1.5m. Tendrils simple. Leaves broadly ovate to reniform, cordate, pubescent, deeply and acutely palmately lobed, to 9–12cm, sharply dentate; petiole pubescent. Flowers solitary; bract ovate-cordate, veined, attached to upper part of peduncle; petals yellow with green venation, to 1.5×1.2cm; ovary fusiform, beaked. Fruit to 7cm, ovoid or ellipsoid, tapering at both ends, covered with ridged, irregular protuberances, green ripening orange and bursting. E Indies, widely naturalized.

M.brachybotrys Poepp. & Endl. See *Cyclanthera brachybotrys*.

M.cardiospermoides Klotz.
Climber to 6m, perennial; rootstock tuberous. Leaves biternately 9–15-foliolate, leaflets ovate-oblong, 0.5–3×0.4–2cm, acute, apiculate. Flowers solitary; male bract usually larger; petals yellow, 1.9–2.6×1–1.5cm. Fruit ellipsoid, irregularly tubercled; seeds rugose or ridged, to 14×9×4mm. Southern Africa.

M.charantia L. BALSAM PEAR; BITTER GOURD; BITTER CUCUMBER; LA-KWA.
Annual, climbing to 5m. Stems rigid. Tendrils simple. Leaves deeply 3–7-lobed, pubescent on nerves, lobes obovate to rhombic, acute and apiculate. Flowers solitary; bract mucronate, entire; petals pale yellow to orange, to 2.2 × 1.5cm, bearing basal scales; ovary ovoid, beaked. Fruit oblong or ovoid, orange yellow, strongly rugose-tuberculate, dehiscent, 7–25cm; seeds sculptured, to 11×6×4mm, with grooved margins, embedded in red pulp. Tropics, introduced to Americas.

M.cochinchinensis (Lour.) Spreng. SPINY BITTER CUCUMBER.
Climbing annual. Leaves orbicular, 3–10cm across, cordate, glabrous, lobes 5–9, deeply divided, acute, apiculate, sometimes obscurely pinnatifid. Flowers solitary; bract entire, inserted half way on peduncle; corolla yellow, lobes to 2cm; ovary fusiform, muricate. Fruit oblong or oval, tapering,

ribbed and warty to subspinose, dehiscent, to 20cm; seeds red. India to Japan and New Guinea.

M.cylindrica L. See *Luffa cylindrica*.

M.foetida Schumacher.
Perennial climber or trailer, to 4.5m, base becoming somewhat woody, Leaves ovate-cordate, simple, apiculate, subentire to dentate, sometimes tomentose on nerves beneath, 1–16 × 1–17cm. Male flowers 1–9 per fascicle; calyx ciliate, dark purple in male; petals caducous, white to pale yellow, obovate, darker with scales at base; ovary ovoid, beaked, softly papillose-spinose. Fruit ellipsoid, softly spiny, to 1.5cm; seeds brown, oblong, about 10×6×3mm. Tropical Africa and America.

M.involucrata E. Mey.
Climber. Stems glabrous. Tendrils simple. Leaves palmate, glabrous, lobes 5, dentate, teeth obtuse, to 2.5cm, mucronate. Flowers solitary; bracteole reniform, entire, to 1cm across, inserted near flower; sepals obtuse-orbicular, about 5mm; petals at least 1cm; stamens 3, free, anthers coherent. Fruit globose-ovoid, attenuate, rugose, orange, about 3cm diam. S Africa.

M.lanata Thunb. See *Citrullus lanatus*.
M.operculata L. See *Luffa operculata*.

M.rostrata Zimm.
Perennial climber; rootstock tuberous. Stems to 7m with pubescent tufts at nodes, becoming woody. Leaves compound, pedate, biternate; leaflets usually 9, elliptic to suborbicular, serrate or dentate, to 5 × 3cm. Male inflorescence subumbellate; female flowers subsessile, solitary, occasionally paired; bract white-pubescent, to 1×1.2cm, usually much smaller, especially female; pedicel white-pubescent; calyx lobes subtriangular; petals oblong-ligulate, to 1.3 × 0.8mm, orange-yellow, darker with 2 scales toward base; stamens 3; ovary slightly ridged. Fruit ovoid, beaked, slightly ridged, scarlet; seeds coated with yellow pulp. E Africa.

Monstera Adans. (From Lat. *monstrum*, a marvel, or *monster*, possibly alluding to curious shape of leaves.) SWISS-CHEESE PLANT; WINDOWLEAF. Araceae. 22 evergreen, epiphytic, perennial lianes, to 20m+. Aerial roots often present, long, corky, negatively phototropic. Stems thick, ascending or sprawling. Leaves in 2 ranks, dimorphic with juvenile and adult phases; juvenile foliage often entire, sometimes overlapping, and held close to tree-trunk, when known as shingle plants (also occurring in other genera of Araceae, as well as other families); adult leaves to 90 × 75cm, entire or pinnatifid, more or less oblong, unequal, often perforated, coriaceous, bright to dark green; petioles long, exceeding lamina, pulvinate at apex, sheathing below. Peduncle short; spathe large, to 45cm, cymbiform, deciduous, usually white or cream; spadix densely covered by hermaphrodite flowers, shorter than spathe; perianth absent; stamens 4; ovary 2-locular, ovules 2 per locule; sterile flowers sometimes present among others, with rudimentary parts. Fruit cone-shaped, composed of tightly packed white berries, sometimes edible when mature, aromatic; seeds soft. Tropical America.

CULTIVATION　*Monstera* species are usually vining climbers of humid tropical America, found scrambling up tall trees. In temperate zones, they are most commonly grown as houseplants, or in hot glasshouses. Under such conditions, poles of sphagnum moss are often provided in imitation of natural hosts, dampened to improve atmospheric humidity and to provide a moist medium for the running aerial roots. Species such as *M.standleyana* are thicker-stemmed and mounding in habit, and will often grow without support. If the necessary draught-free conditions of filtered light and high humidity are not provided, the leaf perforations typical of well grown adult specimens of many species may fail to develop. Too much or too little water will cause rapid leaf yellowing. Plants benefit from frequent sponging of leaves to remove dust.

M.deliciosa, that most popular of houseplants, was once grown in English hothouses for its large, cone-shaped compound fruit, known as ceriman, with a flavour described as somewhere between a pineapple and a banana. The fruits are consumed when completely ripe and are used in fruit salad and for drinks and ices. Fruit is produced only under perfect growing conditions, in a warm moist climate, and plants fruit better when allowed to sprawl along the ground. In the US, vines are cultivated in Florida, under half shade.

Propagate from seed, which must not be allowed to dry out; by internodal cuttings, or from cuttings made from growing tips with one leaf attached, rooted with bottom heat in a sandy propagating mix. Alternatively, propagate by air-layering.

Cultivation otherwise as for *Philodendron*.

M.acuminata K. Koch. SHINGLE PLANT.
Stems flattened. Leaves to 28 × 13cm, ovate (overlapping and pressed to support in juveniles), very unequal, base cordate, entire or pinnatifid with 1–2 segments to 5cm wide, coriaceous; petioles to 15cm, sheath broad, membranous, persistent. Peduncle to 5cm; spathe to 7.5cm, spadix 5cm, oblong-ovate. C America.

M.adansonii Schott (*M.pertusa* (L.) De Vriese, non Schott).
To 8m. Leaves to 90 × 25cm, ovate to oblong-ovate or -elliptic, very unequal, larger half rotund-truncate at base, other half subcuneate, perforations irregular, large, elliptic-oblong, in single series on one or both sides of midrib, seldom breaking margin; petioles shorter than lamina, sheath extending to pulvinus, green, persistent. Spathe to 20cm, white, spadix to 10cm, slender. Northern S America. var. **laniata** (Schott) Madison. Leaves 22–55 × 15–40cm, ovate, membranous with many perforations; petiole sheathe deciduous. Spadix to 13×2cm, yellow. Costa Rica to Brazil.

M.deliciosa Liebm. (*Philodendron pertusum* Kunth & Bouché). CERIMAN; SWISS CHEESE PLANT.
To 20m. Stems stout, climbing or sprawling; aerial roots present, long. Leaves 25–90 × 25–75cm, orbicular-ovate, cordate, entire when juvenile, regularly pinnatifid to halfway to midrib when adult, segments curved, oblong, with one vein, also usually perforate with elliptic to oblong holes between base of marginal perforation and midrib, coriaceous, glossy dark green, veins paler green; petioles equalling or exceeding lamina, sheath becoming scarious, deciduous, pulvinus flattened, winged. Spathe to 30cm, cream, persistent; spadix to 25 × 3cm, swelling in fruit, cream-coloured, aromatic and tasting of banana and pineapple when mature. Mexico to Panama. 'Albovariegata': leaves large, partly rich deep green with other sections a contrasting creamy-white. 'Variegata': leaves and stems irregularly variegated cream or yellow.

M.dubia (HBK) Engl. & K. Krause.
Adult leaves to 130 × 60cm, oblong, base truncate, regularly pinnatisect, segments 12–20, linear; juvenile forms shingle plant, with leaves silver-variegated. Petioles to 45cm, sheath deciduous. Spathe large, white; spadix to 42.5cm, white. C America (Nicaragua, Costa Rica).

M.epipremnoides Engl. (*M.leichtlinii* hort.).
Large climber. Adult leaves to 90 × 55cm, ovate- to oblong-elliptic, base truncate or weakly cordate, pinnatifid, segments to 3.5cm across, perforate with 2–3 ranks of elliptic to linear-oblong holes, outermost holes large, reaching or cutting margin; juvenile leaves broad-ovate, smaller; petioles sheathing nearly to pulvinus, sheath persistent, expanded at apex. Spathe to 40cm, white, spadix to 19cm. Costa Rica.

M.falcifolia Engl. See *M.obliqua*.
M.guttifera hort. See *M.standleyana*.

M.karwinskyi Schott.
Stems to 4m+. Leaves 55–85 × 33–55cm, entire, ovate to oblong-elliptic, base truncate, coriaceous, perforate with 1 narrow-oblong hole between main lateral veins; petioles to 55cm, sheathed to pulvinus, sheath soon becoming scarious, deciduous. Spathe green externally, white within; spadix to 14cm, shorter than spathe, thick, cream-coloured. Tropical Mexico.

M.latiloba K. Krause. See *M.subpinnata*.
M.leichtlinii hort. See *M.epipremnoides*.
M.nechodomii hort. See *Epipremnum pinnatum*.

M.obliqua (Miq.) Walp. (*M.falcifolia* Engl.).
Plant small, stems climbing. Leaves to 20×7cm, entire, elliptic to oblong-lanceolate, sometimes much-perforated, with holes covering more area than laminal tissue, or not perforate, bright green. Peduncle to 7.5cm; spathe short, spadix to 3.5cm, with few flowers. Northern S America.

M.pertusa (L.) De Vriese, non Schott. See *M.adansonii*.

M.punctulata Schott.
Resembling *M.deliciosa* but leaves 120 × 60cm, ovate- to oblong-elliptic, petioles closely white-spotted, pulvinus subcylindric; scarious cataphylls persistent on stem; juvenile phase a shingle plant, leaves ovate, base oblique. Spathe to 14cm, pink-buff externally, white within. Tropical Mexico.

M.standleyana Bunting (*M.guttifera* hort.; *Philodendron guttiferum* hort. non Kunth).
Juvenile phase with slender stems; leaves to 20×5cm, narrow-oblong-lanceolate, main lateral veins emerging from midrib at acute angle; petioles to 12.5 × 1.5cm. Adult stems stout, leaves to 60 × 33cm, entire, oblong-ovate, base obtuse, not perforate, very dark green, lateral veins prominent beneath; petioles 50cm, broadly winged. Peduncle to 30cm; spathe 28cm, cream-coloured; spadix 15cm, cream. Costa Rica.

M.subpinnata (Schott) Engl. (*M.latiloba* K. Krause; *M.uleana* Engl.; *Rhaphidophora laciniosa* hort.).
Leaves to 33cm, orbicular-ovate, pinnatifid with 3–4 pairs of widely separated narrowly oblanceolate segments, each 15 × 2.5cm, with 1 main lateral vein and several parallel subsidiary veins; petiole to 25cm, sheath deciduous. Spathe to 15cm, dull yellow, spadix to 10cm. Peru.

M.uleana Engl. See *M.subpinnata*.

Morinda L. (From Gk *moron*, mulberry, and *inda*, Indian.) INDIAN MULBERRY. Rubiaceae. Some 80 species of shrubs, erect or climbing, or trees. Stems usually glabrous; branches and branchlets terete or 4-angled. Leaves opposite or, rarely, in whorls of 3; stipules united at base, occasionally sheathing with petioles. Flowers hermaphrodite or polygamo-dioecious, long- or short-peduncled or, rarely, sessile, axillary or terminal in dense, often paniculate or umbellate clusters, often united by calyces; calyx tube obovoid or urn-shaped or hemispheric, limb truncate or minutely toothed; corolla tube funnel- or salver-shaped, white or red, lobes 4–7, usually 5, valvate in bud, leathery; stamens 4–7, usually 5, inserted in tube or at throat of corolla, anthers dorsifixed, included or exserted, usually oblong or linear; ovary 2–4-celled (occasionally spuriously), style included or exserted, 2-branched or, rarely, entire; ovules solitary in each cell. Fruit a syncarp, fleshy; pyrenes many, 1-seeded, hard; seeds obovoid or reniform. Tropics.

CULTIVATION   Commonly called 'Indian mulberry', a reference to the resemblance of the aggregated fruits to mulberries, *Morinda* is grown for its dense clusters of creamy or reddish coloured flowers. Cultivate as for *Mussaenda*.

M.umbellata L. (*M.royoc* hort.).
Shrub, erect or trailing or climbing, divaricately branched, to 1m or, when vine-like, 6m high. Branches terete, glabrous or pubescent at first. Leaves to 10×5cm or more, oblong to elliptic, acute at apex, narrowed or acute or obtuse at base, occasionally membranous, glabrous or pubescent beneath, veins 5–6, conspicuous; petioles to 1cm; stipules acute, united or sheathing. Flowers in terminal, umbellate heads; peduncles to 10, to 4cm, glabrous or pubescent; corolla rotate, to 6mm, hairy at throat. Fruit globose, to 1.2cm wide, orange-red. Tropical Asia, Australia.

Mucuna Adans. (Brazilian name for these plants.) Leguminosae (Papilionoideae). Some 100 species of woody lianes, climbing herbs and erect shrubs. Leaves trifoliolate; leaflets stalked; stipules caducous; stipels frequently present. Flowers papilionaceous, large in axillary clusters or racemes, sometimes long-peduncled and pendulous; calyx bilabiate, lobes 4–5, upper pair united; standard rounded, exceeded by other petals, keel hardened at apex, sharply beaked; ovary sessile, ovules few to several; style filiform, stigma tiny, terminal; stamens 10, vexillary stamen free, anthers 2 types, 5 larger, glabrous, basifixed, alternate with 5 shorter, versatile, filaments distended at apex. Fruit ovoid, torulose to linear, often sharply bristly or velvety (causing irritation), thick, usually dehiscent; seeds oblong or spherical, with a hilum and rim-aril, or a longer hilum and no aril. Widespread in the tropics and subtropics of both hemispheres. Z10.

CULTIVATION   *M.bennettii* and *M.novoguineensis* are spectacular flame-flowered climbers for the warm glasshouse or tropical gardens, the first with short, drooping racemes, the second with very long, packed, cylindrical racemes of sharp-beaked flowers. Their cultural requirements are as for *Strongylodon*. *M.pruriens* and *M.sempervirens* are less showy, more intriguing, with racemes and clusters respectively of purple-black or mauve to white flowers. In zones lower than 9, they perform best in cool glasshouses and conservatories, but they might be attempted outdoors in favoured regions, treatment as for the hardier *Millettia* species.

M.aterrima (Piper & Tracy) Holland. See *M.pruriens* var. *utilis*.

M.bennettii F. Muell. NEW GUINEA CREEPER.
Woody climber to 20m. Stems rugose, mostly glabrous. Leaflets 11–13.5×5–7.5cm, elliptic, apex acute, base rounded, glabrous. Flowers to 8.5cm, vivid scarlet or flame-coloured, in a short inflorescence; calyx orange, pubescent and setose, tube 8–10×20mm; keel curved, 11mm diam. New Guinea. Z10.

M.cochinchinensis (Lour.) A. Chev. See *M.pruriens*.
M.deeringiana (Bort) Merrill. See *M.pruriens* var. *utilis*.
M.kraetkei Warb. See *M.novoguineensis*.
M.nivea DC. See *M.pruriens*.

M.novoguineensis R. Scheff. (*M.kraetkei* Warb.).
Liane to 30m; stems to 5cm diam., initially densely hirsute, later glabrous. Leaflets 10–19×8.5–13.5cm, elliptic, glabrous or pubescent throughout. Flowers 5–8cm, flame-coloured to scarlet, in pendulous, conical inflorescence 7–60cm long; calyx 6–13×9–22mm diam., yellow-hued, red-brown, pubescent; keel 4–7mm diam., strongly curved. New Guinea. Z10.

M.pruriens (L.) DC. (*M.cochinchinensis* (Lour.) A. Chev.; *M.nivea* DC.). VELVET BEAN.
Semi-woody, climbing herb, short-lived perennial or annual, to 4m. Stems rugose, initially thickly hirsute, later glabrous. Leaflets 5–19×3.5–17cm, ovate, obovate, rhomboid or elliptic, grey-hirsute. Racemes to 30cm; flowers 3–4cm, damson to pale purple or white; keel 2.8–4cm. Fruit 5–9×0.8–2×0.5cm, oblong, thickly amber- or brown-setose or velutinous, sometimes rugose. Asia; naturalized elsewhere. var. *utilis* (Wallich ex Wight) Bak. ex Burck. (*M.aterrima* (Piper & Tracy) Holland; *M.deeringiana* (Bort) Merrill). VELVET BEAN; FLORIDA BEAN; BENGHAL BEAN. Racemes to 30cm, pendulous; standard purple flushed green, wings dirty red. Fruit darkly velutinous. Z8.

M.sempervirens Hemsl.
Vigorous evergreen climber to 12m. Leaves prominently reticulate-veined; terminal leaflet to 12cm. Flowers waxy, bruised purple-black, malodorous, in short nodding racemes, often several from one axil on old wood; keel 6–8cm, strongly curved. Fruit to 30cm, velutinous. Spring. China (W Hubei, Sichuan). Z8.

Muehlenbeckia Meissn. (For H.G. Muehlenbeck (1798–1845), Swiss physician and student of the flora of Alsace.) Polygonaceae. 15 species of largely dioecious, evergreen climbing or procumbent subshrubs and shrubs. Stems initially robust, erect or stoloniferous, simple, later densely branched with dark, slender, interlacing branchlets. Leaves small, alternate, occasionally absent; stipules sheathing. Flowers minute, fertile and unisexual flowers sometimes produced on same plant, axillary or terminal and clustered, white-green; perianth deeply 5-lobed; stamens 8; styles 3; ovary 3-angled. Fruit a 3-angled achene, surrounded by enlarged fleshy perianth, white. S America, New Zealand, Australia, New Guinea.

CULTIVATION Grown for their intricate habit, minute foliage and small but very sweetly fragrant flowers, *Muehlenbeckia* species are suitable for covering tree stumps and rocky banks, or for scrambling through shrubs. *M.complexa* is also amenable to hanging basket cultivation, forming a mass of intricately tangled dark wiry stems if unsupported and bearing fleshy white fruits where plants of both genders are grown together. This species is sometimes treated as a standard, grown on without support in open beds to promote a number of long stems, then potted in tubs of rich loamy soil with these stems gathered and tied to a stout central cane. Plants grown in this way produce a weeping crown of fine branchlets which contrast superbly with underplanted half-hardy bedding plants such as white marguerites, Senecios and variegated grasses. Despite its delicate appearance, *M.complexa* can match other climbing Polygonaceae in vigour when grown in warmer climates and has become a troublesome invader in parts of California.

Given a position sheltered from cold, drying winds, *M.axillaris* will tolerate temperatures of −15°C/5°F and below. With the exceptions of *M.adpressa* and *M.gunnii*, which require cool glasshouse protection (5°C/40°F) in cool temperate zones, the remaining species show similar cold-tolerance. Grow in well drained soil in sun to part shade. Prune only to restrict to allotted space. Propagate by semi-ripe cuttings in summer, or by seed, *M.axillaris* also by division.

M.adpressa (Labill.) Meissn.
Spreading or climbing shrub, often twining over other plants, to 2m, glabrous. Leaves orbicular to ovate, cordate at base, 1–6cm, margins minutely crisped. Flowers in axillary racemes, 2.5–8cm; perianth segments 2.5–3mm. Fruit perianth enclosing 3-angled ovoid achene. Australia. Z9.

M.adpressa var. *hastata* Meissn. See *M.gunnii*.

M.australis (Forst. f.) Meissn.
Stout vine to 10m; stems much-branched, interlacing, branchlets slender. Leaves ovate to nearly orbicular, 2–8×1–3cm. Flowers 4–5mm diam., in branched panicles to 5cm, tinged green. Fruit glossy, black. Summer–early autumn. New Zealand. Z8.

M.axillaris (Hook. f.) Walp. (*M.nana* Thurst.).
Small deciduous prostrate or straggling shrub, forming clumps to 1m across, stems and branches rooting at nodes, shoots thin, wiry, gold to black, finely grey-pubescent. Leaves 0.5–1 × 0.3–0.6cm oblong to nearly orbicular, glabrous, dark green above, ashy grey beneath. Flowers 1 or 2 in leaf axils, to 4mm diam., yellow-green. Fruit 3mm, glossy, black. Summer–early autumn. Australia, Tasmania, New Zealand. Z8.

M.complexa (Cunn.) Meissn. MAIDENHAIR VINE; WIRE VINE; MATTRESS VINE; NECKLACE VINE.
Deciduous liane, creeping or climbing to 5m; stems interlaced forming dense tangles without support, branchlets slender, wiry, soft, gold-red, white-pubescent when young, later brittle, red-brown to grey-black. Leaves 0.5–2cm, bright green above, purple or silver beneath, variable on same plant, oblong to circular or pandurate, rounded or cordate at base, glabrous. Flowers small, green-white, in axillary or terminal 2.5–3cm spikes. Fruit 2–2.5mm, black, enclosed in fleshy

white cup of perianth. Summer. New Zealand. 'Nana': dwarf; leaves pandurate. var.*microphylla* (Colenso) Ckn. Dense shrub to 60cm. Leaves sparse, rounded, small. var.*triloba* (Colenso) Cheesem.(*M.triloba* Colenso; *M.varians* Meissn.). Leaves deeply pandurately lobed.

M.ephedroides Hook.f.
Prostrate to sprawling shrub, forming a thicket; stems to 1m, rush-like, deeply grooved, glabrous. Leaves linear to sagittate, 0.8–2.5cm, often absent, dark to grey-green. Flowers in small axillary clusters or small spikes, occasionally with a few fertile flowers; perianth segments 2–3.5mm, narrow-triangular. Fruit 3 × 1.5mm, shiny black. Summer. New Zealand. var. *muriculata* (Colenso) Cheesem. (*M.muriculata* Colenso). Small shrub. Stems very slender, almost thread-like. Leaves smaller than type, 0.3–1.2cm. Perianth segments becoming membranous in fruit. Z8.

M.gunnii (Hook. f.) Walp. (*M.adpressa* var. *hastata* Meissn.).
Climbing shrub, resembling *M.adpressa* but stems to 10m; leaves broadly lanceolate-hastate, acute or short-acuminate, 3–8×1–3cm. Perianth segments 4–5mm. Fruit ovoid-oblong, 5mm. Australia. Z9.

M.muriculata Colenso. See *M.ephedroides* var. *muriculata*.
M.nana Thurst. See *M.axillaris*.

M.sagittifolia (Ortega) Meissn.
Liane or climbing shrub. Leaves variable, sagittate or lanceolate, acuminate, 4–9×1.5–2.5cm, upper leaves narrow, linear. Flowers in a slender raceme, white-green, resembling those of *M.complexa*; perianth segments reflexed. Fruit 3–4mm. Summer. S America (Brazil, Paraguay, Uruguay). Z9.

M.triloba Colenso. See *M.complexa* var. *triloba*.
M.varians Meissn. See *M.complexa* var. *triloba*.

Mukia Arn. Cucurbitaceae. 4 species of monoecious climbers. Stems hispid, becoming somewhat woody at base. Tendrils simple. Leaves palmate, ovate to cordate, triangular, petiolate. Inflorescence a sessile cluster; flowers small, unisexual, yellow, subsessile or pedicellate; calyx campanulate, lobed; petals joined at base; male flowers with 3 stamens inserted on calyx and an elevated disc; female flowers sometimes solitary; stigmas 2–3; ovary ellipsoid or globose; staminodes present or absent; disc annular. Fruit a berry, small, subsessile, ellipsoid to globose, sometimes hispid at first, red when ripe, smooth; seeds small, subelliptic, margins raised. Old World Tropics. Z9.

CULTIVATION As for *Momordica*.

M.maderaspatana (L.) Roem. (*Cucumis maderaspatanus L.*).
Perennial climber or trailer to 3m. Rootstock woody. Stems bristly. Leaves ovate, hastate, usually cordate, sometimes dentate or lobulate, 1.5–11 × 1.5–11cm, midlobe triangular, lateral lobes ovate-triangular; petiole rough-pubescent, to 8cm. Flowers pedicellate; calyx to 2cm, lobes 1mm; petals about 2 ×1mm, yellow; ovary green, globose, slightly beaked, bristly. Fruits subsessile, in clusters, scarlet, glabrous, smooth; seeds ovate. Spring–late summer. Africa, India to China and Malaysia, Australia.

Mussaenda L. (From the Sri Lankan name.) Rubiaceae. Some 100 species of shrubs, subshrubs and herbs, sometimes loosely twining. Stems erect or climbing, branched, terete. Leaves ovate or elliptic to oblong, apex more or less acute, subsessile or petiolate, opposite or 3-whorled, membranous, glabrous or pubescent; stipules interpetiolar, persistent or deciduous, truncate or 2-lobed, occasionally connate. Flowers pedicellate in axillary or terminal, few- to many-flowered panicles or cymes; bracts and bracteoles deciduous; calyx tube turbinate to ovoid or oblong, lobes 5, linear or spathulate to lanceolate, often one developed into an enlarged, showy, leaf-shaped limb; corolla tubular to funnelform, tube pubescent at throat, lobes 5, spreading, valvate in bud and often connate, pubescent; stamens 5, attached at throat, anthers dorsifixed, included; style occasionally 2-branched, stigma 2-lobed, included or exserted, ovules many. Fruit a berry, globose to ellipsoid, 2-celled, indehiscent, fleshy, occasionally crowned by persistent calyx limb; seeds many, flat, testa reticulate to spinulose, endosperm fleshy. Tropical Old World. Z10.

CULTIVATION Grown for their colourful enlarged leaf-like sepals, more conspicuous than, but sometimes in vibrant contrast to the flower, as in *M.erythrophylla* with bright red sepals and yellow petal lobes, and *M.frondosa* with orange flowers and white sepals. Hybrids and cultivars such as 'Aurorae' and 'Alicia' with golden flowers and white-veined salmon or brick-red calyx lobes are also available. Grow in the hot glasshouse (min. 16–18°C/60–65°F) in a pH-neutral mix of equal parts loam, peat and leafmould with added sharp sand, with direct sunlight. Water plentifully when in growth, sparingly in winter. Provide support for climbing specimens, and thin out crowded stems or prune to a framework in spring. Propagate from semi-ripe cuttings or air layering in summer, or by seed in spring. Susceptible to attack by white fly. Also by red spider mite.

M.abyssinica Chiov. See *M.arcuata*.

M.albiflora Hayata, non Merrill. See *M.pubescens*.

M.arcuata Poir. (*M.abyssinica* Chiov.).
Shrub, to 7m. Stems erect or climbing, viscid, glabrous or short-pubescent, indistinctly lenticellate. Leaves to 20×10cm, obovate or elliptic to suborbicular, apex narrowly acute to caudate, base obtuse or acute to cuneate, lustrous and leathery glabrous above and sparsely pubescent beneath, 5–7-veined; petioles to 2cm; stipules to 1cm, deciduous, truncate or 2-lobed, glabrous. Flowers yellow, fragrant in loose or dense, few-flowered panicles or cymes; pedicels to 7mm, peduncles to 4cm; bracts to 25×2mm; calyx tube turbinate to ellipsoid, to 4mm, limb deciduous, lobes to 15×3mm, linear or spathulate, margin toothed; corolla tube to 25mm, glabrous or pubescent at throat, lobes to 2×1cm, ovate or elliptic to oblong, apex acute, red stellate-pubescent. Tropical Africa, Madagascar.

M.erythrophylla Schumach. & Thonn.
Shrub, to 8m. Stems erect or climbing, red-pubescent and, occasionally, white-lenticellate. Leaves to 18 × 11cm, ovate or elliptic to suborbicular, apex acute or narrowly acute, base cuneate or obtuse to cordate, pubescent, 7–10-veined; petioles to 5cm; stipules to 1cm, persistent, 2-lobed, pubescent. Flowers in dense, pedunculate panicles or cymes, pink to red and white to yellow or white with a red throat; pedicels to 1cm, peduncles to 3cm, both pubescent; bracts to 2cm, glabrous; calyx tube to 5mm, obovoid, pubescent, limb deciduous, lobes to 2×3mm, lanceolate, enlarged lobes to 6 per inflorescence, ovate to oblong, bright scarlet to deep crimson, pubescent; corolla tube to 3mm, pubescent, lobes to 1 × 1cm, partially connate, orbicular, apex obtuse, glabrous or pubescent. Tropical Africa. 'Queen Sirikit': branches drooping; leaves broad, wavy; valyx lobes deep pink to ivory.

M.formosa Jacq. See *Randia formosa*.

M.frondosa L. WHITE FLAG BUSH.
Shrub, to 3m. Stems erect, glabrous or pubescent to tomentose. Leaves to 15cm, ovate, lanceolate or elliptic to oblong, apex narrowly acute, tomentose beneath, sessile or petiolate; stipules to 6mm, 2-lobed. Flowers yellow in dense, terminal corymbs; calyx to 2cm, enlarged lobe to 5cm, white; corolla funnel-shaped, tube to 25mm, pubescent, lobes ovate, apex acute or narrowly acute. Summer–autumn. Tropical Asia (Indochina to Malaysia).

M.glabra Vahl. COMMON MUSSAENDA.
Shrub, to 3m. Stems ascending to diffuse, more or less glabrous, lenticellate. Leaves to 15×8cm, oblong to lanceolate or elliptic, apex narrowly acute, base attenuate, lustrous and leathery, sparsely pubescent on veins beneath, 5–6-veined;

short-petiolate; stipules truncate to 2-lobed, lanceolate, apex acute. Flowers in terminal, branched, many-flowered cymes, orange to red; bracts persistent, lanceolate, apex subulate; calyx to 6mm, tube campanulate, limb deciduous, lobes lanceolate, apex subulate, developed lobe to 10cm, white, apex acute, base obtuse, glabrous; corolla tube to 25mm, glabrous or pubescent, apex of lobes acute. Tropical Asia (India to Malaysia).

M.incana Wallich.
Shrub, to 1m. Stems erect sometimes sprawling, simple or branched, pubescent. Leaves to 15×8cm, ovate or elliptic to oblong, apex acute or subacute, base acute or obtuse, rigid, pubescent, 9–10-veined, subsessile to short-petiolate; stipules 2-lobed, apex attenuate. Flowers in subsessile corymbs, chrome yellow; calyx lobes filiform, developed lobe to 7cm, pubescent, white to cream or yellow; corolla to 2cm, lobes ovate, apex narrowly acute.   Tropical Asia (India to Malaysia).

M.kotoensis Hayata. See *M.macrophylla*.

M.macrophylla Wallich (*M.kotoensis* Hayata).
Shrub, to 2m. Stems climbing, simple, sparsely pubescent Leaves to 25 × 10cm, ovate to oblong, apex acute to narrowly acute, base obtuse or acute to cuneate, sparsely pubescent on veins; petioles to 4cm; stipules 2-lobed, deltoid. Flowers orange in dense, short-stalked, terminal cymes; calyx tube to 2mm, limb deciduous, lobes lanceolate to oblanceolate, apex obtuse, developed lobe to 12cm, rhomboid, white to yellow; corolla to 3cm, tube pubescent, lobes orbicular. Summer. Tropical Asia (India to Taiwan, Malaysia, Philippines).

M.parviflora Kanehira, non Miq. See *M.pubescens*.

M.pubescens Ait. f. (*M.albiflora* Hayata, non Merrill; *M.parviflora* Kanehira, non Miq.).
Shrub to 2m. Stems erect to climbing, pubescent Leaves to 8×4cm or more, ovate or elliptic to oblong, apex acute to narrowly acute, base acute or obtuse, papery, pubescent, short-petiolate; stipules to 1cm, 2-lobed, connate at base, deltoid or lanceolate to linear. Flowers yellow in dense, terminal cymes or corymbs; bracts linear; calyx tube to 3mm, pubescent, lobes to 6mm, erect, linear, pubesc., developed lobe to 9×5cm, ovate to elliptic, white; corolla tube to 3cm, pubescent, lobes to 6mm, ovate to deltoid or lanceolate, apex narrowly acute, pubescent. Tropical Asia (China, Taiwan). Often confused in cultivation with *M.frondosa*.

M.roxburghii Hook. f.
Shrub to 4m. Stems erect to scrambling, pubescent. Leaves to 30 × 5cm, lanceolate or elliptic to oblong, apex narrowly acute to caudate, base attenuate, membranous, glabrous to pubescent beneath, 8–10-veined; petioles to 2.5cm; stipules

deltoid to lanceolate. Flowers in dense, many-flowered cymes or corymbs; calyx limb persistent, lobes filiform, pubescent, developed lobe to 7cm, glabrous, white; corolla tube to 2cm, silky, lobes filiform, pubescent. Tropical Asia (Himalaya).

M.sanderiana Ridl.
Shrub, to 2m. Stems erect to creeping. Leaves lanceolate, base cordate, sericeous, subsessile. Flowers in terminal cymes, yellow; developed lobe to 8cm, white, sericeous; corolla tubular. Tropical Asia (Indochina).

For illustration see Rubiaceae.

Mutisia L. f. (For José Celestino Mutis of Cadiz (1732–1808), teacher of anatomy and student of South American plants.) Compositae. About 60 species of glabrous to tomentose subshrubs or shrubs, many of them sprawling or twining. Leaves alternate, simple or pinnate, often terminating in a tendril. Capitula radiate, medium to large, terminal, solitary, pedunculate, erect to pendulous; receptacle flat to convex; involucre cylindric to oblong-campanulate; phyllaries imbricate, in several rows, broadly lanceolate, often with leafy appendage; ray florets few, female, purple, rose, yellow, scarlet or orange, rarely white; disc florets numerous, hermaphrodite, fertile or sterile, usually yellow. Fruit a cylindric-fusiform to turbinate, glabrous cypsela; pappus of long, stiff, plumose, tawny or white bristles. S America. Z9 unless specified.

CULTIVATION Showy, semi-woody scramblers and twiners with brilliantly coloured, daisy-like flowers. Given the protection of a south- or southwest-facing wall and good drainage, *M.oligodon* will tolerate temperatures to about −15°C/5°F and *M.decurrens* to about −10°C/14°F; *M.clematis*, *M.ilicifolia*, *M.spinosa* var. *pulchella* and *M.subulata* are almost as hardy. Grow in deep, well drained, moderately fertile soils, in a position with shade at the roots but where top growth will receive full sun; a large rock or deep organic mulch placed over the roots will provide the necessary protection and help conserve moisture in growth. Provide support by means of wire or trellis, or plant at the foot of a wall shrub in a sheltered, sunny position. Under glass, water moderately when in growth, maintain good ventilation with a minimum winter temperature of 7–10°C/40–50°F. Prune to remove weak and overcrowded growth after flowering or in spring in cool climates. Propagate by stem cuttings in summer, rooted in sand in a closed case with gentle bottom heat, by simple layering, or by removal of suckers in species like *M.decurrens*. Also by seed in spring.

M.acuminata Ruiz & Pav. (*M.viciifolia* Cav.).
Much-branched shrub to 1m; branches flexuous. Leaves 8–10cm, pinnatisect, terminating in a trifid tendril; leaflets to 4×1cm in 9–14 pairs, opposite or alternate, elliptic-lanceolate, acuminate, base decurrent, glabrous. Capitula on peduncles to 12cm; involucre cylindric; phyllaries in 6–7 series, ovate to oblong, innermost to 5cm, outer much shorter, grey, tinged red; ray florets 5–8, bright red or scarlet. Fruit to 2cm; pappus to 2cm. Andes (Peru to Bolivia).

M.arachnoidea Mart. ex D. Don. See *M.speciosa*.
M.breviflora Philippi. See *M.ilicifolia*.

M.clematis L. f.
Liane to 10m; branches angular, minutely tomentose at first. Leaves 5–10cm, pinnate; with a long, trifid, terminal tendril; leaflets to 7×3cm, in 4–5 pairs, lowermost reduced to stipules, otherwise opposite, elliptic, tomentose beneath and sometimes also above. Capitula to 6cm diam., pendulous, shortly pedunculate; involucre campanulate; phyllaries in 4–5 series, lanceolate, acute, inner to 4.5cm, outer shortest; ray florets 9–10, bright orange to scarlet or maroon. Fruits 1.5cm; pappus to 1.7cm. Summer–autumn. N Andes (C Colombia and Ecuador).

M.decurrens Cav.
Much-branched, rhizomatous subshrub to 2m. Leaves to 10× 2cm, lanceolate, sessile, acute at apex with long, bifid, terminal tendril, decurrent at base, entire or sharp-toothed, main vein prominent. Capitula to 12cm diam., on peduncles to 10cm; involucre campanulate; phyllaries in 4–5 series, outer *c*1cm, broadly oval, with short linear appendage, inner to 3.5cm, oblong-ovate, acute; ray florets 10–15, brilliant orange. Fruit to 1cm; pappus to 2.5cm, plumose. Summer. S Andes (Chile, Argentina). Z8.

M.ilicifolia Cav. (*M.breviflora* Philippi).
Branched shrub usually climbing to 3m; branches glabrous or somewhat lanate above. Leaves to 6×4cm, ovate to ovate-elliptic, sessile, with a long, simple, terminal tendril, base cordate and semi-amplexicaul, margin spinose-dentate with 10–12 pairs of triangular teeth, subcoriaceous, glabrous above, tomentose or glabrescent beneath. Capitula 2–3cm diam., on peduncles to 4cm; involucre campanulate; phyllar-

ies in 5–6 series, outer reduced to an acute, lanceolate appendage, to 13mm, densely tomentose below, middle almost semicircular with lanceolate appendage, inner broadly oblong-ovate, to 1.5cm, somewhat tomentose near apex, otherwise glabrous; ray florets *c*8, pale pink. Fruit to 1cm, cylindric-fusiform; pappus to 1.8cm, off-white. Chile.

M.latifolia D. Don.
Shrub to 1.5m; branches 2–3-winged, ascending or sprawling, densely leafy. Leaves to 5.5×3.5cm, ovate or elliptic, sessile, apex truncate, base cordate and semi-amplexicaul, spinose-dentate with 10–15 pairs of teeth each side, midrib conspicuously prolonged into a terminal tendril, subcoriaceous, tomentose or glabrescent above, densely tomentose or occasionally subglabrous beneath. Capitula to 7.5cm diam., on peduncles to 4cm; involucre campanulate; phyllaries in 5–7 series, outer broadly ovate-lanceolate, to 1.5cm, acute, tomentose on back, middle semicircular with ovate-lanceolate appendage, inner broadly elliptic, to 2cm, without appendage, glabrous; ray florets 10–15, lilac or deep rose. Fruit glabrous; pappus to 1.8cm, dusky white. Autumn. C Chile.

M.linearifolia Cav.
Dwarf creeping shrub to 30cm; branches densely leafy, ribbed. Leaves to 3×0.5cm, linear, sessile and decurrent, acute and shortly mucronate, entire, strongly revolute, glabrous. Capitula to 6cm diam., shortly pedunculate; involucre campanulate; phyllaries in 4–5 series, ovate to elliptic, shortly mucronate, outer to 0.5cm, occasionally suborbicular, inner to 2cm, tinged red; ray florets 8–10, red. Fruit striate; pappus to 2.5cm, white to pale grey. S Andes (N Argentina, C Chile).

M.oligodon Poepp. & Endl.
Straggling shrub or liane to 1m, decumbent or ascending; branches gently undulate. Leaves to 3.5×1.5cm, oblong to elliptic, acute or obtuse, sessile, base cordate, usually remotely 1–2-dentate near apex, upper leaves few, terminating in a tendril, glabrous above, densely tomentose beneath. Capitula to 7cm diam. on peduncles to 5cm; involucre campanulate; phyllaries in 5–6 series, outer shortest, semicircular with a lanceolate, reflexed and semi-amplexicaul, apical appendage, inner oblong, to 2cm, obtuse; ray florets *c*10, bright red. Fruit 12–14mm, cylindric, somewhat tapered to apex; pappus 18mm, off-white. S Chile, S Argentina.

M.pulchella Speg. See *M.spinosa* var. *pulchella*.
M.retusa Rémy. See *M.spinosa* var. *pulchella*.

M.sinuata Cav.
Low shrub to 30cm, often creeping; branches flexuous, narrowly winged. Leaves close-set, to 3×0.6cm, lanceolate, sessile, acute, base attenuate and decurrent, margins revolute, with 6–8 triangular teeth, glabrous above, minutely tomentose or glabrescent beneath, upper leaves usually terminating in a simple tendril. Capitula to 5cm diam., shortly pedunculate; involucre campanulate; phyllaries in 4–5 series, broadly ovate to oblong, outer to 1cm with a lanceolate terminal appendage, inner minutely mucronate; ray florets 8–10, to 2cm, white to light yellow above, pink or grey below. Fruit cylindric-fusiform, to 15mm; pappus to 15mm, white. S Andes (C Chile and Argentina).

M.speciosa Ait. (*M.arachnoidea* Mart. ex D. Don).
Shrub to 6m; branches prominently ribbed, occasionally narrowly winged. Leaves 4–12cm, pinnate, terminating in a trifid tendril, leaflets in 4–7 pairs, opposite or alternate, lanceolate, generally acute, base cuneate, lowermost leaflets reduced. Capitula to 8cm diam., usually on peduncles to 1.5cm; involucre campanulate; phyllaries in 5–7 series, ovate-lanceolate, outer recurved, inner mucronate; ray florets 13–20, pink to red. Fruit 2.5cm, cylindric-fusiform, glabrous; pappus to 2.5cm, white. Andes of Ecuador, S Brazil.

M.spinosa Ruiz & Pav.
Liane to 6m; young branches spinose-winged. Leaves to 6× 3.5cm, elliptic to ovate-elliptic, sessile, base cordate and semi-amplexicaul, usually entire or with 1–2 pairs of spinose teeth near apex, terminating in a long simple tendril, glabrous above, sparsely lanate or glabrous beneath. Capitula to 6cm diam., on peduncles to 8cm; involucre campanulate; phyllaries in 5 series, outer semicircular, with a linear-lanceolate, generally reflexed, apical appendage, inner to 1.5cm, oblong; ray florets 8–10, pale pink. Fruit to 1.5cm, cylindric, somewhat attenuate toward apex; pappus 2cm, white, tinged grey. S Argentina, Chile. var. *pulchella* (Speg.) Cabr. (*M.retusa* Rémy; *M.pulchella* Speg.). Leaves persistently white-tomentose beneath.

M.subulata Ruiz & Pav. (*M.versicolor* Philippi).
Low, often creeping shrub to 50cm; stems cylindric, undulate. Leaves to 7×0.1cm, linear-subulate, with apical spine or tendril of variable length, sessile, margin revolute, entire, glabrous. Capitula to 7.5cm diam., shortly pedunculate; involucre cylindric; phyllaries in 7–8 series, outer ovate, to 1cm, with short, linear, apical appendage, inner oblong, to 3cm, obtuse; ray florets *c*10, brilliant red to scarlet. Fruit to 1cm; pappus 2–2.5cm, plumose, white. S Andes (C Chile).

M.versicolor Philippi. See *M.subulata*.
M.viciifolia Cav. See *M.acuminata*.

Naravelia DC. (From a Singalese name.) Ranunculaceae. Some 5 species of woody climbers, closely allied to *Clematis*. Leaves opposite, pinnate, lower leaflets normal, others transformed into tendrils at end of rachis. Flowers actinomorphic, in terminal panicles; calyx of, usually 4, valvate, petaloid sepals, purple-green to yellow; corolla 9–14 staminodes, linear to clavate; stamens numerous. Fruit a narrow achene with plumose style and twisted ovary, sometimes beaked, not twisted. India to Malaysia. Z10.

CULTIVATION   See *Clematopsis*.

N.zeylanica DC. (*Atragene zeylanica* L.).
Climbing shrub. Leaves trifoliolate, lower 2 leaflets ovate, acute, glabrous above, sericeous beneath, 5-veined, entire, or 1–2-toothed, central leaflet transformed to tendril, 3-fid at apex; petiole long. Flowers yellow, sepals ovate-lanceolate, caducous; petals 6–12, linear-spathulate, exceeding sepals. Fruit slightly hairy. Autumn–winter. Tropical India, Malaysia, Sri Lanka.

Neoalsomitra Hutch. (From Gk *neos*, new, and *Alsomitra*, a closely allied genus.) Cucurbitaceae. 12 species of dioecious climbers. Tendrils simple or bifid. Leaves simple or 3–5-foliolate. Male flowers in panicles or loose axillary racemes; peduncles very slender; calyx cup-shaped, lobes 5, oblong to oblong-lanceolate; corolla rotate, deeply 5-lobed, lobes oblong; stamens 5, free, with short filaments, anthers oblong, curved; female flowers in racemes; ovary 1–3-locular, ovules numerous, styles 3–4. Fruit clavate to cylindric, terete to bluntly triangular in section, 3-valved; seeds compressed, wing membranous (if present), with sinuate-tuberculous margin. Indomalaya to Australia and W Pacific. Z10.

CULTIVATION   An unusual tropical Cucurbit with gouty stems; cultivation as for *Trichosanthes*, but with a grittier potting medium and watering and humidity greatly reduced in the colder, darker months.

N.podagrica Steenis.
Stems to 30m, glabrous, base fleshy, thickened, fusiform, to 100×10cm, with hard, green spines 1.5–5cm (adapted leaves) in basal regions; branches also thickened at base. Leaflets obovate, blunt, base cuneate, middle leaflet 6–11×4–7cm, petiolule to 2cm, lateral leaflets 5–10×3–6cm, petiolule to 1.5cm; outermost leaflets smaller, arising from petiolule of lateral leaflets. Male flowers green-yellow, in panicles to 40cm, female flowers on pedicels *c*1mm. Fruit in panicles, tubular to cup-shaped, to 1.5–2cm; seeds flat, 4–5×3–3.5mm, with a delicate wing. S Malaysia.

Nepenthes L. (Name used by Homer, meaning grief-assuaging and applied in ancient times to plants capable of inducing euphoria; it was given to these pitcher plants because of their supposed medicinal properties.) PITCHER PLANT; TROPICAL PITCHER PLANT. Nepenthaceae. 70 species of climbing or scrambling, terrestrial or epiphytic dioecious carnivorous perennial shrubs or semi-woody herbs to 15m. Leaves loosely spiralling, ligulate to lanceolate, entire, coriaceous, with midrib prolonged into clasping tendril terminated by swollen pitcher; petiole distinct, sometimes winged, or absent; pitchers to 35cm, held upright from end of pendulous tendril, hollow and usually containing water, cylindric to rounded, often with unequal sides and sometimes sigmoidally curved, usually green with red spots or suffusion, mouth of pitcher with thickened, ribbed and often colourful rim, the peristome; apex prolonged to form a fixed 'lid' projecting over pitcher-mouth, often brightly coloured and with nectar-secreting glands, acting as insect lure and partial shield against excessive entry of water; 2 wings or ridges present on side of pitcher opposite to insertion of lid, often undulate and usually toothed or fringed. Pitchers often dimorphic depending on location on plant (i.e. equal and borne on basal leaf 'whorls' or slender on scrambling stems); all effective insect traps with complex trapping mechanisms; insects are attracted by bright colours and secretions of lid and peristome, enter pitcher but cannot obtain a grip on smooth waxy surface of upper part of inner wall and fall into the liquid below where death and digestion occur. Inflorescence an ebracteate raceme or thyrse; flowers to 3mm across; regular; sepals 4, in 2 whorls of 2, glandular on inner surface, green, bronze or dull red-brown; corolla absent; stamens 8–25, united in column; ovary inferior, 3–4-locular, ovules many, stigma sessile. Fruit a dehiscent leathery capsule, seeds numerous, usually filiform. Madagascar, Seychelles, Tropical Asia to Australia (northern Queensland). Z10.

CULTIVATION   The evolution of the climbing habit has taken many curious twists and turns, threading itself through most reaches of the plant kingdom. In this volume alone, there can be found climbing cacti, orchids and ferns; at the same time, there are isolated families of perhaps just one or a few genera that have developed exclusively as climbers, but no genus listed here has inspired so much awe and speculation as *Nepenthes*. They are carnivores, scattered over an inexplicably wide range of forest and scrub habitats from tropical Asia to New Caledonia, Madagascar and northern Australia, their long woody stems clambering sometimes to considerable heights and hung with trapping pitchers which develop from the leaf tendrils. The appetite of these remarkable plants and their methods of despatch and digestion are lovingly described by the plant collector Frank Kingdon-Ward in his *Pilgrimage for Plants* (1960):

> Into this pool of Siloam honey-loving creatures slither while trying to obtain free board and lodging; unable to swim or to climb out, they are soon drowned. When they are dead, their soft parts are quickly digested and absorbed. That, in a nutshell, is the whole works; the fantastic pitchers, each an open mouth and a ravenous stomach; the enticing sweetness secreted by the pitcher wall; the water-trap below; the deadly active juices. Once lured into the pitcher, escape is impossible. The trap is very efficient. It is not just a curiosity of nature; it is a living, working organism. The green leaves function in the ordinary way, and manufacture carbohydrates, while the highly specialized pitchers ensure a supply of nitrogen for the manufacture of proteins. (Nitrates are usually absent from the sphagnum, or peaty marshes, in which pitcher-plants grow.)

In this last century, *Nepenthes* was a popular ornamental, grown in teak baskets in intermediate to warm orchid house conditions. Many species and hybrids were offered, most of which were lost to cultivation during the decline of the great stove era which began with the First World War. Today the activities of carnivore enthusiasts have restored many of these plants to cultivation; micropropagation has made available once more a wide range of specimen and hybrids, most of them in vigorous, resilient and freely pitcher-bearing clones. Moreover, our enhanced understanding of this genus has done much to dispel their reputation for difficulty. Some, such as *N.alata* and the Highland Hybrids, can be grown with ease in cool conservatories or the home, requiring no more than a bright (not sunny) position and regular watering and misting even with tap water.

In cultural terms, the tropical pitcher-plants fall into two groups, those occurring in the wild below 1000m/3250ft, the 'lowland' species, and the 'highland' species from above this altitude, which in cultivation differ in their temperature requirements. Lowland species require a minimum winter temperature of 18.5°C/65°F, with diurnal temperatures exceeding 27°C/80°F; in summer the nightly minimum should be 21°C/70°F, with diurnal temperatures rising to 38°C/100°F. This also applies to lowland hybrids and hybrids with highland species. A winter nocturnal minimum of between 8.5–12°C/47–54°F is suitable for the highland species with diurnal temperature between 18–22°C/64–72°F: in summer the maximum daytime temperature should not exceed 21°C/70°F, with a nocturnal minimum of 12–15°C/54–60°F. Basic cultivation is similar for the two groups. The compost must be well drained; two parts bark, two parts perlite and one part coir, leafmould or moss peat is a standard compost. Ample moisture and high humidity are required but free drainage is essential; lattice or basket pots are recommended for this reason. Liquid fertilizer is beneficial, applied to the roots or as a foliar feed. Old plants will produce long, clambering stems that will require tying-in to canes, trellis or wires. These tend, however, to become bare and exhausted and will benefit from heavy pruning in spring. Propagation is best performed by air layering, as cuttings seldom succeed.

N.alata Blanco.
To 3.5m. Pitchers numerous, weakly dimorphic; lower 6.5–13cm, cylindric above, constricted at centre, inflated at base, light green with red flecks, or heavily suffused red, mouth oblique, oval, peristome green or occasionally red, lid elliptic with glandular crest at base of inner surface; wings prominent, fimbriate; upper pitchers elongate with wings reduced to ribs. Highland. Philippines, Malaysia, Borneo, Sumatra.

N.albomarginata Lobb.
To 2m. Leaves 20×2.5cm. Pitchers to 12.5cm, cylindric, narrowed to base where it becomes upcurved, green, sometimes spotted red, or pink, with conspicuous white band immediately below peristome, mouth oblique, oval, peristome finely ribbed, narrow, lid oblong, rounded, green, spotted red, wings

narrow, sparsely toothed. Lowland. Malaysia, Sumatra, Borneo.

N.ampullaria Jack.
Tall climber, producing pitchers only at base. Upper leaves to 17.5×5cm, oblong, tendril to 7.5cm. Pitchers produced from subterranean rhizome or rosettes of basal leaves with lamina to 5cm; pitchers similar, to 5cm, rounded, squat, green spotted and blotched deep red, or entirely green or deep red, mouth horizontal, oval to round, peristome with narrow rim, but descending vertically into pitcher-mouth, lid to 3.5cm, narrow, reflexed from mouth, wings broad, widely spreading, strongly toothed. Lowland. Malaysia, Borneo, Sumatra to New Guinea.

N.bicalcarata Hook.f.
Tall climber to 14m. Pitchers dimorphic; lower to 10cm, rounded, green, sometimes suffused rust-red or entirely rust-

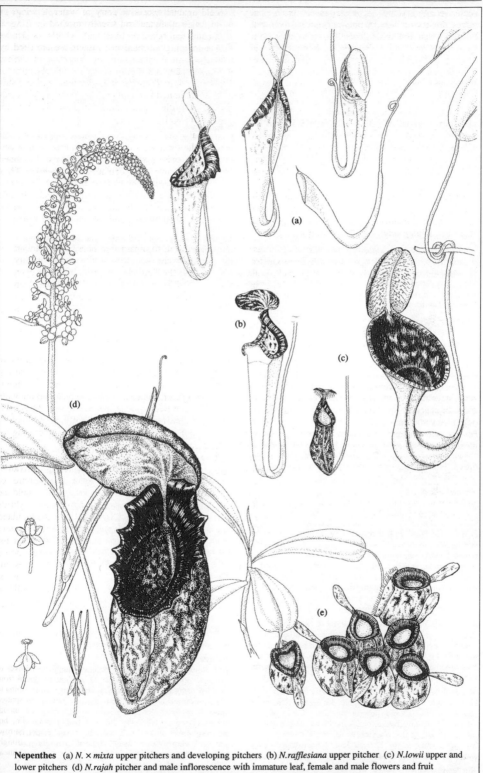

Nepenthes (a) *N. × mixta* upper pitchers and developing pitchers (b) *N.rafflesiana* upper pitcher (c) *N.lowii* upper and lower pitchers (d) *N.rajah* pitcher and male inflorescence with immature leaf, female and male flowers and fruit (e) *N.ampullaria* rosette pitchers (in basal cluster) and climbing stem with pendent pitchers

red, mouth somewhat oblique, round, peristome inclined into pitcher, green, lid well raised above pitcher, reniform, with ends of peristome forming 2 distinct walrus-like tusks pointing downwards, wings broad, toothed; upper pitchers to 13cm, campanulate to funnel-shaped, wings replaced by ribs. Lowland. Borneo.

N.burbidgeae Burb.
Tall climber to 10m. Leaves to 40×10cm, oblong to lanceolate, tendril to 60cm. Pitchers dimorphic; lower to 18×12cm, ovate, pale green to white with red blotches, mouth oblique, round, peristome broad, yellow-white with red bands, lid orbiculate, glandular at base below, margin undulate, wings narrow, toothed; upper pitcher to 13×7cm, funnel-shaped, contracted just below mouth, mouth horizontal, wings reduced to prominent ribs with very short teeth. Highland. Borneo (Mt Kinabalu).

N.× chelsonii hort. Veitch ex Mast. (*N.× dominyi× N.× hookeriana.*)
Intermediate between parents. Pitchers broadly ovoid, yellow-green spotted purple-red, mouth oblique, oval, peristome dark purple, wings broad, toothed. Lowlands. Garden origin

N.×coccinea hort. (*N.× dominyi× N.mirabilis.*)
Pitchers to 15×7.5cm, yellow-green heavily marked purple-red, inflated below middle, cylindric in upper part, mouth oblique, oval, peristome with red and black ridges, lid ovate-oblong, green with red markings, wings broad, toothed. Lowland. Garden origin.

N.curtisii Mast. See *N.maxima.*
N.× dominiana Nichols. See *N.× dominyi.*
N.× dominyi Veitch (*N.× dominiana* Nichols.). (*N.rafflesiana × N.gracilis.*)
Tall climber. Pitchers to 15cm, light green, heavily marked dark red, cylindric but tapering upwards, mouth oblique, oval, peristome narrow, pale green, lid green, suffused red, wings broad, spreading, toothed. Lowland. Garden origin.

N.× dormanniana hort. (*N.mirabilis × N.× sedenii* Veitch (*N.gracilis × N.khasiana*).)
Pitchers 15×7.5cm, green with many red spots and blotches, flask-shaped, somewhat inflated below middle, mouth oblique, oval to rounded, peristome broad, green, finely ridged, lid broadly ovate, wings broad, undulate, toothed. Lowland. Garden origin.

N.gracilis Korth.
Stems slender, prostrate or climbing, to 2m. Leaves to 12.5×2.5cm, linear to elliptic, tendril to 7.5cm. Pitchers dimorphic, numerous; lower to 7.5cm, shortly flask-shaped, rounded below, light green with dark red spots, or suffused pink, or dark maroon to almost black, mouth slightly oblique, oval to rounded, peristome narrow, green; lid orbicular, dark red, wings narrow, shortly toothed; upper pitchers elongated, to 15cm, constricted at middle and somewhat inflated at base, dark mahogany-red or red-brown, with peristome green to red-brown, wings reduced to ridges, interior white or pink-white. Lowland. Indonesia (Borneo to Sulawesi), Philippines.

N.× henryana Nichols. (*N.hookeriana × N.× sedenii.*)
Pitchers to 15cm, irregularly flask-shaped, inflated below with long cylindric neck, predominantly red-purple with few green flecks, mouth oblique, oval, peristome broad, crimson shaded violet, interior green with violet spots, wings narrow, toothed. Lowland. Garden origin.

N.× hookeriana Lindl. (*N.rafflesiana × N.ampullaria.*)
Natural hybrid. Pitchers dimorphic; lower to 11cm, ovoid, pale green with dark red spots, or sometimes heavily blotched red, mouth oblique, round, peristome broad, descending into pitcher, green, lid flat, obovate, wings broad, strongly fimbriate; upper pitchers to 12.5 × 2.5cm, funnel-shaped, wings reduced to ridges. Lowland. Malaysia, Sumatra, Borneo.

N.× intermedia hort. Veitch. (*N.gracilis × N.rafflesiana.*)
Pitchers to 15×6.5cm, green heavily blotched red, subcylindric, tapering gradually above; mouth oblique, ovate, peris-

tome dark red, lid with distinct column, ovate, obtuse, wings broad, long-toothed. Lowland. Garden origin.

N.khasiana Hook.f.
Tall climber to 10m+. Leaves sessile, lanceolate. Pitchers dimorphic; lower 7.5–17.5cm, inflated below, tapering above, green, tinged pink, upper pitchers to 20cm, cylindric, slightly inflated at base, green with red markings, mouth oblique, oval, peristome dark red, lid oval, green externally, red within, wings reduced to ridges. Highland, winter maximum 8°C. Assam (Khasi hills).

N.madagascariensis Poir.
Low shrub, rarely climbing, to 2m. Leaves to 28×8cm, ovate to lanceolate. Pitchers dimorphic; lower to 13cm, squat-cylindric, red or green, spotted red, mouth oblique, ovate, peristome ribbed, red, lid curved over pitcher mouth, orbiculate to reniform; upper pitchers to 17cm, funnel-shaped, bright yellow-green, sometimes suffused red, mouth horizontal, lid erect; wings reduced to ridges. Highland. Madagascar.

N.× mastersiana hort. Veitch ex Mast. (*N.sanguinea × N.khasiana.*)
Pitchers 11×3cm, cylindric with slight constriction at middle, deep claret-red with deeper purple spots, thinly hairy, mouth oblique, ovate, peristome red, interior pink-cream, spotted red, lid rounded, wings narrow, sparsely toothed in lower pitchers, reduced to ridges in upper pitchers. Highland. Garden origin.

N.maxima Reinw. ex Nees (*N.curtisii* Mast.).
Leaves to 20cm, glandular beneath. Pitchers dimorphic; lower to 20×6.5cm, cylindric, pale green, longitudinally streaked red, mouth oblique, ovate, peristome wide, dark red, lid somewhat cordate, green, mottled purple, wings narrow, toothed; upper pitchers to 30×7.5cm, trumpet-shaped, wings reduced to ridges. Highland. Indonesia (Borneo, Sulawesi) to New Guinea.

N.mirabilis (Lour.) Druce (*N.phyllamphora* Willd.). MONKEY CUP.
Shrub or climber to 10m. Leaves to 40×8cm, oblong to lanceolate, margin entire or minutely dentate. Pitchers cylindric or slightly inflated at base, to 18cm, pale green with red spots, or sometimes wholly red, mouth oblique, round, peristome broad, flattened, striped red, lid orbicular to ovate, wings present in lower pitchers, toothed, reduced to prominent ridges in upper pitchers. Lowland. S China, SE Asia to New Guinea and Queensland.

N.× mixta Mast.(*N.northiana × N.maxima.*)
Pitchers weakly dimorphic, 10–35×3.5–7.5cm; lower cylindric, pale green, spotted purple-red, mouth oblique, oval, peristome broad, strongly ribbed, glossy ruby red, lid finely spotted red, wings narrow, toothed; upper pitchers funnel-shaped, with wings reduced to ridges. Lowland. Garden origin.

N.northiana Hook.f.
Pitchers to 30×8.5cm, cylindric, pale green, heavily spotted purple, mouth oblique, oval, peristome very broad, outer margin undulate, yellow, striped purple, lid ovate-oblong, glossy, spotted black on lower surface, wings narrow, toothed. Lowland. Borneo.

N.phyllamphora Willd. See *N.mirabilis.*

N.rafflesiana Jack.
Tall climber, to 9m. Leaves to 25cm, oblong, tendril to 30cm. Pitchers dimorphic; lower to 12.5 × 7.5cm, ventricose, rounded at base, green, heavily spotted red, mouth oblique, oval, peristome broad, crimson, strongly ribbed, narrowing upwards to form elongate process to lid, spiny above, lid oblong-orbicular, wings to 2.5cm broad, spreading, teeth incurved; upper pitchers to 23×7.5cm, funnel-shaped, curved and narrowing to base, wings reduced to ridges. Lowland. Malaysia, Sumatra, Borneo.

N.rajah Hook.f. KING MONKEY CUP.
Stems prostrate. Tendrils emerge from underside of lamina below apex. Pitchers dimorphic, largest in genus; lower to 35×

15cm, rounded, capable of capture and digestion of prey to rat-size, green lightly spotted red, or entirely red to purple externally, spotted red and purple-black within, mouth oblique, oval, peristome broad, outer margin projecting beyond pitcher-walls, undulate, strongly ribbed, crimson with darker bands, lid large, exceeding mouth, ribbed below, wings narrow, toothed; upper pitchers funnel-shaped, narrowing to base, wings reduced to ridges. Highland. Borneo (Mt Kinabalu).

N.reinwardtiana Miq.
Tall climber, to 10m. Leaves to 20×3cm, linear-lanceolate, sessile. Pitchers to 20×5cm, cylindric, somewhat inflated at base with slight constriction at middle, green externally, glaucous blue-green within, mouth oblique, ovate, peristome very narrow, green, lid elliptic, almost flat, to 4cm across; untoothed ridges present. Lowland. Borneo.

N.stenophylla Mast.
Tall climber. Pitchers dimorphic; lower to 15cm, narrow-cylindric, pale yellow-green, longitudinally flecked purple; mouth oblique, oval, peristome narrow, banded red, lid rounded, with narrow connective neck, wings very narrow, sparsely toothed; upper pitchers to 28cm, funnel-shaped, tapering to base, wings reduced to ribs. Highland. Borneo.

N.tentaculata Hook.f.
Stems prostrate, to 2m. Leaves to 18×3cm, lanceolate, sessile. Pitchers dimorphic; lower to 7×3cm, squat, flask-shaped, inflated below, cylindric above, pale green to white, heavily marked with red-purple; mouth oblique, oval, peristome narrow, red, lid with distinct upright bristles on upper surface, wings narrow, toothed; upper pitchers to 15cm, elongate flask-shaped, purple-green to dark-red; wings present, narrow, toothed. Highland. Borneo.

N.veitchii Hook.f.
Epiphytic. Pitchers to 20cm, cylindric, pale green, mouth oblique, ovate, peristome broad, strongly ribbed, canary-yellow, lid small, oblong, wings broad, toothed. Highland. Borneo.

N.ventricosa Blanco.
Terrestrial or epiphytic; stems short. Pitchers numerous, to 18cm, inflated at base with middle constricted, pale to white-green, sometimes flecked red; mouth shallowly oblique, ovate, peristome broad, strongly ribbed, red, or green with red bands; lid ovate; wings absent. Highland. Philippines.

N.cultivars.
'Courtii': leaves leathery; pitchers marbled wine-red towards apex, wings fringed. 'Dir. G.T. Moore': leaves to 45cm; pitchers purple-red marbled green, wings prominent, rim lined purple. 'Henry Shaw': pitchers large, solid, pale green spotted wine-red. 'Lieut. R.B. Pring': pitchers pear-shaped, red-purple acquiring green marbling with age, wings prominent with purple hairs. 'St. Louis': pitchers pear-shaped, dark red becoming paler with age, slightly marbled green, wings mottled. 'Superba': vigorous; leaves deep green, long; pitchers variable from urn-shaped to funnel-shaped, green tinged yellow and splashed maroon, rim ribbed in maroon and crimson, lid striped red, fringe with red hairs.

Norantea Aubl. (Variant of *Gonora antegri*, the Caribbean name for *N.guianensis*.) Marcgraviaceae. 35 species of epiphytic, usually climbing shrubs differing from *Marcgravia* in their long erect racemes or spikes with fertile flowers along their entire length. As in *Marcgravia*, the floral bracts are modified into fleshy, hollow nectaries but tend to be far larger, bladder-like and brilliantly coloured. Tropical America. Z10.

CULTIVATION The Red Hot Poker or Beacon Plant, *N.guianensis* is one of the most spectacular climbing shrubs for subtropical and tropical gardens and large warm glasshouses and conservatories (minimum winter temperature 13°C/55°F). Its robust branches are clothed with large, leathery dark green leaves and terminate in long, straight racemes densely hung with orange-red inflated bracts. Plant in full sun or semi-shade (light summer shading required under glass) in a fertile soil rich in decayed vegetable matter. Regular watering, hosing and manuring are beneficial outdoors. Under glass, the Red Hot Poker requires copious water, liquid feed and frequent misting when in growth, but little attention in winter. *Norantea* is a self-clinging climber and will progress rapidly into the lower boughs of large trees or against the trunks of large palms. It will also cover walls and rocky outcrops and, if unsupported, form massive shrubby hummocks. Well grown plants will become very large and may require pruning after flowering. Root semi-ripe cuttings in a heated case; propagation also by air layering.

N.guianensis Aubl. BEACON PLANT; RED HOT POKER.
Vigorous evergreen shrub to 10×10m, usually climbing by means of adventitious roots. Leaves to 30cm, oblong-elliptic, mucronate, leathery, glossy dark green, midrib conspicuous. Inflorescence a terminal, erect to nodding spike to 1m densely hung with 5–8cm scarlet and orange bladder-like bracts. Guyana.

Odontadenia Benth. (From Gk *odons*, tooth, and *aden*, gland; referring to the 5-toothed glands.) Apocynaceae. 30 species of climbing shrubs, closely related to *Mandevilla*. Leaves entire, opposite, pinnately veined. Flowers borne in large, loose cymes, yellow, showy; calyx 5-lobed; corolla funnelform or slightly salverform. Tropical America. Z10.

CULTIVATION Given moderate watering when in growth and a winter minimum temperature of 15–21°C/60–70°F, cultivation is essentially as for *Allamanda*. Propagate by cuttings of young shoots rooted in a closed case with bottom heat, or by seed.

O.grandiflora (G.Mey.) Kuntze. See *O.macrantha*.

O.macrantha (Roem.& Schult.) Markgr. (*O.grandiflora* (G.Mey.) Kuntze; *O.speciosa* Benth.).
Woody vine. Leaves to 15cm, oblong-ovate, apex acute, smooth, dark green, leathery. Flowers to 8cm diam., delicately scented; corolla bright yellow shaded orange, tube 3.5–5cm. Costa Rica to Peru and N Brazil.

O.speciosa Benth. See *O.macrantha*.

Oxera Labill. (From Gk *oxys*, sour, referring to the acrid sap.) ROYAL CLIMBER. Verbenaceae. Some 20 species of shrubs, often scandent, glabrous. Leaves opposite, coriaceous, simple, entire. Flowers white or yellow-white, in axillary, forked cymes, pedicellate, sometimes forming a panicle; calyx 4-or 5-lobed or dentate; corolla 4-lobed; stamens 2, long-exserted. Fruit a drupe. New Caledonia. Z10.

CULTIVATION   As for *Petraea*.

O.pulchella Labill. SNOWY OXERA.
Scandent, evergreen shrub. Leaves to 12.5cm, entire or dentate, petiolate, upper leaves oblong, lower leaves oblong-lanceolate. Cymes many-flowered; flowers to 5cm, pendent, white or yellow-white; calyx conspicuous; corolla to 5cm, campanulate or infundibular, lobes broadly oblong. New Caledonia.

Paederia L. (Lat. *paedor*, a stench, referring to the foetid odour of *P.foetida* and other species, when crushed.) Rubiaceae. 20 species of climbing shrubs. Leaves opposite, entire. Flowers small in axillary clusters together forming a long slender panicle; corolla tubular or funnel-shaped, 4- or 5-lobed. Fruit globose or compressed, thin-skinned, glossy. SE Asia.

CULTIVATIONA genus containing several attractive climbers, among them *P.foetida* with lilac flowers and the hairy *P.tomentosa* with rose-purple flowers. They tend not to be cultivated, possibly because of the stench the foliage emits if bruised. *P.scandens*, however, is found in some gardens and even used as a vegetable in its native places. A deciduous twiner with narrow, dark green leaves and purple-throated white flowers followed by orange berries, it will scramble through shrubs and trees in sunny, sheltered sites in zones 7 and over. It thrives on most fertile soils. Propagate by semi-ripe cuttings.

P.scandens Merr. (*P.chinensis*; *P.wilsonii*).
Deciduous climber to 5m. Leaves 5–10cm, ovate to ovate-lanceolate, base rounded to cuneate, apex slender-acuminate, dark green above, somewhat downy beneath. Panicles slender, terminal, composed of axillary clusters; corolla to 1.5 × 0.75cm, white with a purple-tinted throat. Fruit to 0.75cm diam., globose, orange. Summer. China, Japan, Korea. Z7.

Pandorea Spach. (For the Gk goddess *Pandora*.) Bignoniaceae. 6 species of lianes. Leaves pinnate, leaflets sparsely glandular beneath, opposite, in 1–7 pairs, oblong to ovate or elliptic. Inflorescences thyrsiform, mostly terminal; peduncle bractless; calyx cupular to campanulate, 5-lobed or truncate; corolla zygomorphic, tube cylindrical or funnelform, tube and lower side hairy, lobes 5, rounded, spreading; stamens hairy at base, unequal; ovary cells with many ovules. Capsule stalked, beaked, cylindrical to flat; valves cymbiform, leathery; seeds rounded, each in a thin wing. Australia, Papuasia, E Malesia, New Caledonia. Z9.

CUJLTIVATION   Grown for their glossy foliage and showy, frequently heavily scented blooms; those of *P.jasminoides* are carried from winter into early summer. The creamy flowers of *P.pandorana* are often very attractively marked with violet speckles and, although small, are carried in abundance. *P.pandorana* is found in the fertile soils of coastal *Nothofagus moorei* woodlands of eastern Australia, in a climate that experiences high summer rainfall and an average winter minimum temperature of 0°C/32°F. Both *P.pandorana* and *P.jasminoides* have experienced short periods of frost, to –3 or –4°C, without severe damage and have proved very drought-tolerant in cultivation. In warm temperate and subtropical gardens they are beautiful climbers for walls and pergolas, and are sometimes used as groundcover on banks. In cool temperate areas, they are grown on the walls of cool glasshouses or conservatories, and trained along the rafters. Cultivate as for *Bignonia*.

P.amboinensis Boerl. See *Tecomanthe dendrophila*.
P.australis Spach. See *P.pandorana*.
P.brycei (N.E. Br.) Rehd. See *Podranea brycei*.
P.dendrophila Boerl. See *Tecomanthe dendrophila*.

P.jasminoides (Lindl.) Schum. (*Tecoma jasminoides* Lindl.).
BOWER OF BEAUTY; BOWER PLANT.
To 5m. Stem stout. Leaflets pale green, 2.5–5× 1–2cm, 4–9, ovate-lanceolate, apex obtuse. Corolla 4–5cm, white, streaked or stained deep, rich pink within, short pubescent Spring–summer. NE Australia. 'Alba': flowers pure white. 'Lady Di': flowers white, throat cream. 'Rosea': flowers pink, throat darker. 'Rosea Superba': flowers large, pink, throat darker, spotted purple.

P.pandorana (Andrews) Steenis (*Bignonia pandorana* Andrews; *Bignonia pandorea* Vent.; *Bignonia pandorae* Sims; *Tecoma australis* R. Br.; *Bignonia australis* Ait.; *Bignonia meonantha* Sweet; *Tecoma diversifolia* G. Don; *P.australis* Spach; *Tecoma floribunda* Cunn. ex DC.). WONGA-WONGA VINE.
Evergreen to 6m (to 30m in habitat). Stem slender. Leaflets 3–10×1.5–6cm, usually in 6 pairs, ovate-lanceolate, glabrous, entire or sometimes crenate. Flowers fragrant; corolla 1–3cm, tube twice length of lobes, tuberculate-puberulent, creamy yellow, streaked and splashed red or purple. Winter–spring. Australia, New Guinea, Pacific Is. 'Rosea': flowers pale pink.

P.ricasoliana (Tenf.) Baill. see *Podranea ricasoliana*.

For illustration see Bignoniaceae.

Papilionanthe Schltr. (From Lat. *papilio*, moth and Gk *anthos*, flower.) Orchidaceae. Some 11 species of monopodial, epiphytic or terrestrial orchids. Stems slender, terete, erect or scrambling, often branching and rooting at nodes. Leaves in 2 ranks, alternate, terete, narrowly tapering, pungent or obtuse, obscurely grooved above, sheathing below. Inflorescence usually a short, axillary raceme or panicle; sepals obovate, obtuse, weakly undulate, lateral sepals clawed; petals suborbicular, spreading, margins more undulate than in lateral sepals; lip trilobed, minutely pubescent, base saccate, midlobe bifid, broad, cuneate, lateral lobes large, often erect; spur saccate, conical. Himalaya to Malaysia.

CULTIVATION   Vigorous scrambling epiphytes. *P.teres* and *P.hookeriana*, formerly included in *Vanda*, require sunny positions in the intermediate or warm house in baskets or beds of open bark mix. Syringe and water freely throughout the year. The former especially is an important garden plant and cut flower in the tropics and subtropics, notably in Singapore and Hawaii. *P.vandarum*, from cool hilly districts, requires lower temperatures (min. 7°C/45°F) and drier conditions in winter. Its stems are more slender than in the other two species listed here, a deep green and decked with short racemes of lace-like flowers. It is one of the most beautiful orchids for cultivation in baskets or on moss-coated poles in the cool house. Propagate all by stem cuttings or division.

P.hookeriana (Rchb. f.) Schltr. (*Vanda hookeriana* Rchb. f.). Stems scrambling, to 2.2m. Leaves 7–10 × 0.3cm. Inflorescence to 30cm; flowers 2–12; dorsal sep. and petals white or pale mauve, chequered deep mauve, faintly spotted, lateral sepals nearly white, lip deep purple, midlobe pale mauve marked purple; dorsal sepals obovate-oblong, obtuse, erect, undulate, crisped, to 2×1.5cm, lateral sep. spreading; petals elliptic to orbicular, undulate, base twisted to reflexed; lip midlobe reniform to flabellate, to 3×4cm, weakly trilobed, lateral lobes triangular-falcate to oblong; spur very short. Malaysia, China, Borneo, Vietnam. Z10.

P.teres (Roxb.) Schltr. (*Vanda teres* (Roxb.) Lindl.). Stems to 1.75m but branching to form scrambling mats. Leaves erect and incurved, to 20×0.4cm. Inflorescence produced in continuous succession, 15–30cm; flowers 3–6 per raceme, 5–10cm diam.; sepals and petals white or ivory deepening to rose or magenta, lip buff to golden, banded or dotted blood-red or mauve; sepals ovate to subrhombic, undulate, obtuse, spreading, to 4×3cm; petals orbicular, undulate, base twisted, to 4.5×4cm; lip midlobe flabellate to obcordate, deeply cleft, lateral lobes enveloping column; spur to 2.5cm, funnel-shaped. Thailand, Burma, Himalaya. Z10.

P.vandarum (Rchb. f.) Garay (*Aerides vandarum* Rchb. f.). Stems to 2m, slender, terete, branching tangentially, sprawling, dark green, freely producing flattened grey roots and cascading or forming densely tangled clumps. Leaves to 10cm, borne at 45° to stem, slender, tapering, pungent, dark green often flushed purple. Inflorescence to 8cm, seldom branching, bearing flowers over several seasons; flowers to 5 at once, nocturnally fragrant, to 5cm diam., crystalline white, often tinted opal or basally flushed lilac to pink; sepals to 3.5 × 1.75cm, obovate, basally clawed, reflexed, undulate to crispate; petals broader, more undulate, strongly reflexed and twisted; lip midlobe clawed, broadly obcordate, apically ruffed and deflexed, claw 3-ridged, lateral lobes falcate, erect, acuminate, apically denticulate with secondary, toothed lobe toward sinus of lateral and midlobes; spur cylindric, to 2cm. India, Burma. Z9.

Parsonsia R. Br. (For John Parsons (1705–70), Scottish physician and naturalist.) Apocynaceae. 80 species of woody climbers. Leaves opposite. Inflorescence a terminal or axillary panicle; flowers small; corolla tubular, often inflated, limb 5-lobed. Asia, Australasia, Pacific.

CULTIVATION   An attractive climber with beautifully tinted and remarkably mutable foliage, it is suitable for the cool glasshouse or, in mild areas, for a sheltered situation outdoors, where it will survive brief winter lows of –10°C/14°F. *P.capsularis* tolerates a range of soils, performing best in a well drained but moisture-retentive position in full sun. Water container-grown plants moderately when in growth and maintain good ventilation with a winter minimum of 5–7°C/40–45°F. Train on wires, through shrubs or, in pots, up a wigwam of canes. Propagate by seed or by soft stem cuttings.

P.capsularis R. Br. Evergreen climber to 5m. Stems slender, twining, glabrous or rough, buff tinted or marked chocolate or purple-green. Leaves highly variable in size and shape: 2–7.5cm, narrow-linear, simple or lobed, buff overlaid chocolate, pink or dark green in juvenile state, adult leaves 2.5–6×1.25–2cm, entire, seldom so beautifully marked as in juveniles. Inflorescence a terminal panicle, usually crowded; corolla to 3mm, white, campanulate, lobes recurved. New Zealand. Z9.

Parthenocissus Planch. (From Gk *parthenos*, virgin, and *kissos*, ivy, a loose translation of 'virginia creeper'.) VIRGINIA CREEPER. Vitaceae. 10 species of generally deciduous woody vines, trailing or ascending with tendrils; tendrils branched, twining, usually with adhesive disks. Leaves alternate, palmately 3–7-lobed or -parted. Inflorescence terminal aggregated clusters or cymose panicles; flowers small, green to cream, bisexual or unisexual; receptacle wanting; petals 4–5, separate, an spreading at anthesis; stamens short, erect. Fruit a berry, dark blue or black, flesh thin; seeds 1–4. N America, E Asia, Himalaya.

CULTIVATION   These attractive and vigorous climbers generally occupy moist soils in woodland or forest in the wild, climbing towards the light by means of tendrils, by their characteristic adhesive pads or, if conditions dictate, by twining and weaving. The most commonly cultivated species have escaped from gardens and naturalized – *P.quinquefolia* on walls and waste ground in Europe whilst *P.tricuspidata* is found in Balkan forests to altitudes of 2100m/6825ft. They are invaluable for growing up and through sturdy trees, for growing over pergolas, walls and fences and for covering unsightly buildings. The twining or tendril-climbing species, such as *P.inserta*, are very effective if allowed to weave through large shrubs, small trees and hedging; they need sup-

Parthenocissus quinquefolia

port if used to cover buildings, but are perhaps at their most beautiful given horizontal support so that they can form an elegant hanging curtain of foliage. The self-clinging species are unsurpassed for covering large areas of bare wall with the proviso that the more vigorous species, in particular *P.tricuspidata* and *P.quinquefolia*, need a structurally sound surface and must be prevented from reaching under house eaves and roof tiles and into window casements.

All are grown for their handsome foliage, that of *P.henryana* is particularly striking, deep velvety green-bronze with contrasting silvery venation. Most give a peerless display of autumnal brilliance in crimson and scarlet, complemented in good seasons by small, plum-coloured fruits. Hardiness varies, ranging from tolerance of temperatures of −25°C/−13°F for *P.quinquefolia* and at least −15°C/5°F for *P.inserta*, *P.tricuspidata* and its cultivars; *P.henryana* withstands cold to between −5 and −10°C/23−14°F. *P.himalayana* is not reliably hardy in zones with prolonged low temperatures, and needs a sheltered position in zones at the limits of its hardiness.

Plant into a moisture-retentive but well drained fertile soil. *Parthenocissus* species require at least partial shade for good colour display; grow *P.quinquefolia*, *P.inserta* and *P.himalayana* in semi-shade on east or west facing walls, give *P.tricuspidata* and *P.henryana* a position in partial shade, or grow on a sunless wall. Give initial support until plants produce adhesive pads. Prune annually to keep growths away from the roof eaves etc., in autumn or early winter. For pergola-trained specimens, cut the current season's growth back to one or two viable buds from the main framework, thus creating a spur system, from which the following season's growth can cascade.

Propagate species by seed, although some such as *P.inserta* and *P.tricuspidata* may hybridize and will not come true. Remove pulp and sow fresh out of doors or in the cold frame, or stratify for 6 weeks at or just below 5°C/40°F, and sow under glass in spring. The fruit pulp may cause skin irritation. Propagate cultivars by leaf-bud cuttings in early to mid summer, and rooted in a closed case with bottom heat; also by 10–12cm/4–5in. basal hardwood cuttings of the current season's growth taken immediately after leaf fall; treat with rooting hormone (0.8–1.0% I.B.A.) and root in individual pots with a bottom heat at 18–21°C/64–70°F. Pot on as soon as rooted to minimize root disturbance. Incease also by simple layering.

P.engelmannii Koehne & Gräbn. ex Gräbn. See *P.quinquefolia* var. *engelmannii*.

P.henryana (Hemsl.) Diels. & Gilg (*P.henryi* hort.; *Vitis henryana* Hemsl.; *Vitis henryi* hort.; *Vitis thomsonii* Veitch non Lawson; *Psedera henryana* (Hemsl.) Schneid.; *Ampelopsis henryana* (Hemsl.) Rehd. in L.H. Bail.; *Cissus henryana* hort.).
Vine, ascending, to 5m, deciduous; stems acutely 4-angled, glabrous; tendrils 5–7-forked. Leaves palmately 5-parted; petiole 4–11cm; leaflets 4–12× 1.5–6cm, obovate to oblanceolate or narrowly ovate, acute at apex, tapered to base, coarsely dentate except near base, dark velvety red- or brown-green with pink and silvery variegations along main veins especially at first, becoming dark green then red in autumn, slightly pubescent on veins beneath, shortly petiolulate. Inflorescence terminal, leafy, a panicle of cymes to 18cm. Fruit dark blue. China. Z7.

P.henryi hort. See *P.henryana*.

P.heptaphylla (Buckl.) Britt. & Small.
Vine, climbing to 9m, deciduous; shoots terete to rather angular, ferruginous when young; tendrils long, forked. Leaves generally 7-parted, coarsely serrate, dark green above, paler beneath, glabrous; leaflets 3–6cm, oblong-obovate, cuneate at base. Inflorescence a lax cyme, 3–7cm diam. Fruit globose, 8–12mm, blue-black. Spring. Texas. Z9.

P.heterophylla (Bl.) Merrill.
Leaves, simple or 2–3-parted, long-petiolate; leaflets 6–25× 3–12cm, 3, or 1–2 on floral branches, coarsely crenate-serrate, lateral leaflets obliquely ovate-oblong, central one oblong, all shortly petiolulate, glabrous or pubescent beneath. Inflorescence widely branched, glabrous. Fruit red tinged black. China. Z8.

P.himalayana (Royle) Planch. (*Ampelopsis himalayana* Royle; *Vitis himalayana* (Royle) Brandis; *Cissus himalayana* Walp.; *Cissus neilgheriensis* Wight).
Vine, ascending, to 18m, deciduous; young stems partially woody, glabrous. Leaves always 3-parted; petiole slender, 5–12cm; leaflets 5–15×4–10cm, shortly petiolulate, central leaflet ovate, oval or obovate, lateral leaflets very obliquely ovate and often somewhat obliquely cordate at base, dentate, abruptly tapered to apex, dark green above (becoming rich red in autumn), paler and somewhat glaucous beneath,

glabrous above, very sparsely pubescent on main vein beneath. Inflorescence laxly clustered, repeatedly forked. Fruit globose, 6mm, black. Late spring–summer. Himalaya. var. **rubrifolia** (Lév. & Vaniot) Gagnep. (*P.sinensis* Diels & Gilg; *Vitis rubrifolia* Lév. & Vaniot). Leaflets smaller and relatively broader, tinged purple when young; inflorescence smaller. Taiwan, W China. Z9.

P.hirsuta Small. See *P.quinquefolia* var. *hirsuta*.
P.inserens Hayek. See *P.inserta*.

P.inserta (A. Kerner) Fritsch (*P.inserens* Hayek; *P.vitacea* (Kerner) Hitchc.; *P.spaethii* Koehne & Gräbn.; *Psedera vitacea* (Kerner) Gray; *Vitis inserta* Kerner; *Vitis vitacea* (Kerner) Bean).
Vine, high-climbing, or shrubby; tendrils 3–5-branched, twining, usually without adhesive disks. Leaves palmately compound, glossy green (richly coloured in autumn), glabrous to thinly pubescent beneath, long-petiolate; leaflets 5, elliptic to obovate, acutely serrate particularly in distal part, abruptly acuminate at apex, cuneate at base, sessile or petiolulate. Inflorescence to 8cm, forked cymose solitary with divergent branches forming a broadly rounded flower cluster. Fruit 6mm diam., almost black. Summer. N America (New England, Quebec west to Manitoba, south to Wyoming and Texas). 'Macrophylla': leaflets to 20cm, elliptic, colouring poorly in autumn. Z3.

P.laetevirens Rehd.
Vine, high-climbing close to *P.quinquefolia*, tendrils thin, 5–8-branched. Leaves 5-parted; leaflets 5–10cm, elliptic to obovate, margins coarsely serrate, light yellow-green, glabrous, or sometimes pubescent on veins beneath. Panicles terminal, 15–25cm. Fruit 8mm diam., globose, dark blue. China (W Hupeh). Z9.

P.quinquefolia (L.) Planch. (*Psedera quinquefolia* Gray; *Ampelopsis hederacea* (Ehrh.) DC.; *Ampelopsis quinquefolia* (L.) Michx.; *Cissus mexicana* DC.; *Vitis hederacea* Ehrh.; *Vitis quinquefolia* (L.) Lam.). VIRGINIA CREEPER; WOODBINE.
Vine to 30m, glabrous throughout; stems slender, tinged red at first; tendrils 5–8-branched with numerous terminal adhesive. Leaves usually 5-parted; petiole 2.5–10cm; leaflets 2.5–10×1.6cm, elliptic to obovate, acutely serrate particularly in distal part, abruptly acuminate at apex, cuneate at base, dull green above (rich crimson in autumn), paler and somewhat

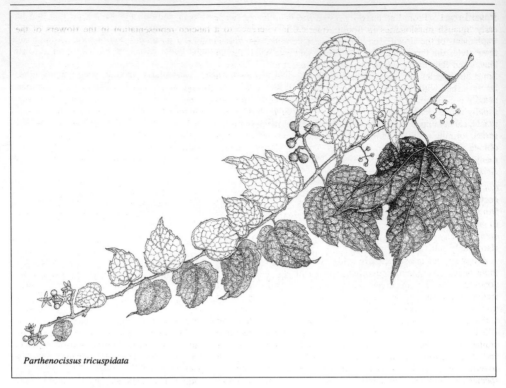

Parthenocissus tricuspidata

glaucous beneath, generally petiolulate. Inflorescence paniculate, terminal and from upper leaf axils, flowers in umbellate cymes of 3–8. Fruit globose, 6mm diam., dark blue-black. Summer. E US (Maine west to Iowa & Kansas, south to Florida & Texas) to Mexico. 'Minor': 10–12 branchlets on tendrils; leaves small, oval to elliptic. 'Murorum': tendrils short, abundant. var. **engelmannii** Rehd. (*P.engelmannii* Koehne & Gräbn. ex Gräbn.; *Ampelopsis engelmannii* hort. ex Rehd. in Bail.). Leaflets smaller. var. **hirsuta** Planch. (*P.hirsuta* Small). Leaves and young stems softly white-pubescent. var. **saint-paulii** (Koehne & Gräbn.) Rehd. (*P.saint-paulii* Koehne & Gräbn.; *Ampelopsis saint-paulii* hort. ex Rehd.). Tendrils 8–12-branched; leaves persistent in autumn, leaflets 12–15cm; inflorescence elongate. Z3.

P.saint-paulii Koehne & Gräbn.. See *P.quinquefolia* var. *saint-paulii*.

P.semicordata (Wallich) Planch. (*Vitis semicordata* Wallich in Roxb.; *Vitis himalayana* var. *semicordata* (Wallich) M. Lawson).
Similar to *P.himalayana* but young shoots pilose; leaves smaller, pilose beneath. Himalaya. Z9.

P.sinensis Diels & Gilg. See *P.himalayana* var. *rubrifolia*.
P.spaethii Koehne & Gräbn. See *P.inserta*

P.thomsonii (Lawson) Planch. (*Vitis thomsonii* Lawson; *Cissus thomsonii* (Lawson) Planch.; *Cayratia thomsonii* (Lawson) Süsseng.).
Vine, climbing, slender, deciduous; tendrils 3–5-branched; stems angular, finely pubescent when young. Leaves 5-parted; leaflets 2.5–10×1–4cm, rather thick-textured, glossy and glabrous above, sparsely downy on main vein beneath, ovate to obovate, acute at apex, tapered to base, shallowly serrate in distal part; petiole slender, 4–11cm, downy, petiolule 3–8mm; leaves, petioles and young shoots bright claret-purple when young, dark shining green tinged purple when mature, ageing to deep maroon. Inflorescence cymose, peduncles elongate and slender. Fruit black. W & C China. Z8.

P.tricuspidata (Sieb. & Zucc.) Planch. in DC. (*Ampelopsis tricuspidata* Sieb. & Zucc.; *Ampelopsis hoggii* Nichols.; *Vitis inconstans* Miq.). JAPANESE CREEPER; BOSTON IVY; VIRGINIA CREEPER.
Vine, stems to 20m, young shoots glabrous; tendrils short, much-branched. Leaves very variable, often so on the same plant, 6–20×3–15cm, broadly ovate and variably 3-lobed with acuminate, serrate lobes or trifoliolate with stalked obovate leaflets, usually shining mid-green and glabrous above, somewhat pubescent on veins beneath or, rarely, above, turning crimson, scarlet or purple in fall. Inflorescence on short shoots, in narrow terminal thyrsoid panicles opposite leaves with several lateral branches. Fruit somewhat flattened, 6–8mm diam., dull dark blue with bloom. Summer. China, Japan. 'Atropurpurea': vigorous growth; leaves large, green tinged blue turning purple, red in spring and autumn. 'Aurata': leaves almost yellow, somewhat marbled green and red, margin rough. 'Beverley Brook': leaves exceptionally small, red in autumn. 'Green Spring': young leaves tinged red, later bright, glossy green above, dull beneath, to 25cm. 'Lowii' (var. *lowii* Rehd.; *Ampelopsis lowii* Cook) (MINIATURE JAPANESE IVY): smaller and more slender; leaves small, 2–3cm, 3–7-lobed, bright green tinged purple when young, colouring brilliant red in autumn; very elegant when young. 'Minutifolia': leaves small, glossy, later purple turning pink. 'Purpurea': leaves persistently red tinged purple. 'Robusta': strong growth; leaves large, glossy, often trifoliate, red and orange in autumn. 'Veitchii' (var. *veitchii* (Gräb) Rehd.; *P.veitchii* Gräbn.) (JAPANESE IVY): leaves small, simple or 3-foliate, leaflets with 1–3 large teeth on each side, purple when young. Z4.

P.veitchii Gräbn. See *P.tricuspidata* 'Veitchii'.
P.vitacea (Kerner) Hitchc. See *P.inserta*.

Passiflora L. (From Lat. *passio*, passion and *flos*, flower, hence 'passion flower'. The name was given by the early Spanish missionaries in South America, in reference to a fancied representation in the flowers of the implements of the Crucifixion; the corona represented the crown of thorns, the five anthers the five wounds, the three styles the three nails, the five sepals and five petals the apostles, less Peter and Judas, and the hand-like leaves and flagellate tendrils the hands and scourges of Christ's persecutors.) PASSION FLOWER. Passifloraceae. Some 500 species of vines or scandent shrubs, sometimes erect herbs, shrubs or small trees. Shoots often angular, furnished with long, tightly spiralling tendrils arising at axils. Leaves alternate, extremely variable in shape, usually 3–5-lobed, sometimes bilobed or entire; petioles often with stalked glands. Flowers regular, usually solitary, sometimes paired and axillary or in very short terminal cymes, usually subtended by 3 green bracts; calyx cupped to tubular, sepals 5, fleshy or membranous; petals 5, sometimes absent; filaments in several series, forming a showy corona between petals and stamens; stamens 5 on a gynophore, anthers linear, ovate or oblong, 2-celled; stigma capitate; styles 3; ovary globose, ovoid or fusiform. Fruit usually a juicy, indehiscent, many-seeded berry; seeds compressed, reticulate, puncticulate or transversely furrowed. Tropical Americas, Asia, Australia, Polynesia.

CULTIVATION   Grown as ornamentals for their exquisitely beautiful, intricately formed and often fragrant and nectar-rich flowers, and for their attractive, sometimes edible fruits; a number are grown commercially for their fruits in the subtropics and in tropical highlands. The fruits of many species are eaten raw, or in some cases used to prepare drinks, ice cream, pies, sauces and so on; some are canned in syrup or candied. *P.ligularis* is considered by many to be the best edible species, while *P.alata*, *P.laurifolia*, *P.mollissima* and *P.quadrangularis* are also widely cultivated for fruit.

A few species are sufficiently cold-tolerant for outdoor cultivation in cool temperate zones. They include the more or less evergreen *P.caerulea*, which with the protection of a sheltered wall will survive occasional lows down to –15°C/5°F; in cooler conditions it may be regarded as a herbaceous perennial since, with sufficient protection at the root, it will resprout from the base in spring. *P.incarnata*, with a truly herbaceous habit, will resprout from the base if given deep mulch protection where temperatures fall to –20°C/–4°F. *P.lutea*, also herbaceous, is the hardiest species, occurring as far north as Pennsylvania, and surviving temperatures as low –25°C/–13°F. They are fairly undemanding in their soil requirements, thriving in any moderately fertile, well-drained and adequately moisture-retentive soil, in sun or part-day shade. Provide the support of wire or trellis and, in less favoured areas, site with shelter from cold, drying winds, mulch with leafmould, bracken litter and a covering of evergreen branches, protecting top-growth with burlap or hessian if necessary. The remaining species need protected cultivation in cool temperate zones, making uniquely handsome and, under suitable conditions, productive specimens for the glasshouse or conservatory. *P.edulis*, *P.×allardii*, *P.antioquiensis*, *P.× caerulea-racemosa*, *P.× exoniensis*, *P.ligularis*, *P.manicata* and *P.mollissima* will tolerate winter temperatures as low as 5°C/40°F, although they may defoliate in these conditions, and are better maintained with minima at 7–10°C/45–50°F. Most of the remaining species require a temperature range of 13–16°C/55–60°F.

When grown for fruit, warm conditions (*c*16°C/60°F) are necessary during flowering to ensure good pollination and fruit set, temperatures thereafter being less critical. Hand pollination using the pollen of unrelated clones, or *P.caerulea*, and spraying with tomato setting hormone in the case of seedless fruit, all help ensure good fruiting; *P.quadrangularis* is self-sterile, and in *P.edulis* pollen is usually shed before the pistils are receptive. *P.coccinea* and *P.vitifolia*, among the most handsome of ornamentals, are also self-sterile but will fruit if hand-pollinated.

Grow all species in a freely draining, fibrous loam-based mix with additional leafmould and sharp sand; *Passiflora* species are generally unfastidious as to soil type, given good drainage, but perform best on soils of only moderate fertility, especially with regard to nitrogen, which encourages foliar growth at the expense of flowering. They are best grown in large pots or tubs, or, if grown in the open border, with some root restriction. Provide full sun with shade from the hottest sun in summer, water plentifully when in growth, sparingly at other times. Prune to prevent overcrowding by removing the weakest shoots in spring, and again if necessary after flowering, pinching out unwanted growth regularly during the growing season; spur back to an established framework in spring. Propagate by heel or nodal cuttings rooted in individual pots in a sandy propagating medium in a closed case or by seed. Evidence suggests that a number of frost-tender species show greater tolerance of low soil temperatures when grafted on to *P.caerulea*, and it may be a worthwhile experiment to grow and fruit *P.edulis*, for example, on *P.caerulea* rootstock in more favoured temperate gardens. Provide a warm south- or southwest-facing wall and train as a single-stemmed specimen on a support low enough to allow winter protection with straw and burlap/hessian or frame lights.

P.actinia Hook.
Stems vining, slender, subcylindric, glabrous. Leaves to 10×8cm, broad-oval or suborbicular, apex usually notched, base rounded or somewhat tapered, subpeltate, entire, glabrous, often glaucous beneath, subcoriaceous or membranous, 5–7-veined; stipules to 4×2cm, ovate; petioles slender to 5cm, 4-glandular. Flowers to 9cm diam., fragrant; pedicels slender, to 3cm; calyx campanulate, glabrous, white inside, green outside, sepals to 1.5cm diam., oblong-lanceolate, obtuse; petals to 2×1cm, white; filaments 4–5-seriate the outermost to 3cm, banded blue, white and red. Fruit glabrous. Spring–summer. SE Brazil. Z10.

P.adenopoda DC.
Stems vining, angular, subglabrous or hispidulous. Leaves to 12×15cm, 3–5-lobed, lobes ovate, apex abruptly acuminate, base cordate, entire or denticulate, hispidulous, 3–5-veined; stipules 1×1.5cm, suborbicular; petioles to 5cm, pubescent, biglandular. Flowers to 7cm diam.; pedicels to 2.5cm; sepals to 4×1cm, oblong-lanceolate, obtuse; petals to 1.2×0.5cm, green-white to ivory, linear-lanceolate; filaments 1-seriate. Fruit to 2.5cm diam., globose, minutely-pubescent; seeds 6×4mm, obcordate, reticulate. Mexico to Venezuela, E Peru. Z10.

P.alata C. Curtis.
Stems vining, stout, glabrous, with 4 winged angles. Leaves to 15 × 10cm, simple, ovate or ovate-oblong, apex acuminate, base rounded to subcuneate, entire or denticulate, membranous, glabrous, penninerved; stipules to 2 × 1cm, linear to ovate-lanceolate, entire or serrulate; petioles to 5cm, canaliculate, 2–4-glandular. Flowers to 12cm diam., fragrant; pedicels to 2.5cm; sepals oblong, obtuse, glabrous green to white beneath, pale crimson above; petals oblong, obtuse brilliant carmine; filaments 4-seriate to 3cm, banded purple red and white. Fruit to 10 × 6cm, obovoid or pyriform, glabrous, yellow. Spring–summer. NE Peru, E Brazil. 'Ruby Glow': fruit yellow, grapefruit-sized. Z10.

P.× alato-caerulea (*P.pfordtii* Mast.). (*P.alata* × *P.caerulea*.)
Stems angular, narrowly winged. Leaves trilobed, entire. Flowers to 10cm diam., pink to purple, white outside; sepals white inside; filaments triseriate, blue-violet, white at apex. Garden origin. 'Imperatrice Eugénie': flowers to 16cm diam., sepals white, petals lilac-pink, filaments white and mauve.

P.alba Link & Otto. See *P.subpeltata*.

P.× allardii Lynch. (*P.caerulea* 'Constance Elliot' × *P.quadrangularis*.)
Vigorous. Leaves usually trilobed. Flowers to 11.5cm diam., white, suffused pink; filaments deep cobalt-blue. Summer–autumn. Z9.

P.× amabilis Lem.
Stems vining, vigorous, slender, cylindric or subcylindric, glabrous. Leaves to 12 × 9cm, ovate-oblong or ovate-lanceolate, apex short-acute, base subcordate, entire, membranous, glabrous, penninerved or subtrinerved; stipules ovate-lanceolate, 1.5 × 0.3cm, acuminate, caducous; petioles to 4cm, slender, 2–4-glandular. Flowers to 9cm diam.; pedicels to 4cm; calyx 1.5 × 1.5cm, short-tubular, glabrous, bright red inside, green outside, sepals 3.5 × 1cm, linear-oblong or linear-lanceolate; petals similar to sepals, bright red; filaments 4-seriate, white. Fruit glabrous. Spring. S Brazil. Z10. cf. *P.violacea.*

P.amethystina Mikan (*P.onychina* Lindl.).
Stems vigorous, vining, slender, cylindric, glabrous or sparsely and weakly downy. Leaves to 6 × 10cm, trilobed, lobes oblong, apex obtuse, base cordate and often peltate, membranous, glabrous, somewhat glaucous beneath, 5-veined; stipules to 1 × 0.4cm, ovate-lanceolate, aristate; petioles to 4.5cm, 5–8-glandular. Flowers to 8cm diam.; pedicels to 5cm; calyx campanulate, green, sepals to 6mm diam., oblong, carinate, sharp-tipped bright blue inside, green outside; petals to 8mm diam., deeper in colour than sepals, oblong, obtuse; filaments 4–5-seriate, to 2.5cm, dark purple; styles connate at base. Fruit ellipsoid, to 6 × 2.5cm, subglabrous. Autumn. E Brazil. Z10.

P.antioquiensis Karst. (*P.van volxemii* Triana & Planch.).
BANANA PASSION FRUIT.
Stems vining or sprawling, slender, cylindric, minutely rusty-pubescent or tomentose. Leaves to 15 × 8cm, dimorphic, ovate to lanceolate, or trilobed, lobes lanceolate, subcordate or rounded at base, irregularly sharp-serrate, pubescent or glabrous, lanuginose beneath; stipules to 0.7cm, subulate; petioles to 4cm, stout, glandular, lanuginose. Flowers to 12.5cm diam.; pedicels to 50cm, lanuginose; calyx to 4cm, narrowly tubular, glabrous, rose-red or magenta, sepals to 6.5 × 2.5cm, oblong-lanceolate, obtuse; petals oblong-lanceolate, obtuse, often of a deeper shade than sepals; filaments 3-seriate, corona small, violet. Fruit ellipsoid. Summer. Colombia.Z9.

P.arborea Spreng.
Tree or shrub to 10m, not usually climbing. Branches cylindric, glabrous, rufous when young. Leaves to 30 × 15cm, oblong or obovate-oblong, apex acute or briefly-acuminate, base rounded or subcuneate, membranous or subcoriaceous, bright green above, glaucous or with minute hairs on veins beneath, penninerved; petioles to 3cm. Flowers to 7.5cm diam. clustered 3–6 on nodding axillary, peduncles to 6cm;

calyx to 1 × 0.5cm, cylindric-campanulate, sepals to 3 × 1.2cm, green-white, linear-oblong, obtuse; petals linear-oblong, obtuse, close to sepals in colour, usually slightly less green; filaments triseriate, yellow. Fruit to 4×2.5cm, ovoid, somewhat yellow. Summer. Colombia. Z10.

P.atomaria Planch. See *P.subpeltata*.

P.× atropurpurea Nichols. (*P.racemosa* × *P.kermesina*.)
Flowers dark blood-red, 7.5cm diam.; sepals purple inside; filaments violet, spotted white.

P.aurantia Forst. f. (*P.banksii* Benth.).
Stems vining, angular, glabrous. Leaves to 7.5cm, shallowly trilobed, lobes ovate, blunt, acute sometimes lobulate. Flowers to 10cm diam., bracts setiform; sepals pale pink deepening to orange-red, linear-oblong; petals orange to brick red; filaments deep red, those of inner series forming a broad tube, those of outer to 2cm, united at base. Fruit 4cm, ovoid. Summer. Australia (Queensland). Z10.

P.banksii Benth. See *P.aurantia*.
P.× belottii Pépin. See *P.× alato-caerulea*.

P.biflora Lam.
Stems vining, 5-angled, furrowed, twisted, green or purple-green, subglabrous. Leaves to 10 × 10cm, narrowly suborbicular to reniform, sometimes bilobed, lobes lanceolate or ovate, apex usually acuminate, base truncate to cuneate, coriaceous, glabrous above, glabrous or minutely pubescent beneath, reticulately 3-veined; stipules narrow linear-subulate or setiform, to 3mm; petioles to 3cm, eglandular. Flowers to 3.5cm diam.; pedicels to 3cm; calyx patelliform or campanulate, white and glabrous inside, green and minutely pubescent or subglabrous outside, sepals to 1.2 × 7cm, ovate-lanceolate, obtuse; petals 8×5mm, white; corona 2.5cm diam., yellow, filaments biseriate. Fruit to 2cm diam., globose. Summer. Mexico to Colombia, Venezuela, Ecuador and Bahamas. Z10.

P.bryonioides HBK.
Stems vining, bluntly angled or subcylindric, hispidulous. Leaves to 7 × 9cm, deeply trilobed, lobes oblong, lateral lobes themselves sometimes bilobed, apex acute or obtuse, base cordate, entire or dentate, hispidulous, 3–5-veined; stipules 0.5 × 2.5cm, semi-ovate, cuspidate, ciliate; petioles to 5cm, biglandular, pubescent Flowers to 3cm diam.; pedicels to 3cm; calyx patelliform or campanulate, green-white, sepals to 1.3 × 0.5cm, ovate-lanceolate, obtuse or subacute; petals 4×1mm, white, linear or linear-lanceolate; corona white, filaments 1-seriate; styles connate at base. Fruit to 3.5 × 2.5cm, ovoid. SW US (Arizona), Mexico. Often confused with *P.morifolia*, which has purple fruits at maturity. Z8.

P.caerulea L. PASSION FLOWER; BLUE PASSION FLOWER.
Stems robust, subangular, striate, furrowed, glabrous, sometimes glaucous. Leaves to 10 × 2.5cm, palmately 5-, sometimes 3-, 7- or 9-, lobed, lobes oblong, apex obtuse or emarginate, base cordate, membranous, glabrous; stipules to 2 × 1cm, ovate; petioles to 4cm, 2–4-, rarely 6-, glandular. Flowers to 10cm diam., faintly fragrant; pedicels to 7cm, usually stout; calyx cupulate, subcoriaceous, glabrous, white or pink-white inside, green outside, sepals to 2 × 1.5cm, oblong, obtuse; petals to 2.5 × 1.5cm, oblong, obtuse, thin-textured, of a slightly clearer colour than sepals filaments 4-seriate, broadly banded, blue at apex, white at centre, purple at base. Fruit 6 × 4cm, ovoid or subglobose, glabrous, orange or yellow. Summer–autumn. Brazil, Argentina. 'Constance Eliott': flowers ivory white. 'Grandiflora': flowers to 15cm diam. Z7.

P.× caerulea-racemosa. (*P.caerulea* × *P.racemosa*.)
Leaves deeply 5-lobed, glabrous. Flowers dark violet, solitary; filaments deep purple-violet. 'Eynsford Gem': flowers pink-mauve; filaments white. Z9.

P.capsularis L.
Stems vining, 3–5-angular, striate, subglabrous or pubescent Leaves to 7 × 10cm, bilobed, lobes downward-pointing, lanceolate, apex acute, base cordate, subglabrous or pilosulous above, lighter and densely-pubescent beneath, 3-veined; stip-

ules linear-subulate, to 7mm; petioles to 3cm, eglandular. Flowers to 6cm diam.; pedicels to 6cm, slender; calyx to 3 × 0.4cm, patelliform or campanulate, pilose, sepals linear-lanceolate, acute, green-white; petals to 1.5 × 0.4cm, ivory, narrow oblong-lanceolate or subspathulate, obtuse; filaments yellow-white, 1–2-seriate. Fruit to 6 × 2cm, ellipsoid or fusiform ridged and angled, ripening purple-red. Summer. Nicaragua to C Brazil to Paraguay, Greater Antilles. Z10.

P.× cardinalis hort. ex Mast.(*P.alata* × *P.racemosa* (?).) Intermediate between parents. Flowers red, 7.5cm diam. Z10.

P.cheilidonea Mast.
Stems vining, angular, striate, lanuginose. Leaves to 14 × 8cm, oblong-lanceolate, bilobed or trilobed, lobes lanceolate, (the central lobe often reduced or merely a mucro in the apical sinus), apex acute, base subcordate or rounded, coriaceous, glabrous; stipules narrow-linear, acuminate; petioles to 2cm, somewhat purple. Flowers to 5cm diam.; peduncles to 2cm; calyx glossy, sepals 2.5 × 1.2cm, yellow green, oblong-lanceolate; petals 1.2 × 0.4cm, of a somewhat clearer colour; filaments biseriate, white, the outermost spotted violet. Fruit 1.5cm diam., globose, seeds 4 × 2.5mm, obovoid, transverse-sulcate. Summer. Colombia, Ecuador. Z10.

P.cinnabarina Lindl.
Stems slender, glabrous. Leaves to 10 × 10cm, usually trilobed, lobes ovate, cordate at base; petioles eglandular. Flowers 6.5cm diam.; bracts setiform; sepals 2.5 × 1cm, bright scarlet, narrow-oblong; petals vivid scarlet, to 1.25cm; filaments erect, corona yellow. Spring–summer. Australia. Z10.

P.coccinea Aubl. (*P.fulgens* Wallis ex Morr.). RED PASSION FLOWER; RED GRANADILLA.
Stems vining, subcylindric, bluntly angled, deep-furrowed, finely rufous minutely-pubescent to tomentose, somewhat purple. Leaves to 14 × 7cm, oblong, rarely suborbicular, apex acute to subobtuse, base subcordate, biserrate or crenate, membranous, subglabrous or minute-pubescent above, tomentose beneath; stipules linear, to 6mm; petioles to 3.5cm, eglandular or biglandular at base. Flowers to 12.5cm diam.; pedicels stout, to 8cm; calyx to 2 × 1.3cm, cylindric-campanulate, sepals to 5 × 1cm, exterior yellow, interior scarlet, linear-lanceolate, acute; petals to 4 × 0.8cm, vivid scarlet, linear, acute; filaments triseriate, pale pink to white at base, deep purple toward apex. Fruit 5cm diam., ovoid or subglobose, finely tomentose, orange or yellow, green-striate and -mottled. Guianas, S Venezuela, Peru, Bolivia, Brazil. Z10.

P.× colvillii Sweet. (*P.caerulea* × *P.incarnata*.)
Leaves deep 3–5-lobed, dentate. Flowers 9cm diam., white, red-spotted; corona filaments banded purple, white and blue. Z7.

P.coriacea Juss. BAT-LEAF PASSION FLOWER.
Stems vining, angular, densely and minutely when young. Leaves to 7 × 25cm, usually 2–3-lobed, lobes oblong-ovate, acute, rarely obtuse, broadly divergent, the whole leaf resembling a bat with outspread wings, peltate, coriaceous, glabrous, reticulately 5-veined. Flowers to 3.5cm diam., solitary and axillary, or in terminal racemes to 6cm; calyx patelliform or campanulate, yellow-green above, sepals to 1.5 × 0.5cm, oblong-lanceolate, obtuse; petals absent; filaments ivory, biseriate. Fruit to 2cm diam., globose, glabrous. Mexico to N Peru and N Bolivia, Guyana. Z10.

P.× decaisneana Planch. (*P.alata* × *P.quadrangularis*.)
Flowers 10cm diam., brilliant carmine; filaments purple and white. Also arising from this cross is *P.× innesii* Mast. (strictly a synonym), with flowers off-white, speckled red; sepals white inside; corona filaments several-seriate, white, banded red at base, spotted violet above, apex white. Garden origin. Z10.

P.edulis Sims. GRANADILLA; PURPLE GRANADILLA; PASSION FRUIT.
Stems vining, bluntly angled, somewhat lanuginose or glabrous. Leaves to 10 × 20cm, deeply trilobed, lobes ovate, glandular-dentate, shiny above, glabrous; petioles biglandular. Flowers to 7.5cm diam.; bracts 12.5mm+; sepals oblong,

spreading, white above, green beneath; petals somewhat narrower and paler than sepals; filaments white banded purple or indigo, strongly wavy towards tips. Fruit 5cm diam., ovoid, green-yellow to dull purple, speckled. Summer. Brazil. f. *edulis*. Fruit yellow. 'Alice': flowers abundant; fruits egg-shaped, purple. 'Crackerjack': fruits large, deep purple to black, abundant. 'Purple Passion': flowers purple. 'Supreme': fruits large, rounded. Additional purple-fruited cvs include 'Black Knight', 'Edgehill','Frederick', 'Purple Giant', 'Red Giant', 'Red Rover' and 'Sunnypash' (usually grafted on *P.caerulea*; very adaptable). f. *flavicarpa* Degen. Yellow-fruited. Cultivars include 'Brazilian Golden' and 'Golden Giant'. Z10.

P.eichleriana Mast.
Stems vining, slender, cylindric, glabrous, somewhat purple. Leaves to 8×10cm, trilobed, lobes oblong, apex mucronate, base cordate and subpeltate, entire, membranous, glabrous, 5-veined; stipules to 3 × 1.5cm, oblong-lanceolate, acuminate; petioles to 6cm, 6–8-glandular. Flowers to 7cm diam.; pedicels to 6cm; calyx campanulate, glabrous, sepals 1cm diam., white-green, oblong, subcoriaceous; petals white, oblong, membranous; filaments 6-seriate. Fruit 3.5cm diam., globose, coriaceous, glabrous. E Brazil, Paraguay. Sometimes confused with *P.subpeltata* or misnamed as its synonym, *P.alba*. Z10.

P.× exoniensis hort. ex L.H. Bail. (*P.antioquiensis* × *P.mollissima*.)
Stems vining, initially lanuginose. Leaves to 10 × 12.5cm, base cordate, lanuginose, deeply trilobed; petioles 2.5cm, biglandular. Flowers to 12.5cm diam., pendulous; calyx 6.5cm, tubular-cylindric, glabrous, exterior brick red, interior rosy pink, sepals oblong-lanceolate; petals bright pink with a violet tint in the throat, oblong-lanceolate; corona small, somewhat white. Z10.

P.filamentosa Cav.
Stems tall, vining, cylindric, lanuginose. Leaves to 8 × 12cm, usually palmately 5–7-lobed, lobes to 3cm diam., oblong-lanceolate, slightly toothed apex acuminate, base cordate, membranous, glossy above, glabrous or minutely villous; stipules to 4 × 1.5mm, aristate, asymmetrically serrulate, caducous; petioles to 4cm, biglandular. Flowers to 8cm diam.; pedicels to 5cm; calyx campanulate, white, sepals to 1cm diam., narrow-oblong, obtuse; petals similar in shape to sepals, white tinted rose filaments several-seriate, white, the outermost banded blue. Fruit 4cm diam., globose. Autumn. C Brazil. Z10.

P.foetida L. RUNNING POP; LOVE-IN-A-MIST; WILD WATER LEMON.
Stems vining, malodorous when crushed. Shoots viscid, densely hairy. Leaves hastate, 3–5-lobed, thin-textured, adpressed-pubescent, glandular-ciliate; petioles to 6cm, eglandular. Flowers to 5cm diam., subtended by 3 showy, deeply and finely glandular-fringed bracts; pedicels to 6cm; calyx white to ivory streaked green, sepals ovate; petals oblong, ivory-lilac; filaments several-seriate white banded violet. Fruit to 2.5cm diam., globose or subglobose, sparsely, rarely densely, hirsute, yellow to bright red. Summer–autumn. South America, Puerto Rico, Jamaica, Lesser Antilles. Z10.

P.fulgens Wallis ex Morr. See *P.coccinea*.

P.galbana Mast.
Stems slender, vining, cylindric, somewhat flexuous, glabrous. Leaves to 13 × 6.5cm, oblong-lanceolate, entire, apex obtuse and mucronulate, base rounded or shallow-cordate, coriaceous, glabrous; stipules to 2 × 1cm, ovate-lanceolate, acute; petioles to 1.5cm, minutely-glandular. Flowers on stout cylindric pedicels to 9cm, fragrant, opening at night; calyx broadly cylindric-campanulate, glabrous, sepals 4 × 0.7cm, narrow-oblong, white, horned; petals 6.5mm diam., narrow-oblong, white to primrose yellow; filaments biseriate, to 12.5mm. Fruit to 7 × 2cm, narrow-ovoid, tapered at apex, glabrous. Winter. E Brazil. Z10.

P.garckei Mast. (*P.pruinosa* Mast.).
Stems vining, cylindric, or somewhat angular above, glabrous. Leaves to 15×25cm, trilobed, lobes oblong-lanceolate, apex acute to obtuse, base truncate or subcordate, subpeltate, entire or subentire, coriaceous, glabrous, reticulately 5–7-veined; stipules to 5 × 2cm, ovate or subreniform, mucronate; petioles to 10cm, 4–6-glandular. Flowers to 8.5cm diam.; pedicels to 6cm; calyx campanulate, glabrous, sepals to 4 × 1cm, blue or purple above, oblong, cucullate; petals to 3.5×1.2cm, lilac, oblong, obtuse; filaments severalseriate, white with a broad central violet band. Fruit subellipsoid, glabrous. Autumn. French Guiana, Guyana, Surinam. Z10.

P.glandulosa Cav. (*P.imthurnii* Mast.).
Stems vining, cylindric or subangular, glabrous or minutepubescent, purple-tinted. Leaves to 15 × 10cm, ovate-oblong to oblong-lanceolate, apex acute or acuminate and mucronulate, base cordate to subacute, entire or somewhat undulate, glaucous, glabrous or minutely-pubescent beneath, coriaceous; stipules linear-subulate or setiform, caducous; petioles to 2.5cm, biglandular. Flowers red or scarlet; peduncles to 8cm; calyx to 2.5 × 1cm, cylindric, sepals to 5 × 1.3cm, oblong; filaments to 1.25cm, biseriate, pink. Fruit to 6×3cm, ovoid. Spring. Guianas, Surinam, E Brazil. Z10.

P.gracilis Jacq. ex Link.
Stems vining, slender, subangular, glabrous. Leaves to 7×10cm, trilobed, lobes obtuse or rounded, cordate at base, entire, membranous, glabrous, glaucous beneath, 3-veined. Flowers 2cm diam.; pedicels to 3cm; calyx patelliform or campanulate, sepals to 1×0.3cm, white to pale green, narrow-oblong, obtuse, concave; petals absent; corona to 2cm diam., filaments biseriate; styles connate at base. Fruit 2.5 × 1.5cm, ellipsoid, glabrous, scarlet. Summer. Venezuela. Z10.

P.grandiflora hort. See *P.caerulea* 'Grandiflora'.

P.hahnii (Fourn.) Mast.
Stems vining, slender, cylindric, angular, striate, glabrous. Leaves to 8 × 7cm, broadly ovate-lanceolate, entire, peltate at base, membranous, glabrous, 3–5-veined, minutely toothed, purple-tinted beneath; stipules to 4 × 2cm, crenate to entire, tinged purple; petioles to 3cm, eglandular. Flowers to 6cm diam., white or cream; pedicels to 7cm; calyx patelliform or campanulate, glabrous, sepals and petals to 3 × 1cm, oblong, obtuse; filaments biseriate, yellow; styles connate at base. Fruit to 3.5cm diam., globose, glabrous. Summer–autumn. C Mexico to Costa Rica, Colombia. Z10.

P.herbertiana Ker-Gawl.
Stems robust, vining or scandent, lanuginose. Leaves 9×9cm, trilobed, lobes triangular, truncate, lanuginose. Flowers to 10cm diam., solitary or paired, white to pale orange-yellow, solitary or paired; sepals 4cm, linear-lanceolate; petals to 2cm; corona broadly tubular, yellow, filaments to 1.25cm. Australia. Z10.

P.holosericea L.
Stems vining, cylindric, striate, corky below, usually lanuginose above. Leaves to 10×7cm, trilobed, lobes rounded, apex mucronulate, base cordate and bidentate, entire, velutinous above, tomentose beneath, reticulately 3-veined; stipules 6mm; petioles to 2.5cm, biglandular. Flowers to 4cm diam., fragrant, solitary or on 2–4-flowered peduncles; calyx patelliform or campanulate, glabrous inside, densely-pubescent outside, sepals to 1.5 × 0.5cm, white, ovate-lanceolate, obtuse; petals to 1.3 × 0.6cm, white spotted red, oblanceolate or spathulate; filaments biseriate, yellow, purple at base; styles connate at base. Fruit 1.5cm diam., globose, glabrous or softpubescent. Mexico, Central America, C & W Cuba, N Colombia, N Venezuela.Z10.

P.imthurnii Mast. See *P.glandulosa*.

P.incarnata L. WILD PASSION FLOWER; MAY POPS; APRICOT VINE; MAY APPLE.
Stems vining, cylindric, angular when young, glabrous or finely lanuginose. Leaves to 15×15cm, trilobed, lobes lanceolate, apex acute or acuminate, base cordate, finely serrate, membranous, deep green above, somewhat glaucous beneath, 3-veined; stipules to 3mm, setiform, caducous; petioles to 8cm, biglandular. Flowers to 7.5cm diam.; sepals pale lavender with a horn-like apical projection; petals white or pale lavender; filaments usually pink to purple. Fruit to 5cm, ovoid, yellow. E US. Z6.

P.× innesii Mast. See *P.× decaisneana*.

P.insignis (Mast.) Hook. (*Tacsonia insignis* Mast.).
Stems vining, cylindric, densely lanuginose. Leaves to 25 × 12cm, ovate-lanceolate, apex acute, base minutely cordate, denticulate, coriaceous, shiny, glabrous and rugulose above, densely rusty-woolly beneath, 3–5-veined; stipules 2 × 1cm, bipinnatisect; petioles to 2cm, 2–4-glandular. Flowers pendulous; pedicels stout, to 20cm; calyx to 4cm×8mm, tubular-cylindric, tomentose, violet-crimson, sepals to 9 × 2cm, oblong, obtuse, concave; petals to 7 × 1.5cm, rose-purple, oblong, obtuse; filaments 12.5mm, 1-seriate, white, mottled blue. Summer–autumn. Bolivia, Peru. Z10.

P.jamesonii (Mast.) L.H. Bail. (*Tacsonia jamesonii* Mast.).
Stems vining, angular, glabrous. Leaves to 8 × 11cm, glabrous, trilobed, lobes subelliptic, apex acute or subobtuse and mucronate, base subcordate, spiny-dentate, subcoriaceous, glossy above; stipules to 2.5 × 0.8cm, oblong-lanceolate, deep-cleft. Flowers to 10cm diam., pendulous; pedicels to 10cm; bracts deeply laciniate; calyx to 10cm, tubular-cylindric, bright rose, sepals to 5×2cm, oblong, obtuse; petals rose to coral pink, oblong, obtuse; corona tinged purple. Fruit glabrous. Ecuador (Andes). Z9.

P.jorullensis HBK (*P.medusae* Lem.).
Stems vining, slender, subtriangular, dense-pubescent Leaves to 8.5 × 8cm, bilobed or trilobed the third lobe often reduced to a mucro in the sinus, lobes rounded or subacute, apex mucronulate, base subcuneate or truncate, minutely pubescent above, glabrous beneath, reticulately 3-veined; stipules setiform, to 3mm; petioles to 4cm, furrowed, eglandular. Flowers to 4cm diam., orange turning pink; pedicels to 3cm; calyx patelliform or campanulate, glabrous, sepals 1.5cm, linear-lanceolate, acute; petals to 4 × 1mm, slender, linear, obtuse; filaments 1-seriate, orange then pink almost equalling sepals; styles connate at base. Fruit 1cm diam., globose, glabrous, glossy black. Autumn. C & S Mexico. Z10.

P.kermesina Link & Otto.
Stems vining, slender, cylindric, glabrous. Leaves to 8 × 10cm, trilobed, lobes oblong-ovate, apex rounded or subacute, base truncate or cordate, membranous, glabrous, deep green above, somewhat glaucous and purple-tinted beneath; stipules to 2.5 × 1.2cm, subreniform, rounded, glaucous beneath; petioles to 4cm, minutely 2–4-glandular. Flowers to 8cm diam.; pedicels to 15cm, slender, tribracteate; calyx 1cm, cylindric-campanulate, glabrous, sepals to 4cm, linear-oblong, scarlet, obtuse, radiate, later reflexed; petals similar to sepals filaments 3–4-seriate, violet-purple; styles connate at base. Fruit glabrous. E Brazil. Z10.

P.× kewensis hort. (*P.caerulea* × *P.kermesina*.)
Flowers 9cm diam., carmine, suffused blue. Z8.

P.laurifolia L. (*P.tinifolia* Juss.). YELLOW GRANADILLA; WATER LEMON; JAMAICA HONEYSUCKLE; BELLE APPLE; VINEGAR PEAR; POMME-DE-LIANE.
Stems vining, cylindric, glabrous. Leaves to 12 × 8cm, ovate-oblong or oblong, subacute to obtuse, apex usually mucronate, base rounded, entire, coriaceous, glossy, glabrous, strongly reticulately 1-veined; stipules to 4mm, narrow-linear, coriaceous; petioles to 1.5cm, stout, biglandular. Flowers to 7cm diam.; pedicels to 3cm, rarely to 8cm; calyx to 1cm, cylindric-campanulate, glabrous, sepals to 2.5 × 1cm, green beneath, red above, oblong, obtuse; petals similar to sepals; filaments 6-seriate, outermost purple banded red, blue and white. Fruit to 8×4cm, ovoid, glabrous, lemon-yellow or orange. Summer. E Brazil, Peru, Venezuela, Guianas, W Indies, Trinidad. Z10.

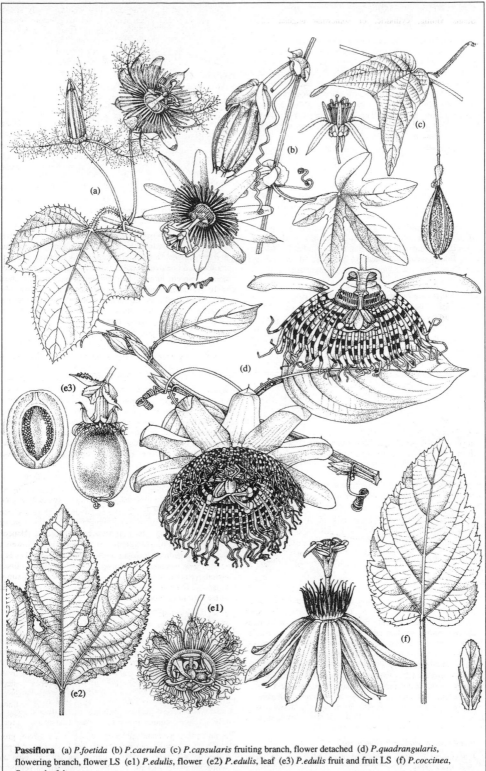

Passiflora   (a) *P.foetida* (b) *P.caerulea* (c) *P.capsularis* fruiting branch, flower detached (d) *P.quadrangularis*, flowering branch, flower LS (e1) *P.edulis*, flower (e2) *P.edulis*, leaf (e3) *P.edulis* fruit and fruit LS (f) *P.coccinea*, flower, leaf, bract

P.× lawsoniana Mast. (*P.alata × P.racemosa.*)
Leaves ovate-oblong, cordate at base. Flowers to 10cm diam., somewhat red; sepals rufous. Z10.

P.ligularis Juss. GRANADILLA; SWEET GRANADILLA.
Stems vining, vigorous, cylindric, glabrous. Leaves to 15 × 13cm, broadly ovate, apex abruptly acuminate, base deeply cordate, entire, membranous, glabrous, blue-green beneath, penninerved; stipules to 2.5 × 1.2cm, lanceolate; petioles to 10cm, 4–6-glandular, with filiform glands. Flowers to 9cm diam., pedicels to 4cm; calyx campanulate, glabrous, sepals to 3.5 × 1.5cm, green-white beneath, white or rosy above, ovate-oblong, acute; petals similar to sepals but smaller; filaments 5–7-seriate, white banded, purple, the outer series equalling petals Fruit to 8×5cm, ovoid, glabrous. Autumn. C Mexico, C America, Venezuela, Peru, W Bolivia. Z10.

P.lutea L.
Stems vining, slender, glabrous or sparsely downy. Leaves to 9×15cm, trilobed, lobes broadly triangular-ovate, apex rounded or obtuse, base rounded to subtruncate, usually membranous, reticulately 3-veined; stipules to 5mm, setiform; petioles to 5cm, eglandular. Flowers to 2cm diam.; pedicels to 4cm, slender, ebracteate; calyx patelliform, light green, sepals to 1 × 0.3cm, linear-oblong, obtuse; petals to 0.5 × 0.1cm, ivory, linear, subacute; filaments biseriate, white, pink at base. Fruit 1.5 × 1cm, globose-ovoid, purple. Summer. E US (Pennsylvania to Texas). Z5.

P.macrocarpa Mast. See *P.quadrangularis.*
P.maculifolia Mast. See *P.organensis.*

P.maliformis L. SWEET CALABASH; SWEETCUP; CONCH APPLE.
Stems vining, cylindric, subangular when young. Leaves to 12 × 10cm, sometimes to 25 × 15cm, ovate, apex acute or abruptly-acuminate, base rounded to cordate, finely serrulate or undulate, membranous; stipules to 1.5×0.2cm, linear; petioles to 5cm, biglandular. Flowers to 8cm diam., fragrant; pedicels to 5cm; calyx 1 × 1.2cm, campanulate, sepals 4 × 1.5cm, oblong, green; petals 3 × 0.5cm, green-white spotted purple, linear-lanceolate; filaments several-seriate, the innermost to 3cm, purple-red banded white, the outermost shorter, banded white and violet. Fruit to 4cm diam., globose, green or orange-green. Summer–autumn. Venezuela, Colombia, N Ecuador, W Indies. Z10.

P.manicata (Juss.) Pers. (*Tacsonia manicata* Juss.). RED PASSION-FLOWER.
Stems vigorously vining, stout, angular, subglabrous or densely strigulose. Leaves to 8 × 9cm, lower leaves to 10 × 14cm, trilobed, lobes ovate, apex obtuse or subacute, base subcordate or rounded, serrate, glabrous or minutely downy above, tomentose beneath; stipules to 2 × 1cm, ovate; petioles to 5cm, 4–10-glandular. Flowers vivid scarlet; pedicels to 7cm; calyx to 2 × 1cm, urceolate-campanulate, green-white inside, green outside, sepals to 3.5cm × 7mm, oblong-lanceolate, obtuse; petals oblong, obtuse; filaments 3–4-seriate, corona blue and white. Fruit to 5×3.5cm, ovoid or suborbicular, shiny deep green, glabrous. Colombia to Peru. Z9.

P.maximiliana Bory. See *P.misera.*
P.medusae Lem. See *P.jorullensis.*

P.membranacea Benth.
Stems vining, cylindric or subangular, striate, glabrous. Leaves to 10 × 10cm, orbicular, obscurely trilobed, base peltate, membranous, glabrous, 3-nerved; stipules to 1.5 × 3cm, cordate-reniform; petioles to 4cm, eglandular. Flowers light green or cream; pedicels slender, to 15cm; calyx 2cm diam., broad-campanulate, glabrous, to 4×1cm, oblong-lanceolate, obtuse; petals to 4×0.8cm, oblanceolate; filaments biseriate; styles connate at base. Fruit 4 × 3cm, ovoid, coriaceous, glabrous. S Mexico to Costa Rica. Z10.

P.mexicana Juss.
Stems vining, obscurely 5-angled, furrowed, glabrous. Leaves to 8cm diam., glabrous, bilobed, lobes to 4cm, oblong, apex obtuse, base truncate or rounded, deep green and glabrous above, paler beneath, 3-veined; stipules to 2mm, setiform or

narrow-linear; petioles to 2cm, eglandular. Flowers to 4cm diam., maroon; pedicels to 3cm; calyx 1cm diam., patelliform, glabrous, interior white, exterior green to red, sepals to 1.5cm, narrow-lanceolate; petals reflexed; filaments biseriate; styles connate at base. Fruit to 1.2cm diam., globose, glabrous. SW US (S Arizona), C Mexico. Z9.

P.miersii Mast.
Stems vining, slender, cylindric, glabrous, often bright yellow. Leaves to 8 × 3cm, lanceolate, apex subacute or rounded, base subpeltate, truncate or rounded, subcoriaceous, glabrous, dark claret or maroon, netted with pale green veins beneath; stipules to 2.5 × 1.2cm, ovate, rounded; petioles to 1.5cm, slender, biglandular. Flowers to 5cm diam.; pedicels to 5cm, slender, articulate; calyx campanulate, glabrous, sepals to 2.5 × 0.7cm, green, oblong, obtuse, aristate; petals white tinted pink, obtuse; filaments 4-seriate, white, the outermost banded violet. Fruit to 4 × 2cm, obovoid or ellipsoid, glabrous. Summer. E Brazil. Z10.

P.× militaris hort. (*P.antioquiensis × P.manicata.*)
Flowers to 12.5cm diam., bright crimson. Z10.

P.misera HBK (*P.maximiliana* Bory).
Stems vining, angular or flattened, striate, glabrous or subglabrous. Leaves to 13cm diam., bilobed, lobes to 2.5cm, apex rounded or subacute, base cordate or subtruncate, membranous, glabrous or pilosulous, flushed purple beneath reticulately 3-veined; stipules to 3.5mm, setiform to narrow-linear; petioles to 3.5cm, eglandular. Flowers to 4cm diam.; pedicels to 10cm, slender; calyx patelliform or campanulate, interior white, exterior green and minutely-pubescent, sepals to 1.8 × 0.5cm, lanceolate-oblong to linear-oblong, obtuse; petals to 1.3×0.4cm, white, linear-oblong, obtuse; filaments biseriate, tinted or marked purple; styles connate at base. Fruit to 13mm diam., globose or ovoid. Autumn. Panama, northern & eastern America to N Argentina. Z9.

P.mixta L. f.
Stems vining, angular, glabrous or grey-pubescent Leaves to 10 ×13cm, sometimes to 17cm, trilobed, lobes ovate-oblong, apex acute or abruptly acuminate, base truncate or subcordate, serrate, glabrous and distinctly veined above, glabrous to velutinous beneath, coriaceous; stipules to 2×1cm, subreniform, cuspidate; petioles to 3cm, 4–8-glandular. Flowers pendulous; pedicels to 6cm, stout; bracts sometimes woolly (var. *eriantha*) calyx to 11 × 1cm, tubular-cylindric, sepals to 4 × 1.5cm, pink to orange-red, oblong, obtuse; petals same colour on sepals obtuse; corona a deep lavender or purple rim composed of 1 or 2 ranks of very short filaments. Fruit to 6 × 2.5cm, ovoid. C Venezuela, Colombia, Ecuador, Peru, Bolivia. Z10.

P.mollissima (HBK) L.H. Bail. (*Tacsonia mollissima* HBK). CURUBA; BANANA PASSION FRUIT.
Stems vining, cylindric, striate, with soft golden hairs. Leaves to 10 × 12cm, trilobed, lobes ovate, apex acute, base subcordate, sharply serrate-dentate, soft-pubescent above, tomentose beneath, membranous; stipules to 9×4mm, subreniform; petioles to 9cm. Flowers pendulous; pedicels to 6cm; calyx to 8 × 1cm, olive-green, glabrous, long-tubular, sepals to 3.5×1.5cm, soft pink, oblong, obtuse; petals obtuse, same colour as sepals; corona reduced to a warty rim. Fruit to 7 × 3.5cm, oblong-ovoid, yellow-soft-pubescent. W Venezuela, Colombia, SE Peru, W Bolivia. Z6.

P.mooreana Hook.f.
Stems vining, subangular, stout, somewhat glaucous and scabrous, glabrous. Leaves to 12 × 10cm, glabrous, trilobed, lobes narrowly oblong-lanceolate, apex mucronate, base cuneate, coriaceous, glaucous beneath, distinctly and reticulately 5-veined; stipules to 4 × 1cm, ovate-lanceolate, acuminate; petioles to 0.7cm, biglandular. Flowers 6cm diam.; pedicels to 1.5cm; calyx campanulate, glabrous, white above, exterior green, sepals to 8mm diam., oblong, obtuse; petals 1cm diam., white oblong, obtuse; filaments biseriate, blue, banded white and indigo. Fruit ovoid, glabrous, yellow. Summer. S Bolivia, Paraguay, N Argentina. Z10.

P.morifolia Mast.
Stems vining, 4-angled, furrowed, subglabrous. Leaves to 11 × 15cm, trilobed, sometimes to 5-lobed, lobes ovate, apex acute, base cordate, dentate or subentire, membranous, deep green and uncinate-hispidulous above, lighter and pilosulous beneath; stipules 6 × 3mm, ovate; petioles to 6cm, biglandular. Flowers to 3cm diam.; pedicels to 2cm; sepals to 1.5 × 0.4cm, white and purple-mottled or uniformly green, linear-oblong, obtuse; petals to 0.8 × 0.4cm, inconspicuous, linear-lanceolate, obtuse; filaments 1-seriate. Fruit 2cm diam., purple, globose, glaucous, hispidulous. Guatemala, Peru, Paraguay, Argentina. Very similar to *P.warmingii*. 'Scarlet Flame': fruit tasting of strawberries. Z10.

P.oerstedii Mast.
Stems vining, slender, subangular when young, later cylindric. Leaves to 13 × 9cm, lanceolate, apex acute or obtuse, only rarely bilobed or trilobed, base usually cordate, subpeltate, green and glabrous above, glaucous and glabrous to dense-tomentose beneath, 5–7-veined; stipules to 4 × 1.5cm, ovate; petioles to 4cm, (2-)4–6-glandular. Flowers to 6cm diam.; pedicels to 4cm, glabrous; calyx to 8mm, campanulate, sepals to 3 × 1.2cm, white, ovate-lanceolate; petals to 1.5 × 0.5cm white tinted pink, linear, obtuse; filaments several-seriate, purple. Fruit to 6 × 3cm, ovoid. S Mexico to Colombia and C Venezuela. Z10.

P.onychina Lindl. See *P.amethystina*.

P.organensis Gardn. (*P.maculifolia* Mast.).
Stems vining, subangular, flattened, glabrous. Leaves shaped like a fishtail, dark green tinted purple to chocolate brown with somewhat jagged-edged regions of silver, cream, pink or lime-green variegation, glabrous, bilobed, rarely trilobed, lobes to 3cm diam., divergent, broad-ovate to lanceolate, apex mucronulate, base rounded, membranous or subcoriaceous, 3–5-veined extrafloral nectaries conspicuous above as dark spots; stipules to 3mm, linear-subulate; petioles to 3cm, slender, eglandular. Flowers to 5cm diam., cream to dull purple, usually solitary; peduncles to 4cm; calyx to 1.5cm diam., broad-patelliform, glabrous, sepals 1.5cm, oblong-lanceolate, obtuse, recurved; petals to 7.5mm, ovate-lanceolate; filaments to three-quarters length of petals, 1-seriate, cream to dark violet to purple. Fruit to 1.5cm diam., globose, glabrous. E Brazil. Z10.

P.peltata Cav. See *P.suberosa*.

P.penduliflora Bertero ex DC.
Stems vining, strongly angular, striate, glabrous. Leaves to 7.5 × 8cm, suborbicular to triangular-obovate, shallowly trilobed with lobes acute or obtuse, sometimes subentire, rounded at base, trinerved, subcoriaceous or membranous; stipules to 4mm; petioles to 2cm, slender, eglandular. Flowers to 4cm diam., pedicels to 10cm; calyx campanulate, sepals to 2 × 0.6cm, yellow-green, oblong-lanceolate, obtuse; petals to 0.7cm, yellow-green to ivory, oblanceolate, short-clawed at base; filaments 1-seriate; styles connate at base. Fruit to 1.5cm diam., globose or ovoid. Spring–summer. E Cuba, Jamaica. Z10.

P.perfoliata L.
Stems vining, angular, striate, glabrous or lanuginose. Leaves to 6 × 2.5cm, oblong, bilobed, lobes widely divergent, rounded-ovate, overlapping at base, perfoliate, subcoriaceous, 3-veined; stipules to 3mm, linear-subulate; petioles to 5mm, eglandular, glabrous or minute-pubescent. Flowers maroon, solitary rarely paired; pedicels to 3cm; calyx to 1.3 × 0.8cm, turbinate-cylindric, sepals to 2 × 0.3cm, linear-subulate; petals to 0.7cm diam., oblanceolate, acute; filaments 1-seriate, corona very short, yellow. Fruit to 1.5cm diam., globose. Summer. Jamaica. Z10.

P.pfordtii Mast. See *P.× alato-caerulea*.

P.picturata Ker-Gawl.
Stems vining, cylindric, glabrous. Leaves to 6 × 7cm, trilobed, lobes ovate, apex rounded or subacute, base subpeltate and usually rounded, glabrous, membranous, bright green above,

somewhat purple beneath; stipules to 2.5 × 1cm, ovate; petioles to 3cm, slender, 2–6-glandular. Flowers to 10cm diam.; pedicels to 12cm, stout; calyx 0.5 × 1.5cm, campanulate, glabrous, interior white, blue or violet, exterior green, sepals 2.5 × 1cm, linear-oblong, somewhat concave; petals smaller than sepals, pale rose or violet, oblong, obtuse; filaments biseriate the outermost white banded blue. Fruit to 3.5cm diam., globose, glabrous. Autumn. Surinam, Brazil. Z10.

P.pinnatistipula Cav.
Stems vining, long, angular, white-tomentose or lanate at first, later subglabrous. Leaves to 10 × 13cm, trilobed, lobes lanceolate, apex acute or acuminate and mucronate, base subcordate, sharp-serrate, rugose and glabrous above, densely grey-white-lanate beneath, coriaceous; stipules to 7 × 5mm, with pinnate, filiform lobes; petioles to 3.5cm, 4–6-glandular. Pedicels to 7cm, nodding; calyx to 5 × 1cm, tubular-cylindric, interior white tinged blue, exterior bright pink, densely-tomentose, sepals to 4 × 1cm, oblong, obtuse; petals bright rosy pink, obtuse; filaments 2.5cm, biseriate, blue. Fruit 5cm diam., subglobose, somewhat tomentose or subglabrous, yellow-green. Peru, Chile. Z10.

P.princeps Lodd. See *P.racemosa*.
P.pruinosa Mast. See *P.garckei*.

P.psilantha (Sodiro) Killip (*Tacsonia psilantha* Sodiro).
Stems vining, cylindric, striate, soft-pubescent. Leaves to 8 × 10cm, trilobed, lobes oblong-lanceolate, apex acuminate, base cordate, serrate-dentate, subglabrous or finely and minutely above, soft-pubescent, especially on veins, beneath; stipules to 1 × 0.5cm, subreniform; petioles to 2.5cm, 8–10-glandular. Flowers pale red or white; pedicels to 2.5cm; calyx to 10 × 0.5cm, tubular-cylindric, glabrous, sepals to 3 × 0.5cm, narrow-oblong, obtuse; petals obtuse. Fruit 5 × 2.5cm, ovoid, soft-pubescent. S Ecuador (mts). Z9.

P.punctata L.
Stems vining, subtriangular, flattened, striate, glabrous. Leaves to 5 × 12cm, oblong, glabrous, shallowly trilobed or bilobed, lobes rounded and emarginate, base truncate or subcordate, membranous, somewhat glaucous beneath, 3–5-veined; stipules to 5mm, linear-falcate; petioles to 6cm, slender, eglandular. Flowers to 4cm diam., green-white; pedicels slender, to 8cm; calyx campanulate, glabrous, glossy light yellow-green, duller inside, sepals to 1.8 × 1cm, oblong-lanceolate, obtuse; petals to 1.2 × 0.6cm, oblong-lanceolate, recurved; filaments biseriate; styles connate at base. Fruit 2cm, ellipsoid, glabrous. Ecuador, N Peru. Sometimes confused with *P.misera*. Z10.

P.quadrangularis L. (*P.macrocarpa* Mast.). GRANADILLA; GIANT GRANADILLA.
Stems vining, stout, 4-angular, angles distinctly winged, glabrous. Leaves to 20 × 15cm, ovate-lanceolate, apex abruptly acuminate, base rounded, to cordate, entire, glabrous, penninerved; stipules to 3.5 × 2cm, ovate, acute; petioles to 5cm, stout, 6-glandular. Flowers to 12cm diam.; pedicels to 3cm; calyx shallowly campanulate, glabrous, sepals to 4 × 2.5cm, green beneath, pearly grey-green tinted flesh pink above, ovate or ovate-oblong, concave; petals to 4.5 × 2cm, fleshy, pale mauve-pink, oblong-ovate to oblong-lanceolate, obtuse; filaments 5-seriate, white, banded blue and red-purple, equalling sepals and strongly twisted. Fruit to 30 × 15cm, oblong-ovoid, glabrous Tropical America. 'Variegata': leaves splotched yellow. Z10.

P.racemosa Brot. (*P.princeps* Lodd.). RED PASSION FLOWER.
Stems scandent or vining, almost 4-angled, striate, light green when young, glabrous. Leaves to 10 × 11cm, polymorphic, ovate and simple, or trilobed, lobes oblong, apex acute or subobtuse, base subpeltate, truncate or cordate, entire, coriaceous, glabrous, 5-veined; stipules to 1.5 × 1cm, broad-ovate; petioles to 4cm, slender, biglandular. Flowers to 12cm diam., scarlet-red or white, in pendulous, 8–13-flowered, racemes to 30cm; pedicels 1cm; calyx to 1.5 × 1.2cm, cylindric, glabrous, throat maroon, sepals to 4 × 1cm, oblong, with keel-like longi-

tudinal wings; petals oblong, obtuse; filaments triseriate, white banded dark purple, inner filaments red and very short. Fruit to 7 × 3cm, narrow-ovoid, obtuse, coriaceous, glabrous. Brazil. Z10.

P.raddiana DC. See *P.kermesina*.

P.rubra L.
Stems vining, 3–5-angled, striate, densely grey-pubescent, rarely subglabrous. Leaves to 8 × 10cm, bilobed (rarely with a far smaller midlobe), cordate at base, membranous, downy; stipules to 8mm, setiform; petioles to 5cm, eglandular. Flowers to 5cm diam.; pedicels ebracteate; calyx patelliform or campanulate, glabrous inside, pubescent outside, distinctly 3-veined, sepals to 3 × 0.6cm, ivory to linear-lanceolate, subacute; petals to 1.5 × 0.4cm, similar to colour to sepals; filaments 1–2-seriate, red-purple or lavender. Fruit to 2.5 × 1.8cm, rarely to 5.5 × 2.5cm, ovoid or obovoid, hirsute, later subglabrous. Autumn. Colombia, Venezuela, Peru, Bolivia, E Brazil, W Indies. Z10.

P.sanguinolenta Mast. & Lind.
Stems vining, angular, densely villous. Leaves densely villous, lunate-bilobed, lobes to 2cm diam., lanceolate, apex mucronulate, base cordate, membranous; stipules setiform, to 5mm; petioles to 1.5cm, eglandular. Flowers dull red or maroon; pedicels to 5cm, slender, ebracteate or bracts caducous; calyx to 2cm, cylindric, distinctly nerved, densely villous-hirsute, sepals to 2 × 0.5cm, linear-oblong; petals to 1 × 0.3cm, linear; filaments biseriate. Fruit densely villous-hirsute. Ecuador. Z9.

P.seemannii Griseb.
Stems vining, cylindric, striate, glaucous, glabrous. Leaves to 9 × 6cm, sometimes to 13 × 15cm, cordate-ovate, apex obtuse or abruptly acuminate and mucronate, base deeply-cordate, subentire, glaucous, glabrous, thin-textured; stipules to 1.5cm, linear, serrulate; petioles to 7cm, biglandular, sometimes 4-glandular. Flowers to 10cm diam.; pedicels to 10cm; calyx 2cm, campanulate-funnelform, glabrous, white, tinged purple or violet, sepals to 4 × 1.5cm, ovate-lanceolate, obtuse, corniculate; petals to 3.5 × 1.2cm, purple, oblong-lanceolate, obtuse; filaments biseriate. Fruit to 5×3.5cm, ovoid, glabrous. S Mexico to Panama, NW Colombia. Z10.

P.serratifolia L.
Stems vining, vigorous, cylindric, striate, minutely hirsute. Leaves to 12 × 7cm, ovate, apex acuminate, base rounded or cordate, serrulate, membranous or subcoriaceous, subglabrous above, minutely hirsute beneath; stipules 7mm, linear-subulate, serrulate; petioles to 12cm, densely and minutely hirsute, 6-glandular. Flowers to 6cm diam., fragrant; pedicels to 7cm; calyx campanulate, sepals to 3 × 0.8cm, pink-purple, lanceolate, carinate; petals to 2×0.6cm, oblong-lanceolate, obtuse, similar to sepals in colour; filaments several-seriate, the outermost to 3cm, blue, dark purple toward base. Fruit to 9 × 5cm, ovoid or subglobose, glabrous, yellow. Spring–autumn. E Mexico to Costa Rica. Z10.

P.sicyoides Schltr. & Cham.
Stems vining, slender, subglabrous or hispidulous. Leaves to 8 × 10cm, trilobed, lobes deltoid-acuminate, the midlobe much the longest, apex mucronate, base cordate, entire or denticulate, membranous, light green above, glaucous beneath, hispidulous, 3-veined; stipules to 7mm, ovate, cuspidate; petioles to 6cm, hispidulous, biglandular. Flowers very fragrant, solitary or paired, to 4cm diam.; pedicels slender, to 3cm; calyx patelliform or campanulate, hispidulous, sepals to 2 × 1cm, yellow-green, oblong-lanceolate, acute downy beneath; petals to 1.2cm, white, ovate-lanceolate; filaments 8.5mm, 1-seriate, white, banded red-purple. Fruit obovoid, glabrous. Summer. C & S Mexico. Z10.

P.stipulata Aubl.
Stems vining, cylindric, glabrous. Leaves to 8 × 10cm, trilobed, lobes broad-ovate, apex briefly acuminate or subacute, base subpeltate and cordate, membranous, glabrous, glaucous beneath, 5-veined; stipules ovate, to 3 × 1cm; peti-

oles to 5cm, 2–5-glandular. Flowers to 6cm diam., fragrant; pedicels to 5cm; calyx obconic-campanulate, glabrous, light green inside, darker outside, sepals to 3×1cm, green beneath, white-green above, oblong-lanceolate; petals white to 3cm; filaments several-seriate, white, violet at base. Fruit glabrous. French Guiana. Z10.

P.suberosa L. (*P.peltata* Cav.).
Stems slender, vining, becoming winged and corky. Leaves entire to deeply trilobed, lobes linear-lanceolate to broad-ovate, apex acute or obtuse, base rounded sometimes peltate, membranous or subcoriaceous; stipules linear-subulate, to 8mm; petioles to 4cm, biglandular. Flowers to 3cm diam., green-yellow to ivory, solitary or paired, axillary, sometimes in terminal, racemes; sepals ovate-lanceolate, subobtuse; petals absent; filaments biseriate. Fruit to 1.5cm diam., globose or ovoid, dark purple or black, glaucous when young. Summer. Tropical America. Z10.

P.subpeltata Ortega (*P.alba* Link & Otto; *P.atomaria* Planch.). GRANADINA.
Stems vining, cylindric, striate, glabrous. Leaves to 9 × 12cm, trilobed, lobes oblong, apex rounded or obtuse, base often subpeltate or subcordate, glabrous; stipules to 4 × 2cm, oblong, mucronate; petioles to 6cm, slender, 2–4-glandular. Flowers to 5cm diam.; pedicels to 6cm; calyx glabrous, sepals to 1cm diam., green beneath, green-white above, oblong, obtuse; petals white, linear-oblong; filaments 5-seriate, white. Fruit to 4cm diam., ovoid or subglobose, glabrous, somewhat green. C Mexico, C America, Colombia, Venezuela. cf. *P.eichleriana*. Z10.

P.tinifolia Juss. See *P.laurifolia*.

P.trifasciata Lem.
Stems vining, angular, striate, glabrous. Leaves to 10 × 10cm, glabrous, trilobed, lobes deltoid, apex acute or subobtuse, base cordate, membranous, dull dark green mottled pale green or yellow on either side of veins or above, maroon or violet beneath; stipules subulate, to 4mm; petioles to 5cm, eglandular. Flowers to 3.5cm diam., fragrant; pedicels slender, to 3cm; bracts setiform; calyx broad-campanulate, glabrous, sepals 1.5 × 0.5cm, yellow-green, oblong, obtuse petals 1 × 0.3cm, ivory-white, linear; filaments biseriate, yellow-green. Fruit to 2.5cm diam., globose, glabrous, glaucous. Peru, Brazil. Z10.

P.tuberosa Jacq.
Tuberous-rooted. Stems vining, glabrous. Leaves to 6 × 12cm, oblong, deeply bilobed, lobes lanceolate, with a mucro in sinus, base rounded, subcoriaceous, glabrous, dark and glossy above, paler beneath, reticulately 3-veined; stipules to 5mm, narrow-linear, coriaceous; petioles to 2cm, eglandular. Flowers to 5cm diam., white, solitary or paired; pedicels to 4cm; calyx patelliform or campanulate, glabrous, sepals to 2 × 0.6cm, oblong-lanceolate, obtuse; petals to 1×0.4cm, ovate-lanceolate, obtuse; filaments white banded purple, biseriate. Fruit glabrous. Summer–autumn. Caribbean (St. Thomas, Trinidad), Northern S America. Z10.

P.tucumanensis Hook.
Stems vining, angular, subcylindric below, glabrous, somewhat glaucous, sulcate. Leaves to 6 × 1.5cm, 3–5-lobed, lobes oblong-lanceolate, apex mucronate, base cordate and finely serrate, membranous, deep green above, somewhat glaucous beneath, glabrous, 3–5-veined; stipules ovate-lanceolate, to 3 × 1.5cm; petioles to 3cm, eglandular. Flowers to 5cm diam., white; pedicels slender, to 2.5cm, eglandular; calyx campanulate, glabrous, white inside, green outside, sepals 5mm diam., oblong-lanceolate, cucullate; petals white; filaments 12.5mm, several-seriate, white, banded violet. Fruit to 5 × 3.5cm, ovoid, glabrous. Summer. NW Argentina. Z10.

P.umbilicata (Griseb.) Harms (*Tacsonia umbilicata* Griseb.).
Stems vining, subcylindric, striate, glabrous. Leaves to 6 × 7.5cm, trilobed, lobes oblong-ovate, apex rounded or subacute and mucronate, base cordate, entire or somewhat undulate, subcoriaceous, 5–7-veined; stipules to 2 × 1cm, ovate,

mucronate; petioles to 3.5cm, slender, eglandular or minutely biglandular. Flowers more or less erect, maroon, violet or dark blue; pedicels to 9cm, stout, cylindric; calyx to 3.5 × 0.9cm, tubular-cylindric, glabrous, sepals to 3×0.6cm, linear-oblong; petals linear-oblong, obtuse; filaments 5-seriate. Fruit to 7×4cm, ovoid, glabrous. C Bolivia, N Argentina. Z10.

P.van volxemii Triana & Planch. See *P.antioquiensis*.

P.violacea Vell.
Stems long, vining, cylindric or subangular, glabrous. Leaves to 12 × 15cm, trilobed, lobes oblong, base cordate and sub-peltate, entire or subentire, membranous or subcoriaceous, glabrous, 5–7-veined, glaucous beneath; stipules ovate-oblong, to 3.5 × 1.5cm; petioles to 5cm, 3–8-glandular. Flowers to 10cm diam., violet; peduncles stout, to 15cm; calyx campanulate, purple inside, pruinose outside, glabrous, sepals to 1cm diam., oblong or oblong-lanceolate, long-awned; petals to 1cm diam., oblong-lanceolate, obtuse; filaments 6–7-seriate, to 4cm, violet, white at apex and base. Fruit glabrous. Autumn. Bolivia, E Brazil, Paraguay. Very similar to *P.amethystina*. Z10.

P.viridiflora Cav.
Stems vining, slender, angular, compressed, glabrous. Leaves to 7 × 9cm, lower leaves to 16 × 25cm, glabrous, deeply trilobed, lobes ovate to suborbicular, apex obtuse, entire, peltate, coriaceous, shiny deep green above, paler beneath, reticulately 3–7-veined; stipules 5mm, linear-lanceolate, acute; petioles to 6cm, biglandular. Flowers green; pedicels to 2cm, ebracteate; calyx cylindric, gibbous, glabrous, sepals to 1.5 × 0.2cm, linear, acute; petals absent; filaments 1-seriate. Fruit to 2cm diam., subglobose, glabrous. S Mexico. Z10.

P.vitifolia HBK.
Stems vining, cylindric, rusty-tomentose. Leaves to 15 × 18cm, trilobed, resembling *Vitis*, lobes acuminate, truncate to cordate at base, dentate or crenate, membranous, shiny above, densely minutely pubescent or minutely tomentose, 3–5-veined; stipules setiform, to 5mm; petioles to 5cm, biglandular at base, densely rusty-tomentose. Flowers to 9cm diam., scarlet, bright red or vermilion; pedicels stout, densely rusty-tomentose; calyx cylindric, subglabrous, sepals to 8 × 2cm, lanceolate, obtuse; petals to 6 × 1.5cm, linear-lanceolate, obtuse; filaments 3-seriate, red to bright yellow. Fruit 5 ×

3cm, ovoid, minutely pubescent. Spring–summer. C America (Nicaragua), Venezuela, Colombia, Ecuador, N Peru. 'Scarlet Flame': fruits tasting of strawberries. Z10.

P.warmingii Mast.
Stems vining, slender, angular, furrowed. Leaves to 5×6cm, trilobed, lobes deltoid, acute, mucronulate, cordate at base, dentate, membranous, hispidulous above, minutely downy beneath, 3-veined; stipules semi-ovate, to 6×3mm; petioles to 5cm, slender, biglandular. Flowers 2.5cm diam., white; peduncles to 1.5cm; calyx green-white, sepals to 1 × 0.5cm, lanceolate-oblong, obtuse; petals to 7 × 3mm, lanceolate-oblong, obtuse; filaments biseriate, white at apex, purple-violet at base. Fruit ovoid, pilose. Colombia, Brazil, Paraguay. Perhaps not distinct from *P.morifolia*, and likely to be sunk into that species. Z10.

P.watsoniana Mast.
Stems vining, slender, cylindric, glabrous, purple-tinted. Leaves to 6×8cm, trilobed, lobes oblong, apex obtuse or sub-acute, base subpeltate and subtruncate, membranous, glabrous, green above, maroon beneath, 5-veined; stipules to 1.5 × 1cm, ovate or subreniform, subacute or rounded and aristulate; petioles to 3cm, slender, 2–5-glandular. Flowers to 8cm diam.; pedicels slender, to 5cm; calyx 4mm, campanulate, glabrous, sepals 7mm diam., green beneath, white tinted violet above oblong-lanceolate, obtuse; petals 4mm diam., white-tinted violet to pale lilac, thin, linear-lanceolate, obtuse; filaments 5-seriate, erect, violet, banded white. Fruit glabrous. Summer–autumn. C & S Brazil. Z10.

P.cultivars. 'Amethyst': stems thin; leaves to 10cm diam., 3-lobed; petals intense blue, corona filaments dark purple. 'Star of Bristol': slender vine; leaves 3–5 lobed; sepals to 5 × 1.5cm, green, purple above; petals mauve, to 4.5×1.6cm, filaments 4–5-seriate, deep mauve at base, centrally banded of lilac, apex mauve; fruits ovoid, bright orange. 'Star of Clevedon': slender vine; sepals white, green and white outside, to 5 × 1.5cm; petals white, to 5×1.5cm; corona filaments 4-seriate, purple at base, centrally banded white then blue-lilac. 'Star of Kingston' (*P.* 'Amethyst' × *P.caerulea*): as 'Star of Clevedon', but sepals tipped mauve inside, petals light mauve, filaments deep mauve base, banded white, apex mauve.

Peniocereus (A. Berger) Britt. & Rose. (From Gk *penios*, a thread, and *Cereus*, alluding to the slender stems.) Cactaceae. About 20 species of prostrate or scandent shrubs; roots thickened, turnip-like or dahlia-like; stems slender, ribbed, sparingly-branched; epidermis hairless or papillose-downy, light green or rather dark; spines conspicuous, or adpressed and short. Flowers nocturnal or diurnal, occasionally terminating the stem; tube long and slender; floral areoles with bristles or spines. Fruit narrowly ovoid, tapered at apex, fleshy red, the spines or bristles more or less deciduous; seed broadly oval, 1.4–4.6×1.2–3.3mm, black-brown, shiny or matt, ruminate or not, periphery undifferentiated or crested with larger cells; relief flat to low-conical. C America to NW Mexico and SW US. Z9.

CULTIVATION Grow in an intermediate greenhouse (min. 10–15°C/50–60°F); use 'standard' cactus compost: moderate to high inorganic content (more than 50% grit), pH 6–7.5; shade in hot weather; maintain low humidity; keep dry from mid-autumn until early spring, except for light misting on warm days in later winter. Few of the species are seen in cultivation, and only *P.viperinus* and *P.serpentinus* flower at all readily.

P.diguetii (F.A.C. Weber) Backeb. See *P.striatus*.

P.greggii (Engelm.) Britt. & Rose (*Cereus greggii* Engelm.).
Root large, turnip-like; stems mostly 30–60 × 1–2cm, dark grey-brown, papillose-downy; ribs 3–6, deep; areoles c4.5–6mm apart; spines 10–13, to 3mm. Flowers 15–21 × 7.5cm, white. C N & NW Mexico, SW US.

P.johnstonii Britt. & Rose.
Perhaps only a variety of *P.greggii*; rootstock tuberous, massive, 10–40×5–20cm; stems 1 or more, unbranched, clambering to 3m, 5–15mm diam.; ribs 3–5; central spines 1–3, to 8mm, subulate; radial spines 9–12, 1.5–9mm, brown to black. Flowers 15cm; tepals white, tinged pink outside. Fruits oblong-ovoid, 5–6cm, red, with black spines. NW Mexico (Baja California).

P.maculatus (Weingart) Cutak.
Shrub to 3m or more, sparsely branched; stems segmented, the segments c50 × 3cm, olive-green, tinged purple, with small white spots; ribs 3–4; areoles 5–20mm apart; spines 6–9, 1–3mm. Flowers 9–11cm, creamy white; outer tepals tinged purple red. Fruit pear-shaped, 5–3cm, red with red pulp. Spring–summer. Mexico (Guerrero).

P.serpentinus (Lagasca & Rodriguez) N.P. Tayl. (*Nyctocereus serpentinus* (Lagasca & Rodriguez) Britt. & Rose).
Rootstock thickened, more or less tuberous; stems 2–3m × 3–5cm, green; ribs 10–17; areoles c10mm apart; spines 10–14, to 30mm long. Flowers 15–20 × 8cm, white, tinged red outside. Summer. Mexico, widely cultivated.

P.striatus (Brandg.) F. Buxb. (*Cereus striatus* Brandg.; *Wilcoxia striata* (Brandg.) Britt. & Rose; *Neoevansia striata* (Brandg.) Sanchez-Mej.; *P.diguetii* (F.A.C. Weber) Backeb.; *Wilcoxia diguetii* (F.A.C. Weber) Peebles). Stems to 1m × 5–8mm, grey or blue-green; ribs 6–9; areoles 5–15mm apart; spines *c*9, to 3mm. Flowers 7.5–15×5–7.5cm, white to pink or purple-tinged. Fruit pear-shaped, 3–4cm, scarlet, with deciduous, bristly spines. NW Mexico, S Arizona.

P.tomentosa Bravo. See *P.viperinus*.

P.viperinus (F.A.C. Weber) Klusac ex Kreuzinger (*Cereus viperinus* F.A.C. Weber; *Wilcoxia viperina* (F.A.C. Weber) Britt. & Rose; *P.tomentosa* Bravo). Rootstock tuberous, dahlia-like; stems to 3m×1–1.5cm, dark grey-brown, papillose-downy; ribs 8–10, very low (stems almost terete); areoles 10–30mm apart; spines 9–12, to 5mm. Flowers to 3–9 × 4cm, bright pink to red. Summer. Central S Mexico. Perhaps referable here is *Wilcoxia papillosa* Britt. & Rose, a poorly understood species from W Mexico (Sinaloa), doubtfully reported as in cultivation. It has 3–5-ribbed stems and areoles with only 6–8 spines.

Pereskia Mill. (For Nicholas Claude Fabry de Peiresc (1580–1637), councillor at Aix and patron of science.) Cactaceae. 16 species of trees, shrubs and woody climbers, some with tuberous roots; stems not conspicuously succulent, terete, unsegmented, not ribbed or tubercled. Leaves present, broad, flat, thin, not or only slightly succulent, deciduous or subpersistent; glochids absent; spines usually numerous. Inflorescence paniculate or corymbose, or flowers clustered or solitary; flowers diurnal, stalked or sessile; epigynal tube none; floral areoles with wool, often hairs, and rarely spines, perianth rotate, spreading or rarely erect, red, pink or white; ovary a cavity at the style-base or inferior. Fruit berry-like to pear-like, sometimes with persistent scales; pericarp juicy or tough, indehiscent; pulp present or absent; seeds more or less circular, 1.7–7.5mm, black-brown, shiny; relief flat. S Mexico, C America, North & West S America, Brazil. Z9.

CULTIVATION   Robust spiny clamberers, scarcely recognizable as cacti because of their woody climbing habit and distinct leaves. They are valued for their leafy cover, drought-resistance and attractive flowers, white in *P.aculeata*, pink in *P.weberiana*; the former also has the cultivar 'Godseffiana', a strikingly attractive foliage plant suitable for home or conservatory. In Mediterrancean and subtropical climates, they will thrive outdoors on walls and pergolas in sunny, sheltered situations. In cooler regions, grow in an intermediate greenhouse (min. 10–15°C/50–60°F); use 'standard' cactus compost: moderate to high inorganic content (more than 50% grit), pH 6–7.5; shade in hot weather; maintain low humidity; keep dry from mid-autumn until early spring, except for light misting on warm days in late winter.

P.aculeata Mill. (*P.pereskia* (L.) Karst.). Woody climber, scrambling to 10m; main stems cane-like, 2–3cm thick; distal branches *c*4mm thick. Leaves lanceolate to elliptic or ovate, to 11×4cm, shortly petiolate, usually with a pair of small, persistent, claw-like spines, 4–8mm, resembling stipular spines, at the base; 'normal' spines developing at areoles on older growth only, numerous on trunk, straight. Flowers numerous, in panicles, 2.5–5cm diam., scented; floral areoles with hairs and often small spines; perianth white or nearly so; ovary a hollow at the style-base. Fruit *c*2cm diam., pale yellow to orange, sometimes spiny, fleshy. Autumn. Tropical America.   'Godseffiana' (*P.godseffiana* hort.): leaves variegated yellow to peach-coloured, purple-tinted beneath.

P.godseffiana hort. See *P.aculeata* 'Godseffiana'.

P.pereskia (L.) Karst. See *P.aculeata*.

P.weberiana Schum.   *P.antoniana* (Backeb.) Rauh; *Rhodocactus antonianus* Backeb.). Slender shrub, 1–3m, sometimes scandent; rootstock large, tuberous; canes 1cm thick; distal branches 2mm thick. Leaves 2.5–8×1–4cm, elliptic to narrowly elliptic-lanceolate, acute, cuneate, fleshy, venation pinnate, lateral veins 2–4, obscure; spines 3–5, 8–13mm, subulate, brown or yellow-brown. Flowers solitary, 1.5–2.5cm diam., or proliferating from the pericarpel to form clusters; floral areoles few, spineless; perianth pink or white; ovary half-inferior. Fruit a nearly globose berry, 5–15mm diam., shiny black, juicy. Spring. Bolivia.

Pereskiopsis Britt. & Rose. (From *Pereskia* and Gk *-opsis*, appearance, resembling.) Cactaceae. About 9 species of sparsely branched or scrambling shrubs, to 4m; stems terete, unsegmented; leaves present, elliptic, obovate to spathulate or almost circular, more or less succulent, deciduous to persistent; glochids present; spines usually 1 to several, acicular. Flowers usually lateral, *Opuntia*-like, sessile, diurnal, rarely nocturnal; floral areoles with leaves, areoles and glochids; ovary inferior; tube none; perianth yellow, pink or red. Fruit fleshy; seeds few, broadly oval, 4–5mm; aril present, enclosing entire seed, light grey, surface trichomatous. Mexico and Guatemala.

CULTIVATION   Clambering leaf cacti with attractive yellow flowers, grow in an intermediate greenhouse (min. 10–15°C/50–60°F); use 'standard' cactus compost: moderate to high inorganic content (more than 50% grit), pH 6–7.5; shade in hot weather; maintain low humidity; keep dry from mid-autumn until early spring, except for light misting on warm days in late winter. All species are of tropical or subtropical origin, and require minimum temperature of about 10°C/50°F for successful cultivation. During the growing season they can be watered as frequently as non-succulent plants.

P.gatesii Baxter. Scandent shrub to 2–3m, glabrous; main stem 15mm diam.; lateral branches numerous, short; leaves obovate, acute, up to 3.5 × 1.8cm, fleshy; glochids numerous, brown; spines 1 to several, 5cm, with thin papery sheath, pale brown at first, eventually deciduous. Flower rotate, 6.5cm diam., lemon-yellow. Fruit cylindric 2–2.7×0.7–1cm, pink, sterile, but producing vegetative shoots from the upper areoles. Summer. NW Mexico (Baja California). Apparently just a sterile clone of *P.porteri*. Instead of producing seeds, the plant propagates itself by the falling of ripened fruits which have developed branchlets at the upper areoles. Z9.

P.porteri (Brandg. ex F.A.C. Weber) Britt. & Rose. Scandent shrub to 1.2m or more, glabrous; main stem to 3cm diam; leaves obovate, acute, 2–3cm, fleshy; glochids numerous, brown; spines 0–2 on young shoots, increasing to 3–8 or more, 3–5cm, on older growth, pale brown. Flower *c*4cm diam., yellow. Fruit oblong, 4–7cm, orange, fertile. Summer. NW Mexico (Sinaloa and Baja California). Z9.

Periploca L. (From Gk *peri*, around, and *ploke*, referring to the twining habit of some species.) Asclepiadaceae. 11 species of glabrous shrubs, sometimes twining. Leaves opposite. Flowers star-like in loose cymes or corymbs. Fruit composed of 2 follicles. Mediterranean to E Asia, Tropical Africa. Z6.

CULTIVATION   A strongly growing climber for arches, fences and pergolas, *P.graeca* is grown for its dark shining foliage, which remains green until leaf fall, and for the interesting if ill-scented flowers; the yellow fruits and sap are poisonous. It is occasionally grown as a wall climber, but requires wire or other support. Easily grown in a warm position in full sun in any moderately fertile and well drained soil. Little pruning is needed other than to remove weak and overcrowded growth in spring. Propagate by seed, division, layers or by semiripe cuttings in summer.

P.graeca L. SILK VINE.
Deciduous twiner to 10m. Leaves 2.5–10cm, ovate to lanceolate, glossy dark green. Flowers 8–12 in long-stalked corymbs, malodorous, exterior yellow-green, interior maroon to chocolate, limb to 2.5cm diam., lobes 5, spreading, downy. Follicles to 12cm, narrowly cylindrical; seeds tufted. SE Europe to Asia Minor.

Petrea L. (For Lord Robert James Petrie (1714–43) of Thorndon, Essex, owner of one of the best private collections of exotics in Europe, supervised by Phillip Miller.) BLUE BIRD VINE; PURPLE WREATH; QUEEN'S WREATH; SANDPAPER VINE. Verbenaceae. 30 species of lianes, shrubs, or small trees. Leaves opposite or whorled, simple, entire, exstipulate, deciduous, often semi-deciduous or evergreen in cultivation, surface rough, veins prominent. Inflorescence racemose, axillary or terminal, elongate, many-flowered; bracts small or absent; flowers hypogenous, bisexual, regular or occasionally zygomorphic, each subtended by 1 to many caducous bracteoles; torus distinct and ring-like, swollen; calyx inferior, gamosepalous, tube campanulate, mostly ribbed, lobes 5, linear-oblong, showy, blue, purple, violet or white; corolla inferior, gamosepalous, hypercrateriform, darker than calyx, slightly zygomorphic, lobes 5, subequal, rounded; stamens 4, included in corolla at or near middle of tube, filaments short, slender, anthers medifixed, oblong or ovate; ovary subglobose or obovoid, bilocular, each

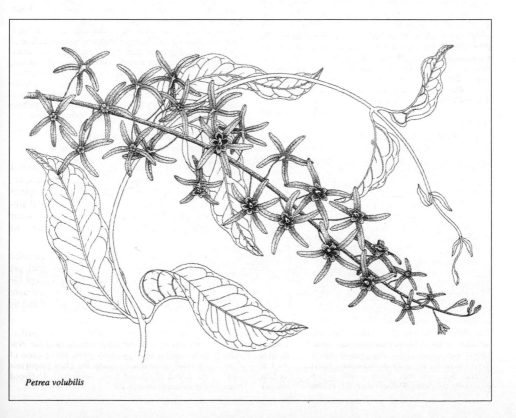

Petrea volubilis

locule uniovulate, stigma small, capitate. Fruit drupaceous, enclosed by accrescent fruiting calyx, containing 2, 1-seeded stones. Tropical America and Mexico; *P.volubilis* naturalized in India. Z10.

CULTIVATION *Petrea* species (particularly *P.volubilis*) are widely cultivated in the Tropics, where the dark green foliage and showy blue racemes account for their popularity both as vigorous climbers and as weeping standards. Plant outside in full sunlight to light shade on freely draining soils tending to low pH. Water and spray copiously during the growing season. Prune hard after flowering (spring in the Tropics) to maintain a simple branch pattern, avoiding congestion and the accumulation of fallen leaves, which are slow to decompose.

In cool-temperate zones, under glass, grow in direct sun or bright filtered light with medium to high humidity and a winter minimum temperature of 10°C/50°F. Mist frequently in warm sunny weather. Plant in large tubs, open beds or under and through staging in a freely draining, lime-free medium enriched with leafmould. Propagate by layering (both simple and air) or semi-hardened nodal cuttings inserted in sand with bottom heat and misted regularly. *Petrea* is afflicted by scale and mealybug. The coarse, tough, upper leaf surfaces and granular-fissured bark favour the secondary problem of sooty mould. Regular hosing down of well established vines should hold this in check.

P.arborea HBK. BLUE PETREA; TREE PETREA.
Subscandent shrub or small tree. Branches slender, grey, conspicuously lenticellate, glabrate; twigs short-pubescent. Leaves to 16×8cm, decussate-opposite, sessile or subsessile, thin-textured, grey-green above, brighter green beneath, elliptic, obtuse or slightly retuse, base cordate or subcordate, slightly asperous on both surfaces. Inflorescence to 16cm, ascending or nodding, densely pubescent; calyx to 1.7cm, blue, lobes longer than tube, to 1.2×0.4cm, obtuse; corolla to 0.7cm, lobes rounded, cambridge blue; filaments glabrous, staminode obsolete; ovary obovoid. Colombia and Venezuela to Guyana and Trinidad. Commonly confused in horticulture with *P.volubilis*. 'Broadway': flowers white.

P.kohautiana Presl. FLEUR DE DIEU.
Liane to 20m. Branches stout, light grey or ashy-white, obtusely tetragonal, glabrate, conspicuously lenticellate; leaf scars prominent. Leaves to 20×11cm, decussate-opposite, petiolate, coriaceous, dark green, broadly elliptic, apex and base variable, glabrate. Inflorescence to 60cm, erect or nodding, scabrous; calyx to 2cm, violet or blue, lobes exceeding tube, acute or obtuse, sometimes emarginate; corolla to 2cm, lobes rounded, violet or blue; filaments pilose, staminode minute; ovary obovoid, glabrous. W Indies, Antilles. var. *anomala* Mold. Flowers white.

P.racemosa Nees. PURPLE WREATH.
Woody vine or shrub, branches grey or brown, densely puberulent. Leaves to 18×8cm, chartaceous, becoming membranous, elliptic, obtuse to subacute, base attenuate or acute,

bright green, serrate or denticulate, glabrous. Inflorescence to 31cm, axillary, erect or nutant, loosely many-flowered; peduncles to 2cm, densely puberulent; pedicels to 2cm, glabrous; calyx purple, violet-blue or lilac, tube to 0.6× 0.2cm, obconic, adpressed-puberulent, lobes to 1.4×0.5cm, narrowly obovate, subglabrous or slightly puberulent; corolla hypocrateriform, tube to 1cm, infundibular, exterior slightly pubescent towards apex, interior densely long-pubescent, lobes to 0.75×0.6cm, broadly ovate, densely short-pubescent. Northern S America.

P.volubilis L. BLUEBIRD VINE, PURPLE WREATH; SAND PAPER VINE.
Woody vine to undershrub, to 12m. Branches and branchlets twining, pale brown to ashy grey, slender, shortly pubescent, conspicuously lenticellate, leaf scars conspicuous. Leaves to 21×11cm, decussate-opposite, oblong-elliptic, apex acute or shortly acuminate, base cuneate, petiolate, subcoriaceous, scurfy, deep green above, lighter green and densely or sparsely pubescent beneath, asperous, thus seeming somewhat viscid. Inflorescence to 22–36cm, an erect, arching or pendent crowded, cylindrical raceme; calyx lilac, lobes longer than tube, to 1.8×0.6cm, narrowly oblong, apex round, tube with spreading hairs; corolla to 0.8cm, tube densely pubescent in upper quarter, lobes broadly elliptic, puberulent, indigo to amethyst; filaments glabrous, staminode obsolete; ovary oblong-obovoid, glabrous. C America and Lesser Antilles, introduced elsewhere. 'Albiflora': flowers white.

Phaseolus L. (Lat. diminutive of Gk *phaselos*, name used by Dioscorides for a kind of bean.) BEAN. Leguminosae (Papilionoideae). Over 20 species of annual or perennial, usually climbing herbs. Leaves trifoliolate; stipules small, not decurrent; leaflets stipellate. Flowers in axillary racemes; calyx campanulate, bilabiate; standard orbicular, symmetric, keel with a spirally coiled beak; stamens diadelphous, uppermost distinct; style pubescent inside, the thickened part twisted more than 360°; stigma oblique. Fruit a linear-oblong, dehiscent legume, usually many-seeded. New World. Closely allied to *Vigna*, which differs from *Phaseolus* in having stipules often basally appendaged, the thickened part of the style less strongly twisted, the keel beak recurved, not spirally coiled, and in several technical characteristics related to pollen and biochemistry.

CULTIVATION *P.coccineus* is the Scarlet Runner Bean and *P.vulgaris* the Green Bean; for detailed cultivation and cultivars, see 'Beans' in *The New RHS Dictionary of Gardening* (1992). Lima beans or butter beans, *P.lunatus*, are vigorous plants usually grown as annuals. They are grown for their edible seeds which must be boiled before eating to destroy hydrocyanic acid. They are available in both bush and climbing forms, the latter generally being more productive. Lima beans are very frost tender, prone to drop their flowers on very nitrogen-rich soils, and are even less tolerant of cold and wet than the Scarlet Runner Bean, *P.coccineus*, although their cultivation requirements are otherwise similar. They are usually grown on ridges, raised beds or mounds to ensure the necessary good drainage, and seed should not be planted until the soil has warmed up; where frosts occur late into the season, they are sometimes started under glass, to be set out when danger of frost is passed. In warm temperate climates, lima beans mature about 12–16 weeks from sowing. In the tropics cultivationis restricted to elevations between 300–1200m/1000–4000ft; temperatures above 27°C/80°F adversely affect fertilization and pod formation is reduced in very hot weather. In cooler maritime climates such as those in the UK, the growing season is usually too short and too cool for the beans to mature and crops are seldom worthwhile.

P.aconitifolius Jacq. See *Vigna aconitifolia.*

P.acutifolius A. Gray.
Annual. Stems short, twining. Leaflets to 6×4cm, thin, linear-lanceolate or lanceolate-ovate, attenuate-acuminate. Flowers white to pale purple, few, on very short peduncles. Fruit to 9 × 1.5cm, 2–10-seeded; seeds 8.5 × 5.5mm, round, variable in colour, white, yellow, black or grey, sometimes speckled brown, blue or black. SW US, Mexico. var. *latifolius* G. Freeman. TEPARY BEAN. Terminal leaflets to 9.9×5cm, lateral leaflets to 8×5cm. Fruit linear. Z10.

P.angularis W. Wight. See *Vigna angularis.*
P.aureus Roxb. See *Vigna radiata.*
P.bipunctatus Jacq. See *P.lunatus.*
P.caracalla L. See *Vigna caracalla.*

P.coccineus L. (*P.multiflorus* Lam.). SCARLET RUNNER BEAN; DUTCH CASE-KNIFE BEAN.
Resembles *P.vulgaris*, but perennial (albeit usually treated as an annual), racemes many-flowered and longer than leaves, corolla to 3cm, scarlet, sometimes with white wings and keel, keel beak forms 1–1¹/₂ turns of a spiral. Leaflets to 13cm, ovate-cordate. Fruit to 30.5cm; seeds broad, to 2.5cm, black, mottled buff to red. Tropical America. 'Albus' (var. *albus* L.H. Bail.) WHITE DUTCH RUNNERS: flowers and seeds white. Z10.

P.giganteus hort. See *Vigna caracalla.*
P.inamuenus L. See *P.lunatus.*
P.limensis Macfad. See *P.lunatus.*

P.lunatus L. (*P.inamuenus* L.; *P.bipunctatus* Jacq.; *P.puberulus* HBK; *P.xuaresii* Zucc.; *P.limensis* Macfad.; *P.saccharatus* Macfad.). LIMA BEAN.
Twining or erect and bushy, grown as an annual. Leaves long-petiolate; rachis to 2.5cm; stipules to 4cm, narrow-triangular; leaflets to 10cm, ovate to rhombic or deltoid, obtuse to acute or subacute; stipels inconspicuous, ovate to linear. Inflorescence to 20cm, axillary; pedicels to 7mm; calyx to 0.3cm, broad-campanulate, pilose; corolla yellow-green or white to lilac, standard 1cm diam., wings 1cm, keel narrow, 1cm. Fruit to 10 × 1.5cm, oblong-lunate, 2–4-seeded; seeds to 1 × 0.5cm, red-brown, reniform. Winter–spring. Tropical S America. Z10.

P.multiflorus Lam. See *P.coccineus.*
P.puberulus HBK. See *P.lunatus.*
P.radiatus L. See *Vigna radiata.*
P.saccharatus Macfad. See *P.lunatus.*
P.sublobatus Roxb. See *Vigna radiata.*

P.vulgaris L. KIDNEY BEAN; GREEN BEAN; SNAP BEAN; HARICOT; COMMON BEAN; FRENCH BEAN; FRIJOL; RUNNER BEAN; STRING BEAN; SALAD BEAN; WAX BEAN.
Erect or climbing annual to 4m. Leaflets to 10 × 6cm, ovate or ovate-orbicular, acuminate. Racemes shorter than leaves, to 6-fld; corolla to 1.8cm, white, pink or purple, keel beak forms 2 turns of a spiral. Fruit to 50×2.5cm, narrow, flat or subcylindric, brown; seeds 1.3cm, elongate or globose, red, brown, black, white, or mottled. Summer. Tropical America. var. *humilis* Alef. The widely grown 'bush' bean. Z10.

P.xuaresii Zucc. See *P.lunatus.* var. *albus* (L.H. Bail.). See *Phaseolus coccineus* 'Albus'.

× **Philageria** Mast. (*Philesia* × *Lapageria.*) Liliaceae (Philesiaceae). Scrambling shrub, habit similar to *Lapageria* but less vigorous and more bushy. Leaves 4.5×1–1.5cm, lanceolate, leathery, 3-veined; petioles 0.5–0.7cm. Flowers solitary or few at ends of branches (as in *Philesia*), drooping, but outer tepals 3.8×1.6cm, not more than two-thirds length of inner, fleshy, dull red deep or magenta with a blue bloom, inner tepals 6× 3cm, bright rose, more faintly bloomed; filaments spotted pink. Summer. Garden origin. Z9.

CULTIVATION   An attractive intergeneric hybrid between the climbing *Lapageria* and its shrubby, compact ally *Philesia*, with cultural requirements as for *Lapageria.*

× *P.veitchii* Mast. (*Lapageria rosea* × *Philesia magellanica.*)

Philodendron Schott. (From Gk *phileo*, to love, and *dendron*, tree, alluding to the climbing or epiphytic habit.) Araceae. 350+ species of epiphytic or terrestrial evergreen perennials, some climbing with long, slender, rooting stems, some with leaves in a dense basal rosette, or along or crowning a stout, unbranched stem; juvenile phase often distinct from adult. Stems stout bearing adventitious roots; internodes very short to elongate. Leaves often large, entire or lobed to pinnatifid to pedate, oblong or ovate, cordate to sagittate, coriaceous, usually dark green, venation pinnate with primary and secondary veins parallel; petioles stout, often equalling or sometimes exceeding lamina, sheathed, often with groove above between longitudinal marginal ridges, occasionally geniculate above or swollen at base, leaf scars very distinct on stem; leaves subtended by membranous cataphylls which sometimes persist, covering stem. Peduncles axillary, spathe, fleshy, forming tube around spadix below, expanded above, hooded to cymbiform, persistent, often with resinous ducts, white to green and yellow, often marked with red and purple; spadix shorter than or subequal to spathe, usually white, densely covered by unisexual flowers, male and female zones adjacent, sometimes fragrant; perianth absent; stamens 2–5, lowest male flowers sterile; ovary 2- to many-locular, ovules 1 to many. Fruit a berry, white to orange or red. Tropical America.

CULTIVATION   Alongside *Epipremnum, Monstera, Rhaphidophora* and *Scindapsus, Philodendron* confirms the Araceae as the family richest in foliage climbers for tropical and subtropical gardens, the home and glasshouses. Few public buildings in the West cannot boast a long-suffering member of one of these genera. *Philodendron scandens*, the Heart-Leaf Vine, ranks among the top five interior plants, so resilient and omnipresent as to be barely worth reproducing in silk or plastic. This species is comparatively small and slender-stemmed; others are altogether bolder, with stout stems and large, tough leaves ranging in form from heart- to sword-shaped, from entire to palmately or pinntely lobed, in texture from high gloss to the silken or velvety and in colour from deep green to purple-red, scarlet and near-black, sometimes variegated and mottled, or with white, silver or gold veins and differently coloured stems and petioles.

Grow in an open, fertile, moisture-retentive mix of loam, coir or bark, leafmould and coarse sand. Maintain a day temperature of 21–27°C/70–80°F, falling to 15–21°C/60–70°F at night when in growth, with a winter minimum of 15°C/60°F. Site in part-shade or in filtered light, ensuring protection from bright summer sun; provide good air circulation but avoid draughts of both cold and warm air (as in central heating vents). Mist frequently when in growth and water moderately, reducing as temperatures fall in winter. When plants are in full growth and roots have filled the pots, feed regularly with 10:10:5 NPK liquid fertilizer. Train on moss poles, wire cylinders filled with the potting medium, or canes. Smaller species will also trail, making good cascade plants for baskets and planters, also groundcover. The larger species may be pruned, or their stem tips frequently repropagated to create bushier, more or less free-standing specimens. Encourage branching by pinching out tips. Propagate by air layering and by stem tip or leaf bud cuttings rooted in individual small pots in a closed case with bottom heat at 21–25°C/70–77°F. Seed when available will germinate at 20°C/68°F, grow seedlings on at 18–21°C/65–70°F. *Pythium* spp. may cause root rots of mature specimens if they are overwatered.

P.andreanum Devansaye. See *P.melanochrysum.*

P.angustisectum Engl. (*P.elegans* K. Krause).
Stems climbing; internodes to 5cm. Leaves to 60 × 45cm, reflexed, ovate in outline, basal sinus triangular, pinnatisect, segments to 2.5cm across, 16 per side, linear, acute, with 1 vein, glossy dark green above; petiole terete, subequal to lamina. Peduncles short; spathe to 15cm, green externally with pink margins, yellow within. Colombia.

P.asperatum K. Koch. See *P.ornatum.*

P.auriculatum Standl. & L.O. Williams.
Stems stout, climbing; internodes short. Leaves to 90 × 35cm, erect, narrow-elliptic-oblong, basally auriculate, veins paler than lamina; petiole shorter than lamina, subcylindric. Peduncle 12.5cm; spathe to 28cm, green-white. Costa Rica.

P.bahiense Engl.
Close to *P.ruizii*, differing in smaller leaves. Lamina to 35 × 12.5cm, main lateral veins 5–6 paired; petiole to 15cm, sheathed in basal half. Brazil (Bahia).

P.barrosoanum Bunting (*P.deflexum* hort. non Poepp. ex Schott).
Stems climbing, internodes 3–6 × 4cm. Leaves 40 × 25cm, reflexed, hastate, 3-lobed, median lobe ovate, apex acuminate or mucronate, lateral lobes 30 × 17.5cm, elliptic-ovate, very unequal, base rounded, sinus very broad, veins broad; petiole to 75cm, cylindric. Peduncles 4–5, to 10cm; spathe to 20cm, green, tinged red, tube red within; spadix equaling spathe, shortly stipitate. S America.

P.bipennifolium Schott (*P.panduraeforme* misapplied). HORSEHEAD PHILODENDRON; FIDDLE-LEAVED PHILODENDRON.
Stems climbing, tall, internodes long. Leaves to 45 × 15cm, reflexed, 5-lobed, glossy dark green, terminal lobe long, to 25 × 10cm, obovate, lateral lobes angular, obtuse, basal lobes broadly oblong-triangular, sinus open; petiole terete, shorter than lamina. Peduncle short; spathe 11cm, green-cream. SE Brazil.

P.brenesii Standl.
Stems climbing. Leaves to 50 × 25cm, lanceolate- to ovate-oblong, base deeply cordate, coriaceous, midrib broad, prominent, main lateral veins to 8+ pairs; petiole subequal to lamina. Spathe to 15cm, tube inflated, green externally, dark-red within. Costa Rica.

P.coerulescens Engl. See *P.inaequilaterum.*

P.cordatum (Vell. Conc.) Kunth. HEART-LEAF PHILODENDRON.
Stems tall, climbing, internodes short. Leaves 45 × 25cm, reflexed, ovate-triangular, base sagittate, basal lobes round-angular, overlapping or with narrow sinus to 15cm, margins undulate; petioles shorter than or exceeding lamina. Spathe to 15cm, green. SE Brazil.

P.× corsinianum Senoner. (Parents unrecorded, probably including *P.verrucosum.*)
Stems climbing, tall, internodes short, fibrous remains of cataphylls persistent at nodes. Leaves to 75 × 60cm, reflexed, ovate, base cordate, shallowly pinnate-lobed, marked metallic red-purple between green veins beneath when young, becoming green; petioles subequal to lamina. Peduncle short, with

white lines; spathe 18cm, tube purple externally, limb green-white, spotted red.

P.crassinervium Lindl.
Stems climbing, tall, internodes to 10cm. Leaves to 60 × 10cm, narrow-elliptic-oblong, long-acuminate, cuneate at base, coriaceous, midrib convex, inflated, to 1.5cm across, lateral veins many; petioles to 18cm, subcylindric. Peduncle exceeding petioles; spathe to 15cm, constricted above tube, green beneath, dull white above, base cherry-red within. SE Brazil.

P.cruentum Poepp. REDLEAF PHILODENDRON.
Close to *P.ruizii* differing in leaf blade narrower, to 40 × 10cm, basal lobes acute; petioles to 18cm. Spathe to 15cm, white externally, red within. Peru.

P.deflexum Poepp. ex Schott. See *P.myrmecophilum.*
P.deflexum hort. non Poepp. ex Schott. See *P.barrosoanum.*

P.devansayeanum Lind.
Stem prostrate or climbing; internodes 3–4 × 8cm. Leaves to 100cm, ovate, cordate, glossy, orange-brown when young, midrib and main lateral veins purple-red beneath; petioles to 150cm, erect, winged below, purple-red. Peduncle to 10cm; spathe to 15cm, white above, light red beneath. Peru, W Ecuador.

P.distantilobum K. Krause.
Stems climbing. Leaves to 40 × 35cm, erect, ovate-oblong in outline, pinnatifid nearly to midrib, seg. 5–6 per side, oblanceolate to linear, acuminate, to 5cm across, entire or basal segment bifid, interstitial sinuses wide, angular; petiole subequal to lamina. Peduncles several, to 12.5cm; spathe to 8.5cm, green-white. Brazil .

P.domesticum Bunting (*P.hastatum* hort. non K. Koch & Sello). SPADE-LEAF PHILODENDRON.
Stems climbing. Leaves to 60 × 30cm, reflexed, elongate-triangular, sagittate, undulate, glossy bright green, basal lobes round-oblong to triangular, main lateral veins in 5–6 pairs; petiole equalling lamina, flattened above toward apex, centrally longitudinally ridged. Peduncle to 15cm; spathe to 18cm, green externally, deep pink-red within with green border. Origin unknown. 'Variegatum': leaves splashed yellow, cream and acid green.

P.dubium hort. non Chodat & Visch. See *P.radiatum.*
P.duisbergii Epple ex Bunting. See *P.fendleri.*
P.elegans K. Krause. See *P.angustisectum.*
P.epipremnum. See *Epipremnum pinnatum.*

P.erubescens K. Koch & Augustin. RED-LEAF PHILODENDRON; BLUSHING PHILODENDRON.
Stems tall, climbing, purple or red-purple when young, with deep pink to pink-brown cataphylls. Leaves to 40cm, reflexed, ovate-triangular, base short sagittate-cordate, somewhat coriaceous, glossy dark green above, coppery-purple beneath; petiole equalling lamina, flattened towards apex, tinged purple. Peduncle purple-red; spathe 15cm, cymbiform, dark purple externally, crimson within, scented; spadix white, equalling spathe. Colombia. 'Burgundy' (hybrid): leaves leathery, to 30cm, base cordate to hastate, flushed red, veins burgundy, stem claret. 'Golden Erubescens': vigorous climber; stems thin, round; leaves gold, tinted pink beneath

and when young. 'Imperial Red': leaves dark purple to red. 'Red Emerald': vigorous; stems claret; leaves long-cordate, to 40cm, dark green with red ribs beneath, shiny, petioles long and rich red.

P.fendleri K. Krause (*P.duisbergii* Epple ex Bunt.).
Stems climbing to 5m, internodes to 2–6×5–6cm, cataphylls becoming scarious, deciduous. Leaves 60cm, reflexed, triangular-ovate in outline, pinnatifid, marginal seg. 11–23 × 3–8cm, 6–9 per side, oblong, obtuse, with 1 main lateral vein per segment, sinus wide, midrib convex; petioles to 90cm, terete, shortly sheathed at base. Peduncles 4, to 18cm; spathe 18cm, green externally, rich dark maroon within, tube 5cm, inflated; spadix shorter than spathe. Colombia, Venezuela, Trinidad.

P. 'Fernleaf'. See *P.pinnatilobum*.

P.fibrillosum Poepp.
Stems climbing, fibrous remains of cataphylls persistent. Leaves 40×18cm, erect, oblong-elliptic, tapering to each end, membranous, main lateral veins many, prominent; petiole 18cm, apex geniculate. Spathe to 7.5cm, purple below. Peru.

P.fibrillosum hort. non Poepp. See *P.grazielae*.

P.fragrantissimum (Hook.) Kunth.
Stems climbing when young, branching above when adult. Adult leaves 45–60cm, oblong-cordate to sagittate, petioles deeply grooved above, juvenile leaves ovate, small, with winged petioles. Spathe to 23cm, convolute and hooded, tube bright red, limb pale cream, very fragrant; spadix subequal to spathe, acute, tapering upwards. Northern S America.

P.giganteum Schott.
Large, stems climbing, to 10cm diam., internodes short, remains of cataphylls persistent. Leaves to 100 × 60cm, reflexed, ovate, cordate or sagittate, basal lobes rounded, overlapping; petioles stout, equalling or much exceeding lamina. Peduncle short, stout; spathe to 23cm, tube inflated, cherry-red, limb oblong, white within, dull red externally; spadix stout, sessile. Caribbean Is. to Trinidad.

P.gloriosum André.
Stems climbing or prostrate, internodes short, with persistent scarious remains of cataphylls. Leaves 40 × 33cm, reflexed, broad-ovate, cordate-sagittate, basal lobes rounded, dark velvety green above, midrib and main veins ivory-white; petioles to 75cm, flattened above, streaked white. Peduncle to 16.5cm, white-lined; spathe 16.5cm, tube pale green, tinged pink, limb pink. Colombia. 'Terciopelo Redondo': leaves sage green with pale green venation, tinted pink beneath.

P.grandifolium (Jacq.) Schott.
Stems climbing, dull green with purple spots, internodes to 5 × 3cm. Leaves 50 × 35cm, entire, lanceolate, base cordate, apex acuminate to cuspidate, subcoriaceous, basal lobes ovate to quadrangular, obtuse; midrib prominent, main lateral veins 7–8 per side; petiole to 45cm, terete, shortly grooved at base. Peduncles 1–2, to 10cm; spathe to 11cm, tube somewhat inflated, yellow-green externally, purple within, limb ovate, cream within. Venezuela, French Guiana, Martinique.

P.grazielae Bunting (*P.fibrillosum* hort. non Poepp.).
Stems climbing, internodes to 5cm. Leaves 8.5 × 10.5cm, reflexed, subreniform, cordate, acuminate, coriaceous, main lateral veins numerous; petioles to 7.5cm, terete, sheathed below in juvenile phase. Peduncle 2cm, spathe 4–5cm, slender, green-white; spadix to 4cm. Amazonian Peru, Brazil.

P.guatemalense Engl. See *P.inaequilaterum*.
P.guttiferum hort. non Kunth. See *Monstera standleyana*.
P.hastatum hort. non K. Koch & Sello. See *P.domesticum*.

P.ilsemannii Sander (*P.sagittifolium* misapplied).
Variegated juvenile phase of undetermined sp., possibly allied to *P.cordatum*. Stems climbing. Leaves reflexed, narrow-ovate, cordate-sagittate, heavily marked white with green and grey-green patches. Origin unknown.

P.imbe Endl.(*P.sellowianum* Kunth).
Stem climbing, red-purple. Leaves 33 × 18cm, reflexed, ovate-oblong, cordate to sagittate, glossy above, basal lobes rounded, sinus narrow, 7.5cm, main lateral veins in 3 pairs, widely spreading; petiole terete, equalling lamina. Peduncle short; spathe 15cm, tube green externally, red within, limb broad-ovate, cream; spadix slender. SE Brazil. 'Goldiana': dense; leaves long-ovate, rich green with gold speckles, red beneath, yellow when young, petioles short. 'Variegatum': leaves irregularly blotched green, dark green and cream. 'Weber's Selfheading': climber; leaves thick, very shiny, oblique oblanceolate, midrib light green, ribs red beneath, petioles red spotted yellow-green.

P.imperiale Schott. See *P.ornatum*.

P.inaequilaterum Liebm. (*P.coerulescens* Engl.; *P.guatemalense* Engl.).
Stems slender, woody, climbing. Leaves to 30 × 15cm, spreading to erect, membranous, ovate to elliptic-oblong, acuminate, base obtuse or truncate, main lateral veins numerous, widely spreading; petioles to 20cm, winged to geniculum. Spathe 15cm, green-white. Mexico to Colombia.

P.inconcinnum Schott.
Stems climbing, internodes 5cm. Leaves 20 × 8.5cm, oblong to narrow-obovate, acuminate, base emarginate, midrib broad, main lateral veins in 5–7 pairs; petioles to 20cm+, flattened above, sometimes winged in basal half. Spathe to 14cm, green-yellow externally, cream within, red at base. Venezuela.

P.krebsii Schott.
Stems climbing, internodes 2.5–10cm. Leaves 35 × 20cm, spreading, ovate to oblong-elliptic or elongate-triangular, base cordate, subcoriaceous, glossy dark green, midrib broad, lateral veins numerous; petioles 12.5cm, terete. Peduncle equalling petiole; spathe 10cm, green. Caribbean Is.

P.lacerum (Jacq.) Schott.
Stems climbing, to 30m, internodes long. Leaves 75cm, reflexed, ovate to round in outline, cordate, pinnatisect to less than halfway to midrib, lobes cuneate, obtuse, midrib and main lateral veins prominent; petioles terete, to 90cm. Peduncles several, 20cm+; spathe 12.5cm, tube inflated, dull red-purple externally, purple within, limb green-yellow. Cuba, Jamaica, Hispaniola.

P.laciniatum (Vell. Conc.) Engl. See *P.pedatum*.
P.laciniosum Schott. See *P.pedatum*.

P.latilobum Schott.
Stems climbing. Juvenile leaves entire; adult leaves 30 × 25cm, ovate-triangular in outline, base obtuse to sub-truncate, 3-lobed toward apex, median lobe to 15cm across, broad-ovate, acute, lateral lobes rounded, with upper margin shorter and somewhat curved, obtuse, main lateral veins 6. Peru.

P.lingulatum (L.) K. Koch.
Stems slender, climbing. Leaves to 40cm, membranous, oblong-elliptic to ovate, acuminate, truncate to emarginate at base, glossy dark green above; petioles slightly exceeding lamina, widely winged except for apical 1.5–6.5cm. Spathe 15cm, cream, becoming green with age. W Indies.

P.maximum K. Krause.
Stems climbing, 5cm diam., internodes short, remains of cataphylls persistent. Leaves 135 × 73cm, reflexed, long-ovate, sagittate, undulate to sinuate, dark green above, midrib and main lateral veins pale; petiole to 105cm, flattened above. Peduncle to 30cm; spathe 20cm, green. Brazil (Acre).

P.melanochrysum Lind. & André (*P.andreanum* Devansaye).
BLACK-GOLD PHILODENDRON.
Stems climbing, internodes long. Leaves 100×30cm, reflexed to pendent, oblong-lanceolate or narrow-ovate, sagittate, acuminate, basal lobes overlapping or sinus narrow, velvety black-green above, veins pale green, copper-coloured when young; petioles to 50cm, scabrous; juvenile leaves smaller, ovate-cordate, basal lobes sometimes connate; petioles

sheathing below. Spathe 20cm, tube green, limb acuminate, white. Colombia.

P.mexicanum Engl.
Stems climbing, internodes long. Leaves reflexed, long-triangular, more or less hastate, median lobe 38 × 18cm, lateral lobes 23×8.5cm, lanceolate to oblong, curved; petioles 60cm. Spathe to 15cm, green externally, ruby-red within. Mexico.

P.micans K. Koch. See *P.scandens* ssp. *scandens* f. *micans*.

P.microstictum Standl. & L.O. Williams.
Stems climbing. Leaves to 23 × 20cm, broad-triangular to nearly reniform, long-acuminate, emarginate or truncate in juvenile phase, coriaceous, main lateral veins numerous; petioles equalling lamina, broadly sheathed at base. Peduncle exceeding petiole; spathe 15cm, green externally, tube dark red within at base. Costa Rica.

P.myrmecophilum Engl. (*P.deflexum* Poepp. ex Schott).
Stems climbing, internodes short. Leaves 25–50 × 17.5–30cm, erect, entire, ovate, cordate to hastate, coriaceous, basal lobes obtuse to rounded, to 17cm, separated by deep sinus; petioles to 50cm, grooved, sheathed beneath, inhabited by ants. Peduncle to 20cm; spathe to 15cm, lanceolate-ovate, white and purple, or purple with margin white. Amazon basin.

P.ochrostemon Schott.
Stems climbing, slender, internodes long. Leaves 28 × 11.5cm, spreading or erect, oblong-elliptic to oblong, base truncate, midrib narrow, main lateral veins in 10–12 pairs; petioles shorter than laminae, narrowly winged, auriculate at apex. Spathe 15cm, tube green externally, yellow-green within, limb yellow. SE Brazil.

P.ornatum Schott (*P.asperatum* K. Koch; *P.sodiroi* hort. ex Bellair & St. Leger (invalid); *P.imperiale* Schott).
Stems climbing, internodes to 10cm when juvenile, 2.5cm when adult, fibrous remains of cataphylls persistent. Leaves 60cm, reflexed, ovate, deeply cordate, glossy dark green, sometimes spotted with grey, veins red beneath; petiole equalling lamina, flattened above toward apex, somewhat scabrous, purple when young. Peduncle short, red with white streaks; spathe 14cm, apex 2cm, long-subulate, cream within, tube green externally, limb white, tinged red externally. Venezuela to Peru & SE Brazil.

P.oxycardium Schott. See *P.scandens* ssp. *oxycardium*.
P.panduraeforme misapplied. See *P.bipennifolium*.

P.pedatum (Hook.) Kunth (*P.laciniatum* (Vell. Conc.) Engl.; *P.laciniosum* Schott).
Stems tall, climbing, internodes long. Leaves reflexed, ovate in outline, irregularly pinnatifid, terminal lobe 45 × 30cm, median seg. elliptic, obovate or rhombic, lateral seg. to 5 per side, oblong, obtuse, with 2 or more main lateral veins each, basal lobes 27 × 17cm, widely spreading; petioles exceeding lamina, terete, sometimes verrucose toward apex; juvenile leaves with 5 lobes. Spathe 12.5cm, green externally, becoming white toward apex, cream within, red-purple at base of tube. S Venezuela, Surinam to SE Brazil. 'Purple Green': leaves flushed red-purple.

P.pertusum Kunth & Bouché. See *Monstera deliciosa*.

P.pinnatilobum Engl. (*P.*'Fernleaf').
Stems climbing, angular, internodes to 3.5cm or to 10cm when juvenile. Leaves to 50cm across, erect, ovate-orbicular, pinnatifid, lateral seg. 1.5cm across, to 13 per side, narrow, acuminate, basal lobes bifid; juvenile leaves with fewer segments and basal lobes reduced; petioles equalling lamina, grooved above. Peduncles clustered, 22cm; spathe 10cm, green, tinged pink at base externally. Brazil (Amazonia).

P.pittieri Engl. See *P.scandens* ssp. *scandens* f. *scandens*.

P.radiatum Schott (*P.dubium* hort. non Chodat & Visch.). DUBIA PHILODENDRON.
Stems climbing. Leaves to 90×70cm, reflexed, ovate in outline, cordate-sagittate, deeply pinnatifid, terminal lobe with 8 pairs oblong or further 3-parted segments, interstitial sinuses narrow, basal lobes 5-parted, lateral veins fused at sinus; petioles exceeding lamina, terete. Peduncles clustered; spathe to 25cm, tube inflated, dull red-purple externally, cherry-red within, limb green externally, white within. C America.

P.rubens Schott.
Stems erect or climbing, stout, internodes long. Leaves 50× 28cm, reflexed, ovate, sagittate-cordate, acuminate, basal lobes rounded; petioles to 60cm, subterete, somewhat scabrous towards apex. Peduncle red with white streaks; spathe 15cm, green, spotted white externally, red-purple within. Venezuela.

P.rugosum Bogner & Bunting.
Stems climbing, internodes 1.5–3×4cm. Leaves to 35×30cm, ovate, cordate, apex cuspidate, coriaceous, bright green, markedly rugose above, smooth beneath, midrib convex, main lateral veins 7–10, inconspicuous; petioles to 40cm, terete, grooved toward base. Peduncles 1–4, to 5cm, red; spathe to 10cm, dark red below, paler red above, apex green; spadix to 9cm, sessile, cream. Ecuador.

P.ruizii Schott.
Stems climbing. Leaves 60 × 23cm, narrowly elliptic- to oblanceolate-oblong, base obtuse, truncate or auriculate, coriaceous, main lateral veins in 10 pairs, scarcely distinct from secondary veins; petioles much shorter than lamina, 25cm. Peduncles clustered; spathe to 10cm, pale green. Peru.

P.sagittatum hort. See *P.sagittifolium*.

P.sagittifolium Liebm. (*P.sagittatum* hort.).
Stems climbing, internodes short. Leaves to 60×30cm, long triangular-oblong, sagittate, subcoriaceous, glossy bright green, basal lobes to 12.5cm, triangular, obtuse, midrib broad, main lateral veins to 6–7-pairs, spreading; petioles subequal to lamina, flattened to convex above. Spathe to 18cm, green, purple at base within. SE Mexico.

P.sagittifolium misapplied. See *P.ilsemannii*.

P.scandens K. Koch & Sello (*P.cordatum* misapplied). HEART-LEAF PHILODENDRON.
ssp. *scandens* f. *scandens* (*P.pittieri* Engl.). Stems slender, climbing, but becoming pendent, internodes long. Leaves 8(–30) × 6–23cm, reflexed, ovate-cordate, acuminate, glossy green above, green or red-purple beneath, main lateral veins in 2–3 pairs; petioles slender, shorter than lamina, subterete, channelled above. Inflorescence borne on pendent shoots; peduncle short; spathe to 19cm, green externally, limb white within, sometimes tinged red. Mexico and W Indies to SE Brazil. f. *micans* (K. Koch) Bunting (*P.micans* K. Koch). Leaves bronze above, red to red brown beneath, basal lobes larger, slightly overlapping. ssp. *oxycardium* (Schott) Bunting (*P.oxycardium* Schott). Juvenile leaves glossy, brown when immature, green when mature. E Mexico. 'Variegatum': leaves dark green marbled off-white and green-grey.

P.schottianum H. Wendl. ex Schott.
Stems climbing, internodes short. Leaves 60×40cm, broad-ovate, cordate, main lateral veins in 5–6 pairs; petioles exceeding lamina, subcylindric. Peduncle red; spathe 12.5cm, green externally, red-purple within. Costa Rica.

P.sellowianum Kunth. See *P.imbe*.

P.sodiroi hort. ex Bellair & St. Leger (invalid). See *P.ornatum*.

P.squamiferum Poepp.
Close to *P.pedatum*. Stems climbing. Leaves 60×45cm, pinnatifid, 5-lobed, lobes entire, median lobe elliptic to rhombic, lateral lobes oblong-triangular, falcate, basal lobes elliptic,

separated by broad sinuses; juvenile leaves entire or 3-lobed; petioles 15–30cm, red, terete, densely covered by fleshy bristles. Peduncles 7.5cm, paired, verrucose, red; spathe to 10cm, tube red-purple, limb green-yellow and red-purple externally, cream within. Eastern S America (Surinam, French Guiana, Brazil). 'Florida' (*P.pedatum* or *P.laciniatum* × *P.squamiferum*): climber; leaves in 5 lobes, midrib pale, ribs indented, brown to red beneath; petioles thin, round, somewhat warty. 'Florida Compacta' (*P.pedatum* var. *palmisectum* or *P.quercifolium* × *P.squamiferum*): non-climbing; leaves thick, deep green; petioles round, marked plum. 'Florida Variegata': leaves irregularly blotched pale cream, often covering half the leaf.

P.tripartitum (Jacq.) Schott.
Stems climbing, internodes long. Leaves more or less reflexed, 3-lobed nearly to base, lobes to 25 × 7.5cm, elongate ovate-elliptic, median sometimes oblanceolate, lateral lobes 25cm, inequilateral, sides rounded; petioles slightly exceeding lamina, terete. Peduncle short, solitary; spathe 15cm, tube green, purple at base within, limb white. S America.

P.trisectum Standl.
Close to *P.tripartitum*, but smaller in all parts. Leaf lobes 19 × 3.5cm, nearly equal, united at base, lateral lobes equilateral, curved; petioles to 33cm. Peduncle 11.5cm; spathe 10cm, green-white. Costa Rica.

P.triumphans hort. See *P.verrucosum*.

P.verrucosum Schott (*P.triumphans* hort.).
Stems climbing, internodes to 15cm. Leaves 60 × 40cm, reflexed, ovate, sagittate-cordate, margins shallowly sinuate, shimmering dark green above with pale green zones along midrib and main lateral veins, red-violet beneath; petioles equalling lamina, flattened above, covered by fleshy red, green or white scales (also covering peduncle, spathe and cataphylls). Peduncle to 20cm; spathe 21cm, red-brown, becoming lime-green above externally, pink-red within, white above. Costa Rica to Ecuador.

P.warscewiczii K. Koch.
Stems very large, climbing. Leaves semi-deciduous, reflexed, membranous, triangular, bipinnatifid, primary lobes few, deeply lobed, ultimate segments occasionally dentate, basal sinus very broad, with lateral veins united. Peduncle 5cm; spathe to 15cm, green externally, cream within; spadix sessile. Guatemala.

P.cultivars. 'Angra dos Reis': leaves thick, broad-sagittate, very glossy; stalks marked red. 'Beleza do Acre': leaves broad, sagittate, to 1m, shiny, margin wavy, ribs lighter. 'Choco': leaves heavy, to 30cm, dark lush green, veins white. 'Edmundo Barroso': creeping; leaves thick, upright, ovate-oblong, midrib raised. 'Emerald King': leaves to 30cm long, spade-shaped, pointed. 'Emerald Queen': leaves bright green, hastate, shiny, petioles short; Fl hybrid. 'New Yorker': leaves sagittate, dipped, thick, dark green, veins lighter, tinted red when young, petioles dotted maroon. 'Painted Lady': leaves sagittate, gold when young, later mottled green; petioles tinted red. 'Red Duchess': leaves to 25cm long, cordate, dark green, shiny, tinted red beneath, petioles red. 'Santa Leopoldana': leaves long sagittate, thick, to 1m, dark green, shiny, ribs white, edges red; petioles and stems red; spathe tinted red. 'Silver Cloud': leaves thick, waved, splattered silver towards edge, pale beneath, petioles broad and flat, finely striped white.

Pholistoma Lilja. (From Gk *pholis*, scale, and *stoma*, mouth.) Hydrophyllaceae. 3 species of prostrate or weakly climbing annual herbs closely related to *Nemophila*, from which it can be distinguished by the retrorse bristly spines on the upper stems. Stems rather succulent and easily broken, usually angled and spiny. Leaves pinnatifid. Flowers white, blue or mauve, borne in cymes or, more rarely, solitary; calyx lobes 5; corolla lobes 5; stamens 5; style shallowly cleft. Fruit a capsule, 1-celled, setose or prickly. Southwest N America.

CULTIVATION A useful half-hardy climber for temporary cover on fences and tree stumps etc., especially in informal situations. Sow seed under glass in early spring. Prick out seedlings when large enough to handle and grow on in individual pots until planted out.

P.auritum (Lindl.) Lilja (*Nemophila aurita* Lindl.). FIESTA FLOWER.
To 1.2m. Leaves oblong in outline, hirsute, expanded and clasping at base, lobes 7–11. Flowers to 2.75cm diam., blue, lilac or violet marked with deeper streaks, grouped 2–5 at shoot tips. California.

Phryganocydia Mart. ex Bur. (From Gk *phryganon*, undershrub, and *kydion*, greater.) Bignoniaceae. 3 species of lianes; pseudostipules absent. Stem without glandular patches. Leaves 2-foliolate, often with simple tendril. Flowers solitary or in lax panicles; calyx spathe-like, split; corolla tubular-funnelform, lilac to magenta, lepidote outside; stamens didynamous; ovary conical to terete, lepidote; disc absent. Capsule linear, flattened, median nerve not prominent, lepidote; seeds with 2 brown wings. Costa Rica to Brazil. Z10.

CULTIVATION A rampant climber found in open, low-lying habitats, often at the roadsides, *P.corymbosa* is one of Trinidad's most beautiful climbers, bearing a profusion of fragrant pink or purple trumpet-shaped blooms, in several flushes over the season. Cultivate as for *Bignonia*.

P.corymbosa (Vent.) Bur. ex Schum. (*Spathodea corymbosa* Vent.).
Stem 5cm diam. Leaves 2-foliolate, usually with an apical tendril; leaflets elliptic to ovate-elliptic, apex obtuse, base rounded, 4–20 × 2–11cm with 3 nerves, principal nerve red-brown beneath; tendrils simple, 7–16cm. Flowers in corymbose panicles, magenta, throat white; calyx 1cm; corolla funnelform, 4–9 × 1–2.5cm. Fruit 12–53 × 1–3cm, linear-oblong, pilose; seeds 1–2 × 4–7cm. Panama to Brazil and Bolivia.

Pileostegia viburnoides

Pileostegia Hook. f. & Thoms. (From Gk *pilos*, felt, and *stege*, roof, referring to the form of the corolla.) Hydrangeaceae. 4 species of climbing or prostrate evergreen shrubs related to *Hydrangea* and *Schizophragma*, distinguished in having flowers all alike in terminal, corymbose panicles. Calyx cup-shaped, 4–5-lobed; petals 4–5; stamens to 0.5cm, inserted in calyx cup with petals; ovary semi-inferior, 5-celled, ovules many, style stout, 5–6-lobed at apex. E Asia.

CULTIVATION   *Pileostegia* is a useful climber for a north- or east-facing wall, although it flowers more profusely in sun. Propagate by nodal stem and tip cuttings taken from young growth as the foliage expands, treat with rooting hormone and root in a closed case with bottom heat; also by seed and layers. Otherwise, cultivate as for *Decumaria*.

P.viburnoides Hook. f. & Thoms. (*Schizophragma viburnoides* (Hook. & Thoms.) Stapf).
6–10m. Stems self-clinging; branchlets initially scurfy, later glabrous. Leaves 5–18cm, narrow-oblong to ovate-lanceolate, opposite, entire, coriaceous, glossy dark green, pitted above, prominently and closely veined beneath. Panicles to 15cm, crowded, borne profusely; flowers 0.8cm diam., white; stamens conspicuous, slender. India, China, Taiwan. Z8.

Piper L. PEPPER. (Classical Latin name from Gk *peperi*, derived in turn from an Indian name.) Piperaceae. More than 1000 species of erect shrubs, tough woody climbers and small trees, sometimes soft-stemmed, often with pungent odour; stems often swollen at nodes. Leaves alternate, lamina often attached asymmetrically to petiole, one side lower than other; stipules absent or attached to petiole. Inflorescence axillary or opposite leaf, a cylindric spike, or rarely compounded of several spikes; flowers small, those of New World species bisexual, of Old World species unisexual, subtended by often concave floral bract; perianth wanting; stamens 2–10; stigmas 2–4, generally 3. Fruit a drupe with this mesocarp; seed 1. Pantropical. Z10 unless stated.

CULTIVATION   Pepper, *P.nigrum*, is cultivated commercially in the rich alluvial soils of the low altitude, wet tropics, either as a second or subsidiary crop in the shade of tree crops or with other species cultivated to provide shade; other than the cultivation of *P.nigrum* and *P.betle* in botanic collections of economically important plants, in temperate zones *Piper* species are more commonly grown as ornamentals. With the exception of *P.kadsura* which will tolerate short-lived light frost in sheltered woodland sites in humus-rich soils, *Piper* species are suitable for the warm glasshouse or conservatory, valued for their often very attractively marbled foliage, notably so in *P.ornatum*. Plant in borders, tubs or baskets in an open mix incorporating composted bark, leafmould and coir. Semi-shade or filtered sunlight is preferred, although most species will tolerate heavy shade and may even be used as creepers under staging or trained on the dark trunks of densely leafy host trees. Water, feed and mist frequently during warm weather, less so in winter. Pruning to remove weak growth and thin congested growth is best done in late winter/early spring before growth commences. Propagate by seed or by semi-ripe cuttings in sand in a closed case.

P.betle L. BETEL; BETLE PEPPER.
Climber to 5m; stem rounded, woody, nodes scarcely swollen, frequently producing adventitious roots, glabrous. Leaves to 13.5 × 7.5cm, broadly ovate to cordate, acute to acuminate at apex, rounded to cordate at base, green, smooth and glabrous, somewhat coriaceous; petiole 13 × 2mm, glabrous, with stipules extending to half its length. Inflorescence leaf-opposed, solitary, male spike 115×5mm, female 55× 8mm, pale green glaucous; peduncle 2cm × 1.5mm. Fruit to 12cm, embedded in rachis and coalescing into a fleshy red mass. Indian to Malay Peninsula. Extensively grown in SE Asia for its leaves ('*pan*') and spikes which are chewed with betel nut (fruit of the palm *Areca catechu*) and lime.

P.crocatum auct. See *P. ornatum*

P.cubeba L.f. CUBEB; CUBEB PEPPER.
Climber to 3m; stems round, smooth, somewhat swollen at nodes, glabrous. Leaves 14×6cm, elliptic to lanceolate, acute to acuminate at apex, broadly tapered, rounded or somewhat cordate at base, and often asymmetric, green above, paler beneath, smooth; petiole 11 × 2mm, grooved above. Inflorescence leaf-opposed, solitary, erect becoming pendulous, spikes unisexual, male 85×4.5mm, female 75×18mm; peduncles 30×2.5mm, glabrous. Fruit loosely arranged, red-brown, long-pedicellate. Indonesia.

P.futokadsura Sieb. See *P.kadsura*.

P.guineense Schum. & Thonn. GUINEA CUBEB; ASHANTI PEPPER; BENIN PEPPER.
Vine, stems climbing over trees to 23m. Leaves alternate, very variable, 10×7cm, suborbicular to ovate on main stem, oval to lanceolate on lateral branches, acuminate at apex, cordate or rounded at base; petioles 3cm on main stem leaves, 1.2cm on those of lateral branches. Spikes erect in flower, pendent in fruit, 3cm; peduncle 7mm, glabrous; bracts ciliate; stamens 2, perhaps rarely 3; stigmas 3–5, sessile. Fruiting spikes 7cm, tomentose; fruit 4.5mm diam., red, dry; pedicel 7mm. Tropical Africa (Guinea to Uganda and Angola).

P.kadsura (Choisy) Ohwi (*P.futokadsura* Sieb.). JAPANESE PEPPER.
Scandent shrub, clambering over rocks and trees; branches slender, with aerial roots. Leaves 6.5 × 3.5cm, ovate, or rounded-cordate on young plants, long-acuminate at apex, rounded at base, entire, dark green, paler beneath, rather stiff and thick, often sparsely pubescent. Spikes 3–8cm, female shorter than male; peduncles pendulous; bracts peltate. Fruit globose, 3.5mm diam., red. Japan, S Korea, Ryukyus. Z8.

P.longum L.
Slender climber, 3m; stems angled or fluted, not or scarcely swollen at nodes, rather hairy. Leaves 7.5 × 4cm, broadly lanceolate to lanceolate-elliptic, broadly acute to obtuse at apex, rarely somewhat acuminate, deeply auriculate at base, very slightly asymmetric, green above, paler beneath, smooth, minutely hairy beneath, densely glandular-punctate; petiole 12×1mm, grooved. Inflorescence leaf-opposed, solitary, erect, male spikes 6cm×2.5mm, female spikes 2cm × 6.5mm; peduncle of male spikes 3cm, of female 11mm, minutely pubescent. Fruit very densely arranged. Tropical E Himalaya.

P.metallicum Hallier f.
Scandent herb to more than 1m; stems 2.5mm diam., red when young, becoming dull deep green with age, glabrous, with adventitious roots from nodes. Leaves alternate, to 15 × 11cm, ovate, apex acuminate and mucronate, scarcely contracted to petiole at base, tinged red when young, beautiful metallic deep green when mature, red with a silvery sheen beneath, thick, veins reticulate, dark red; petioles to 4×0.4cm. Flowers and fruit unknown. Borneo.

P.nigrum L. COMMON PEPPER; PEPPER PLANT; BLACK PEPPER; WHITE PEPPER; MADAGASCAR PEPPER.
Climber to 4m, monoecious or dioecious; stems rounded, swollen at nodes, glabrous. Leaves 9×6cm, broadly ovate to cordate, broadly tapered, rounded or weakly cordate at base, acute to obtuse, often shortly acuminate at apex, green, glabrous; petiole 22 × 2mm, deeply grooved. Inflorescence leaf-opposed, solitary, pendulous, spikes mostly bisexual, 7.5 × 0.6cm; peduncle 15 × 1.5mm, glabrous. Fruit loosely arranged, 5mm diam., dark red when fully ripe. S India & Sri Lanka, naturalised in N Burma and Assam.

P.ornatum N.E. Br. CELEBES PEPPER.
Shrub, extensively spreading, creeping or weakly climbing, to 5m; stem rounded, wiry, dark green or rufescent, glabrous. Leaves 9.5×7.5cm, broadly cordate to suborbicular, peltate with petiole attached 1–2cm from lower margin, obtuse and rounded or acute and attenuate at apex, rounded to somewhat cordate at base, finely mottled dark green, pink and silver above, flushed maroon beneath; petiole 7.5×0.3cm, grooved above, with stipules to 12mm when young. Inflorescence unknown. Sulawesi.

P.porphyrophyllum (Lindl.) N.E. Br.
Shrub very extensively spreading, creeping or sometimes weakly climbing, to 8m; stem rounded with longitudinal grooves, wiry, rufescent, often with lines of hairs. Leaves 12.5 × 10.5cm, broadly cordate to suborbicular, generally obtuse and shortly mucronate at apex, cordate to auriculate at base, thin, dark green above with red and white spots, flushed purple beneath; petiole 33 × 3mm, grooved. Inflorescence leaf-opposed, male spikes 12×0.4cm, female 3 × 0.8cm; peduncles 2.5cm, hairy. Malay Peninsula, Borneo.

P.rubrovenosum hort. ex Rodigas.
Vine; stems flexuous, woody. Leaves obliquely elliptic to cordate, acute to acuminate at apex, entire, bright deep green above, paler beneath, glabrous, rather coriaceous, veins 5, marked by irregular rose lines above; stipules adnate to petiole, pink. Inflorescence and fruit unknown. New Guinea.

P.sylvaticum Roxb. MOUNTAIN LONG PEPPER.
Climber to 4m; stem rounded, becoming woody, with longitudinal lines, nodes somewhat swollen. Leaves 9 × 5cm, ovate to cordate, acute to acuminate at apex, broadly tapered, rounded or cordate at base, often somewhat asymmetric, dark green above, paler beneath, rough, glandular-pubescent on main veins beneath, glandular-punctate on minor veins; petiole 10×1mm, grooved. Inflorescence leaf-opposed, solitary, erect, male spikes 55×3mm, female 19× 6mm; peduncles 9×1.5mm, minutely glandular-pubescent. Fruit densely arranged but individuals distinct. Subtropical E Himalaya.

Pithecoctenium Mart. ex Meissn. (From Gk *pithekos*, ape or monkey, and *ktenion*, comb, referring to the spiny fruits.) Bignoniaceae. 12 species of lianes. Branches hexagonal; pseudostipules falling early. Leaves 2–3-foliolate, terminal leaflet often replaced by trifid tendril, tendril often further divided to 15-fid, some tendril tips form swollen rings. Inflorescence a terminal raceme or panicle; calyx cupular, truncate, thick, 5-denticulate, lepidote, puberulent; corolla white, tubular-campanulate, thick and fleshy, puberulent outside; anthers glabrous; ovary ellipsoid or cylindrical, densely pubescent; ovules multi-seriate; disc annular, pulvinate. Fruit a capsule, flattened-elliptic, woody, valves parallel, densely spiny; seeds winged, surrounded by hyaline membranous wing. Americas, Mexico, to Brazil and Argentina. Z10.

CULTIVATION Slender climbers, attractive in foliage and flower and interesting in fruit; *P.cynanchoides* has felted young growth and large panicles of showy white flowers which produce small, flat seed pods covered in yellow bristles. Cultivate as for *Anemopaegma*.

P.buccinatorium DC. See *Distictis buccinatoria*.

P.carolinae Nichols.
Leaflets with apex acuminate, base cordate, lightly pubescent. Flowers fragrant; corolla white, tube tinted yellow, arcuate, tomentose, lobes slightly recurved, laciniate, crispate, spreading. Brazil.

P.cinereum DC. See *Distictis laxiflora*.
P.clematideum Griseb. See *P.cynanchoides*.

P.crucigerum (L.) A. Gentry (*Bignonia crucigera* L.; *Bignonia echinata* Jacq.; *P.echinatum* (Jacq.) Baill.).
Leaflets 3.3–18cm, ovate to suborbicular, apex acuminate, base cordate, membranous, lepidote, veins pubescent.

Inflorescence to 15-flowered; rachis pubescent; corolla 3.6–6.1 cm, often bent 90° in middle of tube, densely pubescent, yellow in throat, otherwise white. Mexico to N Argentina and Uruguay.

P.cynanchoides DC.
Leaflets 2.5–4cm, ovate, reniform or triangular, apex acuminate, margin ciliate. Corolla 3–6cm, white streaked yellow in throat. Brazil to Argentina.

P.echinatum (Jacq.) Baill. See *Pithecoctenium crucigerum*.
P.laxiflorum DC. See *Distictis laxiflora*.

Pleonotoma Miers. (From Gk *pleios*, many, and *temno*, to cut; the leaves are much divided.) Bignoniaceae.14 species of scrambling lianes. Branches tetragonal, angles sharp. Leaves once or twice pinnate with trifid tendrils. Flowers in racemes, usually terminating branchlets; calyx cylindrical, split one side; corolla tubular-campanulate, ventricose, bilabiate, 5-lobed; stamens 4, didynamous, incurved, included, with fifth rudimentary staminode; ovary cylindrical, glabrous, rugose; disc pulvinate. Fruit a capsule, linear, compressed; seeds flat, in hyaline wings. Americas. Z10.

CULTIVATION As for *Anemopaegma*.

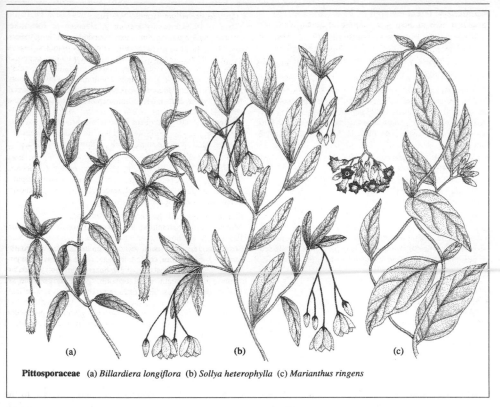

Pittosporaceae   (a) *Billardiera longiflora* (b) *Sollya heterophylla* (c) *Marianthus ringens*

P.variabile(Jacq.) Miers (*Bignonia variabilis* Jacq.).
Trunk to 3cm diam. Lower leaves twice trifoliate, upper leaves ternate, with trifid tendril; leaflets 2–16 ×0.8–1cm, elliptic to ovate-elliptic, apex acute to acuminate, base truncate to cuneate; petioles 2–7cm. Flowers in short racemes; calyx to 9mm, truncate; corolla 6–10×1–3cm at mouth, tubular-funnelform, tube pale yellow, limb white to cream. Fruit 15–30×1.5–3cm, linear to oblong, acute, flattened, verrucose-tuberculate. Guatemala to Venezuela and Trinidad.

Plumbago L. (From Lat. *plumbum*, lead; the plant was thought to be a cure for lead poisoning.) LEADWORT Plumbaginaceae. 15 species of shrubs, perennial or annual herbs. Leaves alternate, simple, entire, often auriculate at base. Inflorescence a spicate terminal raceme, 2–3-bracteate; spikelets usually 1-flowered; calyx tubular, 5-parted, often conical after anthesis, 5-ribbed, scarious between ribs; corolla gamopetalous, tube slender far exceeding calyx, limb 5 lobed, spreading; stamens 5 rarely 4, free, filaments 5, usually dilated at base; ovary superior, oblong, style 1, pubescent below, usually long and slender stigmatic lobes 5. Fruit a capsule, splitting into 5 valves; valves 1-seeded. Warm and tropical regions. Z9.

CULTIVATION   *P.auriculata*, the species most commonly seen in cultivation, makes a beautiful specimen for warm temperate, frost-free gardens, as cover for fence, trellis and pergola, as a free-standing informal hedge or as a container plant; in cooler climates it is suitable for the cool to intermediate glasshouse or conservatory, treated as a climber with support, in the border or as a tub specimen. It is valued for the profusion of sky blue flowers borne on the current season's growth throughout summer into late autumn or, in warm conditions, into early winter. Flowering usually occurs in the second year from seed; since *P.auriculata* is tolerant of a range of environmental conditions and flowers when young, it is sometimes used as a short-term houseplant. *P.scandens* requires similar conditions to *P.auriculata*; the remaining species, including the handsome winter-flowering climber *P.indica*, need warm or tropical glasshouse conditions in temperate zones.

Grow *P.auriculata* in a well drained, high-fertility, loam-based mix in direct sunlight, with a winter minimum of 7°C/45°F, ventilating freely when conditions allow at temperatures above 10°C/50°F. Water plentifully and liquid-feed fortnightly when in full growth, reducing water after flowering to keep just moist in winter. Tie to supports as growth proceeds. Prune hard in late winter, either to the base or by cutting lateral growth hard back to a more permanent framework of branches. Grow tender species such as

P.indica in bright filtered light or in sun, with some shade in summer, maintaining moderate to high humidity, with a minimum temperature 16–18°C/60–65°F. Cut back to within 10–15cm/4–6in. of the base in spring, for flowers in summer; given some heat, unpruned specimens will bloom in late winter. Propagate *P.auriculata* by semi-ripe cuttings of non-flowering lateral growth with a heel, rooted in sand in a closed case with gentle bottom heat. Propagate *P.indica* by basal cuttings and root cuttings; also by seed in spring.

P.auriculata Lam. (*P.capensis* Thunb.). CAPE LEADWORT.
Shrub, evergreen; stems long-arching, somewhat scandent.
Leaves to 7×4cm, oblong to oblong-spathulate, tapering into petiole. Spikes short; calyx lobes triangular; corolla 2.5cm across and 4cm long, pale blue. S Africa, naturalized S Europe. Z9.

P.auriculata Bl. non Lam. See *P.zeylanica*.
P.capensis Thunb. See *P.auriculata*.
P.coccinea Salisb. See *P.indica*.
P.flaccida Moench. See *P.zeylanica*.
P.floridana Nutt. See *P.scandens*.

P.indica L. (*P.coccinea* Salisb.; *P.rosea* L.).
Herb or subshrub, semiscandent or erect, glabrous. Leaves 5–11×2–5cm. Spikes 10–30cm, lax; calyx 8–9mm, glandular-pubescent, tinged red; corolla deep rosy pink to pale red or purple; tube to 2.5cm; style often fringed below. SE Asia.

P.lactea Salisb. See *P.zeylanica*.
P.mexicana HBK. See *P.scandens*.
P.occidentalis Sweet. See *P.scandens*.
P.rosea L. See *P.indica*.

P.scandens L. (*Molubda scandens* (L.) Raf.; *P.floridana* Nutt.; *P.mexicana* HBK; *P.occidentalis* Sweet). DEVIL'S HERB; TOOTHWORT.
Evergreen shrub, decumbent to scandent; branches grooved, glabrous. Leaves to 10cm, oblong to oblong-lanceolate, mucronate, tapering to short petiole. Inflorescence paniculate; calyx tube glandular pubescent; corolla to 2cm, white or blue, lobes mucronulate; stamens 4. Summer. S US to Tropical S America.

P.virginica Hook. f. See *P.zeylanica*.
P.viscosa Blanco. See *P.zeylanica*.

P.zeylanica L. (*P.auriculata* Bl. non Lam.; *P.flaccida* Moench; *P.lactea* Salisb.; *P.virginica* Hook. f.; *P.viscosa* Blanco).
Shrub to 1m, somewhat scandent; branches many-angled. Leaves 3–12×2–5cm, ovate to oblong, acute or obtuse, tapering to petiole. Spikes dense, glandular-pubescent; calyx to 12mm; corolla to 2.5cm, white, lobes ovate; anthers blue to violet; style glabrous. SE Asia to Australia.

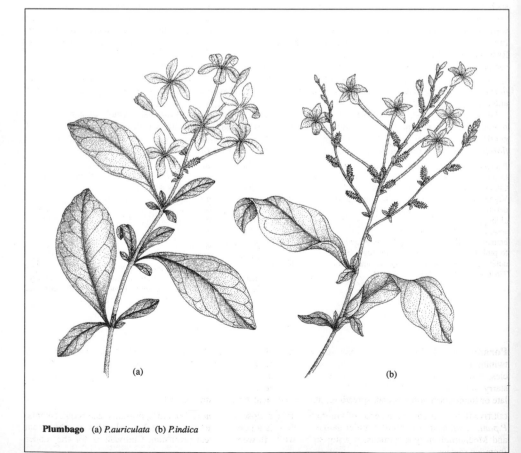

(a) (b)

Plumbago (a) *P.auriculata* (b) *P.indica*

Podranea Sprague. (An anagram of *Pandorea*, with which *Podranea* was once united.) Bignoniaceae. 2 species of climbing shrubs. Leaves imparipinnate; pseudostipules not leafy. Flowers in terminal, pyramidal thyrses; calyx campanulate, lobes regular; corolla showy, funnelform-campanulate, glabrous outside; stamens included, anthers glabrous; staminode very short, glabrous; disc cupular-pulvinate; ovary linear, glabrous, ovules in 9 rows. Capsule linear, rostrate, leathery, valves smooth; seeds small, transverse-oblong, in large membranous wings. S Africa. Z9.

CULTIVATION Grown for their fragrant and pretty, foxglove-like flowers, often carried throughout the summer. In warm temperate and subtropical gardens, *Podranea* species are useful evergreen climbers for pergolas, trellis and walls; established plants are drought-tolerant and will withstand light frosts although they may become partly or wholly deciduous at low temperatures. *Podranea* requires less water but otherwise is cultivated as for *Bignonia*. Propagate by seed in spring or by semi-ripe cuttings.

P.brycei (N.E.Br.) Sprague (*Pandorea brycei* (N.E.Br.) Rehd.). QUEEN OF SHEBA; ZIMBABWE CLIMBER.
Stem quadrangulate, nodes pubescent. Leaflets 9–11, c2–4× 0.6–1.3cm, serrulate. Inflorescence to 10cm, lax; calyx to 1.3 ×1.3cm, scaly, lobes deltoid, mucronate; corolla 3.8×1.8cm at throat, lobes 1.3–2.3cm, pale purple, villous inside tube, lobes ciliate. Capsule to 30×1.5cm. Zimbabwe.

P.ricasoliana (Tanf.) Sprague. PINK TRUMPET VINE; PORT ST JOHN CLIMBER; RICASOL PODRANEA.
Differs from *P.brycei* in leaflets 5–11, entire and flowers to 6cm long, pale pink striped red with a glabrous, not villous throat. S Africa.

Polygonum L. (From Gk *polys* many, and *gonu*, joint; the stems have conspicuously swollen nodes.) KNOTWEED; SMARTWEED; FLEECE VINE; SILVER LACE VINE. Polygonaceae. Some 150 species of mostly annual or perennial herbs, occasionally aquatic or scramblers, or woody subshrubs, stems appearing jointed. Leaves simple, entire; stipules sheathing. Flowers small, sometimes showy, fertile, clustered in axils of leaves or bracts, or in terminal panicles or spikes; perianth funnel- or bell-shaped, segments 3–6, commonly 5, usually equal, petal-like, white, pink or red; stamens 3–9; stigmas 2–3. Fruit a 2–3-angled achene, enclosed by persistent perianth, or protruding to half its length. N temperate regions.

CULTIVATION A diverse genus with species suited to a number of situations in the garden. The climbing species such as *P.baldschuanicum* and *P.aubertii* make vigorous and rapid cover for large tree stumps, and are widely used for clothing unsightly garden structures, especially on poorer soils; they are perhaps better suited to less well manicured areas, being rampant and untidy climbers, although both species are very handsome when in full flower. The dense foliage of well established plants provides excellent cover and nest sites for birds. Russian Vines may be difficult to eradicate once established and will out-compete most other climbers, even robust species such as *Lonicera periclymenum*. They may be confined by the most severe pruning in late winter, sprouting freely from older wood. That said, they should still be used with caution in confined spaces. *P.multiflorum* offers a similar, if rather more pleasing effect, its red herbaceous stems clothed with bright green foliage and lacy white panicles.

Grow in moisture-retentive, not too fertile soils in sun or part shade. Propagate *P.aubertii* and *P. baldschuanicum* by hardwood nodal cuttings of stem pieces with two nodes in late winter; root in close case with gentle bottom heat at 10–12°C/50–55°F; top growth may resume before rooting has occurred. Increase *P.multiflorum* by soft tip cuttings in summer rooted in a closed case with bottom heat. Also by seed.

P.aubertii L. Henry (*Bilderdykia aubertii* (L. Henry) Dumort.; *Fallopia aubertii* (L. Henry) Holub). RUSSIAN VINE; CHINA FLEECE VINE; SILVER LACE VINE.
Vigorous, twining, woody vine to 15m; stems glabrous, slender, becoming thinly woody. Leaves 3–10cm, ovate to ovate-oblong, acute, slightly cordate at base, bronze-red on opening, soon bright green, margins wavy; petioles long. Flowers in branched axillary and terminal panicles, white or green-white to pink in fruit, fragrant; perianth segments 4–6mm in fruit, outer segments winged. Late summer–autumn. W China, Tibet, Russia (Tadzhikistan). Z4.

P.baldschuanicum Reg. (*Bilderdykia baldschuanica* (Reg.) Webb; *Fallopia baldschuanica* (Reg.) Holub). MILE-A-MINUTE VINE; RUSSIAN VINE.
Rampant climber resembling *P.aubertii* but more woody; flowers in broader, drooping panicles, white tinged pink; perianth segments 6–8mm in fruit. Late summer–autumn. Iran (Bukhara). Z4.

P.multiflorum Thunb.
Climbing perennial, 1–2m+; root tuberous; stems slender, branched, red. Leaves 3–6×2.5–4.5cm, ovate-cordate, short-acuminate, green, shiny; petiole long. Inflorescence a loose, branched, tomentose panicle; flowers white; perianth 1.5–2mm, 7–8mm in fruit. Fruit a 3-angled achene, enclosed in perianth, 2.5mm. Autumn. China. Z7.

Porana Burm. f. (Derivation obscure; native name in E Indies.) Convolvulaceae. Some 20 species of slender, twining herbs, or shrubs. Leaves alternate, cordate-ovate, many-nerved, entire. Flowers small, in terminal panicles, cymes or racemes, sometimes solitary and axillary, white, blue or purple; sepals subequal, spreading to starry, some or all becoming enlarged, scarious, prominently veined and falling with the fruit; corolla campanulate or funnelform, lobes broad, spreading, plicate. Tropical Asia, Australia. Z10.

CULTIVATION An attractive genus of vigorous climbers close to *Ipomoea* both in appearance and requirements. *P.paniculata*, as its wealth of popular names testifies, is a popular choice for pergolas and trellis in subtropical and Mediterranean-type gardens, bearing small white flowers in great profusion. Cultivate as for the tender *Ipomoea* species.

P.grandiflora Wallich.
Liane climbing to 5m. Leaves to 10cm, cordate, apex acute. Flowers axillary, produced in succession, sweetly fragrant; corolla broadly funnelform to salverform, 5–6cm diam., purple turning crimson with 5 rosy-mauve stripes extending from throat to limb. Late summer. Nepal to Sikkim.

P.paniculata Roxb. BRIDAL BOUQUET; CHRIST VINE; CHRISTMAS VINE; CLIMBING WHITE LILAC; HORSETAIL CREEPER; INDIAN SILVER CREEPER; MOUNTAIN CREEPER; SNOW CREEPER; SNOW-IN-THE-JUNGLE; WHITE CORALLITA.
Liane to 9m. Leaves cordate, to 15×4cm, slender-acuminate, glabrous above, white-pubescent beneath. Flowers in large, many-flowered, terminal, pendulous, much-branched panicles; 3 sepals enlarged; corolla to 0.8cm, white, tubular-campanulate, obscurely lobed. Summer to autumn. N India, Upper Burma.

P.racemosa Roxb.
Annual or short-lived herb climbing quickly to 10m. Flowers racemose, scented; corolla to 1cm diam., white, funnelform, distinctly lobed. Late summer. Bhutan, Assam, Nepal.

Posadaea Cogn. Cucurbitaceae. 1 species, a climbing, pubescent herb. Tendrils simple to bifid. Leaves ovate to orbicular, entire or shallowly 3–7-lobed, occasionally remotely denticulate, cordate, membranous, to 18 × 19cm. Male inflorescence a raceme, short, few-flowered; calyx tube campanulate, lobulate, to 1cm; corolla yellow, rotate, exterior pubescent, lobes 5, rounded, sparsely dentate, to 1cm; stamens 3, anthers white. Female inflorescence to 5cm; flowers similar to male except staminodes 5; ovary inferior, elliptic-ovoid, pubescent;

P.sphaerocarpa Cogn.

Praecitrullus Pang. (From Lat. *prae*, before, and *Citrullus*.) Cucurbitaceae. 1 species, a climbing or trailing monoecious herb. Stem strongly villous or hispid. Tendrils slender, 2–3-fid. Petiole pubescent. Leaves sparingly pinnately lobed, hispid, slightly denticulate to entire, veins densely hispid beneath; probracts spathulate. Male flowers solitary, yellow; calyx campanulate, pubescent, lobes obconic, to 1cm; stamens 3, 2 connate; pedicel about 1mm; female flowers solitary, yellow; calyx broadly campanulate, lobes about 0.5mm, lanceolate; ovary villous or softly pubescent. Fruit a subspherical berry, to 6cm diam., light or dark green; seeds ovate-oblong, to 8mm, smooth, pale yellow. Early spring–autumn. India, Pakistan. Z10. Distinguished from *Citrullus* by echinate pollen grains, sparingly pinnatifid leaf lobes and chromosome number.

CULTIVATION   As for *Citrullus*.

P.fistulosus (Stocks) Pang. (*Citrullus fistulosus* Stocks).

Prestonia R. Br. (For Charles Preston (*d*1711), Professor of Botany at Edinburgh.) Apocynaceae. 65 species of tall, climbing, woody vines with milky sap. Leaves opposite, stipulate, entire, pinnately-veined. Flowers bisexual, in dense lateral corymbose cymes or umbels, sessile or shortly stalked; corolla funnelform, limb 5-lobed, flaring, with a crown of 5 scale-like segments included in throat; stamens carried on corolla, anthers surrounding and in contact with stigma. Fruit a pair of many-seeded follicles; seeds comose. Tropical America. Z10.

CULTIVATION   A striking climber for the intermediate to warm glasshouse or conservatory, valuable for both its foliage and flowers. Its cultural requirements are as for *Allamanda*.

P.quinquangularis (Jacq.) Spreng. (*Echites rubrovenosa* Lind.).
Leaves to 15cm, oval to oval-ovate, apex pointed, base rounded to obtuse, thin-textured, emerald green net-veined red or purple, veins ultimately golden-yellow to white, glabrous or subglabrous; petioles 2cm. Flowers in clusters of 6–20; calyx lobes abruptly reflexed; corolla 1.2–1.5cm long, 1.8cm across, yellow-green, lobes obovate, abruptly reflexed. Fruit to 35cm, robust, follicles fused at apex; seed hairs yellow-brown. Summer. Lesser Antilles to Guyana, Venezuela.

Prionotes R. Br. (From Gk *prionon*, a small saw, alluding to the serrated leaves.) Epacridaceae. 1 species, a small prostrate or scandent shrub, in habitat a climbing epiphyte, growing on trunks of dead and decaying trees. Branches glabrous, erect, slender, intertwining. Leaves to 2cm, elliptic or oblong, blunt, dark green, thick-textured, short-petiolate, margins minutely callose-serrate. Flowers solitary in upper leaf axils, pendulous on slender glandular pedicels to 1.25cm, corolla to 2.5cm, rose pink to scarlet; inflated-tubular, subventricose at base, constricted at throat. Summer. Tasmania. Z9.

CULTIVATION   Occurring as an understorey epiphyte scrambling over dead or decaying trunks and on rocks on sheltered banks in temperate montane forest or woodland, *Prionotes* is a calcifuge grown for its profusion of richly coloured flowers. Suitable for outdoor cultivation in regions that are frost-free or almost so, in a sheltered situation that approximates to its habitat; otherwise, grow in a moist, acid soil with additional composted bark, in the cool glasshouse in part shade. Propagate by tip cuttings in autumn.

P.cerinthoides R. Br. CLIMBING HEATH.

Pseudogynoxys (Greenman) Cabr. Compositae. About 13 species of perennial shrubs or climbers. Leaves alternate, ovate to oblong, more or less acute, base attenuate or cuneate to cordate, entire to serrate or dentate. Capitula radiate or discoid, solitary or few to many in terminal or axillary corymbose clusters; receptacle flat; involucre campanulate to hemispherical; phyllaries in 1 series, oblong, apex pubescent; florets pale to deep orange or red, ray florets female, disc florets hermaphrodite. Fruit a cylindrical, ribbed cypsela; pappus of hairs. Tropical S America. Z10.

CULTIVATION A vigorous evergreen climber for the cool to intermediate glasshouse or conservatory where it will rapidly cover walls and pillars with deep green foliage and cheerful orange-red daisy flowers. Plant in a moist, but not overwet loam-based fertile mix in semi shade or full sun. Feed fortnightly in spring and summer. Trim back shoots to 2–3 nodes of the main stems after flowering. Increase by seed or semi-ripe nodal cuttings.

P.chenopodioides (Kunth) Cabr. (*Senecio chenopodioides* Kunth; *Senecio confusus* (DC.) Britten). MEXICAN FLAMEVINE; ORANGEGLOW VINE; TRAILING GROUNDSEL; MEXICAN FIREVINE; MEXICAN DAISY.
Liane or climbing shrub to 6m. Leaves narrowly ovate, dentate, light green, glabrous. Capitula radiate, to 5cm diam., bright orange to flame, few, in terminal and axillary corymbs, more or less fragrant. Fruit to 4mm; pappus white. Colombia.

Psiguria Necker ex Arn. Cucurbitaceae. Some 15 species of dioecious or, occasionally, monoecious vines or lianes. Tendrils simple. Leaves 3–5-foliolate or 3–5-lobed to entire. Male flowers clustered; calyx cylindrical, 5-lobed, corolla rotate; stamens 2, filaments short, anthers 2-locular; female flowers usually solitary; staminodes 2; ovary ovoid, carpels 2, style connate, stigma 2-lobed. Fruit indehiscent; seeds numerous, oblong, compressed. Tropical America. Z10.

CULTIVATION As for *Momordica*, but cross-pollination is usually needed for fruit production.

P.warscewiczii (Hook. f.) Wunderlin (*Anguria warscewiczii* Hook. f.).
Stems slender, glabrous. Tendrils simple. Leaves 3-foliolate; central leaflet 11–17 × 5–8cm, obovate-oblong, acuminate, lateral leaflets somewhat hastate, slightly smaller; petioles 3–6cm. Male flowers axillary, in racemes, orange to scarlet, calyx 1–2cm, cylindrical, corolla ventricose, lobes rounded to obovate, 5–8mm, pubescent, anthers 5–6mm; female flowers solitary to few in axils, ovary oblong-fusiform, styles to 8mm. Fruit oblong-ellipsoid, 5.5–7 × 1.8–2.5cm, pale green with darker stripes; seeds numerous, 7–8mm. S Mexico to Colombia.

Pterisanthes Bl. (From Gk *pteron*, wing, and *anthos*, flower, referring to the flattened form of the inflorescence.) Vitaceae. 20 species of vines. Tendrils present. Leaves simple or compound. Inflorescences leaf-opposed, pendulous, of flat fleshy bodies with irregularly lobed margins, attached to rachis along one side, with numerous sessile or immersed bisexual flowers and sometimes with several long-pedicelled sterile, male or bisexual flowers; peduncles long; flowers 4–5-merous; calyx slightly lobed; petals free, broadly ovate; ovary 2-celled, sunk in disc; cells each with 2 ovules; stigma small. Fruit is a berry, exserted; seeds 1–3, furrowed on both sides. Burma, W Malaysia. Z10.

CULTIVATION As for *Cissus*.

P.polita (Miq.) Lawson (*Vitis polita* Miq.).
Vine, climbing extensively, very slender, glabrous throughout. Leaves 10–20×5–9cm, elliptic-oblong to ovate, subcordate at base, acute at apex, entire or remotely spinose-serrate, membranous. Inflorescence body red; flowers 4-merous. Borneo, Sumatra.

Pueraria DC. (For M.N. Puerari (1766–1845), professor at Copenhagen.) Leguminosae (Papilionoideae). Some 20 species of herbaceous or woody twiners. Leaves trifoliolate or, rarely, pinnate; leaflets large, ovate or rhomboid, entire or sinuately lobed, stipellate. Inflorescences long, axillary, or clustered as racemes at branch ends; standard obovate or round, auricles inflexed; bracts small or narrow, caducous. Fruit 2-valved, linear, flat, dehiscent. SE Asia, Japan. Z5.

CULTIVATION *P.lobata*, a deciduous twiner with dense foliage and long racemes of fragrant pea-flowers, is particularly useful as a rapidly growing screen, providing temporary cover for buildings and fences, or, if unsupported, as groundcover. In good soils, growth may exceed 15m/50ft during the season as is evinced by its performance in the SE US, where it was at first planted as a fodder plant and erosion-control but has now become a notorious weed. In areas where winter temperatures fall much below −15°C/5°F, *P.lobata* may be grown as an annual; given adequate protection at the roots, however, it will re-sprout from the base in spring if cut down by frost. Grow in full sun in well drained soils, training the young stems to cover the support. Prune in spring, if necessary, to control spread. Propagate from seed in spring, sown singly in pots in the warm glasshouse; plant out when the danger of frost has passed.

P.lobata (Willd.) Ohwi (*P.thunbergiana* (Sieb. & Zucc.) Benth.). JAPANESE ARROWROOT; KUDZU VINE. Woody, hairy-stemmed vine to 20m; roots tuberous. Leaflets entire or slightly lobed, central leaflet 14–18cm, lateral leaflets smaller, pubescent; petiole 10–20cm. Inflorescence an axillary or terminal raceme, erect, to 25cm; flowers to 1.5cm, purple; calyx 5-toothed; petals 5, nearly regular; stamens 10, monadelphous. Fruit 4–9 × 0.6–1.5cm, hirsute. Autumn. China, Japan.

P.thunbergiana (Sieb. & Zucc.) Benth. See *P.lobata*.

Pyrostegia Presl. (From Gk *pyr*, fire, and *stege*, covering, referring to the fiery corolla.) Bignoniaceae. 3–4 species of lianes climbing by tendrils; branches angled. Leaves bifoliate with or without terminal trifid tendril, or sometimes trifoliate; pseudostipules inconspicuous. Flowers in terminal thyrses; calyx campanulate or denticulate; corolla narrow-tubular to club-shaped, curved, and ventricose above with 5 short, recurved acute lobes; stamens exserted, glabrous; disc annular or cup-shaped; ovary linear, ovaries in 2 rows. Fruit a linear capsule, glabrous, valves parallel; seeds transverse oblong with membranous hyaline wings. Americas. Z10.

CULTIVATION In tropical and subtropical gardens *P.venusta* is a beautiful evergreen for arches, pergolas and fences, climbing by tendrils and by twining stems. In cool temperature zones, it is a handsome vine for the warm glasshouse or conservatory, with spectacular many-flowered panicles of brilliant orange-red blooms, produced in profusion from autumn through to spring. Under glass, grow in full light in large tubs in a fertile, well drained medium with additional organic matter and coarse sand. Maintain a humid atmosphere and a minimum temperature at about 10–13°C/50–55°F, watering plentifully in summer and carefully and sparingly in winter. Prune in late winter early spring, cutting back flowered stems to within 30cm/12in. of the base. *P.venusta* works well if trained to a single overhead stem, with flowered shoots cut back to 2–3 buds each spring. Propagate by semi-ripe cuttings of 2–3 nodes in summer. Red spider mite, scale insect and mealybug may infest plants grown under glass.

P.ignea (Vell.) Presl. See *P.venusta*.

P.venusta (Ker-Gawl.) Miers (*Bignonia ignea* Vell.; *Bignonia venusta* Ker-Gawl.; *P.ignea* (Vell.) Presl). GOLDEN SHOWER; FLAME VINE; FLAMING TRUMPET; ORANGE-FLOWERED STEPHANOTIS; TANGO. Branches glabrous or hairy. Leaflets to 11 × 5cm, ovate to oblong-lanceolate, apex obtuse, base rounded, papery or leathery, glabrous to pubescent and scaly above, glabrous to villous and scaly beneath. Pedicels puberulent to villous; calyx 0.5–0.7 × 0.4–0.5cm, 5–10-nerved, glabrous or puberulent and scaly; corolla tube 3.5–6×0.3cm, curved, orange, glabrous, lobes linear, 1–1.5cm, puberulent; disc campanulate, 1mm; ovary 3–4mm, scaly. Fruit 25–30 × 1.4–1.6cm, smooth, leathery, median line conspicuous; seeds 1 × 3.5cm. Brazil, Paraguay, Bolivia, NE Argentina.

Quisqualis L. (From Lat. *quis*, who and *qualis*, what kind– there was at first some uncertainty as to the family to which this plant belonged.) Combretaceae. Some 17 species of scandent shrubs often climbing by woody hooks (persistent petioles). Leaves usually opposite, simple, entire, glabrous or pubescent; petioles sometimes persisting, becoming woody, thorn-like and hooked. Inflorescence a terminal or axillary raceme or panicle, bracteate, few- to several-flowered; flowers showy, bisexual; calyx tube adnate to ovary, pubescent to glabrous, lobes 5, triangular, caducous; corolla long and narrowly tubular, exceeding calyx lobes, limb spreading, lobes 5, oblong-elliptic, obtuse; stamens 10, in 2 series; ovules 2 to 4. Fruit oblong, 5-angled or 5-winged, tapering at both ends, 1-seeded. Tropical and S Africa, tropical Indomalaysia. Z10.

CULTIVATION Widely cultivated in the tropics and subtropics, and occasionally in frost-free warm temperate climates, although not so floriferous there, *Q.indica* is an extraordinarily handsome climber for arches, pillars, pergolas and trees. Its foliage provides a dense, bright green cover, while the slender, tubular flowers are usually borne in profusion, sweetly if elusively scented and pass through an intriguing range of shades of rose and brick red having opened white to shell pink (this rather deep and sudden flushing gives the plant the popular name Drunken Sailor). In cool temperate zones, it is a beautiful specimen for the larger warm glasshouse or conservatory, preferably planted directly into the border. In warm climates, it is easily grown in sun or part-shade in a range of well drained and not too fertile soils; nitrogen-rich soils encourage foliar growth at the expense of flowering. Under glass, admit bright filtered light or full sun with shade during the hottest summer months and use a freely draining, medium-fertility, sandy loam. Water plentifully when in growth, reducing water in winter, to allow a period of almost dry rest with a minimum temperature of 13°C/55°F. Prune in late winter to thin congested growth and to shorten flowered stems back to the main framework of growth. Propagate by heeled softwood cuttings in a closed case with bottom heat, or by seed; seed-grown plants may take on a bush habit when young before beginning to climb.

Q.indica L. AKAR-DANI; DRUNKEN SAILOR; IRANGAN-MALLI; RANGOON CREEPER. Rampant climber; branchlets tomentose or adpressed-pubescent, sometimes glandular. Leaves to 18.5 × 9cm, elliptic or elliptic-oblong, acuminate, cordate to rounded at base, chartaceous, glabrous to pubescent with vein impressed above; petiole to 5cm, glabrous to pubescent, persistent and becoming a thorny grappling hook. Inflorescence to 10cm, sometimes paniculate, terminal and axillary, pendent; flowers fragrant; calyx lobes to 2mm, acute; corolla lobes enlarging to 20 × 6mm, to 1/3 length of tube, white becoming pink to red on upper surfaces and within throat over a period of days, exterior somewhat silky; filaments to 8mm; ovules 3 or 4. Fruit to 4 × 1.5cm, dark brown, elliptic-ovate, pubescent, 5-winged. Old World Tropics.

Quisqualis indica

Rhaphidophora Hassk. (Name for Gk *raphis*, needle, and *phora*, to bear; the cells contain raphides.) Araceae. (Sometimes spelt *Raphidophora*.) 70 species of evergreen climbers or creepers, sometimes with distinct juvenile and adult phases. Stems stout, bearing adhesive adventitious roots. Leaves in 2 ranks when juvenile (shingle plant, see *Monstera*), entire or pinnatifid, sometimes perforate, the holes large or small, lateral veins all parallel; petioles long, geniculate at apex, sheathed, with sheath soon becoming scarious. Peduncle solitary, subequal to or shorter than petioles; spathe cymbiform, not forming tube, deciduous, yellow to green; spadix shorter than spathe, densely covered by mostly hermaphrodite flowers, some unisexual female flowers also present; perianth absent; stamens 4, ovary unilocular or imperfectly divided into 2–3 locules, ovules numerous. Berries united; seeds soft, straight. SE Asia.

CULTIVATION As for *Philodendron*; best planted directly into the glasshouse border with the support of a stout moss pole, or dead tree stump up which they can climb.

R.aurea (Lind. & André) Birdsey. See *Epipremnum aureum*.

R.celatocaulis (N.E. Br.) Knoll (*Pothos celatocaulis* N.E. Br.). SHINGLE PLANT.
Stems climbing, tall. Leaves of juvenile plants 8.5–10 × 5.5–6.5cm, in 2 ranks, closely adpressed to substrate, overlapping and obscuring stem, entire, elliptic-ovate, coriaceous, blue-green; adult leaves to 40× 30cm, entire, pinnatifid or pinnatisect, occasionally perforate, segments obliquely truncate at apex; petiole equalling lamina. Peduncle to 40cm; spathe to 15×6cm, fleshy. yellow. Borneo.

R.decursiva (Wallich) Schott.
Stems climbing, tall. Leaves (adult; juvenile phase not usually cultivated) 90 × 70cm, pinnatisect, oblong in outline, coriaceous, segments 7–21 per side, lanceolate, attenuate above, constricted at base, each with 1 main lateral vein and 2 secondary veins; petioles 40–50cm. Peduncle much shorter than petioles; spathe 17.5×10cm, ovate-oblong, acuminate, fleshy, yellow; spadix to 15cm, yellow, becoming grey-green. SE Asia (Sri Lanka to N Burma).

Rhektophyllum N.E. Br. (From Gk *rechtos*, torn, and *phyllon*, leaf.) Araceae. 1 species, a tall evergreen climber to 10m+; juvenile and adult phases distinct. Stems rooting at nodes, thick when adult, slender in juvenile phase. Leaves of juvenile phase to 30cm, entire, hastate to sagittate, margin more or less undulate, basal lobes broad, dark green above, handsomely variegated white between veins, markings resembling fern-fronds, primary lateral veins in 2–3 pairs in median lobe; petiole to 40cm; leaves in adult phase ovate to oblong-ovate, perforated or laciniate to form cuneate segments, major veins of basal lobes naked at sinus, minor veins reticulate; petioles to 90cm. Peduncle 5cm; spathe to 10cm, cylindric, scarcely constricted, green externally, red-purple within; spadix shorter than spathe, with male zone three times longer than female zone; flowers unisexual, perianth absent; stamens 3–4; ovary unilocular, ovule solitary. Fruit an obovoid berry, 1cm, red. Tropical West Africa. Sometimes placed in *Cercestis* Schott. Z10.

CULTIVATION   As for *Philodendron*.

R.mirabile N.E. Br.

Rhodochiton Otto & Dietr. (From Gk *rhodon*, rose, and *chiton*, cloak, referring to the large, rosy calyx.) Scrophulariaceae. Some 3 species of perennial, climbing herbs. Stems slender, twining. Leaves cordate to deltoid, serrulate, alternate; petioles twining. Flowers pendulous, solitary in leaf axils; calyx inflated, cup-like, divisions shallow, lobes entire, acute; corolla tube slender, elongate, expanding as 5 obtuse lobes; stamens 4, conspicuous, partly exserted. Fruit an oblong to globose capsule. Summer. Mexico. Z9.

CULTIVATION   *R.atrosanguineum* is a tender perennial vine, inhabiting light, sandy soils in its native Mexico. In frost-free zones, it may be grown in the open garden . It makes twining growth up to 3m/10ft and produces a profusion of striking black-purple flowers with ashy white anthers, hanging from lantern-like purple-pink calyces in its first year from seed. In cold areas, it may be grown outdoors as an annual (sometimes surviving as a herbaceous perennial in favoured situations) or as a perennial in cool glasshouses or conservatories. Grow in a sunny, sheltered spot on rich, well drained soil with additional organic matter at planting. Provide support while plants are still very young. Under glass, grow in a medium-fertility loam-based mix, water plentifully during the growing season, sparingly in winter, and give a minimum temperature of 5°C/40°F; ventilate freely and shade from direct summer sun. Cut back and re-pot in spring. Propagate from seed sown at 15–18°C/60–65°F under glass in early spring or as soon as ripe (fresh seed germinates best, older seed may be erratic, remaining dormant for up to 40 days).

R.atrosanguineum (Zucc.) Rothm. (*R.volubile* Otto & Dietr.).
Scandent, pubescent perennial, to 6m. Leaves to 6cm, alternate, cordate or obscurely 5-lobed, dark green above, pale green beneath. Flowers strongly pendulous; calyx lantern-like, acutely 5-lobed, membranous, shallow-campanulate, persistent after pollination, rose-pink or mauve; corolla blood-red to maroon-black, tubular, elongating to 6.5cm, limb 5-lobed, exterior minutely glandular-pubescent; stamens 4, long, slender, anthers ash-white, conspicuous. Seeds 3–4mm, oblong, orbicular.

R.volubile Otto & Dietr. See *R.atrosanguineum*.

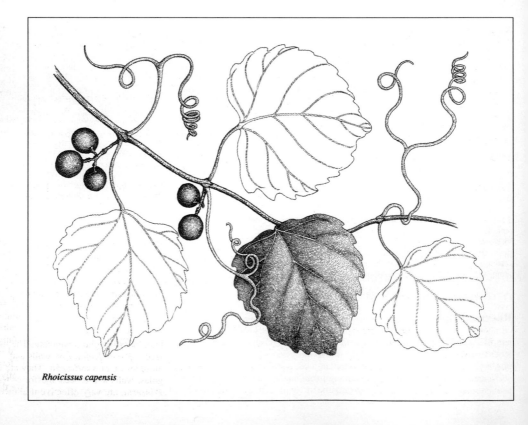

Rhoicissus capensis

Rhoicissus Planch. (From Gk *rhoia*, pomegranate, and *Cissus*.) Vitaceae. 12 species of more or less woody vines. Tendrils generally present, opposite leaves. Leaves simple or 3-foliolate, or rarely digitately 5-foliolate, margins entire to variously dentate; stipules generally present. Inflorescence of thyrsoid, leaf-opposed cymes; peduncles occasionally cirrhous; calyx more or less entire; petals 5–6, more or less thickened or succulent towards apex; stamens bending over gynoecium; disc entire; style simple, entire. Seeds 1–2, occasionally to 4, generally prominently grooved, smooth or rugose. Tropical & Southern Africa. Z9.

CULTIVATION   *R.capensis*, a forest native in the wild, is a useful house or conservatory plant in temperate regions, tolerant of fairly low light levels and grown for its attractive, leathery foliage, a particularly beautiful pale claret colour when young. In frost-free zones it is valuable for covering trellis and fencing. Cultivate as for the more resilient *Cissus* species, with a minimum temperature of 7–10°C/45–50°F.

R.capensis Planch. (*Cissus capensis* (Thunb.) Willd.; *Vitis capensis* Thunb.).
Tuberous evergreen vine, climbing strongly. Stems terete, striate, ferruginous-tomentose when young; tendrils very long, forked. Leaves simple, orbicular to reniform, broadly cordate at base, obtuse at apex, very obtusely 5-angled, strongly repand-dentate, 10–20cm across, coriaceous, ferrugi-nous-tomentose when young, glabrescent above except perhaps along veins, major veins 3, diverging from base; petioles long; stipules ovate. Inflorescence thyrsoid, densely ferruginous-tomentose; peduncles long with several lateral branches; flowers lanate. Fruit globose, very dark red tinged black, glossy. S Africa.

Ripogonum Forst. & Forst. f. (From Gk *rhips*, twig, and *gonu*, knee, joint; the plant is both jointed and twiggy.) Liliaceae (Smilacaceae). 8 species of climbing shrubs, much-branched above. Leaves opposite or nearly so, 3–5-veined with transverse reticulate veins between. Flowers small, in axillary or terminal racemes, sometimes forming a terminal panicle; perianth deciduous, segments 6, free, equal or outer segments shorter; stamens 6, filaments very short, flattened, anthers erect; ovary superior, sessile, 3-celled; styles short, stout; stigmas 3, recurved. Fruit a globose berry, usually 1-seeded; seeds globose. Australia, New Zealand. (Sometimes spelt *Rhipogonum*.)

CULTIVATION   As for the tender *Smilax* species.

R.scandens Forst. & Forst. f.
Tall, glabrous climber; stems knotted at joints, often forming interwoven masses. Leaves 7.5–12.5cm, narrowly ovate-oblong to oblong-lanceolate, acute, or acuminate, coriaceous. Racemes axillary, simple or branched, 7.5–15cm; pedicels slender, spreading; flowers tinged green, 0.8cm diam. Fruit 0.8cm diam., bright red. New Zealand. Z9.

Rosa L. (Lat. name for this plant.) Rosaceae. 100–150 species of deciduous, or sometimes evergreen, shrubs with erect, arching or scrambling, occasionally trailing stems, usually with prickles and/or bristles. Stipules usually present, persistent, usually joined to leaf-stalk for most of their length. Leaves alternate, usually odd-pinnate, rarely 3-foliolate or simple; leaflets toothed. Receptacle (hypanthium) globose to urn-shaped. Flowers solitary or in corymbs, usually borne at the end of short branches, single to double; sepals (4–)5, entire or the 2 outer and half the third one with lateral lobes, and the inner 2 and half the third entire, the tips acute to attenuate or broadened and leafy; petals (4–)5 in single flowers, usually obovate, tip often notched, white, cream, pink, red, purple-pink, orange or yellow; stamens (in single flowers) *c*30–200, in several whorls; ovaries many, each with 1 ovule, free, carried on the base and/or sides of the enclosing receptacle; styles free or united into a column, exserted from mouth of receptacle or not. Fruit (hip or hep) containing many achenes, usually red or orange, sometimes black or green, enclosed by the fleshy receptacle; achenes 1-seeded, bony, often hairy. All the species described are summer-flowering unless otherwise specified. Temperate and subtropical zones of the northern hemisphere. Problems of classification and naming are rife in this genus, many species of which have been cultivated and hybridized for centuries, and some of which are very polymorphic. The last complete account of the genus was by Lindley (*Rosarum Monographia*) in 1820: a new revision is urgently needed which will incorporate investigations into the complex cytology and the problems produced by hybridization.

CULTIVATION   The climbing roses can be broadly split into two types. *Climbers* can be said to be those climbing roses with quite large flowers in small trusses and which, particularly with the modern varieties, are fully remontant. *Ramblers* have small flowers in very large clusters and flower only at midsummer or a little later. Of the two, ramblers have the more flexible canes and so are easier to train over arches, pergolas and on pillars. Climbers can more easily be accommodated on walls and fences, where the shoots should be fanned out and trained on wires as near to the horizontal as possible: this will encourage flowering shoots to form along their entire length and not just at the tips. Many of the less vigorous modern climbers, such as 'Golden Showers', make good pillar roses – with the shoots trained in a spiral around the pillar, flowering can be secured low down. The more vigorous of the climbers and ramblers can be trained over what might otherwise be rather dull shrubs or into trees.

Many climbers and ramblers will succeed with only light, maintenance pruning. They will, however, perform better with some attention. Simply reduce the side shoots by about two-thirds and leave the main shoots alone. Side shoots can be reduced by about half after flowering, when a further flush of blooms will usually be produced. Cut away completely the flowered shoots of ramblers, replacing them with new shoots; these should grow from the base each year. If there are too few new shoots, leave some of the old having, simply having trimmed them back.

Although tolerant of a range of soils and sites, roses will never thrive without full sun for the greater part of the day or if the soil is waterlogged. They like plenty of water, but need soil that is at the same time well drained – a good medium-grade loam for example, preferably of pH6.5. A heavy clay soil deficient in lime can receive a dressing of hydrated lime. Alternatively, apply calcium sulphate or gypsum at a rate of up to $0.9kg/m^2(28oz/yd^2)$, which does not increase the alkalinity. It is always important to incorporate plenty of organic matter before planting – well rotted stable manure, garden compost, leafmould or coir can be dug freely into the top spit, with liberal additions of bonemeal or hoof-and-horn meal at $85g/m^2(2.8oz/yd^2)$, or some other fertilizer which supplies phosphorus, such as superphosphate or basic slag.

Newly planted roses hardly ever flourish in beds where others have been grown or are growing. The new plants lack their predecessors' ability to withstand the harmful soil-borne organisms that cause Replant Syndrome. For this reason, either plant new individuals in holes some 45cm/18in. deep and 60cm/2ft wide, filled with fresh soil in established collections, or, where the whole bed can be refurbished, renew or sterilize the soil to a depth of 45cm/18in.

In a temperate climate, plant any time during winter and early spring. Where the winter temperatures fall below –23°C/–10°F for any length of time, as in many parts of North America and Northern Europe, wait until the spring. Do not, in any case, plant in the middle of a frosty spell. Before planting, inspect the plants and cut away any damaged or dead wood. Shorten the thickest of the main roots by about one half to encourage the production of fine feeding roots from them. Prepare a planting mixture from a 50/50 mixture of loam and leafmould, about half a bucketful per plant, well mixed with a handful per plant of bonemeal or a slow-release rose fertilizer. The budding unions should be planted about 2.5cm/1in. below soil level: this will give them some protection. In very cold areas it may be advisable to double or even treble this depth. Ideally, spread the roots of each rose out evenly all around its hole. Because of the mechanical planting methods used by many nurserymen, the roots may be growing in only one direction, the rose should be placed at one side of the planting hole and the roots fanned out as evenly as possible over the rest of the space. The same principle should be used when planting against a wall, where the soil will be very dry. The hole should be at least 45cm/18in. away from the wall surface and the roots spread towards damper soil. Otherwise, planting, staking and preliminary watering of roses is much as it would be for any other shrub. Sometimes the shoots of newly planted roses are mounded up or wrapped up with turves to prevent their drying out. This protection should be removed when the buds begin to break. Roses should be pruned at the time of planting, cutting them back drastically to only 5–8cm/2–3in. above soil level.

Routine maintenance. Two applications of a granular or powdered fertilizer per year should be all that is needed. A small handful sprinkled around each plant clear of the crown after pruning, and again at midsummer, will produce excellent results. There should be no later application as this will encourage soft autumn growth, liable to be frosted. A 4–8cm/2–3in. layer of mulch, preferably of organic material, should be applied to the surface of a rose bed once the soil has begun to warm up in spring. Eventually it will break down to form humus and provide plant foods if the best of all mulches, farmyard manure or garden compost, is used. If fresh organic material is used, extra nitrogen fertilizer should be added to compensate for the chemicals that the decomposing mulch will extract from the soil.

Deadheading and cutting back. Spent flower heads and flower trusses should be removed regularly to prevent the formation of hips, which discourage the production of late flowers.

Suckers are outgrowths of the rootstock rather than the desirable scion. If allowed to develop unchecked, they will supersede the cultivated rose. The presence of seven leaflets per leaf is a useful indication of a sucker but not a foolproof one, for some cultivated varieties have the odd leaf with seven leaflets. However, a sucker shoot is likely to be of a lighter green and the colour and shape of the thorns can be different too. If in any doubt, try to find the point of origin of the growth, if necessary by scraping away soil: if it comes from below the budding union it is a sucker. Pull the sucker away rather than cutting it, as this will also remove any dormant buds that may have been forming at its base. Cutting a sucker will only encourage strong new growth.

Propagation. Most roses root readily from cuttings, the ramblers especially. Roses produced in this way may lack the vigour of their budded counterparts but at least will not sucker. Hardwood cuttings should be taken in early autumn, choosing shoots of the current year's growth about pencil thickness. Those that have flowered in midsummer are ideal. For the cuttings bed, choose a place in the garden shaded from the midday sun but open and airy; a slit trench about 20cm/8in. deep should be dug for the cuttings. On light soils, simply push a spade vertically into the soil along a marked centre line and then work it backwards and forwards to form a slot. Sprinkle 2.5cm/1in. of coarse sand along the base of the trench or slot. After discarding the soft tip of the shoot, the cuttings should be made about 23cm/9in. long, severed just below and just above a leaf-axil bud. Strip off all but the top pair of leaves and snap off the thorns. Insert each cutting vertically in the trench about 15cm/6in. apart. Only about one-third of each should be left projecting above ground level when they have been trodden firmly in and watered. Keep them watered in dry spells and make sure that they remain firm in the ground after frosts. The following spring they should begin to grow, but it will take three years or more for them to develop into full-size plants.

Budding or bud-grafting not only produces fully-grown plants very quickly but may also confer on the budded rose qualities of vigour and resistance it might not otherwise have possessed. Budding should be performed in midsummer on stocks that were planted the previous autumn. Strong shoots that have finished flowering should provide at least three buds each. Remove the thorns and snip off the leaves, but not the petioles which help make the buds easy to handle. Place the budwood in a plastic bag to keep it from drying out while the stock is prepared. Clear the soil from the neck of the stock and wipe it clean with a damp cloth. Make a T-shaped incision in the side of the neck, just deep enough to penetrate the bark. The cross stroke of the T should be about 5mm/¹/₅in. long and the down stroke 2cm/⁴/₅in. Take a shoot from the plastic bag and, using a scooping action, cut out a bud, on a bark shield about 2.5cm/1in. long. The slither of wood behind the bud shield should be removed, leaving only the bud. Using the tapered end of the budding knife, very gently lift the two flaps of bark on either side of the down-stroke of the T cut. Holding the bud by its leaf-stalk handle, slide it downwards under the bark flaps until the bud itself is just below the level of the cross stroke of the T. Bind or seal the bud in place. The top-growth of the stock can be cut away once the bud is seen to have taken and be growing the following spring, leaving a stump no more than 1cm/¹/₂in. long. Two or even three buds are usual for a standard rose to ensure a balanced head. Insert them into the top of the stem if using Rugosa stocks and close to the stem into equally spaced lateral growths if using briar stocks.

Pests and diseases. Although several diseases and disorders affect the health of roses, only three are serious enough to need regular treatment in most seasons. These are powdery mildew (*Sphaerotheca pannosa*), black spot (*Diplocarpon rosae*) and rose rust (*Phragmidium mucronatum*). How regular the treatment should be depends on geographical location and is largely unpredictable. There can be seasonal differences as well, and preventive spraying may even be needed before the disease is seen, with repeat applications every ten days or so. In general, however, spraying should only be carried out at the first signs of disease.

Rose rust shows first in spring as small orange pustules on the upper surfaces of leaves. This is the least infective stage, but if left untreated the more serious summer stage will follow. This shows as further orange pustules under the leaves, which later turn black, in which form they will overwinter. Rust will spread rapidly and quickly defoliate the plant. A contact fungicide spray in spring should eradicate it for a season. *Canker and crown gall*, caused by the fungi *Coniothyrium fuchelii* and *C.rosarum*, producing brown lesions or deep corrugated cankers, or else brownish swellings near the bud union. In all cases cut away the infected parts. *Rose anthracnose* is a fungus disease which causes white spots with red rims on the leaves, with sometimes brown raised pustules on the stems as well. If left, the red coloration turns yellow and the leaves will fall. Cut away infected shoots. *Purple spotting* is not a disease, although it vaguely resembles black spot. The spots are, however, dark purple, much smaller, less regular in shape, and do not have fringed edges. It is caused by a soil deficiency which improved drainage and a balanced fertilizer should cure. *Dieback* is caused by a fungus which enters as the result of damage by frost or a canker, and further encouraged by a deficiency of potash in the soil so that shoots are slow to ripen. Shoots gradually die back from the tips downwards, becoming brown and wrinkled. Cut infected shoots away to the first healthy bud.

Insect pests likely to be a real problem include aphids (greenfly) on both sides of the Atlantic and, in North America, Japanese beetles and chafers.

The most common aphid species infesting roses is *Macrosiphum rosae*. They are small green or pinkish soft-bodied insects that cluster on the young shoots, flower buds and the undersides of the leaves, sucking the sap. Winged forms migrate to other bushes at certain times of the year and throughout the summer they reproduce with incredible rapidity if unchecked. Shoots will be stunted and distorted and a sticky substance aphids produce will coat rose stems and leaves, attracting both ants and a black fungus known as sooty mould. Spray with a contact or systemic spray. *Ants* will not attack a rose directly but, particularly on sandy soil, may build their nests among the roots, causing the plant to wilt. Apply an ant-nest destroyer. *Capsid bugs* are bright green insects which cause small brown spots on young leaves, and buds to become distorted and wither before opening. Spray as for greenfly. *Chafers, Japanese beetles, rose curculio and fuller beetles* attack roses with the result that the petals and anthers of the roses may be nibbled and irregular holes eaten in the leaves. The grubs of chafers may attack the roots of the roses and weaken the plants. In an area where chafers are a problem, disinfect the soil prior to planting, and for all these beetles spray as for aphids. If not too numerous, beetles may be picked off by hand and destroyed. *Froghoppers* are small, green-yellow insects which hide themselves in blobs of foam. These can be easily seen in early summer on shoots and in leaf axils. They suck sap and can distort the shoots. Wash away foam and then spray as for aphids, or pick off by hand. *Leaf-cutter bees (Megachile centuncularis)* cut small, circular pieces from rose leaves to line their nest tunnels. They are seldom serious pests and no treatment is recommended. *Leafhoppers (Typhlocyba rosae)* are tiny, yellow-green insects that jump like grasshoppers and feed on the undersides of rose leaves, on which their discarded skins can often be seen. The leaves turn a mottled purple and a bad attack can cause leaf-fall. Spray as for aphids. *Leaf-miners* are grubs boring white blisters on the leaves, often in chain formation. Affected leaves should be picked off and burned. Preventive spray as for greenfly. *Leaf-rolling sawflies (Blennocampa pusilla)* are small black flies which lay their eggs in the leaf margins, also injecting a toxin which causes the leaf to roll up longitudinally to protect the grey-green grub when it hatches. A preventive systemic spray in late spring and again four weeks later will help. Otherwise pick off and burn affected leaves. *Rose scale (Aulacapsis rosea)* produces clusters of grey-white scales, mainly on old stems, that hide insects which suck sap and may cause the stems to wilt. If confined to a small area, painting with methylated spirit will prevent spreading; otherwise spray as for aphids. *Rose slugworms (Endelomyin aethiops)* are small grubs which feed on the leaf surfaces early in spring, skeletonizing the leaves in patches, the infected areas turning brown. Spray as for greenfly. *Shoot or pith borers* are grubs of certain sawflies, rose stem girdlers and carpenter bees. They lay eggs in rose stems and the grubs eat the pith. In some countries, pith borers enter through pruning cuts if these are not protected by pruning paint. Cut away wilting shoots and use a contact spray. *Spider mites* (red spider) are most active in hot, dry conditions and tend to be more troublesome under glass. The signs are leaves with brown-bronze patches on the upper surfaces and the finest of webs just visible on the undersides. The mites are almost invisible to the naked eye and control is difficult, although they do not like a cold water spray. A systemic insecticide may also help. *Thrips (Thrips fuscipennis)* are tiny, brown-yellow winged insects thriving in hot weather, when they attack the edges of the petals of roses in bud (particularly pale pink and white varieties) so that the flowers open misshapen. Spray as for greenfly. *Tortrix moths and other caterpillars* eat holes in the leaves, less regular in shape than those of the leaf-cutter bee. Caterpillars can be picked off by hand if not too numerous, but a bad attack can be halted by a contact or systemic spray. The tortrix moth caterpillar is hidden in a rolled-up leaf, the edges held together with silken threads. It may bore into rose buds and feed on them, as may the caterpillar of the lackey moth, which hides in a tent-like silken structure.

R. 'Anemone'. See *R.× anemonoides.*

R. × anemonoides Rehd. (*R.*'Anemone'). (Probably *R.laevigata × R.× odorata.*)
Less vigorous than *R.laevigata*, from which it differs in the stipules being more united and petals pale pink with deeper veins. Early summer. Garden origin. Z8.

R.arvensis Huds. FIELD ROSE.
Shrub with trailing or climbing stems 1–2m tall, bearing sparse, scattered, stout, more or less curved, equal prickles. Stipules narrow. Leaves deciduous; leaflets 1–4cm, (3–)5–7, deep green, elliptic to broadly ovate or rounded, acute or subacute, hairless on both sides, although sometimes downy on veins beneath, margins with simple teeth. Bracts absent. Receptacle smooth or somewhat glandular. Flowers 1–8, single, usually fragrant, 2.5–5cm across; sepals with lateral lobes, smooth or sparsely glandular on the back, reflexed and falling after flowering; petals white to pink; styles united, exserted; stigmas hairless. Fruit 0.6–2.5cm, spherical to ovoid, red, usually smooth. SW & C Europe, S Turkey. Z6.

R.banksiae 'Albo-Plena'. See *R.banksiae* var. *banksiae.*

R.banksiae Ait. BANKSIAN ROSE; BANKSIA ROSE.
Shrub with strong climbing stems up to 12m tall, unarmed or bearing very sparse, hooked prickles. Stipules very narrow, soon falling. Leaves evergreen; leaflets 2–6.5cm, 3–7, oblong-lanceolate to elliptic-ovate, acute or obtuse, glossy and hairless above, sometimes downy beneath on the midrib, margin wavy, with simple teeth. Bracts very small, soon falling. Flowers many in umbels, single or double, fragrant, 2.5–3cm across; sepals entire, reflexed and falling after flowering; petals white or yellow; styles free, not exserted. Fruit *c*0.7cm, spherical, dull red. Early summer. W & C China. var. **banksiae** (*R.banksiae* var. *alboplena* Rehd.; *R.banksiae* 'Banksiae'; *R.banksiae* 'Albo-Plena'). Flowers double, white, violet-scented. var. **normalis** Reg. Flowers single, white, very fragrant, and stems usually bearing hooked prickles. 'Lutea' (var. *lutea* Lindl.): stems generally unarmed; leaflets usually 5; flowers double, yellow, slightly fragrant; the hardest taxon and the most floriferous. 'Lutescens' (f. *lutescens* Voss): flowers single, yellow, highly scented. Z7.

R.banksiae 'Banksiae'. See *R.banksiae* var. *banksiae.*
R.banksiae var. *alboplena* Rehd. See *R.banksiae* var. *banksiae.*
R.banksiae var. *lutea* Lindl. See *R.banksiae* var. *normalis* 'Lutea'.
R.banksiae f. *lutescens* Voss. See *R.banksiae* var. *normalis* 'Lutescens'.

R.beggeriana Schrenk ex Fisch. & Mey.
Shrub with erect, sometimes climbing stems 1.8–3m tall, red-tinged when young, bearing pale, somewhat flattened, hooked prickles usually in pairs at the nodes. Stipule narrow. Leaves deciduous, aromatic; leaflets 0.7–3cm, 5–9, narrowly elliptic to obovate, obtuse, grey-green and hairless above, glandular and sometimes downy beneath, margins with simple teeth. Bracts narrowly ovate. Receptacle smooth. Flowers in clusters of 8 or more at the ends of new shoots, single, slightly malodorous, 2–3.8cm across; sepals entire, hairy or not on the back, glandular or not, erect after flowering but eventually falling; petals white; styles free, not exserted. Fruit 0.6–1cm, more or less spherical, red, turning purple, smooth. SW & C Asia. Z4.

R.bracteata Wendl. MACARTNEY ROSE.
Shrub with procumbent or climbing, brown-downy stems 3–6m tall, bearing stout, broad-based, hooked prickles in pairs at the nodes, and numerous glandular bristles. Stipules united at the base, fringed. Leaves evergreen; leaflets 1.5–5cm, 5–11, dark green, obovate to elliptic or oblong, obtuse, glossy and hairless above, downy beneath at least on midrib, margins with simple teeth. Bracts large, deeply toothed, downy. Receptacle hairy. Flowers usually solitary, single, smelling of fruit, 5–8cm across; sepals entire, brown-hairy on the back, reflexed and falling after flowering; petals white; styles free, not exserted. Fruit 2.5–3.8cm, spherical, orange-red, hairy. Summer–late autumn. SE China, Taiwan; naturalized in US from Virginia to Texas and Florida. Z7.

R.brunonii Lindl. (*R.moschata* var. *napaulensis* Lindl.). HIMALAYAN MUSK ROSE.
Vigorous shrub with arching or climbing stems 5–12m tall, bearing short, stout, hooked prickles. Stipules narrow with spreading tips. Leaves 17–21cm, deciduous, drooping; leaflets 3–6cm, 5–7(–9), narrowly ovate to elliptic or oblong-elliptic, acute or acuminate, grey-green or blue-green and somewhat hairy above, downy beneath at least on veins, sometimes glandular, margins with simple teeth. Bracts absent. Receptacle hairy and usually glandular. Flowers in clusters, often with several clusters combined into a large compound inflorescence, single, fragrant, 2.5–5cm across; sepals with lateral lobes, hairy and slightly glandular on the back, reflexed at flowering time, falling after flowering; petals white; styles united, exserted; stigmas downy. Fruit 0.7–1.8cm, subglobose to obovoid, red-brown, smooth. Himalaya, from Afghanistan to SW China (Yunnan, Sichuan). Many of the plants grown in gardens as *R.moschata* are in fact *R.brunonii*, having been distributed under the wrong name by nurseries. 'La Mortola': a very strong-growing selection. Z7.

R.canina L. DOG ROSE; COMMON BRIER; DOG BRIER.
Vigorous shrub with arching, sometimes climbing stems 1.5–5.5m tall, bearing scattered, strong, hooked, more or less equal prickles; bristles absent. Stipules narrow to broad. Leaves deciduous; leaflets 1.5–4cm, 5–7, narrowly elliptic to ovate, acute or obtuse, usually hairless on both sides, sometimes glandular beneath or downy on veins, margins with simple or compound teeth. Bracts often broad. Receptacle smooth. Flowers solitary or 2–5, single, fragrant, 2.5–5cm across; sepals with lateral lobes, usually hairless on the back, reflexed and falling after flowering; petals white or pale pink; styles free, exserted; stigmas woolly or not. Fruit 1–3cm, ovoid to subglobose, red to orange, smooth. Cooler parts of Europe and SW Asia, NW Africa, naturalized in N America. Z3.

R.cathayensis (Rehd. & Wils.) Bail. See *R.multiflora* var. *cathayensis.*
R.cerasocarpa Rolfe (*R.gentiliana* sensu Rehd. & Wils. pro parte, non Lév. & Vaniot). Shrub with climbing or semi-climbing stems to 4.5m tall, bearing few, stout, scattered, recurved prickles. Stipules narrow. Leaves 17–20cm, deciduous; leaflets 5–10cm, (3–)5, narrowly ovate to elliptic, leathery, acute to acuminate, hairless or more or less so on both sides, margin with simple teeth. Bracts absent. Receptacle downy and glandular. Flowers many in clusters, single, fragrant, 2.5–3.5cm across, opening from abruptly pointed buds; sepals usually with lateral lobes, downy and glandular on the back, reflexed and falling after flowering; petals white; styles united. Fruit 1–1.3cm, spherical, deep red, downy. W & C China. Z5.

R.chinensis Jacq. (*R.indica* Ait. f.). CHINA ROSE; BENGAL ROSE

Shrub, varying in habit from dwarf to semi-climbing up to 6m tall. Stems unarmed or bearing scattered, slightly hooked, somewhat flattened prickles. Stipules narrow. Leaves evergreen; leaflets 2.5–6cm, 3–5, lanceolate to broadly ovate, acuminate, glossy and hairless above, hairless beneath except for downy midrib, margins with simple teeth. Bracts narrow. Receptacle smooth or glandular. Flowers solitary or in clusters, single or semi-double, *c*5cm across, often fragrant; sepals entire or with a few lateral lobes, smooth or glandular on the back, reflexed and falling after flowering; petals pale pink to scarlet or crimson; styles free, somewhat exserted. Fruit 1.5–2cm, ovoid to pear-shaped, green-brown to scarlet. Summer to early autumn. Garden origin (China). A repeat-flowering rose which contributed this feature to European roses when it was introduced around 1800. var. *spontanea* (Rehd. & Wils.) T.T. Yu & Ku (*R.chinensis* f. *spontanea* Rehd. & Wils.). Climber or bush usually 1–2.5m tall. Leaflets lanceolate. Flowers 1–3, single, pink, turning red, 5–6cm across; sepals entire. Fruit orange. W China. The wild type of cultivated *R.chinensis*. Z7.

R.corymbulosa Rolfe.
Shrub with erect or sometimes prostrate or climbing stems to 2m, unarmed or bearing a few straight, slender prickles. Leaves deciduous, turning purple in autumn; leaflets 1.3–5cm, 3–5, elliptic to ovate-oblong, acute, dark green and sparsely downy above, glaucous and downy beneath, margins with compound teeth. Bracts present. Receptacle obovoid, glandular-bristly. Flowers in clusters of up to 12, single, 1.9–2.5cm across; sepals entire, downy and glandular-bristly on the back, erect and persistent in fruit; petals deep pink, paler at the base; styles free, slightly exserted; stigmas downy. Fruit 1–1.3cm, ovoid-spherical to spherical, coral-red, glandular-bristly. China (Hubei, Shensi). Z6.

R.cymosa Tratt.(*R.microcarpa* Lindl., non Besser non Retz.).
Differs from *R.banksiae* in having stems more prickly, inflorescence larger and branched, flowers smaller, always single, white, *c*1.5cm across, with sepals which bear lateral lobes. Early summer. C & S China. Z8.

R. 'Dupontii' (*R.× dupontii* Déségl., in part; *R.nivea* Dup.).
DUPONT ROSE; SNOW-BUSH ROSE
Thought for some time to be a hybrid between *R.moschata* and *R.gallica*, but this seems to be unlikely. Differs from *R.moschata* in its smaller size (2–3m tall), leaflets with compound teeth, flowers single, 6–7.5cm across, creamy pink with sepals glandular on the back, and free styles. Garden origin. Z6.

R.× dupontii Déségl., in part. See *R.* 'Dupontii'.

R.ecae Aitch. (*R.xanthina* var.*ecae* (Aitch.) Boulenger).
Much-branched, erect, suckering shrub. Stems to 1.5m, bearing dense, straight, flattened, red-tinged prickles. Stipules very narrow. Leaves deciduous, aromatic; leaflets 0.4–0.8cm, 5–9, broadly elliptic to obovate or more or less orbicular, obtuse, glandular beneath, margins with simple, often glandular teeth. Bracts absent. Flowers solitary, single, 2–3cm across; sepals entire, hairless, spreading or deflexed in fruit, persistent; petals deep yellow. Fruit 0.5–1cm, spherical, shiny red-brown, smooth and hairless. NE Afghanistan, NW Pakistan and adjacent USSR, N China. 'Golden Chersonese' (*R.ecae* × *R.* 'Canary Bird'): to 2m, with the aromatic leaves and deep yellow flowers of *R.ecae*. 'Helen Knight' (*R.ecae* × *R.pimpinellifolia* 'Grandiflora'): stems red-brown, to 3m against a wall; flowers large, yellow. Z7.

R.ernestii Stapf ex Bean. See *R.rubus*.

R.filipes Rehd. & Wils.
Shrub with arching and climbing stems up to 9m tall, purple when young, bearing few, small, hooked prickles. Stipules narrow. Leaves deciduous, coppery when young; leaflets 3.5–8cm, 5–7, narrowly ovate to narrowly elliptic, acuminate, hairless above and beneath or sometimes downy on veins beneath, margins with simple teeth. Bracts absent. Flowers to 100 or more in large clusters up to 30cm or more wide, single, fragrant, 2–2.5cm across; sepals with a few lateral lobes, glandular and slightly downy or hairless on the back, reflexed and falling after flowering; petals creamy or white, sometimes downy on the back; styles united, exserted; stigmas woolly. Fruit 0.8–1.5cm, spherical to broadly ellipsoidal, orange becoming crimson-scarlet. W China. 'Kiftsgate': inflorescence to 45cm across. Z5.

R.× fortuneana Lindl. (Possibly *R.banksiae* × *R.laevigata*.)
Differs from *R.banksiae* in having 3–5, rather thin leaflets, and solitary, double, creamy white flowers 5–10cm across. Garden origin (China). Z8.

R.gentiliana sensu Rehd. & Wils. pro parte, non Lév. & Vaniot. See *R.cerasocarpa*.

R.gentiliana Lév. & Vaniot. See *R.multiflora* var. *cathayensis*.

R.gigantea Collett ex Crépin (*R.× odorata* var. *gigantea* (Crépin) Rehd. & Wils.; *R.× odorata* 'Gigantea').
Shrub with climbing stems 8–12(–30)m tall, bearing stout, scattered, uniform, hooked prickles. Stipules narrow. Leaves evergreen or semi-evergreen; leaflets 3.8–9cm, 5–7, elliptic to ovate, acuminate, glossy above, hairless on both sides, margins with simple, often glandular teeth. Bracts present. Receptacle smooth. Flowers 1(–3), single, fragrant, 10–15cm across, opening from slender, pale yellow buds; sepals entire, smooth on the back, reflexed and falling after flowering; petals white or cream; styles free; stigmas downy. Fruit 2–3cm, spherical or pear-shaped, red, or yellow flushed with red. Early summer. NE India, Upper Burma, China (Yunnan). Z9.

R.helenae Rehd. & Wils.
Shrub with rambling stems 5–6m tall, purple-brown when young, bearing short, stout, hooked prickles. Leaves deciduous; leaflets 1.9–6cm, (5–)7–9, ovate to elliptic or obovate, acute, bright green and hairless above, grey beneath and downy on the veins, margins with simple teeth. Bracts absent. Receptacle densely glandular. Flowers many in somewhat flat clusters, single, fragrant, 2–4cm across; sepals with lateral lobes, glandular on the back, reflexed after flowering, eventually falling; petals white; styles united into a hairy column, exserted; stigmas hairy. Fruit 1–1.5cm, ovoid, ellipsoidal or pear-shaped, scarlet or orange-red, glandular. C China. Z5.

R.indica Ait. f. See *R.chinensis*.

R.× iwara Sieb. ex Reg. (*R.multiflora* × *R.rugosa*.)
Differs from *R.multiflora* in the stems bearing large, hooked prickles, and the leaflets grey-downy beneath. Flowers single, white. Japan. Z5.

R.× jacksonii Bak.(*R.wichuraiana* × *R.rugosa*.)
Differs from *R.wichuraiana* by its larger, wrinkled leaflets and bright crimson flowers. Garden origin. Z5.

R.jundzillii Besser (*R.marginata* auct., non Wallr.).
Erect or trailing, suckering shrub with stems 1–2.4m, bearing a few slender, scattered, straight or decurved prickles, sometimes intermixed with bristles. Stipules large and broad. Leaves deciduous; leaflets 2.5–4.5cm, 5–7, obovate to broadly elliptic, acute or acuminate, hairless above, somewhat glandular and sometimes downy beneath, margins with compound glandular teeth. Bracts present. Receptacle often glandular-bristly. Flowers usually solitary, sometimes 2–8, single, slightly fragrant, 5–7.5cm across; sepals with lateral lobes, glandular on the back, spreading to reflexed and falling after flowering; petals pale to rosy pink, fading with age; styles united, stigmas woolly. Fruit 1.5–2.5cm, ovoid to spherical, red, smooth and glandular-bristly. W Europe to S Russia (including Caucasus), Turkey. Z5.

R.× kordesii Wulff. (*R.wichuraiana* × *R.rugosa*.)
Tetraploid produced by Wilhelm Kordes who selfed 'Max Graf', used as a parent for a number of repeat-flowering climbers. It differs from *R.wichuraiana* in the deep pink to red, recurrent flowers which are single to semi-double and 7–8cm across. Garden origin. cf. *R.× jacksonii*. Z5.

R.laevigata Michx. CHEROKEE ROSE.
Vigorous shrub with climbing, green stems to 10m or more, bearing scattered, stout, red-brown, hooked prickles. Stipules united at the base, soon falling. Leaves evergreen; leaflets 3–6(–9)cm, 3(–5), lanceolate to elliptic or ovate, rather leathery, acute or acuminate, glossy above, hairless on both sides, midrib sometimes prickly beneath, margins with simple teeth. Bracts absent. Receptacle very bristly. Flowers solitary, single, fragrant, 5–10cm across; sepals entire, bristly on the back, erect and persistent in fruit; petals white or creamy white; styles free, not exserted. Fruit 3.5–4cm, pear-shaped, orange-red to red, bristly. Early summer. S China, Taiwan, Vietnam, Laos, Cambodia, Burma, naturalized S US. 'Cooperi' (COOPER'S BURMA ROSE): stems red rather than green; leaves with 5 or 7 leaflets; petals become pink-spotted with age; possibly hybrid of *R.laevigata × R.gigantea.* Z7.

R.× lheritiana Thory. (Possibly *R.pendulina × R.chinensis.*)
Shrub with red-tinged stems climbing to 4m, unarmed or with a few prickles. Leaves deciduous; leaflets 3–7, ovate-oblong, with simple teeth, hairless on both sides. Bracts present. Receptacle smooth. Flowers many, in clusters, semi-double; sepals entire; petals purple-red, white at the base; styles free, not exserted. Fruit subglobose, smooth. Garden origin. Z4.

R.longicuspis Bertol.(*R.lucens* Rolfe; *R.yunnanensis* (Crépin) Boulenger).
Vigorous shrub with scrambling and climbing stems to 6m or more, tinged red when young, bearing few, short, curved or hooked prickles which may be absent on flowering branches. Stipules narrow. Leaves to 20cm, evergreen or semi-evergreen, tinged red when young; leaflets 5–10cm, (3–)5–7, narrowly ovate to elliptic, leathery, acuminate, hairless on both sides although occasionally downy on midrib beneath, margins with simple teeth. Bracts absent. Receptacle hairy and usually globular. Flowers to 15 in a loose cluster, single, smelling of bananas, c5cm across, opening from narrowly ovoid buds; sepals with lateral lobes, hairy and glandular on the back, reflexed after flowering and eventually falling; petals white, silky on the back; styles united, exserted. Fruit 1.5–2cm, broadly ellipsoidal to spherical, red to orange, often hairy and glandular. Early to mid-summer. NE India, W China, ?Burma. var. *sinowilsonii* (Hemsl.) T.T. Yu & Ku (*R.sinowilsonii* Hemsl.).Leaves to 30cm, leaflets slightly downy beneath, flower-buds broadly ovoid, sepals hairless or nearly so on the back. SW China. Z9.

R.lucens Rolfe. See *R.longicuspis.*

R.luciae Franch. & Rochebr. & Crépin.
Shrub with prostrate or climbing stems up to 3.5m tall, bearing small, scattered, pale brown, rather flattened, slightly hooked prickles. Stipules very thin. Leaves evergreen or semi-evergreen; leaflets 2–4.5cm, 5(–7), rather thin, the terminal one longer than the others, acute to acuminate, both sides hairless or almost so, margins with simple teeth. Bracts absent. Receptacle smooth or glandular. Flowers 3–30 in clusters, single, fragrant, 2–3cm across, opening from short, rounded buds; sepals reflexed and falling after flowering; petals white; styles united, exserted; stigmas woolly. Fruit ovoid to spherical, red to purple, c7mm long, smooth or glandular. Early summer and again in late summer. E China, Japan, Korea. Very similar to *R.wichuraiana* and considered by some botanists to be conspecific: if so then the name *R.luciae* has priority. Z7.

R.× macrantha hort., non Desp.(*R.* 'Macrantha'). (A hybrid between *R. gallica* and possibly *R.canina.*)
Vigorous shrub. Stems 1.5–2m, arching or spreading, green, bearing sparse, scattered, straight or slightly curved prickles, mixed with small straight bristles and stalked glands. Stipules narrow. Leaves deciduous; leaflets 3–5(–7), dull green, ovate to oblong-ovate, acute to acuminate, hairless on both sides but glandular beneath and with tiny prickles on the midrib, margins with simple or compound teeth. Bracts present. Receptacle slightly glandular below. Flowers 2–5 in clusters, single to semi-double, fragrant, c7.5cm across; sepals with many lateral lobes, hairy inside and on margin, slightly glandular on the back, reflexed and falling after flowering; petals pale pink, fading to white; styles free, not or only slightly exserted. Fruit to 1.5cm wide, subspherical, red. Garden origin. Z6.

R. 'Macrantha'. See *R.× macrantha.*

R.maximowicziana Reg.
Shrub with arching and climbing stems bearing few, small, scattered, straight and hooked prickles, with bristles on the young branches. Stipules very narrow. Leaves deciduous; leaflets 2.5–5cm, 7–9, ovate-elliptic to oblong, acute to acuminate, hairless on both sides, margins with simple teeth. Bracts present. Receptacle smooth. Flowers many in small clusters, single, 2.5–3.5cm across; sepals with lateral lobes, reflexed after flowering and finally falling; petals white; styles united; stigmas hairless. Fruit 1–1.2cm, ovoid, red, smooth. Manchuria. Z6.

R.microcarpa Lindl., non Besser non Retz. See *R.cymosa.*

R.moschata Herrm. MUSK ROSE.
Robust shrub with arching or semi-climbing, purple- or red-tinged stems 3–10m tall, bearing few, scattered, straight or slightly curved prickles. Stipules very narrow. Leaves deciduous; leaflets 3–7cm, 5–7, broadly ovate to broadly elliptic, acute or acuminate, shiny and hairless above, downy or not on veins beneath, margins with simple teeth. Bracts absent. Receptacle finely adpressed-hairy, rarely slightly glandular. Flowers in few-flowered loose clusters, single, with a musky scent, 3–5.5cm across; sepals entire or with lateral lobes, hairy on the back, reflexed and persistent after flowering; petals white or cream, reflexing with age; styles united, exserted; stigmas woolly. Fruit 1–1.5cm, subglobose to ovoid, orange-red, usually downy and sometimes glandular. Late summer to autumn. Unknown in the wild; cultivated in S Europe, Mediterranean and SW Asia. var. *nastarana* Christ. Leaflets smaller, always hairless beneath; flowers larger, more numerous, tinged pink. Z6.

R.moschata var. *napaulensis* Lindl. See *R.brunonii.*

R.mulliganii Boulenger.
Similar to *R.rubus,* but stems 6m or more, leaflets 5–7, flowers 4.5–5.5cm across on stalks 2.5–3.5cm long, carried in looser clusters; the sepals always have lateral lobes. W China. Z5.

R.multiflora Thunb. ex Murray. (*R.polyantha* Sieb. & Zucc.). JAPANESE ROSE; BABY ROSE.
Strong-growing shrub with arching, trailing or sometimes climbing stems 3–5m tall, bearing many small, stout, decurved prickles. Stipules with laciniate margins, usually glandular-bristly. Leaves deciduous; leaflets 1.5–5cm, (5–)7–9(–i1), obovate or elliptic, acute, acuminate or obtuse, hairless above, hairless or downy beneath, margins with simple teeth. Bracts usually absent. Receptacle hairy. Flowers few to many in branched clusters, single, fruit-scented, 1.5–3cm across; sepals with lateral lobes, glandular-bristly on the back, shorter than petals even in bud, reflexed and falling after flowering; petals cream, fading to white, occasionally pink; styles united, exserted; stigmas hairless. Fruit 0.6–0.7cm, ovoid to spherical, red. Japan, Korea, naturalized in US. The lower branches root where they touch the soil. Much used as a stock for grafting, especially for ramblers. 'Carnea' (*R.multiflora* var. *carnea* Thory): flowers double, flesh-pink. 'Grevillei' (*R.multiflora* var. *platyphylla* Thory; 'Platyphylla') (SEVEN SISTERS ROSE): leaflets large, wrinkled; flowers in clusters of 25–30(–50), usually double, deep pink-purple fading to white. 'Wilsonii': flowers single, white, c5cm across. var. *cathayensis* Rehd. & Wils.(*R.cathayensis* (Rehd. & Wils.) Bail.; *R.gentiliana* Lév. & Vaniot) Flowers single, rosy pink, to 4cm across, in rather flat clusters. China. Z5.

R.multiflora 'Platyphylla'. See *R.multiflora* 'Grevillei'.
R.multiflora var. *carnea* Thory. See *R.multiflora* 'Carnea'.
R.multiflora var. *platyphylla* Thory. See *R.multiflora* 'Grevillei'.
R.multiflora var. *watsoniana* (Crépin) Matsum. See *R.watsoniana.*

R.nivea Dup. ex Lindl., non DC. See *R.*'Dupontii'.

R.× *odorata* (Andrews) Sweet. TEA ROSE.
Thought to be a hybrid between *R.chinensis* and *R.gigantea*. Differs from *R.gigantea* in the single or double flowers 5–8cm across, with white, pale pink or yellow petals Mid to late summer. Garden origin (China). Z7.

R.× odorata 'Gigantea'. See *R.gigantea*.
R.× od.,rata var. *gigantea* (Collett ex Crépin) Rehd. & Wils. See *R.gigantea*.

R.× *paulii* Rehd.(*R.* 'Paulii').(*R.rugosa × R.arvensis*.)
Stems vigorous, trailing to 4m. Flowers in clusters, single, white, fragrant, to 6cm across; sepals entire, glandular. 'Rosea': flowers pink with paler centres. Z4.

R. 'Paulii'. See *R.× paulii*.

R.*phoenicia* Boiss.
Shrub with slender, climbing stems 3–5m tall, bearing few, short, curved or hooked, broad-based, more or less equal prickles. Stipules glandular-toothed. Leaves deciduous; leaflets 2–4.5cm, (3–)5(–7), elliptic to rounded, acute to obtuse, somewhat downy on both sides, more so beneath, margins with simple or compound teeth. Bracts usually hairy. Receptacle hairless or slightly hairy. Flowers 10–14 in clusters, single, 4–5cm across, opening from ovoid, rounded buds; sepals with lateral lobes, often downy on the back, reflexed and falling after flowering; petals white; styles united, exserted; stigmas hairless. Fruit 1–1.2cm, ovoid, red, smooth. NE Greece, Cyprus, Turkey, Syria, Lebanon. Z9.

R.× *polliniana* Spreng. (*R.arvensis × R.gallica*.)
Differs from *R.arvensis* in its rather leathery, leaflets which are slightly downy beneath, and flowers 5–6cm across. N Italy. Z7.

R.polyantha Sieb. & Zucc. See *R.multiflora*.

R.*rubus* Lév. & Vaniot (*R.ernestii* Stapf ex Bean; *R.ernestii* f. *nudescens* Stapf; *R.ernestii* f. *velutescens* Stapf).
Vigorous shrub with spreading or semi-climbing, often purple-tinged stems, 2.4–5m tall, bearing few, short, hooked prickles (young shoots hairy or more or less hairless). Stipules narrow. Leaves deciduous; leaflets 3–9cm, (3–)5, elliptic-ovate to oblong-obovate, acute, glossy and hairless above, grey-green and usually downy beneath, often purple-tinged when young, margins with simple teeth. Bracts absent. Receptacle glandular-bristly. Flowers to 12 in tight clusters, single, fragrant, 2.5–3.8cm across, on stalks 1–2.5cm long; sepals entire or with lateral lobes, downy and glandular on the back, reflexed after flowering and falling; petals white, yellow at the base; styles united into a shortly exserted downy column; stigmas woolly. Fruit 0.9–1.5cm, spherical or ovoid, dark red, glandular-bristly. Late summer. W & C China. Z8.

R.*sempervirens* L. EVERGREEN ROSE
Shrub with prostrate, trailing or scrambling stems 6–10m tall, unarmed or bearing straight or hooked, broad-based prickles. Stipules narrow. Leaves evergreen or semi-evergreen; leaflets 1.5–6cm, (3–)5–7, narrowly ovate to elliptic, the terminal usually larger than the upper laterals, acuminate, hairless on both sides except for midrib which may be downy beneath, margins with simple teeth. Bracts short, entire, more or less hairless, falling early. Receptacle often glandular-bristly. Flowers (1–)3–10 in clusters, single, slightly fragrant, 2.5–4.5cm across, opening from blunt, ovoid buds; sepals entire, glandular-bristly on the back, reflexed to spreading and falling after flowering; petals white; styles more or less united, exserted; stigmas usually woolly. Fruit 1–1.6cm, ovoid or spherical, orange-red, often glandular-bristly. S Europe, NW Africa, Turkey. Z7.

R.*setigera* Michx. PRAIRIE ROSE; SUNSHINE ROSE; CLIMBING ROSE.
Shrub with slender, spreading, trailing or rambling stems 2–5m tall, bearing stout, more or less straight, broad-based, scattered prickles. Stipules narrow. Leaves deciduous; leaflets 3–8cm, 3–5, ovate to ovate-oblong, long, acute to acuminate,

deep green and hairless above, pale green and downy on the veins beneath, margins with coarse, simple teeth. Bracts absent. Receptacle glandular-bristly. Flowers 5–15 in loose clusters, single, sometimes fragrant, 5–7.5cm across; sepals with lateral lobes, downy and glandular-bristly on the back, reflexed after flowering, then falling; petals deep pink fading to pale pink or nearly white; styles united, exserted; stigmas hairless. Fruit *c*0.8cm, spherical, red to green-brown, glandular-bristly. East & Central N America. Z4.

R.sinowilsonii Hemsl. See *R.longicuspis* var. *sinowilsonii*.

R.*soulieana* Crépin.
Robust shrub with erect, spreading or semi-climbing stems 3–4m tall, bearing scattered, stout, decurved, compressed, broad-based prickles. Stipules narrow. Leaves 6.5–10cm, deciduous; leaflets 1–3cm, (5–)7–9, grey-green, obovate to elliptic, acute to obtuse, hairless on both sides although somewhat downy on midrib beneath, margins with simple teeth. Bracts absent. Receptacle glandular. Flowers in many-flowered branched clusters 10–15cm across, single, with a fruity scent, 2.5–3.8cm across, opening from yellow buds; sepals entire or with a few lateral lobes, hairless or downy and often glandular on the back, reflexed and falling after flowering; petals white; styles united, exserted; stigmas sparsely hairy. Fruit *c*1cm, ovoid to subglobose, pale to dark orange, glandular. W China. Z7.

R.watsoniana Crépin (*R.multiflora* var. *watsoniana* (Crépin) Matsum.).
Shrub with arching, trailing or climbing stems to 1m tall, bearing small, scattered prickles. Stipules very narrow, entire. Leaves deciduous; leaflets 2.5–6.5cm, 3–5, linear-lanceolate, hairless above and mottled with yellow or grey near the midrib, downy beneath, margins wavy and bearing simple teeth. Bracts absent. Flowers in clusters, single, 1–1.7cm across; sepals entire, hairy on the back, reflexed after flowering, finally falling; petals pale pink, occasionally white; styles united, exserted. Fruit 0.6–0.7cm, spherical, red. Garden origin (Japan). The fruit are usually sterile. Any seedlings which are produced are normal *R.multiflora*, suggesting that *R.watsoniana* may be a mutant. Z5.

R.*wichuraiana* Crépin. MEMORIAL ROSE.
Shrub with procumbent, trailing or climbing stems 3–6m tall, bearing strong, curved prickles. Stipules broad, toothed. Leaves evergreen or semi-evergreen; leaflets 5–9, dark green, elliptic to broadly ovate or rounded, obtuse, hairless on both sides except for midrib beneath, margins with simple teeth. Bracts absent. Receptacle sometimes glandular. Flowers 6–10 in loose clusters, single, fragrant, 2.5–5cm across; sepals entire or with a few lateral lobes, often downy or slightly glandular on the back, reflexed and falling after flowering; petals white; styles united, exserted; stigmas woolly. Fruit 1–1.5cm, ovoid or spherical, orange-red to dark red. Summer–early autumn. Japan, Korea, E China, Taiwan, naturalized in N America. 'Variegata': leaflets cream with pink tips when young, turning green, marked with cream. Z5.

R.xanthina var. *ecae* (Aitch.) Boulenger. See *R.ecae*.
R.yunnanensis (Crépin) Boulenger. See *R.longicuspis*.

R.cultivars *Climbers*. (a) *White*. 'White Cockade' ('New Dawn' × 'Circus'): vigorous, to 3m; flowers semi-double, white with flush of cream in folds, scented, sides of petals roll back, grouped, abundant; (Cocker, 1969). 'New Dawn' ('New Dawn' × 'Circus'): vigorous; leaves rich green; flowers very double, white, scented, profuse; recurrent; (L.E. Longley, 1949). (b) *Yellow*. 'Dreaming Spires': tall-growing; leaves shiny; flowers large to 13cm diam., deep butter yellow with light orange hint, scented; (Mattocks, 1973). 'Golden Showers': to 3m; flowers large, semi-double, bright yellow fading to cream, abundant, fragrant; (Lammerts 1956). 'Lawrence Johnston' ('Mme Eugene Verdier' × 'Persian Yellow'): very tall-growing, to 6m; flowers double, loose, bright yellow, scented, grouped, very abundant; (Pernet-Ducher, 1923). 'Leverkussen' (*R.× kordesii* × 'Golden

Glow'): strong-growing, to 3m; leaves shiny light green; flowers large, double, opening to flat, lemon yellow with darker centre, scented, profuse; (Kordes, 1954). 'Mermaid' (*R.bracteata* × double yellow Tea Rose): strong-growing, to 7m; leaves rich green; flowers very large, to 16cm diam., single, very light yellow, anthers dark, scented, sterile; (W. Paul, 1918). 'Royal Sunset' ('Sungold' × 'Sutter's Gold'): tall-growing; flowers to 13cm diam., double, apricot orange, abundant; (Morey/Jackson & Perkins, 1960). (c) *Pink*. 'Albertine' (*R.wichuraiana* × 'Mrs Arthur Robert Waddell'): strong and bushy-growing; leaves dark green; flowers large, double, loose, pale pink, buds flesh pink, profuse, well scented; (Barbier, 1921). 'America' ('Fragrant Cloud' × 'Tradition'): flowers large, double, petals overlap, clear pale rose, grouped, continuous, abundant, buds narrow; (W.A. Warriner, 1967). 'Dream Girl', ('Dr W. van Fleet' × 'Senora Gari'): to 3m high; flowers to 10cm diam., double, flesh pink flushed yellow, scented, recurrent; (Jacobus, 1944). 'Macha' (®Handel, ®Händel, ®Haendel) ('Columbine' × 'Heidelberg'): tall-growing, to 4m; flowers to 8cm diam., double, cupped, warm white with wide carmine edge, scented; (McGredy, 1965). 'New Dawn' (sport of 'Dr W. van Fleet'): vigorous, to 6m; leaves light green; flowers double, pale pink with centre darker, scented, abundant; (Dreer Somerset, 1930). 'Parade' ('New Dawn' seedling × 'Climbing World's Fair'): strong-growing; leaves dark green; flowers to 10cm diam., semi-double, deep vivid pink, scented, abundant, nodding, recurrent; (Boerner/Jackson & Perkins, 1953). 'Pink Perpetue' ('Spectacular' × 'New Dawn'): strong-growing; flowers double, rich soft pink, fragrant, grouped, recurrent, abundant; (Gregory 1965). 'Swan Lake' ('Peace' × ('Signora' × 'Mrs John Laing')): vigorous; leaves dark green; flowers to 10cm diam., double, high-centred, light satin pink fading to white, scented, abundant; (F. Meilland, 1951). (d) *Reds*' Delmur' (®Altissimo) ('Tenor' × ?): strong-growing; young growth red; flowers large, to 13cm diam., single, crimson to deep red, stamens gold, continuous; (Delbard-Chabert, 1966). 'Blaze' ('Paul's Scarlet Climber' × 'Gruss an Teplitz'): vigorous; leaves deep green; flowers semi-double, bright clear red, in large groups; (Kallay, 1932). 'Macdub' (®Dublin Bay) ('Bantry Bay' × 'Altissimo'): leaves dark green; flowers to 10cm diam., double, open, rich red, scented, abundant; (McGredy, 1975). 'Maitam' (®Fugue) ('Alain' × 'Guine'): wide-growing; flowers double, flattening later, deep scarlet, continuous; (Meilland, 1968). ®Joseph's Coat ('Buccaneer' × 'Circus'): tall and strong-growing; flowers double, mixture of orange, yellow and crimson, long-lasting, profuse; (Swim/Armstrong, 1964). ®Parkdirektor Riggers (*R.×kordesii* × 'Our Princess'): vigorous; leaves shiny rich green; flowers to 8cm diam., semi-double, vibrant red, stamens yellow, grouped, continuous, profuse; (Kordes, 1957). 'Scharlachglut' ('Scarlet Fire'), ('Poinsettia' × *R.gallica* 'Grandiflora'): wide-growing; flowers to 13cm diam., single, almost flat, bright red, grouped, abundant; fruit red, abundant; (Kordes, 1952). 'Spectacular' ('Danse de Feu'), ('Paul's Scarlet Climber' × *R.multiflora* seedling): vigorous; leaves shiny; flowers large, double, scarlet, muddy red with age, continuous; (Mallerin, 1953).

Ramblers. (a) *White*. 'Félicité et Perpetué' (*R.sempervirens* × ?): strong-growing, to 5m; leaves somewhat evergreen; flowers to 4cm diam., double, well-shaped, pale pink in bud, opening palest cream, grouped, short-lived, profuse, recur-

rent; (A.A. Jacques, 1827). 'Kiftsgate' (sport of *R.filipes*): very vigorous; flowers small, single, pale cream in bud, opening white, in trusses, non-recurrent, late-flowering; also its palest pink seedling 'Brenda Colvin'; (E. Murrell, 1954). 'Rambling Rector' (probably *R.multiflora* × *R.moschata*): vigorous; flowers small, semi-double, white, stamens yellow, scented, profuse; (1912). 'Seagull' (possibly *R.multiflora* × ?): to 5m; leaves glossy bright green; flowers to 2.5cm diam., flat, to 13 rounded petals, white, stamens yellow; (1907). 'Wedding Day' (seedling of *R.longicuspis* var. *sinowilsonii* × ?): strong-growing; stems thorny; flowers single, edge frilled, cream fading to white, scented, abundant, grouped; (F.C. Stern, 1950). (b) *Yellow*. 'Emily Gray' ('Jersey Beauty' × 'Comtesse du Cayla'): to 6m; leaves shiny dark green; flowers to 3.8cm diam., double, yellow burnished copper, stamens yellow, grouped, non-recurrent; (Williams, 1918). 'Phyllis Bide' (probably 'Perle d'Or' × 'Gloire de Dijon'): flowers small, loose, gold in bud, opening white with yellow and pink flushes; (1923). (c) *Pink*. 'Alexandre Girault' (*R.wichuraiana* × 'Papa Gontier'): leaves bright green; very vigorous, to 6m; flowers very double, dark pink with sunny orange petal base, sweetly scented, grouped, non-recurrent; (Barbier, 1909). 'Dorothy Perkins' (*R.wichuraiana* × 'Mme Gabriel Luizet'): strong-growing; leaves pale green; flowers small, double, pink, abundant; susceptible to mildew; (Jackson & Perkins, 1901). 'François Juranville' (*R.wichuraiana* × 'Mme Laurette Messimy'): strong growing, to 8m; leaves bronze when young; flowers large, double, informal, strong flesh pink with yellow base, sweetly scented, profuse; (Barbier, 1966). 'May Queen' (*R.wichuraiana* × 'Champion of the World'): strong-growing, to 5m; flowers fully double, quartered, soft old rose, developing lilac tints later, scented; (W.A. Manda, 1898). 'Minnehaha' (*R.wichuraiana* × 'Paul Neyron'): strong-growing; leaves small; flowers very small, double, pink fading to white, in large, clusters; (Walsh, 1905). (d) *Red*. 'American Pillar', 'Van Fleet' ((*R.wichuraiana* × *R.setigera*) × Hybrid Perpetual): leaves deep glossy green; flowers to 6cm diam., single, flat, pink-red with white centre, stamens gold, grouped in panicles, late-flowering, profuse; (1902). 'Crimson Showers' (seedling of 'Excelsa'): stems pliant; flowers to 2.5cm diam., double, bright crimson, grouped, abundant, late-flowering, profuse; (Norman, 1951). 'Paul's Scarlet Climber' ('Paul's Carmine Pillar' seedling × ?): bushy; leaves shiny; flowers double, scarlet, abundant, grouped, non-recurrent; (W. Paul, 1916). 'Veilchenblau' ('Crimson Rambler' × 'Erinnerung an Brod'): vigorous, to 4m; stems almost thornless; flowers to 3cm diam., single, deep violet later more blue with white centre, abundant; (J.C. Schmidt, 1909).

Polyantha. (a) *White*. 'Polyantha Grandiflora': climbing or rambling to 6m. Leaves dark glossy green; flowers creamy-white, very fragrant, stamens orange-yellow. Fruit oval, orange-red. 'Yvonne Rabier' (*R.wichuraiana* × Polyantha): low-growing; leaves lush green; flowers small, fully double, white, centre flushed yellow, in tight groups, recurrent; (Turbat, 1910). (b) *Pink*. 'Cécile Brunner' (Polyantha double white × 'Mme de Tartas'), SWEETHEART ROSE: loose-growing, some forms strongly climbing; leaves very small; flowers small, double, flat, palest pink fading at edges, yellow flush at centre, scented; (Veuve Ducher, 1889).

Rubia L. (From Lat. *ruber*, red, referring to the dye extracted from *R.tinctoria*.) Rubiaceae. Some 60 species of herbs or subshrubs. Stems climbing, diffuse, or erect, 4-angled, glabrous to rough and rigidly hairy or prickly. Leaves sessile or petiolate, 4–8-whorled (as, occasionally, are leaf-like stipules), or opposite, linear, lanceolate, obovate, or cordate, often scabrous at margin and on nerves beneath. Flowers pedicellate, bisexual, in axillary or terminal panicles or cymes; pedicels articulate with ovary; calyx tube globose to ovoid, limb obsolete, absent or forming a swollen rim; corolla rotate, bell- or funnel-shaped, lobes 4–5; stamens 4–5, inserted on tube of corolla, anthers exserted; ovary 2-celled, or 1-celled by abortion, styles 2, or 1 and deeply bifid, stigmas capitate, ovules solitary in each cell, erect, basally attached. Fruit berry-like, globose, fleshy. Europe, Africa, Asia.

CULTIVATION The genus *Rubia* is not renowned for ornamental virtue, being of greater interest for its medicinal properties, and for the dye substances, alizarin and purpurin, extracted from the tangled red roots. The roots are harvested from two-year-old plants, in spring and autumn. *R.tinctoria* was once extensively cultivated as a dye plant in Turkey, the Balkans, France and Holland, but has been superseded by the chemical synthesis of alizarin which began in 1868. It is still cultivated commercially in Europe and Central Asia, for medicinal use: when administered internally, the dye colours urine and milk, but particularly young bones, and is used in osteopathic investigations. The species listed below are sometimes encountered in economic, botanic or herbal collections, where they are grown in full sun or partial shade on free-draining soils and trained through canes or cut twigs.

R.conotricha Gand. See *R.cordifolia*.

R.cordifolia L. (*R.conotricha* Gand.; *R.longipetiolata* Bullock). INDIAN MADDER; MUNJEET.
Perennial herb. Stem to 6m, climbing or creeping, usually rough with retrorse prickles and pubescent; branches straggling, flexible, 4-angled, elongate, occasionally glabrous. Leaves to 8×4cm, lanceolate to ovate or cordate, glabrous to rough and pubescent, prickly, 5–7-veined; petioles to 3cm+, pubescent, prickly. Flowers pedicellate, in loose, trichotomous, pedunculate cymes to 3cm or more, cream to yellow or green; pedicels 5mm; calyx 1mm; corolla tube 1mm, lobes ovate or lanceolate to triangular, to 1mm. Fruit to 8mm wide, glabrous, lustrous, black. Europe and Africa (Greece to S Africa), Asia (Siberia, south to India, Indonesia, east to China, Japan). Z6.

R.longipetiolata Bullock. See *R.cordifolia*.

R.peregrina L. WILD MADDER; LEVANT MADDER.
Perennial, evergreen herb. Stem climbing, scrambling, or creeping, to 120cm, lower part woody, persistent, terete, glabrous, upper parts 4-angled, rough, with retrorse prickles.

Leaves to 6×2cm, sessile, linear, lanceolate, elliptic, or ovate, stiffly leathery, lustrous green above, nerves rough and prickly beneath, prickly or toothed and cartilaginous at margin. Flowers, light yellow-green, many in terminal and axillary, cymose panicles, to 10cm; corolla to 6mm wide, lobes to 3mm, acuminate; anthers round to ovate. Fruit to 6mm wide, lustrous black. W & S Europe, N Africa, Middle East. Z7.

R.tinctoria L. MADDER.
Perennial herb. Stem climbing or scrambling, to 1m, woody at base, rough and prickly or hairy; rhizome red. Leaves to 10 × 3cm, subsessile, 4–6-whorled, lanceolate to ovate or oblong, somewhat leathery, rough and prickly or toothed on nerves beneath and at margin, veins obscure above, prominent, pinnate and reticulate beneath; petioles to 3mm. Flowers in loose, much-branched, leafy, thyrsoid cymes to 30cm, pale yellow-green to honey-coloured; calyx tube globose; corolla rotate to bell-shaped, to 3×5mm, lobes lanceolate to ovate; anthers linear-oblong. Fruit globose, to 6mm wide, fleshy, red-brown to black. E Mediterranean to C Asia. Z6.

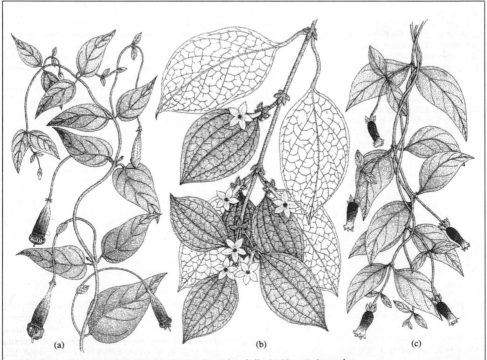

Rubiaceae (a) *Manettia cordifolia* (b) *Mussaenda erythrophylla* (c) *Manettia luteorubra*

Rubus L. (Lat. name for this plant.) Rosaceae. Perhaps 250 species of erect, scrambling, trailing or prostrate shrubs, often with prickles on the stems, petioles and petiolules and inflorescences. Leaves entire, lobed or divided into 3 to many leaflets which are usually toothed and may themselves be lobed; stipules always present, often conspicuous, sometimes falling early. Flowers in clusters, racemes or panicles, sometimes solitary, usually bisexual; sepals 4–5 or rarely more, spreading, erect or reflexed; petals 4–5 or rarely more (occasionally absent), very variable in size, white, pink, red or purple, spreading or erect and adpressed to the stamens; stamens numerous, anthers sometimes hairy; sepals, petals and stamens borne on the edge of a narrow perigynous disc; carpels 5 to many, free, borne on a usually cylindric or conical receptacle. Fruit a 'berry' composed of 5 to many variably coherent fleshy drupelets, which may separate from the receptacle as a (hollow) unit, or may fall from the plant by abscission of the flower-stalk while still attached to the receptacle. Most parts of the temperate world and mountains in the tropics. In most of the species the stems (canes) are biennial, bearing leaves during their first year and shoots bearing leaves and infloresences arising from the axils of the first-year leaves in the second. The leaves of the first and second year may differ considerably in shape and the degree of division and/or lobing. In some plants, shoots borne low down on the second-year stems do not flower, but grow rapidly and mimic first-year shoots; the leaves on these shoots are often aberrant.

CULTIVATION   A large and diverse genus containing many scramblers and climbers, usually attaching and advancing themselves by means of prickly stems and leaf stalks. The Brambles, loosely grouped as microspecies within the aggregate *R.fruticosus*, are vigorous ramblers grown for their fruit, their foliage (*R.laciniatus*, deeply cut; *R.ulmifolius* 'Variegatus', variegated) and flowers (*R.linkianus*; *R.ulmifolius* 'Bellidiflorus'). These hardy shrubs will grow in most situations and soils, either trained on walls or allowed to ramble through trees and shrubs. Their stems should be treated as canes, trained and tied-in through their first season, branching, flowering and fruiting in the second, cut out at the base in their third. All of these species are robust and potentially invasive.

The New Zealand brambles (*R.australis*, *R.cissoides*, *R.squarrosus*) are altogether more tender. They require moist, open soils rich in organic matter and sunny but sheltered positions. These are plants with slender, glossy and densely prickly stems, rather fine foliage and long panicles of small white flowers. The fruits, in tones of orange, pink and red, are also attractive, but tend only to be produced by long-established plants in very favoured sites – a prospect made all the less likely by the persistence of juvenile states in these species and their unisexual flowers. *R.squarrosus* is perhaps the most successful in cool temperate cultivation and the most visually exciting – a low-growing, barbed wire-like tangle of dark glossy stems picked out with pale thorns. Its leaves (at least in the juvenile state) are usually reduced to whip-like petiolules set strongly at angles to one another and tipped with tatters of leaf blade. As one might expect, it harmonizes well with other New Zealand natives such as *Corokia* and *Muehlenbeckia* and in winter looks particularly striking grown as a loose ground cover broken by the strong fountain-like forms of bronze sedges like *Carex buchananii*.

Other *Rubus* species deserving special mention include *R.flagelliflorus*, a graceful evergreen with slender white-felted stems and the narrow-leaved and elegant *R.henryi* var. *bambusarum*. These Chinese natives require a sheltered, rather shady situation and moist, humus-rich soils.

Increase by detaching rooted suckers just before leaf fall or in spring; also by simple layering and by cuttings (semi-ripe for evergreen species, softwood or hardwood for deciduous species) in a closed case with bottom heat.

R.australis Forst.
Evergreen climber (creeping when juvenile); stems long, wiry, prickly. Leaves variable in shape and size, 3–5-foliolate. Flowers small, white in long panicles. New Zealand. Z8. This name is sometimes misapplied to *R.cissoides*. Plants labelled *R.cissoides* may, at the same time, represent the juvenile stage of *R.australis*.

R.australis var. *cissoides* (A.Cunn.) Hook. See *R.cissoides*.
R.bambusarum Focke. See *R.henryi* var.*bambusarum*.

R.chroosepalus Focke.
Semi-evergreen straggling shrub. Stems terete, slender, glabrous, with short, recurved prickles. Leaves simple, to 18 × 10cm, base cordate, apex long-acuminate, very finely and sharply serrate, often shallowly lobed, glabrous, with a few prickles. Flowers to 1.2cm diam., in terminal panicles to 23cm; calyx woolly, purple inside; petals absent. Fruit small, black. C China. Z6.

R.cissoides A.Cunn. (*R.australis* var. *cissoides* (A.Cunn.) Hook.). BUSH LAWYER.
Scandent, evergreen, dioecious shrub. Stems stout, prickles usually absent; branches with reddish prickles. Leaves 3–5-foliolate; leaflets variable, to 15 × 2cm, linear-lanceolate to ovate-lanceolate, slightly cordate, truncate or oblique at the base, glabrous and shiny above, toothed, petioles and petiolules with recurved prickles. Flowers white, to 1.2cm diam., unisexual, in often much-branched panicles to 60cm. Fruit

small, red-orange. New Zealand. Some material cultivated under this name may well belong to the juvenile phase of the true *R.australis* Forst. Z8.

R.clemens Focke. See *R.setchuenensis*.

R.ellipticus Sm.
Strongly-growing, scrambling evergreen shrub to 4.5m, with a narrow, upright habit. Stems densely red- or brown-pubescent, with bristles and short soft hairs as well as stout prickles. All leaves 3-foliolate; leaflets broadly elliptic, rounded at the apex, regularly serrate, grey-tomentose beneath, midrib prickly. Flowers white, small, in few-flowered panicles. Fruit yellow. Himalaya, SW China. Z8.

R.flagelliflorus Focke.
Scrambling or procumbent evergreen shrub to 2m.Stems slender, white-tomentose when young, with minute, recurved prickles. Leaves simple, to 18 × 12cm, broadly ovate, longer than broad, apex acuminate, cordate at base, not or very shallowly lobed, finely and sharply serrate, adpressed-pubescent above, thickly yellow-tomentose beneath; petioles to 5cm, somewhat prickly. Flowers white, in short axillary clusters; sepals purple inside; petals falling early. Fruit to 1.25cm in diam., shining, black. Summer. C & W China. Z7.

R.fruticosus agg. L. BRAMBLE; BLACKBERRY.
A. group name applied as an aggregate to all the species of Subgenus *Rubus* collectively. Those treated here are *Rr.hispidus, laciniatus, linkianus, mirus, trivialis, ulmifolius*. Z6.

R. henryi Hemsl. & Kuntze.
Scrambling evergreen shrub to 6m. Stems slender, with a few reflexed prickles, tomentose-floccose when young. Leaves trilobed, to 15cm, glabrous above, closely white-tomentose beneath, lobes to 2.5cm, narrow, long-acuminate, finely serrate; petiole to 4cm. Flowers pink, to 2cm diam., in 6–10-flowered, terminal and axillary, glandular racemes to 7.5cm; petals acuminate, glandular-pubescent. Fruit 0.65cm diam., shiny, black. C & W China, var. *bambusarum* (Focke) Rehd. (*R.bambusarum* Focke). Branchlets with more, small, hooked prickles; leaves deeply 3-lobed, leaflets narrowly lanceolate, to 12.5×2cm, petioles to 3mm. C China (Hubei). Z7.

R.hispidus L. SWAMP DEWBERRY; RUNNING BLACKBERRY; SWAMP BLACKBERRY.
Semi-evergreen shrub to 1.5m. Stems mostly prostrate, slender, wiry, with minute recurved prickles, bristly. Leaves trifoliolate; leaflets obovate, to 4.5 × 2cm, tapering to the base, sharply and coarsely serrate near the apex, glabrous or subglabrous. Flowers white, to 3cm in diam., in finely pubescent few-flowered corymbs to 30cm; petals obovate, to 8mm. Fruit to 12mm, red, later almost black. Summer. Eastern N America. Z3.

R.hupehensis Oliv. (*R.swinhoei* Hance).
Prostrate or scrambling evergreen shrub, stems terete, thin, dark, woolly when young, with few minute prickles. Leaves simple, to 11.5 × 4cm, oblong-lanceolate, long-acuminate, rounded at base, finely serrate, smooth but with minute setae on the veins above, closely grey-tomentose beneath; petiole to 12mm. Flowers in usually 3–7-flowered, short, terminal, glandular-pubescent racemes; calyx grey-tomentose; petals caducous. Fruit red at first, later purple-black. C China. Z6.

R.laciniatus Willd. (*R.fruticosus* var. *laciniatus* (Willd.) Weston.) CUT-LEAVED BRAMBLE; CUT-LEAF BLACKBERRY; FERN-LEAVED BRAMBLE, PARSLEY-LEAVED BRAMBLE.
Scrambling, deciduous shrub. Stems robust, angled, pubescent with stout, recurved prickles. Leaves 3-5-foliolate; petiole to 7.5cm, with hooked prickles; leaflets divided into pairs of laciniate segments, almost glabrous or pubescent beneath. Flowers pink-white, in large terminal panicles; pedicels prickly, pubescent; sepals to 2cm, narrow, tailed, reflexed, woolly, prickly at the base; petals toothed at apex. Fruit to 2cm, black. Origin unknown. 'Elegans': leaves small, upper leaf surface hairy; flowers and fruit rare. Z5.

R.lambertianus Ser.
Semi-evergreen scandent shrub. Stems angled with few recurved prickles, tomentulose or subglabrous when young; flowering stems glabrous. Leaves to 12cm, ovate or oblong-ovate, cordate at base, crenate-dentate and somewhat lobed or 3-lobed, pilose above, more densely so beneath; petioles to 4cm. Flowers white, to 0.8cm diam., in panicles to 14cm long; sepals ovate-lanceolate, somewhat hairy or glabrous, not glandular. Fruit small, red. Summer. C.China. Z6.

R.lineatus Bl.
Rambling deciduous or semi-evergreen shrub to 3m. Stems woolly, with few minute prickles. Leaves 3–5-foliolate, those on the flowering shoots with 3 leaflets, the terminal not deeply 3-lobed; petioles to 7.5cm, woolly, leaflets to 23 × 6cm, oblanceolate to oblong, shortly acuminate, tapered at base, sharply toothed with triangular teeth, dark green above, glossy, silvery sericeous-woolly beneath, with 30–50 pairs of conspicuous parallel lateral veins. Flowers white, in short axillary clusters; sepals woolly. Fruit small, red or yellow. Himalaya, SW China to Malaysia, Indonesia (Java). Z8.

R.linkianus Ser. (*R.thyrsoideus* Wimm.).
Stems scrambling, robust, grooved, glabrous or almost so, with few reflexed prickles. Leaves 5-foliolate; leaflets elliptic, the lowermost sessile, the other stalked with prickly petiolules, ovate or broadly ovate, acute or shortly acuminate, rounded or subcordate at the base, coarsely serrate, glabrous above, white-tomentose beneath. Flowers white or pink, always double, to 2.5cm diam., in villous, prickly panicles to

18cm; sepals ovate, acuminate, tomentose outside. Origin unknown. Z6.

R.malifolius Focke.
Deciduous shrub to 3m. Stems prostrate or scrambling, with few, short, recurved prickles, glabrous. Leaves simple, ovate, to 12 × 5cm, rounded at base, abruptly pointed at the apex, serrate with broad teeth, glabrous above, woolly on the veins beneath; petiole to 1.6cm. Flowers white, to 2.5 diam., in eglandular terminal racemes to 10cm; sepals ovate, woolly; petals rounded, overlapping; anthers hairy. Fruit black. Summer.W China. Z6.

R.mirus L.H. Bail. MARVEL DEWBERRY.
Arching or scrambling shrub. Stems with stout prickles. Leaves 3–5 foliolate, glabrous; leaflets ovate or elliptic, to 6cm, shortly acuminate, broad or subcordate at the base, finely and closely serrate. Flowers white, to 3cm in diam., in 3–4-flowered racemes; pedicels to 7cm, pubescent, prickly; sepals to 7mm, acute, pubescent. Fruit oblong, 2.5cm or more, black. US (Florida). Z8.

R.moluccanus hort. non L. See *R.reflexus*.
R.omeiensis Rolfe. See *R.setchuenensis*.

R.parkeri Hance.
Scrambling deciduous shrub. Stems terete, thin, with few short recurved prickles, thickly grey glandular-pubescent. Leaves to 18 × 9cm, broadly lanceolate, base cordate, apex acuminate, shallowly and sinuously lobed and sharply and finely serrate, bristly on veins above, reddish woolly beneath; petiole to 2.5cm, pubescent, prickly. Flowers to 0.8cm diam., white in elongate, densely villous and glandular-bristly open panicles; calyx densely glandular-pubescent with red-tinged glands. Fruit small, black with few drupelets. Summer. China. Z6.

R.reflexus Ker-Gawl. (*R.moluccanus* hort. non L.).
Scrambling deciduous shrub. Stems with very dense, close brown hairs and sparse, minute prickles. Leaves simple, rather deeply 3–5 lobed, the lobes triangular or narrowly triangular, acute, finely to coarsely serrate, brown-hairy along the veins above, densely brown-hairy beneath; stipules large and persistent, divided into narrow, hairy lobes. Flowers to 1.5cm diam., almost stalkless in axillary clusters; sepals ovate, densely hairy outside and inside; petals about as long as sepals. Fruit spherical, purple-black. Summer. S. China. The true *R.moluccanus* of Linnaeus is an Indonesian species which is not cultivated. Z8.

R.setchuenensis Bur. & Franch. (*R.clemens* Focke; *R.omeiensis* Rolfe).
Large, straggling, deciduous shrub. Stems terete, shortly stellate-pubescent, without prickles. Leaves 5- or obscurely 7-lobed, to 18 × 8cm, cordate at base, irregularly serrate, stellate-hairy above, more densely so beneath; petiole to 7.5cm; stipules to 2cm, divided into narrow segments. Flowers purple, to 1.2cm diam., in many-flowered, terminal panicles; pedicels woolly; calyx woolly, sepals triangular, acute. Fruit black. Summer. W China. Z5.

R.squarrosus Fritsch.
Sprawling to climbing evergreen shrub, usually tinted dark purple-red throughout. Branchlets wiry, slender, with numerous, small, yellow prickles. Leaves with 3–5 lanceolate to oblong-lanceolate leaflets whose blades are very often reduced or entirely absent, leaving wiry and prickly whip-like petiolules, if present, they are irregularly serrate or lobed. Flowers unisexual, yellow-white, to 0.8cm diam., in panicles to 15cm long; calyx tomentose. Fruit orange-red. New Zealand. Z8.

R.swinhoei Hance. See *R.hupehensis*.
R.thyrsoideus Wimm. See *R.linkianus*.

R.trivialis Michx. SOUTHERN DEWBERRY.
Scrambling shrub to 1m or more. Stems ascending, soon becoming prostrate and woody, branched, prickly, bristly and glandular-pubescent. Leaves 3–5-foliolate, glabrous, those of

the first-year (non-flowering) shoots often leathery and persistent; petioles stout, prickly, often glandular-pubescent; leaflets narrowly elliptic to narrowly ovate, to 7 × 3.5cm,acute, acuminate or obtuse, narrowed at base, sharply serrate or toothed, glabrous. Flowers white to pink, to 3cm diam., solitary; calyx reflexed, glandular or glabrous; petals broad, overlapping, obtuse. Fruit oblong, to 3cm, black. N.America. Z6.

R.ulmifolius Schott. BRAMBLE.
Stems robust, arching to scrambling, conspicuously bloomed, with broadly-based, straight or hooked prickles. Leaves divided into 3 or 5 leaflets, densely white-hairy beneath. Inflorescence raceme-like. Sepals deflexed. Petals pink or white, crumpled. W & C Europe. 'Bellidiflorus': flowers double, usually pink. 'Variegatus': leaves variegated. Z7.

Salpichroa Miers. (From Gk *salpinx*, trumpet, and *chroa*, colour, referring to the appearance of the flowers.) Solanaceae. 17 species of herbs, sometimes scrambling. Stems glabrous or pubescent. Leaves alternate to subopposite, entire, base attenuate, long-petiolate. Flowers solitary or paired in axils; calyx pentamerous, barely accrescent; corolla tubular to urceolate, lobes 5, acute, erect to spreading or recurved; stamens 5, protruding, attached above middle of tube; ovary 2-chambered, stigma capitate. Fruit ovoid to oblong, 2-chambered; seeds disc-shaped. SW US, temperate S America. Z9.

CULTIVATION *Salpichroa* species frequently occur as epiphytes and vining plants in nature, sometimes as prostate specimens on stony soils. *S.origanifolia* is grown for its white flowers and ornamental, 'egg-like' fruit; it also has strongly aromatic foliage and is attractive to bees. In cool, temperate zones, it may be grown as an annual, since it makes rapid growth and flowers from seed in the first year. In warmer regions and in cool glasshouses and conservatories, it is useful for clothing walls, trellising or other supports. Cultivation otherwise as for the tender *Solanum* species.

S.glandulosa Hook.
To 60cm. Stems densely branched. Leaves to 2.5cm, paired, cordate to ovate, glandular-pubescent. Flowers yellow; pedicels filiform; corolla to 3cm, throat to 1.3cm diam. Summer. Chile.

S.origanifolia (Lam.) Baill. (*S.rhomboidea* (Gillies & Hook.) Miers). COCK'S EGGS; PAMPAS LILY OF THE VALLEY.
Aromatic annual or perennial. Root fleshy, stem slender, pubescent, woody at base. Leaves to 1.5 × 1cm, near opposite, rhomboid-ovoid, glabrous to subglabrous, ciliate, base obtuse, attenuate. Flowers solitary or paired, white; pedicel slender, pendulous to 3cm; disc annular, fleshy; calyx campanulate, to 4mm, lobes subulate; corolla to 1cm, lobes triangular, to 2mm. Fruit to 2 × 1cm, ovoid, white or yellow. Argentina.

S.rhomboidea (Gillies & Hook.) Miers. See *S.origanifolia*.

Sandersonia Hook. (For John Sanderson (1820 or 1821–81), honorary secretary of the Horticultural Society of Natal and discoverer of this plant.) Liliaceae (Colchicaceae). 1 species, a perennial herb with tuberous roots. Stems to 75cm, erect or weakly climbing. Leaves to 10cm, sessile, cauline, alternate, often tendril-tipped. Flowers solitary in axils of upper leaves; pedicels 2–3cm, decurved; perianth 2–2.5cm, rounded-campanulate to urceolate, orange, lobes 6, fused except at outward-curving tips, with 6 short nectariferous spurs at base; stamens to 0.8cm, at base of lobes; ovary superior; style trifid. Fruit a capsule. Summer. S Africa (E Cape). Z9.

CULTIVATION A beautiful, erect or loosely twining lily with bright orange bell-like flowers; its cultural requirements are much like those of *Littonia*.

S.aurantiaca Hook. CHINESE LANTERN LILY; CHRISTMAS BELLS.

Sarcostemma R. Br. (From Greek *sarx*, flesh, and *stemma*, crown; the corona is fleshy.) Asclepiadaceae. 10 species of succulent subshrubs; stems jointed, green, usually leafless or with leaves reduced to scales. Flowers in shortly pedunculate umbels or clusters, small, white to pink; corolla usually rotate with projecting lobes; corona double. Tropical & subtropical Africa, Madagascar, India, Malaysia, Australia. Z10.

CULTIVATION As for *Ceropegia*.

S.brunonianum Wight & Arn.
Twining to prostrate shrub, branching dichotomous, internodes 5–6cm, cylindrical, green. Flowers 8–12 in umbels, white. Peninsular India.

S. madagascariense Descoings.
Liana-like, sap milky. Flowers in groups of 2–3, terminal or along the shoots; corolla fleshy. Madagascar.

S.socotranum Lavranos.
Small, shrubby, succulent perennial; stems to 150 × 0.2–0.5cm, minutely pubescent at first, becoming woody with age, trailing or pendulous, nodes much constricted, internodes 2–5cm. Flowers 2–8 per umbel on stout peduncles at the nodes; corolla 7.5mm diam., campanulate, tinted green; corona white. Socotra.

S.tetrapterum Turcz. See *Cyanchum aphyllum*.

Sargentodoxa Rehd. & Wils. (For Charles Sprague Sargent (1841–1927), American dendrologist and first Director of the Arnold Arboretum of Harvard University, and Gk *doxe*, glory, distinction.) Sargentodoxaceae. 1 species, a climbing deciduous shrub to 7m. Leaves alternate, long-petiolate, 3-foliolate, leaflets unequal, median leaflet to 12cm, rhombic-ovate, cuneate at base, with petiolule to 1cm, lateral leaflets semi-ovate, oblique at base, palmately 2–3-veined, subsessile, all short-acuminate at apex, dark glossy green above, pale green beneath. Inflorescence a pendulous raceme to 15cm; flowers to 1.2cm, functionally unisexual, very fragrant; pedicels slender, with 2 bracteoles; sepals in 2 whorls of 3, petaloid, green-yellow; corolla lobes 6, reduced to small, scale-like nectaries; in male plants stamens 6, opposite corolla lobes, vestigial ovary present; in female plants carpels numerous, superior, spirally arranged on enlarged receptacle, ovules solitary, 6 staminodes present. Berries to 0.8cm, stalked, dark blue, in an umbel or head-like arrangement on fleshy receptacle; seed solitary, black. Late spring. China, Laos, Vietnam. Z9.

CULTIVATION Suitable for clothing trellis and fencing in zones that are frost-free or almost so; in mild temperate gardens, *Sargentodoxa* may also be grown against a sunny wall, which will give several degrees of frost protection. This unusual vine is grown for its attractive dark green foliage and showy fruit. It enjoys the distinction of being the sole species of the only genus in the family Sargentodoxaceae, which commemorates the great Harvard dendrologist C.S. Sargent. This family was split from the Lardizabalaceae on the basis of its spirally arranged carpels each with one ovule. In many other respects, it closely resembles the members of that family and its culture and uses are much as for *Holboellia* and *Lardizabala*. Grow in a fertile, freely draining but moisture-retentive soil in full sun or part-day shade. Propagate by seed or stem cuttings.

S.cuneata Rehd. & Wils.

Saritaea Dugand. (Dedicated by Armando Dugand (1906–1971) to his wife, because of its beauty and floriferousness.) Bignoniaceae. 1 species, a liane. Branches subterete, striate, without glandular patches between nodes; pseudostipules leafy, 0.6–4.2×0.4–2cm. Leaves 2-foliate, often with a simple tendril or scar; leaflets 5.2–6.4cm, obovate, obtuse, base cuneate or decurrent, papery, lepidote above and beneath, glandular between nerves beneath; petiole 1.7–2.8cm, lepidote; petiolules 1.3–1.6cm, lepidote. Flowers in terminal or axillary paniculate cymes; calyx 7.8×6.7mm, cupular, truncate, lepidote; corolla red-purple, white in throat inside with purple-red nectaries, tubular-campanulate, 7.9–9.1×1.6–2cm at mouth, tube 5.6–6.3cm, lobes 2.2–3.1cm, glabrous outside, pubescent inside at stamen bases; stamens didynamous; anthers glabrous; ovary cylindrical, lepidote, ovules 2-seriate; disc small, cupular-pulvinate, 1×2mm. Fruit a linear, flattened capsule, valves parallel; seeds 2-winged. Colombia and Ecuador.

CULTIVATION *S.magnifica* is grown for its large, showy, pale purple to rose-pink flowers, streaked with darker shades at the throat, and carried in flushes throughout the year. Grow in bright filtered light in a well drained but moisture-retentive medium, with additional organic matter. Provide a minimum temperature of about 10–15°C/50–60°F with a buoyant atmosphere, watering moderately to keep evenly moist. Propagate by semi-ripe or greenwood cuttings of strong side shoots with 2–3 nodes, root in a closed case with bottom heat at 21–24°C/70–75°F. Sow seed in spring.

S.magnifica (Sprague ex Steenis) Dugand *Arrabidaea magnifica* Sprague ex Steenis). PALO NEGRO.

Schefflera Forst. & Forst. f. (For J.G. Scheffler (1722–1811), physician in Danzig and an acquaintance of the Forsters.) IVY TREE; UMBRELLA TREE. Araliaceae. Over 700 species of unarmed glabrous or pubescent trees, shrubs, subshrubs or vines, very often epiphytic, occasionally also strangling host trees and becoming self-supporting. Leaves usually palmately compound, petiolate, base more or less forming a sheath around the twig and commonly developing 2 stipules, these generally fused into a ligule sometimes up to 10cm; leaflets 3-20 but in a few species reduced to 1 or further subdivided, developing in a single plane or occasionally fascicled, usually stalked; juvenile leaves sometimes differing markedly from adults. Inflorescences compound, paniculate or umbellate, usually leafless, terminal or becoming falsely lateral but never on short shoots, generally solitary on any one twig; flowers in small umbels, heads, racemes or spikes; calyx rim sometimes conspicuous, lobed, toothed, wavy or uniform; petals 4–5 or more, valvate or more or less fused into a cap; stamens as many as the petals or more numerous (up to 500); ovary 2–30-locular (sometimes to 75 locular), the styles free or variously united or entirely reduced. Fruit drupaceous, elongate, round or more or less compressed, inferior or up to half or more superior at maturity; pyrenes smooth; seeds generally with uniform endosperm. Warmer regions of the world, with the greatest numbers of species in the Americas (over 200) and from S & E Asia to the Pacific (500 or more); poorly represented in Africa and with only three species, none endemic, in Australia. Absent from the Mascarene and Hawaiian Is. Z10.

CULTIVATION A large genus of evergreen tropical and subtropical shrubs and trees grown for their attractive, palmately divided leaves. Among the most popular members of the genus are the bold Octopus Tree, *S.actinophylla*, and the fine, dark-leaved *S.elegantissima* (*Dizygotheca elegantissima*), both found in homes, offices and public buildings throughout the world. The species listed here are fast gaining in popularity, especially in their smaller and variegated forms. They are lianes and stranglers for the most part, but are usually treated as free-standing tree or shrub specimens. Young leads of *S.pueckleri* and *S.elliptica* are, however, commonly offered as houseplants, trained on moss poles. Pot in an open, soilless, bark-based mix or treat hydroponically. Maintain minimum winter temperatures between 13–20°C/55–68°F. Give strong, filtered light throughout the year and maintain medium to high humidity by syringing 2–3 times daily in hot weather and (if grown as a houseplant) standing the pot on a tray of moist pebbles. Water moderately, allowing the medium to become slightly dry between times. Avoid direct summer sun, draughts and winter cold spots. Feed monthly during the growing season with a dilute liquid fertilizer. Healthy plants will respond well to hard pruning. Increase by air-layering, sectional stem cuttings and softwood cuttings rooted with 18–21°C/65–70°F bottom heat in spring and summer. Susceptible to infestation by scale insect, whitefly, red spider mite and mealybug.

S.arboricola (Hayata) Hayata.
Glabrous epiphytic shrub or liane, eventually spreading through tree crowns; in cultivation usually grown as a shrub. Leaves with a small stipular ligule; leaflets 7–11, in adults obovate, entire, to 11×4.5cm, stalked, bright green and semiglossy above, apex more or less obtuse, the tip shortly acuminate, lateral veins not numerous, ascending and arching near margin; leaflets in intermediate plants somewhat smaller, narrower, the apex acute; juvenile leaves with short, widely spaced teeth. Inflorescence terminal, paniculate, 2× compound; flowers in small, stalked umbels, racemosely arranged along the primary branches. Fruit ovoid, about 5mm, orange, finally black. Taiwan. Several cultivars formally recognized (e.g. 'Compacta', 'Gold Capella', 'Jacqueline', 'Trinetta'), based on leaflet shape, serration, division and variegation. The narrowly elliptic leaflets of the intermediate stage have been seen in some cultivated plants to persist, though increasing in size. A related species is *S.leucantha* R. Vig. *(S.kwangsiensis* Merrill ex Li) of southern China and Vietnam, with small, rather narrowly elliptic leaflets, widely grown in SE Asia for medicinal purposes and as an ornamental.

S.digitata hort., non Forst. f.& Forst. See *S.venulosa*.

S.elliptica (Bl.) Harms *(S.odorata* (Blanco) Merrill & Rolfe). GALAMAI-AMO.
Glabrous, freely branching liane to 10m or more, ultimately forming large masses; stems comparatively slender, light brown, becoming somewhat cane-like when not finding early support. Leaflets (4)5–7 to 17.5×10cm, elliptic to broadly elliptic or ovate, entire, glossy green above; apex obtuse, the tip shortly acuminate, lateral veins few (leaflets in young plants may be thicker and more obovate); petiole to 15cm. Inflorescence terminal, paniculate, 2× compound to 15cm or more, appearing conical; main axis elongate, primary branches spreading, clustering towards the bottom of the axis; flowers very small, green, in umbels; ovary 5–7-locular, the stigmata sessile on a rising disk, slightly spaced apart from one another. Fruit round, 4–5mm diam., yellow to orange, before ripening black, in numerous sprays in large plants. SE Asia through Malesia to Taiwan, Palau, Philippines, New Britain and NE Australia.

S.odorata (Blanco) Merrill & Rolfe. See *S.elliptica*.

S.pubigera (Brongn. ex Planch.) Frodin *(S.stelzneriana* hort. ex Guillaum.; *S.venulosa* auct., non (Wight & Arn.) Harms; *S.venulosa* var *erythostachys* (Hook.f.) A.Berger).
Large, diffusely branching shrub to 7m, eventually scandent or spreading and sometimes forming massive growths by rooting of lower branches. Young branches and petioles red-purple, glabrous. Leaves 7–9-foliolate, petiole to 20cm; leaflets elliptic to oblong-ovate, glabrous, to 17.5×8cm, stalked, apex acute to obtuse, the tip acuminate to subcaudate, somewhat recurved, base cuneate to rounded, main veins 6-8, ascending, rich green, distinctly reticulated. Inflorescence terminal, paniculate, 2× compound; axes more or less red-purple, puberulous to glabrous, the main axis short to slightly elongate, the primary branches about 10, to 15cm; flowers to 5mm in small, racemosely arranged, pedunculate, head-like umbels; petals 4–5, deep red, cohering into a cap; filiments white, anther cream; ovary 4–5-locular, shallow, the disc pale green, the stigmata sessile, obscure. Winter. Asia (E Himalaya and Naga Hills to SW Yunnan). Only male plants in cultivation.

S.pueckleri (K. Koch) Frodin.
Erect, glabrescent, ultimately short-boled, many-branched and spreading tree to 18×0.6m or scandent and high-climbing but lacking aerial roots; young parts brown-floccose. Leaves in large rosettes, 5–10-foliolate, the stipular ligules small; petioles to 45cm; leaflets narrowly oblong, to 25 × 8cm, resembling *S.actinophylla* but upper surface deeper green and glossier and lateral veins very numerous, closely spaced and spreading, yellow-green beneath, margins always entire. Inflorescence pseudolateral, paniculate, somewhat umbelliform, 2× compound, relatively few-flowered, maturing slowly with up to 5 at once on a single branch; primary branches or rays about 3, extending to 10cm or so from a very short main axis and with large basal bracts; umbels 3–7 per branch, stalked, 3–5 flowered, at branch ends and sometimes also in 1(-2) pairs along them; flowers green, 1.5cm or more diam., mallet-like in bud; corolla forming a cap; stamens to 90 or more; ovary to at least 75-locular, the inferior portion corky, the stigmata sessile in a dog-biscuit pattern on the elevated, concave disc. Fruit to 3.5cm diam., laterally ovoid, one-third or more superior, green when unripe. Winter. S & SE Asia.

S.rotundifolia (Ten.) Frodin.
Related to *S.roxburghii*. Leaflets 5–7, nearly round, on stalks to 5cm. Flowers yellow. Plants most nearly approximating to this have been collected in elevated areas of southern India, particularly in Tamil Nadu, and usually determined as *S.stellata* (Gaertn.) Harms; a species properly limited to Sri Lanka.

S.roxburghii Gamble.
Diffusely branching shrub, eventually scandent or spreading by rooting of branches. Young branches and petioles green, glabrous. Leaves in terminal rosettes, 5-7 foliolate, the petiole to 15cm or so; leaflets narrowly ovate to shortly oblong to oblong-elliptic, glabrous, somewhat smaller than in *S.pubigera*, on stalks to 2.5cm, apex obtuse, the tip acuminate, base obtuse to rounded, main veins few, more or less spreading, surface not markedly reticulate. Inflorescence terminal, paniculate, 2× compound, somewhat open, the axes green, main axis somewhat elongate, the primary branches spreading, to 20cm or more; flowers to 3mm in small, racemosely arranged pedunculate umbels; petals 5, yellow, somewhat cohering in a cap; stamens cream; ovary 5-locular, shallow, disc off-white, stigmata sessile, obscure. Fruit round, 5mm diam., yellow later orange, finally black, remaining almost wholly inferior. Summer. N India.

S.stelzneriana hort. Calif. See *S.venulosa*.
S.stelzneriana hort. ex Guillaum. See *S.pubigera*.

S.venulosa (Wight & Arn.) Harms *(S.digitata* hort., non Forst. f.& Forst.; *S.stelzneriana* hort. Calif.).
See also *Ss. pubigera, roxburghii*. Plants grown in Hawaii and N America (California and Florida) under this name, or as *S.digitata* or *S.stelzneriana*, cannot, however, be referred to either. They are distinguished by obovate or oblong-obovate leaflets, slender inflorescence with small green-white flowers, and a partly superior ovary topped by 5 distinct, sessile stigmata. Only male plants known in cultivation.

S.venulosa auct., non (Wight & Arn.) Harms. See *S.pubigera* and *S.roxburghii*.
S.venulosa var *erythostachys* (Hook.f.) A.Berger. See *S.pubigera*.

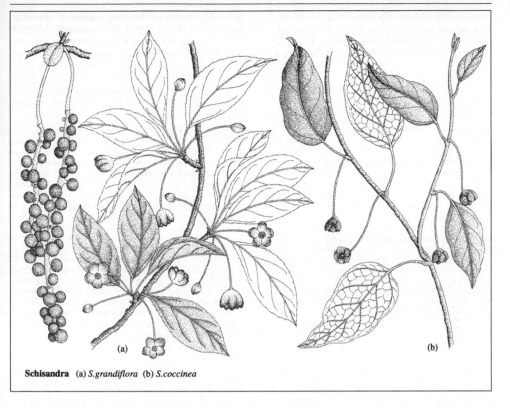

Schisandra   (a) *S.grandiflora*   (b) *S.coccinea*

Schisandra Michx. (*Schizandra* auct.). (From Gk *schizo*, to split, and *aner*, man, referring to the well separated anther cells.) Schisandraceae. 25 species of monoecious or dioecious, deciduous or evergreen climbing shrubs. Stems twining. Leaves alternate, entire or remotely dentate, mostly oblong-lanceolate, cuneate at base, tapering to a slender petiole. Flowers solitary or in axillary clusters; perianth cupped, sepals and petals indistinguishable, 5–12; stamens 5–15. Fruit a number of brightly coloured berry-like carpels, borne on an axis which elongates with ripening to a slender, pendulous spike. E Asia, Eastern N America.

CULTIVATION   Vining shrubs grown for their showy, fragrant if short-lived flowers, and drooping spikes of red or black fruits. They occur naturally as twining climbers of rich forest and woodland and are suitable for growing outdoors in subtropical, warm-temperate and sheltered cool-temperate gardens: the most frost-hardy is the eastern Asian *S.chinensis*, which will tolerate temperatures of –17°C/1°F. Others, such as *S.sphenanthera* and *S.propinqua*, are suitable for cultivation in the cool to intermediate glasshouse in colder areas; where temperatures do not drop much below –7°C/20°F they will thrive if given the protection of a south- or west-facing wall. Plant in spring in any fertile, well drained but moisture-retentive loam with some protection from the most intense sunlight: slightly acid soils are preferred but with the incorporation of plenty of humus-rich material at planting, some alkalinity is tolerated. Topdress annually with organic material and water plentifully during dry periods, particularly wall-grown specimens. In the open, they may be allowed to scramble over rocks, walls or tree stumps, but in the absence of a natural support, trellis or other framework is essential. Prune in late winter or spring to remove dead wood and to train or limit to the allocated space.

Propagate from seed (produced only when both sexes are cultivated) sown in cold frames in the autumn or by semi-ripe cuttings in summer, inserted singly into small pots and given bottom heat of 15–18°C/60–65°F or placed under mist. Grow on in a lime-free loam-based medium. Overwinter in cold frames before planting out direct from pots to minimize root damage. Alternatively, propagate by layering long shoots during the autumn, severing plants from parent material the following year. Susceptible to attack by aphid.

S.chinensis (Turcz.) Baill.
Leaves 5–14×3–10cm, elliptic to obovate, apex acute, base narrow, cuneate, denticulate or serrulate, glossy deep green, glabrous except for young veins. Flowers to 1.25cm diam., pale rose to bright pink, fragrant, borne on pendulous pedicels to 2.5cm; tepals to 9; stamens 4–6, filaments united to near apex forming a column. Fruiting spike to 10cm, crowded with scarlet berries. China. Z4.

S.coccinea Michx. (*S.glabra* (Brickell) Rehd.). BAY STAR VINE; WILD SARSPARILLA.
Leaves 5–14cm, ovate to elliptic, somewhat fleshy, ultimately glabrous, entire or remotely and obscurely waxy-toothed. Flowers to 1cm diam., crimson, borne on slender pedicels to 5cm; tepals 9–12; stamens 5, united to form a disc 4mm diam.; pistils 12–30. Fruiting spike to 3.5cm; fruit to 1cm, oval, red. SE US. Z7.

S.glabra (Brickell) Rehd. See *S.coccinea*.

S.glaucescens Diels.
Leaves 5–10 × 1.5–5cm, obovate, apex acuminate, base cuneate, finely and remotely shallow-toothed, glabrous, glaucous beneath. Flowers to 2cm diam., orange-red on pedicels to 4cm; tepals 6–7; stamens 18–25, filaments largely united, forming a rounded column. Fruiting spike to 10cm; fruit scarlet. W China. Z8.

S.grandiflora Hook. & Thoms.
Leaves 6–15×2–7cm, lanceolate to oblanceolate, obscurely denticulate to subentire, not glaucous. Flowers 2.5cm diam., fragrant, white, cream or pale rose on pedicels to 5cm; tepals 7, rarely 8; stamens 33–60, filaments united only at base. Fruiting spike to 12cm, pendulous; berries red, globose. N India, Bhutan, Nepal. var. **cathayensis** Scheid. Leaves smaller; flowers rose pink. var. **rubriflora** (Rehd. & Wils.) Schneid. (*S.rubriflora* Rehd. & Wils.). Flowers deep scarlet. India, Burma, W China. Z8.

S.henryi C.B. Clarke.
Leaves to 12cm, ovate to ovate-elliptic, denticulate, glaucous beneath. Flowers white on 5cm long pedicels; tepals to 1.5cm, 6–10, broad; stamens 14–40, united at base on a conical-clavate column. Fruit spike to 15cm; berries crowded. C & S China. Z8.

S.propinqua (Wallich) Baill.
Leaves 4–16×0.8–5cm, lanceolate or narrowly ovate-elliptic, apex briefly acuminate, base somewhat rounded, not glaucous, sparsely toothed or entire. Flowers to 1.5cm diam., orange, on slender pedicels to 1.25cm; tepals 6–10; stamens 6–16, filaments fused into a rounded mass into which the anthers are depressed. Fruiting spike to 15cm, crowded with red berries to 1cm long. C & W China, Himalaya. var. *sinensis* Oliv. Leaves narrower; flowers smaller and somewhat yellow. Cold-resistant. Z8.

S.rubriflora Rehd. & Wils. See *S.grandiflora* var. *rubriflora*.
S.sphenandra auct. See *S.sphenanthera*.

S.sphenanthera Rehd. & Wils.(*S.sphenandra* auct.).
Closely resembles *S.glaucescens* but leaves 3–11×3–7cm, obovate to elliptic, not glaucous beneath Flowers orange, concave; stamens 10–15. S & W China. Z7.

Schizophragma Sieb. & Zucc. (From Gk *schizo*, to cut, and *phragma*, fence, referring to the fruits, which split and fragment between the ribs.) Hydrangeaceae. 4 species of deciduous climbing and creeping shrubs, attaching themselves by means of short, adhesive, aerial roots. Branchlets initially firm and smooth, bark ultimately coarse, exfoliating. Leaves opposite, long-petioled, ovate, entire or toothed. Flowers small, white, in flat-topped terminal cymes, each branch bearing a long-stalked peripheral enlarged sepal, these appear petal-like and form a showy outer ring encompassing smaller white fertile flowers; sepals and petals 4–5; stamens 10; ovary inferior, style 1, stigma 4–5-lobed. Fruit a turbinate capsule, dehiscing between the 10 ribs. Himalaya to Japan, Taiwan. Readily distinguished from the similar *Hydrangea anomala* by the single, enlarged, outer sepals. In *Hydrangea*, these are replaced by sterile flowers with 4–5 enlarged sepals. Z7.

CULTIVATION   These magnificent climbing shrubs resemble a larger, showier *Hydrangea petiolaris*, whose cultural requirements they share.

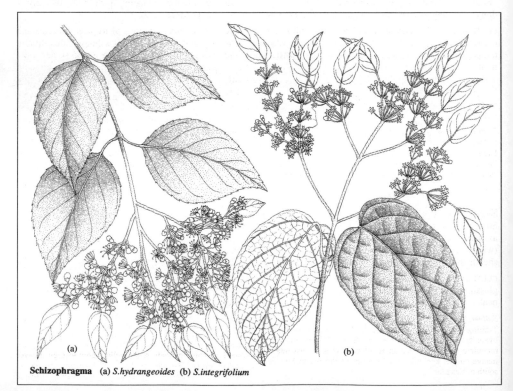

Schizophragma   (a) *S.hydrangeoides*   (b) *S.integrifolium*

S.flueggeoides J. Muell. See *S.integrifolium*.

S.hydrangeoides Sieb. & Zucc.
To 10m. Branchlets initially buff, downy, ripening glabrous, ashy grey-brown. Leaves 8–12.5cm, broadly ovate, apex shortly acuminate, base subcordate, coarsely toothed, ultimately glabrous, pale to mid-green above, paler to silvergreen beneath; petiole 2.5–5cm. Inflorescence to 20cm diam., flat-topped; sterile outer sepals 2.5–3.5cm, ovate, cordate to rhombic, white to ivory. Japan, Korea. 'Roseum': petioles tinted sealing-wax red; sterile outer sepals snow-white blushing rose.

S.integrifolium Oliv. (*S.ramiflora* J. Muell.; *S.flueggeoides* J. Muell.).
10–15m. Leaves 10–18cm, ovate, apex narrowly acuminate, base rounded or cordate, entire or sparsely and irregularly toothed, veins beneath pubescent. Inflorescence to 30cm diam.; sterile outer sepals 6.5–7.25cm, narrowly ovate to rhombic, white. C & W China.

S.ramiflora J. Muell. See *S.integrifolium*.

S.viburnoides (Hook. & Thoms.) Stapf. See *Pileostegia viburnoides*.

Scindapsus Schott. (Name used in Ancient Greece for plant resembling ivy, later applied to this genus of climbing plants.) Araceae. About 40 evergreen climbers. Stems ascending by adhesive adventitious roots. Leaves entire, ovate to oblong or oblong-lanceolate, acuminate, lateral veins parallel; petioles geniculate at apex, often winged. Peduncles solitary or clustered, equalling or shorter than petiole; spathe cymbiform, deciduous, green or white; spadix densely covered with hermaphrodite flowers, equalling or shorter than spathe, enlarging in fruit; perianth absent; stamens 4; ovary unilocular, ovule solitary. Fruit a berry with one hard-coated seed. SE Asia, Pacific, Brazil. Z10.

CULTIVATION   As for the smaller *Philodendron* species.

S.aureus (Lind. & André) Engl. See *Epipremnum aureum*.

S.pictus Hassk.
Stems to 12m+, slender, 2–6mm diam., verrucose. Leaves to 18×12.5cm, ovate-lanceolate to broad-ovate, acute or acuminate, coriaceous, dull green; petiole to 3cm, winged to geniculum. Peduncle 3cm, stout; spathe to 6.5cm, white; spadix green. Probably not frequently cultivated. Java to Borneo. 'Argyraeus' (var. *argyraeus* Engl.) SATIN POTHOS: the juvenile phase, often cultivated. Leaves 7–10 × 5–8cm, ovate-cordate, silky deep green, with silver spots. Flowering does not occur.

Sechium P. Browne. (From *chacha*, W Indian name.) CHAYOTE; CHACO; CHOCHO. Cucurbitaceae. Some 6–8 species of monoecious climbers. Tendrils 1–5-parted. Leaves simple, palmately angled or lobed, base cordate; petiole long. Male flowers in axillary, elongate racemes, calyx 5-lobed, corolla 5-lobed nearly to base, stamens 3, filaments connate, anthers spreading; female flowers 1–2, axillary, calyx and corolla resemble male, ovary oblong with fleshy spines or unarmed. Seed solitary, large, smooth, often germinating in the fruit, the cotyledons extending towards the base, the hypocotyl emerging at its apex. C America. Z10.

CULTIVATION   A tuberous-rooted perennial climber from the cooler, montane regions of tropical America and cultivated there, as in India, for its edible fruits ('chayote' or 'chow-chow'). It requires glasshouse cultivation in temperate regions in intermediate heat, medium humidity and bright, filtered light. Prone to red spider mite: treat as detailed under *Trichosanthes*. Pot in spring in a 2:2:1:1 sterilized loam, well rotted manure, leafmould and grit mixture with good drainage. Water plentifully throughout growth and liquid-feed fortnightly, training the growth on to a trellis or a tripod of strong canes. Propagate by cuttings rooted at 18°C/65°F in spring or by seed. One large seed is produced per fruit and often germinates within it while on the vine. In this case, plant the whole fruit.

S.edule (Jacq.) Sw. CHAYOTE; CHOYOTE, CHOCHO; CHOW CHOW; CHRISTOPHINE; VEGETABLE PEAR.
High-climbing perennial from thickened, tuberous roots. Stems glabrous. Tendrils glabrous. Leaves 5–18cm, ovate to suborbicular, 3–5-angled or -lobed, entire to minutely and remotely toothed, scabrous above, glabrate beneath; petioles 4–14cm, puberulent to glabrous. Male flowers in 10–30cm-long racemes, pale yellow, corolla lobes *c*15mm; female flowers tinged green. Fruit obovoid-pyriform, to 18cm, green-yellow, smooth. Summer. C America.

Securidaca L. (From *securis*, hatchet, referring to the shape of the wing at the end of the pod.) Polygalaceae. 80 species of trees or often scandent shrubs. Leaves alternate, simple, entire, with stipular glands. Flowers in axillary and terminal, often paniculate racemes, irregular, usually pink or purple; sepals 5, the inner 2 petal-like (wings); petals 3, the lower petal usually keeled, clawed, with a fringed crest; stamens 8, filaments united into a sheath split on upper side. Fruit a samara with a dorsal wing. Tropics. Z10.

CULTIVATION   Valued for the showy racemes of fragrant flowers, *Securidaca* species are grown in the warm glasshouse in cool temperate zones. Propagate by semi-ripe cuttings rooted in sand in a closed case with bottom heat.

S.diversifolia (L.) S.F. Blake.
Trailing or climbing shrub. Leaves to 13cm, elliptic-oblong to ovate or elliptic, thick, pubescent, shining and prominently reticulate above; petioles short. Flowers pink to magenta or mauve-purple, keel with a yellow tip. W Indies and Mexico, south to Ecuador.

S.erecta Jacq. See *S.diversifolia*.

S.longipedunculata Fres. VIOLET-TREE.
Slender semi-scandent shrub to tree, 3–10m+; bark light grey, smooth, becoming finely scaly, yellow-grey to grey. Leaves variable, 2.5–5.5(–9)cm, oblong to linear-lanceolate to oblong-ovate, glabrous or glabrescent; petioles short. Flowers

in terminal or axillary racemes to 15cm long, red or purple, fragrant. Tropical Africa. var. *longipedunculata*. Young branches spreading, not transformed or reduced into spines; young shoots slightly pubescent. var. *parvifolia* Oliv. Young branches transformed or reduced to spines that bear leaves and racemes; young shoots densely pubescent.

S.virgata Sw.
High climber. Leaves rounded at both ends or somewhat notched, c2cm wide, but much smaller on flowering branches. Flowers scented, distant,; racemes terminal, filiform, drooping; corolla rosy, wings rosy without, white within. W Indies.

Selaginella Beauv. (Diminutive of *Selago*, the old name for another Lycopod.) LITTLE CLUB MOSS; SPIKE MOSS. Selaginellaceae. Over 700 species of evergreen moss-like plants. Rhizomes long and creeping, much-branched, subterranean or scrambling over surface, wiry; stems with terminal fork usually flabellate-dichotomous, trailing, suberect, sarmentose or scandent; elongate root-like rhizophores produced at nodes along length of trailing stems, often growing through space for some distance before rooting in soil. Leaves numerous, scale-like, very small, in 2 planes or several ranks, most usually with 2 rows in upper plane adpressed and imbricate and 2 rows in lower plane larger and more spreading. Sporophylls either ordinary leaves or modified leaves clustered in strobili; sporangia in axils of sporophylls, dimorphic, as are spores: megasporangia containing 1–4 large megaspores, and microsporangia containing numerous microspores. Tropics and subtropics worldwide, with a few species also in temperate zones, extending rarely to Arctic.

CULTIVATION   The Peacock Fern is one of the most beautiful foliage climbers for the warm glasshouse, growing case or a steamy bathroom. A scrambling 'moss', it produces slender wiry stems, usually to 1.75m tall in cultivation, with remote, ferny branches shifting in colour from bronze-red to brilliant iridescent blue. Plant in clay pots containing a mix of coarse bark, leafmould, charcoal and well rotted garden compost. Position in semi to deep shade with a minimum temperature of 15°C/60°F. Soak thoroughly whenever the compost begins to dry and mist daily (at least twice daily in hot weather) with rain water. Guide loosely through wires or on canes, moss poles or neighbouring plants. Propagate by stem cuttings 6–10cm long and already bearing adventitious roots.

S.willdenovii (Desv. ex Poir) Bak. PEACOCK FERN.
Stems 3–4m, scandent, branched from base; pinnae 30–60cm, deltoid, spreading; pinnules deltoid and decompound, terminal branches contiguous and short. Leaves 1–3mm, scale-like,

crowded, overlapping, emerging red-bronze to green with an iridescent sheen becoming deep bronze-green overlaid with kingfisher blue. Strobili quadrangular, 12–25mm. Old World Tropics. Z10.

Selenicereus (A. Berger) Britt. & Rose. (From Gk *selene*, the moon, and *Cereus*, referring to the nocturnal flowers.) Cactaceae. Some 20 species of scandent, epilithic or epiphytic cacti; stems slender, often bearing aerial roots; ribs 2–12; spines short, bristly or hair-like, rarely acicular or absent. Flowers funnelform, medium-sized to very large, 12–40×10–20cm, nocturnal; floral areoles with hair-spines, bristles or spines; tepals white (red-tinged in *S.wercklei*), or the outer yellow, pink or brown; staminal throat-circle present. Fruit globose, ovoid or oblong, 6–8cm, fleshy, usually red, spination persistent. Seeds oval or broadly oval, 2.2–3.8 × 1.2–2.2mm, black-brown or brown, not or somewhat shiny, keeled (*S.witti*) or not; relief flat to low-domed; mucilage-sheath present, covering entire seed. Tropical America and the Caribbean region.

CULTIVATION   A genus of showy climbing cacti with stems either long and slender or shorter, winged and flattened, attaching themselves in both cases by aerial roots. The flowers are large and funnel-shaped in shades of white, cream and topaz and usually opening with nightfall. Their nocturnal flowering has given these plants (*S. grandiflorus* especially) a mystique and majesty well expressed by the popular name Queen of the Night; it has also captured the imagination of great botanical artists including those working for Thornton's *Temple of Flora* (1799–1807) and Margaret Mee (1988). In frost-free climates, several species will adapt readily to dry, sunny walls and rooftops: large plants of *S.grandiflorus* can be seen in gardens in the Mediterranean and Caribbean.The non-clambering, shorter-stemmed species such as *S.wittii* tend to require some shade, and higher humidity and temperatures – they perform best if attached to bark, tree fern fibre or branches and treated as one would an intermediate growing orchid such as *Cattleya*.

In cool temperate regions, grow all species in an intermediate glasshouse or conservatory (winter minimum temperature 10–15°C/50°–60°F) in an acid, open, bark-based mix. Train the long-stemmed species on wires, shade in summer and maintain high humidity by misting. Rest winter-flowering species in late summer. Reduce water and humidity in winter and admit full light. Propagate by rooted sections of stem.

S.anthonyanus (Alexander) D. Hunt.
Climbing and epiphytic; primary stems clinging by aerial roots, to 2m or more, flattened, shallowly lobed; lateral branches to 1m or more, 2-winged, 7–15cm, broadly and deeply dentate-lobed, the lobes 25–45×10–16mm, 4–6, thick, tapered and curved, apex obtuse; areoles in the sinuses; spines 3, short. Flowers salverform, 12 × 10–15cm, fragrant; pericarpel *c*2 × 2cm, green, with numerous scales 1–2mm and areoles with bristles and pale brown spines 1–3mm; tube cyclindric, 3–1.5cm, stiff, purple, with scales 3–6mm, the

lower areoles with wool and bristles the upper naked; outer tepals purple, inner pale yellow; style stout, 6mm diam.; stigmas 12–14, 16–18mm, widely spreading, white. Summer. Mexico. Z9.

S.atropilosus Kimnach.
Sprawling to scandent, to 3m or more, profusely branched; stems 1.5–2(–4)cm diam.; ribs (3–)4(–6), 4–7mm high, serrate to crenate, obtuse to subacute; areoles 3-6cm apart; spines 2–6, 1–6mm, off-white, red-tinged or almost black. Flowers subapical, funnelform, upcurved, 12×9–11cm; floral

areoles numerous, with brown or black-brown hairs 3–20mm and 1–10 brown or black-brown spines 3–6mm; outer tepals yellow-green, tinged red, inner pale yellow or green-tinged. Fruit subglobose to oblong 5–6×c4cm, purple, with easily deciduous spines; pulp white. Summer. Mexico. Z9.

S.boeckmannii (Otto ex Salm-Dyck) Britt. & Rose. See S.grandiflorus.
S.brevispinus Britt. & Rose. See S.grandiflorus.
S.coniflorus (Weing.) Britt. & Rose. See S.grandiflorus.

S.donkelaarii (Salm-Dyck) Britt. & Rose (S. nelsonii (Weing.) Britt. & Rose).
Stems to 8m × 1cm diam.; ribs 9–10 or fewer, very low, rounded; spines 10–15, 1–4mm, adpressed. Flowers 18cm; floral areoles with spines, but without hairs; outer tepals tinged red, inner white. SE Mexico (Yucatan). Z9.

S.grandiflorus (L.) Britt. & Rose. (S.boeckmannii (Otto ex Salm-Dyck) Britt. & Rose; S.brevispinus Britt. & Rose; S.coniflorus (Weing.) Britt. & Rose; S.hondurensis (Schum.) Britt. & Rose; S.kunthianus (Otto ex Salm-Dyck) Britt. & Rose; S.pringlei Rose; S.vaupelii (Weing.) A. Berger). QUEEN OF THE NIGHT.
Stems 1.2–2.5cm diam.; ribs 5–8(–10), low; areoles 5–20mm apart; spines 6–18, 4.5–15mm, setaceous, and (on young growth) white, pale yellow or brown hairs, these later deciduous. Flowers 17.5–30 × 12.5–17.5cm; outer tepals pale yellow or brown-tinged, inner white. Summer. Jamaica, Cuba, etc. The taxonomy of this species, long-known as the 'Queen of the Night', and its close allies, is hindered by uncertainty as to its original provenance, by its widespread cultivation and naturalization, and by hybridization. Z9.

S.hamatus (Scheidw. ex Pfeiff.) Britt. & Rose.
Stems slender, c1.5cm diam., 3–4-angled, the angles with prominent spurs up to 1cm long beneath the areoles; spines short and weak. Flowers 20–35cm, white. Summer. Mexico. Z9.

S.hondurensis (Schum.) Britt. & Rose. See S.grandiflorus.

S.inermis (Otto ex Pfeiff.) Britt. & Rose.
Stems 1–2cm diam., 3–5-angled or ribbed; ribs compressed, acute, sinuate-crenate, or very low; areoles remote, to 6cm apart; spines usually 0. Flowers 15×c10cm; pericarpel and tube cyclindric, 8×1.5cm, green; scales linear; flc al areoles brown-felted and with 10–15 brown spines to 1cm; outer tepals yellow-green, tinged purple at base; inner tepals white, tinged pink at base. Venezuela, Colombia. Z9.

S. innesii Kimnach.
Stems sprawling and clambering. c12mm diam.; ribs 6, low, tuberculate; areoles c1cm apart; spines 3–9, 1–2mm, the central subulate, yellow-brown, the remainder hair-like, off-white. Flowers perfect or pistillate, 4–4.5cm long, the pistillate not expanding, the perfect rotate, c5cm; pericarpel sub-globose, c7×10cm; tube very short; floral areoles with spines 3–6mm, white, tinged pink, and hair-spines 2–3mm, pale yellow; outer tepals tinged magenta; inner white. Windward Is. (St Vincent). Z9.

S.kunthianus (Otto ex Salm-Dyck) Britt. & Rose. See S.grandiflorus.

S.macdonaldiae (Hook.) Britt. & Rose.
Resembling S.grandiflorus, but the areoles seated on tubercles 2–3mm high. Honduras(?). Z9.

S.maxonii Rose. See S.urbanianus.

S.megalanthus (schaum. ex Vaup.) Moran.
Resembling S.setaceus, but with larger flowers and different fruit. Stem-segments to 1–2×3–6cm, 3-angled or winged; areoles 3–5 cm apart; spines 2–3, 3–5mm, broad-based. Flowers funnelform, 30(–38)cm; tube and pericarpel with narrow scales and bristly spines; tepals white. Fruit not known. Peru, Bolivia. This may be the plant cultivated in

Colombia and Ecuador for the edible fruit, known as 'pitaya', which is exported to the US and Europe. The 'pitaya' fruit is ovoid, to 11 × 6cm, strongly tuberculate; pericarp thick, yellow; spines 5–10mm, deciduous; pulp white, edible. Z9.

S.mirandae Bravo. See Weberocereus glaber.

S.murrillii Britt. & Rose.
Slender vine to 6m or more; stems 8mm diam.; dark green; ribs 7–8, low, obtuse, tinged purple; areoles 1–2 cm apart; spines 5–6, minute, the 2 lowest longer and reflexed, 1–2cm, the others conic, tinged green to black. Flowers 15×15cm; tube tinged purple, with scattered areoles and 1–2 minute spines but no long hairs; outer tepals green-yellow; inner tepals white. Mexico. Z9.

S.nelsonii (Weing.) Britt. & Rose. See S.donkelaarii.
S.nycticalus (Link & Otto) W.T. Marshall. See S.pteranthus.
S.pringlei Rose. See S.grandiflorus.

S.pteranthus (Link & Otto) Britt. & Rose. (S.nycticalus (Link & Otto) W.T. Marshall).
Resembling S.grandiflorus, but stems stouter, 2.5–5cm diam., 4–6-angled; areoles 2–2.5cm apart, with 1–5 short, hard, conic spines 1–3mm. Fruit red. Summer. Mexico. Z9.

S.setaceus (DC.) Werderm.
Stems usually 3- but sometimes 4–5-angled, 2–4(–8) cm diam.; areoles 2–3cm apart; spines 1–3, 1–2mm, conic, brown. Flowers 25–30cm; pericarpel with small scales and areoles with felt and spiny; tube with larger scales. Fruit ovoid, tuberculate and bristly, red. Brazil to Argentina. Z9.

S.spinulosus (DC.) Britt. & Rose.
Stem 1–2cm diam., with 4–5 ribs; areoles 1.5–2.5cm apart; spines 6–8, only 1mm. Flowers 10–12.5×7–8.5cm; areoles or pericarpel shiny, but without silky hairs; outer tepals pale brown-green, inner white to pale pink. Spring-summer. SW US (Texas), Mexico. Z9.

S.testudo (Karw. ex Zucc.) F. Buxb.
Stems clambering or climbing to 5m or more, irregular segmented and ribbed, usually adhering to tree-trunks or rocks by tough aerial roots; segments of very variable form, mostly either elongate, 3–4-ribbed, with more or less equal ribs 2–3cm high, or much broader, sometimes almost semi-ovoid, to 10–15cm, 5–10-ribbed, the ribs very unequal and folded and parted over another, the outer larger and covering those beneath; areoles 1–2cm apart; spines 10 or more, 1–2cm, brown or pale yellow to white. Flowers c28cm, creamy white; tube with hairs and bristles to 3cm. C America (S Mexico to Costa Rica). Z9

S.urbianus (Gürke ex Weing.) Britt. & Rose. (S.maxonii Rose).
Resembling S.grandiflorus. Stems to 3cm diam.; ribs usually 4–5, prominent; areoles c1cm apart; spines several, to 1cm, brown, accompanied by several longer, white hairs. Flowers 20–30cm; pericarpel and tube red-brown with long white hairs; outer tepals brown to orange; inner tepals white. Hispaniola, Cuba. Not described until 1904, but possibly introduced much earlier and taken to be the same as S.grandiflorus. Z9.

S.vagans (Brand) Brit. & Rose.
Stems 1–1.5cm diam.; ribs c10, low; areoles 1–1.5cm apart; spines numerous, less than 1cm, acicular, yellow-brown. Flowers 15cm; tube 9cm, brown-green; floral areoles with 5–8 spines to 8mm; outer tepals white, tinged brown or green; inner tepals white. Fruit ellipsoid, 7×3–5cm, tuberculate, pink. W Mexico (Sinaloa). Z9.

S.vaupelii (Weing.) A. Berger. See S.grandiflorus.

S.wercklei (F.A.C. Weber) Britt. & Rose.
Stems elongate, slender, 5–15mm diam.; ribs 6–12, very low; areoles small; spines 0. Flowers 15–16cm; outer tepals tinged red; inner tepals white. Fruit ovoid, yellow, with brown spines. Costa Rica. Z9.

Semele androgyna

S.wittii (Schum.) G. Rowley.
Epiphyte, clinging by aerial roots from the midrib; stems elongate, 2-winged, c10cm broad, green or becoming red or purple when growing in full sun; areoles marginal, 6–8mm apart; spines numerous, to 12mm, acicular, yellow-brown. Flowers 25cm, white; limb relatively short. Fruit ovoid, 2.5–3.5cm, spiny. Amazonian region of Brazil, Colombia and Peru. Z9.

Semele Kunth. (Named for the daughter of Kadmos and mother of Dionysos.) CLIMBING BUTCHER'S BROOM. Liliaceae (Asparagaceae). 1 species, a robust, climbing, evergreen, perennial herb. Rhizomes short, clump-forming; roots fleshy. Stems 5–7m × 1–2cm, terete, climbing or sprawling, snaking then twining toward summit, glabrous, somewhat rough, becoming rigid; despite their shrubby appearance, these stems are tough and highly developed annual shoots. True leaves mostly borne along main stem, scale-like, soon withering and becoming hard, dry and prickly or, ultimately, disintegrating to chaffy remains; cladophylls arranged subpinnately on branches, leaf-like, dark green, glabrous, rigid to semi-pliable, those near stem base 2.5–7 × 1.5cm, broadly ovate to cordate, upper cladophylls smaller, denser, sharper, ovate-lanceolate. Flowers unisexual, 1 to several, clustered in a notch on margins of cladophylls or, rarely, on upper face of cladophyll, male flowers c9mm diam., females c6.5mm diam.; perianth cream, lobes 6, united for one third of their length, then spreading, often persistent, dry, brown; stamens united into a tube, anthers 6, not opening in female flowers; style with 3 stigmatic lobes emerging from staminal tube. Fruit a berry to 2cm diam., orange-red; seeds usually 1. Early summer. Canary Is. Z9.

CULTIVATION Needing the protection of the cool glasshouse or conservatory in cool temperate zones, *Semele* is a climber with evergreen cladodes bearing small creamy flowers in the marginal notches. Its habit and foliage are striking – a massive *Asparagus*-ally with snaking green stems arising from a basal clump and decked with tough pinnate foliage (in fact cladodes closely arranged on branches). The flowers are insignificant save when they wither and fall leaving an unsightly brown powdering on the glasshouse floor. The berries, however, are attractive and give *Semele* the appearance of a giant Butcher's Broom. Grow in a gritty but fertile medium preferably in filtered light; provide strong support and water moderately when in growth. Flowers are carried on year-old growth and fruit will not ripen for a further twelve months, so pruning should be restricted to removing shoots only where necessary to confine to allotted space. Propagate by division.

S.androgyna (L.) Kunth.

Senecio L. (From Lat. *senex*, an old man, referring to usually white or grey hairy pappus.) Compositae. About 1000 species of trees, shrubs, lianes and herbs. Leaves alternate, entire to variously lobed. Capitula usually in corymbs, rarely solitary, usually radiate; receptacle flat, naked; phyllaries mostly uniseriate, sometimes with shorter subsidiary phyllaries at base of capitulum (calyculus); ray florets usually female; disc florets hermaphrodite, yellow, rarely white or purple. Fruit a more or less cylindric, ribbed cypsela; pappus of simple, rarely subplumose hairs, rarely absent. Cosmopolitan.

CULTIVATION A vast and highly diverse genus, *Senecio* contains several true climbers, attractive perennials for frost-free gardens, the cool to intermediate glasshouse (minimum temperatures 7–10°C/45–50°F), conservatories and the home. The species listed below climb and scramble freely, creating a loose cover of dark green foliage lit up by clusters of daisy-like flowers. The Canary Creeper, *S.tamoides*, produces masses of small orange-yellows against dark green, ivy-like leaves. *S.macroglossus*, the Wax Vine, is still more 'ivy-like', a tough, thinly succulent twiner suitable for tubs and baskets, or for use as a houseplant, trained on a wigwam of canes. It is most often encountered as the cultivar 'Variegatus'. Plant all the species below in a free-draining medium-fertility potting mix in full sun with good ventilation. Water moderately and feed fortnightly with dilute feed when in full growth. Allow a slight dry rest, cut back as necessary and repot after flowering. Propagate by semi-ripe tip cuttings of 2–4 nodes with most of the leaves removed, rooted in a case, or by basal layering.

S.auriculatissimus Britten.
Evergreen, perennial, scandent shrub, climbing to 3m, subglabrous; stems much-branched. Leaves to 7×5cm; transversely oblong or rounded-reniform, petiolate, coarsely, obtusely dentate, petiole to 5cm, base conspicuously auriculate, dilated into 2cm-wide auricle. Capitula to 2.5cm diam., radiate, in lax clusters to 15cm diam.; phyllaries many, calycinal few, small; ray florets 12–15, golden-yellow. Spring. C Africa.

S.chenopodioides Kunth. See *Pseudogynoxys chenopodioides*.
S.confusus (DC.) Britten. See *Pseudogynoxys chenopodioides*.

S.macroglossus DC. NATAL IVY; WAX VINE.
Slender, twining perennial herb to 2m; stems somewhat succulent, glabrous. Leaves to 8×4.5cm, deltoid, hastate, usually 3-lobed, lobes acute to acuminate, lower pair spreading, thinly fleshy; petiole to 3cm. Capitula radiate, solitary or to 3 in a corymb; peduncles to 10cm, with conspicuous bracts; phyllaries to 1cm, c12, calycinal elliptic-lanceolate, to length of involucre, margins often ciliate; ray florets 8 or more cream or pale yellow. Summer. Eastern S Africa to Mozambique and Zimbabwe. 'Variegatus': leaves dark green marked cream-yellow and grey-green. Z10.

S.mikanioides Otto ex Harv. See *Delairea odorata*

S.scandens Buch.-Ham. ex D. Don.
Perennial to 5m, woody at base; stems elongate, branched, scandent, densely pubescent at first, becoming glabrous. Leaves to 10×4.5cm, ovate or elongate-deltoid, acuminate, truncate to hastate at base, irregularly incised-toothed to subentire or lobed, pubescent; petiole to 2cm. Capitula

*c*1.5cm diam., radiate; in a spreading, terminal paniculate corymbs, peduncles to 1cm; densely pubescent; phyllaries 8, lanceolate, acute; ray florets yellow. Winter. E Asia. Z9.

S.subscandens Hochst. ex A. Rich. See *Solanecio angulatus.*

S.tamoides DC. CANARY CREEPER; CLIMBING CINERARIA. Much-branched evergreen scandent shrub to 12m. Leaves to 7cm, ivy-like, basically ovate-orbicular, base cordate or trun-cate with free or ± overlapping lobes, apex acute, margins with 4–6 broad, angular teeth or lobes per side, bright green, glabrous, thinly fleshy. Inflorescence a crowded, stalked, axillary or terminal corymb; capitula to 2cm diam., radiate, ray florets 5, strap-shaped, bright orange-yellow. Summer. S & C Africa.

Seyrigia Keraudren. (For Mr. Seyrig, who assembled a herbarium in Ampandandrava, a mining district of S Madagascar.) Cucurbitaceae. 4 species of dioecious, climbing herbs. Stems slender, occasionally succulent, ribbed, little-branched, often becoming leafless. Tendrils simple, slender. Leaves to 5-lobed, small, usually ephemeral. Male flowers small, in short, few-flowered racemes, with small bracts, calyx campanulate to funnelform, lobes small, petals lanceolate, stamens 2, filaments short, thick, inserted on edge of calyx tube, anthers 2-thecous, connective not prolonged; female flowers solitary, calyx and corolla resemble male, but with 2 staminodes; ovary oval-oblong, 2-locular, ovules 2 per locule, style straight, with 2 stigmas. Fruit a small, fleshy berry, bright red when ripe, glabrous; seeds small, in red pulp, enveloped by transparent aril. Madagascar. Z10.

CULTIVATION As for *Coccinia.*

S.humbertii Keraudren. Stems to 3m, cylindrical, ribbed, densely white-pubescent, internodes 6–8cm. Tendrils 5–20cm, white-pubescent. Leaves 3-lobed, small (these may persist in cultivation). Male flowers 6–8, calyx short, lobes triangular, hairy on outer face; corolla conspicuously nerved, petals pubescent at apex; female flowers with pedicels 7–8mm, petals recurved; ovary 4–6×2mm, style 2mm, stigmas papillose. Fruit indehiscent, ovoid, base truncate, *c*1.5cm. Madagascar.

Sicana Naudin. (Peruvian name.) Cucurbitaceae. 2 species of vigorous climbing perennials. Tendrils 3–5-parted. Leaves alternate, palmately lobed, glabrous; petiole long. Flowers solitary, large, unisexual; male flowers with 5 reflexed calyx lobes, corolla deeply 5-lobed, yellow, stamens 3, inserted in mouth of receptacle, filaments short, connate at base, anthers free; female flowers with 3 staminodes, ovary oblong-ovoid, with 3 carpels, ovules numerous, style connate, stigmas 3. Fruit ellipsoid, fleshy, indehiscent; seeds numerous, oblong-ovate, compressed, marginate. C & S America, W Indies. Z10.

CULTIVATION As for *Trichosanthes*, except that multiple plantings and cross-pollination are not required. Fruit of *S.odorifera* has a pleasant odour, but when raw the flesh is difficult to chew and swallow; often used for scenting clothes and linen, said to ward off insects, and used in preserves and sweets.

S.atropurpurea André. See *S.odorifera.*

S.odorifera (Vell.) Naudin. CURUBÁ; CURUA; COROA; CASSABANANA. Stems to 15m, puberulent when young. Tendrils *c*4-parted. Leaves suborbicular, 3–5-lobed, base cordate, 10–20cm; petiole 4–15cm, margins undulate or denticulate. Corolla fleshy, campanulate, lobes *c*2mm, tomentose; female flowers with staminodes to 5mm, stigma capitate 8–10mm diam. Fruit ellipsoid, to 30cm, yellow turning orange, or purple-red, flesh pale yellow; seeds *c*1cm. S America.

Sicyos L. (From Gk *sikyos*, cucumber.) Cucurbitaceae. About 25 species of monoecious, annual climbers and trailers. Leaves simple or palmately lobed. Tendrils 2–5-fid. Male inflorescence a raceme, sometimes branched; female flowers solitary, smaller than males; flowers small, white to pale green; calyx campanulate, shallow, denticulate; petals 5 occasionally 3–4, fused at base; stamens 2–5, usually 3, inserted at base of tube, filaments and anthers united; ovary ovoid, beaked, fusiform, uniloculate, uniovular. Fruit small, ovoid or fusiform, indehiscent, usually spiny, dry, sometimes woody; seed solitary, subovate to fusiform, smooth. Americas, Pacific Islands, Australasia.

CULTIVATION As for *Coccinia*, but raise as an annual. Multiple planting is not required for fruit set. In cool-temperate regions with hot summers, *S.angulatus* is sometimes used as a screen plant, but may become invasive.

S.angulatus L. BUR CUCUMBER; STAR CUCUMBER. To 6m. Leaves cordate to orbicular, sharply angled or lobed; petiole pubescent. Peduncle pubescent. Fruit in clusters, to 1cm, spiny. E Canada, US. Z6.

S.oreganus Torr. & A. Gray. See *Marah oreganus.*

Sinofranchetia (Diels) Henry. (For Adrien René Franchet (1834–1900), French botanist.) Lardizabalaceae. 1 species, a fast-growing, deciduous, dioecious twining shrub to 10cm, glabrous, with a red-flushed bloom on young shoots. Leaves slender-stalked, trifoliolate; leaflets 6–14cm, ovate, entire, papery, midrib distinct, venation pinnate, dark green above, blue-green beneath, central leaflet larger, rhombic-obovate to broadly ovate, apex short-acuminate, base cuneate, petiolule 2–3cm, lateral leaflets obliquely ovate, petiolules shorter. Inflorescence a pendulous raceme 10–30cm long, including peduncle; flowers white, to 8mm across; sepals 6; nectaries 6; pedicels 2–3mm; males with 6 free stamens, females with 3 carpels. Fruit a globose berry, 1.5–2cm, occurring in threes, lavender-purple, sometimes setting despite the absence of a male pollinator; seeds 5–6mm, black. Summer. C & W China. Z6.

CULTIVATION   A vigorous twining climber grown for its dark and handsome foliage, *Sinofranchetia* is suitable for covering unsightly buildings or for growing through large trees. Cultivate as for *Holboellia*. Propagate by seed.

S.chinensis (Franch.) Hemsl.   *For illustration see Lardizabalaceae.*

Sinomenium Diels. (From *sino*, Chinese, and *men*, moon – Chinese Moonseed.) Menispermaceae. 1 species, a deciduous, glabrous twining shrub to 7m. Leaves to 20cm, variable in shape, ovate-cordate to reniform, entire or shallowly to distinctly 3–5-lobed, deep bright green. Flowers small, yellow, unisexual in slender pyramidal panicles to 20cm long. Fruit to 0.75cm diam., globose, black, pruinose. Summer. E Asia. Z8.

CULTIVATION   As for the related *Menispermum*.

S.acutum (Thunb.) Rehd. & Wils.
var. *cinereum* (Diels) Rehd. & Wils. Leaves grey-downy beneath.

Smilax L. (Gk name for this plant.) GREENBRIER; CATBRIER. Liliaceae (Smilacaceae). Some 200 species of dioecious, perennial, evergreen or deciduous, climbing or scrambling vines, with rhizomes or tubers. Stems terete, angular, branched, spiny, prickly or bristly, at least below. Leaves alternate, the lower reduced to scales, prominently 3- to 9-veined with interconnecting net veins, papery to leathery, sometimes with spiny margins; stalks usually very short; modified stipules and occasionally stipule-like auricles borne in pairs near the base, usually terminated by a curling tendril. Flowers white to pale-green, yellow or brown, lateral, solitary or borne in small axillary umbels or racemes; tepals 6, separate, free; male flowers with 6 free stamens borne at the base of the tepals; female flowers with up to 6 staminodes, and a superior ovary on which 1–3 stigmas are borne directly; anthers basifixed. Fruit a red, blue, or black, spherical or ovoid, 1–6-seeded berry. Tropics, temperate Asia, US. Florists' Smilax is usually *Asparagus asparagoides*.

CULTIVATION   These large climbing perennials are distantly related to the lilies, a fact not evinced by their rather shrubby habit, prickly stems, broad, tough leaves and nugatory flowers. Their wiry, tangled stems arise from a basal clump and progress quickly through surrounding vegetation. Outdoors, they appreciate semi-wooded or woodland locations on damp, leafy soils. The hardiest species (to at least –20°C/–4°F), such as *S.glauca*, the malodorous-flowered *S.herbacea* and *S.rotundifolia*, will scramble through trees and shrubs and over tree stumps; the flowers are not noticeably ornamental but sometimes give rise to a crop of small fruits. *S.discotis*, *S.hispida* and *S.china* are almost as hardy (between –10 and –15°C/14–5°F), the remaining species need glasshouse protection, to 7°C/45°F. The most attractive hardy species are *S.glauca* and *S.aspera* 'Maculata' with bold mottled leaves. Of the tender species, *S. argyraea* with narrow, silvered foliage is outstanding. Tolerant of a range of soil types in sun or part shade. Propagate by division or by seed.

S.argyraea Lind. & Rodigas.
Stems climbing, wiry with short, rigid spines. Leaves to 25cm, bright green with silver-white or pale green spots or streaks, acute or acuminate, 3-veined, short-stalked. Flowers and fruits unknown. Peru, Bolivia. Z9.

S.aspera L
Creeping, climbing, or scrambling evergreen to 15m; stems zigzag, angled, spiny, rarely spineless. Leaves variable, 4–11 ×2–10cm, narrowly to broadly lanceolate, triangular, ovate, oblong or kidney-shaped, abruptly narrowed above the usually cordate base, 5–9-veined, shiny on both surfaces with margins and (usually) main veins prickly; petiole to 2cm, usually spiny. Flowers pale-green, fragrant, in axillary and terminal racemes of 5–30; tepals pale green, 2–4mm. Fruit black or red, to 6mm. Canary Is., S Europe to Ethiopia and India. Z8. 'Maculata': leaves blotched white.

S.china DC.
Deciduous climber to 5m, stems sparsely prickly or unarmed. Leaves to 8cm, broadly ovate to orbicular, sometimes wider than long, apex abruptly acuminate, base somewhat cordate, leathery or papery, 5–7-veined; petioles 8–2.5cm. Flowers yellow-green, in single umbels with peduncles to 2.5cm. Fruit red, globose, to 9mm diam. Korea, Japan. Z6. The source of

'China Root', a drug once used to treat gout.

S.discotis Warb.
Deciduous climber to 7.2m; stems angled, armed with hooked spines to 4mm. Leaves 4–10×2–5cm, ovate, apex acute to obtuse, base cordate, glaucous beneath, 3–5-veined; petiole 2–4cm; auricles as long as petioles. Flowers green-yellow, borne in umbels with slender stalk to 4cm. Fruit blue-black. China. Z9.

S.excelsa L.
Deciduous climber to 20m, sometimes scrambling; stems terete with slightly raised lines, thorny, spines straight, to 7mm. Leaves variable, 5–13cm long, scarcely as wide, broadly ovate to orbicular, apex acuminate, base cordate or truncate, thinly textured or slightly leathery, margins rough or serrulate, 5–7-veined; petioles to 1.5cm. Flowers green, in single umbels of 4–12; peduncles 7–20mm; male tepals 5–7mm, female 4–5mm. Fruit red, 3-seeded, 8–10mm. E Bulgaria to USSR. Z6.

S.glauca Walter. SAWBRIER; WILD SARSPARILLA
Widely climbing deciduous or semi-evergreen shrub; stems spiny, especially below, terete, often glaucous; spines slender, rigid; branches angled, prickly, terete when young, green or brown. Leaves 4–13×3.5–10cm, ovate to lanceolate, broadly

tapered or cordate at base, glaucous and papillose beneath, occasionally above also, 7-veined, often mottled or streaked in a paler or darker silvery tone, auricles shorter than leaf stalks. Flowers yellow to brown, borne in axillary umbels of 5–11, with an arched, flat stalk of 1–1.5cm, usually longer than the petiole. Fruit 5–8mm diam., black, glaucous, spherical berries. SE US. Z4.

S.grandifolia Reg. See *S.regelii*.

S.herbacea L. CARRION FLOWER; JACOB'S LADDER.
Annual climber to 3m; stems glabrous, unarmed, much-branched. Leaves 5–12×3–12cm, triangular-ovate to lanceolate, rounded to shortly acuminate, rounded to truncate or slightly cordate at the base, leathery, 7–9-veined, entire or nearly so; stalk to 8cm. Flowers few to numerous, carrion-scented, green, borne in rounded umbels with a stalk of 10–30cm; tepals 3.5–6mm. Fruit blue-black, subglobose, to 1cm diam. E US. Z4.

S.hispida Muhlenb. BRISTLY GREENBRIER; HAGBRIER; HELLFETTER.
High-climbing deciduous shrub to 15m; stems conspicuously prickly below, terete or slightly angled; branches angled, glabrous, without spines. Leaves 5–15×1.5–2cm, ovate to circular, apex abruptly acuminate, base cordate, 5–9-veined, serrulate, shiny, drying grey; petioles 0.6–1.8cm. Flowers in in 25-flowered axillary umbels, peduncles 1.5–10cm, 1.5× longer than petioles. Fruit blue-black, to 6mm diam. S & C US. Z5.

S.kraussiana Meisn.
Climbing shrub, stems prickly. Leaves to 20cm, elliptic-ovate. Fruit to 1.25cm, nearly globose, purple. Africa.

S.lanceolata L. JACKSON BRIER.
Climbing, evergreen, woody vine, older stems sparsely prickly. Leaves to 8cm, lanceolate-ovate to ovate, glossy above, entire. Fruit to 1cm diam., globose, dull red to brown, on stalks longer than subtending petioles. N Florida to W Indies, Mexico & Panama.

S.laurifolia L. LAUREL-LEAVED GREENBRIER; BLASPHEME VINE; BAMBOO VINE.
Evergreen, tuberous climber, stems terete, green, prickly below; branches angled, mostly unarmed. Leaves 5–20×1–7.5cm, narrowly ovate to oblong-lanceolate, leathery, thick-textured, cuneate, margins inrolled, 3-veined, midrib much more prominent than lateral veins beneath. Flowers green, in single umbels, with peduncles shorter than or equal to petioles. Fruit black, ovoid, 6–8mm diam. SE US. Z8.

S.maculata Roxb. See *S.aspera* 'Maculata'.

S.officinalis F.J. Hanb. & Flueck. See *S.regelii*.
S.ornata Hook. See *S.regelii*.

S.regelii Killip & Morton (*S.grandifolia* Reg.; *S.utilis* Hemsl.; *S.saluberrima* Gilg; *S.ornata* Hook.; *S.officinalis* F.J. Hanb. & Fluck).
Shrub to 15m; stems with 4 sharp angles and spines below, 4 angled or winged above, spines to 1cm. Lower leaves very variable to 30×21cm, ovate to oblong, apex rounded or acuminate, base cordate or hastate, upper leaves much smaller, lanceolate to oblong, gradually tapered at the base; petioles to 7cm. Male flowers solitary or in umbellate racemes to 6.5cm, female flowers solitary, peduncles to 10cm. Fruit black, to 1.5cm diam. NC America. Z9.

S.rotundifolia L. COMMON GREENBRIER; COMMON CATBRIER; BULLBRIER; HORSE BRIER.
High-climbing, woody, deciduous or partly evergreen vine to 10m; stems 4-angled, conspicuously prickly with spines to 8mm on the angles. Leaves 5–15cm, broadly ovate to circular, base round to cordate, thick-textured and leathery, 5-veined, dark green, lustrous, margins entire or roughened; petioles 0.6–1.2cm. Flowers green-yellow, in single umbels on peduncles of 5–15mm, flattened, slightly longer than petioles. Fruit blue to black, 5–8mm diam. E US. Z4.

S.saluberrima Gilg. See *S.regelii*.

S.smallii Morong.
Evergreen shrub. Stems to 3m, terete and glabrous; lower stems with spines 5–6mm, upper stems spineless. Leaves to 15×7cm, usually much smaller, lanceolate to ovate, abruptly acuminate, gradually tapered at the base, thin-textured, glabrous, 5-veined, shiny dark green above, duller and paler beneath without spines; petioles to 1.5cm. Flowers green, few to numerous, in umbels, spikes or racemes, peduncles to 1cm; male tepals 5–6mm, female 3–4mm; styles 3. Fruit black, globose, 5–7mm diam. SE US, C America. Z8.

S.utilis Hemsl. See *S.regelii*.

S.walteri Pursh. RED-BERRIED GREENBRIER; RED-BERRIED BAMBOO.
Deciduous, climbing, slender, woody vine; stems slightly angled, spiny towards base, yellow or brown, older stems often prickly; branches square in section, unarmed. Leaves 5–12×1.5–6.5cm, ovate to ovate-lanceolate, apex obtuse or abruptly acute, base broadly cuneate to cordate, 5–7-veined. Flowers borne in simple umbels of 6–15, yellow, green or brown, drying brown-orange; peduncles 5–15cm, flat, usually shorter than petioles. Fruit red, occasionally white, 8–12mm diam. E US. Z7.

Solandra (L.) Sw. (*Swartzia* Gmel. non Schreb.). (For Daniel Carlsson Solander (1733–82), botanist.) CHALICE VINE. Solanaceae. 8 species of shrubby climbers. Bark ridged. Leaves alternate, simple, entire, usually coriaceous, shiny. Flowers nocturnally fragrant, axillary, solitary, perigynous, short-stipitate; calyx to 5cm, long-tubular, to 5-lobed at apex; corolla tube to 37cm, cylindric to funnel-shaped, longer than calyx, white, yellow or purple-blue, apex campanulate, limb 5-lobed, lobes overlapping in bud, becoming reflexed, white to yellow, occasionally blotched purple; stamens 5, attached to corolla; ovary 4-chambered; stigma dry. Fruit a conic berry, pulpy, 2-chambered, surrounded by calyx; seeds to 7×4mm. Tropical America. Z10.

CULTIVATION Occurring as semi-epiphytes or stout-stemmed lianas, the Chalice Vines often bloom in the crowns of large, buttressed trees growing by streams and rivers: their outsize trumpet-shaped yellow and white flowers are frequently fragrant and ribbed or veined with darker contrasting colours. They are cultivated in the open in tropical and subtropical climates, trained as climbers against walls, fences, trellising, pergolas and pillars; some, such as *S.hartwegii* and *S.longiflora*, may be grown as lawn specimen shrubs or in mixed borders. In cool-temperate areas, give intermediate glasshouse conditions (minimum temperature 10°C/50°F). Plant in well-drained soils in spring in full sun or part shade (*S.longiflora* prefers alkaline conditions). Both in the open and under glass, rich moist soils and full sunlight will promote rapid vegetative growth: a single specimen may cover up to 14m²/17yd² of wall space and plants grown under glass require plenty of room to develop. However, conditions favourable for growth will not promote flowering: after an initial period of shoot growth, reduce watering almost to wilting point to induce flowering. Shorten long, vigorous shoots annually, in late winter/early spring, removing weak shoots altogether (flowering occurs on the current year's wood); excessive pruning tends to make

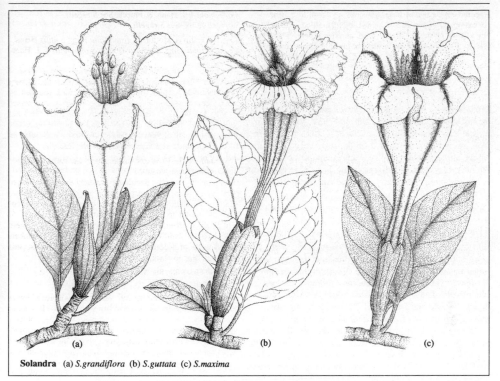

Solandra (a) *S.grandiflora* (b) *S.guttata* (c) *S.maxima*

awkward, unsightly specimens. Under glass, give bright, filtered light and ventilate above 20°C/68°F: water plentifully during the summer months, sparingly in winter. Propagate from seed in spring and by greenwood cuttings in a closed propagating case with bottom heat in summer. Susceptible to mealybug, aphid, scale insect and red spider mite.

S.grandiflora Sw. (*Swartzia grandiflora* (Sw.) J.F. Gmel.).
Evergreen glabrous or pubescent shrub, to 5m+. Leaves to 17cm, elliptic to elliptic-oblong or obovate, apex acute; petiole to 2.5cm. Flowers fragrant; calyx tubular, to 8cm, glabrous or pubescent, appearing 2-lipped; corolla white, becoming yellow to pink tinged yellow, to 23cm, funnel-shaped; limb lobed, lobes undulate to crenate. Fruit ovoid to globose, green. Spring. Jamaica, Puerto Rico, Lesser Antilles.

S.guttata D. Don (*Swartzia guttata* D. Don ex Lindl.).
Evergreen climbing shrub, to 2m+. Leaves to 15×11cm, broad-elliptic to ovate or obovate, soft-pubescent beneath, apex acute to acuminate; petiole to 6cm. Flowers terminal, erect, fragrant; calyx tubular, 3-lobed, to 9cm, soft pubescent; corolla to 26 ×8cm, funnel-shaped, throat pale yellow, spotted or striped purple; limb spreading, crispate; anthers to 1cm. Fruit globose, yellow. Mexico. Much material labelled as *S.guttata* is *S.maxima*.

S.hartwegii N.E. Br. See *S.maxima*.
S.laevis Hook. See *S.longiflora*.

S.longiflora Tussac (*S.laevis* Hook.; *S.macrantha* Dunal).
Resembles *S.grandiflora*, but calyx to half length of corolla tube. Shrub, to 2m. Leaves to 10cm, elliptic to obovate-oblong. Flowers white tinged purple, to 30cm; calyx to 11cm; corolla to 32×8cm, apex contracted; corolla lobed, lobes dentate, undulate; stamens attached 13–19cm from corolla base; anthers to 1cm. Fruit to 3cm diam. Winter. Jamaica, Cuba, Hispaniola.

S.macrantha Dunal. See *S.longiflora*.

S.maxima (Sessé & Moc.) P. Green (*S.hartwegii* N.E. Br.;
S.nitida Zuccagni).
Climbing glabrous shrub, to 4m. Stems branching. Leaves to 15cm, elliptic, glabrous, apex short-acuminate or acute to obtuse; petiole to 7cm. Flowers yellow, to 20cm; calyx to 7cm, glabrous, lobed, lobes to 4, unequal; corolla glabrous, urceolate, to 20cm; cor. tube 5-veined, veins purple, interior 5-ridged, ridges purple; limb lobed, lobes 5, reflexed; stamens attached 10cm from base. Mexico, C America, Colombia, Venezuela.

S.nitida Zuccagni. See *S.grandiflora*.
S.viridiflora Miers. See *Dyssochroma viridiflora*.

Solanecio (Schultz-Bip.) Walp. Compositae. About 15 species of subsucculent or succulent, tuberous-rooted herbs, softly woody shrubs, climbers or epiphytes. Leaves alternate, simple, sometimes deeply lobed, pinnately veined, glabrous, glandular or tomentose. Capitula discoid, several to numerous, in terminal compound cymes, receptacle flat, glabrous; phyllaries in 1 series, with smaller outer bracts (calyculi); florets yellow; anther collars broadened toward base; style arms truncate, fringed with short papillae, or with a central tuft of longer papillae. Fruit an oblong, glabrous or shortly pubescent cypsela; pappus of fine bristles. Tropical Africa, Madagascar, Yemen. Z10.

CULTIVATION   As for *Senecio*.

S.angulatus (Vahl) C. Jeffrey.
Perennial climbing herb to 3m, shrubby below, glabrous, shining. Leaves to 12×6cm, ovate or oval, deeply dissected, often spreading, base auriculate, lobes to 3cm, 2–5 on each side, linear, oblong-ovate or obovate, often spreading or recurved, margins entire, toothed or undulate, terminal lobe largest. Capitula to 1cm, narrowly campanulate, in rounded, often dense cymes; calyculus of few, short, linear to lanceolate bracts; phyllaries to 9mm, 5–8, linear to broadly linear; florets c10, tubular, hermaphrodite. Fruit short, ribbed, setulose. Tropical Africa.

Solanum L. (Lat. name for this plant.) Nightshade. Solanaceae. About 1400 species of herbs, shrubs, trees or, occasionally, vines. Leaves simple, entire, lobed or parted. Inflorescence cymose, umbellate, paniculate or racemose; calyx campanulate or rotate, 5-dentate, sometimes enlarged in fruit; corolla rotate or broadly campanulate, regular, 5-angled or 5-lobed, tube very short, limb plaited in bud; stamens 5, all fertile, filaments very short, anthers oblong to linear, connivent or connannate around style, opening by terminal pores or short terminal clefts; ovary 2-celled, stigma small. Fruit a berry, fleshy or coriaceous; seeds numerous, more or less flattened. Cosmopolitan, particularly Tropical America.

CULTIVATION One of the 'great' genera of flowering plants, at 1400 species strong, it is perhaps unsurprising that *Solanum* should contain some climbers. Among the hardy species, *S.dulcamara*, the Deadly Nightshade, is included here only for reasons of completeness and because it is so often encountered as a weed species. Rather higher value is attached to *S.crispum* and *S.jasminoides*. The first is an exceptionally vigorous semi-scandent shrub hardy to 10°C/14°F. Stout, fast-growing stems are clothed with large, entire, dark green leaves and topped with trusses of mauve-blue 'Nightshade' flowers with contrasting golden anthers. This species will thrive on most reasonably fertile soils in full sunlight. It requires the support of a wall or fence but comparatively little tying-in – the sturdy stems become more or less self-supporting, especially if regularly pruned. Long shoots of established plants of *S.crispum* should be pruned back to within five nodes in early to mid spring to promote a bushy, floriferous framework. The vigorous cultivar 'Glasnevin' may require an additional summer pruning; this may promote successional flushes of flowers.

    S.jasminoides is a more graceful climber, ill deserving its popular name, Potato Vine. It produces a tangled mass of slender, dark-tinted stems densely covered with variably lobed dark green foliage and delicate cymes of white or very pale violet flowers. With the support of wires or trellis, it will soon covered sheltered, sunny walls and fences and will flower throughout the summer, the overall effect – as its specific epithet suggest – being rather like that of a Jasmine.

    The remaining species are hardy only in sheltered locations in zone 9 (they are, for example, seen outdoors in the Mediterranean, New Zealand and California). They are otherwise robust climbing shrubs for walls, posts and rafters in the conservatory and glasshouse (minimum winter temperature –10°C/14°F). *S.donnell-smithii* is a prickly, rather awkward-looking vine with downy white or opal flowers. Also prickly, *S.wendlandii* is a splendid species with large, deeply lobed leaves and heavy trusses of broad lilac flowers with a distinctive if rather evasive perfume. It requires a rich, moist soil and, once a framework is established, careful but decisive pruning in late winter to maintain vigour and free flowering. It its finer forms, *S.pensile* bears large violet-blue flowers with a bright white central star. *S.seaforthianum*, the St Vincent Lilac, is a more slender climber, ubiquitous in tropical and subtropical gardens, where it is valued for its narrow, drooping panicles of lilac Nightshade flowers. Plant the tropical species in a medium- to high-fertility loam-based mix with tubs or borders in the glasshouse. They will tolerate fairly heavy shade, especially in summer, but prefer bright filtered sunlight. Water, feed and mist frequently in summer, sparingly in winter. Increase all species by seed sown in late winter in a heated case, or by semi-ripe stem cuttings. All are highly toxic – which does little to deter whitefly.

S.crispum Ruiz & Pav.
Robust shrub, climbing to 3–4m, stems green and pubescent when young, woody with age. Leaves 7–12cm, ovate to lanceolate, apex acute, base rounded to cordate, margins sometimes undulate-crispate, finely pubescent, persistent in mild climates, petiolate. Inflorescence terminal, corymbs 7–10cm diam.; flowers fragrant; calyx 5-toothed; corolla to 3cm diam., 5-lobed, mauve-blue; anthers yellow. Fruit pea-sized, white tinged yellow. Summer. Chile. 'Glasnevin': habit vigorous; flowers deep mauve-blue with golden yellow anthers, in large clusters. Z8.

S.donnell-smithii J.Coult.
Vine, high-climbing, more or less hispid. Stems woody, densely stellate-hairy, armed with stout recurved yellow spines. Leaves 7–15cm, oblong to elliptic, generally angular-lobed, main vein beneath spiny. Inflorescence axillary, cymose, lax, few-flowered; calyx deeply 5-cleft, lobes acuminate, prickly; corolla deeply parted, 2.5+cm diam., lobes linear-lanceolate, white, sometimes tinged pale blue, densely pubescent, without. Fruit 2cm diam., globose, orange. Mexico to San Salvador. Z10.

S.dulcamara L. BITTERSWEET; CLIMBING NIGHTSHADE; DEADLY NIGHTSHADE; FELONWOOD; POISONOUS NIGHTSHADE.
Perennial scrambler or trailer. Stems 2–4m, becoming rather woody below, shoots grey tinged yellow. Leaves 5–12 × 2–7cm, simple or deeply lobed, deep green above, paler beneath, minutely pubescent to subglabrous, simple leaves ovate, entire, acuminate at apex, rounded or subcordate at base, lobed leaves with terminal lobe ovate, laterals 1–2, lanceolate to ovate, basal, divergent or deflexed, much smaller than terminal; petioles 1–4cm. Inflorescence arising from internodes, or opposite leaves, laxly branched, cymose, pedunculate, drooping; pedicels jointed at base, 1cm; calyx 3–4mm; corolla 1–1.5cm diam., lobes reflexed, pale violet or blue to white, sometimes with green spots at base; anthers 5mm. Fruit ovoid to globose, 8–12mm, bright red; seeds suborbicular, 2mm, pale. Summer. Eurasia, naturalized N America. All parts of the plant are toxic. 'Variegatum': leaves variegated; flowers purple-blue. Z4.

S.jasminoides Paxt. POTATO VINE.
Deciduous or semi-evergreen vine, copiously branched, glabrous; shoots slender, sometimes tinted purple. Leaves

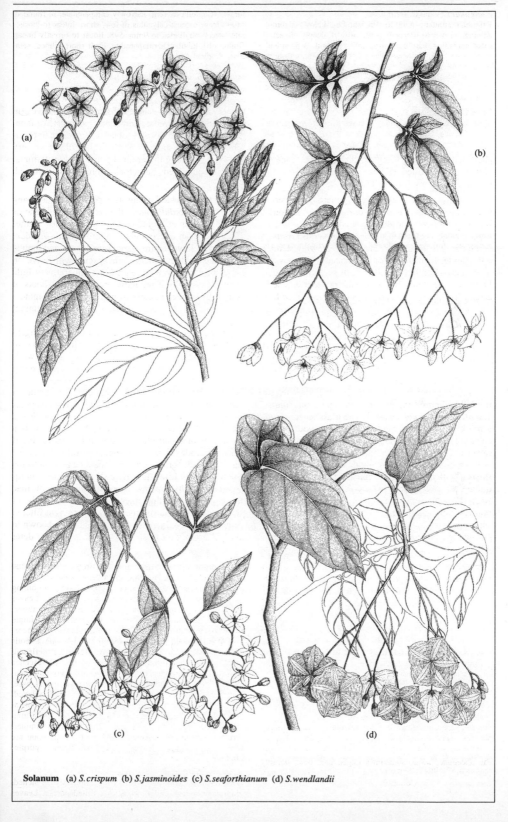

Solanum (a) *S. crispum* (b) *S. jasminoides* (c) *S. seaforthianum* (d) *S. wendlandii*

petiolate, 3–5-parted, leaflets ovate, entire, 4–6cm, reduced upwards, uppermost leaves simple, entire, ovate-lanceolate, subcordate at base. Inflorescence of short racemes 2.5–3cm long, clusters 5–7cm diam.; calyx shallowly 5-toothed; corolla stellate, 2–2.5cm diam., enlarging and becoming bell-like with age, white tinted violet-blue or pure white; stamens lemon yellow. Summer. Brazil. 'Album': vigorous; leaves dark green, flowers pure white, long-lasting. Z8.

S.pensile Sendt.
Vine, branched, high-climbing. Leaves 5–10cm, ovate, cordate at base, glabrous and glossy green above, paler beneath. Inflorescence large, paniculate, pendulous, hairy; corolla to 4cm diam., lobed, lobes incurved at apex, bright violet to pale blue with white centre star. Fruit 1–2cm, globose, pale violet. Guyana, Surinam. Z10.

S.seaforthianum Andrews. BRAZILIAN NIGHTSHADE; ST VINCENT LILAC; GLYCINE; ITALIAN JASMINE; TOMATILLO.
Rather slender vine to 6m, glabrous or sparsely pubescent. Leaves 5–10×3–8cm, broadly elliptic, entire or generally pinnately divided into ovate lobes, base rounded, apex acute to acuminate. Inflorescence lateral or subterminal, narrowly

pyramidal, paniculate, pendulous, few- to many-flowered; pedicels 4–6mm; calyx 1mm, funnelform, minutely dentate, glabrous; corolla star-like, campanulate to rotate, expanding to 2cm diam., lobes 8–12mm, elliptic-oblong, blue, purple, pink or white, ciliolate; anthers 2mm, yellow. Fruit 6–10mm, globose, red. S America; widely cultivated and naturalized in Tropics. Z10.

S.wendlandii Hook.f. POTATO VINE; GIANT POTATO CREEPER; PARADISE FLOWER.
Robust vine to 5m+; stems glabrous, sparsely armed with scattered short, hook-like spines. Leaves variable, 10–25cm, simple to pinnate, bright green, pinnate leaves with large terminal leaflets and 8–12 laterals, upper leaves simple and oblong, or 3-lobed and cordate with lobed or incised lateral leaflets, lobes ovate to oblong, entire. Inflorescence terminal, cymose, pendulous, 15cm+ diam.; corolla rotate, 5cm diam., lilac-blue, scarcely lobed, the margins wavy, 5-pointed and recurved with midpetaline areas narrow, darker or paler stripes, surface undulate, the whole resembling a billowing skirt or inverted parachute; anthers cream. Fruit 1–10cm diam., globose to ovoid. Summer. Costa Rica. 'Albescens': flowers off-white. Z10.

Solena Lour. (From Gk *solen*, tube.) Cucurbitaceae. 1 species, a monoecious climbing herb. Root tuberous. Stems slender, glabrous. Tendrils simple. Leaves subsessile, polymorphic, entire or remotely dentate, ovate to deeply 5- or more lobed, cordate, acute, scabrid and glandular above; petiole slender, exstipulate. Male inflorescence axillary, umbellate; female flowers solitary; flowers yellow to white, about 6×4mm with minute, subulate teeth; corolla triangular-lobed; stamens 3, filaments ciliate; ovary oblong, ovules several. Fruit ovoid, scabrous, occasionally villous, fleshy, 2.5–1.5cm; seeds grey, small. Asia to Malaysia. Z10.

CULTIVATION As for *Coccinia*. The leaves, roots and fruits are edible. Purgatives and stimulants are derived from the seeds and roots.

S.amplexicaulis (Lam.) Gandhi (*Bryonia amplexicaulis* Lam.).

Sollya Lindl. (For R.H. Solly (1778–1858), botanical anatomist and physiologist.) Pittosporaceae. 3 species of perennial, evergreen, slender climbers or scandent shrubs, to 2m. Leaves alternate, simple, small, narrow, margins entire or slightly undulate. Inflorescence a terminal, lax, few-flowered cyme, or flowers sometimes solitary; flowers small, blue, nodding, on slender pedicels; sepals small; petals obovate; anthers longer than filaments, connivent in a conical arrangement around style. Fruit an indehiscent berry. Australia. Z9.

CULTIVATION Elegant twining climbers grown for their clusters of gracefully nodding bell-shaped flowers carried from mid-summer into autumn, *Sollya* species will tolerate temperatures down to freezing, provided their wood is well ripened. In cool regions they may be grown in the cool glasshouse or conservatory. Grow in a humus-rich, moisture-retentive but well drained medium, with full sun to part shade; provide support and pinch out shoot tips on young plants to encourage branching. Under glass, ensure shade from the hottest sun in summer; water moderately when in full growth, less in winter. Repot and prune in spring to remove weak, dead and overcrowded growth. Under glass, maintain a winter minimum temperature of 5–10°C/40–50°F. Propagate by seed sown at 21°C/70°F, by soft heeled cuttings or greenwood in early summer or by leaf bud cuttings in summer; root in a closed case with bottom heat. Red spider mite may be a problem under glass

S.drummondii Morr. See *S.parviflora*.
S.fusiformis (Labill.) Briq. See *S.heterophylla*.

S.heterophylla Lindl. (*S.fusiformis* Payer; *S.fusiformis* (Labill.) Briq.). BLUEBELL CREEPER; AUSTRALIAN BLUEBELL.
Slender, scandent shrub, 0.5–1.5m. Leaves 2.5–5cm, on short petioles, ovate to linear-oblong or oblanceolate, obtuse to acuminate, paler beneath. Inflorescence with 4–8(–12) flowers, terminal or with 1 opposite leaf; petals 8mm, blue. Summer. W Australia.

S.parviflora Turcz. (*S.drummondii* Morr.).
Slender climber to 2m, with a loose, soft pubescence. Leaves to 2.5cm, subsessile, thin, lanceolate to oblong-linear. Inflorescence 2–3-flowered or flowers solitary; pedicels slender; petals c6mm, blue. Summer. W Australia.

S.fusiformis Payer. See *S.heterophylla*.

For illustration see Pittosporaceae.

Stauntonia DC. (For Sir George Staunton (1737–1801), Irish physician, diplomat and naturalist; he accompanied Lord Macartney on his Embassy to China in 1793.) Lardizabalaceae. 16 species of dioecious, evergreen, twining shrubs. Leaves alternate, palmately compound. Inflorescence a few-flowered axillary raceme; flowers unisexual, although, like *Sinofranchetia*, female plants will set fruit in the absence of a male pollinator; sepals 6, fleshy, acuminate; petals and nectaries absent, male flowers with stamens connate (distinguishing them from *Holboellia* in which the stamens are free), female flowers with 3 carpels and stamens reduced to staminodes. Fruit an edible, ellipsoid berry. E Asia (Burma to Taiwan and Japan).

CULTIVATION   A twining climber grown for its attractive foliage, small fragrant flowers and edible egg-shaped fruits, *Stauntonia* is suited to a cool greenhouse or conservatory. In milder regions, where temperatures do not fall below –5°C/23°F for prolonged periods, a warm sheltered site will be suitable, in which case cultivate as for *Akebia*.

S.hexaphylla Decne. (*Rajania hexaphylla* Thunb.; *Holboellia hexaphylla* hort.).
Stems twining to 10m, glabrous. Leaflets 3–7, to 14cm, ovate to elliptic, apex acute to acuminate, dark green, glossy, coriaceous. Flowers to 2cm, white to ivory, with a violet tint, fragrant. Fruit 2.5–5cm, globose to ovoid, purple. Summer. S Korea, Japan, Ryukyu Is. var. *obovata* Wu. Leaflets 6–10cm, obovate to oblong-lanceolate, apex caudate, base obtuse. Mts of Japan and Taiwan. Z8.

For illustration see Lardizabalaceae.

Stenochlaena J. Sm. (From Gk *stenos*, narrow, and *chlaina*, cloak, referring to the absent indusia.) Blechnaceae. Some 5 species of large, tropical, usually epiphytic, climbing ferns. Rhizome indefinitely scandent, with sparse, round or elongate, deciduous scales. Fronds dimorphic; sterile fronds pinnate, lateral pinnae usually articulate to the rachis, with basal glands, firm, glabrous, margin sharply cartilaginous-serrate, veins free; fertile fronds pinnate or very rarely bipinnate, pinnae linear, entire, margin sometimes reflexed, veins forming a single row of narrow areoles on each side of the costa. Sporangia cover a zone extending from the outer side of the costal areole toward or almost to the margin. Tropical Africa, Asia and Australasia. Z10.

CULTIVATION   Tropical terrestrial ferns usually occurring in bog or marshland. Of vigorous habit, the rather coarse, pinnate fronds are widely spaced along the thin rhizomes and quickly cover large areas. Emerging fronds have a pink hue. Excellent for ground cover in situations too wet and shaded for other plants, they are extremely adaptable and will succeed in full sun, although bright filtered sunlight is preferred in the intermediate glasshouse. Although enjoying plentiful watering, they will adapt to drier conditions, and will succeed in a hanging pot or basket where the rhizomes will cascade down and the plant is more easily contained – specimens grown in the border may become invasive, and may frequently need thinning. *S.palustris* has rhizomes with a tendency to climb using adhesive roots. They will also succeed well as indoor plants. A medium suitable for terrestrial ferns is recommended with an acidic pH. Copious watering, good air circulation combined with high humidity and feeding at fortnightly intervals ensures sturdy growth during the growing season. Propagation is from spores, or by division: large divisions tend to establish better than small pieces.

S.heteromorpha J. Sm. See *Blechnum filiforme*.

S.palustris (Burm.) Bedd. (*S.scandens* J. Sm.; *Acrostichum scandens* L.). CLIMBING FERN.
Rhizome woody, widely climbing. Fronds 90×30cm, pinnate, glossy, sterile pinnae 10–20 × 2–6cm, sessile or slightly pedunculate, serrulate, acuminate, base cuneate, articulated, edge thickened, fertile pinnae to 15–30 × 0.3–0.4cm, lower pinnae distant; petioles to 10cm, erect, glabrous, firm. India, S China, Australasia.

S.scandens J. Sm. See *S.palustris*.

S.sorbifolia (L.) J. Sm. (*Acrostichum sorbifolium* L.).
Rhizome thick, woody, often to 12m long, occasionally spiny. Fronds 30–45 × 15–30cm, pinnate, sterile pinnae 3–20 pairs, 12–15 × 1.5cm, entire or dentate, articulated at base, fertile pinnae 5–10 × 1.5cm, 2.5–5cm apart. Tropical America.

S.tenuifolia (Desv.) Moore.
Rhizome widely scandent, woody, slightly scaly. Sterile fronds 90–150 × 30–45cm, pinnate, pinnae 15–23 × 2–4cm, short-peduncled, acuminate, finely and densely serrulate, glossy, edge thickened; fertile fronds bipinnate, glossy, pinnae long-stipitate, with numerous distant pinnules. Tropical Africa.

Stephanotis Thouars. (From Gk *stephanotis*, a name given to the Myrtle used in ancient Greece for making crowns or garlands (a use to which these flowers are put) but the name here to derives from *stephanos*, crown, and *otos*, ear, referring to the auricled staminal corona.) Asclepiadaceae. 5 species of twining, glabrous, evergreen shrubs. Leaves opposite, coriaceous. Flowers large, white, waxy, in umbel-like axillary cymes; calyx 5-parted, segments somewhat leafy; corolla salver- to funnelform, tube cylindrical, often slightly inflated at base, throat dilated, limb with 5 spreading lobes; corona scales 5, erect. Fruit a fleshy follicle. Old World Tropics. Z10.

CULTIVATION   Grown for its glossy evergreen foliage and beautifully fragrant, waxen blooms, carried throughout the summer months, *Stephanotis* is a vigorous climber for pergolas, trellis and fencing in tropical regions. In cooler climates it is a handsome plant for the warm glasshouse, conservatory or home, trained on trellis or wire or especially grown in pots in the traditional manner and trained on wire hoops. Grow in freely draining mediums that are fertile, moisture-retentive, well aerated and rich in organic matter; provide high humidity, bright filtered light during the hottest summer months, but otherwise full light; water plentifully and feed fortnightly with dilute liquid feed when in full growth, misting frequently in warm weather. Reduce water in winter to keep just moist. Blooms are carried on young shoots, so prune in winter before growth commences, thinning

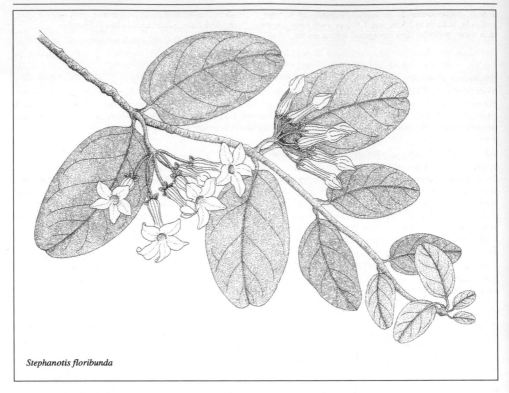

Stephanotis floribunda

out congested shoots. Propagate by seed, layers or semi-ripe cuttings, treat with hormone rooting compound and root in a humid closed case with bottom heat. Sometimes infested by soft scale (*Coccus hesperidum*) and hemispherical scale (*Saissetia coffeae*); root mealybug can also be a troublesome pest.

S.floribunda (R. Br.) Brongn. (*S.jasminoides* hort.). MADAGASCAR JASMINE; BRIDAL WREATH; CHAPLET FLOWER; WAX FLOWER; FLORADORA.
Stems to 4m. Leaves to 15cm, oval to oblong-elliptic, thickly coriaceous, dull sage to dark green above, apex often minutely mucronulate, midvein conspicuous, short-stalked. Flowers in short-stalked, crowded, radial clusters, highly fragrant; corolla to 6cm, pure white to ivory, lobes ovate-oblong. Madagascar.

S.jasminoides hort. See *S.floribunda*.

Stictocardia Hallier f. (From Gk *stiktos*, spotted, and *kardia*, heart, the undersides of the cordate leaves are spotted with glands.) Convolvulaceae. About 12 species of perennial, woody or herbaceous climbers with puberulent or glabrate stems. Leaves petiolate, usually axillary or ovate, base cordate, veins often impressed above, with tiny, black, glandular hairs beneath. Inflorescence 1- to many-flowered, axillary, pedunculate; sepals 5, orbicular to ovate, apex subacute or blunt to emarginate, subequal, sometimes with black glandular hairs; corolla funnel-shaped; stigma 2-lobed. Fruit an indehiscent capsule, globose to subspheroidal, often enclosed by enlarged sepals, with 1–4 short-pubescent seeds. Pantropicaly separated from *Ipomoea* mainly on the basis of its indehiscent capsule and glandular leaf undersides; its pollen is spinulose. Z10.

CULTIVATION   As for the perennial, tender species of *Ipomoea*.

S.beraviensis (Vatke) Hallier f. (*Ipomoea beraviensis* vatke; *Ipomoea pringsheimiriana* Rendle; *Argyreia beraviensis* (Vatke) Bak.). KING'S IPOMOEA.
Woody climber to 10m, young growth densely hairy. Leaves to 16–23cm, ovate, apex mucronate, acute or blunt, base truncate or shallowly cordate, veins deeply impressed; petioles to 17cm. Inflorescence on 8–25mm peduncles, many-flowered; pedicels 6–10mm; sepals 7–13mm, elliptic or suborbicular, bases pubescent, glabrous above, blunt or emarginate with a tiny mucro at apex; corolla 4.5–5cm, bright crimson, tube orange-yellow at base, midpetaline areas with tufts of hairs at apices. Fruit 14 × 13mm; seeds 6mm, black. W Africa to Ethiopia and Zimbabwe, Madagascar.

S.campanulata (L.) Merrill (*S.tiliifolia* (Desv.) Hallier f.; *Argyreia tiliifolia* (Desr.) Wight).
Woody climber to 12m. Leaves 8–25cm, cordate to cordate-ovate, apex acute to short-acuminate, glabrate; petioles 3–14cm. Inflorescence 1–4-flowered; pedicels 1–3.5cm; sepals 1–2cm, pubescent to glabrate; corolla 5–8cm, crimson with orange or yellow stripes inside. Fruit 2.5–3cm diam.; seeds about 8–9mm, grey-brown, minutely hairy. Pantropical.

S.maculosoi (Mattei) Verdc. (*Ipomoea maculosoi* Mattei)
Woody climber to 8m, with ridged, yellow, more or less hairy stems. Leaves 6.5–11cm, broadly ovate to suborbicular, apex rounded to short-acuminate, base deeply cordate; petioles

2–8cm. Inflorescence 2- to several-flowered, on a 5mm peduncle; pedicels to 2.5cm; sep. 1.5–2cm, oval, inner longer than outer, glabrous, apex emarginate with a mucro; corolla 5.5–7cm, scarlet, tube paler, midpetaline areas hairy at apex. Fruit 1.8cm diam.; seeds 6mm, brown. S Somalia.

S.tiliifolia (Desr.) Hallier f. See *S.campanulata*.

Stigmaphyllon A. Juss. (From Gk *stigma*, and *phyllon*, leaf; the stigma is expanded and somewhat leaf-like.)

Malpighiaceae. 60–100 species of lianes. Leaves opposite or pseudo-alternate, simple or lobed, entire or dentate; glands 2, usually on petioles, sometimes below; stipules small or absent. Inflorescences axillary or terminal short dense sessile corymbiform racemes; sepals 5, lateral 4 with 2 glands; petals 5, clawed, glabrous, unequal, usually yellow, lateral 4 concave with margin dentate or fimbriate; stamens 10, filaments connate at base; ovary 3-lobed, 3-locular, styles 3, dilated at apex. Fruit a samara, 1–3 on pyramidal receptacle, wings large, elongated, thick at upper margin. Tropical Americas, Caribbean. Z10.

CULTIVATION   Handsome woody twiners, grown for their foliage and long-stalked clusters of beautiful if short-lived flowers, often carried in succession over several weeks. Some may tolerate a brief light frost when mature, but they are generally suitable for outdoor cultivation only in tropical and subtropical zones; otherwise they make attractive specimens trained up pillars and wires in the intermediate glasshouse or conservatory. Grow in sun or light shade in any moderately fertile soil. Under glass, plant directly into the glasshouse border into a fertile and freely draining medium; admit bright light but ensure shade from the hottest summer sun. Water moderately when in growth and keep almost dry when at rest. Maintain a winter minimum temperature of 13–15°/55–60°F. Prune in late winter/spring or immediately after blooming to confine to bounds and to thin out congested growth. Propagate by semi-ripe cuttings in a sandy propagating mix with gentle bottom heat, or by seed.

S.aristatum Lindl.
Climber to 5m. Leaves sagittate-hastate, acute, glabrous, leaves on young branches oblong, entire; petiole with 2 glands at apex. Flowers few in pedunculate umbels; petals fimbriate. Summer. Brazil.

S.ciliatum (Lam.) A. Juss. AMAZON CLIMBER; GOLDEN VINE.
Liane to 8m. Leaves 4–9.5 × 3.5–7.5cm, broad-ovate, base deeply auriculate with rounded overlapping lobes, apex obtuse or acute or acuminate or mucronate, margin ciliate, often bronze at first. Flowers 3–8; petals golden-yellow, fimbriate. Coast of C & S America (Belize to Uruguay).

S.diversifolium (Kunth) A. Juss.
Tall liane. Leaves 2–8 × 0.5–5cm, suborbicular to ovate or elliptic to linear, base cuneate to rounded or cordate, apex acute to rounded, apiculate, coriaceous, glabrate above, tomentose beneath, margin entire, eglandular. Flowers 6–20; petals dentate. Cuba, Lesser Antilles.

S.fulgens (Lam.) A. Juss.
Climbing shrub or liane, sericeous in all parts when young. Leaves to 17 × 17cm, opposite, orbicular to ovate, base reniform or cordate, apex rounded, short acuminate or apiculate, margin coarsely crenate or subentire, adult leaves glabrous above, silver- or bronze-sericeous beneath. Flowers to 1.7cm diam.; petals terracotta, spotted yellow at middle. N Brazil to Caribbean.

S.heterophyllum Hook.
Tall liane. Leaves opposite, ovate, apex obtuse, mucronate, margin undulate, or sometimes cordate or 3-lobed, lobes oblong. Flowers in axillary umbels; petals orbicular. Argentina (Tucuman).

S.humboldtianum A. Juss.
Liane. Leaves 5–11cm, ovate to suborbicular or cordate, apex acute or rounded, mucronate, base truncate, rounded or cordate, glabrate above, pubescent beneath. C America (Mexico to Panama), northern & eastern S America.

S.jatrophifolium A. Juss.
To 2m. Leaves palmately 5–7-cleft, acute, margin serrate-ciliate, light green; petioles glandular at apex. Flowers may in umbels; petals shell-shaped, fimbriate. Uruguay.

S.littorale A. Juss.
Tall liane. Leaves 5–12.5cm, opposite or alternate, variable in shape, long-petiolate. Flowers many, to 2.5cm across, in axillary corymbs; petals long-clawed. S Brazil.

Stizophyllum Miers. (From Gk *stizo*, to prick, and *phyllon*, leaf: the leaves are hollow pellucid-punctate, as if pricked.)

Bignoniaceae. 3 species of lianes. Branches terete, hollow, without glandular patches between nodes. Leaves trifoliolate, hollow-pellucid-punctate, glandular-scaly beneath, terminal leaflet often replaced by simple or trifid tendril. Flowers in axillary racemes; calyx campanulate, inflated, bilabiate to regularly 5-lobed, pubescent; corolla tubular-campanulate; anthers glabrous or pubescent; ovary linear-tetragonal, scaly; ovules 2-seriate. Fruit a narrow, linear capsule, valves parallel, convex, striate and pubescent; seeds slender, 2-winged, wings membranous. Mexico to Brazil. Z10.

CULTIVATION   As for *Clytostoma*.

S.perforatum Miers (*Bignonia perforata* Cham.).
Leaflets to *c*20cm, ovate, apex subacuminate, tomentose beneath. Calyx margin lacerate; corolla to 5cm, white to cream marked pink, pubescent outside. Brazil.

Streptosolen Miers. (From Gk *streptos* twisted, and *solon*, tube, referring to the twisted corolla tube.)

Solanaceae. 1 species, an erect to weakly climbing or sprawling evergreen, scabrous, pubescent shrub, to 2.5m. Branches slender. Leaves to 5cm, alternate, ovate to elliptic, acute, entire; petiole to 1cm. Inflorescence terminal, corymbose; flowers stipitate, borne at branch apices; calyx to 1cm, tubular, dentate, teeth 5, acute; corolla funnel-shaped, tube long, spirally twisted, yellow to orange yellow, limb orange-red, spreading, appearing 2-lipped, lobes 5, broad-oblong; fertile stamens 4. Fruit capsular, 2-chambered, leathery. Colombia, Peru. Z9.

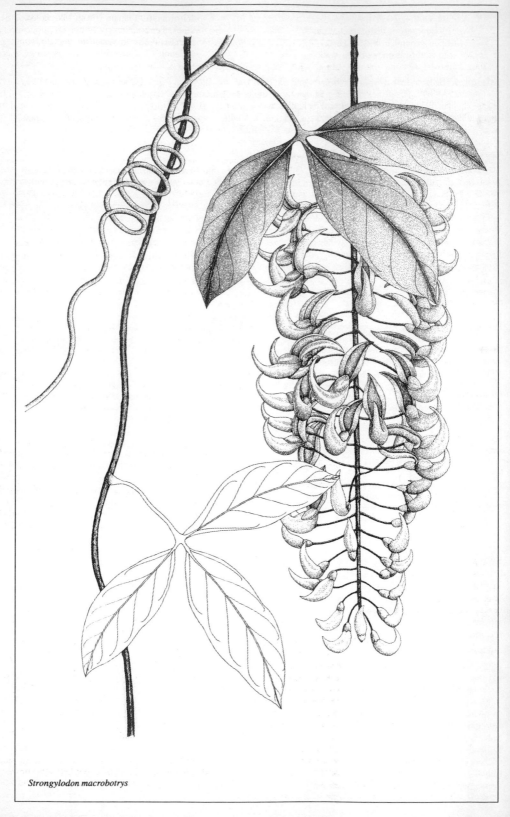

Strongylodon macrobotrys

CULTIVATION Cultivated in dry, virtually frost-free climates as a standard or a wall-trained plant, *S.jamesonii* is valued for its trumpets of yellow to burnt-orange flowers with their twisted and narrow tubes, flaring wide at the mouth. In open ground it will make a shrub of 1.2–1.8m/4–6ft, but by tying its arching to weakly climbing branches into a wire framework on walls, pergolas or pillars it makes a good, leafy screening plant reaching almost 3.5m/11ft. In zone 9, it may succeed against a south or west-facing wall. Plants are occasionally used as informal hedging. Plant out in spring in light, well drained loam in full sun; although fairly drought-tolerant, *Streptosolen* grows best with adequate moisture in the root zone. Prune straggling specimens by cutting back the previous season's growth by one third after flowering, removing weak shoots completely.

In cool temperate areas grow under intermediate glasshouse conditions (min. temperature 7°C/45°F); conservatory plants may be trained to form standards or attractive specimen shrubs for standing out on patios during the summer months. Under glass, grow in a well drained, high-fertility loam-based medium with bright filtered light and medium humidity; water moderately in summer, sparingly in winter, feed established plants monthly with a dilute liquid fertilizer and ventilate when temperatures rise above 20°C/68°F. Repot or top-dress annually. Propagate by 8cm/3in. heeled greenwood cuttings in a closed case with bottom heat in spring/summer: stock plants which are to provide cuttings may be pruned back to 15cm/6in. of the framework in late winter. Pinch young plants to encourage bushy growth or to train to climb stakes and trellising. Susceptible to aphid, red spider mite and whitefly: diseases include tomato spotted wilt virus.

S.jamesonii (Benth.) Miers (*Browállia jamesonii* Benth.).
ORANGE BROWALLIA; MARMELADE BUSH; FIREBUSH.

Strongylodon Vogel. Leguminosae (Papilionoideae). Some 20 species of robust evergreen or deciduous shrubs or lianes. Flowers papilionaceous, with a long, sharp beak-like keel, usually in long racemes. Fruit a large indehiscent legume. SE Asia to Polynesia. Z10.

CULTIVATION Among the most spectacular of all climbing plants, the Jade Vine is festooned with long racemes of jade to aquamarine lobster-claw-like flowers which, seen in a shady stove house or a bower in some tropical garden, assume an eerily luminescent quality. Plant in tubs or greenhouse borders in well drained, neutral to acid soil into which leafmould and well rotted farmyard manure have been incorporated. Water and syringe plentifully during the growing season (avoid wetting flowers); at other times allow a slight drying between waterings to discourage continuous weak growth. A winter minimum of 15°C/60°F is essential as are careful training (along wires but not too near the glass) and light pruning as for young plants of *Wisteria*. Sown in high temperatures (27–30°C/80–85°F) in a closed case, seed is quick to germinate but slow to reach maturity: air layering and stem cuttings taken in early summer will usually produce better results. The Jade Vine is sometimes affected by scale insect and mealybug.

S.macrobotrys A. Gray. JADE VINE; EMERALD CREEPER.
Vigorous evergreen twining liane to 13m. Stems initially glossy, purple-green, hardening to black-brown with finely peeling ashy bark. Leaves dark green, emerging pink-bronze, trifoliolate; leaflets to 12.5 × 6.5cm, oblong-obovate. Inflorescence a pendulous, axillary, cylindrical raceme to 90cm; flowers to 7.5cm, paired or in whorls, long-stalked; corolla waxy aquamarine to luminous jade green, standard strongly recurved, margins inrolled; wings rounded, to one third length of keel, keel tapering finely, apex strongly incurved to hooked. Philippines.

Strophanthus DC. (From Gk *strophos*, twisted cord, and *anthos*, flower, referring to the twisted corolla lobes.) Apocynaceae. 38 species of shrubs and small trees, often climbing. Branches lenticellate. Leaves opposite or whorled, pinnately veined. Flowers bisexual, usually showy, in terminal or lateral, dense and few-flowered corymbose clusters; calyx 5-lobed; corolla funnelform or salverform, with 10 claw-like scales in the mouth, lobes 5, often produced into very long, twisted, thread-like tails; stamens borne in tube mouth, converging into cone around stigma. Fruit of 2, divaricate, fusiform follicles; seeds with a stalked comose appendage. Tropical to S Africa, Tropical Asia. Z10.

CULTIVATION A genus of evergreen tropical trees and shrubs, many of them climbing, *Strophanthus* is grown for its showy flowers, usually in tones of white and cream and often with remarkably long and narrow petals. The fruits, a pair of horn-like follicles, are also of interest, being long and woody and of value to dried flower arrangers. In the wet tropics and subtropics, these plants will thrive on moist, fertile soils in semi-shade, as could be provided by a host tree or a sheltered house wall. In colder climates, they may be grown in tubs or beds of rich loam-based compost in the large intermediate to warm glasshouse or conservatory. Avoid full sunlight and wide fluctuations of temperature. Propagate by semi-ripe cuttings taken in summer and inserted in a case with bottom heat.

S.capensis A. DC. See *S.speciosus*.

S.caudatus (Burm. f.) Kurz.
Trailing or climbing shrub to 6m. Leaves 7.5–20cm, slightly leathery, oblong or oblong-obovate, apex abruptly acuminate, base narrowed. Flowers yellow-white, sometimes stained purple; corolla tube 2.5cm, corolla lobe tails 7.5–20cm. Fruit 12.5–15cm. Tropical Asia.

S.divaricatus (Lour.) Hook. & Arn. (*S.divergens* Graham).
Lax, climbing shrub 1–3m. Leaves 3.5–9cm, glabrous, elliptic-oblong, narrowed to both ends, apex mucronate. Flowers

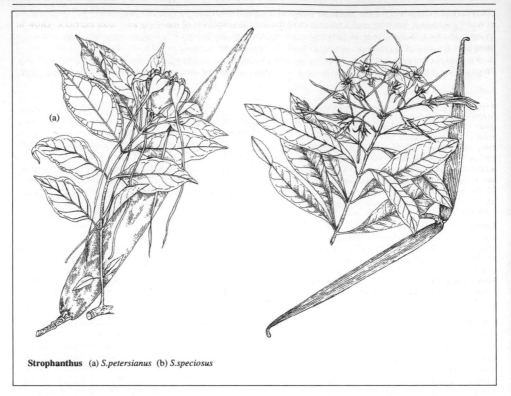

Strophanthus (a) *S.petersianus* (b) *S.speciosus*

malodorous in few-flowered cymes; corolla green-yellow with red stripes in the throat, lobes to 10cm, thread-like. S China and Vietnam.

S.divergens Graham. See *S.divaricatus*.

S.grandiflorus (N.E. Br.) Gilg. See *S.petersianus*.

S.gratus (Wallich & Hook.) Baill. CLIMBING OLEANDER. Robust climber to 8m or more. Leaves 5–18cm, apex shortly acuminate, leathery, olive-green, veins perpendicular to midrib; petiole short, stained red, scarcely dilated at base. Flowers white tinted red or purple, ultimately yellow, in dense cymes; corolla tube 1.5–4.5cm, lobes 1.4–3.5cm, membranous, obovate with obtuse tips, slightly crisped, not prolonged into tails, the scales in the mouth rose-pink, subulate, exserted 7.5mm. Fruit to 40cm. Tropical W Africa.

S.petersianus Klotzsch (*S.grandiflorus* (N.E.Br.) Gilg). Glabrous woody climber. Leaves 2.8–11cm, oblong-acuminate, ± undulate, pale beneath. Flowers dull yellow streaked with red, corolla tube 3cm wide at mouth, tails 15cm or more, reflexed, loosely twisted, yellow stained red. S Tropical Africa.

S.preussii Engl. & Pax. Climber to 4m or more. Branches glabrous, red-brown. Leaves 5–12.5cm, elliptic or oblong, acuminate or abruptly pointed, glabrous. Flowers fragrant, cream to orange with purple spots and streaks in throat; corolla tube 1.5cm, tinged purple near base, lobes ovate, abruptly constricted to purple tails, these often 30cm long; scales in mouth, short, obtuse, deep yellow. Fruit to 25cm. Tropical W Africa.

S.sarmentosus DC. Scrambling shrub. Leaves 2–15cm, ovate to oval, apex acuminate. Flowers solitary or in sparsely flowered cymes. Corolla 10cm, white striped purple in mouth, tube 1.7–4cm, tails 3–11cm, scales in mouth purple, awl-shaped. Fruit 10–28cm. Tropical Africa.

S.speciosus (Ward & Harv.) Reber (*S.capensis* A. DC.). CORKSCREW-FLOWER. Erect or rambling glabrous shrub. Branches olive-green. Leaves 2–11cm, usually small, in whorls of 3(4), oblong-lanceolate to lanceolate, acute or obtuse above, leathery. Flowers cream-yellow spotted red; corolla tube 1–1.5cm, lobes 2–5cm, spirally twisted, scales in mouth awl-shaped, short. Fruit 10–22cm. S Africa.

Syngonium Schott. (From Gk *syn*, together or joined, and *gone*, womb, alluding to united ovaries.) Araceae. 33 species of evergreen epiphytic or terrestrial perennials, usually with distinct juvenile and adult phases. Stems climbing or trailing, rooting from nodes, internodes short when adult; sap milky. Leaves simple, sagittate to ovate when juvenile, becoming larger and more sagittate as pre-mature leaf, adult leaves 3–5-lobed, or pedate, with 3–13 unequal segments, median segment largest, often variegated; petioles long, usually sheathing to at least half length. Inflorescences clustered in axils; peduncle erect at anthesis, drooping in fruit; spathe margins overlapping below forming inflated tube persistent around female flowers, limb expanded, cymbiform, membranous, green to yellow and white, often marked red or purple within; spadix shorter than spathe, covered by unisexual flowers, male and female zones separated by sterile flowers; perianth absent; stamens 4, connate; ovaries united. Fruit a compound group of berries, brown. Flowering seldom or never occurs in cultivation, most plants being sold in juvenile or pre-adult phase. Tropical America. Z10.

CULTIVATION   Attractive foliage plants for pots and hanging baskets for the heated conservatory and intermediate to warm glasshouse, but with useful tolerances of the drier atmospheres of the home and other interiors. Grow in an open and well drained medium, rich in organic matter, and shade from bright direct sunlight; provide a moist moss pole for support, a minimum temperature of 16–18°C/61–65°F, and water moderately, allowing the medium to dry partially between waterings. Pinch out stem tips to encourage branching. Repot in spring if necessary. Propagate by leaf bud or stem tip cuttings taken in summer and rooted in a closed case; also by division.

S.albolineatum Bull. See *S.podophyllum* 'Albolineatum'.

S.angustatum Schott (*S.oerstedianum* Schott).
Juvenile leaves to 6cm, cordate, median lobe ovate, lateral lobes suborbicular, dark green, marked grey-green along veins above; intermediate leaves sagittate to hastate, acuminate; adult leaves pedatisect, segments 3–11, free, median lobe to 31×10cm, elliptic to oblong-elliptic to oblanceolate, acuminate, lateral segments inequilateral, lowermost auriculate, main lateral veins 4–5 per side, impressed above; petiole 15–40cm. Inflorescence 7 per axil; peduncle almost triangular, 10cm; spathe to 14cm, tube elliptic, to 5cm, green, limb acuminate, cream; spadix to 9cm. Mexico to Costa Rica.

S.auritum (L.) Schott.
Juvenile leaves ovate or sagittate to hastate, acute; adult leaves trisect to 5-pedatisect, segments confluent, median lobe 10–30 ×6–20cm, broadly elliptic, acuminate, lateral lobes inequilateral, conspicuously auriculate at base, somewhat glossy above, main lateral veins 5–7 per side; petioles to 48cm. Inflorescence 3 per axil; peduncle to 13cm; spathe tube cylindric, to 8.5cm, dark-green externally, green stained bronze-red within, limb ovate, mucronate, to 18×10cm, cream; spadix to half length limb. Jamaica, Cuba, Hispaniola. 'Fantasy': leaves compound, midlobe with smaller lobes each side, thick, deep green, shiny, mottled white; petiole streaked cream.

S.erythrophyllum Birdsey ex Bunting.
Juvenile leaves 3–9cm, ovate, cordate, lobes rounded, black-green above, pale green soon becoming deep violet-purple beneath; adult leaves trisect, segments free, spreading or slightly overlapping, median segment 10–22 × 4.5 × 10cm, elliptic or lanceolate-elliptic to ovate, lateral segments to 10 × 4.5cm, inequilateral but not auriculate at base, subcoriaceous, glossy dark green above, pale green or violet-purple beneath; petioles to 20cm. Inflorescence 2–3 per axil; peduncle to 11cm; spathe tube ovoid to ellipsoid, to 4cm, green, limb to 11×6cm, white; spadix to 13.5cm. Panama.

S.gracile (Miq.) Schott. See *S.podophyllum*.

S.hoffmannii Schott.
Juvenile leaves sagittate, 4–18cm, green with grey veins; adult leaves trisect, segments free or confluent at base, 9–28× 3.5–11cm, median segments oblong-elliptic to ovate-oblong or lanceolate, acuminate, usually inequilateral, lateral segments to 24×8cm, very inequilateral, distinctly auriculate at base, somewhat glossy above, main lateral veins 5–10 per side, impressed above; petiole to 33cm. Inflorescence 1–3 per axil; peduncle to 9cm; spathe tube ovoid, to 4.5cm, dark green externally, red to violet-purple within, limb ovate, to 8cm, green-white to white; spadix to 12cm. Costa Rica to Panama.

S.macrophyllum Engl.
Juvenile leaves broadly ovate, to 16 × 10cm; adult leaves pedatisect, segments 7–9, free or outermost confluent, median segments 17–47 × 5–18cm, oblanceolate, elliptic to ovate-elliptic, acuminate to acute, downturned at apex, outer segments auriculate, light green above main lateral veins 3–4 per side in median segments; petioles to 60cm. Inflorescence 4–8 per axil; peduncle to 13cm; spathe tube ovate, to 5.5cm, green, limb to 11.5cm, green, becoming cream, apex mucronate. Mexico to Ecuador.

S.mauroanum Birdsey ex Bunting.
Juvenile leaves to 16cm, sagittate, marked grey- or yellow-green along midrib and larger lateral veins; adult leaves usually trisect, occasionally with 5 segments, segments free or sometimes confluent, median segments12–21 × 3.5–10cm,

elliptic to ovate-elliptic, acuminate, lateral segments inequilateral, sometimes auriculate, main lateral veins 6–10 per side, impressed above. Inflorescences to 2 per axil; peduncle to 9cm; spathe tube ellipsoid to narrow-ovoid, to 5cm, green externally, dark violet-purple within, limb to 8cm, ovate-elliptic, acuminate, white; spadix to 10cm. Costa Rica, Panama.

S.oerstedianum Schott. See *S.angustatum*.

S.peliocladum Schott. See *S.podophyllum* var. *peliocladum*.

S.podophyllum Schott (*S.vellozianum* Schott; *S.gracile* (Miq.) Schott; *S.riedelianum* Schott; *S.xanthophilum* Schott).
Juvenile leaves 7–14cm, simple, cordate, acuminate at apex, becoming sagittate or hastate as plant ages, median lobe somewhat constricted at base, basal lobes triangular, pointing downwards or outwards; intermediate leaves to 27cm; adult leaves pedatisect, segments 3–11, confluent to free, median segments 16–38×6–17cm, obovate to broad-elliptic, acuminate, with 3–7 pairs main lateral veins, lowermost segments auriculate, dark green above, pale or sometimes glaucescent beneath; petioles to 60cm. Inflorescence 4–11 per axil; peduncle to 9cm; spathe to 11cm, tube ovoid to ellipsoid, to 4cm, green, limb green-white to cream or sometimes yellow, spadix to 9cm. Mexico to Brazil and Bolivia. 'Albolineatum' (*Nephthytis triphylla* hort.): leaves heart-shaped with white centre and veins when young, later palmate and green. 'Albovirens': leaves slender, hastate when young, ivory flushed green, edge green. 'Atrovirens': leaves hastate when young, dark green with sage green shading around veins. 'Dot Mae': cultigen of 'Albolineatum', with leaves broader and more boldly marked. 'Emerald Gem': leaves fleshy, sagittate when young, shiny dark green; petioles short. 'Emerald Gem Variegated': compact; leaves thin, white to pale grey with irregular variegation. 'Imperial White': leaves tinted blue, veins white. 'Roxanne': rosette form, later creeping; petioles pinky brown; leaves hastate, when young, glossy dull green with muddy green centre and shading along the white ribs. 'Ruth Fraser': selection 'Albolineatum', variegation bolder and longer-lasting. 'Silver Knight': leaves silver-green. 'Tricolor': leaves hastate and trilobed when young, dark green with light green and white variegation; flowers purple, light pink and cream. 'Trileaf Wonder': cultigen; leaves marked ash green along lateral veins and midrib. 'Variegatum': leaves splashed pale green. var. **peliocladum** (Schott) Croat (*S.peliocladum* Schott). Differing only in stems covered by conspicuous tuberculate excrescences (stems smooth in *S.podophyllum*). Leaves trisect to 5-lobed. Costa Rica to Panama.

S.riedelianum Schott. See *S.podophyllum*.

S.salvadorense Schott.
Juvenile leaves to 19 × 11cm, hastate or sagittate, lobes inequilateral; intermediate leaves to 30cm, ovate; adult leaves trisect to almost 5-sect, confluent to almost free, median lobe 14–28×8–18cm, broad-ovate to ovate-elliptic, acuminate, lateral lobes ovate, unequal, auricles usually absent but hastate if present, main lateral veins 2–5 per side; petioles to 42cm. Inflorescence 1–2; peduncle to 18cm; spathe tube ellipsoid, to 8cm, green, tinged red at base within, limb broad-ovate to 10cm, green externally, white within; spadix to 10cm. Mexico to El Salvador.

S.standleyanum Bunting.
Juvenile leaves to 10×4cm, elliptic, acuminate, intermediate leaves elliptic to oblong or lanceolate, subhastate or cordate at base; adult leaves trisect, segments free, median segments 18–28 × 6.5–12cm, inequilateral, elliptic to oblong, acuminate, lateral segments to 24cm, elliptic-oblong, sometimes

slightly auriculate on outer margin; main lateral veins 6 per side; petioles to 35cm. Inflorescence solitary; peduncle 5cm; spathe tube fusiform cylindric, to 5cm, green, limb ovate-elliptic, to 7cm, white; spadix 8cm. Honduras to Costa Rica. 'Lancetilla': leaves matt green, ovate and unequal when young, erect, later 3-lobed.

S.vellozianum Schott. See *S.podophyllum.*

S.wendlandii Schott.
Juvenile leaves to 10cm, cordate, median lobe ovate, acuminate, lateral lobes triangular, velvety green above, veins streaked silver-grey; adult leaves trisect, median segments 8–20×2–8cm, elliptic to oblong-elliptic, acuminate, lateral segments to 15×6cm, oblong-elliptic to narrow-ovate, dark velvety green, main lateral veins 6–10 per side; petioles to 32cm. Inflorescence 1–3 per axil; peduncle to 10cm, triangular; spathe tube ovoid, to 6cm, pale green externally, red within, limb to 10.5cm, acuminate, yellow-green externally, white within; spadix weakly sigmoid, curved outwards below, inward in upper part, to 10.5cm. Costa Rica.

S.xanthophilum Schott. See *S.podophyllum.*

S.cultivars. 'Jenny': leaves pale silver flushed green. 'Maya Red': leaves entirely tinted pink. 'White Butterfly': leaves silver flushed green, edged green.

Tecomanthe Baill. (From *Tecoma,* to which it is closely related and Gk *anthe,* flower.) Bignoniaceae. 5 species of climbing or procumbent lianes. Stems with small, glandular patches on branch nodes. Leaves pinnate; leaflets in 1–7 pairs, entire or dentate, glandular-punctate beneath. Flowers in pendent racemes from old wood; flowers opposite, subtended by narrow bract; calyx to 4cm, 5-lobed, lobes triangular, ciliate; corolla funnelform, tube gradually expanded to apex, lobes 5, triangular, hairy at base of stamens inside; stamens 4, didynamous, usually included; disc annular; ovary glabrous. Fruit a linear capsule, terete or compressed, beaked, valves 2, leathery to woody, smooth; seeds with thin scarious wings. Moluccas, Papuasia, Australia, New Zealand.

CULTIVATION Grown for the foxglove-like flowers, they require the protection of the warm glasshouse in any other than tropical climates. Grow in an open, sandy and rapidly draining mix rich in organic matter and give light shade in summer. Water plentifully when in growth, less at other times, and maintain a minimum temperature of 16–18°C/60–65°F. Tie in stems in summer as growth progresses, and prune in spring to remove weak and overcrowded growths. Propagate by semi-ripe cuttings with three nodes, and root in a closed case with bottom heat at 24–27°C/75–80°F.

T.acutifolia Steenis. See *T.dendrophila.*
T.amboinensis Steenis. See *T.dendrophila.*

T.dendrophila (Bl.) Schum. (*Campana rubra* Rumphius; *Campsis dendrophila* Seem.; *Gelsemium amboinense* Kuntze; *Gelsemium dendrophilum* Kuntze; *Pandorea amboinensis* Boerl.; *Pandorea dendrophila* Boerl.; *T.acutifolia* Steenis; *T.amboinensis* Steenis; *T.gloriosa* S. Moore; *T.venusta* S. Moore).
Leaflets 1–2 pairs, 3–13 ×1.5–7cm, ovate to oblong-lanceolate, papery or herbaceous, margin entire or apex notched; petiolules to 0.8cm. Inflorescence borne on old wood of 6–20 packed flowers; pedicels 1–2cm; calyx 1.25–4cm, green tinted red or purple; corolla 7–11cm, lobes 0.75–1.5×1–2cm, tube pale to deep pink, lobes cream lined purple, or pink throughout, hairy at base of stamens inside. Fruit 17–30 × 3–3.75 ×3cm, woody. Moluccas, New Guinea, Solomon Is. Z10.

T.gloriosa S. Moore. See *T.dendrophila.*

T.speciosa W. Oliv.
Leaflets 2 pairs, 8–18 ×5–11cm, obovate, apex rounded, often divided, base cuneate, leathery, shining; petiolule 2–5cm. Inflorescence borne on old wood; pedicels to 2cm; calyx 1.5–2.5cm, glabrous, 3–5-lobed; corolla 6–8cm, tube 3.5–4.5cm, 1cm diam. in middle, cream to green, hairy inside at base of stamens, lobes 2–2.5 ×1–1.5cm, lanate outside, glabrous inside; stamens exserted. Fruit 17 ×3cm, oblong-linear, curved, woody, slightly flattened. Three Kings Is. (New Zealand). Z9.

T.venusta S. Moore. See *T.dendrophila.*

Tecomaria Spach. (From the genus *Tecoma,* to which these plants are closely related.) Bignoniaceae. 1 species, an erect or scrambling shrub or tree to 7m. Branches with glandular patches between nodes. Leaves imparipinnate; leaflets 2–3×1–3cm, elliptic-ovate to rhombic, ovate or orbicular, rounded to acuminate, cuneate at base, shining above, margins serrate; pseudostipules inconspicuous. Flowers in terminal thyrses or racemes; calyx tubular-campanulate, pubescent to glabrous, lobes triangular-deltoid, ciliate; corolla yellow, orange or scarlet, slender, tube 3–4×0.2–0.3cm at base, often glandular, slightly expanded, curved, glabrous outside, hairy at base of stamens inside, limb to 3cm diam., zygomorphic, deeply bilabiate, lobes 1.5×1cm; stamens exserted; disc cup-shaped; ovary oblong, sparsely scaly; ovules 2-seriate. Fruit an oblong-linear capsule, to 13×1cm; seeds transverse oblong with membranous, hyaline wings. S Africa. Z9.

CULTIVATION A scrambling shrub with tubular flowers in shades of yellow, orange and flame, *T.capensis* thrives in full sun on walls and pergolas in subtropical or Mediterranean climates. In colder regions, it fares better grown as a border or tub specimen in cool conservatories or glasshouses, although it may withstand temperatures as low as −3°C/27°F and might therefore be attempted on sheltered south-facing walls in favoured locations in zones 7 and 8. It will succeed in most soils, provided they are fertile and free-draining. Water and feed generously when in growth, little in winter. Prune after flowering to remove weak, congested or unwanted growth. Propagate by air-layering or by semi-ripe cuttings inserted in a case with bottom heat. *T.capensis* can be pruned and trained to take the form of a standard or free-standing shrub; it has also been used as a hedging plant. The subspecies *nyassae* tends to be more tree-like, seldom scandent, and requires hi ;her temperatures.

T.capensis (Thunb.) Spach. CAPE HONEYSUCKLE. As for the genus. ssp. **capensis** *(Bignonia capensis* Thunb.; *Tecoma capensis* (Thunb.) Lindl.; *T.krebsii* Klotzsch; *T.petersii* Klotzsch).Usually a shrub, often scrambling. Leaflets 2–5 pairs. Calyx 4–8mm, tubular-campanulate. S Africa, Swaziland, S Mozambique. 'Apricot': compact, to 1.5m tall; flowers vivid orange. 'Aurea': rapid-growing; leaves to 5cm long, divided into toothed leaflets, to 9, glossy rich green; flowers funnel-shaped, to 5cm long, stamens protruding, bright gold. 'Coccinea': flowers carlet. 'Lutea': low-growing; flowers strong yellow. 'Salmonea': vigorous; flowers pale pink to orange. ssp. **nyassae** (Oliv.) Brummitt *(Tecoma nyassae* Oliv.; *Tecoma shirensis* Bak.; *T.nyassae* (Oliv.) Schum.;

T.shirensis (Bak.) Schum.; *Tecoma whytei* C.H. Wright; *Tecoma nyikensis* Bak.; *T.rupium* Bullock).Usually trees to 7m. Inflorescence and leaf rachis thickly pubescent to glabrous. Leaflets 3–6 pairs. Calyx 8–23mm, narrowly tubular. Tanzania, Zaire, NE Angola, Zambia, Malawi, N Mozambique.

T.krebsii Klotzsch. See *T.capensis* ssp. *capensis.*
T.nyassae (Oliv.) Schum. See *T.capensis* ssp. *nyassae.*
T.petersii Klotzsch. See *T.capensis* ssp. *capensis.*
T.rupium Bullock. See *T.capensis* ssp. *nyassae.*
T.shirensis (Bak.) Schum. See *T.capensis* ssp. *nyassae.*

Telfairia Hook. (For Charles Telfair (1778–1838), Irish botanist.) Cucurbitaceae.3 species of dioecious, perennial climbers and lianes. Stem usually herbaceous, becoming fibrous- ribbed if persisting. Tendrils bifid, probracteate. Leaves pedate; leaflets 3–7, terminal leaflet largest. Male inflorescence a many-flowered raceme; flowers large, usually purple; calyx tubular, broad, short, toothed; petals 5, free; stamens 5 or 3 when united; female flowers solitary, larger than male; ovary ribbed, inferior; stigma 3-parted. Fruit large, fleshy, ribbed, many-seeded, dehiscent; seeds large, ovate to suborbicular, compressed. Africa. Z9.

CULTIVATION   Vigorous perennial climbers from lowland rainforest and riversides of tropical Africa, grown for their long, 10-ribbed fruits and edible oily seeds. Space is needed for successful cultivation under glass. Plant in spring in a high-fertility soil-based mix. Plants of both sexes will be required for fruit production. Grow on in hot conditions, high humidity and bright filtered light. Liquid feed fortnightly when in growth and train on strong trellis or cable supports. Very prone to red spider mite. Collect seed to start again the following season as cuttings are very difficult to root. If grown as a perennial, reduce watering over winter and then topdress with fresh compost in spring.

T.occidentalis Hook.f. Climber to 15m or more. Stems glabrous or pubescent. Probracts 4–8mm. Leaflets 3–5, elliptic, acuminate, basally acute, entire to sinuate, sometimes sparsely pubescent. Male inflorescence to 30cm; bracts to 8mm; calyx tube densely glandular outside; petals white, purple markings at base, about 2.5 ×1cm; stamens 3, coherent. Fruit white, flesh yellow, ellipsoid; seeds many, obliquely ovate, to 4cm, smooth, fibrous sheath rudimentary or absent. Sierra Leone to Zaire and Angola.

T.pedata (Sims) Hook. *(Fevillea pedata* Sims). Climber, to 30m or more. Roots fleshy, stems glabrous. Probracts spathulate. Leaflets 3–7, lanceolate to elliptic, acuminate, base acute and occasionally lobed, veins sparsely pubescent. Male inflorescence to 25cm; bracts to 10mm; calyx tube pubescent, lobes coarsely dentate; petals to about 2cm; female flowers on pedicels to 14cm; petals larger than male. Fruit green, ellipsoid, ribbed, to 45cm; seeds many, in a fibrous sheath. Mozambique, Tanzania, widely cultivated in Africa.

Tetrastigma (Miq.) Planch. JAVAN GRAPE. (From Gk *tetra*, four, and stigma, referring to the 4-lobed stigma.) Vitaceae. 90 species of deciduous or evergreen dioecious vines. Tendrils entire or bifid, sometimes with adhesive pads. Leaves alternate, palmately or pedately compound. Inflorescence cymose, axillary or opposite leaves; flowers small; calyx lobed, dentate or truncate; petals free, sessile, with broad base and saccate or corniculate apex, green; receptacle distinct or obscure; male flowers with stamens inserted under receptacle, rudimentary ovary present or wanting; female flowers with very minute staminodes, ovary 2-celled with 2 ovules per cell, style short and thick or wanting, stigma broad, generally 4-lobed. Fruit a berry, globose or ellipsoid; seeds 1–4, transversely rugose. Indomalaysia to tropical Australia.

CULTIVATION   A genus of attractive Asian vines grown for their foliage. In the Himalayan species, this resembles a smaller, finer *Parthenocissus quinquefolia:T.obtectum* and *T.serrulatum* are, for example, very beautifully proportioned, 'dwarf' dark green vines ideally suited to ground cover, low walls and baskets in the cold glasshouse and conservatory. They will also succeed outdoors in sheltered places in zones 8 to 9. In the more southerly species, the foliage resembles the larger *Cissus* species. These are plants for the intermediate glasshouse or conservatory, or for large spaces in the home or in public buildings (minimum temperature 10°C/50°F). The *Tetrastigma* most often grown is *T. voinierianum*, a magnificent foliage vine with large, palmately compound leaves, whose resemblance to the Horse Chestnut earns the plant one of its two common names. Swollen terminal sections of stem frequently abscise, fall down, root and proliferate – a further correspondance with *Cissus* and one that earns *T.voinierianum* its other common name, Lizard Plant, a reference to the tail-shedding evasions of some lizards. The fruit of *T.harmandii* is edible, the taste like that of a Muscadine grape. Some of the largest SE Asian species eventually form extremely long and compressed woody stems. These hang like ribbons from the forest canopy. In several cases, the larger species play host to the root parasites, *Rafflesia* and, most spectacularly, to *R.arnoldii*, the reeking heavyweight champion of the plant kingdom.

Guide the larger plants on strong wires, posts and rafters. Grow in pots, tubs or beds in a high-fertility loam-based mix with added garden compost and leafmould. Give bright, filtered light or partial shade; *T.voinierianum* and the diminutive *T.obtectum* will tolerate deep shade. In summer maintain high humidity by syringing or hosing once the foliage is no longer in bright sunshine. Water plentifully when in growth, keeping evenly moist; reduce watering in winter. Cut out overcrowded growth in spring. Increase by stem cuttings in summer, or by simple layers, or by detached stem propagules for *T.voinierianum*.

T.harmandii Planch. AYO.
Stems rather compressed, woody, to 10m, 1–2.5cm diam., rough; tendrils simple. Leaves mostly pedately 5-foliolate, large; leaflets 5–12cm, elliptic-oblong, remotely dentate, acuminate, glabrous and glossy. Inflorescence 4–10 × 4–10cm, axillary, solitary, minutely pubescent, pedunculate; flowers numerous, pale green, faintly fragrant; calyx very small; pedicels short; petals 4, 3.5mm. Fruit globose, fleshy. Indochina, Philippines. Z10.

T.obovatum (Lawson) Gagnep. (*Vitis vomerensis* hort.; *Vitis obovata* Lawson).
Rufous to ferruginous-tomentose throughout. Tendrils simple, long. Leaves digitately 5-foliolate; leaflets 8–25 × 4–6cm, obovate, obtuse to rounded at base, subobtuse to barely acuminate at apex, adpressed mucronate-dentate, firm to chartaceous; petiole 15cm; petiolules robust, 0.8–1.8cm. Inflorescence corymbose, 11cm diam.; peduncles 3cm; pedicels longer than flowers; flowers numerous, white; calyx with 4 triangular teeth; corolla acutely ovoid; petals 4, ovate, attenuate to apex, 3.5mm. Fruit globose. SE Asia. Z10.

T.obtectum (Wallich ex Lawson) Planch. (*Cissus obtectum* Wallich; *Vitis obtecta* Lawson).
Evergreen or semi-evergreen. Stems with minute and short-lived white to pink hairs; tendrils small, often sparingly branched, with adhesive pads. Leaves crowded, palmately 5-foliolate, small, glabrous, long-petiolate; leaflets 5–8cm, obovate to elliptic, acute, remotely mucronate-crenate; petiolule of terminal leaflets shorter than laterals; stipules red to pink. Inflorescence umbellate, slender, pedunculate; flowers tinged green; pedicels slender, pubescent. Himalaya, W & C China. Z9.

T.planicaule (Hook. f.) Gagnep. (*Vitis planicaulis* Hook. f.).
Climbing strongly to tree-tops, subglabrous throughout. Stems conspicuously compressed, on largest plants to 30 × 3cm at base, with thin leafless bands descending from branches; tendrils simple, stout. Leaves membranous to subcoriaceous; petioles 10–17cm; leaflets 12–20 × 5–7.5cm, oblong-lanceolate, obtusely serrate, subacuminate, on 2–4cm petiolules. Inflorescence subcorymbose. Fruit globose, cherry-sized, red. Himalaya (Sikkim). Z9

T.serrulatum (Roxb.) Planch. (*Cissus serrulata* Roxb.; *Cissus capriolata* (D. Don) Royle; *Vitis capriolata* D. Don).
Glabrous throughout. Stems very slender, wiry; tendrils slender, simple or forked. Leaves 5-foliolate; leaflets 4–7.5 × 1.5–3cm, lanceolate to ovate, acute to subacuminate at apex, margins bristly-serrate; petiole 4–6cm. Inflorescence axillary or terminating short lateral branches; peduncles with conspicuous scarious bracts; pedicels 6–8mm. Fruit globose, currant-sized, black. Temperate Himalaya, W China. Z9.

T.voinierianum (Pierre ex Nichols. & Mottet) Gagnep. (*Cissus voinieriana* (Pierre ex Nichols. & Mottet) Viala; *Vitis voinieriana* Pierre ex Nichols. & Mottet). CHESTNUT VINE; LIZARD PLANT.
Very vigorous, densely and softly fulvous-tomentose, especially at first. Stems stout, becoming woody, tendrils simple. Leaves palmately 3–5-foliolate, tough, glabrescent above, somewhat tawny-hairy beneath, leaflets 10–25 × 6–11cm, obovate to broadly rhombic, subcordate to rounded at base, abruptly acuminate at apex, weakly serrate to crenate-serrate; petioles 8–15cm; petiolules 2–5cm. Inflorescence 5cm, corymbose, dense, many-flowered; calyx large, with 4 acutely triangular teeth; corolla 3.5mm, pyramidal in bud; petals 4, triangular-oblong. Laos. Z10.

Thladiantha Bunge. (From Gk *thladias*, eunuch, and *anthos*, flower; type specimens of *T.dubia* had malformed anthers.) Cucurbitaceae. 23 species of tuberous-rooted, dioecious, annual and perennial climbers. Tendrils simple or 2-fid. Leaves simple, ovate, or pedately 3–7-foliolate. Male flowers yellow, in racemes, occasionally solitary; calyx short-campanulate, lobes 5, linear or lanceolate; corolla campanulate, petals 5, free; stamens 5; female flowers solitary or clustered, staminodes 5; calyx with scale-like appendages; ovary oblong, style 3-lobed. Fruit oblong-ovoid, indehiscent, fleshy, red, smooth or ribbed; seeds obovate, flattened, small. E to SE Asia, Africa.

CULTIVATION Prostrate herbs found wild in woodlands and thickets in temperate Eastern Asia, grown for their attractive yellow campanulate flowers. *T.dubia* is hardy in Zone 7 and easy to grow in a sunny sheltered site in any well-drained soil; other species require winter protection.

T.dubia Bunge.
Tall perennial climber or sprawler. Stems villous. Tendrils simple. Leaves 5–10 × 4–9cm, ovate-cordate, short-acuminate, pubescent mucronate-dentate. Male flowers yellow, axillary, solitary, 6–7cm diam.; peduncle 1–3cm, softly hairy; calyx short-campanulate to nearly rotate, lobes recurved, c12mm; petals long-ovate, 2.5cm; female flowers on peduncles to 1.5cm; ovary oblong, pubescent. Fruit oblong to 4 × 2.5cm, red; seeds 4–4.5mm. Summer. Korea, NE China. Z7.

T.nudiflora Hemsl. ex Forbes & Hemsl.
Perennial Stems slender, sulcate. Tendrils 2-fid. Leaves 8–15 × 5–10cm, ovate-cordate or rounded-cordate, denticulate,

acute, acuminate, scabrous above, with brown hairs beneath; petiole 2–6cm. Male flowers yellow, in racemes; calyx lobes ovate-lanceolate, c5mm; petals c12mm; female flowers solitary. Fruit globose, 3–4cm, red; seeds numerous, compressed-obovoid. China). Z9.

T.oliveri Cogn. ex Mottet.
Vigorous annual climber. Stems to 10m, smooth, glabrous. Tendrils 2-fid, long. Leaves c20cm, rounded-cordate, denticulate, scabrous, paler green beneath; petiole 15–20cm. Male flowers bright yellow, 30–40 in cymes; pedicels 5–25mm; calyx c1cm; corolla campanulate, c2.5cm; female flowers solitary. Summer. China. Z9.

Thunbergia Retz. (For Carl Peter Thunberg (1743–1828), Swedish botanist. A student of Linnaeus, he travelled for the Dutch East India Company as a doctor and sent back plants from Japan, Java and South Africa. He became Professor of Botany at Uppsala.) Acanthaceae. 100 species of suberect, scandent or twining annual or perennial herbs and shrubs. Leaves opposite, ovate, lanceolate or elliptic, base cuneate, obtuse or hastate. Flowers solitary in leaf axils or sometimes gathered into terminal racemes, showy, subtended by 2 leafy bracts;

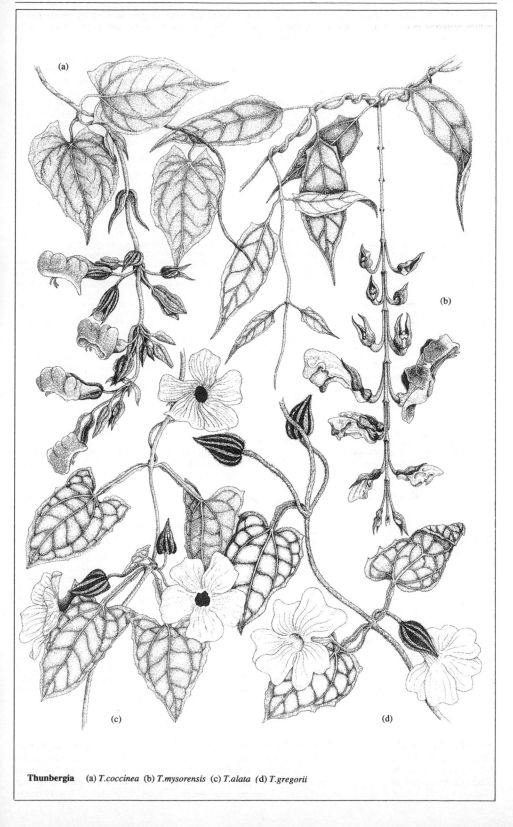

Thunbergia   (a) *T.coccinea* (b) *T.mysorensis* (c) *T.alata* (d) *T.gregorii*

calyx minute, enclosed in bracts, fused into a ring or 10–15-toothed; corolla tube curved, ventricose, lobes 5, rounded; stamens 4, didynamous. Fruit a globose, leathery capsule with an ensiform beak. S & Tropical Africa, Madagascar, warm Asia.

CULTIVATION *Thunbergia* includes some of the most beautiful climbers for the arches and pergolas of tropical and subtropical gardens and some, such as *T.erecta*, which may be used as flowering hedges in similar climates. In cooler zones, many are elegant and vigorous specimens for borders and large containers in the warm glasshouse or conservatory. The long golden chains of *T.mysorensis* are particularly handsome and produced over many months – few garden experiences are so memorable as a walk beneath an arbour of this species when in full bloom. Some, such *T.alata* and *T.gregorii*, flower in their first year from seed and are commonly grown as frost-tender annuals. The latter may overwinter at the base of a warm south-facing wall in mild winter areas, especially if cut back at the end of the season and given mulch protection.

Grow in a fertile loam-based mix with additional sharp sand and screened manure, in direct sun but with shade from the strongest summer sun. Train on wires or trellis. Maintain moderate humidity with good air movement (*T.alata* and *T.gregorii* require lower levels of humidity) and water plentifully when in growth. Reduce water as light and temperature levels fall to keep almost dry in winter. Prune lightly in late winter or early spring before growth resumes; hard pruning will severely reduce the production of flowers. Easily propagated by most types of cuttings rooted in a closed case with bottom heat, by simple layering or by seed.

T.alata Bojer ex Sims. BLACK-EYED SUSAN.
Twining perennial herb, often grown as an annual. Leaves to 7.5cm, ovate-elliptic to cordate, apex acute to acuminate, margin dentate; petiole winged. Flowers solitary on long pedicels; bracts somewhat inflated; calyx 12-toothed; corolla to 3.75×4cm, creamy-white or yellow-orange usually with a dark purple-brown throat. Summer-early autumn. Tropical Africa. 'Alba': flowers white, centre dark. 'Aurantiaca': flowers orange to yellow, centre dark. 'Bakeri': flowers snow white. Suzie Hybrids: flowers orange, yellow or white, eye dark. Z9.

T.angulata Hilsenb. & Boj. ex Hook.
Largely glabrous climbing shrub. Leaves to 5cm, ovate-cordate to sagittate; petioles to 10cm. Flowers long-stalked; bracts to 1cm, ciliate, 1-nerved; calyx lobes many, linear; corolla to 2.5×2cm, pale blue, throat yellow. Madagascar. Z10.

T.battiscombei Turrill in Hook.
Erect or scrambling herb to 4m. Stems tetragonal, glabrous. Leaves to 11×6cm, ovate to obovate-elliptic, apex rounded to blunt and somewhat apiculate, entire, principal veins 3, prominent.Racemes to 10 cm, axillary, to 10-flowered; bracts to 2cm, elliptic-ovate, conspicuously net-veined; calyx more or less 8-lobed, small; corolla to 4.5×1.5cm, blue, obliquely tubular with 5 broad, rounded lobes. East Tropical Africa. Z10.

T.capensis Retz.
Sprawling, usually herbaceous perennial, sometimes grown as an annual. Leaves suborbicular, obscurely toothed, glabrescent above,principal veins 5, setose beneath. Flowers 4–10 together; bracts pilose; calyx lobes 7–11, minute, filiform; corolla to 3cm, creamy yellow. S.Africa (E Cape, Transkei). Z9.

T. chrysops Hook.
Slender herbaceous twiner. Stems slightly hairy. Leaves to 6× 2.5cm, ovate-cordate, acute to subacuminate, angularly lobed to dentate, principal veins 5–7. Flowers solitary, axillary, short-stalked; bracts 2, ovate-cordate; calyx annulate, truncate; corolla to 6×5cm, subcampanulate to infundibular, tube yellow, contracted at base, becoming rich purple toward spreading limb with golden throat, limb broadly 5-lobed and somewhat 2-lipped. Sierra Leone. Z10.

T.coccinea Wallich ex D. Don (*Hexacentris coccinea* (Wallich) Nees).
Perennial climber. Stems woody, 3–8m. Leaves to 15cm, narrowly cordate to ovate-elliptic, apex obtuse to acuminate , margin toothed, thick-textured, with 3 or 5 principal veins , glabrous or subglabrous. Flowers held horizontally in pendent racemes 15–45cm long; calyx a tiny rim; corolla 2.5cm, tubular, ventricose above, orange-red, lobes unequal, reflexed. Winter-spring. India, Nepal, Burma. Z10.

T.dregeana Nees.
Herbaceous climber, ultimately woody. Leaves to 5×4cm, ovate-subcordate, pubescent throughout, minutely pustular, toothed, principal veins 5. Floral bracts pubescent; calyx with many linear lobes; corolla to 2×3cm, salverform, tube swollen in centre, creamy white to dull orange yellow, throat yellow, lobes large, rounded. S Africa (E Cape to Natal and Swaziland). Z9.

T.erecta (Benth.) Anderson (*Meyenia erecta* Benth. in Hook.). KING'S MANTLE; BUSH CLOCK VINE.
Erect or twining shrub to 2m. Branches slender. Leaves 3–6cm, ovate to oblong, subentire to toothed, glabrous, shining; petiole to 1.25cm. Flowers solitary, axillary; calyx with 7–10 teeth; corolla 7cm, tube yellow-cream, lobes dark blue-violet. Summer. Tropical W to S Africa. 'Alba': flowers white. Z10.

T.fragrans Roxb.
Perennial, aromatic climber. Stem woody, glabrous or with retrorse hairs. Leaves 5–7.5cm, triangular-ovate to oblong, base cordate to hastate, margin subentire to toothed; petiole 1.25–3.75cm. Flowers solitary; calyx toothed; corolla to 3 × 5cm,white, lobes spreading.India, Sri Lanka, Australasia. 'Angel Wings': flowers snow white, lightly scented. Z10.

T.gibsonii S. Moore. See *T. gregorii*.

T.grandiflora Roxb. BLUE TRUMPET VINE; CLOCK VINE; BENGAL CLOCK VINE; SKY VINE; SKYFLOWER; BLUE SKYFLOWER.
Large perennial twining shrub. Stems woody, slightly hispid. Leaves 10–20cm, ovate-elliptic, rough-pubescent, apex acute, margin toothed or lobed, principal veins 5–7. Flowers solitary, axillary or rarely clustered in racemes; calyx cupular, subentire; corolla to 7.5 × 7.5cm, blue-violet, lobes broad, somewhat unequal, limb thus appearing two-lipped. Summer. N India. 'Alba': flowers white.

T. gregorii S. Moore.
Perennial twining climber, often cultivated as an annual. Stems usually herbaceous in cultivation, slightly hispid. Leaves to 7.5cm, triangular-ovate, apex acute to acuminate, principal veins 5–7, softly hairy, margin toothed; petiole 2.5–6.25cm, winged. Flowers solitary; bracts hispid, often somewhat red-tinted; calyx 10–13-lobed; corolla 4.5×4.5cm, orange, lobes truncate; pedicel 5–7cm with spreading hairs. Summer. Tropical Africa. Z9.

T.harrisii Hook. See *T. laurifolia*

T.laevis Nees in Wallich.
Differs from *T.fragrans* in its glabrous, not retrorsely hairy stems, leaves with only one lobe per side in lower half, green-tinted corolla tube and puberulous, not glabrous ovary.

T.laurifolia Lindl.
Robust glabrous twiner differing from *T. grandiflora* in its scarcely angled or lobed leaves with 3, not 5 or 7 principal

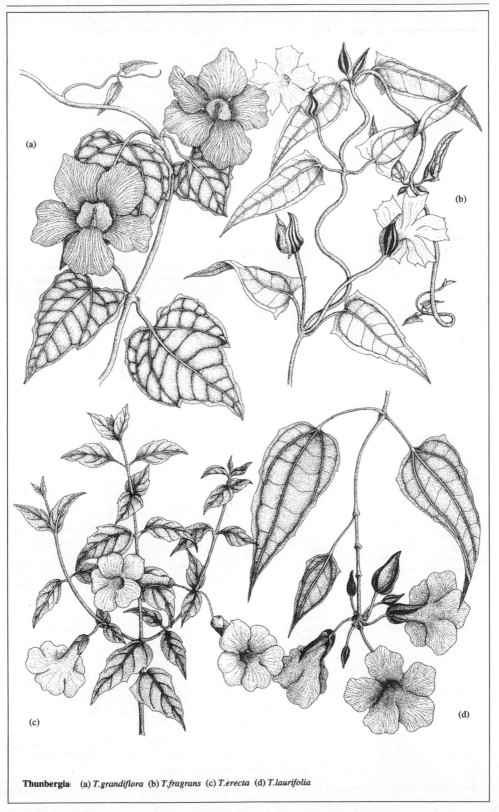

Thunbergia   (a) *T.grandiflora* (b) *T.fragrans* (c) *T.erecta* (d) *T.laurifolia*

veins and flowers with corolla 10–15 × 6.5cm, broadly funnelform,with limb not so conspicuously 2-lipped, ultramarine blue with pale throat. Malaysia. Z10.

T.mysorensis (Wight) Anderson ex Bedd. (*Hexacentris mysorensis* Wight).
Twining climber to 6m. Stems woody. Leaves 10–15cm, narrowly elliptic, apex acuminate, base obtuse to cuneate, margin toothed, glabrate, principal veins 3. Flowers held semi-erect in pendent racemes: bracts 2.5cm, green-purple; calyx a minute rim; corolla 3.75cm,. 5cm across at apex, tube rich golden yellow, lobes strongly unequal, reflexed, often marked

red-brown. Spring. Nilgiri Hills in India. Z10.

T.scandens Pers. ex Nees. See *T.fragrans.*

T.vogeliana Benth. in Hook.
Scandent shrub. Branches angled and somewhat twining when young, glabrous except at nodes. Leaves 7.5–15cm, ovate-oblong, entire to denticulate, base narrowed, papillose-scabrous. Bracts ovate, blunt, hairy, leathery, red-tinted; calyx short, lobes 12, subulate; corolla infundibular, tube white outside, yellow inside, limb violet. Tropical Africa. Z10.

T.volubilis Pers. See *T.fragrans.*

Toxicodendron (Tourn.) Mill. (*Toxicodendrum* Thunb.). (From Gk *toxicos*, poisonous, and *dendron*, tree.) Anacardiaceae. About 9 species of dioecious, deciduous trees, shrubs or lianes. Leaves alternate, palmate to imparipinnate, exstipulate, thin, glabrous to sericeous above, glabrous to tomentose beneath; leaflets opposite. Inflorescence a panicle or raceme, erect, often becoming pendent on fruiting, axillary or lateral; flowers small, cream to yellow-green; bracts lanceolate, deciduous; sepals 5, persistent, imbricate, joined at base; petals ascending, veined, glabrous, imbricate, often apically reflexed; ovary unilocular by abortion, stigma tripartite; stamens 5, inserted below disc, anthers dorsiflexed; disc cupular, nectiferous. Fruit a subglobose or laterally flattened drupe, endocarp bony. N America to northern S America.

CULTIVATION   *T.radicans*, Poison Ivy, and *T.diversilobum*,   Poison Oak, are amongst the most poisonous of the Anacardiaceae. Even indirect contact with *T.diversilobum* and *T.radicans* may produced a severe spreading dermatitis due to the presence of 3-n pentadecycatechnol. In Europe, poisonous species will seldom be encountered except in botanic gardens, labelled and out of reach. In North America an estimated 70% of the population are sensitized to their skin-irritant allergens, which are constituents of the latex-like emulsions present in the schizogenous ducts; neither pollen nor smoke from burnt materials gives rise to allergic reactions. Particular care should be taken by gardeners in wooded areas of North America not to confuse either species with members of *Hedera* or *Parthenocissus*. They should be handled only with gloves. The toxins reach the skin only when the plant tissue has been damaged; immediate and thorough washing may prevent subsequent dermatitis. If they were grown (rather than tolerated) in wooded gardens, it would be for their rich autumn colour.

T.diversilobum (Torr. & A. Gray) Greene (*Rhus diversiloba* Torr. & A. Gray; *Rhus toxicodendron* ssp. *diversiloba* (Torr. & A. Gray) Engl.; *T.radicans* ssp. *diversilobum* (Torr. & A. Gray) Thorne; *Rhus lobata* Hook.; *Rhus quercifolia* Steud.). WESTERN POISON OAK.
Shrub or vine. Branches glabrous to puberulent, slender; aerial roots brown;   bark grey-brown to dark red. Leaves palmate, occasionally pinnate; leaflets 3, occasionally 5 or more, 3–7cm, ovate-oblong to suborbicular, entire, undulate, crenate to dentate, obtuse, usually asymmetric, glabrous above, subpilose beneath. Fruit cream-white, globose to reniform, sometimes laterally flattened. US west coast to Vancouver. Z5.

T.eximium Greene. See *T.radicans* ssp. *eximium.*
T.negundo Greene. See *T.radicans* ssp. *negundo.*
T.orientale Greene. See *T.radicans* ssp. *orientale.*
T.quercifolium Greene. See *T.diversilobum.*

T.radicans (L.) Kuntze (*Rhus toxicodendron* L.; *Rhus radicans* L.). POISON IVY; MARK WEED; POISON MERCURY.
Shrub or vine, rarely an epiphytic tree. Branches slender, twining, puberulent; aerial roots brown. Leaves palmate to

pinnate; leaflets 3, rarely 5 or 7, 2.5–18cm, ovate-elliptic, irregularly serrate, asymmetric, acute, acuminate or cuspidate, terminal leaflet larger. Fruit to 7 × 1mm, cream-yellow to light brown, glabrous to bristly. S Canada and E US to Guatemala, C China to Taiwan and Japan. Z5. ssp. **barkleyi** Gillis. Leaflets entire or subentire, terminal leaflet elliptic or lanceolate. Mexico, Guatemala. Z8. ssp. **eximium** (Greene) Gillis (*T.eximium* Greene). Leaflets deeply incised, base rounded. Mexico. ssp. **hispidum** (Engl.) Gillis (*Rhus toxicodendron* var. *hispida* Engl.).Terminal leaflet twice as long as broad, attenuate. Fruits hispid, hairs to 1mm. ssp. **negundo** (Greene) Gillis(*T.negundo* Greene).Leaflets ovate or lanceolate; petiole puberulent to densely pubescent. US. ssp. **orientale** (Greene) Gillis (*T.orientale* Greene). Terminal leaflet ×1.2–1.7 as long as broad, cuneate. Fruit short-hairy or papillose. Japan. ssp. **pubescens** (Engelm. ex Wats.) Gillis (*Rhus toxicodendron* var. *pubescens* Engelm. ex Wats.). Leaflets serrate, terminal leaflet broadly ovate. ssp. **verrucosum** (Scheele) Gillis (*T.verrucosum* Scheele). Leaflets with lobed or deeply cut margins. Oklahoma, Texas. Z7.

T.verrucosum Scheele. See *T.radicans* ssp. *verrucosum.*

Trachelospermum Lem.(From Gk *trachelos*, neck, and *sperma*, seed.) Apocynaceae. 20 species of evergreen climbing shrubs with milky sap in leaves and stems. Leaves opposite, leathery, entire, markedly veined. Flowers white or pale yellow, in terminal and axillary cymes; calyx 5-lobed; corolla with cylindrical tube and 5 spreading, twisted lobes overlapping to the right; stamens short, anthers united and attached to stigma; ovary of 2 carpels. Fruit a pair of terete follicles; seeds comose. India to Japan. Z8.

CULTIVATION   Grown for their creamy-white, fragrant flowers produced in summer or late summer and for the glossy evergreen foliage, which often colours well in winter, *Trachelospermum* species make handsome self-clinging climbers for warm walls or for the cool glasshouse or conservatory in cool temperate zones. *T.asiaticum* is the hardiest species: well ripened wood will survive temperatures to –15°C/5°F with good drainage and wall shelter. Where temperatures fall much below –5°C/23°F, *T.jasminoides* is more safely grown in the

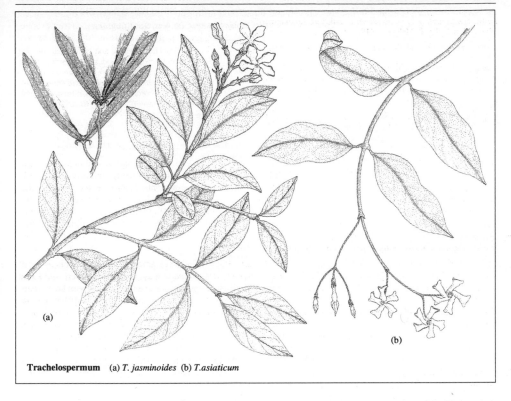

Trachelospermum   (a) *T. jasminoides* (b) *T.asiaticum*

conservatory. Grow in any well drained, moderately retentive soil in sun or with light part dry shade. Water container-grown plants moderately when in growth and maintain good ventilation with a winter minimum of 5–7°C/40–45°F. *Trachelospermum* flowers on short laterals produced on older wood. Prune to remove deadwood and weak growths and cut back excessively long stems almost to flowering wood. Propagate by seed, by simple layering or by semi-ripe cuttings in summer.

T.asiaticum (Sieb. & Zucc.) Nak. (*Rhynchospermum asiaticum* hort.).
Climber, 5–7m, densely branched; shoots persistently hairy. Leaves 2–5×0.9–2cm, elliptic or ovate, dark glossy green, glabrous; petiole 3mm. Flowers in terminal cymes 5–6.5cm across; calyx lobes erect, pointed; corolla yellow-white, tube 0.7–0.8cm, 2cm across limb, lobes obovate; stamens slightly exserted. Summer. Japan, Korea. The name *T.majus* has been misapplied to this species.

T.jasminoides (Lindl.) Lem. (*Rhynchospermum jasminoides* Lindl.).
Evergreen climber to 7m; shoots slender, hairy when young, becoming glabrous. Leaves 4–7.5×1.25–2.5cm, oval-lanceolate, tapered to both ends, dark shining green, downy beneath at first; petiole 3mm. Flowers intensely fragrant, white, in glabrous axillary and terminal cymes; calyx lobes lanceolate, reflexed; corolla tube 0.75–1cm, 2.5cm across limb, lobes narrow, wavy; stamens included. Fruit to 15cm. Summer. China. 'Japonicum': leaves veined white, turning bronze in autumn. 'Minimum': habit dwarf; leaves mottled. 'Variegatum': leaves ovate to almost linear-lanceolate, with white and milk-green stripes, often tinged pink to red-bronze. 'Wilsonii': leaves ovate to linear-lanceolate, veins distinct, flushed red-bronze to maroon in winter.

Trichosanthes L. (From Gk *thrix*, hair, and *anthos*, a flower, referring to the hairs fringing the corolla.) Cucurbitaceae. Some 15 species of monoecious or dioecious, annual or perennial herbs. Stems 3–10m, climbing. Tendrils simple or 2–5-fid. Leaves 3–5-lobed or simple, entire to denticulate. Male flowers white, usually in racemes, sometimes solitary; calyx cylindric, 5-lobed; corolla rotate, 5-lobed, lobes fimbriate; stamens 3, inserted on calyx tube, filaments short, anthers free or connate. Female flowers solitary or a few, clustered; ovary inferior, oblong, 1-locular, ovules numerous, stigmas 3, entire or 2-fid. Fruit indehiscent, ovoid or globose, fleshy, smooth; seeds numerous, mostly smooth. Indomalaya to Pacific. Z10 unless specified.

CULTIVATION   Vigorous tendril climbers from the moist tropics of the Old World, mostly perennial and grown for their attractively fringed white flowers and colourful fruits. The most successful species is the snake gourd, *T.cucumerina* var. *anguina*, with long orange-red streaked fruits tasting (when young) of runner beans. All need glasshouse cultivation as annuals in temperate zones in hot conditions, preferably with bottom heat and high humidity. Bright filtered light is needed and a rich potting mixture of 2:2:1:1 sterilized loam, well-rotted manure, coir and grit, with very good drainage. Plant in early spring; plants of either sex are required for fruit production. Water plentifully throughout growth and liquid feed fortnightly, training the growth on to a strong trellis. Control red spider mite by a proprietary mite-killer or by introducing predatory mite. Ensure fruit production by cross-pollination. Collect seed in the autumn for spring sowing with bottom heat at 20°C/68°F or take softwood cuttings where seed is not produced.

T.anguina L. See *T.cucumerina* var. *anguina*.

T.bracteata (Lam.) Voigt. See *T.tricuspidata*.

T.colubrina Jacq. f. See *T.cucumerina* var. *anguina*.

T.cordata Roxb.
Perennial climber, from tuberous roots. Tendrils robust, puberulous. Leaves 12–20×9–12cm, broadly ovate-cordate, thin-textured, entire to slightly angular-lobed; petioles 5–10cm. Male flowers 4–8, in racemes to 20cm, pedicels 1–2mm, bracts *c*4cm, sparsely villous-hirsute; calyx *c*5cm, lobes erect, 1.5×2–3mm; stamen filaments *c*1mm, anther to 14mm; female flowers solitary, subsessile. Fruit globose, bright red streaked orange; seeds to 1.5×0.5cm, with slightly angular margins. Summer. Indomalaya.

T.cucumerina L.
Annual. Tendrils 2–3-fid. Leaves 6–1.3cm diam., orbicular-reniform to broadly ovate, 5–7-lobed, slightly toothed; petiole 2–7cm. Male flowers in racemes; peduncles to 12cm; bracts minute or absent; pedicels 1–2cm; calyx tube 1.5–2.5cm, lobes erect, spreading, *c*1.5mm; corolla lobes very deeply laciniate; stamen filaments to 1.5mm, anther *c*3mm; female flowers solitary; peduncle to 3–12mm; ovary narrow. Fruit ovoid, conical, 5–6cm; seeds *c*1cm, compressed, undulate. Summer. India to Malaysia, Australia. var. *anguina* (L.) Haines (*T.anguina* L.; *T.colubrina* Jacq. f.). SERPENT CUCUMBER; CLUB GOURD; SNAKE GOURD; VIPER GOURD. Annual. Stems puberulous. Leaves 10–15×12–18cm, shallowly to deeply 3–5-lobed, pubescent to sparsely hairy. Male flowers 8–15; peduncles 10–25cm; corolla lobes finely and deeply laciniate. Fruit 30–200cm, elongate, cylindrical, twisted, striped white when young, orange when ripe; seeds 15–17mm, rugulose. Summer. India to Pakistan.

T.cucumeroides Maxim. ex Franch. & Savat. See *T.ovigera*.

T.dioica Roxb.
Tendrils 2-fid, short. Leaves 7–10×4–8cm, ovate-oblong, lobed, sinuate-dentate, cordate, acute, slightly scabrous; petiole 1–3mm. Male flowers solitary; peduncles paired, 2–3cm; calyx tube *c*4cm, cylindrical, lobes linear; corolla lobes oblong; anther free, *c*3.5mm; female flowers solitary; peduncles to 4mm. Fruit oblong, 5–12cm, orange-red, smooth; seed 6–7×5–6mm, rounded. Summer. Indomalaya.

T.foetidissima Jacq. See *Kedrostis foetidissima*.

T.japonica (Miq.) Reg. See *T.kirilowii* var. *japonica*.

T.kirilowii Maxim.
Perennial. Tendrils 3–5-fid. Leaves 10–12cm, orbicular, often deeply 5-lobed, lobes oblong, with deep sinuses, lobulate, punctate-scabrous above, glabrescent beneath; petiole 3–4cm, scabrous. Male flowers in racemes 15–18cm; pedicels 1–3mm, often with solitary flower on long pedicel; bracts to 2cm, toothed; calyx lobes linear, entire, *c*12mm, finely hairy; corolla lobes obovate, deeply cut; female flowers solitary; pedicel 3mm. Fruit to 10cm, ovoid to oblong, orange-red; seeds to 16×10mm, numerous, pale brown. China, Mongolia, Vietnam. var. *japonica* (Miq.) Kitam. (*Gymnopetalum japonicum* Miq.; *T.japonica* (Miq.) Reg.). Leaves ovate to orbicular, 3–5-lobed. Male flowers in racemes to 20cm, bracts to 2.5cm, coarsely toothed. Fruit to 10cm, ovoid-globose, yellow; peduncles grooved, 2–3cm; seeds 11–14mm, dark brown. Japan. Z9.

T.ovigera Bl. (*T.cucumeroides* Maxim. ex Franch. & Savat.). SNAKE GOURD.
Perennial. Tendrils 2-fid, short. Leaves 10–15×7–12cm, broadly ovate, cordate, basal sinus 2–3cm, entire or 3-lobed, glabrous above, villous beneath, denticulate; petiole 2–5cm. Male flowers 4–12 per raceme; peduncle 5–10cm; bracts *c*5mm; pedicels 5–7mm; calyx tube 2.5–3cm, lobes 3–5mm; anther 3–5mm; female flowers solitary on peduncles *c*4cm. Fruit ovoid, 4–7cm, red; seeds cuneate, 8×8–9mm, with longitudinal band. Summer. India, Burma, Malaysia, Java.

T.palmata Roxb. non L. See *T.tricuspidata*.

T.palmata L. non Roxb. See *Ceratosanthes palmata*.

T.tricuspidata Lour. (*T.bracteata* (Lam.) Voigt; *T.palmata* Roxb.).
Tendrils often 2-fid. Leaves 9–18cm, variable, ovate, pentagonal or deeply 3–5-lobed, thin-textured, glabrescent, denticulate; petiole 3–7cm. Male flowers white, in racemes 10–20cm; pedicels *c*1cm; bracts oval, to 2cm, entire to dentate; calyx lobes 1–2cm, entire to dentate; stamens coherent into head *c*1cm; female flowers solitary. Fruit 6–9×2.5–6cm, subglobose, red streaked orange; peduncle robust, 1–2cm; seeds numerous, *c*12 × 6mm, smooth. Asia, Indomalaya, Australia.

T.tuberosa Roxb. non Willd. See *Ceratosanthes palmata*.

Trichostigma A. Rich. (From Gk *trichos*, hair, and *stigma*, in reference to the hairy stigma.) Phytolaccaceae. 3 species of erect or climbing shrubs. Leaves oval or elliptic, alternate, entire, petiolate. Flowers in racemes; sepals free, ovate or elliptic, reflexed in fruit; petals absent; stamens 8–25; ovary 1-celled. Fruit globose, berry-like. Tropical S America. Z10.

CULTIVATION   *T.peruvianum* is an exceptionally fine foliage plant with long slender stems and large quilted leaves; the whole plant is tinted dark purple, with the exception of the upper leaf surfaces, which have a leaden or bronze lustre. Small white flowers are produced in narrow bottlebrush-like spikes, these elongate and cascade, creating a pleasing contrast with the bold leaves. In cold climates, this plant is sometimes seen in intermediate to warm glasshouses (minimum temperature 13–16°C/55–60°F), where it thrives in a moist, loamy medium in high humidity and shade. Under glass, it is perhaps best treated as a free-standing specimen to a height of 1m/3ft, as – say – three rooted and unstopped cuttings planted together and grown for display over 2–3 seasons prior to repropagation. In warmer climates, or if planted in borders and tubs in the glasshouse, *Trichostigma* will produce long scrambling stems which will require support.

T.peruvianum H. Walter.
Erect to scrambling shrub to 2m. Stems slender, angular, purple-red. Leaves 25 × 18cm, elliptic, slender-pointed, shiny metallic grey-green above, appearing velvety, purple-maroon beneath, veins conspicuous, deeply sunken, giving a corrugated appearance to upper surface. Flowers small, white, in long racemes, ascending at first, soon elongating and hanging; pedicels purple-red. Fruit small. Andes.

Tripterygium Hook. f. (From Gk *tri-*, three, and *pteryx*, wing, in reference to the 3-winged fruit.) Celastraceae. 2 species of deciduous scandent shrubs, winter buds broadly conical, with about 2 pairs of outer scales. Leaves alternate, petiolate, serrate, large; stipules linear, caducous. Flowers polygamous, in large terminal panicles, small; calyx 5-lobed; petals 5; stamens 5, on margin of cupular disc; ovary superior, 3-angled, style short. Fruit 3-winged, wings broad, membranous; seed 1, erect, linear, exarillate. E Asia.

CULTIVATION Climbing or scandent shrubs valued for their autumn display of winged fruits: in *Tripterygium wilfordii* these are brilliant brown-red. In the wild they are commonly seen sprawling over forest vegetation. In cultivation they are well adapted to climbing through sturdy trees or over unsightly walls, where they flower best in full sun. Their soil requirements are not exacting, they thrive in a moist loamy soil and are tolerant of chalk. *T.regelii* is perfectly winter hardy and will tolerate a minimum temperature of –15°C/5°F, but *T.wilfordii* is only suitable for mild areas, where there is protection of a south-facing wall or evergreen cover and the temperature does not fall below –5°C/23°F. Easily propagated by autumn-sown seed.

T.regelii Sprague & Tak.
To 10m; branches slightly angled, rufescent, glabrous, warty. Leaves 5–15cm, ovate to broadly so, or elliptic, abruptly acuminate to acute, rounded at base, obtusely serrate, vivid green, glabrous above, sometimes papillose-pilose on nerves beneath. Flowers to 6mm diam., white tinged green. Fruit broadly lanceolate, retuse to cordate at both ends, with 3 elliptic or cordate wings, to 1.8cm diam. including wings, pale green. Summer. Japan, Korea, Manchuria. Z5.

T.wilfordii Hook. f.
To 13m; shoots angled. Leaves 6 to 15cm, oblong-elliptic to ovate, finely crenate, glabrous, usually glaucous beneath. Flowers to 6mm diam., pale green; anthers red-purple. Fruits crowded in clusters, to 1.2cm diam., purple-red, wings to 5mm wide. Autumn. Taiwan, E China. Z9.

Trochomeria Hook. f. Cucurbitaceae. 7 species of tuberous-rooted perennials. Stems annual, slender, prostrate or climbing, or erect. Tendrils simple or absent. Leaves palmately 3–5-lobed or dissected, occasionally stipulate, ciliate or dentate, short-petioled. Male flowers in nodal or axillary clusters or racemes, or solitary, yellow-green; calyx cylindrical to campanulate, often elongated, lobes minute; corolla commonly rotate, lobes 5, free nearly to base, spreading or reflexed; stamens 3, inserted on calyx tube, filaments free, anthers connate, forming a head; female flowers solitary, with 3 staminodes; ovary ovoid to ellipsoid, ovules horizontal; stigma 3-lobed. Fruit an indehiscent, red berry; seeds ellipsoid to subglobose, white, smooth. Africa. Z10.

CULTIVATION As for *Coccinea*.

T.debilis (Sonder) Hook. f. (*Zehneria debilis* Sonder).
Stems prostrate or climbing, tendrilous, glabrous or slightly pubescent. Leaves variable, 1.5–6 × 2–11cm, commonly deeply 3–7-lobed, lobes elliptic to linear, entire to coarsely pinnatifid, 2–5cm, scabrid; stipule absent or 0.5–2cm, toothed or lobed; petioles to 2cm. Male flowers on pedicels to 2cm; calyx 1–2cm; corolla lobes *c*1cm, recurved; female flowers with ovary 0.7cm. Fruit subglobose to ellipsoid, 2.5–3.5 × 2–2.5cm, red; seeds *c*8 × 5mm, white. S Africa, Namibia.

Tropaeolum L. (Coined by Linnaeus from Gk *tropaion*, Lat. *tropaeum*, trophy, i.e. a sign of victory consisting originally of a tree-trunk set up on the battlefield and hung with captured helmets and shields; as gardeners used to grow *T.majus* up pyramids of poles and netting, Linnaeus compared its rounded leaves to shields and its flowers to spear-pierced blood-stained gold helmets ornamenting such a memorial or statue of victory.) NASTURTIUM; INDIAN CRESS; CANARY BIRD VINE; CANARY BIRD FLOWER; FLAME FLOWER. Tropaeolaceae. Some 86 species of sometimes tuberous-rooted, herbaceous annuals and perennials, usually vines that climb by twisting their leafstalks around suitable supports, or compact and bushy. Leaves alternate, mostly long-stalked, shield-shaped, 5-angled, or variously lobed and dissected. Flowers solitary from the leaf axils, usually long-stalked, asymmetrical, generally colourful and showy, yellow, orange, red, or less commonly purple and blue, spurred; sepals 5; petals usually 5, smooth-edged, lobed or fringed, clawed at base, upper two differ from the others and are commonly smaller; stamens 8. Fruit separates into 3 rounded 1-seeded carpels with a fleshy or spongy outer layer. S Mexico to Brazil and Patagonia.

CULTIVATION The commonly grown Nasturtium, one of the most easily grown of annual flowers, is derived mainly from *T.majus*, although its many cultivars reflect hybridity between this and other species. They range from low-growing dwarf cultivars, such as the crimson-flowered 'Empress of India' and 'Tom Thumb', with a wide colour range, for edging and for the flower border, through semi-trailing types, such as the double-flowered 'Glorious Gleam', especially good for hanging baskets. Taller climbing types are suited to trellis, fence and other supports, as is the undemanding *T.peregrinum*, a rapid climber valued for its yellow, finely fringed flowers. All annuals and those treated as such, grow well in sun in any well drained but moisture-retentive soil, preferably of low or only moderate fertility, since richer substrates produce leaves at the expense of flowering.

The perennial species, most of which have soil requirements similar to those of the annuals, exhibit a range of cold tolerance. *T.polyphyllum* is among the hardiest; given the perfect drainage of a raised bed, where it will trail elegantly over the edge, it is reliable to about –15°C/5°F. The rhizome pulls itself down deep below the soil surface and sometimes travels, the beautiful glaucous foliage emerging in a different situation in subsequent years, densely clothed in summer with a profusion of yellow flowers, thereafter dying back completely. *T.speciosum* and *T.leptophyllum* show similar cold-tolerance.

Tropaeolum (a) *T.speciosum* (b) *T.azureum* (c) *T.peregrinum* (d) *T.polyphyllum* (e) *T.tricolorum*

T.tricolorum and *T.tuberosum* thrive in essentially frost-free gardens, but will survive short-lived, light frost given a warm sheltered situation with good drainage; *T.tuberosum* is a short day plant and in cool temperate gardens the late flowers are likely to be spoiled by frost. The large-tubered cultivar, 'Ken Aslet', begins to bloom much earlier in mid summer and is more desirable for cooler climates. The tubers of these and other slightly tender species, such as *T.pentaphyllum*, may be lifted in autumn and stored in cool, dry conditions for replanting in spring. Alternatively, grow in the cool glasshouse or conservatory. *T.azureum*, *T.tricolorum* and *T.brachyceras* work very well in the cool glasshouse, alpine house or conservatory, trained on pea sticks. Grow in good light, in a neutral or slightly acidic mix of loam, leafmould and sharp sand. Water plentifully when in growth withdrawing moisture gradually as foliage fades, to store the plants more or less dry in their pots over winter.

T.speciosum differs from other species in that it performs best in zones with cool, moist summers. It favours relatively high rainfall on an acid soil enriched with well rotted compost or leafmould; with the incorporation of liberal quantities of humus it may also succeed on deep soils over chalk. Without support, it makes effective, sprawling groundcover. *T.speciosum* may be difficult to establish for reasons that are not entirely clear, although one of the fundamental requirements for success is that the roots and lower stems are cool and shaded.

Sow seed of annual species *in situ* or for earlier blooms under glass in late winter/early spring at 13–16°C/55–60°F. Propagate perennials with fleshy rhizomes, such as *T.polyphyllum* and *T.speciosum* by careful division, tuberous species by separation of small tubers when repotting or by basal stem cuttings in spring. Plants are sometimes infected by virus diseases including spotted wilty virus: small yellow spots which become brown form on the foliage and cause distortion in growth; destroy affected plants.

T.albiflorum Lem. See *T.leptophyllum*.

T.azureum Miers(*T.violiflorum* A. Dietr.).
Glabrous climber to 1.2m, with small tubers. Leaves 5-lobed, to 3cm across, often less, lobes narrow, small, linear-lanceolate to obovate. Flowers purple-blue, 1–2cm in diam.; petals emarginate, obovate, spreading; spur *c*5mm, conical. Chile. Z9.

T.brachyceras Hook. & Arn.
Slender, glabrous climber with small tubers. Leaves 5–7-lobed, to 3cm across, often less, lobes obovate to linear-lanceolate, obtuse. Flowers to 1.3cm, yellow; upper petals with purple lines; pet. more or less emarginate. Chile. Z9.

T.canariense hort. ex Lindl. & Moore. See *T.peregrinum*.
T.chrysanthum Planch. & Lind. See *T.pendulum*.
T.edule Paxt. See *T.leptophyllum*.
T.elegans G. Don. See *T.tricolorum*.

T.hookerianum Barnéoud.
Climber. Leaves 7-lobed, to 1.5cm diam.; petioles slender, to 1.5cm. Pedicels very long, to 8cm; flowers *c*2cm diam., with a musty odour; calyx pale green; petals yellow, spur conical. *c*5mm. Chile. Z9.

T.incisum (Spreng.) Sparre.
Perennial herb, prostrate to procumbent. Leaves 5-lobed, to 2.5cm diam., lobes trilobed. Flowers to 2.5cm diam.; calyx pink; petals yellow, spur conical. *c*1.5cm. Argentina. Z10.

T.jarrattii Paxt. See *T.tricolorum*.

T.×leichtlinii hort Leichtl. (*T.leptophyllum* × *T.polyphyllum*.)
Flowers bright orange-yellow, spotted red. Garden origin. Z8.

T.leptophyllum G. Don (*T.albiflorum* Lem.; *T.edule* Paxt.).
Differs from *T.polyphyllum* in its tubers and climbing habit. Climber with large tubers. Leaves long-stalked, 6- or 7-lobed. Flowers *c*3.5cm, much overtopping leaves, orange, yellow, or pink-white; petals notched; spur straight, *c*1.5cm, narrow, conical Chile and Bolivia. Z8.

T.lobbianum hort. Veitch ex Hook. See *T.peltophorum*.

T.majus L. NASTURTIUM; INDIAN CRESS.
Strong-growing, glabrous annual climber to 2m. Leaves orbicular, nerves not projecting beyond margin, rarely lobed. Flowers large, to 6cm, very variable in colour, in all shades of red, orange, or yellow (orange in wild plant); petals rounded, clawed, claws fimbriate; spur 2cm or more long. Colombia to Bolivia. Cultigen introduced from Peru to Europe in 1684, widely cultivated. Many of the varia-

tions have resulted from the crossing of *T.majus* with *T.peltophorum*, *T.minus* and, less frequently, with *T.moritzianum* and *T.peregrinum*. 'Hermine Grashoff': to 20cm; leaves round, pale green; flowers double, orange-scarlet. 'Peach Melba': compact; flowers cream-yellow blotched at throat, edible. 'Salmon Baby': compact; flowers deep salmon pink, fringed, edible. 'Variegatum': to 1.2m, trailing; leaves variegated; flowers orange or red. Florepleno Series: flowers double. Climbing Hybrids Improved: trailing to 1.8m; flowers in wide range of colours. Double Gleam Hybrids: to 30cm, somewhat trailing; flowers semi-double in golden yellow, orange and scarlet, scented. 'Dwarf Cherry Rose': leaves dark green; flowers semi-double, cerise. 'Fiery Festival': flowers deep scarlet, abundant, fragrant. 'Golden Gleam': flowers double or semi-double, rich yellow. 'Strawberries and Cream': compact; petals cream splashed bright red. Gleam series: semi-trailing habit; flowers double, in single or a mixture of colours that includes scarlet, yellow and orange. 'Nanum': non-climbing, dwarf, compact form with smaller flowers. Alaska Hybrids: leaves light green, marbled and striped cream; flowers in white range of colours. 'Burpeei': flowers fully double. Dwarf Compact Hybrids: habit dwarf, dense; flowers in range of colours. 'Empress of India': leaves deep green; flowers bright scarlet, edible. Tom Thumb Hybrids: habit dwarf, compact; flowers single in wide range of colours. Whirlybird Hybrids: low-growing; flowers semi-double in range of colours.

T.minus L.
Non-climbing glabrous annual. Leaves rounded-reniform, nerves projecting beyond margin in a point. Flowers smaller than in *T.majus*, deep yellow; petals ending in a bristle-like point, lower petals much-spotted; spur distinctly curved, *c*2.5cm, cylindrical. Peru, Ecuador.

T.mucronatum Meyen. See *T.tuberosum*.

T.myriophyllum (Poepp. & Endl.) Sparre.
Climber. Leaves to 9-lobed, to 3cm diam., often less, lobes narrow, lanceolate. Flowers pale yellow-orange, to 3cm diam., spur to 2cm. Chile. Z9.

T.peltophorum Benth. (*T.lobbianum* hort. Veitch ex Hook.).
Pubescent annual climber to 0.3m with a spread of 3m. Leaves rounded, mucronate, long-stalked, veins ending at leaf margins in projecting points. Flowers medium to large, orange-red or yellow; upper petals rounded, lower clawed, toothed, fringed below; spur somewhat curved, *c*3cm, peduncles much longer than leaves. Colombia, Ecuador. 'Spitfire': flowers deep orange-red. Z9.

T.pentaphyllum Lam. (*T.quinatum* Hellen.)
Glabrous perennial climber to 6m with long, beaded tubers; stems and leaf-stalks purple. Leaves 5-lobed, lobes elliptical, usually obtuse, long-stalked. Flowers 2–3cm, in pendent masses; upper sepals spotted, red; petals scarlet, entire; spur conical, *c*2.5cm, red or green. S America. Z8.

T.peregrinum L. (*T.canariense* hort. ex Lindl. & Moore). CANARY CREEPER.
Perennial climber to 2.5m, treated as a half-hardy annual. Leaves usually 5-lobed, to 5cm across, lobes radially veined, pale green. Flowers long-stalked, to 2.5cm diam.; petals sulphur or lemon-yellow, upper erect, red-spotted at base, apex fimbriate-lacerate; spur to 1.2cm, conical, hooked, green. Peru, Ecuador. Z9.

T.polyphyllum Cav.
Grey-green herbaceous annual or perennial with long rhizome and prostrate or climbing leafy stems to 3m. Leaves 3–6cm across, 5- to 7-or more lobed, lobes sometimes cut, variable, glaucous-blue. Flowers long-stalked, freely produced, in long masses; petals yellow, orange or ochre, nearly equal, obovate, upper notched; spur *c*2cm, narrowly conical. Chile, Argentina. Z8.

T.quinatum Hellen. See *T.pentaphyllum*.

T.sessilifolium Poepp. & Endl.
Climber with tuberous roots. Leaves 3–5-lobed, to 1.5cm diam., often less, lobes ovate. Calyx green-yellow; petals dark red shaded with violet, bright red towards the base, to 1.5cm, spur conical, to 1.2cm. Chile. Z9.

T.smithii DC.
Climber, half-hardy annual or perennial. Leaves 5-lobed, to 6cm across, lobes acute, sometimes cut. Flowers bright orange-red, all petals bristle-fringed sometimes with darker nerves, spur somewhat curved, conical, *c*1.8cm. Tropical S America. Z10.

T.speciosum Poepp. & Endl. FLAME NASTURTIUM; SCOTTISH FLAME FLOWER.
Tall climber, perennial, to 3m, with more or less fleshy rhizome Leaves (5–)6(–7) lobed, to 5cm across, hairy, lobes obovate, notched, radially veined, shortly stalked. Flowers of moderate size, petals scarlet, upper narrow-wedge-shaped, lower rounded to square, notched, abruptly clawed; spur narrow, 2–3cm, more or less straight. Fruit blue. Chile. Z8.

T.tricolorum Sw. (*T.elegans* G. Don; *T.jarrattii* Paxt.).
Variable, tall, slender, perennial climber to 2m, with small tubers. Leaves 5–7-lobed, to 3cm across, lobes usually linear-obovate, green. Flowers of various colours; calyx obconical-turbinate, often orange-scarlet, rimmed black, but may be blue, violet, red or yellow with green margin, and yellow within; petals held mostly within calyx, orange, entire, shorter than spur; spur 1.5–2.3cm, straight or somewhat curved, red to yellow with a blue or green tip. Bolivia, Chile. Z8.

T.tuberosum Ruiz & Pav. (*T.mucronatum* Meyen).
Glabrous, perennial climber, 2–3m, with large yellow tubers marbled with purple, and red- or blue-tinged stems, leaf-stalks and peduncles. Leaves 3–5-lobed, truncate at base, long-stalked, grey-green. Flowers long-stalked, cup-shaped. Calyx red; petals about equal to sepals, usually entire, upper rounded, lower narrower, all orange or scarlet; spur straight, abruptly narrowed, scarlet, 1.5–2cm. Peru, Bolivia, Colombia and Ecuador. 'Ken Aslet': flowers orange. Z8.

T.violiflorum A. Dietr. See *T.azureum*.

Tweedia Hook. & Arn. (For J. Tweedie (1775–1862), of Glasgow and Argentina.) Asclepiadaceae. 1 species, a twining subshrub to 90cm. Shoots lax, sparsely branched, densely but minutely white-pubescent throughout. Leaves to 10cm, oblong to oblong- or lanceolate-cordate. Flowers to 2.5cm diam., solitary, or a few clustered in

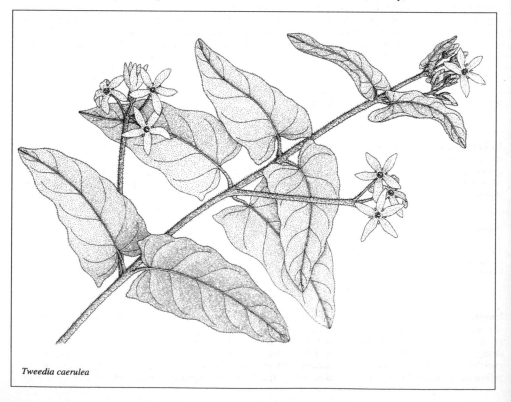

Tweedia caerulea

axils; corolla tube short broadly campanulate, lobes 5, spreading, oblong, powder-blue and tinged green when young, becoming sky blue then lilac with age. S Brazil, Uruguay. Z10.

CULTIVATION   A herbaceous climber for frost-free zones, or under glass in cool temperate zones with a minimum temperature of 5°C/40°F. It may also be grown as an annual, flowering in its first year from seed in late summer/early autumn. Grow in any well drained, moderately fertile soil in sun. Propagate by seed. Pinch back when young to encourage branching. The flowers last well when cut.

T.caerulea D. Don (*Oxypetalum caeruleum* (D. Don) Decne.).

Ullucus Caldas. (From the native name, Ulluco.) Basellaceae. 1 species, a twining procumbent perennial herb; rhizomes slender, subterranean, bearing fleshy tubers to 3cm, rose-purple in wild plants, those of cultivars usually larger and white, yellow or red. Stems to 60cm, angular. Leaves to 20cm across, cordate or reniform, fleshy, lustrous; petioles stout, sulcate above, exceeding blades, often bearing small aerial tubers in axils. Racemes axillary; bracteoles red, orbicular, 2 per flower; flowers small, bisexual; perianth lobes yellow, lustrous, tapering into a filamentous or acicular apex; stamens 5, filaments erect; style simple, stigma 1. Fruit a berry. N Andes, cultivated throughout S America. Z9.

CULTIVATION   *Ullucus* is widely cultivated as a root crop in its native regions and sometimes grown in educational collections elsewhere; it underwent unsuccessful trials in Britain to assess its suitability as an alternative to the potato. Plant in spring in light, humus-rich soils. Earth up the lower stem, as for potatoes, to encourage the formation of tubers. Lift in autumn after frosts have killed the foliage.

U.tuberosus Loz. (*Basella tuberosa* (Caldas) Humb.).

Urechites Muell.Arg. (Gk *oura*, tail, *Echites*, a related genus from which this differs in its coiled, tail-like anther appendages). Apocynaceae. 2 species of climbing subshrubs and shrubs. Leaves opposite, entire. Flowers showy, 2 to several in terminal or axillary scorpioid cymes; calyx 5-parted with numerous small, scale-like appendages at base; corolla funnel-shaped, tube short, cylindrical, throat tubular-campanulate, limb with 5 broad, twisted lobes; stamens 5, attached to top of tube, anthers with slender coiled appendages; seeds beaked and comose. Subtropical and Tropical Americas. Z10.

CULTIVATION   *U.lutea* is a slender, woody-based vine resembling a rather finer *Allamanda*, with downy oval leaves and large bright yellow flowers. In tropical and subtropical locations it will take readily to pergolas, archways and trellises provided it is sheltered from strong winds and planted in a moist, fertile soil. Under glass, it will cover walls and twine through pillars and frameworks given a medium-fertility loam-based soil, shade from scorching sunlight, a regular feed when in growth and a minimum temperature of 13°C/55°F. Propagate by hardwood cuttings inserted in a frame.

U.lutea Britt. (*Echites andrewsii* Chapman; *Echites suberecta*; *U.suberecta* Muell.Arg.; *U.pinetorum*).
Woody-based vine; young shoots loosely twining, softly pubescent. Leaves ovate to oval or elliptic, silky at first.

Flowers 4–6 per terminal cyme; corolla to 5cm, bright yellow. US (Florida), south to Colombia.

U.pinetorum. See *U.lutea*.
U.suberecta Muell.Arg. See *U.lutea*.

Vallaris Burm. f. (From Lat. *vallum*, stake, palisade; the stems are used in Java for fences.) Apocynaceae. 3 species of twining shrubs with milky sap. Leaves opposite, entire, minutely dotted. Flowers bisexual, white in cymes or clusters; calyx 5-lobed, sometimes glandular within; corolla salverform, tube short, throat glabrous, lobes broad; stamens carried at top of tube, filaments very short, club-shaped, anthers exserted, attached to stigma. Fruits many-seeded oblong follicles; seeds comose. Tropical Asia. Z10.

CULTIVATION   As for *Strophanthus*.

V.solanacea (Roth) Kuntze (*V.dichotoma* (Roxb.) Wallich ex A. DC.; *V.heynei* Spreng.).
Tall climbing shrub with pale bark. Leaves 2–15×0.8–6cm, elliptic or linear-oblong, slender-pointed. Flowers white in forked cymes, fragrant, 1.5cm across. India, Sri Lanka.

Vanilla Mill.(From Spanish *vainilla*, a diminutive of *vaina*, a pod or sheath.) Orchidaceae. About 100 species of scandent orchids; roots adventitious, arising at nodes, aerial or clinging, rooting in soil where they touch the ground. Stems succulent, cylindrical, jointed, climbing or trailing, green or brown, often channelled. Leaves fleshy, sessile or shortly petiolate, borne singly at nodes, sometimes absent or reduced to scales. Racemes or panicles usually axillary, occasionally terminal, few to many-flowered; flowers large, usually fragrant, white, yellow or green, the lip sometimes marked with purple or yellow; sepals and petals free, similar; lip usually larger, adnate to column at base and forming a funnel; column long, curved. Capsules cylindrical, dehiscent; seeds relatively large. Tropics and subtropics of Old and New World.

CULTIVATION   The scrambling, vine-like habit of this intermediate to warm-growing genus is highly unusual within Orchidaceae, as is the great non-ornamental value of *V.planifolia*, the vanilla orchid, grown for its pods on support shrubs and trees throughout the tropics. They produce trusses of large, waxy, often highly fragrant flowers in shades of white, green, cream and topaz: the rope-like growth of some (notably the near-leafless species) is also curiously attractive. Leafy species, particularly *V.planifolia*, demand high temperatures and good water supplies throughout the year. The thick-stemmed 'leafless' species will tolerate cooler, drier conditions and bright light once established. In optimum conditions, the stems may become bare and wither at the base, leaving the vines wholly epiphytic and free to clamber through their supports or form large knots: in such cases, regular misting and foliar feeding are essential. Stem cuttings with growing tips should be taken cleanly at a node or constriction and allowed to dry before insertion in damp perlite in a heated case (temperature circa 27°C/80°F). Once the thick, adhesive roots have developed (not to be confused with the smaller, largely inactive 'hook' roots found in several species), the young plants should be moved on to well drained pots of a coarse bark mix with added leafmould and sphagnum moss. Syringe and water freely; maintain high temperatures and light shade. As the stems grow and begin to clamber, furnish support by tying in to a cork slab, moss pole or moss-covered trellis. Sometimes affected by scale insect.

V.anaromatica Griseb. See *V.inodora*.
V.articulata Northr. See *V.barbellata*.

V.barbellata Rchb. f. (*V.articulata* Northr.).
Stems 1cm diam., terete, branching, succulent, of indefinite length. Leaves to 4cm, lanceolate, short-lived. Racemes axillary, to 12-flowered; flowers yellow-green or buff, lip white, purple towards apex; sepals to 4.8×1.5cm, elliptic; petals 4× 1.6cm, elliptic, keeled; lip to 3.5cm long, 4cm wide when flattened, funnel-shaped, the edge undulate, with disc of white hairs, becoming yellow papillae near apex; column to 3cm. Capsule to 10×1cm, pendent, cylindrical. Summer. S Florida, Cuba, W Indies.

V.fragrans (Salisb.) Ames. See *V.planifolia*.
V.grandiflora Lindl. See *V.pompona*.

V.humboldtii Rchb. f.
Stems 1–1.5cm diam., green-brown, of indefinite length. Leaves vestigial, scale-like. Panicles to 30cm, axillary, 12–20-flowered; flowers bright yellow, lip with chestnut-brown patch in throat; sepals 6–7×2cm, lanceolate; petals somewhat longer and broader; lip 6cm, funnel-shaped, the edge undulate, with short brown papillae and rosy red hairs over 1 cm long in throat. Comoros Is.

V.imperialis Kränzl.
Stems green, succulent, very long. Leaves to 28×12cm, subsessile, succulent, elliptic. Racemes to 15cm, densely several-to many-flowered; bracts imbricate, 1–3cm; flowers yellow or cream, lip blotched with rose-pink or purple; sepals and petals 6–8cm, lanceolate or oblanceolate; lip 5–7cm forming a tube narrow at the base, much expanded above with lacerate scales in the centre and long hairs toward apex, apex undulate and reflexed; column 4cm, joined to lip for most of its length. Ivory Coast, Ghana, Cameroun, Congo, Zaire, Uganda, Tanzania.

V.inodora Schiede (*V.anaromatica* Griseb.).
Stem to 0.8cm diam., green, terete, succulent. Leaves to 25× 12cm, broadly ovate, apiculate, yellow-green. Racemes axillary, 5–6-flowered; flowers unscented, yellow-green, lip white with yellow crest; sepals 5.5×2cm, oblong-lanceolate, thick-textured; petals similar but narrower; lip to 5cm long, 3cm white when flattened, funnel-shaped, the edge undulate, with fleshy crest in centre; column 2.5cm. Spring–autumn. Florida, C America, W Indies, NE South America.

V.phaeantha Rchb. f.
Stem to 0.8cm diam., green, terete, of indefinite length. Leaves 10–12×3.5cm, oblong, fleshy. Racemes axillary, several-flowered; flowers short-lived, pale green, the lip white striped with yellow; sepals and petals 9×1.5cm, oblanceolate;

lip adnate to column, tubular, narrow at base, expanded above, undulate and reflexed at apex; disc composed of papillae; column 6.5cm. Capsule 10×1cm, pendent, cylindrical. Late spring–summer. Florida, W Indies.

V.phalaenopsis Rchb. f. (*V.roscheri* Rchb. f.).
Stems 1–2cm diam., succulent, of indefinite length. Leaves vestigial, brown, to 3cm. Raceme to 30cm, many-flowered; flowers white flushed with pink, salmon, coral-pink or yellow in the throat, sweet-scented; sepals to 8×2.5cm, lanceolate-oblong, apiculate; petals similar but wider; lip to 8×4.5cm, funnel-shaped, with 4 rows of laciniate crests and digitate lamellae toward the base; column to 2.5cm long. Capsule to 17.5×0.8cm. Seychelles, Kenya, Tanzania, Mozambique, S Africa (Natal).

V.planifolia Andrews (*V.fragrans* (Salisb.) Ames). VANILLA.
Stems 1cm diam., green, terete, of indefinite length. Leaves 15×5cm, oblong, fleshy. Racemes axillary, densely several-flowered; flowers pale yellow-green, the lip with yellow hairs; sepals and petals 5–6×1cm, oblanceolate; lip 4×3cm, tubular, adnate to column margin fringed, curled back; column 3.5cm. Capsule 15–25cm, pendent, cylindrical. Spring. Florida, W Indies, C & S America. 'Variegata': leaves and stems striped cream to yellow.

V.polylepis Summerh.
Stems to 8m long, 1–1.5cm diam., succulent, bright green. Leaves to 24×6.5cm, fleshy, lanceolate to ovate. Racemes to 20-flowered, with 1–3 flowers opening at a time; flowers white or green-white, the lip yellow in throat and usually maroon-purple towards apex; sepals to 6×2cm, oblanceolate, fleshy; petals similar but slightly wider and less fleshy, with exterior keel terminating in a point about 0.2cm long; lip to 6 × 2.5cm, adnate to column for 3cm at base, funnel-shaped, the edge undulate; disc with up to 12 rows of branched scales 2mm long, the basal 3cm of lip papillose; column to 4.5cm. Capsule to 15 × 1.5cm. Zaire, Kenya, Zambia, Malawi, Zimbabwe, Angola.

V.pompona Schiede (*V.grandiflora* Lindl.).
Scandent, rooting at nodes. Leaves to 25×10cm, fleshy, ovate to oblong; petiole to 2cm. Raceme to 10cm; flowers green-yellow with orange-yellow marks on lip; pedicel and ovary to 5cm; bracts to 1.5cm, ovate; sepals and petals to 8×1cm, spreading, fleshy, narrowly oblanceolate, acute or subobtuse with dorsal keel; lip to 8×4cm, adnate to column at base, more or less tubular, apex undulate, bilobed or emarginate; disc with warty veins and dentate lamellae. Capsule to 15cm, aromatic. C America, tropical S America, Trinidad; naturalized Lesser Antilles.

V.roscheri Rchb. f. See *V.phalaenopsis*.

Vicia L. VETCH; TARE. (From Latin *vincire*, to bind, referring to the clasping tendrils.) Leguminosae (Papilionoideae). Some 140 species of annual or perennial herbs, often climbing by means of tendrils. Leaves alternate, paripinnate or imparipinnate; stipules usually small, leafy. Flowers solitary and axillary or in axillary fascicles and racemes; calyx actinomorphic to bilabiate; standard obovate or oblong, cleft, keel obtuse; stamens 10, 9 united, 1 separate; style downy throughout or on lower side only, or glabrous. Fruit more or less oblong, dehiscent; seeds 2 or more. Europe, S America, Hawaii, tropical E Africa.

CULTIVATION   *Vicia* species occur most frequently in grassy, hedgerow and woodland habitats, often in maritime and montane regions, both on calcareous and slightly acid soils. They have a range of horticultural uses. The field bean, *V.faba*, and *V.sativa* are used as green manure, are efficient nitrogen fixers and offer the advantage of overwintering from autumn sowings on ground that might otherwise remain vacant, except for weeds. They can also be sown in spring and summer. Of the remaining species, all are at least moderately ornamental, having fine pinnate foliage and pea flowers ranging in colour from white through crimson to violet-blue. Many have that delicate beauty characteristic of plants unimproved by breeding and selection; these are perfectly suited to use in the wild and woodland garden or wild flower meadows that approximate to their natural habitats. Those with an upright, non-twining habit, such as the softly pubescent *V.canescens*, the richly coloured *V.onobrychioides*, and *V. oroboides*, are suitable for the herbaceous border; *V.unijuga* is a wiry upright species for the herbaceous border. *V.orobus* and *V.pyrenaica* are suited to the rock garden. Grow in any well drained soil in sun, where soils remain sufficiently moist, or in dappled or part-day shade. For a green manure,*V.faba* is broadcast at a rate of $200g/m^2$ ($6oz/yd^2$); *V.sativa* is sown 8–10cm/3–4in. apart in rows 15–20cm/6–8in. apart. Propagate from scarified seed in spring or autumn.

V.canescens Labill.
Perennial, 38–46cm; stems many, erect, woolly. Leaflets in 8–12 pairs, crowded, linear-elliptic, upper leaves sometimes having a short tendril. Flowers blue in a dense raceme. Summer. Lebanon. Z8.

V.cracca L. (*V.gerardii* (All.) Gaudin; *V.incana* Gouan.) TUFTED VETCH; BIRD VETCH; CANADA PEA.
Scrambling or climbing perennial, stems to 180cm, glabrous or adpressed-pubescent. Leaves with branched tendrils; leaflets 5–30 × 1–6mm in 6–15 pairs, linear to ovate-oblong. Racemes 10–30-flowered, dense; flowers 8–12mm, indigo. Summer. Eurasia, US. Z5.

V.faba L. BROAD BEAN; ENGLISH BEAN; EUROPEAN BEAN; FIELD BEAN. Robust erect annual to 2m, lacking tendrils: stems stout, ridged. Leaflets 4–10 × 1–2cm, alternate or sometimes in 1–3 pairs, oval to oblong, obtuse, glaucous. Flowers to 2.5cm, solitary or in axillary clusters, white with bright to deep purple spot or splash. Fruit 8–20 × 1–2cm, densely pubescent at first, becoming lightly pubescent at maturity; seeds ovoid-oblong, compressed. Late spring–summer. N. Africa, SW Asia.

V.gerardii (All.) Gaudin. See *V.cracca*.

V.hirsuta (L.) S.F. Gray.
Pubescent annual, 20–70cm. Leaflets 5–20 × 1–3mm, in 4–10 pairs, linear- or obovate-oblong. Racemes 1–8-flowered, almost equalling leaves; flowers 2–4mm, buff tinged pale purple. Europe.

V.incana Gouan. See *V.cracca*.

V.onobrychioides L.
Glabrous or pubescent perennial, 30–120cm. Leaflets 10–35 × 1–4mm, 4–11 pairs, linear- or oblong-lanceolate. Racemes 4–12-flowered; flowers 17–24mm, violet with pale keel. S Europe. Z7.

V.oroboides Wulf. in Jacq.
Subglabrous or sparsely pubescent perennial, 25–50cm. Leaves lacking tendrils. Leaflets 40–80 × 15 × 45mm, in 1–4 pairs, ovate, acute. Racemes 2–12-flowered; flowers

14–19mm, pale yellow or blue. Summer. E Alps to W Hungary and C Yugoslavia. Z5.

V.orobus DC. in Lam. and DC. BITTER VETCH.
Pubescent perennial to 60cm. Leaves 5–8cm, abruptly mucronate, lacking tendrils; leaflets 8–23 × 3–8mm, in 6–15 pairs, oblong to elliptic, obtuse, mucronate. Racemes 6–20-flowered; flowers 12–25mm, white veined purple. Summer-early autumn. Europe. Z6.

V.pyrenaica Pourr.
Glabrous or glabrescent, creeping, stoloniferous perennial, 5–30cm. Leaflets 4–12 × 2–6mm, 3–6 pairs, oblong to suborbicular, truncate or emarginate, mucronate; tendrils usually simple; stipules entire. Flowers 16–25mm, solitary, bright violet-purple. Summer. Mts of Spain and France. Z8.

V.sativa L. SPRING VETCH; TARE.
Pubescent annual or biennial to 80cm. Leaflets 6–20 × 1–6mm, in 3–8 pairs, linear to obcordate, acute, mucronate or cleft; stipules usually with a dark spot. Flowers 10–30mm, purple, usually paired at axils. Europe, naturalized N America. Z5.

V.sepium L. BUSH VETCH.
Usually pubescent perennial, 30cm–1m. Leaflets 7–30 × 4–14mm, 3–9 pairs, ovate to ovate-oblong, obtuse, mucronate or emarginate, stipules spotted. Flowers 12–15mm, 2–6 together, dull blue, indigo or violet, sometimes short-stalked. Europe (mts) to Himalaya. Z6.

V.tenuifolia Roth. FINE-LEAVED VETCH.
Stems glabrous or adpressed-pubescent. Leaflets 10–30 × 2–6mm, 5–13 pairs, linear or linear-oblong. Racemes 15–30-flowered, usually dense; flowers 12–18mm, purple, pale lilac or lilac-blue. Europe. Z6.

V.unijuga A. Braun.
Erect perennial; stems slender, 30–38cm, tangled, lacking tendrils. Leaflets to 8cm, 1 pair, lanceolate to ovate. Racemes secund, many-flowered; flowers deep violet-purple or blue. Summer. NE Asia. Z7.

Vigna Savi. (For Dominico Vigna (*d*1647), Professor of Botany at Pisa.) Leguminosae (Papilionoideae). Some 150 species of erect, twining or creeping herbs. Leaflets 3, ovate to elliptic. Flowers clustered or racemose, often on long peduncles, mostly yellow to white, or purple; standard orbicular, sometimes basally auricled, keel incurved and frequently twisted, as is upper part of style, the lower, thickened part of style seldom twisted in excess of 180°; uppermost stamen separate. Fruit linear, straight or curved. Tropical Africa, S & C America, S US, Asia.

CULTIVATION *Vigna* species are used for fodder, green-manuring and ornament. Most are cultivated for their edible seeds, eaten as bean sprouts (especially *V.angularis* and *V.radiata*), and in soups and stews. The pods and young leaves are also eaten as raw or cooked vegetables. *V.angularis*, established for many centuries in the Far East, is now cultivated in South America, Central Africa, India and the southern states of the US. It requires temperatures of 15–30°C/60–86°F with moderate and well-distributed rainfall, although some cultivars are fairly drought-resistant. It is classed as a short-day plant, but cultivars vary in their response to daylength.

V.radiata, Mung Bean, is not known in the wild state, but has long been cultivated in India; it was introduced to southern China and Indonesia at an early date and is now widely grown in many tropical regions. It will tolerate temperatures in the range 30–36°C/86–97°F and moderate rainfall. High rainfall and excessive humidity may reduce yields. Cultivars may be short, long or daylength-neutral. In tropical and subtropical climates, seeds are often sown during the wet season so that plants will mature and ripen during the dry season. Soils should be well drained with a high organic content; a pH of 5.5–7.0 is usually suitable, although some cultivars are alkaline-tolerant. Sow seeds at 20–30cm/8–12in. intervals in rows 40–50cm/16–20in. apart; pre-sowing applications of P and N fertilizers will stimulate growth. Young pods may be harvested 50–70 days from sowing but late-maturing cultivars require 70–120 days to produce mature pods. Since high temperatures and low humidity are required for the development of the pods, cultivation in temperate zones is not practicable.

The Asparagus Bean, *V.unguiculata* ssp. *sesquipedalis*, has a long history of cultivation in tropical Asia. It thrives in conditions of high rainfall, although prolonged downpours will reduce flowering. Climbing forms (reaching 4m/13ft) and dwarf cultivars are available. Most cultivars appear to be daylength-neutral and are adapted to temperatures in the range 20–30°C/68–86°F; a soil temperature of 21°C/70°F is required for successful germination. Well drained soils with a pH 5.5–6.0 are most suitable. Sow seeds in well prepared beds or ridges. Plant climbing cultivars at 30–45cm/12–18in. intervals in rows 70–100cm/28–39in. apart. They may need the support of stakes or trellis to 2.5m/8ft high. At these spacings, yields of 300–500g/m^2 may be obtained. A balanced NPK fertilizer should be applied before sowing, followed by topdressings high in P and K. Harvest young pods 50-70 days from sowing for early-maturing cultivars, and in 100–120 days for late flowerers.

In temperate areas, *V.unguiculata* ssp. *sesquipedalis* may be grown under glass with a temperature range 21–25°C/70–77°F. Sow seed in trays or pots of a soilless propagating mix and transfer to growing bags or 25cm/10in. pots when 10–12cm/4–5in. high.

V.caracalla is grown as an ornamental for its curious fragrant flowers with spiralled standards. Suitable for outdoor cultivation in frost-free zones, in any fertile, well drained soil in sun, otherwise in the warm glasshouse. Propagate by seed.

V.aconitifolia (Jacq.) Maréchal. MOTH BEAN.
Shoots slender,. erect to diffuse, moderately brown-hirsute. Leaflets to 5cm, mostly deeply 3-lobed, thin-textured. Racemes compressed, capitate, on elongate peduncles exceeding lvs; bracteoles exceeding calyx, stiffly ciliate; corolla to 0.6cm. Fruit cylindrical, 2.5–5cm. S Asia.

V.angularis (Willd.) Ohwi and Ohashi (*Phaseolus angularis* W. Wight). ADZUKI BEAN; ADUKI BEAN.
Erect or scandent to 75cm. Leaflets to 10cm, ovate, hairy, terminal leaflet 3-lobed. Flowers *c*2cm. Fruits 10cm, pendent. Seeds pink-red, with small black eye. Asia. Z10.

V.caracalla (L.) Verdc. (*Phaseolus caracallus* L.; *Phaseolus giganteus* hort.). SNAIL FLOWER; CORKSCREW FLOWER; SNAIL BEAN.
Twining perennial to 6m. Leaflets to 13×10cm, ovate, acute, pubescent throughout. Flowers to 5cm, fragrant, white or yellow, wings pink-purple, keel coiled like a small snail's shell. Fruit to 18cm, linear. Tropical S America.

V.catjang (Burm. f.) Walp. See *V.unguiculata* ssp. *cylindrica*.

V.radiata (L.) R. Wilcz. (*Phaseolus aureus* Roxb.; *Phaseolus radiatus* L.). MUNG BEAN; GREEN GRAM; GOLDEN GRAM.
Hirsute annual; shoots freely branching, sparsely leaved, erect, to 90cm or longer. Leaflets to 10cm, ovate to rhomboidal, acuminate. Flowers yellow, few near tips of peduncles equalling petioles. Fruit to 10cm, slender, short-hairy; seeds green. India, Indonesia, US.

V.sinensis (L.) Savi ex Hassk. See *V.unguiculata* ssp. *unguiculata*.

V.unguiculata (L.) Walp. COWPEA; HORSE GRAM; CHERRY BEAN.
Annual; stems to 3.7m erect or scandent. Leaflets to 15cm, glabrous, central leaflet to 12cm, hastate, lateral leaflets unequal. Flowers in axillary racemes. Fruit 10–23cm, pendulous, smooth with thick, decurved beak; seeds 0.4–0.8 × 0.3–0.4cm, 10–15, variable in size and colour. S Asia. ssp. *unguiculata* (*V.sinensis* (L.) Savi ex Hassk.). BLACK-EYED PEA. Fruit pendent, to 25cm; seeds usually with a dark 'eye'. ssp. *cylindrica* (L.) Eselt. ex Verdc.(*V.catjang* (Burm. f.) Walp.). CATJANG; JERUSALEM PEA; MARBLE PEA. Fruits to 12cm; seeds marbled. Africa, India. ssp. *sesquipedalis* (L.) Verdc. ASPARAGUS BEAN; YARDLONG BEAN. Leaflets rhombic. Fruit pendent, to 90cm, soft and swollen. S Asia.

Vincetoxicum Wolf. (From Lat. *vincere*, to conquer, and *toxicum*, poison, referring to their supposed powers as antidotes.) Asclepiadaceae. Some 80 species of erect or twining perennial herbs or subshrubs. Leaves opposite, rarely alternate or in whorls of 4. Inflorescence cymose; flowers green-yellow or tinged purple, occasionally nearly black; calyx 5-parted; corolla round-campanulate, deeply 5-cleft; corona attached to staminal tube, nearly entire, toothed, shortly 5–10-lobed. Temperate & warm regions.

CULTIVATION As for *Periploca*, the stems of those listed below, however, tend to be herbaceous and often only twine in their uppermost regions, making these plants suitable for cultivation in the open border, supported by canes or cut twigs.

V.nigrum (L.) Moench (*Cynanchum nigrum* (L.) Pers.). BLACK SWALLOWORT.
Erect or scrambling to 90cm. Stems twining at apex. Leaves to 12cm, ovate-lanceolate, slender-pointed, finely ciliate. Cymes open, axillary; corolla 1cm diam., purple-black, bearded inside. S Europe, naturalized NE US. *V.medium* from Eastern Europe differs in its broader leaves and white, glabrous corolla.

V.officinale Moench (*Cynanchum vincetoxicum* (L.) Pers.). Differs from *V.nigrum* in its narrower leaves and unbearded green-white corolla. Europe.

Vitis L. (Name used by the Romans for the grapevine.) VINE. Vitaceae. Some 65 species of climbing shrubs. Branches long, slender; bark on older branches dividing into long fibrous strips; tendrils opposite leaves, often lacking at every third node, without adhesive tips but coiling tightly. Leaves more or less lobed. Inflorescence paniculate; flowers small, yellow-green, male on some plants, bisexual on others; calyx minute; petals 5, united at ends into a cap which is shed as flower opens; stamens 5, alternating with 5 nectar-bearing glands; style short. Fruit a berry, often pruinose; seeds 2–4, pear-shaped, pointed at base. Northern Hemisphere, particularly North America.

CULTIVATION   The ornamental species are usually found in rich, damp woodland soils; several inhabit still moister conditions in swamp (e.g.*V.rotundifolia*) and on riverbanks and at lakesides (*V.riparia*). They are mostly vigorous vines climbing by tendrils and ideally suited to clothing pergolas, trellis and fences, and for creating covered walkways; they will climb and cascade through sturdy trees and, with support, make good wall plants.

Ornamental *Vitis* species are grown primarily for their luxuriant and often very attractive foliage although some, such as *V.davidii*, with distinctive prickly stems, *V.riparia*, with sweetly scented flowers, and *V.labrusca*, will also bear edible fruits. *V.vinifera* has given rise to a number of clones with beautiful foliage, for example, 'Incana' with very downy, grey green leaves and 'Purpurea', with claret red leaves turning rich red-purple in autumn. Many other species are valued for their brilliance in autumn, including the spectacular, large-leaved and vigorous *V.coignetiae*, *V.davidii*, *V.amurensis*, and *V.thunbergii*.

Grow in deep, moist, well drained, moderately fertile and preferably calcareous soils. Plant *V.thunbergii* and *V.romanetii* in full sun; others will grow well in partial shade but need a warm situation for fruit ripening and good autumn colours. Prune in mid winter, before the sap begins to rise; in a restricted space, most species can be trained to a permanent framework and cut back to within one or two buds to form a spur system which becomes increasingly picturesque with age. Excessive growth is removed, i.e. stopped at 5–6 leaves in mid-summer as the basal growth begins to ripen, frequently giving rise to attractive contrasts between new and mature foliage. It is essential that any support system, particularly for covered walks, has good sound foundation, to carry the weight of foliage; it is also wise to make generous allowance for height. Vines often make growths in excess of 2m in length during the season, quickly reducing an arbour walk to an impenetrable tunnel.

Propagate by hardwood cuttings in late winter rooted in a closed case with bottom heat at 18–21°C/60–65°F. Propagate *V.coignetiae* also by simple layers or by seed, stratify for six weeks at or below –5°C/23°F, although progeny will be variable. For the cultivars and cultivation of the edible grape, see 'Grapes' in *The New RHS Dictionary of Gardening* (1992).

V.acerifolia Raf. (*V.doaniana* Munson; *V.longii* Prince). BUSH GRAPE.
Climbing vigorously, deciduous; shoots densely white-lanate when young; pith interrupted at nodes by thick diaphragms. Leaves 5–11cm, broadly cordate to reniform, distinctly 3-lobed, coarsely dentate, green tinged blue, white-lanate at first, persistently so beneath and in patches above; petiole one quarter to half length of lamina, white-lanate. Fruit 16mm diam., globose, purple. Late spring to summer. SC US (Oklahoma to Texas). Z6.

V.aconitifolia (Bunge) Hance. See *Ampelopsis aconitifolia*.
V.acuminata (A. Gray) Seem. See *Cayratia acuminata*.
V.aegeriophylla (Bunge) Boiss. See *Ampelopsis vitifolia*.

V.aestivalis Michx. (*V.bourquiniana* Munson). SUMMER GRAPE.
Vigorous, high-climbing; stems sparsely pilose to glabrous when mature; pith interrupted by diaphragms; tendrils lacking opposite every third leaf. Leaves 10–30cm, broadly ovate to subrotund, cordate at base, with narrow to broad basal sinus, more or less deeply 3–5-lobed or rarely entire, dull green, rufescent to ferruginous arachnoid-tomentose on both surfaces when young, persistently ferruginous floccose-tomentose beneath, more or less glaucous above; petioles sparsely pilose or glabrous when mature. Panicles slender, elongate, to 25cm. Fruit 5–10mm diam., globose, dark purple or black, pleasantly flavoured. Summer. NE America (Ontario to Alabama). var. **argentifolia** (Munson) Fern. (*V.argentifolia* Munson; *V.bicolor* Gray). Tomentum on underside of leaves mostly deciduous, revealing blue-green or silvery surface; young twigs blue-white. Northern and inland parts of range. Z3.

V.amurensis Rupr.
Climber or sometimes shrub-like, strong-growing, deciduous, to 15m; young shoots tinged red, tomentose; pith interrupted at nodes by a thick woody diaphragm. Leaves 10–25cm, 5-lobed, often deeply so, with deep, round, broad basal sinus, central lobe broadly ovate with slender, abrupt point, green, rich crimson and purple in autumn, somewhat pubescent beneath. Inflorescence cylindric to conic, axis winged, lax. Fruit 16 × 10mm, subglobose ovoid, black, glaucous, skin thick and dark, flesh succulent, usually bitter. Late spring to midsummer; fruits late summer. NE Asia (N China, Korea, CE Asia). Z4.

V.antarctica (Vent.) Benth. See *Cissus antarctica*.
V.arborea L. See *Ampelopsis arborea*.
V.argentifolia Munson. See *V.aestivalis* var. *argentifolia*.

V.arizonica Engelm. CANYON GRAPE.
Much-branched, not vigorously climbing, somewhat shrubby; stems very slender, angled, grey tomentose when young, bark dark grey to almost black on older stems. Leaves 5–10 × 5–10cm, ovate-cordate, irregularly dentate and generally 3-lobed, tomentose to floccose throughout. Inflorescence tomentose. Fruit 8–10mm diam., ovoid to globose, black, slightly glaucous. Summer. SW US, N Mexico. Z6.

V.armata Diels & Gilg. See *V.davidii*.

V.austrina Small. See *V.cinerea* var. *floridana*.

V.baileyana Munson (*V.virginiana* Munson).
High-climbing; branches angled, arachnoid-tomentose when young, glabrescent when mature. Leaves 6–10cm, unlobed or shortly 3-lobed, sparsely arachnoid-pubescent particularly along veins. Panicle dense. Fruit 4–7mm diam., black. SE US. Z6.

V.berlandieri Planch.
Climbing, robust; young shoots angular, brown tinged grey, hairy, mature shoots minutely floccose; nodal diaphragms thick; tendrils not present at every node, long, 2–3-partite. Leaves 8–10×6–8cm, broadly cordate, notched to shallowly 3-lobed, shallowly dentate with broad teeth, basal sinus V-shaped to U-shaped, dark green and glossy above, grey-pubescent becoming glabrous beneath. Inflorescence large, dense; pedicels long. Fruit small, succulent, black, slightly bitter but pleasant when fully ripe. Summer; fruits late summer. N America (Texas, Arkansas, N Mexico). Z7.

V.betulifolia Diels & Gilg.
Vigorously climbing, deciduous; young shoots lanate at first, later glabrous; tendrils very rarely branching. Leaves to 10cm, generally ovate, simple or rarely slightly 3-lobed, acutely dentate, tinged red when young, becoming dark green when mature, red or bronze in autumn, downy on veins above, somewhat tomentose beneath when young, almost glabrous when mature; petioles half to two thirds length of lamina, tinged purple. Panicle slender, sometimes forked, 10–12cm. Fruit 8mm diam., globose, blue-black, somewhat glaucous. C & W China. Z7.

V.bicolor Le Conte (*V.leconteana* House). BLUE GRAPE.
Climbing vigorously; shoots white tinged blue, glabrous. Leaves 10–30cm, broadly ovate, 3–5-lobed, green above, very glaucous white tinged blue beneath, glabrous or sub-glabrous on both surfaces. Fruit 12mm diam., very dark purple tinged black. C & E US. Z5.

V.bicolor Gray non Le Conte. See *V.aestivalis* var. *argentifolia*.

V.bourquiniana Munson. See *V.aestivalis*.

V. 'Brant'. (*V.* 'Clinton' (*V.labrusca* × *V.riparia*) ×*V.vinifera* 'Black St. Peters').
A popular fruiting vine growing vigorously to 12m. Leaves large, deeply 3–5-lobed, turning deep purple-red in autumn with veins and margins edged yellow-green. Fruit sweet, purple-black, pruinose.

V.californica Benth.
Climbing 6–9m, stout; shoots grey, arachnoid-tomentose when young, later mostly glabrous; diaphragms thick. Leaves 5–10×5–10cm, rounded-cordate or reniform, occasionally 3-lobed, rounded at apex, with broadly rounded basal sinus, regularly dentate to a depth of 3mm, teeth broadly triangular, green, deep crimson in autumn, glabrous above, generally cinereous-tomentose beneath; petiole 2.5–5cm, grey arachnoid-tomentose. Inflorescence 5–15cm; flowers fragrant. Fruit 8mm diam., black, purple-glaucous, flesh rather thin, inedible. Early summer. W US (Oregon to California). Z7.

V.candicans Engelm. ex A. Gray. See *V.mustangensis*.
V.capensis Thunb. See *Rhoicissus capensis*.
V.capriolata D. Don. See *Tetrastigma serrulatum*.
V.chaffanjonii Lév. & Vaniot. See *Ampelopsis chaffanjonii*.

V.cinerea (Engelm. ex A. Gray) Millardet in Bushberg.
SWEET WINTER GRAPE.
High-climbing; branches angular, arachnoid-tomentose when young, twigs densely pubescent when mature; pith interrupted at each node by a diaphragm; tendrils absent opposite every third node. Leaves 10–20cm, broadly ovate to subrotund, shallowly 3-lobed or unlobed, irregularly serrate, when young densely arachnoid-tomentose beneath and partially so above, when mature mostly glabrous above and white to cinereous floccose-tomentose beneath; petioles arachnoid-tomentose when young, pubescent when mature. Panicles slender, elongate, 10–20cm. Fruit 4–6mm diam., almost black, scarcely glaucous. Early summer.

C & E US. var. *floridana* Munson (*V.simpsonii* Small; *V.austrina* Small). Leaves rufescent to ferruginous floccose-tomentose beneath. SE Virginia to Florida. Z5.

V.cirrhosa Thunb. See *Cyphostemma cirrhosum*.
V.citrulloides Dipp. See *Ampelopsis brevipedunculata* var. *maximowiczii* 'Citrulloides'.

V.coignetiae Pull. ex Planch. (*V.thunbergii* hort. non Sieb.).
CRIMSON GLORY VINE.
Climbing vigorously and rapidly to tall treetops, deciduous; young shoots round, ribbed, loosely grey lanate at first; tendrils absent at every third node. Leaves to 30 × 25cm, rounded, obscurely acutely 3- or 5-lobed, dentate, deeply cordate at base, acute at apex, veins impressed, dark green, turning bronze to crimson or scarlet in autumn, glabrous above, thickly ferruginous-tomentose beneath; petiole 5–15cm, lanate. Fruit 12mm diam., black, purple-glaucous, scarcely edible. Japan, Korea. Z5.

V.cordifolia Michx. CHICKEN GRAPE; FROST GRAPE.
Vigorous climber; main stem to 60cm diam. in wild; young shoots smooth or slightly hairy; tendril wanting from every third node. Leaves rounded-ovate, coarsely irregularly dentate, unlobed or obscurely 3-lobed, cordate at base with narrow, pointed sinus, acute at apex, 7–12cm broad, glabrous and glossy above, sometimes pubescent on veins beneath; petiole often to length of lamina. Panicles pendulous, 10–30cm. Fruit 8–12mm diam., globose, black, reasonably palatable after exposure to frost, harsh and acid before. SE US. Z5.

V.davidiana (Carr.) Nichols. See *Ampelopsis brevipedunculata* or *Ampelopsis humulifolia*.

V.davidii (Carr.) Foex (*Spinovitis davidii* Carr.; *V.armata* Diels & Gilg).
Luxuriant climber, deciduous; young shoots very rough with spiny, hooked, glandular bristles, never pubescent Leaves 10–25cm, ovate-lanceolate, base cordate, dentate, apex acuminate, shining dark green above, tinged blue or grey beneath, usually brilliant red in autumn, glabrous above, more or less glandular-setose beneath and somewhat downy in vein axils; petiole half to four-fifths length of lamina, glandular-setose. Fruit 16mm diam., black, pleasantly flavoured. China. 'Veitchii': leaves shiny, tinged bronze in summer. var. *cyanocarpa* (Gagnep.) Sarg. Shoots less prickly; leaves larger, colouring well in autumn; fruit densely blue-white-glaucous. Z7.

V.ficifolia Bunge. See *V.thunbergii*.
V.delavayana (Planch.) Franch. ex Bean. See *Ampelopsis delavayana*.
V.discolor (Bl.) Dalz. See *Cissus discolor*.
V.dissecta Carr. See *Ampelopsis aconitifolia*.
V.doaniana Munson. See *V.acerifolia*.
V.elegans Koch. See *Ampelopsis brevipedunculata* var. *maximowiczii* 'Elegans'.
V.elegantissima Jaeger. See *Ampelopsis brevipedunculata* var. *maximowiczii* 'Elegans'.
V.endresii (Veitch) Nichols. See *Cissus endresii*.
V.erosa Bak. See *Cissus erosa*.
V.ficifolia var. *pentagona* Pamp. See *V.pentagona*.

V.flexuosa Thunb.
Elegant climber; stems slender, curving, slightly striate; shoots downy when young, later glabrous. Leaves 4–10 × 4–8cm, rounded-ovate, cordate or triangular-truncate at base, often contracted at apex to an acute point, shortly deltoid-dentate, thin and firm, glabrous and glossy above, downy in veins and in vein axils beneath with beige hairs. Panicle slender, 5–15×2–4cm. Fruit 7mm diam., globose, black tinged blue. Early summer. E Asia (China, India, Japan, Java, Korea). Z6.

V.flexuosa var. *major* Veitch. See *V.pulchra*.
V.flexuosa var. *parvifolia* (Roxb.) Gagnep. See *V.parvifolia*.
V.flexuosa var. *wilsonii* hort. See *Ampelopsis bodinieri*.

V.girdiana Munson.
Vigorous climber, 2–12m, young parts densely white-tomentose. Leaves 5–10cm, broadly ovate, more or less deeply

lobed and irregularly acutely dentate, triangular at apex, cordate at base with rather deep narrow sinus, green and glabrous above, cinereous-tomentose beneath, rather firm; petioles mostly 3–8cm. Inflorescence decompound-paniculate, 5–10cm, floccose. Fruit globose, 4–7mm diam., black, slightly glaucous. Early summer. California, Baja California. Z8.

V.gongylodes Burchell ex Bak. See *Cissus gongylodes*.
V.hederacea Ehrh. See *Parthenocissus quinquefolia*.
V.henryana Hemsl. See *Parthenocissus henryana*.
V.henryi hort. See *Parthenocissus henryana*.
V.heterophylla Thunb. See *Ampelopsis brevipedunculata*.
V.heterophylla Thunb. See *Ampelopsis brevipedunculata* var. *maximowiczii*.
V.heterophylla var. *maximowiczii* Reg. See *Ampelopsis brevipedunculata* var. *maximowiczii*.
V.himalayana (Royle) Brandis. See *Parthenocissus himalayana*.
V.himalayana var. *semicordata* (Wallich) M. Lawson. See *Parthenocissus semicordata*.
V.hypoglauca (A. Gray) F. Muell. See *Cissus hypoglauca*.
V.inconstans Miq. See *Parthenocissus tricuspidata*.
V.inserta Kerner. See *Parthenocissus inserta*.
V.japonica Thunb. See *Cayratia japonica*.

V.labrusca L. FOX GRAPE; SKUNK GRAPE.
Climbing vigorously; shoots densely lanate when young, branches glabrous when mature; pith interrupted by diaphragm at nodes; tendrils or panicles from every node. Leaves 10–20cm, rounded-cordate, usually shallowly 3-lobed, shallowly serrate, deep green above, thick and firm, glabrous above, densely ferruginous to rufescent-tomentose beneath, occasionally cinereous tomentose when mature; petiole less than half length of lamina. Panicles ovoid, 4–8cm. Fruit 1–2cm diam., globose, dark red to almost black, skin thick, with musky or foxy aroma. Early summer; late summer. NE US (Maine to S Carolina and Tennessee). Z5.

V.labrusca Thunb. non L. See *V.thunbergii*.
V.labrusca var. *sinuata* Reg. See *V.thunbergii* var. *sinuata*.

V.labruscana Bail.
The cultivated form derived from *V.labrusca*, often crossed with *V.vinifera*. Differs from *V.labrusca* in fewer tendrils; inflorescence larger, shouldered and conic, or thyrsoid; fruits larger, with less foxy flavour. Z5.

V.laciniosa L. See *V.vinifera* 'Apiifolia'.

V.lanata Roxb.
Shoots densely ferruginous lanate-tomentose when young. Leaves 8–15×4–8cm, broadly ovate, cordate at base, shortly acute to obtuse at apex, coarsely dentate, occasionally broadly and shortly lobed, green, scarlet in autumn, glabrous above, ferruginous tomentose beneath, rather thick. Inflorescence narrow with 2–4 long spreading branches at base; flowers very small. Fruit 5mm diam., globose, purple. Asia (Himalaya, China, India, Taiwan). Z9.

V.leconteana House. See *V.bicolor*.
V.leeoides Maxim. See *Ampelopsis leeoides*.

V.linecumii Buckl. POSY-OAK GRAPE.
Small to medium climber or forming bushy clumps; stems sparsely pilose to glabrous when mature; pith interrupted by a diaphragm; tendrils absent opposite every third leaf. Leaves to 30cm, broadly ovate to subrotund, cordate at base, with narrow to broad basal sinus, more or less deeply 3–5-lobed or rarely entire, thick, sparsely cinereous tomentose to thinly arachnoid-lanate, sometimes glaucous beneath; petioles sparsely pilose or glabrous when mature. Panicles slender, elongate, 5–15cm. Fruit 1–2.5cm diam., dark purple or black. Summer. Eastern N America (Ontario to Alabama). Z4.

V.longii Prince. See *V.acerifolia*.
V.megalophylla Veitch. See *Ampelopsis megalophylla*.
V.micans (Rehd.) Bean. See *Ampelopsis bodinieri*.
V.monosperma Michx. ex Sarg. See *V.palmata*.

V.monticola Buckl. (*V.texana* Munson).
Climber to 9m; branchlets slender, angled, slightly downy; pith interrupted at nodes by a thin diaphragm. Leaves 5–10 × 5–10cm, rounded, cordate at base with broad rounded basal sinus, more or less tapered to acute apex, coarsely triangular-dentate, slightly 3-lobed, small, rather thin, dark green above, tinged grey beneath, shining both sides, lanate on veins beneath when young; petiole about half length lamina. Fruit 12mm diam., globose, black, sweetly flavoured. SW Texas. Z6.

V.mustangensis Buckl. (*V.candicans* Engelm. ex A. Gray).
MUSTANG GRAPE.
Vigorously climbing, deciduous; shoots densely white lanate; pith interrupted at nodes by thick diaphragms. Leaves 5–11cm, broadly cordate to reniform, entire to sinuate or obscurely 3-lobed, or on young plants sometimes 3-, 5-, or 7-lobed and scarcely or shallowly dentate, dull dark green, white lanate above at first, persistently and thickly white-tomentose beneath; petiole a quarter to half length of lamina, white-lanate. Fruit 16mm diam., globose, purple, unpleasantly flavoured. US (Oklahoma and Arkansas to Texas). Z5.

V.oblonga Benth. See *Cissus oblonga*.
V.obovata Lawson. See *Tetrastigma obovatum*.
V.obtecta Lawson. See *Tetrastigma obtectum*.
V.odoratissima Donn. See *V.vulpina*.
V.oligocarpa Lév. & Vant. See *Cayratia oligocarpa*.
V.oratissima Raf. See *V.riparia*.
V.orientalis (Lam.) Boiss. See *Ampelopsis orientalis*.
V.pagnuccii Romanet. See *V.piasezkii* var. *pagnuccii*.

V.palmata Vahl (*V.monosperma* Michx. ex Sarg.; *V.rubra* Michx.). RED GRAPE; CAT GRAPE.
High-climbing; branches bright maroon to red particularly when young, glabrous. Leaves 8–14cm, triangular-ovate to subrotund, 3–5-lobed often deeply so, sparsely pubescent beneath on veins and in vein axils, 3-lobed leaves with terminal lobe triangular and elongate to acuminate apex, 5-lobed leaves constricted at base to rounded sinuses; petioles bright maroon to red. Panicles 8–15cm. Fruit black, scarcely glaucescent. Early summer. S & C US. Z5.

V.parvifolia Roxb. (*V.flexuosa* var. *parvifolia* (Roxb.) Gagnep.).
Elegant climber; stems slender, slightly striate; shoots laxly tomentose when young, later glabrous. Leaves to 8 × 5cm, rounded-ovate, broadly cordate at base, acuminate at apex, sometimes broadly 3-lobed, coarsely dentate, thin and firm, shining bronze-green above, tinged purple beneath when young, glabrous and glossy above, sometimes downy on veins and in vein axils beneath. Panicle slender oblong, 5–15 ×2–4cm; flowers very small. Fruit 7mm diam., globose, black tinged blue. E Asia (Himalaya to C China and Taiwan). Z7.

V.pentagona Diels & Gilg non Voigt (*V.quadrangularis* Rehd.; *V.ficifolia* var. *pentagona* Pamp.).
Vigorous climber, deciduous; shoots very pale or white-tomentose; tendrils twining, tomentose. Leaves 8–15 × 6–12cm, ovate, cordate or truncate at base, acute at apex, unevenly shallowly dentate, generally shallowly 3–5-lobed, dark green above, persistently white-adpressed-tomentose beneath, veins in 6–9 pairs; petioles 2.5–7.5cm. Panicles slender, 10–15cm. Fruit 8mm diam., globose, blue-black. W & C China. var. *bellula* Rehd. Leaves smaller, 4–6.5cm. Z6.

V.persica Boiss. See *Ampelopsis vitifolia*.

V.piasezkii Maxim. (*Parthenocissus sinensis* (Veitch) Diels & Gilg; *Psedera sinensis* (Diels & Gilg) Schneid.; *V.sinensis* Veitch).
Vigorous climber, deciduous; young shoots lanate at first, later glabrous; tendrils very rarely branching. Leaves 8–15 × 6–12cm, acutely dentate, very variable, generally simple near base of shoot becoming progressively more lobed and divided upwards, scarcely to very deeply 3-lobed and cordate at base, or with 3–5-leaflets, leaflets tapered to base, central leaflets oval or obovate and petiolulate, laterals obliquely ovate and

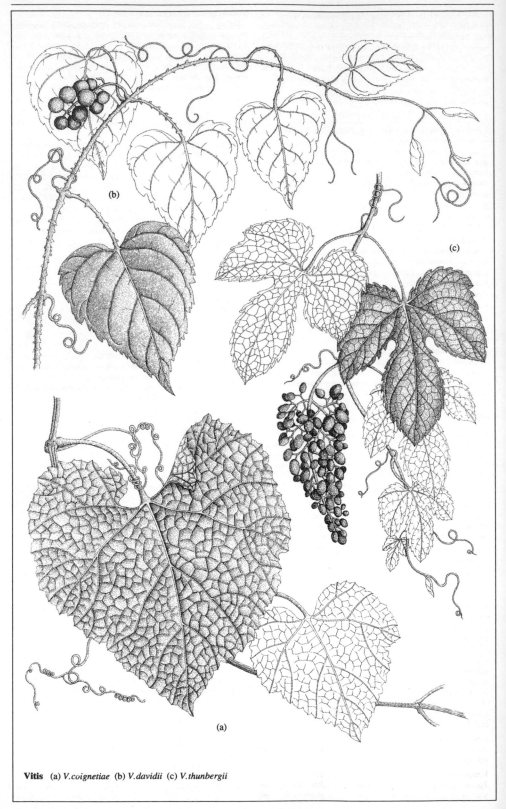

Vitis (a) *V. coignetiae* (b) *V. davidii* (c) *V. thunbergii*

sessile, tinged red when young, dark green when mature, red or bronze in autumn, downy on veins above, brown-tomentose beneath; petioles half to two-thirds length of lamina, tinged purple. Panicle slender, sometimes forked, 10–12cm. Fruit 8mm diam., globose, very dark purple tinged black. W & C China. var. *pagnuccii* (Romanet) Rehd. (*V.pagnuccii* Romanet). Shoots and leaves more or less glabrous. Z6.

V.planicaulis Hook. f. See *Tetrastigma planicaule*.
V.polita Miq. See *Pterisanthes polita*.
V.pterophora Bak. See *Cissus gongylodes*.

V.pulchra Rehd. (*V.flexuosa* var. *major* Veitch). (Possibly *V.amurensis* × *V.coignetiae*.)
Vigorous climber, deciduous; shoots tinged red, soon smooth and glabrous. Leaves 7–15cm, rounded-ovate, sometimes somewhat 3-lobed, more often coarsely dentate, broadly and shallowly cordate at base, acute at apex, tinged red when opening, green when mature, purple and blood-red in autumn, glabrous above or nearly so, grey pubescent beneath; petiole 4–10cm. Panicles slender, to 10cm. Summer. Origin unknown, but probably NE Asia. Z7.

V.quadrangularis Rehd. See *V.pentagona*.
V.quadrangularis (L.) Wallich ex Wight & Arn. non Rehd. See *Cissus quadrangularis*.
V.quinquefolia (L.) Lam. See *Parthenocissus quinquefolia*.
V.repens Veitch. See *Ampelopsis bodinieri*.
V.reticulata Pamp. non M.A. Laws. See *V.wilsoniae*.
V.rhombifolia Bak. See *Cissus rhombifolia*.

V.riparia Michx. (*V.oratissima* Raf.; *V.virginana* Poir.; *V.vulpina* Lecomte non L.). FROST GRAPE; RIVERBANK GRAPE.
High-climbing vine or scrambling bush; young shoots glabrous; pith interrupted by diaphragms, to 2mm thick at maturity. Leaves 10–20cm, broadly cordate, generally 3-lobed, coarsely and acutely serrate, shining green both sides, pubescent beneath when young, persistently pubescent in vein axils and sometimes along veins; petiole half to equal length of lamina. Panicles 5–10cm; flowers sweetly scented of mignonette. Fruit 6–12mm, globose, black tinged purple, heavily blue-glaucous. Early summer. C N America (New Brunswick and Quebec to Montana, south to Texas, Tennessee and Virginia). Z2.

V.romanetii Romanet ex Foex (*V.rutilans* Carr.).
Vigorous climber; young shoots pubescent with scattered erect, glandular setae. Leaves 15–25 × 10–18cm, 3-lobed, shallowly dentate, teeth bristle-tipped, basal sinus deep and narrow, dark green and slightly pubescent along veins or subglabrous above, densely grey-tomentose beneath, with hairs and perhaps a few large glandular setae amongst hairs; petiole one-third to half length of lamina, downy and bristly as shoot but with more copious bristles. Fruit 8–12mm diam., black. China. Z6.

V.rotundifolia Michx. (*V.vulpina* Torr. ex A. Gray non L.; *Muscadinia rotundifolia* (Michx.) Small). MUSCADINE GRAPE; BULLACE; FOX GRAPE.
Vigorously climbing to 28m in wild; bark tight, not shredding; young shoots warted; pith continuous through nodes; tendrils unbranched. Leaves 6–12cm, rounded to broadly ovate, coarsely and irregularly serrate, occasionally slightly lobed, acute to apex, cordate at base, basal sinus 90° wide or wider with entire margins, dark green above, green tinged yellow beneath, glossy on both surfaces, firm, subglabrous at maturity except in vein axils; petiole generally shorter than lamina. Panicles dense, short, 2–5cm. Fruit few in subglobose cluster, 1–2.5cm diam., rounded, dull purple, not at all glaucous, skin thick and tough, flesh musky-flavoured. Early summer. SE US. Z5.

V.rubra Michx. See *V.palmata*.
V.rubrifolia Lév. & Vant. See *Parthenocissus himalayana* var. *rubrifolia*.

V.rupestris Scheele. BUSH GRAPE; SAND GRAPE.
Sprawling vine or shrub to 2m, rarely ascending, usually prostrate or reclining on bushes; young shoots glabrous or nearly

so; tendrils usually wanting, or a few opposite uppermost leaves only. Leaves 5–10 × 6–12cm, reniform to depressed-ovate, usually unlobed, coarsely and irregularly dentate, often more or less folded, abruptly acuminate, with broad basal sinus, green tinged blue, paler beneath, firm, glabrous or sparsely pubescent along main veins beneath; petiole shorter than lamina. Panicles small, occasionally to 10cm. Fruit 6–12mm diam., subglobose, purple-black, slightly glaucous. Early summer; fruits late summer. SC US. Z5.

V.rutilans Carr. See *V.romanetii*.
V.semicordata Wallich in Roxb. See *Parthenocissus semicordata*.
V.serjaniifolia (Reg.) Maxim.. See *Ampelopsis japonica*.
V.sieboldii hort. ex K. Koch. See *V.thunbergii*.
V.simpsonii Small. See *V.cinerea* var. *floridana*.
V.sinensis Veitch. See *V.piasezkii*.
V.striata (Ruiz & Pav.) Miq. See *Cissus striata*.
V.succulenta Galpin. See *Cissus cactiformis*.
V.sylvestris C. Gmel. See *V.vinifera* ssp. *sylvestris*.
V.texana Munson. See *V.monticola*.
V.thomsonii Lawson. See *Cayratia thomsonii*.
V.thomsonii Veitch non Lawson. See *Parthenocissus henryana*.

V.thunbergii Sieb. & Zucc. (*V.ficifolia* Bunge; *V.labrusca* Thunb. non L.; *V.sieboldii* hort. ex K. Koch).
Moderately to vigorously climbing; stems slender; young shoots angled, more or less lanate; tendril lacking at every third node. Leaves 7–10cm, or occasionally to 15cm diam., 3–5-lobed, cordate at base, lobes ovate, irregularly acutely shallowly dentate, sinus between lobes often expanded and rounded at bottom, dull dark green, rich crimson in autumn, glabrous above, ferruginous-tomentose beneath; petiole to half length of lamina. Fruit in bunches 5–8cm long, to 9mm diam., black, purple-glaucous. Summer. China, Japan, Korea, Taiwan. var. *sinuata* (Reg.) Rehd. Leaves deeply lobed, lobes coarsely sinuate. China, Japan. Z6.

V.thunbergii hort. non Sieb. & Zucc. See *V.coignetiae*.
V.tinctoria Poit. & Turpin. See *V.vinifera* 'Purpurea'.

V.treleasei Munson ex L.H. Bail.
Much-branched, somewhat shrubby, rarely climbing; young stems pale green, glabrous or glabrescent; bark on older stems pale grey, fibrous. Leaves 6–10 × 6–12cm, broadly ovate to cordate, generally 3-lobed, lobes sometimes very small, irregularly dentate, bright green and glabrous above, paler and hairy along veins or in vein axils beneath. Inflorescence 5–7cm. Fruit 6–8mm diam., globose, slightly glaucous, skin thin. Late spring–summer. SW US (W Texas to SE Arizona). Z7.

V.veitchii Lynch. See *Parthenocissus tricuspidata* 'Veitchii'.

V.vinifera L. COMMON GRAPE VINE.
High-climbing, stems to 35m in the wild; young shoots glabrous or arachnoid-lanate, tendrils (or panicles on upper part of stem) generally absent opposite every third leaf, branched. Leaves 5–15cm, orbicular, generally palmately 3–7-lobed, irregularly dentate, cordate at base, glabrescent above, often persistently hairy, tomentose or lanate beneath. Panicles rather dense. Late spring to early summer; fruits late summer. S & C Europe. 'Apiifolia' (*V.laciniosa* L.): leaves deeply and finely lobed. 'Brant': see *V*. 'Brant'. 'Ciotat': ornamental; leaves very deeply incised. 'Incana' (DUSTY MILLER GRAPE): leaves 0–3-lobed, covered in fine grey-white cobwebby down. 'Madame Mathias Muscat': ornamental; strong; leaves and shoots glossy purple. 'Purpurea' (*V.vinifera* var. *purpurea* Veitch; var. *purpurea* Bean; *V.tinctoria* Poit. & Turp.) (TEINTURIER GRAPE): leaves white-downy when young, becoming plum-purple, deepening to dark purple in autumn; fruits dark purple, harshly acid. ssp. *vinifera* (ssp. *sativa* Hegi). Fruit 6–22mm, ellipsoid to globose, green, yellow, red or purple-black, sweet; seeds 0–2, pyriform with elongate beak. Found only in cult., mostly in S & C Europe, widely naturalized. ssp. *sylvestris* (C. Gmel.) Hegi (*V.sylvestris* C. Gmel.; *V.vinifera* var. *sylvestris* (C. Gmel.)

Willd.). Foliage dimorphic, more deeply lobed in male plants. Fruit 6mm, ellipsoid, black tinged blue, acid. SE & SC Europe to Asia Minor, Caucasus, N Iran, Turkestan. The original wild grapevine, probably first domesticated towards the east of its distribution. Z6.

V.vinifera ssp. *sativa* Hegi. See *V.vinifera* ssp. *vinifera*.

V.vinifera var. *purpurea* Bean. See *V.vinifera* 'Purpurea'.

V.vinifera var. *purpurea* Veitch. See *V.vinifera* 'Purpurea'.

V.vinifera var. *sylvestris* (C. Gmel.) Willd. See *V.vinifera* ssp. *sylvestris*.

V.virginana Poir. See *V.riparia*.

V.virginiana Munson non Poir. See *V.baileyana*.

V.vitacea (Kerner) Bean. See *Parthenocissus inserta*.

V.voinieriana Pierre ex Nichols. & Mottet. See *Tetrastigma voinierianum*.

V.vomerensis hort. See *Tetrastigma obovatum*.

V.vulpina L. (*V.odoratissima* Donn). FROST GRAPE; CHICKEN GRAPE.
High-climbing, rather robust; pith interrupted by diaphragms 2–5mm thick; tendrils branched, usually rufescent, 2-partite.

Leaves 10–15 × 8cm, rounded, unlobed or slightly 3-lobed, coarsely serrate, with broad shallow basal sinus, pale green and glabrous above, pubescent beneath when young, persistently so in vein axils. Panicles lax, slender, elongate, 10–15cm; flowers fragrant. Fruit 5–10mm, black or dark blue, not glaucescent, very acid, becoming sweet and edible after exposure to frost. Early summer. C & E US. Z5.

V.vulpina Lecomte non L. See *V.riparia*.

V.vulpina Torr. ex A. Gray non L. See *V.rotundifolia*.

V.wilsoniae Veitch (*V.reticulata* Pamp. non M.A. Laws).
Climbing very vigorously; shoots lanate when young. Leaves somewhat rounded-ovate, more or less cordate at base, shortly acute at apex, sinuate-dentate, 7.5–15cm diam., deep red in autumn, lanate both sides when young, becoming glabrous above and somewhat arachnoid-lanate beneath when mature particularly on veins. Flowers in slender, often unbranched clusters 8–12cm long. Fruit 10–12mm, black, purple-glaucous. C China. Z6.

Wagatea Dalz. (For Jakob Waga (1800–1872), Polish botanist.) Leguminosae (Caesalpinioideae).1 species, a robust, climbing shrub to 30m; branches hooked (at least when scrambling); branchlets and main rachis of leaves and inflorescences prickly. Leaves bipinnate; pinnae 4–6 pairs; leaflets oblong in 5–7 pairs, glabrous or thinly pubescent above, pale green, densely pubescent beneath; stipules minute. Inflorescence a densely flowered, spike-like raceme or panicle; peduncles stout; bracts subulate, caducous; bracteoles absent; calyx scarlet, campanulate; petals orange, oblong-spathulate, rounded, overlapping, uppermost petal inside and broadest; stamens 10, free, slightly declinate, not exserted, base thickened and densely pubescent, anthers uniform, longitudinally dehiscent; ovary sessile, 4–6-ovuled, style somewhat expanded at apex, stigma oblique, cleft, concave. Fruit oblong, acute, coriaceous, torulose, sutures thick; seeds 1–4, obovate-oblong. SW India, introduced Java. Z10.

CULTIVATION   As for *Camoensia*.

W.spicata Dalz.

Wisteria Nutt. (For Caspar Wistar (1761–1818), Professor of Anatomy at the University of Pennsylvania.) Leguminosae (Papilionoideae). Some 10 species of deciduous, twining, high-climbing woody vines to 10m, older stems becoming trunk-like, twisted and gnarled; bark grey, fissured. Leaves alternate, imparipinnate; stipules caducous; leaflets entire, opposite, oblong-elliptic, apical leaflet usually largest. Flowers in pendulous terminal or axillary racemes; calyx campanulate, teeth 5, lower teeth longer than upper; standard large, reflexed, often with 2 appendages at base, wings falcate, free, obtuse, basally auricled, coherent at apex, keel obtuse; stamens 10, 9 joined, 1 free; ovary stalked, surrounded by a collar-like glandular disc, multi-ovular, style inflexed, glabrous, stigma small, capitate, terminal. Fruit a loment, elongated, dehiscent, 2-valved, leathery, tardily dehiscent; seeds several, large, reniform. China, Japan, E US.

CULTIVATION   Vigorous climbers of elegant habit grown for their attractive foliage and pendulous racemes of (usually) scented flowers, with a colour range from the pure white of *W.venusta* through pinks, mauves and violet-blue, in the different cultivars of *W.floribunda*, to the darker purple of *W.sinensis* 'Black Dragon'. *W.venusta* is a strong climber of more shrubby habit, noted for its large, slightly fragrant flowers and distinguished by its downy, dark green foliage and seed pods. *W.frutescens*, *W.macrostachys* and *W.floribunda* all occur in damp habitats, the first two from the wet woodland, lake margins and streamsides of eastern and central North America, the last from the streamside thickets and woodland of the southern islands of Japan (Honshu, Shikoku and Kyushu). *W.sinensis* occurs on cliffs and in woodland in West Hubei and East Sichuan.

They are eminently suited to arches, arbours and pergolas, where the picturesque, twining habit of growth is seen to best advantage and where the racemes may cascade to their full length. In its cultivated forms, the fragrant racemes of *W.floribunda* commonly reach 60cm/24in. and more in length. With careful pruning and a little support, *W.floribunda* and *W.sinensis* can also be grown as 'free-standing' lawn specimens. Alternatively, all species may be left unhindered to scramble through tall trees. They can also be trained to cover large expanses of sunny wall; those with less extravagant racemes are especially effective on low terrace walls. In *W.floribunda*, unless trained, the flowers of wall-grown plants may be partially obscured by the foliage. *Wisteria* can also be trained as standards, especially useful for pot cultivation in the glasshouse or conservatory, where they can be forced for early flowers.

Plant in a sunny south- or southwest-facing position, with protection from early morning sun in frosty periods and shelter from cold winds. Even the hardiest species, *W.venusta*, *W.macrostachys*, *W.frutescens* and *W.flori-*

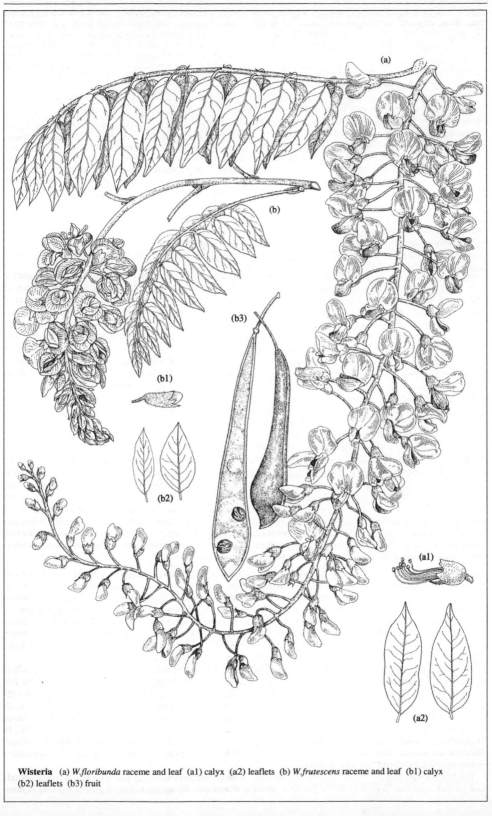

Wisteria   (a) *W. floribunda* raceme and leaf (a1) calyx (a2) leaflets (b) *W. frutescens* raceme and leaf (b1) calyx
(b2) leaflets (b3) fruit

bunda, (which tolerate temperatures to –20°C/–4°F), are more hardy and floriferous if given the additional warmth of a wall; with the possible exception of *W.japonica,* the remaining species are hardy to –15°C/5°F. Grow in a deep, fertile, well drained but moisture-retentive soil; improve very light or chalky soils by incorporating leafmould or garden compost and loam.

Bring container-grown plants into the glasshouse for forcing in late winter, provide a minimum temperature of 10°C/50°F, and spray with lime-free water twice or three times daily. Replace in a sunny position out of doors after blooming and once danger of frost is passed.

Prune initially to form a suitable framework; *Wisteria* can be grown as espaliers, fans, as standards or more informally to cover large walls. In all cases the aim of pruning is to encourage the formation of flowering spurs, close to the main framework of the plant; the primary advantage in training *Wisteria* as an espalier is that the horizontal branches are perfectly suited to the nature of the floral display. First trim back the leading shoot on planting to 75–90cm/30–36in. above ground level. Tie in suitable laterals at about 45° during their first growing season and cut back any sub-laterals to 2–3 buds. During the first winter, the laterals are re-positioned horizontally, and cut back by one third; the leading shoot is cut back to about 90cm/36in. above the point from which the laterals emerge. In subsequent seasons, the extension of the leader and the selection of suitable laterals is repeated until the desired framework is achieved. On an established framework, cut back all shoots to 5–6 buds in mid-summer, about two months after flowering; any subsequent twining growth and late-flowering shoots are again cut back to 2–3 buds in late autumn or winter to form flowering spurs for the following season; the flower buds are quite apparent in winter, being rounder and plumper than the vegetative buds. Any basal shoots not required for propagation by layering should be removed. Old and neglected plants may be rejuvenated by first selecting a suitable framework of well placed branches, and then applying the twice-yearly pruning regime described for established plants.

Propagate by simple layering, or by basal cuttings of side-shoots in early to mid-summer, in a closed case with bottom heat. Also by bench grafting, making an apical wedge graft on to seedling stock of *W.sinensis* in late winter. Plunge the pot in a closed case with bottom heat at 18–21°C/65–70°F; when established, pot on ensuring that the graft union is below the soil surface to encourage the scion to root.

Seed-raised plants are variable and may, in some cases, take up to twenty years to bear flowers of poor quality that are then obscured by foliage. If this method is attempted, sow seed in spring at 10–13°C/50–55°F after pre-soaking in hot water for about 18 hours. Seeds are poisonous.

Chlorosis may occur on alkaline soils; apply sequestered iron as a soil drench or foliar spray. The aphid-borne wisteria vein mosaic virus also causes yellow mottling or spotting of the leaves. Leaf spotting fungi, *Phyllosticta wistariae* and *Septoria wistariae,* cause cosmetic damage.*Wisteria* are also attacked by polyphagous aphids and brown scale, *Parthenolecanium corni.* Birds may consume the flower buds, and on established plants this may be the primary reason for poor flowering, although buds may also be dropped in soils that are too dry, too moist or too fertile, the last resulting in vegetative growth at the expense of flowering. Late frosts will also kill the developing racemes, but, at least in *W.floribunda* and *W.sinensis,* these will often be replaced by a second flush. Insufficient sunlight and misguided pruning will also result in poor flowering.

W.brachybotrys Sieb. & Zucc. See *W.venusta* var. *violacea.*

W.chinensis DC. See *W.sinensis.*

W.floribunda (Willd.) DC. (*W.multijuga* Van Houtte). JAPANESE WISTERIA.
Stems twining clockwise to 8m. Leaves 25–32.5cm; leaflets to 8cm, 11–19, ovate-elliptic to oblong, to 8cm, downy when young, later glossy-glabrous. Inflorescence an axillary raceme 40–120cm, flowering gradually from the base; pedicels to 2.5cm, puberulent; flowers 1.7–1.9cm diam., fragrant, violet, blue, lilac, pink, red or white; calyx to 1cm, pubescent; standard usually less than 2cm diam. Fruit to 15cm, velutinous. Early summer. Japan. A wide range of cultivars has been developed, particularly in Japan, exhibiting variation as follows: raceme length 17cm ('Sekine's Blue') to 90cm ('Macrobotrys'); flowers may be double ('Violacea-plena'), standard from cobalt-violet ('Macrobotrys') to white ('Geisha'), wings and keel blue-violet ('Sekine's Blue') to pale violet ('Naga Noda') to pale rose with a yellow-stained standard ('Rosea') to white ('Alba'), slightly fragrant ('Beni Fugi') to very fragrant ('Naga Noda'). Z4.

W.× formosa Rehd. (*W.floribunda* × *W.sinensis.*)
Stems twining clockwise. Young shoots sericeous. Leaves initially sericeous later bright green throughout and glabrous above; leaflets 9–15, commonly 13. Racemes to 25cm; flowers 2cm diam., deeply fragrant, blooming all at once; pedicels 1.3cm; standard pale violet, wings and keel darker. Early summer. Garden origin. This hybrid was raised in Professor C.S. Sargent's garden at Holm Lea, Brookline, Mass., in 1905; the seed parent was originally *W.floribunda* 'Alba'.

Near-simultaneous flowering distinguishes *W.× formosa* from *W.floribunda,* where blooming starts from base of the raceme. Z5.

W.frutescens (L.) Poir. AMERICAN WISTERIA.
Twining, 10–12m; young shoots yellow. Leaves 20–30cm; leaflets 3–6cm, 9–15, oval-lanceolate, somewhat pubescent when young, later dark green and glabrous above. Racemes 4–10cm, pendulous or sometimes held horizontally to semi-erect, dense, villous; flowers small, to 2cm, mildly fragrant, pale purple-lilac sometimes with a yellow spot on the standard; calyx to 6cm, slender, pubescent; standard auricled at base, wings with short slender auricle on both sides. Fruit 5–10cm, glabrous, compressed. Summer–early autumn. E US. 'Magnifica' (*W.magnifica* Henriq.): flowers lilac with a large sulphur-yellow blotch on the standard. 'Nivea': flowers pure white; stalks short, very pubescent; early-flowering. Z5.

W.japonica Sieb. & Zucc.
Branches slender; young shoots glabrous. Leaves 15–20cm, glabrous, glossy; leaflets 3–6cm, 9–13, ovate, rounded to sub-cordate at base, bright glossy green, glabrous beneath. Raceme 15–30cm, axillary, often branching, crowded; flowers to 1.3cm diam. white or cream, on 4cm stalks; calyx glabrous, except ciliate margin. Fruit 8–10cm, glabrous; seeds 6–7. Summer. Japan, Korea. Japan. Z8.

W.macrostachys (Torr. & A. Gray) Nutt. KENTUCKY WISTERIA.
To 8m; young shoots somewhat villous at first, later glabrous. Leaflets 3–7cm, usually 9, ovate-elliptic to lanceolate, acumi-

Wisteria (a) *W.sinensis* twig, new leaves, raceme (a1) fruit (a2) calyx (a3) leaflets (b) *W.japonica* raceme and leaf
(b1) calyx (b2) fruit (b3) leaflets

nate, initially pubescent, later pubescent only beneath. Racemes 20–30cm, axis and pedicels glandular; flowers to 90, densely packed, opal to rose; calyx teeth longer than tube. Fruit 7–12cm, glabrous, often obscurely twisted. Summer. C US (Missouri, Arkansas, Tennessee). Z6.

W.magnifica Henriq. See *W.frutescens* 'Magnifica'
W.multijuga Van Houtte. See *W.floribunda*.

W.sinensis (Sims) Sweet (*W.chinensis* DC.). CHINESE WISTE-RIA.
Vigorous deciduous climber, twining anti-clockwise to 10m. Shoots glabrous. Leaves 25–30cm; leaflets 5–8cm, 7–13, usually 11, elliptic or ovate, deep green, glabrous above, hirsute beneath, the midrib especially. Flowers to 2.5cm diam., appearing with leaves, faintly scented, pale blue to lilac-mauve, densely packed in 15–30cm racemes, a second, sparser flush of racemes often produced two months after the first; pedicels to 2cm, villous; calyx pubescent; standard to 2.2cm diam., rounded. Fruit 10–15cm, club-shaped, densely velutinous, tapering toward base; seeds 2–3. Late spring. China. 'Alba': flowers white. 'Black Dragon': flowers semi-double, very dark purple. 'Caroline': flowers deep blue-pur-ple, very fragrant. 'Jako': racemes to 30cm, very dense, fragrant; leaflets 11. 'Plena': flowers double, rosette-shaped, lilac. 'Sierra Madre': flowers very fragrant, standard white-tinged, wing and keel, lavender-violet. Z5.

W.venusta Rehd. & Wils. SILKY WISTERIA.
Stems twining anti-clockwise to 9m. Very similar to *W.sinensis*, but shoots pubescent when young. Leaves 20–35cm; leaflets to 10cm, 9–13, elliptic to ovate, apex short-acuminate, rounded at base, pubescent throughout, especially beneath. Racemes 10–15cm, pendulous; pedicels very pubescent; flowers 2–2.5cm diam. white, highly fragrant; calyx cup-shaped, 3 lower teeth subulate; standard stained yellow and auricled at base, keel truncated at apex. Fruit 15–20cm, densely velvety, compressed. Early summer. The typical *W.venusta* is a white-flowered selection long grown in Japan but unknown in the wild. The species' natural condition is represented by var. *violacea* Rehd. (*W.brachybotrys* Sieb. & Zucc.). Inflorescence to 15cm; flowers purple. Japan (W Honshu, Shikoku, Kyushu). Z5.

W.violaceo-plena (C. Schneid.) L.H. Bail. See *W.floribunda* 'Violacea-plena'.

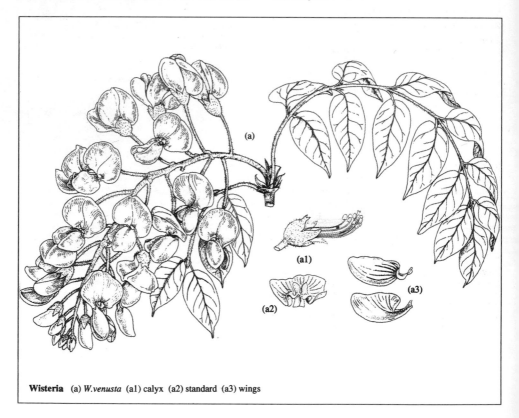

Wisteria (a) *W.venusta* (a1) calyx (a2) standard (a3) wings

Xerosicyos Humbert. Cucurbitaceae. 4 species of climbing perennials. Stems glabrous to sparsely hairy. Tendrils commonly bifid. Leaves alternate, suborbicular to oval, entire, thick, fleshy; petioles short. Flowers unisexual: male flowers small, green-yellow, in axillary, umbelliform clusters, calyx short cup-shaped, lobes 4, lanceolate; petals 4, oval-acuminate, glabrous, stamens 4, alternate to petals, free, equal, anthers reniform; female flowers in umbelliform clusters or loose panicles, calyx long-obconic, staminodes 4, ovary unilocular, ovules 4, styles 2, stigma 2-lobed. Fruit compressed-obconic, apex truncate or broadly emarginate, dry, opening by an upper slit; seeds oblong, compressed, winged. Madagascar. Z10.

CULTIVATION   As for *Coccinea*.

X.danguyi Humbert.
Stems striate, glabrous. Leaves 3.5–5.5×2.5–5cm, suborbicular, thick, fleshy, glaucous above, glabrous; petiole to 1.5cm. Male flowers numerous, yellow-green; petals 3 × 1mm, recurved; female flowers slightly larger than males. Fruit dry, *c*2cm, yellow-brown.

X.decaryi Guill. & Keraudren.
Resembles *X.danguyi*, but leaves 2.5 × 1cm, oblong-elliptic, rounded at apex, light green, petioles 1–2mm.

X.perrieri Humbert.
Tall climber. Stems slightly woody at base. Leaves 1.8–2 × 1.6–2cm, suborbicular, light green, thick, glabrous; petioles 1–1.5mm. Male flowers 3–20, pale green-yellow, petals 10× 6–7mm, female flowers slightly larger than male. Fruit 2.5cm, dry, yellow-brown.

Zehneria Endl. Cucurbitaceae. 30 species of monoecious or dioecious, climbing, perennial herbs. Stems arising annually from rootstock, thickened and woody at base. Tendrils simple. Leaves simple, often palmately lobed, petiolate. Male flowers small, white becoming tinged yellow, solitary or in racemose or subumbelliform clusters, sessile or pedunculate; calyx campanulate, lobes small; corolla lobes 5, connate at base; stamens 3 or 2, filaments inserted on lower haleaf of calyx or subsessile and positioned centrally; female flowers solitary or few to many in axillary clusters; staminodes 3; ovary subglobose to fusiform, smooth, stigma commonly 3-lobed. Fruit solitary or in clusters, small, baccate, red; seeds ovate to elliptic, small, compressed, margins occasionally prominent. Old World Tropics. Z10.

CULTIVATION   As for *Trichosanthes*.

Z.debilis Sonder. See *Trochomeria debilis*.

Z.indica (L.) Keraudren.
Stems woody, striate, sparsely hairy to glabrous. Leaves simple, cordate, pentagonal or 3-lobed, lobes acuminate, sinuate, 3–10cm, bright green, punctate-scabrid above, glabrous beneath but veins pubescent; petiole 1–2cm. Male flowers 3–4-clustered; corolla lobes to 4mm; female flowers 1–4 per axil; pedicels to 10mm. Fruit 10–12mm. E Asia.

Z.scabra (L. f.) Sonder (*Melothria punctata* Cogn.).
Stems to 6m, subglabrous to crisped-pubescent. Leaves 2.5–11cm, ovate to broadly ovate, base cordate to subtruncate, occasionally shallowly 3–5-lobed, scabrid-punctate above, paler and sparsely hairy to densely grey-tomentose beneath; petiole slightly hairy, to 8cm. Male flowers 2–60 in umbelliform clusters, with coaxillary solitary flower; corolla lobes 1.5–3.5mm; stamens 3; female flowers solitary or 2–10, sessile or on peduncles to 2.5cm. Fruit 6–12mm. Distribution as for the genus.

Zygosicyos Humbert. Cucurbitaceae. 2 species of dioecious or monoecious, herbaceous, shrubby climbers. Stems from tubers, slender. Tendrils often bifid. Leaves 3-partite or 3-foliolate. Flowers unisexual: male flowers solitary or in loose racemes, calyx small, lobes 4, lanceolate, small, corolla of 4 free petals, 2 inner slightly longer than outer, stamens 4, filaments forming a central column, connate to half their length, anthers transverse, reniform; female flowers solitary, calyx obconical, staminodes 4, small, inserted at base of petals; ovary unilocular, ovules 2, styles 2, stigmas 2-lobed. Fruit obconical, slightly compressed, leathery, opening by an apical slit; seeds elliptic, compressed, winged. E Asia, Madagascar. Z10.

CULTIVATION   As for *Coccinea*.

Z.tripartitus Humbert.
Stems slightly woody, ribbed, slender. Tendrils simple or bifid, slender. Leaves 25–3 × 1cm, lateral segments divaricate, with 2 or 3 lobes, stiffly pubescent above, especially on veins and margins, glabrescent beneath, entire to sinuate-dentate; petiole furrowed, 0.5–2cm, hairy. Male flowers yellow-green, racemes to 4cm, calyx lobes acute, *c*2mm, petals oblong-linear; female flowers solitary or in small racemes, pedicels 0.7–1.2cm, calyx lobes *c*0.15cm, petals slightly shorter than in male. Fruit pendulous, *c*2×1.5cm; seeds *c*0.8cm, emarginate at base, continuous at apex. Madagascar.

Climbers Listed by Family

Illustrated genera are marked with an asterisk (*).

Acanthaceae
Justicia
Thunbergia*

Actinidiaceae
Actinidia
Clematoclethra

Anacardiaceae
Toxicodendron

Annonaceae
Artabotrys

Apocynaceae
Allamanda*
Beaumontia*
Elytropus
Forsteronia
Gelsemium
Mandevilla*
Odontadenia
Parsonsia
Prestonia
Strophanthus*
Trachelospermum*
Urechites
Vallaris

Araceae
Epipremnum
Monstera
Philodendron
Rhaphidophora
Rhektophyllum
Scindapsus
Syngonium

Araliaceae
Eleutherococcus
× Fatshedera
Hedera*
Schefflera

Aristolochiaceae
Aristolochia*

Asclepiadaceae
Araujia*
Ceropegia*
Cynanchum
Dischidia
Dregea
Fockea
Folotsia
Hoya*
Periploca
Sarcostemma
Stephanotis*
Tweedia*
Vincetoxicum

Basellaceae
Anredera
Ullucus

Bignoniaceae
Adenocalymma
Amphilophium
Anemopaegma
Arrabidaea
Bignonia*
Campsidium*
Campsis*
Clytostoma
Cuspidaria
Cydista
Distictis*
Dolichandra
Eccremocarpus*
Macfadyena
Mansoa
Pandorea*
Phryganocydia
Pithecoctenium
Pleonotoma
Podranea
Pyrostegia
Saritaea
Stizophyllum
Tecomanthe
Tecomaria

Blechnaceae
Blechnum
Stenochlaena

Cactaceae
Acanthocereus
Harrisia
Hylocereus
Leptocereus
Peniocereus
Pereskia
Pereskiopsis
Selenicereus

Campanulaceae
Canarina
Codonopsis

Cannabidaceae
Humulus

Capparidaceae
Capparis

Caprifoliaceae
Lonicera*

Celastraceae
Celastrus
Euonymus
Tripterygium

Combretaceae
Combretum
Quisqualis*

Compositae
Delairea
Hidalgoa
Mikania
Mutisia
Pseudogynoxys
Senecio
Solanecio

Convolvulaceae
Argyreia
Calystegia
Convolvulus*
Ipomoea*
Merremia
Porana
Stictocardia

Cruciferae
Heliophila

Cucurbitaceae
Actinostemma
Benincasa
Bryonia
Ceratosanthes
Cionosicyos
Citrullus
Coccinia
Corallocarpus
Cucumeropsis
Cucumis
Cucurbita
Cyclanthera
Diplocyclos
Echinocystis
Gerrardanthus
Gurania
Gynostemma
Hodgsonia
Ibervillea
Kedrostis
Lagenaria
Luffa
Marah
Melothria
Momordica
Mukia
Neoalsomitra
Posadaea
Praecitrullus
Psiguria
Sechium
Seyrigia
Sicana

Sicyos
Solena
Telfairia
Thladiantha
Trichosanthes
Trochomeria
Xerosicyos
Zehneria
Zygosicyos

Dilleniaceae
Hibbertia

Dioscoreaceae
Dioscorea

Epacridaceae
Prionotes

Ericaceae
Agapetes
Dimorphanthera

Flacourtiaceae
Berberidopsis*

Fumariaceae
Adlumia*
Corydalis*
Dicentra*

Gesneriaceae
Asteranthera
Mitraria

Gleicheniaceae
Diplopterygium

Hydrangeaceae
Decumaria*
Hydrangea
Pileostegia*
Schizophragma*

Hydrophyllaceae
Pholistoma

Lardizabalaceae
Akebia*
Holboellia*
Lardizabala*
Sinofranchetia*
Stauntonia*

Leguminosae
Amphicarpaea
Bauhinia
Caesalpinia
Camoensia
Camptosema
Canavalia
Chorizema
Clianthus
Clitoria*

Derris
Dipogon
Hardenbergia
Kennedya
Lablab
Lathyrus
Millettia
Mucuna
Phaseolus
Pueraria
*Strongylodon**
Vicia
Vigna
Wagatea
*Wisteria**

Liliaceae
Aloe (Aloeaceae)
Asparagus
   (Asparagaceae)
Behnia (Luzuriagaceae)
Bomarea
   (Alstroemeriaceae)
Bowiea (Hyacinthaceae)
Dichelostemma
   (Alliaceae)
Gloriosa
   (Colchicaceae)*
Lapageria
   (Philesiaceae)*
Littonia (Colchicaceae)*
Luzuriaga
   (Luzuriagaceae)
× *Philageria*
   (Philesiaceae)
Ripogonum (Smilacaceae)
Sandersonia
   (Colchicaceae)
Semele (Asparagaceae)*
Smilax (Smilacaceae)

Loasaceae
Caiophora
Loasa

Loganiaceae
Gelsemium

Malpighiaceae
Acridocarpus
Hiptage
Stigmaphyllon

Marcgraviaceae
Marcgravia
Norantea

Menispermaceae
Cocculus
Menispermum
Sinomenium

Moraceae
Ficus

Myrtaceae
Metrosideros

Nepenthaceae
*Nepenthes**

Nyctaginaceae
Bougainvillea

Oleaceae
*Abeliophyllum**
Forsythia
*Jasminum**

Orchidaceae
Papilionanthe
Vanilla

Palmae
Calamus
Chamaedorea

Pandanaceae
Freycinetia

Passifloraceae
Adenia
*Passiflora**

Phytolaccaceae
Ercilla
Trichostigma

Piperaceae
Piper

Pittosporaceae
*Billardiera**
*Marianthus**
*Sollya**

Plumbaginaceae
*Plumbago**

Polemoniaceae
*Cobaea**

Polygalaceae
Securidaca

Polygonaceae
Antigonon
Muehlenbeckia
Polygonum

Ranunculaceae
Aconitum
*Clematis**
Clematopsis
Naravelia

Rhamnaceae
Berchemia

Rosaceae
Rosa
Rubus

Rubiaceae
Chiococca
*Manettia**
Morinda
*Mussaenda**
Paederia
Rubia

Sapindaceae
Cardiospermum

Sargentodoxaceae
Sargentodoxa

Schisandraceae
Kadsura
*Schisandra**

Schizaeaceae
Lygodium

Scrophulariaceae
Asarina
Rhodochiton

Selaginellaceae
Selaginella

Solanaceae
Cestrum
Dyssochroma
Juanulloa
Lycium
Salpichroa
*Solandra**
*Solanum**
Streptosolen

Sterculiaceae
*Fremontodendron**

Tiliaceae
Grewia

Tropaeolaceae
*Tropaeolum**

Verbenaceae
Clerodendrum
Congea
Gmelina
Holmskioldia
Hymenopyramis
Oxera
*Petrea**

Vitaceae
Ampelopsis
Cayratia
*Cissus**
Cyphostemma
*Parthenocissus**
Pterisanthes
*Rhoicissus**
Tetrastigma
*Vitis**

Names no longer in use

Acanthopanax (Decne. & Planch.) Witte
A.giraldii Harms. See *Eleutherococcus giraldii*.
A.gracilistylus W.W. Sm. See *Eleutherococcus gracilistylus*.
A.rehderianus Harms. See *Eleutherococcus rehderianus*.
A.sessiliflorus (Rupr. & Maxim.) Seem. See *Eleutherococcus sessiliflorus*.
A.sieboldianus Mak. See *Eleutherococcus sieboldianus*.
A.pentaphyllus (Sieb. & Zucc.) Marchal. See *Eleutherococcus sieboldianus*.
A.simonii Schneid. See *Eleutherococcus simonii*.
A. spinosus (L.f.) Miq. See *Eleutherococcus spinosus*.
A.trichodon Franch. & Savat. See *Eleutherococcus trichodon*.
A.trifoliatus (L.) Voss. See *Eleutherococcus trifoliatus*.
Adenocalymma Mart. ex Meissn.
A.floribunda DC. See *Cuspidaria floribunda*.
Adhatoda Medik.
A.cydoniifolia Nees. See *Justicia cydoniifolia*.
Aerides Lour.
A.vandarum Rchb. f. See *Papilionanthe vandarum*.
Ampelamus Raf.
A.albidus (Nutt.) Britt. See *Cynanchum laeve*.
Anguria Jacq.
A.makoyana Lem. See *Gurania makoyana*.
A.warscewiczii Hook. f. See *Psiguria warscewiczii*.
Antirrhinum L.
A.asarina L. See *Asarina procumbens*.
A. filipes A.Gray. See *Asarina filipes*.
Asclepias L.
A.aphyllum Thunb. See *Cynanchum aphyllum*.
Atragene L.
A.alpina L. See *Clematis alpina*.
A.americana Sims. See *Clematis verticillaris*.
A.columbiana Nutt. See *Clematis columbiana*.
A.sibirica L. See *Clematis alpina* var. *sibirica*.
A.zeylanica L. See *Naravelia zeylanica*.
Aralia L.
A.pentaphylla Sieb. & Zucc. non Thunb. See *Eleutherococcus sieboldianus*.
Bilderdykia Dumort.
B.aubertii (L. Henry) Dumort. See *Polygonum aubertii*.
B. baldschuanica (Reg.) Webb. See *Polygonum baldschuanicum*.
Blumenbachia Schräd.
B. lateritia (Klotzsch) Griseb. See *Caiophora lateritia*.
Boussingaultia HBK.
B.cordifolia Ten. See *Anredera cordifolia*.
B.gracilis f. *pseudobaselloides* Hauman. See *Anredera cordifolia*.
B.gracilis Miers. See *Anredera cordifolia*.
B.gracilis var. *pseudobaselloides* (Hauman) Bail. See *Anredera cordifolia*.
Bridgesia Bertero ex Cambess.
B. spicata Hook. & Arn. See *Ercilla spicata*.
Brodiaea Sm.
B.volubilis (Kellog) Bak. See *Dichelostemma volubile*.

Browallia L.
B.jamesonii Benth. See *Streptosolen jamesonii*.
Calampelis D. Don.
C. scaber D. Don. See *Eccremocarpus scaber*.
Calonyction Choisy.
C.aculeatum (L.) House. See *Ipomoea alba*.
Campana Rumphius ex Post.
C.rubra Rumphius. See *Tecomanthe dendrophila*.
Campanumoea Bl.
C.cordata Maxim. See *Codonopsis javanica*.
C. japonica Sieb. ex Morr. See *Codonopsis lanceolata*.
C.javanica Bl. See *Codonopsis javanica*.
C. lanceolata Sieb. & Zucc. See *Codonopsis lanceolata*.
Centrostemma (Bl.) Decne.
C. multiflorum (Bl.) Decne. See *Hoya multiflora*.
Cephalandra Schrad. ex Eckl. & Zeyh.
C.palmata Sand. in Harv. & Sand. See *Coccinia palmata*.
Cereus Mill.
C.greggii Engelm. See *Peniocereus greggii*.
C.pentagonus. See *Acanthocereus tetragonus*.
C.pitajaya (Jacq.) DC. See *Acanthocereus colombianus*.
C. viperinus F.A.C. Weber. See *Peniocereus viperinus*.
Childsia J.L. Childs
C.wercklei J.L. Childs. See *Hidalgoa wercklei*.
Chymocormus Harv.
C.edulis (Thunb.) Harv. See *Fockea edulis*.
Cladosicyos Hook.f.
C.edulis Hook. f. See *Cucumeropsis mannii*.
Colocynthis Mill.
C.vulgaris Schräd. See *Citrullus colocynthis*.
Columella Vell.
C. japonica (Thunb.) Alston. See *Cayratia japonica*.
C. oligocarpa (Lév. & Vaniot) Rehd. See *Cayratia oligocarpa*
Dactylicapnos Wall.
D.macrocapnos (Prain) Hutch. See *Dicentra macrocapnos*.
Decaderia
D.grandiflorum Jum. & Perrier. See *Folotsia grandiflora*.
Dioclea Kunth.
D.glycinioides hort. See *Camptosema rubicundum*.
Dipladenia A.DC.
D. boliviensis Hook. f. See *Mandevilla boliviensis*.
D.flava Andrews. See *Urechites lutea*.
D.sanderi Hemsl. See *Mandevilla sanderi*.
D.splendens (Hook. f.) A. DC. See *Mandevilla splendens*.
D. × *amabilis* hort. Buckl. See *Mandevilla* × *amabilis*.
Dolichos L.
D.lablab L. See *Lablab purpureus*.
D. soudanensis hort. See *Lablab purpureus*.
Doxantha Miers.
D. acutistipula Schlecht. See *Macfadyena unguis-cati*.
D. adunca Miers. See *Macfadyena unguis-cati*.
D. capreolata Miers. See *Bignonia capreolata*.

D. dasyonyx (Blake) Blake. See *Macfadyena unguis-cati*.
D. exoleta (Vell.) Miers. See *Macfadyena unguis-cati*.
D. lanuginosa Miers. See *Macfadyena unguis-cati*.
D. mexicana Miers. See *Macfadyena unguis-cati*.
D. praesignis Miers. See *Macfadyena unguis-cati*.
D. serrulata Miers. See *Macfadyena unguis-cati*.
D. tenuicaula Miers. See *Macfadyena unguis-cati*.
D. unguis (L. emend. DC.) Miers. See *Macfadyena unguis-cati*.
Echites P.Browne
E.andrewsii Chapman See *Urechites lutea*
E. laxa Ruiz & Pav. See *Mandevilla laxa*
E. rubrovenosa Lind. See *Prestonia quinquangularis*.
E. splendens Hook.f. See *Mandevilla splendens*
E.suberecta auct. See *Urechites lutea*.
Endoloma Raf.
E.purpureum Raf. See *Amphilophium paniculatum*.
Eriocereus Riccob.
E. tortuosa (Forbes ex Otto & A. Dietr.) Riccob. See *Harrisia tortuosa*
E. adscendens (Gürke) A. Berger. See *Harrisia adscendens*
E. bonplandii (Parmentier ex Pfeiff.) Riccob. See *Harrisia pomanensis*
E. guelichii (Speg.) A. Berger. See *Harrisia guelichii*.
E. jusbertii (Rebut ex Schum.) Riccob. See *Harrisia jusbertii*.
E. martinii (Labouret) Riccob. See *Harrisia martinii*.
E. pomanensis (F.A. Weber) A. Berger. See *Harrisia pomanensis*.
E. regelii Weingart. See *H.regelii*.
Fallopia Adans.
F.aubertii (L. Henry) Holub. See *Polygonum aubertii*.
F. baldschuanica (Reg.) Holub. See *Polygonum baldschuanicum*.
Fevillea L.
F. pedata Sims. See *Telfairia pedata*.
Fremontia Torr.
F.californica Torr. See *Fremontodendron californicum*.
F.mexicana (Davidson) Macbr. See *Fremontodendron mexicanum*.
F.napensis Eastw. See *Fremontodendron californicum* ssp. *napense*.
Fumaria L.
F.fungosa (Ait.) Greene ex BSP. See *Adlumia fungosa*.
Gleichenia Juss.
G.glauca See *Diplopterygium longissimum*.
G.longissima Bl. See *Diplopterygium longissimum*.
Glosocomia D.Don
G.lanceolata Maxim. See *Codonopsis lanceolata*.
G.ussuriensis Rupr. See *Codonopsis lanceolata*.
Gonolobus Michx.
G.laevis Michx. See *Cynanchum laeve*.
Gymnopetalum Arn.
G. japonicum Miq. See *Trichosanthes kirilowii* var. *japonica*.

Habrothamnus Endl.
H.aurantiacus Seem. See *Cestrum aurantiacum.*
H. elegans Brongn. See *Cestrum elegans.*
Hexacentris Nees
H.coccinea (Wallich) Nees. See *Thunbergia coccinea.*
H.mysorensis Wight See *Thunbergia mysorensis.*
Hocquartia Nak.
H.kaempferi (Willd.) Nak. See *Aristolochia kaempferi.*
Isometra Raf.
I.chrysops Stapf. See *Aristolochia chrysops.*
Leptocodon (Hook.f.) Lem.
L.gracilis Lem. See *Codonopsis gracilis.*
Levya Bur. ex Baill.
L. nicaraguensis Bur. ex Baill. See *Cydista aequinoctialis* var. *hirtella.*
Lophospermum D.Don
L.scandens D.Don. See *Asarina lophospermum.*
Macrodiscus Bureau
M. lactiflorus Bur. ex Baill. See *Distictis lactiflora.*
Mahafalia Jum. & Perrier
M.nodosum See *Cynanchum nodosum.*
Maurandya Ortega
M.barclayana Lindl. See *Asarina barclayana.*
M.erubescens (D. Don) A. Gray. See *A.erubescens.*
M.lophospermum L.H. Bail. See *Asarina lophospermum.*
M.purpurea hort. See *Asarina purpusii.*
M.scandens (Cav.) Pers. See *Asarina scandens.*
M.scandens (D. Don) A. Gray non (Cav.) Pers. See *A.lophospermum.*
Melaleuca L.
M.diffusa Forst.f. See *Metrosideros diffusa.*
Medeola L.
M.asparagoides L. See *Asparagus asparagoides*
Meyenia Schdtl.
M. fasciculata Schldl. See *Cestrum fasciculatum.*
Mina La Ll. & Lex.
M.lobata Cerv. See *Ipomoea lobata.*
Muscadinia (Planch.) Small
M. rotundifolia (Michx.) Small. See*Vitis rotundifolia.*
Nacibea Aubl.
N.coccinea Aubl. See *Manettia coccinea.*
Nemophila Nutt.
N.aurita Lindl. See *Pholistoma auritum.*
Neoevansia
N. striata (Brandg.) Sanchez-Mej. See *Peniocereus striatus.*
Nouletia Endl.
N.pterocarpa (Cham.) Pichon. See *Cuspidaria pterocarpa.*
Nyctocereus (A. Berger) Britt. & Rose
N.serpentinus (Lagasca & Rodriguez) Britt. & Rose. See *Peniocereus serpentinus.*
Orobus L.
O.cyaneus Steven. See *Lathyrus cyaneus.*
O.gmelinii Fischer ex DC. See *Lathyrus gmelinii.*
O.luteus L. See *Lathyrus gmelinii.*
O.myrtifolius (Muhlenb.) Hall. See *Lathyrus palustris.*
O.myrtifolius Alef. See *Lathyrus palustris.*
O.niger L. See *Lathyrus niger.*
O.roseus (Stev.) Ledeb. See *Lathyrus roseus.*
O.venetus Mill. See *Lathyrus venetus.*
O.vernus L. See *Lathyrus vernus.*
Oxypetalum R. Br.
O.caeruleum (D. Don) Decne. See *Tweedia caerulea.*
Pentapterygium Klotzsch.
P.rugosum Hook. See *Agapetes rugosa.*
Phaedranthus Miers.
P. buccinatorius (DC.) Miers. See *Distictis buccinatoria.*
Phanera Lour.
P.corymbosa (Roxb. ex DC) Benth. See *Bauhinia corymbosa.*

Pharbitis Choisy.
P.hederacea (L.) Choisy. See *Ipomoea hederacea.*
P. imperialis hort. See *Ipomoea* × *imperialis.*
P. nil (L.) Choisy. See *Ipomoea nil.*
P. purpurea (L.) Choisy. See *Ipomoea purpurea.*
Physianthus Mart.
P.albens G. Don. See *Araujia sericofera.*
P.auricomus Graham. See *Araujia graveolens.*
P.megapotamicus Mart. See *Araujia graveolens.*
Phytolacca L.
P.volubilis Heimerl. See *Ercilla spicata.*
Pothos L.
P.aureus Lind. & André. See *Epipremnum aureum.*
P.celatocaulis N.E. Br. See *Rhaphidophora celatocaulis.*
Prosopostelma Baill.
P.aculeatum Descoings. See *Folotsia aculeata.*
Psedera
P.sinensis (Diels & Gilg) Schneid. See*Vitis pentagona*
P. vitacea (Kerner) Gray. See *Parthenocissus inserta.*
Quamoclit Moench.
Q.coccinea (L.) Moench. See *Ipomoea coccinea.*
Q.coccinea var. *hederifolia* (L.) House. See *Ipomoea hederifolia.*
Q.hederifolia (L.) G. Don. See *Ipomoea hederifolia.*
Q.lobata (Cerv.) House. See *Ipomoea lobata.*
Q.pennata (Desr.) Bojer. See *Ipomoea quamoclit.*
Q.vulgaris Choisy. See *Ipomoea quamoclit.*
Q.× sloteri House. See *Ipomoea × multifida*
Rajania L.
R.hexaphylla Thunb. See *Stauntonia hexaphylla.*
R.quinata Decne. See *Akebia quinata*
Rhodocactus (A. Berger) F. Knuth
R.antonianus Backeb. See *Pereskia weberiana.*
Rhus L.
R.ambigua Lavall. ex Dipp., not Unger. See *Toxicodendron radicans* ssp. *orientale.*
R.diversiloba Torr. & A. Gray. See *Toxicodendron diversilobum.*
R.lobata Hook. See *Toxicodendron diversiloba.*
R.orientalis (Greene) C.K. Scheid. See *Toxicodendron radicans* ssp. *orientale.*
R.quercifiola Steud. See *Toxicodendron diversiloba.*
R.radicans L. See *Toxicodendron radicans.*
R.toxicodendron L. See *Toxicodendron radicans.*
R.toxicodendron ssp. *diversiloba* (Torr. & A. Gray) Engl. See *Toxicodendron diversilobum.*
R.toxicodendron var. *hispida* Engl. See *Toxicodendron radicans* ssp. *hispidum.*
R.toxicodendron var. *pubescens* Engelm. ex Wats. See *Toxicodendron radicans* ssp. *pubescens.*
Rhynchospermum Reinw.
R.asiaticum hort. See *Trachelospermum asiaticum.*
R.jasminoides Lindl. See *Trachelospermum jasminoides.*
Roseocereus Backeb.
R.tetracanthus (Labouret) Backeb. See *Harrisia tetracantha.*
Saelanthus Forssk.
S.rotundifolius. See *Cissus rotundifolius.*
Sarcocyphala Harv.
S.gerrardii Harv. See *Cynanchum aphyllum.*
Schizobasopsis Macbr.
S.kilimandscharica (Mildbr.) Barsc.. See *Bowiea kilimandscharica.*
S.volubilis (Harv. & Hook. f.) J.F. Macbr. See *Bowiea volubilis.*

Schubertia Mart.
S.albens Mart. See *Araujia sericofera.*
S.graveolens Lindl. See *Araujia graveolens.*
Sicydium Schltdl.
S.lindheimeri A. Gray. See *Ibervillea lindheimeri.*
Spathodea Beauv.
S.corymbosa Vent. See *Phryganocydia corymbosa.*
Spinovitis
S.davidii Carr. See *Vitis davidii.*
Stropholirion Torr.
S.californicum Torr. See *Dichelostemma volubile.*
Swartzia Gmel. non Schreb.
S.grandiflora (Sw.) J. Gmel. See *Solandra grandiflora.*
S.guttata D. Don ex Lindl. See *Solandra guttata.*
Systrepha Burchell
S.filiformis Burchell See *Ceropegia infundibuliformis.*
Tacsonia Juss.
T.insignis Mast. See *Passiflora insignis.*
T.jamesonii Mast. See *Passiflora jamesonii.*
T.manicata Juss. See *Passiflora manicata.*
T.mollissima HBK. See *Passiflora mollissima.*
T.psilantha Sodiro. See *Passiflora psilantha.*
T.umbilicata Griseb. See *Passiflora umbilicata.*
Tecoma Juss.
T.australis R.Br. See *Pandorea pandorana.*
T.capensis (Thunb.) Lindl. See *Tecomaria capensis.*
T.floribunda Cunn. ex DC. See *Pandorea pandorana.*
T. jasminoides Lindl. See *Pandorea jasminoides*
T.nyassae Oliv. See *Tecomaria capensis* ssp. *nyassae.*
T.nyikensis Bak. See *Tecomaria capensis* ssp. *nyassae.*
T.shirensis Bak. See *Tecomaria capensis* ssp. *nyassae.*
T.valdiviana Philippi. See *Campsidium valdivianum.*
T.whytei C.H. Wright.See *Tecomaria capensis* ssp. *nyassae.*
Testudinaria Salisb.
T.elephantipes (L'Hérit.) Burchell. See *Dioscorea elephantipes.*
T.macrostachya (Benth.) Rowley. See *Dioscorea macrostachya.*
Trichocereus Riccob.
T. tetracanthus (Labouret) Borg. See *Harrisia tetracantha.*
Tristemon Klotzsch.
T.texanum Scheele. See *Cucurbita texana.*
Vanda Jones ex R.Br.
V.hookeriana Rchb. f. See *Papilionanthe hookeriana.*
V. teres (Roxb.) Lindl. See *Papilionanthe teres.*
Viorna Rchb.
V.baldwinii (Torr. & A. Gray) Small. See *Clematis baldwinii.*
V.fremontii (Wats.) Heller. See *Clematis fremontii.*
V.ochroleuca (Ait.) Small. See *Clematis ochroleuca.*
Volkameria L.
V.aculeata L. See *Clerodendrum aculeatum*
Wattakaka (Decne.) Hassk.
W.sinensis (Hemsl.) Stapf. See *Dregea sinensis.*
Wilcoxia Britt. & Rose
W.diguetii (F.A.C. Weber) Peebles. See *Peniocereus striatus.*
W.striata (Brandg.) Britt. & Rose. See *Peniocereus striatus.*
W.viperina (F.A.C. Weber) Britt. & Rose. See *Peniocereus viperinus.*

Index of Popular Names

JAPANESE WISTERIA *Wisteria floribunda*
JASMINE *Jasminum*
JAVA GLORY BEAN *Clerodendrum × speciosum*
JAVAN GRAPE *Tetrastigma*
JERUSALEM PEA *Vigna unguiculata* ssp. *cylindrica*
JESSAMINE *Jasminum (J.officinale)*

KACHRA *Cucumis melo* ssp. *agrestis* var. *momordica*
KANGAROO VINE *Cissus antarctica*
KENTUCKY WISTERIA *Wisteria macrostachys*
KHESAI *Lathyrus sativus*
KHIRA *Cucumis sativus*
KIDNEY BEAN *Phaseolus vulgaris*
KING MONKEY CUP *Nepenthes rajah*
KING'S IPOMOEA *Stictocardia beraviensis*
KING'S MANTLE *Thunbergia erecta*
KIWI FRUIT *Actinidia deliciosa*
KNOBKERRY *Lagenaria siceraria*
KNOTWEED *Polygonum*
KUDZU VINE *Pueraria lobata*

LA-KWA *Momordica charantia*
LACE FERN *Asparagus setaceus*
LADY OF THE NIGHT *Cestrum nocturnum*
LAUREL-LEAVED GREENBRIER *Smilax laurifolia*
LAVENDER WREATH *Congea tomentosa*
LAWYER CANE *Calamus australis*
LEADWORT *Plumbago*
LEATHER FLOWER *Clematis (C.versicolor; C.viorna; C.virginiana)*
LEVANT MADDER *Rubia peregrina*
LIMA BEAN *Phaseolus lunatus*
LIZARD PLANT *Tetrastigma voinierianum*
LOBSTER CLAW *Clianthus puniceus*
LOOFAH *Luffa (L.cylindrica)*
LORD ANSON'S BLUE PEA *Lathyrus nervosus*
LOVE-CHARM *Clytostoma callistegioides*
LOVE-IN-A-MIST *Passiflora foetida*
LUBIA BEAN *Lablab purpureus*

MACARTNEY ROSE *Rosa bracteata*
MADAGASCAR JASMINE *Stephanotis floribunda*
MADAGASCAR PEPPER *Piper nigrum*
MADDER *Rubia tinctoria*
MADEIRA VINE *Anredera cordifolia*
MAIDENHAIR VINE *Muehlenbeckia complexa*
MALABAR GOURD *Cucurbita ficifolia*
MALAY JEWEL VINE *Derris scandens*
MALU CREEPER *Bauhinia vahlii*
MANDARIN'S-HAT *Holmskioldia sanguinea*
MANGO MELON *Cucumis melo* Chito Group
MANO DE LAGURIJA *Macfadyena unguis-cati*
MANROOT *Marah*
MARBLE PEA *Vigna unguiculata* ssp. *cylindrica*
MARINE IVY *Cissus trifoliata*
MARINE VINE *Cissus trifoliata*
MARK WEED *Toxicodendron radicans*
MARMELADE BUSH *Streptosolen jamesonii*
MARROW *Cucurbita pepo*
MARSH CLEMATIS *Clematis crispa*
MARSH PEA *Lathyrus palustris*
MARVEL DEWBERRY *Rubus mirus*
MATRIMONY VINE *Lycium*
MATTRESS VINE *Muehlenbeckia complexa*
MAY APPLE *Passiflora incarnata*
MAY POPS *Passiflora incarnata*
MEADOW VETCHLING *Lathyrus pratensis*
MELON *Cucumis melo*
MELON APPLE *Cucumis melo* Chito Group
MEMORIAL ROSE *Rosa wichuraiana*
MEXICAN CREEPER *Antigonon leptopus*
MEXICAN DAISY *Pseudogynoxys chenopodioides*
MEXICAN FIREVINE *Pseudogynoxys chenopodioides*
MEXICAN FLAMEVINE *Pseudogynoxys chenopodioides*
MEXICAN IVY *Cobaea scandens*
MIGNONETTE VINE *Anredera cordifolia*
MILE-A-MINUTE VINE *Polygonum baldschuanicum*
MINIATURE GRAPE IVY *Cissus striata*

MINIATURE JAPANESE IVY *Parthenocissus tricuspidata* 'Lowii'
MINORCA HONEYSUCKLE *Lonicera implexa*
MISSOURI GOURD *Cucurbita foetidissima*
MOCK CUCUMBER *Echinocystis lobata*
MONASTRY BELLS *Cobaea scandens*
MONK'S HOOD *Aconitum*
MONKEY CUP *Nepenthes mirabilis*
MOONFLOWER *Beaumontia grandiflora*
MOONSEED *Cocculus; Menispermum*
MOONVINE *Beaumontia grandiflora*
MOROCCAN IVY *Hedera maroccana*
MOSQUITO PLANT *Cynanchum ascyrifolium*
MOTH BEAN *Vigna aconitifolia*
MOUNTAIN CREEPER *Porana paniculata*
MOUNTAIN EBONY *Bauhinia*
MOUNTAIN FRINGE *Adlumia fungosa*
MOUNTAIN LONG PEPPER *Piper sylvaticum*
MUNG BEAN *Vigna radiata*
MUNJEET *Rubia cordifolia*
MUSCADINE GRAPE *Vitis rotundifolia*
MUSK MELON *Cucumis melo* Reticulatus Group; *C.melo* var. *cultus*
MUSK ROSE *Rosa moschata*
MUSTANG GRAPE *Vitis mustangensis*
MYSORE THORN *Caesalpinia decapetala*

NARROW-LEAVED EVERLASTING PEA *Lathyrus sylvestris*
NASTURTIUM *Tropaeolum (T.majus)*
NATAL IVY *Senecio macroglossus*
NATIVE ORANGE *Capparis lasiantha*
NECKLACE VINE *Muehlenbeckia complexa*
NEPAL IVY *Hedera nepalensis*
NEPAL TRUMPET FLOWER *Beaumontia grandiflora*
NETTED MELON *Cucumis melo* Reticulatus Group
NEW GUINEA CREEPER *Mucuna bennettii*
NIGHT JESSAMINE *Cestrum nocturnum*

OLD MAN'S BEARD *Clematis vitalba*
ORANGE BROWALLIA *Streptosolen jamesonii*
ORANGE MELON *Cucumis melo* Chito Group
ORANGE-FLOWERED STEPHANOTIS *Pyrostegia venusta*
ORANGEGLOW VINE *Pseudogynoxys chenopodioides*
ORCHID TREE *Bauhinia*
ORIENTAL BITTERSWEET *Celastrus orbiculatus*
ORIENTAL PICKLING MELON *Cucumis melo* Conomon Group

PAGODA FLOWER *Clerodendrum × speciosum*
PAINTED TRUMPET *Clytostoma callistegioides*
PALO NEGRO *Saritaea magnifica*
PAMPAS LILY OF THE VALLEY *Salpichroa origanifolia*
PAPER FLOWER *Bougainvillea glabra*
PARADISE FLOWER *Solanum wendlandii*
PARLOUR IVY *Delairea odorata*
PARROT'S BEAK *Clianthus puniceus*
PARROT'S BILL *Clianthus puniceus*
PARSLEY-LEAVED BRAMBLE *Rubus laciniatus*
PASSION FLOWER *Passiflora (P.caerulea)*
PASSION FRUIT *Passiflora edulis*
PEACOCK FERN *Selaginella willdenovii*
PELICAN FLOWER *Aristolochia grandiflora*
PEPPER *Piper (P.nigrum)*
PEPPER VINE *Ampelopsis arborea*
PERENNIAL PEA *Lathyrus latifolius*
PERSIAN EVERLASTING PEA *Lathyrus rotundifolius*
PERSIAN IVY *Hedera colchica*
PERSIAN MELON *Cucumis melo* Reticulatus Group
PHANERA *Bauhinia corymbosa*
PHOOT *Cucumis melo* ssp. *agrestis* var. *momordica*
PIGEON WINGS *Clitoria ternatea*
PINE HYACINTH *Clematis baldwinii*
PINK ALLAMANDA *Mandevilla splendens*
PINK CISSUS *Cissus adenopoda*
PINK TRUMPET VINE *Podranea ricasoliana*
PITCHER PLANT *Nepenthes*
POET'S IVY *Hedera helix* ssp. *poetarum*
POISON IVY *Toxicodendron radicans*
POISON MERCURY *Toxicodendron radicans*
POISONOUS NIGHTSHADE *Solanum dulcamara*

TARA VINE   *Actinidia arguta*
TARE   *Vicia* (*V.sativa*)
TEA ROSE   *Rosa × odorata*
TEASEL GOURD   *Cucumis dipsaceus*
TEINTURIER GRAPE   *Vitis vinifera* 'Purpurea'
TEPARY BEAN   *Phaseolus acutifolius* var. *latifolius*
TOMATILLO   *Solanum seaforthianum*
TONGA PLANT   *Epipremnum mirabile*
TOOTHED GUINEA FLOWER   *Hibbertia dentata*
TOOTHWORT   *Plumbago scandens*
TORTOISE PLANT   *Dioscorea elephantipes*
TRAILING GROUNDSEL   *Pseudogynoxys chenopodioides*
TRAILING WOLF'S BANE   *Aconitum reclinatum*
TRAVELLER'S JOY   *Clematis vitalba*
TREEBINE   *Cissus*
TREE PETREA   *Petrea arborea*
TROPICAL PITCHER PLANT   *Nepenthes*
TRUE JASMINE   *Jasminum officinale*
TRUMPET CREEPER   *Campsis* (*C.radicans*)
TRUMPET FLOWER   *Bignonia capreolata*
TRUMPET GOURD   *Lagenaria siceraria*
TRUMPET HONEYSUCKLE   *Lonicera sempervirens*
TRUMPET VINE   *Campsis*
TUBA ROOT   *Derris elliptica*
TUBEROUS PEA   *Lathyrus tuberosus*
TUBEROUS VETCH   *Lathyrus tuberosus*
TUFTED VETCH   *Vicia craca*
TUNKA   *Benincasa hispida*
TWINING BRODIAEA   *Dichelostemma volubile*
TWINING FIRE CRACKER   *Manettia luteorubra*
TWINING SNAPDRAGON   *Asarina*
TWO-FLOWERED PEA   *Lathyrus grandiflorus*

UMBRELLA TREE   *Schefflera*

VANILLA   *Vanilla planifolia*
VAQUERO BLANCO   *Cydista aequinoctialis*
VASE VINE   *Clematis* (*C.viorna*)
VEGETABLE MARROW   *Cucurbita pepo*
VEGETABLE PEAR   *Sechium edule*
VEGETABLE SPONGE   *Luffa cylindrica*
VELVET BEAN   *Mucuna pruriens*; *M.pruriens* var. *utilis*
VENEZUELA TREEBINE   *Cissus rhombifolia*
VETCH   *Vicia* (*V.cracca*)
VETCHLING   *Lathyrus*
VILLOUS FIG   *Ficus villosa*
VINEGAR PEAR   *Passiflora laurifolia*
VINE LILAC   *Hardenbergia violacea*
VINE OF SODOM   *Citrullus colocynthis*
VINE PEACH   *Cucumis melo* Chito Group
VINE RATTANY   *Berchemia scandens*
VIOLET IVY   *Cobaea scandens*
VIOLET TWINING SNAPDRAGON   *Asarina antirrhinifolia*
VIOLET-TREE   *Securidaca longipedunculata*
VIPER GOURD   *Trichosanthes cucumerina* var. *anguina*
VIRGINIA CREEPER   *Parthenocissus quinquefolia*; *P.tricuspidata*
VIRGINIA JASMINE   *Campsis radicans*
VIRGIN'S BOWER   *Clematis* (*C.virginiana*)

WAIT-A-WHILE   *Calamus australis*; *C.muelleri*
WAIT-A-WHILE PALM   *Calamus*
WANGRANGKURA   *Eleutherococcus sessiliflorus*
WATER LEMON   *Passiflora laurifolia*
WATER MELON   *Citrullus lanatus*
WATER YAM   *Dioscorea alata*
WAX BEAN   *Phaseolus vulgaris*

WAX FLOWER   *Hoya*; *Senecio macroglossus*; *Stephanotis floribunda*
WAX GOURD   *Benincasa hispida*
WAX PLANT   *Hoya carnosa*
WAX VINE   *Senecio macroglossus*
WAXWORK   *Celastrus scandens*
WESTERN AUSTRALIA CORAL PEA   *Hardenbergia comptoniana*
WESTERN POISON OAK   *Toxicodendron diversilobum*
WESTERN TRUMPET HONEYSUCKLE   *Lonicera ciliosa*
WEST INDIAN GHERKIN   *Cucumis anguria*
WEST INDIAN SNOW BERRY   *Chiococca alba*
WHITE BRYONY   *Bryonia alba*
WHITE CORALLITA   *Porana paniculata*
WHITE DIPLADENIA   *Mandevilla boliviensis*
WHITE FLAG BUSH   *Mussaenda frondosa*
WHITE-FLOWERED GOURD   *Lagenaria*
WHITE FORSYTHIA   *Abeliophyllum*
WHITE GOURD   *Benincasa hispida*
WHITE HONEYSUCKLE   *Lonicera albiflora*
WHITE PEPPER   *Piper nigrum*
WHITE YAM   *Dioscorea alata*
WILD BALSAM APPLE   *Echinocystis lobata*
WILD BALSAM   *Ibervillea lindheimeri*
WILD CLIMBING HEMP-WEED   *Mikania scandens*
WILD CUCUMBER   *Echinocystis lobata*
WILD HOP   *Bryonia dioica*
WILD MADDER   *Rubia peregrina*
WILD MONK'S HOOD   *Aconitum uncinatum*
WILD MORNING-GLORY   *Calystegia sepium*
WILD PASSION FLOWER   *Passiflora incarnata*
WILD PEA   *Lathyrus*
WILD SAGE   *Gmelina philippensis*
WILD SARSPARILLA   *Schisandra coccinea*; *Smilax glauca*
WILD WATER LEMON   *Passiflora foetida*
WILLOW-LEAVED JESSAMINE   *Cestrum parqui*
WINDMILL JASMINE   *Jasminum laurifolium* f. *nitidum*
WINDOWLEAF   *Monstera*
WINTER JASMINE   *Jasminum nudiflorum*
WINTER MELON   *Cucumis melo* Inodorus Group
WINTER PEA   *Lathyrus hirsutus*
WINTER SQUASH   *Cucurbita maxima*; *C. moschata*
WIRE VINE   *Muehlenbeckia complexa*
WOLF'S BANE   *Aconitum*
WONDER BEAN   *Canavalia ensiformis*
WONGA-WONGA VINE   *Pandorea pandorana*
WOODBINE   *Clematis* (*C.virginiana*); *Lonicera* (*L.periclymenum*); *Parthenocissus quinquefolia*
WOOD ROSE   *Merremia tuberosa*
WOOD VAMP   *Decumaria barbara*
WOOLLY MORNING GLORY   *Argyreia nervosa*

YAMPEE   *Dioscorea trifida*
YANGTAO   *Actinidia arguta*; *A.deliciosa*
YARDLONG BEAN   *Vigna unguiculata* ssp. *sesquipedalis*
YELLOW-EYED FLAME PEA   *Chorizema dicksonii*
YELLOW GRANADILLA   *Passiflora laurifolia*
YELLOW HONEYSUCKLE   *Lonicera flava*
YELLOW JESSAMINE   *Gelsemium*
YELLOW MORNING GLORY   *Merremia tuberosa*
YELLOW PARILLA   *Menispermum canadense*
YELLOW TWINING SNAPDRAGON   *Asarina filipes*
YELLOW VETCHLING   *Lathyrus aphaca*; *L.pratensis*

ZIMBABWE CLIMBER   *Podranea brycei*
ZIT-KWA   *Benincasa hispida*
ZUCCHINI   *Cucurbita pepo*

Bibliography

* all books are published in the UK unless otherwise specified

General

Beckett, K.A. 1983. *Climbing Plants*. (Croom Helm)

Betto, G. 1986. *Le Piante rampicanti*. (Milan: Rizzoli Editore)

Boisset, C. 1989. *Vertical Gardening*. (Mitchell Beazley)

Boucher, G., & S. Mottet. 1898. *Les Clematites, Chevrefeuilles, Bignones, Glycines, Aristoloches et Passiflores*. 160 pp., 30 ill. Paris.

Darwin, C. 1875. *The Movements and Habits of Climbing Plants*. 2nd edn. (John Murray)

Davis, B. 1990. *The Gardener's Illustrated Encyclopaedia of Climbers and Wall Plants*. (Viking)

Genders, R. 1957. *Covering a Wall: The Culture of Climbing Plants*. (The Garden Book Club)

Grey-Wilson, C. and Matthews, V. 1983. *Gardening on Walls*. (Collins)

Griffiths, M. 1994. *Index of Garden Plants*. (Macmillan)

Herklots, G. 1976. *Flowering Tropical Climbers*. (Folkestone: Dawson & Sons)

Huxley, A., Griffiths, M. and Levy, M. 1992. *The New Royal Horticultural Society Dictionary of Gardening*. 4 vols. (Macmillan).

Lucas Philips, C.E. 1967. *Climbing Plants for Walls and Gardens*. (Heinemann)

Menninger, E.A. 1970. *Flowering Vines of the World*. (New York: Hearthside Press)

Olbrich, M. 1983. Ten rare vines for the temperate coast. *Pacific Horticulture*, winter issue.

Rose, P.Q. 1982. *Climbers and Wall Plants*. (Blandford Press)

Susini, E. 1976. *Rampicanti e ricadenti*. (Bologna: Edagricole)

Taylor, J. 1987. *Climbing Plants*. Kew Gardening Guides (Collingridge Books in association with Royal Botanic Gardens, Kew)

—— 1991. *Creative Planting with Climbers*. (Ward Lock)

—— 1993. *Climbers and Wall Plants for Year Round Colour*. (Cassell)

Watson, W. 1920. *Climbing Plants*. (I.C. & E.C.)

Aconitum

Lord, T. 1988. *Aconitum* – notes on the genus. *Hardy Plant* 10: 85–91.

Munz, P.A. 1945. The cultivated Aconites. *Gentes Herbarum* 6: 463–506.

Reichenbach. 1820. *Monograph of the Genus Aconitum*.

—— 1823–7. *Illustrations of the Species Aconitum*.

Acridocarpus

Arenes, J. 1945. Les *Acridocarpus* de Madagascar. *Notul. Syst. Paris* 12: 42–64.

Sprague, T.A. 1906. A revision of *Acridocarpus* . *J. Bot. Lond*. 192–207.

Actinidia

Atkins, A.M. 1948. Introduction of Chinese Gooseberry. *New Zealand Gardener*, vol. 4.

Dunn, S.T. 1911. A revision of the genus *Actinidia*. *J. Linn. Soc. (Bot.)* 39:394–410.

Ferguson, A.R. 1983. *Arnoldia* 3: 24–35.

Gorokhova, G.I. 1974. Introduktsiya *Actinidia kolomikta* v tsentralnom Sibirskom Botanicheskom Sadu. *Byull. Glavn. Bot. Sada* (Moscow) 93: 22–3.

Li, Hui-Lin. 1952. A taxonomic review of the genus *Actinidia*. *Jour. Arn. Arb*. 33: 1–61.

MacMillan Browse, P. 1984. Some notes on Actinidias and their propagation. *Plantsman* 6(3): 167–81.

Milbocker, D.C. 1980. Kiwifruit. *Amer. Horticulturist* 59 (1): 21.

Sutton, S. 1970. *Actinidia chinensis*, the Kiwi Fruit. *Arnoldia* 39: 290–309.

Virkau, V. 1976. Propagation of *Actinidia arguta* and *Actinidia kolomikta*. *Pomona* 9: 130–32.

Warrington, I.J., Weston, G.C. (eds) 1990. *Kiwi fruit: science and management*. Ray Richards in association with the New Zealand Society for Horticultural Science.

Yan, J. 1981. Histoire d'*Actinidia chinensis* Planch. et conditions actuelles de sa production à l'étranger. *J. d'Agriculture Traditionelle et de Botanique Appliquée* 28: 281–90.

Adenia

Glass, C. & Foster, R. 1973. The succulent passion flowers. *Cactus & Succulent J. Amer*. 45:74.

Liebenberg, L.C.C. 1939. A revision of the South African species of *Adenia*. *Bothalia* 3.

Verdcourt, B. 1964. New species of *Adenia* from Eastern Africa. *Bot. Soc. Broteria*, 2 ser., 38: 97–105.

de Wilde, W.J.J.O. 1971. A monograph of the genus *Adenia*. *Meded. Landbouwhogesch. Wageningen* 18.

See also Rowley under Cucurbitaceae.

Agapetes

Argent, G.C.G. and Woods, P.J.B. 1986. *Agapetes* in cultivation. *Plantsman* 8 (2): 65–86.

Sleumer, H. 1967. *Agapetes* (Ericaceae). In *Flora Malesiana*, ser.1, Vol. 6: 878–85.

Stevens, P.F. 1972. Notes on the infrageneric classification of *Agapetes* with four new taxa from New Guinea. *Notes RBG Edinburgh* 32: 13–28.

Stevens, P.F. 1985. Notes on *Vaccinium* and *Agapetes*. *J. Arnold Arboretum* 66: 471–90.

Akebia

Shimizu, T. 1961. Taxonomic study of the genus *Akebia*, with special reference to a new species from Taiwan. *Quart. Jour. Taiwan Mus*. 14:195–202.

Spongberg & Burch. 1979. Lardizabalaceae hardy in temperate North America. *J. Arnold Arboretum* 60:302.

Aloe

Reynolds, G.W. 1969. *The Aloes of South Africa*. Cape Town: A.A. Balkema.

Ampelopsis

Suessenguth, K. 1953. *Vitaceae*. In Engler-Prantl, *Nat. Pflanzenfam*. 20d: 313–15.

Araceae

Bown, D. 1988. *Aroids*. (Hutchinson).

Aristolochia

Ahumada, L.Z. 1978. Novedades sistematicas en el genero *Aristolochia* en Sudamerica I. *Darwiniana* 21(1): 65–80.

Bazzolo, T.M & Pfeifer, H.W.1977. Efimbriate, herbaceous Aristolochias in Brazil and N.W. South America. *Caldasia* 12(56): 19–33.

Bor, N.L. 1939. Some beautiful Indian climbers and shrubs: *Aristolochia. J. Bombay Nat. Hist. Soc.* 203–20.

Boucher G. & Mottet S. (1898). See General above.

Cammerloher, H. 1923. Zur biologia der Blute von *Aristolochia grandiflora. Ost. Bot. Z.* 6–8: 180–98.

Davis, P.H. 1961. *Aristolochia* in the Near East. *Notes R. Bot. Gdn Edinb.* 23: 515–46.

Lecomte, H. 1909. Aristolochiacées d'Indo-Chine. *Not. Syst. Paris* I:72–76.

Lucknow National Botanic Gardens. 1958. *Aristolochia. Bull. Nat. Bot. Gdns Lucknow* 11.

Pauter, J.A. 1981. Notes on *Aristolochia* from Trinidad. *Kew Bull.* 36:231.

Petch, T. 1924. Notes on *Aristolochia. Ann. R. Bot. Gdns Peradeniya* 8: 22–225.

Pfeifer, H.W. 1966. Revision of the North and Central American hexandrous species of *Aristolochia. Ann. Missouri Bot. Gdn* 53: 115–96.

—— 1970. A taxonomic revision of the pentandrous species of *Aristolochia*. Storr, University of Connecticut.

Asarina

De Wolf, G.P. 1956. Notes on cultivated Schrophulariaceae: *Antirrhinum* and *Asarina. Baileya* 4:55.

Asparagus

El-Gazzar, A. & Badawi, A.A. 1975. The taxonomic position of *Asparagus. Phytologia* 29:472.

Huttleston, D.G. 1970. The names of three commonly cultivated ornamental Asparaguses. *Baileya* 17:58–63.

Jessop, J.P. 1966. The genus *Asparagus* in Southern Africa. *Bothalia* 9:31–87.

Valdes, B. 1979. Revision del genero *Asparagus* en Macaronesia. *Lagascalia* 9(1): 65.

Bauhinia

Chen, L. 1939. The Chinese species of *Bauhinia. Lingnan. Sci. Journ.* 18: 261–80, 475–94.

Coetzer & Ross. 1976. *Bauhinia. Trees in South Africa* 28(3): 63.

Soe, M. 1972. Burmese species of *Bauhinia. Union Burma J. Life Sci.* 5 (3): 307–17.

Standley, P.C. & Steyermark, J.A. 1948. Flora of Guatemala. *Fieldiana* 24 (5): 89–96.

De Wit, H.C. 1956. A revision of Malaysian Bauhiniae. *Reinwardtia* 3: 381–539.

Woodson, R.E. et al. 1951. *Bauhinia* in Flora of Panama. *Ann. Mo. Bot. Gdn.* 38: 10–22.

Wunderlin, R.R. 1976. Panamanian species of *Bauhinia. Ann. Miss. Bot. Gdn.* 63:346.

Berberidopsis

Veldkamp, J. 1984. *Berberidopsis* in Australia. *Blumea* 30:29.

Berchemia

Hatusima, S. 1958. On the genus *Berchemia* from Japan; Korea and Formosa. *Jour. Geobot.* 7. 44–47, 69–70.

Suessenguth, K. 1953. Rhamnaceae. In Engler-Prantl, *Nat. Pflanzenfam.* 20d: 141–5.

Bignoniaceae

Boucher, G. & Mottet, S. 1898. See General above.

Blechnum

Jones, D.L. 1987. *Encyclopaedia of Ferns.* (Lothian)

Bougainvillea

Anon. 1959. *Bougainvillea. Bull. Nat. Bot. Gdn Lucknow* No. 41.

Bor, N.L. and Raizada, M.B. 1982. *Some Beautiful Indian Climbers and Shrubs*, 2nd edn (Bombay: Bombay Natural History Society): 291–304.

Gillis, W.T. 1976. Bougainvilleas of cultivation. *Baileya* 20(1): 34–41.

Golby, E. 1970. History of *Bougainvillea* in Florida. In E.A. Menninger, *Flowering Vines of the World*, 238–45.

Holttum, R.E. 1938. The cultivated Bougainvilleas. *Gard. Chron.* Series 3, 103: 164–5.

—— 1938. Bougainvilleas. *M.A.H.A. Magazine* 8: 69–72.

—— 1955. The cultivated Bougainvilleas I. *M.A.H.A. Magazine* 12(2) 2–9.

—— 1955. The cultivated Bougainvilleas II. *Bougainvillea* × *buttiana*, its varieties and hybrids. *M.A.H.A. Magazine* 12(3): 2–11.

—— 1955. The cultivated Bougainvilleas III. Varieties of *Bougainvillea glabra. M.A.H.A. Magazine* 12 (4): 25–36.

—— 1956. The cultivated Bougainvilleas IV. *Bougainvillea spectabilis* and its varieties. *M.A.H.A. Magazine* 13 (1): 13–32.

—— 1956. The cultivated Bougainvilleas V. The recorded hybrids. *M.A.H.A. Magazine* 13 (2): 66–74.

Iredell, J. 1990. *The Bougainvillea Grower's Handbook.* Brookvale, Australia: Simon & Schuster.

MacDaniels, L.H. A study of cultivars of *Bougainvillea. Baileya* 21 (2):77.

Pal, B.P. and Swarup, V. 1974. *Bougainvilleas* (New Delhi: Indian Council of Agricultural Research).

Pancho, J.V. and Bardenas, E.A. 1959. *Bougainvillea* in the Philippines. *Baileya* 7: 91–101.

Williams, R.O. 1950. The White Bougainvillea. *J.R.H.S.* 75 (12): 485–6.

Bowiea

See Rowley under Cucurbitaceae.

Caesalpinia

Schreiber, A. 1980. Die Gattung *Caesalpinia* in Sudwestafrica. *Mitt. Bot. Staatssamuul Munchen* 16:51.

Standley, P.C. & Steyermark, J.A. 1946. Flora of Guatemala. *Fieldiana* 24 (5): 96–105.

Vidal, J.E. & Hulthol, S. 1976. Révision des *Caesalpinia* asiatiques. *Bull. Mus. Nat. Hist. Nat.* 27:69.

Woodson, R.E. 1951. *Caesalpinia* in Flora of Panama. *Ann. Mo. Bot. Gard.* 38: 87–93.

Canavalia

Chatterjee, D. 1949. Indian species of *Canavalia. J. Ind. Bot.* 28:83.

Celastrus

Hou, D. 1955. A revision of *Celastrus. Ann. Miss. Bot.Gdn.* 42:215.

Lander, N.S. & Johnson, L.A.S. 1975. Australian species of *Celastrus. Telopea* 1: 33–9.

Ceropegia

Bruyns, P.V. 1980. Ceropegias of the Pretoria district. *Aloe* 18:21.

—— 1984. *Ceropegia, Brachystelma* and *Tenaris* in S.W. Africa. *Dinteria* 17:3.

Dyer, R.A. 1978. The changing scene of *Ceropegia* and *Brachystelma. Cactus and Succulent J. Amer.* 50:112.

Field, D.V. 1981. *Ceropegia distincta* and some related species in tropical Eastern. & Southern Africa. *Kew Bull.* 36:441.

Field, D.V. & Collenette, I.S.. 1984. *Ceropegia superba*, a new species from Arabia. *Kew Bull.* 39:639.

Huber, H. 1957. Revision der Gattung *Ceropegia*. *Mem. Soc. Bot.* 12.

Lavranos, J.J. 1984. *Ceropegia* species from the winter rainfall area, S.W. Africa. *Dinteria* 17:83.

Lisowski, S. & Malaisse, F. 1974. Le genre *Ceropegia* au Shaba (Zaire). *Bull. Jard. Bot. Nat. Belg.* 44:401.

Scholes, M.A. 1975. Some notes on *Ceropegia*. *Aloe* 13(2):52–6.

Stopp, K. 1964. Die *Ceropegia*-Arten der Umbraticola-Grippe. In Engler, *Bot. Jahrb.* 83:115.

Taylor, N.P. 1980. A new variety of *Ceropegia rupicola*. *Cactus and Succulent J. G.B.* 42:111.

Werdermann, E. 1939. Revision der ostafrikanischen Arten der Gattung *Ceropegia*. In Engler, *Bot. Jahrb.* 70:189.

Cestrum

Beckett, K.A. 1987. *Cestrum* in cultivation. *Plantsman* 9(3): 129–33.

Francey, P. 1935–6. Monographie de genre *Cestrum*. *Candollea* (1935) 146–398; (1936) 1–132.

Chorizema

Meredith, L.D. Crisp, M.D. and Taylor, J.M. 1990. *Chorizema varium* – an extinct Australian species. *Plantsman* 11(4): 246–51.

Cissus

Dress, W.J. 1971. Notes on two cultivated species of *Cissus*. *Baileya* 18:67.

Latiff, A. 1982. The Malay Peninsula species of *Cissus*. *Malayan Nat. J.* 35 (3): 197–207.

Lawrence, G.H.M. 1959.*Cissus* and *Rhoicissus* in cultivation. *Baileya* 7:45-54.

See also Rowley under Cucurbitaceae.

Clematis

Boucher, G., & Mottet, S. 1898. See General above.

Brandenburg, W.A. 1981. Historical background and taxonomy of cultivated large-flowered *Clematis* in Europe. *Kulturpflanze* 29:321.

Erickson, R.O. 1943. Taxonomy of *Clematis* section *Viorna*. *Ann. Mo. Bot. Gard.* 1–62.

Evison, R.J. 1991. *Making the Most of Clematis*. 2nd edn (Floraprint).

Fisk, J. 1989. *Clematis: the Queen of Climbers*. 3rd edn (Cassell).

—— 1991. *Clematis*. Wisley Handbook. 3rd edn (Cassell/RHS.)

Fretwell, B. 1989. *Clematis*. (Collins)

Gardner, R.O. 1981. *Clematis cunninghamii*, the correct name for *C. parviflora*. *N.Z. J. Bot.* 19: 327.

Grey-Wilson, C. 1986. *Clematis orientalis* – a much confused species. *Plantsman* 7(4):193–205.

Handel-Mazzetti, H. 1940. Ranunculaceae. *Acta Hort. Gothob.* 13: 37–219.

Howells, J. 1990. *The Plantsman's Guide to Clematis* (Ward Lock)

—— 1993. *Clematis* wilt: a review of the literature. *Plantsman* 11 (3): 148–61.

Hutchins, G. 1990. New Zealand *Clematis*: hybrids and species in cultivation. *Plantsman* 11(4): 193–209.

Jackman, A.G. 1900. Hybrid *Clematis*. *J.R.H.S.* 24:315.

Jouin, E. 1907. Die in Deutschland kultivierten, winterharten *Clematis*. *Jahrb. DDG.* 228–38.

Kapoor, S.L. 1962, 1964. Flowering plants of India - *Clematis*. *Bull. Nat. Bot. Gdn Lucknow* 78: 1–67; 124: 1–94.

Keener, C.S. 1967. A biosystematic study of *Clematis* subsection *Integrifoliae*. *J. Elisha Mitchell Sci. Soc.* 83:1–41.

Keener, C.S. and Dennis, W.M. 1982. The subgeneric classification of *Clematis* (Ranunculaceae) in temperate North America north of Mexico. *Taxon* 31: 37–44.

Keener, C.S. 1975. Studies in the Ranunculaceae of the southeastern United States III: *Clematis*. *Sida* 6 (1): 33.

Kuntze, O. 1885. Monogr. *Clematis*. *Verh. Bot. Ver. Brandenburg* 83–202.

Lamb, J.G.D. 1990. The propagation of climbing *Clematis*. *Plantsman* 12 (3): 178–80.

Lavallée: Les Clematites à grandes fleurs; Paris 1884.

Lloyd, C. 1989. *Clematis*. 3rd edn (Viking Penguin)

Markham, E. 1951. *The Large and Small Flowered Clematis and their culture in the open air*. 3rd edn.

Moore, T., & Jackman, G. 1977. *The Clematis as a Garden Flower*. New edn.

Pringle, J.S. 1971. Taxonomy and distribution of *Clematis* Sect. *Atragene* in North America. *Brittonia* 23:361–393.

—— 1973. The cultivated taxa of *Clematis* sect. *Atragene*. *Baileya* 19: 49–89.

Riekstina, V. and Riekstins, I. 1990. *Clematis* (Leningrad: Leningradskoie Otdelenie)

Scheller, H. 1981. *Clematis*-wildarten fur unsere Garten. *Gartenpr.* 199.

Shimizu, T. 1973. A new species of *Clematis* from Taiwan. *Taiwania* 18:173.

Snoeijer, W. 1991. *Clematis Index* (Boskoop: J. Fopma)

Spingarn. 1935. The large-flowered *Clematis* hybrids. *Nat. Hort. Magazine* 64 94.

Tamura, M. 1954. Notes on *Clematis* of Eastern Asia I, II. *Acta Phytotax. et Geobot.* 15: 17–20; 117–19.

—— 1987. A classification of the genus *Clematis*. *Acta Phytotax. Geobot.* 38: 33–44.

Tobe, H. 1976. Morphological studies on the genus *Clematis*. *Sci. Rept. Tohoku Univ.* Ser. IV 37: 95–103.

Van de Laar, H.J. 1985. *Clematis* (Grootbloemige Hybriden). *Dendroflora* 22: 33–58.

Clematoclethra

Komarov, V.L. 1908. Revisio critica specierum generis *Clematoclethra* Max. *Acta Hort. Petrop.* 29:83–97.

Clematopsis

Brummitt, R.K. 1976. A reconsideration of *Clematopsis* in Africa, with special reference to Malawi. *Kew Bull.* 31:156.

Exell, A.W., Léonard, J. and Milne-Redhead, E. 1951. Les espèces africaines du genre *Clematopsis*. *Bull. Soc. Roy. Bot. Belgique* 83: 407–27.

Hutchinson, J. 1920. *Clematopsis*, a primitive genus of Clematideae. *Bull. Misc. Inf.* 12–22.

Raynal, J. 1978. *Clematopsis*, genre africano-malagache. *Adansonia* Ser.2, 18:3–18.

—— 1979. The genus *Clematopsis* in Madagascar. In G. Kunkel, *Taxonomic Aspects of African Economic Botany*: 146–9.

Clitoria

Croat, T.B. 1974. Notes on the genus *Clitoria* in Panama. *Phytologia*. 29: 130–34.

Howard, R.A. 1967. Notes on the cultivated woody species of *Clitoria*. *Baileya*. 15:15.

Cobaea

Hemsley, W.B. 1880. The Cobaeas. *The Garden* 17: 352–3.

Standley, P. 1914. A revision of the genus *Cobaea*. *Contributions U.S. National Herbarium* 17: 248.

Herklots, G.A.C. 1986. *Cobaea. Plantsman* 8(1): 36–43.

Cocculus

See under *Menispermum*.

Codonopsis

Anthony, J. 1926. A key to *Codonopsis. Notes RBG Edin*. 15:171–90.

Chipp, T.F. 1908. A revision of the genus *Codonopsis. J. Linn. Soc., Bot*. 38: 374-91.

Finlay, M.K. 1972. On *Codonopsis* which grow at Keillour. *J.R.H.S*. 97: 82-7.

Grey-Wilson, C. 1990. A survey of *Codonopsis* in cultivation. *Plantsman* 12 (pt II): 65-99.

Mathews, Y.S. 1980. The genus *Codonopsis. Quarterly Bull. Alpine Gdn Soc*. 48: 96-108.

Corydalis

Ingwersen, W. 1980. Commendable Corydalises. *Plantsman* 2:129; see also 3:63.

Ludlow, F. & Stearn, W.T. 1975. New Himalayan and Tibetan species of *Corydalis. Bull. Brit. Mus. (Nat. Hist)* 5(2).

Ryberg, M. 1955. A taxonomical survey of the genus *Corydalis. Acta Horti Berg*. 17: 115–75.

Cucurbita and Cucurbitaceae

Bemis, W.P. & Whitaker, T.W. 1969. The xerophytic *Cucurbita* of NW Mexico and SW USA. *Madroño* 20: 33–41.

Bailey, L.H. 1929. The domesticated Cucurbitas. *Gentes Herbarum* 2: 63–115.

—— 1937. *The Garden of Gourds*. (New York:Macmillan).

—— 1943. Species of *Cucurbita. Gentes Herbarum* 6:267–322.

Herklots, G.A.C. 1986. *Cucurbita. Plantsman* 8(2): 86–103.

Jeffrey, C. 1980. A review of the Cucurbitaceae. *Bot. J. Linn. Soc*. 81.

Organ, J. 1963. *Gourds*. (Faber)

Rowley, G.D. 1987. *Caudiciform and Pachycaul Succulents*. (Strawberry Press, California).

Whitaker, T.W. and Bohn, G.W. 1950. The taxonomy, genetics, production and uses of the cultivated species of *Cucurbita. Economic Botany* 4:52–81.

Whitaker, T.W. and Davis, G.N. 1962. *Curcurbits: Botany, Cultivation, and Utilization*. (Leonard Hill).

Whitaker, T.W. and Bemis, W.P. 1975. Origin and evolution of the cultivated *Cucurbita. Bulletin Torrey Botanical Club* 102: 362–8.

Cyphostemma

Hardy & Retief. 1981. The caudiciform *Cyphostemma* species from Southern Africa. *Cactus and Succulent J. Amer*.: 53.

Derris

Thothathri, K. 1961. Revision of *Derris* in India. *Bull. Soc. Surv. Ind*. 3: 179–200.

—— 1976. Studies in Leguminosae (24), Notes on the Indo-Burmese species of *Derris. J. Jap. Bot*. 51(5): 141–50.

Dichelostemma

Hoover, R.F. 1940. The genus *Dichelostemma. Amer. Midl. Nat*. 24: 463–76.

Dimorphanthera

See Sleumer (1967) under *Agapetes*.

Dioscorea

Von Teichman et al. 1979. The genus *Dioscorea* in South Africa. *Boissiera* 24: 215–24.

See also Rowley under Cucurbitaceae.

Diploterygium

See Jones (1987) under *Blechnum*.

Dischidia

Rintz, R.E. The peninsular Malayan species of *Dischidia. Blumea* 26(1).

Distictis

Gentry, A.H. 1974. Studies of Bignoniaceae, 2. A synopsis of the genus *Distictis. Ann. Miss. Bot. Gard*. 61(2).

Euonymus

Blakelock, R.A. 1951. A synopsis of the genus *Euonymus. Kew Bull*. 210–88.

Lancaster, R. 1981. An account of *Euonymus* in cultivation. *Plantsman* 3(3).

Sprague, T.A. 1928. The correct spelling of certain generic names: *Euonymus* or *Evonymus? Kew Bull*. 294–6.

Ficus

Condit & Enderud. 1956. A bibliography of the Fig. *Hilgardia*: 1–663.

Condit, I.J. 1969. *Ficus: The Exotic Species*. Univ. of Calif.

Domke, W. 1935. Der Gummibaum und seine Verwandten. *Gartenflora*. 135–138.

King, G. 1888. *The Species of Ficus of the Indo-Malayan and Chinese Countries*. Calcutta.

Forsythia

Dahlgren, K.V.O. 1946. Om odlade Forsythior och deras fruktsättning. *Lustgarden*: 89–100.

De Wolf, G.P. & R.S. Hebb. 1971. The story of *Forsythia. Arnoldia* 31: 41–63.

Dietrich, H. 1957. Erfahrungen mit *Forsythien-Sorten. Deutsche Baumschule*, 268–75.

Duvernay, J.M. 1953. Le genre *Forsythia. Rev. Hort*. 831–5.

Hyde, B. 1951. Forsythia polyploids. *Journ. Arn. Arb*. 32: 157–8, with plates.

Lingelsheim, A. Oleaceae; *Forsythia*. In Engler, *Pflanzenreich* 72: 109–113.

Markgraf, F. 1930. *Forsythia europaea* und die Forsythien Asiens. *Mitt. DDG*: 1–12.

Sampson, D.R. 1955. Studies on the progeny of triploid *Philadelphus* and *Forsythia. Journ. Arn. Arb*., 369–384.

Seneta, W. 1965. Uber 2 neue *Forsythia*-Hybriden. *Rocznik Dendrol*. 19: 181–92.

Szuszka, B. 1955. Rodzaj Forsythia Vahl w Arboretum Kornickim. *Arboretum Kornickie Rocznik* (Poland) I: 91–110.

—— 1959. Results hitherto obtained in breeding *Forsythia* at Kornik. *Rocznik Arb. Kornik*: 205–25.

Thompson, J.M. 1946. Some features of horticultural interest in the Forsythias *J.R.H.S*. 71: 166–72.

Wyman, D. 1959. Foremost among the Forsythias. *Americ. Nurseryman*, 15 April.

—— 1961. The *Forsythia* story. *Arnoldia* 21: 35–8.

—— 1961. Registration Lists of cultivar names of Forsythias. *Arnoldia* 21: 39–42.

—— 1961. Forsythias. *Amer. Hort. Mag*.: 191–7.

Fremontodendron

Eastwood, A. 1934. New species of *Fremontia. W. Bot*. I(12): 139–41.

Everett, P. 1962. *Fremontia* 'California Glory'. *Lasca Leaves* 12(1): 2–4.

Harvey, M. 1943. A revision of the genus *Fremontia*. *Madroño* 7: 100–110.

Kelman, W.M. 1991. A revision of *Fremontodendron*. *Syst. Bot.* 16(1): 3–20.

MacMillan Browse, P. 1992. Fremontias – California's finest shrubs? *Plantsman* 14 (1): 41–5.

Gloriosa

Ferguson I. 1980. *Gloriosa simplex*. *The Garden* 105 (12): 504.

Field, D.V. The identity of *Gloriosa simplex*. *Kew Bull.* 25(2): 243-5.

—— 1972. The genus *Gloriosa*. *Lilies* 1973, 93–5.

Karihaloo, J.L. 1986. Cytology of three species of *Gloriosa*. *Herbertia* 42:2–13.

Kirtikar, K.R. 1977. The Glory Lily, *Gloriosa superba*. *Hornbill* 6–7.

Narain, P. 1988. *Gloriosa*: cultivars and natural species. *Herbertia* 44: 2–12.

Onderstall, J. The fabulous Flame Lily. *Veld and Flora* 62(3): 24–5.

Percy-Lancaster, S. 1958. *Gloriosa*. *Bull. Nat. Bot. Gdns Lucknow*, No.26.

Percy-Lancaster, S. & A. 1966. *Gloriosa*. *Bull. Nat. Bot. Gdns Lucknow*, No.123.

Hedera

Fortgens, G. et al. 1989. *Hedera* (Winterharde Bodembedekkers). *Dendroflora* 26: 43–66.

Heieck, B.I. 1980. *Hedera Sorten* (Heidelberg: Gärtnerei Abtei Newburg).

Hibberd, S. 1872. *The Ivy, a monograph*. *Ivy Journal* (American Ivy Society)

Jenny, M. 1965. Araliaceae. *Hedera*. *Jahr. Verein ehem. Oeschberger*, 93–102.

Lawrence, G.H.M. and Schulze, A.E. 1942. The cultivated Hederas. *Gentes Herbarum* 6: 107–73.

Lawrence, G.H.M. 1956. The cultivated Ivies. *Morris Arb. Bull.* 7: 19–31.

McAllister, H. 1979. The species of Ivy. *Ivy Exchange Newsletter* 1(4).

McAllister, H. 1988. Canary and Algerian Ivies. *Plantsman* 10(1): 27–30.

McAllister, H. & Rutherford, A. 1983. The species of Ivy. *Ivy Journal* 9(4): 45–54.

Pierot, S.W. 1974. *The Ivy Book* (New York: Macmillan)

Pojarkova, A. 1951. Species Chinensis generis *Hedera* et earum affinitas. *Notulae Systematicae* (Leningrad) 14: 244–64.

Rose, P.Q. 1990. *Ivies*. Rev. edn (Blandford Press)

Rutherford, A. 1984. The history of the Canary Islands ivy and its relatives. *Ivy Journal* 10(4): 13–18.

Rutherford, A. 1989. The ivies of Andalusia. *Ivy Journal* 15(1): 7–17.

Rutherford, A. et al. 1993. New ivies from the Mediterranean area and Macaronesia. *Plantsman* 15 (2): 115–28.

Schaepman, H. 1975. *Preliminary Checklist of Cultivated Hedera*, part I. (American Ivy Society, updated in *Ivy Journal*.)

Seeman, B. 1864. Revision of the Natural Hederaceae. *Journ. Bot.*

Tobler, F. 1912. *Die Gattung Hedera*. Jena.

—— 1927. Die Gartenformen der Gattung *Hedera*. *Mitt. DDG* 1–33.

Heliophila

Schreiber, A. 1979. Die Gattung *Heliophila* in Sudwest Afrika. *Mitt. Bot. Staats. München* 15.

Hodgsonia

Kundu, B.C. A revision of the Indian species of *Hodgsonia* and *Trichosanthes*. *J. Bombay Nat. Hist. Soc.* 43: 362–88.

Hoya

Innes, C. 1988. The genus *Hoya*. *Plantsman* 10: 129–40.

Kloppenburg, D. & Wayman, A. 1992. *The Hoya Handbook: A Guide for the Grower and Collector*. (Oregon: Orca Publishing Co.)

Rintz, R.E. 1978. The Peninsular Malaysian species of *Hoya*. *Malayan Nat. J.* 30(3–4): 467–522.

The Hoyan.

Humulus

Small, E. 1978. Numerical and nomenclatural analysis of morphogeographical taxa of *Humulus*. *Syst. Bot.* 3:37.

Hydrangea

Grootendorst, H.J. 1973. *Hydrangea*. *Dendroflora* 10: 26–40.

Haworth-Booth, M. 1984. *The Hydrangeas*. 5th edn (Constable).

McClintock, E. 1956. The cultivated Hydrangeas. *Baileya* 4: 165–75.

—— 1957. Hydrangeas. *Nat. Hort. Mag.* 36: 270–79.

—— 1957. A monograph of the genus *Hydrangea*. *Proc. Calif. Acad. Sci.* 29: 147–256.

Mallet, C. 1992. *Hydrangeas*. (Varengeville-sur-mer, France: Centre d'Art Floral)

Ibervillea

Moore, H.E. 1953. *Ibervillea*, a Cucurbit newly cultivated in the US. *Baileya* 1:59.

Ipomoea

Austen, D.F. 1978. The *Ipomoea batatas* complex. *Bull. Torrey. Bot. Club* 105:114.

Fosberg, F.R. 1976. *Ipomoea indica* taxonomy: a tangle of Morning Glories. *Bot. Not.* 129:35.

Gunn, C.R. 1972. Moonflowers, *Ipomoea* Sect. *Calonyction* in temperate N. America. *Brittonia* 24: 150–168.

Der Marderosian, A.H. 1965. Nomenclatural history of the Morning Glory, *Ipomoea violacea*. *Taxon* 14: 234.

Jasminum

Decernay, L. 1982. Les Jasmins. *Jard. France.* 10:334–5.

Green, P.S. 1961. Studies in the Genus *Jasminum* I: Section *Alternifolia*. *Notes Roy. Bot. Gard. Edinb.* 23:355–84.

—— 1962. Studies in the genus *Jasminum*: The species from New Caledonia and the Loyalty Islands. *Journ. Arn. Arb.* 43 (2):109–31.

—— 1966. Studies in the genus *Jasminum*: The species in cultivation in North America. *Baileya* 13.4:137–71.

—— 1975. A revision of *Jasminum* in Australia. *Allertonia* 3(6): 403–38.

—— 1984. Studies in the genus *Jasminum*. *Jasminum laurifolium* as a cultivated plant. *Kew Bull.* 39(3):655–6.

—— 1986, Studies in the genus *Jasminum*. *Jasminum* in Arabia. *Kew Bull.* 41(2):413–18.

—— 1987. Studies in the genus *Jasminum*. A long-mis-applied name for a Sino-Indian species of *Jasminum*. *Kew Bull.* 42(2): 437–8.

—— 1988. *Jasminum*. *Plantsman* 10(3): 148–59.

—— 1992. Plant Portraits 196: *Jasminum officinale* 'Inverleith'. *Kew Mag.* 9(2): 63–7.

—— 1993 Plant Portraits 224: *Jasminum sinense*. *Kew Mag.* 10(3):113–6.

Jelitto, C.R. 1978. Winterjasmin, *Jasminum nudiflorum*. *Palmengarten* 42(1): 22–3.

Kobuski, C.E. 1932. Synopsis of the Chinese species of *Jasminum. Journ. Arn. Arb.* 13:145–79.
—— 1959. A revised key to the Chinese species of *Jasminum. Journ. Arn. Arb.* 40:385–90.
Srivastava, S.K. 1986. *Jasminum parkeri:* an endangered endemic taxon from Himachal Pradesh. *J. Econ. Taxon. Bot.* 7(3):709–10.
Wijnands, D.O. 1990. *Jasminum sambac. Bull. Bot. Tuinen Wageningen* 24:11–12.

Kadsura
Smith, A.C. 1947. The Families Illiciaceae and Schisandraceae. *Sargentia* 7:156–211.

Lathyrus
Brunsberg, K. 1977. Biosystematics of the *Lathyrus pratensis* complex. Opera Bot. 41: 1–78.
Chefranova, Z.V. 1978. Summary of the taxonomy of *Lathyrus. Novit. Syst. Pl. Vasc.* 8:205.
Fouzdar, A. & Tandon, S.L. 1975. Cytotaxonomic investigations in the genus *Lathyrus. Nucleus* 18: 24–33.
Gorer, R., Harvey, J.H. and Vickery, R.1991. The mysteries of Lord Anson's Pea. *Plantsman* 13(3): 129–41.
Hitchcock, C.L. 1952. A revision of the N. American species of *Lathyrus. Univ. Wash. Publ. Biol.* 15: 1–104.
Jones, B.R. 1965. *The Complete Guide to Sweet Peas.* (John Gifford)
Norton, S. 1994. All the colours of the rainbow. *The Garden* 119: 216–21.
Unwin, C. 1986. *Sweet Peas: their History, Development and Culture.* (Silent Books)

Lonicera
Bradshaw, D. 1991. Climbing Honeysuckles. *Plantsman*13 (2): 106–11.
Gorer, R. and Harvey, J.H. 1990. The disappearance of *Lonicera × americana. Plantsman* 12 (2): 100–106.
Perkins, C.J. 1991. Virus infection of the genus *Lonicera. Plantsman* 11 (4): 215–21.
Rehder, A. 1903. Synopsis of the genus *Lonicera. Report of the Missouri Botanical Garden,* 27–232.
Van de Laar, H.J. 1988. *Lonicera. Dendroflora* 25:37–54.
Wright, D. 1983. Climbing Honeysuckles. *Plantsman* 4 (4): 236–56.

Lycium
Haegi, L. 1976. Taxonomic account of *Lycium* in Australia. *Austr. J. Bot.* 24: 669–79.
Hitchcock, C.L. 1922. A monographic study of the genus *Lycium* of the Western Hemisphere. *Ann. Miss. Bot. Gard.* 19:179–374.
Pojarkova, A. 1950. Species generis *Lycium,* fructibus rubris ex Asia Media et China. *Not. Syst. (Leningrad)* 13: 238–78.

Lygodium
See Jones (1987) under *Blechnum* above.

Mandevilla
Dress, W.J. 1974. Notes on a *Mandevilla (Dipladenia)* hybrid. *Baileya* 19: 106–9.
Pichon, M. 1950. *Mandevilla: Classification des Apocynacées* XXV: 110–11.
Woodson, R.E. 1933. *Mandevilla. American Echitoideae* 41–173.

Menispermum
Diels, L. 1910. Menispermaceae. In Engler, *Pflanzenreich* 46:1–345.

Merremia
O'Donell, C.A. 1941. Revision de las especies Americanas de *Merremia. Lilloa* 6: 467–554.

Metrosideros
Oliver, W.R.B. 1928. The New Zealand species of *Metrosideros. Trans. and Proc. N.Z. Inst.* 59.

Millettia
Dunn, S.T. 1912. Revision of *Millettia. J. Linn. Soc. Bot.* 41:123.

Monstera
Madison, M. 1977. A Revision of *Monstera. Contrib. Gray. Herb.* 207:3.
See also Bown (1988) under Araceae.

Mucuna
Tateishi & Ohashi. 1981. East Asiatic species of *Mucuna. Bot. Mag. Tokyo* 94:91
Wilmot-Dear, C.M. 1984. Revision of *Mucuna* in China and Japan. *Kew Bull.* 39:23.

Mussaenda
Price, G.R. 1974. Cultivated Mussaendas in the Phillippines. *Kalikasan.* 4(1): 37–55.
Sharma, S.C., Sharga, A.N., Srivastava, S. 1990. Hortotaxonomical studies on some Mussaendas. *Plantsman* 12(3): 184–8.

Mutisia
Cabrera, A.L. 1965. Revision del género *Mutisia. Opera Lilloana* 13: 1–327.
Comber, J. 1949. The hardier Mutisias. *J. RHS* 74: 241–5.
Ingram, J. 1971. *Mutisia* in cultivation. *Baileya* 18: 33–9.

Nepenthes
Juniper, B.E. 1989. *The Carnivorous Plants.* (Academic Press)
Pietropaolo, J. & P. 1986. *Carnivorous Plants of the World.* (Portland, Oregon: Timber Press)
Slack, A. 1979. *Carnivorous Plants.* (Ebury Press)

Pandorea
Lebler, B.A. 1979. Four woody vines. *Queensl. Agric. J.* 105 (4): 374.

Papilionanthe
Garay, L.A. 1974. On the systematics of the monopodial orchids. 2. Key to *Papilionanthe. Bot. Mus. Leafl. Harvard Univ.* 23(10): 369–75.

Parthenocissus
Graebner, P. 1928. Die *Parthenocissus* species. *Mitt. DDG* 1–10.
Rehder, A. 1905. Die amerikanischen Arten der Gattung *Parthenocissus. Mitt. DDG* 469–76.
Van de Laar, H.J. 1981. *Parthenocissus tricuspidata* - Keuringsrapport, *Dendroflora* xviii: 41–50

Passiflora
Boucher, G. & Mottet, S. 1989. See General above.
Jorgensen, P.M. et al. 1984. A guide to collecting passionflowers. *Ann. Miss. B. G.* 71: 1172.
Knock, F. 1965. *Passifloras for your Garden.* Kansas City Missouri.
Lawrence, G.H.M. 1960. Names of *Passiflora* hybrids. *Baileya* 8: 118–120.
—— 1960. Identification of cultivated Passion Flowers. *Baileya* 8: 121–132.
Marshall, E.D. 1973. The Passifloras. *Calif. Hort. Journ.* 34: 146–153.
Vanderplank, J. 1991. *Passion Flowers and Passion Fruit.* (Cassell)

Pereskia
Bleck, M. 1973. *Pereskia* and *Maihuenia. Cactus & Succulent J. Amer.* 45: 214.

Periploca
Browicz, K. 1966. The Periplocaceae in Turkey and Cyprus. *Feddes Rep.* 72: 124–131.
—— 1966. History of the genera *Periploca* and *Cionura*. *Rocznik Dendrol.* 20: 53–73.

Phaseolus
Hassler, E. 1923. Revisio specierum austro-americanarum generis *Phaseoli*. *Candollea* I: 417–72.
Irish, H.C. 1901. Garden beans cultivated as esculents. *Rept. Mo. Bot. Gard.* 12: 81–165.
Leese, B.M. 1958. Identification of Asiatic species of *Phaseolus* by seed characters. *Amer. Midl. Nat.* 40: 132–44.
Leitão, H.F. 1974. Contribuição as estudo taxonomico do genero *Phaseolus* no Brasil. *Bragantia* 33(6): 55–63.
Maréchal, R. et al. 1978. Etude taxonomique d'un groupe complexe d'espèces des genres *Phaseolus* et Vigna (Leg.). *Boissiera* 28.
Piper, C.V. 1926. Studies in American Phaseolineae. *Contr. U.S. Nat. Herb.* 22(9): 663–701.
Standley, P.C. & J.A. Steyermark. 1946. Flora of Guatemala. *Fieldiana* 24(5): 316–35.

Philodendron
See Bown (1988) under Araceae.

Piper
Chew, W-L. 1972. The genus *Piper* (Piperaceae) in New Guinea, Solomon Is. & Australia. *J. Arn. Arb.* 53: 1.
Ichaso, C.L. et al. 1977. Piperaceae do Municipio do Rio de Janeiro, genero *Piper*. *Arq. Jard. Bot. Rio de Janeiro* 20: 145–87.
Yuncker. *Piper* of Brazil. *Hoechnea* 2: 19.

Plumbago
Wood, C.E. 1968. *Plumbago auriculata* versus *P.capensis*. *Baileya* 16:137–9.

Polygonum
Steward, A.N. 1930. The Polygonaceae of Eastern Asia. *Contrib. Gray. Herb.* 80.

Prionotes
Haliwell, B. 1984. *Prionotes cerinthoides*. *Plantsman* 6(1): 42.

Pseudogynoxys
Robinson, H. & Cuatrecasas, J. 1977. Notes on the genus and species limits of *Pseudogynoxys*. *Phytologia* 36(3): 177.

Rhodochiton
Heine, H. 1984. *Rhodochiton atrosanguineum*. *Plantsman* 6(1): 60–61.
Rix, M. 1979. *Rhodochiton volubile*. *Plantsman* 1: 65.
Schultes, R.E. 1940. Notes on the history and distribution of *Rhodochiton volubile*. *Bot. Mus. Leafl. Harvard Univ.* 8:129–33.

Rhoicissus
See Lawrence (1959) under *Cissus*.

Rubus
Bailey, L.H. 1941–5. *Rubus* in North America. *Gentes Herbarum* 5: 1–932.
Focke, W.O. 1910–14. Species Rubrorum. *Bibl. Bot.* 72, 83.

Schisandra
Smith, A.C. 1947. The Families Illiciaceae and Schisandraceae. *Sargentia* 7: 86–156.

Scindapsus
See Bown (1988) under Araceae.

Sinomenium
See under *Menispermum*.

Solandra
De Wolf, G.P. 1955. Notes on cultivated *Solandra*. *Baileya* 3: 173.

Solanum
Edmonds, J.M. 1972. A synopsis of the taxonomy of *Solanum* in S. America. *Kew. Bull.* 27: 95.
Hepper, F.N. 1978. Typification and name changes in some Old World *Solanum* species. *Bot. J. Linn. Soc.* 76: 287–295.
Lawrence, G.H.M. 1960. The cultivated species of *Solanum*. *Baileya* 8: 21, 75.

Stauntonia
Wu, Y.C. 1936. Uber die Gattung *Stauntonia*. *Not. Bot. Gart. Berlin* 13: 364–376.

Stephanotis
Lisitano, N. 1939. Uno dei più bei rampicanti dei paesi caldi: *Stephanotis floribunda*. *Il Giardino Fiorito*, 196.

Strophanthus
Beentje, H.J. 1982. Monograph of *Strophanthus*. *Belmontia* 13.

Thunbergia
Bremekamp, C.E.B. 1955. The *Thunbergia* species of Malesia.*Verh. Akad. Wet. Amst.* (Natuurk) 50.
Hepper, N. 1964. The story of *Thunbergia erecta*. *Nigerian Field* 29.
Marshall, E.D. 1972. The Thunbergias in Southern Californian gardens.*Calif. Hort. J.* 33(1) 35.
Retief, E. & Reyneke, W.F. 1984. The genus *Thunbergia* in Southern Africa. *Bothalia* 15 (1&2).
Shoser, G. 1978. *Thunbergia mysorensis*. *Palmgarten* 42.

Trachelospermum
Hatusima, S. 1940. A revision of Japanese *Trachelospermum*. *Jour. Jap. Bot.* 16: 20–30.

Trichosanthes
See under *Hodgsonia*.

Vallaris
Rudjiman. 1983. Revision of *Vallaris*. *Belmontia* 14:74.

Vitis
Bailey, L.H. 1934. The species of grapes peculiar to North America. *Gent. Herb.* 3: 151–244 (34 ills.)
See also Suessenguth (1953) under *Ampelopsis*.

Wisteria
Bowden, W.M. 1976. A Survey of Wisterias in Southern Ontario gardens. *Roy. Bot. Gard. Hamilton (Ontario, Canada) Techn. Bull.* 8: 1–15.
MacMillan Browse, P. 1984. Some notes on members of the genus *Wisteria* and their propagation. *Plantsman* 6 (2): 109–23.
Sprengel, K. 1911. Neue Mitteilungen uber *Wisteria chinensis*. *Mitt. DDG* 237–240.
Wyman, D. 1961. Showy Wisteria still a problem vine. *American Nurseryman*, (June 1), 10–11, 68–76.

Xerosicyos
Rowley, G.D. *Xerosicyos*. *Ashingtonia* 2: 177.